T0191511

Lecture Notes in Computer Science 13277

More information about this series at https://link.springer.com/bookseries/558

Orr Dunkelman · Stefan Dziembowski (Eds.)

Advances in Cryptology – EUROCRYPT 2022

41st Annual International Conference on the Theory
and Applications of Cryptographic Techniques
Trondheim, Norway, May 30 – June 3, 2022
Proceedings, Part III

 Springer

Editors
Orr Dunkelman ⓘ
University of Haifa
Haifa, Haifa, Israel

Stefan Dziembowski ⓘ
University of Warsaw
Warsaw, Poland

ISSN 0302-9743 ISSN 1611-3349 (electronic)
Lecture Notes in Computer Science
ISBN 978-3-031-07081-5 ISBN 978-3-031-07082-2 (eBook)
https://doi.org/10.1007/978-3-031-07082-2

This Springer imprint is published by the registered company Springer Nature Switzerland AG
The registered company address is: Gewerbestrasse 11, 6330 Cham, Switzerland

Preface

The 41st Annual International Conference on the Theory and Applications of Cryptographic Techniques, Eurocrypt 2022, was held in Trondheim, Norway. Breaking tradition, the conference started on the evening of Monday, May 30, and ended at noon on Friday, June 3, 2022. Eurocrypt is one of the three flagship conferences of the International Association for Cryptologic Research (IACR), which sponsors the event. Colin Boyd (NTNU, Norway) was the general chair of Eurocrypt 2022 who took care of all the local arrangements.

The 372 anonymous submissions we received in the IACR HotCRP system were each reviewed by at least three of the 70 Program Committee members (who were allowed at most two submissions). We used a rebuttal round for all submissions. After a lengthy and thorough review process, 85 submissions were selected for publication. The revised versions of these submissions can be found in these three-volume proceedings.

In addition to these papers, the committee selected the "EpiGRAM: Practical Garbled RAM" by David Heath, Vladimir Kolesnikov, and Rafail Ostrovsky for the best paper award. Two more papers — "On Building Fine-Grained One-Way Functions from Strong Average-Case Hardness" and "Quantum Algorithms for Variants of Average-Case Lattice Problems via Filtering" received an invitation to the Journal of Cryptology. Together with presentions of the 85 accepted papers, the program included two invited talks: The IACR distinguished lecture, carried by Ingrid Verbauwhede, on "Hardware: an essential partner to cryptography", and "Symmetric Cryptography for Long Term Security" by María Naya-Plasancia.

We would like to take this opportunity to thank numerous people. First of all, the authors of all submitted papers, whether they were accepted or rejected. The Program Committee members who read, commented, and debated the papers generating more than 4,500 comments(!) in addition to a large volume of email communications. The review process also relied on 368 subreviewers (some of which submitted more than one subreivew). We cannot thank you all enough for your hard work.

A few individuals were extremely helpful in running the review process. First and foremost, Kevin McCurley, who configured, solved, answered, re-answered, supported, and did all in his (great) power to help with the IACR system. Wkdqn Brx! We are also extremely grateful to Gaëtan Leurent for offering his wonderful tool to make paper assignment an easy task. The wisdom and experience dispensed by Anne Canteaut, Itai Dinur, Bart Preneel, and François-Xavier Standaert are also noteworthy and helped usher the conference into a safe haven. Finally, we wish to thank the area chairs—Sonia Belaïd, Carmit Hazay, Thomas Peyrin, Nigel Smart, and Martijn Stam. You made our work manageable.

Finally, we thank all the people who were involved in the program of Eurocrypt 2022: the rump session chairs, the session chairs, the speakers, and all the technical support staff in Trondheim. We would also like to mention the various sponsors and thank them for the generous support. We wish to thank the continuous support of the Cryptography Research Fund for supporting student speakers.

May 2022

Orr Dunkelman
Stefan Dziembowski

Organization

The 41st Annual International Conference on the Theory
and Applications of Cryptographic Techniques (Eurocrypt 2022)

Sponsored by the *International Association for Cryptologic Research*
Trondheim, Norway
May 30 – June 3, 2022

General Chair

Colin Boyd   NTNU, Norway

Program Chairs

Orr Dunkelman   University of Haifa, Israel
Stefan Dziembowski   University of Warsaw, Poland

Program Committee

Masayuki Abe	NTT Laboratories, Japan
Shashank Agrawal	Western Digital Research, USA
Joël Alwen	AWS Wickr, Austria
Marshall Ball	New York University, USA
Gustavo Banegas	Inria and Institut Polytechnique de Paris, France
Paulo Barreto	University of Washington Tacoma, USA
Sonia Belaïd	CryptoExperts, France
Jean-François Biasse	University of South Florida, USA
Begül Bilgin	Rambus Cryptography Research, The Netherlands
Alex Biryukov	University of Luxembourg, Luxembourg
Olivier Blazy	Ecole Polytechnique, France
Billy Bob Brumley	Tampere University, Finland
Chitchanok Chuengsatiansup	University of Adelaide, Australia
Michele Ciampi	University of Edinburgh, UK
Ran Cohen	IDC Herzliya, Israel
Henry Corrigan-Gibbs	Massachusetts Institute of Technology, USA
Cas Cremers	CISPA Helmholtz Center for Information Security, Germany
Dana Dachman-Soled	University of Maryland, USA
Jean Paul Degabriele	TU Darmstadt, Germany
Itai Dinur	Ben-Gurion University, Israel

Meltem Sönmez Turan	National Institute of Standards and Technology, USA
Daniele Venturi	Sapienza University of Rome, Italy
Ivan Visconti	University of Salerno, Italy
Gaoli Wang	East China Normal University, China
Stefan Wolf	University of Italian Switzerland, Switzerland
Sophia Yakoubov	Aarhus University, Denmark
Avishay Yanai	VMware Research, Israel
Bo-Yin Yang	Academia Sinica, Taiwan
Arkady Yerukhimovich	George Washington University, USA
Yu Yu	Shanghai Jiao Tong University, China
Mark Zhandry	NTT Research and Princeton University, USA

Subreviewers

Behzad Abdolmaleki
Ittai Abraham
Damiano Abram
Anasuya Acharya
Alexandre Adomnicai
Amit Agarwal
Shweta Agrawal
Thomas Agrikola
Akshima
Navid Alamati
Alejandro Cabrera Aldaya
Bar Alon
Miguel Ambrona
Hiroaki Anada
Diego F. Aranha
Victor Arribas
Tomer Ashur
Gennaro Avitabile
Matilda Backendal
Saikrishna Badrinarayanan
Shi Bai
Ero Balsa
Augustin Bariant
James Bartusek
Balthazar Bauer
Carsten Baum
Ämin Baumeler
Arthur Beckers
Charles Bédard

Christof Beierle
Pascal Bemmann
Fabrice Benhamouda
Francesco Berti
Tim Beyne
Rishabh Bhadauria
Adithya Bhat
Sai Lakshmi Bhavana Obbattu
Alexander Bienstock
Erica Blum
Jan Bobolz
Xavier Bonnetain
Cecilia Boschini
Raphael Bost
Vincenzo Botta
Katharina Boudgoust
Christina Boura
Zvika Brakerski
Luís Brandão
Lennart Braun
Jacqueline Brendel
Gianluca Brian
Anne Broadbent
Marek Broll
Christopher Brzuska
Chloe Cachet
Matteo Campanelli
Federico Canale
Anne Canteaut

Ignacio Cascudo
Andre Chailloux
Nishanth Chandran
Donghoon Chang
Binyi Chen
Shan Chen
Weikeng Chen
Yilei Chen
Jung Hee Cheon
Jesus-Javier Chi-Dominguez
Seung Geol Choi
Wutichai Chongchitmate
Arka Rai Choudhuri
Sherman S. M. Chow
Jeremy Clark
Xavier Coiteux-Roy
Andrea Coladangelo
Nan Cui
Benjamin R. Curtis
Jan Czajkowski
Jan-Pieter D'Anvers
Hila Dahari
Thinh Dang
Quang Dao
Poulami Das
Pratish Datta
Bernardo David
Gareth T. Davies
Hannah Davis
Lauren De Meyer
Gabrielle De Micheli
Elke De Mulder
Luke Demarest
Julien Devevey
Siemen Dhooghe
Denis Diemert
Jintai Ding
Jack Doerner
Xiaoyang Dong
Nico Döttling
Benjamin Dowling
Yang Du
Leo Ducas
Julien Duman
Betul Durak

Oğuzhan Ersoy
Andreas Erwig
Daniel Escudero
Muhammed F. Esgin
Saba Eskandarian
Prastudy Fauzi
Patrick Felke
Thibauld Feneuil
Peter Fenteany
Diodato Ferraioli
Marc Fischlin
Nils Fleischhacker
Cody Freitag
Daniele Friolo
Tommaso Gagliardoni
Steven D. Galbraith
Pierre Galissant
Chaya Ganesh
Cesar Pereida García
Romain Gay
Kai Gellert
Craig Gentry
Marilyn George
Hossein Ghodosi
Satrajit Ghosh
Jan Gilcher
Aarushi Goel
Eli Goldin
Junqing Gong
Dov Gordon
Jérôme Govinden
Lorenzo Grassi
Johann Großschädl
Jiaxin Guan
Daniel Guenther
Milos Gujic
Qian Guo
Cyril Guyot
Mohammad Hajiabadi
Ariel Hamlin
Shuai Han
Abida Haque
Patrick Harasser
Dominik Hartmann
Phil Hebborn

Alexandra Henzinger
Javier Herranz
Julia Hesse
Justin Holmgren
Akinori Hosoyamada
Kai Hu
Andreas Hülsing
Shih-Han Hung
Vincenzo Iovino
Joseph Jaeger
Aayush Jain
Christian Janson
Samuel Jaques
Stanislaw Jarecki
Corentin Jeudy
Zhengzhong Jin
Daniel Jost
Saqib Kakvi
Vukašin Karadžić
Angshuman Karmakar
Shuichi Katsumata
Jonathan Katz
Mahimna Kelkar
Nathan Keller
John Kelsey
Mustafa Khairallah
Hamidreza Amini Khorasgani
Dongwoo Kim
Miran Kim
Elena Kirshanova
Fuyuki Kitagawa
Michael Klooß
Sebastian Kolby
Lukas Kölsch
Yashvanth Kondi
David Kretzler
Veronika Kuchta
Marie-Sarah Lacharité
Yi-Fu Lai
Baptiste Lambin
Mario Larangeira
Rio LaVigne
Quoc-Huy Le
Jooyoung Lee
Julia Len

Antonin Leroux
Hanjun Li
Jianwei Li
Yiming Li
Xiao Liang
Damien Ligier
Chengyu Lin
Dongxi Liu
Jiahui Liu
Linsheng Liu
Qipeng Liu
Xiangyu Liu
Chen-Da Liu Zhang
Julian Loss
Vadim Lyubashevsky
Lin Lyu
You Lyu
Fermi Ma
Varun Madathil
Akash Madhusudan
Bernardo Magri
Monosij Maitra
Nikolaos Makriyannis
Mary Maller
Giorgia Marson
Christian Matt
Noam Mazor
Nikolas Melissaris
Bart Mennink
Antonis Michalas
Brice Minaud
Kazuhiko Minematsu
Alberto Montina
Amir Moradi
Marta Mularczyk
Varun Narayanan
Jade Nardi
Patrick Neumann
Ruth Ng
Hai H. Nguyen
Kirill Nikitin
Ryo Nishimaki
Anca Nitulescu
Ariel Nof
Julian Nowakowski

Adam O'Neill
Maciej Obremski
Eran Omri
Maximilian Orlt
Bijeeta Pal
Jiaxin Pan
Omer Paneth
Lorenz Panny
Dimitrios Papadopoulos
Jeongeun Park
Anat Paskin-Cherniavsky
Sikhar Patranabis
Marcin Pawłowski
Hilder Pereira
Ray Perlner
Clara Pernot
Léo Perrin
Giuseppe Persiano
Edoardo Persichetti
Albrecht Petzoldt
Duong Hieu Phan
Krzysztof Pietrzak
Jeroen Pijnenburg
Rachel Player
Antigoni Polychroniadou
Willy Quach
Anaïs Querol
Srinivasan Raghuraman
Adrián Ranea
Simon Rastikian
Divya Ravi
Francesco Regazzoni
Maryam Rezapour
Mir Ali Rezazadeh Baee
Siavash Riahi
Joao Ribeiro
Vincent Rijmen
Bhaskar Roberts
Francisco Rodriguez-Henríquez
Paul Rösler
Arnab Roy
Iftekhar Salam
Paolo Santini
Roozbeh Sarenche
Yu Sasaki

Matteo Scarlata
Tobias Schmalz
Mahdi Sedaghat
Vladimir Sedlacek
Nicolas Sendrier
Jae Hong Seo
Srinath Setty
Yaobin Shen
Sina Shiehian
Omri Shmueli
Janno Siim
Jad Silbak
Leonie Simpson
Rohit Sinha
Daniel Slamanig
Fang Song
Yongsoo Song
Damien Stehle
Ron Steinfeld
Noah Stephens-Davidowitz
Christoph Striecks
Fatih Sulak
Chao Sun
Ling Sun
Siwei Sun
Koutarou Suzuki
Katsuyuki Takashima
Hervé Tale Kalachi
Quan Quan Tan
Yi Tang
Je Sen Teh
Cihangir Tezcan
Aishwarya Thiruvengadam
Orfeas Thyfronitis
Mehdi Tibouchi
Ni Trieu
Yiannis Tselekounis
Michael Tunstall
Nicola Tuveri
Nirvan Tyagi
Sohaib ul Hassan
Wessel van Woerden
Kerem Varc
Prashant Vasudevan
Damien Vergnaud

Contents – Part III

Post-Quantum Cryptography

Information-Theoretic Security

Symmetric-Key Cryptanalysis

Key Guessing Strategies for Linear Key-Schedule Algorithms in Rectangle Attacks

Xiaoyang Dong[1], Lingyue Qin[1(✉)], Siwei Sun[2,3], and Xiaoyun Wang[1,4,5]

[1] Institute for Advanced Study, BNRist, Tsinghua University, Beijing, China
{xiaoyangdong,qinly,xiaoyunwang}@tsinghua.edu.cn
[2] School of Cryptology, University of Chinese Academy of Sciences, Beijing, China
[3] State Key Laboratory of Cryptology, Beijing, China
sunsiwei@ucas.ac.cn
[4] Key Laboratory of Cryptologic Technology and Information Security,
Ministry of Education, Shandong University, Jinan, China
[5] School of Cyber Science and Technology, Shandong University, Qingdao, China

Abstract. When generating quartets for the rectangle attacks on ciphers with linear key-schedule, we find the right quartets which may suggest key candidates have to satisfy some nonlinear relations. However, some quartets generated always violate these relations, so that they will never suggest any key candidates. Inspired by previous rectangle frameworks, we find that guessing certain key cells before generating quartets may reduce the number of invalid quartets. However, guessing a lot of key cells at once may lose the benefit from the early abort technique, which may lead to a higher overall complexity. To get better tradeoff, we build a new rectangle framework on ciphers with linear key-schedule with the purpose of reducing overall complexity or attacking more rounds.

In the tradeoff model, there are many parameters affecting the overall complexity, especially for the choices of the number and positions of key guessing cells before generating quartets. To identify optimal parameters, we build a uniform automatic tool on SKINNY as an example, which includes the optimal rectangle distinguishers for key-recovery phase, the number and positions of key guessing cells before generating quartets, the size of key counters to build that affecting the exhaustive search step, etc. Based on the automatic tool, we identify a 32-round key-recovery attack on SKINNY-128-384 in the related-key setting, which extends the best previous attack by 2 rounds. For other versions with n-$2n$ or n-$3n$, we also achieve one more round than before. In addition, using the previous rectangle distinguishers, we achieve better attacks on round-reduced ForkSkinny, Deoxys-BC-384 and GIFT-64. At last, we discuss the conversion of our rectangle framework from related-key setting into single-key setting and give new single-key rectangle attack on 10-round Serpent.

Keywords: Rectangle · Automated Key-recovery · SKINNY · ForkSkinny · Deoxys-BC · GIFT

The full version of the paper is available at https://ia.cr/2021/856.

O. Dunkelman and S. Dziembowski (Eds.): EUROCRYPT 2022, LNCS 13277, pp. 3–33, 2022.
https://doi.org/10.1007/978-3-031-07082-2_1

1   Introduction

The boomerang attack [60] proposed by Wagner, is an adaptive chosen plaintext and ciphertext attack derived from differential cryptanalysis [15]. Wagner constructed the boomerang distinguisher on E_d by splitting the encryption function into two parts $E_d = E_1 \circ E_0$ as shown in Fig. 1, where two differentials $\alpha \xrightarrow{E_0} \beta$ with probability p and $\gamma \xrightarrow{E_1} \delta$ with probability q are combined into a boomerang distinguisher. The probability of a boomerang distinguisher is estimated by:

$$Pr[E_d^{-1}(E(x) \oplus \delta) \oplus E_d^{-1}(E(x \oplus \alpha) \oplus \delta) = \alpha] = p^2 q^2. \tag{1}$$

The adaptive chosen plaintext and ciphertext of boomerang attack can be converted into a chosen-plaintext attack that is known as amplified boomerang attack [45] or rectangle attack [13]. In rectangle attack, only α and δ are fixed and the internal differences β and γ can be arbitrary values as long as $\beta \neq \gamma$. Hence, the probability would be increased to $2^{-n}\hat{p}^2\hat{q}^2$, where

$$\hat{p} = \sqrt{\sum\nolimits_{\beta_i} Pr^2(\alpha \to \beta_i)} \ \text{ and } \ \hat{q} = \sqrt{\sum\nolimits_{\gamma_j} Pr^2(\gamma_j \to \delta)}. \tag{2}$$

The boomerang attack and rectangle attack have been successfully applied to numerous block ciphers, including Serpent [12,13], AES [14,18], IDEA [11], KASUMI [38], Deoxys-BC [29], etc. Recently, a new variant of boomerang attack was developed and applied to AES, named as retracing boomerang attack [35]. There are two steps when applying the boomerang and rectangle attack, i.e., building distinguishers and performing key-recovery attacks. In building distinguishers, Murphy [51] pointed out that two independently chosen differentials for the boomerang can be incompatible. He also showed that the dependence between two differentials of the boomerang may lead to larger probability, which is also discovered by Biryukov et al. [16]. To further explore the dependence and increase the probability of boomerang, Biryukov and Khovratovich [18] introduced the *boomerang switch* technique including the *ladder switch* and *S-box switch*. Then, those techniques were generalized and formalized by Dunkelman et al. [37,38] as the *sandwich attack*. Recently, Cid et al. [28] introduced the boomerang connectivity table (BCT) to clarify the probability around the boundary of boomerang and compute more accurately. Later, various improvements or further studies [5,21–23,30,57,61] on BCT technique enriched boomerang attacks.

Given a distinguisher, we usually need more complicated key-recovery algorithms to identify the right quartets [13,45] when performing rectangle attack than boomerang attack. Till now, a series of generalized key-recovery algorithms [12–14] for the rectangle attacks are introduced. In this paper, we focus on further exploration on the generalized rectangle attacks. Undoubtedly, generalizing the attack algorithms is very important in the development of cryptanalytic tools, such as the generalizations of the impossible differential attacks [24,25], linear attacks [39], invariant attacks [9], meet-in-the-middle attacks [27,32], etc.

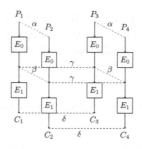

Fig. 1. Boomerang attack.

Our Contributions. When performing the rectangle attacks, we usually add several rounds before and after the rectangle distinguisher. Then, the input and output differences (α, δ) of the rectangle distinguisher propagate to certain truncated form (α', δ') in the plaintext and ciphertext. Similar with the differential attack, in rectangle attack we first collect data and generate quartets whose plaintext difference and ciphertext difference meet (α', δ'). Then the early-abort technique [49] is applied to determine key candidates for each quartet. However, for ciphers with linear key schedule, we find that many quartets meet (α', δ') never suggest any key candidates. In further study, we find the right quartets that suggest key candidates have to meet certain nonlinear relations. However, many quartets meeting (α', δ') always violate those nonlinear relations for all the key guessing, and thereby never suggest any key candidates. This feature is peculiar for rectangle attack on ciphers with linear key schedule, and it rarely appears in other differential-like attack.

Inspired from the previous rectangle attacks [12,13,62], we find that guessing certain key cells before generating quartets may avoid many invalid quartets in advance. However, guessing a lot of key cells as a whole may lose the advantage of early-abort technique [49], which may lead to higher complexity. In addition, we have to take the exhaustive search step into consideration. Hence, to get a tradeoff between so many factors affecting the complexity, we introduce a new generalized rectangle attack framework on ciphers with linear key schedule.

When evaluating dedicated cipher with the tradeoff framework, we have to identify many attack parameters, such as finding an optimal rectangle distinguisher for our new key-recovery attack framework, determining the number and positions of guessed key cells before generating quartets, as well as the size of key counters, etc. Hence, in order to launch the optimal key-recovery attacks with our tradeoff model, we build a uniform automatic tool for SKINNY as an example, which is based on a series of automatic tools [30,41,52] on SKINNY proposed recently, to determine a set of optimal parameters affecting the attack complexity or the number of attacked rounds. Note that in the field of automatic cryptanalysis, there are many works focusing on searching for distinguishers [17,19,20,46,50,54,59], but only a few works [31,52,56] deal with the uniform automatic models that take the distinguisher and key-recovery as a whole optimization model. Thanks to our uniform automatic model, we identify a 32-round key-recovery attack on SKINNY-128-384, which attacks two more rounds than the best previous attacks [41,52]. In addition, for other versions of SKINNY with n-$2n$ or n-$3n$, one more round is achieved.

Table 1. Summary of the cryptanalytic results.

SKINNY							
Version	Rounds	Data	Time	Memory	Approach	Setting	Ref.
	22	$2^{63.5}$	$2^{110.9}$	$2^{63.5}$	Rectangle	RK	[47]
	23	$2^{62.47}$	$2^{125.91}$	2^{124}	ID	RK	[47]
	23	$2^{62.47}$	2^{124}	$2^{77.47}$	ID	RK	[53]
64-128	23	$2^{71.4}$	2^{79}	$2^{64.0}$	ID	RK	[3]
	23	$2^{60.54}$	$2^{120.7}$	$2^{60.9}$	Rectangle	RK	[41]
	24	$2^{61.67}$	$2^{96.83}$	2^{84}	Rectangle	RK	[52]
	25	$2^{61.67}$	$2^{118.43}$	$2^{64.26}$	Rectangle	RK	Full Ver. [33]
	27	$2^{63.5}$	$2^{165.5}$	2^{80}	Rectangle	RK	[47]
64-192	29	$2^{62.92}$	$2^{181.7}$	2^{80}	Rectangle	RK	[41]
	30	$2^{62.87}$	$2^{163.11}$	$2^{68.05}$	Rectangle	RK	[52]
	31	$2^{62.78}$	$2^{182.07}$	$2^{62.79}$	Rectangle	RK	Full Ver. [33]
	22	2^{127}	$2^{235.6}$	2^{127}	Rectangle	RK	[47]
	23	$2^{124.47}$	$2^{251.47}$	2^{248}	ID	RK	[47]
	23	$2^{124.41}$	$2^{243.41}$	$2^{155.41}$	ID	RK	[53]
128-256	24	$2^{125.21}$	$2^{209.85}$	$2^{125.54}$	Rectangle	RK	[41]
	25	$2^{124.48}$	$2^{226.38}$	2^{168}	Rectangle	RK	[52]
	25	$2^{120.25}$	$2^{193.91}$	2^{136}	Rectangle	RK	Full Ver. [33]
	26	$2^{126.53}$	$2^{254.4}$	$2^{128.44}$	Rectangle	RK	Full Ver. [33]
	27	2^{123}	2^{331}	2^{155}	Rectangle	RK	[47]
	28	2^{122}	$2^{315.25}$	$2^{122.32}$	Rectangle	RK	[64]
128-384	30	$2^{125.29}$	$2^{361.68}$	$2^{125.8}$	Rectangle	RK	[41]
	30	2^{122}	$2^{341.11}$	$2^{128.02}$	Rectangle	RK	[52]
	32	$2^{123.54}$	$2^{354.99}$	$2^{123.54}$	Rectangle	RK	Sect. 5.1
ForkSkinny							
	26	2^{125}	$2^{254.6}$	2^{160}	ID	RK	[6]
128-256	26	2^{127}	$2^{250.3}$	2^{160}	ID	RK	[6]
(256-bit key)	28	$2^{118.88}$	$2^{246.98}$	2^{136}	Rectangle	RK	[52]
	28	$2^{118.88}$	$2^{224.76}$	$2^{118.88}$	Rectangle	RK	Full Ver. [33]
Deoxys-BC							
	13	2^{127}	2^{270}	2^{144}	Rectangle	RK	[29]
128-384	14	2^{127}	$2^{286.2}$	2^{136}	Rectangle	RK	[62]
	14	$2^{125.2}$	$2^{282.7}$	2^{136}	Rectangle	RK	[63]
	14	$2^{125.2}$	2^{260}	2^{140}	Rectangle	RK	Full Ver. [33]
GIFT							
	25	$2^{63.78}$	$2^{120.92}$	$2^{64.1}$	Rectangle	RK	[44]
64-128	26	$2^{60.96}$	$2^{123.23}$	$2^{102.86}$	Differential	RK	[58]
	26	$2^{63.78}$	$2^{122.78}$	$2^{63.78}$	Rectangle	RK	Full Ver. [33]

As the second application, we perform our new key-recovery framework on round-reduced ForkSkinny [1,2], Deoxys-BC-384 [43] and GIFT-64 [4] with some previous proposed distinguishers. All the attacks achieve better complexities than before, which also proves the efficiency of our tradeoff model. At last, we discuss the conversion of our attack framework from related-key setting to single-key setting. Since our related-key attack framework is on ciphers with linear key-schedule, it is trivial to convert it into a single-key attack by assigning the key difference as zero. We then apply the new single-key framework to the 10-round Serpent[1] and achieve better complexity than the previous rectangle attack [12]. We summarize our main results in Table 1.

2 Generalized Key-Recovery Algorithms for the Rectangle Attacks

There have been several key-recovery frameworks of rectangle attacks [12–14] introduced before. We briefly recall them with the symbols from [12]. Let E be a cipher which is described as a cascade $E = E_f \circ E_d \circ E_b$ as shown in Fig. 2. The probability of the N_d-round rectangle distinguisher on E_d is given by Eq. (2). E_d is surrounded by the N_b-round E_b and N_f-round E_f. Then the difference α of the distinguisher propagates to a truncated differential form denoted as α' by E_b^{-1}, and δ propagates to δ' by E_f. Denote the number of active bits of the plaintext and ciphertext as r_b and r_f. Denote the subset of subkey bits which is involved in E_b as k_b, which affects the difference of the plaintexts by decrypting the pairs of internal states with difference α. Then denote $m_b = |k_b|$. Let k_f be the subset of subkey bits involved in E_f and $m_f = |k_f|$.

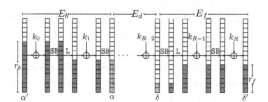

Fig. 2. Framework of rectangle attack on E.

Related-key boomerang and rectangle attacks were proposed by Biham *et al.* in [14]. Assuming one has a related-key differential $\alpha \rightarrow \beta$ over E_0 under a key difference ΔK with probability $\hat{p}$ and another related-key differential $\gamma \rightarrow \delta$ over E_1 under a key difference ∇K with probability $\hat{q}$. If the master key K_1 is known, the other three keys are all determined, where $K_2 = K_1 \oplus \Delta K, K_3 = K_1 \oplus \nabla K$ and $K_4 = K_1 \oplus \Delta K \oplus \nabla K$. A typical example of the successful application of the boomerang attack is the best known related-key attack on the full versions of AES-192 and AES-256, presented by Biryukov and Khovratovich [18].

---

[1] The example attack only wants to prove the efficiency of our model in single-key setting. There are better attacks on Serpent achieved by differential-linear cryptanalysis [34,48].

As shown by Biham, Dunkelman and Keller [11], when the key schedule is linear, the related-key rectangle attack is similar to the single-key rectangle framework. Different from non-linear key schedule, the differences between the subkeys of K_1, K_2, K_3 and K_4 are all determined in each round for linear key schedule. Hence, if we guess parts of the subkeys of K_1, all the corresponding parts of subkeys of K_2, K_3 and K_4 are determined by xoring the differences between the subkeys. In this paper, we focus on the rectangle attacks on ciphers with linear key schedule and list the previous frameworks below. In addition, we give a comparison of different frameworks in Sect. 3.2 and Sect. 6.

2.1 Attack I: Biham-Dunkelman-Keller's Attack

At EUROCRYPT 2001, Biham, Dunkelman and Keller introduced the rectangle attack [13] and applied it to the single-key attack on Serpent [10]. We trivially convert it to a related-key model with linear key schedule:

1. Create and store y structures of 2^{r_b} plaintexts each, and query the 2^{r_b} plaintexts under K_1, K_2, K_3 and K_4 for each structure.
2. Initialize the key counters for the $(m_b + m_f)$-bit subkey involved in E_b and E_f. For each $(m_b + m_f)$-bit subkey, do:
   (a) Partially encrypt plaintext P_1 under K_1 to the position of α by the guessed m_b-bit subkey, and partially decrypt it with K_2 to get the plaintext P_2 within the same structure after xoring the known difference α.
   (b) With m_f-bit subkey, decrypt C_1 to the position of δ of the rectangle distinguisher and encrypt it to the ciphertext C_3 after xoring δ. Similarly, we find C_4 from C_2 and generate the quartet (C_1, C_2, C_3, C_4).
   (c) Check whether ciphertexts (C_3, C_4) exist in our data. If these ciphertexts exist, we partially encrypt corresponding plaintexts (P_3, P_4) under E_b with m_b-bit subkey, and check whether the difference is α. If so, increase the corresponding counter by 1.

Complexity. Choosing
$$y = \sqrt{s} \cdot 2^{n/2-r_b}/\hat{p}\hat{q}, \tag{3}$$
we get about $(y \cdot 2^{2r_b})^2 \cdot 2^{-2r_b} \cdot 2^{-n}\hat{p}^2\hat{q}^2 = s$, where s is the expected number of right quartets. Therefore, the total data complexity for the 4 oracles with K_1, K_2, K_3 and K_4 is
$$4y \cdot 2^{r_b} = \sqrt{s} \cdot 2^{n/2+2}/\hat{p}\hat{q}. \tag{4}$$
In Step 2, the time complexity is about $2^{m_b+m_f} \cdot 4y \cdot 2^{r_b} = 2^{m_b+m_f} \cdot \sqrt{s} \cdot 2^{n/2+2}/\hat{p}\hat{q}$. The memory complexity is $4y \cdot 2^{r_b} + 2^{m_b+m_f}$ to store the data and key counters.

2.2 Attack II: Biham-Dunkelman-Keller's Attack

At FSE 2002, Biham, Dunkelman and Keller introduced a more generic algorithm to perform the rectangle attack [12] in the single-key setting. Later, Liu *et al.* [47] converted the model into related-key setting for ciphers with linear key schedule. The high-level strategy of this model is to generate quartets by birthday paradox without key guessing, whose plaintexts and ciphertexts meet the truncated difference α' and δ', respectively. Then, recover the key candidates for each quartet. The steps are:

1. Create and store y structures of 2^{r_b} plaintexts each, and query the 2^{r_b} plaintexts under K_1, K_2, K_3 and K_4 for each structure.
2. Initialize an array of $2^{m_b+m_f}$ counters, where each corresponds to an $(m_b + m_f)$-bit subkey guess.
3. Insert the 2^{r_b} ciphertexts into a hash table H indexed by the $n - r_f$ inactive ciphertext bits. For each index, there are $2^{r_b} \cdot 2^{r_f-n}$ plaintexts and corresponding ciphertexts for each structure, which collide in the $n - r_f$ bits.
4. In each structure S, we search for a ciphertext pair (C_1, C_2), and choose a ciphertext C_3 by the $n - r_f$ inactive ciphertext bits of C_1 from hash table H. Choose a ciphertext C_4 indexed by the $n - r_f$ inactive ciphertext bits of C_2 from hash table H, where the corresponding plaintexts P_4 and P_3 are in the same structure. Then we obtain a quartet (P_1, P_2, P_3, P_4) and corresponding ciphertexts (C_1, C_2, C_3, C_4).
5. For the quartets obtained above, determine the key candidates involved in E_b and E_f using hash tables and increase the corresponding counters.

Complexity. The data complexity is the same as Eq. (4) given at `Attack I`, with the same y given by Eq. (3).

▶ **Time I**: The time complexity to generate quartets in Step 3 and 4 is about $y^2 \cdot 2^{2r_b} \cdot 2^{r_f-n} + (y \cdot 2^{2r_b+r_f-n})^2 = s \cdot 2^{r_f}/\hat{p}^2\hat{q}^2 + s \cdot 2^{2r_b+2r_f-n}/\hat{p}^2\hat{q}^2$ and $y^2 \cdot 2^{4r_b+2r_f-2n} = s \cdot 2^{2r_b+2r_f-n}/\hat{p}^2\hat{q}^2$ quartets remain.

▶ **Time II**: The time complexity to deduce the right subkey and generate the counters in Step 5 is $y^2 \cdot 2^{4r_b+2r_f-2n} \cdot (2^{m_b-r_b} + 2^{m_f-r_f}) = s \cdot 2^{r_b+r_f-n} \cdot (2^{m_b+r_f} + 2^{m_f+r_b})/\hat{p}^2\hat{q}^2$.

2.3 Attack III: Zhao *et al.*'s Related-Key Attack

For block ciphers with linear key-schedule, Zhao *et al.* [62,64] proposed a new generalized related-key rectangle attack as shown below:

1. Construct y structures of 2^{r_b} plaintexts each. For each structure, query the 2^{r_b} plaintexts under K_1, K_2, K_3 and K_4.
2. Guess the m_b-bit subkey involved in E_b:
   (a) Initialize a list of 2^{m_f} counters.
   (b) Partially encrypt plaintext P_1 with K_1 to obtain the intermediate values at the position of α, and xor the known difference α, and then partially decrypt it to the plaintext P_2 under K_2 within the same structure. Construct the set S_1 and also S_2 in similar way:

$$S_1 = \{(P_1, C_1, P_2, C_2) : E_{b_{K_1}}(P_1) \oplus E_{b_{K_2}}(P_2) = \alpha\},$$
$$S_2 = \{(P_3, C_3, P_4, C_4) : E_{b_{K_3}}(P_3) \oplus E_{b_{K_4}}(P_4) = \alpha\}.$$

(c) The size of S_1 and S_2 is $y \cdot 2^{r_b}$. Insert S_1 into a hash table H_1 indexed by the $n - r_f$ inactive bits of C_1 and $n - r_f$ inactive bits of C_2. Similarly build H_2. Under the same $2(n - r_f)$-bit index, randomly choose (C_1, C_2) from H_1 and (C_3, C_4) from H_2 to construct the quartet (C_1, C_2, C_3, C_4).

(d) We use all the quartets obtained above to determine the key candidates involved in E_f and increase the corresponding counters. This phase is a guess and filter procedure, whose time complexity is denoted as ε.

Complexity. The data complexity is the same as Eq. (4) given by Attack I, with the same y given by Eq. (3).

▶ **Time I**: The time complexity to generate S_1 and S_2 is about $2^{m_b} \cdot y \cdot 2^{r_b}$.

▶ **Time II**: We generate $2^{m_b} \cdot (y2^{r_b})^2 \cdot 2^{-2(n-r_f)} = 2^{m_b} \cdot y^2 \cdot 2^{2r_b - 2(n-r_f)} = s \cdot 2^{m_b - n + 2r_f}/\hat{p}^2\hat{q}^2$ quartets from Step 2(c). The time to generate the key counters is $(s \cdot 2^{m_b - n + 2r_f}/\hat{p}^2\hat{q}^2) \cdot \varepsilon$.

3   Key-Guessing Strategies in the Rectangle Attack

Suppose Fig. 2 shows a framework for differential attack, then E_d is a differential trail $\alpha \mapsto \delta$. In the differential attack, we collect plaintext-ciphertext pairs by traversing the r_b active bits of plaintext to construct a structure. Store the structure indexed by the $n - r_f$ inactive bits of ciphertext in a hash table H. Thereafter, we generate (P_1, C_1, P_2, C_2) by randomly picking (P_1, C_1) and (P_2, C_2) from H within the same index. For each structure, with the birthday paradox, we expect to get $2^{2r_b - 1 - (n - r_f)}$ plaintext pairs, and the differences of plaintexts and ciphertexts in each pair conform to the truncated form α' and δ', respectively. Using the property of truncated differential of the ciphertext to filter wrong pairs in advance due to the birthday paradox is an efficient and generic way in differential attack and its variants, such as impossible differential attack, truncated differential attack, boomerang attack, rectangle attack, etc.

In Attack II of the rectangle attack, Biham, Dunkelman and Keller [12] also generated the quartets using birthday paradox. For each quartet (P_1, P_2, P_3, P_4), the plaintexts and ciphertexts also conform to the truncated forms $(\alpha', \delta'$ in Fig. 2), i.e., $P_1 \oplus P_2$ and $P_3 \oplus P_4$ are of truncated form α', $C_1 \oplus C_3$ and $C_2 \oplus C_4$ are of truncated form δ'. However, when deducing key candidates for each of the generated quartets, we find that the rectangle attack enjoys a very big filter ratio. In other words, the ratio of right quartets which satisfy the input and output differences of the rectangle distinguisher (α, δ in Fig. 2) and suggest key candidates is very small, when compared to the number of the quartets that satisfy the truncated differential (α', δ') in the plaintext and ciphertext.

For the differential attack, given a pair conforming to (α', δ'), it will suggest $2^{m_b + m_f - (r_b + r_f)}$ key candidates. However, for the rectangle attack, given a quartet conforming to (α', δ'), it will suggest $2^{m_b + m_f - 2(r_b + r_f)}$ key candidates due to the filter in both sides of the boomerang. Hence, if $2(r_b + r_f)$ is bigger than $m_b + m_f$, some quartets conforming to (α', δ') may never suggest key candidates.

Here is an example of E_b part in Fig. 3. Since we are considering linear key schedule, we have $k_{2b} = k_{1b} \oplus \Delta$, $k_{3b} = k_{1b} \oplus \nabla$ and $k_{4b} = k_{1b} \oplus \Delta \oplus \nabla$ with fixed (Δ, ∇). Hence, when k_{1b} is known, all other k_{2b}, k_{3b} and k_{4b} are determined. Let S be an Sbox. Then we have

$$S(k_{1b} \oplus P_1) \oplus S(k_{2b} \oplus P_2) = \alpha, \tag{5}$$
$$S(k_{3b} \oplus P_3) \oplus S(k_{4b} \oplus P_4) = \alpha. \tag{6}$$

For a quartet (P_1, P_2, P_3, P_4), when (P_1, P_2) is known, together with $k_{1b} \oplus k_{2b} = \Delta$, we can determine a value for k_{1b} and k_{2b} by Eq. (5). Then k_{3b}, k_{4b} are determined. Hence, by Eq. (6), P_4 is determined by P_3. Hence, P_4 is fully determined by (P_1, P_2, P_3) within a *good* quartet, which may suggest a key. For certain quartets, (P_1, P_2, P_3, P_4) may violate the nonlinear relations (e.g., Eq. (5) and (6)), so that it will never suggest a key.

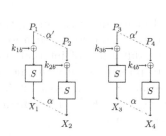

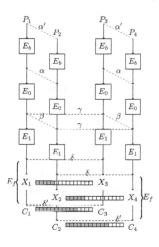

Fig. 3. Nonlinear relations in key-recovery phase.

Fig. 4. Filter with internal state.

According to the analysis of `Attack I` and `Attack III` in Sect. 2, both of them guess (part of) key bits before generating the quartets, i.e., $(m_b + m_f)$-bit and m_b-bit key are guessed in `Attack I` and `Attack III`, respectively. For example in Fig. 3, if we guess k_{1b} in E_b, we can deduce k_{2b}, k_{3b}, k_{4b}. Then, for given P_1 and P_3, we compute P_2 and P_4 with Eq. (5) and (6), respectively. Thereafter, a quartet (P_1, P_2, P_3, P_4) is generated under guessed key k_{1b}, which meets the input difference α. In this way, we can avoid some invalid quartets that never suggest a key in advance.

However, if we guess all the key bits (k_b in E_b and k_f in E_f) at once and then construct quartets as `Attack I`, we may lose the benefit from the early abort technique [49], which tests the key candidates step by step, by reducing the size of the remaining possible quartets at each time, without (significantly) increasing the time complexity. Guessing a lot of key bits at once may reduce the number of invalid quartets, but may also lead to higher overall complexity. To get a better tradeoff, we try to guess all k_b and part of k_f, denoted as k'_f whose size is m'_f. With partial decryption, we may gain more inactive bits (or bits with fixed differences) from the internal state as shown in Fig. 4.

3.1 New Related-Key Rectangle Attack with Linear Key Schedule

With the above analysis, we derive a new tradeoff of the rectangle attack framework with linear key schedule, which tries to obtain better attacks by the overall consideration on various factors affecting the complexity and the number of attacked rounds. We list our tradeoff model in Algorithm 1. Before diving into it, we give Fig. 5 to illustrate which key to guess.

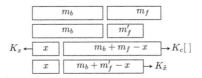

Fig. 5. The guessed key in Algorithm 1

Totally, m_b-bit k_b and m_f-bit k_f are involved in E_b and E_f. Among them, we first guess m_b-bit k_b and m'_f-bit k'_f before generating quartets. Then we use both the inactive bits of the ciphertexts and the difference of internal states computed by k'_f to act as early filters. In order to possibly reduce the memory cost of key counters, we introduce an auxiliary variable x and guess x-bit K_x in Line 3 before initializing the $(m_b + m_f - x)$-bit key counter $K_c[\ ]$. The remaining $(m_b + m'_f - x)$-bit $K_{\tilde{x}}$ is guessed in Line 5 of Algorithm 1.

Complexity. Choosing
$$y = \sqrt{s} \cdot 2^{n/2 - r_b} / \hat{p}\hat{q}, \tag{7}$$
we get about $(y \cdot 2^{2r_b})^2 \cdot 2^{-2r_b} \cdot 2^{-n}\hat{p}^2\hat{q}^2 = s$, where s is the expected number of right quartets. Therefore, the total data complexity for the 4 oracles with K_1, K_2, K_3 and K_4 is
$$4y \cdot 2^{r_b} = \sqrt{s} \cdot 2^{n/2 + 2} / \hat{p}\hat{q}. \tag{8}$$

▶ **Time I (T_1):** In Line 7 to 26 of Algorithm 1, the time complexity is about
$$T_1 = 2^{x + m_b + m'_f - x} \cdot y \cdot 2^{r_b} \cdot 2 = \sqrt{s} \cdot 2^{m_b + m'_f + n/2 + 1} / \hat{p}\hat{q}. \tag{9}$$

▶ **Time II (T_2):** In Line 29, we generate about
$$2^{x + m_b + m'_f - x} \cdot y^2 \cdot 2^{2r_b - 2(n - r_f) - 2h_f} = s \cdot 2^{m_b + m'_f - n + 2r_f - 2h_f} / \hat{p}^2\hat{q}^2 \tag{10}$$
quartets. The time complexity of Line 32 to generate the key counters is
$$T_2 = (s \cdot 2^{m_b + m'_f - n + 2r_f - 2h_f} / \hat{p}^2\hat{q}^2) \cdot \varepsilon. \tag{11}$$

Algorithm 1: Related-key rectangle attack with linear key schedule (Attack IV)

---

1 Construct y structures of 2^{r_b} plaintexts each

2 For structure i $(1 \le i \le y)$, query the 2^{r_b} plaintexts by encryption under K_1, K_2, K_3 and K_4 and store them in $L_1[i]$, $L_2[i]$, $L_3[i]$ and $L_4[i]$

3 **for** *each of the x-bit key K_x, which is a part of $(m_b + m'_f)$-bit K_1* **do**

4 $\quad$ $K_c \leftarrow [\,]$ $\quad$ /* Key counters of size $2^{m_b+m_f-x}$ $\quad$ */

5 $\quad$ **for** *each of $(m_b + m'_f - x)$-bit $K_{\tilde{x}}$ of K_1 involved in E_b and E_f* **do**

6 $\quad\quad$ $S_1 \leftarrow [\,]$, $S_2 \leftarrow [\,]$

7 $\quad\quad$ **for** *i from 1 to y* **do**

8 $\quad\quad\quad$ **for** $(P_1, C_1) \in L_1[i]$ **do**

9 $\quad\quad\quad\quad$ /* Partially encrypt P_1 to α under guessed K_1 and partially decrypt to get the plaintext $P_2 \in L_2[i]$ $\quad$ */

10 $\quad\quad\quad\quad$ $P_2 = E_{b_{K_1 \oplus \Delta K}}^{-1}(E_{b_{K_1}}(P_1) \oplus \alpha)$

11 $\quad\quad\quad\quad$ $S_1 \leftarrow (P_1, C_1, P_2, C_2)$

12 $\quad\quad\quad$ **end**

13 $\quad\quad\quad$ **for** $(P_3, C_3) \in L_3[i]$ **do**

14 $\quad\quad\quad\quad$ $P_4 = E_{b_{K_1 \oplus \Delta K \oplus \nabla K}}^{-1}(E_{b_{K_1 \oplus \nabla K}}(P_3) \oplus \alpha)$

15 $\quad\quad\quad\quad$ $S_2 \leftarrow (P_3, C_3, P_4, C_4)$

16 $\quad\quad\quad$ **end**

17 $\quad\quad$ **end**

18 $\quad\quad$ /* $S_1 = \{(P_1,C_1,P_2,C_2) : (P_1,C_1) \in L_1, (P_2,C_2) \in L_2, E_{b_{K_1}}(P_1) \oplus E_{b_{K_2}}(P_2) = \alpha\}$
$\quad\quad$ $S_2 = \{(P_3,C_3,P_4,C_4) : (P_3,C_3) \in L_3, (P_4,C_4) \in L_4, E_{b_{K_3}}(P_3) \oplus E_{b_{K_4}}(P_4) = \alpha\}$ $\quad$ */

19 $\quad\quad$ $H \leftarrow [\,]$

20 $\quad\quad$ **for** $(P_1, C_1, P_2, C_2) \in S_1$ **do**

21 $\quad\quad\quad$ /* Assuming the first h_f-bit internal states of X_1 and X_2 are derived by decrypting (C_1, C_2) with k'_f $\quad$ */

22 $\quad\quad\quad$ $X_1[1, \cdots, h_f] = E_{f_{K_1}}^{-1}(C_1)$, $X_2[1, \cdots, h_f] = F_{f_{K_1 \oplus \Delta K}}^{-1}(C_2)$

23 $\quad\quad\quad$ /* Assume the inactive bits of δ' are first $n - r_f$ bits $\quad$ */

24 $\quad\quad\quad$ $\tau = (X_1[1,\cdots,h_f], X_2[1,\cdots,h_f], C_1[1,\cdots,n-r_f], C_2[1,\cdots,n-r_f])$

25 $\quad\quad\quad$ $H[\tau] \leftarrow (P_1, C_1, P_2, C_2)$

26 $\quad\quad$ **end**

27 $\quad\quad$ **for** $(P_3, C_3, P_4, C_4) \in S_2$ **do**

28 $\quad\quad\quad$ $X_3[1,\cdots,h_f] = E_{f_{K_1 \oplus \nabla K}}^{-1}(C_3)$, $X_4[1,\cdots,h_f] = E_{f_{K_1 \oplus \Delta K \oplus \nabla K}}^{-1}(C_4)$

29 $\quad\quad\quad$ $\tau' = (X_3[1,\cdots,h_f], X_4[1,\cdots,h_f], C_3[1,\cdots,n-r_f], C_4[1,\cdots,n-r_f])$
$\quad\quad\quad$ Access $H[\tau']$ to find (P_1, C_1, P_2, C_2) to generate quartet (C_1, C_2, C_3, C_4).

30 $\quad\quad\quad$ **for** *each generated quartet* **do**

31 $\quad\quad\quad\quad$ Determine the other $(m_f - m'_f)$-bit key k''_f involved in E_f

32 $\quad\quad\quad\quad$ $K_c[K_{\tilde{x}} \| k''_f] \leftarrow K_c[K_{\tilde{x}} \| k''_f] + 1$ $\quad$ /* Denote the time as ε $\quad$ */

33 $\quad\quad\quad$ **end**

34 $\quad\quad$ **end**

35 $\quad$ **end**

36 $\quad$ /* Exhaustive search step $\quad$ */

37 $\quad$ Select the top $2^{m_b+m_f-x-h}$ hits in the counter to be the candidates, which delivers an h-bit or higher advantage. Guess the remaining $k - (m_b + m_f)$ bit keys combined with the guessed x subkey bits to check the full key.

38 **end**

▶ **Time III** (T_3): The time complexity of the exhaustive search is

$$T_3 = 2^x \cdot 2^{m_b+m_f-x-h} \cdot 2^{k-(m_b+m_f)} = 2^{k-h}. \tag{12}$$

For choosing h (according to the success probability Eq. (14)), the conditions $m_b + m_f - x - h \geq 0$ and $x \leq m_b + m'_f$ have to be satisfied.

The memory to store the key counters and the data structures is

$$2^{m_b+m_f-x} + 4y \cdot 2^{r_b} = 2^{m_b+m_f-x} + \sqrt{s} \cdot 2^{n/2+2}/\hat{p}\hat{q}. \tag{13}$$

3.2   On the Success Probability and Exhaustive Search Phase

The success probability given by Selçuk [55] is evaluated by

$$P_s = \Phi(\frac{\sqrt{sS_N} - \Phi^{-1}(1 - 2^{-h})}{\sqrt{S_N + 1}}), \tag{14}$$

where $S_N = \hat{p}^2\hat{q}^2/2^{-n}$ is the signal-to-noise ratio, with an h-bit or higher advantage. s is the expected number of right quartets, which will be adjusted to achieve a relatively higher P_s, usually $s = 1, 2, 3$. In previous Attack I, II, III and our Attack IV, after generating the k_c-bit key counter, we select the top 2^{k_c-h} hits in the counters to be the candidates, which delivers an h-bit or higher advantage, and determine the right key by exhaustive search.

In Attack I/II, the size of key counters is $2^{m_b+m_f}$. Hence, we have to prepare a memory with size of $2^{m_b+m_f}$ to store the counters. Then the complexity of exhaustive search is $2^{(m_b+m_f-h)} \times 2^{k-(m_b+m_f)} = 2^{k-h}$, where $h \leq m_b + m_f$. Hence, the time of exhaustive search is larger than $2^{k-(m_b+m_f)}$.

In Attack III, the size of key counter is 2^{m_f}, which is smaller than Attack I/II. Then the complexity of the exhaustive search is $2^{m_b} \times 2^{m_f-h} \times 2^{k-(m_b+m_f)} = 2^{k-h}$ for Attack III, where $h < m_f$ because the size of key counters is 2^{m_f}. Hence, the time complexity is larger than 2^{k-m_f}. Compared to Attack I/II, the memory is reduced but the time may be increased.

In Attack IV, the size of key counter is bigger than $2^{m_b+m_f-x}$, which is smaller than Attack I/II, but may be larger than Attack III by choosing x. The time complexity of exhaustive search (T_3 in Attack IV) is $2^x \times 2^{m_b+m_f-x-h} \times 2^{k-(m_b+m_f)} = 2^{k-h}$ with $h < m_b + m_f - x$ and $x \leq m_b + m'_f$. Hence, the time is larger than $2^{k-(m_b+m_f-x)}$ with a key counter of size $2^{m_b+m_f-x}$. Namely, we can further tradeoff the time and memory by tweaking x between the two points achieved by Attack I/II ($x = 0$) and Attack III ($x = m_b$).

As shown in Algorithm 1 and its complexity analysis, we have to determine various parameters to derive a better attack. Many parameters are determined by the boomerang distinguishers, such as m_b, m_f, r_b, r_f and $\hat{p}\hat{q}$. Parameters like x affect the exhaustive search. Moreover, we have to determine the m'_f-bit k'_f including the number of cells and their positions. All these parameters affect the overall complexity of our tradeoff attacks.

To determine a series of optimal parameters, we take SKINNY as an example to build a fully automatic model to identify the boomerang distinguishers with optimal key-recovery parameters in the following section.

4   Automatic Model for SKINNY

SKINNY [7] is a family of lightweight block cipher proposed by Beierle *et al.* at CRYPTO 2016, which follows an SPN structure and a TWEAKEY framework [42]. Denote n as the block size and $\tilde{n}$ as the tweakey size. There are six main versions SKINNY-n-$\tilde{n}$: $n = 64, 128$, $\tilde{n} = n, 2n, 3n$. The internal state is viewed as a 4×4 square array of cells, where c is the cell size. For more details of the cipher's structure, please refer to Section A of the full version of the paper and [7]. The MC operation adopts non-MDS binary matrix:

$$\text{MC} \begin{pmatrix} a \\ b \\ c \\ d \end{pmatrix} = \begin{pmatrix} a \oplus c \oplus d \\ a \\ b \oplus c \\ a \oplus c \end{pmatrix} \quad \text{and} \quad \text{MC}^{-1} \begin{pmatrix} \alpha \\ \beta \\ \gamma \\ \delta \end{pmatrix} = \begin{pmatrix} \beta \\ \beta \oplus \gamma \oplus \delta \\ \beta \oplus \delta \\ \alpha \oplus \delta \end{pmatrix}. \tag{15}$$

Lemma 1. *[6] For any given SKINNY S-box S and any two non-zero differences δ_{in} and δ_{out}, the equation $S_i(y) \oplus S_i(y \oplus \delta_{in}) = \delta_{out}$ has one solution on average.*

4.1   Previous Automatic Search Models for Boomerang Distinguishers on SKINNY

On SKINNY, there are several automatic models on searching for boomerang distinguishers. The designers of SKINNY [7] first gave the Mixed-Integer Linear Programming (MILP) model to search for truncated differentials of SKINNY. Later, Liu *et al.* [47] tweaked the model to search for boomerang distinguishers. At EUROCRYPT 2018, Cid *et al.* [28] introduced the the Boomerang Connectivity Table (BCT) to compute the probability of the boomerang distingusher. Later, Song *et al.* [57] studied the probability of SKINNY's boomerang distinguisher with an extended BCT technique. Hadipour *et al.* [41] introduced a heuristic approach to search for a boomerang distinguisher with a set of new tables. They first searched for truncated differential with the minimum number of active S-boxes with an MILP model based on Cid *et al.*'s [29] model. At the same time, the switching effects in multiple rounds were considered. Then, they used the MILP/SAT models to get actual differential characteristic and experimentally evaluated the probability of the middle part. Almost at the same time, Delaune, Derbez and Vavrille [30] proposed a new automatic tool to search for boomerang distinguishers and provided their source code to facilitate follow-up works. They also introduced a sets of tables which help to calculate the probability of the boomerang distinguisher. With the tables to help roughly evaluate the probability, they used an MILP model to search for the upper and lower trails throughout all rounds by automatically handling the middle rounds. Then a CP model was applied to search for the best possible instantiations. Recently, Qin *et al.* [52] combined the key-recovery attack phase and distinguisher searching phase into one uniform automatic model to attack more rounds. Their extended model tweaked the previous models of Hadipour *et al.* [41] and Delaune *et al.* [30] for searching for the entire $(N_b + N_d + N_f)$ rounds of a boomerang attack.

The aim is to find new boomerang distinguishers in the related-tweakey setting that give a key-recovery attack penetrating more rounds.

4.2   Our Model to Determine the Optimal Distinguisher

In Dunkelman *et al.*'s (related-key) sandwich attack framework [37], the N_d-round cipher E_d is considered as $\tilde{E}_1 \circ E_m \circ \tilde{E}_0$, where $\tilde{E}_0$, E_m, $\tilde{E}_1$ contain r_0, r_m, r_1 rounds, respectively. Let $\tilde{p}$ and $\tilde{q}$ be the probabilities of the upper differential used for $\tilde{E}_0$ and the lower differential used for $\tilde{E}_1$. The middle part E_m specifically handles the dependence and contains a small number of rounds. If the probability of generating a right quartet for E_m is t, the probability of the whole N_d-round boomerang distinguisher is $\tilde{p}^2\tilde{q}^2t$. In the following, we use the above symbols in our search model.

Following the previous automatic models [30,41,52], we introduce a uniform automatic model to search for good distinguishers for the new rectangle attack framework in Algorithm 1. We search for the entire $(N_b + N_d + N_f)$ rounds of a boomerang attack by adding new constraints and new objective function, and takes all the critical factors affecting the complexities into account.

In our extended model searching the entire $(N_b + N_d + N_f)$ rounds of a boomerang attack, we use similar notations as [30,52], where X_r^u and X_r^l denote the internal state before SubCells in round r of the upper and lower differentials. We only list the variables that appear in our new constraints, i.e. DXU$[r][i]$ ($0 \le r \le N_b + r_0 + r_m, 0 \le i \le 15$) and DXL$[r][i]$ ($0 \le r \le r_m + r_1 + N_f, 0 \le i \le 15$) are on behalf of active cells in the internal states, and KnownEnc ($0 \le r \le N_b - 1, 0 \le i \le 15$) is on behalf of the m_b-bit subtweakeys involved in the N_b extended rounds, i.e., $\sum_{0 \le r \le N_b-2, 0 \le i \le 7}$ KnownEnc$[r][i]$ corresponds to the total amount of guessed m_b-bit key in E_b. The constraints in E_b are the same as Qin *et al.*'s [52] model. In the following, we list the differences in our model.

Modelling Propagation of Cells with Known Differences in E_f. Since we are going to filter quartets with certain cells of the internal state with fixed differences, we need to model the propagation of fixed differences in E_f. Taking the key-recovery attack on 32-round SKINNY-128-384 as an example (see Fig. 6), the cells with fixed differences are marked by ▦ and ▩. We define a binary variable DXFixed$[r][i]$ for the i-th cell of X_r and a binary variable DWFixed$[r][i]$ for the i-th cell of W_r ($0 \le r \le N_f - 1, 0 \le i \le 15$), where DXFixed$[r][i] = 1$ and DWFixed$[r][i] = 1$ indicate that the differences of corresponding cells are fixed. For the first extended round after the lower differential, the difference of each cell is fixed: $\forall 0 \le i \le 15, $ DXFixed$[0][i] = 1$.

In the propagation of the fixed differences, after the SC operation, only the differences of inactive cells are fixed. In the ART operation, the subtweakey differences do not affect whether the differences are fixed. Let permutation $P_{SR} = [0, 1, 2, 3, 7, 4, 5, 6, 10, 11, 8, 9, 13, 14, 15, 12]$ represent the SR operation,

$$\text{DWFixed}[r][i] = \neg\text{DXL}[r_m + r_1 + r][P_{SR}[i]], \forall 0 \le r \le N_f - 1, 0 \le i \le 15.$$

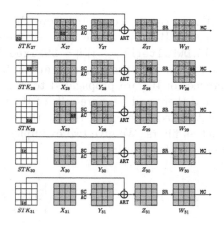

Fig. 6. The cells with fixed differences in N_f-round of the attack on SKINNY-128-384.

The constraints on the impact of the MC operation by Eq. (15) on the internal state are given below: $\forall\ 0 \le r \le N_f - 2, 0 \le i \le 3$,

$$\begin{cases} \texttt{DXFixed}[r+1][i] = \texttt{DWFixed}[r][i] \wedge \texttt{DWFixed}[r][i+8] \wedge \texttt{DWFixed}[r][i+12], \\ \texttt{DXFixed}[r+1][i+4] = \texttt{DWFixed}[r][i], \\ \texttt{DXFixed}[r+1][i+8] = \texttt{DWFixed}[r][i+4] \wedge \texttt{DWFixed}[r][i+8], \\ \texttt{DXFixed}[r+1][i+12] = \texttt{DWFixed}[r][i] \wedge \texttt{DWFixed}[r][i+8]. \end{cases}$$

Modelling Cells that Could be Used to Filter Quartets in E_f. Note that in our attack framework in Algorithm 1, we guess m'_f-bit k'_f of k_f involved in N_f extended rounds to obtain a $2h_f$-bit filter. To identify smaller m'_f with larger h_f, we define a binary variable $\texttt{DXFilter}[r][i]$ for i-th cell of X_r and a binary variable $\texttt{DWFilter}[r][i]$ for i-th cell of W_r ($0 \le r \le N_f - 1, 0 \le i \le 15$), where $\texttt{DXFilter}[r][i] = 1$ and $\texttt{DWFilter}[r][i] = 1$ indicate that the corresponding cells can be used as filters. Note that, the $(n - r_f)$ inactive bits of the ciphertext are also indicated by $\texttt{DWFilter}$. For each cell in X_r, if the difference is nonzero and fixed, we can choose the cell as filter, i.e. ▦ $\xrightarrow{\text{SC}}$ ■. For ▦ $\xrightarrow{\text{SC}}$ ▦, the cell is not a filter because it has been used as filter in W_r. The valid valuations of $\texttt{DXFixed}$, $\texttt{DXL}$ and $\texttt{DXFilter}$ are given in Table 2.

Table 2. All valid valuations of $\texttt{DXFixed}$, $\texttt{DXL}$ and $\texttt{DXFilter}$ for SKINNY.

$\texttt{DXFixed}[r][i]$	$\texttt{DXL}[r_m + r_1 + r][i]$	$\texttt{DXFilter}[r][i]$
0	1	0
1	0	0
1	1	1

In the last round, W_{N_f-1} can be computed from the ciphertexts, and the cells with fixed differences of W_{N_f-1} can be used as filters, i.e., the $(n - r_f)$ inactive bits: $\forall\, 0 \le i \le 15, \texttt{DWFilter}[N_f - 1][i] = \texttt{DWFixed}[N_f - 1][i]$.

Since we extend N_f rounds with probability 1 at the bottom of the distinguisher, then the differences of W_r are propagated to X_{r+1} with probability 1 with the MC operation, and there will be more cells of W_r with fixed differences than the cells of X_{r+1} with fixed differences. Hence, these extra cells with fixed differences in W_r can act as filters. We give two examples of how to determine which cells of W_r can be used for filtering:

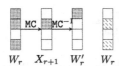

$W_r \quad X_{r+1} \quad W'_r \quad W_r$

Fig. 7. Example (1).

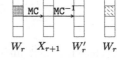

$W_r \quad X_{r+1} \quad W'_r \quad W_r$

Fig. 8. Example (2).

1. Example (1): Figure 7 shows the propagation of fixed differences, i.e., DWFixed and DXFixed, where □ cells denote the unfixed differences. In Fig. 7, the differences of $W_r[0, 1, 3]$ are fixed (marked by ⊞). After the MC operation, only the difference of $X_{r+1}[1]$ is fixed. Since there are three cells with fixed differences in W_r but only one cell with fixed difference in X_{r+1}, we can use two cells of W_r as filters (the one cell of fixed difference in X_{r+1} has been used in the SC computation). To determine which cells acting as filters, we apply the $\texttt{MC}^{-1}$ operation to X_{r+1} and get fixed difference of $W'_r[0]$, which means if $\Delta X_{r+1}[1]$ is fixed, then $\Delta W_r[0]$ will be certainly fixed. Since $X_{r+1}[1]$ has been used as filter in the SC computation, $W_r[0]$ will not act as filter redundantly. Hence, only $W_r[1, 3]$ can be used as filters (marked by ▨).
2. Example (2): In Fig. 8, only the difference of $W_r[1]$ is fixed, which is marked by ⊞. After applying the MC operation, all the differences of X_{r+1} are unfixed. So applying the $\texttt{MC}^{-1}$ operation to X_{r+1}, all the differences of W'_r are unfixed. Hence, the difference of $W_r[1]$ need to be fixed, which can be used for filtering (marked by ▨).

All valid valuations of DWFixed and DWFilter please refer to Section B of the full version of the paper. Note that DXFixed is only used as the intermediate variable to determine DWFilter, since DXFixed is fully determined by DWFixed.

Denoting the sets of all possible valuations listed in Table 2 and Table 8 in the full version of the paper by $\mathbb{P}_i$ and $\mathbb{Q}_i$, there are

$$
\left\{
\begin{aligned}
& (\texttt{DXFixed}[r][i], \texttt{DXL}[r_m + r_1 + r][i], \texttt{DXFilter}[r][i]) \in \mathbb{P}_i, \forall\, 0 \le r \le N_f - 1, 0 \le i \le 15, \\
& (\texttt{DWFixed}[r][i], \texttt{DWFixed}[r][i+4], \texttt{DWFixed}[r][i+8], \texttt{DWFixed}[r][i+12], \\
& \texttt{DWFilter}[r][i], \texttt{DWFilter}[r][i+4], \texttt{DWFilter}[r][i+8], \texttt{DWFilter}[r][i+12]) \in \mathbb{Q}_i, \\
& \hspace{8cm} \forall\, 0 \le r \le N_f - 2, 0 \le i \le 3.
\end{aligned}
\right.
$$

We define a binary variable $\texttt{DXisFilter}[r][i]$ for i-th cell of X_r and a binary variable $\texttt{DWisFilter}[r][i]$ for i-th cell of W_r ($0 \leq r \leq N_f - 1, 0 \leq i \leq 15$), where $\texttt{DXisFilter}[r][i] = 1$ and $\texttt{DWisFilter}[r][i] = 1$ indicate that the corresponding cells are chosen as filters before generating quartets. $\forall\, 0 \leq r \leq N_f - 1, 0 \leq i \leq 15$, $\texttt{DXisFilter}[r][i] \leq \texttt{DXFilter}[r][i], \texttt{DWisFilter}[r][i] \leq \texttt{DWFilter}[r][i]$.

Modeling the Guessed Subtweakey Cells in E_f for Generating the Quartets. We define a binary variable $\texttt{DXGuess}[r][i]$ for i-th cell of X_r and a binary variable $\texttt{DWGuess}[r][i]$ for i-th cell of W_r ($0 \leq r \leq N_f - 1, 0 \leq i \leq 15$), where $\texttt{DXGuess}[r][i] = 1$ and $\texttt{DWGuess}[r][i] = 1$ indicate that the corresponding cells need to be known in decryption from ciphertexts to the cells acting as filters. So whether $STK_r[i]$ should be guessed is also identified by $\texttt{DXGuess}[r][i]$, where $0 \leq r \leq N_f - 1$ and $0 \leq i \leq 7$.

For the round 0, only cells used to be filters in the internal state need to be known: $\forall\, 0 \leq i \leq 15, \texttt{DXGuess}[0][i] = \texttt{DXisFilter}[0][i]$.

From round 0 to round $N_f - 1$, the cells in W_r need to be known involve two types: cells to be known from X_r over the SR operation, and cells used to be filters in W_r:

$$\texttt{DWGuess}[r][i] = \texttt{DWisFilter}[r][i] \vee \texttt{DXGuess}[r][P_{\mathrm{SR}}[i]], \ \forall\, 0 \leq r < N_f - 1,\ 0 \leq i \leq 15.$$

In round 0 to round $N_f - 2$, the cells in X_{r+1} need to be known involve two types: cells to be known from W_r over the MC operation, and cells used to be filters in X_{r+1}: $\forall\, 0 \leq r \leq N_b - 2,\ 0 \leq i \leq 3$

$$
\left\{
\begin{aligned}
&\texttt{DXGuess}[r+1][i] = \texttt{DWGuess}[r][i+12] \vee \texttt{DXisFilter}[r+1][i],\\
&\texttt{DXGuess}[r+1][i+4] = \texttt{DWGuess}[r][i] \vee \texttt{DWGuess}[r][i+4] \vee \texttt{DWGuess}[r][i+8] \vee\\
&\qquad\qquad \texttt{DXisFilter}[r+1][i+4],\\
&\texttt{DXGuess}[r+1][i+8] = \texttt{DWGuess}[r][i+4] \vee \texttt{DXisFilter}[r+1][i+8],\\
&\texttt{DXGuess}[r+1][i+12] = \texttt{DWGuess}[r][i+4] \vee \texttt{DWGuess}[r][i+8] \vee \texttt{DWGuess}[r][i+12] \vee\\
&\qquad\qquad \texttt{DXisFilter}[r+1][i+12].
\end{aligned}
\right.
$$

We have $\sum_{0 \leq r \leq N_f - 1,\ 0 \leq i \leq 7} \texttt{DXGuess}[r][i]$ to indicate the m'_f-bit key guessed for generating quartets.

Modelling the Advantage h in the Key-Recovery Attack. In our Algorithm 1 in Sect. 3.1, the advantage h determines the exhaustive search time, where h should be smaller than the number of key counters, i.e. $h \leq m_b + m_f - x$. The x-bit guessed subkey should satisfy $x \leq m_b + m'_f$, and also determine the size of memory $2^{m_b + m_f - x}$ to store the key counters. So we need a balance between x and h to achieve a low time and memory complexities. We define an integer variable $\texttt{Adv}$ for h and an integer variable $\texttt{x}$. To describe m_f (not m'_f here), we define a binary variable $\texttt{KnownDec}[r][i]$ for i-th cell of Y_r ($0 \leq r \leq N_f - 1, 0 \leq i \leq 15$), where $\texttt{KnownDec}[r][i] = 1$ indicates that the corresponding cell should be known in the decryption from ciphertext to the position of known δ. Then whether $STK_r[i]$ should be guessed is also identified by $\texttt{KnownDec}[r][i]$, where $0 \leq r \leq N_f - 1$ and $0 \leq i \leq 7$. In the first round extended after the distinguisher, only the active cells need to be known: $\forall\, 0 \leq i \leq 15, \texttt{KnownDec}[0][i] = \texttt{DXL}[r_m + r_1][i]$.

In round 1 to round $N_f - 1$, the cells in Y_{r+1} need to be known involve two types: cells to be known from W_r over the MC and SB operation, and active cells in X_{r+1}: $\forall\, 0 \leq r \leq N_b - 2,\ 0 \leq i \leq 3$

$$
\begin{cases}
\texttt{KnownDec}[r+1][i] = \texttt{DXL}[r_m + r_1 + r + 1][i] \vee \texttt{KnownDec}[r][P_{\text{SR}}[i+12]], \\
\texttt{KnownDec}[r+1][i+4] = \texttt{DXL}[r_m + r_1 + r + 1][i+4] \vee \texttt{KnownDec}[r][P_{\text{SR}}[i]] \vee \\
\qquad\qquad \texttt{KnownDec}[r][P_{\text{SR}}[i+4]] \vee \texttt{KnownDec}[r][P_{\text{SR}}[i+8]], \\
\texttt{KnownDec}[r+1][i+8] = \texttt{DXL}[r_m + r_1 + r + 1][i+8] \vee \texttt{KnownDec}[r][P_{\text{SR}}[i+4]], \\
\texttt{KnownDec}[r+1][i+12] = \texttt{DXL}[r_m + r_1 + r + 1][i+12] \vee \texttt{KnownDec}[r][P_{\text{SR}}[i+4]] \vee \\
\qquad\qquad \texttt{KnownDec}[r][P_{\text{SR}}[i+8]] \vee \texttt{KnownDec}[r][P_{\text{SR}}[i+12]].
\end{cases}
$$

We have $\sum_{0 \leq r \leq N_f - 1,\ 0 \leq i \leq 7} \texttt{KnownDec}[r][i]$ to indicate the m_f-bit key.

The Objective Function. As in Sect. 3.1, the time complexities of our new attack framework involve three parts: **Time I** (T_1), **Time II** (T_2) and **Time III** (T_3). We need to balance those time complexities T_1, T_2 and T_3.

The constraints for probability $\tilde{p}^2 t \tilde{q}^2$ of the boomerang distinguisher are same as [30], where DXU, DXL and DXU $\wedge$ DXL are on behalf of $\tilde{p}$, $\tilde{q}$ and t. KnownEnc is on behalf of m_b, and we do not repeat the details here. To describe T_1, we have:

$$
\begin{aligned}
T_1 = &\sum_{0 \leq r \leq r_0 - 1,\ 0 \leq i \leq 15} w_0 \cdot \texttt{DXU}[N_b + r][i] + \sum_{0 \leq r \leq r_1 - 1,\ 0 \leq i \leq 15} w_1 \cdot \texttt{DXL}[r_m + r][i] + \\
&\sum_{0 \leq r \leq r_m - 1,\ 0 \leq i \leq 15} w_m \cdot (\texttt{DXU}[N_b + r_0 + r][i] \wedge \texttt{DXL}[r][i]) + \\
&\sum_{0 \leq r \leq N_b - 2,\ 0 \leq i \leq 7} w_{m_b} \cdot \texttt{KnownEnc}[r][i] + \sum_{0 \leq r \leq N_f - 1,\ 0 \leq i \leq 7} w_{m_f} \cdot \texttt{DXGuess}[r][i] + c_{T_1},
\end{aligned}
$$

where c_{T_1} indicates the constant factor $2^{n/2+1}$, and w_0, w_1, w_m, w_{m_b}, w_{m_f} are weights factors discussed later.

For describing T_2 (let $\varepsilon = 1$), we have:

$$
\begin{aligned}
T_2 = &\sum_{0 \leq r \leq r_0 - 1,\ 0 \leq i \leq 15} 2w_0 \cdot \texttt{DXU}[N_b + r][i] + \sum_{0 \leq r \leq r_1 - 1,\ 0 \leq i \leq 15} 2w_1 \cdot \texttt{DXL}[r_m + r][i] + \\
&\sum_{0 \leq r \leq r_m - 1,\ 0 \leq i \leq 15} 2w_m \cdot (\texttt{DXU}[N_b + r_0 + r][i] \wedge \texttt{DXL}[r][i]) + \\
&\sum_{0 \leq r \leq N_b - 2,\ 0 \leq i \leq 7} w_{m_b} \cdot \texttt{KnownEnc}[r][i] + \sum_{0 \leq r \leq N_f - 1,\ 0 \leq i \leq 7} w_{m_f} \cdot \texttt{DXGuess}[r][i] - \\
&\sum_{0 \leq r \leq N_f - 1,\ 0 \leq i \leq 15} w_{h_f} \cdot (\texttt{DXisFilter}[r][i] + \texttt{DWisFilter}[r][i]) + c_{T_2},
\end{aligned}
$$

where $\sum_{0 \leq r \leq N_f - 1,\ 0 \leq i \leq 15} w_{h_f} \cdot (\texttt{DXisFilter}[r][i] + \texttt{DWisFilter}[r][i])$ corresponds to the total filter $2(n - r_f) + 2h_f$ according to Eq. (10), and c_{T_2} indicates a constant factor 2^n.

For T_3, we have $T_3 = c_{T_3} - \text{Adv}$, where $c_{T_3} = \tilde{n}$ for SKINNY-n-$\tilde{n}$.
For the advantage h and x, we have constraints:

$$
\begin{cases}
\text{x} \leq \displaystyle\sum_{0 \leq r \leq N_b-2,\ 0 \leq i \leq 7} \text{KnownEnc}[r][i] + \sum_{0 \leq r \leq N_f-1,\ 0 \leq i \leq 7} \text{DXGuess}[r][i], \\
\text{Adv} + \text{x} \leq \displaystyle\sum_{0 \leq r \leq N_b-2,\ 0 \leq i \leq 7} \text{KnownEnc}[r][i] + \sum_{0 \leq r \leq N_f-1,\ 0 \leq i \leq 7} \text{KnownDec}[r][i].
\end{cases}
$$

So we get a uniformed objective:

$$\text{Minimize } obj,\ obj \geq T_1,\ obj \geq T_2,\ obj \geq T_2. \tag{16}$$

4.3 Comparisons Between Qin et al.'s Model and Ours

Different from Qin et al.'s [52] uniform automatic key-recovery model, which is about the rectangle attack framework by Zhao et al. [64], our automatic model for Algorithm 1 needs additional constraints to determine h_f-bit internal states acting as filters and m'_f-bit subtweakey needed to guess in the N_f extended rounds. Moreover, in Qin et al.'s [52] model, only the time complexity of (Time II of Zhao et al.'s model [64] in Sect. 2.3) generating quartets is considered. However, in our model we have to consider more time complexity constraints, i.e., Time I, Time II and Time III in Algorithm 1. All these differences lead to better attacks than Qin et al.'s attacks. Especially we gain 32-round attack on SKINNY-128-384, while Qin et al.'s model only achieves 30 rounds.

4.4 New Distinguishers for SKINNY

With our new model, we add such conditions to the automatic searching model in [30,52] to search for new distinguishers. Due to that different parameters have different coefficients in the formula of the time complexity, we give them different weights to model the objective more accurately. For SKINNY, the maximum probability in the DDT table both for 4-bit S-box and 8-bit S-box is 2^{-2}. Then considering the switching effects similar to [41], we adjust the weight $w_{h_f} = 2w_{m_b} = 2w_{m_f} = 4w_0 = 4w_1 = 8w_m = 8$ for $c = 4$ and $w_{h_f} = 2w_{m_b} = 2w_{m_f} = 8w_0 = 8w_1 = 16w_m = 16$ for $c = 8$. Similarly, the constants c_{T_1} and c_{T_2} are set to 33 and 64 for $c = 4$, and to 65 and 128 for $c = 8$. We use different N_b, N_d and N_f. N_b is chosen from 2 to 4 and N_f is 4 or 5 usually. N_d is chosen based on experience, which is shorter than previous longest distinguishers.

By searching for new truncated upper and lower differentials using the MILP model and get instantiations using the CP model following the open source [30], we obtain new distinguishers for SKINNY-128-384, SKINNY-64-192 and SKINNY-128-256. For SKINNY-64-128, we find the distinguisher in [52] is optimal. To get more accurate probabilities of the distinguishers, we calculate the probability $\tilde{p}$ and $\tilde{q}$ considering the clustering effect. For the middle part, we evaluate the probability using the method in [30,41,57] and experimentally verify the probability. The experiments use one computer equipped with one RTX 2080 Ti and the results of our experiments are listed in Table 3. Our source codes are based on the open source by Delaune, Derbez and Vavrille [30], which is provided in https://github.com/key-guess-rectangle/key-guess-rectangle.

Table 3. Experiments on the middle part of boomerang distinguishers for SKINNY.

Version	N_d	r_m	Probability t	Complexity	Time
64-192	22	6	$2^{-17.88}$	2^{30}	21.9s
128-384	23	3	$2^{-20.51}$	2^{31}	30.6s
128-256	18	4	$2^{-35.41}$	2^{40}	16231.8s
128-256	19	4	$2^{-26.71}$	2^{35}	481.2s

We list the 23-round boomerang distinguisher for SKINNY-128-384 in Table 4. For more details of the boomerang distinguishers for other versions of SKINNY, we refer to Section J of the full version of the paper. In addition, we summarize the previous boomerang distinguishers for a few versions of SKINNY in Table 5.

Table 4. The 23-round related-tweakey boomerang distinguisher on SKINNY-128-384.

$r_0 = 11, r_m = 3, r_1 = 9, \tilde{p} = 2^{-32.18}, t = 2^{-20.51}, \tilde{q} = 2^{-15.11}, \tilde{p}^2 t \tilde{q}^2 = 2^{-115.09}$
$\Delta TK1 = $ 00, 00, 00, 00, 00, 00, 00, 00, 24, 00, 00, 00, 00, 00, 00, 00
$\Delta TK2 = $ 00, 00, 00, 00, 00, 00, 00, 00, 07, 00, 00, 00, 00, 00, 00, 00
$\Delta TK3 = $ 00, 00, 00, 00, 00, 00, 00, 00, e3, 00, 00, 00, 00, 00, 00, 00
$\Delta X_0 = $ 00, 00, 00, 00, 00, 00, 00, 00, 00, 00, 00, 00, 00, 00, 00, 20
$\nabla TK1 = $ 00, 8a, 00, 00, 00, 00, 00, 00, 00, 00, 00, 00, 00, 00, 00, 00
$\nabla TK2 = $ 00, 0c, 00, 00, 00, 00, 00, 00, 00, 00, 00, 00, 00, 00, 00, 00
$\nabla TK3 = $ 00, 7f, 00, 00, 00, 00, 00, 00, 00, 00, 00, 00, 00, 00, 00, 00
$\nabla X_{23} = $ 00, 00, 00, 00, 00, 00, 00, 00, 00, 50, 00, 00, 00, 00, 00, 00

5   Improved Attacks on SKINNY

In this section, we give the first 32-round attack on SKINNY-128-384 using the distinguisher in Sect. 4.4 with our new rectangle attack framework. We also give improved attacks on other versions (n-$2n$ and n-$3n$). For more details, please refer to Section D in the full version of the paper.

5.1   Improved Attack on 32-Round SKINNY-128-384

We use the 23-round rectangle distinguisher for SKINNY-128-384 given in Table 4, whose probability is $2^{-n} \tilde{p}^2 t \tilde{q}^2 = 2^{-128-115.09} = 2^{-243.09}$. Prepending

Table 5. Summary of related-tweakey boomerang distinguishers for SKINNY. N_d is the round of distinguishers; $N_b + N_d + N_f$ is the total attacked round.

Version	N_d	Probability $\tilde{p}^2\tilde{q}^2t$	$N_b + N_d + N_f$	Ref.
	17	$2^{-29.78}$	-	[57]
	17	$2^{-48.72}$	21	[47]
64-128	19	$2^{-51.08}$	23	[41]
	19	$2^{-54.36}$	-	[30]
	18	$2^{-55.34}$	24	[52]
	18	$2^{-55.34}$	25	Ours
	22	$2^{-42.98}$	-	[57]
	22	$2^{-54.94}$	26	[47]
64-192	23	$2^{-55.85}$	29	[41]
	23	$2^{-57.93}$	-	[30]
	22	$2^{-57.73}$	30	[52]
	22	$2^{-57.56}$	31	Ours
	18	$2^{-77.83}$	-	[57]
	18	$2^{-103.84}$	22	[47]
	20	$2^{-85.77}$	-	[30]
128-256	21	$2^{-116.43}$	24	[41]
	19	$2^{-116.97}$	25	[52]
	18	$2^{-108.51}$	25	Ours
	19	$2^{-121.07}$	26	Ours
	22	$2^{-48.30}$	-	[57]
	23	2^{-112}	27	[47]
	23	2^{-112}	28	[64]
128-384	24	$2^{-86.09}$	-	[30]
	25	$2^{-116.59}$	30	[41]
	22	$2^{-101.49}$	30	[52]
	23	$2^{-115.09}$	32	Ours

4-round E_b and appending 5-round E_f, we attack 32-round SKINNY-128-384 as illustrated in Fig. 9. As introduced in Sect. 2, the numbers of active bits of the plaintext and ciphertext are denoted as r_b and r_f, and the numbers of sub-key bits involved in E_b and E_f are denoted as m_b and m_f. In the first round, we use subtweakey $ETK_0 = \text{MC} \circ \text{SR}(STK_0)$ instead of STK_0, and there is $ETK_0[i] = ETK_0[i + 4] = ETK_0[i + 12] = STK_0[i]$ for $0 \le i \le 3$. So we have $r_b = 12 \cdot 8 = 96$ by W'_0. As shown in Fig. 9, the ▨ cells are needed to be guessed in E_b, including 3 ▨ cells in STK_2, 7 ▨ cells in STK_1, 8 ▨ cells in ETK_0. Hence, $m_b = 18 \cdot 8 = 144$. In the E_f, we have $r_f = 16 \cdot 8 = 128$ and $m_f = 24 \cdot 8 = 192$. There are 7 cells in STK_{31} and 4 cells STK_{30} marked by red boxes to be guessed in advance, i.e., $m'_f = 11 \cdot 8 = 88$. Then, we get 8 cells in the internal states (marked by red boxes in W_{30}, W_{29} and X_{29}) as additional filters with the guessed m'_f-bit key, i.e., $h_f = 8 \cdot 8 = 64$. Due to the tweakey schedule, we deduce

$STK_{28}[3,7]$ from $ETK_0[1,0]$, $STK_2[0,2]$ and $STK_{30}[7,1]$. So there are only $(m_f - 2c) = 176$-bit subtweakey unknown in E_f after m_b-bit key is guessed in E_b. As shown in Table 6, we have $k'_f = \{STK_{30}[1,3,5,7], STK_{31}[0,2,3,4,5,6,7]\}$ marked in red indexes and $h_f = \{X_{29}[11], W_{29}[5,7,13,15], W_{30}[5,8,15]\}$ marked in bold. Finally, we give the attack according to Algorithm 1 as follows:

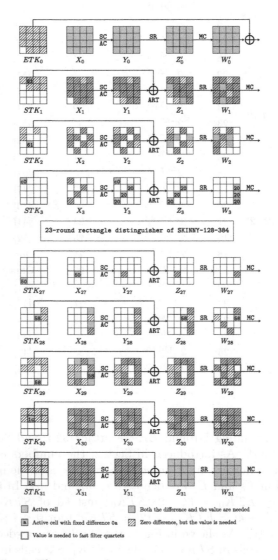

Fig. 9. The 32-round attack against SKINNY-128-384.

1. Construct $y = \sqrt{s} \cdot 2^{n/2-r_b} / \sqrt{\tilde{p}^2 t \tilde{q}^2} = \sqrt{s} \cdot 2^{25.54}$ structures of $2^{r_b} = 2^{96}$ plaintexts each according to Eq. (7). For each structure, query the 2^{96} ciphertexts by encryptions under K_1, K_2, K_3 and K_4. Hence, the data complexity is

Table 6. Internal state used for filtering and involved subtweakeys for 32-round SKINNY-128-384.

Round		Filter	Involved subtweakeys
1		$\Delta W_{30}[5] = 0$	$STK_{31}[5]$
2	30	$\Delta W_{30}[8] = 0$	$STK_{31}[4]$
3		$\Delta W_{30}[15] = 0$	$STK_{31}[3]$
4		$\Delta W_{29}[5] = 0$	$STK_{30}[5], STK_{31}[0,6,7]$
5		$\Delta W_{29}[7] = 0$	$STK_{30}[7], STK_{31}[2,4,5]$
6	29	$\Delta W_{29}[10] = 0$	$STK_{30}[6], STK_{31}[1,7]$
7		$\Delta W_{29}[13] = 0$	$STK_{30}[1], STK_{31}[0,5]$
8		$\Delta W_{29}[15] = 0$	$STK_{30}[3], STK_{31}[2,7]$
9		$\Delta X_{29}[11] = \text{0x58}$	$STK_{30}[5], STK_{31}[0,6]$
10		$\Delta W_{28}[5] = 0$	$STK_{29}[5], STK_{30}[0,6,7], STK_{31}[1,2,3,4,7]$
11	28	$\Delta W_{28}[11] = 0$	$STK_{29}[7], STK_{30}[2,4], STK_{31}[1,3,5,6]$
12		$\Delta W_{28}[13] = 0$	$STK_{29}[1], STK_{30}[0,5], STK_{31}[3,4,6]$
13		$\Delta W_{28}[15] = 0$	$STK_{29}[3], STK_{30}[2,7], STK_{31}[1,4,6]$
14		$\Delta W_{27}[7] = 0$	$STK_{28}[7], STK_{29}[2,4,5], STK_{30}[0,1,3,5,6], STK_{31}[0,1,2,3,4,5,6,7]$
15	27	$\Delta W_{27}[15] = 0$	$STK_{28}[3], STK_{29}[2,7], STK_{30}[1,4,6], STK_{31}[0,3,5,6,7]$
16		$\Delta X_{27}[9] = \text{0x50}$	$STK_{28}[7], STK_{29}[2,4], STK_{30}[1,3,5,6], STK_{31}[0,1,2,5,6,7]$

$\sqrt{s} \cdot 2^{n/2+2}/\sqrt{\tilde{p}^2 t \tilde{q}^2} = \sqrt{s} \cdot 2^{123.54}$ according to Eq. (8). The memory complexity in this step is also $\sqrt{s} \cdot 2^{123.54}$.

2. Guess x-bit key (part of the k_b and k'_f involved in E_b and E_f):

   (a) Initialize a list of $2^{m_b+m_f-2c-x} = 2^{320-x}$ counters. The memory complexity in this step is 2^{320-x}.

   (b) Guess $(m_b + m'_f - x) = (232 - x)$-bit key involved in E_b and E_f:

   i. In each structure, we partially encrypt P_1 under m_b-bit subkey to the positions of known differences of Y_3, and partially decrypt it to the plaintext P_2 (within the same structure) after xoring the known difference α. The details can refer to Section C in the full version of the paper. Do the same for each P_3 to get P_4. Store the pairs in S_1 and S_2. Totally, $m_b = 18 \cdot 8 = 144$-bit key are involved.

   ii. The size of S_1 and S_2 is $y \cdot 2^{r_b} = \sqrt{s} \cdot 2^{121.54}$. For each element in S_1, with $m'_f = 88$-bit k'_f, we can obtain $2h_f = 2 \cdot 64 = 128$ internal state bits as filters. So partially decrypt (C_1, C_2) in S_1 with k'_f to get $\{W_{30}[5,8,15], W_{29}[5,7,13,15], X_{29}[11]\}$ as filters. Insert the element in S_1 into a hash table H indexed by the $h_f = 64$-bit $\{W_{30}[5,8,15], W_{29}[5,7,13,15], X_{29}[11]\}$ of C_1 and $h_f = 64$-bit $\{\bar{W}_{30}[5,8,15], \bar{W}_{29}[5,7,13,15], \bar{X}_{29}[11]\}$ of C_2. For each element (C_3, C_4) in S_2, partially decrypt it with k'_f to get the $2h_f = 128$ internal state bits, and check against H to find the pairs (C_1, C_2), where (C_1, C_3) and (C_2, C_4) collide at the $2h_f = 128$ bits. According to Eq. (9), the data collection process needs $T_1 = \sqrt{s} \cdot 2^{m_b+m'_f+n/2+1}/\sqrt{\tilde{p}^2 t \tilde{q}^2} = \sqrt{s} \cdot 2^{144+88+64+1+57.54} = \sqrt{s} \cdot 2^{354.54}$. We get $s \cdot 2^{m_b+m'_f-2h_f-n+2r_f}/(\tilde{p}^2 t \tilde{q}^2) = s \cdot 2^{144+88-128+128+115.09} = s \cdot 2^{347.09}$ quartets according to Eq. (11).

iii. On ε: for each of $s \cdot 2^{347.09}$ quartets, determine the key candidates and increase the corresponding counters. According to Eq. (11), this step needs $T_2 = s \cdot 2^{347.09} \cdot \varepsilon$. We refer the readers to Table 7 to make the following guess-and-filter steps clearer.

A. **In round 31:** guessing $STK_{31}[1]$ and together with k'_f as shown in Table 7, we compute $Z_{30}[6, 14]$ and peel off round 31. Then $\Delta Y_{30}[6]$ and $\Delta X_{30}[14]$ are deduced. For the 3rd column of X_{30} of (C_1, C_3), we obtain $\Delta X_{30}[6] = \Delta X_{30}[14]$ from Eq. (15). Hence, we obtain $\Delta X_{30}[6]$ and deduce $STK_{30}[6]$ by Lemma 1. Similarly, we deduce $STK'_{30}[6]$ for (C_2, C_4). Since $\Delta STK_{30}[6]$ is fixed, we get an 8-bit filter. $s \cdot 2^{347.09} \cdot 2^8 \cdot 2^{-8} = s \cdot 2^{347.09}$ quartets remain.

B. **In round 30:** guessing $STK_{30}[0]$, we compute $Z_{29}[1, 9, 13]$ as shown in Table 7. Then $\Delta Y_{29}[1]$ and $\Delta X_{29}[9, 13]$ are deduced. For the 2nd column of X_{29} of (C_1, C_3), we can obtain $\Delta X_{29}[1] = \Delta X_{29}[9] = \Delta X_{29}[13]$. Hence, we obtain $\Delta X_{29}[1]$ and deduce $STK_{29}[1]$. Similarly, we deduce $STK'_{29}[1]$ for (C_2, C_4), which is an 8-bit filter. For both (C_1, C_3) and (C_2, C_4), $\Delta X_{29}[9] = \Delta X_{29}[13]$ is an 8-bit filter. $s \cdot 2^{347.09} \cdot 2^8 \cdot 2^{-8} \cdot 2^{-8} \cdot 2^{-8} = s \cdot 2^{331.09}$ quartets remain.

C. Guessing $STK_{30}[2, 4]$, we compute $Z_{29}[3, 7, 15]$ and peel off round 30. Then $\Delta Y_{29}[3, 7]$ and $\Delta X_{29}[15]$ are deduced. For the 4th column of X_{29} of (C_1, C_3), we can obtain $\Delta X_{29}[3] = \Delta X_{29}[7] = \Delta X_{29}[15]$. Hence, we obtain $\Delta X_{29}[3, 7]$ and deduce $STK_{29}[3, 7]$. Similarly, we deduce $STK'_{29}[3, 7]$ for (C_2, C_4), which is a 16-bit filter. $s \cdot 2^{331.09} \cdot 2^{16} \cdot 2^{-16} = s \cdot 2^{331.09}$ quartets remain.

D. **In round 29:** guessing $STK_{29}[2, 5]$, we compute $Z_{28}[3, 11, 15]$. Then $\Delta Y_{28}[3]$ and $\Delta X_{28}[11, 15]$ are deduced. For the 4th column of X_{28} of (C_1, C_3), we can obtain $\Delta X_{28}[3] = \Delta X_{28}[11] = \Delta X_{28}[15]$. Since $STK_{28}[3]$ can be deduced from the known $ETK_0[1]$, $STK_2[0]$ and $STK_{30}[7]$, we can compute $X_{28}[3]$ and $\Delta X_{28}[3]$. For both (C_1, C_3) and (C_2, C_4), $\Delta X_{28}[3] = \Delta X_{28}[15]$ and $\Delta X_{28}[11] = \Delta X_{28}[15]$ are two 8-bit filter. $s \cdot 2^{331.09} \cdot 2^{16} \cdot 2^{-16} \cdot 2^{-16} = s \cdot 2^{315.09}$ quartets remain.

E. Guessing $STK_{29}[4]$, we decrypt two rounds to get $X_{27}[9]$ with known $STK_{28}[7]$. **In round 27**, $\Delta X_{27}[9] = \texttt{0x50}$ is an 8-bit filter for both (C_1, C_3) and (C_2, C_4). $s \cdot 2^{315.09} \cdot 2^8 \cdot 2^{-16} = s \cdot 2^{307.09}$ quartets remain.

So for each quartet, $\varepsilon = 2^8 \cdot \frac{4}{32} + 2^8 \cdot \frac{4}{32} + 2^{-16} \cdot 2^{16} \cdot \frac{4}{32} + 2^{-16} \cdot 2^{16} \cdot \frac{4}{32} + 2^{-32} \cdot 2^8 \cdot \frac{8}{32} \approx 2^{6.01}$ and $T_2 = s \cdot 2^{353.1}$.

(c) (Exhaustive search) Select the top $2^{m_b + m_f - 2c - x - h} = 2^{320 - x - h}$ hits in the counter as the key candidates. Guess the remaining $k - (m_b + m_f - 2c) = 64$-bit key to check the full key. According to Eq. (12), $T_3 = 2^{k-h}$.

In order to balance T_1, T_2, T_3 and memory complexity and achieve a high success probability, we set the excepted number of right quartets $s = 1$, the advantage $h = 40$ and $x = 208$ ($x \le m_b + m'_f = 232$, $h \le m_b + m_f - 2c - x =$

$320 - x$) with Eq. (14). Then we have $T_1 = 2^{354.54}$, $T_2 = 2^{353.1}$ and $T_3 = 2^{344}$. In total, the data complexity is $2^{123.54}$, the memory complexity is $2^{123.54}$, and the time complexity is $2^{354.99}$. The success probability is about 82.1%.

Table 7. Tweakey recovery for 32-round SKINNY-128-384, where the red bytes are among k'_f or obtained in the previous steps.

Step	Internal state	Involved subtweakeys
A	$Z_{30}[6]$	$STK_{31}[7]$
	$Z_{30}[14]$	$STK_{31}[1]$
B	$Z_{29}[1]$	$STK_{30}[5], STK_{31}[6]$
	$Z_{29}[9]$	$STK_{30}[7], STK_{31}[2,4]$
	$Z_{29}[13]$	$STK_{30}[0], STK_{31}[3,4]$
C	$Z_{29}[3]$	$STK_{30}[7], STK_{31}[4]$
	$Z_{29}[7]$	$STK_{30}[4], STK_{31}[3,5,6]$
	$Z_{29}[15]$	$STK_{30}[2], STK_{31}[1,6]$
D	$Z_{28}[3]$	$STK_{29}[7], STK_{30}[4], STK_{31}[3,5,6]$
	$Z_{28}[11]$	$STK_{29}[5], STK_{30}[0,6], STK_{31}[1,3,4,7]$
	$Z_{28}[15]$	$STK_{29}[2], STK_{30}[1,6], STK_{31}[0,5,7]$
E	$X_{27}[9]$	$STK_{28}[7], STK_{29}[2,4], STK_{30}[1,3,5,6], STK_{31}[0,1,2,5,6,7]$

6   Conclusion and Further Disscussion

We introduce a new key-recovery framework for the rectangle attacks on ciphers with linear schedule with the purpose of reducing the overall complexity or attacking more rounds. We give a uniform automatic model on SKINNY to search for distinguishers which are more proper for our key-recovery framework. With the new rectangle distinguishers, we give new attacks on a few versions of SKINNY, which achieve 1 or 2 more rounds than the best previous attacks.

Further Discussion. For ForkSkinny, Deoxys-BC and GIFT, we do not give the automatic models but only apply our new rectangle attack framework in Algorithm 1 with the previous distinguishers. For ForkSkinny, we find that the 21-round distinguisher on ForkSkinny-128-256 in [52] is also optimal for our new rectangle attack model. Our attack on 28-round ForkSkinny-128-256 with 256-bit key reduces the time complexity of [52] by a factor of 2^{22}. For Deoxys-BC-384, our attack reduces the time complexity of the best previous 14-round attack [63] by a factor of $2^{22.7}$ with similar data complexity. For GIFT-64, our rectangle attack uses the same rectangle distinguisher with Ji *et al.* [44], but achieves one more round. Moreover, compared with the best previous attack achieved by differential attack by Sun *et al.* [58], our rectangle attack achieves the same 26 rounds. The details can refer to Section F, G, H of the full version of the paper.

For single-key setting, our tradeoff key-recovery model in Sect. 3 and Zhao *et al.*'s model [62] can be trivially converted into the single-key model by just letting the differences of the keys be 0. We also give an attack on 10-round **Serpent** reusing the rectangle distinguisher by Biham, Dunkelman and Keller [13] and achieving better time complexity (see Section I in the full version of the paper).

Overall Analysis of the Four Attack Models. To better understand different key-recovery rectangle models, we give an overall analysis of the four attack models in Sect. 2 and 3. There are some differences in the four models:

- The **Attack I** of Sect. 2.1 guesses all the $(m_b + m_f)$-bit key at once and generates the quartets;
- The **Attack II** of Sect. 2.2 does not guess the key involved in E_b and E_f when generating quartets, and uses hash tables in the key-recovery process.
- The **Attack III** of Sect. 2.3 only guesses m_b-bit key in E_b to generate quartets and the key-recovery process is just a guess and filter process.
- Our new attack of Sect. 3.1 guesses m_b-bit key in E_b and m'_f-bit key in E_f to generate quartets, which increases the time of generating quartets but reduces the number of quartets to be checked in the key-recovery process.

For all the attack models, the data complexities are the same, which depend on the probability of the rectangle distinguisher and the expected number of right quartets s. To analyze different time complexities, we first compare time complexities of the key-recovery process. Suppose, $\hat{p}\hat{q} = 2^{-t}$ and s is small and ignored, we approximate the four complexities to be

$$
\begin{cases}
\text{Attack I}: T_I = 2^{m_b+m_f+n/2+t+2}, & (17) \\
\text{Attack II}: T_{II} = 2^{m_b+r_b+2r_f-n+2t} + 2^{m_f+2r_b+r_f-n+2t}, & (18) \\
\text{Attack III}: T_{III} = 2^{m_b+2r_f-n+2t} \cdot \varepsilon, & (19) \\
\text{Attack IV}: T_{IV} = 2^{m_b+2r_f-n+m'_f-2h_f+2t} \cdot \varepsilon. & (20)
\end{cases}
$$

To compare T_{II} and T_{III}, when $\varepsilon \leq 2^{r_b}$, the complexity of **Attack III** is lower than **Attack II**. In the key-recovery process of **Attack III**, the early abort technique [49] is usually applied to make the ε very small, i.e., the key-recovery phase on 32-round SKINNY-128-384.

To compare T_{III} and T_{IV}, when $m'_f - 2h_f \leq 0$, the complexity of **Attack IV** is lower than **Attack III**. For the attack where an h_f-bit filter with an m'_f-bit guessed subkey satisfy $m'_f - 2h_f \leq 0$, **Attack IV** is better than **Attack III**.

To compare T_I, T_{II} and T_{III}, we assume that the probability $\hat{p}^2\hat{q}^2$ is larger than 2^{-n} but the gap is small. Then $n/2+t$ can be approximated by n and $2t \approx n$. Thereafter, the complexities can be further estimated as $2^{m_b+m_f+n+2}$ for **Attack I**, $2^{m_b+r_b+2r_f}+2^{m_f+2r_b+r_f}$ for **Attack II** and $2^{m_b+2r_f} \cdot \varepsilon$ for **Attack III**. When $2^{2r_f} \cdot \varepsilon < 2^{m_f+n+2}$, the complexity of **Attack III** is lower than **Attack I**. When $r_b + 2r_f < m_f + n + 2$ and $2r_b + r_f < m_b + n + 2$, the complexity of **Attack II** is lower than **Attack I**.

Hence, different models perform differently for different parameters.

Future Work. Generally, the model is suitable for most block ciphers with linear key schedule. In fact, we also apply our method to CRAFT [8] and Saturnin [26]. For CRAFT, we find a better rectangle attack. However, the attack is inferior to the attack proposed in [40]. For Saturnin, we failed to get any improved attack. We plan to further investigate how to improve the current attacks by applying a more complicated key-bridging technique [36]. For example, in the 32-round attack on SKINNY, "we deduce $STK_{28}[3,7]$ from $ETK_0[1,0]$, $STK_2[0,2]$ and $STK_{30}[7,1]$". The current automatic model does not cover the key-bridging technique. Future work is to adopt this technique into the automatic model to find more effective key relations.

Acknowledgments. This work is supported by National Key R&D Program of China (2018YFA0704701, 2018YFA0704704), the Major Program of Guangdong Basic and Applied Research (2019B030302008), Major Scientific and Technological Innovation Project of Shandong Province, China (2019JZZY010133), Natural Science Foundation of China (61902207, 61772519, 62032014, 62072270) and the Chinese Major Program of National Cryptography Development Foundation (MMJJ20180101, MMJJ20180102).

References

1. Andreeva, E., Lallemand, V., Purnal, A., Reyhanitabar, R., Roy, A., Vizár, D.: Forkcipher: a new primitive for authenticated encryption of very short messages. In: Galbraith, S.D., Moriai, S. (eds.) ASIACRYPT 2019, Part II. LNCS, vol. 11922, pp. 153–182. Springer, Cham (2019). https://doi.org/10.1007/978-3-030-34621-8_6
2. Andreeva, E., Lallemand, V., Purnal, A., Reyhanitabar, R., Roy, A., Vizár, D.: ForkAE v. Submission to NIST Lightweight Cryptography Project (2019)
3. Ankele, R., et al.: Related-key impossible-differential attack on reduced-round SKINNY. In: Gollmann, D., Miyaji, A., Kikuchi, H. (eds.) ACNS 2017. LNCS, vol. 10355, pp. 208–228. Springer, Cham (2017). https://doi.org/10.1007/978-3-319-61204-1_11
4. Banik, S., Pandey, S.K., Peyrin, T., Sasaki, Yu., Sim, S.M., Todo, Y.: GIFT: a small present. In: Fischer, W., Homma, N. (eds.) CHES 2017. LNCS, vol. 10529, pp. 321–345. Springer, Cham (2017). https://doi.org/10.1007/978-3-319-66787-4_16
5. Bar-On, A., Dunkelman, O., Keller, N., Weizman, A.: DLCT: a new tool for differential-linear cryptanalysis. In: Ishai, Y., Rijmen, V. (eds.) EUROCRYPT 2019, Part I. LNCS, vol. 11476, pp. 313–342. Springer, Cham (2019). https://doi.org/10.1007/978-3-030-17653-2_11
6. Bariant, A., David, N., Leurent, G.: Cryptanalysis of forkciphers. IACR Trans. Symmetric Cryptol. **2020**(1), 233–265 (2020)
7. Beierle, C., et al.: The SKINNY family of block ciphers and its low-latency variant MANTIS. In: Robshaw, M., Katz, J. (eds.) CRYPTO 2016, Part II. LNCS, vol. 9815, pp. 123–153. Springer, Heidelberg (2016). https://doi.org/10.1007/978-3-662-53008-5_5
8. Beierle, C., Leander, G., Moradi, A., Rasoolzadeh, S.: CRAFT: lightweight tweakable block cipher with efficient protection against DFA attacks. IACR Trans. Symmetric Cryptol. **2019**(1), 5–45 (2019)
9. Beyne, T.: Block cipher invariants as eigenvectors of correlation matrices. J. Cryptol. **33**(3), 1156–1183 (2020)

10. Biham, E., Anderson, R., Knudsen, L.: Serpent: a new block cipher proposal. In: Vaudenay, S. (ed.) FSE 1998. LNCS, vol. 1372, pp. 222–238. Springer, Heidelberg (1998). https://doi.org/10.1007/3-540-69710-1_15

11. Biham, E., Dunkelman, O., Keller, N.: New cryptanalytic results on IDEA. In: Lai, X., Chen, K. (eds.) ASIACRYPT 2006. LNCS, vol. 4284, pp. 412–427. Springer, Heidelberg (2006). https://doi.org/10.1007/11935230_27

12. Biham, E., Dunkelman, O., Keller, N.: New results on boomerang and rectangle attacks. In: Daemen, J., Rijmen, V. (eds.) FSE 2002. LNCS, vol. 2365, pp. 1–16. Springer, Heidelberg (2002). https://doi.org/10.1007/3-540-45661-9_1

13. Biham, E., Dunkelman, O., Keller, N.: The rectangle attack — rectangling the serpent. In: Pfitzmann, B. (ed.) EUROCRYPT 2001. LNCS, vol. 2045, pp. 340–357. Springer, Heidelberg (2001). https://doi.org/10.1007/3-540-44987-6_21

14. Biham, E., Dunkelman, O., Keller, N.: Related-key boomerang and rectangle attacks. In: Cramer, R. (ed.) EUROCRYPT 2005. LNCS, vol. 3494, pp. 507–525. Springer, Heidelberg (2005). https://doi.org/10.1007/11426639_30

15. Biham, E., Shamir, A.: Differential cryptanalysis of DES-like cryptosystems. J. Cryptol. **4**(1), 3–72 (1991). https://doi.org/10.1007/BF00630563

16. Biryukov, A., De Cannière, C., Dellkrantz, G.: Cryptanalysis of SAFER++. In: Boneh, D. (ed.) CRYPTO 2003. LNCS, vol. 2729, pp. 195–211. Springer, Heidelberg (2003). https://doi.org/10.1007/978-3-540-45146-4_12

17. Biryukov, A., dos Santos, L.C., Feher, D., Velichkov, V., Vitto, G.: Automated truncation of differential trails and trail clustering in ARX. Cryptology ePrint Archive, Report 2021/1194 (2021)

18. Biryukov, A., Khovratovich, D.: Related-key cryptanalysis of the full AES-192 and AES-256. In: Matsui, M. (ed.) ASIACRYPT 2009. LNCS, vol. 5912, pp. 1–18. Springer, Heidelberg (2009). https://doi.org/10.1007/978-3-642-10366-7_1

19. Biryukov, A., Nikolić, I.: Automatic search for related-key differential characteristics in byte-oriented block ciphers: application to AES, Camellia, Khazad and others. In: Gilbert, H. (ed.) EUROCRYPT 2010. LNCS, vol. 6110, pp. 322–344. Springer, Heidelberg (2010). https://doi.org/10.1007/978-3-642-13190-5_17

20. Biryukov, A., Velichkov, V.: Automatic search for differential trails in ARX ciphers. In: Benaloh, J. (ed.) CT-RSA 2014. LNCS, vol. 8366, pp. 227–250. Springer, Cham (2014). https://doi.org/10.1007/978-3-319-04852-9_12

21. Bonnetain, X., Perrin, L., Tian, S.: Anomalies and vector space search: tools for S-box analysis. In: Galbraith, S.D., Moriai, S. (eds.) ASIACRYPT 2019, Part I. LNCS, vol. 11921, pp. 196–223. Springer, Cham (2019). https://doi.org/10.1007/978-3-030-34578-5_8

22. Boukerrou, H., Huynh, P., Lallemand, V., Mandal, B., Minier, M.: On the feistel counterpart of the boomerang connectivity table introduction and analysis of the FBCT. IACR Trans. Symmetric Cryptol. **2020**(1), 331–362 (2020)

23. Boura, C., Canteaut, A.: On the boomerang uniformity of cryptographic sboxes. IACR Trans. Symmetric Cryptol. **2018**(3), 290–310 (2018)

24. Boura, C., Lallemand, V., Naya-Plasencia, M., Suder, V.: Making the impossible possible. J. Cryptol. **31**(1), 101–133 (2018)

25. Boura, C., Naya-Plasencia, M., Suder, V.: Scrutinizing and improving impossible differential attacks: applications to CLEFIA, Camellia, LBlock and SIMON. In: Sarkar, P., Iwata, T. (eds.) ASIACRYPT 2014, Part I. LNCS, vol. 8873, pp. 179–199. Springer, Heidelberg (2014). https://doi.org/10.1007/978-3-662-45611-8_10

26. Canteaut, A., et al.: Saturnin: a suite of lightweight symmetric algorithms for post-quantum security. IACR Trans. Symmetric Cryptol. **2020**(S1), 160–207 (2020)

27. Canteaut, A., Naya-Plasencia, M., Vayssière, B.: Sieve-in-the-middle: improved MITM attacks. In: Canetti, R., Garay, J.A. (eds.) CRYPTO 2013, Part I. LNCS, vol. 8042, pp. 222–240. Springer, Heidelberg (2013). https://doi.org/10.1007/978-3-642-40041-4_13

28. Cid, C., Huang, T., Peyrin, T., Sasaki, Yu., Song, L.: Boomerang connectivity table: a new cryptanalysis tool. In: Nielsen, J.B., Rijmen, V. (eds.) EUROCRYPT 2018, Part II. LNCS, vol. 10821, pp. 683–714. Springer, Cham (2018). https://doi.org/10.1007/978-3-319-78375-8_22

29. Cid, C., Huang, T., Peyrin, T., Sasaki, Y., Song, L.: A security analysis of Deoxys and its internal tweakable block ciphers. IACR Trans. Symmetric Cryptol. 2017(3), 73–107 (2017)

30. Delaune, S., Derbez, P., Vavrille, M.: Catching the fastest boomerangs application to SKINNY. IACR Trans. Symmetric Cryptol. 2020(4), 104–129 (2020)

31. Derbez, P., Fouque, P.-A.: Automatic search of meet-in-the-middle and impossible differential attacks. In: Robshaw, M., Katz, J. (eds.) CRYPTO 2016, Part II. LNCS, vol. 9815, pp. 157–184. Springer, Heidelberg (2016). https://doi.org/10.1007/978-3-662-53008-5_6

32. Derbez, P., Fouque, P.-A., Jean, J.: Improved key recovery attacks on reduced-round AES in the single-key setting. In: Johansson, T., Nguyen, P.Q. (eds.) EUROCRYPT 2013. LNCS, vol. 7881, pp. 371–387. Springer, Heidelberg (2013). https://doi.org/10.1007/978-3-642-38348-9_23

33. Dong, X., Qin, L., Sun, S., Wang, X.: Key guessing strategies for linear key-schedule algorithms in rectangle attacks. Cryptology ePrint Archive, Report 2021/856 (2021). https://ia.cr/2021/856

34. Dunkelman, O., Indesteege, S., Keller, N.: A differential-linear attack on 12-round serpent. In: Chowdhury, D.R., Rijmen, V., Das, A. (eds.) INDOCRYPT 2008. LNCS, vol. 5365, pp. 308–321. Springer, Heidelberg (2008). https://doi.org/10.1007/978-3-540-89754-5_24

35. Dunkelman, O., Keller, N., Ronen, E., Shamir, A.: The retracing boomerang attack. In: Canteaut, A., Ishai, Y. (eds.) EUROCRYPT 2020, Part I. LNCS, vol. 12105, pp. 280–309. Springer, Cham (2020). https://doi.org/10.1007/978-3-030-45721-1_11

36. Dunkelman, O., Keller, N., Shamir, A.: Improved single-key attacks on 8-round AES-192 and AES-256. In: Abe, M. (ed.) ASIACRYPT 2010. LNCS, vol. 6477, pp. 158–176. Springer, Heidelberg (2010). https://doi.org/10.1007/978-3-642-17373-8_10

37. Dunkelman, O., Keller, N., Shamir, A.: A practical-time related-key attack on the KASUMI cryptosystem used in GSM and 3G telephony. In: Rabin, T. (ed.) CRYPTO 2010. LNCS, vol. 6223, pp. 393–410. Springer, Heidelberg (2010). https://doi.org/10.1007/978-3-642-14623-7_21

38. Dunkelman, O., Keller, N., Shamir, A.: A practical-time related-key attack on the KASUMI cryptosystem used in GSM and 3G telephony. J. Cryptol. 27(4), 824–849 (2014)

39. Flórez-Gutiérrez, A., Naya-Plasencia, M.: Improving key-recovery in linear attacks: application to 28-round PRESENT. In: Canteaut, A., Ishai, Y. (eds.) EUROCRYPT 2020, Part I. LNCS, vol. 12105, pp. 221–249. Springer, Cham (2020). https://doi.org/10.1007/978-3-030-45721-1_9

40. Guo, H., et al.: Differential attacks on CRAFT exploiting the involutory s-boxes and tweak additions. IACR Trans. Symmetric Cryptol. 2020(3), 119–151 (2020)

41. Hadipour, H., Bagheri, N., Song, L.: Improved rectangle attacks on SKINNY and CRAFT. IACR Trans. Symmetric Cryptol. 2021(2), 140–198 (2021)

42. Jean, J., Nikolić, I., Peyrin, T.: Tweaks and keys for block ciphers: the TWEAKEY framework. In: Sarkar, P., Iwata, T. (eds.) ASIACRYPT 2014, Part II. LNCS, vol. 8874, pp. 274–288. Springer, Heidelberg (2014). https://doi.org/10.1007/978-3-662-45608-8_15

43. Jean, J., Nikolić, I., Peyrin, T., Seurin, Y.: Submission to CAESAR: Deoxys v1.41, October 2016. http://competitions.cr.yp.to/round3/deoxysv141.pdf

44. Ji, F., Zhang, W., Zhou, C., Ding, T.: Improved (related-key) differential cryptanalysis on GIFT. In: Dunkelman, O., Jacobson, Jr., M.J., O'Flynn, C. (eds.) SAC 2020. LNCS, vol. 12804, pp. 198–228. Springer, Cham (2021). https://doi.org/10.1007/978-3-030-81652-0_8

45. Kelsey, J., Kohno, T., Schneier, B.: Amplified boomerang attacks against reduced-round MARS and serpent. In: Goos, G., Hartmanis, J., van Leeuwen, J., Schneier, B. (eds.) FSE 2000. LNCS, vol. 1978, pp. 75–93. Springer, Heidelberg (2001). https://doi.org/10.1007/3-540-44706-7_6

46. Kölbl, S., Leander, G., Tiessen, T.: Observations on the SIMON block cipher family. In: Gennaro, R., Robshaw, M. (eds.) CRYPTO 2015, Part I. LNCS, vol. 9215, pp. 161–185. Springer, Heidelberg (2015). https://doi.org/10.1007/978-3-662-47989-6_8

47. Liu, G., Ghosh, M., Song, L.: Security analysis of SKINNY under related-tweakey settings. IACR Trans. Symmetric Cryptol. 2017(3), 37–72 (2017)

48. Liu, M., Lu, X., Lin, D.: Differential-linear cryptanalysis from an algebraic perspective. In: Malkin, T., Peikert, C. (eds.) CRYPTO 2021, Part II. LNCS, vol. 12827, pp. 247–277. Springer, Cham (2021). https://doi.org/10.1007/978-3-030-84252-9_9

49. Lu, J., Kim, J., Keller, N., Dunkelman, O.: Improving the efficiency of impossible differential cryptanalysis of reduced camellia and MISTY1. In: Malkin, T. (ed.) CT-RSA 2008. LNCS, vol. 4964, pp. 370–386. Springer, Heidelberg (2008). https://doi.org/10.1007/978-3-540-79263-5_24

50. Mouha, N., Wang, Q., Gu, D., Preneel, B.: Differential and linear cryptanalysis using mixed-integer linear programming. In: Wu, C.-K., Yung, M., Lin, D. (eds.) Inscrypt 2011. LNCS, vol. 7537, pp. 57–76. Springer, Heidelberg (2012). https://doi.org/10.1007/978-3-642-34704-7_5

51. Murphy, S.: The return of the cryptographic boomerang. IEEE Trans. Inf. Theory 57(4), 2517–2521 (2011)

52. Qin, L., Dong, X., Wang, X., Jia, K., Liu, Y.: Automated search oriented to key recovery on ciphers with linear key schedule applications to boomerangs in SKINNY and ForkSkinny. IACR Trans. Symmetric Cryptol. 2021(2), 249–291 (2021)

53. Sadeghi, S., Mohammadi, T., Bagheri, N.: Cryptanalysis of reduced round SKINNY block cipher. IACR Trans. Symmetric Cryptol. 2018(3), 124–162 (2018)

54. Sasaki, Yu., Todo, Y.: New impossible differential search tool from design and cryptanalysis aspects. In: Coron, J.-S., Nielsen, J.B. (eds.) EUROCRYPT 2017, Part III. LNCS, vol. 10212, pp. 185–215. Springer, Cham (2017). https://doi.org/10.1007/978-3-319-56617-7_7

55. Selçuk, A.A.: On probability of success in linear and differential cryptanalysis. J. Cryptol. 21(1), 131–147 (2008)

56. Shi, D., Sun, S., Derbez, P., Todo, Y., Sun, B., Hu, L.: Programming the Demirci-Selçuk meet-in-the-middle attack with constraints. In: Peyrin, T., Galbraith, S. (eds.) ASIACRYPT 2018, Part II. LNCS, vol. 11273, pp. 3–34. Springer, Cham (2018). https://doi.org/10.1007/978-3-030-03329-3_1

57. Song, L., Qin, X., Hu, L.: Boomerang connectivity table revisited. application to SKINNY and AES. IACR Trans. Symmetric Cryptol. **2019**(1), 118–141 (2019)
58. Sun, L., Wang, W., Wang, M.: Accelerating the search of differential and linear characteristics with the SAT method. IACR Trans. Symmetric Cryptol. **2021**(1), 269–315 (2021)
59. Sun, S., Hu, L., Wang, P., Qiao, K., Ma, X., Song, L.: Automatic security evaluation and (related-key) differential characteristic search: application to SIMON, PRESENT, LBlock, DES(L) and other bit-oriented block ciphers. In: Sarkar, P., Iwata, T. (eds.) ASIACRYPT 2014, Part I. LNCS, vol. 8873, pp. 158–178. Springer, Heidelberg (2014). https://doi.org/10.1007/978-3-662-45611-8_9
60. Wagner, D.: The boomerang attack. In: Knudsen, L. (ed.) FSE 1999. LNCS, vol. 1636, pp. 156–170. Springer, Heidelberg (1999). https://doi.org/10.1007/3-540-48519-8_12
61. Wang, H., Peyrin, T.: Boomerang switch in multiple rounds. Application to AES variants and deoxys. IACR Trans. Symmetric Cryptol. **2019**(1), 142–169 (2019)
62. Zhao, B., Dong, X., Jia, K.: New related-tweakey boomerang and rectangle attacks on Deoxys-BC including BDT effect. IACR Trans. Symmetric Cryptol. **2019**(3), 121–151 (2019)
63. Zhao, B., Dong, X., Jia, K., Meier, W.: Improved related-Tweakey rectangle attacks on reduced-round Deoxys-BC-384 and Deoxys-I-256-128. In: Hao, F., Ruj, S., Sen Gupta, S. (eds.) INDOCRYPT 2019. LNCS, vol. 11898, pp. 139–159. Springer, Cham (2019). https://doi.org/10.1007/978-3-030-35423-7_7
64. Zhao, B., Dong, X., Meier, W., Jia, K., Wang, G.: Generalized related-key rectangle attacks on block ciphers with linear key schedule: applications to SKINNY and GIFT. Des. Codes Crypt. **88**(6), 1103–1126 (2020). https://doi.org/10.1007/s10623-020-00730-1

A Correlation Attack on Full SNOW-V and SNOW-Vi

Zhen Shi$^{(\boxtimes)}$ (iD), Chenhui Jin(iD), Jiyan Zhang(iD), Ting Cui(iD), Lin Ding(iD),
and Yu Jin(iD)

PLA SSF Information Engineering University, Zhengzhou 450000, China
shizhenieu@126.com

Abstract. In this paper, a method for searching correlations between
the binary stream of Linear Feedback Shift Register (LFSR) and the
keystream of SNOW-V and SNOW-Vi is presented based on the technique of approximation to composite functions. With the aid of the linear relationship between the four taps of LFSR input into Finite State
Machine (FSM) at three consecutive clocks, we present an automatic
search model based on the SAT/SMT technique and search out a series
of linear approximation trails with high correlation. By exhausting the
intermediate masks, we find a binary linear approximation with a correlation $-2^{-47.76}$. Using such approximation, we propose a correlation
attack on SNOW-V with an expected time complexity $2^{246.53}$, a memory
complexity $2^{238.77}$ and $2^{237.5}$ keystream words generated by the same
key and Initial Vector (IV). For SNOW-Vi, we provide a binary linear
approximation with the same correlation and mount a correlation attack
with the same complexity as that of SNOW-V. To the best of our knowledge, this is the first known attack on full SNOW-V and SNOW-Vi,
which is better than the exhaustive key search with respect to time complexity. The results indicate that neither SNOW-V nor SNOW-Vi can
guarantee the 256-bit security level if we ignore the design constraint
that the maximum length of keystream for a single pair of key and IV is
less than 2^{64}.

Keywords: SNOW-V · SNOW-Vi · Cryptanalysis · Linear
approximation · Automatic search · Correlation attack

1 Introduction

SNOW-V is a new member of the SNOW family stream ciphers following SNOW
1.0 [1], SNOW 2.0 [2] and SNOW 3G [3]. SNOW 3G, which is used as the core of
3G Partnership Project (3GPP) Confidentiality and Integrity Algorithms UEA2
& UIA2 for UMTS and LTE, enhances the security under the 128-bit key. In
2018, SNOW-V, which was proposed for a standard encryption scheme for 5G
mobile communication system by Ekdahl et al. [4], was announced to satisfy the
256-bit security level requirement from 3GPP with a 256-bit key and 128-bit
Initial Vector (IV). Lately, Ekdahl et al. [5] proposed SNOW-Vi as an extreme

© International Association for Cryptologic Research 2022
O. Dunkelman and S. Dziembowski (Eds.): EUROCRYPT 2022, LNCS 13277, pp. 34–56, 2022.
https://doi.org/10.1007/978-3-031-07082-2_2

performance variant of SNOW-V. Compared with SNOW 3G, the structure of SNOW-V and SNOW-Vi keeps the same, except that a couple of Linear Feedback Shift Registers (LFSRs) are used to replace the original one, and the size of registers increases from 32 bits to 128 bits so that the size of internal state rises significantly. This makes SNOW-V and SNOW-Vi difficult to analyze.

Up to now, several security evaluations on various versions of SNOW-V and SNOW-Vi have been published. Jiao et al. [7] proposed a byte-based guess and determine attack on SNOW-V with a time complexity of 2^{406}, using only seven keystream words. At ToSC 2021, Gong and Zhang [8] performed a linear cryptanalysis of SNOW-V and proposed correlation attacks against three reduced variants. For the reduced variant SNOW-V$_{\boxplus_{32},\boxplus_8}$, they mounted a fast correlation attack with a time complexity $2^{377.01}$, a memory complexity 2^{363}, and $2^{253.73}$ keystream outputs. Yang et al. [9] proposed a guess and determine attack against the full SNOW-V with a time complexity of 2^{378}, and a distinguishing attack against the reduced variant SNOW-V$_\oplus$ with complexity 2^{303}. For the initialization phase, Hoki et al. [10] investigated the security of the initialization of SNOW-V at ACISP 2021, using Mixed-integer Linear Programming (MILP) model to efficiently search for integral and differential characteristics. The resulting distinguishing or key recovery attacks are applicable to SNOW-V with reduced initialization rounds of five, out of the original 16 rounds. However, none of these cryptanalysis efforts result in a valid attack against SNOW-V and SNOW-Vi, which is faster than the exhaustive key search.

Our Contributions. In this paper, we focus on the security levels of SNOW-V and SNOW-Vi against correlation attack.

- The search for high correlation binary approximations is quite a challenge in this cryptanalysis. We introduce a newly constructed composite function, which helps to equivalently transform the linear approximation of the Finite State Machine (FSM) part into that of the composition of several simple functions. In this way, the correlation of a linear approximation trail can be computed by multiplying those of sub-functions with no need to consider the dependence between sub-functions, and the correlations of linear approximations based on three consecutive outputs of SNOW-V can be evaluated by the linear approximation trails of the composite function.
- A series of automatic search models have been widely used to search linear trails with high correlations of block ciphers, but just a few for stream ciphers [11] as far as we know. As we have already converted the approximations of FSM into those of a composite function, we can launch a wide range of search for linear trails by taking advantage of automatic search techniques, and approximate the accurate correlations with the correlations of linear trails.
- With the aid of the linear relationship between the four taps of LFSR input into FSM at three consecutive clocks, we present an automatic search model based on SAT/SMT technique and search out a series of linear approximation trails with high correlations. By exhausting the intermediate masks, we find an accurate binary linear approximation with a correlation $-2^{-47.76}$.

– Using the approximation, we mount a correlation attack with an expected time complexity $2^{246.53}$, a memory complexity $2^{238.77}$, and $2^{237.5}$ keystream words, which can recover the internal state of SNOW-V at the clock producing the first keystream word. For SNOW-Vi, we provide a linear approximation with the same correlation, and mount a correlation attack with the same complexity as that on SNOW-V.

As far as we know, it is the first attack with the time complexity less than that of exhaustive attack on SNOW-V and SNOW-Vi (see Table 1).

Table 1. Summary of the attacks on SNOW-V and SNOW-Vi

Version	Technique	Round	Time	Data	References
SNOW-V$_\oplus$	Distinguishing attack	full	2^{303}	2^{303}	[9]
SNOW-V$_{\sigma_0}$	Correlation attack	full	$2^{251.93}$	$2^{103.83}$	[8]
SNOW-V$_{\boxplus_{32},\boxplus_8}$	Correlation attack	full	$2^{377.01}$	$2^{253.73}$	[8]
SNOW-V	Differential attack	4	$2^{153.97}$	$2^{26.96}$	[10]
	Guess and Determine	full	2^{512}	7	[6]
	Guess and Determine	full	2^{406}	7	[7]
	Guess and Determine	full	2^{378}	8	[9]
	Correlation attack	full	$2^{246.53}$	$2^{237.5}$	Sect. 6
SNOW-Vi	Differential attack	4	$2^{233.99}$	$2^{7.94}$	[10]
	Correlation attack	full	$2^{246.53}$	$2^{237.5}$	Sect. 7

Organization. Section 2 lists some notations and briefly introduces SNOW-V and SNOW-Vi. Section 3 proposes the framework of our linear approximation of SNOW-V. Section 4 describes the automatic search models used in this paper in detail. Based on the results of automatic search, Sect. 5 evaluates the complete correlation. Section 6 and 7 show the correlation attacks on SNOW-V and SNOW-Vi, respectively. Section 8 concludes this paper.

2 Preliminaries

2.1 Notations and Definitions

Henceforth, we fix some notations for convenience.

$GF(2)$	the binary field
$GF(2^n)$	the n-dimensional extension field of $GF(2)$
$\oplus$	the bitwise XOR operation
$\boxplus$	the parallel of four additions modulo 2^{32}
$\boxminus$	the parallel of four subtractions modulo 2^{32}
$\bar{x}$	the NOT operation for a given bit x
$wt(x)$	the Hamming weight of a Boolean vector x

Given two binary vectors $a = (a_{n-1}, a_{n-2}, ..., a_0), b = (b_{n-1}, b_{n-2}, ..., b_0)$, the inner product is defined as $a \cdot b = \overset{n-1}{\underset{i=0}{\oplus}} a_i b_i$.

Let x be an element of $GF(2^{16})$ and $y = (y_{m-1}, y_{m-2}, ..., y_0)$ be an m-dimensional vector on the same field, the product of x and y is defined as $x * y = (xy_{m-1}, xy_{m-2}, ..., xy_0)$, where the product xy_i is operated over $GF(2^{16})$.

The correlation of a binary random variable x is defined as

$$\rho(x) = \Pr(x = 0) - \Pr(x = 1),$$

and the absolute correlation of the binary random variable x is defined as $|\rho(x)|$.

For a vectorized Boolean function $f : GF(2^m) \rightarrow GF(2^n)$, the correlation with the input mask α and the output mask β is calculated as

$$\rho(\alpha \rightarrow \beta) = \frac{1}{2^m} \sum_{x \in GF(2^m)} (-1)^{\alpha \cdot x \oplus \beta \cdot f(x)},$$

and we express the approximation process by $\alpha \xrightarrow[\rho(\alpha \rightarrow \beta)]{f} \beta$. Especially, the correlation of $f(x, y) = x \boxplus y$ with the input mask α, β and output mask γ is denoted by $\rho_A(\alpha, \beta \rightarrow \gamma)$, and the correlation of $f(x) = AES^R(x, 0)$ with input mask α and output mask β is denoted by $\rho_E(\alpha \rightarrow \beta)$.

We use the corresponding bold letter to denote the matrix of a linear transformation, e.g., $P(x) = \boldsymbol{P}x$ for a linear transformation P and a column vector x.

2.2   Description of SNOW-V and SNOW-Vi

SNOW-V. Like previous SNOW stream ciphers, SNOW-V consists of LFSR part and FSM part. The LFSR part of SNOW-V is a circular structure consisting of two LFSRs, and the size of each register in FSM part increases to 128 bits. The overall schematic of SNOW-V algorithm is shown in Fig. 1.

The two LFSRs are named LFSR-A and LFSR-B, both with a length of 16 and a cell size of 16 bits. The 32 cells are denoted as $a_{15}, ..., a_0$ and $b_{15}, ..., b_0$ respectively. The elements of LFSR-A are generated by the polynomial

$$g^A(x) = x^{16} + x^{15} + x^{12} + x^{11} + x^8 + x^3 + x^2 + x + 1 \in GF(2)[x],$$

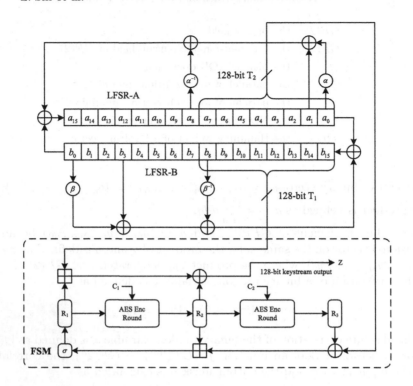

Fig. 1. The keystream generation phase of the SNOW-V stream cipher

while the elements of LFSR-B are generated by

$$g^B(x) = x^{16} + x^{15} + x^{14} + x^{11} + x^8 + x^6 + x^5 + x + 1 \in GF(2)[x].$$

The LFSR part is updated by

$$a^{(t+16)} = b^{(t)} + \alpha a^{(t)} + a^{(t+1)} + \alpha^{-1}a^{(t+8)} \bmod g^A(\alpha),$$
$$b^{(t+16)} = a^{(t)} + \beta b^{(t)} + b^{(t+3)} + \beta^{-1}b^{(t+8)} \bmod g^B(\beta),$$

in which α is a root of $g^A(x)$ and β is a root of $g^B(x)$. Two taps T_1 and T_2 at clock t are given respectively by

$$T_1^{(t)} = (b_{15}^{(8t)}, b_{14}^{(8t)}, ..., b_8^{(8t)}), T_2^{(t)} = (a_7^{(8t)}, a_6^{(8t)}, ..., a_0^{(8t)}).$$

R_1, R_2, R_3 are three 128-bit registers of FSM part, updated by

$$R_1^{(t+1)} = \sigma(R_2^{(t)} \boxplus (R_3^{(t)} \oplus T_2^{(t)})),$$
$$R_2^{(t+1)} = AES^R(R_1^{(t)}, C1),$$
$$R_3^{(t+1)} = AES^R(R_2^{(t)}, C2).$$

$AES^R(input, key)$ denotes the AES encryption round function, C_1 and C_2 are zeros. σ is a byte-oriented permutation:

$$\sigma = [0, 4, 8, 12, 1, 5, 9, 13, 2, 6, 10, 14, 3, 7, 11, 15],$$

and $\sigma^{-1} = \sigma$. The 128 bits keystream at clock t is given by:

$$z^{(t)} = (R_1^{(t)} \boxplus T_1^{(t)}) \oplus R_2^{(t)}.$$

For more details of SNOW-V, please refer to [4].

SNOW-Vi. SNOW-Vi is an extreme performance variant of SNOW-V, and eliminates the linear relationship between $T_1^{(t-1)}, T_1^{(t)}, T_1^{(t+1)}, T_2^{(t)}$. SNOW-Vi is consistent with SNOW-V except that the two fields F_2^A and F_2^B have the generating polynomials:

$$g^A(x) = x^{16} + x^{14} + x^{11} + x^9 + x^6 + x^5 + x^3 + x^2 + 1 \in F_2[x],$$
$$g^B(x) = x^{16} + x^{15} + x^{14} + x^{11} + x^{10} + x^7 + x^2 + x + 1 \in F_2[x],$$

and the LFSR part updates as follows:

$$a^{(t+16)} = b^{(t)} + \alpha a^{(t)} + a^{(t+7)} \bmod g^A(\alpha),$$
$$b^{(t+16)} = a^{(t)} + \beta b^{(t)} + b^{(t+8)} \bmod g^B(\beta).$$

Two taps T_1 and T_2 at clock t are given respectively as

$$T_1^{(t)} = (b_{15}^{(8t)}, b_{14}^{(8t)}, \cdots, b_8^{(8t)}), T_2^{(t)} = (a_{15}^{(8t)}, a_{14}^{(8t)}, \cdots, a_8^{(8t)}).$$

For more details of SNOW-Vi, please refer to [5].

3   Linear Approximation of SNOW-V

Our motivation is to find biased binary approximations of SNOW-V which only relate to the output words and LFSR states. For most stream ciphers, how to evaluate the correlations of linear approximations based on consecutive outputs is a difficult problem. In this section, we convert the linear approximations based on three consecutive outputs of SNOW-V into those of a composite function equivalently. Thus we can evaluate the correlations by the properties of Walsh spectrum, and it is much clearer to investigate the linear approximations from the point of view of composite functions.

SNOW-V employs two LFSRs making up a circular structure. There is a straightforward observation [9] that the four taps at three consecutive clocks satisfy

$$T_2^{(t)} = T_1^{(t+1)} \oplus \beta * T_1^{(t-1)} \oplus \beta^{-1} * T_1^{(t)} \oplus (T_1^{(t-1)} >> 48) \oplus (T_1^{(t)} << 80),$$

and we also confirm it experimentally. The above equation can be rewritten as

$$L(T_1^{(t-1)}, T_1^{(t)}) = T_1^{(t+1)} \oplus T_2^{(t)},$$

where L is a linear mapping recording the linear relationship above. We omit the superscript of $R_1^{(t)}, R_2^{(t)}, R_3^{(t)}$, and simplify them as R_1, R_2, R_3. The keystream outputs in three consecutive clocks can be expressed by

$$z_{t-1} = (T_1^{(t-1)} \boxplus E^{-1}(R_2)) \oplus E^{-1}(R_3),$$
$$z_t = (T_1^{(t)} \boxplus R_1) \oplus R_2,$$
$$z_{t+1} = (T_1^{(t+1)} \boxplus \sigma(R_2 \boxplus (R_3 \oplus T_2^{(t)}))) \oplus E(R_1).$$

Let $\alpha, \beta, \gamma, l, m, n, h$ be 128-bit masks. We observe that the following equation will show a nonzero correlation ρ when the masks take certain values:

$$
\begin{aligned}
(\alpha, &\beta, \gamma, l, m, n, h) \cdot (z_{t-1}, z_t, z_{t+1}, T_1^{(t-1)}, T_1^{(t)}, T_1^{(t+1)}, T_2^{(t)}) \\
&= \alpha \cdot (E^{-1}(R_2) \boxplus T_1^{(t-1)}) \oplus \beta \cdot R_2 \oplus \gamma \cdot (\sigma(R_2 \boxplus (R_3 \oplus T_2^{(t)})) \boxplus T_1^{(t+1)}) \\
&\quad \oplus \alpha \cdot E^{-1}(R_3) \oplus \beta \cdot (R_1 \boxplus T_1^{(t)}) \oplus \gamma \cdot E(R_1) \qquad\qquad (1) \\
&\quad \oplus l \cdot T_1^{(t-1)} \oplus m \cdot T_1^{(t)} \oplus n \cdot T_1^{(t+1)} \oplus h \cdot T_2^{(t)} \\
&\stackrel{\rho}{=} 0.
\end{aligned}
$$

In order to make the linear approximation process more explicit and precise, we divide it into several sub-steps by introducing 6 functions:

$$
\begin{aligned}
f_1(x, y, z, u, v, w) &= (x \boxminus v, y, z, u, L(z, u) \oplus v, w), \\
f_2(x, y, z, u, v, w) &= ((\sigma^{-1}(x) \boxminus y) \oplus v, y, z, u, v, w), \\
f_3(x, y, z, u, v, w) &= (E^{-1}(x), E^{-1}(y), z, u, v, w), \\
f_4(x, y, z, u, v, w) &= (x, (y \boxplus z), u, v, w), \\
f_5(x, y, z, u, v) &= (x, y, z, u, E^{-1}(v)), \\
f_6(x, y, z, u, v) &= (x, y, u, (z \boxplus v)).
\end{aligned}
$$

It is clear that the composite function

$$F(x, y, z, u, v, w) := (f_6 \circ f_5 \circ f_4 \circ f_3 \circ f_2 \circ f_1)(x, y, z, u, v, w)$$

has 6-word input and 4-word output. In the following theorem, we equivalently convert the approximation of FSM part of SNOW-V into that of the composite function F.

Theorem 1. Assume that $R_1, R_2, R_3, T_1^{(t-1)}, T_1^{(t)}, T_1^{(t+1)}$ are independent and uniform distributed. For the binary linear approximation of F

$$(\gamma, \beta, l, m, n, \gamma) \xrightarrow[\rho_F]{F} (\alpha, \alpha, h, \beta),$$

which is under the masks defined by the same $\alpha, \beta, \gamma, l, m, n, h$ as in Eq. (1), we have $\rho = \rho_F$.

Proof. Set

$$(x, y, z, u, v, w) = (\sigma(R_2 \boxplus (R_3 \oplus T_2^{(t)})) \boxplus T_1^{(t+1)}, R_2, T_1^{(t-1)}, T_1^{(t)}, T_1^{(t+1)}, E(R_1)).$$

As $R_1, R_2, R_3, T_1^{(t-1)}, T_1^{(t)}, T_1^{(t+1)}$ are independent and uniform distributed, x, y, z, u, v, w are independent and uniform distributed as well. Recall that

$$L(T_1^{(t-1)}, T_1^{(t)}) = T_1^{(t+1)} \oplus T_2^{(t)},$$

we have

$$F(x, y, z, u, v, w) = (E^{-1}(R_3), E^{-1}(R_2) \boxplus T_1^{(t-1)}, T_2^{(t)}, T_1^{(t)} \boxplus R_1).$$

Thus, the equation of the linear approximation $(\gamma, \beta, l, m, n, \gamma) \xrightarrow{F} (\alpha, \alpha, h, \beta)$ is

$$(\gamma, \beta, l, m, n, \gamma) \cdot (\sigma(R_2 \boxplus (R_3 \oplus T_2^{(t)})) \boxplus T_1^{(t+1)}, R_2, T_1^{(t-1)}, T_1^{(t)}, T_1^{(t+1)}, E(R_1)) \\ \oplus (\alpha, \alpha, h, \beta) \cdot (E^{-1}(R_3), E^{-1}(R_2) \boxplus T_1^{(t-1)}, T_2^{(t)}, T_1^{(t)} \boxplus R_1) \overset{\rho_F}{=} 0. \tag{2}$$

As the linear approximation Eqs. (1) and (2) are exactly the same, it is obvious that the correlation ρ_F of the above approximation is equal to ρ.   □

By Theorem 1, we convert the problem of computing the correlation of Eq. (1) into that of searching for linear approximations of F equivalently. In fact, Theorem 1 also indicates a provable result of the correlations of binary approximations based on three consecutive outputs of SNOW-V. The binary linear approximations of F defined in Theorem 1 by the parameters $\alpha, \beta, \gamma, l, m, n, h$ correspond one-to-one to those of Eq. (1), which have the same correlation. Thus, using the properties of Walsh spectrum of composite functions, we can evaluate the approximations of SNOW-V by measuring the linear trails instead of computing the correlations of approximations directly.

Notice that different choices of l, m, n, h lead to different forms of Eq. (1), i.e., different distinguishers when $\rho \neq 0$. From the linear relation

$$L(T_1^{(t-1)}, T_1^{(t)}) = T_1^{(t+1)} \oplus T_2^{(t)},$$

we know that

$$l \cdot T_1^{(t-1)} \oplus m \cdot T_1^{(t)} \oplus n \cdot T_1^{(t+1)} \oplus h \cdot T_2^{(t)} = 0,$$

when $n\boldsymbol{L} = h\boldsymbol{L} = (l||m)$ holds, in which $||$ represents the cascading operation. Then Eq. (1) shall become

$$(\alpha, \beta, \gamma, l, m, n, h) \cdot (z_{t-1}, z_t, z_{t+1}, T_1^{(t-1)}, T_1^{(t)}, T_1^{(t+1)}, T_2^{(t)}) \\ = \alpha \cdot z_{t-1} \oplus \beta \cdot z_t \oplus \gamma \cdot z_{t+1} \overset{\rho}{=} 0,$$

which contains only the output words z_{t-1}, z_t, z_{t+1}, and indicates a distinguisher for distinguishing attack; otherwise, when

$$l \cdot T_1^{(t-1)} \oplus m \cdot T_1^{(t)} \oplus n \cdot T_1^{(t+1)} \oplus h \cdot T_2^{(t)} \neq 0,$$

we will get a distinguisher for correlation attack which can be used to recover the initial state of the LFSR.

In this paper, we focus on the search of distinguishers for correlation attack. Denoting the intermediate masks as a, b, c, d, e, f, q respectively, the linear approximation trail of F above can be described as

$$(\gamma, \beta, l, m, n, \gamma) \xrightarrow[dL=(e\oplus l)||(f\oplus m), \rho_A(a, n\oplus d\to\gamma)]{f_1} (a, \beta, e, f, d, \gamma) \xrightarrow[\rho_A(b\oplus\beta, d\oplus h\to a\boldsymbol{\sigma})]{f_2}$$

$$(d \oplus h, b, e, f, h, \gamma) \xrightarrow[\rho_E(\alpha\to d\oplus h)\rho_E(c\to b)]{f_3} (\alpha, c, e, f, h, \gamma) \xrightarrow[\rho_A(e, c\to\alpha)]{f_4} (\alpha, \alpha, f, h, \gamma)$$

$$\xrightarrow[\rho_E(q\to\gamma)]{f_5} (\alpha, \alpha, f, h, q) \xrightarrow[\rho_A(f, q\to\beta)]{f_6} (\alpha, \alpha, h, \beta),$$

and its correlation can be evaluated as

$$\rho(a, b, c, d, q) = \rho_A(a, n \oplus d \to \gamma)\rho_A(b \oplus \beta, d \oplus h \to a\boldsymbol{\sigma})\rho_E(\alpha \to d \oplus h)$$
$$\rho_E(c \to b)\rho_A(e, c \to \alpha)\rho_E(q \to \gamma)\rho_A(f, q \to \beta),$$

with the constraint $d\boldsymbol{L} = (e \oplus l)||(f \oplus m)$. This form of approximation enables us to find linear trails with the assistance of automatic search technique. The detailed reasoning process of intermediate masks is given in Appendix A, and there is no need to consider the influence of e and f in later analysis, because they can be generated linearly by d, l, m. According to the properties of Walsh spectrum of composite functions, the accurate correlation of a binary linear approximation with the input and output masks defined by parameters $\alpha, \beta, \gamma, l, m, n, h$ of F should be computed by

$$c(\alpha, \beta, \gamma, l, m, n, h) = \sum_{a, b, c, d, q} \rho(a, b, c, d, q),$$

which means we can get the accurate correlation by exhausting the intermediate masks a, b, c, d, q.

4   Automatic Search of Linear Approximation Trails of SNOW-V

In this section, we model the problem of searching linear approximation trails as STP-based automatic search programs. STP is an SMT solver which encodes the constraints with CVC, SMT-LIB1 and SMT-LIB2 languages [12]. STP has been used to analyze block ciphers [14], but for stream ciphers, there is no precedent as far as we know. Since STP solver can model XOR operations easily, we construct STP-based automatic search program for linear approximation trails of SNOW-V. STP solver will return a solution that meets the conditions if there is one. The model of the linear approximation above contains three substitution layers and four layers of addition modulo 2^{32} operations as the nonlinear part. Here we characterize the linear approximation in the way available for STP solver. For convenience, signs of correlation values are temporarily ignored in the process of characterization, and determined in the verification process.

8-bit S-box. We denote $c(x, y)$ the correlation of an S-box with the input mask $x = (x_7, x_6, ..., x_0)$ and output mask $y = (y_7, y_6, ..., y_0)$. Since the nonzero absolute correlations of the S-box except 1 has 8 values, we split the linear correlation table into multiple Boolean functions like in [13]. Here we construct 8 Boolean functions:

$$f_k(x, y) = \begin{cases} 1, & \text{if } |c(x,y)| = 4k/256; \\ 0, & \text{if } |c(x,y)| \neq 4k/256. \end{cases} \quad k = 1, 2, ..., 8$$

As the expressions longer than 256 characters are not supported by STP solver, $f(x, y)$ needs to be converted into a series of shorter constrains that are fully satisfied. By inputting the truth tables, the software *LogicFriday* can directly give the product-of-sum representation of a Boolean function. For example, the Boolean function with 3 input bits and 1 output bit $h(a_0, a_1, a_2) = a_0 a_1 a_2 \oplus a_0 a_1 \oplus a_2$ has the product-of-sum representation

$$h(a_0, a_1, a_2) = (a_0|a_1|a_2)\&(a_0|\bar{a}_1|a_2)\&(\bar{a}_0|a_1|a_2).$$

Thus, the Boolean function $h(a_0, a_1, a_2)$ has essential conditions

$$\begin{cases} a_0|a_1|a_2 = 0 \Rightarrow h(a_0, a_1, a_2) = 0, \\ a_0|\bar{a}_1|a_2 = 0 \Rightarrow h(a_0, a_1, a_2) = 0, \\ \tilde{a}_0|a_1|a_2 = 0 \Rightarrow h(a_0, a_1, a_2) = 0. \end{cases}$$

In the same way, $f_k(x, y)$ can be converted into a series of logical conditions. With the constraint

$$f_1(x, y)|f_2(x, y)|...|f_8(x, y) = x_0|x_1|...|x_7|y_0|y_1|...|y_7$$

added, we have the observation that $f_k(x, y) = 1$ if and only if $|c(x,y)| = 4k/256$. STP solver does not support the floating-point data type, so we replace the absolute correlation of the i-th S-box $|c^{(i)}(x, y)|$ with [14]

$$S^{(i)} = -\left\lfloor 10^t \log_2 |c^{(i)}(x, y)| \right\rfloor = \sum_{k=1}^{8} \left\lfloor 10^t f_k^{(i)}(x, y) \log_2(256/4k) \right\rfloor,$$

in which t is the precision parameter. Thus we get the absolute correlation of an S-box being accurate to t decimal places.

Addition Modulo 2^{32}. Wallén [15] proposed a recursive method to efficiently compute the correlation with given input and output masks. Then the result was improved by Schulte-Geers [16]. Denoting the output mask as u, the input masks as v, w, the i-th bit of Boolean vector x as x_i, the constraints to obtain a valid linear approximation shall be expressed as

$$\begin{aligned} &z_{n-1} = 0, \\ &z_j = z_{j+1} \oplus u_{j+1} \oplus v_{j+1} \oplus w_{j+1} (0 \leq j < n-1), \\ &z_i \geq u_i \oplus v_i (0 \leq i < n), \\ &z_i \geq u_i \oplus w_i, \end{aligned}$$

in which z is a dummy variable. The correlation of the linear approximation is not zero if and only if z satisfies the constraints, and is given by $\rho_A(v, w \to u) = (-1)^{(u \oplus v) \cdot (u \oplus w)} 2^{-wt(z)}$ when it is not zero. In order to keep consistent with the accuracy of the correlation of S-boxes, we replace the absolute correlation of the j-th modular addition $2^{-wt(z^{(j)})}$ with $Z^{(j)} = 10^t wt(z^{(j)})$ as well.

Objective Function. As there are 48 S-boxes and 16 modular additions taking part in the linear approximation, a trail can be evaluated by $\sum\limits_{i=1}^{48} S^{(i)} + \sum\limits_{j=1}^{16} Z^{(j)}$. A solution returned by the STP solver satisfying the constraint

$$\sum_{i=1}^{48} S^{(i)} + \sum_{j=1}^{16} Z^{(j)} < l$$

represents a trail with the absolute correlation higher than $2^{-10^{-t}l}$.

The Sign. After STP solver returns a linear approximation trail that satisfies all constraints, we verify the trail and determine its sign.

Finding More Trails. As mentioned in Sect. 3, the correlation of a binary linear approximation of SNOW-V can be computed as

$$c(\alpha, \beta, \gamma, l, m, n, h) = \sum_{a,b,c,d,q} \rho(a, b, c, d, q).$$

Assuming that the trail $(\alpha_0, \beta_0, \gamma_0, l_0, m_0, n_0, h_0, a_0, b_0, c_0, d_0, q_0)$ has been found, we can keep searching for other new solutions by introducing the additional constraints:

$$\alpha = \alpha_0, \beta = \beta_0, \gamma = \gamma_0, l = l_0, m = m_0, n = n_0, h = h_0,$$
$$(a \oplus a_0)|(b \oplus b_0)|(c \oplus c_0)|(d \oplus d_0)|(q \oplus q_0) \neq 0.$$

Different solutions can be generated one by one in this way, and the binary correlation gradually approaches its real value by summing up the correlations of linear trails.

We build the automatic search program for the linear approximation above. Labeling different trails with different subscripts, the best result we have found is

$$\alpha_1 = l_1 = c_1 = 0xc, 0, 0, 0$$
$$\beta_1 = m_1 = 0x80, 0, 0, 0$$
$$\gamma_1 = h_1 = b_1 = 0x81ec5a80, 0, 0, 0$$
$$n_1 = 0x81ec5a00, 0, 0, 0$$
$$a_1 = 0xc1000000, 0, 0, 0$$
$$q_1 = 0xa0, 0, 0, 0$$
$$d_1 = 0, 0, 0, 0.$$

with the correlation 2^{-48} (The symbol '0' denotes 32-bit 0, and the leftmost 32-bit word is the most significant word hereafter), meanwhile we also focus on another trail

$$\alpha_2 = l_2 = c_2 = 0xd, 0, 0, 0$$
$$\beta_2 = m_2 = 0x40, 0, 0, 0$$
$$\gamma_2 = h_2 = b_2 = 0x81ec5a80, 0, 0, 0$$
$$n_2 = 0x81ec5a00, 0, 0, 0$$
$$a_2 = 0xc1000000, 0, 0, 0$$
$$q_2 = 0x60, 0, 0, 0$$
$$d_2 = 0, 0, 0, 0.$$

with the correlation $-2^{-49.063}$.

From the expression of $\rho(a, b, c, d, q)$ in Sect. 3, we can see that the common features of both trails are that there is only one active S-box in each substitution layer, and only one active 32-bit word in each layer of addition modulo 2^{32}. Besides, we can see that masks of the two trails are similar. In fact, all of the linear approximation trails we found with high correlations have masks of the same form above. Although these trails can approximate the corresponding linear approximations to some extent, we still want to evaluate the accurate correlations.

5 Evaluating the Accurate Correlations for a Special Type of Binary Linear Approximations

Based on the trails we have searched out, we try to get accurate values of some high correlations. In this section, indeterminate nonzero 8-bit bytes in 128-bit masks are denoted as $*$. Since all the trails we have searched out with absolute correlation higher than 2^{-50} are of the form

$$\alpha = l = 0x000000*, 0, 0, 0$$
$$\beta = m = 0x000000*, 0, 0, 0$$
$$\gamma = h = 0x81ec5a80, 0, 0, 0$$
$$n = 0x81ec5a00, 0, 0, 0,$$

and the accurate correlation of a binary linear approximation should be

$$c(\alpha, \beta, \gamma, l, m, n, h) = \sum_{a,b,c,d,q} \rho(a, b, c, d, q).$$

Thus, we evaluate the accurate correlations of linear trails with parameters

$$\alpha = l = 0x000000X, 0, 0, 0$$
$$\beta = m = 0x000000Y, 0, 0, 0$$
$$\gamma = h = 0x81ec5a80, 0, 0, 0$$
$$n = 0x81ec5a00, 0, 0, 0,$$

by exhausting the intermediate masks a, b, c, d, q for given 8-bit words X and Y.

Mask c and q. Due to the properties of the linear approximation of modular addition, the most significant nonzero bit of an input mask must be in the same position as that of the output mask. Therefore, there is a straightforward observation that c and e have the form $(0x000000*, 0, 0, 0)$, i.e., c and e are zeros except for their 12-th bytes, with the assumption $\alpha = (0x000000X, 0, 0, 0)$ and $\rho_A(c, e \to \alpha) \neq 0$. In a similar way, we can deduce $q = (0x000000*, 0, 0, 0)$ by $\beta = (0x000000Y, 0, 0, 0)$ and $\rho_A(f, q \to \beta) \neq 0$, and so as f. Hence we only need to exhaust at most 255 values of c and q respectively.

Mask d. As l, m, e, f are zeros except for their 12-th bytes, from the linear relation $d\boldsymbol{L} = (e \oplus l) \| (f \oplus m)$ we can get

$$d\boldsymbol{L} = (0x000000*, 0, 0, 0, 0x000000*, 0, 0, 0).$$

This system of linear equations can be confirmed that the unique solution of d is $(0, 0, 0, 0)$. The detailed proof is shown in Appendix B.

Mask b and a. By $\rho_E(c \to b) \neq 0$ and $c = (0x000000*, 0, 0, 0)$, we know that $b\boldsymbol{P} = (0x000000*, 0, 0, 0)$, where $\boldsymbol{P}$ is the binary matrix of the linear transformation of AES round function. So there are 255 values for b to traverse as well. a is constrained by both $\rho_A(a, n \oplus d \to \gamma) \neq 0$ and $\rho_A(b \oplus \beta, d \oplus h \to \sigma^T a) \neq 0$. The first constraint means that the least significant three 32-bit words of a are zeros while the second indicates that the least significant three 32-bit words of $\sigma^T a$ are zeros. Since the 15-th byte is the unique fixed point of σ among the 4 most significant bytes, we have $a = (0x * 000000, 0, 0, 0)$.

Thus, we only need to exhaust 4 bytes to get all the trails with nonzero correlation and reach the accurate correlation of the linear approximation by summing them up when $\alpha, \beta, \gamma, l, m, n, h$ are chosen as above. We could also traverse X and Y to find the optimal approximation of this type. The time complexity is far less than 2^{48}, for most of the cases shall break halfway. Based on the two trails shown in Sect. 4, we compute the correlations and get

$$c(\alpha_1, \beta_1, \gamma_1, l_1, m_1, n_1, h_1) = 2^{-48.06}, c(\alpha_2, \beta_2, \gamma_2, l_2, m_2, n_2, h_2) = -2^{-47.76}.$$

The second one is the optimal approximation of this type, and we can see an interesting aggregation effect: the absolute correlation of the first approximation is lower than the second while the first trail has a higher absolute correlation. For both approximations, there are more trails with negative correlations in the exhaustion process. So the correlation of the first trail 2^{-48} is offset by a large number of negative correlations, resulting in a lower sum $2^{-48.06}$, while the absolute correlation of the second trail $2^{-49.06}$ increases to $2^{-47.76}$ by summing the correlations up.

The involved codes can be found at: https://github.com/acaofsas/SNOW-V.

6   A Correlation Attack on SNOW-V

Based on the generic method of fast correlation attack given in [17], we present a correlation attack on SNOW-V using the linear approximation with the correlation $c = -2^{-47.76}$ given in Sect. 5, and give a more detailed analysis of success probability and complexity.

6.1 General Description of the Presented Correlation Attack on SNOW-V

We call the state of LFSR that produces the first keystream word as the initial state of LFSR. Our aim is to recover the initial state of LFSR. By the result above, we have

$$\alpha \cdot z_{t-1} \oplus \beta \cdot z_t \oplus \gamma \cdot z_{t+1} \oplus l \cdot T_1^{(t-1)} \oplus m \cdot T_1^{(t)} \oplus n \cdot T_1^{(t+1)} \oplus h \cdot T_2^{(t)} \overset{c}{=} 0.$$

We assume that $u = (u_{511}, u_{510}, \cdots, u_0)$ and $\hat{u} = (\hat{u}_{511}, \hat{u}_{510}, \cdots, \hat{u}_0)$ are the initial state and guessed initial state respectively. Since the output of LFSR at clock t can always be expressed as a linear combination of the initial state, i.e., there always exists a $\Gamma_t \in \{0,1\}^{512}$ such that $\Gamma_t \cdot u = l \cdot T_1^{(t-1)} \oplus m \cdot T_1^{(t)} \oplus n \cdot T_1^{(t+1)} \oplus h \cdot T_2^{(t)}$, we can construct a distinguisher with the form

$$\phi_t(\hat{u}) = \alpha \cdot z_{t-1} \oplus \beta \cdot z_t \oplus \gamma \cdot z_{t+1} \oplus \Gamma_t \cdot \hat{u}$$
$$= \alpha \cdot z_{t-1} \oplus \beta \cdot z_t \oplus \gamma \cdot z_{t+1}$$
$$\oplus l \cdot T_1^{(t-1)} \oplus m \cdot T_1^{(t)} \oplus n \cdot T_1^{(t+1)} \oplus h \cdot T_2^{(t)} \oplus \Gamma_t \cdot (u \oplus \hat{u}).$$

$\phi_t(\hat{u})$ will show the correlation $c = -2^{-47.76}$ when $\hat{u} = u$, otherwise $\phi_t(\hat{u})$ is uniform distributed. With this analysis, we recover the initial LFSR state in two steps.

Preprocessing Stage: Let the most significant B bits of binary vector $x = (x_{511}, x_{510}, \cdots, x_0)$ be $x^h = (x_{511}, x_{510}, \cdots, x_{512-B})$, the least significant $512 - B$ bits be $x^l = (x_{511-B}, x_{510-B}, \cdots, x_0)$ and the number of keystream words produced by a pair of key and IV be N. For $1 \leq i_1, i_2 \leq N$, we have

$$(\Gamma_{i_1} \oplus \Gamma_{i_2}) \cdot u = (\Gamma_{i_1}^h \oplus \Gamma_{i_2}^h) \cdot u^h \oplus (\Gamma_{i_1}^l \oplus \Gamma_{i_2}^l) \cdot u^l.$$

If $\Gamma_{i_1}^l = \Gamma_{i_2}^l$, the equation above is converted into $(\Gamma_{i_1} \oplus \Gamma_{i_2}) \cdot u = (\Gamma_{i_1}^h \oplus \Gamma_{i_2}^h) \cdot u^h$. As the event $\phi_{i_1}(u) = 0$ is independent of the event $\phi_{i_2}(u) = 0$ and $p(\phi_{i_1}(u) = 0) = p(\phi_{i_2}(u) = 0) = \frac{1}{2} + \frac{1}{2}c$, we have $p(\phi_{i_1}(u) \oplus \phi_{i_2}(u) = 0) = \frac{1}{2} + \frac{1}{2}c^2$, i.e., $\rho = c^2$. Thus we can get a parity check equation of B bits of the initial state u

$$\alpha \cdot (z_{i_1-1} \oplus z_{i_2-1}) \oplus \beta \cdot (z_{i_1} \oplus z_{i_2}) \oplus \gamma \cdot (z_{i_1+1} \oplus z_{i_2+1}) \oplus (\Gamma_{i_1}^h \oplus \Gamma_{i_2}^h) \cdot u^h \overset{c^2}{=} 0,$$

if $\Gamma_{i_1}^l = \Gamma_{i_2}^l$ holds. Since the probability $p(\Gamma_{i_1}^l = \Gamma_{i_2}^l) = 2^{-(512-B)}$, the expected number of parity check equations with $\Gamma_{i_1}^l = \Gamma_{i_2}^l$ among C_N^2 pairs of Γ_i is $M = C_N^2 2^{-(512-B)} \approx 2^{-(513-B)} N^2$. Thus we can find $2^{-(513-B)} N^2$ parity check equations in preprocessing stage on average.

Processing Stage: Among the M parity check equations we denote the j-th equation $(\alpha, \beta, \gamma) \cdot Z_j \oplus \delta_j \cdot u^h = 0$, where $Z_j = (z_{i_1-1} \oplus z_{i_2-1}, z_{i_1} \oplus z_{i_2}, z_{i_1+1} \oplus z_{i_2+1})$ and $\delta_j = (\Gamma_{i_1}^h \oplus \Gamma_{i_2}^h)$. For each guessed B bits $\hat{u}^h \in \{0,1\}^B$ of the initial state u, we evaluate the parity checks, then get

$$T(\hat{u}^h) = \sum_{j=1}^{M} (-1)^{(\alpha,\beta,\gamma) \cdot Z_j \oplus \delta_j \cdot \hat{u}^h},$$

and predict the $\hat{u}$ that maximizes $T(\hat{u}^h)$ as the correct one. For the remaining $512 - B$ bits, the above process can be repeated when the first B bits are known. Thus, all the initial 512 bits of the LFSR can be recovered.

6.2   Success Probability and Complexity

For linear attacks, we recall the relationship between the probability of success and the number of check equations below:

Definition 1 [18]. *If a B-bit key is attacked and the right key is ranked r-th among all 2^B candidates, $a = B - \log_2 r$ is called the advantage provided by the attack.*

In this paper we refer to the *advantage* defined by Definition 1 as *gain*.

Lemma 1 [18]. *Let p_s be the probability that a linear attack on a B-bit subkey, with a linear approximation of probability $p = \frac{1}{2} + \frac{1}{2}\rho$ and M known parity check equations, delivers an a-bit or higher gain. Assuming that the linear approximation's probability to hold is independent for each guessed key and its probability is equal to $1/2$ for all wrong keys, we have for sufficiently large B and M that*

$$p_s = \Phi\left(2\sqrt{M}\left|p - \frac{1}{2}\right| - \Phi^{-1}(1 - 2^{-a-1})\right),$$

where $\Phi(x) = \frac{1}{\sqrt{2\pi}} \int_{-\infty}^{x} e^{-\frac{t^2}{2}} dt$ is the distribution function of the standard normal distribution.

Corollary 1 [18]. *With the assumptions of Lemma 1,*

$$M = \frac{1}{\rho^2}\left(\Phi^{-1}(p_s) + \Phi^{-1}(1 - 2^{-a-1})\right)^2$$

parity check equations are needed in a linear attack to accomplish an a-bit gain with a success probability of p_s.

By the results of [19], we use the formula $\Phi^{-1}(1 - \lambda) \overset{\lambda \to 0^+}{\approx} \sqrt{-2\ln\lambda}$ to approximate $\Phi^{-1}(1 - 2^{-a-1})$. Hence, we have $M \approx \frac{1}{\rho^2}\left(\Phi^{-1}(p_s) + \sqrt{2(a+1)\ln 2}\right)^2$ for sufficiently large a.

The complexity can be evaluated as follows. In the preprocessing stage, we evaluate and store each $\Gamma_i \in \{0,1\}^{512}$ for $1 \leq i \leq N$. Then we sort Γ_i according to the value of Γ_i^l such that $\Gamma_{i_1}^l = \Gamma_{i_2}^l$ holds for any i_1 and i_2 in the same set. Thus we can construct a series of parity check equations which is only related to the most significant B bits of initial state. The time complexity of preprocessing stage is $O(N) + O(N\log_2 N)$, and memory complexity is $O(N)$.

In the processing stage, $T(\hat{u}^h)$ is computed for each guessed $\hat{u}^h \in \{0,1\}^B$ by evaluating M parity check equations. When $B > \log M$, denoting the most significant $\lceil \log M \rceil$ bits of δ_j and $\hat{u}^h$ as δ_j^{h1} and $\hat{u}^{h1}$, the least significant $B - \lceil \log M \rceil$ bits as δ_j^{h2} and $\hat{u}^{h2}$ respectively, we can accelerate the process using fast Walsh transformation by

$$
\begin{aligned}
T(\hat{u}^h) &= \sum_{j=1}^{M} (-1)^{(\alpha,\beta,\gamma) \cdot Z_j \oplus \delta_j \cdot \hat{u}^h} \\
&= \sum_{\zeta \in \{0,1\}^{\lceil \log M \rceil}} \sum_{j, \delta_j^{h1} = \zeta} (-1)^{(\alpha,\beta,\gamma) \cdot Z_j} \cdot (-1)^{\delta_j^{h1} \cdot \hat{u}^{h1}} \cdot (-1)^{\delta_j^{h2} \cdot \hat{u}^{h2}} \\
&= \sum_{\zeta \in \{0,1\}^{\lceil \log M \rceil}} \sum_{j, \delta_j^{h1} = \zeta} (-1)^{(\alpha,\beta,\gamma) \cdot Z_j} \cdot (-1)^{\delta_j^{h2} \cdot \hat{u}^{h2}} \cdot (-1)^{\zeta \cdot \hat{u}^{h1}} \\
&= \sum_{\zeta \in \{0,1\}^{\lceil \log M \rceil}} (-1)^{\zeta \cdot \hat{u}^{h1}} \sum_{j, \delta_j^{h1} = \zeta} (-1)^{(\alpha,\beta,\gamma) \cdot Z_j} \cdot (-1)^{\delta_j^{h2} \cdot \hat{u}^{h2}} \\
&= \sum_{\zeta \in \{0,1\}^{\lceil \log M \rceil}} (-1)^{\zeta \cdot \hat{u}^{h1}} g_{\hat{u}^{h2}}(\zeta),
\end{aligned}
$$

where $g_{\hat{u}^{h2}}(\zeta) = \sum_{j, \delta_j^{h1} = \zeta} (-1)^{(\alpha,\beta,\gamma) \cdot Z_j \oplus \delta_j^{h2} \cdot \hat{u}^{h2}}$.

For each guessed $\hat{u}^{h2} \in \{0,1\}^{B - \lceil \log M \rceil}$ and $\zeta \in \{0,1\}^{\lceil \log M \rceil}$, we compute $g_{\hat{u}^{h2}}(\zeta)$ and get $T(\hat{u}^h) = \sum_{\zeta \in \{0,1\}^{\lceil \log M \rceil}} (-1)^{\zeta \cdot \hat{u}^{h1}} g_{\hat{u}^{h2}}(\zeta)$ by calculating the Walsh transform of $g_{\hat{u}^{h2}}(\zeta)$. This process can be done with a time complexity

$$
2^{B - \lceil \log M \rceil}(M + \lceil \log M \rceil 2^{\lceil \log M \rceil}) \approx 2^B(1 + \lceil \log M \rceil)
$$

and a memory complexity $O(2^B)$. By Corollary 1, we have

$$
M = \frac{1}{\rho^2}\left(\Phi^{-1}(p_s) + \Phi^{-1}(1 - 2^{-B-1})\right)^2
$$

when the correct u^h is predicted as the top ranked, i.e., $a = B$. Therefore, we can work out M with fixed p_s and B, then compute N by $M \approx 2^{-(513-B)} N^2$. Finally, the values which minimize the time complexity $N(\log N + 1) + 2^B(1 + \lceil \log M \rceil)$ shall be taken to determine the total complexity.

We test different choices for p_s and B and find that $M \approx 2^{200}$ and $N \approx 2^{237.5}$ under $p_s = 0.999992$ and $B = 238$, which makes the total complexity lowest.

The time complexity of the preprocessing stage is $2^{245.40}$, the memory complexity is $2^{237.5}$. In the processing stage the time complexity is $2^{245.65}$, the memory complexity is 2^{238}. Thus, the attack can be done with the total time complexity $2^{246.53}$, memory complexity $2^{238.77}$ and $2^{237.5}$ keystream words given.

After the first 238 bits in the initial state of the LFSR be recovered, one can recover the rest 274 bits of LFSR in the same way. Denoting the most significant 238 bits of binary vector x as $x^{(238)} = (x_{511}, x_{510}, ..., x_{274})$, the following B' bits as $x^{h'} = (x_{273}, ..., x_{274-B'})$ and the least significant $274 - B'$ bits as $x^{l'} = (x_{273-B'}, ..., x_0)$ respectively, for $1 < i_1, i_2 < N'$ we have

$$(\Gamma_{i_1} \oplus \Gamma_{i_2}) \cdot u = (\Gamma_{i_1}^{(238)} \oplus \Gamma_{i_2}^{(238)}) \cdot u^{(238)} \oplus (\Gamma_{i_1}^{(h')} \oplus \Gamma_{i_2}^{(h')}) \cdot u^{(h')} \oplus (\Gamma_{i_1}^{(l')} \oplus \Gamma_{i_2}^{(l')}) \cdot u^{(l')}.$$

As the most significant 238 bits are known, we can get $M' \approx 2^{-(275-B)} N'^2$ parity check equations when $\Gamma_{i_1}^{l'} = \Gamma_{i_2}^{l'}$ holds. By Corollary 1, when $p_s = 0.999992$ and $B' = 199$, we have $M' \approx 2^{200}$ and $N' \approx 2^{138}$, which indicates a much lower time complexity of $2^{206.66}$, and lower data and memory complexities than that of the recovery of the first 238 bits. The remaining 75 bits can be exhausted directly.

It is easy to see that with the recovery of the LFSR state in encryption stage, one can recover the three memories R_1, R_2 and R_3 in encryption stage with a time complexity not more than 2^{128}. In fact, as $z^{(t)} = (R_1^{(t)} \boxplus T_1^{(t)}) \oplus R_2^{(t)}$, the state $R_2^{(t)}, R_1^{(t+1)}, R_2^{(t+1)}$ and $R_3^{(t+1)}$ shall be recovered as soon as $R_1^{(t)}$ is guessed. Thus the initial states are recovered, i.e., we can predict the keystream word at any clock. There remains an open problem of how to recover the original key of SNOW-V effectively if one has recovered the initial states in encryption stage, which is worth being explored in the future.

7 A Correlation Attack on SNOW-Vi

Using the same method, in this section we launch a correlation attack on SNOW-Vi in a similar way.

7.1 Linear Approximation of SNOW-Vi

In WiSec 2021, Ekdahl et al. [5] proposed SNOW-Vi. Besides the field and update transformation of the LFSR, the tap $T_2^{(t)} = (a_7^{(8t)}, a_6^{(8t)}, \cdots, a_0^{(8t)})$ of SNOW-V was changed to $T_2^{(t)} = (a_{15}^{(8t)}, a_{14}^{(8t)}, \cdots, a_8^{(8t)})$ as well. We have experimentally confirmed that, regarding every bit in four taps $T_1^{(t-1)}, T_1^{(t)}, T_1^{(t+1)}$ and $T_2^{(t)}$ as the coefficient vector of the initial state, the 512×512 binary matrix composed of these vectors is full rank, i.e., $T_1^{(t-1)}, T_1^{(t)}, T_1^{(t+1)}$ and $T_2^{(t)}$ do not have linear relationship any more. Thus, we modify the six functions to be

$$
\begin{aligned}
f_1(x, y, z, t, u, v, w) &= ((x \boxminus u), y, z, t, v, w), \\
f_2(x, y, z, u, v, w) &= ((\sigma^{-1}(x) \boxminus y) \oplus v, y, z, u, w), \\
f_3(x, y, z, u, v) &= (E^{-1}(x), E^{-1}(y), z, u, v), \\
f_4(x, y, z, u, v) &= (x, (y \boxplus z), u, v), \\
f_5(x, y, z, u) &= (x, y, z, E^{-1}(u)), \\
f_6(x, y, z, u) &= (x, y, (z \boxplus u)).
\end{aligned}
$$

The composite function becomes

$$F(x, y, z, t, u, v, w) = (f_6 \circ f_5 \circ f_4 \circ f_3 \circ f_2 \circ f_1)(x, y, z, t, u, v, w),$$

with 7 input words and 3 output words. Using the same method and symbols as in Sect. 3, we consider the linear approximation $(\gamma, \beta, l, m, n, h, \gamma) \xrightarrow{F} (\alpha, \alpha, \beta)$. Taking 7 independent and uniform distributed words as the input variables:

$$\begin{aligned} &(x, y, z, t, u, v, w) \\ &= (\sigma(R_2 \boxplus (R_3 \oplus T_2^{(t)})) \boxplus T_1^{(t+1)}, R_2, T_1^{(t-1)}, T_1^{(t)}, T_1^{(t+1)}, T_2^{(t)}, E(R_1)), \end{aligned}$$

we have

$$F(x, y, z, t, u, v, w) = (E^{-1}(R_3), E^{-1}(R_2) \boxplus T_1^{(t-1)}, T_1^{(t)} \boxplus R_1).$$

Then the equation of the linear approximation $(\gamma, \beta, l, m, n, h, \gamma) \xrightarrow{F} (\alpha, \alpha, \beta)$ is

$$\begin{aligned} &(\gamma, \beta, l, m, n, h, \gamma) \\ &\cdot (\sigma(R_2 \boxplus (R_3 \oplus T_2^{(t)})) \boxplus T_1^{(t+1)}, R_2, T_1^{(t-1)}, T_1^{(t)}, T_1^{(t+1)}, T_2^{(t)}, E(R_1)) \\ &\oplus (\alpha, \alpha, \beta) \cdot (E^{-1}(R_3), E^{-1}(R_2) \boxplus T_1^{(t-1)}, T_1^{(t)} \boxplus R_1) \\ &= \alpha \cdot z_{t-1} \oplus \beta \cdot z_t \oplus \gamma \cdot z_{t+1} \oplus l \cdot T_1^{(t-1)} \oplus m \cdot T_1^{(t)} \oplus n \cdot T_1^{(t+1)} \oplus h \cdot T_2^{(t)} \\ &\overset{\rho'}{=} 0. \end{aligned}$$

The linear approximation above can be expressed as

$$\begin{aligned} (\gamma, \beta, l, m, n, h, \gamma) &\xrightarrow[\rho_A(a, n \to \gamma)]{f_1} (a, \beta, l, m, h, \gamma) \xrightarrow[\rho_A(b \oplus \beta, h \to a\sigma)]{f_2} (h, b, l, m, \gamma) \\ &\xrightarrow[\rho_E(\alpha \to h)\rho_E(c \to b)]{f_3} (\alpha, c, l, m, \gamma) \xrightarrow[\rho_A(l, c \to \alpha)]{f_4} (\alpha, \alpha, m, \gamma) \xrightarrow[\rho_E(q \to \gamma)]{f_5} (\alpha, \alpha, m, q) \\ &\xrightarrow[\rho_A(m, q \to \beta)]{f_6} (\alpha, \alpha, \beta), \end{aligned}$$

and the correlation of a linear trail can be computed as

$$\begin{aligned} \rho'(a, b, c, q) = &\rho_A(a, n \to \gamma)\rho_A(b \oplus \beta, h \to a\sigma)\rho_E(\alpha \to h)\rho_E(c \to b) \\ &\rho_A(l, c \to \alpha)\rho_E(q \to \gamma)\rho_A(m, q \to \beta), \end{aligned}$$

where a, b, c, q are the intermediate masks.

7.2 Compared with the Linear Approximation of SNOW-V

The correlation of a linear trail of SNOW-V is

$$\begin{aligned} \rho(a, b, c, d, q) = &\rho_A(a, n \oplus d \to \gamma)\rho_A(b \oplus \beta, d \oplus h \to a\sigma)\rho_E(\alpha \to d \oplus h)\rho_E(c \to b) \\ &\rho_A(e, c \to \alpha)\rho_E(q \to \gamma)\rho_A(f, q \to \beta). \end{aligned}$$

Since $d = 0, e = l, f = m$ holds for the type of linear trails in Sect. 5, the expression can be reduced to

$$\begin{aligned} \rho(a, b, c, 0, q) = &\rho_A(a, n \to \gamma)\rho_A(b \oplus \beta, h \to a\sigma)\rho_E(\alpha \to h)\rho_E(c \to b) \\ &\rho_A(l, c \to \alpha)\rho_E(q \to \gamma)\rho_A(m, q \to \beta), \end{aligned}$$

which is the same as the correlation $\rho'(a, b, c, q)$ of SNOW-Vi. Hence, we have the straightforward observation.

Proposition 1. For any trail of the linear approximation process of SNOW-Vi above, the linear trail of SNOW-V determined by the same parameters

$$(\alpha, \beta, \gamma, l, m, n, h, a, b, c, q)$$

with $d = 0$ has the same correlation as that of SNOW-Vi, i.e.,

$$\rho(a, b, c, 0, q) = \rho'(a, b, c, q).$$

Proposition 1 indicates that the linear approximation trails of SNOW-Vi correspond one-to-one to the trails with $d = 0$ of SNOW-V, and the set consisting of all linear trails of SNOW-Vi is a subset of that of SNOW-V. Therefore, the results of SNOW-V in this paper are also appropriate for SNOW-Vi. We could approximate SNOW-Vi with the same correlation $-2^{-47.76}$ of SNOW-V under

$$\alpha = l = 0xd, 0, 0, 0$$
$$\beta = m = 0x40, 0, 0, 0$$
$$\gamma = h = 0x81ec5a80, 0, 0, 0$$
$$n = 0x81ec5a00, 0, 0, 0.$$

Similarly, the correlation attack presented in Sect. 5 with time complexity $2^{246.53}$, memory complexity $2^{238.77}$ and $2^{237.5}$ words given is effective for SNOW-Vi as well.

8   Conclusion

In this paper, we study the linear approximation of the nonlinear functions of SNOW-V and SNOW-Vi by the composite function technique. By the Walsh spectrum theorem of composite function, we propose a method for searching linear trails with high correlation of SNOW-V and SNOW-Vi in a wide range. As the automatic search technique is available for this framework, the search efficiency has been significantly improved. Based on the results searched out, we manage to evaluate the accurate correlation of a special type of binary linear approximations. For SNOW-V, we find a binary linear approximation with correlation $-2^{-47.76}$, substantially improving the results in the design document. Using the linear approximation we launch a correlation attack with a time complexity $2^{246.53}$, a memory complexity $2^{238.77}$ and $2^{237.5}$ keystream words given. For SNOW-Vi, the binary linear approximation is also valid, and the correlation attack on SNOW-V is effective for SNOW-Vi as well. The results of this paper show that SNOW-V and SNOW-Vi can be attacked with complexity less than key exhaustion when we ignore the design constraint that the maximum of keystream length with a single pair of key and IV is 2^{64}.

Acknowledgement. We thank the anonymous reviewers for their valuable suggestions on how to improve this paper. Also, we thank Alexander Maximov for helpful discussion and verification of our results. This work is supported by National Natural Science Foundation of China (Grant No. 61772547).

A   Detailed Reasoning Process of Intermediate Masks

Based on the linear approximation of F in Sect. 3, we analyze the intermediate masks in the case that the input and output masks are fixed as $(\gamma, \beta, l, m, n, \gamma)$ and $(\alpha, \alpha, h, \beta)$ respectively. We denote ξ_j^i the mask of the j-th output of f_i and ρ_i the correlation of f_i. Then the linear approximation equation of f_1 is

$$
\begin{aligned}
&\gamma \cdot x \oplus \beta \cdot y \oplus l \cdot z \oplus m \cdot u \oplus n \cdot v \oplus \gamma \cdot w, \\
&\overset{\rho_1}{=} \xi_1^1 \cdot (x \boxminus v) \oplus \xi_2^1 \cdot y \oplus \xi_3^1 \cdot z \oplus \xi_4^1 \cdot u \oplus \xi_5^1 \cdot L(z, u) \oplus \xi_5^1 \cdot v \oplus \xi_6^1 \cdot w,
\end{aligned}
\tag{3}
$$

which is equivalent to

$$
\begin{aligned}
&(\beta \oplus \xi_2^1) \cdot y \oplus (\gamma \oplus \xi_6^1) \cdot w \oplus [\xi_5^1 \cdot L(z, u) \oplus (l \oplus \xi_3^1) \cdot z \oplus (\xi_4^1 \oplus m) \cdot u] \\
&\oplus [\xi_1^1 \cdot (x \boxminus v) \oplus \gamma \cdot x \oplus (n \oplus \xi_5^1) \cdot v] \overset{\rho_1}{=} 0.
\end{aligned}
$$

With the assumption that $\rho_1 \neq 0$, we have $\xi_2^1 = \beta, \xi_6^1 = \gamma$. Denoting $\xi_1^1 = a, \xi_3^1 = e, \xi_4^1 = f, \xi_5^1 = d$, we have $d\boldsymbol{L} = (e \oplus l)||(f \oplus m)$ by

$$
d \cdot L(z, u) = d\boldsymbol{L}(z||u)^T = (e \oplus l) \cdot z \oplus (f \oplus m) \cdot u,
$$

and (3) is equivalent to $\gamma \cdot x \overset{\rho_1}{=} a \cdot (x \boxminus v) \oplus (n \oplus d) \cdot v$, which is the linear approximation $a, n \oplus d \to \gamma$ of the addition modulo 2^{32}. Thus the correlation of (3) is $\rho_1 = \rho_A(a, n \oplus d \to \gamma)$.

For f_2, we have

$$
\begin{aligned}
&a \cdot x \oplus \beta \cdot y \oplus e \cdot z \oplus f \cdot u \oplus d \cdot v \oplus \gamma \cdot w \\
&= \xi_1^2 \cdot (\sigma^{-1}(x) \boxminus y) \oplus \xi_1^2 \cdot v \oplus \xi_2^2 \cdot y \oplus \xi_3^2 \cdot z \oplus \xi_4^2 \cdot u \oplus \xi_5^2 \cdot v \oplus \xi_6^2 \cdot w,
\end{aligned}
\tag{4}
$$

which is equivalent to

$$
\begin{aligned}
&[\xi_1^2 \cdot (\sigma^{-1}(x) \boxminus y) \oplus a \cdot x \oplus (\beta \oplus \xi_2^2) \cdot y] \oplus (e \oplus \xi_3^2) \cdot z \oplus (\xi_4^2 \oplus f) \cdot u \\
&\oplus (\xi_1^2 \oplus \xi_5^2 \oplus d) \cdot v \oplus (\xi_6^2 \oplus \gamma) \cdot w \overset{\rho_2}{=} 0.
\end{aligned}
$$

By $\rho_2 \neq 0$ we know that $\xi_3^2 = e, \xi_4^2 = f, \xi_6^2 = \gamma, \xi_1^2 = d \oplus \xi_5^2$. Denoting $\xi_2^2 = b$, then (4) is equivalent to $\xi_1^2 \cdot (\sigma^{-1}(x) \boxminus y) \oplus a \cdot x \oplus (\beta \oplus \xi_2^2) \cdot y = 0$. Let $X = \sigma^{-1}(x)$, then the above equation can be converted to

$$
a \cdot \sigma(X) = (a\boldsymbol{\sigma}) \cdot X \overset{\rho_2}{=} (\beta \oplus b) \cdot y \oplus \xi_1^2 \cdot (X \boxminus y),
$$

which is the linear approximation $\beta \oplus b, d \oplus \xi_5^2 \to a\boldsymbol{\sigma}$ of the addition modulo 2^{32}, hence $\rho_2 = \rho_A(\beta \oplus b, d \oplus \xi_5^2 \to a\boldsymbol{\sigma})$.

For f_3, the following equation holds

$$
\begin{aligned}
&(d \oplus \xi_5^2) \cdot x \oplus b \cdot y \oplus e \cdot z \oplus f \cdot u \oplus \xi_5^2 \cdot v \oplus \gamma \cdot w \\
&\overset{\rho_3}{=} \xi_1^3 \cdot E^{-1}(x) \oplus \xi_2^3 \cdot E^{-1}(y) \oplus \xi_3^3 \cdot z \oplus \xi_4^3 \cdot u \oplus \xi_5^3 \cdot v \oplus \xi_6^3 \cdot w.
\end{aligned}
\tag{5}
$$

It is equivalent to

$$
\begin{aligned}
&[\xi_1^3 \cdot E^{-1}(x) \oplus (d \oplus \xi_5^2) \cdot x] \oplus [\xi_2^3 \cdot E^{-1}(y) \oplus b \cdot y] \oplus (\xi_3^3 \oplus e) \cdot z \oplus (\xi_4^3 \oplus f) \cdot u \\
&\oplus (\xi_5^3 \oplus \xi_5^2) \cdot v \oplus (\xi_6^3 \oplus \gamma) \cdot w \overset{\rho_3}{=} 0.
\end{aligned}
$$

By $\rho_3 \neq 0$ we know that $\xi_3^3 = e, \xi_4^3 = f, \xi_5^3 = \xi_5^2, \xi_6^3 = \gamma$. Let $\xi_2^3 = c$, then (5) is equivalent to $[\xi_1^3 \cdot E^{-1}(x) \oplus (d \oplus \xi_5^2) \cdot x] \oplus [\xi_2^3 \cdot E^{-1}(y) \oplus b \cdot y] \overset{\rho_3}{=} 0$, which is the two linear approximations $\xi_1^3 \overset{AES}{\to} d \oplus \xi_5^2$ and $c \overset{AES}{\to} b$ of AES round function, so we have $\rho_3 = \rho_E(\xi_1^3 \to d \oplus \xi_5^2)\rho_E(c \to b)$.

For f_4, we have

$$\xi_1^3 \cdot x \oplus c \cdot y \oplus e \cdot z \oplus f \cdot u \oplus \xi_5^2 \cdot v \oplus \gamma \cdot w \overset{\rho_4}{=} \xi_1^4 \cdot x \oplus \xi_2^4 \cdot (y \boxplus z) \oplus \xi_3^4 \cdot u \oplus \xi_4^4 \cdot v \oplus \xi_5^4 \cdot w, \quad (6)$$

which is equivalent to

$$(\xi_1^3 \oplus \xi_1^4) \cdot x \oplus [\xi_2^4 \cdot (y \boxplus z) \oplus c \cdot y \oplus e \cdot z] \oplus (f \oplus \xi_3^4) \cdot u \oplus (\xi_5^2 \oplus \xi_4^4) \cdot v \oplus (\gamma \oplus \xi_5^4) \cdot w \overset{\rho_4}{=} 0.$$

By $\rho_4 \neq 0$ we know that $\xi_1^4 = \xi_1^3, \xi_3^4 = f, \xi_4^4 = \xi_5^2, \xi_5^4 = \gamma$, and we can rewrite the above equation as $\xi_2^4 \cdot (y \boxplus z) \overset{\rho_4}{=} c \cdot y \oplus e \cdot z$, which is the approximation $c, e \to \xi_2^4$ of addition modulo 2^{32}. Obviously $\rho_4 = \rho_A(c, e \to \xi_2^4)$.

For f_5, the approximation equation is

$$\xi_1^3 \cdot x \oplus \xi_2^4 \cdot y \oplus f \cdot z \oplus \xi_5^2 \cdot u \oplus \gamma \cdot v \overset{\rho_5}{=} \xi_1^5 \cdot x \oplus \xi_2^5 \cdot y \oplus \xi_3^5 \cdot z \oplus \xi_4^5 \cdot u \oplus \xi_5^5 \cdot E^{-1}(v), \quad (7)$$

which is equivalent to

$$(\xi_1^3 \oplus \xi_1^5) \cdot x \oplus (\xi_2^4 \oplus \xi_2^5) \cdot y \oplus (f \oplus \xi_3^5) \cdot z \oplus (\xi_5^2 \oplus \xi_4^5) \cdot u \oplus [\xi_5^5 \cdot E^{-1}(v) \oplus \gamma \cdot v] \overset{\rho_5}{=} 0.$$

By $\rho_5 \neq 0$ we know that $\xi_1^5 = \xi_1^3, \xi_2^5 = \xi_2^4, \xi_3^5 = f, \xi_4^5 = \xi_5^2$. Denoting $\xi_5^5 = q$, then (7) can be reduced to $q \cdot E^{-1}(v) \oplus \gamma \cdot v \overset{\rho_5}{=} 0$, which is the linear approximation $q \overset{AES}{\to} \gamma$ of AES round function, so $\rho_5 = \rho_E(q \to \gamma)$.

For f_6, we have

$$\xi_1^3 \cdot x \oplus \xi_2^4 \cdot y \oplus f \cdot z \oplus \xi_5^2 \cdot u \oplus q \cdot v \overset{\rho_6}{=} \alpha \cdot x \oplus \alpha \cdot y \oplus h \cdot u \oplus \beta \cdot (z \boxplus v). \quad (8)$$

By $\rho_6 \neq 0$ we know that $\xi_1^3 = \xi_2^4 = \alpha, \xi_5^2 = h$, and (8) can be simplified to $\beta \cdot (z \boxplus v) \oplus f \cdot z \oplus q \cdot v \overset{\rho_6}{=} 0$, which is the linear approximation $f, q \to \beta$ of addition modulo 2^{32}. So we have $\rho_6 = \rho_A(f, q \to \beta)$.

Thus, the linear approximation trail of F can be described as

$$(\gamma, \beta, l, m, n, \gamma) \xrightarrow[dL=(e \oplus l)||(f \oplus m), \rho_A(a, n \oplus d \to \gamma)]{f_1} (a, \beta, e, f, d, \gamma) \xrightarrow[\rho_A(b \oplus \beta, d \oplus h \to a\sigma)]{f_2}$$

$$(d \oplus h, b, e, f, h, \gamma) \xrightarrow[\rho_E(\alpha \to d \oplus h)\rho_E(c \to b)]{f_3} (\alpha, c, e, f, h, \gamma) \xrightarrow[\rho_A(e, c \to \alpha)]{f_4} (\alpha, \alpha, f, h, \gamma)$$

$$\xrightarrow[\rho_E(q \to \gamma)]{f_5} (\alpha, \alpha, f, h, q) \xrightarrow[\rho_A(f, q \to \beta)]{f_6} (\alpha, \alpha, h, \beta).$$

B   The Proof of $d = (0, 0, 0, 0)$ Under $dL = (0x000000*, 0, 0, 0, 0x000000*, 0, 0, 0)$

Here we denote 128-bit vector $d = (d_7, d_6, ..., d_0)$ in which $d_i \in GF(2^{16})$, and β the binary matrix form of $\beta \in GF(2^{16})$. By the relation

$$L(x, y) = \beta * x \oplus \beta^{-1} * y \oplus (x >> 48) \oplus (y << 80),$$

we have

$$d \cdot L(x,y) = d \cdot \beta * x \oplus d \cdot \beta^{-1} * y \oplus d \cdot (x >> 48) \oplus d \cdot (y << 80)$$
$$= d \cdot \beta * x \oplus d \cdot \beta^{-1} * y \oplus [(d << 48) \cdot x] \oplus [(d >> 80) \cdot y],$$

which is equivalent to

$$d\boldsymbol{L} = (d_7\boldsymbol{\beta} \oplus d_4, ..., d_3\boldsymbol{\beta} \oplus d_0, d_2\boldsymbol{\beta}, ..., d_0\boldsymbol{\beta},$$
$$d_7\boldsymbol{\beta}^{-1}, ..., d_3\boldsymbol{\beta}^{-1}, d_2\boldsymbol{\beta}^{-1} \oplus d_7, ..., d_0\boldsymbol{\beta}^{-1} \oplus d_5).$$

Recall

$$d\boldsymbol{L} = (0x000000*, 0, 0, 0, 0x000000*, 0, 0, 0),$$

we can observe that

$$d_2\boldsymbol{\beta} = d_1\boldsymbol{\beta} = d_0\boldsymbol{\beta} = d_7\boldsymbol{\beta}^{-1} = d_5\boldsymbol{\beta}^{-1} = d_4\boldsymbol{\beta}^{-1} = d_3\boldsymbol{\beta}^{-1} = d_1\boldsymbol{\beta}^{-1} \oplus d_6 = 0.$$

As $\boldsymbol{\beta}$ is invertible, we can get $d = (0, 0, 0, 0)$.

References

1. Ekdahl, P., Johansson, T.: SNOW - a new stream cipher. In: Proceedings of First Open NESSIE Workshop, KU-Leuven, pp. 167–168 (2000)
2. Ekdahl, P., Johansson, T.: A new version of the stream cipher SNOW. In: Nyberg, K., Heys, H. (eds.) SAC 2002. LNCS, vol. 2595, pp. 47–61. Springer, Heidelberg (2003). https://doi.org/10.1007/3-540-36492-7_5
3. ETSI/SAGE.: Specification of the 3GPP confidentiality and integrity algorithms UEA2 & UIA2 (2006)
4. Ekdahl, P., Johansson, T., Maximov, A., Yang, J.: A new SNOW stream cipher called SNOW-V. IACR Trans. Symmetric Cryptol. **2019**(3), 1–42 (2019)
5. Ekdahl, P., Maximov, A., Johansson, T., Yang, J.: SNOW-Vi: an extreme performance variant of SNOW-V for lower grade CPUs. In: Pöpper, C., Vanhoef, M., Batina, L., Mayrhofer, R. (eds.) WiSec 2021, pp. 261–272. ACM, New York (2021)
6. Cid, C., Dodd, M., Murphy, S.: A security evaluation of the SNOW-V stream cipher. Quaternion Security Ltd, 4 June 2020. https://www.3gpp.org/ftp/tsg_sa/WG3_Security/TSGS3_101e/Docs/S3-202852.zip
7. Jiao, L., Li, Y., Hao, Y.: A guess-and-determine attack on SNOW-V stream cipher. Comput. J. **63**(12), 1789–1812 (2020)
8. Gong, X., Zhang, B.: Resistance of SNOW-V against fast correlation attacks. IACR Trans. Symmetric Cryptol. **2021**(1), 378–410 (2021)
9. Yang, J., Johansson, T., Maximov, A.: Improved guess-and-determine and distinguishing attacks on SNOW-V. IACR Trans. Symmetric Cryptol. **2021**(3), 54–83 (2021)
10. Hoki, J., Isobe, T., Ito, R., Liu, F., Sakamoto, K.: Distinguishing and key recovery attacks on the reduced-round SNOW-V and SNOW-Vi. Cryptology ePrint Archive, Report 2021/546 (2021)
11. Shi, D., Sun, S., Sasaki, Yu., Li, C., Hu, L.: Correlation of quadratic boolean functions: cryptanalysis of all versions of full MORUS. In: Boldyreva, A., Micciancio, D. (eds.) CRYPTO 2019, Part II. LNCS, vol. 11693, pp. 180–209. Springer, Cham (2019). https://doi.org/10.1007/978-3-030-26951-7_7

12. Ganesh, V., Hansen, T., Soos, M., Liew, D., Govostes, R.: STP constraint solver (2014). https://github.com/stp/stp
13. Abdelkhalek, A., Sasaki, Y., Todo, Y., Tolba, M., Youssef, A.M.: MILP modeling for (large) S-boxes to optimize probability of differential characteristics. IACR Trans. Symmetric Cryptol. **2017**(4), 99–129 (2017)
14. Liu, Yu., Liang, H., Li, M., Huang, L., Hu, K., Yang, C., Wang, M.: STP models of optimal differential and linear trail for S-box based ciphers. SCIENCE CHINA Inf. Sci. **64**(5), 1–3 (2021). https://doi.org/10.1007/s11432-018-9772-0
15. Zhou, C., Feng, X., Wu, C.: Linear approximations of addition modulo 2^n. In: Joux, A. (ed.) FSE 2011. LNCS, vol. 6733, pp. 359–377. Springer, Heidelberg (2011). https://doi.org/10.1007/978-3-642-21702-9_21
16. Schulte-Geers, E.: On CCZ-equivalence of addition mod 2^n. Des. Codes Cryptogr. **66**, 111–127 (2013)
17. Zhang, B., Xu, C., Meier, W.: Fast correlation attacks over extension fields, large-unit linear approximation and cryptanalysis of SNOW 2.0. In: Gennaro, R., Robshaw, M. (eds.) CRYPTO 2015. LNCS, vol. 9215, pp. 643–662. Springer, Heidelberg (2015). https://doi.org/10.1007/978-3-662-47989-6_31
18. Selçuk, A.A.: On probability of success in linear and differential cryptanalysis. J. Cryptol. **21**(1), 131–147 (2008)
19. Blondeau, C., Gérard, B., Tillich, J.P.: Accurate estimates of the data complexity and success probability for various cryptanalyses. Des. Codes Cryptogr. **59**, 3–34 (2011)

Refined Cryptanalysis of the GPRS Ciphers GEA-1 and GEA-2

Dor Amzaleg and Itai Dinur[✉]

Department of Computer Science, Ben-Gurion University, Beersheba, Israel
dinuri@cs.bgu.ac.il

Abstract. At EUROCRYPT 2021, Beierle et al. presented the first public analysis of the GPRS ciphers GEA-1 and GEA-2. They showed that although GEA-1 uses a 64-bit session key, it can be recovered with the knowledge of only 65 bits of keystream in time 2^{40} using 44 GiB of memory. The attack exploits a weakness in the initialization process of the cipher that was presumably hidden intentionally by the designers to reduce its security.

While no such weakness was found for GEA-2, the authors presented an attack on this cipher with time complexity of about 2^{45}. The main practical obstacle is the required knowledge of 12800 bits of keystream used to encrypt a full GPRS frame. Variants of the attack are applicable (but more expensive) when given less consecutive keystream bits, or when the available keystream is fragmented (it contains no long consecutive block).

In this paper, we improve and complement the previous analysis of GEA-1 and GEA-2. For GEA-1, we devise an attack in which the memory complexity is reduced by a factor of about $2^{13} = 8192$ from 44 GiB to about 4 MiB, while the time complexity remains 2^{40}. Our implementation recovers the GEA-1 session key in average time of 2.5 h on a modern laptop.

For GEA-2, we describe two attacks that complement the analysis of Beierle et al. The first attack obtains a linear tradeoff between the number of consecutive keystream bits available to the attacker (denoted by ℓ) and the time complexity. It improves upon the previous attack in the range of (roughly) $\ell \leq 7000$. Specifically, for $\ell = 1100$ the complexity of our attack is about 2^{54}, while the previous one is not faster than the 2^{64} brute force complexity. In case the available keystream is fragmented, our second attack reduces the memory complexity of the previous attack by a factor of 512 from 32 GiB to 64 MiB with no time complexity penalty.

Our attacks are based on new combinations of stream cipher cryptanalytic techniques and algorithmic techniques used in other contexts (such as solving the k-XOR problem).

1 Introduction

GPRS (General Packet Radio Service) is a mobile data standard that was widely deployed in the early 2000s. The standard is based on the GSM (2G) technology established by the European Telecommunications Standards Institute (ETSI).

© International Association for Cryptologic Research 2022
O. Dunkelman and S. Dziembowski (Eds.): EUROCRYPT 2022, LNCS 13277, pp. 57–85, 2022.
https://doi.org/10.1007/978-3-031-07082-2_3

Encryption is used to protect against eavesdropping between the phone and the base station, and two proprietary stream ciphers GEA-1 and GEA-2 were initially designed and used for this purpose.

1.1 First Public Analysis of GEA-1 and GEA-2

Recently, Beierle et al. presented the first public analysis of GEA-1 and GEA-2, which should ideally provide 64-bit security [2]. Remarkably, the authors described a weakness in the initialization process of GEA-1, showing that two of its three internal linear feedback shift registers (LFSRs) can only assume 2^{40} values out of the 2^{64} possible. This led to a practical meet-in-the-middle (MITM) attack in time complexity 2^{40} and memory complexity 44.5 GiB. The attack only needs 65 bits of known keystream (24 from the same frame), which can be easily deduced from the ciphertext assuming knowledge of 65 plaintext bits (that can be obtained from metadata such as headers). The attack is therefore completely practical, as demonstrated by the authors. Since the attack recovers the 64-bit session key, it allows to decrypt the entire GPRS session.

The weakness of GEA-1 is believed to have been intentionally introduced and hidden by the designers, presumably due to strict export regulations on cryptography that were in effect in 1998 when the cipher was designed. To support this hypothesis, [2] carried out extensive experiments on random LFSRs which showed that it is very unlikely that the weakness occurred by chance. In the followup work [3], Beierle, Felke and Leander showed how to construct such a weak cipher efficiently.

The initialization weakness of GEA-1 is not present in the stronger cipher GEA-2 (which also uses a fourth register to produce the output). Yet, the authors of [2] presented an attack on GEA-2 which showed that it does not provide the ideal 64-bit security. Specifically, given 12800 bits of keystream used to encrypt a full GPRS frame, the complexity of the attack is about 2^{45} GEA-2 evaluations and it requires 32 GiB of memory. It is based on a combination of algebraic and MITM attacks.

The main challenge in practice is in obtaining the 12800-bit consecutive keystream, which may require social engineering or additional ad-hoc methods. Therefore, the authors presented a data-time tradeoff curve showing that the crossover point for beating exhaustive search is about 1468 consecutive keystream bits.

A variant of the attack is also applicable in case the known available keystream used to encrypt a frame is fragmented and contains no long consecutive block. In particular, given 11300 bits of fragmented keystream, the time complexity of the attack becomes roughly 2^{55}, while the memory complexity remains 32 GiB.

Impact of Attacks. The ETSI prohibited the implementation of GEA-1 in mobile phones in 2013. On the other hand, it is still mandatory to implement GEA-2 today [10].

Surprisingly, the authors of [2] noticed that modern mobile phones still supported GEA-1, deviating from the specification. As described in [2], this could have severe implications as it opens the door for various types of downgrade attacks. Consequently, after disclosing this vulnerability, test cases were added to verify that the support of GEA-1 is disabled by devices before entering the market.

In contrast, ETSI followed the mid-term goal to remove the support of GEA-2 from the specification. Yet, specification changes require consent of several parties and may take a long time.

1.2   Our Results

In this paper, we describe several attacks on GEA-1 and GEA-2 that improve and complement the ones of [2]. Our attacks are summarized in Table 1.

Attack G1. Attack G1 reduces the memory complexity of the previous attack on GEA-1 by a factor of about $2^{13} = 8192$ to 4 MiB, while the time complexity remains 2^{40} GEA-1 evaluations.[1] We implemented the attack and executed it on a modern laptop. Averaged over 5 runs, it recovers the GEA-1 session key in average time of 2.5 h. In comparison, as it is difficult to run the attack of [2] on a laptop due to its high memory consumption, it was executed on a cluster.

For GEA-2, we present two attacks that focus on scenarios where the attacker obtains limited data which may be easier to acquire in practice. In general, the feasibility of assumptions on the available data depend on the exact attack scenario, and our goal is to describe attacks that optimally utilize this data.

Attack G2-1. Attack G2-1 assumes the attacker obtains ℓ bits of consecutive keystream. The complexity of this attack is about $2^{64}/(\ell - 62)$ GEA-2 evaluations. For example, given $\ell = 126$ (a keystream of moderate length), it already has a non-negligible advantage by a factor of 64 over exhaustive search. For $\ell = 1100$ the complexity of our attack is roughly 2^{54}, while the previous attack is not faster than the 2^{64} brute force complexity. In the range $\ell > 7000$, the attack of [2] is more efficient. Our attacks consume a moderately larger amount of memory than those of [2] (by a factor between 2 and 5, depending on the variant).

Attack G2-2. Attack G2-2 is mostly interesting when the available keystream is fragmented. This may occur if (for example) the eavesdropping communication channel is noisy or not stable, or the attacker only knows parts of the plaintext. In this scenario, our attack reduces the memory complexity of the previous attack by a factor of *at least* $2^9 = 512$ from 2^{35} bytes (32 GiB) to at most 2^{26} bytes (64 MiB) with no penalty in time complexity. For example, given 11300 bits of fragmented keystream in a frame, the complexity of the previous attack is about 2^{55} and it requires about 32 GiB of memory. We reduce the memory complexity to 32 MiB (by a factor of 2^{10}). Since the cost of the attack is largely influenced by its memory complexity, such a reduction is clearly favorable.

---

[1] As in [2], we define a GEA-1 evaluation as the number of bit operations required to generate a 128-bit keystream.

Table 1. Summery of our attacks.

Cipher	Attack	Time	Data (bits)	Memory	Main technique	Section
GEA-1	G1	2^{40}	65	4 MiB	3-XOR	Sect. 3.4
GEA-2	G2-1	$2^{64}/(\ell - 62)$	ℓ consecutive	64 GiB	4-XOR	Sect. 4.3
GEA-2	G2-2†	2^{55}	11320 fragmented	32 MiB	Algebraic + MITM	Sect. 4.4

† Specific parameter set for the attack with 11320 bits of fragmented keystream.

Impact of New Attacks. Unlike the work of [2], our work does not have immediate practical implications. Supposedly, after the measures taken following the work of [2], GEA-1 should no longer be supported by modern mobile phones. Regardless, the attack of [2] on GEA-1 is already practical and there is little more to be gained on this front.

On the other hand, our memory-optimized attack on GEA-1 is still interesting since it shows that the cost of eavesdropping to communication at a large scale (i.e., simultaneously eavesdropping to several GPRS sessions) is even lower than predicted by [2]. Indeed, implementing such an attack that requires several dozens of GiB was not trivial in the early 2000's, when GEA-1 was in wide use. With significantly reduced memory consumption, it is much easier to distribute the attack's workload among many cheap low-end devices.

As for GEA-2, our attacks provide new and interesting scenarios in which the cipher can be broken more efficiently than before. These attacks may have longer-term impact in expediting the removal of GEA-2 from the specification.

Regardless of this work's practical impact, we view its main contribution as technical and summarize it below. Analyzing ciphers that have been in wide use provides additional motivation for this work, yet it is not the only motivation.

1.3   Technical Contributions

GEA-1 and GEA-2 have interesting designs and there is additional insight to be gained from their analysis. Our techniques build on work that was published well after GEA-1 and GEA-2 were designed. However, this does not rule out the possibility that (variants of) these techniques were used (e.g., by intelligence agencies) to break the ciphers in practice. We now overview some of our techniques.

Optimization and Adaptation of k-XOR Algorithms. In the k-XOR problem, we are given access to k random functions $f_1, \ldots, f_k$ and a target value t, and the goal is to find a k-tuple of inputs $(x^{(1)}, \ldots, x^{(k)})$ such that $f_1(x^{(1)}) \oplus \ldots \oplus f_k(x^{(k)}) = t$. Since the outputs of GEA-1 and GEA-2 are calculated by XORing the outputs of their internal registers, using techniques for solving k-XOR in their cryptanalysis is natural (indeed, the MITM attacks of [2] essentially solve a 2-XOR problem). However, in our specific case, we wish to apply additional techniques which are not directly applicable. Consequently, we optimize and adapt them to obtain our attacks.

Attack G1. In cryptanalysis of GEA-1, we use the *clamping through precomputation* technique, proposed to reduce the memory complexity of k-XOR algorithms in [4] by Bernstein. Applying the technique naively results in a penalty in time complexity. Our main observation is that the $k = 3$ functions in the corresponding 3-XOR problem are not random, and we show how to exploit a property of the GEA-1 internal registers to apply the technique with no penalty. Essentially, the property is that it is possible to efficiently enumerate all internal states of a register that output a given prefix string.[2]

Attack G2-1. In Attack G2-1, we attempt to apply Wagner's *k-tree algorithm* [17]. For $k = 4$ it improves upon standard 4-XOR algorithms provided that the domains of f_1, f_2, f_3, f_4 are sufficiently large and many 4-XOR solutions exist. The algorithm exploits this to efficiently find only one of them. However, the k-tree algorithm is not directly applicable to GEA-2, as a standard attack based on 4-XOR can only target a single internal state of GEA-2. Nevertheless, we show how to adapt a technique developed in [2] (and used in another attack) which allows to simultaneously target several internal states of the stream cipher. In our case, this artificially creates more solutions to the 4-XOR problem, and therefore a variant of the k-tree algorithm is applicable.

Application to the Stream Cipher XOR Combiner. Interestingly, unlike the other attacks on GEA-2 (including the ones of [2], which exploit the low algebraic degree of its output), Attack G2-1 does not assume any special property of the 4 internal GEA-2 registers, whose outputs are XORed to produce the keystream. The attack is therefore applicable to a generic XOR combiner of 4 stream ciphers with an arbitrary internal structure.

Optimizing Meet-in-the-Middle Attacks by Subspace Decompositions. A MITM attack is composed of two parts, each iterating over a subspace of vectors. If the vectors of the two subspaces are linearly dependent, we can decompose them and iterate over their common dependent part in a loop. Each iteration consists of a MITM attack on smaller independent subspaces, reducing the memory complexity. This technique is relatively standard (see [1,7,13]), although typically applied in different settings such as hash function cryptanalysis.

Our attacks use subspace decompositions several times. In a few of these cases, they are not initially applicable and only made possible in combination with additional techniques. Specifically, for GEA-1 we use two decompositions and the second one is made possible by exploiting specific properties of its internal registers. Attack G2-2 is based on the combined algebraic and MITM (or

---

[2] This property is somewhat related to the *sampling resistance* property defined in the context of time-memory tradeoffs for stream ciphers with precomputation [5,6]. However, sampling resistance deals with the complexity of efficiently generating a *single* state (specified by some index) that produces an output prefix. On the other hand, we need to efficiently generate *all* states with a different efficiency measure.

2-XOR) attack of [2]. Subspace decomposition is made possible after guessing the values of carefully chosen linear combinations of variables.

1.4   Structure of the Paper

The rest of this paper is structured as follows. Next, in Sect. 2, we give some preliminaries. Our attack on GEA-1 is described in Sect. 3, while our attacks on GEA-2 are given in Sect. 4.

2   Preliminaries

2.1   Description of GEA-1 and GEA-2

We give a short description of the GPRS ciphers GEA-1 and GEA-2, as specified in [2] (which is currently the only public source for their specification). We only describe the relevant components for our analysis.

The input to the encryption process of both ciphers consists of a 12800-bit plaintext (GPRS frame), a 64-bit session key, a direction bit (uplink/downlink), and a 32-bit IV which is a counter incremented for each frame.

GEA-1. GEA-1 uses three linear feedback shift registers (LFSRs) over $\mathbb{F}_2$, named A, B and C of lengths 31, 32 and 33, respectively. The registers operate in Galois mode, namely the bit that is shifted out of a register is XORed to the bits in a specified set of positions. The output of each register is computed by a non-linear Boolean function $f : \mathbb{F}_2^7 \to \mathbb{F}_2$ which has an algebraic degree of 4 (see [2] for its specification).

Initialization. The inputs to the GEA-1 initialization process consist of a 64-bit secret key, a public direction bit, and a 32-bit public IV. The initialization uses a non-linear feedback shift register (NLFSR) of length 64 to which the inputs are loaded while clocking the register (refer to [2] for more details).

The NLFSR's final state is a 64-bit seed. The seed is used to initialize the registers A, B and C via a linear mapping. The exact details of this mapping are irrelevant to this paper. However, the weakness of GEA-1 is based on a crucial property of this mapping (discovered in [2]): the joint 64-bit initial state of the registers A and C can only attain 2^{40} values (out of the 2^{64} possible).

We further note that in the event that one of the registers is set to 0 after initialization, it is reset to a non-zero state. For simplicity, throughout this paper, we will ignore this unlikely event.

Finally, another property of the initialization that we will use (shown in [2]), is that given a 96-bit initial state of the registers and the public IV and direction bits, there is a very simple algorithm that inverts the initialization process and recovers the session key. This implies that recovering the 96-bit initial state in the encryption process of a single plaintext (frame) allows to decrypt the entire session.

Keystream Generation. After initialization, the cipher starts generating keystream. The output of each register is calculated by applying f to 7 bits in specified positions. A keystream bit is computed by XORing the 3 register outputs. After calculating a keystream bit, each register is clocked once before producing the next keystream bit.

The feedback positions of each register and the positions which serve as inputs to f are given in Fig. 1 (taken from [2]).

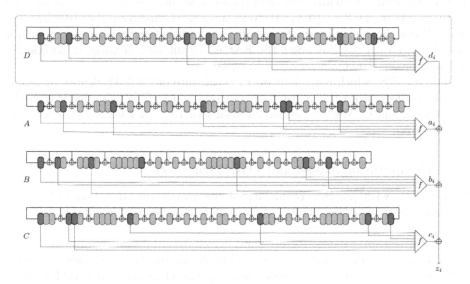

Fig. 1. Keystream generation of GEA-1 and GEA-2. Register D is only present in GEA-2. Credit: [2].

GEA-2. GEA-2 is built similarly to GEA-1, hence we focus on the differences. Besides the registers A, B, C, the GEA-2 state consists of a fourth 29-bit register D (which also uses f to produce the output), as shown in Fig. 1. The GEA-2 keystream is generated by XORing the outputs of the 4 registers.

The initialization process of GEA-2 is similar to that of GEA-1, but it makes use of a longer 97-bit NLFSR which produces a 97-bit seed. The seed is then used to initialize the state of the 4 registers via a linear mapping. Unlike the initialization mapping of GEA-1, the mapping of GEA-2 does not seem to have any noticeable weakness (in particular, one can verify that any pair of registers can assume all possible states). As for GEA-1, given an initial state and the public inputs, it is possible to efficiently recover the session key.

2.2 Notation

We describe the notation used throughout this paper.

For an integer $n > 0$, let $[n] = \{1, \ldots, n\}$. For a vector $x \in \mathbb{F}_2^n$ and $m \in [n]$, $x_{[m]} \in \mathbb{F}_2^m$ denotes the vector composed of the first m bits of x. For $m_1, m_2 \in [n]$ such that $m_1 \leq m_2$, $x_{[m_1,m_2]} \in \mathbb{F}_2^{m_2-m_1+1}$ denotes the vector composed of the bits of x in position m_1 up to m_2 (inclusive).

For a linear transformation T, we denote by $\mathrm{Im}(T)$ its image and by $\ker(T)$ its kernel. For a linear subspace V, we denote by $\dim(V)$ its dimension.

GEA-Related Notation. For the register A, we denote by $\hat{A} \in \mathbb{F}_2^{31}$ its internal state, and by $f_A : \mathbb{F}_2^{31} \to \{0,1\}^*$ the output of A starting from the given internal state. Typically, we will refer to specific bits of this function. In particular, for $m \in \mathbb{N}$, $f_A(\hat{A})_{[m]} \in \mathbb{F}_2^m$ denotes the first m output bits. Analogous notation is defined for the remaining registers B, C, D.

For $v \in \mathbb{F}_2^{96}$ (which represents an internal state of GEA-1), denote by $v_{[B]} \in \mathbb{F}_2^{32}$ its projection on the register B and by $v_{[AC]} \in \mathbb{F}_2^{64}$ its projection on the registers A and C. We use similar notations for the other GEA-1 registers and for GEA-2.

2.3 Computation Model and Data Structures

Consistently with [2], the complexity of the attacks on GEA-1 and GEA-2 is measured in terms of the number of operations required to generate a keystream of 128 bits.

The algorithms we describe use various lookup tables that support the operations of inserting and searching for elements. We assume that each such operation takes unit time (which is a standard assumption when using hash tables). This complexity of lookup table operations will typically be ignored in the total time complexity calculation, as for most attacks, it is proportional to the number of basic operations of evaluating the outputs of GEA registers.[3] We note that [2] used a slightly different computational model, but it does not have a significant impact on the final complexity estimations in our case.

2.4 3-XOR Problem

We define a variant of the well-known 3-XOR problem that is relevant for this paper. For simplicity, we assume the parameter n is divisible by 3.

Definition 1 (3-XOR).   *Given access to 3 random functions f_1, f_2, f_3 : $\mathbb{F}_2^{n/3} \to \mathbb{F}_2^n$ and a target $t \in \mathbb{F}_2^n$, find $(x^{(1)}, x^{(2)}, x^{(3)}) \in (\mathbb{F}_2^{n/3})^3$ such that $f_1(x^{(1)}) \oplus f_2(x^{(2)}) \oplus f_3(x^{(3)}) = t$.*

We note that in a random function the output of every input is chosen uniformly at random from the range, independently of the other inputs. Since the 3-XOR

---

[3] An exception is Attack G2-2, where most calculations involve different operations. For this attack we mainly reuse the analysis of [2].

problem places an n-bit condition on each triplet $(x^{(1)}, x^{(2)}, x^{(3)})$, the average number of solutions is $2^{3 \cdot n/3} \cdot 2^{-n} = 1$.

The naive 3-XOR algorithm based on sort-and-match (or meet-in-the-middle) has time complexity of roughly $2^{2n/3}$. It is a major open problem to improve this complexity significantly.[4] The naive 3-XOR algorithm also requires $2^{n/3}$ words of memory (of length $O(n)$ bits). However, unlike time complexity, we can significantly improve the memory complexity.

Proposition 1 (3-XOR algorithm using enumeration). *Let* $\tau \in \{0, \ldots, n/3\}$ *be a parameter. Assume there is an (enumeration) algorithm that, given* $t' \in \mathbb{F}_2^{\tau}$, *enumerates all the (expected number of)* $2^{2n/3-\tau}$ *pairs* $(x^{(2)}, x^{(3)}) \in (\mathbb{F}_2^{n/3})^2$ *such that* $(f_2(x^{(2)}) \oplus f_3(x^{(3)}))_{[\tau]} = t'$ *in time complexity* $O(2^{2n/3-\tau})$ *and memory complexity* $O(2^{n/3-\tau})$. *Then, there is an algorithm that solves 3-XOR in time* $O(2^{2n/3})$ *and memory* $O(2^{n/3-\tau})$.

Here, the memory complexity is measured in terms of the number of words of length $O(n)$ bits.

The 3-XOR algorithm is based on the *clamping through precomputation* technique that was proposed to reduce the memory complexity of k-XOR algorithms in [4] by Bernstein (and subsequently used in several works such as [9,14]). For 3-XOR, the idea is to build a (partial) table for f_1 that fixes its output prefix to $u \in \mathbb{F}_2^{\tau}$ (XORed with $t_{[\tau]}$), and loop over all prefixes. Specifically, the algorithm below establishes the proposition.

---

1. For all $u \in \mathbb{F}_2^{\tau}$:
   (a) – Initialize a table $\mathcal{T}_1$, storing elements in $\mathbb{F}_2^{n/3}$.
        – For all $x^{(1)} \in \mathbb{F}_2^{n/3}$, if $f_1(x^{(1)})_{[\tau]} \oplus t_{[\tau]} = u$, store $x^{(1)}$ at index[a] $f_1(x^{(1)}) \oplus t$ in $\mathcal{T}_1$.
   (b) Run the algorithm of Proposition 1 on input $t' = u$. For each pair $(x^{(2)}, x^{(3)})$ returned:
        – Search $\mathcal{T}_1$ for $f_2(x^{(2)}) \oplus f_3(x^{(3)})$. If a match $x^{(1)}$ exists, return $(x^{(1)}, x^{(2)}, x^{(3)})$ as a solution to 3-XOR.

---

[a] The index $f_1(x^{(1)}) \oplus t$ is the input to the hash function of $\mathcal{T}_1$.

Analysis

Correctness. A 3-XOR solution satisfies $f_1(x^{(1)}) \oplus t = f_2(x^{(2)}) \oplus f_3(x^{(3)})$, and therefore if $f_1(x^{(1)})_{[\tau]} \oplus t_{[\tau]} = u$, then $(f_2(x^{(2)}) \oplus f_3(x^{(3)}))_{[\tau]} = u$. Thus, for $u = f_1(x^{(1)})_{[\tau]} \oplus t_{[\tau]}$, $(x^{(2)}, x^{(3)})$ is returned by the enumeration algorithm and the solution is output.

---

[4] There are algorithms that save factors polynomial in n for some variants of the problem (e.g. [9,12,14,15]), but these are generally inapplicable in our setting.

Complexity. For each of the 2^τ iterations, Step 1.(a) requires $O(2^{n/3})$ time, while (by the assumption of Proposition 1) Step 1.(b) requires time $O(2^{2n/3-\tau})$. The total time complexity is thus $O(2^{2n/3})$ as claimed. The probability that $f_1(x^{(1)})_{[\tau]} \oplus t_{[\tau]} = u$ is $2^{-\tau}$. The number of elements stored in T_1 in each iteration is therefore $O(2^{n/3-\tau})$ with high probability, and by the assumption of Proposition 1, this dominates the memory complexity of the algorithm.

Enumeration Algorithm for Proposition 1. Below we describe a simple enumeration algorithm[5] for Proposition 1. We do not use this algorithm and it is only described for the sake of completeness.

---

1. For all $u' \in \mathbb{F}_2^\tau$:
   (a) – Initialize a table T_2, storing elements in $\mathbb{F}_2^{n/3}$.
       – For all $x^{(2)} \in \mathbb{F}_2^{n/3}$, if $f_2(x^{(2)})_{[\tau]} \oplus t' = u'$, store $x^{(2)}$ in T_2.
   (b) For all $x^{(3)} \in \mathbb{F}_2^{n/3}$, if $f_3(x^{(3)})_{[\tau]} = u'$:
       – For all $x^{(2)}$ in T_2, output $(x^{(2)}, x^{(3)})$.

Complexity Analysis. The total time complexity is $O(\max(2^{n/3+\tau}, 2^{2n/3-\tau}))$, where $2^{2n/3-\tau}$ represents the expected number of output pairs. The memory complexity is $O(2^{n/3-\tau})$.

Setting $\tau = n/6$ optimizes the time complexity of the algorithm. Combined with Proposition 1, this gives a 3-XOR algorithm with time and memory complexities of $O(2^{2n/3})$ and $O(2^{n/6})$, respectively.

2.5 4-XOR Problem

We consider the following variant of the 4-XOR problem. For simplicity, assume the parameter n is divisible by 4.

Definition 2 (4-XOR). *Given access to 4 random functions* $f_1, f_2, f_3, f_4 :$ $\mathbb{F}_2^{n/4} \to \mathbb{F}_2^n$ *and a target* $t \in \mathbb{F}_2^n$, *find* $(x^{(1)}, x^{(2)}, x^{(3)}, x^{(4)}) \in (\mathbb{F}_2^{n/4})^4$ *such that* $f_1(x^{(1)}) \oplus f_2(x^{(2)}) \oplus f_3(x^{(3)}) \oplus f_4(x^{(4)}) = t$.

As we have an n-bit condition on each quartet $(x^{(1)}, x^{(2)}, x^{(3)}, x^{(4)})$, the average number of solutions is $2^{4 \cdot n/4} \cdot 2^{-n} = 1$.

A naive meet-in-the-middle algorithm has time complexity of about $2^{n/2}$ and requires $2^{n/2}$ words of memory. It is not known how to substantially improve its time complexity. On the other hand, the memory complexity of the naive algorithm can be significantly reduced to $2^{n/4}$ using a variant of the Schroeppel-Shamir algorithm [16], which is described in [11] (for the subset-sum problem). The idea is to enumerate over all $u \in \mathbb{F}_2^{n/4}$, representing the values

$$f_1(x^{(1)})_{[n/4]} \oplus f_2(x^{(2)})_{[n/4]} \oplus t_{[\tau]} \text{ and } f_3(x^{(3)})_{[n/4]} \oplus f_4(x^{(4)})_{[n/4]},$$

---

[5] The full 3-XOR algorithm is similar to the 3-SUM algorithm of Wang [18].

which are equal for a 4-XOR solution. This allows to split the 4-XOR problem into two 2-XOR problems, each solved by a MITM procedure. The solutions of the two 2-XOR problems are then merged to give a solution to the original 4-XOR problem.

Wagner's k-tree algorithm [17] provides an improvement for k-XOR when the domains of the functions are larger. For $k = 4$, if $f_1, f_2, f_3, f_4 : \mathbb{F}_2^{n/3} \to \mathbb{F}_2^n$, then the number of expected solutions is $2^{4 \cdot n/3} \cdot 2^{-n} = 2^{n/3}$ and the k-tree algorithm finds one of them in time and memory complexities of $O(2^{n/3})$. The high-level idea is that we only need to enumerate over a single $u \in \mathbb{F}_2^{n/3}$ to find a solution with high probability.

In the general case where $f_1, f_2, f_3, f_4 : \mathbb{F}_2^\kappa \to \mathbb{F}_2^n$ for $n/4 \leq \kappa \leq n/3$, a full tradeoff algorithm was devised in [11]. Its time complexity is $O(2^{n-2\kappa})$, while its memory complexity is $O(2^\kappa)$.

3 Memory-Optimized Attack on GEA-1

In this section we describe our memory-optimized attack on GEA-1. We begin by describing the findings of [2] regarding the initialization process of GEA-1 in Sect. 3.1, and the corresponding attack in Sect. 3.2. We then optimize the memory complexity in two steps. The first step is based on a simple observation and reduces the memory complexity by a factor of about $2^8 = 256$ to 128 MiB. The second step further reduces the memory complexity by a factor of about $2^5 = 32$ to 4 MiB. While the additional reduction is only by a factor of 32, it is clearly non-negligible and technically more interesting. Furthermore, some of the ideas will be reused in Attack G2-2 on GEA-2.

3.1 Weakness in the GEA-1 Initialization Process

The initialization process of GEA-1 defines an injective mapping $M : \mathbb{F}_2^{64} \to \mathbb{F}_2^{96}$ which maps the seed to an initial state $(\hat{A}, \hat{B}, \hat{C})$. We can decompose the mapping according to its projections on the different registers:

$$M_A : \mathbb{F}_2^{64} \to \mathbb{F}_2^{31}, M_B : \mathbb{F}_2^{64} \to \mathbb{F}_2^{32}, M_C : \mathbb{F}_2^{64} \to \mathbb{F}_2^{33}.$$

Further define

$$M_{AC} : \mathbb{F}_2^{64} \to \mathbb{F}_2^{64}$$

as the projection of M onto $(\hat{A}, \hat{C})$.

Crucially, it was observed in [2] that $\dim(\ker(M_{AC})) = 24$, where ideally it should be 0. This implies that $\dim(\mathrm{Im}(M_{AC})) = 64 - 24 = 40$ and thus the state $(\hat{A}, \hat{C})$ obtained after initialization can only assume 2^{40} values.

Decomposition of the Initialization Mapping. We have $\dim(\mathrm{Im}(M_B)) = 32$ and therefore $\dim(\ker(M_B)) = 64 - 32 = 32$ (and also $\dim(\ker(M_{AC})) = 24$). Furthermore, $\dim(\ker(M_B) \cap \ker(M_{AC})) = 0$.

Hence, $\mathbb{F}_2^{64}$ can be decomposed as a direct sum into

$$\mathbb{F}_2^{64} = W^{(1)} \boxplus \ker(M_{AC}) \boxplus \ker(M_B),$$

where $\dim(W^{(1)}) = 64 - \dim(\ker(M_{AC})) - \dim(\ker(M_B)) = 8$.

It will be more convenient to work directly over $\mathrm{Im}(M)$ rather than over $\mathbb{F}_2^{64}$ (here, we slightly deviate from [2]). Thus, let

$$U^{(B)} = \{(0, x, 0) \in \mathbb{F}_2^{31} \times \mathbb{F}_2^{32} \times \mathbb{F}_2^{33}\} \text{ and } U^{(AC)} = \{(x, 0, y) \in \mathbb{F}_2^{31} \times \mathbb{F}_2^{32} \times \mathbb{F}_2^{33}\}.$$

Define $V^{(1)}$ as the image of $W^{(1)}$ under M, $V^{(2)} \subset U^{(B)}$ as the image of $\ker(M_{AC})$ under M and $V^{(3)} \subset U^{(AC)}$ as the image of $\ker(M_B)$ under M. We have

$$\mathrm{Im}(M) = V^{(1)} \boxplus V^{(2)} \boxplus V^{(3)}, \tag{1}$$

where

$$\dim(V^{(1)}) = 8, \ \dim(V^{(2)}) = 24, \ \dim(V^{(3)}) = 32.$$

The decomposition above implies that every state $(\hat{A}, \hat{B}, \hat{C}) \in \mathrm{Im}(M)$ (obtained after initialization) can be uniquely represented by a triplet

$$(v^{(1)}, v^{(2)}, v^{(3)}) \in V^{(1)} \times V^{(2)} \times V^{(3)}$$

such that

$$(\hat{A}, \hat{B}, \hat{C}) = v^{(1)} \oplus v^{(2)} \oplus v^{(3)}.$$

Since $v^{(2)}_{[AC]} = 0$ and $v^{(3)}_{[B]} = 0$, then

$$\hat{B} = (v^{(1)} \oplus v^{(2)} \oplus v^{(3)})_{[B]} = (v^{(1)} \oplus v^{(2)})_{[B]} \text{ and}$$
$$(\hat{A}, \hat{C}) = (v^{(1)} \oplus v^{(2)} \oplus v^{(3)})_{[AC]} = (v^{(1)} \oplus v^{(3)})_{[AC]}. \tag{2}$$

3.2   Basic Meet-in-the-Middle Attack

Below we describe the basic attack of [2] with minor differences and using somewhat different notation. We assume for simplicity that the algorithm is given as input the consecutive keystream $z_{[32]}$, and additional keystream that allows verifying that the initial state (or key) is correctly recovered. However, as noted in [2], it can be easily adjusted to use only 24 bits from the same frame.

1. For all $v^{(1)} \in V^{(1)}$:
   (a) Initialize a table $T_B^{v^{(1)}}$, storing elements in $\mathbb{F}_2^{32}$.
   (b) For all $v^{(2)} \in V^{(2)}$, let $\hat{B} = (v^{(1)} \oplus v^{(2)})_{[B]}$. Store $\hat{B}$ in $T_B^{v^{(1)}}$ at index $f_B(\hat{B})_{[32]}$.
2. For all $v^{(1)} \in V^{(1)}$:
   (a) For all $v^{(3)} \in V^{(3)}$, let $(\hat{A}, \hat{C}) = (v^{(1)} \oplus v^{(3)})_{[AC]}$. Search $T_B^{v^{(1)}}$ for $f_A(\hat{A})_{[32]} \oplus f_C(\hat{C})_{[32]} \oplus z_{[32]}$. For each match $\hat{B}$:

> – Test the state $(\hat{A}, \hat{B}, \hat{C})$, and if the test succeeds, recover and
>   output the key.

Since the first step is independent of the keystream, in [2] it was performed in preprocessing.

Testing States. A state $(\hat{A}, \hat{B}, \hat{C})$ is tested by using it to produce more output and comparing with the (additional) available keystream. Since there are 2^{64} possible initial states and the attack directly exploits 32 bits of available keystream, the expected number of states to test is $2^{64-32} = 2^{32}$.

Complexity Analysis. The memory complexity is $2^8 \cdot 2^{24} = 2^{32}$ words (dominated by the 2^8 tables $T_B^{v^{(1)}}$, each of size 2^{24}) and the time complexity is 2^{40}, dominated by the second step. It is assumed to dominate the complexity of testing the 2^{32} states.

3.3   Basic Memory-Optimized Attack

In the previous attack the decomposition is only used to obtain a post-filtering condition. Specifically, all vectors in $V^{(1)}$ are iterated over independently in both steps, and $v^{(1)} \in V^{(1)}$ determines which small table to access in the second step. We construct an outer loop over the elements of the common subspace $V^{(1)}$. This allows to divide the computation of the previous attack into 2^8 independent parts, each using a single small table. We remark that unlike the previous attack, the small tables are no longer computed during preprocessing. Nevertheless, the memory-optimized attack seems favorable, as the online complexity is similar to the previous one, while the memory complexity is reduced. The details of the algorithm are provided below. It is given as input the keystream $z_{[32]}$.

> 1. For all $v^{(1)} \in V^{(1)}$:
>   (a) – Initialize a table T_B, storing elements in $\mathbb{F}_2^{32}$.
>   – For all $v^{(2)} \in V^{(2)}$, let $\hat{B} = (v^{(1)} \oplus v^{(2)})_{[B]}$. Store $\hat{B}$ at index
> $f_B(\hat{B})_{[32]} \oplus z_{[32]}$ in T_B.
>   (b) For all $v^{(3)} \in V^{(3)}$, let $(\hat{A}, \hat{C}) = (v^{(1)} \oplus v^{(3)})_{[AC]}$. Search T_B for
> $f_A(\hat{A})_{[32]} \oplus f_C(\hat{C})_{[32]}$. For each match $\hat{B}$:
>   – Test the state $(\hat{A}, \hat{B}, \hat{C})$, and if the test succeeds, recover and
>   output the key.

Analysis

Correctness. Let $(\hat{A}, \hat{B}, \hat{C})$ be the internal state used to produce the keystream. In particular, it satisfies

$$f_B(\hat{B})_{[32]} \oplus z_{[32]} = f_A(\hat{A})_{[32]} \oplus f_C(\hat{C})_{[32]}. \tag{3}$$

Consider its decomposition $(v^{(1)}, v^{(2)}, v^{(3)}) \in V^{(1)} \times V^{(2)} \times V^{(3)}$ such that $\hat{B} = (v^{(1)} \oplus v^{(2)})_{[B]}$ and $(\hat{A}, \hat{C}) = (v^{(1)} \oplus v^{(3)})_{[AC]}$. By (3), this state is tested in Step 1.(b) for the corresponding value of $v^{(1)}$ and the correct key is output.

Complexity. The time complexity of the attack remains $2^8 \cdot 2^{32} = 2^{40}$, dominated by the 2^8 executions of Step 1.(b). The memory complexity (dominated by each T_B) is 2^{24} words.

3.4   Attack G1 – Improved Memory-Optimized Attack

We now revisit the previous attack on GEA-1, with the aim of further improving its memory complexity with only a minor effect on time complexity. Specifically, similarly to 3-XOR algorithms, given a prefix string, we would like to devise an efficient enumeration algorithm for internal states $(\hat{A}, \hat{C})$ that output this prefix (f_A and f_C replace f_2 and f_3 in Definition 1).

For GEA-1 we are only interested in a small fraction of states $(\hat{A}, \hat{C})$ that can be produced by the initialization process. On the other hand, the standard enumeration algorithm used in Sect. 2.4 for the 3-XOR problem does not impose such restrictions and therefore mostly outputs states that are irrelevant for us, rendering it inefficient for our purpose. Therefore, we need to devise a more dedicated algorithm.

High-Level Overview of the Attack. The attack is based on an enumeration algorithm similarly to the 3-XOR algorithm of Sect. 2.4. Specifically, Proposition 2 below is analogous to Proposition 1 for 3-XOR. It isolates the challenge in improving the memory complexity and allows to design the algorithm in a modular way.

Let $V_{[AC]}^{(3)} \subset \mathbb{F}_2^{64}$ be the projection of $V^{(3)}$ in (1) on the registers A and C (since $v_{[B]}^{(3)} = 0$ for all $v^{(3)} \in V^{(3)}$, the projection does not reduce its dimension). Essentially, the challenge is to enumerate all states $(\hat{A}, \hat{C})$ in the 32-dimensional coset $v_{[AC]}^{(1)} \oplus V_{[AC]}^{(3)}$ that produce a given output prefix efficiently with limited memory.

Proposition 2. *Let $\tau \in [8]$ be a parameter. Assume there is a state enumeration algorithm that given a target $u \in \mathbb{F}_2^\tau$ and a vector $v^{(1)} \in V^{(1)}$, enumerates all the (expected number of) $2^{32-\tau}$ states $(\hat{A}, \hat{C})$ such that $(\hat{A}, \hat{C}) \oplus v_{[AC]}^{(1)} \in V_{[AC]}^{(3)}$ and $f_A(\hat{A})_{[\tau]} \oplus f_C(\hat{C})_{[\tau]} = u$ in time complexity $2^{32-\tau}$ and memory complexity 2^m words of 32 bits. Then, there is a key-recovery attack on GEA-1 in time complexity 2^{40} and memory complexity about $2^{24-\tau} + 2^m$ words of 32 bits.*

Obviously, we would like to have $2^m \ll 2^{24-\tau}$ so the overall memory complexity is about $2^{24-\tau}$.

Note that if $(\hat{A}, \hat{C}) = (v^{(1)} \oplus v^{(3)})_{[AC]}$ as in the previous attack, then $(\hat{A}, \hat{C}) \oplus v_{[AC]}^{(1)} \in V_{[AC]}^{(3)}$ as in the above proposition.

We now describe the key-recovery attack that establishes the proposition. It is based on the clamping through precomputation technique similarly to the

3-XOR algorithm of Proposition 1. Yet, it uses the additional constraint on the states (similarly to the basic GEA-1 attack above). As previously, the attack directly utilizes a keystream $z_{[32]}$.

Attack G1

1. For all $v^{(1)} \in V^{(1)}$ and all $u \in \mathbb{F}_2^\tau$:
   (a) – Initialize a table $\mathcal{T}_B$, storing elements in $\mathbb{F}_2^{32}$.
        – For all $v^{(2)} \in V^{(2)}$, let $\hat{B} = (v^{(1)} \oplus v^{(2)})_{[B]}$. If $f_B(\hat{B})_{[\tau]} \oplus z_{[\tau]} = u$, store $\hat{B}$ at index $f_B(\hat{B})_{[32]} \oplus z_{[32]}$ in $\mathcal{T}_B$.
   (b) – Run the algorithm of Proposition 2 on inputs $v^{(1)}$ and u.
        – For each state $(\hat{A}, \hat{C})$ returned (satisfying $(\hat{A}, \hat{C}) \oplus v^{(1)}_{[AC]} \in V^{(3)}_{[AC]}$ and $f_A(\hat{A})_{[\tau]} \oplus f_C(\hat{C})_{[\tau]} = u$), search $\mathcal{T}_B$ for $f_A(\hat{A})_{[32]} \oplus f_C(\hat{C})_{[32]}$. For each match $\hat{B}$:
          • Test the state $(\hat{A}, \hat{B}, \hat{C})$, and if the test succeeds, recover and output the key.

Analysis

Correctness. Let $(\hat{A}, \hat{B}, \hat{C})$ be the internal state used to produce the keystream. In particular

$$f_B(\hat{B})_{[32]} \oplus z_{[32]} = f_A(\hat{A})_{[32]} \oplus f_C(\hat{C})_{[32]}.$$

We show that when iterating over $v^{(1)}$ and u satisfying $u = f_B(\hat{B})_{[\tau]} \oplus z_{[\tau]} = f_A(\hat{A})_{[\tau]} \oplus f_C(\hat{C})_{[\tau]}$, this state is tested and thus the key is returned.

Consider the state's decomposition $(v^{(1)}, v^{(2)}, v^{(3)}) \in V^{(1)} \times V^{(2)} \times V^{(3)}$ such that $\hat{B} = (v^{(1)} \oplus v^{(2)})_{[B]}$ and $(\hat{A}, \hat{C}) = (v^{(1)} \oplus v^{(3)})_{[AC]}$. For $u = f_B(\hat{B})_{[\tau]} \oplus z_{[\tau]}$, $\hat{B}$ is stored at index $f_B(\hat{B})_{[32]} \oplus z_{[32]}$ in $\mathcal{T}_B$.

Since $(\hat{A}, \hat{C}) \oplus v^{(1)}_{[AC]} = v^{(3)}_{[AC]} \in V^{(3)}_{[AC]}$ and $f_A(\hat{A})_{[\tau]} \oplus f_C(\hat{C})_{[\tau]} = u$, the enumeration algorithm returns $(\hat{A}, \hat{C})$ and $(\hat{A}, \hat{B}, \hat{C})$ is tested as claimed.

Complexity. The complexity of all $2^{8+\tau}$ executions of Step 1.(a) is $2^{8+\tau} \cdot 2^{24} = 2^{32+\tau} \leq 2^{40}$ evaluations of (32 bits of) f_B. By Proposition 2, the complexity of all $2^{8+\tau}$ executions of Step 1.(b) is $2^{8+\tau} \cdot 2^{32-\tau} = 2^{40}$ (evaluations of f_A and f_C) and it dominates the complexity of the attack. The memory complexity is dominated by $\mathcal{T}_B$ in addition to 2^m of the enumeration algorithm and is $2^{24-\tau} + 2^m$ words of 32 bits, as claimed.

Devising a State Enumeration Algorithm. We have reduced the goal to devising a state enumeration algorithm. If we assume that f_A, f_C are random functions, then clearly we cannot produce all solutions required by Proposition 2 in $2^{32-\tau} < 2^{32}$ time (regardless of the memory complexity), since the size of the domain of $\hat{C}$ is 2^{33} (and the number of vectors that satisfy $(\hat{A}, \hat{C}) \oplus v^{(1)}_{[AC]} \in V^{(3)}_{[AC]}$ is 2^{32}). Our main observation is that the functions f_A, f_C are not random and we can utilize their specific properties to devise a dedicated algorithm for GEA-1.

Proposition 3 (State enumeration algorithm for GEA-1). *For $\tau = 5$ and $m = 7$, there is a state enumeration algorithm for GEA-1. Specifically, given inputs $v^{(1)} \in V^{(1)}$ and $u \in \mathbb{F}_2^5$, there is an algorithm that enumerates all the $2^{40-8-5} = 2^{27}$ states $(\hat{A}, \hat{C})$ such that $(\hat{A}, \hat{C}) \oplus v_{[AC]}^{(1)} \in V_{[AC]}^{(3)}$ and $f_A(\hat{A})_{[5]} \oplus f_C(\hat{C})_{[5]} = u$ in time complexity 2^{27} using $2^7 \ll 2^{19}$ memory words of 32-bits.*

Therefore, Proposition 2 implies that we can recover the key of GEA-1 in time complexity 2^{40} and memory complexity (slightly more than) $2^{19} + 2^7$ words of 32 bits.[6] Below we describe the details of the algorithm.

Influence of the State on the Output. We observe that for all registers, only a subset of the internal state bits influence the first output bits. Specifically, we will exploit the following property, which is easily deduced from Fig. 1.

Property 1 (Influence of the state on the output).

- $f_A(\hat{A})_{[5]}$ only depends on $31 - 5 = 26$ bits of $\hat{A}$.
- $f_B(\hat{B})_{[5]}$ only depends on $32 - 7 = 25$ bits of $\hat{B}$.
- $f_B(\hat{C})_{[5]}$ only depends on $33 - 11 = 22$ bits of $\hat{C}$.

Denote these 26 (resp. 25, 22) state bit indices of A (resp. B, C) by J_A (resp. J_B, J_C). We note that we use the above property only for registers A and C.

Initial Attempt. An initial idea that exploits Property 1 is to prepare a table for all possible 2^{22} values of J_C. Then, enumerate over the 2^{26} bits of J_A and merge the (partial) states according to the linear constraints imposed by $V^{(3)}$ via the relation $(\hat{A}, \hat{C}) \oplus v_{[AC]}^{(1)} \in V_{[AC]}^{(3)}$ and the output constraint $f_A(\hat{A})_{[5]} \oplus f_C(\hat{C})_{[5]} = u$. While this algorithm satisfies the required time complexity, it does not give the desired memory saving.

Decomposition by Influential Bits. Let $V_{[J_A J_C]}^{(3)} \subset \mathbb{F}_2^{48}$ denote the projection of $V^{(3)}$ on the 48 influential bits $J_A \cup J_C$. Using a computer program, we calculated $\dim(V_{[J_A J_C]}^{(3)}) = \dim(V^{(3)}) = 32$.

Recall that we are only interested in states $(\hat{A}, \hat{C})$ that satisfy $(\hat{A}, \hat{C}) \oplus v_{[AC]}^{(1)} \in V_{[AC]}^{(3)}$, namely contained in the 32-dimensional coset $(v^{(1)} \oplus V^{(3)})_{[AC]}$. Moreover, as we are only interested in the first 5 output bits, it is sufficient to consider only 48-bit partial states in the projected coset $(v^{(1)} \oplus V^{(3)})_{[J_A J_C]}$ and then complement them to full 64-bit states $(\hat{A}, \hat{C})$.

Since $\dim(V_{[J_A J_C]}^{(3)}) = 32$, it is not efficient to iterate over its elements directly, but the main observation is that we can decompose it according to the bits of

---

[6] Based on this computation, the algorithm requires about 2 MiB of memory. However, if we use the data structure used in the GEA-1 attack of [2], the memory complexity would be 4 MiB (which is what we claim).

J_A and J_C and perform a MITM procedure as in the initial attempt above, but with less memory.

We restrict the discussion to the 48-bit subspace spanned by $J_A \cup J_C$ (viewed as unit vectors). Let $U^{(J_A)} \subset \mathbb{F}_2^{48}$ be the 26-dimensional subspace whose vectors are zero on the bits of J_C. Define the 22-dimensional subspace $U^{(J_C)}$ similarly.

We have

$$\dim(V_{[J_A J_C]}^{(3)} \cap U^{(J_A)}) \geq$$

$$\dim(V_{[J_A J_C]}^{(3)}) + \dim(U^{(J_A)}) - 48 = 32 + 26 - 48 = 10,$$

and similarly, $\dim(V_{[J_A J_C]}^{(3)} \cap U^{(J_C)}) \geq 32 + 22 - 48 = 6$ (both hold with equality, as verified by our program). Since $\dim(U^{(J_A)} \cap U^{(J_C)}) = 0$, we can decompose

$$V_{[J_A J_C]}^{(3)} = V^{(4)} \boxplus V^{(A)} \boxplus V^{(C)}, \tag{4}$$

where $V^{(A)} \subset U^{(J_A)}$ and $\dim(V^{(A)}) = 10$, while $V^{(C)} \subset U^{(J_C)}$ and $\dim(V^{(C)}) = 6$. Therefore, $\dim(V^{(4)}) = 32 - 10 - 6 = 16$.

The additional decomposition allows to divide the computation of the MITM procedure in the initial attempt above into 2^{16} independent smaller procedures, one for each $v^{(4)} \in V^{(4)}$. Consequently, the size of the table for J_C is reduced to $2^{22-16} = 2^6$, while we need to enumerate over $2^{26-16} = 2^{10}$ values for the bits of J_A and match with the table on the 5-bit output u. The average number of matches in the table per $v^{(4)} \in V^{(4)}$ is $2^{6+10-5} = 2^{11}$, and this matching phase dominates the complexity (which is $2^{16} \cdot 2^{11} = 2^{27}$ as required by Proposition 3). We give the details below.

State Enumeration Algorithm for GEA-1. Based on the decomposition

$$V_{[J_A J_C]}^{(3)} = V^{(4)} \boxplus V^{(A)} \boxplus V^{(C)},$$

given in (4), any partial state $(x_A, y_C) \in V_{[J_A J_C]}^{(3)}$ is decomposed as

$$x_A = v_{[J_A]}^{(4)} \oplus v_{[J_A]}^{(A)} \oplus v_{[J_A]}^{(C)} = v_{[J_A]}^{(4)} \oplus v_{[J_A]}^{(A)} \text{ and}$$

$$y_C = v_{[J_C]}^{(4)} \oplus v_{[J_C]}^{(A)} \oplus v_{[J_C]}^{(C)} = v_{[J_C]}^{(4)} \oplus v_{[J_C]}^{(C)}.$$

Partial states relevant for the MITM procedure in the coset $(\tilde{A}, \tilde{C}) \in (v^{(1)} \oplus V^{(3)})_{[J_A J_C]}$ are similarly decomposed as

$$\tilde{A} = v_{[J_A]}^{(1)} \oplus v_{[J_A]}^{(4)} \oplus v_{[J_A]}^{(A)} \text{ and } \tilde{C} = v_{[J_C]}^{(1)} \oplus v_{[J_C]}^{(4)} \oplus v_{[J_C]}^{(C)}.$$

This is the main decomposition used by the algorithm.

Yet, as the algorithm needs to return full 64-bit states and not partial states, it will be more convenient to directly work with 64-bit vectors and project them to partial states when needed. For this purpose, note that since $\dim(V^{(3)}_{[J_A J_C]}) = \dim(V^{(3)}) = 32$, then any 48-bit vector $v \in V^{(3)}_{[J_A J_C]}$ can be uniquely extended via linear algebra to a 64-bit vector $v' \in V^{(3)}_{[AC]}$ such that $v = v'_{[J_A J_C]}$.

Similarly, the subspaces $V^{(4)}, V^{(A)}, V^{(C)}$ (of $V^{(3)}_{[J_A J_C]}$) can be uniquely extended to subspaces $V^{(4')}, V^{(A')}, V^{(C')}$ (of $V^{(3)}_{[AC]}$) such that $V^{(4')}_{[J_A J_C]} = V^{(4)}, V^{(A')}_{[J_A J_C]} = V^{(A)}, V^{(C')}_{[J_A J_C]} = V^{(C)}$. Moreover, any $v^{(3')} \in V^{(3)}_{[AC]}$ can be uniquely written as

$$v^{(3')} = v^{(4')} \oplus v^{(A')} \oplus v^{(C')}, \tag{5}$$

where $(v^{(4')}, v^{(A')}, v^{(C')}) \in V^{(4')} \times V^{(A')} \times V^{(C')}$.

Details of the State Enumeration Algorithm. We extend the output functions $f_A(\hat{A})_{[5]}$ and $f_C(\hat{C})_{[5]}$ to work with partial states $\tilde{A} \in \mathbb{F}_2^{26}$ and $\tilde{C} \in \mathbb{F}_2^{22}$, respectively.

Recall that the state enumeration algorithm receives inputs $v^{(1)} \in V^{(1)}$ and $u \in \mathbb{F}_2^5$ and enumerates all $2^{40-8-5} = 2^{27}$ states $(\hat{A}, \hat{C})$ such that $(\hat{A}, \hat{C}) \oplus v^{(1)}_{[AC]} \in V^{(3)}_{[AC]}$ and $f_A(\hat{A})_{[5]} \oplus f_C(\hat{C})_{[5]} = u$. The algorithm is given below.

---

1. For all $v^{(4')} \in V^{(4')}$:
   (a) – Initialize a table $\mathcal{T}_C$, storing elements in $\mathbb{F}_2^{64}$.
        – For all $v^{(C')} \in V^{(C')}$, let $\tilde{C} = v^{(1)}_{[J_C]} \oplus v^{(4')}_{[J_C]} \oplus v^{(C')}_{[J_C]}$. Store $v^{(C')}$ at index $f_C(\tilde{C})_{[5]} \oplus u$ in $\mathcal{T}_C$.
   (b) For all $v^{(A')} \in V^{(A')}$, let $\tilde{A} = v^{(1)}_{[J_A]} \oplus v^{(4')}_{[J_A]} \oplus v^{(A')}_{[J_A]}$. Search $\mathcal{T}_C$ for $f_A(\tilde{A})_{[5]}$. For each match $v^{(C')}$:
        – Let $v^{(3')} = v^{(4')} \oplus v^{(A')} \oplus v^{(C')}$ and return $(\hat{A}, \hat{C}) = v^{(1)}_{[AC]} \oplus v^{(3')}$.

Analysis

Correctness. Let $(\hat{A}, \hat{C})$ be such that $(\hat{A}, \hat{C}) \oplus v^{(1)}_{[AC]} \in V^{(3)}_{[AC]}$ and $f_A(\hat{A})_{[5]} \oplus f_C(\hat{C})_{[5]} = u$. Then, we can write $(\hat{A}, \hat{C}) = v^{(1)}_{[AC]} \oplus v^{(3')}$, where $v^{(3')} \in V^{(3)}_{[AC]}$, and $v^{(3')} = v^{(4')} \oplus v^{(A')} \oplus v^{(C')}$ as in (5). Then, the partial state $(\tilde{A}, \tilde{C}) = (\hat{A}, \hat{C})_{[J_A J_C]}$ is considered when iterating over $v^{(4')}$, and $(\hat{A}, \hat{C})$ is returned as required.

Complexity. The heaviest step is 1.(b). For each $v^{(4')} \in V^{(4')}$, its complexity is 2^{10} for iterating over $v^{(A')} \in V^{(A')}$. The expected number of matches in $\mathcal{T}_C$ is $2^{10} \cdot 2^6 \cdot 2^{-5} = 2^{11}$ (it is a 5-bit matching). Hence, the total complexity of each iteration is about 2^{11}, while the total complexity is $2^{16} \cdot 2^{11} = 2^{27}$ as claimed in Proposition 3. In terms of memory, table $\mathcal{T}_C$ requires 2^6 words of 64 bits.

Implementation. We implemented the attack in C++ and experimentally verified it on a laptop with an AMD Ryzen-7 5800H processor. The program recovered the GEA-1 session key in 153 min, averaged over 5 runs. As the attack of [2] was implemented on a cluster, it cannot be directly compared to ours. Nevertheless, we give a rough comparison in terms of CPU time: our attack takes 6× time using 32× less cores which are 1.5× faster. This seems favorable and is possibly a consequence of the reduced allocated memory fitting in cache.

4   Attacks on GEA-2

In this section we analyze the GEA-2 cipher. We begin by giving an overview of the attacks of [2], as our attacks reuse some of their techniques.

We then describe a simple attack that is based on the Schroeppel-Shamir variant for 4-XOR. This attack needs only a small amount of keystream. Its time complexity is about 2^{63} and it requires roughly 32 GiB of memory. We subsequently describe Attack G2-1 that improves the simple attack in a scenario where a longer keystream sequence is available: given a consecutive keystream of ℓ bits, the time complexity is about $2^{64}/(\ell - 62)$, while the memory complexity is about 64 GiB accessed randomly (and additional 96 GiB of storage accessed sequentially, which can be eliminated at a small cost).

Finally, we describe Attack G2-2 that targets the initialization of GEA-2. As we explain, for technical reasons the current results are mostly interesting in case the attacker obtains a long yet fragmented keystream (not containing a long window of consecutive known bits). Compared to [2], Attack G2-2 provides an improvement by a factor of (at least) $2^9 = 512$ in memory complexity in the considered scenario.

4.1   Previous Attacks on GEA-2

Let $(\hat{A}, \hat{B}, \hat{C}, \hat{D})$ be an internal state. Since the algebraic degree of the filter function f is 4, any consequent output bit can be symbolically represented as a polynomial of algebraic degree 4 over $\mathbb{F}_2$ in terms of the 125 bits of $(\hat{A}, \hat{B}, \hat{C}, \hat{D})$, treated as variables.

Assume we receive the encryption of a fully known GEA-2 frame, thus obtaining 12800 keystream bits. Hence, we can construct a system of 12800 polynomial equations of degree 4 in 125 variables. Since the registers are independent, the number of monomials that appear in the polynomials is upper bounded by

$$1 + \sum_{i=1}^{4} \binom{29}{i} + \binom{31}{i} + \binom{32}{i} + \binom{33}{i} = 152682.$$

Attempting to apply a linearization attack, we replace every monomial in each polynomial equation with an independent variable and try to eliminate variables by Gaussian elimination on the 12800 linearized polynomial representations of the keystream bits. Unfortunately, the number of variables is much larger than the 12800 available equations, rendering this straightforward approach useless.

Therefore, [2] considers a hybrid approach in which we guess some variables in order to reduce the number of monomials. However reducing the number of monomials to 12800 seems to require guessing at least 58 variables.[7] Each such guess requires additional linear algebra computations which make the attack slower than exhaustive search.

Hybrid with Meet-in-the-Middle. The main idea of [2] is to combine the hybrid approach with a MITM procedure. More specifically, the idea is to guess some bits of the internal states of the shorter registers A and D and eliminate their contribution from the keystream by linearization. Then, perform a MITM procedure on the registers B and C.

We give a high-level overview of this attack. Let $(\hat{A}, \hat{B}, \hat{C}, \hat{D})$ be an unknown internal state that produces $z_{[12800]}$. Guess 11 bits of $\hat{A}$ and 9 bits of $\hat{D}$. This reduces the number of monomials in the remaining $20 + 20$ unknown variables in these registers to $\sum_{i=1}^{4} \binom{20}{i} + \binom{20}{i} = 12390$. By Gaussian elimination, find $12800 - 12390 = 410$ linear expressions (masks) of length 12800, each eliminating the contributions of $\hat{A}$ and $\hat{D}$ from the keystream. The attack essentially only needs 64 of these masks.

Next, apply the 64 masks to the keystream to derive a 64-bit masked keystream (that should depend only on $\hat{B}$ and $\hat{C}$ if the initial guess is correct). Finally, perform a MITM procedure: for each possible value of $\hat{B}$, compute $f_B(\hat{B})_{[12800]}$ and apply the 64 masks. Store $\hat{B}$ indexed by the 64-bit results (after XORing with the masked keystream) in a table. Then, for each possible value of $\hat{C}$, compute $f_C(\hat{C})_{[12800]}$, apply the 64 masks and search the table for the 64-bit value. After additional tests, a match allows to easily construct the full state of GEA-2 and to recover the key if the state is correct. In order to perform all these $2^{32} + 2^{33}$ computations of 64 bits efficiently (without expanding the full 12800-bit output and applying the 64 masks), the attack first interpolates the symbolic representations of the 64 masked outputs of $\hat{B}$ and $\hat{C}$ (which are Boolean functions of degree 4). Then, the fast polynomial evaluation algorithm of [8] is used.

There are two optimizations applied to the attack. The first optimization uses the observation that degree 4 monomials produced by the $20+20$ eliminated variables of $\hat{A}$ and $\hat{D}$ are unchanged by the guesses (as they are not multiplied by any other variable in the original polynomial representations that involve the guessed variables). This allows to perform the Gaussian elimination only once on these $\binom{20}{4} + \binom{20}{4} = 9690$ linearized variables and reduces the complexity of the remaining work for computing the 410 masks.

Overall, the 2^{9+11} performed MITM procedures dominate the time and memory complexities of the attack, which the authors estimate as (about) 2^{54} GEA-2 evaluations, and roughly 2^{32} words, respectively.

---

[7] The authors of [2] showed how to reduce the number of monomials to 12800 by guessing 59 variables. We have found a way to do it by guessing only 58 variables, but this does not have a substantial effect on the attack.

Shifted Keystreams. The second optimization produces 753 internal state targets for the attack at different clocks. This allows to reduce the number of guesses by a factor of (roughly) 753 (after $2^{20}/753$ guesses, we expect to hit one of the internal state targets). Specifically, the idea is to produce from the 12800-bit keystream 753 shifted consecutive keysteams of length 12047 (keystream i starts from position i). Then, by linear algebra, compute $12047 - 753 + 1 = 11295$ masks (linear expressions), each having a constant value on all 753 keystreams. These 11295 constant bits serve as the keystream input to the previous attack and allows to simultaneously target all 753 shifted keystreams. Since the effective keystream size is reduced to 11295, we now have to guess 21 variables instead of 20 to perform linearization, but we are expected to hit one of the targets much faster. The authors estimate the complexity of this attack by about 2^{45} GEA-2 evaluations. The memory complexity remains roughly 2^{32} words (32 GiB).

The authors also calculated the complexity of the optimized attack when given less data and estimated that it beats exhaustive search given at least 1468 consecutive keystream bits.

Attack on Fragmented Keystream. We note that the final optimization can only be applied if the attacker obtains a long sequence of consecutive keystream bits. On the other hand, assume the attacker obtains a frame in which 11300 bits of keystream at arbitrary locations are known. In this case, the best attack is the previous one (without the final optimization) that can be adjusted to work in slightly higher complexity of 2^{55} GEA-2 evaluations (instead of 2^{54}), and 2^{32} words of memory.

4.2   Basic 4-XOR Attack

Our first attack adapts the Schroeppel-Shamir variant for 4-XOR (summarized in Sect. 2.5) to an attack on GEA-2. As in the Schroeppel-Shamir variant, we partition the functions f_A, f_B, f_C, f_D into pairs during the merging process. The time complexity will be dominated by the pair of registers that has the maximal number of possible states. In order to optimize the attack, we consider the pairs (f_C, f_D) and (f_A, f_B) to obtain time complexity of about $2^{31+32} = 2^{63}$ (the number of internal states of registers A and B). This complexity is very close to exhaustive search, and we describe it below mainly as an exposition to Attack G2-1 that follows.

Let $\tau \leq 64$ be a parameter. We enumerate over all $u \in \mathbb{F}_2^\tau$, representing the values of

$$f_C(\hat{C})_{[\tau]} \oplus f_D(\hat{D})_{[\tau]} \oplus z_{[\tau]} \text{ and } f_A(\hat{A})_{[\tau]} \oplus f_B(\hat{B})_{[\tau]}.$$

These values are equal for the correct state $(\hat{A}, \hat{B}, \hat{C}, \hat{D})$.

We assume that we have a 64-bit keystream $z_{[64]}$ (although the attack can be applied in additional scenarios).

---

1. – Initialize a table $\mathcal{T}_D$, storing elements in $\mathbb{F}_2^{29}$.
    – For all $\hat{D} \in \mathbb{F}_2^{29}$, store $\hat{D}$ at index $f_D(\hat{D})_{[\tau]}$ in $\mathcal{T}_D$.
2. – Initialize a table $\mathcal{T}_A$, storing elements in $\mathbb{F}_2^{31}$.
    – For all $\hat{A} \in \mathbb{F}_2^{31}$, store $\hat{A}$ at index $f_A(\hat{A})_{[\tau]}$ in $\mathcal{T}_A$.
3. For each $u \in \mathbb{F}_2^{\tau}$:
    (a) – Initialize a table $\mathcal{T}_{CD}$, storing pairs in $\mathbb{F}_2^{33} \times \mathbb{F}_2^{29}$.
         – For all $\hat{C} \in \mathbb{F}_2^{33}$, search $\mathcal{T}_D$ for $f_C(\hat{C})_{[\tau]} \oplus u \oplus z_{[\tau]}$. For each match $\hat{D}$:
           • Let $v_{CD} = f_C(\hat{C})_{[\tau+1,64]} \oplus f_D(\hat{D})_{[\tau+1,64]} \oplus z_{[\tau+1,64]}$. Store $(\hat{C}, \hat{D})$ at index v_{CD} in $\mathcal{T}_{CD}$.
    (b) For all $\hat{B} \in \mathbb{F}_2^{32}$, search $\mathcal{T}_A$ for $f_B(\hat{B})_{[\tau]} \oplus u$. For each match $\hat{A}$:
         – Let $v_{AB} = f_A(\hat{A})_{[\tau+1,64]} \oplus f_B(\hat{B})_{[\tau+1,64]}$. Search v_{AB} in $\mathcal{T}_{CD}$. For each match $(\hat{C}, \hat{D})$:
           • Test the state $(\hat{A}, \hat{B}, \hat{C}, \hat{D})$ and if the test succeeds, recover and output the corresponding key.

Testing States. A 125-bit state $(\hat{A}, \hat{B}, \hat{C}, \hat{D})$ can be tested by computing more output bits and comparing them against additional available keystream bits (a total of 125 bits suffice on average). Since we impose a 64-bit condition on the 125-bit internal state, the expected number of states to test is $2^{125-64} = 2^{61}$. As the total complexity will be about 2^{63}, we consider the testing time as negligible.

Analysis

Correctness. Fix any $(\hat{C}, \hat{D})$. Then, for

$$u = f_C(\hat{C})_{[\tau]} \oplus f_D(\hat{D})_{[\tau]} \oplus z_{[\tau]},$$

$f_C(\hat{C})_{[\tau]} \oplus u \oplus z_{[\tau]} = f_D(\hat{D})_{[\tau]}$ is searched in $\mathcal{T}_D$ and $\hat{D}$ is retrieved. Therefore, $(\hat{C}, \hat{D})$ is stored at index v_{CD} in $\mathcal{T}_{CD}$. If $(\hat{A}, \hat{B}, \hat{C}, \hat{D})$ is the correct state, then

$$u = f_A(\hat{A})_{[\tau]} \oplus f_B(\hat{B})_{[\tau]}$$

holds as well, implying that when searching $\mathcal{T}_A$ for $f_B(\hat{B})_{[\tau]} \oplus u$, the state $\hat{A}$ is retrieved and $v_{AB} = f_A(\hat{A})_{[\tau+1,64]} \oplus f_B(\hat{B})_{[\tau+1,64]}$ is searched in $\mathcal{T}_{CD}$. Finally, since $v_{AB} = v_{CD}$ for the correct state $(\hat{A}, \hat{B}, \hat{C}, \hat{D})$, then it is tested.

Complexity Analysis. The complexity of generating the outputs $\hat{D}$ in the first step and building the table is about 2^{29} (in terms of τ-bit computations of f_D). Similarly, the complexity of the second step for A is about 2^{31}.

For each of the 2^{τ} iterations of Step 3, the complexity of generating the outputs $\hat{C}$ in Step 3.(a) is about 2^{33}. The expected number of matches in $\mathcal{T}_D$ is $2^{29} \cdot 2^{33} \cdot 2^{-\tau} = 2^{62-\tau}$ (as we match on τ bits), which gives the expected number of entries in $\mathcal{T}_{CD}$. For Step 3.(b), the complexity of generating the outputs $f_B(\hat{B})$ is about 2^{32}. The expected number of matches in T_A is $2^{31} \cdot 2^{32} \cdot 2^{-\tau} = 2^{63-\tau}$. Overall, we estimate the total time complexity per $u \in \mathbb{F}_2^\tau$ by about $\max(2^{33}, 2^{63-\tau})$ GEA-2 evaluations (producing a 128-bit keystream). To optimize the time complexity (and minimize memory complexity for this choice), we choose $\tau = 30$. This gives total time complexity of $2^{30+33} = 2^{63}$.

The memory complexity of all the 3 tables is $2^{29} + 2^{31} + 2^{32} < 2^{33}$ words.

4.3 Attack G2-1 – Extended 4-XOR Attack

The basic attack requires a short keystream and we would like to optimize it in case additional keystream data is available to the attacker.

We show how to apply a variant of Wagner's k-tree algorithm that solves 4-XOR more efficiently than the Schroeppel-Shamir variant in case there are many solutions. For this purpose, we use the idea of [2] and combine several (shifted) keystreams by computing common masks. This allows to combine multiple targets (internal states at different clocks) for the attack, and has an analogous (although not identical) effect to enlarging the domains of the functions in the original 4-XOR problem.

In this attack, the value $u \in \mathbb{F}_2^\tau$ that we iterate over in the loop will represent the values of the linear masks applied to $f_C(\hat{C}) \oplus f_D(\hat{D}) \oplus z$.

Linear Masks. We assume that we have a keystream of length $\ell \geq 64$ bits denoted by $z_{[\ell]}$. For convenience, we assume that ℓ is even. Let $\ell' = (\ell - 62)/2$, and for $j \in [\ell']$ define shifted streams $z^{(j)} = z_{[j,j+\ell'+62]} \in \mathbb{F}_2^{\ell'+63}$. Note that the last index of $z^{(\ell')}$ is keystream bit number $\ell' + \ell' + 62 = \ell$, which is the last index of the stream.

We have ℓ' shifted sequences, each of length $\ell' + 63$ bits, and can compute 64 linearly independent masks $m^{(1)}, \ldots, m^{(64)}$ where $m^{(i)} \in \mathbb{F}_2^{\ell'+63}$ such that for each $i \in [64]$, $m^{(i)} \cdot z^{(j)} = c^{(i)}$ for all $j \in [\ell']$, where $c^{(i)} \in \mathbb{F}_2$ is a constant independent of j (the symbol $\cdot$ denotes inner product mod 2).

Concretely, define a $(\ell' - 1) \times (\ell' + 63)$-dimensional matrix (denoted by Z), where the j'th row is $z^{(j)} \oplus z^{(\ell')}$. The kernel of this matrix is of dimension (at least) $(\ell' + 63) - (\ell' - 1) = 64$. The masks are a basis of the kernel and can be computed by Gaussian elimination. The 64 constants $c^{(i)}$ are determined by application of the 64 masks to $z^{(\ell')}$.

Before describing the attack, we define some additional notation: given the masks $m^{(1)}, \ldots, m^{(64)}$ (as an implicit input), and a state $\hat{A}$, let

$$g_A(\hat{A}) = \{m^{(i)} \cdot f_A(\hat{A})_{[\ell'+63]}\}_{i \in [64]} \in \mathbb{F}_2^{64}$$

denote the concatenations of the applications of the 64 masks to the $(\ell' + 63)$-bit output prefix produced by $\hat{A}$. Similar notation is defined for the registers B, C, D. Finally, let $c \in \mathbb{F}_2^{64}$ denote the concatenation of all the constants $c^{(i)}$.

Details of the Algorithm. The algorithm is given as input the keystream $z_{[\ell]}$. Let $\tau \leq 64$ be a parameter.

Attack G2-1

1. Given $z_{[\ell]}$, compute the matrix $Z \in \mathbb{F}_2^{(\ell'-1)\times(\ell'+63)}$ defined above. Then, derive the masks $m^{(1)}, \ldots, m^{(64)} \in \mathbb{F}_2^{\ell'+63}$ and $c \in \mathbb{F}_2^{64}$ by Gaussian elimination.

2.   – Initialize a table $\mathcal{T}_D$, storing pairs in $\mathbb{F}_2^{29} \times \mathbb{F}_2^{64}$.
    – For all $\hat{D} \in \mathbb{F}_2^{29}$, store $(\hat{D}, g_D(\hat{D}))$ at index $g_D(\hat{D})_{[\tau]}$ in $\mathcal{T}_D$.
    – Build a similar table $\mathcal{T}_A$ for A, storing $(\hat{A}, g_A(\hat{A})) \in \mathbb{F}_2^{31} \times \mathbb{F}_2^{64}$ at index $g_A(\hat{A})_{[\tau]}$.

3.   – Initialize a sequential table (array) $\mathcal{T}_B$, storing elements in $\mathbb{F}_2^{64}$.
    – For all $\hat{B} \in \mathbb{F}_2^{32}$, store $g_B(\hat{B})$ in $\mathcal{T}_B$ in entry $\hat{B}$.
    – Build a similar table $\mathcal{T}_C$ for C, storing $g_C(\hat{C}) \in \mathbb{F}_2^{64}$ in entry $\hat{C}$.

4. For each $u \in \mathbb{F}_2^{7}$:
  (a)   – Initialize a table $\mathcal{T}_{CD}$, storing pairs in $\mathbb{F}_2^{33} \times \mathbb{F}_2^{29}$.
      – For all $\hat{C} \in \mathbb{F}_2^{33}$, retrieve $g_C(\hat{C})$ from $\mathcal{T}_C$. Search $\mathcal{T}_D$ for $g_C(\hat{C})_{[\tau]} \oplus u \oplus c_{[\tau]}$. For each match $(\hat{D}, g_D(\hat{D}))$:
        • Let $v_{CD} = g_C(\hat{C})_{[\tau+1,64]} \oplus g_D(\hat{D})_{[\tau+1,64]} \oplus c_{[\tau+1,64]}$. Store $(\hat{C}, \hat{D})$ at index v_{CD} in $\mathcal{T}_{CD}$.
  (b) For all $\hat{B} \in \mathbb{F}_2^{32}$, retrieve $g_B(\hat{B})$ from $\mathcal{T}_B$. Search $\mathcal{T}_A$ for $g_B(\hat{B})_{[\tau]} \oplus u$. For each match $(\hat{A}, g_A(\hat{A}))$:
      – Let $v_{AB} = g_A(\hat{A})_{[\tau+1,64]} \oplus g_B(\hat{B})_{[\tau+1,64]}$. Search v_{AB} in $\mathcal{T}_{CD}$. For each match $(\hat{C}, \hat{D})$:
        • Test the state $(\hat{A}, \hat{B}, \hat{C}, \hat{D})$. If the test succeeds, recover and output the corresponding key.

Testing a state is done by computing output bits and comparing with $z_{[\ell]}$ at all indices $j \in [\ell']$ (on average, we need to compute about $\lceil \log \ell' \rceil < \lceil \log \ell \rceil \leq 14$ output bits). We note that the attack involves precomputation of additional tables $\mathcal{T}_B, \mathcal{T}_C$ in order to avoid recomputing the masks in each iteration.

Analysis

Correctness. Fixing $(\hat{C}, \hat{D})$, for $u = g_C(\hat{C})_{[\tau]} \oplus g_D(\hat{D})_{[\tau]} \oplus c_{[\tau]}$, $(\hat{C}, \hat{D})$ is stored at index v_{CD} in $\mathcal{T}_{CD}$. If $(\hat{A}, \hat{B}, \hat{C}, \hat{D})$ is a state that produced the shifted keystream $z^{(j)}$ for $j \in [\ell']$, then for every $i \in [64]$,

$$(g_A(\hat{A}) \oplus g_B(\hat{B}) \oplus g_C(\hat{C}) \oplus g_D(\hat{D}))_i =$$
$$m^{(i)} \cdot (f_A(\hat{A}) \oplus f_B(\hat{B}) \oplus f_C(\hat{C}) \oplus f_D(\hat{D}))_{[\ell'+63]} =$$
$$m^{(i)} \cdot z^{(j)} = c^{(i)},$$

where the final equality holds by the properties of the masks. Equivalently,

$$c = g_A(\hat{A}) \oplus g_B(\hat{B}) \oplus g_C(\hat{C}) \oplus g_D(\hat{D}).$$

Specifically,

$$g_C(\hat{C})_{[\tau]} \oplus g_D(\hat{D})_{[\tau]} \oplus c_{[\tau]} = g_A(\hat{A})_{[\tau]} \oplus g_B(\hat{B})_{[\tau]}.$$

This implies that if the algorithm iterates over $u = g_C(\hat{C})_{[\tau]} \oplus g_D(\hat{D})_{[\tau]} \oplus c_{[\tau]}$, then v_{AB} is searched in $\mathcal{T}_{CD}$ and the key is output.

Complexity. Since there are ℓ' shifted keystreams $z^{(j)}$, then the expected number of corresponding $u \in \mathbb{F}_2^\tau$ values is about ℓ' (assuming $\ell' < 2^\tau$) and hence the algorithm is expected to recover the key in about $2^\tau/\ell'$ iterations.

In terms of time complexity, computing the masks in Step 1 by naive Gaussian elimination requires time complexity of roughly ℓ^3 bit operations. Naively applying the masks to the outputs of all states of each register and building the tables $\mathcal{T}_A, \mathcal{T}_B, \mathcal{T}_C, \mathcal{T}_D$ requires about $64 \cdot (2^{29} + 2^{31} + 2^{32} + 2^{33}) \cdot \ell \le 2^{40} \cdot \ell$ bit operations.

Since for GEA-2 we have $\ell \le 12800 < 2^{14}$, then the linear algebra complexity is upper bounded by roughly $2^{14 \cdot 3} + 2^{54} \approx 2^{54}$ bit operations, which is 2^{47} operations on 128-bit words (an upper bound on the complexity in GEA-2 evaluations).

Choosing $\tau = 30$ as in the basic attack, the complexity of each iteration remains about 2^{33} and their total complexity is

$$2^{33} \cdot 2^{30}/\ell' = 2^{64}/(\ell - 62).$$

Since $\ell \le 12800$, this term dominates the complexity of the attack.

The memory complexity of the attack is calculated as follows: the matrix Z requires about ℓ^2 bits of storage, but this will be negligible. The hash tables $\mathcal{T}_A$ and $\mathcal{T}_D$ require about $2^{29} + 2^{31}$ words of 96 bits. The hash table $\mathcal{T}_{CD}$ requires memory of about 2^{32} words of 64 bits. Altogether, the hash tables require memory of about 64 GiB. The sequential tables $\mathcal{T}_B, \mathcal{T}_C$ require storage of $2^{32} + 2^{33} = 3 \cdot 2^{32}$ words of 64 bits or 96 GiB.

Note that this attack does not exploit any special property of the internal GEA-2 shift registers, and is thus applicable to any construction that combines the outputs of 4 independent stream ciphers by a simple XOR operation.

Recomputation of Masked Outputs. It is possible to eliminate the sequential tables and recompute the masked outputs for B and C on-the-fly at a modest penalty in time complexity. For GEA-2, this can be done (for example), with the fast polynomial evaluation algorithm of [8] (as also used in [2]), exploiting the low degree representation of the output of its registers.

4.4 Attacks Targeting the GEA-2 Initialization

We consider attacks that target the GEA-2 initialization process. Although this process does not have a significant weakness as in GEA-1, it linearly maps a 97-bit seed to a 125-bit internal state. Therefore, this state resides in a 97-dimensional linear subspace. Our previous attacks (and the ones of [2]) do not exploit this property and it is interesting to investigate whether it leads to improved attacks. On the other hand, we note that attacks which target the initialization process cannot benefit from the optimization that allows targeting multiple states using a consecutive keystream. While such attacks can target multiple initial states obtained by different GEA-2 frames using similar ideas, this requires more data and is therefore less practical.

Exploiting the GEA-2 Initialization. Our goal is to exploit the fact that the state obtained after initialization resides in a 97-dimensional linear subspace to optimize attacks of GEA-2. This seems difficult at first, as the linear relations among the registers are complex and each register (and pair of registers) can attain all possible values. However, a careful examination will allow optimizations, as described next.

Note that any valid state obtained after initialization must satisfy $125 - 97 = 28$ linear equations (masks). Denote these masks by $m^{(1)}, \ldots, m^{(28)}$, where $m^{(i)} \in \mathbb{F}_2^{125}$ for $i \in [28]$. Let $(\hat{A}, \hat{B}, \hat{C}, \hat{D})$ be a state obtained after initialization. Then, for all $i \in [28]$, $m^{(i)} \cdot (\hat{A}, \hat{B}, \hat{C}, \hat{D}) = 0$.

Suppose we wish to eliminate $g \leq 28$ variables from each register of an unknown state $(\hat{A}, \hat{B}, \hat{C}, \hat{D})$. Consider $m^{(1)}, \ldots, m^{(g)}$ and for each $i \in [g]$, guess the 3 bits

$$m_{[A]}^{(i)} \cdot \hat{A}, \ m_{[B]}^{(i)} \cdot \hat{B}, \ m_{[C]}^{(i)} \cdot \hat{C}.$$

This immediately gives

$$m_{[D]}^{(i)} \cdot \hat{D} = m_{[A]}^{(i)} \cdot \hat{A} \oplus m_{[B]}^{(i)} \cdot \hat{B} \oplus m_{[C]}^{(i)} \cdot \hat{C}.$$

Therefore, we have g linear equations per register ($4g$ in total), and by guessing the values of $3g$ of them we reduce the dimension of the subspace spanned by any register by g. We can thus symbolically represent the value of any b-bit register with only $b - g$ variables, which has an identical effect to guessing g variables per register. Overall, we have eliminated $4g$ variables at the cost of guessing $3g$ bits.

Attack G2-2 – Hybrid with Meet-in-the-Middle. The guessing strategy described above can be used to optimize the hybrid attack on GEA-2, yet it is still not very efficient. We now show how to use the guessing strategy to improve the memory complexity of the hybrid with meet-in-the-middle attack of [2] with no penalty in time complexity. This results in the most efficient attack on GEA-2 given a fragmented keystream.

Assume that we have a frame with 12800 known keystream bits. The analysis can be easily adjusted to a fragmented keystream with less known bits. Recall that the goal in this attack is to eliminate the contributions of the two registers A and D from the keystream, and then perform a meet-in-the-middle attack on registers B and C.

Consider $m^{(1)}, \ldots, m^{(9)}$ as defined in the guessing strategy. For each $i \in [9]$ guess the 2 bits

$$m^{(i)}_{[A]} \cdot \hat{A}, \ m^{(i)}_{[D]} \cdot \hat{D}.$$

Moreover, guess additional 2 arbitrary bits of $\hat{A}$. This has an identical effect to guessing 11 bits of $\hat{A}$ and 9 bits of $\hat{D}$, and now the attack of [2] described above (without exploiting shifted keystreams) is directly applicable.

Optimizing Memory Complexity Using Additional Linear Equations. For each $i \in [9]$, we have

$$m^{(i)}_{[B]} \cdot \hat{B} \oplus m^{(i)}_{[C]} \cdot \hat{C} = m^{(i)}_{[A]} \cdot \hat{A} \oplus m^{(i)}_{[D]} \cdot \hat{D}, \tag{6}$$

where the right hand side is known. These 9 linear equations reduce the dimension of the subspace of states $(\hat{B}, \hat{C})$ relevant to the MITM attack. The main observation is that we can exploit the reduced dimension of this subspace to save memory by decomposing it, similarly to the attacks on GEA-1.
    Let

$$U^{(B)} = \{(x,0) \in \mathbb{F}_2^{32} \times \mathbb{F}_2^{33}\} \text{ and } U^{(C)} = \{(0,x) \in \mathbb{F}_2^{32} \times \mathbb{F}_2^{33}\}.$$

In addition, define

$$V^{(BC)} = \{(x,y) \in \mathbb{F}_2^{32} \times \mathbb{F}_2^{33} \mid \forall i \in [9] : m^{(i)}_{[B]} \cdot x \oplus m^{(i)}_{[C]} \cdot y = 0\}.$$

The states relevant for the attack form an affine subspace $w \oplus V^{(BC)}$, where $w \subset \mathbb{F}_2^{32} \times \mathbb{F}_2^{33}$ depends on the guesses on the right hand side of (6).
    We have $\dim(V^{(BC)}) = 65 - 9 = 56$. Moreover, as all relevant subspaces are in a 65-dimensional subspace,

$$\dim(V^{(BC)} \cap U^{(B)}) \geq 56 + 32 - 65 = 23 \text{ and } \dim(V^{(BC)} \cap U^{(C)}) \geq 56 + 33 - 65 = 24$$

(we chose the masks so both hold with equality, as verified by our program). Since $\dim(U^{(B)} \cap U^{(C)}) = 0$, similarly to the attacks on GEA-1, we can decompose the 56-dimensional subspace $V^{(BC)}$ as a direct sum

$$V^{(BC)} = V^{(1)} \boxplus V^{(2)} \boxplus V^{(3)},$$

where $\dim(V^{(1)}) = 9$, $\dim(V^{(2)}) = 23$, $\dim(V^{(3)}) = 24$, such that for any $(\hat{B}, \hat{C}) \in V^{(BC)}$, we have $\hat{B} = (v^{(1)} \oplus v^{(2)})_{[B]}$ and $\hat{C} = (v^{(1)} \oplus v^{(3)})_{[C]}$.
    By considering the affine subspace $w \oplus V^{(BC)}$, similarly to the attacks on GEA-1, this decomposition allows to reduce the memory complexity by a factor of $2^{\dim(V^{(1)})} = 2^9$ to about 2^{23} words (it still dominates the memory complexity of the attack).
    Interestingly, our advantage in terms of memory complexity *increases* as the number of available keystream bits decreases. This is because more variables are guessed, implying that $\dim(V^{(1)})$ and $2^{\dim(V^{(1)})}$ (which is the advantage factor in memory complexity) increase. For example, given 11300 bits of fragmented keystream, the memory complexity is reduced by a factor of 2^{10}.

Implementation. We implemented the attack in `sage`, assuming 11300 keystream bits are available. We executed several iterations, each with a different guess for the linear expressions described above. An iteration took about 50 min to execute on a laptop using a single thread. While our implementation can be significantly optimized, its main purpose was to verify correctness by checking that the attack indeed returns the correct state for the correct guess.

Acknowledgements. This work was supported by the Israel Science Foundation grant no. 1903/20 and by the European Research Council under the ERC starting grant agreement no. 757731 (LightCrypt).

References

1. Aoki, K., Sasaki, Y.: Meet-in-the-middle preimage attacks against reduced SHA-0 and SHA-1. In: Halevi, S. (ed.) CRYPTO 2009. LNCS, vol. 5677, pp. 70–89. Springer, Heidelberg (2009). https://doi.org/10.1007/978-3-642-03356-8_5
2. Beierle, C., et al.: Cryptanalysis of the GPRS encryption algorithms GEA-1 and GEA-2. In: Canteaut, A., Standaert, F.-X. (eds.) EUROCRYPT 2021, Part II. LNCS, vol. 12697, pp. 155–183. Springer, Cham (2021). https://doi.org/10.1007/978-3-030-77886-6_6
3. Beierle, C., Felke, P., Leander, G.: To Shift or Not to Shift: Understanding GEA-1. IACR Cryptology ePrint Archive, p. 829 (2021). https://eprint.iacr.org/2021/829
4. Bernstein, D.J.: Better price-performance ratios for generalized birthday attacks (2007). https://cr.yp.to/rumba20/genbday-20070904.pdf
5. Biryukov, A., Shamir, A.: Cryptanalytic time/memory/data tradeoffs for stream ciphers. In: Okamoto, T. (ed.) ASIACRYPT 2000. LNCS, vol. 1976, pp. 1–13. Springer, Heidelberg (2000). https://doi.org/10.1007/3-540-44448-3_1
6. Biryukov, A., Shamir, A., Wagner, D.: Real time cryptanalysis of A5/1 on a PC. In: Goos, G., Hartmanis, J., van Leeuwen, J., Schneier, B. (eds.) FSE 2000. LNCS, vol. 1978, pp. 1–18. Springer, Heidelberg (2001). https://doi.org/10.1007/3-540-44706-7_1
7. Bogdanov, A., Rechberger, C.: A 3-subset meet-in-the-middle attack: cryptanalysis of the lightweight block cipher KTANTAN. In: Biryukov, A., Gong, G., Stinson, D.R. (eds.) SAC 2010. LNCS, vol. 6544, pp. 229–240. Springer, Heidelberg (2011). https://doi.org/10.1007/978-3-642-19574-7_16
8. Bouillaguet, C., et al.: Fast exhaustive search for polynomial systems in $\mathbb{F}_2$. In: Mangard, S., Standaert, F.-X. (eds.) CHES 2010. LNCS, vol. 6225, pp. 203–218. Springer, Heidelberg (2010). https://doi.org/10.1007/978-3-642-15031-9_14
9. Bouillaguet, C., Delaplace, C., Fouque, P.: Revisiting and improving algorithms for the 3XOR problem. IACR Trans. Symmetric Cryptol. **2018**(1), 254–276 (2018)
10. ETSI: Digital cellular telecommunications system (Phase 2+) (GSM); 3GPP TS 24.008 version 16.7.0 Release 16: (2021). https://www.etsi.org/deliver/etsi_ts/124000_124099/124008/16.07.00_60/ts_124008v160700p.pdf
11. Howgrave-Graham, N., Joux, A.: New generic algorithms for hard knapsacks. In: Gilbert, H. (ed.) EUROCRYPT 2010. LNCS, vol. 6110, pp. 235–256. Springer, Heidelberg (2010). https://doi.org/10.1007/978-3-642-13190-5_12
12. Joux, A.: Algorithmic Cryptanalysis. Chapman & Hall/CRC, Boca Raton (2009)

13. Knellwolf, S., Khovratovich, D.: New preimage attacks against reduced SHA-1. In: Safavi-Naini, R., Canetti, R. (eds.) CRYPTO 2012. LNCS, vol. 7417, pp. 367–383. Springer, Heidelberg (2012). https://doi.org/10.1007/978-3-642-32009-5_22

14. Leurent, G., Sibleyras, F.: Low-memory attacks against two-round even-mansour using the 3-XOR problem. In: Boldyreva, A., Micciancio, D. (eds.) CRYPTO 2019, Part II. LNCS, vol. 11693, pp. 210–235. Springer, Cham (2019). https://doi.org/10.1007/978-3-030-26951-7_8

15. Nikolić, I., Sasaki, Yu.: Refinements of the k-tree algorithm for the generalized birthday problem. In: Iwata, T., Cheon, J.H. (eds.) ASIACRYPT 2015, Part II. LNCS, vol. 9453, pp. 683–703. Springer, Heidelberg (2015). https://doi.org/10.1007/978-3-662-48800-3_28

16. Schroeppel, R., Shamir, A.: A $T=O(2^{n/2})$, $S=O(2^{n/4})$ algorithm for certain NP-complete problems. SIAM J. Comput. **10**(3), 456–464 (1981)

17. Wagner, D.: A generalized birthday problem. In: Yung, M. (ed.) CRYPTO 2002. LNCS, vol. 2442, pp. 288–304. Springer, Heidelberg (2002). https://doi.org/10.1007/3-540-45708-9_19

18. Wang, J.R.: Space-efficient randomized algorithms for K-SUM. In: Schulz, A.S., Wagner, D. (eds.) ESA 2014. LNCS, vol. 8737, pp. 810–829. Springer, Heidelberg (2014). https://doi.org/10.1007/978-3-662-44777-2_67

Revamped Differential-Linear Cryptanalysis on Reduced Round ChaCha

Sabyasachi Dey[1], Hirendra Kumar Garai[1], Santanu Sarkar[2(✉)] (iD),
and Nitin Kumar Sharma[1]

[1] Department of Mathematics, Birla Institute of Technology and Science Pilani,
Hyderabad, Jawahar Nagar, Hyderabad 500078, India
[2] Department of Mathematics, Indian Institute of Technology Madras,
Chennai, India
santanu@iitm.ac.in

Abstract. In this paper, we provide several improvements over the
existing differential-linear attacks on ChaCha. ChaCha is a stream cipher
which has 20 rounds. At CRYPTO 2020, Beierle et al. observed a differential in the 3.5-th round if the right pairs are chosen. They produced
an improved attack using this, but showed that to achieve a right pair,
we need 2^5 iterations on average. In this direction, we provide a technique to find the right pairs with the help of listing. Also, we provide a
strategical improvement in PNB construction, modification of complexity calculation and an alternative attack method using two input-output
pairs. Using these, we improve the time complexity, reducing it to $2^{221.95}$
from $2^{230.86}$ reported by Beierle et al. for 256 bit version of ChaCha. Also,
after a decade, we improve existing complexity (Shi et al. ICISC 2012)
for a 6-round of 128 bit version of ChaCha by more than 11 million
times and produce the first-ever attack on 6.5-round ChaCha128 with
time complexity $2^{123.04}$.

Keywords: Stream cipher · ARX · ChaCha · Probabilistic Neutral
Bits (PNBs) · Differential attack

1 Introduction

Symmetric key cryptography is an essential element of communication networks
that protects data secrecy by using a secret key. Symmetric key cryptosystems
have the enormous performance advantage of symmetric primitives, such as
tweakable block ciphers, stream ciphers, hash functions, or cryptographic permutations, which is the primary reason for their widespread use. Surprisingly,
the only way to trust these ciphers is to run a continuous analysis that con-
stantly updates the security margin. With quantum computers on the horizon
in the not-too-distant future, the security of today's ciphers has been called
into doubt. While most of the commonly used asymmetric primitives would
be destroyed, doubling the key size of symmetric constructions offers the same
degree of security when searching for keys exhaustively.

© International Association for Cryptologic Research 2022
O. Dunkelman and S. Dziembowski (Eds.): EUROCRYPT 2022, LNCS 13277, pp. 86–114, 2022.
https://doi.org/10.1007/978-3-031-07082-2_4

The ARX based designs are of immense interest in cryptography. ARX stands for Addition, Rotation, and XOR, which is a family of lightweight symmetric-key algorithms that are primarily designed with elementary operations: Modular addition ($x \boxplus y$), bitwise constant distance rotation ($x \lll n$)and exclusive-OR (XOR, $x \oplus y$). Despite not having the best trade-off in hardware, inexplicit security against the renowned linear and differential cryptanalytic tools [5,18], the encryption developed by ARX has a good software efficiency with compact implementation and fast performance in real life.

The concept of ARX is quite old and dates back to 1987 when the block cipher FEAL [21] used it. ARX machinery is used for both block ciphers (e.g., TEA, Speck) and stream ciphers (e.g., Salsa20, ChaCha). Hash functions and MAC algorithms also utilise the ARX machinery. When applying differential/-linear attacks, the only nonlinear operation, *viz.* modular addition needs special attention in ARX. Although the linear and differential properties of modular addition have already been studied [16,19,23], their extension up to the last round is not very simple. As this design is very speedy, designers use many rounds to secure it against linear and differential cryptanalysis.

Both Salsa [3] and ChaCha [4] are well-known symmetric stream ciphers based on ARX machinery. These ciphers have attracted researchers for analysis as well as various companies for commercial use [25]. Salsa with 12-rounds was put forward by Bernstein in the year 2005 as a candidate for the eSTREAM [13] project and was shortlisted among the four finalists in its software profile in April 2007. Bernstein later in 2008 introduced ChaCha [4] as a Salsa variant, which aims at speeding up the diffusion without slowing down encryption. The changes from Salsa to ChaCha are designed to improve the diffusion per turn, increasing resistance to differential cryptanalysis while preserving the time per turn [4]. These designs have a total of 20 rounds. These ciphers also have reduced round variants, of 12-rounds for example. Both these ciphers have 256-bit key version and 128-bit key version. For ChaCha, we use the notation ChaCha256 and ChaCha128 to denote the 256-bit key version and 128-bit key version respectively.

ChaCha encryption extends a 256-bit key to 64 bytes keystream. This cipher has a more conservative design than the AES, and the community quickly gained trust in the safety of the code. Unlike traditional stream ciphers, Salsa and ChaCha both use Pseudo Random Functions (PRFs). Google replaced RC4 with ChaCha in their encryption schemes. ChaCha is in one of the cipher suits of the new TLS 1.3. Google has developed a specific encryption solution called Adiantum for lower-cost entry-level handsets. According to Google [25], Adiantum enables it to use the ChaCha stream cipher in a length-preserving mode that incorporates ideas from AES-based proposals such as HCTR and HCH.
List of protocols and software that implement ChaCha are given in [24].

Previous Works: Since ChaCha is a variant of Salsa, we start with the first cryptanalysis of Salsa in 2005. This attack was designed by Crowley [7], where he cryptanalysed the 5-th round reduced version of Salsa using differential attack.

Table 1. Known full key recovery attacks.

Cipher	Rounds	Time	Data	Memory	Ref.
ChaCha128		2^{128}	0	0	Brute-force attack
		2^{107}	2^{30}	0	[1]
		2^{105}	2^{28}	0	[20]
	6	$2^{84.39}$	$2^{38.66}$	0	[our work]
		$2^{81.58}$	$2^{43.59}$	0	[our work]
	6.5	$2^{123.04}$	$2^{66.94}$	2^{31}	[our work]
ChaCha256		2^{256}	0	0	Brute-force attack
		2^{248}	2^{27}	0	[1]
		$2^{246.5}$	2^{27}	0	[20]
		$2^{238.9}$	2^{96}	2^{96}	[17]
	7	$2^{237.7}$	2^{96}	2^{96}	[6]
		$2^{235.22}$	-	-	[10]
		$2^{230.86}$	$2^{48.83}$	0	[2]
		$2^{221.95}$	$2^{90.20}$	$2^{47.31}$	[our work]

He received a reward from Bernstein for this attack. After that, a further improvement was proposed in the next year by Fischer et al. [14], where they extended the attack to the 6-th round.

In 2008 FSE, the same year in which ChaCha was proposed, Aumasson et al. [1] introduced a concept called 'Probabilistic Neutral Bits'(PNBs) to provide a vital step in the cryptanalysis of both Salsa and ChaCha. Their idea used a meet-in-the-middle approach, in which they identified a set of key bits that have less influence over the position of the output difference at some middle round when we go back from the final state. This idea has been explained in detail in Sect. 3.2. This approach led to the first attack on 8-round Salsa256 and 7-round ChaCha256. Also, they attacked the 7-round Salsa128 and 6-round ChaCha128. Most of the attacks, hitherto on Salsa and ChaCha became dependent on the premise of PNBs. Interestingly, for the next 13 years, even after several improvements in the cryptanalysis, there is no increment of rounds in the attacks against both the ciphers. Some further improvements have been proposed in this direction by Shi et al. [20] using column chaining distinguisher (CCD) for both 128 and 256-bit version of the ciphers. In 2015, Maitra [17] provided the idea of chosen IV cryptanalysis to provide a good improvement in the key recovery of both the ciphers.

Another important contribution in this direction is by Choudhuri et al. [6], where the single-bit distinguisher of a round was extended to a multiple bit distinguisher of a few next rounds using the linear relation. This differential-linear approach provided the first 6-round distinguisher for Salsa and 5-round distinguisher for ChaCha. This contribution resulted in a massive improvement in the key recovery complexity for smaller rounds. However, for higher rounds, it was not that effective. After this, Dey et al. [10] improved the set of probabilistic neutral bits for those attacks and then in [12] they provided a theoretical justification of the distinguisher of these ciphers.

Another significant step in this direction came in CRYPTO 2020, where Beierle et al. [2] provided the first 3.5-th round single bit distinguisher for ChaCha. Using this, they provided a partial key recovery of 36 bits for 6-round of ChaCha256 with complexity only 2^{77} and improved the complexity for the 7-round ChaCha. This distinguisher was also observed by Coutinho et al. [8] independently. Soon after that, in Eurocrypt 2021, Coutinho et al. [9] provided a set of a few more distinguishers for 3.5-th round and provided a further improvement using one of the distinguishers. However, in recent work of [11] it is demonstrated that the used distinguisher for the key recovery is incorrect, which makes the attack invalid. This makes the result of [2] the best-known attack till date against 7-round ChaCha256, which has a complexity of $2^{230.86}$.

Our Contribution

This paper significantly improves the existing differential-linear attacks on ChaCha128 and ChaCha256. The contribution of this paper can be divided into several parts.

At CRYPTO 2020, Beierle et al. [2] demonstrated that by minimizing the Hamming weight of the difference matrix after the first round, we could observe a good differential in the 3.5-th round. However, to achieve one right pair (X, X'), which would produce the minimum difference, we need an average of 2^5 iterations. Also, this is applicable for 70% of the keys, and the other ones cannot produce a proper pair. In this direction, we have two contributions.

First of all, we show that if we slightly modify (relax) the criteria of a suitable pair and allow the Hamming weight to be up to 12 (instead of 10), any key can form a right pair. Also, on average, 8.94 iterations are required to achieve one such IV. We use this result to produce an attack on 6-round of ChaCha128.

Next, we show that we can decompose the key space of the input difference column into two subspaces and construct a memory based on one of these subspaces, which would contain for each member of the list at least one IV with some unique property. This would help to reduce the effort of the 2^5 iterations to achieve the right pair.

Our third contribution is based on improving the PNBs. We provide a three-stage strategy to get a good set of PNBs. Using this strategy in the attack of [9] which achieved their result using 74 PNBs, we have been able to reach up to 79 PNBs to get our best attack. Also, we applied this to produce the first attack on 6.5-round of ChaCha128.

We revisit the complexity calculation formula given by Aumasson et al. [1], which has been followed afterwards by all the works using PNBs on ChaCha and Salsa. We provide a modified formula that gives an accurate complexity.

We explain the scenario in which the previous formula is not applicable. We apply the new formula in one of the attacks against 6-round of ChaCha128. We also provide an alternative attack on the 6-round of ChaCha128, which is more effective than the first one.

Coming to the improvements of the results in the existing attacks, we provide an improvement in 7-round of ChaCha256 by $2^{8.91}$ in the time complexity over the attack in [2]. We improve the 6-round of ChaCha128 attack by $2^{19.44}$. Also, we provide the first-ever attack on 6.5-round of ChaCha128. We provide our attack complexities along with the previous attack complexities in Table 1. Overall, for ChaCha256 with 7 rounds, our attack is as follows: Given an encryption device with a 256 bit secret key, we run it on $2^{90.20}$ different initial vectors, collecting $2^{90.20}$ bits of keystream, from which we recover all the key bits (177 bits in the first stage and the remaining 79 bits in the second stage). The total time complexity required for this attack is $2^{221.95}$ and memory required is $2^{47.31}$. Similarly, for the other versions of the cipher also one can find out the attack setting from the Table 1.

Paper Outline: Our paper consists of 10 sections. In Sect. 1, we have given an introduction about our work and previous works. In Sect. 2, we describe the detailed structure of ChaCha256 and ChaCha128. Section 3 describes the idea of differential-linear cryptanalysis on ChaCha, briefly revisit the work of [2], introduce the idea of attack using Probabilistic neutral bits and the complexity calculation. In Sect. 4, we provide our alternative way of choosing the right pair. In Sect. 5, we explain the modification of complexity estimation. In Sect. 6, we propose an idea for improving the PNBs. In Sect. 7, we explain how using the construction of memory, we can reduce the complexity. In Sect. 8, we present our results for 7-round ChaCha256. Next in Sect. 9, we present our results on ChaCha128. Section 10 concludes the paper.

2   Structure of ChaCha

First, we take a look at the algorithm of the stream cipher ChaCha. The R-round variant of ChaCha256 is denoted by R-round ChaCha256. The original cipher design is of 20 rounds.

The cipher works on sixteen 32-bit words and generates a sequence of 512-bit keystream blocks. The ChaCha function takes a 256-bit key $k = (k_0, k_1, \ldots, k_7)$, a 96-bit nonce (number used once) $v = (v_0, v_1, v_2)$ and a 32-bit counter $t = t_0$ as input and produces the keystream blocks Z. There is also a variant of ChaCha which takes 128-bit keys as input. In that case the key is extended to 256-bit by simply putting the key twice. The operations of this cipher includes XOR ($\oplus$), left rotation ($\lll$) and modulo 2^{32} addition ($\boxplus$). Naturally the r-th keystream block, $0 \leqslant r \leqslant 2^{64} - 1$ of the ChaCha function is dependent on the eight keywords, three nonces and one counter word.

The ChaCha function works on the matrix which consists of 16 words (32-bit bit-string) arranged in the form of 4×4 matrix. Among the 4 rows the first row is a constant string "expand 32-byte k" which is cut into 4 words or constants c_0, c_1, c_2, and c_3, next two rows have the 8 key words $(k_0, k_1, \ldots, k_7)$ of key k and the last row has 1 block counter t_0 and 3 nonces v_0, v_1, and v_2 (for 256-bit key structure). For 128-bit key structure, 4 keywords make a copy of itself and fill up the matrix's second and third row. The four constants for 256-bit key structure are $c_0 = 0x61707865, c_1 = 0x3320646e, c_2 = 0x79622d32, c_3 = 0x6b206574$. There is a slight change in the constants for 128-bit key structure. The four constants for 128-bit key structure are $c_0 = 0x61707865, c_1 = 0x3120646e$, $c_2 = 0x79622d36, c_3 = 0x6b206574$. The matrix looks as follows.

$$X = \begin{pmatrix} X_0 & X_1 & X_2 & X_3 \\ X_4 & X_5 & X_6 & X_7 \\ X_8 & X_9 & X_{10} & X_{11} \\ X_{12} & X_{13} & X_{14} & X_{15} \end{pmatrix} = \begin{pmatrix} c_0 & c_1 & c_2 & c_3 \\ k_0 & k_1 & k_2 & k_3 \\ k_4 & k_5 & k_6 & k_7 \\ t_0 & v_0 & v_1 & v_2 \end{pmatrix}.$$

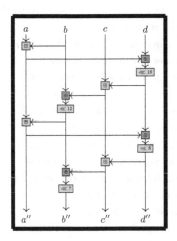

Fig. 1. One quarterround function in ChaCha

In ChaCha, the $\texttt{Round}_R$ function is a nonlinear operation ($\texttt{quarterround}$ function) which transforms a vector (a, b, c, d) into (a'', b'', c'', d'') via an intermediate vector (a', b', c', d') by successively calculating (see Fig. 2).

$$\begin{aligned}
a' &= a \boxplus b; & d' &= ((d \oplus a') \lll 16); \\
c' &= c \boxplus d'; & b' &= ((b \oplus c') \lll 12); \\
a'' &= a' \boxplus b'; & d'' &= ((d' \oplus a'') \lll 8); \\
c'' &= c' \boxplus d''; & b'' &= ((b' \oplus c'') \lll 7);
\end{aligned} \tag{1}$$

For an initial state matrix X, $X^{(r)}$ is determined after r-rounds, and rounds are counted from 1, reforming X after every round. Now in the odd rounds the `quarterround` function acts on the four columns of X, *viz.* $(X_0, X_4, X_8, X_{12}), (X_1, X_5, X_9, X_{13}), (X_2, X_6, X_{10}, X_{14})$, and $(X_3, X_7, X_{11}, X_{15})$. That is why the odd number rounds are also called `column rounds`. In the even number of rounds the nonlinear operations of `Round` function is applied to the four   diagonals $(X_0, X_5, X_{10}, X_{15}), (X_1, X_6, X_{11}, X_{12}), (X_2, X_7, X_8, X_{13})$,   and (X_3, X_4, X_9, X_{14}). Consequently these rounds are called `diagonal rounds`.

Finally the keystream block Z after the R-rounds is computed as $Z = X^{(0)} + X^{(R)}$, where $X^{(0)}$ is denoted as the initial state and $X^{(R)}$ is the state after R-rounds of X. Every round of ChaCha is reversible. From any round $(r + 1)$, $X^{(r)}$ can be obtained by operating the reverse quarterround on $X^{(r+1)}$. Interested readers can refer to [4] for more design details. List of symbols and notations are given in Table 2.

We provide the quarterround function in a diagram form in Fig. 1.

Table 2. List of symbols

Symbol	Description
X	The state matrix of the cipher consisting of 16 words
$X^{(0)}$	Initial state matrix
$X^{(r)}$	State matrix after application of r-round functions
X_i	i-th word of the state matrix X
$X_i[j]$	j-th bit of i-th word in matrix X
$x \boxplus y$	Addition of x and y modulo 2^{32}
$x \boxminus y$	Subtraction of x and y modulo 2^{32}
$x \oplus y$	Bitwise XOR of x and y
$x \lll n$	Rotation of x by n bits to the left
$x \ggg n$	Rotation of x by n bits to the right
$\Delta X_i^{(r)}[j]$	XOR difference after r-th round of the j-th bit of the i-th word of X and X'
$\dim(K)$	Dimension of the space K
K_{mem}	Set of significant bits/Non-PNBs
K_{nmem}	Set of PNBs
$\mathbb{K}_{mem}$	Key Space corresponding to K_{mem}
$\mathbb{K}_{nmem}$	Key Space corresponding to K_{nmem}
ChaCha256	256-key bit version of ChaCha
ChaCha128	128-key bit version of ChaCha
$\mathcal{ID}$ Column	Column in which input difference is given

3   Idea of Differential-Linear Cryptanalysis

Before going to the attack let us first observe the adversary model. The adversary has access to the IVs. He can verify a guess by supplying his own key to the algorithm and check the key's validity by running the algorithm. He can analyse the output of the keystream and examine the key guess.

The differential attack was discovered by Biham and Shamir [5] in 1990. This attack was used initially on block ciphers, but later, it found significant applications in stream ciphers and hash functions. This is a chosen plaintext attack. In this attack, the output of the cipher is observed on the basis of changes in the input. Let P and P' be two plaintexts along with their ciphertexts C and C' respectively. In a differential attack, a correlation between C and C' might be observed. This correlation, in turn, might be exploited to find out the key.

The linear attack was thought up by Matsui [18] in 1992. In this method, the attacker first constructs linear relations between plaintext, ciphertext and key terms with high bias. He then uses these relations together with known plaintext-ciphertext pairs to find the key.

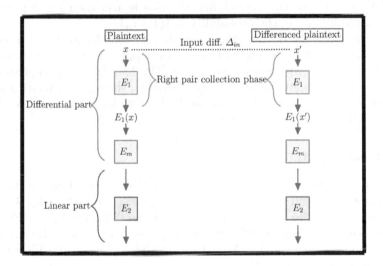

Fig. 2. Differential-linear cryptanalysis

The idea of differential-linear cryptanalysis was introduced by Langford and Hellman [15] in 1994. Here, the cipher E is split into two parts E_1 and E_2 $(E = E_2 \circ E_1)$ such that differential and linear cryptanalyses are applied on the subciphers, respectively. Suppose a substantial differential exists in the first subcipher E_1 and linear approximation in the second subcipher E_2. The combination of these two attacks on $E_2 \circ E_1$ is the differential-linear analysis. See Fig. 2. In differential-linear cryptanalysis for each sample, we require two initial states with the same key but different IVs.

Let X and $X' = X \oplus \Delta_{in}$ be two initial states of subcipher E_1 where, Δ_{in} is called input differential ($\mathcal{ID}$). Also ΔX denotes the difference between two states X, X'. The difference after r_1-rounds is observed between the two states. This is called the output differential $\mathcal{OD}$. If a good bias is observed for this, that is exploited to attack the ciphers.

Differential Linear Attack in the Context of ChaCha: Though these attack methods were initially developed for block ciphers, they have since been successfully applied to stream ciphers. However, the situation is slightly different in the context of stream ciphers. ChaCha being a stream cipher, we explain the scenario in its context. Particularly for ChaCha, where the state can be divided into several words, we denote the j-th bit of the i-th word of X, X' by $X_i[j]$ and $X_i'[j]$ respectively. Here, instead of looking at the output difference of the entire matrices X, X', we choose a particular bit of both the matrices as the position of the output differential. If this is q-th bit of p-th word, then $\Delta X_p[q] = X_p[q] \oplus X_p'[q]$ denotes the difference. Now, instead of plaintexts, we consider the IVs for introducing the input difference. Usually it is given at a single bit of the IV. In the Output difference, we compute the probability of the event $\Delta X_p[q] = 0$. For this probability, the bias is also known as forward bias and is denoted by ϵ_d, i.e. the probability is $\frac{1}{2}(1 + \epsilon_d)$.

After obtaining the output difference after r_1-rounds, we have to look for linear relation on output differential. The linear approximation is observed from r_1-rounds to $(r_1 + r_2)$-rounds of the cipher. The bias for linear approximation is denoted by ϵ_l. Usually for linear approximation, the term correlation is used instead of bias. The linear approximation is observed for both X and X'. So the combined differential-linear bias for $(r_1 + r_2)$-rounds is given as $\epsilon_d \epsilon_l^2$.

3.1   Choosing a Right Pair

In [2], instead of two subciphers E_1, E_2 the authors divided cipher into three subciphers E_2, E_m and E_1 such that $E = E_2 \circ E_m \circ E_1$. Here E_2 is the linear extension as before and $E_m \circ E_1$ construct the differential part (Fig. 3). In E_1, they look for a desired difference in $E_1(x) \oplus E_1(x \oplus \Delta_{in})$. Let us denote this intended difference as Δ_m. Now, the underlying aim of this difference is to improve the bias after $E_m \circ E_1$.

The set of initial states X, $X \oplus \Delta_{in} \in \mathbb{F}_2^n$ which satisfy this desired differential Δ_m after the E_1 are called right pairs. Formally, the set of right pairs is defined as $\chi = \{X \in \mathbb{F}_2^n | E_1(X) \oplus E_1(X \oplus \Delta_{in}) = \Delta_m\}$. The differential bias after E_m is found experimentally, assigning the input difference Δ_m before E_m. Particularly for ChaCha, E_1 consists of 1 round and Δ_m is taken as the minimum possible Hamming weight of the difference matrix $X \oplus X'$ after the 1st round, which is 10.

Now, let p be the probability to achieve a right pair when the initial states are randomly chosen, i.e., $\Pr_{X \in \mathbb{F}_2^n}[\, E_1(X) \oplus E_1(X \oplus \Delta_{in}) = \Delta_m] = p$. Then the complexity of the attack is computed with the assumption that the initial states are all right pairs. Finally this complexity is multiplied by p^{-1} to get the actual complexity, since on average p^{-1} randomly chosen $(X, X \oplus \Delta_{in})$ pairs give one right pair on average.

In their attack, they mentioned that in a column of ChaCha, there are approximately 30% keys which do not have any IVs to form a right pair. These keys are named as strong keys. For the remaining keys, the probability is $\Pr_{X_i \in \mathbb{F}_2^n}[\, E_1(X_i) \oplus E_1(X_i \oplus \Delta_{in}) = \Delta_m] = p \approx \frac{1}{2^5}$.

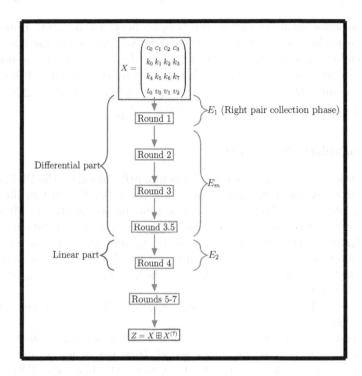

Fig. 3. Differential-linear cryptanalysis of 7-round ChaCha

$\mathcal{ID-OD}$ **Pair:** In [2] the input difference is $\Delta X_{13}^{(0)}[6] = 1$ and the output difference is observed at $\Delta X_2^{(3.5)}[0]$. Due to column wise symmetric structure one can consider input difference at any of the four columns of X i.e., $\Delta X_{12}^{(0)}[6], \Delta X_{13}^{(0)}[6]$, $\Delta X_{14}^{(0)}[6], \Delta X_{15}^{(0)}[6]$ as they will give same approximations after 3.5-th rounds at $\Delta X_1^{(3.5)}[0], \Delta X_2^{(3.5)}[0], \Delta X_3^{(3.5)}[0], \Delta X_0^{(3.5)}[0]$ respectively.

According to the $E_2 \circ E_m \circ E_1$ approach, for ChaCha E_1 is the first round. As right pairs we consider those initial states for which after the 1st round we obtain the difference at only the 10 positions shown below:

$$\Delta X_1^{(1)}[2], \ \Delta X_5^{(1)}[5], \ \Delta X_5^{(1)}[29], \ \Delta X_5^{(1)}[17], \ \Delta X_5^{(1)}[9], \ \Delta X_9^{(1)}[30], \ \Delta X_9^{(1)}[22],$$
$$\Delta X_9^{(1)}[10], \ \Delta X_{13}^{(1)}[30], \ \Delta X_{13}^{(1)}[10].$$

For E_m the cipher is considered after the first round to 3.5-rounds. For this, the observed forward bias is $\epsilon_d = 2^{-8.3} = 0.00317$ [2] given that the number of differences after the 1st round is 10. In the next stage E_2, a linear relation between 3.5-th round and 4-th round is found as:

$$X_2^{(3.5)}[0] = X_2^{(4)}[0] \oplus X_7^{(4)}[7] \oplus X_8^{(4)}[0] \text{ with } \epsilon_l = 1.$$

In [2], the authors obtained a linear relationship between the 3.5-th round and 5-th round. Nevertheless, as we apply the idea of PNBs, we do not use this relation. So we extend the linear relation only up to the 4-th round with the linear bias of $\epsilon_l = 1$. In our paper, we use the linear combination of bits obtained after 4-th round as our $\mathcal{OD}$ pair. In this paper, input difference ($\mathcal{ID}$) is $\Delta X_{13}^{(0)}[6]$ and output difference ($\mathcal{OD}$) is $X_2^{(4)}[0] \oplus X_7^{(4)}[7] \oplus X_8^{(4)}[0]$.

3.2   Probabilistic Neutral Bits

The differential cryptanalysis of ChaCha is primarily based on the PNB concept, which was first proposed by Aumasson et al. [1] in 2008. We explain the concept assuming a key size of 256. The concept of probabilistic neutrality allows us to divide the secret key bits into two categories: significant key bits (of size m) and non-significant key bits (of size $256 - m$). Significant key bits are those that have a large influence on the position at which the differential is observed. Non-significant key bits, on the other hand, are the polar opposite of significant key bits with a low influence.

To detect the PNBs, we focus on the degree of influence each key bit has on the cipher's output.

If we know the full key, we can compute backwards from a given output to observe the skewed differential bit of round. However, if we do not know the key, we may have to guess it in order to discover the bias. The PNBs' goal is to guess the key in two parts. That is, we make educated guesses about the important bits. That is to say, we guess the key bits that are significant. Even if the remaining key bits are incorrectly predicted, the bias must be visible when we compute backwards bias.

To be more specific, we want to find key bits whose values, if arbitrarily changed, have no effect on the output on a large scale. These neutral bits are thought to have a negligible impact. The traditional method of determining the secret key entails a thorough examination of all 2^{256} feasible possibilities. However, if the remaining $(256 - m)$ bits are PNBs, we can only search over the sub key of size m. As a result, the maximum number of guesses is reduced to 2^m.

In the cipher machinery, after a few rounds, we look for output differentials in the state matrix to use the PNB approach.

General Idea of PNB and the Formal Definition: Let X be the initial state matrix of size 4×4. Assume we have found a suitable non-zero input difference ($\mathcal{ID}$) at the j-th bit of the i-th word in the IV say, $\Delta X_i^{(0)}[j]$. Applying this input difference to X we get another state X'. Running X, X' for r-rounds $(1 \leqslant r < R)$ we observe the output difference $(\mathcal{OD})$ at position (p, q), i.e., $\Delta X_p^{(r)}[q]$. The bias is given by ϵ_d, i.e.,

$$\Pr_{v,t}\left[\Delta X_p^{(r)}[q] = 1 \,\middle|\, \Delta X_i^{(0)}[j] = 1\right] = \frac{1}{2}(1 + \epsilon_d), \tag{2}$$

here v, t are IVs and the counter respectively which are considered as random variables.

Keep in mind that after R-round we have the keystream block generated by X as $Z = X + X^{(R)}$. Similarly for initial state X' we have another keystream block after R-rounds, $viz.$ Z' we have $Z' = X' + X'^{(R)}$. So, $\Delta X_p^{(r)}[q] = \left(X_p^{(r)} \oplus X'_p^{(r)}\right)[q]$, where the $\oplus$ is the word-wise XOR of the two matrices X and X'.

In this situation, we alter one key bit, say the l-th bit, where $0 \leqslant l \leqslant 255$, of the key. Consequently, we again have two states Y and Y'. Now, we apply the reverse algorithm of ChaCha on $Z - Y$ and $Z' - Y'$ by $(R - r)$ rounds, and achieve the states S and S' respectively. (Since we apply reverse algorithm, we name the S matrices in reverse order).

Let $\Delta S_p[q] = (S_p \oplus S'_p)[q]$. If for the choice of l we have $\Delta S_p[q] = \Delta X_p^{(r)}[q]$ holding with high probability then we assume the key bit to be non-significant. For this, in the initial approach, a threshold value used to be determined, and all the key bits for which the above mentioned probability was higher than the threshold were considered to be non-significant or probabilistically neutral bit.

In that approach, a formal definition for PNB can be given as follows: For a given input difference $\Delta X_i[j] = 1$ and a predetermined threshold value γ, suppose for a key bit l, $\Pr\left[\Delta X_p^{(r)}[q] = \Delta S_p[q] \,\middle|\, \Delta X_i^{(0)}[j] = 1\right] = \frac{1}{2}(1 + \gamma_l)$. Then, l is a PNB if for that particular bit, $\gamma_l > \gamma$.

In the context of PNB, we come across Neutrality Measure, which is defined as γ_l, where $\frac{1}{2}(1 + \gamma_l)$ is the chance that changing the l-th bit of the key does not impact the output. The key bit with neutrality measure 1 does not have any effect on the output, while having a neutrality measure of 0 means that the key bit has high influence. We, in general, create a threshold value of γ, where $0 \leqslant \gamma \leqslant 1$ such that any key bit l with neutrality measure $\gamma_l > \gamma$ is PNB. Naturally, the bigger the γ is, the more negligible effect the PNBs have. We must choose the γ very optimally so that the time complexity is minimised.

3.3   Complexity Computation

In the actual attack the attacker guesses the significant bits and puts random values in the PNBs and run both the states in backward directions. The actual attack algorithm using PNBs as given in [1] is as follows:

1. For an unknown key guess, collect N pairs of keystream blocks, each of which is generated by states with a random nonce and counter (satisfying the relevant $\mathcal{ID}$).
2. For each choice of the m significant key bits do:
   (a) Compute the bias of $\mathcal{OD}$ using the N keystream block pairs.
   (b) Conduct an extra exhaustive search over the $256 - m$ non-significant key bits to test the validity of this filtered significant key bits and to identify the non-significant key bits if the optimum distinguisher certifies the candidate as a potentially correct one.
   (c) If the correct key is found, stop and output the recovered key.

In this attack the bias in the backward direction when the PNBs are assigned random values is called backward bias and is denoted by ϵ_a. Suppose we have m functional or relatively non PNBs, so there is a list of 2^m possible random variables among which only one option is correct, and others are not. We take the null hypothesis H_0 as the selected variable is not correct. Hence $2^m - 1$ variables satisfy H_0 and only one variable satisfies H_1, the alternative hypothesis (the selected is correct). There can be two types of errors in this attack:

1. Non-detection - The selected variable is correct but it is not detected. The probability of this event is $\Pr_{nd}$.
2. The variable selected is incorrect but it gives significant bias, so an incorrect variable is chosen. The probability of the event is $\Pr_{fa}$.

Using the Neyman-Pearson lemma, for $\Pr_{fa} = 2^{-\alpha}$ and $\Pr_{nd} = 1.3 \times 10^{-2}$, required number of samples N to achieve a bound on these probabilities is

$$N \approx \left(\frac{\sqrt{\alpha \log 4} + 3\sqrt{1 - \epsilon_a \epsilon_d^2}}{\epsilon_a \epsilon_d} \right)^2 .$$

The complexity of the attack is given by the equation

$$2^m(N + 2^{(256-m)}\Pr_{fa}) = 2^m N + 2^{(256-\alpha)}. \tag{3}$$

4   Modification in the Criteria for a Right Pair

As already mentioned, in [2] the right pair is considered for those key-IVs, for which the Hamming weight of Δ_m is 10 after the first round. It helps to get a high bias after 3.5-rounds, though the two major drawbacks are the low value of p and unavailability of IVs for 30% of keys. In this context, we dig a little deeper inside the structure and try to find whether some modification is possible so that without significant loss in complexity, the attack can be applicable for all keys.

Now, if we look at the quarterround operation, it has four addition operations, out of which the first one does not involve any bit with a difference. So, the minimum Hamming weight is possible if no difference propagates to the next bit in the remaining three addition operations. Now, in the third addition operation $a'' = a' \boxplus b'$, there is a difference at $b'[2]$, whose propagation cannot be fully controlled for any key just by choosing a good IV. Except that, in all the remaining addition operations, the difference propagation can be controlled. However, if we allow a difference propagation to the next bit only (i.e., up to $a''[3]$), proper IVs can control further propagation. This we have proved in the following proposition:

Proposition 1. *In the quarterround function of ChaCha on a tuple (a, b, c, d), for any value of b, c there exists d such that $a'[3] = b'[3]$.*

Proof. As we know (a, b, c, d) denotes elements of m-round and (a', b', c', d') denotes elements of $m + 0.5$-round. Considering the second ARX round of the quarterround function we have

$$b'[3] = b[23] \oplus c'[23]$$
$$= b[23] \oplus c[23] \oplus d'[23] \oplus Carry_{(c,d')}[23].$$

where $Carry_{(c,d')}[i]$ denotes i-th carry bit of the sum of c and $d'(c \boxplus d')$.

Using the first ARX round of the quarterround function, $d' = (d \oplus a') \lll 16$. Therefore $d'[23] = d[7] \oplus a'[7]$. This implies

$$b'[3] = b[23] \oplus c[23] \oplus a'[7] \oplus d[7] \oplus Carry_{(c,d')}[23].$$

Case 1. If $c[22] = 0$, we make $d'[22] = 0$ by choosing $d[6] = a'[6]$ implies that $Carry_{(c,d')}[23] = 0$. Hence,

$$b'[3] = b[23] \oplus c[23] \oplus a'[7] \oplus d[7].$$

$\therefore$ If we select $d[7] = a[3] \oplus b[3] \oplus c[23] \oplus a'[7]$, we get $b'[3] = a'[3]$.

Case 2. If $c[22] = 1$ and if $d[6]$ is chosen as $a'[6] \oplus 1$, then $d'[22] = 1$ implies that $Carry_{(c,d')}[23] = 0$. So, $b'[3] = b[23] \oplus c[23] \oplus a'[7] \oplus d[7] \oplus 1$. $\therefore$ If we choose $d[7] = a'[3] \oplus 1 \oplus a'[7] \oplus c[23] \oplus b[23]$, we get $b'[3] = a'[3]$.

Thus for both the cases we have $b'[3] = a'[3]$. $\qquad\square$

However, if there is a difference in $a''[3]$, then in the immediate next XOR, an extra difference would propagate in $b'[11]$. In the next addition, the difference propagation can be controlled by proper IV.

Therefore, if we consider the correct pairs with Hamming weight at most 12, we can find IVs for any key that constructs a suitable pair. We have experimentally verified over randomly chosen keys that become a right pair under this relation of the criteria, 100% of the keys become weak. We experimented with randomly chosen 10^6 keys, and for each of them, we selected 4×10^6 IVs randomly. We observed that at least one IV exists for each key, which, after the first round, gives differences at 12 positions at most. In Fig. 4, we provide in graphical form the side by side comparison of the biases after 3.5-rounds between the case when the difference is 10 vs the difference is at most 12 after the first round. We give this result for 10^2 randomly chosen keys, and for each of them we experimented over 2^{28} random IVs. Out of these we computed the bias only for those which forms the right

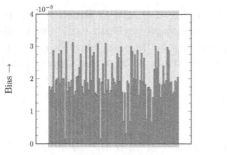
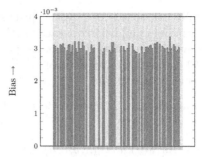

Fig. 4. Comparison of the biases for the case when Hamming weight of Δ_m is 12 (left) vs 10 (right) after the first round. The experiment is done for 100 random keys k_i ($i = 1, 2, \ldots, 100$). Along x-axis, the i-th vertical line represents the bias corresponding to k_i. For each random key the probability is calculated over 2^{28} random IVs.

pair. It is clearly visible that for Hamming weight $\leqslant 12$ (left), the biases are lower, but it exists for every key. On the other hand, for Hamming weight $= 10$ (right), though the biases are higher, but suitable IVs do not exist for some keys to form right pair. These are represented by blank.

The second benefit of this relaxation is that the probability of achieving the right pair becomes higher, which influence the complexity reduction up to some extent. If we look at the three addition operations where a word with difference is involved, there are five positions where the difference may propagate to the next bit. In each of second and third addition there is one such position and in the last addition there are three such positions. In case of minimum Hamming weight all these five propagation should be restricted. On average, out of 2^5 IVs, on average one satisfies all the five restrictions.

On the other hand, if we allow 12 differences, then the permission to propagate the difference at $a''[2]$ to $a''[3]$ relaxes the restriction. We experimentally observe over 10^5 random keys that this relaxation improves the probability p of achieving a proper IV for right-pair construction to $\frac{1}{8.94} \approx \frac{1}{9}$. In other words, for randomly chosen 9 IVs, on average, one qualifies to form a right pair. Please note that this probability is computed over any randomly chosen keys, unlike the previous scenario where p has been computed only over the 70% weak keys.

Besides these two advantages, definitely the apparent disadvantage is that the bias ϵ_d after the 3.5-th round comes down from 0.00317 to 0.0021 (see Table 3). However, p^{-1} decreases from 2^5 to $2^{3.17}$. It is worth noting that the attack complexity is inversely proportional to $p \cdot \epsilon_d^2$. Thus, even though e_d in case 12 is less than in case of 10 difference, the disadvantage does not affect the time complexity because p^{-1} is also less in the first case. Therefore, the product $p \cdot \epsilon_d^2$ is almost same in both the cases. In fact, from the table one can observe that it is slightly higher for the second case ($\leqslant 12$), which will actually improve the complexity.

Table 3. Comparison between the two criteria for right pair on the Hamming weights of the output difference after one round

Hamming weight	$= 10$	$\leqslant 12$
ϵ_d	0.00317	0.0021
percentage of weak keys	70	100
probability of satisfying(p)	2^{-5}	$2^{-3.17}$
$p \cdot \epsilon_d^2$	$2^{-21.602}$	$2^{-20.96}$

5   Modification of the Time Complexity Estimation

In the Sect. 3.3, we have discussed the technique of complexity computation which has been provided by [1]. Here we provide a modification in the formula of the complexity to make it more accurate. This modification gives a better measurement of complexity for any size of PNB.

As we know, only one is correct among 2^m possible sequences of significant keys, so we compute the total number of iterations separately for both the cases.

i. If the guessed key is correct, we run it for N samples to achieve the m significant key bits. Then in the next step, we run an exhaustive search to find n PNBs ($m + n =$ total size of the key), which takes 2^n iterations. So the complexity in this case is $N + 2^n$.
ii. If the guessed key is any of the remaining $2^m - 1$, then for each such guess, we have to run it for N samples first. Assuming the probability of false alarm $= 2^{-\alpha}$, we can say $(2^m - 1) \cdot 2^{-\alpha}$ keys would give false alarm. For these many keys, we perform a thorough search over 2^n sequences of the PNBs. So the complexity in this case is

$$(2^m - 1) \cdot N + (2^m - 1) \cdot 2^{-\alpha} \cdot 2^n = (2^m - 1) \cdot N + (2^m - 1) \cdot 2^{n-\alpha}.$$

Therefore the total time complexity is

$$N + 2^n + (2^m - 1) \cdot N + (2^m - 1) \cdot 2^{n-\alpha}$$
$$= 2^m \cdot N + 2^n + 2^{m+n-\alpha} - 2^{n-\alpha}$$
$$\approx 2^m \cdot N + 2^n + 2^{m+n-\alpha} \text{ (Since } 2^{n-\alpha} \text{ is negligible compared } to \text{ } 2^{m+n-\alpha})$$

Since $n =$ keysize $- m$, we can also write the complexity as

$$2^m \cdot N + 2^{\text{keysize}-m} + 2^{\text{keysize}-\alpha}.$$

Now in the final expression of complexity, we observe an extra $2^{\text{keysize}-m}$ term, which was not there in the formula given by [1]. The reason is since in their attack and all other attacks given so forth against ChaCha, m is significantly higher than α, which makes $2^{\text{keysize}-m}$ a negligible term compared to $2^{\text{keysize}-\alpha}$, therefore it can be ignored.

However, if we arrive in a scenario where m and α are close, i.e., $2^{\text{keysize}-m}$ is not negligible compared to $2^{\text{keysize}-\alpha}$, then we have to consider both the terms in the complexity. On the other hand if m is considerably smaller than α, then instead of $2^{\text{keysize}-m}$, the $2^{\text{keysize}-\alpha}$ can be ignored and the formula becomes $2^m N + 2^{\text{keysize}-m}$.

6   Improving the PNBs

In [2], the authors assigned threshold bias γ to find the PNBs. They received 74 key bits, which gave higher biases than the threshold. This is the conventional method of searching the PNBs, which was given by Aumasson et al. [1]. In this work, we provide a systematic three-step strategy to find a good set of PNBs, which provides better PNBs than the conventional method, and requires significantly less computation than [10].

*Stage 1: **Preliminary Shortlisting and Direct inclusion***
In this stage we shortlist a number of possible candidates for the PNB. This is done by assigning a threshold bias γ_{prelim} and selecting the ones which give a higher bias than the threshold. This step is pretty similar to the conventional method. However, it is not the final set of PNBs. So, in this case, we keep the threshold slightly lower than the conventional method. Suppose n_{prelim} candidates are selected in this step. Among them, we assign a second threshold γ_{direct} which is higher than the previous one. Key bits with higher biases than this threshold are directly included in the PNB set. Let the number of such PNBs is n_1.

*Stage 2: **Selection of the best candidate in each iteration***
Now after the first stage we include some more PNBs (say n_2) as follows: In the i-th iteration we assign random values to the n_1 PNBs selected in Stage 1 and $(i-1)$ PNBs selected in Stage 2. After that, among the remaining $(n_{prelim} - n_1)$ key bits, we alter the value one at a time and observe the backward bias. The key bit with the highest bias is selected as the i-th PNB of Stage 2. This iteration is repeated n_2 times. So we have $(n_1 + n_2)$ PNBs so far.

*Stage 3: **Cherry-pick from the remaining while randomising the selected ones***
The requirement of the third stage comes when the computed biases of the Stage 2 becomes very small. In this scenario, if we further use the technique of Stage 2, not only do we need a significantly huge number of iterations, but also there is a chance of getting the wrong candidate. So, in the third stage, we assign random values to the already selected PNBs in the first and second stage $(n_1 + n_2$ bits) and randomly change one of the remaining shortlisted $n_{prelim} - (n_1 + n_2)$ candidates. Then we compute the backward bias. Up to this, it is similar to Stage 2. Nevertheless, instead of choosing the best one only, we arrange all the candidates in descending order of their biases and choose the required number of PNBs (suppose n_3) from the top.

7   Construction of Memory

Here we propose an alternate method of getting a right pair $\big((k, v), (k, v')\big)$ with the use of memory. At first, we partition the set of key bit positions of the $\mathcal{ID}$ column into two subsets K_{mem} and K_{nmem}. We aim to partition them in such a way that for a key, only by looking at the values of K_{mem} bits, we can find out an IV which would construct a right pair for this key. The benefit of this is, we can construct a list containing the possible values of only the K_{mem} bit position and their corresponding IVs. If it can be done, for an attacker it is no more required to run p^{-1} random IVs to get one IV to construct a right pair because based on their guess of key they can look up in the list to find a proper IV.

Issue of PNB: In this approach, the probabilistic neutral bits in the $\mathcal{ID}$ column become a vital issue. Since the attacker puts random values on the PNBs, the favourable IV that the attacker chooses from the list is based on his guess of key. If the actual values at the PNB positions are different from their assigned values, the IV chosen by the attacker from the list may not construct a right pair with the actual key. Suppose k is the actual key and k' is the key guessed by the attacker whose significant bits are correct, i.e., same with k. Now, the IV v which he chooses based on his guess k', may not work for actual key k to form right pair. In that case, even though the significant bit guess is correct, bias would not be observed.

So, we have to construct our K_{mem} and K_{nmem} subsets in such a way that this problem mentioned above can be solved. The easiest solution to this is to include the PNBs in the K_{nmem} subset. How does it help us we explain it explicitly in Sect. 7.2.

7.1   Decomposition into Memory and Non-memory Subspace

In the first round all the columns work independently, and the difference propagation is within the input difference column only. So, for convenience, we take our E_1 as the `quarterround` of the column in which the input difference is given. Let $K_{\mathcal{ID}}$ be the set of key bit positions and $\mathbb{K}_{\mathcal{ID}}$ be the key space corresponding to the input difference column. So, $|K_{\mathcal{ID}}| = \dim(\mathbb{K}_{\mathcal{ID}})$. Hence, any key in $\mathbb{K}_{\mathcal{ID}}$ is of the form $(x_0, x_1, \ldots, x_{|K_{\mathcal{ID}}|})$.

Here we introduce one term along with its notation. For any subset K' of $K_{\mathcal{ID}}$, we denote $\mathbb{K}'$ to be the subspace corresponding to K', which we define as the collection of keywords $\{(x_0, x_1, \ldots, x_{|K_{\mathcal{ID}}|})\}$ for which the values corresponding to the bit position which are not in K' are 0, i.e.,

$$\mathbb{K}' = \big\{(x_0, x_1, \ldots, x_{|K_{\mathcal{ID}}|}) \mid x_i = 0 \text{ when } i \notin K'\big\}.$$

Thus the partition of the key bits into K_{mem} and K_{nmem} subsets actually provides a decomposition of the key space into the direct sum of two subspaces. This means, each of the subsets K_{mem} and K_{nmem} corresponds to a subspace of the entire key space of the column. We refer to these subspaces as $\mathbb{K}_{mem}$ subspace and $\mathbb{K}_{nmem}$ subspace.

Then, according to our partition we break the key space into the direct sum of the two subspaces $\mathbb{K}_{mem}$ and $\mathbb{K}_{nmem}$,

$$\mathbb{F}_2^{\dim(\mathbb{K}_{\mathcal{ID}})} = \mathbb{K}_{mem} \oplus \mathbb{K}_{nmem}.$$

Example: Consider a 5 bit key $(x_0, x_1, x_2, x_3, x_4)$. Then the entire key space contains a total 2^5 keys. Now suppose $x_0, x_1, x_2 \in K_{mem}$ and $x_3, x_4 \in K_{nmem}$. Then, $\mathbb{K}_{mem}$ is the collection of keys for which $x_3 = x_4 = 0$, i.e.,

$$\mathbb{K}_{mem} = \big\{(x_0, x_1, x_2, 0, 0)\big\}$$

and $\mathbb{K}_{nmem}$ is the collection of keys for which $x_0 = x_1 = x_2 = 0$, i.e.,

$$\mathbb{K}_{nmem} = \big\{(0, 0, 0, x_3, x_4)\big\}$$

Now a right pair $\big((k, v), (k, v')\big)$ in that column should satisfy

$$E_1(k, v) \oplus E_1(k, v') = \Delta_m \text{ where } v' = v \oplus \Delta_{in}. \tag{4}$$

Now for any $k \in \mathbb{K}_{mem}$, $k \oplus \mathbb{K}_{nmem}$ is a coset which contains $2^{\dim(\mathbb{K}_{nmem})}$ elements. We aim to find at least one IV v such that $\forall\ k' \in k \oplus \mathbb{K}_{nmem}$, $\big((k', v), (k', v')\big)$ is a right pair, i.e., for every $k' \in k \oplus \mathbb{K}_{nmem}$, $E_1(k', v) \oplus E_1(k', v') = \Delta_m$. In this context we define two terms:

Exploitable Key: A key $k \in K_{\mathcal{ID}}$ is a exploitable key with respect to the $\mathbb{K}_{nmem}$ subspace if there exists at least one IV v such that for any key $k' \in k \oplus \mathbb{K}_{nmem}$, $\big((k', v), (k', v')\big)$ forms a right pair. It is easy to note that an exploitable key is definitely a weak key.

Favourable IV: For an exploitable key k, an IV v is a favourable IV if for any key $k' \in k \oplus \mathbb{K}_{nmem}$, $\big((k', v), (k', v')\big)$ forms a right pair.

Let p_{exp} be the probability of getting a key k which has at least one favourable IV, i.e., among all possible elements of $\mathbb{K}_{mem}$, p_{exp} is the fraction of keys for which such IV exist. We form a list of such keys along with at least one of their favourable IVs. The memory required for this is $p_{exp} \times 2^{\dim(\mathbb{K}_{mem})}$.

Now, we use these exploitable keys in our attack with the help of favourable IVs. So we have to construct the direct sum $\mathbb{K}_{nmem}$ and $\mathbb{K}_{mem}$ in such a way that this p_{exp} is high, i.e., a considerable fraction of the keys are exploitable. Secondly, as the size of the memory required depends on the dimension of $\mathbb{K}_{mem}$, therefore, our aim also is to increase the dimension of $\mathbb{K}_{nmem}$ because it would reduce the memory size. However, it can be understood from the definition of an exploitable key that more the dimension of $\mathbb{K}_{nmem}$, more is the elements in a coset $k \oplus \mathbb{K}_{nmem}$. To become an exploitable key, one IV should construct the right pair with all the keys in the coset. So the fraction of exploitable keys p_{exp} decreases as $\dim(\mathbb{K}_{nmem})$ increases.

7.1.1   Construction of the K_{nmem} Subset

Here we provide a heuristic algorithm for how to choose the key bits which would construct a good K_{nmem} subset whose corresponding $\mathbb{K}_{nmem}$ subspace contains a huge fraction of exploitable keys. We begin with the PNBs which are in the input difference column. We call this set $PNB_{\mathcal{ID}}$. We include the PNBs directly into the K_{nmem} subset. For the purpose of this construction we define a temporary subset $K_{nmem}^{temp} \subseteq K_{\mathcal{ID}}$ and the corresponding subspace of $\mathbb{K}_{nmem}^{temp}$. We use this temporary subset to construct the actual K_{nmem} subset. Consider this temporary subset K_{nmem}^{temp} is a variable subset where we assign different elements at different steps according to our requirement.

We start with $K_{nmem}^{temp} = PNB_{\mathcal{ID}}$. Note that, the $PNB_{\mathcal{ID}}$ should be such that for $K_{nmem}^{temp} = PNB_{\mathcal{ID}}$, a huge fraction of weak keys are exploitable keys with respect to the corresponding $\mathbb{K}_{nmem}^{temp}$ subspace. If we don't have such properties for $PNB_{\mathcal{ID}}$, we have to reject some PNBs and start with a smaller PNB set. Now, once we have such a suitable $PNB_{\mathcal{ID}}$, to include further key bits into K_{nmem}, for each of the remaining key bit positions i, we do as follows: We take $K_{nmem}^{temp} = PNB_{\mathcal{ID}} \cup \{i\}$ and consider the corresponding $\mathbb{K}_{nmem}^{temp}$. For a randomly chosen exploitable key and its favourable IV with respect to $\mathbb{K}_{nmem}^{temp}$ which corresponds to $K_{nmem}^{temp} = PNB_{\mathcal{ID}}$, we find the probability that this key is an exploitable key with the same IV as favourable IV for $\mathbb{K}_{nmem}^{temp}$ where $K_{nmem}^{temp} = PNB_{\mathcal{ID}} \cup \{i\}$. If this probability is higher than some predetermined threshold, we include i into K_{nmem}. We write this in a proper algorithm form in Algorithm 1.

Algorithm 1: Construction of K_{nmem} subset

Input: A set of PNBs in the input difference column ($PNB_{\mathcal{ID}}$), a threshold probability p_{thres}, a collection L of ξ exploitable key-favourable IV combinations for $\mathbb{K}_{nmem}^{temp}$ corresponding to $K_{nmem}^{temp} = PNB_{\mathcal{ID}}$, a counter.

1   **for** *each $i \in K_{\mathcal{ID}}$ such that $i \notin PNB_{\mathcal{ID}}$* **do**
2   counter = 0.
3      $K_{nmem}^{temp} = PNB_{\mathcal{ID}} \bigcup \{i\}$
4   **for** *each exploitable key-favourable IV combination $(k, v) \in L$* **do**
5   **if** *k is an exploitable key with v as its favourable IV for $\mathbb{K}_{nmem}^{temp}$* **then**
6   increase the counter.
7   **end**
8   **end**
9   **if** $\frac{counter}{\xi} \geq p_{thres}$ **then**
10   include i in the K_{nmem}.
11   **end**
12 **end**

7.2   How to Construct the Attack

In the PNB based attack, the attacker assigns random values to the PNBs and tries to guess the significant key bits correctly. In our approach, we propose that while guessing the significant key bits, the attacker finds the member from the list of exploitable keys. The list also contains at least one favourable IV for each of the keys. Keep in mind that for each key of the list, we can construct $2^{|K_{nmem}|}$ different keys by changing the values of the K_{nmem} key bits, and the same favourable key would form a right pair with each one of those keys.

In [2], the authors mentioned that instead of having many strong keys which do not form a right pair, we would have with high probability at least one column which has weak keys. Similarly, here if we can keep the percentage of exploitable key high in each column, then with high probability, we will have at least one column in which we have an exploitable key. Let the member be k. As already mentioned, k actually represents a coset $k \oplus \mathbb{K}_{nmem}$. Now, the list also contains at least one favourable IV $v_{\mathcal{ID}}$ for k.

Now, while generating the data for N different IVs, the attackers always use the same $v_{\mathcal{ID}}$ for the input difference column and change the values of the IVs in the remaining columns. According to the structure of ChaCha, we still have 2^{96} different IVs, which ensures that a sufficient number of IVs are always available to get N data samples.

Now according to our construction of K_{nmem} subset, $PNB_{\mathcal{ID}} \subseteq K_{nmem}$. Therefore, the set of significant key bits in the $\mathcal{ID}$ column i.e., Non-$PNB_{\mathcal{ID}} \supseteq \mathbb{K}_{mem}$. Consequently if our guessed non-PNBs/significant bits are correct, this implies that even if the PNBs are incorrectly guessed, the actual key still lies in $k \oplus \mathbb{K}_{nmem}$. Thus we write in a form of a proposition below.

Proposition 2. *If $PNB_{\mathcal{ID}} \subseteq K_{nmem}$, then for any exploitable key k and its favourable IV v with respect to $\mathbb{K}_{nmem}$, if random values are assigned in the bit positions of $PNB_{\mathcal{ID}}$ to form a key k', then v is a favourable IV for k' as well.*

The reason for this is if k, k' is the guessed key and actual key, respectively, both lie in the same coset. Therefore the favourable IV $v_{\mathcal{ID}}$ gives minimum difference after the first round for k' as well. So, if we guess only the non-PNBs correctly, we can find a favourable IV for both the actual key and the guessed key.

Example: Suppose a cipher uses a 10-bit key $(k_0, k_1, k_2, k_3, k_4, k_5, k_6, k_7, k_8, k_9)$ where k_8 and k_9 are PNBs and $K_{nmem} = \{k_7, k_8, k_9\}$. While guessing the significant key bits we look at the list of exploitable keys. Suppose, we choose $(k_0, k_1, k_2, k_3, k_4, k_5, k_6, k_7, k_8, k_9) = (0, 0, \ldots, 0)$ from the list of exploitable keys. Therefore our guess of significant key bits $(k_0, k_1, k_2, k_3, k_4, k_5, k_6, k_7)$ is $(0, 0, 0, 0, 0, 0, 0, 0)$.

Suppose the favourable IV of $(0, 0, 0, 0, 0, 0, 0, 0, 0, 0)$ is v. Therefore v forms a right pair with each key of $(0, 0, 0, 0, 0, 0, 0, 0, 0, 0) \oplus \mathbb{K}_{nmem}$, i.e. $(0, 0, 0, 0, 0, 0, 0, 0, 0, 0), (0, 0, 0, 0, 0, 0, 0, 0, 0, 1), (0, 0, 0, 0, 0, 0, 0, 0, 1, 0), \ldots, (0, 0, 0, 0, 0, 0, 0, 1, 1, 1)$. So in the attack, the attacker uses v as its IV. If the guess $(0, 0, 0, 0, 0, 0, 0, 0)$ as the significant key bits is correct then whatever be the actual value of k_8, k_9, v will form a right pair with the key $(0, 0, 0, 0, 0, 0, 0, 0, k_8, k_9)$. So the attacker will achieve the desired bias for the correct guess of the significant key bits.

8   Attack on 7-round ChaCha256

In our simulations, we used the GCC compiler version 9.3.0 and the drand48() function in the programmes for 32-bit random number generation.

In reference to [2] taking the input difference as $\Delta X_{13}^{(0)}[6]$ and obtaining output difference at $\Delta X_{2}^{(4)}[0] \oplus \Delta X_{7}^{(4)}[7] \oplus \Delta X_{8}^{(4)}[0]$, we have bias $2^{-8.3} = 0.00317$. Here we will go 4-rounds forward and 3-rounds backward. In ChaCha256 we apply our proposed strategy from Sect. 6 in the following manner.

Preliminary Shortlisting of PNB: In the first step we shortlist the preliminary candidates for the PNB by assigning threshold $\gamma_{prelim} = 0.2$. We achieve total $n_{prelim} = 96$ candidates with higher bias than this. Among this, the bits which are in the input difference column are $\{39, 47, 48, 49, 51, 52, 59, 168, 169, 191\}$.

Construction of K_{nmem}: We apply Algorithm 1 to find the key bits which are from K_{nmem}. For this, we have to start with the PNBs of this column. We observe that if we include all the 9 bits mentioned above, we do not get any favourable IVs for any key. So we reject some PNBs and consider only 5 PNBs in that column which are $PNB_{ID} = \{39, 47, 48, 168, 191\}$. We assign the threshold $p_{thres} = 0.8$ and find out total 13 bits which gives higher values than p_{thres}. Including these into the K_{nmem} set along with the PNBs we achieve $K_{nmem} = PNB_{ID} \bigcup \{163, 164, 165, 171, 172, 173, 174, 175, 176, 183, 184, 185, 186\}$.

Therefore, the dimension of K_{mem} is $64 - 18 = 46$. We observe that among all the keys of K_{ID} approximately 62% are exploitable keys. Please note that only 70% keys are weak keys anyway, so only 8% weak keys do not qualify as exploitable keys. So for each column, we have to construct a list of approximately $0.62 \times 2^{46} = 2^{45.31}$ possible keys along with their favourable IVs. Hence the total memory required is $2^{47.31}$.

Remaining PNB Construction: Among them, by assigning the second threshold as $\gamma_{direct} = 0.45$, we achieve $n_1 = 67$ bits which we include directly in the PNB set. Next, in stage 2, we include $n_2 = 9$ more candidates by choosing the best candidate at each iteration. In stage 3, we assign random values to the chosen 76 PNBs. Now, along with this, we alter the value of one bit at a time from the remaining shortlisted candidates. We choose the best $n_3 = 3$ bits among them. Finally, we have a set of 79 PNBs which we provide below:

$\{219, 220, 221, 222, 223, 255, 77, 78, 79, 66, 67, 80, 68, 81, 69, 102, 82, 103, 70, 104, 83, 105, 71, 84, 106, 123, 124, 72, 85, 107, 125, 244, 126, 127, 225, 86, 109, 199, 47, 192, 207, 155, 2, 156, 3, 157, 224, 245, 108, 4, 158, 159, 168, 73, 246, 226, 193, 90, 211, 74, 200, 48, 87, 208, 95, 91, 191, 5, 6, 110, 212, 111, 227, 213, 92, 194, 115, 201, 39\}$.

In Fig. 5, we mark the achieved PNBs according to their position in the key. The PNBs selected as direct inclusion (Stage 1), best Candidate in each iteration (Stage 2) and Cherry-picked (Stage 3) are respectively denoted by the colors red, blue and green. Also, for each category, the intensity of the color of the PNB signifies their influence as PNB. For example, among the Stage 1 PNBs (red), highest intensity of red denotes the bit which was included at first into the PNB set, and lowest intensity of red denotes the last (67-th) PNB (in Stage 1). Same is true for Stage 2 and Stage 3 as well.

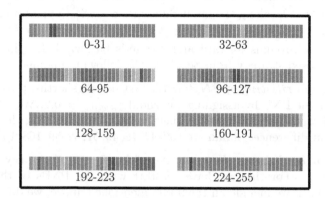

Fig. 5. ▮: Non-PNBs, ▮: Stage 1 PNBs, ▮: Stage 2 PNBs, ▮:Stage 3 PNBs

Complexity: We have the backward bias $\epsilon_a = 0.00057$ for these 79 PNBs. As already mentioned, $\epsilon_d = 0.00317$. For $\alpha = 38.8$, this gives $N = 2^{44.89}$ and time complexity $2^{221.95}$. Now, since we have $2^{45.31}$ exploitable keys in the input difference column, and for each guess we need $N = 2^{44.89}$ data the overall data complexity becomes $2^{44.89} \times 2^{45.31} = 2^{90.2}$.

8.1 Practical Observations to Confirm the Theoretical Estimations

To validate statistical assumptions, we performed experiments for 2^{32} many random keys. We take 25 PNBs.

1. In this case we see $\epsilon_a = 0.84822$. Since $\epsilon_d = 0.00317$, the estimated bias is $\epsilon_a \cdot \epsilon_d = 0.00269$. We verify this by experimental observation, which gives the value 0.00266, which is very close to estimated value.
2. Next we take $\Pr_{fa} = 2^{-\alpha}$ for $\alpha = 5.9$. Then, according to the formula, N will be $4749558 = 2^{22.18}$. We assign a fixed value to non-PNBs and random value to PNBs and perform experiment for N times. We need another parameter T to check whether the assigned non-PNBs are correct or not. For more details one can see [22, Section II]. One can check from [22], $\Pr_{fa} = Q(|\frac{T}{\sqrt{N}}|)$ and $\Pr_{nd} = Q(|\frac{2N\epsilon_a\epsilon_d - T}{2\sqrt{N(\frac{1}{4} - \epsilon_a^2\epsilon_d^2)}}|)$, where $Q(x) = \frac{1}{\sqrt{2\pi}} \int_x^\infty y^2 \, dy$. For $T = 4930$, according to these two error formulas, theoretically we get $\Pr_{fa} < 2^{-\alpha}$ and $\Pr_{nd} < 1.3 \times 10^{-2}$.
   Now, to verify these error probabilities experimentally, we perform our experiment on 2^{14} random keys. We achieve $\Pr_{fa} = \frac{93}{2^{14}} < 2^{-\alpha}$ and $\Pr_{nd} = \frac{7}{2^{14}} < 1.3 \times 10^{-2}$.

Therefore, this experimental verification validates the theoretical estimations.

9 Results on ChaCha128

9.1 Attack on 6.5-round ChaCha128

Now we provide the first-ever key recovery attack on a 6.5-round of ChaCha128. For this we use the memory approach and consider as right pairs those which have Hamming weight 10 after the first round with input difference at $\Delta X_6^{(0)}[13]$ and output difference at $\Delta X_2^{(4)}[0] \oplus \Delta X_7^{(4)}[7] \oplus \Delta X_8^{(4)}[0]$.

Preliminary Shortlisting of PNB: At first we assign a threshold $\gamma_{prelim} = 0.15$ to shortlist the PNBs for the attack. Total 53 bits surpassed γ_{prelim}. Among them there are 5 bits (*viz.* $32, 40, 41, 52, 63$), which comes from the $\mathcal{ID}$ column. Since we have to construct an appropriate K_{nmem} subset containing the PNBs of $\mathcal{ID}$ columns before finalizing the PNBs, we construct the K_{nmem} subspace first.

K_{nmem} ***Construction:*** Among the 5 shortlisted PNBs from $\mathcal{ID}$ column, we can only include $63, 40$, and 41 into our K_{nmem} subset. If we include any of the remaining two, we do not get a high fraction of exploitable keys. We can neither extend this set. The reason for such a small size of K_{nmem} is that in ChaCha128 if we recall the initial state matrix, then we see that X_5 and X_9 are the same, and if any particular key bit is a good candidate for K_{nmem}, then it should be from both X_5 and X_9. In other words, there are very few bits i for which $X_5[i]$ and $X_9[i]$ both are good candidates for K_{nmem}. The key space of ChaCha128 is of dimension 32 only for each column. This helps to make a list of keys of K_{mem} of size 2^{29} only for each column. So, the memory required is 2^{31}.

Final PNB Construction: So from our 53 shortlisted PNBs, we reject $\{32, 40\}$ since those reduces the fraction of exploitable keys. From the remaining 51 bits, at first we directly include 41 bits into the PNB set by assigning threshold $\gamma_{direct} - 0.27$. After that, we use the second step of our strategy to include 2 more PNBs. The third stage is not used here. The list of 43 PNBs is

$\{7, 12, 13, 14, 26, 27, 28, 29, 30, 31, 40, 63, 64, 65, 66, 71, 72, 79, 80, 83, 84, 85, 86, 91, 92, 93, 94, 95, 96, 97, 98, 99, 104, 105, 115, 116, 117, 118, 119, 124, 127, 87, 15\}$

Complexity: The forward bias for this PNB set is $\epsilon_d = 0.00317$ as before. The backward bias is $\epsilon_a = 0.0040$. For $\alpha = 8.5$, $N = 2^{37.94}$ the time complexity is $2^{123.04}$. Since there are 2^{29} exploitable keys for the input difference column, the data complexity is $2^{37.94} \times 2^{29} = 2^{66.94}$.

9.2 Attack on 6-round ChaCha128

We provide two attacks on the 6-round ChaCha128 using our PNB search strategy and new criteria for correct pairs. The first attack goes with the usual 2-step technique where we first find the significant bit values and then find the PNB values. In the second attack, we propose an alternative 3-step attack which further reduces the complexity.

9.2.1   First Attack Method on 6-round ChaCha128

Preliminary shortlisting of PNB: In the first step, we shortlist the preliminary candidates for the PNB by assigning threshold $\gamma_{prelim} = 0.35$. We achieve $n_{prelim} = 88$ candidates with higher bias than this. Among them, by assigning the second threshold as $\gamma_{direct} = 0.65$, we achieve $n_1 = 73$ bits which we include directly in the PNB set.

Next in step 2, we start with $n_{prelim} - n_1 = 15$ remaining key bits. From there, we include $n_2 = 10$ more candidates by choosing the best candidate at each iteration. We do not go to stage 3 of PNB construction in this attack. So, our total PNB size is $n = 83$. Exploitable keys are unavailable because of the huge number of PNBs with high backward biases in the input difference column. If we reject a significant number of PNBs from this column, the complexity will get affected. This is why go back to the technique proposed in [2] where we randomly guess IVs to achieve the right pairs. However, we choose the criterion of the right pair to be at most 12 differences after the first round. This brings down the forward bias from 0.00317 to 0.0021. However, on the other hand, now, in a column, all the keys are weak.

Complexity: In 6-round ChaCha128 we will go 4 rounds forward and 2-rounds backward. Here, we have forward bias $\epsilon_d = 0.00217$. The PNB set we get is

{0, 1, 7, 12, 13, 14, 15, 16, 17,18, 19, 20, 21, 26, 27, 28, 29, 30, 31, 32, 33, 34, 46, 51, 52, 53, 54, 55, 56, 57, 58, 59, 60, 61, 62, 63, 79, 80, 81, 82, 83, 84, 85, 90, 91, 92, 93, 94, 95, 96, 104, 115, 116, 117, 118, 119, 120, 121, 122, 127, 35, 86, 22, 123, 47, 8, 105, 97, 109, 2, 39, 64, 40, 65, 71, 98, 124, 87, 36, 110, 48, 41, 9, 23}.

For 83 PNBs we get backward bias $\epsilon_a = 0.025$. Now, on average, we need $p^{-1} = 2^{3.18}$ iterations we achieve the right pair. So, our formula becomes $p^{-1} \cdot (2^m \cdot N + 2^{(128-\alpha)}) + 2^n$. Please note that the p^{-1} does not need to be multiplied with 2^n because this term comes in the second step of only for the case when the significant key bits are correctly guessed, and a favourable IV is achieved to form a right pair. We achieve our best result for $\alpha = 52$. This gives $N = 2^{35.48}$. However, since we have to multiply it by p^{-1}, so the final data complexity is $2^{38.66}$. The time complexity is $2^{84.39}$. If we increase the number of PNBs further, the attack complexity starts increasing. The reason for this is the additional 2^n terms involved in the attack. This affects the overall complexity even though the remaining complexity decreases up to a few more PNBs. We provide in Table 4 the complexities for different sizes of the PNB set.

Table 4. Complexities for 6-Round ChaCha for different PNB sizes using the first attack method

PNB size	ϵ_a	α	Complexity
80	0.042	65	$2^{85.39}$
81	0.035	50	$2^{84.84}$
82	0.030	55	$2^{84.46}$
83	0.025	52	$2^{84.39}$
84	0.021	53	$2^{84.65}$
85	0.018	54	$2^{85.26}$

9.2.2   Alternative Attack on 6-round ChaCha128

Now we propose a slightly modified model of attack. This attack is beneficial when the PNB set size is very high. Instead of finding the significant key bits for a fixed input-output pair, we consider two input-output positions. Due to the column wise symmetric structure of ChaCha, we observe similar biases for the $\mathcal{ID} - \mathcal{OD}$ pairs $(\Delta X_{13}^{(0)}[6],\ X_2^{(4)}[0] \oplus X_7^{(4)}[7] \oplus X_8^{(4)}[0])$ and $(\Delta X_{12}^{(0)}[6],\ X_1^{(4)}[0] \oplus X_6^{(4)}[7] \oplus X_{11}^{(4)}[0])$. we involve both of them into our attack.

Attack Procedure: Suppose the two input-output positions are denoted as $\mathcal{ID} - \mathcal{OD}_1$ and $\mathcal{ID} - \mathcal{OD}_2$. Suppose, we consider m_1 significant key bits and remaining keysize $- m_1$ PNBs for $\mathcal{ID} - \mathcal{OD}_1$. Similarly, for the other input-output difference position, we have a different set of significant bits and PNBs. Among the significant key bits of $\mathcal{ID} - \mathcal{OD}_2$, we consider only those which are not common with the significant key bits of $\mathcal{ID} - \mathcal{OD}_1$. Let there be m_2 such bits. Instead of the usual two-step key recovery technique where we first find the significant key bits and then find PNBs, we propose a 3-step technique. In this, we first find the significant key bits corresponding to $\mathcal{ID} - \mathcal{OD}_1$. Once we achieve it, we go for the remaining m_2 significant key bits corresponding to $\mathcal{ID} - \mathcal{OD}_2$ pair. Once we achieve them, we go for the usual exhaustive search over the remaining bits in the third step. The attack is provided below in an algorithm form in Algorithm 2.

Algorithm 2:

Input: N_1 pairs of keystream (Z, Z') corresponding to $\mathcal{ID} - \mathcal{OD}_1$, N_2 pair of keystream (Z, Z'') corresponding to $\mathcal{ID} - \mathcal{OD}_2$.

1 **for** *each possible 2^{m_1} values of significant key bits of $\mathcal{ID} - \mathcal{OD}_1$* **do**
2   Assign random values to $128 - m_1$ PNBs and run the reverse round by 2 rounds on $Z - X$ and $Z' - X'$.
3   **if** *the bias observed for the $\mathcal{OD}$ position higher than the predetermined threshold* **then**
4   **for** *each possible 2^{m_2} values of the significant key of $\mathcal{ID} - \mathcal{OD}_2$* **do**
5   Keep the same values of m, significant key bits of $\mathcal{ID} - \mathcal{OD}_1$ pair.
6   Assign random values to the PNBs corresponding to $\mathcal{ID} - \mathcal{OD}_2$.
7   For N_2 samples of $Z - X, Z'' - X''$ run the reverse round for 2 rounds.
8   **if** *the bias at second $\mathcal{OD}$ position is higher than the predetermined threshold* **then**
9   perform an exhaustive search over $128 - (m_1 + m_2)$ remaining key bits, and stop if the correct key is found.
10   **end**
11   **end**
12   **end**
13 **end**

Complexity: For each of the 2^{m_1} possible values of the significant bits, we have to run N_1 pairs. So, we have $2^{m_1} \cdot N_1$ operations. Now, if the probability of false alarm is $2^{-\alpha}$, then for $2^{m_1-\alpha}$ possible wrong keys we receive false alarm. However, if α is considerably higher than m_1, we can ignore the occurrence of any false alarm, i.e., only the right key gives a higher bias than the threshold. In the next step, we go through 2^{m_2} possible key bit values, each run on N_2 samples, which gives a complexity $2^{m_2} \cdot N_2$. Here also, we ignore the occurrence of false alarms since α is high. In the final step, we run an exhaustive search over $2^{128-(m_1+m_2)}$ possible values of non PNBs.

Therefore, if p is the probability of getting a right pair in case of both the $\mathcal{ID} - \mathcal{OD}$ pairs, then the overall complexity $p^{-1}(2^{m_1} \cdot N_1 + 2^{m_2} \cdot N_2) + 2^{128-(m_1+m_2)}$. The data complexity is $p^{-1}(N_1 + N_2)$.

Application on ChaCha128: We consider total 89 PNBs for each $\mathcal{ID} - \mathcal{OD}$ pair. So, we have 39 significant bits for each pair. Instead of listing down the PNBs, we list the significant bits since they are less in numbers.

$\mathcal{ID} - \mathcal{OD}_1$:

$$\mathcal{ID} := \Delta X_{13}^{(0)}[6] \quad \mathcal{OD} := (X_2^{(4)}[0] \oplus X_7^{(4)}[7] \oplus X_8^{(4)}[0]).$$

Significant key bits
{3, 4, 5, 6, 10, 11, 25, 37, 38, 43, 44, 45, 49, 50, 67, 68, 69, 70, 72, 73, 74, 75, 76, 77, 78, 88, 89, 99, 100, 101, 102, 103, 107, 108, 112, 113, 114, 125, 126}

$\mathcal{ID} - \mathcal{OD}_2$:

$$\mathcal{ID} := \Delta X_{12}^{(0)}[6] \quad \mathcal{OD} := (X_1^{(4)}[0] \oplus X_6^{(4)}[7] \oplus X_{11}^{(4)}[0]).$$

Significant key bits
{5, 6, 11, 12, 13, 17, 18, 35, 36, 37, 38, 41, 42, 43, 44, 45, 46, 55, 56, 57, 67, 68, 69, 70, 71, 75, 76, 80, 81, 82, 94, 99, 100, 101, 102, 106, 107, 120, 121}

One can see that 19 bits are common. So in our notations, $m_1 = 39, m_2 = 20$. We consider α to be significantly higher than m_1. Here, for $\alpha = 50$, we see that, on average, among 2^{50} keys, only one key is there, which will give a false alarm. However, since our total number of guesses is 2^{m_1}, therefore we can ignore the influence of any false alarm. By the same logic, in the second step, also we ignore the false alarm. For 89 PNBs we get $\epsilon_a = 0.0063$ in both the cases. For $\alpha = 50$, $N_1 = N_2 = 2^{39.41}$. However, to get the right pair, we have to go for $2^{3.18}$ random IVs. So, the data complexity is $2^{3.18} \times 2 \times 2^{39.41} = 2^{43.59}$ and the time complexity is $2^{81.58}$.

10   Conclusion

In this paper, we first present an idea to improve the forward bias by the help of list. Also, we show how one can choose a suitable IV to reduce the memory size of this list. Next, we present a new technique to construct probabilistic neutral bit set. This choice gives a significant improvement in the backward bias. As a result, we get around $2^{8.91}$ times better time complexity than [2] for 7-round of ChaCha256. Also, we obtain $2^{23.42}$ times better complexity for 6-round ChaCha128 than the existing work [20], and we report first-time cryptanalysis for 6.5-round ChaCha128. We are very hopeful that our ideas can work on other ARX designs.

Acknowledgement. We are very grateful to Dmitry Khovratovich and EURO-CRYPT 2022 reviewers for their detailed comments and helpful suggestions.

References

1. Aumasson, J.-P., Fischer, S., Khazaei, S., Meier, W., Rechberger, C.: New features of Latin dances: analysis of Salsa, ChaCha, and Rumba. In: Nyberg, K. (ed.) FSE 2008. LNCS, vol. 5086, pp. 470–488. Springer, Heidelberg (2008). https://doi.org/10.1007/978-3-540-71039-4_30

2. Beierle, C., Leander, G., Todo, Y.: Improved differential-linear attacks with applications to ARX ciphers. In: Micciancio, D., Ristenpart, T. (eds.) CRYPTO 2020. LNCS, vol. 12172, pp. 329–358. Springer, Cham (2020). https://doi.org/10.1007/978-3-030-56877-1_12

3. Bernstein, D.J.: Salsa20. Technical report 2005/025, eSTREAM, ECRYPT Stream Cipher Project (2005). https://www.ecrypt.eu.org/stream/papers.html

4. Bernstein, D.J.: ChaCha, a variant of Salsa20 (2008). http://cr.yp.to/chacha.html

5. Biham, E., Shamir, A.: Differential cryptanalysis of DES-like cryptosystems. In: Menezes, A.J., Vanstone, S.A. (eds.) CRYPTO 1990. LNCS, vol. 537, pp. 2–21. Springer, Heidelberg (1991). https://doi.org/10.1007/3-540-38424-3_1

6. Choudhuri, A.R., Maitra, S.: Significantly improved multi-bit differentials for reduced round Salsa and ChaCha. IACR Trans. Symmetric Cryptol. **2016**(2), 261–287 (2016). https://doi.org/10.13154/tosc.v2016.i2.261-287

7. Crowley, P.: Truncated differential cryptanalysis of five rounds of Salsa20. In: SASC 2006 - Stream Ciphers Revisited (2006). http://eprint.iacr.org/2005/375

8. Coutinho, M., Neto, T. C. S.: New multi-bit differentials to improve attacks against chacha. IACR Cryptol. ePrint Arch. **2020**, 350 (2020). https://eprint.iacr.org/2020/350

9. Coutinho, M., Souza Neto, T.C.: Improved linear approximations to ARX ciphers and attacks against ChaCha. In: Canteaut, A., Standaert, F.-X. (eds.) EURO-CRYPT 2021. LNCS, vol. 12696, pp. 711–740. Springer, Cham (2021). https://doi.org/10.1007/978-3-030-77870-5_25

10. Dey, S., Sarkar, S.: Improved analysis for reduced round Salsa and Chacha. Discr. Appl. Math. **227**, 58–69 (2017). https://doi.org/10.1016/j.dam.2017.04.034

11. Dey, S., Dey, C., Sarkar, S., Meier, W.: Revisiting cryptanalysis on ChaCha from CRYPTO 2020 and Eurocrypt 2021. https://eprint.iacr.org/2021/1059.pdf

12. Dey, S., Sarkar, S.: Proving the biases of Salsa and ChaCha in differential attack. Des. Codes Cryptogr. **88**(9), 1827–1856 (2020). https://doi.org/10.1007/s10623-020-00736-9
13. ECRYPT: eSTREAM, the ECRYPT Stream Cipher Project. See https://www.ecrypt.eu.org/stream/
14. Fischer, S., Meier, W., Berbain, C., Biasse, J.-F., Robshaw, M.J.B.: Non-randomness in eSTREAM candidates Salsa20 and TSC-4. In: Barua, R., Lange, T. (eds.) INDOCRYPT 2006. LNCS, vol. 4329, pp. 2–16. Springer, Heidelberg (2006). https://doi.org/10.1007/11941378_2
15. Langford, S.K., Hellman, M.E.: Differential-linear cryptanalysis. In: Desmedt, Y.G. (ed.) CRYPTO 1994. LNCS, vol. 839, pp. 17–25. Springer, Heidelberg (1994). https://doi.org/10.1007/3-540-48658-5_3
16. Lipmaa, H., Moriai, S.: Efficient algorithms for computing differential properties of addition. In: Matsui, M. (ed.) FSE 2001. LNCS, vol. 2355, pp. 336–350. Springer, Heidelberg (2002). https://doi.org/10.1007/3-540-45473-X_28
17. Maitra, S.: Chosen IV Cryptanalysis on reduced round ChaCha and Salsa. Disc. Appl. Math. **208**, 88–97 (2016). https://doi.org/10.1016/j.dam.2016.02.020
18. Matsui, M., Yamagishi, A.: A new method for known plaintext attack of FEAL cipher. In: Rueppel, R.A. (ed.) EUROCRYPT 1992. LNCS, vol. 658, pp. 81–91. Springer, Heidelberg (1993). https://doi.org/10.1007/3-540-47555-9_7
19. Miyano, H.: Addend dependency of differential/linear probability of addition. IEICE Trans. Fundam. Electron. Commun. Comput. Sci. **81**(1), 106–109 (1998). https://search.ieice.org/bin/summary.php?id=e81-a_1_106
20. Shi, Z., Zhang, B., Feng, D., Wu, W.: Improved key recovery attacks on reduced-round Salsa20 and ChaCha. In: Kwon, T., Lee, M.-K., Kwon, D. (eds.) ICISC 2012. LNCS, vol. 7839, pp. 337–351. Springer, Heidelberg (2013). https://doi.org/10.1007/978-3-642-37682-5_24
21. Shimizu, A., Miyaguchi, S.: Fast data encipherment algorithm FEAL. In: Chaum, D., Price, W.L. (eds.) EUROCRYPT 1987. LNCS, vol. 304, pp. 267–278. Springer, Heidelberg (1988). https://doi.org/10.1007/3-540-39118-5_24
22. Siegenthaler, T.: Decrypting a class of stream ciphers using ciphertext only. IEEE Trans. Comput. **34**(1), 81–85 (1985). https://doi.org/10.1109/TC.1985.1676518
23. Wallén, J.: Linear approximations of addition modulo 2^n. In: Johansson, T. (ed.) FSE 2003. LNCS, vol. 2887, pp. 261–273. Springer, Heidelberg (2003). https://doi.org/10.1007/978-3-540-39887-5_20
24. https://ianix.com/pub/chacha-deployment.html
25. https://varindia.com/news/for-the-entry-level-smartphones-google-announced-a-new-encryption-solution-adiantum

A Greater GIFT: Strengthening GIFT Against Statistical Cryptanalysis

Ling Sun[1,2,3], Bart Preneel[4], Wei Wang[1,3], and Meiqin Wang[1,3,5(✉)]

[1] Key Laboratory of Cryptologic Technology and Information Security,
Ministry of Education, Shandong University, Jinan, China
{lingsun,weiwangsdu,mqwang}@sdu.edu.cn
[2] State Key Laboratory of Cryptology, P.O.Box 5159, Beijing 100878, China
[3] School of Cyber Science and Technology, Shandong University, Qingdao, China
[4] Department of Electrical Engineering-ESAT, KU Leuven and imec,
Leuven, Belgium
bart.preneel@kuleuven.be
[5] Quan Cheng Shandong Laboratory, Jinan, China

Abstract. GIFT-64 is a 64-bit block cipher with a 128-bit key that is more lightweight than PRESENT. This paper provides a detailed analysis of GIFT-64 against differential and linear attacks. Our work complements automatic search methods for the best differential and linear characteristics with a careful manual analysis. This hybrid approach leads to new insights. In the differential setting, we theoretically explain the existence of differential characteristics with two active S-boxes per round and derive some novel properties of these characteristics. Furthermore, we prove that all optimal differential characteristics of GIFT-64 covering more than seven rounds must activate two S-boxes per round. We can construct all optimal characteristics by hand. In parallel to the work in the differential setting, we conduct a similar analysis in the linear setting. However, unlike the clear view in differential setting, the optimal linear characteristics of GIFT-64 must have at least one round activating only one S-box. Moreover, with the assistance of automatic searching methods, we identify 24 GIFT-64 variants achieving better resistance against differential attack while maintaining a similar security level against a linear attack. Since the new variants strengthen GIFT-64 against statistical cryptanalysis, we claim that the number of rounds could be reduced from 28 to 26 for the variants. This observation enables us to create a cipher with lower energy consumption than GIFT-64. Similarly to the case in GIFT-64, we do not claim any related-key security for the round-reduced variant as this is not relevant for most applications.

1 Introduction

The expanded deployment of small computing devices that have limited resources (e.g., Radio-Frequency IDentification (RFID) tags, industrial controllers, intra-body sensors) strongly push the evolution of lightweight cryptography. There has been a significant amount of work done by the research

O. Dunkelman and S. Dziembowski (Eds.): EUROCRYPT 2022, LNCS 13277, pp. 115–144, 2022.
https://doi.org/10.1007/978-3-031-07082-2_5

community related to this topic. New lightweight algorithms are being proposed on a regular basis. Some lightweight algorithms such as PRESENT [12], PHOTON [19], and SPONGENT [11] have already been included in ISO standards (ISO/IEC 29192-2:2012 and ISO/IEC 29192-5:2016).

Among the numerous lightweight primitives, PRESENT is probably one of the first candidates particularly designed for efficient hardware implementations. Although the security margin of PRESENT has been reduced by exploiting the clustering effect of linear characteristics [14], it is one of the first generation lightweight ciphers. Notably, NOEKEON [17], which has good hardware performance, was designed in 2000 also before the term lightweight cryptography was widely used.

Ten years after the publication of PRESENT, Banik *et al.* [4,5] revisit the design strategy of PRESENT and propose a new design, named GIFT, that gains much-increased efficiency in hardware and software implementations. In order to avoid some of the potential weaknesses of PRESENT, the designers develop a construction paradigm called "Bad Output must go to Good Input (BOGI)" to guide the selection of bit permutations in PRESENT-like ciphers. GIFT outperforms a vast number of lightweight designs and remains a competitive cipher to date.

Design and cryptanalysis are two inseparable aspects in the development of cryptography and can bring out the best in each other. In the past decade, automatic methods [23, 26–28, 32] gradually develop into powerful tools facilitating the analyses of symmetric-key primitives. This approach has been very successful in developing better attacks and security bounds.

However, tempted by the convenient and fast usage of automatic tools, researchers may spend less attention on a careful study of the primitives themselves. Our research shows that such an analysis can identify new properties and lead to a better understanding of the strength and weaknesses of a design.

This paper studies GIFT-64 with both automatic methods and mathematical analysis; this "hybrid" method uncovers new insights into the security of GIFT-64 and some of its variants.

1.1 Our Results

Motivated by some new observations on differential and linear attacks of GIFT-64, we attempt to explain the results and propose in-depth cryptanalyses of the cipher. The results of this paper can be summarised as follows.

Properties of Differential Characteristics Activating Two S-boxes per Round. For the crucial role of differential characteristics with two active S-boxes in each round, we try to infer more properties of these characteristics. An alternative description for the round function of GIFT-64 is introduced, where internal states are viewed as 4×4 matrices. With the help of the alternative description, we first show that, for differential characteristics activating two S-boxes per round, the two active S-boxes in one of the first two rounds must be located in the same column of the matrix state. Then, we derive some conditions on the differential propagation for the bit permutation operating on the column of the state, and 26 candidate differential propagations are discovered. After evaluating the compatibilities among these candidates, we prove the existence of differential characteristics with two active S-boxes per round. Beyond that, we also confirm that any differential characteristics covering more than seven rounds and activating two S-boxes in each round must utilise some of the 26 candidate differential propagations.

Explicit Formula for the Differential Probability of the Optimal Characteristic. We propose an explicit formula for the differential probability of the optimal characteristic. Precisely, the probability $\Pr(r)$ of r-round optimal differential characteristics with $r \geqslant 8$ can be calculated with the following equation

$$- \log_2\left(\Pr(r)\right) = \begin{cases} [(r-3)/2] \cdot 10 + 12 & \text{if } r \bmod 2 \equiv 1, \\ [(r-2)/2] \cdot 10 + 8 & \text{otherwise.} \end{cases}$$

All Optimal Differential Characteristics of GIFT-64. All optimal differential characteristics covering more than seven rounds with the maximum probability can be constructed starting from the 26 candidate differential propagations. In other words, all optimal differential characteristics of GIFT-64 must activate two S-boxes per round. In addition, we show that for the round-reduced variant with an odd number of rounds, the number of optimal characteristics is 288; otherwise, the number of optimal characteristics is 10400.

Properties of Linear Characteristics with Two Active S-boxes per Round. In parallel to the analysis in the differential setting, we also investigate linear characteristics activating two S-boxes in each round. Moreover, we present some properties for this kind of characteristic, and verify that they can be constructed. However, unlike the clear view in the differential setting, the optimal linear characteristics for GIFT-64 must contain at least one round with only one active S-box.

Variants with Comparable Differential and Linear Properties. Considering the gap between the upper bounds on the differential probability and the linear correlation, we wonder whether we can find a variant of GIFT-64 with analogous security levels under the differential and linear settings. To facilitate the investigation, we devise a sufficient condition for two GIFT-64-like ciphers to be equivalent to each other, enabling us to create an equivalence relation over the set of all GIFT-64-like ciphers. Based on the equivalence relation, we identify 168 equivalence classes; the variants in each class share the same cryptographic properties. In other words, it is sufficient to carefully analyse 167 representative variants. After performing an automatic searching method, we recognise one equivalence class, denoted as GIFT-64[2021], with both lengths of the optimal effective differential and linear characteristics equal to 12. In other words, comparing to GIFT-64, all the 24 variants in GIFT-64[2021] achieve better resistance against differential cryptanalysis while maintaining a similar security level against linear cryptanalysis.

Resistance Against Other Attacks. The security of variants in GIFT-64[2021] w.r.t. the impossible differential attack [9,21], the zero-correlation attack [13], and the integral attack [22] were checked with automatic methods in [15,16,28,33]. Since the new variants strengthen GIFT-64 against statistical cryptanalysis, we claim that 26 rounds could be used rather than 28 rounds for the variants. On this basis, we create a 26-round variant without related-key security, which is more energy-efficient than GIFT-64[1]. Nevertheless, we find that the performance of the 24 variants in the related-key differential attack setting is inferior to that of GIFT-64. This observation suggests that the designers have evaluated the security of the cipher under the related-key differential attacks, although they do not claim security in this setting. For most applications, this security is not required; for the few applications where this is required, the key schedule of the newly proposed variant could be redesigned.

Outline. In Sect. 2, we review the target cipher GIFT-64 and recall the automatic searching method exploited in this paper. Motivated by some observations on the experimental results, Sect. 3 presents a series of new differential properties of GIFT-64. In parallel to the search in Sect. 3, we present in-depth analytic results in the linear setting in Sect. 4. Section 5 argues why GIFT-64 can indeed be improved by creating a variant. At last, we conclude the paper and list future work in Sect. 6.

2 Preliminary

In this section, we first review the overall structure and the design philosophy of GIFT-64. Then, an automatic searching method, utilised to assist the following analyses, is briefly recalled.

2.1 Specification of GIFT-64

GIFT [4] is a family of lightweight block ciphers composed of two versions. In this paper, we only focus on GIFT-64, a 64-bit block cipher with a 128-bit key and with 28 rounds.

The cipher initialises the cipher state S with a 64-bit plaintext $b_0 b_1 \cdots b_{63}$, where b_0 stands for the most significant bit. Alternatively, the cipher state can be expressed as sixteen 4-bit nibbles $S = w_0 \| w_1 \| \cdots \| w_{15}$. Apart from the plaintext, the 128-bit key $K = k_0 \| k_1 \| \cdots \| k_7$ acts as the other input of the cipher. After initialising as above, the cipher iteratively uses the round function to update the cipher state. Each round of GIFT-64 consists of three steps.

SubCells(SC). GIFT-64 applies an invertible 4-bit S-box GS to every nibble of the cipher state.

---

[1] The GIFT designers also did not claim related-key security.

PermBits(PB). This operation maps the bit from the position i of the cipher state to the position $P_{64}(i)$ as

$$b_{P_{64}(i)} \leftarrow b_i, \ i \in \{0, 1, \ldots, 63\},$$

where $P_{64}(i)$ can be calculated as

$$63 - \left\{ 4 \left\lfloor \frac{63 - i}{16} \right\rfloor + 16 \left[3 \left\lfloor \frac{(63 - i) \bmod 16}{4} \right\rfloor + (63 - i) \bmod 16 \right] + (63 - i) \bmod 4 \right\} \bmod 64.$$

AddRoundKey(ARK$_{RK_r}$). This step adds the round key and the round constant. Since the round constant does not affect the analysis in this paper, we only pay attention to the round key. In the r-th round, a 32-bit round key RK_r is extracted from the key state and is further partitioned into two 16-bit words as $RK_r = U \| V = u_0 u_1 \cdots u_{15} \| v_0 v_1 \cdots v_{15}$. Then, U and V are XORed to the cipher state as

$$b_{4 \cdot i + 2} \leftarrow b_{4 \cdot i + 2} \oplus u_i, \ b_{4 \cdot i + 3} \leftarrow b_{4 \cdot i + 3} \oplus v_i, \ i \in \{0, 1, \ldots, 15\}.$$

The design of the key schedule realises the goals of minimising the hardware area and supporting efficient software implementation simultaneously. It only involves the key state rotation in blocks of 16-bit and the bit rotation within some 16-bit blocks.

Key Schedule. Before the key state updates, a round key is first extracted from it. To be precise, two 16-bit words of the key state are set as the round key $RK = U \| V$, where

$$U \leftarrow k_6, \ V \leftarrow k_7.$$

After generating the round key, GIFT-64 employs the following transformation to update the key state,

$$k_0 \| k_1 \| \cdots \| k_7 \leftarrow (k_6 \ggg 2) \| (k_7 \ggg 12) \| k_0 \| k_1 \| \cdots \| k_5,$$

where '$\ggg i$' represents an i-bit right rotation within a 16-bit word.

For more details about the cipher, see Banik et al. [5].

2.2 Bit Permutation in PermBits Operation of GIFT-64

After fixing the overall structure of the cipher as a PRESENT-like [12] one, the designers set out a small area goal and manage to use an S-box with a lower implementation cost than that of RECTANGLE [34]. However, the S-box GS with low cost cannot reach the differential and linear branching numbers of three. In other words, for GS, *1-1 bit transitions*, which are referred to as differential/linear propagations with input and output differences/masks being unit vectors, are possible in both the differential and linear settings. Note that the 1-1 bit transition may result in long differential and linear characteristics with a single active S-box per round. Hence, to ensure the nonexistence of consecutive 1-1 bit differential and linear transitions in the cipher, the designers propose a new construction paradigm called *"Bad Output must go to Good Input (BOGI)"* to design the bit permutation.

Denote the sixteen S-boxes in the i-th round as GS_0^i, GS_1^i, ..., GS_{15}^i. The S-boxes can be grouped into two different ways:

▷ the Quotient group $Q_x^i = \{GS_{4 \cdot x}^i, GS_{4 \cdot x+1}^i, GS_{4 \cdot x+2}^i, GS_{4 \cdot x+3}^i\}$, $0 \leqslant x \leqslant 3$;
▷ the Remainder group $R_x^i = \{GS_x^i, GS_{x+4}^i, GS_{x+8}^i, GS_{x+12}^i\}$, $0 \leqslant x \leqslant 3$.

With this notation, the design of the 64-bit permutation in PermBits operation boils down to the construction of four independent and identical 16-bit permutations that map the output bits of Q_x^i to the input bits of R_x^{i+1}. In this sense, the BOGI paradigm can be viewed as a guideline for the creation of the 16-bit group mapping. It determines the rule to map the output bits of S-boxes in Q_x^i to the input bits of S-boxes in R_x^{i+1} and is analysed in differential and linear setting parallelly.

In the differential setting, we consider the *1-1 bit DDT* [4], a sub-table of the differential distribution table (DDT) [10], composed of differential transitions with input and output differences being unit vectors (cf. Table 4 in Supplementary Material A of the long version for the 1-1 bit DDT of GIFT). Given the 1-1 bit DDT, an input (resp., output) difference $\Delta x = x_0 x_1 x_2 x_3$ (resp., $\Delta y = y_0 y_1 y_2 y_3$) is named as a *good input* (resp., *good output*) if the corresponding row (resp., column) has all zero entries; otherwise, it is called a *bad input* (resp., *bad output*). Denote GI, GO, BI, and BO the sets of positions for the nonzero bits in the good inputs, good outputs, bad inputs, and bad outputs, respectively. Then, based on the 1-1 bit DDT of GIFT, we have $GI = \{0, 1, 2\}$, $GO = \{1, 2, 3\}$, $BI = \{3\}$, and $BO = \{0\}$.

Notice that a bad output could come from a 1-1 bit transition through a certain S-box in the current round. The primary purpose of BOGI is to ensure that the existing 1-1 bit transition will not head to another 1-1 bit transition in the succeeding round, which is realised by artificially mapping the active bit of the (potentially) bad output to an active bit of some good inputs in the next round. Concretely, regarding a 1-1 bit DDT with $|BO| \leqslant |GI|$, the *differential BOGI permutation* is defined as a permutation $\pi : BO \cup GO \rightarrow BI \cup GI$ with $\pi(BO) = \{\pi(i) \mid i \in BO\} \subseteq GI$. Likewise, in the linear case, the *linear BOGI permutation* can be derived regarding the *1-1 bit LAT* (cf. Table 5 in Supplementary Material A of the long version), which is the dual notion of 1-1 bit DDT in the linear approximation table (LAT) [24].

For the purpose of increasing the security of the cipher regarding differential and linear cryptanalyses at the same time, the *BOGI permutation* exploited in the cipher should belong to the intersection of the set of differential BOGI permutations and the set of linear BOGI permutations. For GIFT, the BOGI permutation is fixed as the identity mapping $\pi(i) = i$. After determining the BOGI permutation, during the construction of the group mapping, the i-th output bits of the S-boxes in Q_x^i must be connected to the $\pi(i)$-th input bits of the S-boxes in R_x^{i+1}. This mandatory requirement breaks the existence of consecutive 1-1 bit transitions. Hence, the cipher assembled with this kind of group mappings does not exhibit long differential and linear characteristics activating a single S-box per round.

Except for the above countermeasure to enhance the security, the group mapping should also validate the following four rules to guarantee the bijectivity of the linear layer and attain an optimal full diffusion[2].

1. The input bits of an S-box in R_x^{i+1} come from 4 distinct S-boxes in Q_x^i.
2. The output bits of an S-box in Q_x^i go to 4 distinct S-boxes in R_x^{i+1}.
3. The input bits of 4 S-boxes from the same Q_x^{i+1} come from 16 different S-boxes.
4. The output bits of 4 S-boxes from the same R_x^i go to 16 different S-boxes.

2.3   Accelerated Automatic Search with the SAT Method

This section briefly reviews the accelerated automatic searching method in [30], which will be used to examine the soundnesses of some theoretical results in the coming sections.

The automatic search is realised via the Boolean satisfiability problem (SAT), which intends to determine if there exists an instantiation that satisfies a given Boolean formula. In practice, we transform cryptanalytic problems into SAT problems and employ the same SAT solver CiDiCaL [8] as in [30] to solve all concerned SAT problems.

To facilitate a SAT solver to detect desired differential and linear characteristics, we should first create Boolean formulas to translate the cryptanalytic properties of the cipher. Due to the concise structure of GIFT, descriptions of cryptanalytic properties (e.g., the number of differential/linear active S-boxes, the differential probability, and the linear correlation) are reduced to characterisations of properties for the S-box GS. We refer readers to [30] for a detailed approach to generate differential and linear models of a given S-box.

Because we always target characteristics with good cryptanalytic properties (e.g., a small number of active S-boxes, a relatively high differential probability/linear correlation), a cardinality constraint in the form of $\sum_{j=0}^{\omega-1} x_j \leqslant k$ should be integrated into the SAT problem, where x_j's stand for Boolean variables representing cryptanalytic properties of S-boxes, w is the number of x_j's in the cipher, and k is a predicted value for the cryptanalytic property of the cipher. This cardinality constraint can be viewed as an objective function: it tells the SAT solver what kind of characteristics we want to find. With the sequential encoding method [29], the cardinality constraint can be converted into $\mathcal{O}(\omega \cdot k)$ Boolean formulas by introducing $\mathcal{O}(\omega \cdot k)$ auxiliary variables.

The Boolean expressions specifying the cryptanalytic properties of S-boxes and the objective function constitute a basic SAT problem for searching distinguishers. Next, Sun *et al.* [30] managed to incorporate Matsui's bounding conditions abstracted from the branch-and-bound depth-first searching algorithm

---

[2] GIFT-64 achieves full diffusion after three rounds.

[25] into the SAT problem to accelerate the automatic search. The efficiency arises from the manipulation of the knowledge of cryptanalytic properties of short characteristics. For instance, suppose that we are checking the existence of R-round differential characteristics $(\Delta_0, \Delta_1, \ldots, \Delta_R)$ with probability no less than $\mathrm{Pr_{Ini}}(R)$, where Δ_i implies the input difference of the i-th round. Given the maximum probability $\mathrm{Pr_{Max}}(i)$ achieved by i-round differential characteristics for all $1 \leqslant i \leqslant R - 1$, the bounding condition $\mathcal{C}_{(r_1, r_2)}$, originating from the r_1-th round and terminating with the r_2-th round, forces the SAT solver to concentrate on characteristics validating the following inequality

$$\mathrm{Pr_{Max}}(r_1) \cdot \left[\prod_{i=r_1}^{r_2-1} \mathrm{Pr}\left(\Delta_i \rightarrow \Delta_{i+1} \right) \right] \cdot \mathrm{Pr_{Max}}(R - r_2 - 1) \leqslant \mathrm{Pr_{Ini}}(R),$$

where $\mathrm{Pr}\left(\Delta_i \rightarrow \Delta_{i+1} \right)$ stands for the probability of the differential propagation $\Delta_i \rightarrow \Delta_{i+1}$ in the i-th round. The adjunction of the bounding condition [30] shrinks the solution space of the basic SAT problem and results in a notable speedup.

3   Differential Property of GIFT-64

Through analysing the automatic searching results related to differential and linear cryptanalyses of GIFT-64, we attempt to develop an in-depth understanding on the security of the cipher. Therefore, we reimplement the search for GIFT-64 with the publicly available source code provided in [30], even if the authors of [30] have already completed the full picture on the number of active S-boxes, the differential probability, as well as the linear correlation.

Based on the results shown in Fig. 1, this section presents some novel differential properties of GIFT-64. In the following, the minimum numbers of differential and linear active S-boxes for r-round characteristics are denoted as #SD(r) and #SL(r), respectively. The maximum differential probability and linear correlation for r-round characteristics are represented as $\mathrm{Pr}(r)$ and $\mathrm{Cor}(r)$.

3.1   Observations on Experimental Results

In Fig. 1, the minimum number of differential active S-boxes #SD(r) is linearly dependent on r for all $r \geqslant 8$. Starting from the eighth round, #SD(r) strictly increases by two per round. Further, after decoding the optimal differential characteristic with the maximum probability from the output of the SAT solver, we observe that the optimal characteristics covering more than seven rounds always maintain two active S-boxes in each round. Thus, we wonder whether a characteristic with a single active S-box in some rounds achieving the maximum differential probability exists. The research in this section provides an answer for this issue.

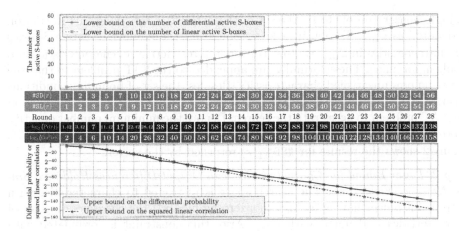

Fig. 1. Bounds reflecting differential and linear properties of GIFT-64.

3.2   Lifted Bounds on the Number of Differential Active S-boxes

Let $\mathbb{D}_{\texttt{0x1}}$ be the set of differential characteristics with at least one round activating a single S-box, and the value 0x1 equals the input difference of the active S-box. We manage to calculate a lower bound on the number of active S-boxes for characteristics in $\mathbb{D}_{\texttt{0x1}}$.

The accelerated automatic method reviewed in Sect. 2.3 is applied to accomplish this task, and we split the search into three steps. To begin with, we explore the lower bound for characteristics with input differences having a single nonzero nibble 0x1. Then, the characteristics with output differences having a single nonzero nibble 0x1 are considered. Note that the characteristics in $\mathbb{D}_{\texttt{0x1}}$ can be created with the characteristics in the first two steps. Therefore, the lower bound for characteristics in $\mathbb{D}_{\texttt{0x1}}$ is derived from the experimental results in the first two steps.

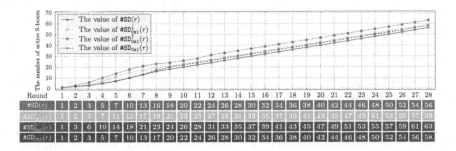

Fig. 2. Minimum numbers of differential active S-boxes in different settings.

Step 1: Lower Bound for Characteristics with Input Differences Having a Single Nonzero Nibble 0x1. We focus on characteristics with input differences having a single nonzero nibble 0x1. The set of characteristics satisfying this restriction is denoted as $\mathbb{D}_{0x1}^{\downarrow}$. To obtain a lower bound on the number of active S-boxes for characteristics in $\mathbb{D}_{0x1}^{\downarrow}$, we first convert the restriction on characteristics into Boolean formulas. These formulas are appended to the SAT problem so that the solver ignores unsatisfied characteristics. Besides, the set of bounding conditions terminating with the last round $\mathcal{C}_{(*,R)} = \{\mathcal{C}_{(r,R)} \mid 1 \leqslant r \leqslant R - 1\}$ is included in the SAT problem to accelerate the search. Denote the minimum number of active S-boxes for r-round characteristics in $\mathbb{D}_{0x1}^{\downarrow}$ with $\#\mathrm{SD}_{0x1}^{\downarrow}(r)$, where $1 \leqslant r \leqslant 28$. Figure 2 shows the results for $\#\mathrm{SD}_{0x1}^{\downarrow}(r)$ returned by the solver.

Step 2: Lower Bound for Characteristics with Output Differences Holding a Single Nonzero Nibble 0x1. The search space is restricted to characteristics with output differences having a single nonzero nibble 0x1; the corresponding set of characteristics is denoted with $\mathbb{D}_{0x1}^{\uparrow}$. Also, this constraint is formulated with Boolean expressions, which are added to the basic SAT problem. To simultaneously speed up the search and guarantee the correctness of the test, in this step, we employ the set of bounding conditions starting from the first round $\mathcal{C}_{(0,*)} = \{\mathcal{C}_{(0,r)} \mid 1 \leqslant r \leqslant R - 1\}$. Let $\#\mathrm{SD}_{0x1}^{\uparrow}(r)$ denote the minimum number of active S-boxes for r-round characteristics in $\mathbb{D}_{0x1}^{\uparrow}$. Figure 2 shows the values for $\#\mathrm{SD}_{0x1}^{\uparrow}(r)$.

Step 3: Lower Bound for Characteristics in $\mathbb{D}_{0x1}$. Let $\#\mathrm{SD}_{0x1}(r)$ be the minimum number of active S-boxes for r-round characteristics in $\mathbb{D}_{0x1}$. Since the characteristic in $\mathbb{D}_{0x1}$ can be created with characteristics in $\mathbb{D}_{0x1}^{\uparrow}$ and $\mathbb{D}_{0x1}^{\downarrow}$, a lower bound for the value of $\#\mathrm{SD}_{0x1}(r)$ can be calculated with $\#\mathrm{SD}_{0x1}^{\uparrow}(*)$ and $\#\mathrm{SD}_{0x1}^{\downarrow}(*)$. Specifically, we have

$$\#\mathrm{SD}_{0x1}(r) \geqslant \min\left\{\#\mathrm{SD}_{0x1}^{\uparrow}(r_1) + \#\mathrm{SD}_{0x1}^{\downarrow}(r_2) \;\middle|\; r_1 + r_2 = r,\; r_1 \geqslant 0,\; r_2 \geqslant 0\right\}, \quad (1)$$

and the value of the right-hand side expression is known from the outputs in *Step 1* and *Step 2*. Additionally, as we find the characteristic with the number of active S-boxes exactly matching the lower bound, we ensure that the bound for $\#\mathrm{SD}_{0x1}(r)$ in Eq. (1) is strict. The values of $\#\mathrm{SD}_{0x1}(r)$ for all $1 \leqslant r \leqslant 28$ can be found in Fig. 2.

Figure 2 reveals that $\#\mathrm{SD}_{0x1}(r) > \#\mathrm{SD}(r)$ for all $r \geqslant 8$. Moreover, after exploiting the three-step test to evaluate all sets $\mathbb{D}_i$ for $i \in \{0x2, \ldots, 0xf\}$ representing the sets of characteristics with at least one round activating a single S-box with the input difference i, we find that $\#\mathrm{SD}_i(r) > \#\mathrm{SD}(r)$ for all $r \geqslant 8$ and $i \in \mathbb{F}_2^4 \setminus \{0x0\}$ (cf. Supplementary Material B.1 of the long version). That is, from the eighth round, the optimal differential characteristic with the minimum number of active S-boxes definitely activates more than one S-box in each round. In other words, the optimal characteristic contains at least two active S-boxes per round. Because the characteristics decoded from the solver evidence the existence of differential characteristics with two active S-boxes in each round, we draw the following proposition.

Proposition 1. If $r \geqslant 8$, the optimal r-round differential characteristic of GIFT-64 with the minimum number of active S-boxes must have two active S-boxes in each round.

3.3   Decreased Upper Bound on the Differential Probability

After obtaining lower bounds on the number of active S-boxes for characteristics in $\mathbb{D}_i$, we attempt to check the differential probability for characteristics in $\mathbb{D}_i$, where i traverses all nonzero 4-bit values. The test is also accomplished with three steps as in Sect. 3.2, and we only accommodate the objective function from the number of active S-boxes to the differential probability. Denote the maximum differential probability for r-round characteristics in $\mathbb{D}_i^\downarrow$ (resp., $\mathbb{D}_i^\uparrow$, $\mathbb{D}_i$) with $\text{Pr}_i^\downarrow(r)$ (resp., $\text{Pr}_i^\uparrow(r)$, $\text{Pr}_i(r)$). The results for $\text{Pr}_i^\downarrow(r)$, $\text{Pr}_i^\uparrow(r)$, and $\text{Pr}_i(r)$ are given in Supplementary Material B.2 of the long version. The following proposition is based on the observation $\text{Pr}_i(r) < \text{Pr}(r)$ for all $i \in \mathbb{F}_2^4 \setminus \{\texttt{0x0}\}$ and $r \geqslant 8$.

Proposition 2. If $r \geqslant 8$, the optimal r-round differential characteristic with the maximum probability must activate at least two S-boxes per round.

From Sect. 3.2–3.3, we notice that differential characteristics activating two S-boxes in each round play a crucial role in the security evaluation for GIFT-64. Consequently, a natural question is whether one can infer more properties of these characteristics, apart from the quantitative information about active S-boxes. Before looking into these characteristics, we first devise an alternative description for the round function of GIFT-64, which facilitates the analyses in the upcoming sections. Note that the designers of GIFT proposed a cubic representation of GIFT-64 [4], which reorganises the 64-bit state as a $4 \times 4 \times 4$ cube. Based on the observation on the cubic representation, Adomnicai *et al.* [1] developed a new GIFT representation called *fixslicing* that allows extremely efficient software bitsliced implementations of GIFT. The new description in the following is based on a 2-dimensional matrix.

3.4   Alternative Description for the Round Function of GIFT-64

In the alternative description, we keep SubCells and AddRoundKey operations and further decompose PermBits operation into two sub-operations. Please find Fig. 3(a) for an illustration.

GroupMaps(GM). Denote the 16-bit group mapping utilised in GIFT-64 as g_0,

$$g_0 = (12, 1, 6, 11,\ 8, 13, 2, 7,\ 4, 9, 14, 3,\ 0, 5, 10, 15).$$

It moves the i-th bit of the input to the $g_0(i)$-th bit for all $0 \leqslant i \leqslant 15$. GroupMaps operation invokes g_0 and independently applies it on each of the 16-bit words $w_{4 \cdot j}^{\text{SC},r} \| w_{4 \cdot j+1}^{\text{SC},r} \| w_{4 \cdot j+2}^{\text{SC},r} \| w_{4 \cdot j+3}^{\text{SC},r}$ of the cipher state, where $w_*^{\text{SC},r}$ stands for nibbles at the output of the SubCells operation and $0 \leqslant j \leqslant 3$.

TransNibbles(TN). This operation works in nibbles. It shifts the nibble from position i of the cipher state to position $T(i)$ for all $0 \leqslant i \leqslant 15$, and

$$T = (0, 4, 8, 12,\ 1, 5, 9, 13,\ 2, 6, 10, 14,\ 3, 7, 11, 15).$$

Equivalently, if we reorganise the cipher state as a 4×4 matrix of nibbles, the bit-oriented description in Fig. 3(a) can be replaced with a nibble-oriented one as in Fig. 3(b), which is a more concise representation. In this description, the 32-bit round key RK_r also should be fitted into a 4×4 matrix of nibbles. In the following, we employ the nibble-oriented description.

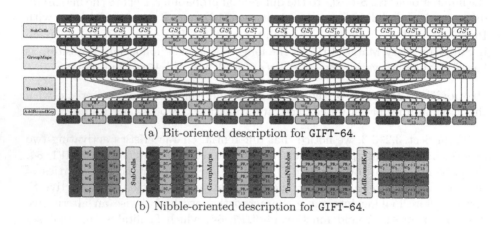

(a) Bit-oriented description for GIFT-64.

(b) Nibble-oriented description for GIFT-64.

Fig. 3. Alternative descriptions for GIFT-64.

3.5   Differential Characteristics with Two Active S-boxes per Round

Next, we study the properties of differential characteristics activating two S-boxes per round. Besides, we temporarily omit AddRoundKey operation as it does not influence the differential property in the single-key attack setting.

Lemma 1. *For* GIFT-64, *if a differential characteristic activates two S-boxes per round, then the two active S-boxes in one of the first two rounds must be located in the same column of the matrix state.*

For the proof of Lemma 1, see Supplementary Material B.3 of the long version.

Now, given a differential characteristic with two active S-boxes per round; we assume that the two active S-boxes in the r-th round are located in the same column. Without loss of generality, the column is set as the first one. Denote the differential propagation of the group mapping g_0 in the r-th round operating on the first column as $\alpha_0 \| \alpha_1 \| \alpha_2 \| \alpha_3 \xrightarrow{g_0} \beta_0 \| \beta_1 \| \beta_2 \| \beta_3$, where two nibbles in

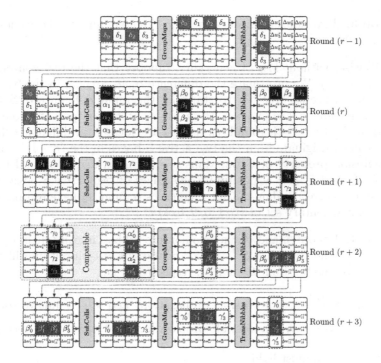

Fig. 4. Illustration for conditions on the group mapping g_0.

$\alpha_0 \| \alpha_1 \| \alpha_2 \| \alpha_3$ are nonzero. In the following, we will see that this propagation should meet some conditions so that the differential characteristic based on it can sustain two active S-boxes in rounds $(r-1)$ and $(r+1)$.

Condition 1. The output difference $\beta_0 \| \beta_1 \| \beta_2 \| \beta_3$ of g_0 has two nonzero nibbles.

Proof. As in Fig. 4, the cipher structure guarantees that $\beta_0 \| \beta_1 \| \beta_2 \| \beta_3$ equals the first row of input difference for the $(r+1)$-th round, which is the composition of input differences for four S-boxes. Because we are analysing characteristics with two active S-boxes in each round, two nibbles among β_0, β_1, β_2, and β_3 have to be nonzero. ■

Condition 2. Two nonzero nibbles in $\beta_0 \| \beta_1 \| \beta_2 \| \beta_3$ cannot take values from the set $\{0x2, 0x4, 0x8\}$.

Proof. Without loss of generality, suppose that the two nonzero nibbles are β_1 and β_3. As in Fig. 4, β_0, β_1, β_2, and β_3 are input differences of four S-boxes in the $(r+1)$-th round, and we denote the corresponding output differences as γ_0, γ_1, γ_2, and γ_3. Based on the diffusion property of GroupMaps operation, to maintain two active S-boxes in the $(r+2)$-nd round, γ_1 and γ_3 should be unit vectors. Accordingly, the input differences β_1 and β_3 regarding γ_1 and γ_3 must be different from 0x2, 0x4, or 0x8, for these input differences cannot perform the 1-1 bit transition. The proof is complete. ■

Condition 3. Two nonzero nibbles in $\alpha_0\|\alpha_1\|\alpha_2\|\alpha_3$ cannot take values from the set $\{\texttt{0x1}, \texttt{0x2}, \texttt{0x4}\}$.

Proof. Likewise, without loss of generality, suppose that the two nonzero nibbles are α_0 and α_2. We propagate the difference $\alpha_0\|\alpha_1\|\alpha_2\|\alpha_3$ in the backward direction and utilise $\delta_0\|\delta_1\|\delta_2\|\delta_3$ to stand for the input difference of SubCells operation regarding $\alpha_0\|\alpha_1\|\alpha_2\|\alpha_3$. As in Fig. 4, at the output of GroupMaps operation in the $(r-1)$-th round, δ_0 and δ_2 are located in different columns. Thus, they must originate from the two active S-boxes in the $(r-1)$-th round. By the diffusion property of GroupMaps operation, δ_0 and δ_2 should be unit vectors. As δ_0 and δ_2 also act as input differences of two active S-boxes in the r-th round, the corresponding output differences α_0 and α_2 have to take values from the complementary set of $\{\texttt{0x1}, \texttt{0x2}, \texttt{0x4}\} \subset \mathbb{F}_2^4$. ∎

Condition 4. Denote β_i and β_j the two nonzero nibbles in $\beta_0\|\beta_1\|\beta_2\|\beta_3$, where $i, j \in \{0, 1, 2, 3\}$ and $i \neq j$. Let $\mathcal{S}_i^D$ and $\mathcal{S}_j^D$ be the sets of 1-bit output differences that can be propagated from β_i and β_j, respectively, i.e.,

$$\mathcal{S}_i^D = \{\gamma_i \mid \beta_i \xrightarrow{GS} \gamma_i \text{ is a possible propagation, and } \gamma_i \text{ is a unit vector}\},$$
$$\mathcal{S}_j^D = \{\gamma_j \mid \beta_j \xrightarrow{GS} \gamma_j \text{ is a possible propagation, and } \gamma_j \text{ is a unit vector}\}.$$

Then, $\mathcal{S}_i^D \cap \mathcal{S}_j^D \neq \emptyset$ must hold.

Proof. Without loss of generality, suppose that $i = 1$ and $j = 3$. We have already proved in Condition 2 that the output differences γ_1 and γ_3 corresponding to β_1 and β_3 must be unit vectors. As in Fig. 4, γ_1 and γ_3 at the input of GroupMaps operation in the $(r+1)$-th round are located in different columns but the same row. If $\gamma_1 \neq \gamma_3$, then at least one of them differs from $\texttt{0x1}$. Since the following GroupMaps operation shifts the two nonzero bits in γ_1 and γ_3 to different rows, the inequality incurs at least three active S-boxes in the $(r+3)$-rd round for sure. So, the preset condition on the characteristic determines that the output differences corresponding to β_1 and β_3 must be an identical unit vector. ∎

Summarising all analyses in the proofs for Condition 1–4, we derive the following proposition.

Proposition 3. For an R-round differential characteristic activating two S-boxes per round, if the two active S-boxes in the r-th round are located in the same column, then, for all i with $0 \leqslant r + 2 \cdot i < R$, the two active S-boxes in the $(r + 2 \cdot i)$-th round are also located in the same column.

Based on Lemma 1 and Proposition 3, we conclude that all differential characteristics with two active S-boxes per round can be decomposed into several pieces of 2-round characteristics, for which the two active S-boxes in the first round are located in the same column. Furthermore, the differential propagations of the form $\alpha_0\|\alpha_1\|\alpha_2\|\alpha_3 \xrightarrow{g_0} \beta_0\|\beta_1\|\beta_2\|\beta_3 \xrightarrow{GS} \gamma_0\|\gamma_1\|\gamma_2\|\gamma_3$ abstracted from these 2-round characteristics fulfil Condition 1–4.

On the contrary, consider two differential propagations validating Condition 1–4,

$$\alpha_0\|\alpha_1\|\alpha_2\|\alpha_3 \xrightarrow{g_0} \beta_0\|\beta_1\|\beta_2\|\beta_3 \xrightarrow{GS} \gamma_0\|\gamma_1\|\gamma_2\|\gamma_3,$$

$$\alpha_0'\|\alpha_1'\|\alpha_2'\|\alpha_3' \xrightarrow{g_0} \beta_0'\|\beta_1'\|\beta_2'\|\beta_3' \xrightarrow{GS} \gamma_0'\|\gamma_1'\|\gamma_2'\|\gamma_3',$$

if the positions of nonzero nibbles in $\gamma_0\|\gamma_1\|\gamma_2\|\gamma_3$ and $\alpha_0'\|\alpha_1'\|\alpha_2'\|\alpha_3'$ are the same, and $\gamma_i \xrightarrow{GS} \alpha_i'$ are possible transitions for all $0 \leqslant i \leqslant 3$, then the two propagations are said to be *compatible* with each other. As shown in Fig. 4, we can craft long differential characteristics that activate two S-boxes per round with compatible propagations.

As a result, to figure out the structure of the differential characteristic activating two S-boxes in each round, we should find out all possible propagations of the form $\alpha_0\|\alpha_1\|\alpha_2\|\alpha_3 \xrightarrow{g_0} \beta_0\|\beta_1\|\beta_2\|\beta_3 \xrightarrow{GS} \gamma_0\|\gamma_1\|\gamma_2\|\gamma_3$. We implement a test and find that 26 propagations validate Condition 1–4 simultaneously (cf. Table 1). Then, we evaluate the compatibilities among them and illustrate the result in Fig. 5(a).

The graph in Fig. 5(a) contains some isolated nodes and short paths, and the corresponding propagations cannot be manipulated to create long differential characteristics. Thus, we remove these nodes and picture a more succinct graph as in Fig. 5(b), which manifests several cycles. On the one hand, these cycles theoretically explain the existence of long differential characteristics with two active S-boxes per round. On the other hand, accompanied by the preceding analyses, we conclude that any differential characteristics covering more than seven rounds with two active S-boxes per round must utilise certain paths in Fig. 5(b).

In particular, from Fig. 5(b), we identify three categories of 4-round iterative differential characteristics with probability 2^{-20}, which are demonstrated in Fig. 6. Note that the three categories cover the eight 4-round iterative differential characteristics with probability 2^{-20} proposed in [35].

Table 1. Candidate propagations $\alpha_0\|\alpha_1\|\alpha_2\|\alpha_3 \xrightarrow{g_0} \beta_0\|\beta_1\|\beta_2\|\beta_3 \xrightarrow{GS} \gamma_0\|\gamma_1\|\gamma_2\|\gamma_3$.

Index	$\alpha_0\|\alpha_1\|\alpha_2\|\alpha_3 \xrightarrow{g_0} \beta_0\|\beta_1\|\beta_2\|\beta_3 \xrightarrow{GS} \gamma_0\|\gamma_1\|\gamma_2\|\gamma_3$	Probability	Index	$\alpha_0\|\alpha_1\|\alpha_2\|\alpha_3 \xrightarrow{g_0} \beta_0\|\beta_1\|\beta_2\|\beta_3 \xrightarrow{GS} \gamma_0\|\gamma_1\|\gamma_2\|\gamma_3$	Probability
D00	0x0039 $\xrightarrow{g_0}$ 0x9003 $\xrightarrow{GS}$ 0x8008	2^{-6}	D13	0x3900 $\xrightarrow{g_0}$ 0x0390 $\xrightarrow{GS}$ 0x0880	2^{-6}
D01	0x0085 $\xrightarrow{g_0}$ 0x0c01 $\xrightarrow{GS}$ 0x0808	2^{-6}	D14	0x5008 $\xrightarrow{g_0}$ 0xc010 $\xrightarrow{GS}$ 0x8080	2^{-6}
D02	0x009c $\xrightarrow{g_0}$ 0x9c00 $\xrightarrow{GS}$ 0x8800	2^{-6}	D15	0x500a $\xrightarrow{g_0}$ 0xc030 $\xrightarrow{GS}$ 0x8080	2^{-6}
D03	0x00a5 $\xrightarrow{g_0}$ 0x0c03 $\xrightarrow{GS}$ 0x0808	2^{-6}	D16	0x5050 $\xrightarrow{g_0}$ 0x5050 $\xrightarrow{GS}$ 0x2020	2^{-6}
D04	0x00c6 $\xrightarrow{g_0}$ 0x0c60 $\xrightarrow{GS}$ 0x0220	2^{-4}	D17	0x5050 $\xrightarrow{g_0}$ 0x5050 $\xrightarrow{GS}$ 0x8080	2^{-6}
D05	0x0390 $\xrightarrow{g_0}$ 0x3900 $\xrightarrow{GS}$ 0x8800	2^{-6}	D18	0x600c $\xrightarrow{g_0}$ 0xc600 $\xrightarrow{GS}$ 0x2200	2^{-4}
D06	0x0505 $\xrightarrow{g_0}$ 0x0505 $\xrightarrow{GS}$ 0x0202	2^{-6}	D19	0x8500 $\xrightarrow{g_0}$ 0x010c $\xrightarrow{GS}$ 0x0808	2^{-6}
D07	0x0505 $\xrightarrow{g_0}$ 0x0505 $\xrightarrow{GS}$ 0x0808	2^{-6}	D20	0x9003 $\xrightarrow{g_0}$ 0x0039 $\xrightarrow{GS}$ 0x0088	2^{-6}
D08	0x0850 $\xrightarrow{g_0}$ 0x10c0 $\xrightarrow{GS}$ 0x8080	2^{-6}	D21	0x9c00 $\xrightarrow{g_0}$ 0x009c $\xrightarrow{GS}$ 0x0088	2^{-6}
D09	0x09c0 $\xrightarrow{g_0}$ 0x09c0 $\xrightarrow{GS}$ 0x0880	2^{-6}	D22	0xa0a0 $\xrightarrow{g_0}$ 0x0a0a $\xrightarrow{GS}$ 0x0101	2^{-4}
D10	0x0a0a $\xrightarrow{g_0}$ 0xa0a0 $\xrightarrow{GS}$ 0x1010	2^{-4}	D23	0xa500 $\xrightarrow{g_0}$ 0x030c $\xrightarrow{GS}$ 0x0808	2^{-6}
D11	0x0a50 $\xrightarrow{g_0}$ 0x30c0 $\xrightarrow{GS}$ 0x8080	2^{-6}	D24	0xc009 $\xrightarrow{g_0}$ 0xc009 $\xrightarrow{GS}$ 0x8008	2^{-6}
D12	0x0c60 $\xrightarrow{g_0}$ 0x00c6 $\xrightarrow{GS}$ 0x0022	2^{-4}	D25	0xc600 $\xrightarrow{g_0}$ 0x600c $\xrightarrow{GS}$ 0x2002	2^{-4}

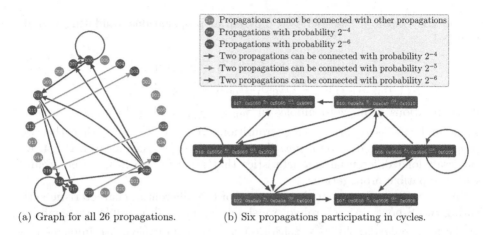

(a) Graph for all 26 propagations.   (b) Six propagations participating in cycles.

Fig. 5. Compatibilities among 26 candidate differential propagations.

3.6 Enumerating All Optimal Differential Characteristics

This section reveals that all optimal r-round differential characteristics ($r \geqslant 8$) with the maximum probabilities can be created with the two cycles 'D06 → D06 → D06' and 'D16 → D16 → D16' in Fig. 5(b).

In Fig. 1, we note that the probability of r-round optimal differential characteristics with $r \geqslant 8$ satisfies the following equation

$$- \log_2 \left(\Pr(r) \right) = \begin{cases} [(r-3)/2] \cdot 10 + 12 & \text{if } r \bmod 2 \equiv 1, \\ [(r-2)/2] \cdot 10 + 8 & \text{otherwise.} \end{cases}$$

which is a linear function when the independent variable r is restricted to even or odd numbers. The two restrictions of the function have a slope of 5 ($= 10/2$). Meanwhile, for all 4-round iterative differential characteristics in Fig. 6, the probabilities of any two consecutive rounds of characteristics are 2^{-10}. Prompted by these two observations, we attempt to construct optimal differential characteristics with cycles of propagations in Fig. 5.

If we only apply the six differential propagations in Fig. 5(b) to compose characteristics, the maximum probability $\underline{\Pr}(r)$ obtained in this case can be calculated via the following formula

$$- \log_2 \left(\underline{\Pr}(r) \right) = \begin{cases} [(r-1)/2] \cdot 10 + 4 & \text{if } r \bmod 2 \equiv 1, \\ (r/2) \cdot 10 & \text{otherwise.} \end{cases}$$

It can be verified that $\underline{\Pr}(r) = \Pr(r) \cdot 2^{-2}$ for all $r \geqslant 8$. To rectify this gap, we fine-tune the head and(or) the tail of the characteristics generated with the cycles and devise numerous characteristics achieving the optimal probability. The adjustment differs depending on the number r of rounds.

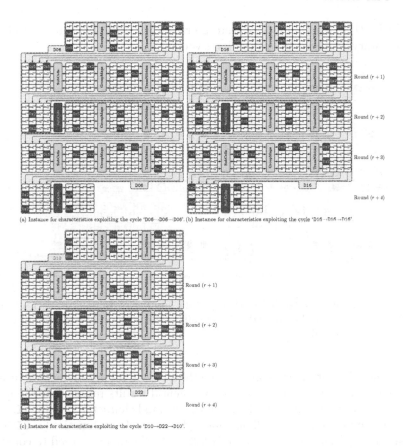

(a) Instance for characteristics exploiting the cycle 'D06→D06→D06'. (b) Instance for characteristics exploiting the cycle 'D16→D16→D16'

(c) Instance for characteristics exploiting the cycle 'D10→D22→D10'.

Fig. 6. Three categories of 4-round iterative differential characteristics with probability 2^{-20}. In each category, more characteristics can be created by cyclically shifting the columns/rows of the differences for the internal states.

288 Optimal Characteristics with an odd Number of Rounds. If $r \bmod 2 \equiv 1$, we can formulate two categories of optimal differential characteristics with the probability being $2^{-\{[(r-3)/2] \cdot 10 + 12\}}$. As in Fig. 7, the first category is based on the cycle 'D06 $\rightarrow$ D06 $\rightarrow$ D06', while the second category iteratively utilises the cycle 'D16 $\rightarrow$ D16 $\rightarrow$ D16'. In both categories, to lift the differential probability in the last round, the differential propagations of the two active S-boxes are replaced from 0x5 $\xrightarrow{GS}$ 0x2 to 0x5 $\xrightarrow{GS}$ 0xf. Also, at the head of the characteristic, we devise two kinds of extensions and ensure that the probabilities of the four active S-boxes in the first two rounds are all equal to 2^{-2}. Each category is composed of 144 characteristics. Thus, in total, we manually identify 288 optimal characteristics.

10400 Optimal Characteristics with an Even Number of Rounds. If $r \bmod 2 \equiv 0$, we construct four categories of optimal differential characteristics with probability

$2^{-\{[(r-2)/2]\cdot10+8\}}$. The number of characteristics is 10400. For more details, see Supplementary Material B.4 of the long version.

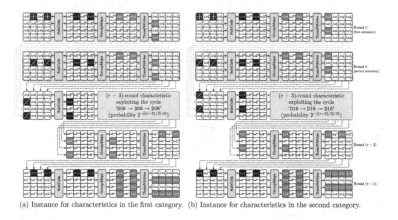

(a) Instance for characteristics in the first category. (b) Instance for characteristics in the second category.

Fig. 7. 288 optimal characteristics with an odd number of rounds. In each category, more characteristics can be created by cyclically shifting the columns/rows of the differences for the internal states.

We utilise the automatic searching method to find all optimal characteristics with the maximum probability. The experimental results reflect that the manually created characteristics constitute all the optimal characteristics for GIFT-64. That is, we know the looks of all optimal differential characteristics for GIFT-64.

Last but not least, the cycle 'D10 → D22 → D10' cannot be used to construct optimal characteristics, although it can be employed to create 4-round iterative characteristics. We explain this with the case illustrated in Fig. 7(a). Note that the extension at the head of the characteristic should ensure that the four active S-boxes in the first two rounds have a differential probability being equal to 2^{-2}. On the other side, the two nonzero nibbles in the input difference of D10 are equal to 0xa. It can be observed from the DDT of GS that the probabilities of all possible transitions with 0xa as the output difference are equal to 2^{-3}, which explains why we cannot create optimal characteristics with this cycle.

4   Linear Property of GIFT-64

In parallel to the case of differential setting investigated in Sect. 3, we derive some in-depth analytic results in the linear setting.

4.1   Fluctuant Bounds in Linear Cryptanalysis Setting

Since we wonder about the performances of linear characteristics with a single active S-box in some rounds, we apply the same method in Sect. 3.2 to determine the lower bound on the number of linear active S-boxes of these characteristics. Denote $\#\mathtt{SL}_{\mathtt{i}}(r)$ the minimum number of active S-boxes for r-round linear characteristics with at least one round activating a single S-box with the input mask $\mathtt{i}$, where $\mathtt{i} \in \mathbb{F}_2^4 \setminus \{\mathtt{0x0}\}$. The corresponding test results are given in Supplementary Material C.1 of the long version. It can be noticed that for all $\mathtt{i} \in \mathbb{F}_2^4 \setminus \{\mathtt{0x0}\}$, $\#\mathtt{SL}_{\mathtt{i}}(r)$ diverges from the initial bound $\#\mathtt{SL}(r)$ from the tenth round. So, we introduce the following proposition.

Proposition 4. If $r \geqslant 10$, then the optimal r-round linear characteristic of GIFT-64 with the minimum number of active S-boxes must activate two S-boxes per round.

Next, the linear correlation bound is studied. Denote $\mathrm{Cor}_{\mathtt{i}}(r)$ the maximum linear correlation for r-round characteristics with at least one round activating a single S-box with the input mask $\mathtt{i}$, where $\mathtt{i} \in \mathbb{F}_2^4 \setminus \{\mathtt{0x0}\}$. The test result about $\mathrm{Cor}_{\mathtt{i}}(r)$ can be found in Supplementary Material C.2 of the long version. It can be noticed that some points of curves for $\mathrm{Cor}_{\mathtt{0x1}}(r)$, $\mathrm{Cor}_{\mathtt{0x2}}(r)$, $\mathrm{Cor}_{\mathtt{0x8}}(r)$, $\mathrm{Cor}_{\mathtt{0xa}}(r)$, $\mathrm{Cor}_{\mathtt{0xc}}(r)$ overlap with those of the curve for $\mathrm{Cor}(r)$ when $r \geqslant 10$. Thus, unlike the case in differential setting, the optimal linear characteristic with the maximum correlation can contain characteristics with a single active S-box in some rounds.

4.2   Linear Characteristics with Two Active S-boxes per Round

It can be observed from Fig. 1 that the minimum number of linear active S-boxes $\#\mathtt{SL}(r)$ is also linearly dependent on r for all $r \geqslant 9$. Hence, we adjust the approach in Sect. 3.5 to the linear setting and look into properties of linear characteristics with two active S-boxes in each round. The ideas to prove lemmas and conditions in this section are similar to those in Sect. 3.5, and we omit proofs.

Lemma 2. For GIFT-64, if a linear characteristic has two active S-boxes per round, then the two active S-boxes in one of the first two rounds must be located in the same column of the matrix state.

Given a linear characteristic activating two S-boxes per round, suppose that the two active S-boxes in the r-th round are located in the same column. Also, without loss of generality, the column is fixed as the first one. Let $\zeta_0\|\zeta_1\|\zeta_2\|\zeta_3 \xrightarrow{\mathtt{g}_0} \eta_0\|\eta_1\|\eta_2\|\eta_3$ be the linear propagation of the group mapping $\mathtt{g}_0$ in the r-th round operating on the first column. Two nibbles in the vector $\zeta_0\|\zeta_1\|\zeta_2\|\zeta_3$ are nonzero. Then, the propagation should satisfy the following conditions so that the linear characteristic exploiting it keeps two active S-boxes in rounds $(r-1)$ and $(r+1)$.

Condition 5. The output mask $\eta_0\|\eta_1\|\eta_2\|\eta_3$ of $\mathtt{g}_0$ has two nonzero nibbles.

Condition 6. Two nonzero nibbles in $\eta_0\|\eta_1\|\eta_2\|\eta_3$ cannot take values from the set $\{\mathtt{0x4}, \mathtt{0x8}\}$.

Condition 7. Two nonzero nibbles in $\zeta_0\|\zeta_1\|\zeta_2\|\zeta_3$ cannot take values from the set $\{\texttt{0x1}, \texttt{0x2}\}$.

Condition 8. Let η_i and η_j be the two nonzero nibbles in $\eta_0\|\eta_1\|\eta_2\|\eta_3$, where $i, j \in \{0, 1, 2, 3\}$ and $i \neq j$. Define two sets $\mathcal{S}_i^L$ and $\mathcal{S}_j^L$ as

$$\mathcal{S}_i^L = \{\lambda_i \mid \eta_i \xrightarrow{GS} \lambda_i \text{ is a possible propagation, and } \lambda_i \text{ is a unit vector}\},$$
$$\mathcal{S}_j^L = \{\lambda_j \mid \eta_j \xrightarrow{GS} \lambda_j \text{ is a possible propagation, and } \lambda_j \text{ is a unit vector}\}.$$

Then, $\mathcal{S}_i^L \cap \mathcal{S}_j^L \neq \emptyset$ must hold.

A dual proposition of Proposition 3 can now be formulated.

Proposition 5. For an R-round linear characteristic with two active S-boxes per round, if the two active S-boxes in the r-th round are located in the same column, the two active S-boxes in the $(r + 2 \cdot i)$-th round are also located in the same column for all i with $0 \leqslant r + 2 \cdot i < R$.

We find that 46 propagations of the form $\zeta_0\|\zeta_1\|\zeta_2\|\zeta_3 \xrightarrow{g_0} \eta_0\|\eta_1\|\eta_2\|\eta_3 \xrightarrow{GS} \lambda_0\|\lambda_1\|\lambda_2\|\lambda_3$ satisfy Condition 5–8, which are listed in Table 6 of Supplementary Material C.3 of the long version. The compatibilities among the 46 candidates are demonstrated in Fig. 17 of Supplementary Material C.4 of the long version. Based on the cycle in the graph, we also theoretically explain the existence of long linear characteristics with two active S-boxes per round.

5   Can We Improve GIFT-64?

The results in Fig. 1 reflect that the differential and linear properties of GIFT-64 are comparable if we only consider the number of differential and linear active S-boxes. However, when it comes to the differential probability and the linear correlation, the resistance of the cipher regarding these two cryptanalytic methods is inconsistent. In particular, the longest effective differential characteristics with probability greater than 2^{-64} covers 13 rounds, while the longest effective linear characteristics covers 12 rounds. We also notice that besides the group mapping g_0 applied in GIFT-64, numerous candidates validate BOGI requirement and the four rules in Sect. 2.2. So, we wonder whether we can find a variant of GIFT-64 constructed with a new group mapping that possesses comparable upper bounds on the differential probability and the linear correlation. The content in this section constitutes our answer to this question.

5.1   Candidate Variants

Among the 24 permutations over the set $\{0, 1, 2, 3\}$, four permutations are BOGI permutations. After taking the four rules in Sect. 2.2 into consideration, we can generate 2304 group mappings (including g_0 in GIFT-64) meeting all requirements for the one in GIFT-64. We call the corresponding 2303 candidate variants, constructed with the 2303 group mappings, GIFT-64-like ciphers. In theory, we should evaluate the differential and linear properties of 2303 variants.

Note that the nibble-oriented description in Sect. 3.4 for GIFT-64 can be used to represent GIFT-64-like ciphers, and the unique modification lies in the group mapping exploited in GroupMaps operation. The GroupMaps operation based on the group mapping g is denoted as GM_g, and we use GM to stand for the set of 2304 GroupMaps operations in GIFT-64-like ciphers.

5.2   Classifying the Variants of GIFT-64

With the alternative description in Sect. 3.4, we are able to create a sufficient condition for two GIFT-64-like ciphers to be equivalent to each other. We start by introducing two special categories of linear transformations over the 4×4 matrix of nibbles, which will be utilised to derive the sufficient condition.

Definition 1 (Row Transformation). Let $\mathbb{P}$ be the set of all permutations over the set $\{0, 1, 2, 3\}$. Given ϱ in $\mathbb{P}$, the *row transformation generated with ϱ,* denoted by RT_ϱ, is a permutation over the 4×4 matrix that transfers the i-th row of the input to the $\varrho(i)$-th row for all $0 \leqslant i \leqslant 3$.

Definition 2 (Column Transformation). Given ϱ in $\mathbb{P}$, the *column transformation generated with ϱ,* denoted by CT_ϱ, is a permutation over the 4×4 matrix that shifts the i-th column of the input to the $\varrho(i)$-th column for all $0 \leqslant i \leqslant 3$.

With the simple definitions of the two kinds of transformations, we can quickly write their inverse operations.

Lemma 3. If $\varrho \in \mathbb{P}$ and ϱ^{-1} is the inverse permutation of ϱ, then the inverse operation of RT_ϱ is $RT_{\varrho^{-1}}$. In symbols, $(RT_\varrho)^{-1} = RT_{\varrho^{-1}}$. Likewise, CT_ϱ and $CT_{\varrho^{-1}}$ are inverse of each other.

Because the row and column transformations only involve permutations over rows and columns of the input matrix, the composition of these two categories of transformations is commutative.

Lemma 4. If ϱ_1 and $\varrho_2 \in \mathbb{P}$, then $RT_{\varrho_1} \circ CT_{\varrho_2} = CT_{\varrho_2} \circ RT_{\varrho_1}$.

To establish the equivalence among GIFT-64-like ciphers, we also investigate the commutativity of the composition between these artificial transformations and the operations in the round function of the GIFT-64-like cipher.

As RT_ϱ and CT_ϱ do not change the values of the entries in the input matrix, the composition between RT_ϱ/CT_ϱ and SubCells operation is commutative.

Lemma 5. If $\varrho \in \mathbb{P}$, then $RT_\varrho \circ SC = SC \circ RT_\varrho$ and $CT_\varrho \circ SC = SC \circ CT_\varrho$.

Since the column transformation CT_ϱ only alter the positions of the columns and do not touch on any permutations within columns, the composition between CT_ϱ and GroupMaps operation is commutative.

Lemma 6. If $\varrho \in \mathbb{P}$ and $\mathrm{GM}_g \in \mathbb{GM}$, then $\mathrm{CT}_\varrho \circ \mathrm{GM}_g = \mathrm{GM}_g \circ \mathrm{CT}_\varrho$.

Note that RT_ϱ and CT_ϱ apply the same permutation ϱ to realise the diffusion of the input matrix in the vertical and horizontal directions, respectively. Recall that TransNibbles operation over the input matrix works like a transposition. Taken together, we obtain the following lemma.

Lemma 7. If $\varrho \in \mathbb{P}$, then $\mathrm{RT}_\varrho \circ \mathrm{TN} = \mathrm{TN} \circ \mathrm{CT}_\varrho$ and $\mathrm{CT}_\varrho \circ \mathrm{TN} = \mathrm{TN} \circ \mathrm{RT}_\varrho$.

Under a permutation of the round keys, the commutativity of the composition between $\mathrm{RT}_\varrho/\mathrm{CT}_\varrho$ and AddRoundKey operation can be constructed.

Lemma 8. If $\varrho \in \mathbb{P}$ and $k \in \left(\mathbb{F}_2^4\right)^{4 \times 4}$, then $\mathrm{RT}_\varrho \circ \mathrm{ARK}_k = \mathrm{ARK}_{\mathrm{RT}_\varrho(k)} \circ \mathrm{RT}_\varrho$ and $\mathrm{CT}_\varrho \circ \mathrm{ARK}_k = \mathrm{ARK}_{\mathrm{CT}_\varrho(k)} \circ \mathrm{CT}_\varrho$.

For simplicity, denote the r-th round function of a GIFT-64-like cipher with the group mapping g as $\mathcal{F}(g, k_r)$, i.e., $\mathcal{F}(g, k_r) = \mathrm{ARK}_{k_r} \circ \mathrm{TN} \circ \mathrm{GM}_g \circ \mathrm{SC}$. Note that the following result is an easy consequence by combining all properties of row and column transformations in Lemma 4–8.

Proposition 6. If $\varrho \in \mathbb{P}$, then $\mathrm{RT}_\varrho \circ \mathcal{F}(g, k_r) = \mathcal{F}\big(g, \mathrm{RT}_\varrho(k_r)\big) \circ \mathrm{CT}_\varrho$.

The following proposition points out a sufficient condition for two GIFT-64-like ciphers being equivalent to each other.

Proposition 7. Let GIFT-64$[g_1]$ and GIFT-64$[g_2]$ be two GIFT-64-like ciphers respectively instantiated with group mappings g_1 and g_2. If there exists an element $\varrho \in \mathbb{P}$ such that $\mathrm{GM}_{g_2} = \mathrm{RT}_\varrho \circ \mathrm{GM}_{g_1} \circ \mathrm{RT}_{\varrho^{-1}}$, then GIFT-64$[g_1]$ and GIFT-64$[g_2]$ differ only by a permutation on the plaintext and ciphertext and a corresponding permutation of the round keys.

For the proofs of Proposition 6–7, see Supplementary Material D of the long version.

Definition 3 (GM-equivalence). Given two elements GM_{g_1} and GM_{g_2} of the set $\mathbb{GM}$, GM_{g_1} and GM_{g_2} are called GM-equivalence, if there exists a $\varrho \in \mathbb{P}$ such that $\mathrm{GM}_{g_2} = \mathrm{RT}_\varrho \circ \mathrm{GM}_{g_1} \circ \mathrm{RT}_{\varrho^{-1}}$. In symbols, $\mathrm{GM}_{g_1} \sim \mathrm{GM}_{g_2}$.

It can be verified that the binary relation '$\sim$' on the set $\mathbb{GM}$ is reflexive, symmetric and transitive. Hence, '$\sim$' is an equivalence relation on $\mathbb{GM}$. Because of the conclusion in Proposition 7, if GM_{g_1} and GM_{g_2} are GM-equivalent permutations, the two GIFT-64-like ciphers implemented with GM_{g_1} and GM_{g_2} share the same cryptographic properties. In particular, this fact holds for the case of differential and linear cryptanalyses.

We classify all permutations in $\mathbb{GM}$ up to GM-equivalence and split the set $\mathbb{GM}$ into 168 distinct equivalence classes. Accordingly, the set of 2304 GIFT-64-like ciphers is partitioned into 168 equivalence classes. Therefore, we only need to check the property of one representative in each possible equivalence class, and the number of candidates is reduced from 2303 to 167. Note that we do not count in the equivalence class containing GIFT-64.

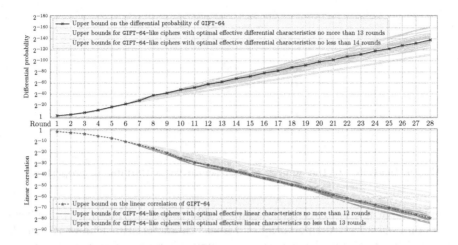

Fig. 8. Test results for 167 representatives.

5.3   Differential and Linear Properties of GIFT-64-like Ciphers

We apply the accelerated automatic method to search for upper bounds on differential probabilities and linear correlations of 167 representative variants. The test results are illustrated in Fig. 8. As the longest effective differential characteristics of GIFT-64 achieve 13 rounds, we split all the 168 representatives into two groups, according to whether the length of the optimal effective differential characteristic is longer than 13 rounds. To make a distinction, in Fig. 8, we use blue curves to exhibit variants with optimal effective differential characteristics no more than 13 rounds. For variants with effective differential characteristics covering more than 13 rounds, the differential probability curves are coloured in red. Since a cipher with short effective differential characteristics is more likely to withstand a differential attack, then, we conclude from Fig. 8 that the security of GIFT-64 against the differential cryptanalysis is moderate among all the 168 representatives.

Similarly, in the linear setting, the 168 representatives are classified according to whether the optimal effective linear characteristic goes beyond 12 rounds. In Fig. 8, the purple curves correspond to GIFT-64-like ciphers with optimal effective linear characteristics no more than 12 rounds, while the variants with yellow curves have longer effective linear characteristics than that of GIFT-64. Unlike the case in differential cryptanalysis, the capability of GIFT-64 against linear cryptanalysis is almost among the best of candidates.

Then, we consider the combination of differential and linear properties. According to the lengths of the optimal effective differential and linear characteristics, the 168 representatives can be divided into 17 groups, and the results can be found in Fig. 9. It can be notified that the performance of GIFT-64 resisting differential and linear attacks is good, and 40 representatives achieve similar security levels to GIFT-64. Moreover, we identify that one representative may

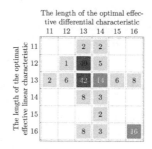

Fig. 9. Heatmap for the number of representatives with different properties.

possess comparable security levels against differential and linear cryptanalyses, and its optimal effective differential and linear characteristics achieve 12 rounds. For simplicity, the equivalence class containing this representative is denoted as GIFT-64[2021]. Next, we discuss the cryptanalytic properties of GIFT-64-like ciphers in GIFT-64[2021].

5.4   Properties of Variants in GIFT-64[2021]

The equivalence class GIFT-64[2021] contains 24 elements, and 24 underlying group mappings can be found in Table 7 of Supplementary Material E.1 of the long version. All variants belonging to GIFT-64[2021] share the same differential and linear properties, which are illustrated in Fig. 10. The clustering effects of differential and linear characteristics are evaluated (cf. Supplementary Material E.3–E.4 of the long version). Similarly to the case of GIFT-64, the differential and linear hull properties of GIFT-64[2021] are not significant.

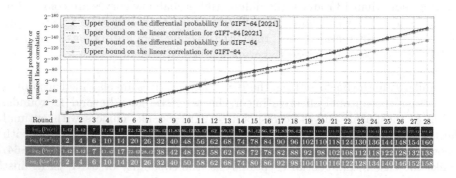

Fig. 10. Cryptanalytic properties of GIFT-64[2021]. A detailed comparison between GIFT-64[2021] and GIFT-64 is given in Supplementary Material E.2 of the long version.

Beyond that, we implement the automatic search of impossible differential distinguishers [28], zero-correlation linear distinguishers [15,16], and integral distinguishers [33] for the variants belonging to GIFT-64[2021]. The experimental results indicate that the security levels of the variants in GIFT-64[2021] withstanding impossible differential (ID) attack, zero-correlation linear attack, and integral attack are similar to those of GIFT-64.

Table 2. Attack results on GIFT-64 and GIFT-64[g_0^c].

Method	GIFT-64					GIFT-64[g_0^c]			
	Round	Time	Data	Memory	Ref.	Round	Time	Data	Memory
Differential	20	$2^{125.50}$	$2^{62.58}$	$2^{62.58}$	[31]	18[†]	$2^{125.16}$	$2^{62.27}$	$2^{62.27}$
Linear	19	$2^{127.11}$	$2^{62.96}$	$2^{60.00}$	[31]	18[‡]	$2^{126.60}$	$2^{62.96}$	$2^{53.00}$
Integral	14	$2^{97.00}$	$2^{63.00}$	-	[5]	14	$2^{97.00}$	$2^{63.00}$	-
ID*	6	-	-	-	[5]	6	-	-	-

[†]: The differential attack is realised with the 12-round differential in the long version.
[‡]: The linear attack is realised with the 12-round linear hull in the long version.
*: The number of rounds is the length of the distinguisher.

In Table 2, we compare the attack results in the single-key attack setting on GIFT-64 and GIFT-64[g_0^c], which is the representative of GIFT-64[2021] instantiated with the group mapping g_0^c in Table 7 of the long version. Note that the best attack on GIFT-64[g_0^c] achieves 18 rounds, which is two rounds less than the length of the best attack on GIFT-64. Furthermore, in the design document, the designer of GIFT-64 expected that the differential probability of 14-round differential would be lower than 2^{-63}. For this reason, they believed 28-round GIFT-64 is enough to resist differential cryptanalysis. Taken these observations together, we claim that for the variant GIFT-64[g_0^c], if the security in the related-key attack setting is not required, 26 rounds could be used rather than 28 rounds.

As mentioned by the designers, for the simple and clean design strategy, GIFT offers extremely good performances and even surpasses both SKINNY [7] and SIMON [6] for round-based implementations. On this basis, 26-round GIFT-64[g_0^c] may become one of the most energy-efficient ciphers as of today and is probably more suitable for the low-energy consumption use cases than GIFT-64. In Table 3, we compare the hardware performance of 26-round GIFT-64[g_0^c] with other lightweight ciphers. The new variant achieves higher throughput and requires a lower energy consumption than GIFT-64.

Although GIFT designer did not claim any related-key security, the security of the cipher in the related-key attack setting was investigated in recent years [18,20,31]. We also check the security of the 24 variants in GIFT-64[2021] in the related-key attack setting. The key schedule remains the same as the one in GIFT-64. We test the lower bound on the number of active S-boxes for up to 18 rounds with the accelerated automatic method. Figure 19 of Supplementary Material E.5 of the long version contains the experimental results. For all 24 variants, the number of active S-boxes in the related-key differential attack setting is always lower than that of GIFT-64. Thus, we believe GIFT-64 maintains

Table 3. Comparison of performance metrics for round-based implementations synthesised with TSMC 90 nm standard cell library.

	Area (GE)	Delay (ns)	Cycle	TP_{MAX} (MBit/s)	Power (μW)	Energy (pJ)
GIFT-64[g_0^c]	1769	0.55	26	4475.5	36.7	95.4
GIFT-64	1770	0.56	28	4081.6	36.7	102.7
SKINNY-64-128	1804	0.86	36	2067.2	36.8	132.5
SIMON-64-128	1829	0.81	44	1795.7	36.5	160.5

a relatively good performance against the related-key differential attack, even though the designers do not claim its security in the related-key attack setting.

To sum up, we find a greater GIFT-64, which strengthens GIFT-64 against statistical cryptanalysis. In this sense, a variant GIFT-64[g_0^c] with 26 rounds is created and achieves better performance than GIFT-64. Likewise, we do not claim any related-key security for the new variant since most applications do not need related-key security. For the few applications where this security is required, the key schedule of the variant could be redesigned.

A probable explanation for the improved resistance against the differential cryptanalysis of GIFT-64[g_0^c] is provided in Supplementary Material E.6 of the long version. As we prepare the paper, we notice that Baek et al. [2] also created a variant for GIFT-64. The distinction between [2] and this paper is explained in Supplementary Material E.7 of the long version.

6   Conclusion and Future Work

6.1   Conclusion

This paper targets the cryptanalysis of GIFT-64 and combines automatic and manual methods to evaluate its security. In the differential setting, we theoretically explain the existence of differential characteristics with two active S-boxes per round and derive some properties of these characteristics, apart from the quantitative information about active S-boxes. Furthermore, all optimal differential characteristics covering more than seven rounds are identified. Parallel work is conducted in the linear setting. Considering the gap between the upper bounds on the differential probability and the linear correlation, we study a variant of GIFT-64 with comparable security levels in the differential and linear settings. With the support of automatic searching methods, we identify 24 variants achieving better resistance against differential cryptanalysis than GIFT-64 while maintaining a similar security level against linear cryptanalysis. As the new variants strengthen GIFT-64 against statistical cryptanalysis, we claim that for the variant GIFT-64[g_0^c], if the security in the related-key attack setting is not required, 26 rounds could be used rather than 28 rounds. This observation results in a cipher more suitable for the low-energy consumption use cases than

GIFT-64. The performance of the 24 variants in the related-key differential attack setting is inferior to that of GIFT-64. However, most applications do not need related-key security.

6.2   Future Work

If one is concerned with related-key attacks, we conjecture that the resistance of variants in GIFT-64[2021] regarding related-key differential attack can be lifted by carefully crafting the key schedule. However, many parameters should be fine-tuned. Thus, we left it as future work.

Secondly, in the construction of GIFT-64-like cipher, we apply the same 16-bit group mapping to each column of the state. How to efficiently evaluate the cases where the group mappings operating on different columns are distinct is an open problem.

Lastly, for GIFT-128, the security levels regarding differential and linear cryptanalyses are also not comparable. We attempt to create an equivalence relation among all variants for GIFT-128. Nevertheless, the number of equivalence classes is 1344. In addition, due to the considerable state size, investigating the security of the variants for GIFT-128 is much more complicated than that of GIFT-64. Still, considering the significant status of GIFT-128 among the lightweight block ciphers and its supporting role in a series of Authenticated Encryptions with Associated Data (AEADs), especially in one of the finalists GIFT-COFB [3] of NIST Lightweight Cryptography project[3], we believe checking the existence of a balanced variant for GIFT-128 will be interesting future work. For more details about the test of GIFT-128, see Supplementary Material F of the long version.

Acknowledgements. The authors would like to thank the anonymous reviewers for their valuable comments and suggestions to improve the quality of the paper. The research leading to these results has received funding from the National Natural Science Foundation of China (Grant No. 62002201, Grant No. 62032014), the National Key Research and Development Program of China (Grant No. 2018YFA0704702), and the Major Basic Research Project of Natural Science Foundation of Shandong Province, China (Grant No. ZR202010220025). Bart Preneel was supported by CyberSecurity Research Flanders with reference number VR20192203.

References

1. Adomnicai, A., Najm, Z., Peyrin, T.: Fixslicing: a new GIFT representation fast constant-time implementations of GIFT and GIFT-COFB on ARM cortex-m. IACR Trans. Cryptogr. Hardw. Embed. Syst. **2020**(3), 402–427 (2020). https://doi.org/10.13154/tches.v2020.i3.402-427
2. Baek, S., Kim, H., Kim, J.: Development and security analysis of GIFT-64-variant that can be efficiently implemented by bit-slice technique. J. Korea Inst. Inf. Secur. Cryptol. **30**(3), 349–356 (2020)

---

[3] https://csrc.nist.gov/Projects/Lightweight-Cryptography.

3. Banik, S., et al.: GIFT-COFB. IACR Cryptol. ePrint Arch. **2020**, 738 (2020). https://eprint.iacr.org/2020/738

4. Banik, S., Pandey, S.K., Peyrin, T., Sasaki, Y., Sim, S.M., Todo, Y.: GIFT: a small present - towards reaching the limit of lightweight encryption. In: Cryptographic Hardware and Embedded Systems - CHES 2017–19th International Conference, Taipei, Taiwan, 25–28 September 2017, Proceedings, pp. 321–345 (2017). https://doi.org/10.1007/978-3-319-66787-4_16

5. Banik, S., Pandey, S.K., Peyrin, T., Sim, S.M., Todo, Y., Sasaki, Y.: GIFT: a small present. IACR Cryptol. ePrint Arch. **2017**, 622 (2017). http://eprint.iacr.org/2017/622

6. Beaulieu, R., Shors, D., Smith, J., Treatman-Clark, S., Weeks, B., Wingers, L.: The SIMON and SPECK families of lightweight block ciphers. IACR Cryptol. ePrint Arch. **2013**, 404 (2013)

7. Beierle, C., et al.: The SKINNY family of block ciphers and its low-latency variant MANTIS. In: Robshaw, M., Katz, J. (eds.) CRYPTO 2016, Part II. LNCS, vol. 9815, pp. 123–153. Springer, Heidelberg (2016). https://doi.org/10.1007/978-3-662-53008-5_5

8. Biere, A.: CaDiCaL at the SAT Race 2019. In: Heule, M., Järvisalo, M., Suda, M. (eds.) Proceedings of SAT Race 2019 - Solver and Benchmark Descriptions. Department of Computer Science Series of Publications B, vol. B-2019-1, pp. 8–9. University of Helsinki (2019)

9. Biham, E., Biryukov, A., Shamir, A.: Cryptanalysis of skipjack reduced to 31 rounds using impossible differentials. In: Stern, J. (ed.) EUROCRYPT 1999. LNCS, vol. 1592, pp. 12–23. Springer, Heidelberg (1999). https://doi.org/10.1007/3-540-48910-X_2

10. Biham, E., Shamir, A.: Differential cryptanalysis of DES-like cryptosystems. In: Advances in Cryptology - CRYPTO 1990, 10th Annual International Cryptology Conference, Santa Barbara, California, USA, 11–15 August 1990, Proceedings, pp. 2–21 (1990). https://doi.org/10.1007/3-540-38424-3_1

11. Bogdanov, A., Knežević, M., Leander, G., Toz, D., Varıcı, K., Verbauwhede, I.: SPONGENT: a lightweight hash function. In: Preneel, B., Takagi, T. (eds.) CHES 2011. LNCS, vol. 6917, pp. 312–325. Springer, Heidelberg (2011). https://doi.org/10.1007/978-3-642-23951-9_21

12. Bogdanov, A., et al.: PRESENT: an ultra-lightweight block cipher. In: Paillier, P., Verbauwhede, I. (eds.) CHES 2007. LNCS, vol. 4727, pp. 450–466. Springer, Heidelberg (2007). https://doi.org/10.1007/978-3-540-74735-2_31

13. Bogdanov, A., Rijmen, V.: Linear hulls with correlation zero and linear cryptanalysis of block ciphers. Des. Codes Crypt. **70**(3), 369–383 (2012). https://doi.org/10.1007/s10623-012-9697-z

14. Cho, J.Y.: Linear cryptanalysis of reduced-round PRESENT. In: Pieprzyk, J. (ed.) CT-RSA 2010. LNCS, vol. 5985, pp. 302–317. Springer, Heidelberg (2010). https://doi.org/10.1007/978-3-642-11925-5_21

15. Cui, T., Chen, S., Fu, K., Wang, M., Jia, K.: New automatic tool for finding impossible differentials and zero-correlation linear approximations. Sci. China Inf. Sci. **64**(2), 1–3 (2020). https://doi.org/10.1007/s11432-018-1506-4

16. Cui, T., Jia, K., Fu, K., Chen, S., Wang, M.: New automatic search tool for impossible differentials and zero-correlation linear approximations. IACR Cryptol. ePrint Arch. **2016**, 689 (2016). http://eprint.iacr.org/2016/689

17. Daemen, J., Peeters, M., Van Assche, G., Rijmen, V.: Nessie proposal: NOEKEON. In: First Open NESSIE Workshop, pp. 213–230 (2000)

18. Dong, X., Qin, L., Sun, S., Wang, X.: Key guessing strategies for linear key-schedule algorithms in rectangle attacks. Cryptology ePrint Archive, Report 2021/856 (2021). https://ia.cr/2021/856

19. Guo, J., Peyrin, T., Poschmann, A.: The PHOTON family of lightweight hash functions. In: Rogaway, P. (ed.) CRYPTO 2011. LNCS, vol. 6841, pp. 222–239. Springer, Heidelberg (2011). https://doi.org/10.1007/978-3-642-22792-9_13

20. Ji, F., Zhang, W., Zhou, C., Ding, T.: Improved (related-key) differential cryptanalysis on GIFT. IACR Cryptol. ePrint Arch. **2020**, 1242 (2020). https://eprint.iacr.org/2020/1242

21. Knudsen, L.: DEAL-A 128-bit block cipher. Complexity **258**(2), 216 (1998)

22. Knudsen, L.R., Wagner, D.A.: Integral cryptanalysis. In: Daemen, J., Rijmen, V. (eds.) FSE 2002. LNCS, vol. 2365, pp. 112–127. Springer, Heidelberg (2002). https://doi.org/10.1007/3-540-45661-9_9

23. Kölbl, S., Leander, G., Tiessen, T.: Observations on the SIMON block cipher family. In: Gennaro, R., Robshaw, M. (eds.) CRYPTO 2015, Part I. LNCS, vol. 9215, pp. 161–185. Springer, Heidelberg (2015). https://doi.org/10.1007/978-3-662-47989-6_8

24. Matsui, M.: Linear cryptanalysis method for DES cipher. In: Helleseth, T. (ed.) EUROCRYPT 1993. LNCS, vol. 765, pp. 386–397. Springer, Heidelberg (1994). https://doi.org/10.1007/3-540-48285-7_33

25. Matsui, M.: On correlation between the order of S-boxes and the strength of DES. In: De Santis, A. (ed.) EUROCRYPT 1994. LNCS, vol. 950, pp. 366–375. Springer, Heidelberg (1995). https://doi.org/10.1007/BFb0053451

26. Mouha, N., Preneel, B.: Towards finding optimal differential characteristics for ARX: application to Salsa20. Technical report, Cryptology ePrint Archive, Report 2013/328 (2013)

27. Mouha, N., Wang, Q., Gu, D., Preneel, B.: Differential and linear cryptanalysis using mixed-integer linear programming. In: Wu, C.-K., Yung, M., Lin, D. (eds.) Inscrypt 2011. LNCS, vol. 7537, pp. 57–76. Springer, Heidelberg (2012). https://doi.org/10.1007/978-3-642-34704-7_5

28. Sasaki, Y., Todo, Y.: New impossible differential search tool from design and cryptanalysis aspects. In: Coron, J.-S., Nielsen, J.B. (eds.) EUROCRYPT 2017, Part III. LNCS, vol. 10212, pp. 185–215. Springer, Cham (2017). https://doi.org/10.1007/978-3-319-56617-7_7

29. Sinz, C.: Towards an optimal CNF encoding of boolean cardinality constraints. In: van Beek, P. (ed.) CP 2005. LNCS, vol. 3709, pp. 827–831. Springer, Heidelberg (2005). https://doi.org/10.1007/11564751_73

30. Sun, L., Wang, W., Wang, M.: Accelerating the search of differential and linear characteristics with the SAT method. IACR Trans. Symmetric Cryptol. **2021**(1), 269–315 (2021). https://doi.org/10.46586/tosc.v2021.i1.269-315

31. Sun, L., Wang, W., Wang, M.: Improved attacks on GIFT-64. Cryptology ePrint Archive, Report 2021/1179 (2021). https://ia.cr/2021/1179

32. Sun, S., Hu, L., Wang, P., Qiao, K., Ma, X., Song, L.: Automatic security evaluation and (related-key) differential characteristic search: application to SIMON, PRESENT, LBlock, DES(L) and other bit-oriented block ciphers. In: Sarkar, P., Iwata, T. (eds.) ASIACRYPT 2014, Part I. LNCS, vol. 8873, pp. 158–178. Springer, Heidelberg (2014). https://doi.org/10.1007/978-3-662-45611-8_9

33. Xiang, Z., Zhang, W., Bao, Z., Lin, D.: Applying MILP method to searching integral distinguishers based on division property for 6 lightweight block ciphers. In: Cheon, J.H., Takagi, T. (eds.) ASIACRYPT 2016, Part I. LNCS, vol. 10031, pp. 648–678. Springer, Heidelberg (2016). https://doi.org/10.1007/978-3-662-53887-6_24

34. Zhang, W., Bao, Z., Lin, D., Rijmen, V., Yang, B., Verbauwhede, I.: RECTANGLE: a bit-slice lightweight block cipher suitable for multiple platforms. Sci. China Inf. Sci. **58**(12), 1–15 (2015). https://doi.org/10.1007/s11432-015-5459-7

35. Zhu, B., Dong, X., Yu, H.: MILP-based differential attack on round-reduced GIFT. In: Matsui, M. (ed.) CT-RSA 2019. LNCS, vol. 11405, pp. 372–390. Springer, Cham (2019). https://doi.org/10.1007/978-3-030-12612-4_19

Side Channel Attacks and Masking

Approximate Divisor Multiples – Factoring with Only a Third of the Secret CRT-Exponents

Alexander May[1] , Julian Nowakowski[1]([✉]) , and Santanu Sarkar[2]

[1] Ruhr-University Bochum, Bochum, Germany
{alex.may,julian.nowakowski}@rub.de
[2] Indian Institute of Technology Madras, Chennai, India

Abstract. We address Partial Key Exposure attacks on CRT-RSA on secret exponents d_p, d_q with small public exponent e. For constant e it is known that the knowledge of half of the bits of one of d_p, d_q suffices to factor the RSA modulus N by Coppersmith's famous *factoring with a hint* result. We extend this setting to non-constant e. Somewhat surprisingly, our attack shows that RSA with e of size $N^{\frac{1}{12}}$ is most vulnerable to Partial Key Exposure, since in this case only a third of the bits of both d_p, d_q suffices to factor N in polynomial time, knowing either most significant bits (MSB) or least significant bits (LSB).

Let $ed_p = 1+k(p-1)$ and $ed_q = 1+\ell(q-1)$. On the technical side, we find the factorization of N in a novel two-step approach. In a first step we recover k and ℓ in polynomial time, in the MSB case completely clementary and in the LSB case using Coppersmith's lattice-based method. We then obtain the prime factorization of N by computing the root of a univariate polynomial modulo kp for our known k. This can be seen as an extension of Howgrave-Graham's *approximate divisor* algorithm to the case of *approximate divisor multiples* for some known multiple k of an unknown divisor p of N. The point of *approximate divisor multiples* is that the unknown that is recoverable in polynomial time grows linearly with the size of the multiple k.

Our resulting Partial Key Exposure attack with known MSBs is completely rigorous, whereas in the LSB case we rely on a standard Coppersmith-type heuristic. We experimentally verify our heuristic, thereby showing that in practice we reach our asymptotic bounds already using small lattice dimensions. Thus, our attack is highly efficient.

Keywords: Coppersmith's method · CRT-RSA · Partial Key Exposure

---

A. May—Funded by DFG under Germany's Excellence Strategy - EXC-2092 CASA - 390781972.
S. Sarkar—Funded by a Humboldt Research Fellowship for experienced researchers, while visiting Ruhr-University Bochum.

O. Dunkelman and S. Dziembowski (Eds.): EUROCRYPT 2022, LNCS 13277, pp. 147–167, 2022.
https://doi.org/10.1007/978-3-031-07082-2_6

1   Introduction

RSA. As opposed to other cryptosystems, RSA has the disadvantage that it suffers from *Partial Key Exposure* (PKE) attacks. Given only a constant fraction of the secret key, in many settings RSA can be broken in polynomial time. Coppersmith's *factoring with a hint* [6] that factors RSA moduli $N = pq$ in polynomial time given only half of the bits of p can be considered the pioneer work in the area, from which many other results where derived [2,5,11,13]. A direct application of *factoring with a hint* is the Boneh-Durfee-Frankel (BDF) attack [5], that factors N given only a quarter of the least significant bits (LSB) of the RSA secret exponent, provided that e is constant. For larger values of e and known most significant bits (MSB) of d, the BDF attack requires the knowledge of a larger fraction of d.

In the case of full-size e, denoted $e \approx N$, and small d, it was shown by Ernst, May, Jochemsz, de Weger [9], Aono [1] and Takayasu and Kunihiro [20] that there exist Partial Key Exposure attacks that require no bits for $d \leq N^{0.284}$ respectively $d \leq N^{0.292}$, coinciding with the results of Boneh and Durfee [4], and work up to full-size d, coinciding with the result of Coron and May [8,15].

CRT-RSA. In practice, basically all RSA implementations use CRT secret exponents $d_p = d \bmod p - 1, d_q = d \bmod q - 1$ in combination with a small public exponent e. The first PKE for CRT-RSA was shown by Blömer and May [2] – also derived from *factoring with a hint* – that factors N given half of either LSBs or MSBs of one of d_p, d_q, provided that e is constant.

Sarkar and Maitra [18] and later Takayasu-Kunihiro [19] showed that there exist Partial Key Exposure attacks for all e up to full-size, where naturally the larger e the more LSBs/MSBs of d_p, d_q one has to know, see Fig. 1.

In the small CRT-exponent setting, May, Nowakowski and Sarkar [17] recently showed that there exist PKE for known LSB that require no knowledge of bits for $d_p, d_q \leq N^{0.122}$, coinciding with Takayasu, Lu, Peng [21], and work up to full-size CRT-exponents.

Discussion of Takayasu-Kunihiro (TK) [19]. From Fig. 1, one observes that the TK attack converges for small e to only a known $\frac{1}{3}$-fraction of the bits of d_p, d_q. We strongly question this result of the TK attack in the small e regime. First, we show that knowledge of a known $\frac{1}{3}$-fraction of p (LSBs/MSBs) implies knowledge of a $\frac{1}{3}$-fraction of d_p, d_q (for constant e), which in turn by the TK-result would imply polynomial time factoring (see Theorem 4). Thus, if TK works in the small e setting, then this result immediately implies that we can factor with only $\frac{1}{3}$ of the bits of p, a major improvement over Coppersmith's famous *factoring with hint*. Second, we give also strong experimental evidence that TK fails to recover the factorization in the small e regime.

Notice that we do not question the TK analysis in general. The point is that the TK attack uses the standard Coppersmith-type heuristic (see Assumption 1) for extracting roots of multivariate polynomials. Takayasu and Kunihiro did not provide experimental verification of this heuristic in [19]. Our experimental results in Sect. 5 show that the heuristic systematically fails when less than

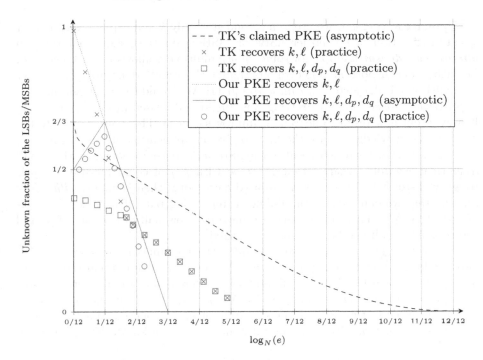

Fig. 1. Comparison between the Takayasu-Kunihiro attack and our attack.

half of the bits of d_p, d_q are known. We conjecture that the TK attack works for $e \leq N^{\frac{1}{8}}$ (asymptotically, for sufficiently large lattice dimension), if at least half of the bits of d_p, d_q are known, see also Fig. 1. We also believe that the asymptotic TK attack area is correct for $e \geq N^{\frac{1}{8}}$, thereby coinciding with our new attack at the point $e = N^{\frac{1}{8}}$.

Our Contributions. We take as starting point the two CRT-exponent equations

$$ed_p = 1 + k(p - 1), \tag{1}$$
$$ed_q = 1 + \ell(q - 1).$$

We then introduce a novel two-step procedure to factor N. In a first step, for $e \leq N^{\frac{1}{4}}$ we efficiently recover k, ℓ given sufficiently many LSBs/MSBs of d_p, d_q. For constant-size e we do not need any bits of d_p, d_q, whereas for $e = N^{\frac{1}{4}}$ we need all bits. We would like to stress that as opposed to the results of Blömer, May [2] our algorithm really requires the knowledge of LSBs/MSBs of *both* d_p, d_q. It is open how to recover k efficiently given only bits of d_p.

Our algorithm for recovering k and ℓ in the case of MSBs of d_p, d_q is completely elementary and rigorous, whereas we recover k, ℓ in the LSB case using Coppersmith's method under the usual heuristic for extracting roots for multivariate modular polynomial equations. We verify our heuristic experimentally in Sect. 5.

Upon recovering k, ℓ, we use in a second step only k and Eq. (1) to construct an approximation of kp (either LSBs or MSBs). We then show that such an *approximate divisor multiple* for some *known* multiple k allows reconstruction of kp with a smaller portion of known bits than in the standard *approximate divisor* case with $k = 1$ aka *factoring with a hint* [6,11]. We would like to stress that the *approximate divisor multiple* setting was already addressed in [3, Theorem 13]. However, our new result (Theorem 3) improves over [3, Theorem 13], and to the best of our knowledge we are the first to give an application of this setting.

Let us illustrate our new result for *approximate divisor multiples* with a small numerical example. Assume that $N = pq$ with p, q of equal bit-size, i.e. p is roughly of size $N^{\frac{1}{2}}$. If we know an approximation of p, then *factoring with a hint* tells us that we can recover the unknown remaining part of p, as long as it is bounded by $N^{\frac{1}{4}}$. This implies that we have to know half of the bits of p, and the remaining half can be efficiently recovered.

Now in the *approximate divisor multiple* setting assume that we know $k \approx N^{\frac{1}{4}}$ and in addition an approximation of $kp \approx N^{\frac{3}{4}}$. Our result shows that the amount of required known bits is then still only $N^{\frac{1}{4}}$, whereas we can efficiently recover the unknown remaining part of kp of size $N^{\frac{1}{2}}$. In other words, in the *approximate divisor multiple* setting we only need a *third* of kp as opposed to a *half* of p in *factoring with a hint*. However, the total amount $N^{\frac{1}{4}}$ of known bits is identical in both settings.

This effect helps us to improve Partial Key Exposure Attacks in the public exponent regime $e \leq N^{\frac{1}{12}}$, and explains the *bump shape* in Fig. 1. Since k grows with larger e, we obtain approximations of kp that allow for more efficient factorizations. This leads to the – maybe somewhat couterintertuitive – result that for $e \approx N^{\frac{1}{12}}$ we need the least amount of d_p, d_q to efficiently factor. Namely, in this case only a third of the bits of d_p, d_q is sufficient to factor N. For $e > N^{\frac{1}{12}}$ our two-step approach requires again more bits, since the reconstruction of k, ℓ in the first step requires more than a third of the bits of d_p, d_q, see Fig. 1. Eventually, based on our conjecture we expect that for $e \geq N^{\frac{1}{8}}$ our approach is superseded by the (heuristic) Takayasu-Kunihiro attack.

Notice that our MSB attack is rigorous in both steps, leading to a fully provable factorization algorithm. In the LSB case we require the usual Coppersmith-type heuristic only for the first step that computes k, ℓ. We verify the validity of this heuristic for our LSB case, and for TK in the case $e \geq N^{\frac{1}{8}}$ experimentally in Sect. 5.

Discussion of Our Result. Since our result suggests that RSA with $e \approx N^{\frac{1}{12}}$ is most vulnerable to Partial Key Exposure attacks, this strange behaviour might ask for further discussion. In our opinion, constant-size e is still weakest in the PKE setting. In fact, whereas the Blömer-May result requires only half of either d_p or d_q, we require at least a third of d_p and d_q. As a (rough) numerical example for n-bit d_p, d_q one requires in Blömer-May $\frac{1}{2}n$ bits to factor N, whereas we require $\frac{2}{3}n$ bits. Nevertheless, there might be side-channel scenarios that allow for easier recovery of a third of both d_p, d_q than for a half of a single CRT-exponent. In such a case, our results indicate that $e \approx N^{\frac{1}{12}}$ is indeed weakest.

2   Coppersmith's Method

We briefly recall Coppersmith's lattice-based method for computing small modular roots of polynomials [7]. For a more thorough introduction we refer to [16].

Suppose we are given a k-variate polynomial $f(x_1, \ldots, x_k)$, which has a small root $r = (r_1, \ldots, r_k)$ modulo some integer M, where for $i = 1, \ldots, k$ and known bounds X_i we have $|r_i| \leq X_i$. Our goal is to compute r in polynomial time.

We fix an $m \in \mathbb{N}$ and define a collection of so-called *shift-polynomials*

$$g_{[i_0, \ldots, i_k]}(x_1, \ldots, x_k) := f^{i_0}(x_1, \ldots, x_k) \cdot x_1^{i_1} \cdot \ldots \cdot x_k^{i_k} \cdot M^{m-i_0}$$

with indices $i_0, \ldots, i_k \in \mathbb{N}$. By construction the shift-polynomials have the root r modulo M^m.

Next we select a subset of polynomials $g_{[i_0, \ldots, i_k]}(X_1 x_1, \ldots, X_k x_k)$, whose coefficient vectors generate an n-dimensional lattice with triangular basis matrix $\mathbf{B}$. If m is chosen sufficiently large and the so-called *enabling condition*

$$|\det \mathbf{B}| \leq M^{mn} \tag{2}$$

is satisfied, then we can compute k polynomials $h_1(x_1, \ldots, x_k), \ldots, h_k(x_1, \ldots, x_k)$ in polynomial time, which have the root r not only modulo M^m, but also over the integers.

If our polynomial f is univariate, i.e. $k = 1$, then we can easily obtain r from h_1, using standard techniques such as Newton's method. In the case of a multivariate polynomial f, i.e. $k > 1$, the polynomials $h_1, \ldots, h_k$ however do not necessarily reveal the root r. Nevertheless, in practice the polynomials $h_1, \ldots, h_k$ usually generate an ideal $\mathfrak{a} = \langle h_1, \ldots, h_k \rangle$ of zero-dimensional variety – in which case we can still obtain r in polynomial time by computing the Gröbner basis of $\mathfrak{a}$. There is, however, no provable guarantee that the variety of $\mathfrak{a}$ is zero-dimensional. Therefore, many Coppersmith-type results rely on the following heuristic assumption.

Assumption 1. *Coppersmith's method for the multivariate setting yields polynomials, which generate an ideal of zero-dimensional variety.*

As Assumption 1 might fail in some instances (e.g. in the small e regime of the TK attack), it is crucial to verify its validity experimentally.

3   Our Two-Step Partial Key Exposure Attack

Let (N, e) be an RSA public key, where $N = pq$ and $e = N^\alpha$. As usual in practice, we assume that p and q have the same bit-size, which lets us bound $p, q = \Theta(N^{1/2})$. Let d_p and d_q be the corresponding CRT-exponents. We assume that d_p and d_q are full-size, i.e., $d_p, d_q = \Theta(N^{1/2})$. We write

$$d_p = d_p^{(M)} 2^i + d_p^{(L)},$$
$$d_q = d_q^{(M)} 2^i + d_q^{(L)},$$

for MSBs $d_p^{(M)}, d_q^{(M)}$ and LSBs $d_p^{(L)}, d_q^{(L)}$. We call knowledge of the bits of $d_p^{(M)}, d_q^{(M)}$ the *MSB case*, where knowledge of $d_p^{(L)}, d_q^{(L)}$ is called the *LSB case*.

Let us first state our main result that already explains the *bump shape* of our attack region in Fig. 1.

Theorem 1. *Let N be sufficiently large. Suppose we are given the public key (N, e) with $e = N^\alpha$ and additionally the MSBs $d_p^{(M)}, d_q^{(M)}$ or the LSBs $d_p^{(M)}, d_q^{(M)}$ of the CRT-exponents d_p, d_q. If the unknown parts of d_p and d_q are upper bounded by N^δ, where*

$$\delta < \min\left\{\frac{1}{4} + \alpha, \frac{1}{2} - 2\alpha\right\},$$

then we can factor N in polynomial time (under Assumption 1 for the LSB case).

Proof. The CRT-exponents d_p, d_q fulfill the RSA key equations

$$ed_p = k(p-1) + 1, \tag{3}$$
$$ed_q = \ell(q-1) + 1. \tag{4}$$

We follow a two-step strategy for factoring N.

Step 1. We show that we can compute the two parameters k and ℓ both in the MSB case (Sect. 3.1) and the LSB case (Sect. 3.2) if the unknown parts of the CRT-exponents are upper bounded by $N^{\frac{1}{2}-2\alpha}$. The MSB algorithm is completely elementary, whereas the LSB algorithm is based on Coppersmith's (heuristic) method for multivariate polynomials, and therefore requires Assumption 1.

Step 2. Given k and MSBs/LBSs of d_p with unknown part bounded by $N^{\frac{1}{4}+\alpha}$, we then provide in Sect. 3.3 a completely rigorous factoring algorithm based on a novel result on *approximate divisor multiples* (Theorem 3) that we prove using Coppersmith's method for univariate modular polynomials.   □

3.1   Step 1: Computing (k, ℓ), Given MSBs

We first show how to compute (k, ℓ), given the MSBs of the CRT-exponents. For this scenario, our algorithm is particularly simple and efficient, as it uses only elementary arithmetic.

Lemma 1 ((k, ℓ) from MSB). *Let N be sufficiently large. Suppose we are given the public key (N, e) with $e = N^\alpha$ and the MSBs $d_p^{(M)}, d_q^{(M)}$. If the unknown LSBs are upper bounded by $d_p^{(L)}, d_q^{(L)} \leq N^\delta$, where*

$$\delta < \frac{1}{2} - 2\alpha,$$

then we can compute (k, ℓ) in time $\mathcal{O}(\log^2 N)$.

Proof. We rewrite Eqs. (3) and (4) as

$$kp = k - 1 + ed_p,$$
$$\ell q = \ell - 1 + ed_q.$$

Multiplying kp with ℓq, we obtain the identity

$$k\ell N = (k-1)(\ell-1) + ed_p(\ell-1) + ed_q(k-1) + e^2 d_p d_q. \tag{5}$$

Let

$$\widetilde{A} := \frac{2^{2i} e^2 d_p^{(M)} d_q^{(M)}}{N}.$$

Since we are given the MSBs $d_p^{(M)} d_q^{(M)}$, $\widetilde{A}$ can efficiently be computed. Using $\delta < \frac{1}{2} - 2\alpha$, we now show $\lceil \widetilde{A} \rceil = k\ell - o(1)$. Hence, for sufficiently large N (which already holds for standard RSA moduli) we have $\lceil \widetilde{A} \rceil = k\ell$.

Let us rewrite (5) as

$$\begin{aligned}
k\ell N - \widetilde{A}N =&(k-1)(\ell-1) + ed_p(\ell-1) + ed_q(k-1) + e^2 d_p d_q - \widetilde{A}N \\
=&(k-1)(\ell-1) + ed_p(\ell-1) + ed_q(k-1) \\
&+ 2^i e^2 (d_p^{(M)} d_q^{(L)} + d_p^{(L)} d_q^{(M)}) + e^2 d_p^{(L)} d_q^{(L)}.
\end{aligned}$$

Using

$$d_p, d_q = \Theta(N^{1/2}), \quad d_p^{(M)}, d_q^{(M)} = \Theta(N^{1/2-\delta}), \quad 2^i = \Theta(N^\delta),$$

and

$$\begin{aligned}
k &= \frac{ed_p - 1}{p - 1} < \frac{ed_p}{p - 1} < \frac{e(p-1)}{p-1} = e, \\
\ell &= \frac{ed_q - 1}{q - 1} < \frac{ed_q}{q - 1} < \frac{e(q-1)}{q-1} = e,
\end{aligned} \tag{6}$$

we obtain

$$\begin{aligned}
k\ell N - \widetilde{A}N &= \mathcal{O}(N^{2\alpha}) + \mathcal{O}(N^{2\alpha+1/2}) + \mathcal{O}(N^{2\alpha+1/2+\delta}) + \mathcal{O}(N^{2\alpha+2\delta}) \\
&= \mathcal{O}(N^{2\alpha+1/2+\delta}),
\end{aligned}$$

and therefore

$$k\ell - \widetilde{A} = \mathcal{O}(N^{\delta+2\alpha-1/2}) = o(1).$$

Thus, given the MSBs, we can compute $k\ell$ in time $\mathcal{O}(\log^2 N)$.

It remains to show that knowledge of $k\ell$ yields k and ℓ. Using Eq. (5) we have

$$k + \ell = 1 - k\ell(N - 1) \bmod e, \tag{7}$$

where the right-hand side is known. By (6) we know that the left-hand side satisfies $0 \le k + \ell < 2e$. Thus, either $0 \le k + \ell < e$ or $0 \le k + \ell - e < e$.

Assume for a moment that $0 \leq k + \ell < e$. Then Eq. (7) holds over the integers. Thus, k, ℓ are the two solutions of the quadratic polynomial equation

$$0 = (x - k)(x - \ell) = x^2 - (k + \ell)x + k\ell = x^2 + (1 - k\ell(N - 1))x + k\ell.$$

We check whether the product of the solutions equals $k\ell$. If it does, we have recovered k and ℓ. If not, we are in the case $0 \leq k + \ell - e < e$. We then recover k and ℓ as the integer solutions of

$$0 = x^2 + (1 - k\ell(N - 1) + e)x + k\ell.$$

This can again be done in time $\mathcal{O}(\log^2 N)$.   □

3.2   Step 1: Computing (k, ℓ), Given LSBs

In Sect. 3.1, the computation of k, ℓ from known MSBs of d_p, d_q within the bound of Lemma 1 was elementary, efficient and provable. Although we achieve in the LSB case the same bound as in Lemma 1, the approach is quite different. We use Coppersmith's lattice-based method in combination with Assumption 1, which makes the recovery of k, ℓ heuristic and a bit less efficient, but we still come close to the bound in a matter of seconds, see Sect. 5.

Lemma 2 $((k, \ell)$ from LSB). *Let N be sufficiently large. Suppose we are given the public key (N, e) with $e = N^\alpha$ and the LSBs $d_p^{(L)}, d_q^{(L)}$. If the unknown MSBs are upper bounded by $d_p^{(M)}, d_q^{(M)} \leq N^\delta$, where*

$$\delta < \frac{1}{2} - 2\alpha,$$

then we can compute (k, ℓ) in polynomial time (under Assumption 1).

Proof. Let us recall Eq. (5):

$$k\ell N = (k - 1)(\ell - 1) + ed_p(\ell - 1) + ed_q(k - 1) + e^2 d_p d_q.$$

Plugging in $d_p = d_p^{(M)} 2^i + d_p^{(L)}$ and $d_q = d_q^{(M)} 2^i + d_q^{(L)}$ we obtain

$$k\ell N \equiv (k - 1)(\ell - 1) + ed_p^{(L)}(\ell - 1) + ed_q^{(L)}(k - 1) + e^2 d_p^{(L)} d_q^{(L)} \quad \text{mod } 2^i e,$$

and equivalently

$$k\ell(N - 1) - k(ed_q^{(L)} - 1) - \ell(ed_p^{(L)} - 1) + A \equiv 0 \quad \text{mod } 2^i e, \quad (8)$$

where

$$A := -e^2 d_p^{(L)} d_q^{(L)} + ed_p^{(L)} + ed_q^{(L)} - 1.$$

We derive from (8) a polynomial

$$f(x, y) := (N - 1)xy - (ed_q^{(L)} - 1)x - (ed_p^{(L)} - 1)y + A,$$

which has the root (k, ℓ) modulo $2^i e$. Notice that all coefficients of f are known.

Now we apply Coppersmith's method to f to compute k and ℓ. To this end, we need to transform f into a polynomial g, which also has the root (k, ℓ) modulo $2^i e$, but additionally has at least one *small* coefficient (in the sense that it does not grow as function of N). This ensures that for sufficiently large N the coefficients of the polynomial do not affect the enabling condition from Eq. (2) in Coppersmith's method.

It is not hard to see that $\gcd(ed_q^{(L)} - 1, 2^i e) = \gcd(ed_q^{(L)} - 1, 2^i)$ is (for randomly chosen RSA keys) a small power of 2. Hence, we may define g by replacing the coefficient of x in f by $\gcd(ed_q^{(L)} - 1, 2^i)$ and multiplying all other coefficients by the multiplicative inverse of

$$\frac{ed_q^{(L)} - 1}{\gcd(ed_q^{(L)} - 1, 2^i)}$$

modulo $2^i e$.

As shown in (6), both k and ℓ can be upper bounded by $k, \ell < e$. It is known (see, for instance, the *generalized rectangle* construction in [12, Appendix A]) that under Assumption 1 we can compute *all* roots (x_0, y_0) of g modulo $2^i e$, that satisfy $|x_0|, |y_0| < e$, in polynomial time, provided that

$$e^2 < (2^i e)^{\frac{2}{3}}. \tag{9}$$

Plugging in $e = N^\alpha$ and $2^i = \Theta(N^{1/2-\delta})$, we find that (9) is asymptotically equivalent to

$$\delta < \frac{1}{2} - 2\alpha,$$

which concludes the proof. $\square$

3.3   Step 2: Factoring N, Given k

In Sects. 3.1 and 3.2 we described Step 1, the computation of k, ℓ from either known MSBs or LSBs of the CRT-exponents. Step 2 now finishes the factorization of N in polynomial time.

To this end, we recall a result of Howgrave-Graham [11] for computing small roots of linear polynomials modulo unknown divisors, which can be seen as a generalization of Coppersmith's *factoring with a hint* result.

Theorem 2 (Howgrave-Graham).   *Suppose we are given a polynomial $f(x) := x + a$ and an integer $N \in \mathbb{N}$ of unknown factorization. Let $p \geq N^\beta \in \mathbb{N}, \beta \in [0, 1]$ be an unknown divisor of N. In time polynomial in $\log N$ and $\log a$, we can compute all integers x_0, satisfying*

$$f(x_0) \equiv 0 \mod p \quad and \quad |x_0| \leq N^{\beta^2}.$$

Factoring with a hint follows when we set $\beta = \frac{1}{2}$ and the coefficient a to either the LSBs or MSBs of p. Then we can efficiently recover the unknown part of size $N^{\frac{1}{4}}$, i.e., half the of p's bits.

We prove the following generalization of Theorem 2.

Theorem 3. *Suppose we are given a polynomial $f(x) := x + a$ and integers $k, N \in \mathbb{N}$, where $k = N^\mu$ for some $\mu \geq 0$. Let $p \geq N^\beta \in \mathbb{N}, \beta \in [0,1]$ be an unknown divisor of N. In time polynomial in $\log N$, $\log k$ and $\log a$, we can compute all integers x_0, satisfying*

$$f(x_0) \equiv 0 \mod kp \quad and \quad |x_0| \leq N^{\beta^2 + \mu}.$$

Remark 1. Blömer, May [3, Theorem 13] already showed a similar generalization with $|x_0| \leq N^{\frac{(\beta+\mu)^2}{1+\mu}}$. However, their bound is for $\mu > 0$ strictly weaker than ours, since

$$\frac{(\beta + \mu)^2}{1 + \mu} = \beta^2 + \mu - \mu \cdot \frac{(\beta - 1)^2}{1 + \mu} < \beta^2 + \mu.$$

Proof. For integers $m, t \in \mathbb{N}$ and $i = 0, \ldots, m$, we define a collection of polynomials

$$g_i(x) := f^i(x) k^{m-i} N^{\max\{0, t-i\}}.$$

Notice that for every root $x_0 \in \mathbb{Z}$ of $f(x)$ modulo kp we have for any i that

$$g_i(x_0) \equiv 0 \mod k^m p^t.$$

Let us set the bound for the size of the root x_0 as

$$X = N^{\beta^2 + \mu}. \tag{10}$$

We construct an $(m + 1) \times (m + 1)$ lattice basis matrix $\mathbf{B}$, where the i-th row corresponds to the coefficient vector of $g_i(xX)$ and the i-th row corresponds to the monomial x^i, see Fig. 2 for an example.

$$
\begin{array}{c}
\\
g_0 \\
g_1 \\
g_2 \\
g_3 \\
g_4
\end{array}
\begin{array}{cccccc}
1 & x & x^2 & x^3 & x^4 \\
\left(\begin{array}{ccccc}
k^4 N^2 & & & & \\
ak^3 N & k^3 NX & & & \\
a^2 k^2 & 2ak^2 X & k^2 X^2 & & \\
a^3 k & 3a^2 kX & 3akX^2 & kX^3 & \\
a^4 & 4a^3 X & 6a^2 X^2 & 4aX^3 & X^4
\end{array}\right)
\end{array}
$$

Fig. 2. Example of our basis matrix $\mathbf{B}$ with $m = 4, t = 2$. Empty entries are zero.

Using Eq. (2), we can compute a univariate polynomial $h(x)$ with all the roots $x_0, |x_0| \leq X$ over the integers, provided that the following enabling condition holds

$$|\det \mathbf{B}| \leq \left(k^m p^t\right)^{m+1}. \tag{11}$$

From $h(x)$ we derive the roots in polynomial time using standard root finding algorithms. (For instance, as noted by Coppersmith [7], the Sturm sequence will suffice, see [14].)

It is not hard to see that

$$\det \mathbf{B} = (kX)^{\frac{m^2+m}{2}} N^{\frac{t^2+t}{2}}.$$

We plug $\det \mathbf{B}$ into (11), set $t = \beta m$, and take the m^2-th root on both sides. Ignoring low order terms, the condition becomes

$$(kX)^{\frac{1}{2}} N^{\frac{\beta^2}{2}} \leq p^\beta k.$$

Solving for X yields

$$X \leq p^{2\beta} N^{-\beta^2} k.$$

Using $p \geq N^\beta$, we obtain the more restrictive condition $X \leq N^{\beta^2+\mu}$, which is satisfied by our definition of X in Eq. (10). $\qquad \square$

Theorem 3 shows that in the case of *approximate divisor multiples* for some known multiple k the size of the efficiently recoverable root grows linearly in k. This might seem quite surprising at first sight, but let us also look at the *known part a*. In Theorem 2 the coefficient a has to be of size at least $N^{\beta-\beta^2}$, whereas in Theorem 3 it has to be of size at least $N^{(\beta+\gamma)-(\beta^2+\gamma)} = N^{\beta-\beta^2}$, i.e., the amount of required known bits stays constant for every k.

Since in Partial Key Exposure attacks for CRT-exponents we get an approximation of kp for some known k (by Step 1), we profit from the *approximate divisor multiple* setting. This is shown in the following Lemma 3, that is a direct application of Theorem 3, and completes the proof of our main Theorem 1.

Lemma 3. *Let N be sufficiently large. Suppose we are given the public key (N, e) with $e = N^\alpha$, the value k and additionally the MSBs $d_p^{(M)}, d_q^{(M)}$ or the LSBs $d_p^{(L)}, d_q^{(L)}$. If the unknown parts of d_p and d_q are upper bounded by N^δ, where*

$$\delta < \frac{1}{4} + \alpha,$$

then we can factor N in polynomial time.

Proof. Let us first prove the MSB case. Using

$$e d_p = 1 + k(p-1) \quad \text{and} \quad d_p = d_p^{(L)} + d_p^{(M)} 2^i$$

with unknown $d_p^{(L)}$, we obtain

$$ed_p^{(L)} + ed_p^{(M)}2^i + k - 1 = kp.$$

This equation yields a polynomial $f_{\mathsf{MSB}}(x) = x + a \bmod kp$ with known coefficient

$$a = \left(ed_p^{(M)}2^i + k - 1\right) \cdot \left(e^{-1} \bmod kN\right) \text{ and root } x_0 = d_p^{(L)}.$$

Using $k = \Theta(N^\alpha)$ and $p = \Theta(N^{1/2})$, we conclude from Theorem 3 that we can compute $d_p^{(L)}$ in polynomial time, provided that

$$d_p^{(L)} < N^{\frac{1}{4}+\alpha},$$

which is satisfied, since $d_p^{(L)} \leq N^\delta$. Eventually, the prime factorization follows from $d_p^{(L)}$ via $\gcd(f_{\mathsf{MSB}}(d_p^{(L)}), N) = p$.

The LSB case follow completely analogous using the polynomial

$$f_{\mathsf{LSB}}(x) = x + \left(ed_p^{(L)} + k - 1\right) \cdot \left((2^i e)^{-1} \bmod kN\right).$$

$\square$

Notice that for $e \geq N^{\frac{1}{4}}$, the unknown part in Lemma 3 of d_p, d_q can be as large as $N^{\frac{1}{4}+\alpha} \geq N^{\frac{1}{2}}$, i.e., we can factor without knowing any bits of d_p, d_q. Thus, our two-step approach cannot work for $e \geq N^{\frac{1}{4}}$, unless factoring is easy, coinciding with Galbraith, Heneghan, McKee [10, Theorem 1].

Corollary 1. *For $e \geq N^{\frac{1}{4}}$ computation of k, ℓ is as hard as factoring.*

3.4   On the Limits of Improving Our Attack

Our two step approach first computes k and ℓ, but the second step only requires k to factor N. One may ask whether the computation of k alone in Step 1 leads to an improved Partial Key Exposure attack. The following lemma answers this in the negative, since the computation of k, ℓ is no more difficult than the computation of k alone.

Lemma 4. *Suppose there exists a polynomial time algorithm, which on input (N, e) outputs k. Then there also exists a polynomial time algorithm, which on input (N, e) outputs (k, ℓ).*

Proof. We rewrite the congruence

$$k(p - 1) + 1 \equiv 0 \quad \bmod e, \tag{12}$$

as

$$p \equiv (k - 1)k^{-1} \quad \bmod e. \tag{13}$$

Notice that from (12) it follows that k is indeed invertible modulo e, as its inverse is $(1 - p)$.

Arguing analogously for ℓ, it follows that the inverse of ℓ modulo e is $(1 - q)$. Combining this observation with (13) and assuming that p is w.l.o.g. invertible modulo e yields

$$\ell \equiv \left(1 - q\right)^{-1} \equiv \left(1 - Np^{-1}\right)^{-1} \equiv \left(1 - Nk(k-1)^{-1}\right)^{-1} \quad \mod e.$$

Hence ℓ can be efficiently computed from (N, e, k). □

4 Limits of the Takayasu-Kunihiro PKE for Small e

In [19, Theorem 7] Takayasu and Kunihiro claim the following result for CRT-exponents $d_p, d_q \approx N^{1/2}$.

Claim 1 (Takayasu, Kunihiro). *Let N be sufficiently large. Suppose we are given the public key (N, e) with $e = N^\alpha$ and additionally the MSBs $d_p^{(M)}, d_q^{(M)}$ or the LSBs $d_p^{(M)}, d_q^{(M)}$ of the CRT-exponents d_p, d_q. If the unknown parts of d_p and d_q are upper bounded by N^δ, where*

1. $\delta < \frac{(12-12\alpha)\tau^2 + (12-16\alpha)\tau + 3 - 4\alpha}{24\tau^3 + 54\tau^2 + 40\tau + 10}$, $\frac{7}{16} < \alpha < 1, \tau > 0$ or,
2. $\delta < \frac{3-4\alpha}{10}$, $0 < \alpha \le \frac{3}{4}$ or,
3. $\delta < \frac{-24\alpha\tau^3 + (12-30\alpha)\tau^2 + (12-16\alpha)\tau + 3 - 4\alpha}{36\tau^2 + 40\tau + 10}$, $0 < \alpha < \frac{1}{13}, \tau > 0$,

then we can factor N in polynomial time.

When numerically optimizing the value of τ, we obtain the results shown in Table 1. We see that for α approaching 0, the value of δ converges to $\frac{1}{3}$. Hence, for constant e, the TK attack claims to succeed for unknown bits of size $N^{1/3}$, or equivalently for known bits of size $N^{1/2-1/3} = N^{1/6}$, i.e., only a third of the bits of the CRT-exponents $d_p, d_q \approx N^{1/2}$ have to be known.

Table 1. Values of α and δ, for which the TK attack claims to succeed.

α	10^{-8}	10^{-4}	0.05	0.10	0.15	0.20	0.25	0.30	0.35	0.40	0.45
δ	0.333	0.330	0.280	0.260	0.240	0.220	0.200	0.180	0.160	0.140	0.120

α	0.50	0.55	0.60	0.65	0.70	0.75	0.80	0.85	0.90	0.95	1.00
δ	0.100	0.082	0.065	0.049	0.036	0.025	0.016	0.009	0.004	0.001	0.000

This is caused by the fact that for $\alpha \to 0$ the third condition of Claim 1 converges to

$$\delta < \frac{12\tau^2 + 12\tau + 3}{36\tau^2 + 40\tau + 10},$$

whose right-hand side gets arbitrarily close to $\frac{12}{36} = \frac{1}{3}$, when choosing τ sufficiently large.

We show in the following that any PKE attack, that succeeds in the very small e regime with only a third of the CRT-exponent bits, leads to an improvement of *factoring with a hint* with also only a third of the prime factor bits. This already casts severe doubts on the validity of the asymptotics of the Takayasu-Kunihiro attack in the small e regime. In the subsequent Sect. 4.1, we give further arguments, why the TK attack fails for $e \leq N^{1/8}$.

We confirm this observation experimentally in Sect. 5. TK fails in the $e \leq N^{1/8}$ regime, but works perfectly for $e > N^{1/8}$.

Theorem 4. *Suppose there exists a polynomial time algorithm* A, *which on input* $(N, e, \widetilde{d_p}, \widetilde{d_q})$ *with* $e = \mathcal{O}(\log N)$ *outputs the prime factors of* N, *where* $\widetilde{d_p}, \widetilde{d_q}$ *are μ-fractions of the MSBs or LSBs of the CRT-exponents for some* $\mu \in [0, 1]$. *Then there also exists a polynomial time algorithm* B, *which on input* $(N, \widetilde{p})$ *outputs the prime factors of* N, *where* $\widetilde{p}$ *is a μ-fraction of the MSBs or LSBs of* p.

Proof. Let $p = p^{(M)}2^i + p^{(L)}$ for MSBs $p^{(M)}$ and LSBs $p^{(L)}$. We first prove the result for the case $\widetilde{p} = p^{(L)}$.

We define B as follows. Given $(N, \widetilde{p})$, we iterate over all odd candidate public exponents $e = 3, 5, 7, \ldots$ and for every e we test all tuples $(k, \ell) \in \{1, 2, \ldots e-1\}^2$. For every (e, k, ℓ), we compute

$$\widetilde{d_p} := (k(\widetilde{p} - 1) + 1)e^{-1} \mod 2^i,$$
$$\widetilde{d_q} := (\ell(N\widetilde{p}^{-1} - 1) + 1)e^{-1} \mod 2^i,$$

and then run A on input $(N, e, \widetilde{d_p}, \widetilde{d_q})$. Notice, if (N, e) is a valid RSA public key and furthermore k and ℓ are the corresponding parameters in the sense of the CRT key equations (3) and (4), then from (3) and (4) it easily follows that $\widetilde{d_p}$ and $\widetilde{d_q}$ are indeed μ-fractions of the LSBs of the CRT-exponents. Hence, whenever (N, e) is valid, A outputs the prime factors of N and we terminate B.

As any $n \in \mathbb{N}$ has at most $\log_2 n$ prime factors, it follows that after $\mathcal{O}(\log \phi(N)) = \mathcal{O}(\log N)$ iterations, we choose an e coprime to $\phi(N)$. This implies that (N, e) is a valid public key. Thus, B terminates after at most $\mathcal{O}(\log N)$ choices of e, from which we conclude that B calls A at most $\mathcal{O}(\log^3 N)$ times.

It remains to prove the MSB case, i.e., $\widetilde{p} = p^{(M)}$. We first note that given $\widetilde{p}$, we immediately obtain from the MSBs of $\frac{N}{\widetilde{p}2^i}$ a μ-fraction of the MSBs of the other prime factor q. Let us denote these MSBs by $\widetilde{q}$.

We iterate, analogous to the LSB case, over all tuples (e, k, ℓ). As before, we are guaranteed to obtain a valid tuple in time $\mathcal{O}(\log^3 N)$. For a valid tuple (e, k, ℓ), we rewrite (3) as

$$d_p^{(M)} = \frac{k(\widetilde{p}2^i - 1) + 1}{2^i e} + \frac{kp^{(L)} - ed_p^{(L)}}{2^i e},$$

where we may bound

$$\left| \frac{kp^{(L)} - ed_p^{(L)}}{2^i e} \right| \leq \frac{kp^{(L)}}{2^i e} + \frac{ed_p^{(L)}}{2^i e} < \frac{2^i e}{2^i e} + \frac{2^i e}{2^i e} = 2.$$

It follows that given $\widetilde{p}$ and a valid tuple (e, k, ℓ), we compute the MSBs of the corresponding d_p as

$$\widetilde{d}_p = \left\lceil \frac{k(\widetilde{p}2^i - 1) + 1}{2^i e} \right\rceil \pm \epsilon_p,$$

where $\epsilon_p \in \{0, 1, 2\}$. Analogous, we compute the MSBs of d_q as

$$\widetilde{d}_q = \left\lceil \frac{\ell(\widetilde{q}2^i - 1) + 1}{2^i e} \right\rceil \pm \epsilon_q,$$

where $\epsilon_q \in \{0, 1, 2\}$.

Analogous to the LSB case we now simply run for all candidates algorithm A on input $(N, e, \widetilde{d}_p, \widetilde{d}_q)$.   □

4.1 Why TK Fails for $e \leq N^{1/8}$

In the MSB case, the TK attack uses Coppersmith's method to compute the integer root $(d_p^{(L)}, d_q^{(L)}, k, \ell)$ of the polynomial

$$\begin{aligned}
f_{\mathsf{MSB}}(x_1, x_2, y_1, y_2) := {}& e^2 x_1 x_2 + (e^2 d_q^{(M)} 2^i - e) x_1 + (e^2 d_p^{(M)} 2^i - e) x_2 \\
& + e x_1 y_2 + e x_2 y_1 + (e d_q^{(M)} 2^i - 1) y_1 + (e d_p^{(M)} 2^i - 1) y_2 \\
& - (N - 1) y_1 y_2 + c_{\mathsf{MSB}},
\end{aligned}$$

where $c_{\mathsf{MSB}} \in \mathbb{Z}$ is some constant. Similarly, in the LSB case, the TK attack uses Coppersmith's method to compute the integer root $(d_p^{(M)}, d_q^{(M)}, k, \ell)$ of the polynomial

$$\begin{aligned}
f_{\mathsf{LSB}}(x_1, x_2, y_1, y_2) := {}& e^2 2^{2i} x_1 x_2 + (e^2 d_q^{(L)} - e) 2^i x_1 + (e^2 d_p^{(L)} - e) 2^i x_2 \\
& + e 2^i x_1 y_2 + e 2^i x_2 y_1 + (e d_q^{(L)} - 1) y_1 + (e d_p^{(L)} - 1) y_2 \\
& - (N - 1) y_1 y_2 + c_{\mathsf{LSB}},
\end{aligned}$$

where $c_{\mathsf{LSB}} \in \mathbb{Z}$ is some constant.

From Fig. 1, we see that our attacks for recovering k and ℓ from Lemmas 1 and 2 require for $e \leq N^{1/8}$ less known bits than the TK attack. Thus, in the very small e regime, it does not seem useful to treat k and ℓ as unknowns in the TK attack. Instead, we should use in a first step our attacks from Lemmas 1 and 2 to obtain k and ℓ and after that plug them into $f_{\mathsf{MSB}}(x_1, x_2, y_1, y_2)$ and $f_{\mathsf{LSB}}(x_1, x_2, y_1, y_2)$ to eliminate the variables y_1 and y_2. By that, we obtain two new polynomials

$$f_{\mathsf{MSB}}(x_1, x_2) := e^2 x_1 x_2 + (e^2 d_q^{(M)} 2^i - e)x_1 + (e^2 d_p^{(M)} 2^i - e)x_2$$
$$+ e\ell x_1 + ek x_2 + c_{\mathsf{MSB}}^*,$$
$$f_{\mathsf{LSB}}(x_1, x_2) := e^2 2^{2i} x_1 x_2 + (e^2 d_q^{(L)} - e)2^i x_1 + (e^2 d_p^{(L)} - e)2^i x_2$$
$$+ e2^i \ell x_1 + e2^i k x_2 + c_{\mathsf{LSB}}^*,$$

for some constants $c_{\mathsf{MSB}}^*, c_{\mathsf{LSB}}^* \in \mathbb{Z}$. Intuitively, this should only improve the TK attack, because then we have to recover only two unknowns instead of four.

Unfortunately, the bi-variate polynomials $f_{\mathsf{MSB}}(x_1, x_2)$ and $f_{\mathsf{LSB}}(x_1, x_2)$ are (unlike their four-variate counterparts) not irreducible over the integers. Indeed, all coefficients of $f_{\mathsf{MSB}}(x_1, x_2)$ are divisble by e and all coefficients of $f_{\mathsf{LSB}}(x_1, x_2)$ are divisible by $e2^i$. Hence, we can not directly apply Coppersmith's method here, as Coppersmith's method only works with irreducible polynomials. Instead, we first have to divide $f_{\mathsf{MSB}}(x_1, x_2)$ by e and $f_{\mathsf{LSB}}(x_1, x_2)$ by $e2^i$.

After that, we can apply the following standard result by Coppersmith [6].

Theorem 5 (Coppersmith). *Let $f(x,y) \in \mathbb{Z}[x,y]$ be an irreducible polynomial of degree one in each variable separately. Let $X, Y \in \mathbb{N}$ and let $W \in \mathbb{N}$ denote the largest coefficient of $f(Xx, Yy)$. Given f, X and Y, we can compute all integer pairs $(x_0, y_0) \in \mathbb{Z}$ satisfying*

$$f(x_0, y_0) = 0 \quad and \quad |x_0| \leq X, |y_0| \leq Y$$

in time polynomial in $\log W$, provided that

$$XY < W^{2/3}.$$

A standard computation shows that Theorem 5 yields for both $f_{\mathsf{MSB}}(x_1, x_2)/e$ and $f_{\mathsf{LSB}}(x_1, x_2)/(e2^i)$ the bound

$$\delta < \frac{1}{4} + \frac{\alpha}{2}.$$

Notice that this bound is for $\alpha \to 0$ inferior to the claimed TK result (Claim 1), and for every $\alpha > 0$ inferior to our result from Lemma 3.

5   Experimental Results

Since it is crucial to verify the validity of Assumption 1, we present in this section some experimental data for our PKE. Additionally, we present experimental evidence that the Takayasu-Kunihiro PKE [19] fails in the small e regime.

We implemented our experiments in SAGE 9.3 using Linux Ubuntu 18.04.4 with an Intel® Core™ i7-7920HQ CPU 3.67 GHz. Our source codes are publicly available on GitHub.[1]

---

[1]   https://github.com/juliannowakowski/crtrsa-small-e-pke.

Table 2. Experimental results for Step 1 of our PKE: Recovering k and ℓ, given the LSBs of the CRT-exponents for 1024 bit N.

Bit-size of e	#Unknown MSBs	Lattice Dim.	LLL time
16	256	9	< 1s
32	275	9	< 1s
48	290	9	< 1s
64	302	9	< 1s
85	315	64	5s
96	294	64	6s
112	258	64	6s
128	226	64	7s
144	186	64	9s
160	155	64	12s
176	118	64	14s
192	82	64	16s

Table 3. Experimental results for Step 2 of our PKE: Factoring N, given k and the LSBs of the CRT-exponents for 1024 bit N.

Bit-size of e	#Unknown MSBs	Lattice Dim.	LLL time
16	256	41	34s
32	275	41	28s
48	290	41	39s
64	302	41	49s
85	315	15	< 1s
96	294	7	< 1s
112	258	7	< 1s
128	226	7	< 1s
144	186	5	< 1s
160	155	5	< 1s
176	118	5	< 1s
192	82	5	< 1s

Our PKE. While Step 2 of our PKE is in both the MSB and LSB case rigorous, Step 1 is in the case LSB case heuristic. For every instance in Table 2 we ran 100 experiments. Assumption 1 was valid in every run, i.e., we could always extract the root (k, ℓ) using a Gröbner basis in a matter of seconds.

For the sake of completeness, we give in Table 3 also some experimental data for Step 2 of our attack. As in Step 1, our PKE requires here only small lattice dimensions to succeed, especially for e larger than 80 bit – making our PKE very efficient. Notice that our attack is best, in the sense of allowing a maximum of unknown bits, for 85-bit e which is a $\frac{1}{12}$-fraction of N's bit-size. In this case, we require $512 - 315 = 197$ known bits for lattice dimension 64, being roughly 38% of the bits of d_p, d_q.

In Fig. 3, we compare our experimental data with our asymptotic result. We see that with our small lattice dimensions we already closely reach the asymptotic bound. The reason is that we use the Coppersmith technique in the MSB case with univariate polynomials only, and in the LSB case with bivariate polynomials.

Compare e.g. in Fig. 3 with the experimental data of the TK attack that uses 4-variate polynomials, and is for similar lattice dimensions far off from the asymptotic bounds.

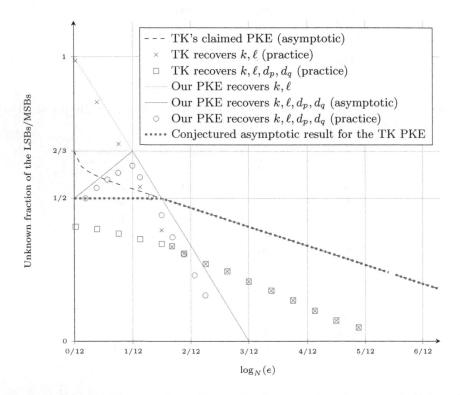

Fig. 3. Comparison between the Takayasu-Kunihiro attack and our attack (enlarged version of Fig. 1).

TK PKE [19]. In Tables 4 and 5 we show our experimental results for the TK attack, as also plotted in Fig. 3. TK succeeds to find the factorization when it recovers (k, ℓ, d_p, d_q). We only ran TK successfully, when providing (significantly) more than half of the bits of d_p, d_q, see Table 4. When providing less than half of the bits of d_p, d_q in the small e regime, the Gröbner basis reveals only k, ℓ, see Table 5. Thus, the polynomials obtained from the TK attack generate an ideal of non-zero variety, as opposed to our heuristic in Assumption 1.

The reason that TK still recovers k, ℓ is that the TK lattice contains as a sublattice our construction from Step 1 (at least in the LSB case).

Notice that Fig. 3 shows that the graph of TK's asymptotic result becomes the steeper the closer it gets to constant e. In contrast, the graph of our experimental results for the TK PKE flattens in the small e regime. We see this as evidence that the TK attack converges for small e actually to a $\frac{1}{2}$-fraction of unknown bits, instead of a $\frac{2}{3}$-fraction. Indeed, we conjecture that for sufficiently large lattice dimensions the TK PKE works until the second intersection with our result, i.e. the point $(\frac{1}{8}, \frac{1}{2})$, for a $\frac{1}{2}$-fraction of unknown bits and after that coincides with the claimed asymptotic result, see also Fig. 3.

Table 4. Experimental results for the TK attack, recovering k, ℓ, d_p, d_q, given the LSBs of the CRT-exponents for 1024 bit N.

Bit-size of e	#Unknown MSBs	Lattice Dim.	LLL time
2	204	64	19s
16	202	64	21s
32	200	64	23s
64	192	64	30s
96	182	64	39s
128	174	64	47s
144	166	64	53s
160	156	64	70s
192	138	64	141s
224	122	64	197s
256	106	64	253s
288	88	64	290s
320	72	64	320s
352	54	64	358s
384	36	64	375s
416	24	64	402s

Table 5. Experimental results for the TK attack, recovering *only* k and ℓ, given the LSBs of the CRT-exponents for 1024 bit N.

Bit-size of e	#Unknown MSBs	Lattice Dim.	LLL time
2	504	64	1s
16	479	64	5s
32	430	64	13s
64	354	64	25s
96	276	64	43s
128	198	64	65s

References

1. Aono, Y.: A new lattice construction for partial key exposure attack for RSA. In: Jarecki, S., Tsudik, G. (eds.) PKC 2009. LNCS, vol. 5443, pp. 34–53. Springer, Heidelberg (2009). https://doi.org/10.1007/978-3-642-00468-1_3
2. Blömer, J., May, A.: New partial key exposure attacks on RSA. In: Boneh, D. (ed.) CRYPTO 2003. LNCS, vol. 2729, pp. 27–43. Springer, Heidelberg (2003). https://doi.org/10.1007/978-3-540-45146-4_2
3. Blömer, J., May, A.: A tool kit for finding small roots of bivariate polynomials over the integers. In: Cramer, R. (ed.) EUROCRYPT 2005. LNCS, vol. 3494, pp. 251–267. Springer, Heidelberg (2005). https://doi.org/10.1007/11426639_15
4. Boneh, D., Durfee, G.: Cryptanalysis of RSA with private key d less than $N^{0.292}$. In: Stern, J. (ed.) EUROCRYPT 1999. LNCS, vol. 1592, pp. 1–11. Springer, Heidelberg (1999). https://doi.org/10.1007/3-540-48910-X_1
5. Boneh, D., Durfee, G., Frankel, Y.: An attack on RSA given a small fraction of the private key bits. In: Ohta, K., Pei, D. (eds.) ASIACRYPT 1998. LNCS, vol. 1514, pp. 25–34. Springer, Heidelberg (1998). https://doi.org/10.1007/3-540-49649-1_3
6. Coppersmith, D.: Finding a small root of a bivariate integer equation; factoring with high bits known. In: Maurer, U. (ed.) EUROCRYPT 1996. LNCS, vol. 1070, pp. 178–189. Springer, Heidelberg (1996). https://doi.org/10.1007/3-540-68339-9_16
7. Coppersmith, D.: Small solutions to polynomial equations, and low exponent RSA vulnerabilities. J. Cryptol. **10**(4), 233–260 (1997)
8. Coron, J., May, A.: Deterministic polynomial-time equivalence of computing the RSA secret key and factoring. J. Cryptol. **20**(1), 39–50 (2007)
9. Ernst, M., Jochemsz, E., May, A., de Weger, B.: Partial key exposure attacks on RSA up to full size exponents. In: Cramer, R. (ed.) EUROCRYPT 2005. LNCS, vol. 3494, pp. 371–386. Springer, Heidelberg (2005). https://doi.org/10.1007/11426639_22
10. Galbraith, S.D., Heneghan, C., McKee, J.F.: Tunable balancing of RSA. In: Boyd, C., González Nieto, J.M. (eds.) ACISP 2005. LNCS, vol. 3574, pp. 280–292. Springer, Heidelberg (2005). https://doi.org/10.1007/11506157_24
11. Howgrave-Graham, N.: Approximate integer common divisors. In: Silverman, J.H. (ed.) CaLC 2001. LNCS, vol. 2146, pp. 51–66. Springer, Heidelberg (2001). https://doi.org/10.1007/3-540-44670-2_6
12. Jochemsz, E., May, A.: A strategy for finding roots of multivariate polynomials with new applications in attacking RSA variants. In: Lai, X., Chen, K. (eds.) ASIACRYPT 2006. LNCS, vol. 4284, pp. 267–282. Springer, Heidelberg (2006). https://doi.org/10.1007/11935230_18
13. Kakvi, S.A., Kiltz, E., May, A.: Certifying RSA. In: Wang, X., Sako, K. (eds.) ASIACRYPT 2012. LNCS, vol. 7658, pp. 404–414. Springer, Heidelberg (2012). https://doi.org/10.1007/978-3-642-34961-4_25
14. Knuth, D.E.: The Art of Computer Programming, Volume II: Seminumerical Algorithms. Addison-Wesley, New York (1969)
15. May, A.: Computing the RSA secret key is deterministic polynomial time equivalent to factoring. In: Franklin, M. (ed.) CRYPTO 2004. LNCS, vol. 3152, pp. 213–219. Springer, Heidelberg (2004). https://doi.org/10.1007/978-3-540-28628-8_13
16. May, A.: Using LLL-reduction for solving RSA and factorization problems. In: Nguyen, P., Vallee, B. (eds.) The LLL Algorithm. Information Security and Cryptography. Springer, Berlin (2009). https://doi.org/10.1007/978-3-642-02295-1_10

17. May, A., Nowakowski, J., Sarkar, S.: Partial key exposure attack on short secret exponent CRT-RSA. In: Tibouchi, M., Wang, H. (eds.) ASIACRYPT 2021, Part I. LNCS, vol. 13090, pp. 99–129. Springer, Cham (2021). https://doi.org/10.1007/978-3-030-92062-3_4

18. Sarkar, S., Maitra, S.: Partial key exposure attack on CRT-RSA. In: Abdalla, M., Pointcheval, D., Fouque, P.-A., Vergnaud, D. (eds.) ACNS 2009. LNCS, vol. 5536, pp. 473–484. Springer, Heidelberg (2009). https://doi.org/10.1007/978-3-642-01957-9_29

19. Takayasu, A., Kunihiro, N.: Partial key exposure attacks on CRT-RSA: better cryptanalysis to full size encryption exponents. In: Malkin, T., Kolesnikov, V., Lewko, A.B., Polychronakis, M. (eds.) ACNS 2015. LNCS, vol. 9092, pp. 518–537. Springer, Cham (2015). https://doi.org/10.1007/978-3-319-28166-7_25

20. Takayasu, A., Kunihiro, N.: Partial key exposure attacks on RSA: achieving the Boneh-Durfee bound. Theor. Comput. Sci. **761**, 51–77 (2019)

21. Takayasu, A., Lu, Y., Peng, L.: Small CRT-exponent RSA revisited. J. Cryptol. **32**(4), 1337–1382 (2019)

Information-Combining Differential Fault Attacks on DEFAULT

Marcel Nageler[1]($\boxtimes$) (iD), Christoph Dobraunig[2] (iD), and Maria Eichlseder[1] (iD)

[1] Graz University of Technology, Graz, Austria
{marcel.nageler,maria.eichlseder}@iaik.tugraz.at
[2] Lamarr Security Research, Graz, Austria
christoph@dobraunig.com

Abstract. Differential fault analysis (DFA) is a very powerful attack vector for implementations of symmetric cryptography. Most counter-measures are applied at the implementation level. At ASIACRYPT 2021, Baksi et al. proposed a design strategy that aims to provide inherent cipher level resistance against DFA by using S-boxes with linear structures. They argue that in their instantiation, the block cipher DEFAULT, a DFA adversary can learn at most 64 of the 128 key bits, so the remaining brute-force complexity of 2^{64} is impractical.

In this paper, we show that a DFA adversary can combine information across rounds to recover the full key, invalidating their security claim. In particular, we observe that such ciphers exhibit large classes of equivalent keys that can be represented efficiently in normalized form using linear equations. We exploit this in combination with the specifics of DEFAULT's strong key schedule to recover the key using less than 100 faulty computation and negligible time complexity. Moreover, we show that even an idealized version of DEFAULT with independent round keys is vulnerable to our information-combining attacks based on normalized keys.

Keywords: Differential Fault Attacks (DFA) · Cryptanalysis · Linear structures · DEFAULT

1 Introduction

Differential fault analysis (DFA) [6] is one of the earliest and most powerful attack vectors on symmetric cryptography if an adversary is capable of inducing physical faults. DFA is a significant threat for cryptographic implementations as it often requires just a few precise faults to recover the key, e.g., only two or three in the case of AES [11, 15]. This underlines the importance of research on countermeasures against this attack vector.

Most of the research in countermeasures focuses on defenses applied on the implementation level that do not require any changes in the protected primitive, mode of operation, or protocol. Among the earliest proposals are duplication-based countermeasures, where the encryption algorithm is computed twice, or encryption and decryption are computed and the results are compared. If the

© International Association for Cryptologic Research 2022
O. Dunkelman and S. Dziembowski (Eds.): EUROCRYPT 2022, LNCS 13277, pp. 168–191, 2022.
https://doi.org/10.1007/978-3-031-07082-2_7

results do no match, no output is released; see Bar-El et al. [3] for an overview. A different line of research deals with infective countermeasures [10,14,17]. This class of defenses always generates an output, but aims to amplify the effect of a fault to the extent that the output becomes useless for an adversary. Other approaches aim to mitigate fault attacks on the mode of operation or on protocol level. The underlying idea of such countermeasures is to limit the observations an attacker can make per static secret to a small number, in the extreme case to one, to preclude the evaluation performed by DFA in the first place, or at least increase the burden in precision to induce the faults. Examples in this direction include fresh re-keying [13] as well as tamper- and leakage-resilient permutation-based cryptography [9]. Many modes for nonce-based authenticated encryption also provide a certain level of implicit protection [8]. Finally, some recent designs propose dedicated cryptographic primitives with features to facilitate protected implementations. Examples include the permutation FRIET [16] and the tweakable block cipher CRAFT [4], which permit efficient implementations with error detection. The most recent proposal in this category, DEFAULT, follows a more radical, fundamental approach by aiming to preclude DFA by design.

DEFAULT is a block cipher design following an interesting new design approach proposed by Baksi et al. [1] at ASIACRYPT 2021. The design approach aims to provide inherent cipher-level protection against DFA by using a fault protecting layer called DEFAULT-LAYER. This layer uses special S-boxes with *linear structures*. Because these linear structures imply that certain groups of keys are differentially equivalent, a DFA adversary cannot learn more than half of the key bits from attacking the S-box layer. The designers argue that an adversary can thus only recover 64 bits of DEFAULT's 128-bit key using DFA, and the remaining key space of 2^{64} candidates is too large to brute-force easily. For a larger security margin, the design approach can easily be scaled for a larger master key size. To provide resistance against cryptanalytic attacks, DEFAULT-LAYER is combined with a more conventional DEFAULT-CORE cipher design.

DEFAULT was originally proposed with a simple key schedule where each round key is identical to the master key [2]. The final published design [1] features a much stronger rotating key schedule. Here, consecutive round keys are derived using a 4-round function with full diffusion; after four round keys, the round keys start rotating. The purpose of this unusually strong construction is to thwart potential attacks that try to combine information learned from consecutive rounds.

Our Contributions. In this paper, we show that an attacker can indeed combine information from multiple rounds, contradicting the claim. We propose attacks on DEFAULT-LAYER for both for the original simple key schedule and the final strong, rotating key schedule, summarized in Table 1. We even show how an idealized key schedule of completely independent round keys could be attacked. Our attacks follow the same classical attacker model as the design paper: we assume the attacker can induce single bitflip faults on the state between rounds and uses only DFA-style evaluation to learn key information. In summary:

Table 1. Overview of DFA attacks on `DEFAULT-LAYER` with different key schedules (simple key schedule, strong key schedule, idealized with independent round keys) and attack strategies (IC: information-combining; NK: normalized-key). ✓: attack is applicable (✓*: but fault complexity differs) ⧗: impractical (2^{64}).

Approach	Faults	Offline time	Key Schedule			Reference
			simple	strong	ideal	
DFA	64	2^{64}	⧗	⧗		[1]
Enc-Dec IC-DFA	16	$\leq 2^{39}$	✓			Section 3.2, 6.1
Multi-round IC-DFA	16	$\leq 2^{20}$	✓			Section 3.3, 6.2
Generic NK-DFA	1728	2^{0}	✓	✓	✓	Section 4.3
Enc-Dec IC-NK-DFA	288	2^{32}	✓*	✓		Section 5.1
Multi-round IC-NK-DFA	84 ± 15	2^{0}	✓*	✓		Section 5.2, 6.3

- We first target the original simple key schedule and show why and how an attacker can *combine information* from multiple DFAs with faults in different rounds. This allows us to learn more than half the key bits, contrary to the intuition underlying the original `DEFAULT` design that the attacker seems to learn the same information in each round. We demonstrate two possible approaches: combining information from *encryption and decryption*, or combining information from *multiple consecutive rounds* (IC-DFA in Table 1).
- To tackle the strong key schedule with full diffusion between round keys, we consider an idealized version with fully independent round keys. We identify large classes of *equivalent keys* that produce the same permutation and then show how to recover a *normalized* version of the correct key, i.e., a representative of the key's equivalence class. We derive a generic attack strategy using these normalized keys that is applicable to all `DEFAULT`-style ciphers with linear structures in their S-boxes (Generic NK-DFA in Table 1).
- We show that we can exploit the specifics of the strong `DEFAULT` key schedule in combination with the normalized-key attack strategy to build an even more powerful attack and recover the `DEFAULT` key (IC-NK-DFA in Table 1).
- Finally, we propose an optimization strategy to minimize the number of required faulty computations for the proposed attacks. We experimentally verified the attacks in simulations. Our source code is available online at https://extgit.iaik.tugraz.at/castle/tool/dfa_on_default.

Outline. In Sect. 2, we provide more background on DFA and relevant countermeasures. Additionally, we recall the specification of `DEFAULT`. In Sect. 3 we show attacks on the original `DEFAULT` design with a simple key schedule. In Sect. 4, we present the concept of equivalent keys. Based on this concept, we propose attacks on the updated `DEFAULT` design with 4 rotating keys in Sect. 5. In Sect. 6, we show optimized attacks that require fewer faulted computations. Finally, we discuss potential mitigations of the attack in Sect. 7.

2   Background

In this section, we recall the preliminaries on Differential fault analysis and other fault attacks, previously proposed countermeasures, and the design strategy of DEFAULT to prevent DFA by design.

2.1   Differential Fault Analysis

For cryptanalysis, the easiest way to see differential fault analysis is to see it as a short-cut differential [5] or truncated differential [12] attack. However, in contrast to cryptanalysis, where only inputs of an algorithm are manipulated, DFA makes use of the ability to insert (bitwise or truncated) differences anywhere during the computation of a cipher.

An easy example is the following differential fault attack on AES. Assume that we have an attacker that can insert a fault during the computation of a single S-box during the penultimate round of AES. For the attack, it does not matter which S-box is faulted; it just matters that only a single one is faulted. Then, at the output of AES, we see that 4 bytes have a difference. We can guess 4 bytes of the last round key associated with these differences and partially decrypt backwards to 4 S-box outputs of the penultimate round. If we observe a difference in more than one S-box, we know that this partial key guess is definitely wrong.

A similar attack can also be carried out on bit-level. Consider an S-box S followed by a key addition in the last round of any cipher. An attacker who is able to trigger precise bitflip faults can fault a bit right before the S-box, thus inducing an *input difference* $\Delta_{in} = u \oplus u'$ between the original value u in the correct computation and the faulty u' in the faulted computation. For example, if they flip the least significant bit, $\Delta_{in} = 1$. This will cause two different output values after the S-box with an *output difference* $\Delta_{out} = v \oplus v' = S(u) \oplus S(u')$. The resulting ciphertext bits will be $c = v \oplus k$ and $c' = v' \oplus k$. As the differential behaviour of S depends on the values of u and thus of v, the attacker can now try for each key candidate k whether $S^{-1}(c \oplus k) \oplus S^{-1}(c' \oplus k) = \Delta_{in}$ and reject all key candidates that do not satisfy this. The number of remaining key candidates is given by the corresponding entry for $(\Delta_{in}, \Delta_{out})$ in the differential distribution table (DDT) of the S-box S [5]. Thus, small entries in the DDT – which are otherwise desired for strong S-boxes against differential cryptanalysis – permit the attacker to learn more information about the key bits k.

Differential fault attacks can not only be performed by observing differences of outputs. They can also be mounted by inserting differences at inputs aiming to cancel them with faults. Whether or not this cancellation is possible reveals information on the propagation of the inserted differences, which in turn reveals information about the actual values in the computation, which reveals information about the key. These attacks are known as fault-based collision attacks [7].

2.2 Design and Specification of DEFAULT

DEFAULT [1] is a 128-bit block cipher designed to inherently resist DFA by limiting the amount of information a DFA attacker can learn about the key. The designers of DEFAULT specify two building blocks: DEFAULT-LAYER to provide security against DFA and DEFAULT-CORE to provide security against classical cryptanalysis. They propose a construction, where DEFAULT-CORE is sandwiched between two applications of DEFAULT-LAYER. So, the encryption function E can be expressed by

$$E = E_{\text{DEFAULT-LAYER}} \circ E_{\text{CORE}} \circ E_{\text{DEFAULT-LAYER}} .$$

DEFAULT-LAYER uses a 128-bit state and applies a round function $\mathcal{R}$ with successive key addition 28 times. DEFAULT-CORE uses the same round function with a different S-box 24 times. Each round consists of the same steps (Fig. 1):

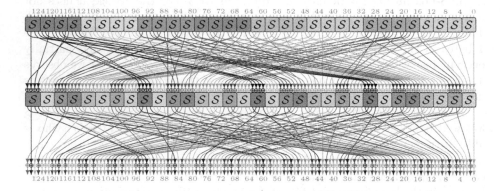

Fig. 1. Two rounds of DEFAULT-LAYER, illustrating the S-box grouping.

SubCells. For DEFAULT-LAYER, the S-box $\mathcal{S}$ from Table 2a is applied to every 4-bit nibble of the state. While DEFAULT-CORE uses the S-box $\mathcal{S}_{\text{core}}$ from Table 2b. The differential properties of the S-box $\mathcal{S}$ are what makes differential fault analysis difficult. As evident from Table 2c, the S-box contains 4 so-called linear structures: $0 \rightarrow 0$, $6 \rightarrow a$, $9 \rightarrow f$, and $f \rightarrow 5$. A linear structure $\alpha \rightarrow \beta$ is a differential transition that happens with 100% probability. In other words, $\mathcal{S}(u) = v$ implies $\mathcal{S}(u \oplus \alpha) = v \oplus \beta$. While this is an undesirable property when considering classical adversaries, it does make differential fault analysis harder. In the usual DFA setup, we obtain $c = k \oplus \mathcal{S}(u)$ and $c' = k \oplus \mathcal{S}(u \oplus \Delta_{\text{in}})$, where Δ_{in} is known but u is unknown. We solve these equations for the key k and the unknown internal value u. However, if (k, u) is a solution each non-trivial linear structure $\alpha \rightarrow \beta$ leads to an additional solution $(k \oplus \beta, u \oplus \alpha)$. Therefore, when applying this setup to DEFAULT-LAYER, the key space can only be reduced to 2^{64} candidates as 4 candidates per key nibble will always remain.

Table 2. Differential Distribution Tables (DDT) of the S-boxes used in DEFAULT.

(a) The DEFAULT-LAYER S-box $\mathcal{S}$

u	0	1	2	3	4	5	6	7	8	9	a	b	c	d	e	f
$\mathcal{S}(u)$	0	3	7	e	d	4	a	9	c	f	1	8	b	2	6	5

(b) The DEFAULT-CORE S-box $\mathcal{S}_{\text{core}}$

u	0	1	2	3	4	5	6	7	8	9	a	b	c	d	e	f
$\mathcal{S}_{\text{core}}(u)$	1	9	6	f	7	c	8	2	a	e	d	0	4	3	b	5

(c) DDT of $\mathcal{S}$.

in\out	0	1	2	3	4	5	6	7	8	9	a	b	c	d	e	f
0	16	·	·	·	·	·	·	·	·	·	·	·	·	·	·	·
1	·	·	·	8	·	·	·	·	·	8	·	·	·	·	·	·
2	·	·	·	·	·	·	·	8	·	·	·	·	·	8	·	·
3	·	·	·	·	8	·	·	·	·	·	·	·	·	·	8	·
4	·	·	·	·	·	·	·	8	·	·	·	·	·	8	·	·
5	·	·	·	·	8	·	·	·	·	·	·	·	·	·	8	·
6	·	·	·	·	·	·	·	·	·	·	16	·	·	·	·	·
7	·	·	·	8	·	·	·	·	·	8	·	·	·	·	·	·
8	·	·	·	·	·	·	8	·	·	·	·	·	8	·	·	·
9	·	·	·	·	·	·	·	·	·	·	·	·	·	·	·	16
a	·	8	·	·	·	·	·	·	·	·	·	8	·	·	·	·
b	·	·	8	·	·	·	·	·	8	·	·	·	·	·	·	·
c	·	8	·	·	·	·	·	·	·	·	·	8	·	·	·	·
d	·	·	8	·	·	·	·	·	8	·	·	·	·	·	·	·
e	·	·	·	·	·	·	8	·	·	·	·	·	8	·	·	·
f	·	·	·	·	·	16	·	·	·	·	·	·	·	·	·	·

(d) DDT of $\mathcal{S}_{\text{core}}$.

in\out	0	1	2	3	4	5	6	7	8	9	a	b	c	d	e	f
0	16	·	·	·	·	·	·	·	·	·	·	·	·	·	·	·
1	·	·	·	·	2	·	·	2	2	2	2	2	·	2	2	·
2	·	·	·	·	·	·	4	4	·	·	·	·	·	·	4	4
3	·	2	·	2	2	2	·	·	2	·	2	·	·	·	2	2
4	·	·	·	·	·	4	4	·	·	·	·	·	·	4	4	·
5	·	·	·	·	2	·	·	2	2	2	2	2	·	2	2	·
6	·	4	·	4	·	·	·	·	·	4	·	4	·	·	·	·
7	·	2	·	2	2	2	·	·	2	·	2	·	·	·	2	2
8	·	·	·	4	·	·	·	4	·	·	·	4	·	·	·	4
9	·	·	2	2	2	·	2	·	2	2	·	·	·	2	·	2
a	·	4	·	·	·	·	·	·	·	4	·	·	8	·	·	·
b	·	2	2	·	2	2	2	2	2	·	·	2	·	·	·	·
c	·	·	4	·	·	4	·	·	·	·	4	·	·	4	·	·
d	·	·	2	2	2	·	2	·	2	2	·	·	·	2	·	2
e	·	·	4	·	·	·	·	·	·	·	4	·	8	·	·	·
f	·	2	2	·	2	2	2	2	2	·	·	2	·	·	·	·

PermBits. A bit permutation is applied to the 128-bit state as depicted in Fig. 1. The design uses the same bit permutation as GIFT-128. Note that the position of a bit within a nibble is invariant for this bit permutation, i.e., if bit i is mapped to bit j we have $i \equiv j \bmod 4$. Additionally, when examining two rounds of DEFAULT, there are groups of 8 S-boxes that do not interact with other groups. Each color in Fig. 1 corresponds to one such group.

AddRoundConstants. A 6-bit constant is xored onto the state at indices 23, 19, 15, 11, 7 and 3. Additionally, the bit at index 127 is flipped.

AddRoundKey. The 128-bit state is xored with the 128-bit round key which is calculated according to the key schedule. In the first preprint version of DEFAULT a simple key schedule where all round keys equal the master key was proposed [2]. This simple key schedule is vulnerable to the information combining attacks we present in Sect. 3. To prevent these attacks, the DEFAULT designers propose a very strong key schedule in their final design. In their theoretical analysis, they first consider an idealized long-key cipher with independent round keys $K_0, K_1, \ldots, K_{27}$, corresponding to a 28×128-bit key K. For that idealized key schedule, no information combining attacks are possible since each round uses a completely independent key. For the practical instantiation, they suggest to generate 4 distinct round keys $K_0, \ldots, K_3$ where $K_0 = K$ and

$K_i = \mathcal{R}(\mathcal{R}(\mathcal{R}(\mathcal{R}(K_{i-1}))))$ for $i \in \{1, 2, 3\}$, where $\mathcal{R}$ is the unkeyed round function. The rounds are then keyed iteratively with $K_0, K_1, K_2, K_3, K_0, K_1, \ldots$. The designers argue that this definition is a reasonable approximation of the idealized version since 4 rounds provide full diffusion, and according to their analysis, combining information throughout 4 rounds is very difficult [1, Section 6.1]. The approach can be parametrized more generally with a variable number of x keys $K_0, \ldots, K_{x-1}$ generated using a variable number of rounds $\mathcal{R}^y$ for a more conservative choice at a higher performance cost. For a full specification, we refer to the design paper [1].

Note that the design does not specify a key addition before the first application of the round function. To simplify the following descriptions, we assume the initial unkeyed round is not present as it can be trivially removed.

Claims About DEFAULT. In summary, DEFAULT-LAYER is designed to limit the information available to a DFA adversary for each round and to prevent combining information across rounds. The linear structures in the S-boxes ensure that for each round at least 2^{64} key candidates remain, while the strong key schedule is designed to prevent combining information across rounds.

3   Information-Combining DFA on Simple Key Schedule

In this section, we consider a simplified version of DEFAULT with a simple key schedule, where each round key equals the master key K. Such a simple key schedule was proposed in the first preprint version of DEFAULT [2]. We argue that for this design variant, the security claim is only valid for attackers targeting only the first or last round key of the cipher. We demonstrate how an attacker can efficiently combine key information learned from multiple different rounds of the cipher, for example from encryption and decryption rounds or from multiple consecutive rounds. This observation relies crucially on the structure of the bits of key information that can be derived by attacking a single S-box.

3.1   Limited Information Learned via DFA

As DEFAULT's designers show, we can only learn a limited amount of information when inducing bit flips before the S-box. In particular, when faulting encryption, we can restrict the key at the output of the S-box to a space of $\{\beta, \beta \oplus 5, \beta \oplus a, \beta \oplus f\}$ for some β. This allows to effectively reduce the key space for the corresponding key bits from 4 bits to 2 bits, but not further, since we cannot distinguish the four values in each set based on the differential behaviour.

However, we can also target an implementation of the decryption algorithm. When faulting decryption, we can restrict the key at the output of the inverse S-box to $\{\alpha, \alpha \oplus 6, \alpha \oplus a, \alpha \oplus f\}$ for some α. Note that this set is spanned by different basis vectors: $\{6, 9\}$ for decryption compared to $\{5, a\}$ for encryption. Nevertheless, combining the knowledge from these two sets is not trivial as, during decryption, we learn information about the nibbles of the base key, while during encryption, we learn information about the nibbles of the inversely permuted key due to the bit permutation layer of the final round.

To efficiently represent the information we learn, we observe that we can express these sets of possible values in terms of linear equations. When faulting the final S-boxes during encryption, we learn the values of $k_0 \oplus k_2$ and $k_1 \oplus k_3$, where (k_0, k_1, k_2, k_3) is any nibble of the inversely permuted key. For example, when we observe the transition $2 \to 7$ in an S-box, we can restrict the output to the set of $\{0, 2, 5, 7, 8, \mathsf{a}, \mathsf{d}, \mathsf{f}\}$. This is equivalent to learning $v_0 \oplus v_2 = 0$, where (v_0, v_1, v_2, v_3) are the output bits of the S-box. Similarly, if we observe the transition $2 \to \mathsf{d}$, we learn $v_0 \oplus v_2 = 1$. With the knowledge of the ciphertext, we can then use this knowledge to learn something about the key. In Table 3, we summarize which expression over the key bits can be learned based on the input difference of the S-box or inverse S-box.

As evident from Table 3, when faulting decryption, we can learn the values of $k_1 \oplus k_2$ and $k_0 \oplus k_3$, where (k_0, k_1, k_2, k_3) is any nibble of the base key. We can complement this information by faulting encryption, which allows us to learn $k'_0 \oplus k'_2$ and $k'_1 \oplus k'_3$, where (k'_0, k'_1, k'_2, k'_3) is any nibble of inversely permuted key. When structured using linear equations, we can transform the equations about the inversely permuted key into equations about the base key by multiplying with the permutation matrix. Because the position of a bit within a nibble is invariant for the bit permutation, we can learn 3 linearly independent equations for each nibble of the key.

Table 3. Information learned when injecting a fault Δ_{in} / Δ_{out}.

Δ_{in}	Learned expression (Enc)	Δ_{out}	Learned expression (Dec)
0	1	0	1
1	$k_0 \oplus k_1 \oplus k_2 \oplus k_3$	1	$k_0 \oplus k_1 \oplus k_2 \oplus k_3$
2	$k_0 \oplus k_2$	2	$k_0 \oplus k_3$
3	$k_1 \oplus k_3$	3	$k_1 \oplus k_2$
4	$k_0 \oplus k_2$	4	$k_0 \oplus k_1 \oplus k_2 \oplus k_3$
5	$k_1 \oplus k_3$	5	1
6	1	6	$k_1 \oplus k_2$
7	$k_0 \oplus k_1 \oplus k_2 \oplus k_3$	7	$k_0 \oplus k_3$
8	$k_0 \oplus k_1 \oplus k_2 \oplus k_3$	8	$k_0 \oplus k_3$
9	1	9	$k_1 \oplus k_2$
a	$k_1 \oplus k_3$	a	1
b	$k_0 \oplus k_2$	b	$k_0 \oplus k_1 \oplus k_2 \oplus k_3$
c	$k_1 \oplus k_3$	c	$k_1 \oplus k_2$
d	$k_0 \oplus k_2$	d	$k_0 \oplus k_3$
e	$k_0 \oplus k_1 \oplus k_2 \oplus k_3$	e	$k_0 \oplus k_1 \oplus k_2 \oplus k_3$
f	1	f	1

3.2   Basic Encrypt-Decrypt Attack on Simple Key Schedule

These observations allow us to reduce the key space to 32 bits by inducing 96 single-bit-flip faults. During encryption, we induce a difference of 2 and 8 for each S-box to learn $k_0 \oplus k_2$ and $k_0 \oplus k_1 \oplus k_2 \oplus k_3$ for each nibble of the inversely permuted key. Additionally, we induce a difference of 2 before each S-box during the final round of decryption to learn $k_0 \oplus k_3$. Then, we combine the information from these faults as explained above to obtain 96 linearly independent equations about the key. Iterating over the remaining 2^{32} key candidates can be performed efficiently by computing the kernel of the matrix. We show in Sect. 6.1 that a similar reduction in key space can be achieved by using only 16 faults.

3.3   Basic Multi-round Attack on Simple Key Schedule

An even more powerful attack can be derived by performing the key-recovery over multiple rounds. The main advantage of targeting multiple rounds is the higher nonlinearity. This allows us to reduce the key space much more. For example, when attacking 3 rounds, we can reduce the key space to a set of 2^{16} keys. This also has the advantage that only a single direction needs to be faulted, i.e., either encryption or decryption. For this attack, we are targeting encryption. Thus, we learn information about the inversely permuted key, which is equivalent to learning information about the base key.

To implement this attack, we first reduce the key space to 64 bits by performing the basic differential fault attack on the final round. In the next step, we expand our analysis to two rounds and analyze each group of $4 + 4$ S-boxes, i.e., each color in Fig. 1, separately. Due to the S-box grouping, these 8 S-boxes do not interact with any other S-boxes in the first 2 rounds. An example of fault propagation is illustrated in Fig. 2b. We place a single fault before each of the 4 considered S-boxes in the penultimate round leading to 5 active S-boxes. For each fault, we have to guess 4 key nibbles in the final round. As the previous step restricts each nibble to 4 candidates, we need to try 2^8 key candidates. For the key addition right after the faulted S-box, we can pick any of the 4 candidates identified in the previous attack step as all of them lead to the same subset of the 2^8 key candidates of the final round. We analyze this property in more detail in Sect. 4. For each of these key guesses, we verify whether the difference before the penultimate round matches the induced fault. We repeat this attack for each of the 8 groups of $4 + 4$ S-boxes each, thus faulting all 32 S-boxes once. This reduces the key space to 16 potential keys per S-box group or 2^{32} keys in total.

Finally, we can reduce the overall key space to 2^{16} keys by attacking 3 rounds. As with 2 rounds, we only need to consider a subset of S-boxes at a time. Because we are dealing with 3 rounds of diffusion, a single fault influences all even- or all odd-numbered S-boxes in the final round. We place our faults in such a way that the keys we guess for the final round overlap with the keys needed for the additional two rounds. Thus, we fault each S-box S_i with $i \in \{0, 2, 8, 10, 21, 23, 29, 31\}$ twice: once by flipping the bit at index 1 and once by flipping the bit at index 2. For example, when faulting the S-box S_0, the fault

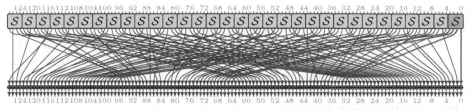

(a) 1-round propagation: learn 64 bits of information (2 per target S-box)

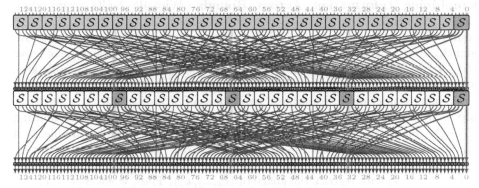

(b) 2-round propagation: learn 32 additional bits of information

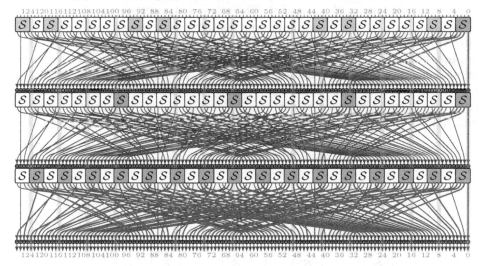

(c) 3-round propagation: learn 16 additional bits of information

Fig. 2. Target S-boxes (▨) and fault propagation example (▨) in the multi-round information-combining DFA on **DEFAULT** with simple key schedule.

propagates as shown in Fig. 2c. As before, we only iterate over the keys which are left from the previous step. Because each fault affects 4 S-box groups from the previous step, we need to try 2^{16} key candidates per fault. The 16 faults we perform for this step of the attack allow us to reliably reduce the key space for each half to 256 keys or 2^{16} keys in total.

Overall, we perform $64 + 32 + 16 = 112$ faults during this attack. The computational complexity is negligible as we store the key sets efficiently using Cartesian products: our straightforward simulated implementation finishes in a few seconds. We show in Sect. 6.2 that a similar reduction in key space can be achieved by using only 16 faults.

Combining Information Across Rounds. Why do faults propagating through multiple rounds divulge more information than only faulting a single round? Note that even after reducing the key space to 16 bits as in the above attack, we are unable to constrain any single nibble of the key to a space of fewer than 4 keys. However, we are able to heavily restrict the space of possible keys when considering larger parts of the key at once.

When considering the example of two rounds of S-boxes applied to a single bit flip as depicted in Fig. 3, we can observe exactly that effect. Based on faulting a single round, we have already reduced the space for each key nibble to 4 candidates. Now, we will use the correct ciphertext C and the faulted ciphertext C' to further reduce the key space. Concretely, we will show that if we pick one value for k_0, we can restrict the space of (k_1, k_2, k_3). Thus, when repeating this process, we can restrict the overall space of (k_0, k_1, k_2, k_3). With the knowledge of k_0, we can calculate v_0, v_0', u_0, and u_0'. Therefore, we know the most significant bit of t_0, t_0', s_0, and s_0'. When examining the faulted S-box, we can easily derive the output difference by examining the ciphertext. Due to the DDT, we know only 8 input/output pairs (r, r', s, s') are compatible with that differential transition. When combining this with the knowledge of k_0 and the most significant bit of t_0, we can halve the space of (r, r', s, s') and thus (t, t') to 4 potential pairs. In turn, this halves the space of potential values for (u_1, u_2, u_3) which translates into halving the space of (k_1, k_2, k_3).

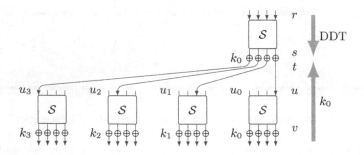

Fig. 3. Information gained by faulting two rounds of single-key DEFAULT.

For the case where a different key is XORed after the application of the S-box in the penultimate round, a very similar reasoning applies. All 4 candidates will lead to the same restricted set for (t_0, t_0') and, thus, the same restricted set for (k_1, k_2, k_3). This is because any difference between the chosen key and the actual key can be compensated by a difference in the unknown input to the S-box.

4   Exploiting Equivalence Classes of Keys

Most block cipher designs use relatively simple key schedules, such as the simple key schedule with $K_i = K$, linear key schedules where $K_i = L(K)$ for some bit permutation or linear function $L(\cdot)$, or key update functions with similarly weak diffusion properties as a single cipher round. In such designs, it is usually easy to combine partial key information from one round with partial information from the next round and thus derive the full key, as we demonstrated in Sect. 3.

Therefore, the final DEFAULT design uses a stronger key schedule, as discussed in Sect. 2.2. To reasonably approximate a long-key cipher with independent round keys, it uses 4 round keys K_0, K_1, K_2, and K_3 in a rotating fashion.

In this section, we observe that the idealized long-key cipher permits classes of equivalent keys that generate the same permutation. We characterize these classes based on the linear structures of the S-box and normalize them, i.e., define a unique representative for each class. Finally, we propose a generic attack strategy for ciphers with linear structures based on this observation. This strategy will be the basis for the concrete, optimized attacks we present in Sect. 5.

4.1   Equivalent Keys in the DEFAULT Framework

In ciphers with linear structures in its S-boxes and independent round keys, there exist large classes of keys that lead to exactly identical behavior. As a small example, consider a toy cipher consisting of one DEFAULT-LAYER S-box with a key addition before and after: $v = S(u \oplus k_0) \oplus k_1$, with $(k_0, k_1) \in \mathcal{K} \times \mathcal{K} = \mathbb{F}_2^4 \times \mathbb{F}_2^4$ (Fig. 4). In that case, we have $(k_0, k_1) \equiv (k_0 \oplus 6, k_1 \oplus \mathsf{a}) \equiv (k_0 \oplus 9, k_1 \oplus \mathsf{f}) \equiv (k_0 \oplus \mathsf{f}, k_1 \oplus 5)$. This works because a difference of, for example, 6 at the input of the S-box always leads to a difference of a at the output which is cancelled by the other key. These classes of equivalent keys allow us to define normalized keys $(\bar{k}_0, \bar{k}_1) \in \mathbb{F}_2^4 \times \mathcal{N}$, where $\mathcal{N} = \{0, 1, 2, 3\}$, thus heavily constraining the choices

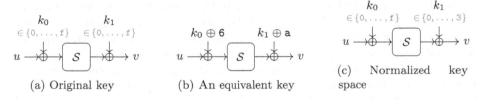

(a) Original key   (b) An equivalent key   (c) Normalized key
                                                                    space

Fig. 4. Equivalent keys for a toy cipher with the DEFAULT S-box S.

for k_1. Crucially, every possible original key maps to one such normalized key. The same logic applies if there is a linear layer before the second key addition; the only difference being that the linear layer changes the output differences of the linear structures.

These linear structures form a linear subspace that we call the linear space of the round function. We use $\mathcal{L}$ to denote the linear space of all $n - 1$ round functions. In the case of DEFAULT-LAYER, there are 32 S-boxes with 2^2 linear structures each. Thus, one round has a linear space of size 2^{64} and $|\mathcal{L}| = 2^{64(n-1)}$.

As the effect of a key is invariant under addition of elements from the linear space, we can partition the key space into equivalence classes. We assign each key k to the set of keys that can be obtained by XORing k with $l \in \mathcal{L}$. In other words, we consider the quotient space of the space of independent round keys modulo the linear space, $\mathcal{K}^n / \mathcal{L}$. Note that if we consider $n - 1$ rounds of a cipher with n independent keys, the effective key space is reduced by all $n - 1$ linear spaces of the individual rounds. Thus, in the case of DEFAULT-LAYER with 4 independent keys, there are $|\mathcal{L}| = 2^{192}$ linear structures, so we can reduce the space of $|\mathcal{K}^4| = 2^{4 \times 128} = 2^{512}$ keys to the space of $|\mathcal{K}^4 / \mathcal{L}| = 2^{128+3 \times 64} = 2^{320}$ equivalence classes.

4.2   Normalized Keys

As working with linear spaces of equivalent keys can be quite tedious, we define one representative per equivalence class. We refer to this set of class representatives as the normalized keys $\mathcal{N}^{(n)}$, where n is the number of round keys. This choice is arbitrary but does influence the computational complexity of the following attacks. Concretely, we want to reduce the potential choices for the parts of the key we have to guess at first. If we examine this at a per-S-box level, we can observe that for each of the equivalent keys, we can select a single one and compensate with the help of the key of the following round (see Fig. 4). We can repeat this process for the first $n - 1$ round keys and thus restrict these keys significantly. Thus, we only need to leave the final round key unconstrained. Therefore, we are able to restrict the space for the first $n - 1$ round keys to a much smaller set $\mathcal{N}$. As the last key is unconstrained we have

$$(\bar{K}_0, \bar{K}_1, \dots, \bar{K}_{n-1}) \in \mathcal{N}^{(n)} = \underbrace{\mathcal{N} \times \dots \times \mathcal{N}}_{n-1 \text{ times}} \times \mathcal{K},$$

where $\bar{K} = (\bar{K}_0, \bar{K}_1, \dots, \bar{K}_{n-1})$ denotes such a normalized key.

In the case of DEFAULT-LAYER with 4 independent keys, this leads to a set of representatives where the nibbles of the first 3 rounds are constrained to the space $\{0, 1, 2, 3\}$ while the final key is unconstrained. For example, the sequence of round keys shown in Fig. 5a is equivalent to the one shown in Fig. 5b. The algorithm used to normalize a given sequence of round keys schedule is outlined in Fig. 6. Note that the mapping from $\mathcal{K}^n$, the set of sequences of round keys of length n, to the set of normalized keys $\mathcal{N}^{(n)}$ is linear. Thus, it can be represented using a $128n \times 128n$ matrix $\mathbf{A}_{\mathcal{K} \to \mathcal{N}, n}$ of rank $64n + 64$.

K_0: 922d8799645a197240612627adac008c $\bar{K}_0$: 02221100023310122001202132330013
K_1: fd034fb83d3f82087ecb3d36ebd5b311 $\bar{K}_1$: 22312310332022020103310210031312
K_2: 6c6ebe434de58a603140168a0cbcea2f $\bar{K}_2$: 31012322123322300020111133332110
K_3: ab6472a5fc49ba97a6504da4acaa8113 $\bar{K}_3$: 1f95f3c6f75987f847a46938a2ea468c

   (a) Sequence of round keys K.   (b) Equivalent normalized key $\bar{K}$.

Fig. 5. An exemplary sequence of round keys and its normalized equivalent.

```
def normalize_key_sequence(key_sequence: List[List[int]]):
    for round_idx, round_key in enumerate(key_sequence[:-1]):
        next_delta = [0] * 32
        for nibble_idx, nibble in enumerate(round_key):
            for delta_in, delta_out in linear_structures:
                if (nibble ^ delta_in) < 4:
                    round_key[nibble_idx] ^= delta_in
                    next_delta[nibble_idx] ^= delta_out
                    break
        next_delta = permute_bits(next_delta)
        for nibble_idx, delta in enumerate(next_delta):
            key_sequence[round_idx + 1][nibble_idx] ^= delta
    return key_sequence
```

Fig. 6. Normalizing a sequence of round keys for DEFAULT-LAYER

4.3 Generic Attack Strategy for Ciphers with Linear Structures

We can use the observation about equivalence classes to recover $n-1$ equivalent round keys by performing DFA on $n-1$ rounds with linear structures and examining the ciphertext. The model which we use for this generic attack is a cipher with a long key consisting of n independent rounds keys for $n-1$ rounds, as illustrated in Fig. 7. Additionally, we assume that the input to these $n-1$ rounds is unknown, as is the case for DEFAULT-LAYER. Note that one of the n keys remains unknown as we do not know the input and no more S-boxes remain to be faulted. In the case of DEFAULT, we can fault the S-boxes of DEFAULT-CORE to recover this final key $\bar{K}_{n-1}$ using classical DFA. We would need 64 additional faults to recover $\bar{K}_{n-1}$ using the most basic technique.

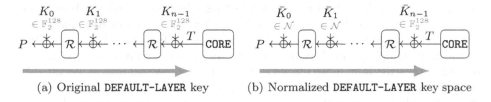

   (a) Original DEFAULT-LAYER key   (b) Normalized DEFAULT-LAYER key space

Fig. 7. Attack scenario for the generally applicable attack strategy.

Instead of recovering the original key $K = (K_0, \ldots, K_{n-1})$, we recover the first $n-1$ round keys of the normalized key $\bar{K} = (\bar{K}_0, \ldots, \bar{K}_{n-1})$. We describe the attack strategy in terms of decryption. However, the attack on encryption is analogous with the only difference being that we need a different set of normalized keys and different indexing. We perform this attack by placing single bit flips before each S-box of the final round of decryption to recover $\bar{K}_0$ uniquely. Once we have recovered the final round key, we can repeat the process to recover $\bar{K}_1$ to $\bar{K}_{n-2}$ uniquely. Thus, only a single round key, $\bar{K}_{n-1}$, remains unknown.

Consider the toy cipher in Fig. 8 which encrypts an unknown internal value t by using $c = k_0 \oplus (\mathcal{S}(k_1 \oplus \mathcal{S}(k_2 \oplus (k_3 \oplus t))))$ with $(k_0, k_1, k_2, k_3) = (2, \mathtt{b}, \mathtt{a}, \mathtt{c})$. By inducing two faults after the XOR of k_1, we can reduce the space of $\bar{k}_0$ to $\{2, 7, 8, \mathtt{d}\}$. This set corresponds to the linear space at the output of $\mathcal{S}$ as it equals $2 \oplus \{0, 5, \mathtt{a}, \mathtt{f}\}$. Therefore, we pick $\bar{k}_0 = 2$. Now we fault after the XOR of k_2 to reduce the space of $\bar{k}_1$ to $\{1, 4, \mathtt{b}, \mathtt{e}\}$. Again, this corresponds to the linear space and we can pick $\bar{k}_1 = 1$. Now we observe a difference between the normalized key and the actual key: $\bar{k}_1 \oplus k_1 = \mathtt{a}$. However, due to the linear structure $6 \rightarrow \mathtt{a}$, we can compensate this by a difference of 6 in k_2. Thus, when faulting after the XOR of k_3, we can reduce the space of $\bar{k}_2$ to $\{3, 6, 9, \mathtt{c}\}$. Note that this includes $k_2 \oplus 6 = \mathtt{c}$. We pick $\bar{k}_2 = 3$. Now the difference $\bar{k}_2 \oplus (k_2 \oplus 6) = \mathtt{f}$ can be compensated by the linear structure $9 \rightarrow \mathtt{f}$. Thus, if we knew the value of t, we would calculate $\bar{k}_3 = 5$. Alternatively, we can fault the components that are used to calculate t to get more information about k_3. For example, if another application of $\mathcal{S}$ was performed before t, we would be able to reduce $\bar{k}_3$ to a space of $\{0, 5, \mathtt{a}, \mathtt{f}\}$. In practice, it is not necessary to carry out all these calculations; instead, it is sufficient to restrict the guessed keys as described in Sect. 4.2.

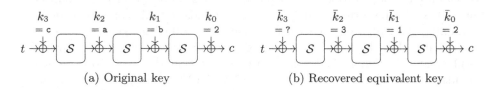

(a) Original key   (b) Recovered equivalent key

Fig. 8. Toy example for the generic attack.

When applying this attack to DEFAULT, we can recover 27 of the 28 normalized keys used by the idealized DEFAULT-LAYER. Once we have these keys, we can continue our attack by faulting DEFAULT-CORE which uses strong S-boxes that contain no non-trivial linear structures. This allows us to recover $\bar{K}_{27}$, and subsequently, the actual key that was used for the cipher. This attack breaks DEFAULT in the fault model specified by the authors. As this attack needs a large amount of faults, we will show more efficient attacks in the next section. Alternatively, we can apply this strategy to $n < 28$ independent round keys in which case we would be able to recover the normalized $(\bar{K}_0, \ldots, \bar{K}_{n-2})$ uniquely and $\bar{K}_{n-1}$ up to a space of 64 bits by faulting the preceding round of DEFAULT-LAYER.

5 Information-Combining DFA on Rotating Key Schedule

So far, we have shown generic attacks that apply to idealized ciphers with independent round keys and exploit only the linear structures of the round function. In this section, we exploit the specifics of the rotating key schedule in DEFAULT to build attacks that require much fewer faults.

5.1 Basic Encrypt-Decrypt Attack on Rotating Key Schedule

We can combine the ideas of Sect. 3.2 and Sect. 4. By using equivalence classes, we can recover the normalized key up to 64 bits by faulting decryption. Then, we can combine this with another 32 bits of information gained by faulting encryption.

In this attack, we target the normalized key consisting of 4 round keys: $\bar{K} = (\bar{K}_0, \bar{K}_1, \bar{K}_2, \bar{K}_3)$. First, we recover $\bar{K}_0$, $\bar{K}_1$, and $\bar{K}_2$ by placing faults before the S-boxes preceding the key addition. Due to the restrictions of the normalized key schedule, we can recover them uniquely by using 192 faults. Then, we place 64 faults before the S-boxes preceding the addition of K_3 to recover $\bar{K}_3$ up to a space of 2^{64} candidates. As in the attack on DEFAULT-LAYER with a simple key schedule, we can represent this set of candidates as a system of linear equations. Next, we perform 32 faults just before the S-boxes in the final round of encryption to gain 32 additional equations about $\bar{K}_3$. Thus, we can reduce the space for $\bar{K}$ to a set of 2^{32} normalized key candidates.

With the normalized key schedule reduced to a space that can be brute-forced, we still need a way to validate each key candidate. In this case, a plaintext-ciphertext pair is not sufficient as a normalized key does not uniquely identify the key used in DEFAULT-CORE. Therefore, we inject a single fault just after DEFAULT-CORE. By using the correct and faulty ciphertexts we obtain, we can validate each of the 2^{32} key guesses to identify the correct normalized key. Once the normalized key is recovered, we can invert DEFAULT-LAYER to recover the intermediate value right after DEFAULT-CORE. Now, we can target DEFAULT-CORE using classical DFA on the strong S-boxes. The downside of this approach is the brute-force complexity of searching the 2^{32} normalized key candidates.

5.2 Basic Multi-round Attack on Rotating Key Schedule

So far, we combined Sect. 4 and Sect. 3.2. Similarly, we can also combine the idea of equivalence classes from Sect. 4 with the multi-round attack of Sect. 3.3. This has the advantage of allowing us to uniquely identify the normalized key, thus eliminating the brute-force complexity. However, this attack is more challenging as the identical round keys are so far apart due to the strong key schedule.

The main idea of this attack is to first recover the first $n = 6$ keys under the assumption that they are chosen independently. Then, we want to equate $K_0 = K_4$ and $K_1 = K_5$. However, when using the attack strategy from Sect. 4.3 we only recover a set of normalized keys $(\bar{K}_0, \ldots, \bar{K}_5)$ up to 64 bits. We cannot add the equality relations $\bar{K}_0 = \bar{K}_4$ and $\bar{K}_1 = \bar{K}_5$ as this set of normalized keys is only a subset of the much larger set of possible non-normalized keys. Therefore, we need to transform the set of normalized keys to the set of non-normalized keys before applying the equations. After adding the equations, we can transform back to the set of normalized candidates for $(\bar{K}_0, \bar{K}_1, \bar{K}_2, \bar{K}_3)$.

This leads to an attack that is performed in 4 steps. We store these spaces of key candidates using systems of linear equations which allows us to perform this attack with negligible runtime complexity. These spaces are depicted in Fig. 9. In step (1), we assume the first $n = 6$ round keys $K_0, \ldots, K_5$ are independently chosen. We can restrict these six keys to a space of 2^{64} normalized candidates by faulting decryption according to the strategy from Sect. 4.3. In step (2), we remove the condition that the round keys need to be normalized and obtain a set of 2^{384} keys. In step (3), we restrict the set of non-normalized keys to only those where the conditions of the rotating key schedule are met, i.e., $K_0 = K_4$ and $K_1 = K_5$. Finally, in step (4), we add the restriction that the first 4 keys form a normalized sequence of round keys and receive a single result.

In the following description, we use k to denote the column vector corresponding to the bits of $(K_0, K_1, \ldots, K_5)$. Similarly, we use $\bar{k}$ to denote the column vector corresponding to the bits of the normalized key $(\bar{K}_0, \bar{K}_1, \ldots, \bar{K}_5)$.

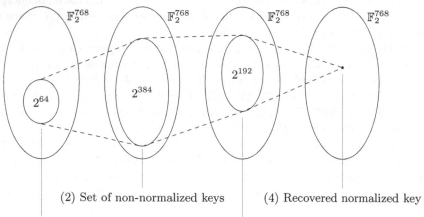

(2) Set of non-normalized keys   (4) Recovered normalized key

(1) Set of normalized keys   (3) Restricted set of non-normalized keys

Fig. 9. The linear spaces used in the attack on DEFAULT.

(1) Creating an equation system for the normalized key $\bar{K}$: We start our attack by assuming the first $n = 6$ keys $K = (K_0, \ldots, K_5) \in \mathcal{K}^6$ are chosen independently and applying the strategy of Sect. 4.3 on the first 6 keys. For now, we ignore the fact that $K_0 = K_4$ and $K_1 = K_5$. Thus, we obtain the normalized keys $\bar{K}_0, \ldots, \bar{K}_4$ uniquely using DFA. We need to fault each S-box in these 5 rounds twice to achieve this reduction. For example, we can inject a difference of 1 and 2 before each S-box. Furthermore, we can limit $\bar{K}_5$ to a space of 2^{64} candidates by faulting the S-boxes before K_5 is added. Again, we need to fault each S-box twice, thus, arriving at a total of 384 faults.

Converting the information about $\bar{K}_0$ to $\bar{K}_4$ into linear equations is trivial as we uniquely know their value. For K_5, we know only know 2 bits of information per nibble, which we can represent using two linear equations from Table 3 each. Therefore, we get the following equation, where A is a $128n \times 128n$ matrix of rank $128n - 64$ and $\bar{k}$, b are column vectors:

$$A \cdot \bar{k} = b .$$

(2) Converting the equation system to all possible keys K: The space of 2^{64} candidates for the normalized key $\bar{K}$ corresponds to a much larger space of candidates for the unrestricted key $K = (K_0, K_1, \ldots, K_5)$. To describe this larger space using linear equations, we note that $A_{\mathcal{K} \rightarrow \mathcal{N}, n} \cdot k = \bar{k}$ and substitute accordingly, where the matrix product is of rank $64n$:

$$A \cdot A_{\mathcal{K} \rightarrow \mathcal{N}, n} \cdot k = b .$$

(3) Adding additional constraints due to the rotating key schedule: Because we know $K_0 = K_4$ and $K_1 = K_5$, we can add 256 additional equations. This restricts the space of solutions to 2^{192} candidates which corresponds to one equivalence class for 4 independent round keys.

(4) Adding constraints to normalize the keys: Finally, we require that the first four round keys are normalized: $(K_0, K_1, K_2, K_3) \in \mathcal{N}^{(4)}$. In matrix notation, this is equivalent to $A_{\mathcal{K} \rightarrow \mathcal{N}, 4} \cdot k_{0 \ldots 3} = k_{0 \ldots 3}$. Note that we use a matrix that is related to but distinct from the normalization matrix used earlier. Therefore, we add the following linear equations:

$$\left(A_{\mathcal{K} \rightarrow \mathcal{N}, 4} + I \mid 0 \right) \cdot k = 0 ,$$

where I is the identity matrix. Then, we get a full-rank system, which we can solve uniquely.

Thus, we are able to recover an equivalent key for DEFAULT-LAYER. As in Sect. 4.3, we still need to recover the key for DEFAULT-CORE which we can achieve by using classical DFA.

We note that this attack is not limited to a rotating key schedule with only 4 distinct round keys: it is applicable to any number of independent round keys, as long as we have two round keys which are used more than once. For example, this attack can also be used to recover the key in case the simple key schedule is used by faulting 3 keys. In general, attacking DEFAULT-LAYER with x rotating keys requires us to recover 64 bits of information about $x + 2$ keys each.

6   Reducing the Number of Faults

While the attacks discussed so far achieve their goals, they are not optimized for efficiency and require quite a number of faulted computations with different fault positions. We can improve the attacks by placing the faults earlier, further from the known plaintext or ciphertext. For this purpose, we need a differential model of the cipher that predicts how these faults propagate.

Differential Model. To store the set of possible differences for a state of the cipher, we use a dictionary that maps from one 128-bit difference to its associated probability. We then examine how this set of possible differences changes round by round. For each round, we examine all possible differences individually and see how they propagate through the round function. To achieve this, we look at each S-box and note the set of possible output difference by examining the differential distribution table. Then, the set of possible differences after the S-box is the Cartesian product of all the individual differences. We do not explicitly keep track of the probability as all transitions for a given input difference are equally likely, as is evident from the differential distribution table. For each of these differences, we apply the bit permutation and add them to the set of differences after the round. To calculate the probability, we divide the probability of observing the difference before the round by the number of potential differences. If an entry already exists, we increase the probability by the calculated amount.

Using the Model to Find Suitable Fault Targets. We can use this model to calculate the expected amount of information learned from a sequence of faults which allows us to search for suitable fault targets. We first calculate the set of 128-bit differences before the final S-boxes and their probabilities. We then convert this set into the set of possible differences for each nibble with associated probabilities. Now, we examine all 32 nibbles independently. For each nibble and each fault, we have a list of possible differences. We examine the Cartesian product of these lists over all faults. Each element in the product is one possible outcome. We calculate its probability as the product of the individual probabilities. For each fault, we look up the information we learn according to Table 3 and enter that into a matrix. The rank of the matrix tells us the overall amount of information we learn. By repeating that process for every element in the Cartesian product and each nibble, we can calculate the expected amount of information learned from that sequence of faults.

In general, we find that placing the faults such that they are processed by 4 S-boxes with successive key-additions, leads to enough diffusion such that most S-boxes in the final round are active while still allowing us to determine the input difference of the final S-box by examining the output difference. Therefore, we apply this model to all possible pairs of fault indices for encryption and decryption to find suitable targets. We find that when each fault is repeated 3 times, flipping the bits at index 2 and 22 during encryption and 33 and 39 during decryption provides the best results.

6.1 Optimized Encrypt-Decrypt Attack on Simple Key Schedule

According to the results of Sect. 6, we place our faults such that they are processed by 4 S-boxes. We then combine faulting the bits at index 2 and 22 during encryption with faulting the bits at index 33 and 37 during decryption.

To decrease the size of the remaining key space, we repeat each fault 4 times, thus performing 16 faults in total. Using these faults, we gather enough information to reduce the size of the key space to between 2^{33} and 2^{39} in 95% of all cases. Figure 10a shows the distribution of the size of the key space after this attack.

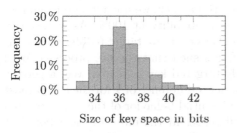
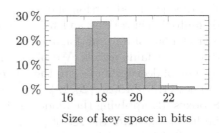

(a) Encrypt-decrypt attack (Section 6.1)   (b) Multi-round attack (Section 6.2)

Fig. 10. Distribution of the size of the remaining key space ($n = 1000$).

6.2 Optimized Multi-round Attack on Simple Key Schedule

To reduce the number of required faults, we can use tricks similar to those in Sect. 6.1. Additionally, we can reuse faults instead of gathering new ones for each round. The following attack applies when faulting the decryption; for encryption, an analogous attack is possible.

We start the attack by inducing 16 separate faults at the S-boxes S_i with $i \in \{0, 2, 8, 10, 21, 23, 29, 31\}$ such that each fault is processed by 4 key-dependent rounds of the cipher. Now, we can analyze these faulted encryptions based on the differential model similar to before and calculate the set of possible differences before each S-box in each round. We start by analyzing the final round: for each S-box, we try all 16 keys and verify whether the key is compatible with the set of possible differences. This reduces the key space per 4-bit key to a set of about 4 candidates: we can reduce the overall key space to a size of 2^{64} in 50% of all cases and to at most 2^{66} in about 90% of all cases.

Next, we analyze all faults across 2 rounds: for each fault and each potentially active S-box in the penultimate round, we try all keys and filter based on the possible differences calculated earlier. Usually, we need to iterate over 2^8 keys. This step reduces the size of the overall key space to 2^{32} in about 75% of all cases and to at most 2^{34} in about 99% of all cases.

Finally, we analyze the faults across 3 rounds: we can again filter based on all potentially active S-boxes in our targeted round. As in Sect. 3.3, however, we do not filter based on those S-boxes where we would need to guess the keys for more than 16 S-boxes. Thus, we usually need to iterate over 2^{16} keys for each potentially active S-box and fault. After this step, we are left with at most 2^{20} keys in about 90% of all cases. Figure 10b shows the distribution of the size of the key space after this attack.

6.3   Optimized Multi-round Attack on Rotating Key Schedule

For the optimized version of our most powerful attack, we use a dynamic number of faulted encryptions and fix the success probability at 100%. As we need to learn 64 bits of information about 6 round keys each, we target 6 different rounds during our fault attack. We place the faults such that the are processed by 4 rounds of decryption before the currently targeted key is XORed. We target the indices $\{1, 5, 9, 13, \ldots, 25, 29\}$, i.e., we induce a difference of 2 for the 8 rightmost S-boxes. By applying the model of the differential behavior of the cipher to each fault, we calculate the set of possible differences at the input of the S-box that is applied before the targeted key is XORed. Then, we can filter each nibble of the targeted key based on this expected difference. As in the basic attack, we restrict these 6 keys to form a normalized sequence of keys, i.e., the nibbles of the first 5 keys are restricted to $\{0, 1, 2, 3\}$. We repeat faulting these 8 S-boxes until we learn 64 bits of additional information about the key. Once we have gathered all the required key information, we continue the attack as in Sect. 5.2.

When performing this attack, we find that we need 83.6 ± 14.8 faults on average to recover an equivalent key for DEFAULT-LAYER. As before, we can continue by performing classical DFA on DEFAULT-CORE. The histogram of needed faults is depicted in Fig. 11. We believe the fault complexity of this attack can be reduced even further by removing the requirement that each normalized round key needs to be recovered uniquely.

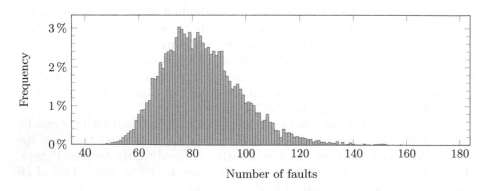

Fig. 11. Number of faults needed to recover the key ($n = 10\,000$).

7   Discussion

We now discuss several potential mitigations for our attack and argue why each of them is not sufficient to preclude information-combining normalized-key DFA attacks.

Inverting one DEFAULT-LAYER. The attacks combining information from encryption and decryption work because we combine information from a DFA on the DEFAULT-LAYER, $E_{\text{DEFAULT-LAYER}}$, with information from a DFA on the inverse DEFAULT-LAYER, $E_{\text{DEFAULT-LAYER}}^{-1}$. Therefore, a possible mitigation for these attacks is to change one DEFAULT-LAYER to its inverse, so that a DFA during encryption and decryption is always mounted on the same function:

$$E_{\text{DEFAULT-LAYER}} \circ E_{\text{CORE}} \circ E_{\text{DEFAULT-LAYER}}^{-1}.$$

However, even then, it is possible to combine information of differential-based fault attacks of $E_{\text{DEFAULT-LAYER}}$ and $E_{\text{DEFAULT-LAYER}}^{-1}$ by combining a DFA with a collision fault attack [7].

Note that this attack is also a threat in the following scenario proposed by the designers [1, Sect. 4.1]: they suggest that the cipher could also only be protected by one DEFAULT-LAYER if the attacker model is limited to a single direction (either encryption or decryption), e.g., $E_{\text{DEFAULT-LAYER}} \circ E_{\text{CORE}}$ for an adversary who targets only encryption. As discussed, this enables differential-based fault attacks on the core cipher using fault-based collision attacks.

Involutive S-box. Another way to achieve a similar result is to replace the S-box used in DEFAULT-LAYER with an involutive S-box. This would prevent the attacks combining information from encryption and decryption. Note that for this countermeasure to work, care must be taken when choosing the linear layer, as a different linear layer could lead to more linearly independent equations about the key. This does not protect against the multi-round or the generic attack.

Strong Linear Layer. A potential mitigation for the information combining attacks on DEFAULT with a simple key schedule is to use a strong linear layer. This would greatly increase the computational complexity of the multi-round attack from Sect. 3.3. However, the attacks based on normalized keys including the attack from Sect. 5.2 would still apply. Additionally, a strong linear layer would make attacks combining information from encryption and decryption easier.

Independent Round Keys. In their design paper, the authors note that using 28 independent round keys for DEFAULT-LAYER would make information combining attacks useless [1, Section 6.1]. While this is true for combining information across rounds, the ideas of equivalent keys from Sect. 4 still apply. In particular, the generic attack from Sect. 4.3 defeats this construction.

8   Conclusion

Due to the practical impact of DFA style attacks, strategies for protecting ciphers are highly relevant and different strategies have been explored in the past years.

The authors of DEFAULT propose an interesting design strategy to inherently limit the amount of information an attacker can learn.

In this paper we showed that while indeed only a limited amount of information can be gained each round, we can combine information across rounds. While it intuitively appears that a simple key schedule prevents information-combining attacks, as the same key is used each round, we show that this is possible. For this reason, the designers proposed a strong key schedule with full diffusion, to ensure that it is infeasible to combine information from neighboring rounds. This indeed helps to prevent straight-forward information-combining DFA attacks.

Unfortunately, we can use the properties of the round function to characterize large classes of equivalent keys by identifying a set of normalized keys. These normalized keys permit us to combine information across many rounds, thus breaking DEFAULT with the proposed strong key schedule and even an idealized key schedule with independent round keys. The key observation is that starting from the ciphertext, in each round, the adversary can either learn additional information about the round key or arbitrarily pick one of the remaining candidates and move on to the next round. By optimizing the placement of faults, we can reduce the fault complexity to less than 100 faulted computations to recover an equivalent key for DEFAULT-LAYER with no additional brute-force cost.

Our analysis shows how challenging it is to prevent these implementation attacks. While cipher-level protection would be a great solution as it does not offload the responsibility to implementers, it seems substantial ideas beyond linear structures are necessary. This raises the question of how the DEFAULT design strategy can be adapted to achieve inherent protection against DFA.

Acknowledgments. We thank the DEFAULT designers for their comments. Additional funding was provided by a generous gift from Google. Any findings expressed in this paper are those of the authors and do not necessarily reflect the views of the funding parties.

References

1. Baksi, A., Bhasin, S., Breier, J., Khairallah, M., Peyrin, T., Sarkar, S., Sim, S.M.: DEFAULT: Cipher level resistance against differential fault attack. In: Tibouchi, M., Wang, H. (eds.) ASIACRYPT 2021. LNCS, vol. 13091, pp. 124–156. Springer, Cham (2021). https://doi.org/10.1007/978-3-030-92075-3_5
2. Baksi, A., et al.: DEFAULT: Cipher level resistance against differential fault attack. IACR Cryptology ePrint Archive, Report 2021/712 (2021), https://eprint.iacr.org/2021/712/20210528:092448
3. Bar-El, H., Choukri, H., Naccache, D., Tunstall, M., Whelan, C.: The sorcerer's apprentice guide to fault attacks. Proc. IEEE **94**(2), 370–382 (2006). https://doi.org/10.1109/JPROC.2005.862424
4. Beierle, C., Leander, G., Moradi, A., Rasoolzadeh, S.: CRAFT: lightweight tweakable block cipher with efficient protection against DFA attacks. IACR Trans. Symmet. Cryptol. **2019**(1), 5–45 (2019). https://doi.org/10.13154/tosc.v2019.i1.5-45
5. Biham, E., Shamir, A.: Differential cryptanalysis of DES-like cryptosystems. In: Menezes, A., Vanstone, S.A. (eds.) CRYPTO 1990. LNCS, vol. 537, pp. 2–21. Springer, Berlin (1990). https://doi.org/10.1007/3-540-38424-3_1

6. Biham, E., Shamir, A.: Differential fault analysis of secret key cryptosystems. In: Kaliski, B.S. (ed.) CRYPTO 1997. LNCS, vol. 1294, pp. 513–525. Springer, Heidelberg (1997). https://doi.org/10.1007/BFb0052259
7. Blömer, J., Krummel, V.: Fault based collision attacks on AES. In: Breveglieri, L., Koren, I., Naccache, D., Seifert, J.P. (eds.) FDTC 2006. LNCS, vol. 4236, pp. 106–120. Springer, Berlin (2006). https://doi.org/10.1007/11889700_11
8. Dobraunig, C., Eichlseder, M., Korak, T., Lomné, V., Mendel, F.: Statistical fault attacks on nonce-based authenticated encryption schemes. In: Cheon, J.H., Takagi, T. (eds.) ASIACRYPT 2016. LNCS, vol. 10031, pp. 369–395. Springer, Berlin (2016). https://doi.org/10.1007/978-3-662-53887-6_14
9. Dobraunig, C., Mennink, B., Primas, R.: Leakage and tamper resilient permutation-based cryptography. IACR Cryptology ePrint Archive, Report 2020/200 (2020). https://ia.cr/2020/200
10. Gierlichs, B., Schmidt, J.M., Tunstall, M.: Infective computation and dummy rounds: fault protection for block ciphers without check-before-output. In: Hevia, A., Neven, G. (eds.) LATINCRYPT 2012. LNCS, vol. 7533, pp. 305–321. Springer, Berlin (2012). https://doi.org/10.1007/978-3-642-33481-8_17
11. Giraud, C., Thillard, A.: Piret and quisquater's DFA on AES revisited. IACR Cryptology ePrint Archive, Report 2010/440 (2010). https://ia.cr/2010/440
12. Knudsen, L.R.: Truncated and higher order differentials. In: Preneel, B. (ed.) FSE 1994. LNCS, vol. 1008, pp. 196–211. Springer, Berlin (1994). https://doi.org/10.1007/3-540-60590-8_16
13. Medwed, M., Standaert, F.X., Großschädl, J., Regazzoni, F.: Fresh re-keying: Security against side-channel and fault attacks for low-cost devices. In: Bernstein, D.J., Lange, T. (eds.) AFRICACRYPT 2010. LNCS, vol. 6055, pp. 279–296. Springer, Berlin (2010). https://doi.org/10.1007/978-3-642-12678-9_17
14. Patranabis, S., Chakraborty, A., Mukhopadhyay, D.: Fault tolerant infective countermeasure for AES. In: Chakraborty, R.S., Schwabe, P., Solworth, J.A. (eds.) SPACE 2015. LNCS, vol. 9354, pp. 190–209. Springer, Berlin (2015). https://doi.org/10.1007/978-3-319-24126-5_12
15. Piret, G., Quisquater, J.J.: A differential fault attack technique against SPN structures, with application to the AES and KHAZAD. In: Walter, C.D., Koç, Ç.K., Paar, C. (eds.) CHES 2003. LNCS, vol. 2779, pp. 77–88. Springer, Heidelberg (2003). https://doi.org/10.1007/978-3-540-45238-6_7
16. Simon, T., Batina, L., Daemen, J., Grosso, V., Massolino, P.M.C., Papagiannopoulos, K., Regazzoni, F., Samwel, N.: Friet: An authenticated encryption scheme with built-in fault detection. In: Canteaut, A., Ishai, Y. (eds.) EUROCRYPT 2020. LNCS, vol. 12105, pp. 581–611. Springer, Cham (2020). https://doi.org/10.1007/978-3-030-45721-1_21
17. Tupsamudre, H., Bisht, S., Mukhopadhyay, D.: Destroying fault invariant with randomization - A countermeasure for AES against differential fault attacks. In: Batina, L., Robshaw, M. (eds.) CHES 2014. LNCS, vol. 8731, pp. 93–111. Springer, Berlin (2014). https://doi.org/10.1007/978-3-662-44709-3_6

Private Circuits with Quasilinear Randomness

Vipul Goyal[1,2], Yuval Ishai[3(✉)], and Yifan Song[1]

[1] Carnegie Mellon University, Pittsburgh, USA
vipul@cmu.edu, yifans2@andrew.cmu.edu
[2] NTT Research, Palo Alto, USA
[3] Technion, Haifa, Israel
yuvali@cs.technion.ac.il

Abstract. A *t-private* circuit for a function f is a randomized Boolean circuit C that maps a randomized encoding of an input x to an encoding of the output $f(x)$, such that probing t wires anywhere in C reveals nothing about x. Private circuits can be used to protect embedded devices against side-channel attacks. Motivated by the high cost of generating fresh randomness in such devices, several works have studied the question of minimizing the randomness complexity of private circuits.

The best known upper bound, due to Coron et al. (Eurocrypt 2020), is $O(t^2 \cdot \log ts)$ random bits, where s is the circuit size of f. We improve this to $O(t \cdot \log ts)$, including the randomness used by the input encoder, and extend this bound to the stateful variant of private circuits. Our constructions are semi-explicit in the sense that there is an efficient randomized algorithm that generates the private circuit C from a circuit for f with negligible failure probability.

1 Introduction

The notion of *private circuits*, due to Ishai, Sahai, and Wagner (ISW) [9], is a simple abstraction of leakage-resilience computation. It is simple both in terms of the underlying computational model, namely Boolean circuits, and in terms of the class of leakage attacks it should protect against.

ISW defined two flavors of private circuits: stateless and stateful. The former captures a one-time computation that maps an encoded (or "secret-shared") input to an encoded output, whereas the latter captures an evolving computation that may update a secret internal state. We will start by considering the simpler stateless model and later discuss an extension to the stateful case.

A (stateless) t-private circuit for a function f is defined by a triple (I, C, O), where I is a trusted, randomized input encoder, mapping an input x to an encoded input $\hat{x}$, C is a randomized Boolean circuit mapping $\hat{x}$ to an encoded output $\hat{y}$, and O is a trusted, deterministic output decoder mapping the encoding $\hat{y}$ to an output y. The natural correctness requirement is that for every input x, we have $O(C(I(x))) = f(x)$ (with probability 1). The security requirement asserts that an adversary who can probe any set of t wires of C learns nothing

O. Dunkelman and S. Dziembowski (Eds.): EUROCRYPT 2022, LNCS 13277, pp. 192–221, 2022.
https://doi.org/10.1007/978-3-031-07082-2_8

about x. Moreover, it is required that I and O be *universal* in the sense that they are independent of (and are typically much smaller than) C and may depend only on the input length and t. This rules out trivial solutions in which I or O compute f. The default encoder I, referred to as the *canonical* encoder, independently splits each input bit x_i into $t+1$ random bits whose parity is x_i.

The simplicity of the private circuits model makes it attractive as an object of theoretical study, enabling a clean and rigorous analysis of the achievable tradeoffs between security and efficiency. On the downside, the same simplicity that makes the model theoretically appealing also makes it a very crude approximation of reality. In particular, the bounded probing attacks that private circuits are designed to protect against are much too restrictive to capture real-life side-channel attacks.

Somewhat unexpectedly, private circuits have gained popularity as a practical method for "higher-order masking" countermeasures that protect embedded devices against realistic side-channel attacks. A partial theoretical explanation was given by Duc et al. [6], who showed that the security of private circuits against probing attacks is enough to also guarantee security against a certain level of *noisy leakage*, which independently leaks a small amount information about each wire.

Minimizing Randomness Complexity. A natural complexity measure for private circuits is their *randomness complexity*, measured by default as the total number of random bits used by the randomized circuit C. (We will later also address the goal of minimizing the randomness used by the input encoder.) The question of minimizing the randomness complexity of private circuits is not only a natural theoretical question, but is also motivated by the high costs of generating fresh randomness on embedded devices.[1] This question has also found unexpected applications to efficiently mitigating selective failure attacks in secure computation protocols based on garbled circuits [8].

The original ISW construction [9] used $O(t^2)$ fresh random bits to compute each AND gate in a circuit computing f. This gives an upper bound of $O(t^2 \cdot s)$ where s is the circuit size of f. Several subsequent works obtained improvements to this bound, with the canonical encoder described above.

Ishai et al. [8], in the broader context of studying robust pseudorandomness generators, show how to reduce the randomness complexity to $O(t^{3+\epsilon} \cdot \log ts)$, for any $\epsilon > 0$, thus making it almost independent of the circuit size s. Belaïd et al. [2] focus on the randomness complexity of implementing a single AND gate, for which they present a probabilistic construction of a gadget that requires only $O(t \log t)$ random bits, compared to $O(t^2)$ in ISW. However, their technique does not efficiently extend to multiple gates, and their construction is not composable in the sense of [1,3] (see Sect. 2 for further discussion). Faust et al. [7]

---

[1] Even if one settles for computational security, alternative approaches based on cryptographic pseudorandom generators (PRGs) are also quite expensive, especially since the PRG computation itself is subject to leakage [9].

present a practically-oriented approach for reusing randomness across multiple AND gadgets, reducing the total amount of randomness for small values of t ($t \leq 7$) by a constant factor. The current state of the art was obtained by the recent construction of Coron et al. [5], which uses $O(t^2 \cdot \log ts)$ random bits. This construction not only improves the bound of [8] by more than a factor of t, but also eliminates the use of low-degree expander graphs that hurts concrete efficiency.

1.1 Our Contribution

In this work, we improve the best previous asymptotic bound of Coron et al. [5] by an additional factor of t. Concretely, we show that any function f computed by a Boolean circuit of size s admits a t-private circuit which uses only $O(t \cdot \log ts)$ random bits.

Our construction is only semi-explicit in the sense that there is an efficient randomized algorithm that generates C from a Boolean circuit for f with negligible failure probability. However, similarly to the construction from [5] (and unlike the earlier construction from [8]), our construction does not require the circuit C to use a good low-degree expander, and we do not see inherent barriers to good concrete efficiency (which we did not attempt to optimize).

We also present the following additional extensions of our main result:

- **Randomness-efficient input encoder.** By using a randomness-efficient encoder I instead of the canonical one, we can obtain the same $O(t \cdot \log ts)$ bound *even when counting the internal randomness of the input encoder*. This is optimal up to the logarithmic factor.
- **Leakage-tolerant circuits.** We can get the same bound in the (stronger) model of *leakage-tolerant* private circuits [8]. In this model there are no trusted input encoder or output decoder, and an adversary probing t wires of C is allowed to learn a similar number of input and output bits.
- **Stateful private circuits.** Finally, our $O(t \cdot \log ts)$ bound applies also to the standard *stateful* model of private circuits from [9] (see the full version), counting the number of fresh random bits in each invocation.

Open Questions. We conjecture that our $O(t \cdot \log ts)$ upper bound is asymptotically optimal in all of the above settings, and leave open the question of proving (or disproving) this conjecture. We also leave open the existence of a fully explicit variant of our constructions.

2   Technical Overview

In this section, we give a detailed technical overview of our main results, starting with some necessary background.

Background: Leakage-Resilient and Leakage-Tolerant Private Circuits. In [9], Ishai et al. introduced the fundamental notion of private circuits. This notion comes in two flavors, a stateful variant and a simpler stateless variant. Here we will start by focusing on the latter for simplicity, but will later show how to extend our results to the stateful model.

Informally, for a function f, a private (stateless) circuit consists of an input encoder I, a compiled circuit C, and an output decoder O. The compiled circuit C takes an encoded input $\hat{x}$ generated by $I(x)$ and computes an encoded output $\hat{y}$ such that $O(y) = f(x)$. The security requires that any t wires in C should be independent of the function input. This notion is also referred to as leakage-resilient private circuits. We focus by default on the canonical encoder: I encodes each input bit x_i by a vector of $t+1$ random bits with parity x_i (Later we will consider a different encoder, in the context of minimizing the randomness complexity of the encoder.). As to the decoder, we consider by default a relaxation of the canonical decoder: To decode each output bit, O takes the parity of a block of bits (which are not restricted to be $t + 1$ bits).

- As noted in [8], without any requirement on I and O, a trivial solution is having I compute a secret sharing of $f(x)$ which is passed by C to the decoder.
- In this work, we focus on the additional randomness used in the compiled circuit C. We want to avoid encoders which output a large amount of randomness.

We may also define the notion of leakage-tolerant private circuits. In this setting, the input and output are not encoded. I.e., the encoder and the decoder are the identity function. The security requires that any set of at most t wires in C can be simulated by the *same number* of input and output wires.

In this work, we show that for any function f with circuit size s, there is a (leakage-resilient) private circuit which uses $O(t \cdot \log ts)$ random bits.

Background: (Strong) t-Wise Independent Pseudo-random Generator. Our construction makes use of the notion of (strong) t-wise independent pseudo-random generators (PRG). Informally, a function $G:\{0,1\}^n \to \{0,1\}^m$ is a t-wise independent PRG if any t bits in $G(x)$ are independent and uniformly random when the input x is uniformly distributed in $\{0,1\}^n$. Moreover, if any t bits in $(x, G(x))$ are independent and uniformly random, then we say G is a *strong* t-wise independent PRG.

We say that G is linear if any output bit of G is equal to the XOR of a subset of its input bits. See Sect. 3.2 for an explicit construction of a *linear and strong* t-wise independent PRG with input size $n = O(t \cdot \log m)$.

Limitations of Previous Approaches. We first recall the definition of robust t-wise independent PRGs introduced in [8]. Intuitively, any probing attack towards a robust t-wise independent PRG is equivalent to a probing attack towards the output bits. The following definition corresponds to the strong robust t-wise independent PRGs in [8].

Definition 1 (Robust t-wise Independent PRGs [8]). *A circuit implementation C of a function $G : \{0,1\}^m \to \{0,1\}^n$ is a (t, k, q)-robust pseudo-random generator if the following holds. Let $\boldsymbol{u}$ be a vector of m uniformly random bits,* and $r = G(u)$. For any set S of at most k wires in C, there is a set T of at most $q|S|$ output bits such that conditioned on any fixing of the values C_S of the wires in S and r_I, where $I = \{i : r_i \in T\}$, the values $r_{\bar{I}}$ of the output bits not in T are t-wise independent.

A generic approach of derandomizing a private circuit introduced in [8] works as follows:

1. First, derandomize a private circuit by assuming an access to t-wise independent random source. This is achieved by considering the notion of randomness locality of a private circuit. The randomness locality of a private circuit is the number of random bits that are used to compute each wire. If each wire uses at most ℓ random bits (i.e., the randomness locality is ℓ), then we may replace the uniform random source by a $(\ell \cdot t)$-wise independent random source to protect against t-probing attacks. It is because any t wires depend on at most $\ell \cdot t$ random bits, and therefore, the distribution of these t wires when using uniform random source is identical to that when using $(\ell \cdot t)$-wise independent random source.
2. Then, replace the $(\ell \cdot t)$-wise independent random source by a robust $(\ell \cdot t)$-wise independent PRG.

In [8], Ishai et al. constructed a private circuit with randomness locality $O(t^2)$ based on the private circuit constructed in [9]. The recent work of Coron et al. [5] further improves the randomness locality to $O(t)$. Combined with a robust $O(t^2)$-wise independent PRG from [8], this gives a private circuit which uses only $\tilde{O}(t^{2+\epsilon})^2$ random bits, for any constant $\epsilon > 0$. Moreover, they also show that in their construction the robust $O(t^2)$-wise independent PRG can be replaced by $O(t)$ independent $O(t)$-wise independent PRGs. This reduces the randomness complexity to $\tilde{O}(t^2)$ and results in better concrete efficiency.

However, the approach of using randomness locality inherently requires $\Omega(t^2)$ random bits. Intuitively, the randomness locality of a private circuit cannot be smaller than t, or otherwise, an adversary may learn extra information about the input by probing a wire and all random bits that are used to compute this wire. It means that the random source should be at least t^2-wise independent, which requires $\Omega(t^2)$ random bits.

To overcome this bottleneck:

1. We first switch the view from computing secret shared wire values, the mainstream method in the literature of private circuits [5,8,9], to computing *masked* wire values. We note that computing masked wire values is commonly used in the literature on secure multi-party computation. However, to the best of our knowledge, this method was not used in the literature on private circuits. We use this to bypass the limitation of using randomness locality and reduce the problem of constructing a private circuit to that of constructing a leakage-tolerant private circuit for the XOR function, which

---

[2] In this paper, we use $\tilde{O}$ notation to hide logarithmic factors in either a PRG output size or a circuit size.

we refer to as a leakage-tolerant XOR gadget. Specifically, assuming the existence of a leakage-tolerant XOR gadget, we construct a private circuit which uses $\tilde{O}(t)$ random bits (excluding the randomness used in the leakage-tolerant XOR gadgets).

2. Then, we focus on the leakage-tolerant XOR gadget. We start with a straightforward construction of a leakage-tolerant XOR gadget assuming the access to correlated random bits. Then we use a special kind of robust PRG, which we refer to as a *robust parity sharing generator*, to generate the correlated random bits. Compared with [8], we extend the notion of robust PRGs in the following two directions: (1) the output bits of the robust PRG should be *correlated* as required by the basic construction of the XOR gadget, and (2) unlike the robust t-wise independent PRG [8], which only focuses on the *number* of random bits on which the probed wires depend, we also take into account the concrete dependence on the random bits induced by the construction of the XOR gadget. This more fine-grained approach allows us to bypass the limitation of using randomness locality when constructing leakage-tolerant XOR gadgets. By using probabilistic arguments, we obtain a semi-explicit construction of a robust parity sharing generator which uses $\tilde{O}(t)$ random bits. This yields a leakage-tolerant XOR gadget with randomness complexity $\tilde{O}(t)$.

Combining the above two steps, we obtain a private circuit in the plain model which uses $\tilde{O}(t)$ random bits. We note that a similar approach is used in [2] to reduce the randomness complexity of a single multiplication gate. Concretely, Belaïd et al. [2] use probabilistic arguments and show the existence of a t-private multiplication circuit, which takes *shared inputs* and produces *shared output*, with randomness complexity $O(t \log t)$. However there are three key differences which make their technique difficult to work for a general circuit (i.e., not restricting to a single multiplication gate):

- The solution in [2] only reduces the randomness complexity for a single multiplication gate. However, to obtain our result, we have to reuse the randomness across all gadgets or otherwise the randomness complexity will be proportional to the circuit size. It is unclear how their result can be extended to reducing the randomness complexity for multiple multiplication gates. Our solution, on the other hand, reuses the randomness across all leakage-tolerant XOR gadgets. See more discussion in Remark 2.
- As discussed in Section 7.2 in [2], their private multiplication circuit is not composable. As a result, Belaïd et al. [2] cannot obtain a private circuit for a general function from their private multiplication circuit without affecting the achieved randomness complexity per gate.
- The construction in [2] takes *shared inputs* and computes *shared output*. As discussed above, derandomizing shared wire values may require at least $\Omega(t^2)$ random bits.

Extensions. Beyond the basic construction, we consider the following two extensions:

1. The first extension is replacing the canonical encoder by a randomness-efficient encoder. Note that the canonical encoder requires $t \cdot n_i$ random bits to encode n_i input bits. We construct a randomness-efficient encoder which reduces the randomness complexity to $O(t \cdot \log n_i)$. As a result, for any function with circuit size s, we obtain a private circuit which uses $O(t \cdot \log ts)$ random bits *including the randomness used in the encoder*.

2. The second extension is to construct a private *stateful* circuit. A stateful circuit models the scenario where the circuit has an internal state. In each invocation, the circuit computes the function which takes as input its internal state and the external input, outputs the result of the function, and stores its new internal state. The security of a private stateful circuit requires that an adversary, which has control over the external input, cannot learn any information about the internal state of the circuit over multiple executions of the circuit with the power of adaptively choosing a set of t internal wires before each execution depending on the output values and the wire values observed in previous executions. We show how to extend our basic construction to a private stateful circuit which uses $O(t \cdot \log t|C|)$ random bits for any stateful circuit C in each invocation.

More details can be found in Sect. 2.3.

2.1 Outer Construction: Private Circuits via Leakage-Tolerant XOR Gadgets

For a boolean function $f : \{0,1\}^{n_i} \to \{0,1\}^{n_o}$, let $\tilde{C}$ denote a circuit that computes the function f. To protect the wire values in $\tilde{C}$, our idea is to mask each wire value in $\tilde{C}$ by an output bit of a t-wise independent PRG. Since any t output bits of a t-wise independent PRG are independent and uniformly distributed, any t masked wire values in $\tilde{C}$ leak no information about the input.

In our construction, we choose to use a linear and strong $2t$-wise independent PRG $G : \{0,1\}^m \to \{0,1\}^{|\tilde{C}|}$. Informally, this is because

- A probing attack can not only probe the masked wire values in $\tilde{C}$, but also the input random bits of G. We need to protect the input random bits of G by using a *strong* $2t$-wise independent PRG.
- A linear PRG allows us to compute each output bit of G by simply computing the XOR of a subset of its input bits. As we will show later, our construction directly uses a leakage-tolerant XOR gadget to compute each masked wire value. In this way, the implementation of G is hidden in the leakage-tolerant XOR gadgets and we do not need to worry about the intermediate wires in the implementation of G.
- As we will see later, our construction may leak at most $2t$ masked wire values within t probes. It requires us to use a $2t$-wise independent PRG.

We use $\boldsymbol{u} = (u_1, u_2, \ldots, u_m)$ to denote the input of G and $\boldsymbol{r} = (r_1, r_2, \ldots, r_{|\tilde{C}|})$ to denote the output of G. Since G is linear, each output bit r_i is the XOR of a subset of $\{u_1, u_2, \ldots, u_m\}$. We refer to this set as the support of r_i, denoted by $\mathsf{supp}(r_i)$. For the circuit $\tilde{C}$, all wires are denoted by $g_1, g_2, \ldots, g_{|\tilde{C}|}$ (including input wires and output wires). The goal is to compute $g_i \oplus r_i$ for all $i \in \{1, 2, \ldots, |\tilde{C}|\}$. Note that we can view $\{g_i \oplus r_i\} \bigcup \mathsf{supp}(r_i)$ as an additive sharing of g_i since the XOR of the bits in $\mathsf{supp}(r_i)$ is equal to r_i. We use $[g_i]$ to represent the set $\{g_i \oplus r_i\} \bigcup \mathsf{supp}(r_i)$. At first glance, one may think that our approach is very similar to the generic approach of constructing private circuits in [5,8,9] since the latter also computes an additive sharing for each wire value. However, we would like to point out that there are two key differences between our approach and the generic approach:

- First, for each additive sharing $[g_i]$ in our approach, the number of shares depends on the size of $\mathsf{supp}(r_i)$, which may vary for different i. On the other hand, the additive sharings in the generic approach all have the same number of shares.
- Second, in our approach, the shares are reused among different additive sharings, which is not the case in the generic approach.

As a result, our approach does not need to derandomize the shares of additive sharings since they reuse the input random bits of the PRG G, which is of size $O(t \log |\tilde{C}|)$. It allows us to bypass the limitation of using randomness locality.

In the outer construction, we assume the existence of a leakage-tolerant XOR gadget (or equivalently, a leakage-tolerant private circuit for the XOR function). Recall that the input encoder is the canonical encoder, which encodes each input bit x_i by a vector of $t+1$ random bits with parity x_i. We may view the encoding of x_i as an additive sharing of x_i, denoted by $[x_i]$. The outer construction works as follows:

1. We first transform the input encoding $[x_i]$ to the masked input bit. Let g_i be the input wire of $\tilde{C}$ which is initialized to x_i. Then we want to compute $g_i \oplus r_i = x_i \oplus r_i$. This is done by using a leakage-tolerant XOR gadget to XOR the bits in $[x_i] \bigcup \mathsf{supp}(r_i)$.
2. For each addition gate with input wires g_a, g_b and output wire g_c in $\tilde{C}$, the masked output wire $g_c \oplus r_c$ is computed by using a leakage-tolerant XOR gadget to XOR the bits in $[g_a] \bigcup [g_b] \bigcup \mathsf{supp}(r_c)$.
3. For each multiplication gate with input wires g_a, g_b and output wire g_c in $\tilde{C}$, we first define $[g_a] \otimes [g_b] = \{u \cdot v : u \in [g_a], v \in [g_b]\}$. Note that $g_a = \oplus_{u \in [g_a]} u$ and $g_b = \oplus_{v \in [g_b]} v$. Therefore

$$g_c = g_a \cdot g_b = (\oplus_{u \in [g_a]} u) \cdot (\oplus_{v \in [g_b]} v) = \oplus_{u \in [g_a], v \in [g_b]} u \cdot v,$$

which means that g_c is equal to the XOR of the bits in $[g_a] \otimes [g_b]$. The circuit first computes $u \cdot v$ for all $u \in [g_a]$ and $v \in [g_b]$. The masked output wire $g_c \oplus r_c$ is then computed by using a leakage-tolerant XOR gadget to XOR the bits in $([g_a] \otimes [g_b]) \bigcup \mathsf{supp}(r_c)$.

4. For each output gate with input wire g_a in $\tilde{C}$, we have computed $g_a \oplus r_a$. Recall that $[g_a] = \{g_a \oplus r_a\} \bigcup \mathsf{supp}(r_a)$ and the XOR of bits in $[g_a]$ is equal to g_a. The circuit simply outputs bits in $[g_a]$.

Let C denote the circuit constructed above. The correctness of C is straightforward from the description. The security follows from the following three facts:

- By the definition of leakage-tolerant private circuits, any probing attack towards a leakage-tolerant XOR gadget is equivalent to a probing attack (that probes the same number of wires) towards the input wires and the output wire of this gadget. Therefore, we only need to focus on two kinds of wires: (1) the input wires of C, and (2) the rest of wires which excludes the internal wires of leakage-tolerant XOR gadgets. The second kind contains the input bits of the PRG G and the masked wire values, i.e., $\{u_i\}_{i=1}^m \bigcup \{g_i \oplus r_i\}_{i=1}^{|\tilde{C}|}$, and the values in $[g_a] \otimes [g_b]$ for all multiplication gate with input wires g_a and g_b in $\tilde{C}$.
- For input wires of C, since each input bit x is encoded by $t+1$ random bits with parity x, any t bits are uniformly random. Therefore, the input wires are leakage resilient.
- For the second kind of wires, note that each value $u \cdot v \in [g_a] \otimes [g_b]$ can be computed by $u \in [g_a]$ and $v \in [g_b]$. Thus, any t wires can be determined by at most $2t$ values in $\{u_i\}_{i=1}^m \bigcup \{g_i \oplus r_i\}_{i=1}^{|\tilde{C}|}$. The security follows from that G is a strong $2t$-wise independent PRG.

We refer the readers to Sect. 4 for more details.

2.2   Inner Construction and Robust Parity Sharing Generator

Given the outer construction in Sect. 2.1, it is sufficient to move our focus to the construction of a leakage-tolerant XOR gadget. Our main technical contribution is a new notion of robust PRGs which we refer to as robust parity sharing generators.

Basic Construction of Leakage-Tolerant XOR Gadgets. We first introduce a straightforward construction of leakage-tolerant XOR gadgets assuming access to ideal correlated random bits, which is adapted from the basic MPC protocol for XOR of Kushilevitz and Mansour [10]. Let $x_1, x_2, \ldots, x_n$ denote the input bits of the gadget $\mathcal{G}$. The goal is to compute the output $\oplus_{i=1}^n x_i$. The circuit is given access to n random bits $r_1, r_2, \ldots, r_n$ with parity 0. (Note that here x_i's and r_i's are different variables from those in Sect. 2.1.)

The basic construction works as follows:

1. For all $i \in \{1, 2, \ldots, n\}$, the circuit computes $g_i := x_i \oplus r_i$ in parallel. (Here too, g_i is a different variable from that in Sect. 2.1.)
2. Then the circuit computes the XOR of $g_1, g_2, \ldots, g_n$ by using a $\lceil \log n \rceil$-depth addition circuit: In each round, the addition circuit partitions the input bits into groups of size 2. For each group, the addition circuit computes the XOR of the bits in this group. The output bits are provided as input bits to the next round.

In fact, our construction works for any addition circuit with the same randomness complexity. Here we choose to use the addition circuit with the smallest depth so as to minimize the depth of the private circuit. In [10], the basic protocol computes $\oplus_{i=1}^n g_i$ by adding up $\{g_i\}_{i=1}^n$ from g_1 to g_n.

We show that this simple construction is leakage-tolerant. First note that the input wires and output wires of the gadget can always be simulated by having access to the corresponding wires. In the following, we only focus on the intermediate wires in $\mathcal{G}$.

We may divide the intermediate wires in $\mathcal{G}$ into two sets: (1) the first set contains the correlated random bits $r_1, r_2, \ldots, r_n$, and (2) the second set contains all wires in the addition circuit, which is either g_i for some $i \in \{1, 2, \ldots, n\}$ or a linear combination of $\{g_1, g_2, \ldots, g_n\}$. If all probed wires are in the first set, the simulator can simply sample the random bits $r_1, r_2 \ldots, r_n$ with parity 0 and output the probed wires. This requires no information about the input and output bits. Suppose at least one wire in the second set is probed. The main observation is that, after mask x_i by r_i, $g_1, g_2, \ldots, g_n$ are uniformly random bits with parity $\oplus_{i=1}^n x_i$. Thus, the simulator works as follows:

1. The simulator first queries the output bit $\oplus_{i=1}^n x_i$, and then randomly samples $g_1, g_2, \ldots, g_n$ with parity $\oplus_{i=1}^n x_i$. In this way, any probed wire in the second set can be simulated.
2. For each wire r_i in the first set, the simulator queries x_i and computes $r_i = g_i \oplus x_i$.

Note that the number of input and output wires queried by the simulator is bounded by the number of probed wires. The main issue of the basic construction is that it uses too many random bits: it requires $n - 1$ uniformly random bits to compute the XOR of n input bits. To reduce the randomness complexity, we first analyse what kind of random source is sufficient for the basic construction. We note that the analysis in [10] is specific to their order of computing $\{g_i\}_{i=1}^n$ and appears difficult to generalize to other orders. Our analysis uses a different argument, described below.

Sufficient Conditions for the Random Source in the Basic Construction. First of all, the correctness of our construction requires that the random variables $(r_1, r_2, \ldots, r_n)$ have parity 0. Now we want to relax the requirement that $r_1, r_2, \ldots, r_n$ are uniformly random bits with parity 0. Going forward, let $r_1, r_2, \ldots, r_n$ be arbitrary possibly correlated bits with parity 0. Let $\tilde{r}_1, \tilde{r}_2, \ldots, \tilde{r}_n$ be uniformly random bits with parity 0.

We observe that a direct sufficient condition is that the distribution of the probed wires when using $r_1, r_2, \ldots, r_n$ is identical to the distribution of the probed wires when using $\tilde{r}_1, \tilde{r}_2, \ldots, \tilde{r}_n$. This is because we have shown that the basic protocol is leakage-tolerant when using uniformly random bits $\tilde{r}_1, \tilde{r}_2, \ldots, \tilde{r}_n$ with parity 0. With the above sufficient condition, we can simulate the probed wires in the same way as that for the basic construction when replacing $\tilde{r}_1, \tilde{r}_2, \ldots, \tilde{r}_n$ with $r_1, r_2, \ldots, r_n$.

More concretely, let $r = (r_1, r_2, \ldots, r_n)$, $x = (x_1, x_2, \ldots, x_n)$, and $\tilde{r} = (\tilde{r}_1, \tilde{r}_2, \ldots, \tilde{r}_n)$. For a set W of at most t intermediate wires in $\mathcal{G}$, the above sufficient condition requires that

$$\texttt{Dist}((x, r), W) = \texttt{Dist}((x, \tilde{r}), W),$$

where $\texttt{Dist}((x, r), W)$ refers to the distribution of W when instantiated by (x, r). We will reduce this to a requirement on the random source r.

Recall that there are two sets of intermediate variables in $\mathcal{G}$: (1) the first set contains the correlated random bits $r_1, r_2, \ldots, r_n$, and (2) the second set contains all wires in the addition circuit, which is either g_i for some $i \in \{1, 2, \ldots, n\}$ or a linear combination of $\{g_1, g_2, \ldots, g_n\}$. Note that each bit in the second set can be written as $\oplus_{i \in L} g_i = (\oplus_{i \in L} x_i) \oplus (\oplus_{i \in L} r_i)$ for some set $L \subset \{1, 2, \ldots, n\}$. Since x are fixed input bits, it is sufficient to only consider the distribution of $\oplus_{i \in L} r_i$. Therefore, consider the set $\mathcal{A}$ defined as:

$$\mathcal{A} = \{r_1, r_2, \ldots, r_n\} \bigcup \{\oplus_{i \in L} r_i : \oplus_{i \in L} g_i \text{ is an intermediate wire in } \mathcal{G}\}.$$

Each variable in $\mathcal{A}$ is a linear combination of $\{r_1, r_2, \ldots, r_n\}$. The sufficient condition above can be transformed to that, for any set W of at most t variables in $\mathcal{A}$, $\texttt{Dist}(r, W) = \texttt{Dist}(\tilde{r}, W)$ holds.

We refer to $\mathcal{A}$ as the access structure of the random variables $\{r_1, r_2, \ldots, r_n\}$. Formally, an access structure $\mathcal{A}$ of a set of variables $\{r_1, r_2, \ldots, r_n\}$ is a set which satisfies that (1) for all $i \in \{1, 2, \ldots, n\}$, $r_i \in \mathcal{A}$, and (2) every variable in $\mathcal{A}$ is a linear combination of $(r_1, r_2, \ldots, r_n)$. One may think that a probing attack can only probe variables in $\mathcal{A}$.

Therefore, we can summarize the sufficient conditions for the distribution of the random source r in the basic construction as follows:

1. The parity of $(r_1, r_2, \ldots, r_n)$ is 0.
2. Let $\mathcal{A}$ be the access structure of $(r_1, r_2, \ldots, r_n)$ as defined above. Let $\tilde{r} = (\tilde{r}_1, \tilde{r}_2, \ldots, \tilde{r}_n)$ be uniformly random bits with parity 0. For any set W of at most t variables in $\mathcal{A}$, $\texttt{Dist}(r, W) = \texttt{Dist}(\tilde{r}, W)$.

Robust Parity Sharing Generator. Now we consider to use a robust PRG to generate the above correlated random bits. We follow the notion of robust t-wise independent PRGs in [8] and define what we refer to as robust parity sharing generators as follows.

Definition 2 (Robust Parity Sharing Generators). *Let $G : \{0, 1\}^m \to \{0, 1\}^n$ be a function and $\mathcal{A}$ be an access structure of the output bits of G. Let u be a vector of m uniformly random bits, and $r = G(u)$. A circuit implementation C of the function G is a (t, k, q)-robust parity sharing generator with respect to $\mathcal{A}$ if the following holds:*

- *The parity of the output bits r is 0.*
- *Let $\tilde{r} \in \{0,1\}^n$ be uniformly random bits with parity 0. For any set S of at most k wires in C, there is a set T of at most $q|S|$ output bits such that for any set W of t variables in $\mathcal{A}$ and for any fixing of the values C_S of the wires in S and r_I, where $I = \{i : r_i \in T\}$,*

$$\texttt{Dist}(r|_{C_S, r_I}, W) = \texttt{Dist}(\tilde{r}|_{\tilde{r}_I = r_I}, W),$$

where $\texttt{Dist}(r, W)$ is the distribution of the variables in W when they are instantiated by r, $r|_{C_S, r_I}$ is the random variable r conditioned on C_S and r_I, and $\tilde{r}|_{\tilde{r}_I = r_I}$ is the random variable $\tilde{r}$ conditioned on $\tilde{r}_I = r_I$.

Informally, a robust parity sharing generator outputs n random bits with parity 0. The output of a robust parity sharing generator satisfies that any t variables in the access structure $\mathcal{A}$ have the same distribution when these t variables are instantiated by n uniformly random bits with parity 0. As a robust t-wise independent PRG, any probing attack towards a robust parity sharing generator is equivalent to a probing attack towards the output bits. In Lemma 1, we formally prove that by replacing the randomness source by a robust parity sharing generator in the basic construction, we obtain a leakage-tolerant XOR gadget in the plain model.

Remark 1. The notion of robust parity sharing generators extends the notion of robust t-wise independent PRGs in the following two directions: (1) the parity of the output bits should be 0, and (2) an adversary may access to the output bits by learning not only a single output bit, but also a linear combination specified in the access structure $\mathcal{A}$.

If $\mathcal{A}$ only contains all the output bits, we may obtain a robust t-wise independent PRG from a robust parity sharing generator by removing the last output bit.

Remark 2. Recall that the outer construction uses the leakage-tolerant XOR gadget to compute each masked wire value. We note that if we use fresh randomness for each leakage-tolerant XOR gadget, then the total number of random bits will depend on the circuit size. To solve it, our construction uses a *single* leakage-tolerant private circuit for all XOR functions, which we refer to as a multi-phase leakage-tolerant XOR gadget, to replace the leakage-tolerant XOR gadgets invoked in the outer construction. Note that it is sufficient for our purpose since the number of probed wires is bounded by t in the whole circuit. Correspondingly, we also extend the notion of robust parity sharing generators to what we refer to as multi-phase robust parity sharing generators. We refer the readers to Sect. 5.2 for more details.

In the following, however, we still focus on robust parity sharing generators for simplicity. The idea can be easily extended to the multi-phase version.

Construction of a Robust Parity Sharing Generator. Let $u = (u_1, u_2, \ldots, u_m)$ denote the input random bits of the generator G. Our idea is to use a matrix M of size $n \times m$ to compute the output correlated random bits $r = (r_1, r_2, \ldots, r_n) = M \cdot u$. To compute r_i,

1. For all $w \in \{1, 2, \ldots, m\}$, G computes $M_{i,w} \cdot u_w$ in parallel. Here $M_{i,w}$ is the entry at i-th row and w-th column in $\boldsymbol{M}$.
2. G computes the $r_i = \oplus_{w=1}^{m} M_{i,w} \cdot u_w$ by using a $\lceil \log m \rceil$-depth addition circuit (see Sect. 2.2 for more details about the addition circuit).

Requiring that the parity of $r_1, r_2, \ldots, r_n$ is 0 is equivalent to requiring that $\sum_{i=1}^{n} \boldsymbol{M}_i = \boldsymbol{0}$.

Our idea is to use a random matrix $\boldsymbol{M}$ and show that the construction of G is a robust parity sharing generator with high probability when $m = O(t \cdot \log tn)$. Note that the structure of G is independent of the matrix $\boldsymbol{M}$. Although a probing attack can depending on $\boldsymbol{M}$, the set of all possible probing attacks is independent of $\boldsymbol{M}$. This allows us to first analyse the probability that G is secure against a fixed probing attack and then apply the union bound on all possible probing attacks.

Therefore, the problem becomes that for a fixed set S of at most k wires in G and a fixed set W of at most t variables in $\mathcal{A}$, there is a set T of at most $q|S|$ output bits (where T only depends on S) such that for any fixing of the values G_S of the wires in S and $\boldsymbol{r}_I$, where $I = \{i : r_i \in T\}$,

$$\mathrm{Dist}(\boldsymbol{r}|_{G_S, \boldsymbol{r}_I}, W) = \mathrm{Dist}(\tilde{\boldsymbol{r}}|_{\tilde{\boldsymbol{r}}_I = \boldsymbol{r}_I}, W).$$

At a high-level, the proof works as follows:

1. We first determine the set T. For each wire in S, if it is r_i or an intermediate wire when computing r_i, we insert r_i in T. Then T contains at most $|S|$ output bits. Intuitively, T corresponds to the set of output bits whose distributions are affected by the wires in S.
2. We note that if a variable w in W is a linear combination of other variables in $W \bigcup T$, then we can safely remove w and only consider $W \backslash \{w\}$. Note that if the argument holds for $W \backslash \{w\}$, then it also holds for W since w is fully determined by the variables in $W \bigcup T \backslash \{w\}$. Therefore, our second step is to find $\tilde{W} \subset W$ such that no variable in $\tilde{W}$ is a linear combination of other variables in $\tilde{W} \bigcup T$.
3. Recall that $\tilde{W} \subset W \subset \mathcal{A}$ and $T \subset \mathcal{A}$. Thus, all variables in $\tilde{W} \bigcup T$ are linear combinations of $r_1, r_2, \ldots, r_n$. We show that the distribution $\mathrm{Dist}(\tilde{\boldsymbol{r}}|_{\tilde{\boldsymbol{r}}_I = \boldsymbol{r}_I}, \tilde{W})$ is the same as the distribution of $|\tilde{W}|$ uniform bits. Therefore, the problem is reduced to analyse the probability that the distribution $\mathrm{Dist}(\boldsymbol{r}|_{G_S, \boldsymbol{r}_I}, \tilde{W})$ is the distribution of $|\tilde{W}|$ uniform bits.
4. We prove that this is equivalent to showing that the probability that for all *non-empty* subset $X \subset \tilde{W}$ and for all subset $Y \subset S \bigcup T$, the XOR of all bits in $X \bigcup Y$ is uniformly distributed. To this end, we first analyse the probability for fixed sets X, Y and then apply the union bound on all possible X, Y.
5. Finally, we note that all variables in $S \bigcup T \bigcup \tilde{W}$ are linear combinations of the input random bits $u_1, u_2, \ldots, u_m$. Therefore, there exists a vector $\boldsymbol{v}(w)$ for all $w \in S \bigcup T \bigcup \tilde{W}$ such that $w = \boldsymbol{v}(w) \cdot \boldsymbol{u}$. The XOR of all bits in $X \bigcup Y$ is uniformly distributed if and only if the summation of the vectors $\boldsymbol{v}(w)$ for all $w \in X \bigcup Y$ is a non-zero vector. Since $\boldsymbol{M}$ is a uniformly random matrix, we show that this holds with overwhelming probability.

We refer the readers to Sect. 6 for more details. Combining all the components we construct, we have the following theorem.

Theorem 1. *Any function f with circuit size s and output size n_o admits a t-private implementation (I, C, O) with the canonical encoder I and the decoder O which, for each output bit, takes the parity of a block of bits (which are not restricted to $t + 1$ bits), where C uses $O(t \cdot \log ts)$ random bits. Moreover, there exists a PPT algorithm which takes $(\tilde{C}_f, 1^t, 1^\lambda)$ as input, where $\tilde{C}_f$ is a circuit of size s that computes f, and outputs, except with $\leq 2^{-\lambda}$ probability, a t-private implementation (I, C, O) such that C uses $O(t \cdot \log ts + \lambda)$ random bits.*

In the full version, we show how to construct a t-leakate-resilient private circuit with the canonical decoder at the cost of $O(t \cdot \log \lambda)$ extra random bits.

Randomness Complexity of t-leakage-Tolerant Private Circuits. In Remark 3, we show that a t-leakage-tolerant private circuit can be obtained from our outer construction with small modifications. When the leakage-tolerant XOR gadgets are instantiated by a multi-phase leakage-tolerant XOR gadget, we have the following theorem.

Theorem 2. *Any function f with circuit size s admits a t-leakage-tolerant private implementation C, where C uses $O(t \cdot \log ts)$ random bits. Moreover, there exists a PPT algorithm which takes $(\tilde{C}_f, 1^t, 1^\lambda)$ as input, where $\tilde{C}_f$ is a circuit of size s that computes f, and outputs, except with $\leq 2^{-\lambda}$ probability, a t-leakage-tolerant implementation C such that C uses $O(t \cdot \log ts + \lambda)$ random bits.*

2.3   Extensions

Replacing the Canonical Encoder with a Randomness-Efficient Encoder. We note that the canonical encoder has already required $t \cdot n_i$ random bits for the input in I. When $n_i \geq t$, it means that the encoding of the input has already contained $O(t^2)$ random bits. It may lead to the following objection: a potential solution may reuse the randomness output by the encoder and may even be deterministic due to the large amount of randomness output by the encoder. We show that we can replace the canonical encoder by a randomness-efficient encoder, and achieve randomness complexity of $O(t \cdot \log ts)$ including the input encoder.

We first construct an encoder which only requires $O(t \cdot \log n_i)$ random bits to encode n_i bits by using a linear and strong t-wise independent PRG $G :$ $\{0, 1\}^m \rightarrow \{0, 1\}^{n_i}$. The construction works as follows:

1. The encoder Enc takes $x \in \{0, 1\}^{n_i}$ as input and $\rho \in \{0, 1\}^m$ as randomness.
2. The encoder Enc first computes $r = G(\rho)$. Then it computes $x \oplus r$.
3. The output of Enc is $(\rho, x \oplus r)$.

Note that it follows the same idea as the outer construction. We then show that we can directly replace the canonical encoder with this construction. Informally, this is because each input bit x_i is equal to the XOR of a subset of output bits of the encoder. To see this, since G is linear, each output bit r_i of G is equal to the XOR of a subset $\mathsf{supp}(r_i)$ of bits of the input ρ. Therefore, each output bit x_i is equal to the XOR of the bits in $\mathsf{supp}(r_i) \bigcup \{x_i \oplus r_i\}$ which are all in the output of the encoder. Thus, we may define $[x_i] = \mathsf{supp}(r_i) \bigcup \{x_i \oplus r_i\}$ and we can use the same outer construction to transform the input encoding to the masked input bits.

As a result, we have the following theorem. We refer the readers to the full version for more details.

Theorem 3. *Any function f with circuit size s and input size n_i admits a t-private implementation (I, C, O), where I uses $O(t \cdot \log n_i)$ random bits and C uses $O(t \cdot \log ts)$ random bits. Moreover, there exists a PPT algorithm which takes $(\tilde{C}_f, 1^t, 1^\lambda)$ as input, where $\tilde{C}_f$ is a circuit of size s that computes f, and outputs, except with $\leq 2^{-\lambda}$ probability, a t-private implementation (I, C, O) such that C uses $O(t \cdot \log ts + \lambda)$ random bits.*

Private Stateful Circuit. We follow the same argument as [9] to transform our basic construction to a private stateful circuit. Concretely, in the first step, we extend our construction to support unprotected input bits and output bits. The unprotected input bits and output bits are not encoded and can be observed by the public. Note that for an unprotected input x_i, we may set $[x_i] = \{x_i\}$ so that we can continue to use our basic construction.

In the second step, we use the randomness-efficient encoder Enc constructed above to encode the initial state. In each invocation, we use the private circuit which takes as input the encoded state and the unprotected external input, and outputs the encoded updated state and the external output. Note that since Enc follows from the same idea as the outer construction, the encoded updated state produced by our private circuit has the same form as that computed by Enc. Therefore, the encoded updated state produced by our private circuit is stored and will be used in the next invocation. The security directly follows from the private circuit that supporting unprotected input bits and output bits.

As a result, we have the following theorem. We refer the readers to the full version for more details.

Theorem 4. *Any stateful circuit C with initial state s_0 admits a t-private implementation $C'[s_0']$ which uses $O(t \cdot \log t|C|)$ random bits. Moreover, there exists a PPT algorithm which takes $(C, s_0, 1^t, 1^\lambda)$ as input and outputs, except with $\leq 2^{-\lambda}$ probability, a t-private implementation $C'[s_0']$ such that C' uses $O(t \cdot \log t|C| + \lambda)$ random bits.*

3 Preliminaries

3.1 Private Circuits

We start by defining the simple "stateless" variant of private circuits.

Definition 3 (Private Circuit [9]). *A private (stateless) circuit for* f : $\{0,1\}^{n_i} \rightarrow \{0,1\}^{n_o}$ *is a triple* (I, C, O) *where* $I : \{0,1\}^{n_i} \rightarrow \{0,1\}^{\hat{n}_i}$ *is a randomized input encoder,* C *is a randomized boolean circuit with input* $\hat{x} \in \{0,1\}^{\hat{n}_i}$, *output* $\hat{y} \in \{0,1\}^{\hat{n}_o}$, *and randomness* $\rho \in \{0,1\}^m$, *and* $O : \{0,1\}^{\hat{n}_o} \rightarrow \{0,1\}^{n_o}$ *is an output decoder, such that for any input* $x \in \{0,1\}^{n_i}$, *we have*

$$\Pr[O(C(I(x), \rho)) = f(x)] = 1,$$

where the probability is over the randomness of I *and* ρ.

In this work, the term "private circuit" will refer to the above stateless notion by default. In the full version, we also discuss the stateful variant and show how to extend our main result to this stronger model.

We will be interested in two different notions of security for private circuits: the standard notion of *leakage-resilience* (against probing attacks) and a more refined notion of *leakage-tolerance*. We define both notions below.

Leakage-Resilient Private Circuit. In the setting of leakage-resilient private circuits, we consider the canonical encoder: I encodes each input bit x_i by a vector of $t + 1$ random bits with parity x_i. This is mainly to avoid encoders which are function-dependent or provide large amount of randomness. For each input bit x, we use $[x_i]$ to denote the set of bits in the encoding of x_i. As to the decoder, we consider a relaxation of the canonical decoder: To decode each output bit, O takes the parity of a block of bits (which are not restricted to be $t + 1$ bits).

We note that the canonical encoder consumes $O(t \cdot n_i)$ random bits to encode an input $x \in \{0,1\}^{n_i}$. Later on, we will also consider a randomness-efficient encoder which only uses $O(t \log n_i)$ random bits.

Definition 4 (*t*-leakage-Resilient Privacy [9]). *We say that* C *is a* t*-leakage-resilient private implementation of* f *with encoder* I *and decoder* O *if for any* $x, x' \in \{0,1\}^{n_i}$ *and any set* P *of* t *wires in* C, *the distributions* $C_P(I(x), \rho)$ *and* $C_P(I(x'), \rho)$ *are identical, where* C_P *denotes the set of* t *bits on the wires from* P.

In the following, whenever we say t-private circuit, we refer to a t-leakage-resilient private circuit.

Leakage-Tolerant Private Circuit. In the setting of leakage-tolerant private circuits, we restrict the encoder and the decoder to be the identity function. The security requires that any set of at most t wires in C should leak at most the *same number* of input and output bits. Formally,

Definition 5 (*t*-leakage-Tolerant Privacy). *We say that* C *is a* t*-leakage-tolerant private implementation of* f *if there exists a simulator* $\mathcal{S} = (\mathcal{S}_1, \mathcal{S}_2)$ *such that for all* x *and any set* P *of at most* t *wires in* C, $\mathcal{S}_1(C, P)$ *outputs a set* P' *of* $|P|$ *input and output wires in* C *such that*

$$C_P(x, \rho) = \mathcal{S}_2(C, C_{P'}(x, \rho)),$$

where C_P *(w.r.t.* $C_{P'}$*) denotes the set of bits on the wires from* P *(w.r.t.* P'*).*

We note that the input wires and output wires can be naively simulated by having access to those wires. Therefore, it is sufficient to only consider the intermediate wires in C. We have the following equivalent definition.

Definition 6. *We say that C is a t-leakage-tolerant private implementation of f if there exists a simulator $S = (S_1, S_2)$ such that for all x and any set P of at most t intermediate wires in C, $S_1(C, P)$ outputs a set P' of $|P|$ input and output wires in C such that*

$$C_P(x, \rho) = S_2(C, C_{P'}(x, \rho)),$$

where C_P (w.r.t. $C_{P'}$) denotes the set of bits on the wires from P (w.r.t. P').

3.2 Strong t-wise Independent Pseudo-Random Generator

Our work will make use of the following notion of (strong) t-wise independent pseudo-random generator.

Definition 7 ((Strong) t-wise Independent PRG). *A function $G : \{0,1\}^n \to \{0,1\}^m$ is a t-wise independent pseudo-random generator (or PRG for short) if any subset of t bits of $G(x)$ is uniformly random and independently distributed when x is uniformly sampled from $\{0,1\}^n$.*

If any subset of t bits of $(x, G(x))$ is uniformly random and independently distributed when x is uniformly sampled from $\{0,1\}^n$, then we say G is a strong t-wise independent PRG.

We say a (strong) t-wise independent PRG G is linear if any output bit of $G(x)$ is equal to the XOR of a subset of bits in x.

Generic Construction of Linear and Strong t-wise Independent PRGs. In [4], Chor et al. introduce the notion of t-resilient functions. A t-resilient function $\mathtt{Ext} : \{0,1\}^n \to \{0,1\}^{n'}$ satisfies that the output of $\mathtt{Ext}$ is uniformly random given any t bits from the input.

A generic approach of constructing a linear and strong t-wise independent PRG is to combine a *linear* t-resilient function $\mathtt{Ext} : \{0,1\}^n \to \{0,1\}^{n'}$ and a *linear* t-wise independent PRG $G' : \{0,1\}^{n'} \to \{0,1\}^m$. Consider the function $G : \{0,1\}^n \to \{0,1\}^m$ which is defined to be $G(x) = G'(\mathtt{Ext}(x))$. Since $\mathtt{Ext}$ and G' are linear, G is also linear. Note that after fixing at most t bits in x, the output of $\mathtt{Ext}(x)$ is uniformly distributed, which means that the output of $G(x) = G'(\mathtt{Ext}(x))$ is t-wise independent. Therefore, any subset of t bits of $(x, G(x))$ is uniformly random and independently distributed, which means that G is a linear and strong t-wise independent PRG.

A Concrete Instance. For our purposes, it will suffice to use the following simple construction using polynomial evaluation over a finite field $\mathbb{F}_{2^k}$. We use $\alpha_0, \alpha_1, \ldots, \alpha_{2^k-1}$ to represent field elements in $\mathbb{F}_{2^k}$. Let $r = (r_0, r_1, \ldots, r_{t-1}) \in \mathbb{F}_{2^k}^t$. Consider the degree-$(t-1)$ polynomial $h_r(\cdot)$ which satisfies that $h_r(\alpha_i) = r_i$ for all $i \in \{0, 1, \ldots, t-1\}$. That is

$$r = (h_r(\alpha_0), h_r(\alpha_1), \ldots, h_r(\alpha_{t-1})).$$

If r is a uniform vector in $\mathbb{F}_{2^k}^t$, then $h_r(\cdot)$ is a random degree-$(t-1)$ polynomial, which means that any t distinct evaluation points of $h_r(\cdot)$ are uniformly random and independently distributed. Thus, for all $\ell \le 2^k - t$ we may define $G : \mathbb{F}_{2^k}^t \to \mathbb{F}_{2^k}^\ell$ by:

$$G(r) = (h_r(\alpha_t), h_r(\alpha_{t+1}), \ldots, h_r(\alpha_{\ell+t-1})).$$

To see why G is a strong t-wise independent PRG, note that $(r, G(r)) = (h_r(\alpha_0), h_r(\alpha_1), \ldots, h_r(\alpha_{\ell+t-1}))$, and any t distinct evaluation points of $h_r(\cdot)$ are uniformly random and independently distributed when r is uniformly sampled from $\mathbb{F}_{2^k}^t$.

Since every element in $\mathbb{F}_{2^k}$ can be represented by k bits, it gives us a strong t-wise independent PRG which takes as input $t \cdot k$ bits and outputs $\ell \cdot k$ bits. Note that ℓ can be as large as $2^k - t + 1$. Therefore, to construct a strong t-wise independent PRG which outputs m bits, we only need to use a field of size $O(m)$, which means that the input size can be as small as $O(t \cdot \log m)$.

We note that in the above construction, each output element $h_r(\alpha_i)$ can be written as a linear combination of r. Since we are in an extension field of the binary field where addition is equivalent to coordinate-wise XOR, it implies that every output bit of G is the XOR of a subset of its input. Therefore, for all m, we obtain a linear and strong t-wise independent PRG which takes as input $O(t \cdot \log m)$ bits.

4   Outer Construction: t-private Circuit via Leakage-Tolerant XOR Gadgets

For a boolean function $f : \{0,1\}^{n_i} \to \{0,1\}^{n_o}$, let $\tilde{C}$ denote a circuit that computes the function f. Let G be a linear and strong $2t$-wise independent PRG $G : \{0,1\}^m \to \{0,1\}^{|\tilde{C}|}$. We use $u = (u_1, u_2, \ldots, u_m)$ to denote the input of G and $r = (r_1, r_2, \ldots, r_{|\tilde{C}|})$ to denote the output of G. Since G is linear, each output bit r_i is the XOR of a subset of the input bits in $u_1, u_2, \ldots, u_m$. We refer to this set as the support of r_i, denoted by $\mathsf{supp}(r_i)$.

Our idea is to compute a masked bit for each wire value in $\tilde{C}$ using the output bit of G. Concretely, suppose all the wire values in $\tilde{C}$ are denoted by $g_1, g_2, \ldots, g_{|\tilde{C}|}$ (including input wires and output wires). For all $i \in 1, 2, \ldots, |\tilde{C}|$, we want to compute $g_i \oplus r_i$, where r_i is the i-th output bit of G. Intuitively, any set of t bits in $\{u_1, u_2, \ldots, u_m, g_1 \oplus r_1, g_2 \oplus r_2, \ldots, g_{|\tilde{C}|} \oplus r_{|\tilde{C}|}\}$ are uniformly random and independently distributed and therefore can be simulated by simply choosing t uniform bits. Note that for each wire value g_i, we can view $\{g_i \oplus r_i\} \bigcup \mathsf{supp}(r_i)$ as an additive sharing of g_i since the XOR of the bits in $\mathsf{supp}(r_i)$ is equal to r_i. We use $[g_i]$ to represent the set $\{g_i \oplus r_i\} \bigcup \mathsf{supp}(r_i)$.

We will first construct a t-private circuit by using a t-leakage-tolerant private circuit for the XOR function, which we referred to as a t-leakage-tolerant XOR gadget.

Intuitively, a leakage-tolerant XOR gadget satisfies that any probing attack towards the gadget is equivalent to a probing attack (that probes the same number of wires) towards the input wires and the output wire of this gadget. The construction of the circuit C works as follows.

1. The circuit C takes as input the input encoding $[x_1], [x_2], \ldots, [x_{n_i}]$ and the randomness $\rho \in \{0,1\}^m$. We use ρ as the input of the PRG G.
2. Transforming Input Encoding: We first transform the input encoding to the masked input bits using the corresponding output bits from G. For each input x_i, let g_i denote the input wire in $\tilde{C}$ that takes x_i as input. Then we want to compute the bit $g_i \oplus r_i$ in the circuit C. This is done by using a t-leakage-tolerant XOR gadget $\mathcal{G}$ with input bits in $[x_i]$ and $\mathsf{supp}(r_i)$.
3. Evaluating Addition Gates in $\tilde{C}$: For each addition gate in $\tilde{C}$ with input wires g_a, g_b and output wire g_c. Suppose we have constructed the circuit to compute $g_a \oplus r_a$ and $g_b \oplus r_b$ in C. To compute $g_c \oplus r_c$, we insert a t-leakage-tolerant XOR gadget $\mathcal{G}$ with input bits in $[g_a], [g_b]$ and $\mathsf{supp}(r_c)$.
4. Evaluating Multiplication Gates in $\tilde{C}$: For each multiplication gate in $\tilde{C}$ with input wires g_a, g_b and output wire g_c. Suppose we have constructed the circuit to compute $g_a \oplus r_a$ and $g_b \oplus r_b$ in C. Recall that $[g_a] = \{g_a \oplus r_a\} \bigcup \mathsf{supp}(r_a)$ and $[g_b] = \{g_b \oplus r_b\} \bigcup \mathsf{supp}(r_b)$. Let $[g_a] \otimes [g_b] := \{u \cdot v : u \in [g_a], v \in [g_b]\}$. Then the XOR of all bits in $[g_a] \otimes [g_b]$ is equal to $g_a \cdot g_b = g_c$. Thus, to compute $g_c \oplus r_c$, we first compute $u \cdot v$ for all $u \in [g_a], v \in [g_b]$ and then insert a t-leakage-tolerant XOR gadget $\mathcal{G}$ with input bits in $[g_a] \otimes [g_b]$ and $\mathsf{supp}(r_c)$.
5. Transforming to Output Encoding: The last step is to transform each masked output bit to the encoding of this output bit. For each output wire g_a in $\tilde{C}$, suppose we have constructed the circuit to compute $g_a \oplus r_a$ in C. Recall that $[g_a] = \{g_a \oplus r_a\} \bigcup \mathsf{supp}(r_a)$. Therefore, the XOR of the bits in $[g_a]$ is equal to g_a. The circuit simply outputs the wires in $[g_a]$ as the encoding of the output bit g_a.

Theorem 5. *Assume $\mathcal{G}$ is a t-leakage-tolerant XOR gadget. The circuit C constructed above is a t-private implementation of the function f.*

Proof. Following the definition of the t-privacy in Definition 4, it is sufficient to show that, for any $\boldsymbol{x}, \boldsymbol{x}' \in \{0,1\}^{n_i}$ and any set P of t wires in C, the distributions $C_P(I(\boldsymbol{x}), \boldsymbol{\rho})$ and $C_P(I(\boldsymbol{x}'), \boldsymbol{\rho})$ are identical, where C_P denotes the set of t bits on the wires from P. Since $\mathcal{G}$ is t-leakage-tolerant, any set of at most t intermediate variables within $\mathcal{G}$ can be perfectly simulated by probing the same number of the input wires and the output wire of $\mathcal{G}$. Therefore, it is sufficient to only focus on the set of t wires in C that does not include intermediate wires in the gadgets.

We first divide the wires in C (excluding the intermediate wires in the gadgets) into two disjoint sets:

1. The set of input wires of C: $\{[x_1], [x_2], \ldots, [x_{n_i}]\}$.
2. The set of the rest of wires in C. It is consist of the random bits $\boldsymbol{\rho} \in \{0,1\}^m$, the masked bits of the wire values $g_1 \oplus r_1, g_2 \oplus r_2, \ldots, g_{|\tilde{C}|} \oplus r_{|\tilde{C}|}$, and the bits in the set $[g_a] \otimes [g_b]$ for each multiplication gate in $\tilde{C}$ with input wires g_a and g_b.

Note that the output wires are included in the second set. We strengthen the argument by allowing to choose t wires in each of these two sets and show that these $2t$ wires can be simulated without knowing the input and the output of f.

For the first set, note that each sharing of $x_1, \ldots, x_{n_i}$ is a random additive sharing with $t+1$ shares. Therefore, any t shares in the first set are uniformly random. We can simulate the bits on the t wires chosen in the first set by uniform values.

For the second set, let $\rho = (u_1, u_2, \ldots, u_m) \in \{0,1\}^m$. Note that any wire $u \cdot v \in [g_a] \otimes [g_b]$, where $u \in [g_a]$ and $v \in [g_b]$, is determined by u and v. Therefore, any t wires in the third set are determined by at most $2t$ wires in the set $T = \{u_1, u_2, \ldots, u_m, g_1 \oplus r_1, g_2 \oplus r_2, \ldots, g_{|\tilde{C}|} \oplus r_{|\tilde{C}|}\}$. Recall that $(r_1, r_2, \ldots, r_{|\tilde{C}|})$ is the output of G on input $\rho = (u_1, u_2, \ldots, u_m) \in \{0,1\}^m$. Since G is a strong $2t$-wise independent PRG, when $\rho = (u_1, u_2, \ldots, u_m) \in \{0,1\}^m$ is chosen uniformly, $(u_1, u_2, \ldots, u_m, r_1, r_2, \ldots, r_{|\tilde{C}|})$ are $2t$-wise independent. Thus, we can simulate the bits on the t wires chosen in the third set by first sampling $2t$ random bits for the wires in T that determine these t wires and then compute the bits on these t wires.

Remark 3. Recall that in the setting of leakage-tolerant private circuits, function input and output are not encoded. We note that the above construction with small modifications gives a *t-leakage-tolerant* private implementation of f: (1) for each input bit x_i, we use $[x_i] = \{x_i\}$ in the above construction; and (2) for each output bit y_i, we use an additional leakage-tolerant XOR gadget with bits in $[y_i]$ to compute y_i.

Recall that in the setting of leakage-tolerant private circuits, the security requires that any set of t wires in C can be simulated by the same number of input and output bits. To show security, we divide the wires in C (after the modifications) into two disjoint sets: (1) the set of all input wires and output wires, and (2) the set of the rest of wires. Note that the second set is consist of the random bits $\rho \in \{0,1\}^m$, the masked bits of the wire values $g_1 \oplus r_1, g_2 \oplus r_2, \ldots, g_{|\tilde{C}|} \oplus r_{|\tilde{C}|}$, and the bits in the set $[g_a] \otimes [g_b]$ for each multiplication gate in $\tilde{C}$ with input wires g_a and g_b. The simulator works by querying the corresponding input and output wires in the first set and simulating the wires in the second set in the same way as described in the proof of Theorem 5.

5   Inner Construction: Leakage-Tolerant XOR Gadget

Following from Theorem 5, it is sufficient to construct a leakage-tolerant XOR Gadget. We first start with a basic construction which is given access to correlated randomness.

5.1   Basic Construction via Correlated Randomness

Let $x_1, x_2, \ldots, x_n$ denote the input bits of the gadget $\mathcal{G}$. The goal is to compute the output $\oplus_{i=1}^n x_i$. The construction of the circuit works as follows:

1. The circuit takes as input n bits $x_1, x_2, \ldots, x_n$. The circuit is given an access to n correlated random variables $r_1, r_2, \ldots, r_n$ which are uniformly random bits with parity 0.
2. The circuit first computes $g_i = x_i \oplus r_i$ for all $i \in \{1, 2, \ldots, n\}$ in parallel.
3. The circuit computes $\oplus_{i=1}^n g_i$ using a $\lceil \log n \rceil$-depth addition circuit. Concretely, in each iteration, all input bits are divided into groups of size 2 and then, for each group, we compute the XOR of the two bits in this group. The results are provided as input bits for the next iteration. Note that in each iteration, we reduce the number of input bits by a factor of 2. The whole process will end after $\lceil \log n \rceil$ iterations.

We show that this simple construction is t-leakage-tolerant given the correlated random variables $r_1, r_2, \ldots, r_n$.

First note that there are two different kinds of intermediate variables: (1) the first kind contains the correlated random variables $\{r_1, r_2, \ldots, r_n\}$, (2) the second kind contains the variables $\{g_1, g_2, \ldots, g_n\}$ computed in Step 2, and all intermediate variables when computing the addition circuit. Note that they are all in the form of $\oplus_{i \in L} g_i$ where $L \subset \{1, 2, \ldots, n\}$.

For any set W of $t_1 (\leq t)$ intermediate variables, we first determine the set $T \subset \{x_1, x_2, \ldots, x_n, \oplus_{i=1}^n x_i\}$ of size at most t_1 that will be used to simulate the intermediate variables in W. We first define I to be a subset of the indices $\{1, 2, \ldots, n\}$ such that for all $r_i \in W$, $i \in I$; or equivalently $I := \{i : r_i \in W\}$. Initially, we set T to be an empty set.

- For all $i \in I$, we insert the i-th input bit x_i in T.
- If W contains any intermediate variable of the second kind (i.e., an intermediate bit in the form of $\oplus_{i \in L} g_i$ where $L \subset \{1, 2, \ldots, n\}$), we insert the output bit $\oplus_{i=1}^n x_i$ in T.

Note that the size of T is at most t_1.

Now we show how to simulate the intermediate variables in W using the input bits and the output bit in T. For all $r_i \in W$, we sample a random bit as r_i. Since $x_i \in T$, we also compute $g_i = x_i \oplus r_i$. If W does not contain any intermediate variable of the second kind, then we are done. Otherwise, the rest of variables in W are all in the form of $\oplus_{i \in L} g_i$ where $L \subset \{1, 2, \ldots, n\}$. If we can generate g_i for all $i \in \{1, 2, \ldots, n\}$, then we can simulate the rest of variables in W. Since we have computed g_i for all $i \in I$, it is sufficient to focus on g_i where $i \notin I$.

Recall that for all $i \in I$, we have $x_i \in T$. Also recall that if W contains any intermediate variable of the second kind, then $\oplus_{i=1}^n x_i \in T$. Therefore, we can compute the parity of $\{x_i : i \notin I\}$ by $\oplus_{i \notin I} x_i = (\oplus_{i \in I} x_i) \oplus (\oplus_{i=1}^n x_i)$. Note that $\{r_i : i \notin I\}$ are random bits with parity $\oplus_{i \notin I} r_i = \oplus_{i \in I} r_i$. For all $i \notin I$, since we use r_i to mask the bit x_i, $\{g_i : i \notin I\}$ are random bits with parity $\oplus_{i \notin I} g_i$. Thus, we first compute

$$\oplus_{i \notin I} g_i = (\oplus_{i \notin I} x_i) \oplus (\oplus_{i \notin I} r_i) = (\oplus_{i \in I} x_i) \oplus (\oplus_{i=1}^n x_i) \oplus (\oplus_{i \in I} r_i).$$

Then, we sample $n - |I|$ random bits with parity $\oplus_{i \notin I} g_i$ as $\{g_i : i \notin I\}$. Finally, we compute the intermediate variables of the second kind in W using $\{g_1, g_2, \ldots, g_n\}$.

5.2   Robust Parity Sharing Generator

Now, we consider to use a generation circuit G for correlated random variables $r_1, r_2, \ldots, r_n$ in the basic construction. In this case, an adversary can also probe wires in G. We first review the definition of robust t-wise independent PRGs introduced in [8]. Then we will extend the notion of robust t-wise independent PRGs to what we refer to as robust parity sharing generators. The following definition corresponds to the strong robust t-wise independent PRGs in [8].

Definition 1 (Robust t-wise Independent PRGs [8]). *A circuit implementation C of a function $G : \{0,1\}^m \to \{0,1\}^n$ is a (t, k, q)-robust pseudo-random generator if the following holds. Let u be a vector of m uniformly random bits, and $r = G(u)$. For any set S of at most k wires in C, there is a set T of at most $q|S|$ output bits such that conditioned on any fixing of the values C_S of the wires in S and r_I, where $I = \{i : r_i \in T\}$, the values $r_{\bar{I}}$ of the output bits not in T are t-wise independent.*

Intuitively, any probing attack towards a robust t-wise independent PRG is equivalent to a probing attack towards the output bits. In [8], Ishai, et al. show that a private circuit can be derandomized by the following two steps:

1. First, derandomzie a private circuit by assuming an access to t-wise independent random source. This is achieved by considering the notion of randomness locality of a private circuit. The randomness locality of a private circuit is the number of random bits that are used to compute each wire. If each wire uses at most ℓ random bits (i.e., the randomness locality is ℓ), then we may replace the uniform random source by a $(\ell \cdot t)$-wise independent random source to protect against t-probing attacks. It is because any t wires depend on at most $\ell \cdot t$ random bits, and therefore, the distribution of these t wires when using uniform random source is identical to that when using $(\ell \cdot t)$-wise independent random source.
2. Then, replace the $(\ell \cdot t)$-wise independent random source by a robust $(\ell \cdot t)$-wise independent PRG.

However, this approach may inherently requires $\Omega(t^2)$ random bits. Intuitively, the randomness locality of a private circuit cannot be smaller than t, or otherwise, an adversary may learn extra information about the input by probing a wire and all random bits that are used to compute this wire. It means that the random source should be at least t^2-wise independent, which requires $\Omega(t^2)$ uniform random bits.

To overcome this bottleneck, our idea is to use a different approach to derandomize our basic construction of the leakage-tolerant XOR gadget. We first analyse what random source we need in our construction.

Sufficient Conditions of the Random Source in the Basic Construction. First of all, the correctness of our construction requires that the random variables $(r_1, r_2, \ldots, r_n)$ should have parity 0. Now we want to relax the requirement that $(r_1, r_2, \ldots, r_n)$ are uniformly random bits with parity 0.

We use r to denote the random variables $(r_1, r_2, \ldots, r_n)$ and x to denote the input bits $(x_1, x_2, \ldots, x_n)$. For a set W of intermediate variables in $\mathcal{G}$, we use $\mathtt{Dist}((x, r), W)$ to denote the distribution of the variables in W when they are instantiated by (x, r). Let $\tilde{r} = (\tilde{r}_1, \tilde{r}_2, \ldots, \tilde{r}_n)$ be uniformly random bits with parity 0. Since we have shown that $\mathcal{G}$ is a leakage-tolerant XOR gadget when using $\tilde{r}$ as random source, a straightforward sufficient condition of the distribution of r is that, for any set W of $t_1(\leq t)$ intermediate variables, $\mathtt{Dist}((x, r), W) = \mathtt{Dist}((x, \tilde{r}), W)$ holds for all x. With this condition, when using r as the random source in $\mathcal{G}$, we can simulate the intermediate variables in W by using the same way as that when the random source is $\tilde{r}$.

Recall that in our construction, there are two kinds of intermediate variables: (1) the first kind contains the random variables $\{r_1, r_2, \ldots, r_n\}$, (2) the second kind contains the variables $\{g_1, g_2, \ldots, g_n\}$ computed in Step 2, and all intermediate bits when computing the addition circuit, which are in the form of $\oplus_{i \in L} g_i$ where $L \subset \{1, 2, \ldots, n\}$. Note that $\oplus_{i \in L} g_i = (\oplus_{i \in L} x_i) \oplus (\oplus_{i \in L} r_i)$. Since x are fixed input bits, it is sufficient to only consider the distribution of $\oplus_{i \in L} r_i$. Therefore, consider the set $\mathcal{A}$ defined as:

$$\mathcal{A} = \{r_1, r_2, \ldots, r_n\} \bigcup \{\oplus_{i \in L} r_i : \oplus_{i \in L} g_i \text{ is an intermediate wire in } \mathcal{G}\}.$$

Each variable in $\mathcal{A}$ is a linear combination of $\{r_1, r_2, \ldots, r_n\}$. The sufficient condition above can be transformed to that, for any set W of $t_1(\leq t)$ variables in $\mathcal{A}$, $\mathtt{Dist}(r, W) = \mathtt{Dist}(\tilde{r}, W)$ holds, where $\mathtt{Dist}(r, W)$ refers to the distribution of the variables in W when they are instantiated by r. We refer to $\mathcal{A}$ as the access structure of the random variables $\{r_1, r_2, \ldots, r_n\}$. Formally, an access structure $\mathcal{A}$ of a set of variables $\{r_1, r_2, \ldots, r_n\}$ is a set which satisfies that (1) for all $i \in \{1, 2, \ldots, n\}$, $r_i \in \mathcal{A}$, and (2) every variable in $\mathcal{A}$ is a linear combination of $(r_1, r_2, \ldots, r_n)$. One may think that an probing attack can only probe variables in $\mathcal{A}$.

Therefore, we can summarize the sufficient conditions of the distribution of the random source r in the basic construction as follows:

1. The parity of $(r_1, r_2, \ldots, r_n)$ is 0.
2. Let $\mathcal{A}$ be the access structure of $(r_1, r_2, \ldots, r_n)$ as defined above. Let $\tilde{r} = (\tilde{r}_1, \tilde{r}_2, \ldots, \tilde{r}_n)$ be uniformly random bits with parity 0. For any set W of $t_1(\leq t)$ variables in $\mathcal{A}$, $\mathtt{Dist}(r, W) = \mathtt{Dist}(\tilde{r}, W)$.

Robust Parity Sharing Generator. Now we are ready to define the notion of robust parity sharing generators.

Definition 2 (Robust Parity Sharing Generators). *Let* $G : \{0,1\}^m \to \{0,1\}^n$ *be a function and* $\mathcal{A}$ *be an access structure of the output bits of* G. *Let* u

be a vector of m uniformly random bits, and $\boldsymbol{r} = G(\boldsymbol{u})$. A circuit implementation C of the function G is a (t, k, q)-robust parity sharing generator with respect to $\mathcal{A}$ if the following holds:

- The parity of the output bits $\boldsymbol{r}$ is 0.
- Let $\tilde{\boldsymbol{r}} \in \{0, 1\}^n$ be uniformly random bits with parity 0. For any set S of at most k wires in C, there is a set T of at most $q|S|$ output bits such that for any set W of t variables in $\mathcal{A}$ and for any fixing of the values C_S of the wires in S and $\boldsymbol{r}_I$, where $I = \{i : r_i \in T\}$,

$$\mathtt{Dist}(\boldsymbol{r}|_{C_S, \boldsymbol{r}_I}, W) = \mathtt{Dist}(\tilde{\boldsymbol{r}}|_{\tilde{\boldsymbol{r}}_I = \boldsymbol{r}_I}, W),$$

where $\mathtt{Dist}(\boldsymbol{r}, W)$ is the distribution of the variables in W when they are instantiated by $\boldsymbol{r}$, $\boldsymbol{r}|_{C_S, \boldsymbol{r}_I}$ is the random variable $\boldsymbol{r}$ conditioned on C_S and $\boldsymbol{r}_I$, and $\tilde{\boldsymbol{r}}|_{\tilde{\boldsymbol{r}}_I = \boldsymbol{r}_I}$ is the random variable $\tilde{\boldsymbol{r}}$ conditioned on $\tilde{\boldsymbol{r}}_I = \boldsymbol{r}_I$.

Let $\mathcal{G}$ be the t-leakage-tolerant XOR gadget we constructed in Sect. 5.1 that uses correlated randomness. Recall that $(x_1, x_2, \ldots, x_n)$ are input bits, $(r_1, r_2, \ldots, r_n)$ are random bits with parity 0, and $g_i = x_i \oplus r_i$ for all $i \in \{1, 2, \ldots, n\}$. Also recall that the access structure $\mathcal{A}$ of $\{r_1, r_2, \ldots, r_n\}$ is defined by

$$\mathcal{A} = \{r_1, r_2, \ldots, r_n\} \bigcup \{\oplus_{i \in L} r_i : \oplus_{i \in L} g_i \text{ is an intermediate wire in } \mathcal{G}\}.$$

We show how to construct a t-leakage-tolerant XOR gadget $\mathcal{G}'$ in the plain model (i.e., without access to correlated randomness) by using a $(t, t, 1)$-robust parity sharing generator with respect to $\mathcal{A}$. The construction simply uses a $(t, t, 1)$-robust parity sharing generator with respect to $\mathcal{A}$ to generate correlated randomness $(r_1, r_2, \ldots, r_n)$ for $\mathcal{G}$ and then uses $\mathcal{G}$ to compute the output.

Lemma 1. *The gadget $\mathcal{G}'$ constructed above is a t-leakage-tolerant XOR gadget.*

Proof. It is sufficient to show that for any $t_1 \leq t$ and any set W of t_1 intermediate variables, there exists a subset $T \subset \{x_1, x_2, \ldots, x_n, \oplus_{i=1}^n x_i\}$ of size at most t_1 such that the t_1 intermediate variables in W can be perfectly simulated from the bits in T. In the following, we use G to denote the $(t, t, 1)$-robust parity sharing generator.

We first divide the intermediate variables in $\mathcal{G}'$ into two categories:

- The first category contains all the wires in G, including the input random source $(u_1, u_2, \ldots, u_m)$ and the output correlated random variables $(r_1, r_2, \ldots, r_n)$.
- The second category contains the rest of intermediate wires in $\mathcal{G}'$. In other words, the second category contains all intermediate wires in $\mathcal{G}$ except the correlated randomness $(r_1, r_2, \ldots, r_n)$. For all $i \in \{1, 2, \ldots, n\}$, let $g_i = x_i \oplus r_i$. By the construction of $\mathcal{G}$, each variable in the second category is a linear combination of $(g_1, g_2, \ldots, g_n)$.

Let S be the set of intermediate variables in W that belong to the first category, and W' be the set of intermediate variables in W that belong to the second category. Then $|W| = |S| + |W'|$, and $|S|, |W'| \leq t$.

We first determine the set $T \subset \{x_1, x_2, \ldots, x_n, \oplus_{i=1}^n x_i\}$ that is used to simulate the intermediate variables in W. Let T' be the set of output bits of G in Definition 2. Then $|T'| = |S|$. There are two cases.

- If $W' = \emptyset$, then $T = \{x_i : r_i \in T'\}$. In this case $|T| = |T'| = |S| = |W| = t_1$.
- If $W' \neq \emptyset$, then $T = \{x_i : r_i \in T'\} \bigcup \{\oplus_{i=1}^n x_i\}$. In this case, $|T| = |T'| + 1 \leq |S| + |W'| = |W| = t_1$.

Now we describe the simulation of intermediate wires in W.

- For all intermediate wires in S, we sample uniformly random bits as $u_1, u_2, \ldots, u_m$ and compute G by taking $u_1, u_2, \ldots, u_m$ as input. Then we output the values associated with the intermediate wires in S.
- The following step is only done if $W' \neq \emptyset$. In this case, $T = \{x_i : r_i \in T'\} \bigcup \{\oplus_{i=1}^n x_i\}$. Let $I = \{i : r_i \in T'\}$. Then T is also equal to $\{x_i : i \in I\} \bigcup \{\oplus_{i=1}^n x_i\}$
  For all intermediate wires in W', let $\tilde{W} = \{\oplus_{i \in L} r_i : \oplus_{i \in L} g_i$ is in $W'\}$. Then $\tilde{W} \subset \mathcal{A}$ and $|\tilde{W}| = |W'| \leq t$. Since G is a $(t, t, 1)$-robust parity sharing generator, by Definition 2,

$$\mathrm{Dist}(r|_{G_S, r_I}, \tilde{W}) = \mathrm{Dist}(\tilde{r}|_{\tilde{r}_I = r_I}, \tilde{W}).$$

Since $(x_1, x_2, \ldots, x_n)$ are fixed input bits, we have $\mathrm{Dist}(r|_{C_S, r_I}, W') = \mathrm{Dist}(\tilde{r}|_{\tilde{r}_I = r_I}, W')$. Therefore, it is sufficient to simulate the intermediate wires in W' by using correlated randomness $\tilde{r}$ subject to $\tilde{r}_I = r_I$.

Recall that each variable in W' is a linear combination of $(g_1, g_2, \ldots, g_n)$. Therefore, we first generate $g_1, g_2, \ldots, g_n$ and then compute the variables in W'. For all $i \in I$, we compute $g_i = x_i \oplus \tilde{r}_i$. Note that $\{\tilde{r}_i : i \notin I\}$ are uniformly random bits with parity $\oplus_{i \notin I} \tilde{r}_i = \oplus_{i \in I} \tilde{r}_i$. Also note that we can compute the parity of $\{x_i : i \notin I\}$ by $(\oplus_{i=1}^n x_i) \oplus (\oplus_{i \in I} x_i)$. Therefore, $\{g_i = x_i \oplus \tilde{r}_i : i \notin I\}$ are uniformly random bits with parity $(\oplus_{i \notin I} \tilde{r}_i) \oplus (\oplus_{i \notin I} x_i)$. We generate uniformly random bits with parity $(\oplus_{i \notin I} \tilde{r}_i) \oplus (\oplus_{i \notin I} x_i)$ as $\{g_i : i \notin I\}$. Now we can compute variables in W' by using $(g_1, g_2, \ldots, g_n)$.

Multi-phase Leakage-Tolerant XOR Gadget and Multi-phase Robust Parity Sharing Generator. We note that if we use a robust parity sharing generator for each gadget $\mathcal{G}$, then the total number of random bits will depend on the circuit size. To solve it, we first consider what we call multi-phase leakage-tolerant XOR gadgets, which can compute a bounded number of XOR functions. Formally,

Definition 8 (Multi-phase Leakage-Tolerant XOR Gadget). *Let p and $n_1, n_2, \ldots, n_p$ be positive integers. For all $j \in \{1, 2, \ldots, p\}$, the function f takes as input a sequence of n_j bits $x_1^{(j)}, x_2^{(j)}, \ldots, x_{n_j}^{(j)}$ and outputs $\oplus_{i=1}^{n_j} x_i^{(j)}$. We say $\mathcal{G}$ is a multi-phase t-leakage-tolerant XOR gadget if it is a t-leakage-tolerant private implementation of f.*

Note that it is strictly weaker than p compositions of t-leakage-tolerant XOR gadgets since a multi-phase t-leakage-tolerant XOR gadget can only tolerate t probes across all phases while p compositions of t-leakage-tolerant XOR gadgets can tolerate t probes for each gadget, i.e., $p \cdot t$ probes in total. However, a multi-phase t-leakage-tolerant XOR gadget is sufficient to replace the t-leakage-tolerant XOR gadgets used in the outer protocol (see Sect. 4) since the number of probed wires is bounded by t in the whole circuit.

To construct a multi-phase t-leakage-tolerant XOR gadget, we extend the t-robust parity sharing generator to the multi-phase version as follows.

Definition 9 (Multi-phase Robust Parity Sharing Generators). *Let p and $n_1, n_2, \ldots, n_p$ be positive integers, $G : \{0,1\}^m \to \{0,1\}^{n_1} \times \{0,1\}^{n_2} \times \ldots \times \{0,1\}^{n_p}$ be a function, $\boldsymbol{u}$ be a vector of m uniformly random bits, and $\boldsymbol{r} = (\boldsymbol{r}^{(1)}, \boldsymbol{r}^{(2)}, \ldots, \boldsymbol{r}^{(p)}) = G(\boldsymbol{u})$, where $\boldsymbol{r}^{(j)} \in \{0,1\}^{n_j}$ for all $j \in \{1, 2, \ldots, p\}$. For each $\boldsymbol{r}^{(j)}$, let $\mathcal{A}_j$ be an access structure of the output bits $\{r_1^{(j)}, r_2^{(j)}, \ldots, r_{n_j}^{(j)}\}$. Let $\mathcal{A} = \bigcup_{j=1}^p \mathcal{A}_j$. A circuit implementation C of the function G is a multi-phase (t, k, q)-robust parity sharing generator with respect to $\mathcal{A}$ if the following holds:*

- *For all $j \in \{1, 2, \ldots, p\}$, the parity of the output bits $\boldsymbol{r}^{(j)}$ is 0.*
- *Let $\tilde{\boldsymbol{r}} = (\tilde{\boldsymbol{r}}^{(1)}, \tilde{\boldsymbol{r}}^{(2)}, \ldots, \tilde{\boldsymbol{r}}^{(p)}) \in \{0,1\}^{n_1} \times \{0,1\}^{n_2} \times \ldots \times \{0,1\}^{n_p}$ be uniformly random bits such that for all $j \in \{1, 2, \ldots, p\}$, the parity of $\{\tilde{r}_1^{(j)}, \tilde{r}_2^{(j)}, \ldots, \tilde{r}_{n_j}^{(j)}\}$ is 0. For any set S of at most k wires in C, there is a set T of at most $q|S|$ output bits such that for any set W of t variables in $\mathcal{A}$ and for any fixing of the values C_S of the wires in S and $\boldsymbol{r}_I$, where $I = \{(j, i) : r_i^{(j)} \in T\}$ and $\boldsymbol{r}_I$ is the vector that contains all bits in $\{r_i^{(j)} : (j, i) \in I\}$,*

$$\mathtt{Dist}(\boldsymbol{r}|_{C_S, \boldsymbol{r}_I}, W) = \mathtt{Dist}(\tilde{\boldsymbol{r}}|_{\tilde{\boldsymbol{r}}_I = \boldsymbol{r}_I}, W),$$

where $\mathtt{Dist}(\boldsymbol{r}, W)$ is the distribution of the variables in W when they are instantiated by $\boldsymbol{r}$, $\boldsymbol{r}|_{C_S, \boldsymbol{r}_I}$ is the random variable $\boldsymbol{r}$ conditioned on C_S and $\boldsymbol{r}_I$, and $\tilde{\boldsymbol{r}}|_{\tilde{\boldsymbol{r}}_I = \boldsymbol{r}_I}$ is the random variable $\tilde{\boldsymbol{r}}$ conditioned on $\tilde{\boldsymbol{r}}_I = \boldsymbol{r}_I$.

Let $\mathcal{G}$ be the t-leakage-tolerant XOR gadget we constructed in Sect. 5.1 that uses correlated randomness. We construct a multi-phase t-leakage-tolerant XOR gadget $\mathcal{G}'$ as follows:

1. First, we use a multi-phase t-robust parity sharing generator G with respect to a proper access structure $\mathcal{A}$ to prepare the correlated randomness for all phases.
2. Then, we use $\mathcal{G}$ to compute the XOR function in each phase.

The access structure $\mathcal{A}$ is defined as follows. For all $j \in \{1, 2, \ldots, p\}$, let $\boldsymbol{x}^{(j)} = (x_1^{(j)}, x_2^{(j)}, \ldots, x_{n_j}^{(j)})$ be the input bits and $\boldsymbol{r}^{(j)} = (r_1^{(j)}, r_2^{(j)}, \ldots, r_{n_j}^{(j)})$ be the random bits with parity 0, and $g_i^{(j)} = x_i^{(j)} \oplus r_i^{(j)}$ for all $i \in \{1, 2, \ldots, n\}$. We define the access structure $\mathcal{A}_j$ of $\{r_1^{(j)}, r_2^{(j)}, \ldots, r_{n_j}^{(j)}\}$ to be

$$\mathcal{A}_j = \{r_1^{(j)}, r_2^{(j)}, \ldots, r_{n_j}^{(j)}\} \bigcup \{\oplus_{i \in L} r_i^{(j)} : \oplus_{i \in L} g_i^{(j)} \text{ is an intermediate wire of } \mathcal{G}(\boldsymbol{x}^{(j)}; \boldsymbol{r}^{(j)})\}.$$

Then, the access structure $\mathcal{A} = \bigcup_{j=1}^{p} \mathcal{A}_j$. We show that this simple construction $\mathcal{G}'$ is a multi-phase t-leakage-tolerant XOR gadget.

Lemma 2. *The gadget $\mathcal{G}'$ constructed above is a multi-phase t-leakage-tolerant XOR gadget.*

The proof can be found in the full version.

Randomness Complexity of Our t-Private Circuit. In Sect. 6, we will show the following theorem.

Theorem 6. *For all positive integers p and $n_1, n_2, \ldots, n_p$, let $N = \sum_{i=1}^{p} n_i$ and $\mathcal{A}$ be the access structure defined above. There exists a PPT algorithm which takes $(1^t, 1^\lambda, \mathcal{A})$ as input, and outputs a multi-phase $(t, t, 1)$-robust parity sharing generator with respect to $\mathcal{A}$ with probability $1 - 2^{-\lambda}$ such that the input size $m = O(t \cdot \log tN + \lambda)$.*

The proof follows from Lemma 3 in Sect. 6.

We analyse the randomness complexity of our t-private circuit. Recall that f is the function we want to compute and n_i is the input size of f.

- Recall that in the outer construction, the random bits are used as input of a linear and strong $2t$-wise independent PRG G with output size $|\tilde{C}|$, where $\tilde{C}$ is a circuit that computes the function f. By using the construction in Sect. 3.2, the number of random bits that are used in G is bounded by $O(t \cdot \log |\tilde{C}|)$.
- For the inner construction, we only need to use random bits to instantiate the multi-phase $(t, t, 1)$-robust parity sharing generator in Theorem 6. To this end, we analyse the number of phases and the input size of each phase.
  In the outer construction, we invoke the leakage-tolerant XOR gadget for each wire in $\tilde{C}$. Therefore, the number of phases $p = |\tilde{C}|$.
  Recall that for each wire value g_i in the outer construction, we use $[g_i]$ to represent the set $\{g_i \oplus r_i\} \bigcup \mathsf{supp}(r_i)$, where r_i is the output bit of the $2t$-wise independent PRG G that is associated with g_i. Since the input size of G is bounded by $O(t \cdot \log |\tilde{C}|)$, the size of $[g_i]$ is also bounded by $O(t \cdot \log |\tilde{C}|)$. Note that:
  - For an input wire which carries the value x_i, the input size of the leakage-tolerant XOR gadget is $|[x_i]| + |\mathsf{supp}(r_i)| = O(t \cdot \log |\tilde{C}|)$.
  - For an addition gate with input wires g_a, g_b and output wire g_c, the input size of the leakage-tolerant XOR gadget is $|[g_a]| + |[g_b]| + |\mathsf{supp}(r_c)| = O(t \cdot \log |\tilde{C}|)$.
  - For a multiplication gate with input wires g_a, g_b and output wire g_c, the input size of the leakage-tolerant XOR gadget is $|[g_a] \otimes [g_b]| + |\mathsf{supp}(r_c)| = O(t^2 \log^2 |\tilde{C}|)$.
  Therefore, $N \le p \cdot \max\{n_1, n_2, \ldots, n_p\} = O(|\tilde{C}| \cdot t^2 \log^2 |\tilde{C}|)$. Thus, inner construction requires $O(t \cdot \log(t|\tilde{C}| \cdot t^2 \log^2 |\tilde{C}|) + \lambda) = O(t \cdot \log t|\tilde{C}| + \lambda)$ random bits.

In summary, the randomness complexity of our t-private circuit is $O(t \cdot \log t|\tilde{C}| + \lambda)$.

Theorem 1. *Any function f with circuit size s and output size n_o admits a t-private implementation (I, C, O) with the canonical encoder I and the decoder O which, for each output bit, takes the parity of a block of bits (which are not restricted to $t + 1$ bits), where C uses $O(t \cdot \log ts)$ random bits. Moreover, there exists a PPT algorithm which takes $(\tilde{C}_f, 1^t, 1^\lambda)$ as input, where $\tilde{C}_f$ is a circuit of size s that computes f, and outputs, except with $\leq 2^{-\lambda}$ probability, a t-private implementation (I, C, O) such that C uses $O(t \cdot \log ts + \lambda)$ random bits.*

Randomness Complexity of t-leakage-Tolerant Private Circuits. As we discussed in Remark 2, we can obtain a t-leakage-tolerant private circuit from our outer construction with small modifications. As for the randomness complexity, we need to invoke one more time of the leakage-tolerant XOR gadget for each output bit and the input size of the XOR gadget is bounded by $O(t \cdot \log |\tilde{C}|)$. When the leakage-tolerant XOR gadgets are instantiated by a multi-phase leakage-tolerant XOR gadget, the number of phases $p = |\tilde{C}| + n_o = O(|\tilde{C}|)$, where n_o is the number of output bits of f, and $N \leq p \cdot \max\{n_1, n_2, \ldots, n_p\} = O(|\tilde{C}| \cdot t^2 \log^2 |\tilde{C}|)$. We have the following theorem.

Theorem 2. *Any function f with circuit size s admits a t-leakage-tolerant private implementation C, where C uses $O(t \cdot \log ts)$ random bits. Moreover, there exists a PPT algorithm which takes $(\tilde{C}_f, 1^t, 1^\lambda)$ as input, where $\tilde{C}_f$ is a circuit of size s that computes f, and outputs, except with $\leq 2^{-\lambda}$ probability, a t-leakage-tolerant implementation C such that C uses $O(t \cdot \log ts + \lambda)$ random bits.*

Circuit Size. Our construction can be viewed as a composition of two parts: (1) the computation of a multi-phase $(t, t, 1)$-robust parity sharing generator in the inner construction, and (2) the computation for input wires, addition gates, multiplication gates, and the leakage-tolerant XOR gadgets (and for output wires in the leakage-tolerant variant).

For the first part, our construction of the multi-phase robust parity sharing generator has size $O(m \cdot N)$, where m is the input size of the generator, and N is the output size (see Sect. 6). Let s denote the circuit size of $\tilde{C}$ that computes f. Thus, the first part has size $O((t \cdot \log ts + \lambda) \cdot t^2 s \cdot \log^2 s) = O(t^3 s \cdot \log^2 s \cdot \log ts + \lambda \cdot t^2 s \cdot \log^2 s)$.

For the second part, for each input wire and addition gate (and output wire in the leakage-tolerant variant), we use the leakage-tolerant XOR gadget with input size $O(t \cdot \log s)$. For each multiplication gate, we first compute $O(t^2 \cdot \log^2 s)$ multiplications and then use the leakage-tolerant XOR gadget with input size $O(t^2 \cdot \log^2 s)$. Thus, the second part has size $O(t^2 s \cdot \log^2 s)$.

Thus, the overall circuit size is $O(t^3 s \cdot \log^2 s \cdot \log ts + \lambda \cdot t^2 s \cdot \log^2 s)$. Thus, assuming $\lambda \leq \tilde{O}(t)$, the circuit size is $\tilde{O}(t^3 s)$.

6 Construction of Multi-phase Robust Parity Sharing Generator

In this section, we show that there exists a multi-phase $(t, t, 1)$-robust parity sharing generator with randomness complexity $O(t \cdot \log tN)$, where $N = \sum_{j=1}^{p} n_j$. In the following, addition and multiplication operations are in the binary field $\mathbb{Z}_2$.

Let $\boldsymbol{u} = (u_1, u_2, \ldots, u_m)$ denote the input of G. For all $j \in \{1, 2, \ldots, p\}$, our idea is to use a matrix $\boldsymbol{M}^{(j)} \in \{0, 1\}^{n_j \times m}$ to compute $\boldsymbol{r}^{(j)} = (r_1^{(j)}, r_2^{(j)}, \ldots, r_{n_j}^{(j)}) = \boldsymbol{M}^{(j)} \cdot \boldsymbol{u}$. Specifically, to compute $r_i^{(j)}$,

1. The circuit G first computes the coordinate-wise multiplication $\boldsymbol{M}_i^{(j)} * \boldsymbol{u}$, where $\boldsymbol{M}_i^{(j)}$ is the i-th row of $\boldsymbol{M}^{(j)}$. That is, the circuit G computes $\boldsymbol{M}_{i,w}^{(j)} \cdot u_w$ for all $w \in \{1, 2, \ldots, m\}$.
2. Then, the circuit G computes $r_i^{(j)} = \sum_{w=1}^{m} \boldsymbol{M}_{i,w}^{(j)} \cdot u_w$ by using a $\lceil \log m \rceil$-depth addition circuit.

The requirement that the parity of $\boldsymbol{r}^{(j)}$ is 0 is equivalent to $\sum_{i=1}^{n_j} \boldsymbol{M}_i^{(j)} = \boldsymbol{0}$.

Let $\mathcal{A}$ be the access structure defined in the construction of the multi-phase t-leakage-tolerant gadget in Sect. 5.2. We will show that when using random matrices for $\{\boldsymbol{M}^{(j)}\}_{j=1}^{p}$ (with $m = O(t \log tN + \log(1/\epsilon))$) which are subject to $\sum_{i=1}^{n_j} \boldsymbol{M}_i^{(j)} = \boldsymbol{0}$ for all $j \in \{1, 2, \ldots, p\}$, with probability $1 - \epsilon$, the above construction is a multi-phase $(t, t, 1)$-robust parity sharing generator with respect to the access structure $\mathcal{A}$.

To this end, for any set S of at most t wires in G, we first determine the set T of at most $|S|$ output bits. For each wire in S, if it is $r_i^{(j)}$ or an intermediate wire when computing $r_i^{(j)}$, we insert $r_i^{(j)}$ in T. Then, it is clear that the size of T is bounded by $|S|$. We will prove the following argument in the full version.

Lemma 3. *Let $\{\boldsymbol{M}^{(j)}\}_{j=1}^{p}$ be random matrices subject to $\sum_{i=1}^{n_j} \boldsymbol{M}_i^{(j)} = \boldsymbol{0}$ for all $j \in \{1, 2, \ldots, p\}$, and G be the circuit constructed above. Let $\mathcal{A}$ be the access structure defined in the construction of the multi-phase t-leakage-tolerant gadget in Sect. 5.2. For any set S of at most t wires in G, let T be the set of at most $|S|$ output bits defined above.*

Then, when $m = O(t \log tN + \log(1/\epsilon))$, where $N = \sum_{j=1}^{p} n_j$, with probability $1 - \epsilon$, for any set S of at most t wires in G, any set W of t variables in $\mathcal{A}$ and for any fixing of the values G_S of the wires in S and $\boldsymbol{r}_I$, where $I = \{(j, i) : r_i^{(j)} \in T\}$ and $\boldsymbol{r}_I$ is the vector that contains all bits in $\{r_i^{(j)} : (j, i) \in I\}$,

$$\mathrm{Dist}(\boldsymbol{r}|_{G_S, \boldsymbol{r}_I}, W) = \mathrm{Dist}(\tilde{\boldsymbol{r}}|_{\tilde{\boldsymbol{r}}_I = \boldsymbol{r}_I}, W),$$

where $\mathrm{Dist}(\boldsymbol{r}, W)$ is the distribution of the variables in W when they are instantiated by $\boldsymbol{r}$, $\boldsymbol{r}|_{G_S, \boldsymbol{r}_I}$ is the random variable $\boldsymbol{r}$ conditioned on G_S and $\boldsymbol{r}_I$, and $\tilde{\boldsymbol{r}}|_{\tilde{\boldsymbol{r}}_I = \boldsymbol{r}_I}$ is the random variable $\tilde{\boldsymbol{r}}$ conditioned on $\tilde{\boldsymbol{r}}_I = \boldsymbol{r}_I$.

Acknowledgements. Y. Ishai supported by ERC Project NTSC (742754), BSF grant 2018393, and ISF grant 2774/20. V. Goyal and Y. Song were supported by the NSF award 1916939, DARPA SIEVE program, a gift from Ripple, a DoE NETL award, a JP Morgan Faculty Fellowship, a PNC center for financial services innovation award, and a Cylab seed funding award. Y. Song was also supported by a Cylab Presidential Fellowship.

References

1. Barthe, G., et al.: Strong non-interference and type-directed higher-order masking. In: Proceedings of the 2016 ACM SIGSAC Conference on Computer and Communications Security, CCS 2016, New York, NY, USA, pp. 116–129. Association for Computing Machinery (2016)

2. Belaïd, S., Benhamouda, F., Passelègue, A., Prouff, E., Thillard, A., Vergnaud, D.: Randomness complexity of private circuits for multiplication. In: Fischlin, M., Coron, J.-S. (eds.) EUROCRYPT 2016. LNCS, vol. 9666, pp. 616–648. Springer, Heidelberg (2016). https://doi.org/10.1007/978-3-662-49896-5_22

3. Cassiers, G., Standaert, F.-X.: Trivially and efficiently composing masked gadgets with probe isolating non-interference. IEEE Trans. Inf. Forensics Secur. **15**, 2542–2555 (2020)

4. Chor, B., Goldreich, O., Hasted, J., Freidmann, J., Rudich, S., molensky, R.: The bit extraction problem or t-resilient functions. In: 26th Annual Symposium on Foundations of Computer Science (SFCS 1985), pp. 396–407 (1985)

5. Coron, J.-S., Greuet, A., Zeitoun, R.: Side-channel masking with pseudo-random generator. In: Canteaut, A., Ishai, Y. (eds.) EUROCRYPT 2020. LNCS, vol. 12107, pp. 342–375. Springer, Cham (2020). https://doi.org/10.1007/978-3-030-45727-3_12

6. Duc, A., Dziembowski, S., Faust, S.: Unifying leakage models: from probing attacks to noisy leakage. In: Nguyen, P.Q., Oswald, E. (eds.) EUROCRYPT 2014. LNCS, vol. 8441, pp. 423–440. Springer, Heidelberg (2014). https://doi.org/10.1007/978-3-642-55220-5_24

7. Faust, S., Paglialonga, C., Schneider, T.: Amortizing randomness complexity in private circuits. In: Takagi, T., Peyrin, T. (eds.) ASIACRYPT 2017. LNCS, vol. 10624, pp. 781–810. Springer, Cham (2017). https://doi.org/10.1007/978-3-319-70694-8_27

8. Ishai, Y., et al.: Robust pseudorandom generators. In: Fomin, F.V., Freivalds, R., Kwiatkowska, M., Peleg, D. (eds.) Automata, Languages, and Programming, pp. 576–588. Springer, Berlin (2013). https://doi.org/10.1007/3-540-13345-3

9. Ishai, Y., Sahai, A., Wagner, D.: Private circuits: securing hardware against probing attacks. In: Boneh, D. (ed.) CRYPTO 2003. LNCS, vol. 2729, pp. 463–481. Springer, Heidelberg (2003). https://doi.org/10.1007/978-3-540-45146-4_27

10. Kushilevitz, E., Mansour, Y.: Randomness in private computations. SIAM J. Discrete Math. **10**(1997), 647–661. Earlier version in PODC (1996)

MITAKA: A Simpler, Parallelizable, Maskable Variant of FALCON

Thomas Espitau[1], Pierre-Alain Fouque[2], François Gérard[3],
Mélissa Rossi[4], Akira Takahashi[5], Mehdi Tibouchi[1],
Alexandre Wallet[2], and Yang Yu[6(✉)]

[1] NTT Corporation, Tokyo, Japan
{thomas.espitau.ax,mehdi.tibouchi.br}@hco.ntt.co.jp
[2] IRISA, Univ Rennes 1, Inria, Rennes Bretagne-Atlantique Center, Rennes, France
pa.fouque@gmail.com, alexandre.wallet@inria.fr
[3] University of Luxembourg, Esch-sur-Alzette, Luxembourg
francois.gerard@uni.lu
[4] ANSSI, Paris, France
melissa.rossi@ssi.gouv.fr
[5] Aarhus University, Aarhus, Denmark
takahashi@cs.au.dk
[6] BNRist, Tsinghua University, Beijing, China
yu-yang@mail.tsinghua.edu.cn

Abstract. This work describes the MITAKA signature scheme: a new hash-and-sign signature scheme over NTRU lattices which can be seen as a variant of NIST finalist FALCON. It achieves comparable efficiency but is considerably simpler, online/offline, and easier to parallelize and protect against side-channels, thus offering significant advantages from an implementation standpoint. It is also much more versatile in terms of parameter selection.

We obtain this signature scheme by replacing the FFO lattice Gaussian sampler in FALCON by the "hybrid" sampler of Ducas and Prest, for which we carry out a detailed and corrected security analysis. In principle, such a change can result in a substantial security loss, but we show that this loss can be largely mitigated using new techniques in key generation that allow us to construct much higher quality lattice trapdoors for the hybrid sampler relatively cheaply. This new approach can also be instantiated on a wide variety of base fields, in contrast with FALCON's restriction to power-of-two cyclotomics.

We also introduce a new lattice Gaussian sampler with the same quality and efficiency, but which is moreover compatible with the integral matrix Gram root technique of Ducas et al., allowing us to avoid floating point arithmetic. This makes it possible to realize the *same* signature scheme as MITAKA efficiently on platforms with poor support for floating point numbers.

Finally, we describe a provably secure masking of MITAKA. More precisely, we introduce novel gadgets that allow provable masking at any order at much lower cost than previous masking techniques for Gaussian sampling-based signature schemes, for cheap and dependable side-channel protection.

O. Dunkelman and S. Dziembowski (Eds.): EUROCRYPT 2022, LNCS 13277, pp. 222–253, 2022.
https://doi.org/10.1007/978-3-031-07082-2_9

1   Introduction

The third round finalists for signatures in the NIST postquantum standardization process consist of just three candidates: Rainbow [9], a multivariate scheme, Dilithium [12,29], a lattice-based scheme in the Fiat–Shamir with aborts framework, and Falcon [38], a hash-and-sign signature over NTRU lattices. They occupy fairly different positions within the design space of post-quantum signature schemes, and it is therefore important to understand, for each of them, to what extent they could possibly be improved by exploring similar designs that overcome some of their limitations. This paper aims at doing so for the Falcon signature scheme.

Hash-and-Sign Lattice-Based Signatures. Falcon fits within the long and hectic history of hash-and-sign signatures based on lattices. In those schemes, the signing key is a "good" representation of a lattice, the *trapdoor*, which makes it possible, given an arbitrary point in the ambient space, to find lattice points that are relatively close to it (i.e. solve the *approximate closest vector* problem, ApproxCVP[1]); the verification key, on the other hand, is a "bad" representation: it allows anyone to check if a point is in the lattice, but not to solve ApproxCVP. In order to sign a message, it is then hashed to a random point in the ambient space, and the signature is a lattice point close to it, obtained using the trapdoor. To verify, one checks that the signature is in the lattice and sufficiently close to the hash digest.

Early constructions along those lines, such as the GGH signature scheme [20] and multiple iterations of NTRUSign [21,22], were later shown to be insecure due to a common critical vulnerability: the lattice points obtained as signatures would leak information about the trapdoor used to compute them, which could then be recovered using more or less advanced statistical techniques [14,33]. One of the first round NIST candidates was in fact broken using the same idea [40].

It is thus crucial for security to prove that signatures are sampled according to a distribution that is *statistically independent* of the trapdoor. The first approach to do so, which remains the state of the art,[2] is due to Gentry, Peikert and Vaikuntanathan (GPV) [18]: sample the ApproxCVP solution according to a discrete Gaussian distribution centered at the target point and supported over the lattice, with covariance independent from the trapdoor (usually spherical). This type of lattice discrete Gaussian sampling can be carried out by randomizing known deterministic algorithms for ApproxCVP, like Babai rounding and Babai's nearest plane algorithm.

---

[1] Sometimes, this is also seen as a *bounded distance decoding* problem, BDD, but with large enough decoding bound that there are exponentially many solutions, instead of a unique one as is typically the case in the traditional formulation of BDD.

[2] Other techniques have been proposed that avoid Gaussian distributions, as in [30], but they tend not to be competitive.

Within the overall GPV framework, specific signature schemes vary according to the lattices over which they are instantiated, the construction of the corresponding trapdoors, and the lattice Gaussian sampling algorithms they rely on based on those trapdoors. The security level achieved by such a scheme is then essentially determined by the *quality* of the trapdoor and of the Gaussian sampling algorithm, defined as the minimal standard deviation achievable in Gaussian sampling, while still preserving the statistical independence of the output.

A complete overview of existing proposals for each of those elements is beyond the scope of the current work. We focus instead on the particular case of NTRU lattices with the usual NTRU trapdoors first considered in NTRUSign, as those lattices appear to offer the most efficient implementations by a significant margin, thanks to their compact trapdoors.

Hash-and-Sign Signatures over NTRU Lattices. NTRU lattices are, in essence, free rank 2 module lattices over cyclotomic rings, and the NTRU designers showed how to construct good trapdoors for them, even though the original signature schemes based on them proved insecure.

They were brought within the GPV framework (and thus gained provable security) thanks to the work of Ducas, Lyubashevsky and Prest (DLP) [13], who combined them with the Gaussian sampling algorithm obtained by randomizing Babai's nearest plane algorithm (this randomization is sometimes called the *Klein sampler* for lattice Gaussians). They analyzed the security of the construction and provided what became the first reasonably efficient implementation of a signature scheme in the GPV framework.

This DLP signature scheme offers relatively compact keys and signatures, but suffers from a relatively long signing time, quadratic in the $\mathbb{Z}$-rank of the underlying lattice. This is because the nearest plane computation is carried out after descending to $\mathbb{Z}$, essentially ignoring the module structure of the lattice.

FALCON is a direct improvement of this scheme, obtained by replacing this quadratic Gaussian sampling by a quasilinear one, derived from the quasilinear nearest plane algorithm described in the Fast Fourier Orthogonalization paper of Ducas and Prest [15] (and refining the parameter selection using a tighter statistical analysis based on the Rényi divergence). The computation still ultimately descends to $\mathbb{Z}$, but takes advantage of the tower field structure of the underlying number field (assumed to be a power-of-two cyclotomic) to achieve a better complexity.

These two approaches are equivalent in terms of the quality of the resulting Gaussian sampler, which is essentially the best possible for the given NTRU lattice. However, DLP does so at the cost of a slow signing algorithm, whereas FALCON, while fast, suffers from a very complex signing algorithm that is hard to implement, poorly suited for parallelization and difficult to protect against side-channel attacks. On the last point, both schemes have been shown to suffer from potential vulnerabilities with respect to side-channel leakage [17,25], and even though the most recent implementation of FALCON appears to be protected against timing attacks [23,35], countermeasures against stronger side-channel attacks like DPA seem difficult to achieve. FALCON is also limited to NTRU lattices over power-of-two cyclotomic fields, which limits its flexibility in terms of parameter selection. That latter limitation can be overcome to some extent by extending the construction to higher rank modules, as done in MODFALCON [7], but the other drawbacks remain.

Another possibility is to instantiate the randomized ApproxCVP algorithm directly over the underlying ring, instead of doing so over $\mathbb{Z}$. For the randomized version of Babai rounding, this gives rise to (the ring version of) Peikert's sampler, as introduced in [34]. This can also be done for Babai's nearest plane algorithm, leading to what Ducas and Prest call the *hybrid sampler*. The resulting algorithms consist of a constant number of ring multiplications, so that quasilinear complexity is obtained "for free" as long as the underlying ring has a fast multiplication algorithm (as certainly holds for arbitrary cyclotomics). This makes them highly versatile in terms of parameter selection. They are also much simpler than FALCON, easy to parallelize, and support fairly inexpensive masking for side-channel protection.

Their downside, however, is the lower quality of the corresponding samplers compared to FALCON and DLP. Indeed, by not descending to $\mathbb{Z}$ but only to the ring itself, the ApproxCVP algorithm achieves less tight of a bound compared to the Klein sampler, and hence the Gaussian sampling has a larger standard deviation. This is analyzed in details in Prest's Ph.D. thesis [37] (although certain heuristic assumptions are incorrect), and results in a substantially lower security level than FALCON and DLP.

Our Contributions: The MITAKA *Signature Scheme.* In this work, we revisit in particular the hybrid sampler mentioned above, and show that the security loss compared to FALCON can be largely mitigated using a novel technique to generate higher quality trapdoors. The resulting scheme, MITAKA,[3] offers an attractive alternative to FALCON in many settings since:

- it is considerably simpler from an algorithmic and an implementation standpoint, while keeping the same complexity (in fact, it is likely faster at the same dimension due to better cache locality);
- signature generation is parallel(izable);
- like Peikert's sampler, it has an online/offline structure, with the online part requiring only one-dimensional discrete Gaussian sampling with very small, constant standard deviation and simple linear operations;
- it can be instantiated over arbitrary cyclotomic fields[4], which makes it quite versatile in terms of parameter selection;

---

[3] Trivia: Mitaka is a neighborhood in Tokyo, Japan whose name means "the three falcons". It sounded fitting considering the maskable, parallelizable nature of our scheme and its strong points compared to FALCON.

[4] In principle, even more general number fields are possible as well, provided a good basis is known for their canonical embedding. The corresponding security analysis is cumbersome, however.

– it is easier to protect against side-channels and can be cheaply masked even at high order.

The main idea that allows us to achieve higher security than previously expected is as follows. It is well-known that, given NTRU generators (f, g), it is easy to compute the quality of the corresponding NTRU trapdoor for the hybrid sampler (in particular, it can be done without computing the whole trapdoor). It is thus very easy to check whether a given (f, g) reaches a certain threshold in terms of bit security, and as a result, the costly part of key generation is the sampling of the random ring elements f and g themselves (with discrete Gaussian coefficients). One can therefore achieve a greatly improved security level at the same cost in terms of randomness and not much more computation time if one can "recycle" already sampled ring elements f and g.

We propose several ways of doing so. The simplest one is to generate lists $\{f_i\}$, $\{g_j\}$ of candidate elements for f and g, and test the pairs (f_i, g_j): this increases the space of candidates quadratically, instead of linearly, in the amount of generated randomness. One can also generate the f_i's, g_j's themselves as sums of Gaussians with smaller standard deviation (as long as it remains above the smoothing parameters), and consider the Galois conjugates of a given g_j. By combining these techniques appropriately, we achieve a substantial security increase, of around 15 bits for typical parameter sizes. Concretely, we achieve the same security level as Dilithium–II [12] (which was argued to reach NIST Level-I) in dimension $d = 512$, and attain roughly NIST Level–V in dimension $d = 1024$, with intermediate parameter settings possible.

We also provide a detailed security analysis of our construction, and while most of the presentation focuses on power-of-two cyclotomics for simplicity's sake and easier comparison with previous work, we also show that intermediate NIST security levels can be conveniently achieved using other base fields, e.g. of dimension 648 (same security as FALCON–512), 768 (NIST Level–II), 864 (NIST Level–III) and 972 (NIST Level–IV).

As an additional contribution, we also introduce a novel, alternate lattice Gaussian sampler for MITAKA that achieves the same complexity and the same quality as the hybrid sampler, but has a different structure, closer to Peikert's sampler. The advantage of that alternate sampler is that it is compatible with the integral lattice Gram root technique of Ducas et al. [11], making it possible to instantiate it *without floating point arithmetic*. We call the resulting construction MITAKA$_{\mathbb{Z}}$. We stress that MITAKA and MITAKA$_{\mathbb{Z}}$ are two different approaches to implement the *same* signature scheme (in the sense that the generated signatures have statistically close distributions), and one can choose one or the other as preferred depending on whether the target platform has fast floating point arithmetic or not.

Finally, we introduce a new, concrete approach to mask those signature generation algorithms efficiently. In previous work, efficiently masking signature schemes using Gaussian sampling has proved quite challenging: even for the case of 1-dimensional *centered* discrete Gaussians, as in the BLISS signature scheme [10], this is far from straightforward [4]. Since MITAKA and MITAKA$_{\mathbb{Z}}$, like FALCON and DLP, require discrete Gaussian sampling with *variable* centers, a naive approach to masking is unlikely to yield fast results. Instead, we introduce and prove a novel gadget for sampling Gaussian distribution with an arithmetically masked center and a fixed standard deviation. This allows us to completely avoid masking Gaussian sampling operations in the online phase:[5] this works for a masked center, because picking a uniform center in $[0, M)$ with fixed denominator and sampling a discrete Gaussian around that center results in a close to uniform distribution modulo M. Carrying out this share-by-share sampling directly causes a slight decrease in the quality of the resulting sampler (depending on the number of shares), but this can be overcome completely with careful use of rejection sampling. Combining these statistical techniques with usual provable masking methodology, we achieve very efficient side-channel protection for both MITAKA and MITAKA$_{\mathbb{Z}}$.

Organization of the Paper. We start in Sect. 2 with preliminary material. In Sect. 3, we show some Gaussian samplers over modules that are the building blocks of MITAKA. Section 4 introduces the techniques to improve the quality of NTRU trapdoors, which elevates the security level achievable using MITAKA's samplers. The security analysis and preliminary implementation results of MITAKA are respectively provided in Sects. 5 and 6. In Sect. 7, we describe a provably secure masking of MITAKA. Finally, Sect. 8 provides some concluding remarks.

2   Preliminaries

For any $a \in \mathbb{R}$ and $q > 0$, let $[a]_q = \lfloor aq \rceil / q \in (1/q)\mathbb{Z}$.

2.1   Linear Algebra and Lattices

Write $\mathbf{A}^t$ for the transpose of any matrix $\mathbf{A}$. Let $s_1(\mathbf{A}) = \max_{\mathbf{x} \neq 0} \frac{\|\mathbf{A}\mathbf{x}\|}{\|\mathbf{x}\|}$ the largest singular value of $\mathbf{A}$. Let $\Sigma \in \mathbb{R}^{n \times n}$ be a symmetric matrix. We write $\Sigma \succ 0$ when Σ is *positive definite*, i.e. $\mathbf{x}^t \Sigma \mathbf{x} > 0$ for all non-zero $\mathbf{x} \in \mathbb{R}^n$. We also write $\Sigma_1 \succ \Sigma_2$ when $\Sigma_1 - \Sigma_2 \succ 0$. It holds that $\Sigma \succ 0$ if and only if $\Sigma^{-1} \succ 0$ and that $\Sigma_1 \succ \Sigma_2 \succ 0$ if and only if $\Sigma_2^{-1} \succ \Sigma_1^{-1} \succ 0$. A lattice $\mathscr{L}$ is a discrete additive subgroup of a Euclidean space. When the space is $\mathbb{R}^m$, and if it is generated by (the columns of) $\mathbf{B} \in \mathbb{R}^{m \times d}$, we also write $\mathscr{L}(\mathbf{B}) = \{\mathbf{B}\mathbf{x} \mid \mathbf{x} \in \mathbb{Z}^d\}$. If $\mathbf{B}$ has full column rank, then we call $\mathbf{B}$ a basis and d the rank of $\mathscr{L}$. The volume of $\mathscr{L}$ is $\mathrm{Vol}(\mathscr{L}) = \det(\mathbf{B}^t \mathbf{B})^{\frac{1}{2}}$ for any basis $\mathbf{B}$.

---

[5] The same idea can be adapted to the offline phase by masking the zero center. This is a bit less compelling, however, as it requires more shares, and replaces centered Gaussian sampling by variable center sampling.

2.2   Power-of-Two Cyclotomic Fields

For the sake of simplicity and readability, we focus in the rest of this article on the case where the number field is a cyclotomic field of conductor a power of 2. In any case, the content of this section generalizes straightforwardly to other cyclotomic number fields, as well as most of our results. Besides, the use of cyclotomic fields is nowadays pervasive in lattice-based cryptography. In this section we therefore keep only the minimum amount of notation and definitions to follow the article. More details can be found in the full version [16].

Let $d = 2^\ell$ for some integer $\ell \geqslant 1$ and ζ_d to be a $2d$-th primitive root of 1. Then for a fixed d, $\mathscr{K} := \mathbb{Q}(\zeta_d)$ is the d-th power-of-two cyclotomic field, and its ring of algebraic integers is $\mathscr{R} := \mathbb{Z}[\zeta_d]$. The field automorphism $\zeta_d \mapsto \zeta_d^{-1} = \overline{\zeta_d}$ corresponds to the complex conjugation, and we write the image f^* of f under this automorphism. We have $\mathscr{K} \simeq \mathbb{Q}[x]/(x^d+1)$ and $\mathscr{R} \simeq \mathbb{Z}[x]/(x^d+1)$, and both are contained in $\mathscr{K}_\mathbb{R} := \mathscr{K} \otimes \mathbb{R} \simeq \mathbb{R}[x]/(x^d+1)$. Each $f = \sum_{i=0}^{d-1} f_i \zeta_d^i \in \mathscr{K}_\mathbb{R}$ can be identified[6] with its coefficient vector $(f_0, \ldots, f_{d-1}) \in \mathbb{R}^d$. The adjoint operation extends naturally to $\mathscr{K}_\mathbb{R}$, and $\mathscr{K}_\mathbb{R}^+$ is the subspace of elements satisfying $f^* = f$.

The cyclotomic field $\mathscr{K}$ comes with d complex field embeddings $\varphi_i : \mathscr{K} \to \mathbb{C}$ which map f seen as a polynomial to its evaluations at the odd powers of ζ_d. This defines the so-called *canonical embedding* $\varphi(f) := (\varphi_1(f), \ldots, \varphi_d(f))$. It extends straightforwardly to $\mathscr{K}_\mathbb{R}$ and identifies it to the space $\mathcal{H} = \{\mathbf{v} \in \mathbb{C}^d : v_i = \overline{v_{d/2+i}}, 1 \leqslant i \leqslant d/2\}$. Note that $\varphi(fg) = (\varphi_i(f)\varphi_i(g))_{i \leqslant d}$. When needed, this embedding extends entry-wise to vectors or matrices over $\mathscr{K}_\mathbb{R}$. We let $\mathscr{K}_\mathbb{R}^{++}$ be the subset of $\mathscr{K}_\mathbb{R}^+$ which have all positive coordinates in the canonical embedding.

2.3   Matrices of Algebraic Numbers and NTRU Modules

2.3.1 2×2 $\mathscr{K}$-Valued Matrices

This work deals with free $\mathscr{R}$-modules of rank 2 in $\mathscr{K}^2$, or in other words, groups of the form $\mathscr{R}\mathbf{x} + \mathscr{R}\mathbf{y}$ where $\mathbf{x} = (x_1, x_2), \mathbf{y} = (y_1, y_2)$ span $\mathscr{K}^2$. There is a natural $\mathscr{K}$-bilinear form over $\mathscr{K}^2$ defined by $\langle \mathbf{x}, \mathbf{y} \rangle_\mathscr{K} := x_1^* y_1 + x_2^* y_2 \in \mathscr{K}$. It can be checked that for all $\mathbf{x} \in \mathscr{K}^2$, $\langle \mathbf{x}, \mathbf{x} \rangle_\mathscr{K} \in \mathscr{K}_\mathbb{R}^{++}$. This form comes with a corresponding notion of orthogonality. In particular, the well-known Gram-Schmidt orthogonalization procedure for a pair of linearly independent vectors $\mathbf{b}_1, \mathbf{b}_2 \in \mathscr{K}^2$ is defined as

$$\tilde{\mathbf{b}}_1 := \mathbf{b}_1, \quad \tilde{\mathbf{b}}_2 := \mathbf{b}_2 - \frac{\langle \mathbf{b}_1, \mathbf{b}_2 \rangle_\mathscr{K}}{\langle \mathbf{b}_1, \mathbf{b}_1 \rangle_\mathscr{K}} \cdot \tilde{\mathbf{b}}_1.$$

One readily checks that $\langle \tilde{\mathbf{b}}_1, \tilde{\mathbf{b}}_2 \rangle_\mathscr{K} = 0$. The Gram-Schmidt matrix with columns $\tilde{\mathbf{b}}_1, \tilde{\mathbf{b}}_2$ is denoted by $\tilde{\mathbf{B}}$ and we have $\det \tilde{\mathbf{B}} = \det \mathbf{B}$.

For $\Sigma \in \mathscr{K}_\mathbb{R}^{2\times 2}$, we write Σ^* its conjugate-transpose, where $*$ is the conjugation in $\mathscr{K}_\mathbb{R}$. We extend the notion of positive definiteness for matrices with entries in $\mathscr{K}_\mathbb{R}$: $\Sigma \in \mathscr{K}_\mathbb{R}^{2\times 2}$ is positive definite when $\Sigma = \Sigma^*$ and all the d matrices

---

[6] This is the so-called coefficient embedding.

induced by the field embeddings are positive definite. We then write $\Sigma \succ 0$. For example, $\mathbf{B}^*\mathbf{B}$ is a positive definite matrix for all $\mathbf{B} \in \mathscr{K}_\mathbb{R}^{2 \times 2}$. Positive definite matrices admit "square roots", that is, matrices $\sqrt{\Sigma}$ such that $\sqrt{\Sigma}\sqrt{\Sigma}^* = \Sigma$.

This work uses fundamental quantities for matrices over $\mathscr{K}$. The first is defined as $|\mathbf{B}|_\mathscr{K} := \max_{1 \leqslant i \leqslant 2} \|\varphi(\langle \tilde{\mathbf{b}}_i, \tilde{\mathbf{b}}_i \rangle_\mathscr{K})\|_\infty^{1/2}$. Since the eigenvalues λ_1, λ_2 of $\mathbf{B}^*\mathbf{B}$ are all in $\mathscr{K}^{++}$, coordinate-wise square roots are well-defined. The largest singular value of (the embeddings of) $\mathbf{B}$ is recovered as $s_1(\mathbf{B}) := \max_{1 \leqslant i \leqslant 2} \|\varphi(\sqrt{\lambda_i})\|_\infty$.

NTRU Modules. Given $f, g \in \mathscr{R}$ such that f is invertible modulo some prime $q \in \mathbb{Z}$, we let $h = f^{-1}g \bmod q$. The NTRU module determined by h is $\mathscr{L}_{\mathrm{NTRU}} = \{(u, v) \in \mathscr{R}^2 : uh - v = 0 \bmod q\}$. Two bases of this free module are of particular interest for cryptography:

$$\mathbf{B}_h = \begin{bmatrix} 1 & 0 \\ h & q \end{bmatrix} \text{ and } \mathbf{B}_{f,g} = \begin{bmatrix} f & F \\ g & G \end{bmatrix},$$

where $F, G \in \mathscr{R}$ are such that $fG - gF = q$. This module is usually seen as a lattice of volume q^d in $\mathbb{R}^{2d}$ thanks to the coefficient embedding. Lemma 1 shows the formulas for the associated quality parameters of $\mathbf{B}_{f,g}$.

Lemma 1 ([37], adapted). *Let $\mathbf{B}_{f,g}$ be a basis of an NTRU module. We have $\sqrt{q} \leqslant |\mathbf{B}_{f,g}|_\mathscr{K} \leqslant s_1(\mathbf{B}_{f,g})$ and :*

$$|\mathbf{B}_{f,g}|_\mathscr{K}^2 = \max\left(\|\varphi(ff^* + gg^*)\|_\infty, \left\|\frac{q^2}{\varphi(ff^* + gg^*)}\right\|_\infty\right),$$

$$s_1(\mathbf{B}_{f,g})^2 = \frac{1}{2}\|\varphi\left(T + \sqrt{T^2 - 4q^2}\right)\|_\infty,$$

where $T := ff^* + gg^* + FF^* + GG^*$. We have $|\mathbf{B}_{f,g}|_\mathscr{K} = s_1(\tilde{\mathbf{B}})$, where $\tilde{\mathbf{B}}$ is the Gram-Schmidt orthogonalization (over $\mathscr{K}$) of $\mathbf{B}_{f,g}$.

2.4   Gaussians over Rings

The Gaussian function on $\mathbb{R}^d$ centered at $\mathbf{c}$ and with covariance matrix $\Sigma \succ 0$ is defined as $\rho_{\mathbf{c}, \Sigma}(\mathbf{x}) = \exp(-\frac{1}{2}(\mathbf{x} - \mathbf{c})^t \Sigma^{-1}(\mathbf{x} - \mathbf{c}))$. If $\Sigma = s^2 \mathbf{I}_d$, we write also $\rho_{\mathbf{c}, s} = \exp(-\|\mathbf{x} - \mathbf{c}\|^2/(2s^2))$ and call the associated Gaussian *spherical*. We omit $\mathbf{c}$ if it is $\mathbf{0}$. The normal distribution $\mathcal{N}_\Sigma$ of covariance Σ then has density probability function $((2\pi)^d \cdot \det \Sigma)^{-1/2}\rho_\Sigma$. When we write $\mathcal{N}_{\mathscr{K}_\mathbb{R}, s}$, we mean that $(z_1, \ldots, z_d) \leftarrow (\mathcal{N}_{s/\sqrt{d}})^d$ is sampled and $(z_1 + iz_2, \ldots, z_{d-1} + iz_d)$ is outputted.

The discrete Gaussian distribution over a full rank lattice $\mathscr{L}$, centered at $\mathbf{c}$ and with covariance matrix $\Sigma \succ 0$ has density function given by

$$\forall \mathbf{x} \in \mathscr{L}, D_{\mathscr{L}, \mathbf{c}, \Sigma}(\mathbf{x}) = \frac{\rho_{\mathbf{c}, \Sigma}(\mathbf{x})}{\rho_{\mathbf{c}, \Sigma}(\mathscr{L})}.$$

For $c \in \mathscr{K}_\mathbb{R}$ and $s > 0$, we also use the notation $\lfloor c \rceil_s$ to denote the distribution $D_{\varphi(\mathscr{R}), \varphi(c), s}$. It extends coordinate-wise to vectors in $\mathscr{K}_\mathbb{R}^2$. For $\varepsilon > 0$, the smoothing parameter of a lattice $\mathscr{L}$ is $\eta_\varepsilon(\mathscr{L}) = \min\{s > 0 : \rho_{1/s}(\mathscr{L}^\vee) \leqslant 1 + \varepsilon\}$, where

---

Algorithm 1: RingPeikert sampler

Input: A matrix $\mathbf{B} \in \mathscr{K}^{2\times 2}$ such that $\mathscr{L} = \varphi(\mathbf{B}\mathscr{R}^2)$ and a target center $\mathbf{c} \in \mathscr{K}_{\mathbb{R}}^2$.

Result: $\mathbf{z} \in \mathscr{L}$ with distribution negligibly far from $D_{\mathscr{L},\mathbf{c},\Sigma}$.

1 *Precomputed: a parameter* $r \geqslant \eta_\varepsilon(\mathscr{R}^2)$, *and* $\Sigma_0 \in \mathscr{K}_{\mathbb{R}}^{2\times 2}$ *such that* $\Sigma_0\Sigma_0^* = \Sigma - r^2\mathbf{B}\mathbf{B}^*$

2 $\mathbf{x} \leftarrow \Sigma_0 \cdot (\mathcal{N}_{\mathscr{K}_{\mathbb{R}}, 1})^2$

3 $\mathbf{z} \leftarrow \lceil \mathbf{B}^{-1}(\mathbf{c} - \mathbf{x}) \rfloor_r$

4 **return** $\mathbf{B}\mathbf{z}$

$\mathscr{L}^\vee$ is the dual lattice. The exact definition of the lattice dual is not needed in this work, and when $\mathscr{L} = \mathscr{L}(\mathbf{B}) \subset \mathbb{R}^d$, it is enough to know the matrix $\mathbf{B}^{-t}$ encodes it. We say that $\sqrt{\Sigma} \geqslant \eta_\varepsilon(\mathscr{L})$ when $\rho_1(\sqrt{\Sigma}^*\mathscr{L}^\vee) = \rho_{\Sigma^{-1}}(\mathscr{L}^\vee) \leqslant 1 + \varepsilon$. In particular, one checks that $r\mathbf{B} \succ \eta_\varepsilon(\varphi(\mathbf{B}\mathscr{R}^2))$ when $r \geqslant \eta_\varepsilon(\mathscr{R}^2)$. We use the following bound.

Lemma 2 (Adapted from [18]). *Let* $\mathbf{B}\mathscr{R}^2$ *be free* $\mathscr{R}$*-module, and let* $\mathscr{L} = M(\mathbf{B})\mathbb{Z}^{2d}$ *be the associated rank* d *lattice in* $\mathbb{R}^{2d}$*. For all* $\varepsilon > 0$,

$$\eta_\varepsilon(\mathscr{L}) \leqslant |\mathbf{B}|_{\mathscr{K}} \cdot \frac{1}{\pi}\sqrt{\frac{\log(2d(1+1/\varepsilon))}{2}}.$$

3   Sampling Discrete Gaussians in $\mathscr{R}$-Modules

We present three approaches to sample discrete Gaussian over rings. The first two are respectively Peikert's perturbative approach adapted from [34], and the hybrid sampler of Ducas and Prest [37], which is core to MITAKA and uses the first as a subroutine. Then we describe a new sampler based on [11] which can involve integer arithmetic only and combines the ideas of the other two others.

3.1   Peikert's Sampler

In [34], Peikert presented an efficient algorithm to sample discrete Gaussians in a target lattice, using small continuous Gaussian perturbation. On a high level, it can be thought of as a randomized version of Babai's round-off algorithm, using random (normal) perturbations to hide the lattice structure, and can be formulated directly over the algebra $\mathscr{K}_{\mathbb{R}}$. The pseudo-code in Algorithm 1 outputs discrete Gaussians in a free rank 2 $\mathscr{R}$-module $\mathscr{L}$ described by a basis $\mathbf{B} \in \mathscr{K}^{2\times 2}$, with an arbitrary center in $\mathscr{K}_{\mathbb{R}}^2$. When $\Sigma \succ r^2\mathbf{B}\mathbf{B}^*$, the existence of Σ_0 below is guaranteed.

Algorithm 2: RingPeikert, one-dimensional version

Input: A target center $c \in \mathcal{K}_{\mathbb{R}}$.
Result: $z \in \mathcal{R}$ with distribution negligibly far from $D_{\mathcal{R},c,\Sigma}$.

1 *Precomputed: a parameter* $r \geqslant \eta_\varepsilon(\mathcal{R})$*, and* $\sigma_0 \in \mathcal{K}_{\mathbb{R}}$ *such that*
$\sigma_0^* \sigma_0 = \Sigma - r^2$

2 $x \leftarrow \sigma_0 \cdot \mathcal{N}_{\mathcal{K}_{\mathbb{R}},1}$

3 **return** $\lceil c - x \rfloor_r$

Theorem 1 ([34], adapted). *Let $\mathscr{D}$ be the output distribution of Algorithm 1. If $\varepsilon \leqslant 1/2$ and $\sqrt{\Sigma} \geqslant s_1(\mathbf{B}) \cdot \eta_\varepsilon(\mathcal{R}^2)$, then the statistical distance between $\mathscr{D}$ and $D_{\mathscr{L},c,\Sigma}$ is bounded by 2ε. Moreover, we have*

$$\sup_{\mathbf{x} \in \mathbf{B}\mathscr{R}^2} \left| \frac{\mathscr{D}(\mathbf{x})}{D_{\mathscr{L}(\mathbf{B}),c,\Sigma}(\mathbf{x})} - 1 \right| \leqslant 4\varepsilon.$$

From Lemma 1 and Lemma 2, note that the condition in the statement ensures that we are above the smoothing parameter of the target lattice. In practice, the covariance parameter is a scalar multiple of the identity matrix, or a positive real "constant" if seen in $\mathcal{K}_{\mathbb{R}}^{++}$. We highlight in Algorithm 2 the one-dimensional version of Peikert's sampler, that is, outputting discrete Gaussians in $\mathcal{R}$, because it appears as a subroutine of the hybrid sampler in the next section.

3.2   Ducas and Prest's Hybrid Sampler

In [37], a so-called hybrid sampler is presented that outputs discrete Gaussians in free $\mathcal{R}$ modules of finite rank. On a high level, this hybrid sampler follows Klein's approach, which is a randomized version of the Nearest Plane algorithm. In the ring context, the randomization subroutine happens "at the ring level" thanks to a ring Gaussian sampler, instead of "at the integer level". To again hide the lattice structure, perturbations are also involved but their distribution now depends on the target center. The hybrid sampler is described in Algorithm 3, which makes use of floating-point arithmetic, and is core to the Mitaka scheme.

It relies on a ring sampler which can be instantiated by Algorithm 2. For the sake of clarity, these "Peikert sampling" steps are made explicit in lines 4–6 and 9–11. We restrict to "totally spherical" standard deviation parameters (that is, scalar matrices) as they are the main use-case of this work.

Theorem 2 ([37], Theorem 5.10, adapted). *Let $\mathscr{D}$ be the output distribution of Algorithm 3. If $\varepsilon \leqslant 2^{-5}$ and $\sqrt{\Sigma} \geqslant |\mathbf{B}|_{\mathcal{K}} \cdot \eta_\varepsilon(\mathcal{R}^2)$, then the statistical distance between $\mathscr{D}$ and $D_{\mathscr{L},c,\Sigma}$ is bounded by 7ε. Moreover, we have*

$$\sup_{\mathbf{x} \in \mathbf{B}\mathscr{R}^2} \left| \frac{\mathscr{D}(\mathbf{x})}{D_{\mathscr{L},c,\Sigma}(\mathbf{x})} - 1 \right| \leqslant 14\varepsilon.$$

Algorithm 3: Hybrid Gaussian sampler

Input: A target center $c \in \mathscr{K}_{\mathbb{R}}^2$, a matrix $\mathbf{B} = [\mathbf{b}_1, \mathbf{b}_2]$ such that $\mathscr{L} = \varphi(\mathbf{B}\mathscr{R}^2)$ and its GSO $[\tilde{\mathbf{b}}_1, \tilde{\mathbf{b}}_2]$ over $\mathscr{K}$, a parameter $\sigma > 0$ (corresponding to $(\sigma, \ldots, \sigma) \in \mathscr{K}_{\mathbb{R}}$).

Result: z with distribution negligibly far from $D_{\mathscr{L}, c, \sigma^2 \mathbf{I}_{2d}}$.

1 *Precomputed:* $\sigma_i := \sqrt{\frac{\sigma^2}{\langle \tilde{\mathbf{b}}_i, \tilde{\mathbf{b}}_i \rangle} - r^2} \in \mathscr{K}_{\mathbb{R}}^{++}$.

2 $\mathbf{c}_2 \leftarrow \mathbf{c}, \mathbf{v}_2 \leftarrow 0$

3 $d_2 \leftarrow \frac{\langle \tilde{\mathbf{b}}_2, \mathbf{c}_2 \rangle_{\mathscr{K}}}{\langle \tilde{\mathbf{b}}_2, \tilde{\mathbf{b}}_2 \rangle_{\mathscr{K}}}$

4 $u_2 \leftarrow \mathcal{N}_{\mathscr{K}_{\mathbb{R}}, 1}$

5 $y_2 \leftarrow \sigma_2 \cdot u_2$

6 $x_2 \leftarrow \lfloor d_2 - y_2 \rceil_r$

7 $\mathbf{c}_1 \leftarrow \mathbf{c}_2 - x_2 \mathbf{b}_2, \mathbf{v}_1 \leftarrow x_2 \mathbf{b}_2$

8 $d_1 \leftarrow \frac{\langle \tilde{\mathbf{b}}_1, \mathbf{c}_1 \rangle_{\mathscr{K}}}{\langle \tilde{\mathbf{b}}_1, \tilde{\mathbf{b}}_1 \rangle_{\mathscr{K}}}$

9 $u_1 \leftarrow \mathcal{N}_{\mathscr{K}_{\mathbb{R}}, 1}$

10 $y_1 \leftarrow \sigma_1 \cdot u_1$

11 $x_1 \leftarrow \lfloor d_1 - y_1 \rceil_r$

12 $\mathbf{v}_0 \leftarrow \mathbf{v}_1 + x_1 \mathbf{b}_1$

13 **return** $\mathbf{v}_0$

In our integer arithmetic friendly sampler presented in the next section, we rely on a specific variant where the target lattice is described by an upper triangular matrix $\mathbf{U}$, or equivalently, when the Gram-Schmidt orthogonalization is the identity matrix. It is presented in Algorithm 4, and is core to MITAKA$_{\mathbb{Z}}$. In particular, in MITAKA$_{\mathbb{Z}}$, the ring sampler becomes a *discrete* Gaussian sampler that can be emulated in integer arithmetic. This is emphasized below by RingSampler$_{\mathbb{Z}}$.

3.3 An Integer Arithmetic Friendly Sampler

To clarify the presentation, in this section we identify matrices over $\mathscr{K}$ to their structured version over $\mathbb{Q}$. Fundamentally, our new sampler for $D_{\mathscr{L}(\mathbf{B}), c, s}$ combines Peikert's approach of Algorithm 1 and hybrid sampling in the case where the Gram-Schmidt is the identity. What allows us to restrict to integer arithmetic is to rely on the work of [11]. There, the authors showed how to generate small *integral* perturbation vectors, relying on a generalization of the Cholesky decomposition that can be also computed purely in integer arithmetic.

On the "hybrid side", as observed in the previous section, it is enough for us to have access to a discrete Gaussian sampler in integer arithmetic. Multiplying the output of Algorithm 4 by the Gram-Schmidt orthogonalization $\tilde{\mathbf{B}} = \mathbf{B}\mathbf{U}^{-1}$ of the target lattice basis, one would obtain vector with the correct support. The Gram-Schmidt basis may however contain entries in $\mathscr{K}$ that may have very large denominators. We avoid this thanks to an approximation $\hat{\mathbf{B}} \in (1/(pq))\mathscr{R}^{2 \times 2}$ of

---

Algorithm 4: Hybrid Gaussian sampler, $\mathbf{U}$ version

Input: A target center $\mathbf{c} = (c_1, c_2) \in \mathcal{K}^2$, an upper triangular matrix
$\mathbf{U} = [(1,0),(u,1)]$ with $u \in \mathcal{K}$, a parameter $r > 0$ (corresponding
to $(r, \dots, r) \in \mathcal{K}_\mathbb{R}$).

Result: $\mathbf{z}$ with distribution negligibly far from $D_{\mathscr{L}(\mathbf{U}),\mathbf{c},r}$.

1   $z_2 \leftarrow \mathsf{RingSampler}_{\mathbb{Z}}(c_2, r)$
2   $c_1' \leftarrow c_1 - z_2 u$
3   $z_1 \leftarrow \mathsf{RingSampler}_{\mathbb{Z}}(c_1', r)$
4   **return** $\mathbf{z} = \mathbf{U}(z_1, z_2)$.

Algorithm 5: Integer arithmetic ring Gaussian sampler

Input: a matrix $\widehat{\mathbf{B}} \in \mathscr{R}^{2 \times 2}$ such that $\widehat{\mathbf{B}}\mathbf{U}_{\hat{u}} = \mathbf{B} = \widetilde{\mathbf{B}}\mathbf{U}_u$, where
$\hat{u} = [u]_p \in \frac{1}{p}\mathscr{R}$, a center $\mathbf{c} \in \mathscr{R}^2$, and parameters $r, s > 0$.

Result: $\mathbf{z}$ with distribution negligibly far from $D_{\mathscr{L}(\mathbf{B}),\mathbf{c},rs}$.

1   *Precomputed:* $\Sigma_p = s^2 \mathbf{I} - \widehat{\mathbf{B}}\widehat{\mathbf{B}}^t$ and $\mathbf{A} \leftarrow \mathsf{IntGram}(p^2(\Sigma_p - \mathbf{I}))$
    /* $\mathbf{A}\mathbf{A}^t = p^2(\Sigma_p - \mathbf{I})$ */
2   $\mathbf{p} \leftarrow$ Algorithm 6$(p, \mathbf{A})$ /* $\mathbf{p} \sim D_{\mathscr{R}^2, r^2 \Sigma_p}$ */
3   $\hat{\mathbf{c}} \leftarrow \widehat{\mathbf{B}}^{-1}(\mathbf{c} - \mathbf{p})$
4   $\mathbf{z}' \leftarrow$ Algorithm 4$(\hat{u}, \hat{\mathbf{c}}, s)$ /* $\mathbf{z}' \sim D_{\mathscr{L}(\mathbf{U}_{\hat{u}}),\hat{\mathbf{c}},s}$ */
5   **return** $\mathbf{z} = \widehat{\mathbf{B}}\mathbf{z}'$

$\widetilde{\mathbf{B}}$, obtained by p-rounding of the upper right coefficient of $\mathbf{U}$. The quality of this approach is essentially driven by $|\mathbf{B}_{f,g}|_{\mathscr{K}} = s_1(\widetilde{\mathbf{B}})$.

Algorithm 5 describes this approach. The notation $\mathbf{U}_{\hat{u}}$ denotes that the upper-right coefficient of the matrix is $\hat{u}$. The procedure IntGram is fully described in [11], and impacts the choice of parameters for the algorithm to be actually correct. On a high level, given in input a positive definite matrix $\Sigma \in \mathscr{R}^{2 \times 2}$, it outputs a matrix $\mathbf{A} \in \mathscr{R}^{2 \times m}$ such that $\mathbf{A}\mathbf{A}^t = \Sigma$, and where $m \geqslant 2$. In our context, the input is a small perturbation covariance matrix $\Sigma_p = s^2 \mathbf{I} - \widehat{\mathbf{B}}\widehat{\mathbf{B}}^t$, where s is a large enough integer.

The offline sampler in Algorithm 6 is adapted from [11] and outputs from the expected distribution as long as $\mathbf{A}$ has been suitably computed. In terms of notation, recall that $\Lambda(\mathbf{A})^\perp \subset \mathscr{R}^m$ is the lattice of integer solutions of $\mathbf{A}\mathbf{x} = \mathbf{0}$.

We now state the correctness of Algorithm 5, stressing that the statement is correct as long as the integral root decomposition could be carried out and $p \geqslant d$.

Theorem 3. *Keep the notation of Algorithm 5, assuming also that IntGram correctly computes $\mathbf{A}$. For $\varepsilon \in (0,1)$, let $s > |\mathbf{B}_{f,g}|_{\mathscr{K}}(1 + \sqrt{2d/p}) + 1$ be an*

Algorithm 6: Offline sampler

Input: An integer $p > 0$, a matrix $\mathbf{A} \in \mathscr{R}^{2 \times m}$.
Result: $\mathbf{p} \in \mathscr{R}^2$ with distribution negligibly far from $D_{\mathscr{R}^2, r^2 \Sigma}$, where $\Sigma = \frac{1}{p^2} \mathbf{A}\mathbf{A}^t + \mathbf{I}$.

1 *Precomputed:* integers $r > \eta_\varepsilon(\mathscr{R}^2)$ and L such that $Lr \geqslant \eta_\varepsilon(\Lambda(A)^\perp)$.
2 $\mathbf{x} \leftarrow (\lfloor 0 \rceil_{Lr})^m$
3 $\mathbf{p}' \leftarrow \frac{1}{pL} \mathbf{A}\mathbf{x}$
4 $\mathbf{p} \leftarrow \lfloor \mathbf{p}' \rceil_r$
5 **return** $\mathbf{p}$.

---

integer and $r \geqslant \eta_\varepsilon(\mathbb{Z}^{2d})$. Then the distribution $\mathscr{D}$ of the output of Algorithm 5 is at statistical distance at most 15ε from $D_{\mathscr{L}(\mathbf{B}),\mathbf{c},sr}$. Moreover, we have

$$\sup_{\mathbf{z} \in \mathscr{L}(\mathbf{B})} \left| \frac{\mathscr{D}(\mathbf{z})}{D_{\mathscr{L}(\mathbf{B}),\mathbf{c},sr}(\mathbf{z})} - 1 \right| \leqslant 30\varepsilon.$$

3.4 Asymptotic Security of the Samplers

Hash-and-sign signatures over lattices are constructed, following the GPV framework [18], by hashing a message to the ambient space of the lattice, and returning as a signature a lattice point close to that hash digest. This is done using a "good" representation of the lattice, called the *trapdoor*, that enables the signer to solve the ApproxCVP problem with a relatively small approximation factor. Moreover, to prevent signatures from leaking information about the secret trapdoor, the close lattice points need to be sampled according to a distribution that is statistically independent of the trapdoor: usually a spherical discrete Gaussian distribution supported over the lattice and centered at the hash digest. This is where the algorithms from the previous sections come into play.

The security of the resulting signature scheme depends on the standard deviation of the discrete Gaussian distribution output by the sampler: the smaller the standard deviation, the closer the distance to the hash digest, the harder the corresponding ApproxCVP problem, and hence the higher the security level. As we have seen, however, there is a lower bound (depending on the trapdoor) to how small of a standard deviation the sampler can achieve while remaining statistically close to the desired spherical Gaussian: lower than that, and the distribution may start to deviate from that Gaussians in ways that could expose information about the secret trapdoor, and thus compromise the security of the signing key.

In the case of NTRU lattices, the trapdoor is the secret basis: $\mathbf{B}_{f,g} = \begin{bmatrix} f & F \\ g & G \end{bmatrix}$, and the standard deviation of the discrete Gaussian obtained from this trapdoor varies depending on the sampling algorithm, as discussed in particular in [37, §6]. It can be written as:

$$\sigma = \alpha \cdot \eta_\varepsilon(\mathscr{R}^2) \cdot \sqrt{q} \tag{1}$$

Table 1. Comparison of the best achievable trapdoor quality α for the various Gaussian samplers over NTRU lattices.

Sampler	$\alpha\sqrt{q}$	Best achievable α
Peikert	$s_1(\mathbf{B}_{f,g})$	$O(d^{1/4}\sqrt{\log d})$ [37, §6.5.2]
Hybrid (MITAKA)	$\|\mathbf{B}_{f,g}\|_{\mathscr{K}}$	$O(d^{1/8}\log^{1/4} d)$ [full version of this paper [16]]
Klein (FALCON)	$\|\mathbf{B}_{f,g}\|_{\mathrm{GS}}$	$O(1)$ [37, §6.5.1]

where the factor $\alpha \geqslant 1$, which we call the *quality*, depends on the sampler for a given trapdoor.

For the so-called Klein sampler used in DLP and FALCON, $\alpha\sqrt{q}$ is the Gram–Schmidt norm $\|\mathbf{B}_{f,g}\|_{\mathrm{GS}} := \max_{1\leqslant i\leqslant 2d} \|\widetilde{\mathbf{b}_i^{\mathbb{Z}}}\|_2$ of $\mathbf{B}_{f,g}$ *over the integers*. For the Peikert sampler over $\mathscr{K}$, Theorem 1 shows that $\alpha\sqrt{q} = s_1(\mathbf{B}_{f,g})$. Finally, for the hybrid sampler, Theorem 2 shows that $\alpha\sqrt{q} = \|\mathbf{B}_{f,g}\|_{\mathscr{K}}$.

For a given sampler, the generators f, g should be sampled appropriately to minimize the corresponding α. In his thesis [37], Prest analyzed the optimal choices both theoretically (under suitable heuristics) and experimentally. The resulting optimal choices for α are as follows (after correcting the flawed heuristic analysis of Prest in the case of the hybrid sampler; detailed discussion is in the full version [16]):

- heuristically, the quality of the Peikert sampler satisfies $\alpha = O(d^{1/4}\sqrt{\log d})$ [37, §6.5.2];
  for the hybrid sampler, we show $\alpha = O(d^{1/8}\log^{1/4} d)$ (and not $O(\sqrt{\log d})$ contrary to what was claimed in [37, §6.5.2] based on flawed heuristics);
- for the Klein sampler (used in DLP, and in modified form, FALCON), the heuristic analysis in [37, §6.5.1] show that it can be taken as low as $\sqrt{e/2} \approx 1.17$ independently of the dimension, and in particular $\alpha = O(1)$.

These properties are summarized in Table 1.

3.5 The MITAKA Signature Scheme

The previous samplers can be plugged directly into the GPV framework [18] to construct secure hash-and-sign signature schemes in the random oracle model. The idea is to sign a message by first hashing it as a point in the ambient space of the lattice, and then using the sampler to construct a lattice point close to that target. The signature is then the difference between the target and the lattice point (a small vector in the lattice coset defined by the target). The signing procedure is described more precisely in Algorithm 8. Both MITAKA and MITAKA$_{\mathbb{Z}}$ are specific instantiations of this paradigm, using the samplers of Algorithms 3 and 5 respectively. MITAKA generates the key pair in a similar manner to FALCON, but some techniques are introduced to improve the quality of the trapdoor (see Sect. 4 for details). In particular, as done in FALCON, it is also possible to trade secret-key size for efficiency by giving only 3 of the

---

Algorithm 7: Key generation

Input: Global parameter $\Psi = (\mathscr{R}, q, \sigma, r)$, quality parameter α.
Result: A key pair (pk, sk).

1 $(f, g) \leftarrow$ FirstVec(Ψ, α) satisfying $|\mathbf{B}_{f,g}|^2_{\mathscr{K}} \leqslant \alpha^2 q$ /* Algorithm 10 */
2 **if** f *is not invertible* mod q **then** restart
3 $(F, G) \leftarrow$ NTRUSolve$(\Psi, (f, g))$ satisfying $fG - gF = q$
4 $[\mathbf{b}_1, \mathbf{b}_2] \leftarrow [(f, g), (F, G)]$
5 $\widetilde{\mathbf{b}}_2 \leftarrow \mathbf{b}_2 - \frac{\langle \mathbf{b}_1, \mathbf{b}_2 \rangle_{\mathscr{K}}}{\langle \mathbf{b}_1, \mathbf{b}_1 \rangle_{\mathscr{K}}} \mathbf{b}_1 \in \mathscr{K}^2$
6 $n_i \leftarrow \langle \widetilde{\mathbf{b}}_i, \widetilde{\mathbf{b}}_i \rangle_{\mathscr{K}} \in \mathscr{K}_{\mathbb{R}}^{++}$ for $i = 1, 2$
7 $\sigma_i \leftarrow \sqrt{\frac{\sigma^2}{n_i} - r^2} \in \mathscr{K}_{\mathbb{R}}^{++}$ for $i = 1, 2$
8 pk $\leftarrow f^{-1}g \bmod q$, sk $= (\mathbf{b}_1, \mathbf{b}_2, n_1^{-1}\widetilde{\mathbf{b}}_1, n_2^{-1}\widetilde{\mathbf{b}}_2, \sigma_1, \sigma_2)$
9 **return** (pk, sk)

---

4 polynomials in the basis and enough information to recover Gram-Schmidt data by on-the-fly computations, all in Fast Fourier format. The verification algorithms of MITAKA and FALCON are exactly the same. For completeness, we describe the key generation and verification in Algorithms 7 and 9.

In Algorithm 8, the acceptance bound γ for signatures is chosen slightly larger than $\sigma\sqrt{d}$, for σ the standard deviation of the sampler given by Eq. (1) above, in order to ensure a low repetition rate for signature generation. (In the concrete security evaluation of Sect. 5, γ is selected so as to ensure $<10\%$ rejection; this gives e.g. $\gamma = 1.042\sigma\sqrt{2d}$ for $d = 512$). Signature verification simply recovers the second component $s_2 = s_1 \cdot h + c \bmod q$ and checks that the vector $\mathbf{s} = (s_1, s_2)$ is of length at most γ.

The security argument of Gentry, Peikert, and Vaikuntanathan reduces the security of the signature scheme to the hardness of SIS in the underlying lattice up to bound 2γ. It is therefore invalidated if an attacker can obtain two distinct outputs of the sampler with the same center (since their difference would be a solution to this SIS problem) [18, Section 6.1]. This is avoided in the signature scheme by randomizing the hash value associated with the message using a sufficiently long random salt $r \in \{0, 1\}^k$. To avoid collisions, it suffices to pick $k \geqslant \lambda + \log_2 q_s$ for λ bits of security and q_s signature queries. The choice of $k = 320$ as in [7, 38] suffices for up to 256 bits of security.

4 Improved Trapdoor Generation

The Peikert, hybrid and FALCON samplers for an NTRU basis $\mathbf{B}_{f,g}$ all have essentially the same complexity, and the first two are significantly simpler, easier to implement, slightly faster in the same dimension, and offer better avenues for parallelization and side-channel resistance (see Sect. 7). It would therefore be desirable to adopt one of the first two for practical implementations.

Algorithm 8: Signing

Input: A message m, a secret key sk, a bound γ.
Result: A signature sig of m.

1 **do**
2 $\quad$ $r \xleftarrow{\$} \{0,1\}^k$, $c \leftarrow H(r\|m)$
3 $\quad$ $z \leftarrow \mathsf{Sampler}(\mathsf{sk}, (0, c))$ $\qquad$ /* Algorithm 3 or 5 */
4 $\quad$ $s \leftarrow (s_1, s_2) = (0, c) - z$ $\qquad$ /* $s_1 \cdot h - s_2 \equiv -c \bmod q$ */
5 **while** $\|s\|^2 > \gamma^2$
6 **return** sig $= (r, s_1)$.

Algorithm 9: Verification

Input: A signature sig $= (r, s_1)$ of m, a public key pk $= h$, a bound γ.
Result: Accept or reject.

1 $c \leftarrow H(r\|m)$
2 $s_2 \leftarrow c + s_1 \cdot h \bmod q$
3 **if** $\|(s_1, s_2)\|^2 > \gamma^2$ **then** **return** Reject.
4 **return** Accept.

However, as seen in Sect. 3.4, the FALCON sampler has a substantial advantage in terms of security, since its Gaussian standard deviation is proportional to $\|\mathbf{B}_{f,g}\|_{\mathrm{GS}}$, whereas the Peikert and hybrid samplers are proportional to $s_1(\mathbf{B}_{f,g})$ and $|\mathbf{B}_{f,g}|_{\mathscr{K}}$ respectively, which are both larger. This results in a significant difference in asymptotic terms, as shown in Table 1, and also in bit security terms as will become apparent in the next section.

To increase the security level achievable using the first two samplers, and in particular the hybrid sampler, we propose a new technique to significantly improve the quality of NTRU trapdoors. We note in passing that it also applies to FALCON: while it cannot yield significant improvements in terms of security, since the standard deviation it achieves is already a very small factor away from the theoretical optimum, it can be used to speed up key generation substantially. The idea is as follows.

Recall that NTRU trapdoor generation for FALCON, say, works by sampling f, g with discrete Gaussian coefficient, computing the $\|\mathbf{B}_{f,g}\|_{\mathrm{GS}}$ of the resulting NTRU basis, and checking if this value is below the desired quality threshold. If not, we try again, and if so, the NTRU basis is completed and kept as the secret key. Trapdoor sampling for the hybrid sampler is similar. (On the other hand, for Peikert, completion has to be recomputed at each step to evaluate $s_1(\mathbf{B}_{f,g})$).

In this process, the costly operations are, on the one hand, the generation of the discrete Gaussian randomness, which has to be repeated several dozen times over in order to reach the desired threshold (this is not explicitly quantified by the authors of FALCON, but experiments suggest that, in many instances, upwards of 50 iterations are necessary), and, on the other hand, the completion of the basis (still costly despite recent optimizations [36]), which is only carried out once at the end and not for each iteration[7].

To optimize the process, our idea is to amortize the cost of discrete Gaussian sampling, by constructing several candidate trapdoors from the same randomness. We propose three main ideas to do so.

Lists of Candidates for f and g. The usual key generation algorithm for FALCON, as already mentioned, normally ends up generating many pairs (f_i, g_i), and tests each of them as a candidate first vector for the NTRU lattice.

Since we are generating Gaussian vectors f_i and g_i anyway, we can easily recycle this generated randomness by testing all the mixed pairs (f_i, g_j) instead: this results in a set of possible candidates which increases quadratically with the number of random vectors we generate, instead of just linearly.

Generating the Gaussian Vectors as Linear Combinations. Independently, one can generate each candidate vector f as a linear combination $\sum_{k=1}^{\ell} f^{(k)}$ where each $f^{(k)}$ is sampled from a discrete Gaussian of standard deviation $\sigma_0/\sqrt{\ell}$, for σ_0 the desired standard deviation of f. It is well-known that this results in the correct distribution provided that $\sigma_0/\sqrt{\ell}$ remains above the smoothing parameter of $\mathbb{Z}$ [32]. In fact, the FALCON implementation already does so for $d = 512$, where the candidate vectors are sums of two Gaussians vectors of standard deviation $\sqrt{2}$ times lower.

Now, when generating several f_i's, one obtains ℓ lists $L_k = \{f_i^{(k)}\}_i$ of Gaussian vectors. It is again possible to recycle this generated randomness by mixing and matching among those lists, and constructing candidates f of the form $\sum f_{i_k}^{(k)}$ for varying indices i_k, so that the total set of candidates is in bijection with $\prod_k L_k$. Its size increases like the ℓ-th power of the size of the lists.

Using the Galois Action. Finally, one can expand the set of candidates for g, say, by applying the action of the Galois group. In principle, other unitary transformations of g, even less structured ones like randomly permuting the coefficients in the power basis, could also be considered, but the Galois action in particular is convenient as it is expressed as a circular permutation on the embeddings $\varphi_i(g)$ of g (i.e., the Fourier coefficients), and for the hybrid sampler, the computation of the quality is entirely carried out in the Fourier domain.

Concretely, recall from Lemma 1 that the quality parameter α of the hybrid sampler associated with $\mathbf{B}_{f,g}$ satisfies:

$$\alpha^2 = \frac{|\mathbf{B}_{f,g}|_{\mathscr{K}}^2}{q} = \max\left(\frac{\max_i z_i}{q}, \frac{q}{\min_i z_i}\right)$$
$$\text{where } z_i = \varphi_i(ff^* + gg^*) = |\varphi_i(f)|^2 + |\varphi_i(g)|^2 \in \mathbb{R}^+.$$

---

[7] This is the case at least for FALCON and for the hybrid sampler, as for both of them, one can compute the quality of the trapdoor given only (f, g). This is especially fast for the hybrid sampler. For the Peikert sampler, however, doing so without also obtaining (F, G) seems difficult, and is left as an open problem.

It is easy to compute the embeddings z_i^τ associated to $\mathbf{B}_{f,\tau(g)}$ for some Galois automorphism τ of $\mathscr{K}$ simply by applying the corresponding permutation on the components of $\varphi(g)$. Moreover, we see from this representation that the conjugation $\tau_* : g \mapsto g^*$ leaves this quality invariant, so the relevant Galois elements to consider are a set of representatives of $\mathrm{Gal}(\mathscr{K}/\mathbb{Q})/\langle\tau_*\rangle$. For power-of-two cyclotomics, one can for example use τ_5^k for $k = 0, \ldots, d/2 - 1$, where $\tau_5(\zeta_d) = \zeta_d^5$.

Security Considerations. The techniques above can potentially skew the distribution of f and g somewhat compared to the case when each tested (f, g) that fails to pass the security threshold is thrown away. However, this is not really cause for concern: the precise distribution of f and g is not known to affect the security of the signature scheme other than in two ways:

- the extent to which it affects the geometry of the trapdoor, as encoded in the quality parameter α already; and
- the length of (f, g) itself as it affects key recovery security, but this length is always at least as large in our setting as in Falcon.

This indicates that our optimized secret keys do not weaken the scheme.

Concrete Example. In Algorithm 10, we describe an example key generation procedure that combines all three techniques presented above: we construct lists of candidates for f and g and test all possible pairs. Moreover, each f and g itself is sampled as a sum of $\ell = 2$ narrower Gaussians, and the list of g's is expanded using the Galois action. Of course, different combinations of the techniques are also possible, but this particular one offers a good balance between efficiency and achievable security.

Using this approach, as shown in Fig. 1, we are able to efficiently generate trapdoors with $\alpha \leqslant 2.04$ for $d = 512$, and $\alpha \leqslant 2.33$ for $d = 1024$ by $m \approx 16$ (corresponding to generating 64 narrow Gaussian vectors to select one candidate (f, g), largely in line with Falcon).

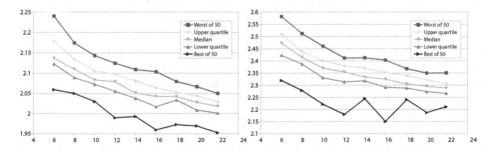

Fig. 1. Quality α reached by the optimized sampler of Algorithm 10 for various choices of m (50 trials each, $\sigma_0 = 1.17\sqrt{q/2d}$, G coset representatives of $\mathrm{Gal}(\mathscr{K}/\mathbb{Q})/\langle\tau_*\rangle$). Reachable α in dimension 512 (left) and 1024 (right).

Algorithm 10: MITAKA optimized key generation

Input: Desired standard deviation σ_0 of f and g, target quality α of the Gaussian, number of samples m to generate, set G of Galois automorphisms to apply. The total search space is of size $\#G \cdot m^4$ for $4m$ generated discrete Gaussian vectors.
Result: NTRU first trapdoor vector (f, g) with quality better than α.

1 **for** $i \in [1, m]$ **do**
2 $\quad\big|\quad f_i' \leftarrow D_{\mathcal{R}, \sigma_0/\sqrt{2}}, f_i'' \leftarrow D_{\mathcal{R}, \sigma_0/\sqrt{2}}$
3 $\quad\big|\quad g_i' \leftarrow D_{\mathcal{R}, \sigma_0/\sqrt{2}}, g_i'' \leftarrow D_{\mathcal{R}, \sigma_0/\sqrt{2}}$
4 **end for**
5 $L_f \leftarrow \{f_i' + f_j'' \mid i, j \in [1, m]\}$
6 $L_g \leftarrow \{\tau(g_k' + g_\ell'') \mid k, \ell \in [1, m], \tau \in G\}$
7 $L_u \leftarrow \{(f, \varphi(ff^*)) \mid f \in L_f\}$
8 $L_v \leftarrow \{(g, \varphi(gg^*)) \mid g \in L_g\}$
9 **for** $(f, u) \in L_u, (g, v) \in L_v$ **do**
10 $\quad\big|\quad z \leftarrow u + v$
11 $\quad\big|\quad$ **if** $q/\alpha^2 \leqslant z_i \leqslant \alpha^2 q$ *for all* i **then** **return** (f, g)
12 **end for**
13 **restart**

Improved Search via Early Aborts and Filtering. Key generation using the technique above involves an exhaustive search in a relatively large set of candidates $L_u \times L_v$, and testing each candidate involves $O(d)$ comparisons:

$$q/\alpha^2 \leqslant u_i + v_i \leqslant \alpha^2 q \quad \text{for } 1 \leqslant i \leqslant d/2,$$

as done in Step 11 of Algorithm 10. One can of course reject a candidate immediately as soon as one of the comparison fails, but this can happen arbitrarily late in the loop through the indices.

However, the lower bound condition is much more likely to fail than the upper bound for a given candidate (see the full version [16] for detailed analysis). Moreover, if we fix u, then it is more likely to fail on any given v for the indices i such that u_i is small. One can therefore improve the algorithm by a wide margin by carrying out a simple precomputation on u: extract the list of indices $S_u(w)$ of the w smallest elements of u for some $w \ll d/2$ (this can be done without sorting, in time $O(d)$). Then, for each corresponding candidate v, first check in time $O(w)$ whether the lower bound condition holds on the indices in $S_u(w)$: if so, the comparison is carried out normally, and otherwise v is rejected early.

Picking for example $w = 25$, we find that around 99.8% of candidates are rejected early in that way for our parameters, greatly reducing the number of full-fledged comparisons. All in all, this lets us achieve a speed-up of more than 5- to 10-fold as d ranges from 512 to 1024.

An additional, very simple optimization is to filter out values u, v such that $\|u\|_\infty > \alpha^2 q$ (and similarly for v) from the lists L_u and L_v, since such candidates clearly cannot satisfy the comparison.

5   Security Analysis of MITAKA

Concrete Security. In order to assess the concrete security of our signature scheme, we proceed using the usual cryptanalytic methodology of estimating the complexity of the best attacks against *key recovery attacks* on the one hand, and *signature forgery* on the other. For the parameter choices relevant to our scheme (in which the vectors of the trapdoor basis are not unusually small), key recovery is always harder than signature forgery, and therefore the cost of signature forgery is what determines the security level. The security of the forgery is a function of the standard deviation of the lattice Gaussian sampler used in the signature function, which itself depends on the quality α of the trapdoor, as discussed in Sect. 3.4. This analysis translates into concrete bit-security estimates following the methodology of NEWHOPE [1], sometimes called "core-SVP methodology". In this model [5,26], the bit complexity of lattice sieving (which is asymptotically the best SVP oracle) is taken as $\lfloor 0.292\beta \rfloor$ in the classical setting and $\lfloor 0.265\beta \rfloor$ in the quantum setting in dimension β. The resulting security in terms of α is given in Fig. 2 in dimensions 512 and 1024. This allows us to compare MITAKA with FALCON as well as with a "naive" version of the hybrid sampler that would omit the optimizations of Sect. 4; the results are presented in Table 2. Detailed and comprehensive analysis is given in the full version [16].

In addition, as mentioned earlier, our construction can be instantiated over more general base fields than power-of-two cyclotomics, which enables us to choose security level in a much more flexible way than FALCON. Example security levels which can be reached in this way are presented in Table 3. For such fields, we can choose the modulus q to be the first prime which is congurant to 1 modulo the conductor. Again, detailed analysis is given in the full version [16].

Asymptotic Security. As for all signature schemes in the GPV framework, the EUF–CMA security of our scheme in an asymptotic sense reduces, both in the classical [18] and quantum random oracle models [6], to the SIS problem in the underlying lattice (in this case, an instance of Module–SIS [27]). However, as is the case for FALCON (and as holds, similarly, for Dilithium), the SIS bound

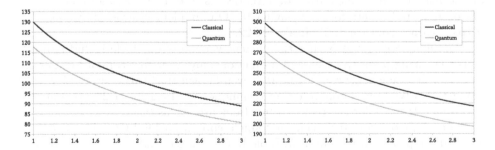

Fig. 2. Security (classical and quantum) against forgery as a function of the quality $1 \leqslant \alpha \leqslant 3$ of the lattice sampler (left: dimension 512 and right: dimension 1024).

Table 2. Concrete values for sampler quality and associated bit security level.

	$d = 512$				$d = 1024$			
	Quality α	Classical	Quantum	NIST Level	Quality α	Classical	Quantum	NIST Level
FALCON	1.17	124	112	I	1.17	285	258	V
Naive Hybrid[a]	3.03	90	82	below I	3.58	207	188	IV
MITAKA	2.04	**102**	**92**	I[b]	2.33	**233**	**211**	V

[a] Key generation with the same median amount of randomness as MITAKA Algorithm 10 with $m = 16$, but without the optimizations of Sect. 4.
[b] Taking into account the heavy memory cost of sieving. This is the same level as Dilithium–II; see [28, §5.3].

Table 3. Intermediate parameters and security levels for MITAKA.

	$d = 512$	$d = 648$	$d = 768$	$d = 864$	$d = 972$	$d = 1024$
Conductor	2^{10}	$2^3 \cdot 3^5$	$2^8 \cdot 3^2$	$2^5 \cdot 3^4$	$2^2 \cdot 3^6$	2^{11}
Security (C/Q)	102/92	136/123	167/151	192/174	220/199	233/211
NIST level	I$^{-\,(a)}$	I$^{(b)}$	II	III	IV	V
Modulus q	12289	3889	18433	10369	17497	12289
Quality α	2.04	2.13	2.20	2.25	2.30	2.33
Sig. size (bytes)	713	827	1080	1176	1359	1405

[a] Above round 2 Dilithium–II.
[b] Above FALCON–512; arguably NIST level II.

in Euclidean norm for the standard parameter choice ($q = 12289$) makes the underlying assumption vacuous. This is not known to lead to any attack, and can be addressed by increasing q if so desired, or reducing to the SIS problem in infinity norm instead.

6   Implementation Results

In order to assess the practicality of MITAKA, we carried out a preliminary, pure C implementation of the scheme (using the sampler described in Algorithm 3). For easier and fairer comparison, we reused the polynomial arithmetic and FFT of the reference implementation of FALCON, as well as its pseudorandom generator (an implementation of ChaCha20). Our implementation is available at https://github.com/espitau/Mitaka-EC22.

An important caveat is that the current version of our code includes direct calls to floating point transcendental functions, and therefore cannot be guaranteed to run in constant time as is. It is well-known that this can be addressed using the polynomial approximation techniques used e.g. in [4,23,41], but full precision estimates for the required functions are left as future work.

The result of those tests run on a single core of an Intel Core i7–1065G7 @ 1.30 GHz laptop can be found in Table 4. We can see that MITAKA is approximately twice as fast as the other lattice-based candidates. However, it should be noted that all those tests were performed using reference implementations. While the comparison with FALCON can be seen as fair due to the shared code,

Table 4. Performance comparisons of MITAKA with FALCON and Dilithium at the lowest and highest security levels. The private key size corresponds to the expanded key for all schemes (including the FALCON tree for FALCON, the expanded public matrix for Dilithium, and the precomputed sampling data for MITAKA).

	Lowest security level			Highest security level		
	FALCON–512	Dilithium–2	MITAKA–512	FALCON–1024	Dilithium–5	MITAKA–1024
Security (C/Q)	124/112	121/110	102/92	285/258	230/210	233/209
Claimed NIST level	I	II	I⁻	V	V	V
Sig. size (bytes)	666	2420	713	1280	4595	1405
Pub. key size (bytes)	896	1312	896	1792	2592	1792
Priv. key size (kB)	56	18	16	120	82	32
Sig. time (kcycles)	502	466	248	1191	931	514

the comparison with a non-optimized implementation of Dilithium is somewhat less relevant. Still, we believe that these preliminary results are quite promising for MITAKA.

Furthermore, performance is mainly driven by the cost of the continuous and discrete one-dimensional Gaussian samplers. Since signature generation can be split in an offline part and an online part, MITAKA can offer even better speed results if some computations can be performed between signatures. While these results are favorable to MITAKA, optimized implementations on specific architectures would be needed for a definitive comparison to FALCON and Dilithium.

7   Side-Channel Countermeasure

First, our signature scheme can be easily made isochronous. According to [23], isochrony ensures independence between the running time of the algorithm and the secret values. For our signature, the absence of conditional branches implies that one can implement our signature isochronously using standard techniques.

In a second step, we turn our signature scheme into an equivalent one which is protected against more powerful side-channel attacks that exploit the leakage of several executions. More precisely, following the seminal work due to Ishai, Sahai, and Wagner [24], we aim to protect our samplers for MITAKA and MITAKA$_{\mathbb{Z}}$ alternative described in Sect. 3 from the so-called *t-probing side-channel adversary*, who is able to peek at up to t intermediate variables per each invocation of an algorithm. The *masking* countermeasure is a technique to mitigate such attacks, by additively *secret-sharing* every sensitive variables into $t + 1$ values in $\mathcal{R}$. The integer t is often referred to as *masking order*. Essentially, we will provide two functionally equivalent alternative algorithms for MITAKA and MITAKA$_{\mathbb{Z}}$ where any set of at most t intermediate variables is independent from the secret. In this paper, we consider the masking order as a—potentially large—arbitrary variable t. Clearly, high masking order allows a side-channel protected implementation to tolerate stronger probing attacks with larger number of probes. For a ring element $a \in \mathcal{R}$, we say that a vector $(a_i)_{0 \leqslant i \leqslant t} \in \mathcal{R}^{t+1}$ is an arithmetic masking of a if $a = \sum_{i \in [0,t]} a_i$. For readability, we often write $[\![a]\!] := (a_i)_{0 \leqslant i \leqslant t}$.

The masking of our signature presents three unprecedented difficulties in masked lattice-based schemes:

1. Compared to Fiat-Shamir with aborts, masking the Gaussian sampling is unavoidable. We here present a novel technique to efficiently mask Gaussian sampling in Sect. 7.2.1. Notably, our approach only requires arithmetic masking, allowing us to avoid any conversion between arithmetic and Boolean shares during the online phase.
2. The computations are performed in $\mathbb{Z}$ instead of a modular ring. This feature does not appear in any other lattice-based scheme. Thus, we need to fix a bound on the size of the masks and make sure that the computations will never pass this bound. Let Q^{mask} be the bound on the largest manipulated integer, the shares of $[\![a]\!]$ are implicitly reduced modulo Q^{mask}. Sometimes we refine the notation $[\![\cdot]\!]$ into $[\![\cdot]\!]_M$ to explicitly specify a modulus $M < Q^{\mathrm{mask}}$ for secret-sharing.
3. Some polynomial multiplications need both inputs to be masked. This unusual operation does not appear in LWE-based schemes where the multiplications are performed between a public matrix of polynomial and a masked vector. We handle this problem with a function in Sect. 7.2.2.

7.1 Preliminaries on Masking Countermeasure

The most basic security notion for a masking countermeasure is the t-*privacy* of a gadget G [24]. This notion guarantees that any set of at most t intermediate variables observed during the computation is independent of the secret input. While the idea behind the notion is relatively simple, t-private gadgets are unfortunately not composable, meaning that a gadget consisting of multiple t-private sub-gadgets may not be necessarily secure. Hence in this work we rely on the following more handy security notions introduced by Barthe et al. [2].

Definition 1 (t-NI, t-SNI). *Let G be a gadget with inputs $(x_i)_{0 \leqslant i \leqslant t} \in \mathcal{R}^{t+1}$ and outputs $(y_i)_{0 \leqslant i \leqslant t} \in \mathcal{R}^{t+1}$. Suppose that for any set of t_1 intermediate variables and any subset of $O \subseteq [1, t]$ of output indices with $t_1 + |O| \leqslant t$, there exists a subset of indices $I \subseteq [1, t]$ such that the output distribution of the t_1 intermediate variables and the output variables $(y_i)_{i \in O}$ can be simulated from $(x_i)_{i \in I}$. Then*

– *if $|I| \leqslant t_1 + |O|$ we say G is t-non-interfering (t-NI); and*
– *if $|I| \leqslant t_1$ we say G is t-strong-non-interfering (t-SNI).*

It is easy to check that t-SNI implies t-NI which implies t-probing security. The above notion can be naturally extended for a gadget with multiple input and output sharings. Note that *linear* operations performed share-wise (such as addition of two sharings, or multiplication by a constant) are trivially t-NI, as each computation on share i can be simulated from the input share x_i. Building blocks satisfying either NI or SNI can be easily composed with each other, by inserting the Refresh gadgets at suitable locations to re-randomize shares [2, Proposition 4]. It is also internally used in the Unmask gadget before taking the sum of

Table 5. Masking properties of known and new gadgets

Gadget name	Security property	Reference
SecMult	t-SNI	[2, 24, 39]
Refresh	t-SNI	[2, 8]
Unmask	t-NIo	[3]
MaskedCDT	t-NI	[4, 19]
SecNTTMult	t-SNI	This work, Lemma 4
GaussShareByShare	t-NIo	This work, Lemma 3

shares, so that a probe on any partial sum doesn't leak more information than one input share [3].

Typically, the non-interference notions only deal with gadgets where all of the inputs and outputs are sensitive. To also handle public, non-sensitive values, a weaker notion called NI *with public output* (t-NIo) was proposed in [3]. As stated in [3, Lemma 1], if a gadget G is t-NI secure it is also t-NIo secure for any public outputs.

In the sequel, we use the SecMult gadget that computes the multiplication of two masked inputs. It is one of the key building blocks of masking theory and has been introduced in [24, 39] and proved t-SNI in [2].

We also use the MaskedCDT gadget that generates a masked sample that follows a tabulated Gaussian distribution of a fixed center c and a fixed standard deviation r. The table values are not sensitive so they are the same as for the unmasked implementation. This masked CDT algorithm was introduced in [4, 19] and proved t-NI.

7.2 Two New Gadgets

In Table 5, we introduce the known and new gadgets necessary for our sampler along with their properties. These properties will be proved in the following subsections.

7.2.1 Share-by-Share Gaussian Sampling

In this section, we present a novel technique for generating a masked Gaussian sampling with an arbitrary masked center $[\![c]\!]$ of $c \in 1/C \cdot \mathbb{Z}$ for some fixed integer C. Note that $1/C \cdot \mathbb{Z}$ is not a ring, and thus the multiplication is not well-defined for shares in $1/C \cdot \mathbb{Z}$. This is not an issue in our application, since we never carry out multiplication of two sharings in this form.

We aim at considering a share by share generation. A direct and fast approach is to generate $z_i \leftarrow D_{\mathbb{Z}, c_i, r/\sqrt{t+1}}$ for each share of c and to output $(z_0, \cdots, z_t)$ as $[\![z]\!]$. To ensure $z \sim D_{\mathbb{Z}, c, r}$, it requires $r \geq \sqrt{2(t+1)}\eta_\epsilon(\mathbb{Z})$ according to [31], which yields a considerable security loss. To overcome this issue, we propose a different

---

Algorithm 11: GaussShareByShare

Input: An unmasked standard deviation r. An arithmetic masking $[\![c]\!]$ of the center $c \in 1/C \cdot \mathbb{Z}$. Let $B := \lceil \sqrt{2(t+1)} \rceil$.

Result: An arithmetic masking $[\![z]\!]$ with z's distribution negligibly far from $D_{\mathbb{Z},c,r}$.

1 **for** $i \in [0,t]$ **do**
2 $\quad$ $z_i \leftarrow D_{1/B \cdot \mathbb{Z}, c_i, r/\sqrt{t+1}}$
3 **end for**
$\quad$ /* Extracting the fractional part of z */
4 $[\![\bar{z}]\!]_1 \leftarrow (z_0 \bmod 1, \dots, z_t \bmod 1)$ $\quad$ /* secret-sharing in $(\frac{1}{B} \cdot \mathbb{Z})/\mathbb{Z}$ */
5 **if** Unmask$([\![\bar{z}]\!]_1) \neq 0$ **then**
6 $\quad$ **restart** to step 1
7 **end if**
8 **return** $(z_0, \dots, z_t)$

---

approach sampling shares over $1/B \cdot \mathbb{Z}$ with $B := \lceil \sqrt{2(t+1)} \rceil$ and utilizing rejection sampling to keep the masked output over $\mathbb{Z}$. Our masked Gaussian sampling algorithm is presented in Algorithm 11.

Correctness. We now show that Algorithm 11 is correct for $r \geq \eta_\epsilon(\mathbb{Z})$. Since $r \geq \eta_\epsilon(\mathbb{Z}) \geq \frac{\sqrt{2(t+1)}}{B} \eta_\epsilon(\mathbb{Z})$, by [31, Theorem 3], in step 4, $z = \sum_{i=0}^{t} z_i$ follows $D_{1/B \cdot \mathbb{Z}, c, r}$. Thanks to the rejection sampling, the support of the final output z is $\mathbb{Z}$ and noticing that the probability of each output z is proportional to $\rho_{r,c}(z)$, it follows that the distribution of z is $D_{\mathbb{Z},c,r}$. The rejection rate is $\frac{\rho_{r,c}(\mathbb{Z})}{\rho_{r,c}(1/B \cdot \mathbb{Z})} \approx 1/B$ as $r \geq \eta_\epsilon(\mathbb{Z}) \geq \eta_\epsilon(1/B \cdot \mathbb{Z})$. All in all, we have shown that Algorithm 11 provides $[\![z]\!] \sim D_{\mathbb{Z},c,r}$ at the cost of about $\sqrt{2(t+1)}$ average rejections.

Masking Security. Let $\bar{z} = \sum_i \bar{z}_i \bmod 1$. As the Unmask gadget is only NIo secure with public output $\bar{z}$, we need to show that $\bar{z}$ does not leak sensitive information, i.e. the output z and the center c. Indeed, the output only occurs when $\bar{z} = 0$, hence $\bar{z}$ is independent of the output. The support of $\bar{z}$ is $\frac{1}{B}\{0, 1, \cdots, B-1\}$ and $\Pr[\bar{z} = \frac{i}{B}] \propto \rho_{c,r}(\mathbb{Z} + \frac{i}{B}) = \rho_{c-\frac{i}{B}, r}(\mathbb{Z}) \in [\frac{1-\epsilon}{1+\epsilon}, 1]\rho_r(\mathbb{Z})$ due to the smoothness condition $r \geq \eta_\epsilon(\mathbb{Z})$. Therefore the distribution of $\bar{z}$ is negligibly close to uniform independent of c. Consequently, $\bar{z}$ can be securely unmasked. As all the operations are performed share by share and assuming uniformly distributed shares of the input center c, we can deduce the following lemma.

Lemma 3. *The gadget* GaussShareByShare *is t-NIo secure with public output* $\bar{z}$.

In the implementation, one needs to instantiate an unmasked Gaussian sampling with arbitrary center and fixed standard deviation (line 2 of Algorithm 11). We chose a table based approach and follow the technique of [32] to use a reduced number of tables.

7.2.2   Polynomial Multiplication

In some lattice-based schemes such as Kyber or Dilithium, polynomial multiplication is always performed between a sensitive and a public polynomial. This means that, using polynomials protected with arithmetic masking, one can multiply each share independently by the public unmasked polynomial and obtain an arithmetic sharing of the result of the multiplication. In this work, we have polynomials multiplications with both operand in arithmetic masked form. Given $[\![a]\!]$ and $[\![b]\!] \in \mathscr{R}^{t+1}$, we want to compute $[\![c]\!] \in \mathscr{R}^{t+1}$ such that $\sum_{i=0}^{t} c_i = \left(\sum_{i=0}^{t} a_i \right) \cdot \left(\sum_{i=0}^{t} b_i \right)$. To perform this masked polynomial multiplication, we propose to rely on an NTT-based multiplication. Using NTT, the product of two polynomials $a, b \in \mathbb{Z}_{Q^{\mathrm{mask}}}[x]/(x^d + 1)$ is given by

$$\mathsf{NTT}^{-1}(\mathsf{NTT}(a) \circ \mathsf{NTT}(b))$$

with $\circ$ the *coefficient-wise* product between two vectors in $\mathbb{Z}_{Q^{\mathrm{mask}}}$. Since the NTT is linear, it can be applied on each share independently and we only have to mask the coefficient-wise multiplication between elements of $\mathbb{Z}_{Q^{\mathrm{mask}}}$ using the technique of [24]. While a naive multiplication algorithm would require d^2 ISW multiplications, we only need d of them. Since we want to multiply the polynomials in $\mathbb{Z}$ and not in $\mathbb{Z}_{Q^{\mathrm{mask}}}$, we need to work with a modulus large enough to avoid any reduction in the result. Recall that it is also possible to use several Q^{mask} with CRT techniques to reduce the size.

Let us define SecNTTMult, the masked product of two polynomials $[\![a]\!], [\![b]\!]$ arithmetically masked in $\mathbb{Z}_{Q^{\mathrm{mask}}}[x]/(x^d + 1)$ by

$$\mathsf{NTT}^{-1}((\mathsf{SecMult}(\mathsf{NTT}([\![a]\!])_j, \mathsf{NTT}([\![b]\!])_j)_{0 \le j \le d-1}).$$

The algorithm for this product is detailed in the full version of our paper [16].

Lemma 4. SecNTTMult *is t-SNI secure.*

Note that here the shares are entire polynomials containing d coefficients. So, t probes actually provide $t \times d$ coefficients to the attacker.

Proof. Let $\delta \le t$ be the number of observations made by the attacker. Assume the following distribution of the attacker δ observations of intermediate shared polynomials: δ_1 observations on the first NTT computation on $\hat{a}$, δ_2 observations on the first NTT computation on $\hat{b}$, δ_3 observations on the SecMult part (which provides the knowledge of the $d \times \delta_3$ *coefficients* of the probed polynomials), δ_4 observations on the last NTT^{-1} computation, and δ_5 observations of the returned values. Finally, we have $\sum_{i=1}^{5} \delta_i \le \delta$. The algorithm NTT^{-1} is linear, thus it is t-NI and all the observations on steps 6 and 7 can be perfectly simulated with at most $\delta_4 + \delta_5$ shares of $\hat{c}$. The algorithm SecMult is applied coefficient-wise, thus each i-th execution has δ_3 observations of intermediate values (here coefficients) and $\delta_4 + \delta_5$ observations on the outputs (here coefficients too). By applying d times the t-SNI property for each SecMult operation, we can conclude that every observation from steps 3 to 7 can be perfectly simulated with at most δ_3 shared (polynomials) of $\hat{a}$ and $\hat{b}$. The linearity of the NTT with arithmetic

---

Algorithm 12: MaskedMITAKA$_\mathbb{Z}$Sampler

Input: A masked secret key in the following form:
$([\widetilde{\mathbf{B}^*}], [\widetilde{\mathbf{B}^*}^{-1}], [\widetilde{v}], [\mathbf{A}])$ and a masked vector $[\mathbf{c}]$ for a center
$\mathbf{c} \in \mathscr{R}^2$, both arithmetically masked mod Q^{mask}.
Result: An unmasked sample $\mathbf{z} \sim D_{\mathscr{L}(\mathbf{B}),s,\mathbf{c}}$.

1 **Offline**
2 $[\mathbf{p}] \leftarrow$ MaskedOfflineSampling($[\mathbf{A}]$)
3 **Online**
4 $[\mathbf{c}^{\mathrm{pert}}] \leftarrow [\mathbf{c}] - [\mathbf{p}]$
5 $[\mathbf{c}^{\mathrm{pert}}] \leftarrow$ SecNTTMult($[\widetilde{\mathbf{B}^*}^{-1}], [\mathbf{c}^{\mathrm{pert}}]$)
6 $[\mathbf{v}] \leftarrow$ MaskedOnlineSampling($[\widetilde{v}], [\mathbf{c}^{\mathrm{pert}}]$)
7 $[\mathbf{z}] \leftarrow$ SecNTTMult($[\widetilde{\mathbf{B}^*}], [\mathbf{v}]$)
8 **return** $\sum_{i=0}^{t} \mathbf{z}_i \bmod Q^{\mathrm{mask}}$

---

masking allows to finish proving that every set of size at most t observations containing $\sum_{i=1}^{4} \delta_i$ (resp. δ_5) intermediate (resp. returned) *polynomial shares* can be perfectly simulated with at most $\sum_{i=1}^{4} \delta_i$ polynomial shares of each input.

In the following, we extrapolate this polynomial multiplication technique to matrices of polynomials and keep the same notation SecNTTMult. We also remark that although SecNTTMult are sometimes called back-to-back in the masked samplers, this can be further optimized in practice: to minimize the number of NTT/NTT^{-1} invocations in an implementation, one could keep the NTT representation as much as possible, and then bring it back to the coefficient domain whenever it encounters GaussShareByShare, as explicitly described in the full version of our paper [16].

7.3 Masking the MITAKA$_\mathbb{Z}$ Sampler

The detailed overall structure of the sampler is presented in Algorithm 12; the algorithms for the online and offline samplings are detailed in the full version of this paper [16]. We remark that Algorithm 12 consists in a linear succession of gadgets with no dependency cycle, i.e. each line depends on freshly computed masked inputs. Thus, one can show that this algorithm is t-NI, as proved in Theorem 4 below. The proof is detailed in the full version of our paper [16].

Theorem 4. *The masked* MITAKA$_\mathbb{Z}$ *sampler (Algorithm 12) is t-NIo with public output* $\mathbf{z}$.

7.4 Masking the MITAKA Samplers

Our masked version of the RingPeikert sampler of Algorithm 1 and of the Hybrid sampler of Algorithm 3 are provided in the full version [16]. Although masked MITAKA is instantiated with the MaskedHybrid sampler, we also include MaskedRingPeikert for completeness because the former can be essentially obtained by extending the basic masking paradigm outlined in the latter.

Contrary to $\text{MITAKA}_\mathbb{Z}$, one can remark that we here need to mask floating-point arithmetic. However, we can avoid it by representing each sensitive variable from $\mathscr{K}_\mathbb{R}$ as a fixed-point number. Concretely, an element $x \in \mathscr{K}_\mathbb{R}$ is approximated by $\tilde{x} \in \mathscr{K}_\mathbb{R}$ such that every coefficient of $q^k\tilde{x}$ is an integer, where k is a parameter determining the precision. Then we can secret-share $q^k\tilde{x}$ in $\mathbb{Z}^d_{\text{Q}^{\text{mask}}}$ for $\text{Q}^{\text{mask}} \gg q^k$. Since we do not perform many multiplication operations, an accumulated scaling factor does not break the correctness of sampler if we choose sufficiently large Q^{mask}.

We also remark that a secret-shared center in fixed-point representation must be divided by a scaling factor q^k for the following 1-dimensional discrete Gaussian sampling to work share-by-share. This division can be performed in floating-point arithmetic in practice. For the sum of shares to represent the correct center in the MaskedRingPeikert sampler, we further set $\text{Q}^{\text{mask}} = q^{k+\ell}$ for some $\ell > 0$. The resulting shares after division form a sharing of $\mathbf{v} = [(v_{1,j})_{j\in[0,d-1]}, (v_{2,j})_{j\in[0,d-1]}]$ over $(\mathbb{Q}/q^\ell\mathbb{Z})^{2d}$. Thanks to our GaussShareByShare introduced earlier, we are able to perform the discrete Gaussian sampling independently w.r.t each share of the center, while avoiding a factor of $\sqrt{t+1}$ overhead incurred in the standard deviation. As a result we obtain shares of discrete Gaussian samples $[\![z_{i,j}]\!]_{q^\ell}$ such that the distribution of $z_{i,j}$ is statistically close to $D_{\mathbb{Z},v_{i,j},r} \mod q^\ell$ for every $i = 1,2$ and $j \in [0, d-1]$. Since the output values of the signature are defined mod q we can further map the shares to $[\![\cdot]\!]_q$ and the remaining computations can be performed mod q.

Since we invoke the above routine twice in the MaskedHybrid sampler, the initial masking modulus needs to be increased so that no wrap-around occurs during the masked computation of the second nearest plane. Concretely, the first nearest plane operations are computed with modulus $\text{Q}^{\text{mask}} = q^{2k+\ell}$; the second nearest plane operations are performed on $[\![\cdot]\!]_{q^{k+\ell}}$, with corresponding arithmetic shares of sensitive inputs; the output values can be represented in $[\![\cdot]\!]_q$ as in the MaskedRingPeikert.

Although a naive implementation of the MITAKA sampler should rely on floating-point arithmetic and thus naturally carry out FFT-based polynomial multiplications, we instead make use of NTT in our masked algorithms. Notice that the masked instances only deal with a multiplication between polynomials mapped to $\mathbb{Z}_{\text{Q}^{\text{mask}}}[x]/(x^d + 1)$ (or $\mathbb{Z}_{q^{\ell+k}}[x]/(x^d + 1)$ during the second nearest plane of the Hybrid sampler) thanks to the fixed-point representation. This allows us to exploit SecNTTMult as in MaskedMITAKA$_\mathbb{Z}$Sampler. One caveat is that in the current setting Q^{mask} is restricted to a *power* of q, but we are able to show such a choice is indeed NTT-friendly. Recall that the prime q is usually chosen such that $q = 1 \mod 2d$, so that $x^d + 1$ has exactly d roots $(\zeta, \zeta^3, \ldots, \zeta^{2d-1})$ over $\mathbb{Z}_q$. Now thanks to the Hensel lifting, one can construct another set of d roots $(\omega, \omega^3, \ldots, \omega^{2d-1})$ over $\mathbb{Z}_{q^2}$, such that $\omega = \zeta \mod q$. By iterating this procedure until the roots for a sufficiently large modulus Q^{mask} are obtained, we can indeed utilize the NTT for evaluating $f(x) \in \mathbb{Z}_{Q^{mask}}[x]/(x^d + 1)$ on the primitive $2d$-th roots of unity.

We are able to prove that both masked samplers meet the standard security notion (t-NIo) for masked signature schemes. The proof is detailed in the full version [16].

Theorem 5. *The masked* MITAKA *sampler is t-NIo secure with public output* $\mathbf{v}_0$.

8 Conclusion

The FALCON signature scheme, one of the NIST round 3 finalists, is a very attractive postquantum scheme for real-world deployment: it has fast signing and verification, the best bandwidth requirements (as measured in combined verification key and signature size) of all round 2 signatures, as well as a solid, well-understood security. However, it suffers from a number of short-comings: it has a complex structure that makes it hard to implement correctly; it is not flexible in terms of parameter selection (only supporting NIST security levels I and V, and no intermediate level); it is inefficient on architectures without fast native floating point arithmetic; and it is difficult to protect against side-channels.

In this paper, we introduced MITAKA, a simpler variant based on similar design principles, which manages to maintain the advantages of FALCON while largely mitigating those shortcomings: as we have seen, it has performance on par or superior to FALCON, its bandwidth requirements are similar (not quite as good as FALCON, but still far better than all other NIST candidates), and its security relies on the same assumptions. However, unlike FALCON, it is also relatively simple to implement; it supports a wide range of parameter settings covering all NIST security levels; it can be implemented using the MITAKA$_{\mathbb{Z}}$ sampler in a way that avoids floating-point arithmetic; and it can be efficiently protected against side-channel attacks, for example with our proposed masking countermeasure. It also has nice additional properties such as its online/offline structure.

Thus, we showed that NTRU-based hash-and-sign signatures have even more potential than previously expected to replace, e.g., elliptic curve-based schemes in a postquantum world. Some questions remain for future work, such as:

– to what extent can signature size be reduced? (while smaller than other lattice schemes, it is substantially larger than classical elliptic curve-based signatures, or postquantum candidates based on multivariate cryptography and isogenies);
– can security for the hybrid sampler be improved further with better trapdoor generation? (there is still a substantial gap between the hybrid sampler and Klein–GPV);
– how fast can MITAKA perform with a fully optimized, constant-time implementation on, e.g., Intel CPUs with AVX2? What about embedded microcontrollers with and without masking?

Acknowledgements. We would like to thank Léo Ducas, Thomas Prest and Damien Stehlé for valuable comments and discussions. The second and seventh authors were supported by the European Union H2020 Research and Innovation Program Grant 780701 (PROMETHEUS). The third author was supported by the ERC Advanced Grant No. 787390. The fifth author has been supported by the Carlsberg Foundation under the Semper Ardens Research Project CF18-112 (BCM); the European Research Council (ERC) under the European Unions's Horizon 2020 research and innovation programme under grant agreement No. 803096 (SPEC). The eighth author has been supported by the National Natural Science Foundation of China (No. 62102216), the National Key Research and Development Program of China (Grant No. 2018YFA0704701), the Major Program of Guangdong Basic and Applied Research (Grant No. 2019B030302008) and Major Scientific and Techological Innovation Project of Shandong Province, China (Grant No. 2019JZZY010133).

References

1. Alkim, E., Ducas, L., Pöppelmann, T., Schwabe, P.: Post-quantum key exchange - a new hope. In: Holz, T., Savage, S. (eds.) USENIX Security 2016, pp. 327–343. USENIX Association, August 2016

2. Barthe, G., et al.: Strong non-interference and type-directed higher-order masking. In: Weippl, E.R., Katzenbeisser, S., Kruegel, C., Myers, A.C., Halevi, S. (eds.) ACM CCS 2016, pp. 116–129. ACM Press, October 2016. https://doi.org/10.1145/2976749.2978427

3. Barthe, G., et al.: Masking the GLP lattice-based signature scheme at any order. In: Nielsen, J.B., Rijmen, V. (eds.) EUROCRYPT 2018. LNCS, vol. 10821, pp. 354–384. Springer, Cham (2018). https://doi.org/10.1007/978-3-319-78375-8_12

4. Barthe, G., Belaïd, S., Espitau, T., Fouque, P.A., Rossi, M., Tibouchi, M.: GALACTICS: Gaussian sampling for lattice-based constant- time implementation of cryptographic signatures, revisited. In: Cavallaro, L., Kinder, J., Wang, X., Katz, J. (eds.) ACM CCS 2019, pp. 2147–2164. ACM Press, November 2019. https://doi.org/10.1145/3319535.3363223

5. Becker, A., Ducas, L., Gama, N., Laarhoven, T.: New directions in nearest neighbor searching with applications to lattice sieving. In: Krauthgamer, R. (ed.) 27th SODA, pp. 10–24. ACM-SIAM, January 2016. https://doi.org/10.1137/1.9781611974331.ch2

6. Boneh, D., Dagdelen, Ö., Fischlin, M., Lehmann, A., Schaffner, C., Zhandry, M.: Random oracles in a quantum world. In: Lee, D.H., Wang, X. (eds.) ASIACRYPT 2011. LNCS, vol. 7073, pp. 41–69. Springer, Heidelberg (2011). https://doi.org/10.1007/978-3-642-25385-0_3

7. Chuengsatiansup, C., Prest, T., Stehlé, D., Wallet, A., Xagawa, K.: ModFalcon: compact signatures based on module-NTRU lattices. In: Sun, H.M., Shieh, S.P., Gu, G., Ateniese, G. (eds.) ASIACCS 2020, pp. 853–866. ACM Press, October 2020. https://doi.org/10.1145/3320269.3384758

8. Coron, J.-S.: Higher order masking of look-up tables. In: Nguyen, P.Q., Oswald, E. (eds.) EUROCRYPT 2014. LNCS, vol. 8441, pp. 441–458. Springer, Heidelberg (2014). https://doi.org/10.1007/978-3-642-55220-5_25

9. Ding, J., et al.: Rainbow. Technical report, National Institute of Standards and Technology (2020). https://csrc.nist.gov/projects/post-quantum-cryptography/round-3-submissions

10. Ducas, L., Durmus, A., Lepoint, T., Lyubashevsky, V.: Lattice signatures and bimodal Gaussians. In: Canetti, R., Garay, J.A. (eds.) CRYPTO 2013. LNCS, vol. 8042, pp. 40–56. Springer, Heidelberg (2013). https://doi.org/10.1007/978-3-642-40041-4_3

11. Ducas, L., Galbraith, S., Prest, T., Yu, Y.: Integral matrix gram root and lattice Gaussian sampling without floats. In: Canteaut, A., Ishai, Y. (eds.) EUROCRYPT 2020. LNCS, vol. 12106, pp. 608–637. Springer, Cham (2020). https://doi.org/10.1007/978-3-030-45724-2_21

12. Ducas, L., et al.: CRYSTALS-Dilithium: a lattice-based digital signature scheme. IACR TCHES **2018**(1), 238–268 (2018). https://doi.org/10.13154/tches.v2018.i1.238-268. https://tches.iacr.org/index.php/TCHES/article/view/839

13. Ducas, L., Lyubashevsky, V., Prest, T.: Efficient identity-based encryption over NTRU lattices. In: Sarkar, P., Iwata, T. (eds.) ASIACRYPT 2014. LNCS, vol. 8874, pp. 22–41. Springer, Heidelberg (2014). https://doi.org/10.1007/978-3-662-45608-8_2

14. Ducas, L., Nguyen, P.Q.: Learning a zonotope and more: cryptanalysis of NTRUSign countermeasures. In: Wang, X., Sako, K. (eds.) ASIACRYPT 2012. LNCS, vol. 7658, pp. 433–450. Springer, Heidelberg (2012). https://doi.org/10.1007/978-3-642-34961-4_27

15. Ducas, L., Prest, T.: Fast Fourier orthogonalization. Cryptology ePrint Archive Report 2015/1014 (2015). https://eprint.iacr.org/2015/1014

16. Espitau, T., et al.: MITAKA: a simpler, parallelizable, maskable variant of falcon. Cryptology ePrint Archive Report 2021/1486 (2021). https://ia.cr/2021/1486

17. Fouque, P.-A., Kirchner, P., Tibouchi, M., Wallet, A., Yu, Y.: Key recovery from gram–schmidt norm leakage in hash-and-sign signatures over NTRU lattices. In: Canteaut, A., Ishai, Y. (eds.) EUROCRYPT 2020. LNCS, vol. 12107, pp. 34–63. Springer, Cham (2020). https://doi.org/10.1007/978-3-030-45727-3_2

18. Gentry, C., Peikert, C., Vaikuntanathan, V.: Trapdoors for hard lattices and new cryptographic constructions. In: Ladner, R.E., Dwork, C. (eds.) 40th ACM STOC, pp. 197–206. ACM Press, May 2008. https://doi.org/10.1145/1374376.1374407

19. Gérard, F., Rossi, M.: An efficient and provable masked implementation of qTESLA. In: Belaïd, S., Güneysu, T. (eds.) CARDIS 2019. LNCS, vol. 11833, pp. 74–91. Springer, Cham (2020). https://doi.org/10.1007/978-3-030-42068-0_5

20. Goldreich, O., Goldwasser, S., Halevi, S.: Public-key cryptosystems from lattice reduction problems. In: Kaliski, B.S. (ed.) CRYPTO 1997. LNCS, vol. 1294, pp. 112–131. Springer, Heidelberg (1997). https://doi.org/10.1007/BFb0052231

21. Hoffstein, J., Howgrave-Graham, N., Pipher, J., Silverman, J.H., Whyte, W.: Performance improvements and a baseline parameter generation algorithm for NTRUSign. Cryptology ePrint Archive Report 2005/274 (2005). https://eprint.iacr.org/2005/274

22. Hoffstein, J., Howgrave-Graham, N., Pipher, J., Silverman, J.H., Whyte, W.: NTRUSign: digital signatures using the NTRU lattice. In: Joye, M. (ed.) CT-RSA 2003. LNCS, vol. 2612, pp. 122–140. Springer, Heidelberg (2003). https://doi.org/10.1007/3-540-36563-X_9

23. Howe, J., Prest, T., Ricosset, T., Rossi, M.: Isochronous Gaussian sampling: from inception to implementation. In: Ding, J., Tillich, J.-P. (eds.) PQCrypto 2020. LNCS, vol. 12100, pp. 53–71. Springer, Cham (2020). https://doi.org/10.1007/978-3-030-44223-1_4

24. Ishai, Y., Sahai, A., Wagner, D.: Private circuits: securing hardware against probing attacks. In: Boneh, D. (ed.) CRYPTO 2003. LNCS, vol. 2729, pp. 463–481. Springer, Heidelberg (2003). https://doi.org/10.1007/978-3-540-45146-4_27

25. Karabulut, E., Aysu, A.: Falcon down: breaking falcon post-quantum signature scheme through side-channel attacks (2021)
26. Laarhoven, T.: Search problems in cryptography. Ph.D. thesis, Eindhoven University of Technology (2015)
27. Langlois, A., Stehlé, D.: Worst-case to average-case reductions for module lattices. Des. Codes Crypt. **75**(3), 565–599 (2014). https://doi.org/10.1007/s10623-014-9938-4
28. Lyubashevsky, V., et al.: CRYSTALS-DILITHIUM. Technical report, National Institute of Standards and Technology (2019). https://csrc.nist.gov/projects/post-quantum-cryptography/round-2-submissions
29. Lyubashevsky, V., et al.: CRYSTALS-DILITHIUM. Technical report, National Institute of Standards and Technology (2020). https://csrc.nist.gov/projects/post-quantum-cryptography/round-3-submissions
30. Lyubashevsky, V., Wichs, D.: Simple lattice trapdoor sampling from a broad class of distributions. In: Katz, J. (ed.) PKC 2015. LNCS, vol. 9020, pp. 716–730. Springer, Heidelberg (2015). https://doi.org/10.1007/978-3-662-46447-2_32
31. Micciancio, D., Peikert, C.: Hardness of SIS and LWE with small parameters. In: Canetti, R., Garay, J.A. (eds.) CRYPTO 2013. LNCS, vol. 8042, pp. 21–39. Springer, Heidelberg (2013). https://doi.org/10.1007/978-3-642-40041-4_2
32. Micciancio, D., Walter, M.: Gaussian sampling over the integers: efficient, generic, constant-time. In: Katz, J., Shacham, H. (eds.) CRYPTO 2017. LNCS, vol. 10402, pp. 455–485. Springer, Cham (2017). https://doi.org/10.1007/978-3-319-63715-0_16
33. Nguyen, P.Q., Regev, O.: Learning a parallelepiped: cryptanalysis of GGH and NTRU signatures. J. Cryptol. **22**(2), 139–160 (2008). https://doi.org/10.1007/s00145-008-9031-0
34. Peikert, C.: An efficient and parallel Gaussian sampler for lattices. In: Rabin, T. (ed.) CRYPTO 2010. LNCS, vol. 6223, pp. 80–97. Springer, Heidelberg (2010). https://doi.org/10.1007/978-3-642-14623-7_5
35. Pornin, T.: New efficient, constant-time implementations of Falcon. Cryptology ePrint Archive Report 2019/893 (2019). https://eprint.iacr.org/2019/893
36. Pornin, T., Prest, T.: More efficient algorithms for the NTRU key generation using the field norm. In: Lin, D., Sako, K. (eds.) PKC 2019. LNCS, vol. 11443, pp. 504–533. Springer, Cham (2019). https://doi.org/10.1007/978-3-030-17259-6_17
37. Prest, T.: Gaussian sampling in lattice-based cryptography. Ph.D. thesis, École Normale Supérieure, Paris, France (2015)
38. Prest, T., et al.: FALCON. Technical report, National Institute of Standards and Technology (2020). https://csrc.nist.gov/projects/post-quantum-cryptography/round-3-submissions
39. Rivain, M., Prouff, E.: Provably secure higher-order masking of AES. In: Mangard, S., Standaert, F.-X. (eds.) CHES 2010. LNCS, vol. 6225, pp. 413–427. Springer, Heidelberg (2010). https://doi.org/10.1007/978-3-642-15031-9_28
40. Yu, Y., Ducas, L.: Learning strikes again: the case of the DRS signature scheme. In: Peyrin, T., Galbraith, S. (eds.) ASIACRYPT 2018. LNCS, vol. 11273, pp. 525–543. Springer, Cham (2018). https://doi.org/10.1007/978-3-030-03329-3_18
41. Zhao, R.K., Steinfeld, R., Sakzad, A.: FACCT: fast, compact, and constant-time discrete gaussian sampler over integers. IEEE Trans. Comput. **69**(1), 126–137 (2020)

A Novel Completeness Test for Leakage Models and Its Application to Side Channel Attacks and Responsibly Engineered Simulators

Si Gao[✉][iD] and Elisabeth Oswald[✉][iD]

Digital Age Research Center (D!ARC), University of Klagenfurt, Klagenfurt, Austria
{si.gao,elisabeth.oswald}@aau.at

Abstract. Today's side channel attack targets are often complex devices in which instructions are processed in parallel and work on 32-bit data words. Consequently, the *state* that is involved in producing leakage in these modern devices is not only large, but also hard to predict due to various micro-architectural factors that users might not be aware of. On the other hand, security evaluations—basing on worst case attacks or simulators—explicitly rely on the underlying *state*: a potentially *incomplete state* can easily lead to wrong conclusions.

We put forward a novel notion for the "completeness" of an assumed state, together with an efficient statistical test that is based on "collapsed models". Our novel test can be used to recover a *state* that contains multiple 32-bit variables in a grey box setting. We illustrate how our novel test can help to guide side channel attacks and we reveal new attack vectors for existing implementations. We then demonstrate the application of this test in the context of leakage modelling for leakage simulators and confirm that even the most recent leakage simulators do not capture all available leakage of their respective target devices. Our new test enables finding nominal models that capture all available leakage but do not give a helping hand to adversaries. Thereby we make a first step towards leakage simulators that are responsibly engineered.

1 Introduction

Leakage models are crucial not only for attacks and leakage simulators, but also for implementing masking schemes. Having a complete, accurate leakage model, experienced cryptographic engineers can diligently examine if the security assumptions are respected and avoid potential implementation pitfalls.

But what does a leakage model constitute of? Informally, most of the existing literature understands a leakage model to be a *leakage function* that maps a collection of device internal variables (*the state*) to a real value (if it is a univariate model). Considering this informal definition in the context of attacks, it is clearly desirable to try and find a function that offers good predictions for the true device leakage, because it enables successful attacks with few traces.

© International Association for Cryptologic Research 2022
O. Dunkelman and S. Dziembowski (Eds.): EUROCRYPT 2022, LNCS 13277, pp. 254–283, 2022.
https://doi.org/10.1007/978-3-031-07082-2_10

Thus, a lot of research has gone into deriving good proportional or direct estimates for leakage functions from real device data [1–5]. However, the leakage function itself is only part of what constitutes a leakage model: the *state* that is being leaked on is equally relevant.

In a realistic setting (such as typical 32-bit processors based on the ARM Cortex M architecture, or dedicated hardware implementations of cryptographic algorithms), finding the *state* is far from easy—not only because they tend to be closed source. Even if open source descriptions are available, e.g. ARM released some semi-obfuscated VHDL descriptions of the M0 and a non-obfuscated VHDL description of an implementation of their M3 architecture, these are not necessarily micro-architecturally equivalent to the corresponding commercial products on the market. Micro-architectural effects have been explored and exploited across many recent works [6–10]. These papers show how a wrong assumption about the *state* renders provably secure masking schemes completely insecure in practice. Leakage models matter thus for implementing provably secure masking schemes because they help engineers to ensure the security assumptions are respected. Leakage models can also guide an evaluator to demonstrate attacks for specific implementations. Last but not least, they are fundamental to a prevalent type of early-stage evaluation tool—leakage simulators.

1.1 State of the Art

Leakage modelling, or profiling, has been an active area of research within the side channel community since its very beginning. Typical models are based on some assumption about what leaks (the *state*) and how it leaks (the function form in regression models, or the number of templates in direct parameter estimation), and then the corresponding coefficients are determined from the data. Typical examples of such profiling approaches are [1–5].

A leakage simulator is a tool that takes a software implementation of a cryptographic algorithm (in e.g. C or Assembly) as input, then outputs a leakage trace that is meant to capture (ideally) all the leakage characteristics of a target device. Various leakage simulators have been built within the last decade, e.g. industrial examples include PINPAS [11] (no device specific leakage model, limited to simple 8 bit devices), esDynamic [12] (multiple platforms and leakage models, but no device specificity), Virtualyzr [13] (needs the HDL description, no specific leakage model); academic examples include [14,15] and [16]. Both sides develop the concept and recognise the importance of both accurate device emulation as well as leakage models.

Only relatively recently, a profiling approach was developed in the context of the ELMO simulator [5], which enabled some progress towards capturing complex leaks[1]. According to the authors' estimation, the ELMO model captures over 80% of the data dependent power consumption of the modelled processor [5,17]. However the ELMO approach cannot be pushed further, as it only

---

[1] Estimating leakage profiles in the context of multiple interacting 32-bit variables requires a non-trivial approach because the implied data complexity for naively estimating templates is infeasible.

captures limited micro-architecture states (e.g. operand buses and bitflips [5]) and their "lower order" interactions. There is another potential drawback: the ELMO model demonstrates (in [5]) various non-trivial leaks (i.e. from covert micro-architecture operations) that can be efficiently exploited by attackers in practice. The natural question is then: is it ethical to make highly accurate predictive leakage models publicly available (in other words, release them to potential adversaries)?

1.2   Our Contributions

We stress that finding the exact intermediate state from a typical processor in a grey box setting is a long-standing problem: like many (statistical learning) problems, a universally optimal solution is unlikely to exist. Thus, whilst we do not claim optimality of our work, we claim the following contributions:

1. We clearly state the identification of the actual *state* as a fundamental problem and discuss its impact on attacks and leakage simulators.
2. We put forward a novel notion for models—denoted as *"completeness"*— which flags whether the tested model has captured all relevant state.
3. We put forward a novel statistical methodology based on what we call "collapsed" models: using the nested *F-test*, we can test whether a leakage model is *complete* in a "collapsed" setup and infer whether it is *complete* in the original un-collapsed setup.
4. We show how our approach can find subtle leakage that can be easily overlooked. Although such leakage does not necessarily contribute to more effective attacks, it plays an important role in comprehensive security evaluations.
5. We discuss the importance of *completeness* in the context of leakage simulators and demonstrate that our approach can lead to better models for simulations.
6. We discuss the importance of responsibly engineering leakage simulators and put forward a first promising step in this direction.

Organisation. We start our discussion with clarifying some definitions and introducing a few useful statistical tools in Sect. 2. Section 3 introduces the concept of *completeness* and proposes a necessary (but not sufficient) test to verify *completeness*. We further show how our novel test can be applied when analysing the leakage from both unprotected and masked implementations (Sect. 4), revealing subtle leakage that is otherwise difficult to find. Section 5 confirms *completeness* is also critical for leakage simulators, demonstrating how an incomplete leakage model can jeopardise the following detection accuracy. We summarise our discussion and emphasise a few important lessons learned in Sect. 6.

2   Preliminaries

2.1   Notation and Background to Leakage Modelling

We aim for a simple notation throughout this paper: observed leakage is treated in a univariate fashion, therefore we drop indices for time points[2].

We call the set $\mathbf{X}$ the entire device state (at some time point). $\mathbf{X}$ is comprised of all input/key dependent variables that the leakage function L acts on. The variable $Y = \{y\} \in \mathbf{Y}$ is a leakage observation that is available to an adversary. We also follow the usual convention that traces are noisy, whereby the leakage contribution $L(\mathbf{X})$ and the (Gaussian) noise $N(0, \sigma^2)$ are independent:

$$y = L(\mathbf{X}) + N(0, \sigma^2)$$

The leakage model is an approximation of the real device leakage. It consists of a function and a state: the function maps the state to a (set of) real value(-s). Following the trajectory of [5,18], we consider univariate models, thus we write $L : \mathbb{F}_2^n \to \mathbf{R}$ and $x \in \mathbb{F}_2^n$.

Throughout this work we assume that we are working in a "grey box" setting, i.e. we have some basic knowledge about the device/implementation (e.g. the Instruction Set Architecture, ISA) and we can execute arbitrary code during profiling, but we do not have the concrete gate-level hardware details (i.e. a typical software implementation with a commercial core). The relevant device state $\mathbf{X}$ (for a certain time index) is unknown in this setting, as $\mathbf{X}$ may contain various micro-architecture elements that are transparent to developers. We can of course, build an overly conservative model using all possible states $\hat{\mathbf{X}}$ where $\mathbf{X} \subset \hat{\mathbf{X}}$[3]. However, such a model is clearly undesirable for both attacks/evaluations (because it requires guessing the entire key) and simulators (because its estimation requires an impractical amount of real device data).

The de facto practice in all attacks/evaluations, when building leakage models, is to divide the model building process into two steps. The first step is identifying a concise (i.e. easily enumerable) state $\mathbf{Z}$. For instance, a popular assumption is that the intermediate state depends completely on the output of an S-box (denoted by S_{out}) computation, which leads to a state with small cardinality (e.g. $\#\{\mathbf{Z}\} = 2^8$ for AES).

The second step is to estimate the coefficients of the leakage function assuming it only acts on $\mathbf{Z}$. We use the standard notation $\tilde{L}$ to indicate the estimation of L. Various techniques have been proposed, including naive templating [1], regression-based modelling [2,3], step-wise regression [19], etc. Previous works [2,19,20] have also proposed various metrics to evaluate/certificate the device's leakage (as well as the quality of model that built from the measurements). As many will be utilised later, the next two subsections explain these

---

[2] We use the concept of "time points" for readability, but one could equally use the concept of clock cycles or instructions instead.

[3] $\hat{\mathbf{X}}$ contains all intermediate variables that occur during the *entire* execution of an instruction sequence or algorithm.

techniques in details, then we move on to our main topic: *what should we do about the first step?*

2.2 Leakage Modelling: Approaches

Already in the early days of side channel research, the concept of profiling (aka leakage modelling, aka templating) was introduced by Chari et al. [1]. In their original paper, the idea was to assume that the distribution of the measurements from the same state value should follow a (multivariate) normal distribution, and an adversary with *a priori* access to a device can simply estimate the parameters of this distribution.

An alternative to the direct parameter estimation is using regression techniques to derive an equivalent model. A paper by Schindler et al. [2] proposes the use of regression to derive a linear model of a considered state.

The basis of building regression models is that we can express any real valued function of $\mathbf{Z}$ as a polynomial $\tilde{L} = \sum_j \beta_j u_j(\mathbf{Z})$ [21]. In this polynomial the explanatory variables u_j are monomials of the form $\prod_{i=0}^{n-1} z_i^{j_i}$ where z_i denotes the i-th bit of $\mathbf{Z}$ and j_i denote the i-th bit of j (with n the number of bits needed to represent $\mathbf{Z}$ in binary). For clarity, we further define a mapping function $\mathbf{U}$ that maps the n-bit state $\mathbf{Z}$ to a 2^n-length vector:

$$\mathbf{U}(\mathbf{Z}) = (u_0(\mathbf{Z}), u_1(\mathbf{Z}), ..., u_{2^n-1}(\mathbf{Z}))$$

In the following, we can simply use $\tilde{L}(\mathbf{Z}) = \vec{\beta}\mathbf{U}(\mathbf{Z})$ instead of $\tilde{L}(\mathbf{Z}) = \sum_j \beta_j u_j(\mathbf{Z})$.

Regression then estimates the coefficients β_j. The explanatory variables u_j simply represent the different values that $\mathbf{Z}$ can take. If we do not restrict the u_j then the resulting model is typically called the *full model*. If no subscript is given, we implicitly mean the *full* model. In many previous attacks, the leakage model is restricted to just contain the linear terms. We denote this particular *linear model* as

$$\tilde{L}_l(\mathbf{Z}) = \vec{\beta}\mathbf{U}_l(\mathbf{Z}) = \vec{\beta}(u_{2^0}(\mathbf{Z}), u_{2^1}(\mathbf{Z}), ..., u_{2^{n-1}}(\mathbf{Z}))$$

2.3 Judging Model Quality

Any model is only an approximation: there is a gap between the model output and the observed reality. Statistical models are built for at least two purposes [22]. They are either used to predict events in the future, in which case the model quality relates to its predictive power; or they are used to help explain reality, in which case the model quality relates to how many of the relevant factors it can identify. In the context of leakage attacks/evaluations, models are used to predict side channel leaks. Therefore we use metrics such as the coefficient of determination, and cross validation to judge the quality. In the context of leakage simulators, the goal of building these models is to include as many relevant leakage sources as possible. Therefore, the quality relates how two (or more) models compared with each other in terms of explaining the realistic leakage.

Coefficient of Determination. For any model $\tilde{L}(\mathbf{Z})$ that is estimated from the side channel measurements $\mathbf{Y}$, the "modelling error" can be defined as the *residual sum of squares, RSS* (aka the *sum of squared estimate of errors, SSE*),

$$RSS = \sum_{i=1}^{q}(y^{(i)} - \tilde{L}(z^{(i)}))^2,$$

where q represents the number of traces and $z^{(i)}$ represents the value of z for the i-th measurement. Meanwhile, the explained data-variance can be interpreted as the *explained sum of squares, ESS* (aka the *sum of squares due to regression, SSR*),

$$ESS = \sum_{i=1}^{q}\left(\tilde{L}(z^{(i)}) - \bar{y}\right)^2,$$

where $\bar{y}$ represents the mean of measured values $\mathbf{Y}$. If $\tilde{L}$ is derived from linear regression on $\mathbf{Y}$, RSS and ESS should sum up to the *total sum of squares, TSS* (aka SST),

$$TSS = \sum_{i=1}^{q}\left(y^{(i)} - \bar{y}\right)^2.$$

Then, the *coefficient of determination* (R^2) is defined as[4]:

$$R^2 = \frac{ESS}{TSS} = 1 - \frac{RSS}{TSS}.$$

Given two estimated models $\tilde{L}_1$ and $\tilde{L}_2$, whereby both models are assumed to have the same number of terms (i.e. same restrictions on $u_j(\mathbf{Z})$ in Sect. 2.2), intuitively, the model with the higher R^2 value would be considered as better. The crucial point here is that both models need the same number of terms, because the R^2 increases with the number of terms that are included in the model. Consequently, the R^2 does not lend itself to investigate models that represent approximations in different numbers of terms.

Cross-validation. An important aspect in model validation is to check if a model overfits the data. If a model overfits the data, it will generalise badly, which means it is bad in terms of predicting new data. Therefore using cross-validation of any chosen metric (e.g. the RSS) is essential [20] when aiming for models with a high *predictive power*. Given two models, one can compute via cross validation both RSS values and then judge their relative predictive power.

F-Tests. Given two "nested" models (i.e. there is a so called *full* model and a *restricted* model which only contains a subset of the terms of the full model), the *F-test* is the most natural way to decide whether the *restricted* model is missing

---

[4] Alternatively, it can also be written as $R^2 = 1 - \frac{SSE}{SST}$. Note the distinction between RSS (i.e. "R" for *residue*) and SSR (i.e. "R" for *regression*).

significant contribution compared with the *full* model. More specifically, assuming a *full* model $\tilde{L}_f(\mathbf{Z}_f)$ and a *restricted* model $\tilde{L}_r(\mathbf{Z}_r)$, where $\mathbf{Z}_r$ is constructed by removing $z_f - z_r$ explanatory variables (set regression coefficients to 0) from $\mathbf{Z}_f$, one can compute the F-statistic as

$$F = \frac{\frac{RSS_r - RSS_f}{z_f - z_r}}{\frac{RSS_f}{q - z_f}}.$$

The resulting F follows the F distribution with $(z_f - z_r, q - z_f)$ degree of freedom. A p-value below a statistically motivated threshold rejects the null hypothesis (the two models are equivalent) and hence suggests that at least one of the removed variables is potentially useful. This approach was used in [5] to derive relatively fine grained models on selected intermediate states.

2.4   Leakage Certification Techniques

Leakage certification techniques, e.g. "assumption error" and "estimation error" [20] are also designed under the assumption that $\mathbf{Z}$ is given. One could be tempted to use such techniques to test if the selected state $\mathbf{Z}$ is "good enough": however, neither does this fit with the original intention of [20] nor is the statistical power of the "leakage certification" techniques sufficient. In the interest of flow we provide the reasoning for this statement in Appendix A.

3   Model Quality: Is My Leakage Model Complete?

It is critical to remember that all approaches for judging model quality assume that the state $\mathbf{Z}$ has already been found. As we argued in the introduction, in practice, this state is not only unknown but also non-trivial to determine.

In existing publications, the suitable state $\mathbf{Z}$ is often found through an *ad hoc* procedure: one tries some set $\mathbf{Z}$, and then evaluates the leakage model (using $\mathbf{Z}$) via R^2 or cross-validation (or alternatively, performs attacks with CPA). If the evaluation/attack result is not successful, it suggests the current $\mathbf{Z}$ is unlikely to be correct. Otherwise, $\mathbf{Z}$ might be a part of $\mathbf{X}$, but it remains unclear if $\mathbf{Z}$ already contains all variables that leak (in relation to the code sequence that the attack/evaluation relates to). In this section, we introduce the novel concept of model completeness, and an associated test to measure it efficiently.

3.1   Completeness

We make the important observation that the task of finding the *state* is the same as the task of deciding whether some variables contribute significantly to a model. This implies that we can find the state by testing nested models via an F-test to determine if the "bigger" model explains the real data better than the "smaller" model. This approach has been used before in the side channel literatures for deciding if low degree terms should be included in $\tilde{L}(\mathbf{Z})$ in [5,19]. We thus suggest to use this idea to define the notion of model completeness.

Definition 1. *We consider two nested models $\tilde{L}(\mathbf{Z}_f)$ and $\tilde{L}(\mathbf{Z}_r)$, and a corresponding F-test with*

$$H_0: \tilde{L}_f(\mathbf{Z}_f) \text{ and } \tilde{L}_r(\mathbf{Z}_r) \text{ explain the observations equally well, and} \qquad (1)$$

$$H_1: \tilde{L}_f(\mathbf{Z}_f) \text{ explains the observations better than } \tilde{L}_r(\mathbf{Z}_r). \qquad (2)$$

*We call $\mathbf{Z}_r$ as **complete** (with respect to $\mathbf{Z}_f$) if the null hypothesis of the F-test cannot be rejected.*

The notion of model completeness (of a reduced model with respect to some full model) means that the reduced model does not miss any (statistically) significantly contributing factor when compared with the full model.

Toy Example. Suppose that $\tilde{L}(\hat{\mathbf{X}})$ contains the variables $\{x_0, x_1, x_2, x_3\}$ and the model $\tilde{L}(\mathbf{Z})$ contains the variables $\{x_0, x_1, x_2\}$. Following our discussion in Sect. 2.2, we estimate the model coefficients from realistic measurements:

$$\tilde{L}_f = \vec{\beta}_f \mathbf{U}(\hat{\mathbf{X}}),$$

$$\tilde{L}_r = \vec{\beta}_r \mathbf{U}(\mathbf{Z}).$$

We subject these models (which are nested as $\mathbf{Z}$ is included in $\hat{\mathbf{X}}$) to the F-test. If the F-test reports a *p-value* lower than the significance level α, we can conclude at least one of the regression terms that depends on x_3 is contributing significantly, and therefore we reject the null hypothesis. Thus, according to our definition, $\mathbf{Z}$ is not complete with respect to $\hat{\mathbf{X}}$.

Towards Finding the State in Practice. In practice we have limited information about the state (at any point in time during a computation). Thus our main challenge is to define a conservative set $\hat{\mathbf{X}}$ that satisfies $\mathbf{X} \subseteq \hat{\mathbf{X}}$, then drop terms from $\hat{\mathbf{X}}$ to see which (combinations of) terms actually matter (i.e. find an approximation $\mathbf{Z}$ for $\mathbf{X}$).

As $\hat{\mathbf{X}}$ is a superset of $\mathbf{X}$, it is not hard to see that if $\mathbf{Z}$ is *complete* w.r.t. $\hat{\mathbf{X}}$, it should also be *complete* w.r.t. $\mathbf{X}$. Informally, this means if we can first explicitly define $\hat{\mathbf{X}}$, then test our selected $\mathbf{Z}$ against it, the F-test result will illustrate whether $\mathbf{Z}$ is *complete* or not (up to some statistical power), even if the true $\mathbf{X}$ remains unknown. The remaining challenges are firstly how to define a complete $\hat{\mathbf{X}}$ at the first place, and secondly how can we test $\mathbf{Z}$ against $\hat{\mathbf{X}}$ in an F-test.

For deterministic block cipher implementations with a constant key (a case frequently considered in the side channel literature), a conservative state assumption would be based on the entire plaintext. If an implementation is masked, then also the masks need to be included. The F-test then checks the contribution of all resulting explanatory variables[5]. Because of the large block size, this is a

---

[5] Note that this is not the same application scenario as leakage detection tests, which consider only the unshared secret. We did not propose the F-test as a leakage detection test here, therefore "which statistical moment the corresponding leakage detection is" is out of the scope.

starting point that is in fact unworkable from a statistical point of view (i.e. requires too many observations for model estimation). We explain a statistical trick in the next section, that makes this seemingly infeasible problem, practical.

3.2   Collapsed F-Test for Completeness

As we explained before, the *full* model is often too large in relevant practical scenarios: it consists of many large variables. In statistical terminology such models are called factorial designs, and the challenge is how to reduce the number of factors. Techniques such as aliasing or identifying confounding variables (i.e. variables that impact on multiple factors, or identifying factors that are known to be related) are well known in statistical model building. These techniques rely on *a priori* knowledge about the model (potentially because of prior work, or other sources of information), which we do not have in our setting.

However, we identified two ideas/observations that enable us to define a novel strategy to deal with factorial designs in our setting. The first observation (we mention this before in the text) is that the F-test, although often used to deal with proportional models, actually tests for the inclusion/exclusion of explanatory variables in *nested* models. This implies that the test is agnostic to the actual value of the regression coefficient, thus we can set them to 0/1 and work with nominal models.

The second observation is that although our explanatory variable contains n independent bits, their leakages often share a similar form (e.g. the standard HW model can be written as the sum of every single bit), because the underlying circuit treats them as "a word". Furthermore, for leakage modelling, we want to include any variable in our model if a single bit of that variable contributes to leakage. Based on these observations we show an elegant trick to bound our explanatory variables to a small space.

Bounding the Explanatory Variables. We demonstrate our trick based on an example at first: assume we know the leakage can be conservatively determined by four n-bit values A, B, A' and B' (i.e. $\tilde{L}(\hat{\mathbf{X}}) = \vec{\beta}\mathbf{U}(\hat{\mathbf{X}})$, where $\hat{\mathbf{X}} = \{\hat{x}|\hat{x} = a||b||a'||b'\}$). In order to test if a chosen partial state $\mathbf{Z} \subset \hat{\mathbf{X}}$ is *complete* w.r.t $\hat{\mathbf{X}}$, following our previous discussion, we should test the following two regression models:

$$\tilde{L}_f(\hat{\mathbf{X}}) = \vec{\beta}\mathbf{U}(\hat{\mathbf{X}}),$$

$$\tilde{L}_r(\mathbf{Z}) = \vec{\beta}\mathbf{U}(\mathbf{Z}).$$

The nested F-test then applies to verify the following hypotheses:

H_0: $\tilde{L}_r(\mathbf{Z})$ *explains the observations as well as* $\tilde{L}_f(\hat{\mathbf{X}})$.
H_1: $\tilde{L}_f(\hat{\mathbf{X}})$ *explains the observations significantly better than* $\tilde{L}_r(\mathbf{Z})$.

Unfortunately, testing $\tilde{L}_f(\hat{\mathbf{X}})$ would require 2^{4n} explanatory variables in $\mathbf{U}(\hat{\mathbf{X}})$ as $\hat{x}$ is a $4n$-bit state. For $n \geq 32$, it requires an infeasible number of observations to properly estimate $\tilde{L}_f(\hat{\mathbf{X}})$. However, via setting $a_i = a_0$ (a_i stands for the i-th bit of a, a_0 drawn at random from $\{0,1\}$), we can bound the variable A to a much smaller space:

$$a = (a_0, a_0, ..., a_0), a_0 \in \mathbb{F}_2.$$

Since a_0 is a binary variable that satisfies $a_0^i = a_0$, $i > 0$, $\hat{\mathbf{X}} = \{\hat{x}|\hat{x} = a||b||a'||b'\}$ now "collapses" to a $(3n+1)$-bit state set $\hat{\mathbf{X}}_c = \{\hat{x}_c|\hat{x}_c = a_0||b||a'||b'\}$. Applying this restriction to the other 3 variables, the collapsed leakage function $\tilde{L}_c(\hat{\mathbf{X}}_c) = \vec{\beta}\mathbf{U}(\hat{\mathbf{X}}_c)$, $\hat{\mathbf{X}}_c = \{\hat{x}_c|\hat{x}_c = a_0||b_0||a'_0||b'_0\}$ contains only 2^4 explanatory variables, which makes it easy to work with.

Of course, such a restriction is not for free: originally, there could be many interaction terms between the explanatory variables. In the model $\tilde{L}_c$ these terms are "collapsed" and "added" to the remaining terms, e.g. $a_1 a_0$ becomes a_0 as $a_1 = a_0$. In fact, as there is only 1 bit randomness, a_0 now becomes an alias for the operand A: having this term in $\tilde{L}_c$ suggests A appears in $\tilde{L}$, but certainly not in the same way as in $\tilde{L}_c$. We can expand this idea by allowing two (or more) bits of randomness: this enables us to differentiate between linear and non-linear models[6].

Slightly formalising this idea, we define a mapping called "collapse" $Coll$ that converts a term $u_j(\hat{\mathbf{X}})$ in the original "un-collapsed" setup to $u_{Coll(j)}(\hat{\mathbf{X}}_c)$. Recall that $u_j(\hat{\mathbf{X}})$ is defined (Sect. 2.2) as:

$$u_j(\hat{\mathbf{X}}) = \prod \hat{x}_i^{j_i},$$

where j_i represents the i-th bit of the binary representation of j. For any $j \in [0, 2^{4n})$, we define the $2^{4n} \to 2^4$ map $Coll$ as:

$$Coll(j) = j_{coll} = j_a||j_{a'}||j_b||j_{b'} \in [0, 2^4),$$

where $j_a = \bigvee_{i=0}^{n-1} j_i$, $j_{a'} = \bigvee_{i=n}^{2n-1} j_i$, $j_b - \bigvee_{i=2n}^{3n-1} j_i$, $j_{b'} = \bigvee_{i=3n}^{4n-1} j_i$. It is clear that when all operands are bounded to 1-bit, we have that

$$u_j(\hat{\mathbf{X}}) = u_{j_{coll}}(\hat{\mathbf{X}}_c), \hat{\mathbf{X}}_c = \{\hat{x}_c|\hat{x}_c = a_0||a'_0||b_0||b'_0\}.$$

The latter can be easily tested in an F-test. In the following, we show that the test model passes the F-test in our "collapsed" case is a necessary (but not sufficient) condition for passing the F-test in the original setup.

Theorem 1. *If a collapsed term $u_{j_{coll}}(\hat{\mathbf{X}}_c)$ cannot be ignored from $\tilde{L}_c$ (i.e. $\beta_{j_{coll}} \neq 0$), at least one of the corresponding $u_j(\hat{\mathbf{X}})$ cannot be ignored from $\tilde{L}$ (i.e. $\beta_j \neq 0$).*

Proof. In the original case, any leakage model can always be written as

$$\tilde{L}(\hat{\mathbf{X}}) = \sum_{j=0}^{2^{4n}-1} \beta_j u_j(\hat{\mathbf{X}})$$

---

[6] We could take this further and include more "intra-variable" interactions, but we left this for future considerations. The "inter-variable" interactions remain in $\tilde{L}_c$ anyway.

However, considering the inputs have been bounded, such model collapses to:

$$\tilde{L}(\hat{\mathbf{X}}) = \sum_{j_{coll}=0}^{2^4-1} \left(\sum_{\forall j, Coll(j)=j_{coll}} \beta_j \right) u_{j_{coll}}(\hat{\mathbf{X}}_c)$$

Thus, if a certain collapsed term $u_{j_{coll}}(\hat{\mathbf{X}}_c)$ has a significant contribution to $\tilde{L}_c$ (i.e. $\beta_{j_{coll}} \neq 0$), one can conclude that:

$$\sum_{\forall j, Coll(j)=j_{coll}} \beta_j \neq 0 \Rightarrow \exists j, \beta_j \neq 0$$

Clearly nothing can be concluded if the above sum equals 0, which suggests this is only a necessary condition.

Theorem 1 implies that whilst we still cannot directly test $\tilde{L}_f = \vec{\beta}\mathbf{U}(\hat{\mathbf{X}})$, given a partial state $\mathbf{Z}$, we can test:

$$\tilde{L}_{cf}(\hat{\mathbf{X}}_c) = \vec{\beta}\mathbf{U}(\hat{\mathbf{X}}_c),$$

$$\tilde{L}_{cr}(\mathbf{Z}_c) = \vec{\beta}\mathbf{U}(\mathbf{Z}_c),$$

as the cardinalities of both $\mathbf{U}(\hat{\mathbf{X}}_c)$ and $\mathbf{U}(\mathbf{Z}_c)$ are at most 2^4. Then the nested F-test applies to:

H_0: $\tilde{L}_{cr}(\mathbf{Z}_c)$ *explains the observations as well as* $\tilde{L}_{cf}(\hat{\mathbf{X}}_c)$,
H_1: $\tilde{L}_{cf}(\hat{\mathbf{X}}_c)$ *explains the observations significantly better than* $\tilde{L}_{cr}(\mathbf{Z}_c)$.

If this F-test rejects H_0, we can also conclude that in the original un-collapsed setup, $\tilde{L}_f(\hat{\mathbf{X}})$ fits the observations significantly better than $\tilde{L}_r(\mathbf{Z})$. Thus, we learn that $\mathbf{Z}$ is not complete with respect to $\hat{\mathbf{X}}$ without testing it explicitly.

Toy Example. Suppose we want to test $\tilde{L}_r = \vec{\beta}\mathbf{U}(\mathbf{Z}), \vec{\beta} \in \mathbb{R}^{2^{2n}}$ where $\mathbf{Z} = \{z | z = a || b\}$ against $\tilde{L}_f = \vec{\beta}\mathbf{U}(\hat{\mathbf{X}}), \vec{\beta} \in \mathbb{R}^{2^{4n}}$ where $\hat{\mathbf{X}} = \{\hat{x} | \hat{x} = a || b || a' || b'\}$. As mentioned before, for $n = 32$, direct testing is not an option. However, we can bound the inputs and test the collapsed models instead:

$$\tilde{L}_{cr} = \beta_0 + \beta_1 a_0 + \beta_2 b_0 + \beta_3 a_0 b_0$$

$$\tilde{L}_{cf} = \beta_0 + \beta_1 a_0 + \beta_2 a'_0 + \beta_3 b_0 + \beta_4 b'_0$$
$$+ \beta_5 a_0 b_0 + \beta_6 a'_0 b'_0 + \beta_7 a'_0 b_0 + \beta_8 a_0 b'_0 + \beta_9 b_0 b'_0 + \beta_{10} a_0 a'_0$$
$$+ \beta_{11} a_0 a'_0 b'_0 + \beta_{12} a_0 a'_0 b_0 + \beta_{13} a_0 b'_0 b_0 + \beta_{14} a'_0 b'_0 b_0$$
$$+ \beta_{15} a_0 a'_0 b_0 b'_0$$

If the F-test rejects the null hypothesis, then we know that the missing terms make a difference not only in $\tilde{L}_c$ but also in $\tilde{L}$. Therefore, we can conclude $\mathbf{Z}$ is also not complete (w.r.t. to $\hat{\mathbf{X}}$) in the original setup, without explicitly testing it. The price to pay is that unlike the original F-test, our collapsed test becomes a necessary condition instead of a sufficient condition. Nevertheless, any $\mathbf{Z}$ that fails our test presents a genuine concern, as it directly suggests the selected $\mathbf{Z}$ is unlikely to be complete.

In the remainder of this paper we will *always* work with collapsed models, thus the subscript c will be dropped from all models.

3.3   Statistical Power of the Nested F-Test

It is imperative to understand the power of any statistical test. The power of a test is the probability that it detects an effect if the effect is present. To compute the power of a collapsed F-test, we first need to consider the *effect size* that we are dealing with. The *effect size* in our case relates to the difference between the *restricted* model and the *full* model, which can be computed (according to Cohen [23]) as:

$$f^2 = \frac{R_F^2 - R_R^2}{1 - R_F^2} = \frac{RSS_R - RSS_F}{RSS_F}.$$

Under the alternative hypothesis, the computed F-statistic follows a non-central F distribution with non-centrality parameter λ and two degrees of freedom from the numerator df_1 and the denominator df_2. When $f^2 = 0$, this becomes the null distribution of the central F-distribution. Thus, when the false positive rate is set to α, the threshold of the F-statistic is

$$F stat_{th} = Q_F(df_1, df_2, 1 - \alpha),$$

where Q_F is the quantile function of the central F distribution. The *false-negative* rate β can be computed as

$$\beta = F_{nc}(F stat_{th}, df_1, df_2, \lambda),$$
$$\lambda = f^2(df_1 + df_2 + 1),$$

where F_{nc} is the CDF function of the non-central F distribution. The statistical power for effect size f^2 is then $1 - \beta$. Our 3 tests in Sect. 5.1 have $df_1 = \{256 - 7, 256 - 19, 256 - 16\}$, $df_2 = q - 256$, $q = 20000$, per-test $\alpha = 10^{-3.7}$, which all come to $1 - \beta \approx 1$ for the *small effect size* $f^2 = 0.02$ in [23]. According to [24] this corresponds indeed to what they observed in similar experiments.

Summarising, assuming sufficient traces (20k in our calculation), the F-test on collapsed models has high power for relevant side channel scenarios according to [24].

4   Dissecting Attacks: Towards Worst-Case Adversaries

A recent paper by Bronchain and Standaert [25] demonstrated impressively how knowledge of an implementation (affine masking implementation from ANSSI [26] on an off-the-shelf, thus "grey box" processor) can help to derive extremely powerful profiled attack strategies. We wondered if our novel technique of the collapsed F-test could reveal further leakage that they might have missed (they did not explicitly consider if or not they had included all leaking variables).

To this end, we investigate the leakage of this implementation[7]. Our measurement setup consists of an ARM Cortex M3 core (NXP LPC1313). As the code is written in C, the compiling toolchain and commercial core create a grey-box scenario: we can locate the S-box computation in the power traces, but we have no full state information. The working frequency is set to 12 MHz, while our oscilloscope (Picoscope 5243D) captures 10k traces at 250 MSa/s (for both the collapsed case and the un-collapsed case). We are analysing the masked table look-ups of the first 4 S-boxes in the first round. Altogether the 4 S-box computations take 17 μs, which amounts to around 204 clock cycles and 4250 samples on the power trace.

Note that the original implementation also includes hiding techniques, such as random shuffling. Unless stated otherwise, our following analysis always assume shuffling is not presented (i.e. "#define NO_SHUFFLE" in the code, which corresponds to the non-shuffling analysis in [26]). Alternatively one can take our analysis as a "follow-up" after the shuffling permutation has been already recovered using the technique in [25].

Affine Masking. As this implementation is specific to AES, each data byte is protected as an element on the Galois Field $\mathbb{GF}(2^8)$. More specifically, each data byte x is presented as:

$$C(x; rm, ra) = (rm \otimes x) \oplus ra$$

where C is the encoding function, rm is called the *multiplicative mask* and ra the additive mask. Note that by definition, rm is uniform on $[1, 255]$ (i.e. cannot be 0). For the i-th state byte x_i, the implementation stores the additive mask ra_i accordingly in a mask array ra. The *multiplicative mask* rm, on the other hand, is shared among all 16 bytes within this encryption. Each linear operation (e.g. ShiftRow, MixColumn) can be done separately on each share. Meanwhile, the masked S-box is pre-computed according to the *multiplicative mask* rm and the S-box input/output mask r_{in} and r_{out}:

$$S'(rm \otimes x \oplus r_{in}) = rm \otimes S(x) \oplus r_{out}$$

Code Snippet for the S-Box. In order to compute the S-box's output using the pre-computed table, one must transfer the additive mask ra_i to r_{in}, then after the table look-up, transfer r_{out} back to ra_i. The *SubBytesWithMask* function performs this task as follow:

```
SubBytesWithMask:
...                          //r3=C(x) r10=ra
...                          //r0=i r8=S'
```

---

[7] The original *Compute_GTab* function contains a few instructions (e.g. *uadd8*) that are not available on our platform. We had rewritten an equivalent version in pure Thumb-16 assembly. This makes no difference in our leakage analysis as we are not targeting this part.

```
ldrb r4, [r3, r0]      //(1) r4=C(x)_i^rin
ldrb r6, [r10, r0]     //(2) r6=ra_i
eor  r4, r6            //(3) r4=C(x)_i^rin^ra_i
ldrb r4, [r8, r4]      //(4) r4=rmS(x)^rout
eor  r4, r6            //(5) r4=rmS(x)^rout^ra_i
strb r4, [r3, r0]      //(6) store r4 to state
...                    //removing rout later
```

Note that the r_{in} is added before this function, therefore line (1)–(3) purely focus on removing ra_i. Similarly, removing r_{out} is postponed to the end of the S-box calculation, therefore not presented in this code.

Initial Analysis. We first analyse the leakage of the first S-box look-up and use 1 bit to represent each x_i. All random masks (used within the captured 4 Sbox computation) must also be considered in our leakage analysis: we use 6 bits to represent $ra_{0:3}$, r_{in} and r_{out} respectively. When collapsed to 1 bit, rm is restricted to 1 (i.e. nullifies the protection of rm)[8]. Thus, we exclude this bit from our F-test and analyse the leakage where rm is set to 1. This means we will not cover any potential unexpected leakage introduced by rm in our experiment: of course, one can always switch to the 2-bit version and use more traces to cover rm.

The complete model is therefore defined as

$$\tilde{L}_f(\hat{\mathbf{X}}) = \vec{\beta}\{\forall j \; u_j(\hat{\mathbf{X}})|\hat{x} = x_{0:3}||ra_{0:3}||r_{in}||r_{out}, \hat{x} \in \hat{\mathbf{X}}\}$$

Targeting the leakage from the first S-box computation, we assume that all the computed values are leaking plus their transitions (i.e. following the spirit of [27]). Thus we first define a coarse-grained model capturing all possible computations for the first S-box:

$$\tilde{L}_r(\mathbf{Z}) = \vec{\beta}\{\forall j \; u_j(\mathbf{Z})|z = x_0||ra_0||r_{in}||r_{out}, z \in \mathbf{Z}\}$$

One can check that all the intermediate values that appear in the code snippet can be expressed by this restricted model $\tilde{L}_r(\mathbf{Z})$. Applying the F-test between $\tilde{L}_f(\hat{\mathbf{X}})$ and $\tilde{L}_r(\mathbf{Z})$ to the leakage measurements from computing the first S-box, our analysis finds that this x_0-only model fails in the collapsed F-test. As Fig. 1 shows, the blue line clearly passes the threshold (i.e. $-log_{10}(pv) > th \Rightarrow pv < 10^{-pv}$), which implies that the realistic leakage contains much more than what $\tilde{L}_r(\mathbf{Z})$ can express.

One Step Further. We notice that the *ldrb* instruction probably loads not only the target byte, but also the other bytes within the same word (see also in Section 5.2 of [10]). Thus, our line (1) loads:

$$\{rm \otimes x_0 \oplus ra_0 \oplus r_{in}, rm \otimes x_1 \oplus ra_1 \oplus r_{in}, rm \otimes x_2 \oplus ra_2 \oplus r_{in}, rm \otimes x_3 \oplus ra_3 \oplus r_{in}\},$$

---

[8] Note that this only applies to the collapsed case and the F-test: the following regression analyses and attacks are performed on the un-collapsed traces, where the protection of rm still applies.

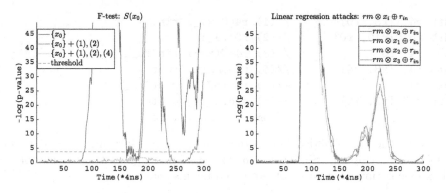

Fig. 1. Leakage analysis for the first S-box (Color figure online)

Line (2) loads

$$\{ra_0, ra_1, ra_2, ra_3\}.$$

As a consequence, the transition from Line (1) to Line (2) presents

$$\{rm \otimes x_0 \oplus r_{in}, rm \otimes x_1 \oplus r_{in}, rm \otimes x_2 \oplus r_{in}, rm \otimes x_3 \oplus r_{in}\}.$$

If we add both these values (plus their transitions) into $\tilde{L}(\mathbf{Z})$, the red lines show that the first peak around 100–150 is gone, suggesting the leakage has been safely captured in the collapsed model. However, the second half of the trace still presents some extra leakage.

Let us further consider line (4): if it also loads a word, then the observed leakage depends not only on the target byte, but also on 3 adjacent bytes,

$$\{S'(rm \otimes x_0 \oplus rin), S'(rm \otimes x_0 \oplus rin \oplus 1),$$
$$S'(rm \otimes x_0 \oplus rin \oplus 2), S'(rm \otimes x_0 \oplus rin \oplus 3)\}.$$

Unfortunately, the expression above does not follows high-to-low byte-order: as the memory address is masked by rin, the byte-order in this word varies from trace to trace. Therefore, if we calculate the memory bus transition leakage from line (2) to (4), the correct form can be complicated. Nonetheless, we can always create a conservative term $\mathbf{Z}_{a1}$ where $za_1 = x_0 || r_{in} || r_{out} || ra_1$: adding $\vec{\beta}\mathbf{U}(\mathbf{Z}_{a1})$ covers all possible transitions between ra_1 and the S-box output bytes from line (4), despite which byte it is transmitting to. Similarly, we add $\mathbf{Z}_{a2}$ and $\mathbf{Z}_{a3}$ to $\tilde{L}(\mathbf{Z})$ and construct a model that passes the F-test (i.e. the cyan line in the left half of Fig. 1).

We further verify our inference from the F-test—*ldrb loads word and causes word-wise transitions*. In order to confirm such leakage does exist, we go back to the original un-collapsed implementation and perform a linear regression attack [3] on $rm \otimes x_i \oplus r_{in}$. In theory, *ldrb* should load x_0 only, which means only $rm \otimes x_0 \oplus r_{in}$ should be loaded for the masked table look-up. However, we did observe that the other 3 bytes also contribute to peaks on the regression results

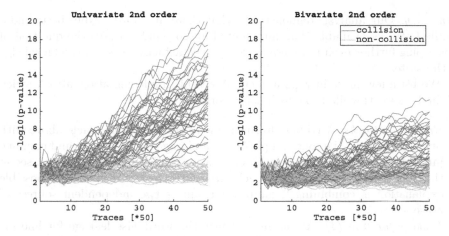

Fig. 2. Collision oracle

in the right half of Fig. 1. To our knowledge, the most reasonable explanation is that such leakage is from the transition from line (1) and (2), where the entire 32-bit word is loaded in both cases.

A Novel Non-profiled Attack Option. The existence of leakage for multiple $rm \otimes x_i \oplus r_{in}$ provides a clue for a novel non-profiled attack strategy for this implementation: as all 4 bytes leak simultaneously around point 100, we can raise our measurements to their 2nd power (i.e. a univariate 2nd order attack), which cancels the influence of r_{in}. However, unlike the trivial Boolean masking schemes, now x_i (or $x_i \oplus x_{i+1}$) is still protected by rm. That being said, considering if we have a "collision" (aka $x_i = x_j$) within a word, we know for sure $rm \otimes x_i \oplus r_{in} = rm \otimes x_j \oplus r_{in}$ as both rm and r_{in} are shared among all bytes. Such restriction further affects the variance of the measured leakage, which could be exploited through 2nd order attacks.

Implementing this idea, we have tested 50 plaintexts that have collisions and 50 plaintexts without collision in the first word. Within each test, we perform a fixed-versus-random t-test and plot the minimal p-value in Fig. 2. After 2500 fixed traces and 2500 random traces, nearly 90% of the collision cases can be identified, which confirms the validity of our analysis above.

It is not hard to see that such an oracle provides a link between each key bytes: in a chosen plaintext setup, attackers can manipulate the plaintext and learn information about the secret key. Ideally, if we find 3 collisions[9] within the same word and determine their collision indices through adaptive testing, the key space for each word can be reduced to 2^8. Similar procedure can be applied to the other 3 32-bit words. Consequently, to recover the master key, we only need to enumerate the remaining 2^{32} key guess space. We leave the question of *what is the most efficient attack strategy* open, as it is out of the scope of this paper.

---

[9] 4 bytes in one word, therefore there are at most $\binom{4}{2} = 6$ collisions.

Summary. Our analysis demonstrates that there are considerably better non-profiled attacks available than anticipated in [26], and it raises the question of developing further even more advanced profiled attacks based on the knowledge of the state.

We list a few more intriguing facts about this implementation/attack which might be a worthwhile topic for future works:

- *Bivariate attacks.* A trivial alternative is to construct our oracle above with bivariate leakage (i.e. one sample for x_0 and one sample for x_1) and combine multiple points on the trace with the "mean-free" product. As we can see in the right half of Fig. 2, this approach turns out to be less efficient. One possible explanation is combining 2 samples introduces two independent sources of noise.
- *Leakage for line (4).* At the first glance, the word-wise leakage for line (4) seems to be a better target. The entire word is masked with 1 byte rm, 1 byte r_{out} and contains 8-bit of secret key. In our experiment, we found the influence of rm to be onerous, at least in a non-profiled setup. However, as this leakage reveals a certain key-byte's value (versus reveals the key byte's relation to other key bytes), we leave the exploitability of such leakage as an open problem.
- *Avoiding leakage.* The exploited leakage above can be easily prevented, if the implementation loads something else between line (1) and (2). In other words, this is a specific implementation pitfall, not linked to the masking scheme itself. As a comparison, the bivariate version in the right half of Fig. 2 is not affected by these subtle implementation details.
- *Link to t-test.* The exploited leakage can be found through 2nd order fixed-versus-random (or fixed-versus-fixed) t-test, suppose the selected fixed constant contains a "collision". For a randomly selected constant, the probability that it has a "collision" in the first word is around 0.04, which poses again a question on the "coverage" of using 1 or 2 fixed constant(-s) in leakage detections [28].

5   Application to Leakage Simulators

In recent years, various leakage simulators have been proposed in order to enable early-stage leakage awareness in the context of software implementations on off-the-shelf processors [29]. Using a leakage simulator, developers can identify and patch potential leaks at an early stage, even if they have no physical access to the target device. In this section, we utilise our new test to challenge existing leakage simulators that have either asserted models or estimated models.

Throughout this section, we use the same ARM Cortex M3 core as our target software platform. Each profiling trace set includes 20k traces to estimate and evaluate models, in line with the statistical analysis that we provided for our novel test. The measurement setup is the same as in Sect. 4, except for the working frequency which we reduced to 1 MHz: a lower frequency helps to provide a clearer cycle-to-cycle view, which is essential for model building. Any model is ultimately data dependent: a proportional leakage model such as [5] represents the device leakage as captured by a specific setup. In particular, the explanatory variables in a leakage model relate to the (micro)architecture of the modelled processor, and the coefficients relate to the measurement setup. With our novel technique the emphasis is to build nominal models, i.e. models that only have 0/non-0 coefficients, at least initially[10].

5.1   Modelling Leakage of Individual Instructions

As pointed out in [29], one of the remaining challenge for grey-box simulators is "(they) target relatively simple architectures". In fact, many tools only target algorithmic variables that may correspond to multiple intermediate states. Even if the simulator takes binary code as its input (e.g. ELMO [5]), the undocumented micro-architectural effects can still cause all sorts of issues [10]. Our novel statistical tool can help to identify missed leakage: if the leakage model utilised by a leakage simulator fails our novel test, it suggests that some contributing factor is missing.

The most sophisticated grey-box simulators that exist at the moment have all been built for the ARM Cortex M family, including ELMO [5] and its extension ELMO* [18], as well as MAPS [30]. ELMO derives its models from profiling traces from an actual Cortex M0 processor. The ELMO*/ROSITA [18] tools extend the ELMO model to cover various memory related leaks. The MAPS simulator does not have a profiled power model, since it uses value/transition-based models that are derived directly from the hardware description of an Cortex M3 core (provided by ARM under an educational licence). Technically speaking, there is no guarantee that this example core is identical to the IP cores that ARM sold to the manufacturers.

The code snippet that we will use in the following does not utilise any memory instruction. Thus, any observed difference is purely down to how the simulators model the leakage within the data processing unit. Considering that ELMO* extends ELMO mainly in the memory sub-system, in most cases below, they should produce the same result as ELMO (therefore omitted in the comparison). The ELMO repository offeres a range of leakage models all sitting on top of a Thumb instruction set emulator: there is a power model for an M0 by STM, an EM model derived from an M4, and an additional power model derived from an M3 [17]. This last model/version corresponds to the processor in our setup (an NXP LPC1313). In the following, our comparison is always on this M3 version of ELMO. Our comparision also include the simulator MAPS, which is also designed for a Cortex M3 [30].

Simplified Instruction-Wise Model. A common simplification in the three grey-box simulators ELMO, ELMO* and MAPS is that they all focus on the leakage

---

[10] To build a proportional model on top of the recovered nominal model is possible. One would need to estimate coefficients based on further measurement data (adjusted to the frequency that the target would run on in the wild).

within the ALU. This is a sensible choice: even if the processor has a multi-stage pipeline, we do not necessarily care about the leakage from fetching or decoding the instructions (as it is often not data-dependent[11]).

Sticking with the same notation as before, we describe the full model for instructions with two inputs (current A and B, previous A' and B') as $\tilde{L}_f = \vec{\beta}\mathbf{U}(\hat{\mathbf{X}})$, where $\hat{\mathbf{X}} = \{AA'BB'\} = \{\forall \hat{x}|\hat{x} = a||a'||b||b'\}$. The output value of an instruction, denoted as C (previous C'), is completely determined by A and B, therefore there is no need to add C (or C') into $\tilde{L}_f$. However, if restrictions on the inputs are added (e.g. the leakage of A is linear, denoted as $\mathbf{U}_l(A) = \{u_j(A)|HW(j) < 2\} = \{1, a_0, ..., a_{n-1}\}$), we might need to add the instruction output C to our model. In our experiments, we also consider the following leakage models that correspond to the most commonly used models in the existing literature:

$\tilde{L}_l = \vec{\beta}(\mathbf{U}_l(A)), \mathbf{U}_l(B), \mathbf{U}_l(C))$: this model is a linear function of the current inputs and output. Because of the linearity of this model, it is imperative to include the output here. For instance, if the circuit implements the bitwise-and function, the leakage on ab cannot be described by any linear function of a and b. In the existing literature this is often further simplified to the Hamming weight of just the output (aka the HW model).

$\tilde{L}_{le}$:

$$\tilde{L}_{le} = \vec{\beta}(\mathbf{U}_l(A), \mathbf{U}_l(B), \mathbf{U}_l(C), \mathbf{U}_l(A'), \mathbf{U}_l(B'), \mathbf{U}_l(C'),$$
$$\mathbf{U}_l(A \oplus A'), \mathbf{U}_l(B \oplus B), \mathbf{U}_l(C \oplus C'))$$

this model further includes Hamming distance information, which can be regarded as an extension for both the Hamming weight and the Hamming distance model (used in the MAPS simulator [30]); it therefore also generalises the ELMO model [5] which only fits a single dummy for the Hamming distance leakage.

$\tilde{L}_{TA} = \vec{\beta}\mathbf{U}(\{AB\})$: this model represents template attacks [1], where all relevant current inputs are taken into consideration. In this model the output does not have to be included because we allow interactions between the input variables. This model can also be taken as a faithful interpretation of "only computation leaks" [31].

Challenge Code Snippet. Before any further analysis, we craft a code snippet that can trigger core leakage in the execute cycle, while not causing any other type of data-dependent leakage from other pipeline stages (i.e. *fetch* and *decode*):

```
eors   r2,r2            //r2=0
eors   r1,r3            //r1=a', r3=b'
nop
```

---

[11] Otherwise, the program has data-dependent branches, which should be checked through information flow analysis first.

```
nop
eors   r5,r7                    //r5=a,   r7=b **Target**
nop
nop
```

eors r5, r7 represents the cycle we are targeting: the 2 pipeline registers are set to value a and b, where the previous values are a' and b'. a' and b' are set by *eors r1, r3*: since both lines use *eors*, a (b) and a' (b') should share the same pipeline register.

The 2 *nop*-s before/after ensure all data-dependent leakage should be caused by *eors r5, r7*: in a 3-stage pipeline micro-processor, the previous XOR-s should already been committed and retired, while the fetcher/decoder should be executing *nop*-s (which in theory, does not cause any data-dependent leakage[12]).

Collapsed F-Test. Although we are working at an instruction level, because each operand has 32 bits, building the full model $\tilde{L}_f$ is still infeasible. Thus, we need to "collapse" $\tilde{L}_f$ to a smaller space. More specifically, we allow each operand to contain 2-bit randomness ($a = \{a_1 a_2 .... a_1 a_2\}$): comparing with the 1-bit strategy in Sect. 3.2, this option needs more traces to achieve reasonable statistical power. However, with 2-bit random operands we can distinguish whether the contribution of a specific term is linear or not, which is of interest when comparing existing simulators.

Figure 3 shows the F-test results: clearly, models that exclude transitions in the inputs massively exceed the rejection threshold. This means that in these cases we can conclude that the dropped transition terms have a statistically significant impact on the model. The linear model with transitions $\tilde{L}_{le}$ only marginally fails the test: thus it again demonstrates how significant the transitions are, but it also indicates that dropping higher-order terms does impact the quality of the leakage model.

Clearly, none of the three conventional models can be regarded as complete. As a consequence, existing simulators that built on $\tilde{L}_{le}$ (e.g. ELMO/ELMO* and MAPS) are expected to miss leakage, due to the limited explanatory power of the respective leakage models. Various effects could be contributing here (including the bit-interaction [9]).

5.2   Modelling Leakage of Complex Instruction Sequences

Our novel methodology clearly shows that conventional models are not sufficient even when just considering a single instruction, dispatched in a way that respects the simulator assumptions (no fetch or decode leakage, no memory leakage). Two questions follow immediately: can we develop better models and what do existing simulators miss when it comes to complex code sequences?

---

[12] In practice, this may depend on the content of $r8$ in ARM cores; our experiments had already set $r8$ to 0 beforehand.

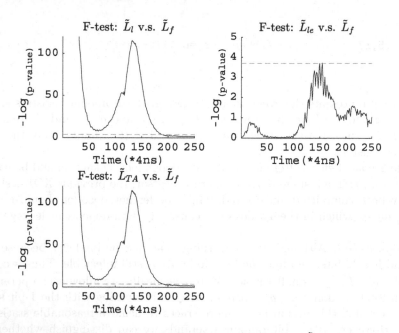

Fig. 3. Comparing various models against $\tilde{L}_f$

We answer these questions based on an Assembly sequence that implements a 2-share ISW (bitwise) multiplication gadget. Such a multiplication gadget is an integral part of a typical masking scheme.

More specifically, we consider the Thumb-encoded 2-share ISW multiplication gadget that is given in the second column (under the header "Instruction") of Table 1. To avoid overloading notation, we denote the first share of input a as $a_{(1)}$. To define the full model we assume that the inputs to the gadget, a and b, and the randomness r, are collapsed to 2-bit variables. The *full* model is then given as

$$\tilde{L}_f = \vec{\beta}\mathbf{U}(\{A_{(1)}A_{(2)}B_{(1)}B_{(2)}R\})$$

Working with this larger code sequence implies that we must expect leakage from the pipeline registers and the fetch and decode stages (i.e. leakage that we prohibited in our much simpler analysis before).

Collapsed F-Test. We recall that both $\tilde{L}_l$ and $\tilde{L}_{TA}$ were already clearly rejected by the F-test for just a single instruction (as shown in Fig. 3), thus we only challenge the completeness of $\tilde{L}_{le}$ (with respect to $\tilde{L}_f$) in the context of the more complex code snippet. $\tilde{L}_{le}$ is of particular interest because ELMO/ELMO* [5, 18] and MAPS [30] use a subset of $\tilde{L}_{le}$. The result is shown in the left picture in Fig. 4. We can see, unlike in Fig. 3, the linear extended model is clearly rejected by our test for multiple instructions.

Table 1. Leakage detection results on a 2-share ISW multiplication gadget

	Instruction	Device	ELMO	MAPS	$\tilde{L}_b$
0	$//r1 = a_{(1)}, r2 = a_{(2)}$ $//r3 = b_{(1)}, r4 = b_{(2)}, r5 = r$				
1	mov r6, r1(mov.w r6, r1 for MAPS)				
2	ands r6, r3$//r6 = a_{(1)}b_{(1)}$				
3	mov r7, r4(mov.w r7, r4 for MAPS)			✓	
4	ands r7, r2$//r7 = a_{(2)}b_{(2)}$				
5	ands r1, r4$//r1 = a_{(1)}b_{(2)}$	✓			✓
6	eors r1, r5$//r1 = a_{(1)}b_{(2)} \oplus r$	✓			✓
7	ands r2, r3$//r2 = a_{(2)}b_{(1)}$	✓	✓	✓	✓
8	eors r1, r2$//r1 = a_{(1)}b_{(2)} \oplus r \oplus a_{(2)}b_{(1)}$				
9	eors r6, r1$//c_{(1)} = a_{(1)}b_{(2)} \oplus r \oplus a_{(2)}b_{(1)} \oplus a_{(1)}b_{(1)}$	✓			✓
10	eors r7, r5$//c_2 = r \oplus a_{(2)}b_{(2)}$	✓	✓	✓	✓

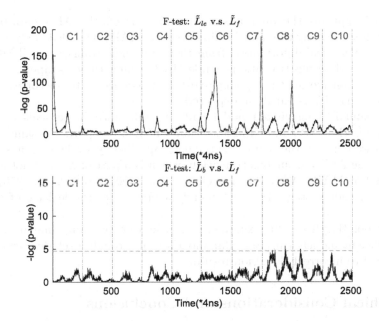

Fig. 4. Model comparison based on a 2-share ISW multiplication in software

Building a Better Model $\tilde{L}_b$. Similar to Sect. 4, we can try to build a better leakage model by adding terms and re-evaluating the model quality through the collapsed F-test. We call the final model out of this *ad-hoc* procedure $\tilde{L}_b$. We derived this model by observing that most operands influence the leakage for at least 2 cycles, which suggests that the decoding stage does significantly contribute to the data-dependent leakage. Consequently we include data from the decoding stage in $\tilde{L}_b$. Developing an architectural reasoning for this model is beyond the scope of this paper. However, Fig. 4 shows that $\tilde{L}_b$ only marginally fails our test, and thus is considerably better than the linear extended model that simulators like ELMO/ELMO* and MAPS use.

Challenging $\tilde{L}_b$. Whilst we now have a model that explains the device leakage of our Cortex M3 for a relatively complex gadget, it is still open if this better model helps to actually improve the simulator-based leakage detections. Thus we perform a leakage detection test (first order t-test) for the 2-share ISW implementation above, on realistic traces measured from our M3 core, traces from ELMO, traces from MAPS, and traces where we use $\tilde{L}_b$ to predict leakage. The last four columns in Table 1 show the resulting leakage detection test results.

MAPS captures all register transitions, including the pipeline registers in the micro-architecture (command line option "-p") [30]. MAPS reports 3 leaking instructions in our experiments: 2 are verified by the realistic 1st order t-test, while cycle 3 is not. Technically, this may not be a *false-positive* because MAPS is using the 32-bit instruction *mov.w* instead of the tested 16-bit instruction mov^{13}.

ELMO captures the operands and transitions on the ALU data-bus [5]: ELMO reports exactly the same leaking cycles as MAPS. Detailed analysis shows that both cycles leak information from their operands' transitions: ELMO captures these as data-bus transitions, while MAPS claims these as pipeline register transitions. Considering the pipeline registers are connected to the corresponding ALU data-bus, this is hardly unexpected.

Our manually constructed model leads to significantly better leakage predictions than both MAPS and ELMO as Table 1 shows. It reports the same leaking cycles as we found in the real measurements. Specifically, cycle 5 reports a leakage from the ALU output bus transition, which is a part of $\tilde{L}_{le}$ but not covered by ELMO or MAPS. We suspect cycle 6 (1250–1500) and 9 (2000–2250) come from the decoding stage: they are merely a preview of the leakage of cycle 7 and 10.

Extrapolating from this example, it is clear that building simulators based on insufficient models (in particular models that wrongly exclude parts of the state) lead to incorrect detection results.

6   Ethical Considerations and Conclusions

This paper puts the *state* that is captured by a leakage model at the centre stage. Knowledge of this state matters: in the case where we want to argue that we have the "best possible attack" (perhaps in the context of an evaluation where we try to argue that the evaluation result corresponds to the worst-case adversary), and in the case where we want to build an accurate leakage simulator (perhaps to evaluate software countermeasures such as masking).

---

[13] For some reason, MAPS seems to have a problem with the 16-bit *mov* instruction in our experiments.

In our paper we put forward the novel notion of *"completeness"* for a model. A model is *complete* if it captures all relevant state information, thus suitable to be the basis for leakage simulators or security evaluations. Deciding if a model is *complete* initially seems like a computationally infeasible task in the case of modern processors: even for a 2-operand instruction, if we take previous values into account, there are 2^{4n} possible values. For $n = 8$ (i.e. in a small micro-controller), it is computationally expensive; but for $n = 32$ (i.e. in a modern microprocessor), it becomes clearly infeasible. We overcome this problem by introducing a novel statistical technique using *collapsed* models as part of a nested F-test methodology. Our novel technique is robust and effective, and works in a grey box setting, as we illustrate based on a range of concrete experiments.

The leakage models that result from our test are qualitatively different to leakage models that are currently in use: they are nominal models, which means that the coefficients in these models only describe if a variable (or an interaction term of multiple variables) contributes to the device leakage, or not. The models thus are no longer proportional to the real device leakage, consequently they are of less use for proportional attack techniques (e.g. correlation or template attacks). Our approach trades off less complete proportional models for nominal models that are statistically closer to a complete model—one could consider combining both modelling techniques to reintroduce some proportionality.

However, we argue that nominal models represent an important option also from a research ethics perspective. Research into modelling techniques leads to a dual-use question: techniques that are explicitly developed to work on off-the-shelf processors, and potentially released as part of open source projects such as ELMO and ROSITA may play in the hands of adversaries. Indeed the ELMO paper already shows an example of using ELMO's leakage model in a correlation based attack on a physical M0: it considerably improves the attack performance and does clearly have potential for dual use. Nominal models, on the other hand, can help to develop more sophisticated attacks (in the sense that more leakage can be included in an attack), or confirm that the best attack has already been found (again in the sense that all leakage was included). However, they do not lead to an immediate improvement for simple model based attacks (such as correlation attacks). Finally research ethics also ties in with practice: when discussing the possibility of developing models for processors with commercial vendors, an immediate concern is that of "helping adversaries" by supplying high quality leakage models that can be readily used in attacks. Therefore, the option to supply nominal models that can be used for leakage detection (or potentially for automated leakage proofs) is seen as a potential way forward for the practical deployment of simulators.

Acknowledgments. We would like to thank all anonymous reviewers for their constructive comments. The authors were funded in part by the ERC via the grant SEAL (Project Reference 725042).

A   PI, HI and Assumption Error

Leakage certification approaches such as described in [20,32,33] (based on the general framework introduced by Standaert, Malkin and Yung [34]) aim at providing guarantees about the quality of an evaluation, based on estimating the amount of information leaked by a target device.

In order to estimate the amount of leaked information (i.e. the mutual information), the intermediate state must be selected as a first step. In our notation, this means the user must correctly provide an enumerable state $\mathbf{Z}$ that ensures the corresponding model $\tilde{L}(\mathbf{Z})$ is close to the *full* model $\tilde{L}(\mathbf{X})$ w.r.t. its explanatory power. Then, one can estimate the mutual information of $MI(\mathbf{Z}; L)$ using concepts like perceived information (PI) or hypothetical information (HI) [33].

The common choice for $\mathbf{Z}$ is often a variable that relates to a single S-box [20,32,33]: because the MI calculation runs through all possible values of $\mathbf{Z}$, it corresponds to a template attack. This extremely popular choice is potentially inadequate because the device state is likely to be considerably more complex (as we have argued before), and it will likely include at least transition leaks, which cannot be captured in this way. Consequently, prior to any of these leakage certification approaches, it is imperative to test what state must be considered.

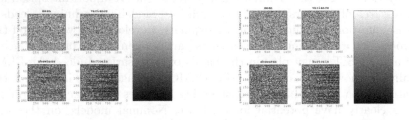

(a) HD leakage without any noise   (b) HD leakage with noise variance 0.1

Fig. 5. Moment based detection of "assumption error"

A.1   Estimating "Assumption Errors"

In [20] Durvaux et al. proposed a technique to test for (the so-called) assumption errors in the leakage model [20]. One could be tempted to regard this as an alternative solution for testing *completeness*. Unlike our *F-test*, their approach is based on checking if the distance between pairs of simulated samples (generated with a profiled model) and the distance between simulated and actual samples behave differently.

However, their technique of checking assumption errors is about ensuring that the estimation of MI is accurate. In order words, their technique is not an effective way to test whether $\mathbf{Z}$ is complete or not. To demonstrate this, we present a simple experiment that is based on the common example of leakage from an AES S-box output ($S(p_1 \oplus k_1)$, where p_1 is the plaintext byte and k_1 is the corresponding key byte). Let us further assume that the leakage function L depends on not only on $S(p_1 \oplus k_1)$, but also the previous S-box output $S(p_0 \oplus k_0)$:

$$L = HW(S(p_1 \oplus k_1)) + HD(S(p_1 \oplus k_1), S(p_0 \oplus k_0)).$$

Taking advantage of the code from [32], we can validate the power of detecting the above "assumption error": Fig. 5a portrays the moment-based estimation on the leakage function above in a noise free setting.

Each line corresponds to a model value, and if any value leads to a line that keeps getting "darker", it would suggest the p-value is small enough to confidently report an "assumption error". Even if there is no noise (left figure), only the *kurtosis* marginally reports errors. With some small noise added in (Fig. 5b), the situation remains the same. Only the *kurtosis* gives some small p-values, but there is no statistical decision criterion that enables us to draw a firm conclusion here. This outcome should not be surprising. Because p_0 is an independent random variable, the Hamming distance part follows Binomial

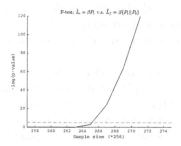

Fig. 6. F-test with noise variance 0.1

distribution $B\left(\frac{n}{2}, \frac{n}{4}\right)$ where n is the bit-length of p_0 (for AES, $n = 8$). With $Z = P_1$, the estimated model would be:

$$M = HW(S(p_1 \oplus k_1)) + \mathcal{N}\left(\frac{n}{2}, \frac{n}{4}\right)$$

where $\mathcal{N}(\mu, \sigma^2)$ represents the Gaussian distribution. For any fixed value of $p_1 \oplus k_1$, the "distance between pairs of simulated samples" becomes

$$D_M = \left\{l_1 - l_2 | l_1 \in \mathcal{N}\left(\frac{n}{2}, \frac{n}{4}\right), l_2 \in \mathcal{N}\left(\frac{n}{2}, \frac{n}{4}\right)\right\}$$

Meanwhile, "the distance between simulated and actual samples" becomes:

$$D_{LM} = \left\{l_1 - l_2 | l_1 \in \mathcal{N}\left(\frac{n}{2}, \frac{n}{4}\right), l_2 \in B(0.5, n)\right\}$$

It is well-known that with reasonably large n, the binomial distribution will asymptotically approximate the Gaussian distribution. The idea behind this test in [20] is based on an expected inconsistency between the unexplained leakage distribution and estimated Gaussian distribution: the test becomes powerless if the former equals/stays close to Gaussian, which is not really a rare case in side channel applications.

In contrast, our *F-test* can detect such an "error" with ease, see Fig. 6. The advantage here requires though to explicitly assign $\mathbf{X} = \{P_1 P_0\}$. Without some guess work (or a priori knowledge) one may need to use a *collapsed full* model instead, say using 1 bit for each plaintext byte and testing on a trace set larger than 2^{16}.

We want to emphasize at this point that these previous works did not aim for testing the *completeness* of the state as such, so our findings do not invalidate their statements. We merely wish to point out that there is a difference between their ideas of "assumption errors" and our notion of "*completeness*".

A.2   HI and PI

Bronchain, Hendrickx and Massart et al. proposed that using the concepts of *Perceived Information* (PI) and *Hypothetical Information* (HI), one can "bound the information loss due to model errors quantitatively" by comparing these two metrics, estimate the true unknown MI and obtain the "close to worst-case" evaluations [33].

It is critical to remember the "worse-case" are restricted the computed MI: back to previous our example, estimating HI and PI still bound the correct mutual information $MI(K_1; P_1, L)$. The additional Hamming distance term affects how we should interpret this metric: when combing multiple key-bytes to obtains the overall security-level, $MI(K_1; P_1, L)$ might not be as helpful as one may hope.

More concretely, we tested our example simulation leakage with the code provided in [33]: as we can see in Fig. 7, PI and HI still bounds the correct MI. The only difference here is MI itself decreases as P_0 and K_0 are not taken into consideration.

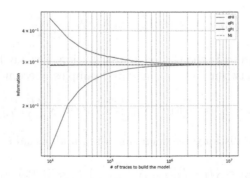

Fig. 7. PI and HI estimation for the leakage function

A.3   Bias-Variance Decomposition

Lerman, Veshchikov and Markowitch et al. also proposed a diagnosis tool based on the bias-variance decomposition [35]. The goal of their tool is purely predictive—"guiding the design of the best profiled attack". In other words, the "syndrome to diagnose" is still restricted to the specific selected intermediate state. In our example, the additional Hamming distance will be taken as part of the random noise. Admittedly, unless the missing Hamming distance is taken into the model building procedure, any corresponding leakage will always end up in the noise. Therefore, any model can be perfectly estimated, yet that does not guarantee it is *complete*, as the estimated noise is not necessarily pure *measurement noise*.

References

1. Chari, S., Rao, J.R., Rohatgi, P.: Template attacks. In: Kaliski, B.S., Koç, K., Paar, C. (eds.) CHES 2002. LNCS, vol. 2523, pp. 13–28. Springer, Heidelberg (2003). https://doi.org/10.1007/3-540-36400-5_3
2. Schindler, W., Lemke, K., Paar, C.: A stochastic model for differential side channel cryptanalysis. In: Rao, J.R., Sunar, B. (eds.) CHES 2005. LNCS, vol. 3659, pp. 30–46. Springer, Heidelberg (2005). https://doi.org/10.1007/11545262_3
3. Doget, J., Prouff, E., Rivain, M., Standaert, F.: Univariate side channel attacks and leakage modeling. J. Cryptogr. Eng. 1(2), 123–144 (2011). https://doi.org/10.1007/s13389-011-0010-2
4. Whitnall, C., Oswald, E.: Profiling DPA: efficacy and efficiency trade-offs. In: Bertoni, G., Coron, J.-S. (eds.) CHES 2013. LNCS, vol. 8086, pp. 37–54. Springer, Heidelberg (2013). https://doi.org/10.1007/978-3-642-40349-1_3
5. McCann, D., Oswald, E., Whitnall, C.: Towards practical tools for side channel aware software engineering: 'grey box' modelling for instruction leakages. In: 26th USENIX Security Symposium (USENIX Security 2017), Vancouver, BC, pp. 199–216. USENIX Association (2017)
6. Papagiannopoulos, K., Veshchikov, N.: Mind the gap: towards secure 1st-order masking in software. In: Guilley, S. (ed.) COSADE 2017. LNCS, vol. 10348, pp. 282–297. Springer, Cham (2017). https://doi.org/10.1007/978-3-319-64647-3_17
7. Gigerl, B., Hadzic, V., Primas, R., Mangard, S., Bloem, R.: COCO: co-design and co-verification of masked software implementations on CPUs. IACR Cryptology ePrint Archive 2020/1294 (2020)
8. De Meyer, L., De Mulder, E., Tunstall, M.: On the effect of the (micro) architecture on the development of side-channel resistant software. IACR Cryptology ePrint Archive 2020/1297 (2020)
9. Gao, S., Marshall, B., Page, D., Oswald, E.: Share-slicing: friend or foe? IACR Trans. Cryptogr. Hardw. Embed. Syst. **2020**(1), 152–174 (2019)
10. Marshall, B., Page, D., Webb, J.: MIRACLE: MIcRo-ArChitectural leakage evaluation. IACR Cryptology ePrint Archive (2021). https://eprint.iacr.org/2021/261
11. den Hartog, J., Verschuren, J., de Vink, E., de Vos, J., Wiersma, W.: PINPAS: a tool for power analysis of smartcards. In: Gritzalis, D., De Capitani di Vimercati, S., Samarati, P., Katsikas, S. (eds.) SEC 2003. ITIFIP, vol. 122, pp. 453–457. Springer, Boston, MA (2003). https://doi.org/10.1007/978-0-387-35691-4_45

12. eshard: esDynamic. https://www.eshard.com/product/esdynamic/. Accessed June 2018
13. Secure-IC: Virtualyzr. http://www.secure-ic.com/solutions/virtualyzr/. Accessed June 2018
14. Thuillet, C., Andouard, P., Ly, O.: A smart card power analysis simulator. In: Proceedings of the 12th IEEE International Conference on Computational Science and Engineering, CSE 2009, pp. 847–852. IEEE Computer Society (2009)
15. Debande, N., Berthier, M., Bocktaels, Y., Le, T.H.: Profiled model based power simulator for side channel evaluation. Cryptology ePrint Archive Report 2012/703 (2012)
16. Gagnerot, G.: Étude des attaques et des contre-mesures assoccées sur composants embarqués. Ph.D. thesis, Université de Limoges (2013)
17. McCann, D.: ELMO (2017). https://github.com/bristol-sca/ELMO
18. Shelton, M.A., Samwel, N., Batina, L., Regazzoni, F., Wagner, M., Yarom, Y.: ROSITA: towards automatic elimination of power-analysis leakage in ciphers. In: NDSS 2022 (2022)
19. Whitnall, C., Oswald, E., Standaert, F.-X.: The myth of generic DPA...and the magic of learning. In: Benaloh, J. (ed.) CT-RSA 2014. LNCS, vol. 8366, pp. 183–205. Springer, Cham (2014). https://doi.org/10.1007/978-3-319-04852-9_10
20. Durvaux, F., Standaert, F.-X., Veyrat-Charvillon, N.: How to certify the leakage of a chip? In: Nguyen, P.Q., Oswald, E. (eds.) EUROCRYPT 2014. LNCS, vol. 8441, pp. 459–476. Springer, Heidelberg (2014). https://doi.org/10.1007/978-3-642-55220-5_26
21. Crama, Y., Hammer, P.L. (eds.): Boolean Models and Methods in Mathematics, Computer Science, and Engineering. Cambridge University Press, Cambridge (2010)
22. Shmueli, G.: To explain or to predict? Stat. Sci. 25(3), 289–310 (2010)
23. Cohen, J.: F tests of variance proportions in multiple regression/correlation analysis. In: Cohen, J. (ed.) Statistical Power Analysis for the Behavioral Sciences, pp. 407–453. Academic Press (1977)
24. Whitnall, C., Oswald, E.: A critical analysis of ISO 17825 ('testing methods for the mitigation of non-invasive attack classes against cryptographic modules'). In: Galbraith, S.D., Moriai, S. (eds.) ASIACRYPT 2019. LNCS, vol. 11923, pp. 256–284. Springer, Cham (2019). https://doi.org/10.1007/978-3-030-34618-8_9
25. Bronchain, O., Standaert, F.: Side-channel countermeasures' dissection and the limits of closed source security evaluations. IACR Trans. Cryptogr. Hardw. Embed. Syst. 2020(2), 1–25 (2020)
26. Benadjila, R., Khati, L., Prouff, E., Thillard, A.: Hardened library for AES-128 encryption/decryption on ARM cortex M4 achitecture. https://github.com/ANSSI-FR/SecAESSTM32
27. Balasch, J., Gierlichs, B., Grosso, V., Reparaz, O., Standaert, F.-X.: On the cost of lazy engineering for masked software implementations. In: Joye, M., Moradi, A. (eds.) CARDIS 2014. LNCS, vol. 8968, pp. 64–81. Springer, Cham (2015). https://doi.org/10.1007/978-3-319-16763-3_5
28. Whitnall, C., Oswald, E.: A cautionary note regarding the usage of leakage detection tests in security evaluation. Cryptology ePrint Archive Report 2019/703 (2019)
29. Buhan, I., Batina, L., Yarom, Y., Schaumont, P.: SoK: design tools for side-channel-aware implementations (2021)

30. Le Corre, Y., Großschädl, J., Dinu, D.: Micro-architectural power simulator for leakage assessment of cryptographic software on ARM cortex-M3 processors. In: Fan, J., Gierlichs, B. (eds.) COSADE 2018. LNCS, vol. 10815, pp. 82–98. Springer, Cham (2018). https://doi.org/10.1007/978-3-319-89641-0_5

31. Micali, S., Reyzin, L.: Physically observable cryptography. In: Naor, M. (ed.) TCC 2004. LNCS, vol. 2951, pp. 278–296. Springer, Heidelberg (2004). https://doi.org/10.1007/978-3-540-24638-1_16

32. Durvaux, F., Standaert, F.-X., Del Pozo, S.M.: Towards easy leakage certification: extended version. J. Cryptogr. Eng. 7(2), 129–147 (2017). https://doi.org/10.1007/s13389-017-0150-0

33. Bronchain, O., Hendrickx, J.M., Massart, C., Olshevsky, A., Standaert, F.-X.: Leakage certification revisited: bounding model errors in side-channel security evaluations. In: Boldyreva, A., Micciancio, D. (eds.) CRYPTO 2019. LNCS, vol. 11692, pp. 713–737. Springer, Cham (2019). https://doi.org/10.1007/978-3-030-26948-7_25

34. Standaert, F.-X., Malkin, T.G., Yung, M.: A unified framework for the analysis of side-channel key recovery attacks. In: Joux, A. (ed.) EUROCRYPT 2009. LNCS, vol. 5479, pp. 443–461. Springer, Heidelberg (2009). https://doi.org/10.1007/978-3-642-01001-9_26

35. Lerman, L., Veshchikov, N., Markowitch, O., Standaert, F.: Start simple and then refine: bias-variance decomposition as a diagnosis tool for leakage profiling. IEEE Trans. Comput. 67(2), 268–283 (2018)

Towards Micro-architectural Leakage Simulators: Reverse Engineering Micro-architectural Leakage Features Is Practical

Si Gao[1]([⊠]) [iD], Elisabeth Oswald[1]([⊠]) [iD], and Dan Page[2]([⊠]) [iD]

[1] Digital Age Research Center (D!ARC), University of Klagenfurt,
Klagenfurt, Austria
{si.gao,elisabeth.oswald}@aau.at
[2] Department of Computer Science, University of Bristol, Bristol, UK
daniel.page@bristol.ac.uk

Abstract. Leakage simulators offer the tantalising promise of easy and quick testing of software with respect to the presence of side channel leakage. The quality of their build in leakage models is therefore crucial, this includes the faithful inclusion of micro-architectural leakage. Micro-architectural leakage is a reality even on low- to mid-range commercial processors, such as the ARM Cortex M series. Dealing with it seems initially infeasible in a "grey box" setting: how should we describe it if micro-architectural elements are not publicly known?

We demonstrate, for the first time, that it is feasible, using a recent leakage modelling technique, to reverse engineer significant elements of the micro-architectural leakage of a commercial processor. Our approach first recovers the micro-architectural leakage of each stage in the pipeline, and the leakage of elements that are known to produce glitches. Using the reverse engineered leakage features we build an enhanced version of the popular leakage simulator ELMO.

1 Introduction

Securing a specific implementation of a cryptographic algorithm on a concrete device is never a trivial task. In recent years, a proposal to help with this challenge has emerged: instead of testing implementations in a costly lab setup, leakage simulators like ELMO [1], MAPS [2], and ROSITA [3] have surfaced, which all claim to capture significant leakage of the respective devices that they apply to. A comprehensive survey of existing simulators was recently published [4]. This survey puts forward a range of challenges that are yet to be solved, among which is the inclusion of more micro-architectural effects (of the resp. processor).

Micro-architectural leakage can render the provable properties of modern masking schemes meaningless in practice. Let us consider for instance an implementation of a masked multiplication using the 2-share masking scheme originally proposed in [5]. We consider its implementation using Thumb Assembly on a microprocessor with the ARM Cortex M3 architecture (see the program code

O. Dunkelman and S. Dziembowski (Eds.): EUROCRYPT 2022, LNCS 13277, pp. 284–311, 2022.
https://doi.org/10.1007/978-3-031-07082-2_11

in this section). The masked multiplication computes the shared out product $c = (c_1, c_2)$ of two shared out numbers a, b (with $a = (a_1, a_2)$ and $b = (b_1, b_2)$) using an independent random number r.

```
1        ISWd2:
2        ...
3        //r1=a(1),  r2=a(2),  a(1)+a(2)=a
4        //r3=b(1),r4=b(2),  r5=r,  b(1)+b(2)=b
5        mov   r6, r1   //r6=a(1)
6        ands  r6, r3   //r6=a(1)b(1)
7        mov   r7, r4   //r7=b(2)
8        ands  r7, r2   //r7=a(2)b(2)
9        ands  r1, r4   //r1=a(1)b(2)
10       eors  r1, r5   //r1=a(1)b(2)+r
11       ands  r3, r2   //r3=a(2)b(1)
12       eors  r1, r3   //r1=a(1)b(2)+r+a(2)b(1)
13       eors  r6, r1   //c(1)=a(1)b(2)+r+a(2)b(1)+a(1)b(1)
14       mov   r0, r9   //r0=output address
15       eors  r7, r5   //c(2)=r+a(2)b(2)
16       ...
```

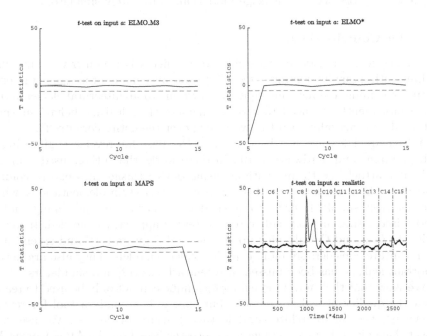

Fig. 1. 1st order TVLA on input a on existing simulators and realistic measurements

The multiplication rule produces the shared out product in a manner that guarantees that no information is revealed about a or b assuming individual intermediate values do not leak jointly. Consequently in practice it typically shows leakage because this assumption is often not justified. Using a leakage simulator, we can pinpoint the instructions that violate the assumption, then try to avoid the leakage via revising the corresponding instructions.

With real measurements, the first order fixed-versus-random t-test on the input a show leakage during the execution of the instructions in line 9 and 15 (the bottom right corner in Fig. 1). But when we execute the same piece of code in ELMO (we use the recently released M3 version of ELMO [6]), no leakage can be found (see the upper left graph in Fig. 1). The ROSITA tool uses an "upgraded version" of ELMO, which they call ELMO* [3]. Leakage detection reports leakage for the instruction on line 5 (upper right in Fig. 1). According to the realistic detection, this is a false-positive leak, while the true leaks in line 9 and 15 are not reported. The white-box M3 simulator MAPS [2] reports leakage for the instruction on line 15, but fails to report leakage for line 9 (bottom left in Fig. 1).

All three simulators fail to capture some leak(-s) in this example, and one finds a leak where there is none. Our motivation is thus to develop a technique that leads to more accurate leakage models and ultimately simulators.

1.1 Our Contributions

The challenge to include micro-architectural effects is a non-trivial one when working with many interesting cores. This is because many processors of interest feature pipelining and have multiple unknown micro-architectural elements that leak. Consequently we need to reverse engineer their leakage behaviour (note that we do not actually need to reverse engineer the entire core itself).

Side-channel leakage has been used in the past for reverse engineering of both programs and hardware [7–10]. In these works the authors used standard DPA style attacks (with and without using device leakage models) to confirm hypotheses about the internals of the respective devices/implementations, which were relatively simple. In order to tackle devices that feature pipelining, and/or a more interesting memory subsystem, a better approach is needed. In recent work [11], Gao and Oswald pick up the methodology from [1] and extend it so it can capture considerably more complex leakage models. They also argue that important leakage has been missed in recent attacks [12] and simulators.

We show that their novel modelling technique can not only be used to reason about the quality of leakage models, but that it is actually a tool for reverse engineering the micro-architectural leakage features of devices. We use it to dissect the leakage from a commercial processor based on the ARM Cortex M3 architecture and reveal its micro-architectural leakage characteristics. Doing so is all but straightforward: [11] are clear that the test itself provides "clues" about the internal mechanisms, but one needs to design additional confirmatory experiments to actually verify the micro-architectural meaning of these clues (this ties in with another recent paper [13]).

To put our results into the context of the existing leakage simulation literature, we then compare leakage predictions that are based on the reverse-engineered micro-architectural leakage with the predictions of the most sophisticated simulators ELMO and MAPS[1].

Whilst our methodology currently involves intensive manual effort, we argue such effort is worthwhile, because:

- it enriches our understanding of micro-architecture effects in relevant processor architectures,
- it significantly improves the state-of-the-art leakage modelling of micro-architectural elements,
- it showcases that many existing leakage models and tools miss significant micro-architectural effects.

1.2   Methodology and Paper Organisation

In the following three sections, we discuss step by step how to reverse engineer the micro-architectural leakage elements of a close-sourced commercial processor. In contrast to previous works that captured only simple micro-architectural leakage, and led to the simulators ELMO, ELMO* and MAPS, we aim to comprehensively recover all micro-architectural leakage.

In a grey-box setting, we cannot take advantage of a detailed hardware description, but we can utilise publicly available architectural information to guide our analysis. Therefore, our methodology is based on the following key steps:

1. Build an abstract diagram from the public available information (e.g. architecture reference [14], ISA [15], etc.) and make some safe architectural inferences (Sect. 2).
2. Recover the relevant micro-architectural details through analysing the side-channel leakage. Specify the data flow for each instruction and construct a micro-architectural leakage model for each pipeline stage (Sect. 3).
3. Evaluate the overall micro-architectural leakage for the target processor, further adding more subtle micro-architectural leakages (e.g. glitches) or discarding non-significant factors (Sect. 4).

We then challenge the resulting micro-architectural leakage model of our M3 by a comprehensive comparison in Sect. 5, and we conclude this paper in Sect. 6.

---

[1] ELMO* [3] offers an extension to ELMO that captures some more leakage from the memory subsystem. ELMO offers also such an extension (in the follow-up development), yet both are drawn from experimental guesses. Nevertheless, our focus in this paper still lies in pipelined core, where the entire ELMO family sticks with the original ELMO model [1].

Experimental Setup. Throughout this paper, we preserve the same experimental setup:

- Target: NXP LPC1313 (ARM Cortex-M3) running at 1 MHz with only Thumb instructions
- Measurement point: voltage at a 100 Ω shunt resistor at the VCC end
- Pre-processing: on-board 22db amplifier (NXP BGA2801)
- Oscilloscope: Picoscope 5243D running at 250 MSa/s

Unless stated otherwise, each tested code snippet takes 50k traces. Our setup ensures leakage does not last for more than 1 cycle, which helps to identify how leakage changes from cycle to cycle. Thus, most experimental results in the following two sections have been cropped to the exact cycle, which contains 250 sample points.

Statistical Reverse Engineering Methodology. As a reverse engineering tool we use the methodology from [11]. Their methodology extends the modelling technique of ELMO. We provide an informative explanation of their technique, which essentially enables to "compare" two leakage models. A leakage model consists of a function and some variables that correspond to actual leakage elements (e.g. architectural registers, buffers, etc.). The models that we compare consist of the same function (which includes possible interactions between variables), but they contain different variables. Specifically we reduce a model by removing a variable (or the interaction between variables) that represents an unknown leakage element. The statistical test from [11] then checks if this additional variable explains statistically significantly more of the observable leakage. If so, then we conclude that the removed variable represents a significant leakage element in the processor.

To facilitate explaining our research in the following sections, we need to introduce some notation and formalism around the leakage modelling and testing process. We will refer to any model that we test with M and if there are multiple models we distinguish them by their subscript, e.g. we may want to test two models M_0 and M_1. A leakage model consists of a function and some variables. The function defines if and how the included variables interact with each other. The methodology in [11] works with nominal models, thus all coefficients are either 0 or non-0 in the resulting functions. Thus we drop these coefficients for readability, and instead use a set notation to indicate how variables interact with each other: if two variables X, and Y fully interact with each other then we write their respective model as $\{XY\}$; if the two variables only leak independently then we write their respective model as $\{X, Y\}$.

In our work we hope to find if a simpler model $M_1 = \{X, Y\}$ already suffices, or if a fully interactive model $M_0 = \{XY\}$ is necessary. We note at this point that the simpler model M_1 is indeed included in M_0: in fact, M_0 includes all interaction terms and also the individual variables X, Y. A statistical test can be applied to tell whether M_0 is a "better" model than M_1, which implies whether X and Y interact with each other in the measurements. The problem of this approach is that the variables that we consider are all "large" in the sense that statistically every 32-bit variable (the M3 operates on 32 bit data words) leads to 32 independent statistical variables. Testing multiple large variables then leads to the problem that a test requires a large number of leakage observations to produce statistically significant results. To circumvent this problem we use the trick of "collapsing models" from [11].

2   Step 1: Identifying Safe Architectural Assumptions

Although exploring every concrete detail is not possible in a grey-box scenario, there is always some public information available that can be used to construct an initial, abstract architectural view. For instance, from Fig. 2, reproduced from [14, Figure 1.2], we know the Cortex-M3 processors use a 3-stage pipeline [14]: the stages are termed **Fe(tch)**, **De(code)**, and **Ex(ecute)**. More specifically, while executing instruction $i - 2$, instruction $i - 1$ is being decoded by the instruction decoder, and instruction i is being fetched from the memory to the instruction register. Since there is no dedicate write-back stage, the Arithmetic Logic Unit (ALU) output is written-back to the register file (or memory) immediately after the **Execute** stage.

Although not directly provided in [14], we believe the following details can be safely inferred

- A set of pipeline registers exists between stages, meaning, for example, an instruction register between **Fetch** and **Decode** and pipeline register(s) between **Decode** and **Execute**.
- Figure 2 explicitly claims that "register read" occurs within the **Decode** stage; this implies the pipeline registers between **Decode** and **Execute** stores control signals *and* operands read from the register file.
- Many Thumb instructions [15] use 2 operands, which suggests the register file should have at least 2 read ports; this implies there are (at least) 2 operand pipeline registers between **Decode** and **Execute**.

3   Step 2: Recovering Major Micro-architectural Leakage Elements

Previous works such as [13,16] have shown that side-channel leakage can reveal some micro-architectural details. In this spirit, but utilising the F-test methodology for nested models, we set out to recover the major micro-architectural leakage elements of our Cortex-M3 core. We do so by analysing each of three pipeline stages separately.

3.1   Fetch

The **Fetch** stage fetches one or several instructions from the memory to the instruction register (i.e. block **Fe** in Fig. 2). Based on the publicly information

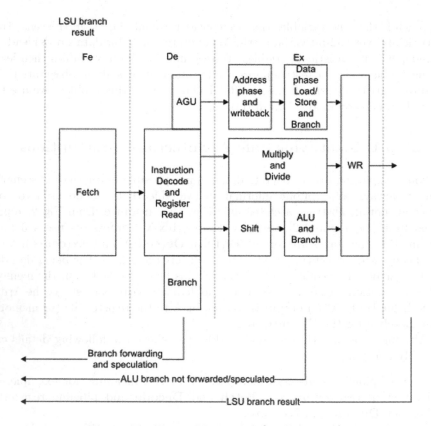

Fig. 2. The Cortex-M3 pipeline [14, Figure 1.2].

provided in the ARM reference manual, we envision the micro-architecture of the **Fetch** stage to look as depicted in Fig. 3a.

Functionally, the fetched instruction's address is stored in Program Counter (PC, aka R15 in ARM): therefore we plot F.1 which sends PC value to the instruction memory. PC can be incremented automatically (F.2), or accepts new address for branching (from ALU or decoder). F.3 loads the instruction(-s) to the instruction register, which marks the beginning of **Decode**. We plot all wires in this stage as blue lines in Fig. 3a.

In terms of micro-architectural ambiguity, there is none in Fig. 3a. In fact, the wires F.1–3 are fully determined by the value of PC. Unless the program performs data dependent branches, all leakage from this stage is constant between executions. We further exclude the leakage from data dependent branches in our analysis: compared with leakage modelling, information flow analysis is a much easier solution for that issue.

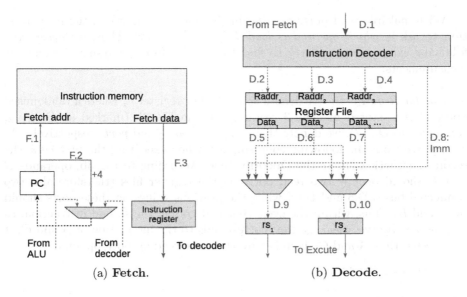

(a) **Fetch**.   (b) **Decode**.

Fig. 3. Hypothetical micro-architecture: **Fetch** and **Decode**. (Color figure online)

3.2   Decode

The **Decode** stage starts from translating the fetched instruction into the control logic, and ends with sending the pre-loaded operand(-s) to the pipeline register(-s) (i.e. block **De** in Fig. 2).

Figure 3b plots our view of the micro-architecture for the **Decode** stage. The decoder translates the instruction (D.1) into control signals, including the register indices for the pre-loaded operands (D.2 D.4) and potential immediate numbers (D.8). The corresponding operands are loaded from the register file (D.5–D.7), then sent to the pipeline registers (D.9–D.10). The pipeline registers rs_1 and rs_2 mark the beginning of **Execute**. All the wires in this stage are plotted as purple lines: if the signal is directly read from a register, we use solid line; otherwise, we use dash line to represent the fact that this signal might be affected by glitches (analysed in Sect. 4.2). Note that there should also be a few pipeline registers storing the control signals and the immediate number: as they are not data-dependent, we simply omit those in Fig. 3b.

Unlike **Fetch**, there are a few ambiguities in the **Decode** stage: first, it is unclear how many read ports/operands should exist in Fig. 3b. Considering most Thumb instructions take at most 2 operands, previous tools often assume the register file has 2 read ports [1,2] (i.e. connected to D.5 and D.6). We also started with a similar architecture, but some instructions (e.g. *adds Rd, Rn, Rm*) produced leakage that access more than 2 registers. From side-channel leakage alone, we cannot conclude whether there is another read port (i.e. D.7), or such leakage is from a multiplexing route of the existing ports or even an unexpected access from glitches. Either way, we proceed our analysis assuming there are 3 read ports (which is leakage equivalent to the other options).

With multiple read ports existing in the micro-architecture, the next question to ask is *which operand is loaded from which port*. Thus, we design the following experiments and try to find the answer from analysing the realistic measurements.

Testing the Read Ports. We denote $a as the low register r_a where a randomised operand A is stored in. The 3 reading ports in Fig. 3b (marked as $Data_{1-3}$, connected to D.5–7), we denote them as $port_1$, $port_2$ and $port_3$ respectively. As we can see from the following code snippet, when executing the first *eors*, the second instruction enters the **Decode** stage. According to Fig. 3b, operands C and D should occupy two read ports on the register files (therefore also two connected buses D.5 and D.6), while the previous values on these ports should be A and B. Thus, within the cycle that is decoding the second instruction, as long as we observe a leakage that corresponds to the interaction of A and C, it is expected that A and C should share the same reading port/operand bus.

```
1 Testing_port:
2 ...
3 eors $a,$b
4 INSTR $c, $d
5 nop
6 eors $0,$0  //$0=register that stores 0
7 ...
```

Specifically, let us assume in *eors $a,$b*, A takes port 1 (i.e. D.5)[2]. From here, whenever an interaction is detected between A and C, we set C to port 1. Otherwise, if an interaction is detected between A and D, we set D to port 1.

This leads to testing the following two models using real device data:

– $M_0 = \{AC\}$, $AC = \{x|x = a||c, a \in A, c \in C\}$
– $M_1 = \{A, C\}$ (similarly BD, AD, BC)

If the test concludes that there is no enough evidence that M_1 is significantly worse than M_0, we conclude that there is no strong evidence of A and C interact with each other, therefore it is less likely A and C shares the same reading port/operand bus in the micro-architecture. Otherwise, A is clearly interacting with C: if the interaction is indeed coming from the micro-architecture[3], it is likely A and C share the same reading port/operand bus.

Altogether we tested 55 Thumb instructions, which covers almost the entire instruction set (versus 23 cryptography-relevant instructions in ELMO [1]).

---

[2] If it is the other way around, what we learned is a "mirrored specification", which will be remedied by a *mirrored* leakage model later.

[3] In theory, it is also possible that the interaction is caused by glitches, or physical defaults such as coupling [17]. In our experiments, we find the magnitude of wire transition leakage is usually larger than the other options, which makes it possible to make a distinction.

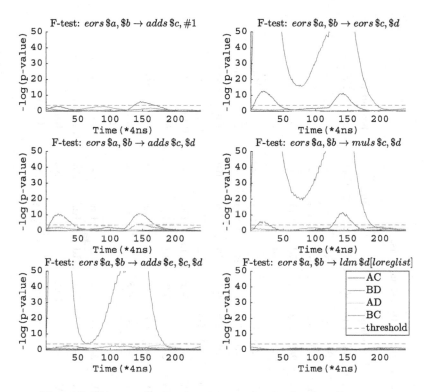

Fig. 4. Leakage analysis on register access in the decoding stage.

Table 1 gives a concise summary of the instructions and our findings through leakage analysis, which we explain subsequently.

Results. Our analysis shows that the decoding leakage (i.e. which operand is loaded through which port) strongly depends on the instruction encoding. More specifically, the column *Encoding* in Table 1 demonstrates the encoding bit-field of each instruction: ARM often uses R_d to represent the destination register and R_m/R_n represent the source registers. The assembler instruction uses those explicitly, yet did not explicitly explain the distinction (especially for R_m and R_n), or whether it links to any micro-architecture element. From our following analysis, it seems there is at least some connection.

Let us first look at some concrete F-test results as given in Fig. 4. In this figure, the black dashed line gives the F-test threshold, and any of the coloured lines that exceed the threshold indicates that the corresponding term cannot be dropped (or in other words, it needs to be included as a micro-architectural leakage element).

There are six sub-figures, which correspond to different cases:

- *adds* $c, \#1$ (Type I): only interaction AC appears, which suggests C is loaded to port 1.

Table 1. Summary of tested Thumb-16 instructions.

Group		Assembler	Encoding				Decoding			Executing	
	Operand		Type	Rd	Rm	Rn	Port 1	Port 2	Port 3	RS_1	RS_2
ALU	0	MOVS Rd, #<imm8>	I	10-8	-	-	Rd	-	-	-	-
	1	INSTR.a Rd, Rm(, #<imm3/5>)	II	2-0	5-3	-	Rd	Rm	-	Rm	-
		INSTR.b Rd, Rm(, #<imm3/5>)	II	2-0	5-3	-	Rd	Rm	-	-	Rm
		INSTR Rd, Rd, #<imm8>	I	10-8	-	-	Rd	-	-	Rd	-
		INSTR Rd, Rm	III	7,2-0	6-3	-	Rd	Rm	-	-	Rm
		INSTR Rd, Rm	II	2-0	5-3	-	Rd	Rm	-	Rd	Rm
	2	INSTR Rd, Rn, Rm	IV	2-0	8-6	5-3	Rd	Rm	Rn	Rn	Rm
		ADD Rdn, Rm	III	7,2-0	6-3	-	Rdn	Rm	-	Rdn	Rm
		MUL Rdm, Rn	IV	2-0	-	5-3	Rdm	Rn	-	Rdm	Rn
LOAD	Imm	LDR(H/B) Rd, [Rn, #<imm>]	IV	2-0	-	5-3	Rd	Rn	-	Rn	-
	Reg	LDR(H/B) Rd, [Rn, Rm]	IV	2-0	8-6	5-3	Rd	Rn	Rm	Rn	Rm
	Multiple	LDM Rn!, <loreglist>	V	-	-	10-8	-	-	Rn	Rn	-
	Pop	POP <loreglist>	V	-	-	-	-	-	-	C	-
STORE	Imm	STR(H/B) Rd, [Rn, #<imm>]	IV	2-0	-	5-3	Rd	Rn	-	Rn	Rd
	Reg	STR Rd, [Rn, Rm]	IV	2-0	8-6	5-3	Rd	Rn	Rm	Rn->Rd	Rm
	Multiple	STM Rn!, <loreglist>	V	-	-	10-8	-	-	Rn	Rn	-
	Push	PUSH <loreglist>	V	-	-	-	-	-	-	C	-

- $eors\,\$c,\$d$ (Type II): as expected, this group shows interaction AC and BD, even if R_d is not required by the functionality (e.g. $rsbs\,R_d, R_m$). Required or not, C/D is loaded to port 1/2 respectively.
- $adds\,\$c,\$d$ (Type III): as showed in Table 1, the only difference here is both C and D can come from a high register (R_{8-13}). Although the interaction is significantly weaker, we saw the same interaction as Type II in Fig. 4 (i.e. $A \rightarrow C$ and $B \rightarrow D$).
- $muls\,\$c,\$d$ (Type IV): unlike the previous cases, Type IV explicitly uses another register R_n (see Table 1). For mul and ldr, the leakage form is consistent: R_d (C) is connected to port 1 and R_n (D) is connected to port 2, therefore all transitions of AC and BD remain the same. We assume R_m (if used) is loaded from the extra port 3.
- $adds\,\$e,\$c,\$d$ (Type IV, exceptional): 3 register instructions (i.e. $adds, subs$) are exceptional: they connect R_m instead of R_n to port 2. R_d is still loaded, yet not interacting with operand A or B. Although no concrete evidence, we set R_d to port 1 and leave R_n to port 3.
- $eors\,\$a,\$b \rightarrow ldm\,\$d, [loreglist]$ (Type V): this group shows no interaction; we assume R_n connects to port 3.

$push$ and pop do not load any operand (other than the non-data-dependent stack register SP) in the decoding stage, therefore have been excluded from the decoding part of Table 1. Corresponding to the 3 purple dash lines (D.5–D.7) in Fig. 3b, Table 1 documents the operand on each port for each instruction. Note that in a grey-box scenario, Table 1 represents the "reasonable conjectures" from leakage analysis: without reviewing the source code, this is the best possible guess we come up with. D.9 and D.10 connect to the pipeline registers rs_1 and rs_2, which will be inspected in the **Execute** stage.

3.3   Execute

On the contrary, the **Execute** stage is relatively simple: preloaded operands start from the pipeline register (E.1 and E.2 in Fig. 5a), then go through the computation logic within the ALU. The ALU's output (E.4) is then sent back to the register file or memory, depending on the specific instruction. There might be some more complicated computation logic (e.g. the multiplier in Fig. 2), but from a leakage point of view, since they all connect to the pipeline registers, we simply combine everything into the equivalent ALU. Most previous tools assume there are two pipeline registers that store the operands: in our analysis, we found that 2 registers could already explain our observed leakage, therefore we stick with 2 registers in Fig. 5a.

In previous tools, **Execute** is often regarded as the critical part: for instance, ELMO [1] captures the leakage/transition leakage from the 2 operands on the data buses E.1 and E.2 in Fig. 5a. MAPS [2] on the other hand, captures the transition leakage on the pipeline registers rs_1 and rs_2, as well as the destination register transition in the register file (the assignment for rs_1 and rs_2 may or may not be identical to NXP's implementation). Both tools ignore the **Fetch**

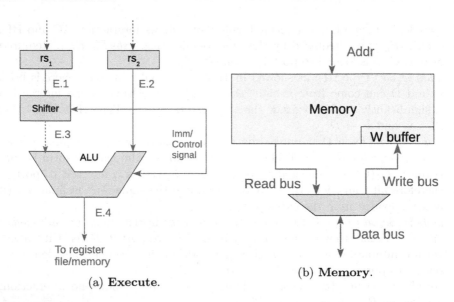

(a) **Execute.**

(b) **Memory.**

Fig. 5. Hypothetical micro-architecture: **Execute** and **Memory**. (Color figure online)

and **Decode** stage and focus on part of the **Execute** stage's leakage. Recall that our analysis in the previous section did not reveal D.9 or D.10. Even if we knew what appears on D.9 and D.10, the pipeline registers rs_1 and rs_2 could still preserve their own values (driven by their control signal). Thus, the fundamental question to answer in this stage, is *which value enters rs_1/rs_2?*

We can perform a similar analysis as for the **Decode** stage. Specifically, let us consider the same code snippet, but targeting at the latter *eors.*

```
1 Testing_rs1rs2:
2 ...
3 eors $a,$b
4 INSTR $c,$d
5 nop
6 eors $0,$0  //$0=register that stores 0
7 ...
```

Assuming *eors* sets rs_1 to A and rs_2 to B, as the latter *eors* should have the same micro-architectural effect as the previous one, thus it would set both rs_1 and rs_2 to 0. We have tested beforehand that *nop* does not touch the pipeline registers in our target core, which is also confirmed in [13]. The purpose of having this *nop* is separating the pipelined leakage: in a 3-stage processor, when executing the latter *eors*, it is expected that the target instruction *INSTR* has already committed its result, therefore does not further affect the leakage. Thus, we can test if the operands A or B still affects the leakage for the latter *eors*: if so, the pipeline register transits as

$$rs_1 : A \to A \to 0, HD = A$$

otherwise, we further test whether C or D affects the leakage. If C is presented in the leakage, it suggests:

$$rs_1 : A \to C \to 0, HD = C$$

Considering that the observed leakage for executing the latter *eors* is not affected by the decoding stage of $INSTR$, we can have a higher confidence that C enters rs_1.

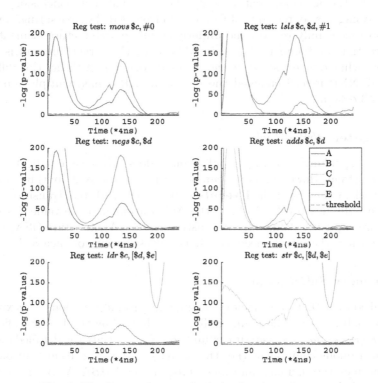

Fig. 6. Pipeline register analysis in the executing stage.

Following this approach, we have tested all instructions in Table 1. A few representative results are presented in Fig. 6, namely:

- *movs $c, #imm* does not store the immediate in pipeline registers, therefore both rs_1 and rs_2 keep their previous values (i.e. A and B).
- There are two types of 1-operand ALU instructions (Table 1): *mov*, *shift*-s, and *add/sub* use only rs_1, while *neg/mvn*, *reverse*, and *extend* instructions utilise only rs_2.
- 2-operand ALU instructions always use both rs_1 and rs_2. Further analysing the transition shows that the left operand always goes to rs_1: that is to say, R_d goes to rs_1 if R_d contains a necessary operand; otherwise R_n enters rs_1 (i.e. *INSTR Rd, Rn, Rm*).

- For *ldr*-s, the base address (R_n) enters rs_1, while the offset (if not constant), goes to rs_2. If the offset is constant, rs_2 preserves its previous value.
- For *str*-s, the first cycle works the same way as *ldr*, while the second cycle sends R_d to rs_1.
- *pop* and *push* clear rs_1 with the address in SP, which according to our assumption, should be a constant.

It is worthwhile to mention that most our results in Table 1 regarding the pipeline registers are consistent with [2][4]. The fact that their conclusion is drawn from analysing the source code of Cortex-M3 from ARM is reassuring: our technique did successfully recover the underlying micro-architecture elements. The only exception we found is shift-s: in MAPS [2], the target operand is always set to rs_2; while our test suggests the operand goes to rs_1. Either this difference is because NXP indeed changed the design, or ARM has multiple versions of Cortex-M3 design.

3.4   Register Write-Back

Technically speaking, a 3-stage pipeline often does not have a dedicate register write-back stage. However, as we can see in Fig. 2, the ALU output has to be written back at the end of the **Execute** cycle, which leads to a transition leakage that affects the next cycle. As both the ALU output and the value destination register are explicitly defined by the Instruction Set Architecture (ISA) and the executing code, there is no need for further investigation for such leakage.

3.5   Memory Sub-system

It is well known that the memory subsystem produces various "unexpected" issues [3,13,16,18,19]. The main challenge is that while the ISA specifies *what should happen in the processor*, it certainly does not specify the detailed design of any asynchronous component (i.e. the memory). More specifically, in our case, ARM specifies the memory interface through the AMBA APB Protocol [20]: the protocol defines how the processor should communicate with the peripheral, performing read/write operations. However, the peripheral is asynchronous (aka self-timed) to the processor, therefore the response time as well as internal interactions are completely up to the peripheral. Take *ldr/str* instructions for instance, although it is often assumed they take 2 cycles, in practice, the situation is much more complicated. The peripheral can prolong the transfer by adding wait states [20], or for certain instructions, the ALU can proceed without the peripheral finishing its task.

As a consequence, without a timing-accurate memory simulator, the chance of constructing a timing-accurate leakage model for the memory sub-system seems gloomy. In Fig. 5b, we construct a hypothetical view that captures various known issues (e.g. from [3,13]). Specifically, we assume our memory system works as follows:

---

[4] Available in their code repository, not in the paper.

- Each load/store produces leakage on the entire word (32-bit), even if the target is only one byte (see Sect. 5.2 [13]).
- The memory system has only one (shared) address bus (specified by [20]).
- The memory buses preserve their values until the next access (recommended in [20]).
- Read and write share the same data bus (consistent with Sect. 5.1 [13]).
- There is also a dedicate bus/buffer that holds the write value (our own experiments).

Although Fig. 5b does not specify the timing behaviour, fortunately, the accurate timing is not required for many application scenarios (e.g. leakage simulators [1–3]/verifiers [21]): for developers, it is essential to learn *why such leakage appears*, but less crucial *when*.

Take two adjacent store instructions for instance, as long as we know there exists a transition leakage on the write bus, we do not necessarily care about *whether this leakage appears at clock cycle x or $x + y$*. Whilst a more detailed investigation on timing characteristics might be possible, they becomes increasingly unrewarding in a grey-box setting.

4   Step 3: Refining the Micro-architectural Leakage Model

In the previous section, we reverse engineered where operands are stored in the micro-architecture, and we developed a first understanding of the interactions between operands across the three pipeline stages. Now we set out to refine this understanding and characterise the interactions.

4.1   Considering Components with Stable Signals

Fetch. Stable signals are from micro-architectural components that do not have glitches. Because we assume our target program does not contain any "data-dependent branches", we do not need to consider elements from this stage.

Decode. Because we do not consider data dependent instructions, we can also exclude all purple wires before the register file (D.1–4, D.8) as they do not produce data-dependent leakage (i.e. remain the same between each execution). After accessing the register file, each purple wire must be considered, as it carries an operand that varies from trace to trace.

Based on the information in Table 1, we can build a simplified micro-architectural leakage model that only contains the "stable" signals in the circuit for D.5–D.7 (aka read ports 1–3). The outputs of two operand MUX-s are trickier: when rs_1 is updated, D.9 carries the updated value. However, when rs_1 preserves its previous value (e.g. *rsbs Rd, Rm*), we cannot determine the value on D.9 easily. Considering the same leakage could come from various equivalent micro-architectures, we consider them separately in Sect. 4.2.

Thus, the assumed micro-architectural leakage for the decoding stage is:

$$L_d = \{port_1 \otimes port_1', port_2 \otimes port_2', port_3 \otimes port_3'\}$$

where $port_1'$ represents the value on port 1 from the previous instruction decoding. If both values on port 1 are not constant,

$$port_1 \otimes port_1' = \{(x||y)|x \in port_1, y \in port_1'\}$$

Otherwise, if one of the values is a constant, this term can be simplified to only $port_1$ or $port_1'$. This leakage is a super set of both the standard HW and HD model, covering not only the leakage of the values but also any transition occurring on the wire.

Using again the *collapsed F-test* [11], we can interrogate if this model explains all observable leakage (in the decoding stage). Figure 7 plots the evaluation for the same instructions in Fig. 4: for all but one instruction L_d is correct. Only for the 3-operand *adds*, the test result suggests L_d cannot explain all the observed leakage within this decoding stage (which will be further studied in Sect. 4.2).

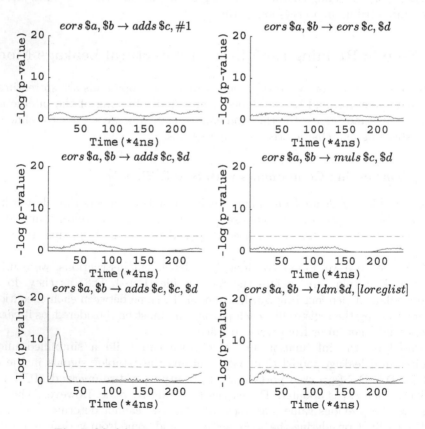

Fig. 7. Model completeness analysis in the decoding stage.

Execute. Similarly, for the **Execute** stage, we ignore the immediate number and the control signals, and focus on the wires E.1, E.2 and E.4. Obviously, the entire leakage of this stage depends on the two operands in rs_1 and rs_2.

Unlike the **Decode** stage, these two operands deliberately interact with each other in the ALU. Thus, it is expected that there is some cross-operand leakage. Considering that the ALU is a relatively complicated piece of combinational logic where multiple computations run in parallel (i.e. not "gated" [18,19]), finding the exact form of L_E presents its own challenge. Therefore, we leave L_E conservatively as:

$$L_E = \{rs_1 \otimes rs_2 \otimes rs_1' \otimes rs_2'\}$$

Clearly L_E includes all possible glitchy states on the red wires in Fig. 5a. The data-dependent bits in the Current Program Status Register (CPSR) rely on the ALU's output, and are therefore also covered by L_E. For conciseness we refer to [11] where one of the examples analyses just this situation; besides, Fig. 9 also evaluates the entire leakage model, including the execute leakage here.

Register Write-Back. Although a write-back stage does not exist in this 3-stage pipeline, updating the destination register still happens after the **Execute** stage: thus, we need a separate micro-architectural leakage element L_{WB} to capture such leakage. Denote the ALU output from the last cycle as Res and the previous value of the destination register as R_d. The register write-back leakage element L_{WB} can be written as:

$$L_{WB} = \{Res \otimes R_d\}$$

Note that Res is defined by the ISA and R_d is architecturally visible, therefore does not take any further investigation.

Memory. Following Sect. 3.5, we denote Bus as the shared bus and Bus_w as the dedicate write bus, where $Addr$ represents the address bus. The micro-architectural leakage of the memory subsystem is:

$$L_M = \{Bus \otimes Bus', Bus_w \otimes Bus_w', Addr \otimes Addr'\}$$

Although some of above leakage only appears for memory access instructions, considering the APB protocol explicitly recommends to keep the remaining values on the bus [20], we always keep L_M as part of the leakage model, even if the instruction does not access memory.

4.2   Glitch and Multiplexer

Glitchy Register Access. The lower left figure in Fig. 7 suggests that considering only the stable signals is not always enough. In a more realistic scenario, the situation can be even worse: in order to achieve a concrete understanding of *which operand is read from which port*, we deliberately designed our setup (see Sect. 3.2) to avoid various "known issues". For instance, it is reported back in

2017 by Papagiannopoulos and Veshchikov that some processors might implicitly access an adjacent register while accessing a target register [16]. It was latter explained in [18] such leakage is likely to be caused by the address decoding in the register file. When setting up our experiments, we deliberately use only the odd registers (i.e. r_1, r_3, r_5, r_7): although there is no guarantee that such LSB-neighbouring effect is the only type of neighbouring effect in our target processor, within 50k traces, we did not find this effect in our analysis.

Nonetheless, the so-called "neighbouring effect" [16] can be extended to more general glitchy accesses within the register file: in a 3-stage core, considering the decoding and operand pre-loading are happening in the same cycle, it is expected that the signal glitch starts even earlier, say from the decoded register addresses (i.e. D.2–D.4 in Fig. 3b). Back to our exceptional *adds*: as one can see in Table 1, the previous *eors* loaded R_m from bit 5-3 of the instruction, while the current *adds* requires R_m from bit 8-6 instead. Considering this change of field needs to be initiated by the decoder, we can expect that for a short time after the clock edge, the decoder still outputs R_m as the bit 5-3 of the new *adds* instruction (i.e. $R_n = C$), and then switches back to bit 8-6, which gives $R_m = D$. In other words, although the stable signal on $port_2$ changes as:

$$B \to D$$

the glitchy signal switches through:

$$B \to C \to D$$

which might give the transition of $B \otimes C$ and $C \otimes D$.

As we can see in Fig. 8, the interaction $C \otimes D$ is clearly visible in the upper-left. Without including this micro-architectural leakage our constructed leakage model does not fully explain the observed leakage.

The lower half of Fig. 8 demonstrates another case of this effect. Specifically, if we try the following code:

```
1  glitchy_reg:
2  ...
3  eors  r5,r7    //r5=C,  r7=D
4  adds  r3,#1    //r1=A,  r3=B
5  ...
```

Following our discussion above, when decoding *adds*, there might be a short time period when the decoder still decodes in the style of *eors*. According to Table 1, this means the immediate number 1 will be taken as register r_1 (bit 2-0 from the instruction *eors*). In the lower left of Fig. 8, clearly value A is loaded in this cycle. In fact, as the signal transition goes $C \to A \to B$, there could be interaction of $C \otimes A$ and $A \otimes B$, which is exactly what we see in Fig. 8. Our completeness test confirms that we can capture all of this micro-architectural leakage as long as these terms are added in.

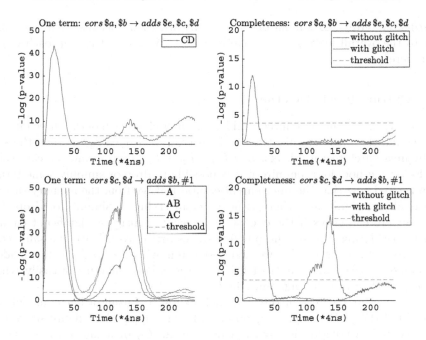

Fig. 8. Glitchy register access in the decoding stage.

Taking glitches into consideration, we add one glitchy term for each port: for port 1, denoted as $port_{1g}$, representing the glitchy accessed value on port 1. The glitchy decoding stage leakage can be regarded as

$$L_{Dg} = L_D + \{port_{1g} \otimes port_1, port_{1g} \otimes port'_1\}$$

where $port_{1g}$ could be:

- Implicitly access caused by decoding: decoding the current instruction in the previous style
- Implicitly access caused by register address: the neighbouring effect, needs to be tested on the specific device

$port_{2g}$ can be added following the similar rules. Considering such an effect has a relatively small magnitude and enormous test space (i.e. the entire decoding space must be considered), we did not further identify which factor must be added and which can perhaps be ignored. A conservative micro-architectural leakage model will include everything, if more implementation details were available then certain elements could be excluded (with the resulting model checked via the F-test).

Multiplexer. Grey-box simulators usually discard them, because their contribution to the overall leakage is relatively limited. We follow this approach in our work here[5].

4.3   Putting It All Together

We constructed a micro-architectural leakage model for each of the three pipeline stages, and the memory subsystem. The overall device leakage is then the sum of the micro-architectural leaks: $L = L_D + L_E + L_M + L_{WB}$, and we can, using the F-test methodology, enquire if it is possible to drop or simplify some terms. Because we know that the micro-architectural leakage from the memory subsystem is always significant, there is no point in trying to simplify or drop this. However, we can check if the decode and execute leakage is significant enough (when considering it as all the pipeline stages are active). With the same code in Sect. 3.2 ("Testing_port"), we first test if removing L_D or L_E can provide a valid model: as we can see in the left half of Fig. 9, both fail our test easily, which suggests both stages' leakage must be kept.

Thus, we further test in the right half of Fig. 9 if using a linear model (i.e. a weighted HW/HD model) is good enough. The upper right figure suggests if the executed instruction is *eors*, having a linear L_D or a linear L_E passes F-test, although L_D and L_E cannot be linear at the same time. This is in fact consistent with the observations in [11]: if the instruction is relatively simple, using a linear model of the ALU inputs/output can be a valid option. The lower right of Fig. 9 shows that for an *adds* instruction, the execute stage must utilise a non-linear model. But, the decoding leakage L_D can always be set to linear in our experiments: considering the decoding stage only contains buses that load values and flip from one value to another, this is quite natural. Hence we always restrict the decoding leakage L_D to be a linear micro-architectural leakage element, denoted as L_{Dl}. Similarly, as the write-back logic is relatively simple, we also simplify L_{WB} to be a linear micro-architectural leakage element (L_{WBl}). Because of the known byte-wise interactions on the memory bus [13], L_M is left without any restriction.

$$L = L_{Dl} + L_E + L_{WBl} + L_M$$

5   Putting Our Micro-architectural Model to the Test

In this section, we further show how existing simulators fail to find leakage, but our new micro-architectural model reveals it, and helps to develop concrete attacks to exploit it. Then we report on our integration of the new model in the existing emulator ELMO.

---

[5] One recent white-box tool, Coco [18]), takes a conservative approach: if we have MUX(s, a, b) (where s is the selecting signal), they simply allow any possible leakage by considering $a \otimes b \otimes s$.

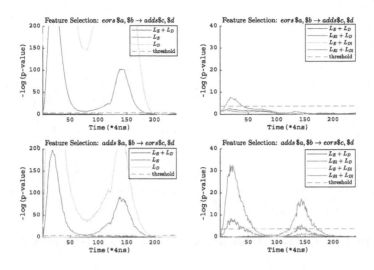

Fig. 9. Feature selection for our leakage model.

5.1   Exploiting Decoding Port Leakage

Existing simulators typically do not define any explicit decoding leakage. In particular, ELMO (and ELMO*) always set $rs_1 = R_d$ and $rs_2 = R_m$, even if R_d is never used in certain instructions (e.g. *movs* R_d, R_m in Table 1). This is not correct (at least on the core that we utilised), but if we consider the "operand buses" in ELMO to be the decoding read ports, then decoding leakage is captured by ELMO (and ELMO*), albeit in a different clock cycle.

The following code snippet is from another 2-share bitwise ISW multiplication [5], where $a_1(b_1)$ and $a_2(b_2)$ represent the two input shares of $a(b)$. Leakage reports from ELMO[6] and MAPS are:

- ELMO. Line 7 is leaking from the first operand's bit-flip ($r_2 = a_2 * b_1 \rightarrow r_6 = a_1 * b_1$).
- MAPS. No leakage.

```
1  ISWd2:
2  ...              // r1=a1*b2+r,  r2=a2,  r3=b1,
3  ...              // r6=a1*b1, r9=output address
4  ands  r2, r3  // r2=a2*b1
5  eors  r1, r2  // r1=a1*b2+r+a2*b1
6  mov   r2, r9  // Get back output address
7  eors  r6, r1  // r6=a1*b1+a1*b2+r+a2*b1
8  ...
```

---

[6] The ELMO* [3] extension does not find any additional leakage.

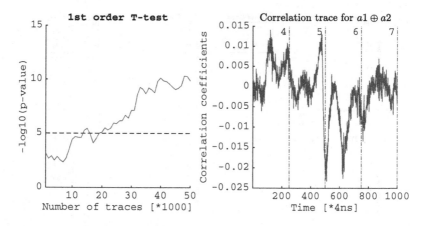

Fig. 10. Experiments with 50k traces on 2-share bitwise ISW multiplication.

According to Table 1, line 7 should not show any leakage from rs_1, since line 6 never loaded r_2 to rs_1. However, the decoding stages of line 6 and 7 load these operands into $port_1$, which suggests a leakage can be found in the decoding cycle of line 7. The right half of Fig. 10 illustrates the correlation trace using $HW(a_1 \oplus a_2)$: the correlation peaks appear in the execute cycle of line 6 (i.e. the decoding cycle of line 7). Besides, the TVLA trend in the left half of Fig. 10 shows such leakage is relatively weak: it takes more than 20k traces before the leakage can be stably detected.

To show that missing out on the explicit inclusion of decoding leakage matters, we further investigate a 3-share bitwise ISW multiplication (where no first order leakage can be found in this implementation).

```
1 ISWd3:
2 ...
3 mov   r7, r9       //r7=a3
4 mov   r5, r11      //r5=b3
5 ands  r5, r7       //r5=a3*b3
6 ands  r4, r6       //r6=a2*b2
7 ands  r3, r1       //r3=a1*b1
8 ldr   r7, [r0, #0] //r7=r12
9 ...
```

In theory, there should not be any attack that combines less than three intermediates (leakage points), which increases the required number of traces. We show that a third order attack indeed does not succeed with a too limited number of traces in the upper-left of Fig. 11)[7].

---

[7] Our implementation only uses LSB to compute the bit-sliced S-box; therefore the measured trace has been averaged 50 times before analysis, in order the increase the SNR.

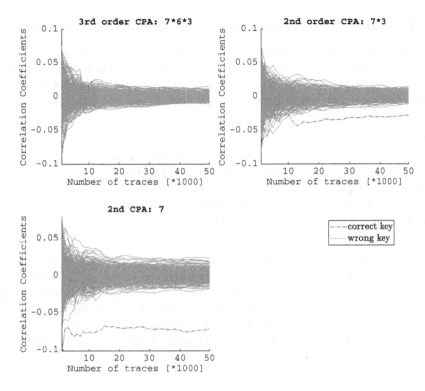

Fig. 11. Experiments with 50k traces on 3-share bitwise ISW multiplication.

However, given our micro-architectural leakage model we may safely assume that the processor will inadvertently combine masking shares for us. Indeed, even the simpler ELMO model can predict such leakage: specifically, the first operand bit-flip from line 6 and 7 gives the leakage of $a_1 \oplus a_2$, which should reveal the secret a if combined with the leakage of line 3 (i.e. a_3). We have also confirmed this leakage in Fig. 11: the upper-right figure shows using this combination, the correct key can be found within 10k traces.

With the decoding leakage added in, our micro-architectural leakage model extensively expands the region of potential leakage: considering the execute cycle of line 7, we know from Table 1 that ldr does load r_7 in the decoding cycle, which provides the leakage of a_3. As a consequence, we can use the second order moment of the measurements from line 7 alone, which avoids the combination of noise from different time samples. In our experiments, this is indeed the best option: the correct key guess can be found with only 1k traces. In other words, the supposedly provably secure scheme can be attacked in a univariate manner, but none of the existing simulators would reveal this weakness.

5.2   Consequences of Incorrectly Assigning Pipeline Registers

When it comes to the pipeline registers, many instructions do not follow the default $rs_1 = R_d$ and $rs_2 = R_m$ setup as Table 1 shows. Considering the pipeline registers may even be preserved through a few instructions, this is clearly an issue if some previous operand is believed to be cleared out of the context while in reality it is sitting somewhere within the processor.

```
1 Scverif_Ref:
2 ...                    // r1=output address
3 ...                    // r5=a2+r, r3=a1+r
4 str   r5, [r1, #4]  //
5 pop   {r4-r5}        // Reload r4 and r5
6 eors  r3, r3         // Clear r3
7 ...
```

The above code is from a 2-share refreshing gadget verified by scVerif [21]. Clearly, any transition between r_3 and r_5 leaks the secret a. Let us focus on line 5: scVerif treats *pop* as several *load*-s, where each *load* clears both rs_1 and rs_2 (see [21, Alg.3]). According to Table 1, *pop* on our target device only clears rs_1, but not rs_2. Thus, when executing line 6, rs_2 remains the previous value set by line 4. According to Table 1, there is a transition between $a_2 + r$ and $a_1 + r$ on rs_2. Leakage reports from ELMO and MAPS are:

- ELMO/ELMO*. No leakage.
- MAPS. Leakage from line 6, pipeline registers[8].

Here we begin to witness the benefit of having the accurate pipeline register assignment: MAPS clearly points out this leakage, while neither ELMO nor ELMO* finds any leakage. This is because both ELMO and ELMO* stick with ELMO's leakage model, which also believes *pop* clears both rs_1 and rs_2. At least on our M3 core, this is not the case: as we can see in the right half of Fig. 12, a clear correlation peak in line 6 suggests rs_2 still keeps the value from line 4. Since this transition is from rs_2 (versus the port transition in Fig. 10), the left half of Fig. 12 shows its leakage is much easier to detect compared with Fig. 10.

5.3   Towards a Micro-architectural Simulator: μElmo

Our goal is to extract micro-architectural leakage to improve simulation tools: thus we included the reverse engineered micro-architectural leakage elements into the instruction set simulator that underpins ELMO and created an upgraded version of ELMO, denoted as μELMO. The original ELMO already emulate rs_1 and rs_2 (in two variables $op1$ and $op2$), therefore the required revisions are a) updating rs_1 and rs_2 according to Table 1 and b) adding the decoding ports/memory buses as new variables in μELMO.

---

[8] MAPS needs the command line argument "-p" to calculate the pipeline registers' leakage.

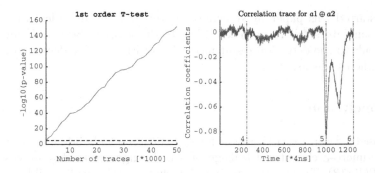

Fig. 12. Experiments with 50k traces on 2-share mask refresh from scVerif.

With μELMO, we now revisit the 2-share ISW multiplication in Sect. 1. We study the simple case where only a single bit is actually encoded in each processor word (recent work has shown that any more clever form of bit or share-slicing would be insecure [12]). Thus except for a single bit (representing a share) the other bits are always constant 0. This implies that any term $rs_1 \otimes rs_2$ can easily be simplified as $\{rs_1, rs_2, rs_1 \oplus rs_2\}$: in the 1-bit version, the later can express any joint leakage from $rs_1 \otimes rs_2$. Using similar converting rules for the entire L, we can easily derive a model that only contains xor-sum terms, not any joint term. We then perform 1st order t-test on each individual term within this cycle separately (e.g. rs_1, rs_2 and $rs_1 \oplus rs_2$) and summarise the leakage of the entire cycle from multiple t-statistics.

Of course, this masking implementation is inefficient: instead one would attempt to simultaneously compute other 1-bit multiplications. If it was possible to ensure their mutual independence we can still simplify the multi-bit $\{rs_1 \otimes rs_2\}$ as $\{HW(rs_1), HW(rs_2), HW(rs_1 \oplus rs_2)\}$ as before (if not then their interaction terms would need to be considered as well).

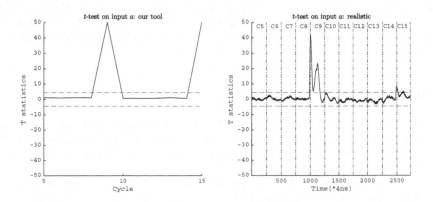

Fig. 13. Comparison of our tool and realistic measurements.

We started this paper by showing how this ISW example leaks in practice but all simulators fail to correctly identify the leaks in Sect. 1. Using μElmo traces leads to the detection result in the left of Fig. 13. The detection correctly idenfies the two leaks.

6   Conclusion

We utilised a recent statistical tool for statistical model building to reverse engineer the micro-architectural leakage of a mid-range commodity processor (the NXP LPC1313). This reverse engineering effort enables us to build more accurate leakage models, which are essential for accurate leakage simulators. As a side effect our model provides, to some extent, an in-depth picture of how the ARM Cortex M3 architecture is implemented in the LPC1313.

Our research was motivated by the observation that the most recent leakage simulators are inaccurate and consequently traces produced by them will not show all leaks that can be found in real devices (or they show leaks where in actual fact are none). We integrate our reverse engineered micro-architectural elements into the simulator that underpins ELMO and then demonstrate that the resulting simulator produces leakage traces that are more faithful to real device traces in the context of enabling the detection of leaks and when they occur.

Our methodology is generic in the sense that it relies on a statistical test that can deal with large numbers of variables (with limited data). For now we need to manually instrument the statistical tests to recover micro-architectural leakage information. However, merging our results with the recently introduced idea of software kernels in [13] could enable automation of our method in the future. This would be a significant step towards being able to produce highly accurate leakage simulators for a range of off-the-shelf processors.

Acknowledgments. We would like to thank Ben Marshall for his invaluable insights, which guided us through various mazes in our leakage modelling efforts. Si Gao and Elisabeth Oswald were funded in part by the ERC via the grant SEAL (Project Reference 725042). This work has been supported in part by EPSRC via grant EP/R012288/1, under the RISE (http://www.ukrise.org) programme.

References

1. McCann, D., Oswald, E., Whitnall, C.: Towards practical tools for side channel aware software engineering: 'grey box' modelling for instruction leakages. In: 26th USENIX Security Symposium (USENIX Security 2017), Vancouver, BC, pp. 199–216. USENIX Association (2017)
2. Le Corre, Y., Großschädl, J., Dinu, D.: Micro-architectural power simulator for leakage assessment of cryptographic software on ARM Cortex-M3 processors. In: Fan, J., Gierlichs, B. (eds.) COSADE 2018. LNCS, vol. 10815, pp. 82–98. Springer, Cham (2018). https://doi.org/10.1007/978-3-319-89641-0_5

3. Shelton, M.A., Samwel, N., Batina, L., Regazzoni, F., Wagner, M., Yarom, Y.: ROSITA: towards automatic elimination of power-analysis leakage in ciphers. CoRR abs/1912.05183 (2019)
4. Buhan, I., Batina, L., Yarom, Y., Schaumont, P.: SoK: design tools for side-channel-aware implementations (2021). https://arxiv.org/abs/2104.08593
5. Ishai, Y., Sahai, A., Wagner, D.: Private circuits: securing hardware against probing attacks. In: Boneh, D. (ed.) CRYPTO 2003. LNCS, vol. 2729, pp. 463–481. Springer, Heidelberg (2003). https://doi.org/10.1007/978-3-540-45146-4_27
6. McCann, D.: ELMO (2017). https://github.com/bristol-sca/ELMO
7. Clavier, C.: Side channel analysis for reverse engineering (SCARE) - an improved attack against a secret A3/A8 GSM algorithm. IACR Cryptology ePrint Archive 2004/49 (2004)
8. Goldack, M.: Side-channel based reverse engineering for microcontrollers (2008)
9. Wang, X., Narasimhan, S., Krishna, A., Bhunia, S.: SCARE: side-channel analysis based reverse engineering for post-silicon validation. In: 2012 25th International Conference on VLSI Design, pp. 304–309 (2012)
10. Oswald, D., Strobel, D., Schellenberg, F., Kasper, T., Paar, C.: When reverse-engineering meets side-channel analysis – digital lockpicking in practice. In: Lange, T., Lauter, K., Lisoněk, P. (eds.) SAC 2013. LNCS, vol. 8282, pp. 571–588. Springer, Heidelberg (2014). https://doi.org/10.1007/978-3-662-43414-7_29
11. Gao, S., Oswald, E.: A novel completeness test and its application to side channel attacks and simulators. IACR Cryptology ePrint Archive (2021). https://eprint.iacr.org/2021/756
12. Gao, S., Marshall, B., Page, D., Oswald, E.: Share-slicing: friend or foe? IACR Trans. Cryptogr. Hardw. Embed. Syst. **2020**(1), 152–174 (2019)
13. Marshall, B., Page, D., Webb, J.: MIRACLE: MIcro-ArChitectural leakage evaluation. IACR Cryptology ePrint Archive (2021). https://eprint.iacr.org/2021/261
14. ARM Limited: ARM®v7-M Architecture Reference Manual (2005). https://developer.arm.com/documentation/ddi0337/e
15. ARM Limited: Thumb® 16-bit Instruction Set Quick Reference Card (2008). https://developer.arm.com/documentation/qrc0006/e
16. Papagiannopoulos, K., Veshchikov, N.: Mind the gap: towards secure 1st-order masking in software. In: Guilley, S. (ed.) COSADE 2017. LNCS, vol. 10348, pp. 282–297. Springer, Cham (2017). https://doi.org/10.1007/978-3-319-64647-3_17
17. De Cnudde, T., Ender, M., Moradi, A.: Hardware masking, revisited. IACR Trans. Cryptogr. Hardw. Embed. Syst. **2018**(2), 123–148 (2018)
18. Gigerl, B., Hadzic, V., Primas, R., Mangard, S., Bloem, R.: COCO: co-design and co-verification of masked software implementations on CPUs. In: Bailey, M., Greenstadt, R. (eds.) 30th USENIX Security Symposium, USENIX Security 2021, 11–13 August 2021, pp. 1469–1468. USENIX Association (2021)
19. De Meyer, L., De Mulder, E., Tunstall, M.: On the effect of the (micro) architecture on the development of side-channel resistant software. IACR Cryptology ePrint Archive 2020/1297 (2020)
20. ARM Limited: AMBA® APB Protocol (2010). https://developer.arm.com/documentation/ihi0024/c/
21. Barthe, G., Gourjon, M., Grégoire, B., Orlt, M., Paglialonga, C., Porth, L.: Masking in fine-grained leakage models: construction, implementation and verification. IACR Trans. Cryptogr. Hardw. Embed. Syst. **2021**(2), 189–228 (2021)

Post-Quantum Cryptography

Beyond Quadratic Speedups in Quantum Attacks on Symmetric Schemes

Xavier Bonnetain[1], André Schrottenloher[2($\boxtimes$)], and Ferdinand Sibleyras[3]

[1] Université de Lorraine, CNRS, Inria, Nancy, France
[2] Cryptology Group, CWI, Amsterdam, The Netherlands
andre.schrottenloher@m4x.org
[3] NTT Social Informatics Laboratories, Tokyo, Japan

Abstract. In this paper, we report the first quantum key-recovery attack on a symmetric block cipher design, using classical queries only, with a more than quadratic time speedup compared to the best classical attack.

We study the 2XOR-Cascade construction of Gaži and Tessaro (EUROCRYPT 2012). It is a key length extension technique which provides an n-bit block cipher with $\frac{5n}{2}$ bits of security out of an n-bit block cipher with $2n$ bits of key, with a security proof in the ideal model. We show that the offline-Simon algorithm of Bonnetain et al. (ASIACRYPT 2019) can be extended to, in particular, attack this construction in quantum time $\widetilde{\mathcal{O}}(2^n)$, providing a 2.5 quantum speedup over the best classical attack.

Regarding post-quantum security of symmetric ciphers, it is commonly assumed that doubling the key sizes is a sufficient precaution. This is because Grover's quantum search algorithm, and its derivatives, can only reach a quadratic speedup at most. Our attack shows that the structure of some symmetric constructions can be exploited to overcome this limit. In particular, the 2XOR-Cascade cannot be used to generically strengthen block ciphers against quantum adversaries, as it would offer only the same security as the block cipher itself.

Keywords: Post-quantum cryptography · Quantum cryptanalysis · Key-length extension · 2XOR-Cascade · Simon's algorithm · Quantum search · Offline-simon

1 Introduction

In 1994, Shor [47] designed polynomial-time quantum algorithms for factoring and computing discrete logarithms, both believed to be classically intractable. This showed that a large-scale quantum computer could break public-key cryptosystems based on these problems, such as RSA and ECC, which unluckily are the most widely used to date.

The impact of quantum computers on secret-key cryptography is, at first sight, much more limited. The lack of *structure* in secret-key cryptosystems seems to defeat most exponential quantum speedups. It can be expected to

© International Association for Cryptologic Research 2022
O. Dunkelman and S. Dziembowski (Eds.): EUROCRYPT 2022, LNCS 13277, pp. 315–344, 2022.
https://doi.org/10.1007/978-3-031-07082-2_12

do so, as it was shown in [8] that relative to an oracle, quantum speedups for worst-case algorithms can be polynomial at most, unless the oracle satisfies some additional structure. This structure, that is essential for exponential speedups, is usually known as a "promise". For example, in Shor's abelian period-finding algorithm [47], the promise is that the oracle is a periodic function.

Another well-known quantum algorithm, Grover's quantum search [26], can speed up an exhaustive key search by a quadratic factor. That is, an attacker equipped with a quantum computer can find the κ-bit key of a strong block cipher in about $\mathcal{O}(2^{\kappa/2})$ operations instead of the $\mathcal{O}(2^\kappa)$ trials necessary for a classical attacker. Despite being merely polynomial, this is already an interesting advantage for this hypothetical attacker. Due to Grover's search, symmetric cryptosystems are commonly assumed to retain roughly half of their classical bits of security, and it is recommended to double their key length when aiming at post-quantum security [44].

Superposition Attacks. In [39], Kuwakado and Morii designed a polynomial-time *quantum distinguisher* on the three-round Luby-Rackoff construction, although it has a classical security proof. Later on, they showed a polynomial-time key-recovery attack on the Even-Mansour construction [40], a classically proven block cipher constructed from a public permutation [23].

Both of these attacks can assume ideal building blocks (random functions in the case of the Luby-Rackoff construction, a random permutation in the case of Even-Mansour), as they focus on the *algebraic structure* of the construction. The target problem (distinguishing or key-recovery) is simply reduced to the problem of finding the hidden period of a periodic function, which can be solved efficiently.

However, in order to run these attacks, the quantum adversary needs to access the construction as a *quantum oracle* (in *superposition*). This means that the black-box must be part of a quantum circuit. When it comes to provable security in the quantum setting, this is a natural assumption, followed by most of the works in this direction (see [6,49] for instance). However, it does not seem too hard to avoid quantum queries at the implementation level[1].

Many other symmetric constructions have been shown to be broken under superposition queries in the past few years [10,14,34,41]. All these attacks have been exploiting the algebraic structure of their targets in similar ways, using different period or shift-finding algorithms.

Attacks Based on Quantum Search. *Quantum search*, the equivalent of classical exhaustive search, is a very versatile tool that allows to design many algorithms beyond a mere exhaustive search of the key. However, by only combining quantum search with itself, one cannot obtain a better speedup than quadratic. More precisely[2]:

---

[1] Though it seems also impossible in some restricted cases, for example *white-box encryption*. Here the adversary tries to recover the key of a block cipher whose specification is completely given to him. He can realize the quantum oracle using this specification.

[2] For completeness, we include a short proof of this claim in the full version of the paper [15].

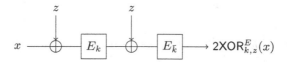

Fig. 1. The 2XOR construction of [25]. E is an ideal n-bit block cipher, z is an n-bit key, k is a κ-bit key and $\bar{k}$ is $\pi(k)$ for some chosen permutation π without fixpoints.

Let $\mathcal{A}$ be a quantum algorithm, with a final measurement, that is built by combining a constant number of quantum search procedures. Let $\mathcal{T}$ be its time complexity and $\mathcal{M}$ its memory complexity. Then there exists a classical randomized algorithm $\mathcal{A}'$ that returns the same results using $\mathcal{M}$ memory and time $\mathcal{O}(\mathcal{T}^2)$.

In other words, if our only quantum algorithmic tool is quantum search, then any quantum attack admits an equivalent classical attack of squared complexity, and that uses a similar memory. In particular, if the quantum procedure goes below the exhaustive key search ($\mathcal{O}(2^{\kappa/2})$), then the corresponding classical procedure can be expected to go below the classical exhaustive key search ($\mathcal{O}(2^{\kappa})$).

Attacks Beyond Quantum Search. So far, when superposition queries are forbidden, all known quantum attacks on symmetric designs (e.g., key-recovery attacks on block ciphers, forgery attacks on MACs) have only been confirmed to reach time speedups less than (or equal to) quadratic: the best that quantum search, and other extended frameworks [43], can offer.

At ASIACRYPT 2019, Bonnetain *et al.* [12] presented new attacks on the Even-Mansour and FX block ciphers that somehow went "beyond quantum search only". Their algorithm combines Simon's algorithm [48] and quantum search, inspired by an attack of Leander and May [41]. In some scenarios, it allows to reach a quadratic speedup *and* an asymptotic memory improvement at the same time. For example, they obtained an attack on an n-bit Even-Mansour cipher, with $2^{n/3}$ classical queries, in quantum time $\tilde{\mathcal{O}}(2^{n/3})$, and memory $\mathsf{poly}(n)$, instead of a classical attack with time $\mathcal{O}(2^{2n/3})$ *and memory* $2^{n/3}$.

Contributions of this Paper. In this paper, we show that the offline-Simon algorithm of [12] can be extended to attack some symmetric constructions with a (provable) quantum time speedup 2.5. Our main example is the *double-XOR Cascade construction* (2XOR in what follows) of Fig. 1, introduced by Gazi and Tessaro [25].

From an n-bit block cipher with key length κ, the 2XOR builds a block cipher with key length $n + \kappa$. It can be seen as a strengthening of the FX construction (which would have a single block cipher call) that enhances the security when the adversary can make many queries. Indeed, in the ideal cipher model, any classical key-recovery of $\mathsf{2XOR}_{k,z}^E$ requires at least $\mathcal{O}(2^{\kappa+n/2})$ evaluations of E, even in a regime where the adversary has access to the full codebook of $\mathsf{2XOR}_{k,z}^E$.

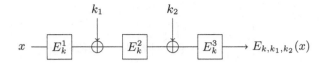

Fig. 2. *Doubly-extended FX* (DEFX) construction. E^1, E^2, E^3 are possibly independent block ciphers, but using the same κ-bit key k. k_1 and k_2 are independent n-bit whitening keys.

In the quantum setting, one can prove (see Sect. 5.3) that a quantum adversary needs at least $\mathcal{O}(2^{\kappa/2})$ quantum queries to either E, $2\mathsf{XOR}^E_{k,z}$ or their inverses. In Sect. 4.2, we show the following:

Given 2^u classical chosen-plaintext queries to $2\mathsf{XOR}^E_{k,z}$, a quantum attacker can retrieve the key k, z in quantum time $\mathcal{O}(n2^u + n^3 2^{(\kappa+n-u)/2})$.

In particular, when $\kappa = 2n$, a classical adversary knowing the full codebook needs a time $\mathcal{O}(2^{\frac{5n}{2}})$ to recover the key, whereas a quantum adversary requires only $\widetilde{\mathcal{O}}(2^n)$. In that case, $2\mathsf{XOR}^E_{k,z}$ offers actually *no improvement* over the *FX* construction, in the quantum setting.

Beyond 2XOR, we use offline-Simon to attack the extended construction of Fig. 2 with the same complexity. We identify other settings where a quantum adversary can gain this 2.5 advantage, e.g., a key-recovery on ECBC-MAC where part of the plaintext is unknown. We also extend our study to the case of *known plaintext queries*, where all but a fraction of the codebook is known, and show that offline-Simon still works in this setting.

This 2.5 speedup was not observed before in [12] because the authors considered constructions such as FX, which would omit the calls to E^1_k and E^3_k. In that case, there exists improved classical time-data trade-offs that allow to reach precisely the square of the quantum time complexities, and offline-Simon only improves the memory consumption.

Whether this 2.5 speedup is the best achievable is an interesting question. We conjecture that variants of offline-Simon could reach a cubic speedup on appropriate problems, but we have not identified any corresponding cryptographic scenario.

Organization of the Paper. We start in Sect. 2 by defining most of the block cipher constructions that will be considered in this paper, and their classical security results. We include results of quantum cryptanalysis for comparison. Details of the attacks are deferred to Sect. 3, where we also cover some definitions and necessary background of quantum cryptanalysis, notably quantum search, Simon's algorithm and offline-Simon.

We regroup our results and applications in Sect. 4. We introduce a construction similar to 2XOR (EFX) and propose self-contained proofs of classical and quantum security. Next, we detail our quantum attack in a chosen-plaintext setting. We also show that when almost all the codebook is known, known-plaintext queries can replace chosen-plaintext queries in offline-Simon. This allows us to devise an attack against EFX and a strengthened variant which we call DEFX.

We discuss the limits of these results in Sect. 6. We conjecture that a variant of offline-Simon could reach a cubic gap, though no corresponding cryptographic problem has been identified for now. We also discuss the apparent similarity of this 2.5 speedup with a 2.5 gap in query complexity [4].

Notations. Throughout this paper, we will use the following notation:

- E will be an n-bit state, κ-bit key block cipher: a family of 2^κ efficiently computable (and invertible) permutations of $\{0,1\}^n$. Security proofs consider the *ideal model*, where E is selected uniformly at random. Attacks (distinguishers, key-recoveries) are randomized algorithms whose success probability is studied on average over the random choice of E. We will also use E^i to denote independent block ciphers.
- Π is a permutation of $\{0,1\}^n$, also selected uniformly at random.
- ω is the matrix multiplication exponent. In practical examples, we can replace ω by 3 since the matrices considered are quite small (at most 256×256 for standard values of n).

2   Classical Constructions and Previous Results

In this section, we recapitulate the constructions considered in this paper. For each of them, we recall classical security bounds, quantum security bounds when they exist, and corresponding quantum attacks. These results are summarized in Table 1 [and Fig. 3]. The quantum attacks will be detailed in Sect. 3.

2.1   Context

We will use, for its simplicity, the Q1/Q2 terminology of [12,29,35], which is the most common in quantum cryptanalysis works. Alternative names exist, such as "quantum chosen-plaintext attack" (qCPA) instead of Q2, found in most provable security works (e.g., [6]) and [17,32].

- A "Q2" attacker has access to a black-box quantum oracle holding some secret. We let O_f denote a quantum oracle for f (we will use the "standard" oracle representation, defined in Sect. 3).
- A "Q1" attacker can only query a black-box *classically*. Naturally, Q2 attackers are stronger than Q1, since one can always emulate a classical oracle with a quantum one (it suffices to prepare the queries in computational basis states). The Q1 setting also encompasses any situation where there is no secret, for example preimage search in hash functions.

The constructions studied in this paper are block ciphers, studied in the *ideal* (cipher or permutation) model. In particular, if $F = F_k[E]$ is the construction and E is its internal component, we assume that E is drawn uniformly at random, and let an attacker query F and E separately. The security proofs show lower bounds on the number of queries to F and E that an attacker must make to

Table 1. Summary of classical and quantum attacks considered in this paper. D is the amount of classical queries to the construction. CPA = classical chosen-plaintext with classical computations. Q1 = classical chosen-plaintext with quantum computations (non adaptive). Q2 = quantum queries. KPA = classical known-plaintext. In quantum attacks, classical bits and qubits of memory are counted together for simplicity. We stress that all the quantum attacks considered here have only polynomial memory requirements. Complexities are displayed up to a constant. We do not consider attacks with preprocessing, or multi-user attacks. We assume $\kappa \geq n$.

Target	Setting	Queries	Time	Mem.	Ref.
EM	Adaptive CPA	$2^{n/2}$	$2^{n/2}$	negl	[22]
	KPA	$D \leq 2^{n/2}$	$2^n/D$	D	[22]
	Q2	n	n^ω	n^2	[40]
	Q1	$D \leq 2^{n/3}$	$\sqrt{2^n/D}$	n^2	[12]
FX	KPA	$D \leq 2^n$	$2^{\kappa+n}/D$	D	[22]
	Adaptive CPA	$D \leq 2^{n/2}$	$2^{\kappa+n}/D$	negl	[19]
	Adaptive CPA	$D \geq 2^{n/2}$	$2^{\kappa+n}/D$	$D^2 2^{-n}$	[19]
	Q2	n	$n^\omega 2^{\kappa/2}$	n^2	[12]
	Q1	$D \leq 2^n$	$\max(D, \sqrt{2^{\kappa+n}/D})$	n^2	[12]
2XOR	KPA	$D \leq 2^{n/2}$	$2^{\kappa+n}/D$	D	[25] (adapted)
	Q2	n	$n^\omega 2^{\kappa/2}$	n^2	Section 4
	Q1	$D \leq 2^n$	$\max(D, \sqrt{2^{\kappa+n}/D})$	n^2	Section 4

succeed. Such bounds can be proven for classical and quantum attackers alike. A Q2 attacker will have access to both F and E in superposition. Though a Q1 attacker will have only classical access to F, *he still has quantum access to E.* Indeed, although supposedly chosen at random, E remains a public component, with a public implementation. Thus, in the ideal model, Q1 attackers still make black-box quantum queries to E.

Attack Scenarios. Usually, an idealized cipher construction is proven to be a *strong pseudorandom permutation* (sPRP, see Definition 1 in Supplementary Material 5). In this security notion, an adversary is asked to distinguish the construction $F_k[E]$ for a random k, from a random permutation, by making either forward or backward queries.

Obviously, a key-recovery attack is also a valid sPRP distinguisher. For all the constructions recalled in Table 1, the security is proven with the sPRP game, and the attacks are key-recovery attacks.

2.2   The Even-Mansour Cipher

The Even-Mansour cipher [23] is a minimalistic construction which is ubiquitous in idealized designs. It starts from a public n-bit permutation $\Pi : \{0,1\}^n \to$

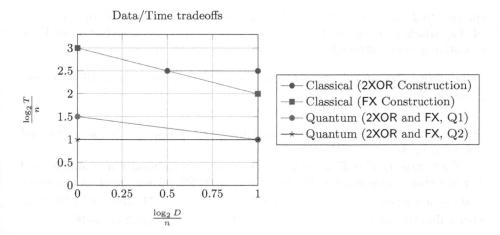

Fig. 3. Detail of Table 1: comparison of the FX and 2XOR security in function of the number of queries for $\kappa = 2n$.

$\{0, 1\}^n$ and two n-bit keys k_1, k_2 ($k_1 = k_2$ would be enough). The cipher is defined as: $\mathsf{EM}_{k_1,k_2}(x) = \Pi(x \oplus k_1) \oplus k_2$. If Π is a random permutation, then an adversary making T queries to Π and D queries to EM cannot recover the key with success probability more than $\mathcal{O}(TD/2^n)$. Matching attacks are known [18,22]. The quantum security was first studied by Kuwakado and Morii [40], who gave a $\mathcal{O}(n^\omega)$ Q2 attack using $\mathcal{O}(n)$ queries (the attack will be presented later on). Several Q1 attacks were given in [12,28,40]. Only the latter (the most efficient) is displayed in Table 1.

2.3 Key-Length Extension Techniques

Different ways of extending the key lengths of block ciphers have been proposed in the literature. Two well-known examples are the *FX construction* and the *Cascade* construction (or multiple-encryption).

FX-Construction. In [36], Kilian and Rogaway proposed key whitenings as a solution to increase the effective key length of a block cipher E:

$$\mathsf{FX}_{k_1,k_2,k}(x) = E_k(x \oplus k_1) \oplus k_2.$$

They showed that in the ideal model, an adversary making D queries to FX needs to make $T = 2^{n+\kappa}/D$ to E to recover the key. This is matched by the attacks of [19,22].

   The FX construction can also be seen as an Even-Mansour cipher where the public permutation Π is replaced by an n-bit block cipher of unknown κ-bit key. This is why the attack strategies are similar.

Quantum Security of FX. In [33], it was shown that given D *non-adaptive* classical chosen-plaintext queries, a quantum adversary needs at least $\sqrt{2^{n+\kappa}/D}$

queries to E to recover the key of FX. This bound is matched by an attack of [12], which is also non-adaptive. It seems likely that the same bound holds for adaptive queries, although this has not been formally proven.

Randomized Cascades. The *double-XOR Cascade construction* (2XOR) was proposed in [25]:

$$2\text{XOR}_{k,z}^{E}(m) = E_{\bar{k}}(E_k(m \oplus z) \oplus z)$$

where $\bar{k}$ is $\pi(k)$ for some known fixpoint-free permutation π, k is a κ-bit key and z is an n-bit key.

They show that if E is an ideal cipher (drawn uniformly at random) and k, z are chosen uniformly at random, then the sPRP advantage of an adversary making q queries to E is bounded by: $4\left(\frac{q}{2^{\kappa+n/2}}\right)^{2/3}$ (Theorem 3 in [25]). In particular, the adversary is free to query the whole codebook of $2\text{XOR}_{k,z}^{E}$.

3XOR and 3XSK. Adding a third whitening key in the output of 2XOR yields the 3XOR construction of [24], which has an improved security. The authors also propose a construction without rekeying, where the two block ciphers are the same:

$$3\text{XSK}_{k,z}[E](x) = E_k(E_k(x \oplus z) \oplus \pi(z)) \oplus z$$

where π is a permutation such that $z \mapsto z \oplus \pi(z)$ is also a permutation. As far as we know, the addition of the third whitening key actually renders the offline-Simon attack inoperable.

3   Quantum Preliminaries

In this section, we recall some background of quantum cryptanalysis, going from Simon's algorithm to the offline-Simon algorithm from [12]. We assume that the reader is familiar with the basics of quantum computing [45] such as: the definitions of qubits, gates (Hadamard, Toffoli), quantum states and the ket notation $|\psi\rangle$. Note that we write quantum states without their global amplitude factors, e.g., $\frac{1}{\sqrt{2^n}}\sum_{x\in\{0,1\}^n}|x\rangle$ will be written $\sum_x |x\rangle$.

We will consider algorithms making oracle calls. A *quantum* (or *superposition*) oracle for a function f will be represented as a black box unitary operator O_f: $O_f|x\rangle|y\rangle = |x\rangle|y \oplus f(x)\rangle$.

Any classical reversible algorithm $\mathcal{A}$ can be written as a circuit using only Toffoli gates. Then, there exists a quantum circuit $\mathcal{A}'$ that uses the same amount of gates, but instead of computing $\mathcal{A}(x)$ on an input x, it computes $\mathcal{A}$ in superposition: $\mathcal{A}'|x\rangle = \mathcal{A}(x)$. We call $\mathcal{A}'$ a *quantum embedding* of $\mathcal{A}$. Classical algorithms are rarely written with reversibility in mind, but they can always be made reversible up to some trade-off between memory and time complexity overhead [9,38,42].

3.1   Quantum Search

It is well known that Grover's algorithm [26] provides a quadratic speedup on any classical algorithm that can be reframed as a black-box search problem.

Amplitude Amplification [16] further allows to speed up the search for a "good" output in any probabilistic algorithm, including another quantum algorithm.

Let $\mathcal{A}$ be a classical probabilistic algorithm with no input, and whose output has a probability p to be "good"; let f a boolean function that effectively tests if the output is good. We are searching for a good output.

Classical exhaustive search consists in running $\mathcal{A}$ until the output is good, and we will do that $\mathcal{O}\left(\frac{1}{p}\right)$ times. Quantum search is a *stateful* procedure using $\mathcal{O}\left(\frac{1}{\sqrt{p}}\right)$ iterations of a quantum circuit that contains: a quantum implementation of $\mathcal{A}$, and a quantum implementation of f. In the case of Grover's algorithm, the search space is trivial, e.g., $\{0,1\}^n$. Here $\mathcal{A}$ has only to sample an n-bit string at random; the corresponding quantum algorithm is a Hadamard transform $H^{\otimes n}|0\rangle = \sum_{x \in \{0,1\}^n} |x\rangle$.

Theorem 1 (From [16]). *Assume that there exists a quantum circuit for $\mathcal{A}$ using T_A operations, and a quantum circuit for f using T_f operations. Then there exists a circuit* QSearch$(\mathcal{A}, f)$ *that, with no input, produces a good output of $\mathcal{A}$. It runs in time:* $\left\lfloor \frac{\pi}{4} \frac{1}{\arcsin\sqrt{p}} \right\rfloor (2T_A + T_f)$ *and succeeds with probability* $\max(p, 1-p)$.

3.2 Simon's Algorithm

In [48], Simon gave the first example of an exponential quantum time speedup relative to an oracle.

Problem 1 (Boolean period-finding). Given access to an oracle $f : \{0,1\}^n \to \{0,1\}^m$ and the promise that:

- (Periodic case) $\exists s \neq 0, \forall x, \forall y \neq x, [f(x) = f(y) \Leftrightarrow y = x \oplus s]$; or:
- (Injective case) f is injective (i.e., $s = 0$).

Find s.

Simon showed that when f is a black-box classical oracle, this problem requires $\Omega(2^{n/2})$ queries, after which a classical adversary will find a collision of f, i.e., a pair x, y such that $f(x) = f(y)$. He can then set $s = x \oplus y$ and verify his guess with a few more queries.

However, given access to a quantum oracle O_f, a very simple algorithm solves this problem in $\mathcal{O}(n)$ quantum queries and $\mathcal{O}(n^\omega)$ classical postprocessing, where ω is the matrix multiplication exponent. This algorithm consists in repeating $\mathcal{O}(n)$ times a subroutine (Algorithm 1) which: • samples a random n-bit value y in the injective case; • samples a random n-bit value y such that $y \cdot s = 0$ in the periodic case. After $\mathcal{O}(n)$ samples, we can solve a linear system to find the case and recover s.

In the injective case, Step 4 gives us a value $f(x_0)$ and makes the state collapse on $|x_0\rangle$ for some unknown x_0. The next Hadamard transform turns this into: $\sum_y (-1)^{x_0 \cdot y}|y\rangle$, and so, all y are measured with the same probability

Algorithm 1. Simon's subroutine.

1: Start in the state   ▷ $|0_n\rangle|0_m\rangle$
2: Apply a Hadamard transform   ▷ $\sum_x |x\rangle|0_m\rangle$
3: Query f ▷ $\sum_x |x\rangle|f(x)\rangle$
4: Measure the output register
5: Apply another Hadamard transform
6: Measure the input register, return the value y obtained

In the periodic case, the state collapses to a superposition of the two preimages x_0 and $x_0 \oplus s$: $\frac{1}{\sqrt{2}}(|x_0\rangle + |x_0 \oplus s\rangle)$. The next Hadamard transform turns this into:

$$\sum_y \left((-1)^{x_0 \cdot y} + (-1)^{(x_0 \oplus s) \cdot y}\right) |y\rangle,$$

and thus, the amplitudes of some of the y turn to zero. These y *cannot* be measured. They are such that: $(-1)^{x_0 \cdot y} + (-1)^{(x_0 \oplus s) \cdot y} = 0 \implies s \cdot y = 1$, which means that we only measure random orthogonal vectors (besides, they all have the same amplitude).

Simon's Algorithm in Cryptanalysis. A typical example is the polynomial-time key-recovery on Even-Mansour of Kuwakado and Morii [40]. Given access to an Even-Mansour cipher EM_{k_1,k_2} of unknown key, define $f(x) = \mathsf{EM}_{k_1,k_2}(x) \oplus \Pi(x)$. It is periodic of period k_1. Π is public, thus quantum-accessible. Given quantum oracle access to EM, we can recover k_1.

Here, as most of the time in crypanalysis, the function f cannot be promised to be *exactly* injective or periodic, and additional collisions will occur. Still, in our case, the output size of the periodic function is too large for these collisions to have any influence on the query cost [11].

The same principle is used in most of the known quantum polynomial-time attacks in symmetric cryptography [10,14,34,39–41]. A cryptanalysis problem, such as the recovery of the key or of an internal value, is encoded as a period-recovery problem.

3.3   Grover-Meet-Simon

In [41], Leander and May proposed to combine Simon's algorithm with quantum search to attack the FX construction:

$$\mathsf{FX}_{k,k_1,k_2}(x) = E_k(x \oplus k_1) \oplus k_2.$$

Indeed, if we guess correctly the internal key k, then we can break the resulting Even-Mansour cipher. In fact, one can actually *recognize the good k* by running an Even-Mansour attack: it will be successful only with the correct k.

More generally, the *Grover-meet-Simon* algorithm solves the following problem.

Problem 2. Given access to a function $F(x, y) : \{0,1\}^n \times \{0,1\}^\kappa \rightarrow \{0,1\}^n$ such that there exists a unique y_0 such that $F(\cdot, y_0)$ is periodic, find y_0 and the corresponding period.

The algorithm is a quantum search over the value $y \in \{0,1\}^\kappa$. In order to guess a key y, it runs Simon's algorithm internally on the function $F(\cdot, y)$. It ends after $\mathcal{O}(n2^{\kappa/2})$ quantum queries to F and $\mathcal{O}(n^\omega 2^{\kappa/2})$ quantum time.

Having no interfering periods for *all the functions* of the family $F(\cdot, y)$ allows to obtain an overwhelming probability of success for each test, and ensures the correctness of the algorithm. Again, this condition is satisfied for objects of cryptographic interest, and a tighter analysis is given in [11]. In the case of FX, we define $F(x, y) = \mathsf{FX}_{k_1,k_2,k}(x) \oplus E_y(x)$.

Reversible Simon's Algorithm. Let us focus on the test used inside the FX attack: it is a quantum circuit that, on input $|y\rangle|0\rangle$, returns $|y\rangle|b\rangle$ where $b = 1$ iff $x \mapsto F(y, x) = \mathsf{FX}_{k_1,k_2,k}(x) \oplus E_y(x)$ is periodic.

This quantum circuit first makes $c = \mathcal{O}(n)$ oracle queries to $F(y, x)$, building the state:

$$\bigotimes_{1 \le i \le c} \sum_x |x\rangle|F(y, x)\rangle = \bigotimes_{1 \le i \le c} \sum_x |x\rangle|\mathsf{FX}_{k_1,k_2,k}(x) \oplus E_y(x)\rangle. \tag{1}$$

These c queries are all uniform superpositions over x, and require to query FX. From this state, Simon's algorithm is run reversibly, without measurements. After a Hadamard transform, the input registers contain a family of $\mathcal{O}(n)$ vectors, whose dimension is computed. If the dimension is smaller than n, then the function is likely to be periodic.

We say "likely" because there is some probability to fail. These failures do not disrupt the algorithm, as shown in [11,12,41].

These computations can be reverted and the state of Eq. 1 is obtained again. It can now be reverted to $|0\rangle$ by doing the same oracle queries to $F(y, x)$.

3.4   Offline-Simon

The offline-Simon algorithm of [12] can be seen as an optimization of Grover-meet-Simon, where all queries to $\mathsf{FX}_{k_1,k_2,k}$ are removed from the algorithm, except for the very first ones.

Crucially, the FX queries remain independent of the internal key guess y, and they are always made on the same uniform superposition $\sum_x |x\rangle$. Thus, we can consider that the following state:

$$|\psi\rangle = \bigotimes_{1 \le i \le c} \sum_x |x\rangle|\mathsf{FX}_{k_1,k_2,k}(x)\rangle,$$

is given to the test circuit and returned afterwards. Intuitively, the state $|\psi\rangle$ stores all the data on FX that is required to run the attack, in a very compact way, since it fits in $\mathcal{O}(n^2)$ qubits.

With the queries done once beforehand and reused through the algorithm, the analysis is slightly different, but $\mathcal{O}(n)$ queries are still sufficient to succeed [11,12].

Requirements. Not all Grover-meet-Simon instances can be made "offline". For this, we need the function $F(x, y)$ to have a special form, such as $F(x, y) = f(x) \oplus g(x, y)$ where f (FX in our case) is be the *offline* function, and g (E in our case) the *online* one. In that case, to find the single y_0 for which $F(\cdot, y_0)$ is periodic, it suffices to make $\mathcal{O}(n)$ queries to f at the beginning of the algorithm.

Offline-Simon and Q1 Attacks. As Offline-Simon uses only a polynomial number of queries, such queries can become very costly without significantly increasing the time cost of the algorithm. In particular, we can now replace the quantum queries by *classical queries* and obtain interesting time-data trade-offs. We will keep the example of FX, taken from [12], with a κ-bit internal key and a block size of n bits. We assume that the adversary can make $D \leq 2^n$ chosen-plaintext queries to FX.

With the offline-Simon algorithm, we proceed as follows. We let $D = 2^u$ for some u, and $k_1 = k_1^l \| k_1^r$, where k_1^l is a subkey of u bits. We define a function with a "reduced codebook":

$$\begin{cases} G : \{0,1\}^u \times \{0,1\}^{n-u} \times \{0,1\}^n \to \{0,1\}^n \\ x, y_1, y_2 \mapsto \mathsf{FX}_{k_1,k_2,k}(x\|0_{n-u}) \oplus E_{y_2}(x\|y_1) \end{cases}$$

The key observation is that $G(\cdot, y_1, y_2)$ is periodic if and only if $y_1, y_2 = k_1^r, k$. In other words, part of the key will be handled by the quantum search, and part of it by the Simon subroutine.

We query $\mathsf{FX}_{k_1,k_2,k}(x\|0_{n-u})$ for all x. We use this data to produce "manually" the query states. This requires $\widetilde{\mathcal{O}}(2^u)$ operations, but *in fine*, no Q2 queries at all. Next, the offline-Simon algorithm searches for the right value of k_1^r, k. This requires $\mathcal{O}(2^{(n+\kappa-u)/2})$ iterations and $\mathcal{O}(n^\omega 2^{(n+\kappa-u)/2})$ total time.

We end up with a time-data trade-off $D \cdot T^2 = \widetilde{\mathcal{O}}(2^{n+\kappa})$, valid for $D \leq 2^n$. This means that for a given D, we get a time $T = \widetilde{\mathcal{O}}\left(\sqrt{\frac{2^{n+\kappa}}{D}}\right)$, the square-root of the classical $T = \mathcal{O}(2^{n+\kappa}/D)$. However, while the classical attacks need D memory, the quantum attack uses only $\mathcal{O}(n^2)$ qubits to store the database. This shows that Simon's algorithm is a crucial tool for this attack.

4   New Result and Applications

In this section, we show the 2.5 gap between a classical security proof (in the ideal model) and a quantum attack. Our target is a slightly more general construction than 2XOR, that we denote by EFX, for "extended FX".

4.1   The EFX Construction and Its Security

Given two independent n-bit block ciphers E^1, E^2, of key size κ, and two n-bit whitening keys k_1, k_2, $\mathsf{EFX}_{k,k_1,k_2}[E^1, E^2]$ (or EFX_{k,k_1,k_2} for short) is an n-bit block cipher with $2n + \kappa$ bits of key (Fig. 4):

$$\mathsf{EFX}_{k,k_1,k_2}(x) = E_k^2\left(k_2 \oplus E_k^1(k_1 \oplus x)\right).$$

The 2XOR construction is a special case of EFX in which E^1 and E^2 are the same block cipher E under different keys $k, k' = \pi(k)$.

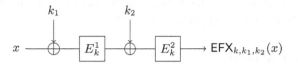

Fig. 4. The "extended FX" construction EFX.

Classical Attack on EFX. The best attack on EFX runs in time $\mathcal{O}(2^{\kappa+n/2})$: one guesses the key k, then attacks the Even-Mansour cipher in time $2^{n/2}$. In fact, this is the same classical attack as for the FX construction with a slight change: after guessing the key, one has to perform reverse queries of the additional block cipher on the known ciphertext values.

Just like the attack on FX, only $2^{n/2}$ known-plaintext queries are required for this (using the slidex attack on Even-Mansour [22]). However, having access to the whole codebook of EFX does not seem to bring any improvement on the key-recovery since we'll still have to make matching queries to the additional block cipher.

More generally, let D and T be the number of online and offline queries respectively, the best attack runs in $DT = \mathcal{O}(2^{\kappa+n})$ for $D \leq 2^{n/2}$ or else $T = \mathcal{O}(2^{\kappa+n/2})$ for $D \geq 2^{n/2}$.

Classical Proof of Security. The classical attack that we sketched above is essentially the best possible in the ideal cipher model. This can be deduced by the combination of the classical FX security bound [37] and the one derived by Gaži and Tessaro [25]. In Sect. 5 we also give a new proof of Theorem 2 that derives both of these bounds in a single go.

Theorem 2. *Consider the EFX construction (Fig. 4) and its sPRP game with n-bit state size and κ-bit ideal blockcipher key. An adversary $\mathcal{A}$ making D online queries and T offline queries has an advantage bounded by both:*

$$\mathbf{Adv}^{sprp}(\mathcal{A}) \leq \frac{3}{2} \cdot \frac{TD}{2^{\kappa+n}} + \left(\frac{T^2D}{2^{2\kappa+2n}}\right)^{\frac{1}{3}}$$

$$+ \left(\frac{2^{4n}T^2D}{2^{2(\kappa+1)}(2^n - D + 1)^3(2^n - (T/D \cdot 2^{2n}/2^\kappa)^{1/3} - D + 1)^3}\right)^{\frac{1}{3}}$$

and:

$$\mathbf{Adv}^{sprp}(\mathcal{A}) \leq \frac{3}{2} \cdot \frac{T}{2^{\kappa+n/2}}$$

Corollary 1. *Consider the EFX construction (Fig. 4) and its sPRP game. To obtain an $\Omega(1)$ advantage, it is required to have both $DT = \Omega(2^{\kappa+n})$ and $T = \Omega(2^{\kappa+n/2})$.*

Quantum Proof of Security. In Sect. 5.3, we study analogously the security in the *quantum ideal cipher model*. We show that any quantum algorithm must make at least $\mathcal{O}(2^{\kappa/2})$ queries to EFX and its block ciphers to distinguish EFX from a random permutation, with constant probability of success. Our attack matches the bound (up to a polynomial factor).

4.2 Quantum Attacks

We can now explain how to attack EFX in the quantum setting.

Theorem 3. *There exists a quantum attack that, given 2^u classical chosen-plaintext queries to EFX, finds the complete key k, k_1, k_2 of the cipher in quantum time $\mathcal{O}\left(n2^u + n^\omega 2^{(\kappa+n-u)/2}\right)$. It succeeds with overwhelming probability when E^1, E^2 are chosen u.a.r.*

Proof. The attack is very similar to the offline-Simon attack on FX given in Sect. 3.4. We write $k_1 = k_1^l \| k_1^r$ where k_1^l is of u bits and k_1^r is of $n - u$ bits. We query the cipher on inputs of the form $x = * \| 0_{n-u}$, which take all u-bit prefixes, and are zero otherwise. We then use a quantum search over the complete key k (κ bits) and k_1^r.

The only difference with the FX attack is in the way we test a guess y_1, y_2 of k_1^r, k. The database of queries now contains:

$$\bigotimes_i \sum_{x \in \{0,1\}^u} |x\rangle |\mathsf{EFX}(x \| 0_{n-u})\rangle = \bigotimes_i \sum_{x \in \{0,1\}^u} |x\rangle |E_k^2(k_2 \oplus E_k^1(k_1^l \oplus x \| k_1^r))\rangle.$$

This means that given our guess y_1, y_2, we cannot just XOR the value of $E_{y_2}^1(x \| y_1)$ in place as we did before, because of the call to E_k^2.

Fortunately, since we have guessed y_2 (that is, the key k), we can map *in place*:

$$\sum_{x \in \{0,1\}^u} |x\rangle |E_k^2(k_2 \oplus E_k^1(k_1^l \oplus x \| k_1^r))\rangle$$

$$\mapsto \sum_{x \in \{0,1\}^u} |x\rangle |(E_{y_2}^2)^{-1}\left(E_k^2(k_2 \oplus E_k^1(k_1^l \oplus x \| k_1^r))\right)\rangle,$$

which, when $y_2 = k$, is exactly:

$$\sum_{x \in \{0,1\}^u} |x\rangle |k_2 \oplus E_k^1(k_1^l \oplus x \| k_1^r)\rangle.$$

From there, we can XOR $E_{y_2}^1(x \| y_1)$ into the register and see if the function obtained is periodic. Both operations (the XOR and the permutation) are reversed afterwards, and we can move on to the next iteration.

While the periodic function can have additional collisions, its output size (n bits) is actually larger than its input size (u bits). Thus, with overwhelming probability, these collisions have no influence on the algorithm [11].   □

In particular, when $\kappa = 2n$ and using 2^{n-1} classical queries, the attack would run in time $\mathcal{O}(n^\omega 2^n)$, compared to the classical $\mathcal{O}(2^{5n/2})$.

Remark 1. For a given y_2, E_{y_2} is a permutation of known specification, of which we can compute the inverse. Thus the mapping $|z\rangle \mapsto |E_{y_2}(z)\rangle$ can be done in two steps using an ancillary register:

$$|z\rangle|0\rangle \mapsto |z\rangle|E_{y_2}(z)\rangle \mapsto |z \oplus E_{y_2}^{-1}(E_{y_2}(z))\rangle|E_{y_2}(z)\rangle = |0\rangle|E_{y_2}(z)\rangle.$$

For more details on the implementation of such functions, see [11].

Remark 2. If the second block cipher call is done at the beginning, and not at the end, the same attack can be done with chosen-ciphertext queries.

Let us note that within this attack, we are actually using offline-Simon to solve the following problem.

Problem 3. Given access to a function $f : \{0,1\}^n \rightarrow \{0,1\}^n$ and a family of permutations $g_y : \{0,1\}^n \rightarrow \{0,1\}^n$, indexed by $y \in \{0,1\}^\kappa$, such that there exists a single $y_0 \in \{0,1\}^\kappa$ such that $g_{y_0}(f)$ is periodic, find y_0.

In the FX attack, g_y was the permutation: $x \mapsto g_y(x) = x \oplus E_y(x)$. Here we simply apply in place another block cipher call, before XORing.

4.3 Attack with Known-Plaintext Queries

The presentation of offline-Simon in [11–13], which we followed in the previous section, constructs an *exact* starting database, that is, a superposition of tuples $(x, f(x))$ with all $x$es forming an affine space. Note that to construct such a vector space, there are some constraints on the queries. There are three scenarios to efficiently achieve this:

- The full codebook is queried,
- The queries are chosen,
- The queries are predictible and regular (for example, queries with a nonce incremented each time).

Hence, if we only have access to random known queries, we need to get the full codebook for our attack, which is a drastic limitation. In this section, we show that the algorithm still works if some values *are missing*. That is, instead of:

$$|\psi\rangle = \bigotimes_{i=0}^{c} \sum_{x \in \{0,1\}^n} |x\rangle|f(x)\rangle,$$

we start from $|\psi'\rangle = \bigotimes_{i=0}^{c} \sum_{x \in X} |x\rangle|f(x)\rangle + \sum_{x \notin X} |x\rangle|0\rangle,$

where $X \subsetneq \{0,1\}^n$ is the set of queries that we were allowed to make. In other words, we replace the missing output by the value 0.

Intuitively, if X is close to $\{0,1\}^n$, the algorithm should not see that. It is actually easy to show by treating offline-Simon as a black-box.

Lemma 1. *Consider an instance of* offline-Simon *with a starting database of* $c = \mathcal{O}(n)$ *states, that succeeds with probability p. Suppose that we now start from a database where a proportion α of queries is missing (that is, $|X| = (1 - \alpha)2^n$). Then* offline-Simon *still succeeds with probability at least $p(1 - \sqrt{2c\alpha})^2$.*

Proof. We can bound the distance between $|\psi\rangle$ and the $|\psi'\rangle$ defined above. Both are sums of 2^{nc} basis vectors with uniform amplitudes. There are less than $c\alpha2^{nc}$ such vectors that appear in $|\psi\rangle$ and that do not appear in $|\psi'\rangle$, and vice-versa, as the value of $f(x)$ is incorrect in each c states in $|\psi'\rangle$ for at most $\alpha2^n$ values. Thus:

$$\||\psi\rangle - |\psi'\rangle\|^2 \leq 2c\alpha \implies \||\psi\rangle - |\psi'\rangle\| \leq \sqrt{2c\alpha}.$$

Let $|\phi\rangle$ and $|\phi'\rangle$ be the states obtained after running offline-Simon with respectively $|\psi\rangle$ and $|\psi'\rangle$. We know that if we measure $|\phi\rangle$, we succeed with probability p. However, we are actually measuring $|\phi'\rangle$. We let $|\phi_e\rangle = |\phi'\rangle - |\phi\rangle$ the (non-normalized) error vector. We bound:

$$\langle\phi|\phi_e\rangle \leq \||\phi\rangle\|\||\phi'\rangle - |\phi\rangle\| = \||\psi'\rangle - |\psi\rangle\| \leq \sqrt{2c\alpha},$$

using the fact that a unitary operator (such as offline-Simon) preserves the euclidean distance. When measuring $|\phi'\rangle$, we project onto $|\phi\rangle$ with probability:

$$(1 - \langle\phi|\phi_e\rangle)^2 \geq (1 - \sqrt{2c\alpha})^2,$$

and in that case we succeed with probability p.

Remark 3. If $\alpha = \mathcal{O}(1/n)$, then offline-Simon succeeds with constant probability.

Note that Lemma 1 only matters when we cannot choose the missing queries, i.e., in a known-plaintext setting. In a chosen-plaintext setting, it would always be more efficient to directly query an affine space.

Attack on EFX. Thanks to Lemma 1, we can attack EFX with known-plaintext queries provided that we have almost all the codebook, bypassing the need for a vector space in the inputs.

Theorem 4. *There exists a quantum attack that, given $(1 - \mathcal{O}(1/n))2^n$ classical* known-plaintext *queries to* EFX*, finds the complete key k, k_1, k_2 of the cipher in quantum time $\mathcal{O}\left(n2^n + n^\omega 2^{\kappa/2}\right)$.*

In particular, we can also attack an even more generic version of EFX, with three calls to independent block ciphers E^1, E^2, E^3. We call it DEFX, for *doubly-extended FX* (see Fig. 2):

$$\mathsf{DEFX}(x) = E_k^3(k_2 \oplus E_k^2(k_1 \oplus E_k^1(x))).$$

In this version, it suffices to remark that $\mathsf{DEFX}(x) = \mathsf{EFX}(E_k^1(x))$. We build states of the form $\sum_x |x\rangle|\mathsf{DEFX}(x)\rangle$ containing almost all the codebook. When we have guessed the right key k, we can map these states to:

$$\sum_x |E_k^1(x)\rangle|\mathsf{EFX}(E_k^1(x))\rangle = \sum_{x'} |x'\rangle|\mathsf{EFX}(x')\rangle,$$

by applying E_k^1 in place on the first register, and continue the attack as before.

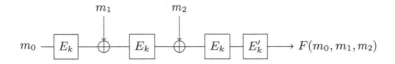

Fig. 5. Three-block ECBC-MAC.

4.4 Applications

The 2XOR-Cascade (2XOR for short) of [25] is an instance of EFX, and the results of Sect. 4.2 immediately apply. This construction can also appear in other situations.

Encrypt-Last-Block-CBC-MAC with Unknown Plaintexts. ECBC-MAC is an ISO standard [31, MAC algorithm 2], variant of CBC-MAC, where the output of CBC-MAC is reencrypted.

Let us consider a three-block ECBC-MAC (Fig. 5):

$$m_0, m_1, m_2 \mapsto F(m_0, m_1, m_2) = E'_k(E_k(m_2 \oplus E_k(m_1 \oplus E_k(m_0)))),$$

with a block cipher E of n bits, $2n$ bits of key k, and $k' = \phi(k)$ is derived from k. Assume that the adversary observes $F(m_0, m_1, m_2)$ for known values of m_0 (for example, a nonce) and *fixed, but unknown* values of m_1, m_2.

Then the problem of recovering k, m_1, m_2 altogether is equivalent to attacking a DEFX construction where the cascade encryption with two different keys derived from k is seen as another blockcipher with key k: $E'_k(E_k(x)) = E_k^2(x)$. More precisely, we assume that the adversary can query for $2^n(1 - \alpha)$ values of m_0, where $\alpha = \mathcal{O}(1/n)$. In that case, Corollary 1 implies that any classical attack will require $\mathcal{O}(2^{5n/2})$ computations. Our quantum attack has a time complexity $\mathcal{O}(n^\omega 2^n)$.

This means that, up to a polynomial factor, it is no harder for the quantum adversary to recover the key of this ECBC-MAC instance, although only the first block is known, than it would be in a chosen-plaintext scenario (where a direct quantum search of k becomes possible).

This enhanced key-recovery attack applies as well if the first block is a nonce that the adversary does not choose (as soon as he is allowed $(1 - \mathcal{O}(1/n))2^n$ queries).

Iterated Even-Mansour Ciphers. A natural setting where this construction will occur is with iterated Even-Mansour ciphers with r rounds, such as the one represented in Fig. 6. They have been considered in a variety of contexts. In particular, a classical cryptanalysis of all 4-round such ciphers with two keys k_0, k_1, for all sequences of k_0 and k_1, is given in [21] (Table 2). For 4 rounds and two keys, offline-Simon does not seem to bring a more than quadratic improvement in any case. However, if the number of rounds increases, we can schedule the keys in order to reproduce a DEFX construction, for example with:

$$k_0, k_0, k_1, k_0, k_1, k_0.$$

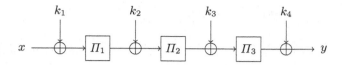

Fig. 6. An iterated Even-Mansour cipher with 4 keys. The Π_i are independent n-bit permutations.

Here the best classical attack seems to be guessing k_0, then breaking the Even-Mansour scheme, in time $2^{3n/2}$. By Theorem 3, the quantum attack runs in time $\widetilde{\mathcal{O}}(2^{2n/3})$ which represents a more-than-quadratic speedup.

While such constructions have been proposed, they tend to avoid these unfavorable key schedules. The LED-128 block cipher [27], which can be analyzed as an iterated Even-Mansour scheme [20], alternates only between its two subkeys k_0 and k_1. Also, note that in these applications, the quantum attacks do not go below the classical query complexity lower bound ($\mathcal{O}(2^{nr/(r+1)})$ for r-round Even-Mansour ciphers).

5   Proving Security

In this section, we show classical and quantum lower bounds on the security of EFX. We start with a classical proof of sPRP security.

5.1   Security Game

We want to prove the super Pseudorandom property of the EFX construction based on ideal ciphers. That means we allow an hypothetic adversary to do forward and inverse queries to ideal cipher oracles as well as an encryption oracle. In the real world, the three keys k, k_1, k_2 are first randomly drawn then the encryption oracle also makes use of the ideal cipher oracles to compute the output. In the ideal world, a new permutation is randomly drawn and used to produce the output. This is the sPRP security game as in Definition 1.

Definition 1 (sPRP Security). *Let $E_{1,k}(a)$ and $E_{2,k}(a)$ be two ideal ciphers with κ-bit key k and n-bit input a, and $\mathcal{P}$ be the set of all n to n bit permutations. The sPRP security game advantage of an adversary for the EFX construction is defined as:*

$$\mathbf{Adv}_{EFX}^{sprp}(\mathcal{A}) = \mathbf{Pr}(\mathcal{A}^{E_{\cdot,\cdot}^{1/-1}(\cdot),EFX_{k,k_1,k_2}^{1/-1}(\cdot)} \to 1) - \mathbf{Pr}(\mathcal{A}^{E_{\cdot,\cdot}^{1/-1}(\cdot),p^{1/-1}(\cdot)} \to 1) .$$

with the randomness of $k, k_1, k_2 \xleftarrow{\$} \{0,1\}^{\kappa+2n}$, $p \xleftarrow{\$} \mathcal{P}$, the ideal ciphers E_1, E_2, and $\mathcal{A}$.

Then, the sPRP security is the maximum advantage over all adversaries $\mathcal{A}$.

Transcript. As the adversary makes queries to the oracles we record the interactions in a transcript. We denote $\mathcal{X}$ the set of all inputs of encryption queries and outputs of decryption queries with $D = |\mathcal{X}|$ the number of online queries. Conversely, $\mathcal{Y}$ is the set of all outputs of encryption and input of decryption. And $\mathcal{Q}_i^j$ is the set of all inputs of forward queries and output of backward queries to the ideal cipher E_j parametrized with the key i with $T_i^j = |\mathcal{Q}_i^j|$ and $T = \sum_{i \in \{0,1\}^\kappa; j \in \{1,2\}} T_i^j$ the total number of offline queries.

At the end of the interaction with the oracles, we help the adversary by providing additional information before the output decision. Hence we define the final transcript τ as:

$$\tau = \{k, k_1, k_2\} \cup \{(x, u, y), \forall x \in \mathcal{X}\} \cup \bigcup_{i \in \{0,1\}^\kappa; j \in \{1,2\}} \{(a, b), \forall a \in \mathcal{Q}_i^j\}$$

where $b = E_{j,i}(a)$ in both real and ideal worlds. In the real world,

$$y = \text{EFX}_{k,k_1,k_2}(x) = k_2 \oplus E_{2,k}(k_1 \oplus E_{1,k}(x))$$

and, after interaction, we provide for the keys k, k_1, k_2 as well as the intermediary values $u = E_{1,k}(x)$ for all $x \in \mathcal{X}$. In the ideal world, $y = p(x)$ that is the output of a randomly chosen permutation and we simulate the keys and intermediate values after interaction as in Algorithm 2.

5.2   H-coefficient Technique

To prove Theorem 2, we will use the H-coefficient technique of Theorem 5.

Theorem 5 (H-coefficient technique). *Let $\mathcal{A}$ be a fixed computationally unbounded deterministic adversary that has access to either the real world oracle $\mathcal{O}_{\text{re}}$ or the ideal world oracle $\mathcal{O}_{\text{id}}$. Let $\Theta = \Theta_g \sqcup \Theta_b$ be some partition of the set of all attainable transcripts into* good *and* bad *transcripts. Suppose there exists $\epsilon_{\text{ratio}} \geq 0$ such that for any $\tau \in \Theta_g$,*

$$\frac{\mathbf{Pr}(X_{\text{re}} = \tau)}{\mathbf{Pr}(X_{\text{id}} = \tau)} \geq 1 - \epsilon_{\text{ratio}},$$

and there exists $\epsilon_{\text{bad}} \geq 0$ such that $\mathbf{Pr}(X_{\text{id}} \in \Theta_b) \leq \epsilon_{\text{bad}}$. Then,

$$\mathbf{Pr}(\mathcal{A}^{\mathcal{O}_{\text{re}}} \to 1) - \mathbf{Pr}(\mathcal{A}^{\mathcal{O}_{\text{id}}} \to 1) \leq \epsilon_{\text{ratio}} + \epsilon_{\text{bad}}. \tag{2}$$

Bad Transcripts. A transcript is said to be bad when Algorithm 2 return the empty set or when $T_k^1 + T_k^2 > \alpha T/2^\kappa$ for some value α to be determined later. Equivalently, a transcript is said to be bad when either $T_k^1 + T_k^2 > \alpha T/2^\kappa$ or $\exists (a, b, x) \in \mathcal{Q}_k^1 \times \mathcal{Q}_k^2 \times \mathcal{X} : a = b \oplus k_1, E_{1,k}(x) = a$ or $\exists (a, b, y) \in \mathcal{Q}_k^1 \times \mathcal{Q}_k^2 \times \mathcal{Y} :$ $a = b \oplus k_1, y = E_{2,k}(b)$ or $\exists (x, a) \in (\mathcal{X} \cap \mathcal{Q}_k^1) \times \mathcal{Q}_k^2 : E_{1,k}(a) = p(x) \oplus k_2$.

Firstly, we bound the probability of $T_k^1 + T_k^2 > \alpha T/2^\kappa$ with the randomness of k using the Markov inequality:

$$\mathbf{Pr}(T_k^1 + T_k^2 > \alpha T/2^\kappa) \leq 1/\alpha \tag{3}$$

Algorithm 2. Building Ideal Transcripts

1: **input:** $\{(x, p(x)), \forall x \in \mathcal{X}\} \cup \bigcup_{i \in \{0,1\}^\kappa} \{(a, E_{t,i}(a)), \forall a \in \mathcal{Q}_i^t, t \in \{1,2\}\}$.
2: **output:** $\{k, k_1, k_2\} \cup \{(x, u), \forall x \in \mathcal{X}\}$.
3: **procedure** IDEALTRANSCRIPT
4:      $\{k, k_1, k_2\} \xleftarrow{\$} \{0,1\}^{n+2\kappa}$
5:      $\tau^* \leftarrow \{k, k_1, k_2\}$
6:      $\mathcal{U} \leftarrow \emptyset$
7:      **for all** $a \in \mathcal{Q}_k^1$ **do**
8:          $\mathcal{U} \leftarrow \mathcal{U} \cup \{E_{1,k}(a)\}$
9:      **end for**
10:     **for all** $a \in \mathcal{Q}_k^2$ **do**
11:         **if** $a \oplus k_1 \in \mathcal{U}$ **then**
12:             **if** $E_{1,k}^{-1}(a \oplus k_1) \in \mathcal{X}$ or $\exists x \in \mathcal{X} : E_{2,k}(a) \oplus k_2 = p(x)$ **then**
13:                 **return** $\emptyset$ ▷ Bad Event
14:             **end if**
15:         **else**
16:             $\mathcal{U} \leftarrow \mathcal{U} \cup \{a \oplus k_1\}$
17:         **end if**
18:     **end for**
19:     **for all** $x \in \mathcal{X}$ **do**
20:         **if** $x \in \mathcal{Q}_k^1$ and $\exists a \in \mathcal{Q}_k^2 : E_{2,k}(a) = p(x) \oplus k_2$ **then**
21:             **return** $\emptyset$ ▷ Bad Event
22:         **else if** $x \in \mathcal{Q}_k^1$ **then**
23:             $\tau^* \leftarrow \tau^* \cup \{(x, E_{1,k}(x))\}$
24:         **else if** $\exists a \in \mathcal{Q}_k^2 : E_k(a) = p(x) \oplus k_2$ **then**
25:             $\tau^* \leftarrow \tau^* \cup \{(x, a \oplus k_1)\}$
26:         **else**
27:             $u \xleftarrow{\$} \{0,1\}^n / \mathcal{U}$
28:             $\mathcal{U} \leftarrow \mathcal{U} \cup \{u\}$
29:             $\tau^* \leftarrow \tau^* \cup \{(x, u)\}$
30:         **end if**
31:     **end for**
32:     **return** τ^*
33: **end procedure**

Then we bound the probability of $\exists (a, b, x) \in \mathcal{Q}_k^1 \times \mathcal{Q}_k^2 \times \mathcal{X} : a = b \oplus k_1, E_{1,k}(x) = a$ with the randomness of k and k_1:

$$\mathbf{Pr}(\exists (a, b, x) \in \mathcal{Q}_k^1 \times \mathcal{Q}_k^2 \times \mathcal{X} : a = b \oplus k_1, E_{1,k}(x) = a)$$

$$= \sum_{i \in \{0,1\}^\kappa} \mathbf{Pr}(\exists (a, b, x) \in \mathcal{Q}_i^1 \times \mathcal{Q}_i^2 \times \mathcal{X} : a = b \oplus k_1, E_{1,i}(x) = a)\mathbf{Pr}(k = i)$$

$$\leq 2^{-\kappa} \sum_{i \in \{0,1\}^\kappa} \min\left(\frac{\min(T_i^1, D) \cdot T_i^2}{2^n}, 1\right)$$

$$\leq 2^{-\kappa-n} \sum_{i \in \{0,1\}^\kappa} \min\left(T_i^1 \cdot T_i^2, D \cdot T_i^2, 2^n\right)$$

As we wish to get a born depending on T but not on the repartition of the offline queries T_i^j, we assume the worst case that is the repartition giving the highest value. Notice that $\sum_i (T_i^1 \cdot T_i^2)$ can be optimized by maximizing a few terms. In our case, we obtain an upper-bound by letting $T_i^1 = T_i^2 = \min(D, 2^{n/2})$ for $T/(2 \cdot \min(D, 2^{n/2}))$ different values of i and $T_i^1 = T_i^2 = 0$ otherwise (the strategy of optimizing the values up to $\max(2^n/D, 2^{n/2})$ gives the same bound.):

$$\mathbf{Pr}(\exists (a, b, x) \in \mathcal{Q}_k^1 \times \mathcal{Q}_k^2 \times \mathcal{X} : a = b \oplus k_1, E_{1,k}(x) = a) \leq \frac{T \cdot \min(D, 2^{n/2})}{2^{\kappa+n+1}} \quad (4)$$

We can derive the same bound the same way for the two remaining bad events $\exists (a, b, y) \in \mathcal{Q}_k^1 \times \mathcal{Q}_k^2 \times \mathcal{Y} : a = b \oplus k_1, y = E_{2,k}(b)$ and $\exists (x, a) \in (\mathcal{X} \cap \mathcal{Q}_k^1) \times \mathcal{Q}_k^2 : E_{1,k}(a) = p(x) \oplus k_2$. Putting it together:

$$\epsilon_{\text{bad}} = \mathbf{Pr}(\tau \text{ is bad}) \leq \frac{1}{\alpha} + 3 \frac{T \cdot \min(D, 2^{n/2})}{2^{\kappa+n+1}} \quad (5)$$

Good Transcripts. Assuming that τ is a good transcript, we want to upper-bound the ratio between the probabilities of τ happening in the real world and in the ideal world. Let $\mathcal{A} = \{E_{2,k}(a) \oplus k_2 : a \in \mathcal{Q}_k^2\}$ and $\mathcal{B} = \{E_{1,k}(b) \oplus k_1 : b \in \mathcal{Q}_k^1\}$.

In the real world, the probability comes from the drawing of the keys and from every fresh queries to the ideal block cipher oracles:

$$1/\mathbf{Pr}(X_{\text{re}} = \tau) =$$

$$2^{\kappa+2n} \left(\prod_{i \in \{0,1\}^n/\{k\}; j \in \{1,2\}} (2^n)_{(T_i^j)} \right) \left((2^n)_{(|\mathcal{Q}_k^1 \cup \mathcal{X}|)} \cdot (2^n)_{(|\mathcal{A} \cup \mathcal{Y}|)} \right)$$

In the ideal world, the probability comes from the ideal block cipher oracles, the encryption oracle and Algorithm 2:

$$1/\mathbf{Pr}(X_{\text{id}} = \tau) =$$

$$2^{\kappa+2n} \left(\prod_{i \in \{0,1\}^\kappa; j \in \{1,2\}} (2^n)_{(T_i^j)} \right) \left((2^n)_{(D)} \cdot (2^n - |\mathcal{B} \cup \mathcal{Q}_k^2|)_{(D - |\mathcal{Q}_k^1 \cap \mathcal{X}| - |\mathcal{A} \cap \mathcal{Y}|)} \right)$$

Putting it together:

$$\frac{\mathbf{Pr}(X_{\text{re}} = \tau)}{\mathbf{Pr}(X_{\text{id}} = \tau)} \geq \frac{(2^n)_{(T_k^1)} (2^n)_{(T_k^2)} (2^n)_{(D)} (2^n - |\mathcal{B} \cup \mathcal{Q}_k^2|)_{(D - |\mathcal{Q}_k^1 \cap \mathcal{X}| - |\mathcal{A} \cap \mathcal{Y}|)}}{(2^n)_{(|\mathcal{Q}_k^1 \cup \mathcal{X}|)} (2^n)_{(|\mathcal{A} \cup \mathcal{Y}|)}}$$

$$\geq \frac{(2^n)_{(T_k^1)} (2^n)_{(T_k^2)} (2^n)_{(D)} (2^n - T_k^1 - T_k^2 + |\mathcal{B} \cap \mathcal{Q}_k^2|)_{(D - |\mathcal{Q}_k^1 \cap \mathcal{X}| - |\mathcal{A} \cap \mathcal{Y}|)}}{(2^n)_{(D + T_k^1 - |\mathcal{Q}_k^1 \cap \mathcal{X}|)} (2^n)_{(D + T_k^2 - |\mathcal{A} \cap \mathcal{Y}|)}}$$

$$\geq \frac{(2^n)_{(T_k^1)} (2^n)_{(T_k^2)} (2^n)_{(D)} (2^n - T_k^1 - T_k^2)_{(D - |\mathcal{Q}_k^1 \cap \mathcal{X}| - |\mathcal{A} \cap \mathcal{Y}|)}}{(2^n)_{(D + T_k^1 - |\mathcal{Q}_k^1 \cap \mathcal{X}|)} (2^n)_{(D + T_k^2 - |\mathcal{A} \cap \mathcal{Y}|)}}$$

First notice that when $D = 2^n$ then $\mathcal{X} = \mathcal{Y} = \{0,1\}^n$ and we have $\frac{\Pr(X_{\mathrm{re}}=\tau)}{\Pr(X_{\mathrm{id}}=\tau)} \geq 1$. Thus we can derive a first bound independent of D ignoring the first bad event (or taking a very high α):

$$\mathbf{Adv}^{\mathrm{sprp}}_{\mathrm{EFX}}(\mathcal{A}) \leq 3\frac{T}{2^{\kappa+n/2+1}}$$

We have to work a bit more to get a bound for when $D \leq 2^{n/2}$:

$$\begin{aligned}
\frac{\Pr(X_{\mathrm{re}}=\tau)}{\Pr(X_{\mathrm{id}}=\tau)} &\geq \frac{(2^n)_{(T_k^1)}(2^n)_{(T_k^2)}(2^n)_{(D)}(2^n-T_k^1-T_k^2)_{(D)}}{(2^n)_{(D+T_k^1)}(2^n)_{(D+T_k^2)}} \\[2mm]
&\geq \frac{(2^n)_{(D)}(2^n-T_k^1-T_k^2)_{(D)}}{(2^n-T_k^1)_{(D)}(2^n-T_k^2)_{(D)}} \\[2mm]
&\geq \left(\frac{(2^n-D+1)(2^n-T_k^1-T_k^2-D+1)}{(2^n-T_k^1-D+1)(2^n-T_k^2-D+1)}\right)^D \\[2mm]
&\geq \left(1+\frac{T_k^1\cdot T_k^2}{(2^n-D+1)(2^n-T_k^1-T_k^2-D+1)}\right)^{-D} \\[2mm]
&\geq 1-\frac{D\cdot T_k^1\cdot T_k^2}{(2^n-D+1)(2^n-T_k^1-T_k^2-D+1)}
\end{aligned}$$

Adding the fact that $T_k^1 + T_k^2$ is upper-bounded by $\alpha T/2^\kappa$ we get:

$$\epsilon_{\mathrm{ratio}} \leq \frac{\alpha^2 T^2 D}{2^{2\kappa+2}(2^n-D+1)(2^n-\alpha T/2^\kappa-D+1)} \tag{6}$$

Conclusion. Hence using the H-coefficient Technique of Theorem 5 we get two upper-bound for the advantage of a classical information theoretic adversary. One mostly useful for $D \leq 2^{n/2}$:

$$\mathbf{Adv}^{\mathrm{sprp}}_{\mathrm{EFX}}(\mathcal{A}) \leq \frac{1}{\alpha}+3\frac{T\cdot\min(D,2^{n/2})}{2^{\kappa+n+1}}+\frac{\alpha^2 T^2 D}{2^{2\kappa+2}(2^n-D+1)(2^n-\alpha T/2^\kappa-D+1)}$$

And one independent of D:

$$\mathbf{Adv}^{\mathrm{sprp}}_{\mathrm{EFX}}(\mathcal{A}) \leq 3\frac{T}{2^{\kappa+n/2+1}}$$

Note that we are free to choose the value α to optimize the bound. We decided to take $1/\alpha = \left(T^2D/2^{2(\kappa+n)}\right)^{\frac{1}{3}}$ and that concludes the proof of Theorem 3.

5.3   Quantum Lower Bound

For completeness, we also prove quantum lower bounds on the security of EFX. The bounds we obtain are weak, in the sense that the security of the construct matches the security of its underlying primitive. However, they are also tight, as the offline-Simon algorithm makes for a matching upper bound.

We prove security in the *quantum ideal cipher model*, introduced in [30]. As for the ideal cipher model, we allow encryption and decryption queries to the block cipher $E^\pm$ and to the construction $C^\pm$. The only difference is that quantum queries are allowed, instead of classical queries. This means we prove security with quantum access to the construction $C^\pm$, which implies the bound when access to $C^\pm$ is only classical.

We note $\mathcal{C}(k, n)$ the distributions of n-bit block, k-bit key block ciphers, and $\mathcal{P}(n)$ the distribution of n-bit permutations. We will prove in this section the indistiguishability between $E^\pm, C^\pm$ with $E^\pm \in \mathcal{C}(k, n)$ and $E^\pm, P^\pm$ with $E^\pm \in \mathcal{C}(m, n)$ and $P^\pm \in \mathcal{P}(n)$ up to $2^{\kappa/2}$ queries.

We rely on the hardness of unstructured search:

Lemma 2 (Optimality of Grover's algorithm [50]). *Let D_0 be the degenerate distribution containing only the κ-bit input all-zero function, and D_1 be the distribution of κ-bit input boolean functions with only one output equal to 1. Then, for any quantum adversary $\mathcal{A}$ that does at most q queries,*

$$\mathbf{Adv}^{dist}_{D_0, D_1}(\mathcal{A}) \le \frac{4q^2}{2^\kappa}.$$

We will now reduce the problem of distinguishing the construction from a random permutation to the unstructured search distinguisher.

Lemma 3 (Distinguishing the EFX construction). *Let $E_1, E_2 \xleftarrow{\$} \mathcal{C}(\kappa, n)^2$, $P \xleftarrow{\$} \mathcal{P}(n)$, $K_1, K_2 \xleftarrow{\$} \{0, 1\}^{\kappa+n}$, $\mathsf{EFX} = E_2(K_1, E_1(K_1, x \oplus K_2) \oplus K_2)$. Then for any quantum adversary $\mathcal{A}$ that does at most q queries,*

$$\mathbf{Adv}^{dist}_{(E_1, E_2, \mathsf{EFX}),(E_1, E_2, P)}(\mathcal{A}) \le \frac{4q^2}{2^\kappa}.$$

Proof. We want to reduce this distinguishing problem to the previous one. First, as in the classical proof, we can remark that the distributions of E_1, E_2, EFX is equal to the distribution of F, E_2, P with $E_2 \xleftarrow{\$} \mathcal{C}(k, n)$, $P \xleftarrow{\$} \mathcal{P}(n)$, $F(K_1, x) = P(E_2^{-1}(K_1, x \oplus K_2) \oplus K_2)$, and for other K, $F(K, x) \xleftarrow{\$} \mathcal{P}(n)$.

Hence, we can consider the following construction: we take $E_1, E_2 \in \mathcal{C}(\kappa, n)^2$, $P \in \mathcal{P}(n)$, $f \in \{0, 1\}^\kappa \to \{0, 1\}$, $K_2 \in \{0, 1\}^n$. We can construct

$$F(K, x) = \begin{cases} P(E_2^{-1}(K, x \oplus K_2) \oplus K_2) & \text{if } f(K) = 1 \\ E_1(K, x) & \text{otherwise} \end{cases}.$$

Now, we can leverage Lemma 2 on the distribution of (F, E_2, P): if f is all-zero, we have the distribution of (E_1, E_2, P). If f has a unique 1, we have the distribution of (E_1, E_2, EFX). Hence, any adversary that distinguishes EFX can also distinguish unstructured search.

Remark 4. This proof can be directly adapted to the case where we only have one cipher, but two related keys are used.

Remark 5 (Tightness). This bound is tight when quantum query access is allowed. With only classical query access, the attack matches the bound only when $n \leq \kappa/2$. To prove security for smaller n (or with a lower amount of classical data), one could adapt the quantum security proofs for the FX construction [33], as the construction of interest is FX plus an additional encryption.

6   On the Maximal Gap

As we have recalled above, exponential speedups can be obtained when the quantum adversary can make superposition queries. For classical queries in symmetric cryptography, the best speedup remained quadratic for a long time. It is likely to remain polynomial, but as we manage to reach a 2.5 gap, it is natural to ask by how much we might extend it. In this section, we connect this question to known results in quantum query complexity. We show that the offline-Simon technique should be able to reach a cubic speedup, but without any cryptographic application at the moment.

Note that if we formulate the question only as "largest speedup when only classical queries are given", it will not properly represent the class of symmetric cryptography attacks that we are interested in. Indeed, Shor's algorithm provides an exponential speedup on a problem with only classical queries.

However, there is still a major difference, in that we are interested in constructions *with security proofs in the ideal model* (e.g., ideal ciphers, random oracles, random permutations). Here the definition of a *largest gap* is more reasonable: all the quantum speedups known are polynomial at best. Besides, we can focus on *query complexity* only, without making any consideration on the memory used or time efficiency of the algorithms.

6.1   Relation with Query Complexity

The question of finding the *largest possible gap* in our context bears some similarities with the question of comparing randomized and quantum query complexities of total boolean functions. In this setting, the best gap known is cubic, which follows from [2] and [7,46]. Initially, the technique of *cheat sheets* developed in [2] allowed the authors to obtain a gap 2.5. We will explain the reasons behind this coincidence.

Definitions. First of all, we need to recapitulate some essential definitions and results of query complexity. We will focus only on a very restricted subset of results. Let us consider a boolean function $f : \{0,1\}^N \rightarrow \{0,1\}$. The definition of f is known, and the only way to evaluate it is then to know some bits of its input string $x_0, \ldots, x_{N-1}$. Here, N can be thought of as an exponential number.

When f is defined over all its input, we call it a *total* function, as opposed to a *partial* function defined only over some domain $D \subseteq \{0,1\}^N$. For example, the $\mathsf{or}_N : \{0,1\}^n \to \{0,1\}$ function computes the OR of all its bits.

For any f, we define:

- the *deterministic* query complexity $D(f)$: the minimum number of queries that have to be made by a deterministic algorithm computing $f(x)$ on every input x;
- the *bounded-error randomized* query complexity $R(f)$: the minimum number of queries made by a randomized algorithm that outputs $f(x)$ with probability at least $2/3$ *on every input x*;
- the *quantum* query complexity $Q(f)$: the minimum number of queries made by a quantum algorithm that outputs $f(x)$ with probability $2/3$.

For example, the classical query complexity of or_N is N, and its quantum query complexity is $\Theta(\sqrt{N})$ (thanks to Grover's algorithm and its matching lower bound).

Clearly, we have in general $Q(f) \leq R(f) \leq D(f)$. In classical cryptography we are usually interested in the measure $R(f)$, and in post-quantum cryptography in $Q(f)$. It has been known for a long time that for *total* boolean functions, polynomial relations hold between these measures. In particular, Beals et al. [8] showed that for any total function f, $D(f) = \mathcal{O}(Q(f)^6)$, and so $R(f) = \mathcal{O}(Q(f)^6)$. This was improved very recently in [3] to $D(f) = \mathcal{O}(Q(f)^4)$ (and so $R(f) = \mathcal{O}(Q(f)^4)$). The quartic relation with $D(f)$ is tight (by a separation given in [4]), but the best proven gap with $R(f)$ is cubic only, and this is conjectured in [4] to be optimal.

Promise Problems. These results underlie the idea that quantum speedups "need structure": indeed, an exponential quantum speedup can occur only if f assumes some *promise* on its input (for example for Simon's algorithm, that it encodes a periodic function). Let us now take an example: the attack on EFX of Theorem 3.

Recovering the key of an EFX instance *could* be seen as computing a boolean function f with a promise. It would be done as follows: the input of the function encodes $\mathsf{EFX}_{k,k_1,k_2}[E](x)$ for all x and $E_z(x)$ for all (z,x); that is, the complete tables of the EFX cipher and the ideal cipher upon which it is built. The function must compute the key k, k_1, k_2 used in EFX. Although the second table (E) could be any value, since any block cipher can be selected at random, the function satisfies the promise that the first table actually encodes $\mathsf{EFX}[E]$.

There is, however, a significant difference between the query complexity of f and the security of EFX. The proof of security in the ideal cipher model reasons about adversaries as *average-case* algorithms. Similarly, the classical and quantum attacks work *on average* over all ciphers E. Typically, when running the Grover-meet-Simon attack, there are bad cases, corresponding to some rare choices of E, in which the algorithm will not be able to return the key. But the relations in query complexity concern only worst-case complexities. Indeed, it was shown in [5] that no polynomial relation holds between the average-case complexities of total functions. Our attack is an average-case algorithm, and so, we cannot say anything about $Q(f)$.

2.5 Separation Result. In [2], the authors proved the existence of a total function f for which $R(f) = \widetilde{\Omega}\left(N^{2.5}\right)$ and $Q(f) = \widetilde{\mathcal{O}}(N)$. Since this 2.5 exponent is reminiscent of ours, we briefly review how it was obtained.

The authors start by defining a function with a promise, by composing Forrelation (a promise problem) and And-Or (a boolean function which has a provable quadratic quantum speedup). We do not need to define Forrelation here. Simon's problem could have been used instead, as a speedup poly(n) vs. $\mathcal{O}\left(2^{n/2}\right)$ is sufficient.

By combining And-Ors of size N^2 with a Forrelation of size N, one obtains a quantum algorithm running in time $Q(f) = \widetilde{\mathcal{O}}(N)$, because Forrelation requires $\widetilde{\mathcal{O}}(1)$ queries and And-Or requires $\mathcal{O}(N)$ queries using Grover's algorithm. The corresponding classical algorithm runs in time $\widetilde{\mathcal{O}}\left(N^{2.5}\right)$, due to the gap in both problems. Next, the authors introduce a generic *cheat sheet* framework which allows to turn partial functions into total ones. The *cheat sheet* variant of a function f, f_{CS}, is more costly. But this additional cost comes from a *certificate* function, which checks if the input satisfies the promise. In the case studied in [2], the certificate simply consists in checking the outputs of the And-Ors, and checking that the Forrelation instance satisfies its promise: all of this can be done in quantum time $\widetilde{\mathcal{O}}(N)$. So the *cheat sheet* variant of the above function provides the said query complexity gap.

The offline-Simon attack does actually the opposite of the function above. Instead of computing a Simon instance out of many individual And-Or results, it computes an Or of many independent Simon instances: we are looking for the single periodic function in a family of functions. This is why the 2.5 exponents coincide.

Besides, since we want to make only classical queries, we have to pay an additional cost N corresponding to the classical queries to EFX. This additional cost coincides with the cost of verifying the Forrelation instance. This is why, similarly to the cheat sheet technique, the offline-Simon structure will allow a cubic gap at most. Yet, these are only similarities, as there is no connection between worst-case and average-case algorithms.

Cubic Separation Result. As written above, only a quartic relation between $Q(f)$ and $R(f)$ for total functions is proven, while the best separation known at the moment is cubic (and this is conjectured to be optimal). It stems from replacing the Forrelation problem in [2] by *k-fold forrelation* [1]. For any k, *k-fold forrelation* has a classical query complexity $\widetilde{\Omega}\left(2^{n(1-1/k)}\right)$ and a quantum query complexity $\mathcal{O}(k)$. This gap was conjectured in [1] and recently proven in [7,46]. Note that *k-fold forrelation* realizes an *optimal gap* between randomized and quantum query complexities for *partial* functions.

6.2   Improving the Gap in Offline-Simon

In full generality, the offline-Simon algorithm can be seen as an algorithm that:

- queries a construction F with unknown key, and populates a table with these queries
- searches for some secret key k using a quantum search where, in order to test a given k, queries to the table are made, and a *superposition attack* on some construction is launched.

In particular, when attacking FX with classical queries only, each iteration of the quantum search reproduces the attack on the Even-Mansour cipher – and uses Simon's algorithm. But we could take this design more generally, and replace the Even-Mansour attack by any other attack using superposition queries. Thus, there is a link between the maximal gap achievable by the offline strategy and the maximal gap of superposition attacks.

The gap in the Even-Mansour attack is $\mathsf{poly}(n)$ vs. $\mathcal{O}\big(2^{n/2}\big)$. We could try to increase it up to $\mathsf{poly}(n)$ vs. $\mathcal{O}(2^n)$. This is the best we can hope for, because we consider an n-bit construction: $\mathcal{O}(2^n)$ is its maximal query complexity. All exponential speedups in quantum cryptanalysis that we know to date, including Q2 attacks on symmetric primitives, and attacks on asymmetric schemes, are based on variants of Simon's and Shor's algorithms. The classical counterpart of these algorithm is a collision search and, as such, they only reach a speedup $\mathsf{poly}(n)$ vs. $\mathcal{O}\big(2^{n/2}\big)$ at best.

However, we can replace this problem by *k-fold forrelation*, and take advantage of its enhanced gap $\mathsf{poly}(n)$ vs. $\mathcal{O}\big(2^{n(1-\epsilon)}\big)$. We conjecture that this gives us a cubic speedup. However, forrelation is not a problem that arises naturally in cryptography. Finding a cryptographically relevant example of a gap between 2.5 and 3 is an interesting open question.

7   Conclusion

In this paper, we gave the first example of a more than quadratic speedup of a symmetric cryptanalytic attack in the classical query model. This 2.5 speedup is actually provable in the ideal cipher model. It is a direct counterexample to the folklore belief that *doubling the key sizes* of symmetric constructions is sufficient to protect against quantum attackers. In particular, generic key-length extension techniques should be carefully analyzed: the 2XOR Cascade proposed in [25] offers practically no additional security in the quantum setting.

The most obvious open question is by how much this gap may be increased. The algorithm we used, offline-Simon, does not seem capable of reaching more than a 2.5 gap. Although a cubic separation seems achievable, we couldn't manage to obtain one with problems of cryptographic interest. This is reminiscent of the cubic gap which is conjectured to be the best achievable between the randomized and quantum query complexities of total functions [2]. However, there is a stark difference between the problems at stake, and in our case, it is not even known if a polynomial relation holds in general.

References

1. Aaronson, S., Ambainis, A.: Forrelation: a problem that optimally separates quantum from classical computing. SIAM J. Comput. **47**(3), 982–1038 (2018)
2. Aaronson, S., Ben-David, S., Kothari, R.: Separations in query complexity using cheat sheets. In: STOC, pp. 863–876. ACM (2016)
3. Aaronson, S., Ben-David, S., Kothari, R., Tal, A.: Quantum implications of huang's sensitivity theorem. Electron. Colloquium Comput. Complex. **27**, 66 (2020)
4. Ambainis, A., Balodis, K., Belovs, A., Lee, T., Santha, M., Smotrovs, J.: Separations in query complexity based on pointer functions. In: STOC, pp. 800–813. ACM (2016)
5. Ambainis, A., de Wolf, R.: Average-case quantum query complexity. In: Reichel, H., Tison, S. (eds.) STACS 2000. LNCS, vol. 1770, pp. 133–144. Springer, Heidelberg (2000). https://doi.org/10.1007/3-540-46541-3_11
6. Anand, M.V., Targhi, E.E., Tabia, G.N., Unruh, D.: Post-quantum security of the CBC, CFB, OFB, CTR, and XTS modes of operation. In: Takagi, T. (ed.) PQCrypto 2016. LNCS, vol. 9606, pp. 44–63. Springer, Cham (2016). https://doi.org/10.1007/978-3-319-29360-8_4
7. Bansal, N., Sinha, M.: k-forrelation optimally separates quantum and classical query complexity. In: STOC, pp. 1303–1316. ACM (2021)
8. Beals, R., Buhrman, H., Cleve, R., Mosca, M., de Wolf, R.: Quantum lower bounds by polynomials. J. ACM **48**(4), 778–797 (2001)
9. Bennett, C.H.: Time/space trade-offs for reversible computation. SIAM J. Comput. **18**(4), 766–776 (1989)
10. Bonnetain, X.: Quantum key-recovery on Full AEZ. In: Adams, C., Camenisch, J. (eds.) SAC 2017. LNCS, vol. 10719, pp. 394–406. Springer, Cham (2018). https://doi.org/10.1007/978-3-319-72565-9_20
11. Bonnetain, X.: Tight bounds for Simon's algorithm. In: Longa, P., Ràfols, C. (eds.) LATINCRYPT 2021. LNCS, vol. 12912, pp. 3–23. Springer, Cham (2021). https://doi.org/10.1007/978-3-030-88238-9_1
12. Bonnetain, X., Hosoyamada, A., Naya-Plasencia, M., Sasaki, Yu., Schrottenloher, A.: Quantum attacks without superposition queries: the offline Simon's algorithm. In: Galbraith, S.D., Moriai, S. (eds.) ASIACRYPT 2019. LNCS, vol. 11921, pp. 552–583. Springer, Cham (2019). https://doi.org/10.1007/978-3-030-34578-5_20
13. Bonnetain, X., Jaques, S.: Quantum period finding against symmetric primitives in practice. IACR Trans. Cryptogr. Hardw. Embed. Syst. **2022**(1) (2021)
14. Bonnetain, X., Naya-Plasencia, M., Schrottenloher, A.: On quantum slide attacks. In: Paterson, K.G., Stebila, D. (eds.) SAC 2019. LNCS, vol. 11959, pp. 492–519. Springer, Cham (2020). https://doi.org/10.1007/978-3-030-38471-5_20
15. Bonnetain, X., Schrottenloher, A., Sibleyras, F.: Beyond quadratic speedups in quantum attacks on symmetric schemes. IACR Cryptology ePrint Archive, p. 1348 (2021)
16. Brassard, G., Hoyer, P., Mosca, M., Tapp, A.: Quantum amplitude amplification and estimation. Contemp. Math. **305**, 53–74 (2002)
17. Cid, C., Hosoyamada, A., Liu, Y., Sim, S.M.: Quantum cryptanalysis on contracting Feistel structures and observation on related-key settings. In: Bhargavan, K., Oswald, E., Prabhakaran, M. (eds.) INDOCRYPT 2020. LNCS, vol. 12578, pp. 373–394. Springer, Cham (2020). https://doi.org/10.1007/978-3-030-65277-7_17
18. Daemen, J.: Limitations of the Even-Mansour construction. In: Imai, H., Rivest, R.L., Matsumoto, T. (eds.) ASIACRYPT 1991. LNCS, vol. 739, pp. 495–498. Springer, Heidelberg (1993). https://doi.org/10.1007/3-540-57332-1_46

19. Dinur, I.: Cryptanalytic time-memory-data tradeoffs for FX-constructions with applications to PRINCE and PRIDE. In: Oswald, E., Fischlin, M. (eds.) EUROCRYPT 2015. LNCS, vol. 9056, pp. 231–253. Springer, Heidelberg (2015). https://doi.org/10.1007/978-3-662-46800-5_10

20. Dinur, I., Dunkelman, O., Keller, N., Shamir, A.: Key recovery attacks on 3-round Even-Mansour, 8-step LED-128, and Full AES[2]. In: Sako, K., Sarkar, P. (eds.) ASIACRYPT 2013. LNCS, vol. 8269, pp. 337–356. Springer, Heidelberg (2013). https://doi.org/10.1007/978-3-642-42033-7_18

21. Dinur, I., Dunkelman, O., Keller, N., Shamir, A.: Cryptanalysis of iterated Even-Mansour schemes with two keys. In: Sarkar, P., Iwata, T. (eds.) ASIACRYPT 2014. LNCS, vol. 8873, pp. 439–457. Springer, Heidelberg (2014). https://doi.org/10.1007/978-3-662-45611-8_23

22. Dunkelman, O., Keller, N., Shamir, A.: Minimalism in cryptography: the Even-Mansour scheme revisited. In: Pointcheval, D., Johansson, T. (eds.) EUROCRYPT 2012. LNCS, vol. 7237, pp. 336–354. Springer, Heidelberg (2012). https://doi.org/10.1007/978-3-642-29011-4_21

23. Even, S., Mansour, Y.: A construction of a cipher from a single pseudorandom permutation. J. Cryptol. 10(3), 151–161 (1997). https://doi.org/10.1007/s001459900025

24. Gaži, P., Lee, J., Seurin, Y., Steinberger, J., Tessaro, S.: Relaxing full-codebook security: a refined analysis of key-length extension schemes. In: Leander, G. (ed.) FSE 2015. LNCS, vol. 9054, pp. 319–341. Springer, Heidelberg (2015). https://doi.org/10.1007/978-3-662-48116-5_16

25. Gaži, P., Tessaro, S.: Efficient and optimally secure key-length extension for block ciphers via randomized cascading. In: Pointcheval, D., Johansson, T. (eds.) EUROCRYPT 2012. LNCS, vol. 7237, pp. 63–80. Springer, Heidelberg (2012). https://doi.org/10.1007/978-3-642-29011-4_6

26. Grover, L.K.: A fast quantum mechanical algorithm for database search. In: STOC, pp. 212–219. ACM (1996)

27. Guo, J., Peyrin, T., Poschmann, A., Robshaw, M.: The LED block cipher. In: Preneel, B., Takagi, T. (eds.) CHES 2011. LNCS, vol. 6917, pp. 326–341. Springer, Heidelberg (2011). https://doi.org/10.1007/978-3-642-23951-9_22

28. Hosoyamada, A., Sasaki, Y.: Cryptanalysis against symmetric-key schemes with online classical queries and offline quantum computations. In: Smart, N.P. (ed.) CT-RSA 2018. LNCS, vol. 10808, pp. 198–218. Springer, Cham (2018). https://doi.org/10.1007/978-3-319-76953-0_11

29. Hosoyamada, A., Sasaki, Y.: Quantum Demiric-Selçuk meet-in-the-middle attacks: applications to 6-round generic feistel constructions. In: Catalano, D., De Prisco, R. (eds.) SCN 2018. LNCS, vol. 11035, pp. 386–403. Springer, Cham (2018). https://doi.org/10.1007/978-3-319-98113-0_21

30. Hosoyamada, A., Yasuda, K.: Building quantum-one-way functions from block ciphers: Davies-Meyer and Merkle-Damgård constructions. In: Peyrin, T., Galbraith, S. (eds.) ASIACRYPT 2018. LNCS, vol. 11272, pp. 275–304. Springer, Cham (2018). https://doi.org/10.1007/978-3-030-03326-2_10

31. ISO Central Secretary: Information technology - Security techniques - Message Authentication Codes (MACs) - Part 1: Mechanisms using a block cipher. Standard ISO/IEC 9797–1:2011, International Organization for Standardization, Geneva, CH, March 2011. https://www.iso.org/standard/50375.html

32. Ito, G., Hosoyamada, A., Matsumoto, R., Sasaki, Y., Iwata, T.: Quantum chosen-ciphertext attacks against feistel ciphers. In: Matsui, M. (ed.) CT-RSA 2019. LNCS, vol. 11405, pp. 391–411. Springer, Cham (2019). https://doi.org/10.1007/978-3-030-12612-4_20

33. Jaeger, J., Song, F., Tessaro, S.: Quantum key-length extension. CoRR abs/2105.01242 (2021)

34. Kaplan, M., Leurent, G., Leverrier, A., Naya-Plasencia, M.: Breaking symmetric cryptosystems using quantum period finding. In: Robshaw, M., Katz, J. (eds.) CRYPTO 2016. LNCS, vol. 9815, pp. 207–237. Springer, Heidelberg (2016). https://doi.org/10.1007/978-3-662-53008-5_8

35. Kaplan, M., Leurent, G., Leverrier, A., Naya-Plasencia, M.: Quantum differential and linear cryptanalysis. IACR Trans. Symmetric Cryptol. **2016**(1), 71–94 (2016)

36. Kilian, J., Rogaway, P.: How to protect DES against exhaustive key search. In: Koblitz, N. (ed.) CRYPTO 1996. LNCS, vol. 1109, pp. 252–267. Springer, Heidelberg (1996). https://doi.org/10.1007/3-540-68697-5_20

37. Kilian, J., Rogaway, P.: How to protect DES against exhaustive key search (an analysis of DESX). J. Cryptol. **14**(1), 17–35 (2001)

38. Knill, E.: An analysis of bennett's pebble game. CoRR abs/math/9508218 (1995)

39. Kuwakado, H., Morii, M.: Quantum distinguisher between the 3-round feistel cipher and the random permutation. In: ISIT, pp. 2682–2685. IEEE (2010)

40. Kuwakado, H., Morii, M.: Security on the quantum-type even-mansour cipher. In: ISITA, pp. 312–316. IEEE (2012)

41. Leander, G., May, A.: Grover meets simon – quantumly attacking the FX-construction. In: Takagi, T., Peyrin, T. (eds.) ASIACRYPT 2017. LNCS, vol. 10625, pp. 161–178. Springer, Cham (2017). https://doi.org/10.1007/978-3-319-70697-9_6

42. Levin, R.Y., Sherman, A.T.: A note on Bennett's time-space tradeoff for reversible computation. SIAM J. Comput. **19**(4), 673–677 (1990)

43. Magniez, F., Nayak, A., Roland, J., Santha, M.: Search via quantum walk. SIAM J. Comput. **40**(1), 142–164 (2011)

44. National Academies of Sciences: Engineering, and Medicine: Quantum Computing: Progress and Prospects. The National Academies Press, Washington, DC (2018)

45. Nielsen, M.A., Chuang, I.: Quantum computation and quantum information (2002)

46. Sherstov, A.A., Storozhenko, A.A., Wu, P.: An optimal separation of randomized and quantum query complexity. In: STOC, pp. 1289–1302. ACM (2021)

47. Shor, P.W.: Algorithms for quantum computation: Discrete logarithms and factoring. In: FOCS, pp. 124–134. IEEE Computer Society (1994)

48. Simon, D.R.: On the power of quantum computation. SIAM J. Comput. **26**(5), 1474–1483 (1997)

49. Song, F., Yun, A.: Quantum security of NMAC and related constructions. In: Katz, J., Shacham, H. (eds.) CRYPTO 2017. LNCS, vol. 10402, pp. 283–309. Springer, Cham (2017). https://doi.org/10.1007/978-3-319-63715-0_10

50. Zalka, C.: Grover's quantum searching algorithm is optimal. Phys. Rev. A **60**(4), 2746 (1999)

Orientations and the Supersingular Endomorphism Ring Problem

Benjamin Wesolowski[1,2]([✉]) [ID]

[1] Univ. Bordeaux, CNRS, Bordeaux INP, IMB, UMR 5251, 33400 Talence, France
benjamin.wesolowski@math.u-bordeaux.fr
[2] INRIA, IMB, UMR 5251, 33400 Talence, France

Abstract. We study two important families of problems in isogeny-based cryptography and how they relate to each other: computing the endomorphism ring of supersingular elliptic curves, and inverting the action of class groups on oriented supersingular curves. We prove that these two families of problems are closely related through polynomial-time reductions, assuming the generalised Riemann hypothesis.

We identify two classes of essentially equivalent problems. The first class corresponds to the problem of computing the endomorphism ring of *oriented curves*. The security of a large family of cryptosystems (such as CSIDH) reduces to (and sometimes from) this class, for which there are heuristic quantum algorithms running in subexponential time. The second class corresponds to computing the endomorphism ring of *orientable curves*. The security of essentially all isogeny-based cryptosystems reduces to (and sometimes from) this second class, for which the best known algorithms are still exponential.

Some of our reductions not only generalise, but also strengthen previously known results. For instance, it was known that in the particular case of curves defined over $\mathbf{F}_p$, the security of CSIDH reduces to the endomorphism ring problem in subexponential time. Our reductions imply that the security of CSIDH is actually equivalent to the endomorphism ring problem, under polynomial time reductions (circumventing arguments that proved such reductions unlikely).

1 Introduction

We study two families of computational problems at the heart of isogeny-based cryptography, and how they relate to each other: computing the endomorphism ring of supersingular elliptic curves, and inverting the action of class groups on oriented supersingular curves. On one hand, the problem of computing endomorphism rings is of foundational importance to the field: its presumed hardness is necessary [GPST16, CPV20, FKM21] (and sometimes sufficient [CLG09, GPS20]) for the security of essentially all isogeny-based cryptosystems. On the other hand, the action of *ideal class groups* on sets of elliptic curves induces presumably hard inversion problems. This action, and the presumed hardness of its inversion, is the fertile ground upon which many cryptosystems have been built—from the

© International Association for Cryptologic Research 2022
O. Dunkelman and S. Dziembowski (Eds.): EUROCRYPT 2022, LNCS 13277, pp. 345–371, 2022.
https://doi.org/10.1007/978-3-031-07082-2_13

early work of Couveignes [Cou06], to CSIDH [CLM+18] and its many variants [CD20,BKV19,CS21]. Thanks to the notion of *orientation* introduced by Colò and Kohel [CK20], it has recently become clear that such actions play a ubiquitous role in isogeny-based cryptography. On one hand, orientations provide a framework that directly generalises the family of CSIDH-like cryptosystems. On the other hand, it has been identified [DDF+21] that even the security of cryptosystems where group actions were not expected, such as SIDH [JD11] and its variants, reduces to an action inversion problem, called the *Uber isogeny problem*, opening a new cryptanalytic avenue.

1.1   Oriented Endomorphism Ring Problems

Isogenies are morphisms between elliptic curves, and endomorphisms of an elliptic curve E are isogenies from E to itself. They form a ring, written $\mathrm{End}(E)$. Given a supersingular elliptic curve E over $\overline{\mathbf{F}}_p$, the endomorphism ring problem EndRing consists in computing a basis of $\mathrm{End}(E)$. This EndRing problem was proved in [Wes22] (and heuristically since [EHL+18]) to be equivalent to the problem of finding isogenies between supersingular elliptic curves, assuming the generalised Riemann hypothesis. Let $\mathfrak{O}$ be an order in a quadratic number field K. An orientation is an embedding

$$\iota : \mathfrak{O} \longhookrightarrow \mathrm{End}(E)$$

which cannot be extended to a superorder of $\mathfrak{O}$. We call (E, ι) an $\mathfrak{O}$-oriented elliptic curve, and E is $\mathfrak{O}$-orientable. We introduce three *oriented* variants of the endomorphism ring problem, in increasing order of hardness (precise definitions are provided in Sect. 4):

- $\mathfrak{O}$-EndRing: given an $\mathfrak{O}$-oriented elliptic curve (E, ι), compute a basis of $\mathrm{End}(E)$. It is presumably easier than EndRing since ι provides additional information.
- EndRing$|_{\mathfrak{O}}$: given an $\mathfrak{O}$-orientable elliptic curve E, compute a basis of $\mathrm{End}(E)$. It is simply the restriction of EndRing to $\mathfrak{O}$-orientable inputs.
- $\mathfrak{O}$-EndRing*: given an $\mathfrak{O}$-orientable E, compute a basis of $\mathrm{End}(E)$ together with an $\mathfrak{O}$-orientation expressed in this basis.

1.2   Class Group Action Problems

A key feature of $\mathfrak{O}$-orientations is that they induce a group action. Given an $\mathfrak{O}$-oriented (E, ι), and an invertible $\mathfrak{O}$-ideal $\mathfrak{a}$, one can construct another $\mathfrak{O}$-oriented elliptic curve $\mathfrak{a} \star (E, \iota) = (E^{\mathfrak{a}}, \iota^{\mathfrak{a}})$, and an isogeny $\varphi_{\mathfrak{a}} : E \to E^{\mathfrak{a}}$ connecting them. This construction induces a free action of the ideal class group $\mathrm{Cl}(\mathfrak{O})$ on $\mathfrak{O}$-oriented curves up to isomorphism. We define four variants of the problem of inverting this group action (precise definitions are provided in Sect. 3):

- $\mathfrak{O}$-Vectorization: given two $\mathfrak{O}$-oriented elliptic curves (E, ι) and (E', ι'), find an ideal $\mathfrak{a}$ such that E' is isomorphic to $E^{\mathfrak{a}}$. The *effective* variant asks for

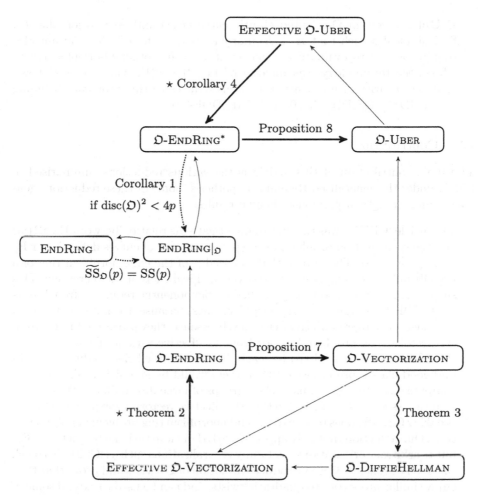

Fig. 1. Arrows represent probabilistic polynomial time reductions in the length of the instance (i.e., $\log p$, $\log(\mathrm{disc}(\mathfrak{O}))$, and the length of the provided $\mathfrak{O}$-orientations), and for those marked by a star $\star$, in $\#(\mathrm{Cl}(\mathfrak{O})[2])$, the size of the 2-torsion of the class group. Arrows with no reference (thin or dotted) are trivial reductions. Thick arrows assume that the factorisation of $\mathrm{disc}(\mathfrak{O})$ is known. Dotted arrows assume the stated condition. The "snake" arrow is a quantum reduction. $\mathrm{SS}(p)$ is the set of all supersingular elliptic curves over $\mathbf{F}_{p^2}$ (up to isomorphism), and $\widetilde{\mathrm{SS}}_{\mathfrak{O}}(p)$ is the subset of $\mathfrak{O}$-orientable curves. Non-trivial reductions assume the generalised Riemann hypothesis.

the isomorphism to preserve the orientation, and also requires a way to evaluate the action of $\mathfrak{a}$ on any other $\mathfrak{O}$-oriented curve. The *vectorization* terminology comes from Couveignes' work [Cou06]. The security of many cryptosystems reduces to this problem, such as CSIDH [CLM+18], CSI-FiSh [BKV19], CSURF [CD20], or generalisations to other orientations [CS21].

– $\mathfrak{O}$-UBER: given an $\mathfrak{O}$-oriented elliptic curve (E, ι) and an $\mathfrak{O}$-orientable E', find an ideal $\mathfrak{a}$ such that E' is isomorphic to $E^{\mathfrak{a}}$. The *effective* variant also requires a way to evaluate the action of $\mathfrak{a}$ on any other $\mathfrak{O}$-oriented curve. This *Uber* terminology was introduced in [DDF+21], where it was shown that the security of many cryptosystems reduces to this problem, including SIDH [JD11], OSIDH [CK20] and Séta [DDF+21].

1.3   Contribution

The main contribution of this article is the various reductions summarised in Fig. 1, under the generalised Riemann hypothesis. Some of these reductions generalise and strengthen previously known results:

– The article [CPV20] was the first to investigate the relation between ENDRING and the vectorisation problem, in the particular case of curves defined over $\mathbf{F}_p$ (i.e., $\sqrt{-p} \in \mathfrak{O}$). They prove that knowledge of the endomorphism ring of a CSIDH public key allows one to recover the ideal class of the secret key. This surprising result, however, only implies a subexponential reduction from breaking CSIDH to computing endomorphism rings, because it is not easy to find a *good* ideal class representative of the key. In essence, they prove a reduction from the vectorisation problem, but not from its effective variant. They argue that this effectiveness seems hard to reach, because if an efficient reduction could find good class representatives, then there would be an efficient algorithm to compute discrete logarithms in class groups of large discriminant. We circumvent this issue, proving in Sect. 6 that the effective vectorisation problem (hence breaking CSIDH) does reduce to the endomorphism ring problem in polynomial time. Our reductions not only apply to CSIDH or close variants restricted to $\mathbf{F}_p$, but to arbitrary orientations, including generalisations such as [CS21]. To reach this level of generality, we introduce the notion of $\mathfrak{O}$-twists and prove that they enjoy similar properties to quadratic twists, and can be used to extend some of the techniques introduced in [CPV20].

– Considering vectorisation as a group-action analog of the discrete logarithm problem, there is a corresponding Diffie–Hellman analog, $\mathfrak{O}$-DIFFIEHELLMAN (sometimes called *parallelisation*). Properly instantiated, it corresponds to the problem of recovering the shared secret in CSIDH. In [GPSV21], it was proved that if the action of $\mathrm{Cl}(\mathfrak{O})$ is efficiently computable, then the (non-effective) $\mathfrak{O}$-VECTORIZATION problem reduces to $\mathfrak{O}$-DIFFIEHELLMAN in quantum polynomial time. This result hit a similar wall as [CPV20]: the action is only efficiently computable for hard-to-find good ideal class representatives. Here again, our reductions bypass this obstacle, proving in Sect. 7 that $\mathfrak{O}$-DIFFIEHELLMAN is actually equivalent to $\mathfrak{O}$-VECTORIZATION (and to its effective variant, and to $\mathfrak{O}$-ENDRING) under quantum polynomial time reductions.

Finally, we focus in Sect. 8 on the case where $\mathfrak{O}$ is a non-maximal order, proving reductions from our problems of interest to their *a priori* easier counterpart for superorders (with smaller discriminants and class groups).

1.4 Notation

We denote by $\mathbf{Z}$ and $\mathbf{Q}$ the ring of integers and the field of rational numbers. For any prime power q, we denote by $\mathbf{F}_q$ the finite field with q elements, and $\overline{\mathbf{F}}_q$ its algebraic closure. We write $f = O(g)$ for the classic big O notation, which is equivalent to $g = \Omega(f)$. The size of a set S is denoted by $\#S$. Let a and b be two integers. We write $a \mid b$ if a divides b, and $a \parallel b$ if $a \mid b$ and $\gcd(a, b/a) = 1$. All statements containing the mention (GRH) assume the generalised Riemann hypothesis.

2 Preliminaries

In this section, we recall relevant notions related to quaternion algebras, supersingular elliptic curves, their endomorphism rings, and orientations.

2.1 Quadratic Fields and Orders

Let K be a quadratic number field. We write $\alpha \mapsto \overline{\alpha}$ for the conjugation, i.e., the unique non-trivial involution of K. Given any $\alpha \in K$, we write its norm $N(\alpha) = \alpha\overline{\alpha}$, and its trace $\mathrm{Tr}(\alpha) = \alpha + \overline{\alpha}$. An *order* in K is a discrete subring $\mathfrak{O} \subset K$ such that $K = \mathbf{Q}\mathfrak{O}$. A *generator* of $\mathfrak{O}$ is an element ω such that $\mathfrak{O} = \mathbf{Z}[\omega]$. The ring of integers $\mathfrak{O}_K$ of K is the unique maximal order in K. Given an order $\mathfrak{O}$, the (ideal) class group $\mathrm{Cl}(\mathfrak{O})$ consists of the invertible ideals of $\mathfrak{O}$ modulo principal ideals. The class of an ideal $\mathfrak{a}$ is denoted $[\mathfrak{a}]$.

2.2 Quaternion Algebras

To any prime number p, one can associate a quaternion algebra $B_{p,\infty}$ defined as

$$B_{p,\infty} = \mathbf{Q} + \mathbf{Q}i + \mathbf{Q}j + \mathbf{Q}ij,$$

with the multiplication rules $i^2 = -q$, $j^2 = -p$ and $ji = -ij$, where q is a positive integer that depends on p. More precisely, the latter is given by

$$q = \begin{cases} 1 & \text{if } p \equiv 3 \bmod 4, \\ 2 & \text{if } p \equiv 5 \bmod 8, \\ q_p & \text{if } p \equiv 1 \bmod 8, \end{cases}$$

where q_p is the smallest prime such that $q_p \equiv 3 \bmod 4$ and $\left(\frac{p}{q_p}\right) = -1$ (see [Piz80]). Assuming GRH, it follows from [LO77] that $q_p = O((\log p)^2)$, which can thus be computed in polynomial time in $\log p$. For the general theory of quaternion algebras, we refer the reader to [Vig06] or [Voi21].

Conjugation, Trace and Norm. Let $\alpha = x_1 + x_2 i + x_3 j + x_4 ij$ be a generic element in $B_{p,\infty}$. The algebra $B_{p,\infty}$ has a canonical involution $\alpha \mapsto \overline{\alpha} = x_1 - x_2 i - x_3 j - x_4 ij$. It induces the *reduced trace* and the *reduced norm*

$$\mathrm{Trd}(\alpha) = \alpha + \overline{\alpha} = 2x_1, \text{ and}$$
$$\mathrm{Nrd}(\alpha) = \alpha\overline{\alpha} = x_1^2 + qx_2^2 + p(x_3^2 + qx_4^2).$$

The latter is a positive definite quadratic map, which makes $B_{p,\infty}$ a quadratic space, and endows its finitely generated **Z**-submodules with a lattice structure.

Maximal Orders. An *order* in $B_{p,\infty}$ is a full-rank lattice that is also a subring. It is *maximal* if it is not contained in any other order. For any full-rank lattice $\Lambda \subset B_{p,\infty}$, the *left order* and the *right order of* Λ are

$$\mathcal{O}_L(\Lambda) = \{\alpha \in B_{p,\infty} \mid \alpha\Lambda \subseteq \Lambda\}, \text{ and}$$
$$\mathcal{O}_R(\Lambda) = \{\alpha \in B_{p,\infty} \mid \Lambda\alpha \subseteq \Lambda\}.$$

Let $\mathcal{O}$ be an order. A lattice $I \subseteq \mathcal{O}$ is a left $\mathcal{O}$-ideal if $\mathcal{O}I \subseteq I$, or a right $\mathcal{O}$-ideal if $I\mathcal{O} \subseteq I$. If $\mathcal{O}$ is a maximal order, and I is a left ideal in $\mathcal{O}$, then $\mathcal{O}_L(I) = \mathcal{O}$ and $\mathcal{O}_R(I)$ is another maximal order. Given two maximal orders $\mathcal{O}_1$ and $\mathcal{O}_2$, their *connecting ideal* is the ideal

$$I(\mathcal{O}_1, \mathcal{O}_2) = \{\alpha \in B_{p,\infty} \mid \alpha\mathcal{O}_2\overline{\alpha} \subseteq [\mathcal{O}_2 : \mathcal{O}_1 \cap \mathcal{O}_2]\mathcal{O}_1\},$$

which satisfies $\mathcal{O}_L(I(\mathcal{O}_1, \mathcal{O}_2)) = \mathcal{O}_1$ and $\mathcal{O}_R(I(\mathcal{O}_1, \mathcal{O}_2)) = \mathcal{O}_2$. Let $\mathcal{O}$ be a maximal order. Two left $\mathcal{O}$-ideals I and J are *equivalent* if there exists $\alpha \in B_{p,\infty}$ such that $I = \alpha J$. If I and J are equivalent, then $\mathcal{O}_R(I) \cong \mathcal{O}_R(J)$.

2.3   Elliptic Curves

Recall that an elliptic curve is an abelian variety of dimension 1, isogenies are non-trivial morphisms between them, and endomorphisms are isogenies from a curve to itself. For a detailed reference on elliptic curves, we refer the reader to [Sil86].

Isogenies and Endomorphisms. The set of all isogenies from E to E' (over the algebraic closure of the field of definition), together with the trivial map of kernel E, is written $\mathrm{Hom}(E, E')$. It forms a **Z**-module for point-wise addition $+$. The *endomorphism ring* $\mathrm{End}(E)$ of an elliptic curve E is the **Z**-module $\mathrm{Hom}(E, E)$ together with the composition of maps $\circ$. We have an embedding $\mathbf{Z} \hookrightarrow \mathrm{End}(E) : m \mapsto [m]$, where $[m]$ is the multiplication-by-m map. *Dividing by m* means finding a preimage through $[m]$, which in general is not unique.

The *degree* $\deg(\varphi)$ of an isogeny $\varphi : E \mapsto E'$ is the smallest positive element in $\mathbf{Z} \cap (\mathrm{Hom}(E', E) \circ \varphi)$. There is a unique isogeny $\hat{\varphi}$ such that $\hat{\varphi} \circ \varphi = [\deg(\varphi)]$, called the *dual* of φ. The degree is an integral quadratic map; it thereby endows the $\mathbf{Z}$-module $\mathrm{Hom}(E, E')$ with the structure of a lattice, with associated bilinear form

$$\langle \varphi, \psi \rangle = \frac{1}{2} \left(\hat{\varphi} \circ \psi + \hat{\psi} \circ \varphi \right).$$

If $\alpha \in \mathrm{End}(E)$, we write $E[\alpha] = \ker(\alpha)$. We also write $E[m] = \ker([m])$ for $m \in \mathbf{Z}$, and $E[S] = \cap_{\alpha \in S} E[\alpha]$ for $S \subseteq \mathrm{End}(E)$.

Efficient Representation of Isogenies. There are many ways to computationally represent isogenies. Rather that imposing a particular encoding, let us specify the required properties. As in [Wes22], we say that an isogeny $\varphi : E \to E'$ is given in an *efficient representation* if there is an algorithm to evaluate $\varphi(P)$ for any $P \in E(\mathbf{F}_{p^k})$ in time polynomial in the length of the representation of φ and in $k \log(p)$. We also assume that an efficient representation of φ has length $\Omega(\log(\deg(\varphi)))$. With these properties, the quadratic structure of $\mathrm{Hom}(E, E')$ is computationally available, thanks to the following lemma.

Lemma 1. *Given* $\varphi, \psi \in \mathrm{Hom}(E, E')$ *in efficient representation, one can compute* $\langle \varphi, \psi \rangle$ *in time polynomial in the length of the representation of* φ *and* ψ, *and in* $\log p$.

Proof. This is a straightforward generalisation of [EHL+18, Lemma 4].   □

Supersingular Curves. Fix a prime number p. If E is an elliptic curve defined over $\overline{\mathbf{F}}_p$, it is supersingular if and only if its endomorphism ring $\mathrm{End}(E)$ is isomorphic to a maximal order in the quaternion algebra $B_{p,\infty}$ (hence $B_{p,\infty} \cong \mathrm{End}(E) \otimes \mathbf{Q}$). Up to $\overline{\mathbf{F}}_p$-isomorphism, all supersingular elliptic curves over $\overline{\mathbf{F}}_p$ are defined over $\mathbf{F}_{p^2}$, and there are $\lfloor p/12 \rfloor + \varepsilon$ of them, with $\varepsilon \in \{0, 1, 2\}$.

To any isogeny $\varphi : E_1 \to E_2$, one associates a left $\mathrm{End}(E_1)$-ideal $I_\varphi = \mathrm{Hom}(E_2, E_1)\varphi$, which satisfies $\mathrm{End}(E_2) \cong \mathcal{O}_R(I_\varphi)$. Reciprocally, given a left $\mathrm{End}(E_1)$-ideal I, one can construct an isogeny $\varphi_I : E_1 \to E_2$ of kernel $E[I] = \cap_{\alpha \in I} \ker(\alpha)$ and degree $\mathrm{Nrd}(I)$. These two constructions are mutual inverses, meaning that for any I and φ, we have $I_{\varphi_I} = I$ and $\varphi_{I_\varphi} = \varphi$ (up to an isomorphism of the target).

Remark 1. If I and J are coprime to p, we have $E[I] \subseteq E[J]$ if and only if $J \subseteq I$.

Remark 2. An equivalent definition of supersingular is that $E[p^n]$ is trivial for any n. Then, for any isogeny φ, the size of its kernel (i.e., its separable degree) is the largest factor of $\deg(\varphi)$ coprime with p. In particular, given an ideal I, we have that $\#E[I]$ is equal to the largest factor of $N(I)$ coprime with p.

2.4 Orientations

Let K be a quadratic number field, with ring of integers $\mathcal{O}_K$, and let $\mathcal{O}$ be an arbitrary order in K.

Definition 1. (Orientation). A K-*orientation* on an elliptic curve E is an embedding $\iota : K \hookrightarrow \mathrm{End}(E) \otimes \mathbf{Q}$. It is an $\mathfrak{O}$-*orientation* if $\iota(\mathfrak{O}) = \iota(K) \cap \mathrm{End}(E)$. Such a pair (E, ι) is called an $\mathfrak{O}$-*oriented* elliptic curve, and we say that E is $\mathfrak{O}$-*orientable*.

Note that $\mathfrak{O}$-orientations as defined above correspond to the *primitive* $\mathfrak{O}$-orientations of [CK20]. If (E, ι) is an $\mathfrak{O}$-oriented elliptic curve, we will often consider ι as an embedding of $\mathfrak{O}$ into $\mathrm{End}(E)$ (which naturally extends to an embedding of K into $\mathrm{End}(E) \otimes \mathbf{Q}$). This relates to the notion of primitive embedding.

Definition 2. Given two lattices Λ_1 and Λ_2, an embedding $\jmath : \Lambda_1 \hookrightarrow \Lambda_2$ is *primitive* if the group $\Lambda_2 / \jmath(\Lambda_1)$ is torsion-free.

Then, one can equivalently define the notion of $\mathfrak{O}$-orientation as a primitive embedding $\iota : \mathfrak{O} \hookrightarrow \mathrm{End}(E)$.

Given a K-oriented elliptic curve (E, ι), any isogeny $\varphi : E \to E'$ induces a K-orientation $\varphi_*(\iota)$ on E' defined as

$$\varphi_*(\iota)(\alpha) = (\varphi \circ \iota(\alpha) \circ \hat{\varphi}) \otimes \frac{1}{\deg(\varphi)}.$$

From an oriented curve (E, ι), one can naturally define two others. First, its twist $(E, \bar{\iota})$, defined by $\bar{\iota}(\alpha) = \iota(\bar{\alpha})$, further studied in Sect. 6.1. Second, its Frobenius $(E, \bar{\iota})^{(p)} = (E^{(p)}, (\phi_p)_*(\bar{\iota}))$, where $\phi_p : E \to E^{(p)}$ is the Frobenius isogeny.

Definition 3. (Oriented isogeny). Given two K-oriented elliptic curves (E, ι) and (E', ι'), an isogeny $\varphi : (E, \iota) \to (E', \iota')$ is K-*oriented* if $\iota' = \varphi_*(\iota)$. If $\deg(\varphi)$ is prime, ι is an $\mathfrak{O}$-orientation and ι' an $\mathfrak{O}'$-orientation, then the isogeny is *horizontal* when $\mathfrak{O} = \mathfrak{O}'$, *ascending* when $\mathfrak{O} \subsetneq \mathfrak{O}'$, and *descending* when $\mathfrak{O} \supsetneq \mathfrak{O}'$. We say that an isogeny of composite degree is horizontal, ascending or descending if it factors as prime degree isogenies all of that type.

We write $\mathrm{SS}_{\mathfrak{O}}(p)$ the set of $\mathfrak{O}$-oriented supersingular elliptic curves over $\overline{\mathbf{F}}_p$ up to K-oriented isomorphism. We write $(E, \iota) \cong (E', \iota')$ if there is a K-oriented isomorphism between them. Abusing notation, we often write $(E, \iota) \in \mathrm{SS}_{\mathfrak{O}}(p)$ to mean that (E, ι) is a representative of an isomorphism class in $\mathrm{SS}_{\mathfrak{O}}(p)$.

Proposition 1 ([Onu21, **Proposition 3.2**]). *The set* $\mathrm{SS}_{\mathfrak{O}}(p)$ *is not empty if and only if p does not split in K and does not divide the conductor of $\mathfrak{O}$.*

Throughout, we suppose that p does not split in K and does not divide the conductor of $\mathfrak{O}$.

Encoding Orientations. Computationally, an orientation is encoded by a generator ω of $\mathfrak{O}$ (i.e., $\mathfrak{O} = \mathbf{Z}[\omega]$) together with an efficient representation of the endomorphism $\iota(\omega)$. We call this an *efficient representation* of ι.

Volcanoes. The following classification of horizontal, ascending or descending isogenies is commonly referred to as the *volcano* structure of oriented ℓ-isogeny graphs. Let $(E, \iota) \in SS_{\mathfrak{O}}(p)$, let $\ell \neq p$ be a prime, and let Δ be the discriminant of $\mathfrak{O}$. Let $\left(\frac{\Delta}{\ell}\right)$ be the Legendre symbol. From [CK20], the K-oriented isogenies of degree ℓ from (E, ι) are distributed as follows:

- There are $\ell - \left(\frac{\Delta}{\ell}\right)$ descending isogenies,
- If $\mathfrak{O}$ is maximal at ℓ, there are $\left(\frac{\Delta}{\ell}\right) + 1$ horizontal, and no ascending isogeny.
- If $\mathfrak{O}$ is non-maximal at ℓ, there is no horizontal, and one ascending isogeny.

This result implies that each connected component of the K-oriented ℓ-isogeny graph (with vertices $SS_{\mathfrak{O}}(p)$ and with edges for each isogeny of degree ℓ) consists of a cycle of horizontal isogenies (called the *surface*, or the *crater*), to each vertex of which is attached an infinite tree of vertical isogenies. The *volcano* terminology refers to the shape of this graph.

3 Class Groups Acting on Sets of Elliptic Curves

Fix an oriented curve $(E, \iota) \in SS_{\mathfrak{O}}(p)$. An $\mathfrak{O}$-ideal $\mathfrak{a}$ induces a subgroup

$$E[\mathfrak{a}] = \bigcap_{\alpha \in \mathfrak{a}} \ker(\iota(\alpha)),$$

and an isogeny $\varphi_{\mathfrak{a}} : E \rightarrow E^{\mathfrak{a}}$ of kernel $E[\mathfrak{a}]$ and degree $N(\mathfrak{a})$ called the $\mathfrak{a}$-multiplication. The target $E^{\mathfrak{a}}$ is the $\mathfrak{a}$-transform of (E, ι). This construction induces an action of $\mathfrak{O}$-ideals on the set $SS_{\mathfrak{O}}(p)$, defined by

$$\mathfrak{a} \star (E, \iota) = (E^{\mathfrak{a}}, (\varphi_{\mathfrak{a}})_*(\iota)),$$

which factors through $Cl(\mathfrak{O})$. This action, well understood for ordinary elliptic curves with complex multiplication, was first studied in the context of oriented supersingular curves in [CK20] and [Onu21].

Theorem 1 ([Onu21]). *The action*

$$Cl(\mathfrak{O}) \times SS_{\mathfrak{O}}(p) \longrightarrow SS_{\mathfrak{O}}(p) : ([\mathfrak{a}], (E, \iota)) \longmapsto \mathfrak{a} \star (E, \iota)$$

is free and has at most two orbits. For any orbit A, and any $(E, \iota) \in SS_{\mathfrak{O}}(p)$, either $(E, \iota) \in A$, or both $(E, \bar{\iota})$ and $(E^{(p)}, \iota^{(p)})$ are in A.

Proof. This theorem combines [Onu21, Proposition 3.3] and [Onu21, Theorem 3.4]. The statement about $(E, \bar{\iota})$ is from the proof of [Onu21, Proposition 3.3]. □

Computing the Action. The image $\mathfrak{a} \star (E, \iota)$ can be computed in time polynomial in the length of the encoding of (E, ι), in $\log(N(\mathfrak{a}))$ and in the largest prime-power factor of $N(\mathfrak{a})$. This is done by evaluating the action of $\iota(\mathfrak{a})$ on $E[N(\mathfrak{a})]$ to deduce $E[\mathfrak{a}]$, as in [CK20]. Evaluating the induced orientation $(\varphi_\mathfrak{a})_*(\iota)$ requires a division by $\deg(\varphi_\mathfrak{a})$, which can be done in time polynomial in B if $N(\mathfrak{a})$ is B-powersmooth (meaning that all its prime-power factors are smaller than B). Yet, it should be noted that the efficiency of this representation degrades after applying the action of several such ideals, say n, because their product may only be B^n-powersmooth. This will not be an issue when only a constant number of actions are applied in this way (as in our forthcoming reductions), or when the endomorphism ring of the curves are known (in which case an efficient representation of the orientation can be recomputed, that does not depend on the ideal).

3.1 Computational Problems

We now define two problems that translate whether or not the action is *one-way*.

Problem 1 ($\mathfrak{O}$-VECTORIZATION). Given $(E, \iota), (E', \iota') \in \mathrm{SS}_\mathfrak{O}(p)$, find an $\mathfrak{O}$-ideal $\mathfrak{a}$ such that $E' \cong E^\mathfrak{a}$.

Per Theorem 1, a solution $\mathfrak{a}$ of $\mathfrak{O}$-VECTORIZATION always exists since the isomorphism $E' \cong E^\mathfrak{a}$ does not care about the orientation. The *vectorization* terminology comes from Couveignes' work [Cou06], even though proper use of this terminology should require $(E', \iota') \cong \mathfrak{a} \star (E, \iota)$. We will see that this modification makes little difference, as $\mathfrak{O}$-VECTORIZATION will turn out to be equivalent to the following stronger problem.

Problem 2 (EFFECTIVE $\mathfrak{O}$-VECTORIZATION). Given three $\mathfrak{O}$-oriented supersingular curves $(E, \iota), (E', \iota'), (F, \jmath) \in \mathrm{SS}_\mathfrak{O}(p)$, find an $\mathfrak{O}$-ideal $\mathfrak{a}$ (or decide that it does not exist) such that $(E', \iota') \cong \mathfrak{a} \star (E, \iota)$, and an efficient representation of $\varphi_\mathfrak{a} : (F, \jmath) \to \mathfrak{a} \star (F, \jmath)$.

Now, a solution to EFFECTIVE $\mathfrak{O}$-VECTORIZATION does not necessarily exist, since (E, ι) and (E', ι') could be in the two distincts orbits described in Theorem 1. At first glance, the EFFECTIVE $\mathfrak{O}$-VECTORIZATION problem seems harder than $\mathfrak{O}$-VECTORIZATION for two reasons. First, an arbitrary ideal $\mathfrak{a}$ is unlikely to induce an efficient representation of $\varphi_\mathfrak{a}$. This has already proved to be a serious obstacle in the litterature [CPV20, GPSV21], where given an ideal class $[\mathfrak{a}]$, heavy work goes into finding a *good* representative of $[\mathfrak{a}]$ by a *smoothing* step which we do not know how to solve in polynomial time. Second, an isomorphism $E' \cong E^\mathfrak{a}$ does not imply that $(E', \iota') \cong \mathfrak{a} \star (E, \iota)$, and the information lost may be substantial as $h(\mathfrak{O})$ can be arbitrarily large while there are only approximately $p/12$ supersingular curves up to isomorphism. Despite these obstacles, we will show that these two problems are equivalent, by showing they are both equivalent to an oriented version of the endomorphism ring problem.

These two vectorisation problems are closely related to the following analog of the Diffie-Hellman problem.

Problem 3 ($\mathfrak{O}$-DIFFIEHELLMAN). Given an oriented curve $(E, \iota) \in SS_{\mathfrak{O}}(p)$, and its images $\mathfrak{a} \star (E, \iota)$ and $\mathfrak{b} \star (E, \iota)$ for the action of two unknown ideals $\mathfrak{a}$ and $\mathfrak{b}$, compute $\mathfrak{a}\mathfrak{b} \star (E, \iota)$.

In Couveignes' terminology, this is the *parallelisation* problem. It is clear that both problems $\mathfrak{O}$-VECTORIZATION and $\mathfrak{O}$-DIFFIEHELLMAN reduce to the EFFECTIVE $\mathfrak{O}$-VECTORIZATION problem, and the converse reductions are the object of Sects. 5, 6 and 7.

Now, one may consider the same problems when no orientation ι' for E' is provided. This modification seems to make the problems much harder, and this presumed hardness (for large disc($\mathfrak{O}$)) has been introduced in [DDF+21] as the *Uber isogeny assumption.*

Problem 4 ($\mathfrak{O}$-UBER). Given $(E, \iota) \in SS_{\mathfrak{O}}(p)$ and an $\mathfrak{O}$-orientable elliptic curve E', find an $\mathfrak{O}$-ideal $\mathfrak{a}$ such that $E' \cong E^{\mathfrak{a}}$.

The original Uber isogeny assumption from [DDF+21] also asks for an effective way to apply the action of $\mathfrak{a}$, as in the following effective variant.

Problem 5 (EFFECTIVE $\mathfrak{O}$-UBER). Given two $\mathfrak{O}$-oriented curves $(E, \iota), (F, \jmath) \in SS_{\mathfrak{O}}(p)$ and an $\mathfrak{O}$-orientable curve E', find an $\mathfrak{O}$-ideal $\mathfrak{a}$ such that $E' \cong E^{\mathfrak{a}}$, and an efficient representation of $\varphi_{\mathfrak{a}} : (F, \jmath) \to \mathfrak{a} \star (F, \jmath)$.

The main interest for these *Uber* problems is that the security of most isogeny based cryptosystems reduce to them [DDF+21, Section 5], even systems such as SIDH [JD11] for which no class group action is immediately visible. For instance, SIKEp434 [JAC+17] could be broken by solving an instance of EFFECTIVE $\mathfrak{O}$-UBER with $\mathfrak{O} = \mathbf{Z} + 2^n\mathbf{Z}[\sqrt{-1}]$, for some $n \leq 217$.

Remark 3. Complexities will often be expressed as a function of the length of the input. Whenever the input contains an $\mathcal{O}$-orientable elliptic curve over $\mathbf{F}_{p^2}$, we assume that p and $\mathcal{O}$ are part of the input, so its length is always $\Omega(\log p + \log(\text{disc}(\mathfrak{O})))$. For $\mathcal{O}$-oriented curves, the length may be longer, depending on the quality of the provided orientations.

3.2 Some Known or Simple Algorithms

Let us briefly present algorithms to solve some of the problems introduced above.

Proposition 2. *The EFFECTIVE $\mathfrak{O}$-UBER problem can heuristically be solved in expected time $l^{O(1)}\text{disc}(\mathfrak{O})$, with l the length of the input.*

Proof. This is the running time of an exhaustive search restricted to powersmooth ideals, as discussed in [DDF+21, Section 5.3].   □

Proposition 3. *The $\mathfrak{O}$-VECTORIZATION problem can heuristically be solved in expected time $l^{O(1)}\text{disc}(\mathfrak{O})^{1/2}$, with l the length of the input.*

Proof. This is the running time of the meet-in-the-middle approach, as described for instance in [DG16, CLM+18], but using only powersmooth walks.   □

In the following, we use the classic notation

$$L_x(\alpha) = \exp\left(O\left((\log x)^\alpha (\log\log x)^{1-\alpha}\right)\right)$$

for subexponential complexities.

Proposition 4. *The $\mathfrak{O}$-VECTORIZATION problem can heuristically be solved in quantum subexponential time $l^{O(1)} L_{\mathrm{disc}(\mathfrak{O})}(1/2)$, with l the length of the input.*

Proof. The $\mathfrak{O}$-VECTORIZATION problem reduces to the hidden shift problem with respect to the functions $f, f' : \mathrm{Cl}(\mathfrak{O}) \to \mathbf{F}_{p^2}$ defined by $f([\mathfrak{a}]) = j(\mathfrak{a}\star(E,\iota))$ and $f'([\mathfrak{a}]) = j(\mathfrak{a}\star(E',\iota'))$. It only remains to prove that the action can be evaluated in quantum subexponential time, then apply Kuperberg's algorithm [Kup05]. It is tempting to simply adapt the method of [CJS14], but they find smooth class representatives, when we need powersmooth class representatives. We take a cruder, simpler, but heuristic route. One can randomize the class representative of $[\mathfrak{a}]$, until it has a powersmooth norm. The number of $L_x(1/2)$-powersmooth numbers at most x is $L_x(1/2)$ (see [CN00, Section 3.1]), so under the heuristic assumption that norms of random class representatives behave like random integers of the same size, we may find an $L_d(1/2)$-powersmooth representative in time $L_d(1/2)$, with $d = \mathrm{disc}(\mathfrak{O})$. Its action can then be evaluated in time $L_d(1/2)$.   □

4   Oriented Versions of the Endomorphism Ring Problem

4.1   The Endomorphism Ring Problem

To define the endomorphism ring problem in its strongest form, we introduce the notion of ε-basis, thereby unifying the two variants ENDRING and MAXORDER proved to be equivalent under the generalised Riemann hypothesis in [Wes22] (and heuristically since [EHL+18]).

Definition 4 (ε-basis). Let $\varepsilon : B_{p,\infty} \to \mathrm{End}(E)\otimes\mathbf{Q}$ be an isomorphism. Given a lattice $L \subseteq B_{p,\infty}$, an ε-basis of L is a pair (α, θ) where $(\alpha_i)_{i=1}^{\mathrm{rank}(L)}$ is a basis of L and $\theta_i = \varepsilon(\alpha_i)$. Abusing language, we also call (α, θ) an ε-basis of the image lattice $\varepsilon(L)$.

Remark 4. We will often talk about an ε-basis without specifying a priori an isomorphism ε. The ε is then implicit, and when L has full rank, it is uniquely determined by the ε-basis.

Encoding. Computationally, we suppose that elements in $B_{p,\infty}$ are encoded as vectors of rational numbers with respect to the basis $(1, i, j, ij)$. We assume that elements $\eta \otimes n^{-1}$ of $\mathrm{End}(E) \otimes \mathbf{Q}$ are encoded as pairs (η, n) where n is an integer and η is an endomorphism in efficient representation.

The endomorphism ring problem can be defined as either finding a basis of a maximal order $\mathcal{O}$ of $B_{p,\infty}$ isomorphic to $\mathrm{End}(E)$, or finding four endomorphisms that generate $\mathrm{End}(E)$. Both have their own advantages. On one hand, knowledge of the order $\mathcal{O}$ enables the use of powerful algorithms for orders in quaternion algebras (notably, finding ideals connecting orders is much easier that finding isogenies connecting elliptic curves [KLPT14]). On the other hand, an explicit basis of $\mathrm{End}(E)$ provides actual endomorphisms that can be evaluated. It was proved in [Wes22] that a basis of either $\mathcal{O}$ or $\mathrm{End}(E)$ can be transformed into an ε-basis of $\mathrm{End}(E)$, assuming GRH. We therefore define the endomorphism ring problem as follows.

Problem 6 (ENDRING). Given a supersingular elliptic curve E over $\mathbf{F}_{p^2}$, find an ε-basis of $\mathrm{End}(E)$.

Proposition 5. *The ENDRING problem can heuristically be solved in expected time* $(\log p)^{O(1)} p^{1/2}$.

Proof. This is the running time of the best known algorithms for ENDRING, for instance [DG16] and [EHL+20]. □

4.2 Oriented Variants of the Endomorphism Ring Problem

The ENDRING problem can naturally be restricted to $\mathfrak{O}$-orientable curves, resulting in the following problem.

Problem 7 (ENDRING$|_{\mathfrak{O}}$). Given an $\mathfrak{O}$-orientable E, find an ε-basis of $\mathrm{End}(E)$.

Now, if an orientation is provided, we obtain the following variant.

Problem 8 ($\mathfrak{O}$-ENDRING). Given $(E, \iota) \in SS_{\mathfrak{O}}(p)$, find an ε-basis of $\mathrm{End}(E)$.

One could require solutions to $\mathfrak{O}$-ENDRING to be in some way compatible with the orientation. It is unnecessary: as formalised in the following lemma, it is actually easy to express a given orientation in terms of a given ε-basis.

Lemma 2. *Given $(E, \iota) \in SS_{\mathfrak{O}}(p)$ and an ε-basis of $\mathrm{End}(E)$, one can find an embedding $\jmath : \mathfrak{O} \hookrightarrow B_{p,\infty}$ such that $\varepsilon \circ \jmath = \iota$ in time polynomial in the length of the input.*

Proof. We can compute scalar products between endomorphisms with Lemma 1, so we can express the orientation ι in terms of the ε-basis. □

Finally, we consider the seemingly harder problem of computing the endomorphism ring *and* an orientation.

Problem 9 ($\mathfrak{O}$-ENDRING*). Given a supersingular $\mathfrak{O}$-orientable curve E, find an ε-basis of $\mathrm{End}(E)$ and an embedding $\jmath : \mathfrak{O} \hookrightarrow B_{p,\infty}$ such that $\varepsilon \circ \jmath$ is an $\mathfrak{O}$-orientation.

Clearly, $\mathfrak{O}$-ENDRING reduces to ENDRING$|_{\mathfrak{O}}$, which reduces to $\mathfrak{O}$-ENDRING*.

4.3   Computing an Orientation from the Endomorphism Ring

While ENDRING$|_{\mathfrak{O}}$ reduces to $\mathfrak{O}$-ENDRING*, the converse boils down to the following question.

Question 1. Given an $\mathfrak{O}$-orientable curve E and an ε-basis of its endomorphism ring, can one compute an $\mathfrak{O}$-orientation of E in probabilistic polynomial time in $\log(p)$ and $\log(\mathrm{disc}(\mathfrak{O}))$?

We only provide a positive answer to this question when the discriminant of the order $\mathfrak{O}$ is small enough, in Proposition 6. The general case may be more difficult.

Proposition 6. *Given an $\mathfrak{O}$-orientable curve E and an ε-basis of its endomorphism ring, if $|\mathrm{disc}(\mathfrak{O})| < 2p^{1/2} - 1$, then one can compute an $\mathfrak{O}$-orientation of E in probabilistic polynomial time in $\log(p)$.*

Proof. Let ι be an $\mathfrak{O}$-orientation of E. Let $d = \mathrm{disc}(\mathfrak{O})$. Let ω be a Minkowski reduced generator of $\mathfrak{O}$ (of trace either 0 or 1). Then, we have $\mathrm{Nrd}(\omega) \leq (d+1)/4$. For any $\beta \in \mathrm{End}(E)$, we have $|\mathrm{disc}(\mathbf{Z}[\beta])| = 4\mathrm{Nrd}(\beta) - \mathrm{Trd}(\beta)^2 \leq 4\mathrm{Nrd}(\beta)$. Also, for any $\beta \in \mathrm{End}(E) \setminus \iota(\mathfrak{O})$, it follows from [Kan89, Theorem 2'] that $\mathrm{disc}(\mathfrak{O})\mathrm{disc}(\mathbf{Z}[\beta]) \geq 4p$, hence

$$\mathrm{Nrd}(\beta) \geq \frac{p}{d} > \frac{d+1}{4} \geq \mathrm{Nrd}(\omega).$$

This proves that the shortest vector in $\mathrm{End}(E) \setminus \mathbf{Z}$ is a generator of $\iota(\mathfrak{O})$, which can be recovered in polynomial time. Expressing this generator as a linear combination of the ε-basis of $\mathrm{End}(E)$ provides an efficient representation of the orientation ι.   □

Proposition 6 has the following immediate consequence.

Corollary 1. *If $|\mathrm{disc}(\mathfrak{O})| < 2p^{1/2} - 1$, then $\mathfrak{O}$-ENDRING* and ENDRING$|_{\mathfrak{O}}$ are equivalent.*

5   Endomorphism Rings from Orientations

In this section, we prove reductions from the family of endomorphism ring problems to the family of vectorisation problems. A key ingredient is the constructive Deuring correspondence in the 'order-to-curve' direction, Lemma 3, a result first heuristically proved in [EHL+18, Proposition 13]. Observing that it is easy to produce orders with a primitive embedding of $\mathfrak{O}$, we deduce in Lemma 4 that we can construct $\mathfrak{O}$-oriented elliptic curves of known endomorphism ring, to be used as starting points for vectorisation problems.

Lemma 3 (GRH). *There is an algorithm that given p and a maximal order $\mathcal{O} \subset B_{p,\infty}$, returns an elliptic curve E such that $\operatorname{End}(E) \cong \mathcal{O}$ together with an ε-basis of $\operatorname{End}(E)$, and runs in time polynomial in $\log(p)$ and the length of the basis of $\mathcal{O}$.*

Proof. From [EHL+18, Proposition 13] (but using [Wes22] instead of [KLPT14] to get rid of the heuristic assumptions), we get an elliptic curve E such that $\operatorname{End}(E) \cong \mathcal{O}$. From [Wes22, Algorithm 6], we deduce an ε-basis of $\operatorname{End}(E)$. $\square$

Definition 5. Let $\mathcal{O}$ be a maximal order in an algebra $B \cong B_{p,\infty}$, and $\jmath : \mathfrak{O} \hookrightarrow \mathcal{O}$ a primitive embedding. Let I be a left $\mathcal{O}$-ideal of prime norm ℓ, and let $\mathfrak{O}' = \mathcal{O}_R(I) \cap (\jmath(\mathfrak{O}) \otimes \mathbf{Q})$. The ideal I is $\jmath$-descending if $\mathfrak{O}' \subsetneq \jmath(\mathfrak{O})$, $\jmath$-horizontal if $\mathfrak{O}' = \jmath(\mathfrak{O})$, and $\jmath$-ascending if $\mathfrak{O}' \supsetneq \jmath(\mathfrak{O})$.

Remark 5. It immediately follows that an $\mathcal{O}$-oriented isogeny $\varphi : (E, \iota) \to (E, \iota')$ of prime degree is descending (respectively horizontal or ascending) if and only if the kernel ideal $I_\varphi = \{\alpha \in \operatorname{End}(E) | \ker \varphi \subseteq \ker \alpha\}$ is ι-descending (respectively ι-horizontal or ι-ascending). In particular, given $\mathcal{O}$ and $\jmath$, almost all ideals of norm ℓ are $\jmath$-descending, with at most two exceptions [Onu21, Proposition 4.1]. Therefore, a $\jmath$-descending ideal can be found in time polynomial in $\log(\ell)$ by listing three ideals of norm ℓ, and testing them using [Rón92, Theorem 3.2].

Lemma 4 (GRH). *Given $\mathfrak{O}$ and the factorisation of its discriminant, one can find some $\mathfrak{O}$-oriented curve $(E, \iota) \in \operatorname{SS}_\mathfrak{O}(p)$ together with an ε-basis of $\operatorname{End}(E)$ in probabilistic polynomial time in $\log(p)$ and $\log(\operatorname{disc}(\mathfrak{O}))$.*

Remark 6. There is a heuristic algorithm [LB20, Algorithm 1] that solves this task in the case where $\mathfrak{O}$ is maximal. Our approach in the proof below is different, assumes only GRH, and avoids potentially hard factorisations.

Proof. We start by computing some arbitrary maximal order $\mathcal{O}_0$ in $B_{p,\infty}$ (for instance, a special order as in [KLPT14, Section 2.3]). Let K be the quadratic field containing $\mathfrak{O}$, with ring of integers $\mathfrak{O}_K$. Let ω_K be a Minkowski reduced generator of $\mathfrak{O}_K$, with minimal polynomial $x^2 - tx + n$. To find a quaternion $\omega \in B_{p,\infty}$ with the same minimal polynomial, solve

$$(t/2)^2 + qb^2 + p(c^2 + qd^2) = n$$

for $b, c, d \in \mathbf{Q}$ with [Sim06] (using the factorisation of $\operatorname{disc}(\mathfrak{O})$). Let $\omega = t/2 + bi + cj + dij$, which has same norm and trace as ω_K, hence same minimal polynomial. Let a be the smallest integer such that $a\omega \in \mathcal{O}_0$. Let $I = \mathcal{O}_0\omega a + \mathcal{O}_0 a$. We have $I\omega \subseteq I$, so $\omega \in \mathcal{O}_R(I)$, and $\mathcal{O}_R(I)$ can be computed with [Rón92, Theorem 3.2]. The corresponding embedding $\jmath : \mathfrak{O}_K \hookrightarrow \mathcal{O}_R(I) : \omega_K \mapsto \omega$ is primitive since $\mathfrak{O}_K$ is maximal, and it remains to descend to $\mathfrak{O}$. Let c be the conductor of $\mathfrak{O}$. For any prime power $\ell^k \| c$,

- let $\tilde{J}_\ell$ be any $\jmath$-descending $\mathcal{O}_R(I)$-ideal of norm ℓ (see Remark 5), and
- let $J_\ell \subseteq \tilde{J}_\ell$ an ideal of norm ℓ^k such that $J_\ell \not\subseteq \ell\mathcal{O}_R(I)$.

By construction, each J_ℓ is the kernel ideal of a cyclic isogeny of norm ℓ^k whose first step (hence all steps, because of the volcano structure) is descending. The cyclicity of each J_ℓ comes from $J_\ell \not\subseteq \ell\mathcal{O}_R(I)$ and Remark ??. Then, $J = \cap_{\ell|c} J_\ell$ is the kernel ideal of a descending isogeny of degree c, hence $\mathfrak{O} \hookrightarrow \mathcal{O}_R(J) : c\omega_K \mapsto c\omega$ is a primitive embedding. So we define $\mathcal{O} = \mathcal{O}_R(J)$. Applying Lemma 3, we can construct E with an ε-basis of $\text{End}(E) \cong \mathcal{O}$. The orientation ι is provided by the induced efficient representation of the endomorphism $\iota(c\omega_K) = \varepsilon(c\omega)$. $\square$

Proposition 7 (GRH). *Given the factorisation of* $\text{disc}(\mathfrak{O})$, *the* $\mathfrak{O}$-ENDRING *problem reduces to* $\mathfrak{O}$-VECTORIZATION *in probabilistic polynomial time in the length of the instance.*

Proof. Suppose we are given an instance $(E, \iota) \in \text{SS}_\mathfrak{O}(p)$ of $\mathfrak{O}$-ENDRING. Find $(E', \iota') \in \text{SS}_\mathfrak{O}(p)$ together with an ε-basis of $\mathcal{O}' \cong \text{End}(E')$ using Lemma 4. Solving $\mathfrak{O}$-VECTORIZATION, find an $\mathfrak{O}$-ideal $\mathfrak{a}$ such that $(E', \iota') = \mathfrak{a} \star (E, \iota)$. Then $I = \mathcal{O}' \cdot \iota'(\mathfrak{a})$, the kernel ideal of $\varphi_\mathfrak{a}$, is a connecting ideal between $\mathcal{O}' \cong \text{End}(E')$ and $\mathcal{O}_R(I) \cong \text{End}(E)$. The right-order $\mathcal{O}_R(I)$ can be computed with [Rón92, Theorem 3.2], thereby solving $\mathfrak{O}$-ENDRING for (E, ι). $\square$

Proposition 8 (GRH). *Given the factorisation of* $\text{disc}(\mathfrak{O})$, $\mathfrak{O}$-ENDRING* *reduces to* $\mathfrak{O}$-UBER *in probabilistic polynomial time in the length of the instance.*

Proof. We proceed as in Proposition 7, except that no $\mathfrak{O}$-orientation of E is provided, which still allows us to apply $\mathfrak{O}$-UBER instead of $\mathfrak{O}$-VECTORIZATION.

$\square$

6   Reducing Vectorisation to Endomorphism Ring

It is shown in [CPV20] that in the particular case of curves defined over $\mathbf{F}_p$, and $\sqrt{-p} \in \mathfrak{O}$, solving the endomorphism ring problem allows one to solve the $\mathfrak{O}$-VECTORIZATION problem. They note however that in general, the resulting ideal does not necessarily have a smooth norm, so it is hard to compute its action. They conclude that this approach necessitates an expensive smoothing step, hence only provides a sub-exponential reduction of the security of CSIDH to the endomorphism ring problem. A priori, their methods seem very specific to the CSIDH setting, exploiting the action of Frobenius and quadratic twists. Introducing an appropriate generalisation of twisting, we prove in this section that $\mathfrak{O}$-VECTORIZATION reduces to $\mathfrak{O}$-ENDRING in all generality. Pushing the results farther, we circumvent the smoothness obstruction by proving polynomial time reductions between these problems and EFFECTIVE $\mathfrak{O}$-VECTORIZATION, observing that the action of non-smooth ideals can be efficiently evaluated on elliptic curves of known endomorphism ring. The idea that endomorphisms allow one to evaluate non-smooth isogenies had been observed in [FKM21], and the following proposition extends it to the action of ideals on oriented curves.

Proposition 9 (GRH). *Given* $(E, \iota) \in SS_\mathfrak{O}(p)$, *an* ε*-basis of* $\mathrm{End}(E)$, *and an* $\mathfrak{O}$*-ideal* $\mathfrak{a}$, *one can compute* $\mathfrak{a} \star (E, \iota)$ *and an efficient representation of* $\varphi_\mathfrak{a}$ *in probabilistic polynomial time in the length of the input (i.e.,* $\log p$, $\log(\mathrm{disc}(\mathfrak{O}))$, $\log(N(\mathfrak{a}))$ *and the length of* ι *and of the* ε*-basis of* $\mathrm{End}(E)$*).*

Proof. We are given an isomorphism $\varepsilon : \mathcal{O} \to \mathrm{End}(E)$. Let $\jmath : \mathfrak{O} \to \mathcal{O}$ such that $\varepsilon \circ \jmath = \iota$ (see Lemma 2). Let $I = \mathcal{O}\jmath(\mathfrak{a})$, and use [Wes22, Theorem 6.4] to find $\alpha \in I$ such that $J = I\overline{\alpha}/N(\mathfrak{a})$ has powersmooth norm. Then, J is the kernel ideal of an efficiently computable isogeny φ_J (for instance by adapting [GPS20, Lemma 5] to the provided ε-basis instead of the special $\mathcal{O}_0{}^1$). We have $\varphi_\mathfrak{a} \circ [\mathrm{Nrd}(J)] = \varphi_J \circ \varepsilon(\alpha)$, so $E^\mathfrak{a} = \varphi_J(E)$. It only remains to compute the $\mathfrak{O}$-orientation on $E^\mathfrak{a}$, i.e., an efficient representation of $((\varphi_\mathfrak{a})_*(\iota))(\omega)$ for some generator ω of $\mathfrak{O}$. We have

$$((\varphi_\mathfrak{a})_*(\iota))(\omega) = (\varphi_\mathfrak{a} \circ \iota(\omega) \circ \hat{\varphi}_\mathfrak{a})/N(\mathfrak{a}) = (\varphi_J \circ \varepsilon(\alpha\jmath(\omega)\overline{\alpha}) \circ \hat{\varphi}_J)/\mathrm{Nrd}(J).$$

One can compute the quaternion $\alpha\jmath(\omega)\overline{\alpha}$, and deduce an efficient representation of the numerator $\gamma = \varphi_J \circ \varepsilon(\alpha\jmath(\omega)\overline{\alpha}) \circ \hat{\varphi}_J$ thanks to the ε-basis. One can evaluate $((\varphi_\mathfrak{a})_*(\iota))(\omega)$ at any point P by first finding a point P' such that $\mathrm{Nrd}(J)P' = P$ (in polynomial time because $\mathrm{Nrd}(J)$ is powersmooth), then returning $\gamma(P')$. Therefore we have an efficient representation of the orientation $(\varphi_\mathfrak{a})_*(\iota)$. $\square$

6.1 $\mathfrak{O}$-twists, a Generalisation of Quadratic Twists

We now introduce the notion of $\mathfrak{O}$-twists, that enjoys properties similar to quadratic twists.

Definition 6 ($\mathfrak{O}$-twist). We define the $\mathfrak{O}$-twisting involution as the map $\tau :$ $SS_\mathfrak{O}(p) \to SS_\mathfrak{O}(p)$ defined as $\tau(E, \iota) = (E, \overline{\iota})$, where $\overline{\iota}(\alpha) = \iota(\overline{\alpha})$. The oriented curve $\tau(E, \iota)$ is the $\mathfrak{O}$-twist of (E, ι).

Lemma 5. *For any* $(E, \iota) \in SS_\mathfrak{O}(p)$ *and* $\mathcal{O}$*-ideal* $\mathfrak{a}$, *we have* $\tau(\mathfrak{a} \star (E, \iota)) = \overline{\mathfrak{a}} \star \tau(E, \iota)$.

Proof. It follows from the fact that $\cap_{\alpha \in \overline{\mathfrak{a}}} \ker(\iota(\alpha)) = \cap_{\alpha \in \mathfrak{a}} \ker(\overline{\iota}(\alpha))$. $\square$

Recall that sets of isogenies $\mathrm{Hom}(E, E')$ (and in particular $\mathrm{End}(E)$) are lattices. They have a quadratic structure, hence an associated notion of orthogonality. Given $S \subseteq \mathrm{Hom}(E, E')$, we write $S^\perp \subseteq \mathrm{Hom}(E, E')$ the set of isogenies orthogonal to all elements of S.

The following lemma can be seen as an analog of [CPV20, Lemma 11].

Lemma 6. *Let* $(E, \iota) \in SS_\mathfrak{O}(p)$. *For any non-zero* $\theta \in \mathrm{End}(E)$, *we have* $\theta \in$ $\iota(\mathfrak{O})^\perp$ *if and only if* $\theta_*(\iota) = \overline{\iota}$.

---

[1] Alternatively, one can observe that the treatment of $\mathcal{O}_0$ in [GPS20, Lemma 5] is sufficient. Indeed, the ideal J is constructed in [Wes22, Theorem 6.4] as a composition of two $\mathcal{O}_0$-ideals, which can each be translated to an isogeny via [GPS20, Lemma 5].

Proof. First suppose $\theta \in \iota(\mathfrak{O})^{\perp}$. Since $1 \in \mathfrak{O}$, we have $\theta \in 1^{\perp}$, i.e., $\theta = -\hat{\theta}$. Then, for any $\alpha \in \mathfrak{O}$, we have $0 = \theta \circ \bar{\iota}(\alpha) + \iota(\alpha) \circ \hat{\theta} = \theta \circ \bar{\iota}(\alpha) - \iota(\alpha) \circ \theta$. We get

$$\theta_*(\iota)(\alpha) = (\theta \circ \iota(\alpha) \circ \hat{\theta}) \otimes \frac{1}{\deg(\theta)} = (\bar{\iota}(\alpha) \circ \theta \circ \hat{\theta}) \otimes \frac{1}{\deg(\theta)} = \bar{\iota}(\alpha),$$

which proves the first implication. For the converse, suppose that $\theta_*(\iota) = \bar{\iota}$. Then, $\theta \circ \iota(\alpha) = \iota(\bar{\alpha}) \circ \theta$ for any $\alpha \in \mathfrak{O}$. Let $\omega \in \mathfrak{O}$ be a non-zero element of trace 0, so $\bar{\omega} = -\omega$. Write $\theta = x + \theta_0$ where $x \in \mathbf{Q}$ and $\hat{\theta}_0 = -\theta_0$ (concretely, $x = \mathrm{Trd}(\theta)/2$ and $\theta_0 = (\theta - \hat{\theta})/2$). Then,

$$[x] \circ \iota(\omega) + \theta_0 \circ \iota(\omega) = \theta \circ \iota(\omega) = \iota(\bar{\omega}) \circ \theta = -\iota(\omega) \circ \theta$$
$$= -\iota(\omega) \circ [x] - \iota(\omega) \circ \theta_0,$$

hence $[2x] \circ \iota(\omega) = \mathrm{Trd}(\hat{\theta}_0 \circ \iota(\omega)) \in \mathbf{Q}$, which implies $x = 0$ because $\iota(\omega) \notin \mathbf{Q}$. This proves $\theta = \theta_0$, which is orthogonal to 1. The above also implies that $\theta \circ \iota(\omega) = -\iota(\omega) \circ \theta$, which means that θ is orthogonal to $\iota(\omega)$, so $\theta \in \iota(\mathfrak{O})^{\perp}$. $\square$

An issue with $\mathfrak{O}$-twisting is that it might not preserve $\mathrm{Cl}(\mathfrak{O})$-orbits. We introduce the following involution to resolve this.

Definition 7. We define the involution $\tau_p : \mathrm{SS}_{\mathfrak{O}}(p) \to \mathrm{SS}_{\mathfrak{O}}(p)$ as $\tau_p(E, \iota) = (E, \bar{\iota})^{(p)}$, with $(E, \bar{\iota})^{(p)} = (E^{(p)}, (\phi_p)_*(\bar{\iota}))$ where $\phi_p : E \to E^{(p)}$ is the Frobenius isogeny.

Proposition 10. *There exists an ideal $\mathfrak{a}$ such that $\tau_p(E, \iota) = \mathfrak{a} \star (E, \iota)$.*

Proof. The only troublesome case is if $\mathrm{SS}_{\mathfrak{O}}(p)$ partitions into two $\mathrm{Cl}(\mathfrak{O})$-orbits A and B. In that case, both τ and the Frobenius involution interchange A and B (Theorem 1). It follows that τ_p stabilizes A and B. $\square$

It still enjoys some of the useful properties of $\mathfrak{O}$-twisting.

Lemma 7. *We have $\tau_p(\mathfrak{a} \star (E, \iota)) = \bar{\mathfrak{a}} \star \tau_p(E, \iota)$.*

Proof. It follows from Lemma 5 and the fact that $\mathfrak{a} \star (E, \iota)^{(p)} = (\mathfrak{a} \star (E, \iota))^{(p)}$. $\square$

Corollary 2. *An isogeny $\varphi : (E, \iota) \to \tau_p(E, \iota)$ is K-oriented if and only if $\varphi \in (\phi_p \circ \iota(\mathfrak{O}))^{\perp}$, where $\phi_p : E \to E^{(p)}$ is the Frobenius isogeny.*

Proof. By the definition of τ_p, the isogeny φ is K-oriented if and only if $\varphi_*(\iota) = (\phi_p)_*(\bar{\iota})$. The latter is equivalent to $(\hat{\phi}_p)_*(\varphi_*(\iota)) = (\hat{\phi}_p)_*((\phi_p)_*(\bar{\iota}))$. Since

$$(\hat{\phi}_p)_*(\varphi_*(\iota)) = (\hat{\phi}_p \circ \varphi)_*(\iota), \text{ and}$$
$$(\hat{\phi}_p)_*((\phi_p)_*(\bar{\iota})) = [p]_*(\bar{\iota}) = \bar{\iota},$$

we deduce that $(\hat{\phi}_p \circ \varphi)_*(\iota) = \bar{\iota}$. From Lemma 6, this is equivalent to $\hat{\phi}_p \circ \varphi \in \iota(\mathfrak{O})^{\perp}$, i.e., $\varphi \in \phi_p \circ (\iota(\mathfrak{O}))^{\perp} = (\phi_p \circ \iota(\mathfrak{O}))^{\perp}$. $\square$

Corollary 3. *The integral lattice* $(\phi_p \circ \iota(\mathfrak{O}))^\perp \subset \mathrm{Hom}(E, E^{(p)})$ *is primitive (i.e., the greatest common divisor of the integers represented by the associated integral quadratic form is 1).*

Proof. There exist two coprime ideals $\mathfrak{a}$ and $\mathfrak{b}$ such that $\tau_p(E, \iota) = \mathfrak{a} \star (E, \iota) = \mathfrak{b} \star (E, \iota)$ (see for instance [Cox11, Corollary 7.17]). We deduce from Corollary 2 that there are two lattice vectors $\varphi_\mathfrak{a}, \varphi_\mathfrak{b} \in (\phi_p \circ \iota(\mathfrak{O}))^\perp \subset \mathrm{Hom}(E, E^{(p)})$ of coprime norm. □

6.2   Vectorisation Problems from Endomorphism Rings

We now prove that vectorisation problems reduce to endomorphism ring problems, with a strategy similar to that of [CPV20].

Lemma 8. *Let* $(E, \iota) \in SS_\mathfrak{O}(p)$, *a non-zero* $\mathfrak{O}$-*ideal* $\mathfrak{a}$, *and a left* $\mathrm{End}(E)$-*ideal* I *such that* $E[\mathfrak{a}] = E[I]$. *Then,* $I \cap \iota(\mathfrak{O}) = \iota(\mathfrak{p}^k \mathfrak{a})$ *for some* $k \in \mathbf{Z}$, *where* $\mathfrak{p}$ *is the prime ideal above* p.

Proof. This lemma is a generalisation of [CPV20, Lemma 14], from which we adapt the proof. Write $\mathfrak{a} = \mathfrak{p}^i \mathfrak{b}$ where $\mathfrak{b}$ is coprime to p. Similarly, write $I = I_p \cap J$, where $I_p = I + p^{\mathrm{val}_p(\mathrm{Nrd}(I))} \mathcal{O}$ is the p-part of I (i.e., $\mathrm{Nrd}(I_p)$ is a power of p), and $\mathrm{Nrd}(J)$ is not divisible by p. Following the observation of Remark 2, we have $\#E[\mathfrak{a}] = \#E[\mathfrak{b}]$ and $\#E[I] = \#E[J]$, hence

$$E[\mathfrak{b}] = E[\mathfrak{a}] = E[I] = E[J].$$

From the correspondence between ideals coprime to p and kernels of separable isogenies, we have

$$\mathfrak{b} = \{\alpha \in \mathfrak{O} \mid E[\mathfrak{b}] \subseteq \ker(\iota(\alpha))\}, \text{ and}$$
$$J = \{\theta \in \mathrm{End}(E) \mid E[J] \subseteq \ker(\theta)\}.$$

Together with $E[\mathfrak{b}] = E[J]$, we deduce that

$$J \cap \iota(\mathfrak{O}) = \{\theta \in \iota(\mathfrak{O}) \mid E[\mathfrak{b}] \subseteq \ker(\theta)\} = \iota(\mathfrak{b}).$$

There exists j such that $I_p \cap \iota(\mathfrak{O}) = \iota(\mathfrak{p}^j)$, hence $I \cap \iota(\mathfrak{O}) = \iota(\mathfrak{p}^{j-i} \mathfrak{a})$, proving the lemma. □

Lemma 9. *A separable* K-*oriented isogeny of prime degree is horizontal if and only if it is of the form* $\psi \circ \varphi_\mathfrak{a}$ *where* ψ *is a* K-*isomorphism and* $\mathfrak{a}$ *is an invertible ideal in an order of* K.

Proof. Let $\varphi : (E, \iota) \to (E', \iota')$ be a separable K-oriented isogeny of prime degree ℓ. It can be written as $\varphi = \psi \circ \varphi_0$ where $\varphi_0 : E \to E/\ker(\varphi)$ is the canonical projection, and ψ is a K-isomorphism. Suppose it is horizontal. Then, its kernel is of the form $E[\mathfrak{a}]$ with $N(\mathfrak{a}) = \ell$, so $\varphi_0 = \varphi_\mathfrak{a}$. We have

$$\psi_*((\varphi_\mathfrak{a})_*(\iota)) = (\psi \varphi_\mathfrak{a})_*(\iota) = \varphi_*(\iota) = \iota',$$

so $\psi : \mathfrak{a} \star (E, \iota) \to (E', \iota')$ is a K-isomorphism. The converse is clear. □

Proposition 11 (GRH). *Given $(E, \iota) \in SS_{\mathfrak{O}}(p)$ and an ε-basis of $\mathrm{End}(E)$, one can find $\mathfrak{a}$ such that $\tau_p(E, \iota) = \mathfrak{a} \star (E, \iota)$ in probabilistic polynomial time in the length of the input.*

Proof. From Corollary 3, the lattice $\Lambda = (\phi_p \circ \iota(\mathfrak{O}))^\perp \cap \mathrm{Hom}(E, E^{(p)})$ is primitive, so one can find $\varphi \in \Lambda$ of prime degree coprime to p and to the conductor of $\mathfrak{O}$ (for instance with the algorithm [Wes22, Proposition 3.6], which ensures that $\deg(\varphi)$ is a large enough prime, assuming GRH). The algorithm returns

$$\mathfrak{a} = \iota^{-1}((\mathrm{Hom}(E^{(p)}, E) \circ \varphi) \cap \iota(\mathfrak{O})).$$

It remains to show that this output is correct. From Corollary 2, we have that $\varphi : (E, \iota) \to \tau_p(E, \iota)$ is an $\mathfrak{O}$-isogeny, and it is horizontal. Applying Lemma 9, the isogeny φ is induced by an invertible $\mathfrak{O}$-ideal $\mathfrak{b}$. We have $E[\mathfrak{b}] = \ker(\varphi) = E[(\mathrm{Hom}(E^{(p)}, E) \circ \varphi]$, so from Lemma 8, we have $\iota(\mathfrak{a}) = \iota(\mathfrak{p}^k \mathfrak{b})$ for some $k \in \mathbf{Z}$. But $N(\mathfrak{b}) = \deg(\varphi)$ is coprime with p, and $\mathfrak{b} \subseteq \mathfrak{a}$, so $k = 0$. Therefore $\mathfrak{a} = \mathfrak{b}$, hence $\tau_p(E, \iota) = \mathfrak{b} \star (E, \iota) = \mathfrak{a} \star (E, \iota)$. □

Lemma 10. *Suppose $\tau_p(E_1, \iota_1) = \mathfrak{a} \star (E_1, \iota_1)$ and $\tau_p(E_2, \iota_2) = \mathfrak{b} \star (E_2, \iota_2)$. Any ideal $\mathfrak{c}$ such that $\mathfrak{c} \star (E_1, \iota_1) = (E_2, \iota_2)$ satisfies $[\mathfrak{c}^2] = [\mathfrak{a}\mathfrak{b}]$.*

Proof. We have the chain of equalities

$$\begin{aligned}
\overline{\mathfrak{b}}\mathfrak{a} \star (E_1, \iota_1) &= \overline{\mathfrak{b}} \star \tau_p(E_1, \iota_1) = \overline{\mathfrak{b}} \star \tau_p(\overline{\mathfrak{c}} \star (E_2, \iota_2)) \\
&= \mathfrak{c}\overline{\mathfrak{b}} \star \tau_p(E_2, \iota_2) = \mathfrak{c} \star (E_2, \iota_2) \\
&= \mathfrak{c}^2 \star (E_1, \iota_1),
\end{aligned}$$

and we conclude from the fact that the action of the class group is free. □

Theorem 2. (GRH, EFFECTIVE $\mathfrak{O}$-VECTORIZATION reduces to $\mathfrak{O}$-ENDRING). *Given $\mathfrak{O}$ and the factorisation of its discriminant, three $\mathfrak{O}$-oriented elliptic curves $(E, \iota), (E', \iota'), (F, \jmath) \in SS_{\mathfrak{O}}(p)$, together with ε-bases of $\mathrm{End}(E)$, $\mathrm{End}(E')$ and $\mathrm{End}(F)$, one can compute (or assert that it does not exist) an $\mathfrak{O}$-ideal $\mathfrak{c}$ such that $(E', \iota') = \mathfrak{c} \star (E, \iota)$ and an efficient representation of $\varphi_{\mathfrak{c}} : (F, \jmath) \to \mathfrak{c} \star (F, \jmath)$ in probabilistic polynomial time in the length of the input and in $\#(\mathrm{Cl}(\mathfrak{O})[2])$.*

Proof. Suppose we are given $(E, \iota), (E', \iota') \in SS_{\mathfrak{O}}(p)$, together with $\mathrm{End}(E)$ and $\mathrm{End}(E')$. We can compute $\mathfrak{a}$ and $\mathfrak{b}$ such that $\tau_p(E, \iota) = \mathfrak{a} \star (E, \iota)$ and $\tau_p(E', \iota') = \mathfrak{b} \star (E', \iota')$ with Proposition 11. From Lemma 10, the ideal class of $\mathfrak{c}$ is one of the $\#(\mathrm{Cl}(\mathfrak{O})[2])$ square roots of $[\mathfrak{a}\overline{\mathfrak{b}}]$. They can be enumerated following [BS96, Section 6], and each of them can efficiently be checked for correctness with Propositon 9. Once the ideal $\mathfrak{c}$ has been found, compute an efficient representation of $\varphi_{\mathfrak{c}} : (F, \jmath) \to \mathfrak{c} \star (F, \jmath)$ with Proposition 9. □

Corollary 4 (GRH). *Given the factorisation of $\mathrm{disc}(\mathfrak{O})$, EFFECTIVE $\mathfrak{O}$-UBER reduces to $\mathfrak{O}$-ENDRING* in probabilistic polynomial time in the length of the instance and in $\#(\mathrm{Cl}(\mathfrak{O})[2])$.*

Proof. Suppose we are given $(E, \iota), (F, \jmath) \in SS_{\mathfrak{O}}(p)$ and an $\mathfrak{O}$-orientable elliptic curve E'. Solving $\mathfrak{O}$-ENDRING*, one can find ε-bases of End(E), End(F) and End(E'), and an $\mathfrak{O}$-orientation ι' of E'. The result follows from Theorem 2. □

7 The Oriented Diffie-Hellman Problem

In this section, we study the relation of $\mathfrak{O}$-DIFFIEHELLMAN with other $\mathfrak{O}$-oriented problems, proving that it is essentially quantum-equivalent to the problem $\mathfrak{O}$-ENDRING. First, we have the following simple reduction from the problem $\mathfrak{O}$-DIFFIEHELLMAN to EFFECTIVE $\mathfrak{O}$-VECTORIZATION.

Proposition 12.
$\mathfrak{O}$-DIFFIEHELLMAN *reduces to* EFFECTIVE $\mathfrak{O}$-VECTORIZATION *in probabilistic polynomial time in the length of the instance.*

Proof. Suppose we are given an oriented curve $(E, \iota) \in SS_{\mathfrak{O}}(p)$, and its images $\mathfrak{a} \star (E, \iota)$ and $\mathfrak{b} \star (E, \iota)$. Solving EFFECTIVE $\mathfrak{O}$-VECTORIZATION, one can recover the class of $\mathfrak{a}$, and apply its action on $\mathfrak{b} \star (E, \iota)$, thereby obtaining $(\mathfrak{a}\mathfrak{b}) \star (E, \iota)$.
□

Now, it remains to prove that the EFFECTIVE $\mathfrak{O}$-VECTORIZATION problem reduces to $\mathfrak{O}$-DIFFIEHELLMAN. In [GPSV21], it was proved that if the action of $Cl(\mathfrak{O})$ is efficiently computable, then (non-effective) $\mathfrak{O}$-VECTORIZATION reduces to $\mathfrak{O}$-DIFFIEHELLMAN in quantum polynomial time. Unfortunately, the action of $Cl(\mathfrak{O})$ is not efficiently computable in general, since only the action of *smooth* class representatives can be computed efficiently. Therefore the reduction does not run in polynomial time, and it does not apply to the effective variant of $\mathfrak{O}$-VECTORIZATION. We resolve both limitations. First, we prove that the $\mathfrak{O}$-VECTORIZATION problem does reduce to $\mathfrak{O}$-DIFFIEHELLMAN in quantum polynomial time because an oracle for $\mathfrak{O}$-DIFFIEHELLMAN provides an efficient way to evaluate the group action (by a trick similar to what is done in [GPSV21, Lemma 1]). Second, Proposition 7 and Theorem 2 immediately enhance the reduction from $\mathfrak{O}$-VECTORIZATION to a reduction from EFFECTIVE $\mathfrak{O}$-VECTORIZATION.

Theorem 3. (GRH). $\mathfrak{O}$-VECTORIZATION *reduces to* $\mathfrak{O}$-DIFFIEHELLMAN *in quantum polynomial time in the length of the instance.*

Proof. This is essentially an application of a generalisation of Shor's algorithm for the discrete logarithm problem [Sho97], with the observation that an oracle for $\mathfrak{O}$-DIFFIEHELLMAN makes the implicit group structure of a $Cl(\mathfrak{O})$-orbit efficiently computable. More precisely, let $(E, \iota) \in SS_{\mathfrak{O}}(p)$, and $(E', \iota') = \mathfrak{a} \star (E, \iota)$ be an instance of $\mathfrak{O}$-VECTORIZATION. From [Bac90], assuming GRH, there is a bound B polynomial in $\log(\mathrm{disc}(\mathfrak{O}))$ such that $\mathfrak{B} = \{\mathfrak{p} \mid N(\mathfrak{p}) < B$ is prime$\}$ is a generating set of the group $Cl(\mathfrak{O})$. Let

$$f : \mathbf{Z}^{\mathfrak{B}} \times \mathbf{Z} \times SS_{\mathfrak{O}}(p) \longrightarrow SS_{\mathfrak{O}}(p)$$

$$((e_{\mathfrak{p}})_{\mathfrak{p}}, k, (F, \iota_F)) \longmapsto \left(\mathfrak{a}^k \cdot \prod_{\mathfrak{p}} \mathfrak{p}^{e_{\mathfrak{p}}} \right) \star (F, \iota_F).$$

From [Kit95], if one can evaluate f in quantum polynomial time, then one can solve the corresponding Abelian Stabilizer Problem and recover $(e_\mathfrak{p})_\mathfrak{p}$ such that $\mathfrak{a} \sim \prod_\mathfrak{p} \mathfrak{p}^{e_\mathfrak{p}}$ (thereby solving the $\mathfrak{O}$-VECTORIZATION instance). It remains to prove that f can indeed be computed in polynomial time. This is only feasible thanks to the $\mathfrak{O}$-DIFFIEHELLMAN oracle $\mathscr{O}$, which makes the implicit group multiplication $\odot$ on the orbit $\mathrm{Cl}(\mathfrak{O}) \star (E, \iota)$ efficiently computable, as

$$(\mathfrak{b} \star (E, \iota)) \odot (\mathfrak{c} \star (E, \iota)) = (\mathfrak{bc}) \star (E, \iota) = \mathscr{O}((E, \iota), \mathfrak{b} \star (E, \iota), \mathfrak{c} \star (E, \iota)).$$

Therefore, given any $k \geq 0$ and $\mathfrak{b} \star (E, \iota)$, one can compute $\mathfrak{b}^k \star (E, \iota) = (\mathfrak{b} \star (E, \iota))^{\odot k}$ by square-and-multiply. Then, for any $(e_\mathfrak{p})_\mathfrak{p} \in \mathbf{Z}_{\geq 0}^{\mathfrak{B}}$ and $k \geq 0$, one can efficiently compute

$$f((e_\mathfrak{p})_\mathfrak{p}, k, (F, \iota_F)) = \left(\bigodot_\mathfrak{p} (\mathfrak{p} \star (E, \iota))^{\odot e_\mathfrak{p}} \right) \odot (E', \iota')^{\odot k} \odot (F, \iota_F),$$

given the oriented curves $\mathfrak{p} \star (E, \iota)$. Since each $\mathfrak{p}$ has small norm, these $\mathfrak{p} \star (E, \iota)$ can be computed in polynomial time. To deal with negative exponents, we note that the class number $h(\mathfrak{O})$ is computable in quantum polynomial time [BS16], so all exponents can be reduced modulo $h(\mathfrak{O})$.   □

Corollary 5 (GRH). *The problem* CSIDH-DIFFIEHELLMAN *of recovering CSIDH shared secrets reduces to the problem* ENDRING$_{\mathbf{F}_p}$ *of computing the full endomorphism ring of supersingular elliptic curves defined over* $\mathbf{F}_p$, *under a probabilistic polynomial time reduction in* $\log p$. *Conversely,* ENDRING$_{\mathbf{F}_p}$ *reduces to* CSIDH-DIFFIEHELLMAN *in quantum polynomial time in* $\log p$.

Proof. The problem CSIDH-DIFFIEHELLMAN is equal to $\mathfrak{O}$-DIFFIEHELLMAN for some order $\mathfrak{O}$ containing $\sqrt{-p}$. There are at most two possibilities for $\mathfrak{O}$: either $\mathbf{Z}[\sqrt{-p}]$ or $\mathbf{Z}[(1+\sqrt{-p})/2]$. The latter is only possible when $p \equiv 3 \mod 4$. They differ by an index 2, and correspond to CSIDH on the *floor* or on the *surface*—see CSURF [CD20].

In either case, for such an order $\mathfrak{O}$, we now prove that ENDRING$_\mathfrak{O}$ reduces to ENDRING$_{\mathbf{F}_p}$. Let E be an ENDRING$_\mathfrak{O}$-instance. Since E is $\mathfrak{O}$-orientable, there exists $\alpha \in \mathrm{End}(E)$ of degree p. Since E is supersingular, α is purely inseparable, so it factors as $\alpha = \beta \circ \phi_p^E$ where $\phi_p^E : E \to E^{(p)}$ is the Frobenius and $\beta : E^{(p)} \to E$ is an isomorphism. This proves that $E \cong E^{(p)}$, hence $j(E) \in \mathbf{F}_p$ and one can compute an isomorphism $\gamma : E \to E'$ to a curve E' defined over $\mathbf{F}_p$. Therefore, the ENDRING$_\mathfrak{O}$-instance E reduces to the ENDRING$_{\mathbf{F}_p}$-instance E'.

Finally, we prove that ENDRING$_{\mathbf{F}_p}$ reduces to $\mathfrak{O}$-ENDRING. If E is defined over $\mathbf{F}_p$, then either $\iota : \sqrt{-p} \to \phi_p^E$ is an $\mathfrak{O}$-orientation on E, or there exists an isogeny $\varphi : E \to E'$ of degree 2 such that $\varphi_*(\iota)$ is an $\mathfrak{O}$-orientation on E' (see [DG16, Theorem 2.7]). So ENDRING$_{\mathbf{F}_p}$ for E reduces to $\mathfrak{O}$-ENDRING either for E or for one of its three 2-neighbours.

These new reductions at hand, the corollary follows from the other reductions summarised in Fig. 1, given that the factorisation of disc($\mathfrak{O}$) is either $-p$ or $-4p$, and from genus theory, $\#(\mathrm{Cl}(\mathfrak{O})[2]) \leq 2$.   □

8   The Case of Non-maximal Orders

The OSIDH cryptosystem [CK20] exploits elliptic curves oriented by an order of the form $\mathbf{Z} + \ell^e \mathfrak{O}$, where ℓ is a small prime, and $\mathfrak{O}$ has small discriminant. It is observed however that with such parameters, the $(\mathbf{Z} + \ell^e \mathfrak{O})$-VECTORIZATION problem is not hard, hence it would be unsafe for the protocol to provide full efficient encodings of $(\mathbf{Z} + \ell^e \mathfrak{O})$-orientations. In this section, we generalise this fact and study its consequences for relevant variants of the endomorphism ring problem.

Lemma 11. *Let c be a positive integer. Given $(E, \iota) \in \mathrm{SS}_{\mathbf{Z}+c\mathfrak{O}}(p)$ in efficient representation, one can compute the kernel of an isogeny $\varphi : E \to E'$ of degree c such that $\varphi_*(\iota)$ is an $\mathfrak{O}$-orientation of E' in probabilistic polynomial time in the length of the input, the largest prime factor of c, and, for each $\ell^e \parallel c$, the degree of the extension of $\mathbf{F}_p$ over which $E[\ell^e]$ is defined.*

Proof. Let $\varphi : (E, \iota) \to (E', \iota')$ be the unique ascending K-isogeny of degree c, where $\iota' = \varphi_*(\iota)$ is an $\mathfrak{O}$-orientation. We are given a generator ω of $\mathbf{Z} + c\mathfrak{O}$ and an efficient representation of $\iota(\omega)$. The generator is of the form $\omega = a + c\omega_0$ where ω_0 is a generator of $\mathfrak{O}$ and without loss of generality, $a = 0$. We have

$$\iota(\omega) = (\hat{\varphi}_*(\iota'))(\omega) = \frac{\hat{\varphi} \circ \iota'(\omega) \circ \varphi}{c} = \hat{\varphi} \circ \iota'(\omega_0) \circ \varphi.$$

It implies $\ker(\varphi) \subseteq \ker(\iota(\omega))$. Now $\ker(\iota(\omega))$ is cyclic (otherwise $\iota(\omega)$ would be divisible by an integer, hence ι would not be a primitive embedding), so $\ker(\varphi) = \ker(\iota(\omega)) \cap E[c] = \cap_{\ell^e \parallel c}(\ker(\iota(\omega)) \cap E[\ell^e])$ can be recovered in time polynomial in the largest prime factor of c, and, for each $\ell^e \parallel c$, in the degree of the extension of $\mathbf{F}_p$ over which $E[\ell^e]$ is defined. $\qquad \square$

In particular, if c is smooth and $E[c]$ is defined over a small extension of $\mathbf{F}_p$, given $(E, \iota) \in \mathrm{SS}_{\mathbf{Z}+c\mathfrak{O}}(p)$, it is easy to find the unique isogeny ascending to an $\mathfrak{O}$-orientable curve. This is the crux of so-called *torsion point attacks* on SIDH-like cryptosystems [Pet17, KMP+21], which can be reinterpreted as an attempt to recover a $(\mathbf{Z} + c\mathfrak{O})$-orientation from some information on the action of isogenies on torsion points, and some carefully chosen $\mathfrak{O}$.

Lemma 12 (GRH). *Given the kernel of an isogeny $\varphi : E \to E'$, and an ε-basis of $\mathrm{End}(E)$, one can compute an ε-basis of $\mathrm{End}(E')$ in probabilistic polynomial time in the length of the input and the largest prime factor of $\deg(\varphi)$.*

Proof. This statement seems folklore; we give a proof for completeness. Let us describe a simple (and certainly not optimal) algorithm. We may assume that $\ker(\varphi)$ is cyclic. Choose any prime $\ell \mid \deg(\varphi)$, and let $\varphi_1 : E \to E_1 = E/(\ker(\varphi) \cap E[\ell])$. One can compute the left $\mathrm{End}(E)$-ideals I_1 of norm ℓ corresponding to φ_1 (for instance with an exhaustive search among the $\ell + 1$ possibilities, checking each guess by evaluating a basis on the kernel of φ_1). Now, $\mathcal{O}_R(I_1) \cong \mathrm{End}(E_1)$, and one can find an ε-basis of $\mathrm{End}(E_1)$ (for instance with [Wes22, Algorithm 6]). The isogeny φ factors as $\varphi' \circ \varphi_1$ with $\deg(\varphi') = \deg(\varphi)/\ell$, and one can iterate the procedure. $\qquad \square$

Theorem 4 (GRH). $(\mathbf{Z} + c\mathfrak{O})$-ENDRING *reduces to* $\mathfrak{O}$-ENDRING* *in proba-bilistic polynomial time polynomial in the length of the input, the largest prime factor of c, and, for each* $\ell^e \parallel c$, *the degree of the extension of* $\mathbf{F}_p$ *over which* $E[\ell^e]$ *is defined.*

Proof. Let $(E, \iota) \in \mathrm{SS}_{\mathbf{Z}+c\mathfrak{O}}(p)$ be an instance of $(\mathbf{Z} + c\mathfrak{O})$-ENDRING. From Lemma 11, we can compute (within the claimed running time) an isogeny $\varphi : E \to E'$ where E' is $\mathfrak{O}$-orientable. One can solve $\mathfrak{O}$-ENDRING* for E' to find an ε-basis of $\mathrm{End}(E')$. Now, Lemma 12 allows us to find an ε-basis of $\mathrm{End}(E)$ thanks to the ε-basis of $\mathrm{End}(E')$ and the kernel of $\hat{\varphi}$. $\qquad\square$

Lemma 13. *The* $\mathfrak{O}$-ENDRING* *problem can heuristically be solved in expected time* $l^{O(1)}\mathrm{disc}(\mathfrak{O})$, *where* l *is the length of the input.*

Proof. By Proposition 8, one can reduce $\mathfrak{O}$-ENDRING* to $\mathfrak{O}$-UBER in time poly-nomial in $\log p$ and $\log(\mathrm{disc}(\mathfrak{O}))$. Then, one can solve $\mathfrak{O}$-UBER with Proposi-tion 2, under the same heuristics. $\qquad\square$

Corollary 6. $(\mathbf{Z} + c\mathfrak{O})$-ENDRING *can heuristically be solved in probabilistic polynomial time in the length of the input,* $\mathrm{disc}(\mathfrak{O})$, *the largest prime factor of c, and, for each* $\ell^e \parallel c$, *the degree of the extension of* $\mathbf{F}_p$ *over which* $E[\ell^e]$ *is defined.*

Proof. It immediately follows from Theorem 4 and Lemma 13. $\qquad\square$

This corollary implies that if $\mathfrak{O}$ has small discriminant and c is powersmooth, then knowledge of a $(\mathbf{Z} + c\mathfrak{O})$-orientation leaks the whole endomorphism ring.

Theorem 5 (GRH). *Suppose c is* $(\log p)^{O(1)}$-*powersmooth. Then, the problem* $(\mathbf{Z} + c\mathfrak{O})$-ENDRING *reduces to* $\mathfrak{O}$-ENDRING *in probabilistic polynomial time in the length of the input.*

Proof. We proceed as in the proof of Theorem 4, but reducing to $\mathfrak{O}$-ENDRING using the $\mathfrak{O}$-orientation $\varphi_*(\iota)$ on E'. The efficient representation of ι implies that one can efficiently evaluate $\hat{\varphi} \circ \iota(\alpha) \circ \varphi$, and the powersmoothness of c allows one to divide by c, so we have an efficient representation of $\varphi_*(\iota)$ to be used by the $\mathfrak{O}$-ENDRING solver. $\qquad\square$

Acknowledgements. This work was supported by the Agence Nationale de la Recherche under grants ANR MELODIA (ANR-20-CE40-0013) and ANR CIAO (ANR-19-CE48-0008). The author would like to thank Katherine E. Stange and Jean-François Biasse for valuable discussions, feedback and corrections, that helped improve the qual-ity of this work.

References

[Bac90] Bach, E.: Explicit bounds for primality testing and related problems. Math. Comput. **55**(191), 355–380 (1990)

[BKV19] Beullens, W., Kleinjung, T., Vercauteren, F.: CSI-FiSh: efficient isogeny based signatures through class group computations. In: Galbraith, S.D., Moriai, S. (eds.) ASIACRYPT 2019. LNCS, vol. 11921, pp. 227–247. Springer, Cham (2019). https://doi.org/10.1007/978-3-030-34578-5_9

[BS96] Bosma, W., Stevenhagen, P.: On the computation of quadratic 2-class groups. J. de théorie des nombres de Bordeaux 8(2), 283–313 (1996)

[BS16] Biasse, J.-F., Song, F.: Efficient quantum algorithms for computing class groups and solving the principal ideal problem in arbitrary degree number fields. In: Krauthgamer, R. (ed.) Proceedings of the Twenty-Seventh Annual ACM-SIAM Symposium on Discrete Algorithms - SODA 2016, pp. 893–902. SIAM (2016)

[CD20] Castryck, W., Decru, T.: CSIDH on the surface. In: Ding, J., Tillich, J.-P. (eds.) PQCrypto 2020. LNCS, vol. 12100, pp. 111–129. Springer, Cham (2020). https://doi.org/10.1007/978-3-030-44223-1_7

[CJS14] Childs, A., Jao, D., Soukharev, V.: Constructing elliptic curve isogenies in quantum subexponential time. J. Math. Cryptol. 8(1), 1–29 (2014)

[CK20] Colò, L., Kohel, D.: Orienting supersingular isogeny graphs. J. Math. Cryptol. 14(1), 414–437 (2020)

[CLG09] Charles, D.X., Lauter, K.E., Goren, E.Z.: Cryptographic hash functions from expander graphs. J. Cryptol. 22(1), 93–113 (2009)

[CLM+18] Castryck, W., Lange, T., Martindale, C., Panny, L., Renes, J.: CSIDH: an efficient post-quantum commutative group action. In: Peyrin, T., Galbraith, S. (eds.) ASIACRYPT 2018. LNCS, vol. 11274, pp. 395–427. Springer, Cham (2018). https://doi.org/10.1007/978-3-030-03332-3_15

[CN00] Coron, J.-S., Naccache, D.: Security analysis of the gennaro-halevi-rabin signature scheme. In: Preneel, B. (ed.) EUROCRYPT 2000. LNCS, vol. 1807, pp. 91–101. Springer, Heidelberg (2000). https://doi.org/10.1007/3-540-45539-6_7

[Cou06] Couveignes, J.M.: Hard homogeneous spaces. IACR Cryptology ePrint Archive, Report 2006/291 (2006). https://eprint.iacr.org/2006/291

[Cox11] Cox, D.A.: Primes of the Form x2+ ny2: Fermat, Class Field Theory, and Complex Multiplication, vol. 34. John Wiley & Sons, Hoboken (2011)

[CPV20] Castryck, W., Panny, L., Vercauteren, F.: Rational isogenies from irrational endomorphisms. In: Canteaut, A., Ishai, Y. (eds.) EUROCRYPT 2020. LNCS, vol. 12106, pp. 523–548. Springer, Cham (2020). https://doi.org/10.1007/978-3-030-45724-2_18

[CS21] Chenu, M., Smith, B.: Higher-degree supersingular group actions. In: MathCrypt 2021 - Mathematical Cryptology (2021)

[DDF+21] De Feo, L.: Séta: supersingular encryption from torsion attacks. In: Tibouchi, M., Wang, H. (eds.) ASIACRYPT 2021. LNCS, vol. 13093, pp. 249–278. Springer, Cham (2021). https://doi.org/10.1007/978-3-030-92068-5_9

[DG16] Delfs, C., Galbraith, S.D.: Computing isogenies between supersingular elliptic curves over $\mathbb{F}_p$. Designs Codes Cryptogr. 78(2), 425–440 (2014). https://doi.org/10.1007/s10623-014-0010-1

[EHL+18] Eisenträger, K., Hallgren, S., Lauter, K., Morrison, T., Petit, C.: Supersingular isogeny graphs and endomorphism rings: reductions and solutions. In: Nielsen, J.B., Rijmen, V. (eds.) EUROCRYPT 2018. LNCS, vol. 10822, pp. 329–368. Springer, Cham (2018). https://doi.org/10.1007/978-3-319-78372-7_11

[EHL+20] Eisenträger, K., Hallgren, S., Leonardi, C., Morrison, T., Park, J.: Computing endomorphism rings of supersingular elliptic curves and connections to path-finding in isogeny graphs. Open Book Series 4(1), 215–232 (2020)

[FKM21]   Fouotsa, T.B., Kutas, P., Merz, S.-P.: On the isogeny problem with torsion point information. IACR Cryptology ePrint Archive, Report 2021/153 (2021). https://eprint.iacr.org/2021/153

[GPS20]   Galbraith, S.D., Petit, C., Silva, J.: Identification protocols and signature schemes based on supersingular isogeny problems. J. Cryptol. 33(1), 130–175 (2020)

[GPST16] Galbraith, S.D., Petit, C., Shani, B., Ti, Y.B.: On the security of supersingular isogeny cryptosystems. In: Cheon, J.H., Takagi, T. (eds.) ASIACRYPT 2016. LNCS, vol. 10031, pp. 63–91. Springer, Heidelberg (2016). https://doi.org/10.1007/978-3-662-53887-6_3

[GPSV21] Galbraith, S., Panny, L., Smith, B., Vercauteren, F.: Quantum equivalence of the DLP and CDHP for group actions. Math. Cryptol. 1(1), 40–44 (2021)

[JAC+17] Jao, D., et al. SIKE: Supersingular isogeny key encapsulation (2017)

[JD11]   Jao, D., De Feo, L.: Towards quantum-resistant cryptosystems from supersingular elliptic curve isogenies. In: Yang, B.-Y. (ed.) PQCrypto 2011. LNCS, vol. 7071, pp. 19–34. Springer, Heidelberg (2011). https://doi.org/10.1007/978-3-642-25405-5_2

[Kan89]   Kaneko, M.: Supersingular j-invariants as singular moduli mod p. Osaka J. Math. 26(4), 849–855 (1989)

[Kit95]   Kitaev, A.Y.: Quantum measurements and the abelian stabilizer problem. arXiv preprint quant-ph/9511026 (1995)

[KLPT14] Kohel, D., Lauter, K., Petit, C., Tignol, J.A.: On the quaternion ℓ-isogeny path problem. LMS J. Comput. Math. 17(A), 418–432 (2014)

[KMP+21] Kutas, P., Martindale, C., Panny, L., Petit, C., Stange, E.: Weak instances of SIDH variants under improved torsion-point attacks. In: To appear in Advances in Cryptology - CRYPTO 2021, Lecture Notes in Computer Science (2021)

[Kup05]   Kuperberg, G.: A subexponential-time quantum algorithm for the dihedral hidden subgroup problem. SIAM J. Comp. 35(1), 170–188 (2005)

[LB20]   Love, J., Boneh, D.: Supersingular curves with small noninteger endomorphisms. Open Book Series 4(1), 7–22 (2020)

[LO77]   Lagarias, J.C., Odlyzko, A.M.: Effective versions of the Chebotarev density theorem. In: Algebraic number fields: L-functions and Galois properties (Proceedings of Symposium, University of Durham, Durham, 1975), pp. 409–464. Academic Press, London (1977)

[Onu21]   Onuki, H.: On oriented supersingular elliptic curves. Finite Fields and Their Appl. 69, 101777 (2021)

[Pet17]   Petit, C.: Faster algorithms for isogeny problems using torsion point images. In: Takagi, T., Peyrin, T. (eds.) ASIACRYPT 2017. LNCS, vol. 10625, pp. 330–353. Springer, Cham (2017). https://doi.org/10.1007/978-3-319-70697-9_12

[Piz80]   Pizer, A.: An algorithm for computing modular forms on $\gamma_0(n)$. J. Algebra 64(2), 340–390 (1980)

[Rón92]   Rónyai, L.: Algorithmic properties of maximal orders in simple algebras over **Q**. Comput. Compl. 2(3), 225–243 (1992)

[Sho97]   Shor, P.W.: Polynomial-time algorithms for prime factorization and discrete logarithms on a quantum computer. SIAM J. Comput. 26(5), 1484–1509 (1997)

[Sil86] Silverman, J.H.: The Arithmetic of Elliptic Curves, volume 106 of Gradute Texts in Mathematics. Springer, Heidelberg (1986)

[Sim06] Simon, D.: Quadratic equations in dimensions 4, 5 and more. Preprint (2006). See [?] for a published review

[Vig06] Vignéras, M.-F.: Arithmétique des algèbres de quaternions, vol. 800. Springer, Heidelberg (2006)

[Voi21] Voight, J.: Quaternion algebras. In: Graduate Texts in Mathematics, no. 288. Springer, Heidelberg (2021)

[Wes22] Wesolowski, B.: The supersingular isogeny path and endomorphism ring problems are equivalent. In: FOCS 2021–62nd Annual IEEE Symposium on Foundations of Computer Science (2022)

Quantum Algorithms for Variants of Average-Case Lattice Problems via Filtering

Yilei Chen[1]([✉]), Qipeng Liu[2], and Mark Zhandry[3,4]

[1] Tsinghua University, Beijing 100084, China
chenyilei.ra@gmail.com
[2] Simons Institute for the Theory of Computing, Berkeley, USA
[3] NTT Research, Palo Alto, USA
[4] Princeton University, Princeton, USA

Abstract. We show polynomial-time quantum algorithms for the following problems:

1. Short integer solution (SIS) problem under the *infinity* norm, where the public matrix is very wide, the modulus is a polynomially large prime, and the bound of infinity norm is set to be half of the modulus minus a constant.
2. Learning with errors (LWE) problem given LWE-like quantum states with polynomially large moduli and certain error distributions, including bounded uniform distributions and Laplace distributions.
3. Extrapolated dihedral coset problem (EDCP) with certain parameters.

The SIS, LWE, and EDCP problems in their standard forms are as hard as solving lattice problems in the worst case. However, the variants that we can solve are not in the parameter regimes known to be as hard as solving worst-case lattice problems. Still, no classical or quantum polynomial-time algorithms were known for the variants of SIS and LWE we consider. For EDCP, our quantum algorithm slightly extends the result of Ivanyos et al. (2018).

Our algorithms for variants of SIS and EDCP use the existing quantum reductions from those problems to LWE, or more precisely, to the problem of solving LWE given LWE-like quantum states. Our main contribution is solving LWE given LWE-like quantum states with interesting parameters using a filtering technique.

1 Introduction

Solving the shortest vector problem (SVP) over lattices has been a target for designing efficient quantum algorithms for decades. In the literature, solving approximate SVP for *all* lattices has been (classically or quantumly) reduced to the following problems:

1. The short integer solution (SIS) problem, classically, initially shown by Ajtai [Ajt96].

© International Association for Cryptologic Research 2022
O. Dunkelman and S. Dziembowski (Eds.): EUROCRYPT 2022, LNCS 13277, pp. 372–401, 2022.
https://doi.org/10.1007/978-3-031-07082-2_14

2. The dihedral coset problem (DCP), quantumly, initially shown by Regev [Reg02].
3. The learning with errors problem (LWE), quantumly, initially shown by Regev [Reg05].

Therefore, to show an efficient quantum algorithm for approximate SVP in the worst-case, it suffices to construct an efficient quantum algorithm for any one of those average-case problems. However, no polynomial (or even subexponential) time quantum algorithms are known for SIS or LWE. For DCP, a subexponential quantum algorithm is given by Kuperberg [Kup05]. But the quantum reduction shown by Regev [Reg02] requires the DCP algorithm to be noise-tolerant, while the algorithm of Kuperberg is not. Let us also mention that over the past few years, efficient quantum algorithms for SVP for ideal lattices in certain parameter regimes have been shown in [CGS14, EHKS14, BS16, CDPR16, CDW17]. Still, showing a polynomial (or even subexponential) time quantum algorithm for SVP with polynomial approximation factors for *all* lattices is widely open.

The SIS and LWE problems are powerful tools for building cryptosystems, thus understanding the quantum hardness of those two problems is interesting in its own right. The SIS problem is typically used in constructing elementary cryptographic primitives such as one-way functions [Ajt96], collision-resistant hash functions [GGH96] digital signatures [GPV08]. The LWE problem is extremely versatile, yielding public-key cryptosystems [Reg05], and advanced cryptographic capabilities such as fully homomorphic encryption (FHE) [BV11], attribute-based encryption [GVW13], and quantum FHE [Mah18]. The conjectured quantum hardness of SIS and LWE has also made lattice-based cryptosystems popular candidates for post-quantum cryptography standardization [DKRV18, BDK+18, DKL+18].

1.1 Background of SIS, LWE, DCP, and Our Main Results

We show polynomial-time quantum algorithms for certain variants of SIS, LWE, and DCP. Our quantum algorithms for the variants of SIS and DCP go through the existing quantum reductions from those problems to LWE, or more precisely, to the problems of *Constructing quantum LWE states* (C|LWE⟩) and *Solving LWE given LWE-like quantum states* (S|LWE⟩). In fact, the heart of our results is showing a quantum filtering technique for solving those quantum versions of LWE (Fig. 1).

Let us now provide more background of SIS, LWE, and DCP, then state our main results.

SIS. Let us first recall the standard definition of the SIS problem.

Definition 1 (Short integer solution (SIS) problem [Ajt96]). *Let n, m, q be integers such that $m = \Omega(n \log q) \subseteq \text{poly}(n)$. Let β be a positive real number such that $\beta < q$. Let A be a uniformly random matrix over $\mathbb{Z}_q^{n \times m}$. The SIS problem $\text{SIS}_{n,m,q,\beta}$ asks to find a nonzero vector $x \in \mathbb{Z}^m$ such that $\|x\|_2 \leq \beta$ and $Ax \equiv 0 \pmod{q}$.*

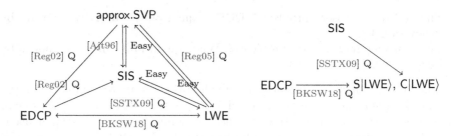

Fig. 1. Left: An overview of the reductions between SVP, SIS, EDCP, and LWE. "$A \to B$" means Problem A reduces to Problem B. "Q" means quantum. Right: The reductions used in our quantum algorithms.

The SIS problem is shown to be as hard as solving approximate SVP for all lattices [Ajt96]. The reductions are improved via a series of works [CN97, Mic02, MR07, GPV08, MP13]. Several variants of the SIS problem are studied in the literature. The most common variant is the one that changes the restriction of the solution. The solution is bounded in ℓ_p norm for some $p \geq 0$, or even the ℓ_∞ norm, instead of bounded in ℓ_2 norm. In this paper, we look at the variant where the solution is bounded by its ℓ_∞ norm. More precisely, we use $\mathsf{SIS}^\infty_{n,m,q,\beta}$ to denote the variant of SIS where the solution x is required to satisfy $\|x\|_\infty \leq \beta$. When $\beta = 1$, it corresponds to the subset-sum problem where the solution is bounded in $\{-1, 0, 1\}$.

Bounding the SIS solution in its ℓ_∞ norm is used quite commonly in cryptography due to its simplicity (it is used, e.g., in [BV15]). When the parameters are set so that $\beta\sqrt{m} > q$, i.e., when m is relatively large compared to q/β, we are not aware of any worst-case problem that is reducible to $\mathsf{SIS}^\infty_{n,m,q,\beta}$. Still, such parameter settings are used in cryptosystems. In a recent practical signature scheme proposed by Ducas et al. [DKL+18], the security of the scheme relies on (the "Module" version of) $\mathsf{SIS}^\infty_{n,m,q,\beta}$ with $\beta\sqrt{m} > q$. In their security analysis, the authors mention that the problem of SIS^∞ by itself has not been studied in-depth. Most of the algorithms they can think of for SIS^∞ are the ones designed for solving SIS or SVP in the ℓ_2 norm, such as BKZ [SE94].

To date, the only algorithm we are aware of that takes advantage of the ℓ_∞-norm bound has the following features. It solves $\mathsf{SIS}^\infty_{n,m,q,\beta}$ with a highly composite q and a very large m. For example, it is a polynomial-time algorithm for $\mathsf{SIS}^\infty_{n,O(n^c),2^c,1}$ when c is a constant. The algorithm is classical, folklore, and we include a formal description of the algorithm in the full version. It was not clear how to solve $\mathsf{SIS}^\infty_{n,m,q,\beta}$ when q is a polynomial prime and β is just slightly smaller than $q/2$, even if m is allowed to be an arbitrary polynomial.

We show a polynomial-time quantum algorithm for $\mathsf{SIS}^\infty_{n,m,q,\beta}$ where q is a polynomial prime modulus, $\beta = \frac{q-c}{2}$ for some constant c, and m is a large polynomial.

Theorem 1. *Let $c > 0$ be a constant integer, $q > c$ be a polynomially large prime modulus. Let $m \in \Omega\left((q - c)^3 \cdot n^{c+1} \cdot q \cdot \log q\right) \subseteq \mathsf{poly}(n)$, there is a polynomial-time quantum algorithm that solves $\mathsf{SIS}^{\infty}_{n,m,q,\frac{q-c}{2}}$.*

Remark 1. Note that if $\beta = q/2$, then a solution can be found classically by simply solving $Ax \equiv 0 \pmod{q}$ over $\mathbb{Z}_q$ using Gaussian elimination. Then for each entry in x, pick the representative over $\mathbb{Z}$ that lies in the range $[-q/2, q/2)$. This classical algorithm also extends to $\beta = \frac{q-c}{2}$ when $q = \Omega(n)$. In particular, as long as all the entries of x are at least $c/2$ far from $q/2$, x will be a valid solution. In the regime $q = \Omega(n)$, a random solution to $Ax \equiv 0 \pmod{q}$ will satisfy this with probability at least $O((1 - c/n)^n) = O(e^{-c})$, a constant. Theorem 1 thus gives a non-trivial algorithm for $\mathsf{SIS}^{\infty}_{n,m,q,\frac{q-c}{2}}$ when $q \in o(n)$, for which (to the best of our knowledge), no prior classical or quantum algorithm was known.

Remark 2. Our algorithm can also solve a variant of SIS where the each entry of the solution is required to be in an arbitrary subset S of $\mathbb{Z}_q$ such that $q - |S| = c$, where c is a constant (instead of the subset $[-\beta, \beta] \cap \mathbb{Z}$ of $\mathbb{Z}_q$). The width of the A matrix is required to satisfy $m \in \Omega\left((q - c)^3 \cdot n^{c+1} \cdot q \cdot \log q\right) \subseteq \mathsf{poly}(n)$. For example, suppose $q = 3$ and $m \in \Omega(n^2)$, our algorithm is able to provide a $\{0, 1\}$-solution for SIS.

Let us remark that our algorithm does not improve upon the existing algorithms for breaking the signature scheme in [DKL+18] since we require m to be very large, while the m used in [DKL+18] is fairly small.

LWE. Let us first recall the classical definition of the LWE problem.

Definition 2 (Learning with errors (LWE) [Reg05]**).** *Let n, m, q be positive integers. Let $u \in \mathbb{Z}_q^n$ be a secret vector. The learning with errors problem $\mathsf{LWE}_{n,m,q,\mathcal{D}_{\text{noise}}}$ asks to find the secret vector u given access to an oracle that outputs a_i, $a_i \cdot u + e_i \pmod{q}$ on its ith query, for $i = 1, ..., m$. Here each a_i is a uniformly random vector in $\mathbb{Z}_q^n$, and each error term e_i is sampled from a distribution $\mathcal{D}_{\text{noise}}$ over $\mathbb{Z}_q$.*

Regev [Reg05] shows if there is a polynomial-time algorithm that solves $\mathsf{LWE}_{n,m,q,\mathcal{D}_{\text{noise}}}$ where $\mathcal{D}_{\text{noise}}$ is Gaussian and m can be an arbitrary polynomial, then there is a quantum algorithm that solves worst-case approximate SVP. Note that in Regev's definition, the LWE samples are completely classical. In the variants of LWE we consider, the error distribution appears in the amplitude of some quantum states. Those quantum variants of LWE were implicitly used in the quantum reductions in [SSTX09,BKSW18], but they have not been made formal. Looking ahead, our new quantum algorithms make explicit use of the quantum nature of the noise distribution.

Our quantum algorithm for SIS^{∞} adapts the quantum reduction from SIS to the problem of *constructing LWE states* implicitly used in [SSTX09].

Definition 3. *Let n, m, q be positive integers. Let f be a function from $\mathbb{Z}_q$ to $\mathbb{R}$. The problem of constructing LWE states $\mathsf{C|LWE}\rangle_{n,m,q,f}$ asks to construct a quantum state of the form $\sum_{u \in \mathbb{Z}_q^n} \bigotimes_{i=1}^{m} \left(\sum_{e_i \in \mathbb{Z}_q} f(e_i)|a_i \cdot u + e_i \bmod q\rangle \right)$, given the input $\{a_i\}_{i=1,\dots,m}$ where each a_i is a uniformly random vector in $\mathbb{Z}_q^n$.*

Our quantum algorithm for EDCP adapts the quantum reduction from EDCP to the problem of *solving LWE given LWE-like quantum states* implicitly used in [BKSW18].

Definition 4. *Let n, m, q be positive integers. Let f be a function from $\mathbb{Z}_q$ to $\mathbb{R}$. Let $u \in \mathbb{Z}_q^n$ be a secret vector. The problem of solving LWE given LWE-like states $\mathsf{S|LWE}\rangle_{n,m,q,f}$ asks to find u given access to an oracle that outputs independent samples a_i, $\sum_{e_i \in \mathbb{Z}_q} f(e_i)|a_i \cdot u + e_i \bmod q\rangle$ on its ith query, for $i = 1, \dots, m$. Here each a_i is a uniformly random vector in $\mathbb{Z}_q^n$.*

We would like to remark that in the problem $\mathsf{C|LWE}\rangle$, there is no secret vector u; the goal is to construct an equal superposition of all LWE states for all possible u. Whereas for the problem $\mathsf{S|LWE}\rangle$, the goal is to find the secret vector u given samples of LWE states for this particular secret vector.

Let us briefly discuss the relations among LWE, $\mathsf{S|LWE}\rangle$, and $\mathsf{C|LWE}\rangle$. If we set f as $\sqrt{\mathcal{D}_{\mathsf{noise}}}$, then an efficient algorithm for solving $\mathsf{LWE}_{n,m,q,\mathcal{D}_{\mathsf{noise}}}$ implies efficient algorithms for solving $\mathsf{C|LWE}\rangle_{n,m,q,f}$ and $\mathsf{S|LWE}\rangle_{n,m,q,f}$. However, solving $\mathsf{C|LWE}\rangle_{n,m,q,f}$ or $\mathsf{S|LWE}\rangle_{n,m,q,f}$ does not necessarily imply solving $\mathsf{LWE}_{n,m,q,\mathcal{D}_{\mathsf{noise}}}$ in general. An algorithm for solving $\mathsf{C|LWE}\rangle_{n,m,q,f}$ only implies an efficient algorithm for solving $\mathsf{LWE}_{n,m,q,\mathcal{D}_{\mathsf{noise}}}$ when m is small compared to the ratio of the "widths" of f and $\mathcal{D}_{\mathsf{noise}}$; we will explain in details in Sect. 1.4.

Let us also remark that the $\mathsf{C|LWE}\rangle$ and $\mathsf{S|LWE}\rangle$ problems we define are different from the problem of "LWE with quantum samples" defined in [GKZ19]. In their definition, the quantum LWE samples are of the form $\sum_{a \in \mathbb{Z}_q^n} |a\rangle|a \cdot u + e\rangle$, where the error e is classical and a is in the quantum state. This variant of quantum LWE is easy to solve [GKZ19], but the idea in the algorithm does not carry to the quantum LWE variants we are interested in.

In [Reg05] (followed by [SSTX09, BKSW18] and most of the papers that use LWE), the noise distribution $\mathcal{D}_{\mathsf{noise}}$ or f is chosen to be Gaussian. One of the nice features of a Gaussian function f is that both f and its discrete Fourier transform (DFT) (over $\mathbb{Z}_q$), defined as

$$\hat{f} : \mathbb{Z}_q \to \mathbb{C}, \quad \hat{f} : y \mapsto \sum_{x \in \mathbb{Z}_q} \frac{1}{\sqrt{q}} \cdot e^{\frac{2\pi i x y}{q}} \cdot f(x),$$

are negligible beyond their centers. Such a feature of $\hat{f}$ is crucial in establishing the quantum reductions among lattice problems in [Reg05, SSTX09, BKSW18].

Other choices of noise distribution are also used for LWE in the literature. One popular option is to let f be the bounded uniform distribution over $[-B, B]$ for some $0 < B < \frac{q}{2}$. For certain choices of n, m, q, B, (classical) LWE with B-bounded uniform error is proven to be as hard as LWE with Gaussian noise [DM13]. On the other hand, Arora and Ge [AG11] present a classical algorithm for breaking LWE with a prime modulus q when the support S of the LWE error distribution is very small. It requires $m \in \Omega(n^{|S|})$ and runs in time $\mathsf{poly}(n^{|S|})$. When $B \in \omega(1)$ and q is a prime, no polynomial-time quantum algorithm has been published for LWE, C|LWE⟩, or S|LWE⟩.

We show when the noise distribution f is chosen such that $\hat{f}$ is *non-negligible* over $\mathbb{Z}_q$, then we can solve both C|LWE⟩ and S|LWE⟩ in quantum polynomial-time.

Theorem 2. *Let $n \in \mathbb{N}$ and $q \in \mathsf{poly}(n)$. Let $f : \mathbb{Z}_q \to \mathbb{R}$ be the amplitude for the error state such that the state $\sum_{e \in \mathbb{Z}_q} f(e)|e\rangle$ is efficiently constructible and $\eta := \min_{y \in \mathbb{Z}_q} |\hat{f}(y)|$ is non-negligible. Let $m \in \Omega\left(n \cdot q/\eta^2\right) \subseteq \mathsf{poly}(n)$, there exist polynomial-time quantum algorithms that solve $\mathsf{C|LWE\rangle}_{n,m,q,f}$ and $\mathsf{S|LWE\rangle}_{n,m,q,f}$.*

Although the theorem does not cover the case where f is Gaussian, it does cover some interesting error distributions f, such as when f is super-Gaussian (i.e., when $f(x) = e^{-|x/B|^p}$, for $0 < p < 2$, $0 < B < q$). It also covers the case where f is the bounded uniform distribution. The following is a corollary of Theorem 2 given that the DFT of bounded uniform distribution is non-negligible over $\mathbb{Z}_q$.

Corollary 1. *Let $n \in \mathbb{N}$ and $q \in \mathsf{poly}(n)$. Let $B \in \mathbb{Z}$ such that $0 < 2B + 1 < q$ and $\gcd(2B + 1, q) = 1$. Let $f : \mathbb{Z}_q \to \mathbb{R}$ be $f(x) := 1/\sqrt{2B+1}$ when $x \in [-B, B] \cap \mathbb{Z}$ and 0 elsewhere. Let $m \in \Omega\left(n \cdot q^4 \cdot (2B + 1)\right) \subseteq \mathsf{poly}(n)$, there exist polynomial-time quantum algorithms that solve $\mathsf{C|LWE\rangle}_{n,m,q,f}$ and $\mathsf{S|LWE\rangle}_{n,m,q,f}$.*

Our quantum algorithms for $\mathsf{SIS^{\infty}}$ and EDCP (i.e., Theorem 1 and Theorem 5) are obtained from the following variant of Theorem 2, where the noise amplitude for the quantum LWE problems is set to be the DFT of the bounded uniform distribution.

Theorem 3. *Let q be a polynomially large prime modulus. Let $B \in \mathbb{Z}$ be such that $q - (2B + 1) = c$ is a constant. Let $f : \mathbb{Z}_q \to \mathbb{R}$ be the bounded uniform distribution over $[-B, B] \cap \mathbb{Z}$. Let $m \in \Omega\left((q - c)^3 \cdot n^{c+1} \cdot q \cdot \log q\right) \subseteq \mathsf{poly}(n)$. There exist polynomial-time quantum algorithms that solve $\mathsf{C|LWE\rangle}_{n,m,q,\hat{f}}$ and $\mathsf{S|LWE\rangle}_{n,m,q,\hat{f}}$.*

DCP. Let us introduce the variant of DCP defined by Brakerski et al. [BKSW18].

Definition 5 (Extrapolated Dihedral Coset Problem (EDCP)). *Let $n \in \mathbb{N}$ be the dimension, $q \geq 2$ be the modulus, and a function $D : \mathbb{Z}_q \to \mathbb{R}$, consists of m input states of the form*

$$\sum_{j \in \mathbb{Z}_q} D(j)|j\rangle|x + j \cdot s\rangle,$$

where $x \in \mathbb{Z}_q^n$ is arbitrary and $s \in \mathbb{Z}_q^n$ is fixed for all m states. We say that an algorithm solves $\mathsf{EDCP}_{n,m,q,D}$ if it outputs s with probability $\mathsf{poly}(1/(n \log q))$ in time $\mathsf{poly}(n \log q)$.

In this paper we are interested in the parameter setting where n is the security parameter and $q \in \mathsf{poly}(n)$. Although not strictly needed in this paper, let us briefly recall how the variants of the dihedral coset problem evolve. The original dihedral coset problem is a special case of EDCP where $n = 1$, q is exponentially large, and D is the uniform distribution over $\{0, 1\}$. Solving DCP implies solving the dihedral hidden subgroup problem. The two-point problem defined by Regev [Reg02] is another special case of EDCP where D is the uniform distribution over $\{0, 1\}$, and n is the security parameter. It was used as an intermediate step for establishing the reduction from approximate SVP to DCP. When the distribution D is non-zero beyond $\{0, 1\}$, the EDCP problem does not necessarily correspond to any versions of the hidden subgroup problem. The reason that Brakerski et al. [BKSW18] considers a distribution D supported beyond $\{0, 1\}$ is to establish a reduction from EDCP to LWE. Therefore, combining with the reduction from LWE to EDCP (by adapting Regev's reduction [Reg02]), they show that EDCP, as a natural generalization of DCP, is equivalent to LWE.

Efficient quantum algorithms are known for variants of EDCP when the modulus q and the distribution D satisfy certain conditions [FIM+03, CvD07, IPS18]. Let us remark that EDCP with those parameter settings are not known to be as hard as worse-case SVP or LWE through the reductions of [Reg02] or [BKSW18].

In this paper we show polynomial-time quantum algorithms that solve EDCP with the following parameter settings.

Theorem 4. *Let $n \in \mathbb{N}$ and $q \in \mathsf{poly}(n)$. Let $f : \mathbb{Z}_q \to \mathbb{R}$ be such that the state $\sum_{e \in \mathbb{Z}_q} f(e)|e\rangle$ is efficiently constructible and $\eta := \min_{z \in \mathbb{Z}_q} |\hat{f}(z)|$ is nonnegligible. Let $m \in \Omega\left(n \cdot q/\eta^2\right) \subseteq \mathsf{poly}(n)$. There is a polynomial time quantum algorithm that solves $\mathsf{EDCP}_{n,m,q,\hat{f}}$.*

Theorem 5. *Let $n \in \mathbb{N}$ and $q \in \mathsf{poly}(n)$. Let c be a constant integer such that $0 < c < q$. Let $m \in \Omega\left((q-c)^3 \cdot n^{c+1} \cdot q \cdot \log q\right) \subseteq \mathsf{poly}(n)$, there is a quantum algorithm running in time $\mathsf{poly}(n)$ that solves $\mathsf{EDCP}_{n,m,q,D}$ where D is the uniform distribution over $[0, q-c) \cap \mathbb{Z}$.*

We note that EDCP with the parameters in Theorem 5 has already been solved in the work of Ivanyos et al. [IPS18] by a quantum algorithm with similar complexity. The parameters in Theorem 4 are not covered by the result in [IPS18], but the implication of such a parameter setting is unclear. Nevertheless, we include our result to demonstrate the wide applicability of our techniques. We will compare our algorithm with the one in [IPS18] in Sect. 1.3.

1.2   Solving the Quantum Versions of LWE via Filtering

As mentioned, our main technical contribution is to solve $\mathsf{S}|\mathsf{LWE}\rangle$ and $\mathsf{C}|\mathsf{LWE}\rangle$ (the quantum versions of LWE we define) with interesting parameters using a *filtering* technique. Let us first explain the basic idea of filtering, then extend it to the general case.

The basic idea of filtering. To illustrate the basic idea of filtering, let us focus on how to use it to solve $\mathsf{S|LWE\rangle}$, namely, learning the secret $u \in \mathbb{Z}_q^n$ given a uniformly random matrix $A \in \mathbb{Z}_q^{n \times m}$ and the following state:

$$|\phi_u\rangle := \bigotimes_{i=1}^{m} \sum_{e_i \in \mathbb{Z}_q} f(e_i)| (u^T A)_i + e_i \pmod q \rangle. \tag{1}$$

Let us remark that an efficient quantum algorithm for $\mathsf{S|LWE\rangle}_{n,m,q,f}$ does not necessarily imply an efficient quantum algorithm for $\mathsf{C|LWE\rangle}_{n,m,q,f}$, since the quantum algorithm for $\mathsf{S|LWE\rangle}_{n,m,q,f}$ may, for example, destroy the input state. However, the quantum algorithm we show for $\mathsf{S|LWE\rangle}_{n,m,q,f}$ directly works for $\mathsf{C|LWE\rangle}_{n,m,q,f}$, so we focus on $\mathsf{S|LWE\rangle}_{n,m,q,f}$.

Let us assume m can be an arbitrary polynomial of n, q is a constant prime. The readers can think of f as any distribution. For readers who would like to have a concrete example, you can think of f as the QFT of bounded uniform distribution, i.e., let $g(z) := 1/\sqrt{2\beta+1}$ for $z \in [-\beta, \beta] \cap \mathbb{Z}$ and 0 elsewhere, then set $f := \hat{g}$ (f is then the discrete sinc function, but in the analysis we will not use the expression of f at all, we will only use g). By solving $\mathsf{S|LWE\rangle}_{n,m,q,f}$ and $\mathsf{C|LWE\rangle}_{n,m,q,f}$ with such a choice of f, we can get a polynomial quantum algorithm for $\mathsf{SIS}_{n,m,q,\beta}^{\infty}$ with a constant prime q and any $\beta \in [1, q/2)$, which was not known before. All the details of the analysis will be given in Sect. 3. Here let us explain the basic idea of filtering using this example.

Let us define

$$\text{for } v \in \mathbb{Z}_q, \ |\psi_v\rangle := \sum_{e \in \mathbb{Z}_q} f(e)|(v+e) \pmod q\rangle.$$

Therefore the input state in Eq. (1) can also be written as

$$|\phi_u\rangle = \bigotimes_{i=1}^{m} |\psi_{(u^T A)_i}\rangle.$$

To learn u from $|\phi_u\rangle$, our algorithm proceeds in two stages: first we look at each coordinate $|\psi_{(u^T A)_i}\rangle$ for $i = 1, ..., m$ separately, with the goal of learning some classical information about each coordinate of $u^T A$. We then continue with a classical step, which uses the information obtained about each coordinate of $u^T A$ to learn u.

Warm-up 1: Orthogonal states. Suppose the vectors in the set $\{|\psi_v\rangle\}_{v \in \mathbb{Z}_q}$ were orthogonal. Then we could define a unitary U such that $U|\psi_v\rangle = |v\rangle$. We could then apply this unitary component-wise to $|\phi_u\rangle$ and measure the results in the computational basis, learning $u^T A$. Gaussian elimination then recovers u.

Warm-up 2: Filtering out a single value. Unfortunately, the $|\psi_v\rangle$ will typically not be orthogonal, so such a unitary as above will not exist. This means we cannot learn v with certainty from $|\psi_v\rangle$.

Nevertheless, we can learn *some* information about v from $|\psi_v\rangle$. Concretely, pick some value $y \in \mathbb{Z}_q$, and consider an arbitrary unitary U_y such that

$$U_y|\psi_y\rangle = |0\rangle.$$

Now imagine applying U_y to $|\psi_v\rangle$, and measuring in the computational basis. If $v = y$, then the measurement will always give 0. Unfortunately, since the $|\psi_v\rangle$ are not orthogonal, measuring $U_y|\psi_v\rangle$ for $v \neq y$ may also give 0. Therefore, while a 0 outcome gives us some prior on the value of v, it does not let us conclude anything for certain.

On the other hand, if a measurement gives a *non-zero* value, then we know for certain that $v \neq y$. This is the basic idea of our filtering approach: we filter out the case where $v = y$, learning an inequality constraint on v. This can be seen as a weak form of unambiguous state discrimination [Per88], where the measurement either gives unambiguous information about the unknowns or is thrown away. It turns out that, in some parameter regimes, learning such non-equality constraints will let us compute u.

Concretely, given an unknown state $|\phi_u\rangle$, we choose an independent random y_i for each coordinate, apply the unitary U_{y_i} to the ith coordinate, and measure. Any measurement result that gives 0, we throw away; for typical $|\psi_v\rangle$, few measurements will give 0. The remaining results yield inequality constraints of the form $(u^T A)_i \neq y_i$. We then apply the classical Arora-Ge algorithm [AG11] to these constraints. This algorithm works by viewing the inequality constraints as degree $q - 1$ constraints and then re-linearizing them. This process converts the inequality constraints into equality constraints, but at the cost of blowing up the number of unknowns to $\approx n^{q-1}$. In the regime where q is a constant and m is a sufficiently large polynomial, the system can be solved in polynomial-time using Gaussian elimination.

Our algorithm: filtering out multiple values. Our algorithm so far is limited to filtering out a single value, which in turn limits us to a constant q, due to our use of Arora-Ge.

In order to get a polynomial-time algorithm for larger q, we must filter out more points; in fact, in order to use Arora-Ge, we need our constraints to have constant degree, which in turn means we must filter out all but a constant number of elements of $\mathbb{Z}_q$. Filtering out so many points requires care.

Consider the goal of filtering out two values. If there exists, for $y_0, y_1 \in \mathbb{Z}_q$, a unitary U_{y_0,y_1} such that

$$U_{y_0,y_1}|\psi_{y_b}\rangle = |b\rangle,$$

then we could apply U_{y_0,y_1} and measure in the computational basis. If the result is not equal to 0 or 1, then we know that $v \notin \{y_0, y_1\}$, thus filtering out two values.

In general such a unitary does not exist, as it would require $|\psi_{y_0}\rangle$ and $|\psi_{y_1}\rangle$ to be orthogonal. Instead what we do is to define a unitary U_{y_0,y_1} such that

$$U_{y_0,y_1}|\psi_{y_b}\rangle \in \mathrm{Span}(|0\rangle, |1\rangle) \ .$$

This method also naturally extends to filtering a larger number of y values. The limitation is that, as the number of y increases, the probability of getting a successful measurement (where "success" means, e.g. getting a result other than 0,1) decreases. For example, suppose the $|\psi_v\rangle$ all lie in the space of dimension $d \ll q$. Then after excluding d values, the probability of a successful measurement will be 0. Even if the vectors are technically linear independent but close to a d-dimensional subspace, the probability will be non-zero but negligible. This, for example, rules out an algorithm for the case where f is discrete Gaussian.

Therefore, whether or not the algorithm will succeed depends crucially on the "shape" of the states $|\psi_v\rangle$, and in particular, the distribution f. Our applications roughly follow the outline above, analyzing specific cases of $|\psi_v\rangle$. Our main observation is that, since all the vectors $|\psi_v\rangle$ are just shifts of a single fixed vector, we can construct a unitary operator by taking the normalized Gram-Schmidt orthogonalization of a circulant matrix M_f, defined by

$$M_f := [|\psi_v\rangle, |\psi_{v+1}\rangle, ..., |\psi_{v+q-1}\rangle]. \tag{2}$$

This allows us to relate the success probability of filtering out $q - 1$ values to the length of the last Gram-Schmidt vector of M_f (before normalization). The length of the last Gram-Schmidt vector is related to the eigenvalues of the circulant matrix M_f, and it can be bounded in terms of the discrete Fourier transform $\hat{f}$ of f. Our calculation suggests that when $\hat{f}$ is *non-negligible* over all the values in $\mathbb{Z}_q$, the success probability of correctly guessing each coordinate is non-negligible. Therefore when m is a sufficiently large polynomial, we get a polynomial-time algorithm for $\mathsf{S}|\mathsf{LWE}\rangle_{n,m,q,f}$. In Fig. 2 we give four examples of error amplitudes. It shows that if the minimum of $\hat{f}$ is non-negligible, then the length of the last Gram-Schmidt of M_f is non-negligible.

1.3   The Related Work of Ivanyos et al.

Let us briefly compare our paper with the work of Ivanyos et al. [IPS18][1]. As mentioned in Sect. 1.1, EDCP with the parameters in Theorem 5 has already been solved in [IPS18] by a quantum algorithm with similar complexity. While we solve EDCP using the quantum reduction from EDCP to $\mathsf{S}|\mathsf{LWE}\rangle$ with sinc error distribution, Ivanyos et al. used a reduction from EDCP to a problem called "learning from disequations" (LSF), defined as follows: the goal is to learn a secret $s \in \mathbb{Z}_q^n$ by querying an oracle which outputs some $a \in \mathbb{Z}_q^n$ such that $\langle a, s \rangle \in A$, where A is a known subset of $\mathbb{Z}_q$. Given the set A and $m \in n^{O(|A|)}$

---

[1] In the initial version of our paper (August 25, 2021) we were not aware of the results in [IPS18]. We sincerely thank Gábor Ivanyos for telling us the results in [IPS18].

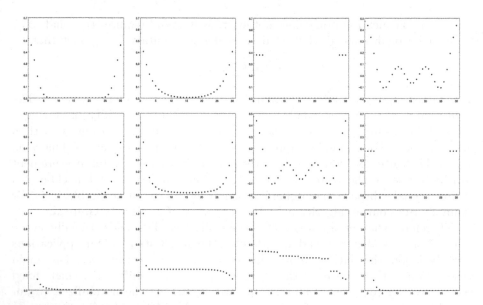

Fig. 2. Examples of error amplitude f (top), its DFT $\hat{f}$ (middle), and the length of the ith Gram-Schmidt vector of M_f in Eqn. (2) for $0 \le i < q$ (bottom). Let $q = 31$ for all examples. The error amplitude f is (from left to right): (1) Gaussian: $f(x) = \exp(-(x/3)^2)$; (2) Laplacian: $f(x) = \exp(-|x/3|)$; (3) Uniform over $[-3,3] \cap \mathbb{Z}$; (4) The DFT of Uniform over $[-3,3] \cap \mathbb{Z}$.

samples $a_1, ..., a_m$, they solve LSF in time $n^{O(|A|)}$ classically (using the Arora-Ge algorithm). This means when $|A|$ is a constant, the problem of LSF is solvable in poly(n) time.

In their algorithm they also used an idea similar to what we called "filtering". While we use filtering to solve S|LWE⟩, they used the idea of filtering in the quantum reduction from EDCP to the LSF problem.

Overall, both papers use the idea of filtering to solve EDCP for the parameters settings in Theorem 5, but the intermediate problems we reduced to are different. It appears that solving S|LWE⟩ allows us to obtain a richer variety of algorithms. In particular, it allows us to obtain a quantum algorithm for SIS$^\infty$, which was not achieved in [IPS18]. Furthermore, our results give evidence that the S|LWE⟩ and C|LWE⟩ problems are quantumly easier to solve than the classical LWE problem, which shows another hope of solving the worst-case lattice problems. Let us elaborate on this point in the next section.

1.4   Future Directions

Our results show polynomial time quantum algorithms for variants of average-case lattice problems. They do not appear to affect the security of any lattice-based cryptosystems in use. One may ask how far are we from solving standard LWE or approximate SVP for all lattices? Here we discuss two potential approaches of extending our results towards those ultimate goals.

Our first observation is that in order to solve standard LWE, "all" what we need to do is to solve $C|LWE\rangle_{n,m,q,f}$ with a smaller m than what we have achieved in Theorem 2 or Corollary 1. For the simplicity of explanation, assume the parameters σ, B, q satisfy $\sigma < B \ll q \in \text{poly}(n)$. To solve decisional $LWE_{n,m,q,D}$ where the noise distribution D is uniform over $[-\sigma, \sigma] \cap \mathbb{Z}$, it suffices to solve $C|LWE\rangle_{n,m,q,f}$ where f is the uniform distribution over $[-B, B] \cap \mathbb{Z}$, and with $m \leq B/\sigma$. Currently, using our result in Corollary 1, we need $m \in \Omega\left(n \cdot q^4 \cdot (2B+1)\right)$, which is polynomial in n but way larger than B/σ.

The algorithm of breaking decisional LWE via solving $C|LWE\rangle$ is well-known and was implicitly used in the attempt of designing quantum algorithms for lattice problems in [ES16]. Let the decisional $LWE_{n,m,q,D}$ instance be $(A \in \mathbb{Z}_q^{n \times m}, y \in \mathbb{Z}_q^m)$ where y is either an LWE sample or uniformly random. We solve $C|LWE\rangle_{n,m,q,f}$, i.e., construct a state

$$|\rho\rangle := \sum_{u \in \mathbb{Z}_q^n} \bigotimes_{i=1}^m \left(\sum_{e_i \in \mathbb{Z}_q} f(e_i) |a_i \cdot u + e_i \pmod{q}\rangle \right).$$

Let U_y denote a unitary operator that maps any $x \in \mathbb{Z}_q^m$ to $x + y$. Then we compute $\langle \rho | U_y | \rho \rangle$ by performing a Hadamard test. If y is an LWE sample, we expect the overlap between $|\rho\rangle$ and $|\rho + y\rangle$ to be at least $(1 - \sigma/B)^m$, whereas if y is uniform, we expect the overlap to be 0. Therefore, if we are able to solve $C|LWE\rangle_{n,m,q,f}$ with $m \leq B/\sigma$, then we can solve decisional $LWE_{n,m,q,D}$. The distributions f and D in the example can be changed to other ones, but all of them require m to be relatively small in order to break standard LWE.

If we are not able to decrease the number of samples in our solutions of $C|LWE\rangle_{n,m,q,f}$ or $S|LWE\rangle_{n,m,q,f}$, another hope of solving worst-case approximate SVP is to modify Regev's reduction [Reg05]. Recall that Regev reduces worst-case approximate SVP to LWE with Gaussian noise and *arbitrarily polynomially* many classical samples. Suppose we can replace LWE with classical samples by its quantum variants $C|LWE\rangle$ or $S|LWE\rangle$, and replace Gaussian distribution by distributions with non-negligible DFT (like bounded uniform or Laplace distributions). Then approximate SVP can be solved using Theorem 2 without decreasing the number of samples. However, it is not clear to us whether modifying Regev's reduction is feasible or not.

2   Preliminaries

Notation and terminology. Let $\mathbb{R}, \mathbb{Z}, \mathbb{N}$ be the set of real numbers, integers and positive integers. For $q \in \mathbb{N}_{\geq 2}$, denote $\mathbb{Z}/q\mathbb{Z}$ by $\mathbb{Z}_q$. For $n \in \mathbb{N}$, $[n] := \{1, ..., n\}$. When a variable v is drawn uniformly at random from the set S, we denote by $v \leftarrow U(S)$.

A vector in $\mathbb{R}^n$ is represented in column form by default. For a vector v, the ith component of v will be denoted by v_i. For a matrix A, the ith column vector of A is denoted a_i. We use A^T to denote the transpose of A, A^H to denote the conjugate transpose of A. The length of a vector is the ℓ_p-norm $\|v\|_p := (\sum v_i^p)^{1/p}$, or the infinity norm given by its largest entry $\|v\|_\infty := \max_i\{|v_i|\}$. The length of a matrix is the norm of its longest column: $\|A\|_p := \max_i \|a_i\|_p$. By default, we use ℓ_2-norm unless explicitly mentioned.

2.1 Quantum Background

We assume the readers are familiar with the basic concepts of quantum computation. All the background we need in this paper is available in standard textbooks of quantum computation, e.g., [NC16]. When writing a quantum state such as $\sum_{x \in S} f(x)|x\rangle$, we typically omit the normalization factor except when needed. When a state can be approximately constructed within a negligible distance, we sometimes say the state is constructible and not mention the negligible distance.

Efficiently constructible unitary operators. In this paper we will use the fact that all the unitary matrices of polynomial dimension can be efficiently approximated within exponentially small distance.

Proposition 1 (Page 191 of [NC16]). *Any unitary matrix U on an n-qubit system can be written as a product of at most $2^{n-1}(2^n - 1)$ two-level unitary matrices.*

Then, using Solovay-Kitaev Theorem, all the unitary matrices of $\mathsf{poly}(n)$ dimensions (therefore, applied on $O(\log n)$ qubits) can be approximated by $2^{O(\log n)} \in \mathsf{poly}(n)$ elementary quantum gates.

Proposition 2. *Let $\mathcal{G}$ denote set of unitary matrices that are universal for two-level gates. Given a unitary matrix $U \in \mathbb{C}^{d \times d}$, there is a classical algorithm that runs in time $\mathsf{poly}(d)$, outputs a sequence of two-level unitary matrices $U_1, ..., U_m \in \mathcal{G}$ such that $\prod_{i=1}^m U_i$ approximates U within distance negligible in d, and $m \in \mathsf{poly}(d)$.*

Looking ahead, the quantum algorithms in this work require quantum Fourier transform, superposition evaluations of classical circuits on quantum states and quantum gates that operate on $O(\log n)$ qubits. Thus, all quantum algorithms in the work can be efficiently approximated.

Quantum Fourier Transform. For any integer $q \geq 2$, let $\omega_q = e^{2\pi i/q}$ denote a primitive q-th root of unity. Define a unitary matrix $F_q \in \mathbb{C}^{q \times q}$ where $(F_q)_{i,j} := \frac{1}{\sqrt{q}} \cdot \omega_n^{ij}$, for $i, j \in \mathbb{Z}_q$.

Theorem 6 (QFT). *The unitary operator $\mathsf{QFT}_q := F_q$ can be implemented by $\mathsf{poly}(\log q)$ elementary quantum gates. When QFT_q is applied on a quantum state $|\phi\rangle := \sum_{x \in \mathbb{Z}_q} f(x)|x\rangle$, we have*

$$\mathsf{QFT}_q|\phi\rangle = \sum_{y \in \mathbb{Z}_q} \hat{f}(y)|y\rangle := \sum_{y \in \mathbb{Z}_q} \sum_{x \in \mathbb{Z}_q} \frac{1}{\sqrt{q}} \cdot \omega_q^{xy} \cdot f(x)|y\rangle.$$

2.2 Arora-Ge Algorithm for Solving LWE

We have defined the SIS, DCP, and LWE problems in the introduction. Here let us mention the Arora-Ge algorithm for solving LWE when the support of the error distribution is small. The following theorem is implicitly proven in [AG11, Section 3].

Theorem 7. *Let q be a prime, n be an integer. Let $\mathcal{D}_{\mathsf{noise}}$ be an error distribution which satisfies:*

1. *The support of $\mathcal{D}_{\mathsf{noise}}$ is of size $D < q$.*
2. $\Pr[e = 0, e \leftarrow \mathcal{D}_{\mathsf{noise}}] = \frac{1}{\delta}$ *for some $\delta > 1$.*

Then, let N be $\binom{n+D}{D}$ and C be a sufficiently large constant. Let $m :=$ $CN\delta q \log q$. There is a classical algorithm that solves $\mathsf{LWE}_{n,m,q,\mathcal{D}_{\mathsf{noise}}}$ in time $\mathsf{poly}(m)$ and succeeds with probability $1 - q^{-N}$.

Note that the probability is only taken over the randomness of samples. The algorithm is deterministic.

Suppose the error distribution $\mathcal{D}_{\mathsf{noise}}$ is known (which is always the case in our application). We can remove the second condition in Theorem 7 by shifting the error distribution such that the probability of getting 0 is maximized. More precisely, suppose $\mathcal{D}_{\mathsf{noise}}$ outputs some $e' \in \mathbb{Z}_q$ with the highest probability; we can always change an LWE sample (a_i, y_i) to $(a_i, y_i - e')$, and apply Arora-Ge on the shifted samples. Thus, we can shift the error distribution so that the probability of getting zero error is at least $1/q$. This transformation gives the following simple corollary.

Corollary 2. *Let q be a prime, n be an integer. Let $\mathcal{D}_{\mathsf{noise}}$ be an error distribution whose support is of size $D < q$ and known to the algorithm. Let $m := C \cdot n^D q^2 \log q$ where C is a sufficiently large constant. There is a classical algorithm that solves $\mathsf{LWE}_{n,m,q,\mathcal{D}_{\mathsf{noise}}}$ in time $\mathsf{poly}(m)$ and succeeds with probability $1 - O(q^{-n^D})$.*

3 The Idea of Filtering and a Mini Result for SIS^∞

In this section we give more details of the basic idea of *filtering*. Using the basic filtering technique, we obtain a polynomial-time quantum algorithm for $\mathsf{SIS}^\infty_{n,m,q,\beta}$ with q being a constant prime, m being as large as $\Omega(n^{q-1})$, and $1 \leq \beta < q/2$. Quantum polynomial-time algorithms for SIS^∞ with such parameter settings have not been given before.

Theorem 8. *Let n be an integer, q be a constant prime modulus. There is a quantum algorithm running in time $\mathsf{poly}(n)$ that solves $\mathsf{SIS}^\infty_{n,m,q,\beta}$ with $m \in$ $\Omega\left(\frac{n^{q-1}q^2 \log q}{0.9 - 1/(2\beta+1)}\right) \subseteq \mathsf{poly}(n)$ and any $\beta \in \mathbb{Z}$ such that $1 \leq \beta < q/2$.*

Note that in the above theorem, $0.9 - 1/(2\beta + 1)$ is at least 0.56 for $\beta \geq 1$. Thus, m is in the order of $n^{q-1}q^2 \log q$.

Let us first recall the existing quantum reduction from SIS to the problem of constructing certain LWE states presented implicitly in [SSTX09], then show the filtering technique and explain how to construct the required LWE states.

3.1   Recalling the Quantum Reduction from SIS to LWE

To give a quantum algorithm for solving $\mathsf{SIS}^{\infty}_{n,m,q,\beta}$ w.r.t. a uniformly random matrix $A \in \mathbb{Z}_q^{n \times m}$, it suffices to produce a state $|\sum_{z \in ([-\beta,\beta] \cap \mathbb{Z})^m \text{ s.t. } Az=0 \pmod q} |z\rangle|$. As long as the set $([-\beta, \beta] \cap \mathbb{Z})^m$ contains a non-zero solution for $Az = 0 \pmod q$, we can solve $\mathsf{SIS}^{\infty}_{n,m,q,\beta}$ with probability $\geq 1/2$ by simply measuring the state.

The following is a quantum reduction from SIS to LWE where the distribution of z is general. Let $f : \mathbb{Z}_q \to \mathbb{R}$ be a function (in the example above, f is the uniform distribution over $[-\beta, \beta] \cap \mathbb{Z}$). We abuse the notation to let $f : \mathbb{Z}_q^m \to R$ be defined as $f(x) = \prod_{i=1}^m f(x_i)$ (we will clearly state the domain when using f).

Proposition 3. *To construct an SIS state of the form*

$$|\phi_{\mathsf{SIS}}\rangle := \sum_{z \in \mathbb{Z}_q^m \text{ s.t. } Az=0 \pmod q} f(z)|z\rangle.$$

It suffices to construct an LWE state of the following form

$$|\phi_{\mathsf{LWE}}\rangle := \sum_{u \in \mathbb{Z}_q^n} \sum_{e \in \mathbb{Z}_q^m} \hat{f}(e)|u^T A + e^T \pmod q\rangle,$$

where $\hat{f}(e_i) = \sum_{x_i \in \mathbb{Z}_q} \frac{1}{\sqrt{q}} \cdot \omega_q^{e_i x_i} f(x_i)$, *for* $i = 1, ..., m$, *and* $\hat{f}(e) = \prod_{i=1,...,m} \hat{f}(e_i) = \sum_{x \in \mathbb{Z}_q^m} \frac{1}{\sqrt{q^m}} \cdot \omega_q^{\langle e, x \rangle} f(x)$.

Proof. $\mathsf{QFT}_q^m |\phi_{\mathsf{LWE}}\rangle = |\phi_{\mathsf{SIS}}\rangle$.   □

The following lemma is immediate from Proposition 3.

Lemma 1. *Let* n, m, q *be any integers such that* $m \in \Omega(n \log q) \subseteq \mathsf{poly}(n)$. *Let* $0 < \beta < q/2$. *Let* f *be the uniform distribution over* $([-\beta, \beta] \cap \mathbb{Z})^m$. *Let* A *be a matrix in* $\mathbb{Z}_q^{n \times m}$. *If there is a polynomial-time quantum algorithm that generates a state negligibly close to* $\sum_{u \in \mathbb{Z}_q^n} \sum_{e \in \mathbb{Z}_q^m} \hat{f}(e)|u^T A + e\rangle$, *then there is a polynomial-time quantum algorithm that solves* $\mathsf{SIS}^{\infty}_{n,m,q,\beta}$ *for* A.

3.2   Constructing the LWE State via Filtering

Now let us describe an algorithm for $C|\mathsf{LWE}\rangle$.

1. The algorithm first prepares the following state:

$$\sum_{x \in \mathbb{Z}_q^m} f(x)|x\rangle \otimes \sum_{u \in \mathbb{Z}_q^n} |u\rangle,$$

where we assume we work with a function f such that $\sum_{x \in \mathbb{Z}_q^m} f(x)|x\rangle$ can be efficiently generated. If so, then the whole state can be efficiently generated.

2. It then applies QFT_q^m on the x registers and gets:

$$\left(\mathsf{QFT}_q^m \sum_{x \in \mathbb{Z}_q^m} f(x)|x\rangle\right) \otimes \sum_{u \in \mathbb{Z}_q^n} |u\rangle = \left(\sum_{e \in \mathbb{Z}_q^m} \hat{f}(e)|e\rangle\right) \otimes \left(\sum_u |u\rangle\right).$$

3. It then adds $u^T A$ to the e registers in superposition, the state becomes:

$$\sum_{u \in \mathbb{Z}_q^n} \sum_{e \in \mathbb{Z}_q^m} \hat{f}(e)|u^T A + e\rangle \otimes |u\rangle. \tag{3}$$

4. Suppose there is a quantum algorithm that takes a state $|\sum_{u \in \mathbb{Z}_q^n} \sum_{e \in \mathbb{Z}_q^m} \hat{f}(e)|u^T A + e\rangle \otimes |u\rangle|$, outputs a state that is negligibly close to

$$\sum_{u \in \mathbb{Z}_q^n} \sum_{e \in \mathbb{Z}_q^m} \hat{f}(e)|u^T A + e\rangle \otimes |0\rangle, \tag{4}$$

then we are done.

Let us now explain how to learn the secret u from the following state

$$|\phi_u\rangle := \sum_{e \in \mathbb{Z}_q^m} \hat{f}(e)|u^T A + e\rangle. \tag{5}$$

For convenience, although $|\phi_u\rangle$ depends on Λ, we ignore the subscript since A will be clear from the context. We focus on the case where q is a constant prime, and for $i = 1, ..., m$, $f(e_i) = 1/\sqrt{2\beta + 1}$ for $e_i \in [-\beta, \beta] \cap \mathbb{Z}$ and 0 elsewhere. At the end of this subsection we will prove Theorem 8.

For the convenience of the rest of the presentation, let us also define

$$\text{for } v \in \mathbb{Z}_q, |\psi_v\rangle := \sum_{e \in \mathbb{Z}_q} \hat{f}(e)|(v + e) \bmod q\rangle. \tag{6}$$

Therefore Eq. (3) can also be written as

$$\sum_{u \in \mathbb{Z}_q^n} (|\phi_u\rangle \otimes |u\rangle) = \sum_{u \in \mathbb{Z}_q^n} \left(\bigotimes_{i=1,...,m} |\psi_{(u^T A)_i}\rangle \otimes |u\rangle\right). \tag{7}$$

Now let us fix a vector $u \in \mathbb{Z}_q^n$. To learn u from $|\phi_u\rangle$, we look at each coordinate $|\psi_{(u^T A)_i}\rangle$ for $i = 1, ..., m$ separately. Let us (classically) pick a uniformly random $y_i \in \mathbb{Z}_q$, then define a q-dimensional unitary matrix that always maps $|\psi_{y_i}\rangle$ to $|0\rangle$; more precisely,

$$U_{y_i} := \sum_{j=0}^{q-1} |j\rangle\langle\alpha_{i,j}|,$$

where $|\alpha_{i,0}\rangle := |\psi_{y_i}\rangle$ and the rest of the vectors $\{|\alpha_{i,j}\rangle\}_{j=1}^{q-1}$ are picked arbitrarily as long as U_{y_i} is unitary.

Looking ahead, we will apply U_{y_i} on $|\psi_{(u^T A)_i}\rangle$. Suppose we measure $U_{y_i}|\psi_{(u^T A)_i}\rangle$ and get an outcome in $\{0, 1, ..., q-1\}$. If the outcome is not 0, then we are 100% sure that $(u^T A)_i \neq y_i$. This is the basic idea of *filtering*, namely, we will filter out the case where $(u^T A)_i = y_i$ for a randomly chosen $y_i \in \mathbb{Z}_q$. Then we will handle the rest of the $q-1$ possibilities of $(u^T A)_i$ using the Arora-Ge algorithm (recall that we assume q is a constant in this subsection).

To explain why filtering works, consider for any $x, y \in \mathbb{Z}_q$. Let $U_y := \sum_{j=0}^{q-1} |j\rangle\langle\alpha_j|$ where $|\alpha_0\rangle := |\psi_y\rangle$ and the rest of the vectors $\{|\alpha_j\rangle\}_{j=1}^{q-1}$ span the rest of the space which are orthogonal to $|\alpha_0\rangle$. Then for any x, $|\psi_x\rangle$ can be written as a linear combination of basis $\{|\alpha_j\rangle\}_{j=0}^{q-1}$ (which contains $|\psi_y\rangle$), i.e.,

$$|\psi_x\rangle = \sum_{j=0}^{q-1} \langle\alpha_j|\psi_x\rangle \cdot |\alpha_j\rangle.$$

Imagine if we apply U_y on $|\psi_x\rangle$ and measure, we will get q different possible outcomes.

- If the outcome is 0, we know that both $x = y$ and $x \neq y$ can happen.
  - If $x = y$, the outcome is 0 with probability 1;
  - Otherwise, the outcome is 0 with probability $|\langle\psi_x|\psi_y\rangle|^2$, which can still be non-zero.
- If the outcome is not 0, we know that it can only be the case: $x \neq y$. Because when $x = y$, the measurement will always give outcome 0.

In the next lemma, we show that if we choose y uniformly at random, the above measurement will give a non-zero outcome with "good" probability.

Lemma 2. *Let y be a uniformly random value in $\mathbb{Z}_q$. Then for any $x \in \mathbb{Z}_q$, the probability of measuring $U_y|\psi_x\rangle$ and getting an outcome not equal to 0 is at least $1 - 1/(2\beta + 1)$:*

$$\forall x, \Pr_{y \in \mathbb{Z}_q}\left[s \neq 0 \wedge s \leftarrow M_{\mathsf{st}} \circ U_y|\psi_x\rangle\right] \geq 1 - \frac{1}{2\beta + 1},$$

where M_{st} is the measurement operator in the computational basis.

Proof. Fixing y, the probability of getting outcome 0 is $|\langle\psi_y|\psi_x\rangle|^2$. The probability of getting a non-zero outcome (when y is chosen uniformly at random) is: $\frac{1}{q}\sum_{y=0}^{q-1}\left(1 - |\langle\psi_y|\psi_x\rangle|^2\right)$.

To bound the probability, we define $|\hat{\psi}_a\rangle = \sum_{x=0}^{q-1} f(x)\omega_q^{-xa}|x\rangle$, we have $|\psi_a\rangle = \mathsf{QFT}_q|\hat{\psi}_a\rangle$. For any x, y, the inner product $\langle\psi_x|\psi_y\rangle = \langle\hat{\psi}_x|\hat{\psi}_y\rangle$. The probability we want to bound is,

$$1 - \frac{1}{q}\sum_{y=0}^{q-1}\langle\psi_y|\psi_x\rangle\langle\psi_x|\psi_y\rangle = 1 - \frac{1}{q}\sum_{y=0}^{q-1}\mathrm{Tr}\left[|\hat{\psi}_x\rangle\langle\hat{\psi}_x|\,|\hat{\psi}_y\rangle\langle\hat{\psi}_y|\right]$$

$$= 1 - \frac{1}{q}\cdot\mathrm{Tr}\left[|\hat{\psi}_x\rangle\langle\hat{\psi}_x|\left(\sum_{y=0}^{q-1}|\hat{\psi}_y\rangle\langle\hat{\psi}_y|\right)\right].$$

Let $\psi := \sum_{y=0}^{q-1} |\hat{\psi}_y\rangle\langle\hat{\psi}_y|$. It can be simplified as follows:

$$\psi = \sum_{y=0}^{q-1} |\hat{\psi}_y\rangle\langle\hat{\psi}_y| = \sum_{y=0}^{q-1} \sum_{x\in\mathbb{Z}_q, x'\in\mathbb{Z}_q} f(x)f(x')\omega_q^{(x'-x)y} |x\rangle\langle x'|$$

$$= \sum_{x\in\mathbb{Z}_q, x'\in\mathbb{Z}_q} f(x)f(x') \sum_{y=0}^{q-1} \omega_q^{(x'-x)y} |x\rangle\langle x'|$$

$$= q \cdot \sum_{x=0}^{q-1} f(x)^2 |x\rangle\langle x|$$

$$= \frac{q}{2\beta+1} \sum_{x=-\beta}^{\beta} |x\rangle\langle x|.$$

Here, we use the fact that $f(x) = 1/\sqrt{2\beta+1}$ for any $x \in [-\beta, \beta] \cap \mathbb{Z}$ and $f(x) = 0$ otherwise. Therefore,

$$1 - \frac{1}{q}\mathrm{Tr}\left[|\hat{\psi}_x\rangle\langle\hat{\psi}_x| \left(\sum_{y=0}^{q-1}|\hat{\psi}_y\rangle\langle\hat{\psi}_y|\right)\right] = 1 - \frac{1}{2\beta+1}\mathrm{Tr}\left[|\hat{\psi}_x\rangle\langle\hat{\psi}_x| \left(\sum_{x=-\beta}^{\beta} |x\rangle\langle x|\right)\right],$$

which is at least $1 - \frac{1}{2\beta+1}$. This follows from $\mathrm{Tr}\left[|\hat{\psi}_x\rangle\langle\hat{\psi}_x| \left(\sum_{x=-\beta}^{\beta} |x\rangle\langle x|\right)\right] \le 1$.

□

Thus, if we measure the superposition $|\phi_u\rangle$ entry-by-entry, with overwhelming probability, we will get at least $(1 - 1/(2\beta + 1) - \varepsilon)m$ outcomes which are not 0 and at most $(1/(2\beta + 1) + \varepsilon)m$ outcomes are 0 (for any constant $\varepsilon > 0$). Here we choose $\varepsilon = 0.1$.

Lemma 3. *For any fixed $x_1, \cdots, x_m \in \mathbb{Z}_q$, uniformly random $y_1, \cdots, y_m \in \mathbb{Z}_q$, the probability of measuring $U_{y_i}|\psi_{x_i}\rangle$ for all $i \in [m]$ and at least $(0.9 - 1/(2\beta+1))m$ outcomes being non-zero is at least $1 - O(e^{-m})$. Namely, for any fixed $x_1, \cdots, x_m \in \mathbb{Z}_q$,*

$$\Pr_{y_1, \cdots, y_m \in \mathbb{Z}_q}\left[z \ge \left(0.9 - \frac{1}{2\beta+1}\right) \cdot m \wedge \forall i, s_i \leftarrow M_{\mathsf{st}} \circ U_{y_i}|\psi_{x_i}\rangle\right] \ge 1 - O(e^{-m}),$$

where z is defined as the number of non-zero outcomes among all $s_1, \cdots, s_m$ and M_{st} is the measurement operator in the computational basis.

Proof. This is a direct consequence of Lemma 2 and Chernoff bound.   □

By union bound, it can also be shown that, with probability at least $1 - O(q^n e^{-m})$, when the measurements on each bit are chosen uniformly at random, we will get at least $(0.9 - 1/(2\beta + 1)) \cdot m$ non-zeros for all $u \in \mathbb{Z}_q^n$.

Corollary 3. *For any fixed A in $\mathbb{Z}_q^{n \times m}$, the probability that for all $u \in \mathbb{Z}_q^n$, measuring $U_{y_i} |\psi_{(u^T A)_i}\rangle$ for all $i \in [m]$ and at least $(0.9 - 1/(2\beta+1))m$ outcomes being non-zero is at least $1 - O(q^n e^{-m})$. Namely,*

$$\Pr_{y_1, \cdots, y_m \in \mathbb{Z}_q} \left[\forall u \in \mathbb{Z}_q^n, z_u \geq \left(0.9 - \frac{1}{2\beta+1} \right) m \right] \geq 1 - O(q^n e^{-m}),$$

where z_u is defined as the number of non-zero outcomes among all $s_{u,1}, \cdots, s_{u,m}$, each $s_{u,i}$ is defined as the measurement outcome of $U_{y_i} |\psi_{(u^T A)_i}\rangle$.

The above corollary implies that, for an overwhelming fraction (at least $1 - O(q^n e^{-m})$) of $y_1, \cdots, y_m$, the following event happens with probability at least $1 - O(q^n e^{-m})$: for all $u \in \mathbb{Z}_q^n$, measuring $U_{y_i} |\psi_{(u^T A))_i}\rangle$ for all $i \in [m]$ and getting at least $(0.9 - 1/(2\beta+1))m$ outcomes being non-zero.

We are now ready to state the main theorem.

Theorem 9. *Let n be an integer, q be a constant prime, C be a sufficiently large constant. Let $m \geq (0.9 - 1/(2\beta+1))^{-1} \cdot C \cdot n^{q-1} q^2 \log q$. Then there exists a QPT algorithm that with overwhelming probability, given a random $A \in \mathbb{Z}_q^{n \times m}$ and $\sum_{u \in \mathbb{Z}_q^n} |\phi_u\rangle \otimes |u\rangle$, outputs a state negligibly close to $\sum_{u \in \mathbb{Z}_q^n} |\phi_u\rangle$. Here $|\phi_u\rangle$ is defined in Eq. (5).*

Proof. Our algorithm works as follows on state $\sum_{u \in \mathbb{Z}_q^n} |\phi_u\rangle |u\rangle = \sum_u \bigotimes_{i=1}^m |\psi_{(u^T A)_i}\rangle |u\rangle$:

1. Pick m uniformly random values $y_1, ..., y_m \in \mathbb{Z}_q$. For each $i \in [m]$, construct a unitary $U_i := \sum_{j=0}^{q-1} |j\rangle \langle \alpha_{i,j}|$ where for $j = 0, ..., q-1$,

$$|\alpha_{i,j}\rangle := \begin{cases} |\psi_{y_i}\rangle, & \text{when } j = 0; \\ \text{Arbitrary } q\text{-dim unit vector orthogonal to } \{|\alpha_{i,k}\rangle\}_{k=0}^{j-1}, & \text{for } j \geq 1; \end{cases} \quad (8)$$

2. For $i = 1, ..., m$, apply U_i to the ith register, we get

$$U_i |\psi_{(u^T A)_i}\rangle = U_i \left(\sum_{j=0}^{q-1} \langle \alpha_{i,j} | \psi_{(u^T A)_i}\rangle \cdot |\alpha_{i,j}\rangle \right)$$

$$= \left(\sum_{j=0}^{q-1} \langle \alpha_{i,j} | \psi_{(u^T A)_i}\rangle \cdot |j\rangle \right) =: \sum_{s_{u,i} \in \mathbb{Z}_q} w_{s_{u,i}} |s_{u,i}\rangle.$$

Here, $s_{u,i}$ denotes the 'measurement outcome' of $U_i |\psi_{(u^T A)_i}\rangle$, but we do not physically measure the register $s_{u,i}$. We denote the vector $(s_{u,1}, \cdots, s_{u,m})$ by s_u.

3. Then we apply the quantum unitary implementation of the classical algorithm in [AG11] to $\sum_u \sum_{s_u \in \mathbb{Z}_q^m} w_{s_u} |s_u\rangle \otimes |u\rangle := \sum_u \bigotimes_{i=1}^m \sum_{s_{u,i} \in \mathbb{Z}_q} w_{s_{u,i}} |s_{u,i}\rangle \otimes |u\rangle$. Let the algorithm $D_{y_1, y_2, \cdots, y_m}$ be the following in Fig 1:

Algorithm 1. Learning u from $u^T A$

1: **procedure** $D_{y_1, y_2, \cdots, y_m}(s_u)$
2:     **for** each $i = 1, 2, \cdots, m$ **do**
3:         **if** $s_{u,i} \neq 0$ (meaning that $(u^T A)_i \neq y_i$) **then**
4:             Let a_i and $y_i \pmod q$ be a sample of LWE
5:         **end if**
6:     **end for**
7:     If there are more than $m' = (0.9 - 1/(2\beta + 1))m$ samples, it runs Arora-Ge algorithm over those samples to learn u and outputs u.
8: **end procedure**

For any $y_1, \cdots, y_m \in Z_q$ and $u \in \mathbb{Z}_q^n$, if $s_{u,i} \neq 0$, then $(u^T A)_i \neq y_i$; moreover, the LWE sample (a_i, y_i) has an error distribution with support $\{1, ..., q-1\}$, so Corollary 2 applies here.

We apply $D_{y_1, y_2, \cdots, y_m}$ in superposition to $\sum_u \sum_{s_u \in \mathbb{Z}_q^m} w_{s_u} |s_u\rangle \otimes |u\rangle$. For every fixed $u \in \mathbb{Z}_q^n$, let Bad_u be the set such that if all $s_u \in \mathsf{Bad}_u$, when we apply this algorithm to s_u, it does not compute u correctly.

By Corollaries 3 and 2, for an overwhelming fraction $(1 - O(q^n e^{-m}))$ of $y_1, \cdots, y_m$, for every u, $\sum_{s_u \in \mathsf{Bad}_u} |w_{s_u}|^2 \leq \mathsf{negl}(n)$. This is because:

(a) By Corollary 3, for an overwhelming fraction of $y_1, \cdots, y_m$, for every u, s_u provides at least $(0.9 - 1/(2\beta + 1))m = C \cdot n^{q-1} q^2 \log q$ samples with probability more than $1 - O(q^n e^{-m})$. Since $m \gg n$, it happens with overwhelming probability.

(b) By Corollary 2, as long as there are more than $C \cdot n^{q-1} q^2 \log q$ random samples, Arora-Ge algorithm succeeds with probability more than $1 - O(q^{-n^{q-1}})$. Note that the probability is taken over these random samples; in our case, the probability is taken over $A, y_1, \cdots, y_m$.

Thus, for an overwhelming fraction of $A, y_1, \cdots, y_m$, for every u, the weight $\sum_{s_u \in \mathsf{Bad}_u} |w_{s_u}|^2 \leq O(q^n e^{-m} + q^{-n^{q-1}}) = \mathsf{negl}(n)$.

Therefore, for an overwhelming fraction of $A, y_1, \cdots, y_m$, the resulting state is:

$$|\phi\rangle := D_{y_1, y_2, \cdots, y_m} \cdot q^{-n/2} \sum_{u \in \mathbb{Z}_q^n} \sum_{s_u \in \mathbb{Z}_q^m} w_{s_u} |s_u, u\rangle$$

$$= q^{-n/2} \sum_{u \in \mathbb{Z}_q^n} \left(\sum_{s_u \notin \mathsf{Bad}_u} w_{s_u} |s_u, 0\rangle + \sum_{s_u \in \mathsf{Bad}_u} w_{s_u} |s_u, D_{y_1, \cdots, y_m}(s_u)\rangle \right)$$

$$= q^{-n/2} \sum_{u \in \mathbb{Z}_q^n} \left(\sum_{s_u} w_{s_u} |s_u, 0\rangle + \mathsf{negl}_u(n) |\mathsf{err}_u\rangle \right)$$

$$= q^{-n/2} \sum_{u \in \mathbb{Z}_q^n} \sum_{s_u} w_{s_u} |s_u, 0\rangle + \mathsf{negl}(n) |\mathsf{err}\rangle.$$

Here $\mathsf{negl}_u(n)$ is a complex number whose norm is negligible in n, $|\mathsf{err}_u\rangle$ is some unit vector. Similarly, it is the case for $\mathsf{negl}(n)$ and $|\mathsf{err}\rangle$.

4. Finally, we apply $\bigotimes_{i=1}^m U_i^{-1}$ to uncompute the projections and get

$$\bigotimes_{i=1}^m U_i^{-1}|\phi\rangle = \sum_{u\in\mathbb{Z}_q^n}\bigotimes_{i=1,\ldots,m}|\psi_{(u^T A)_i}\rangle\otimes|0\rangle + \mathsf{negl}(n)|\mathsf{err}'\rangle = \sum_{u\in\mathbb{Z}_q^n}|\phi_u\rangle\otimes|0\rangle + \mathsf{negl}(n)|\mathsf{err}'\rangle.$$

Therefore we get a state negligibly close to $\sum_{u\in\mathbb{Z}_q^n}|\phi_u\rangle$ $=$ $\sum_{u\in\mathbb{Z}_q^n}\sum_{e\in\mathbb{Z}_q^m}\hat{f}(e)|u^T A + e\rangle$. This completes the proof of Theorem 9.   □

Finally, by Lemma 1 and Theorem 9, we complete the proof of Theorem 8.

4   Gram-Schmidt for Circulant Matrices

The general filtering algorithms used later in this paper construct unitary matrices obtained from applying the normalized Gram-Schmidt orthogonalization (GSO) on circulant matrices. The success probabilities of the general filtering algorithms are related to the norm of the columns in the matrices obtained from GSO. Thus, let us provide some related mathematical background in this section.

Given an ordered set of $k \le n$ linearly independent vectors $\{b_0, ..., b_{k-1}\}$ in $\mathbb{R}^n$, let $B := (b_0, ..., b_{k-1}) \in \mathbb{R}^{n\times k}$. For convenience, we sometimes denote b_i by B_i. Recall the Gram-Schmidt orthogonalization process.

Definition 6 (GSO). *The Gram-Schmidt orthogonalization of B, denoted as* $\mathsf{GS}(B) = (\mathsf{GS}(b_0), \cdots, \mathsf{GS}(b_{k-1}))$*, is defined iteratively for $i = 0, ..., k-1$ as*

$$\mathsf{GS}(b_i) = b_i - \sum_{j=0}^{i-1}\frac{\langle b_i, \mathsf{GS}(b_j)\rangle}{\langle \mathsf{GS}(b_j), \mathsf{GS}(b_j)\rangle}\cdot \mathsf{GS}(b_j).$$

Let us also define the normalized version of Gram-Schmidt orthogonalization.

Definition 7. *Given an ordered set of $k \le n$ linearly independent vectors $\{b_0, ..., b_{k-1}\}$ in $\mathbb{R}^n$, let $B := (b_0, ..., b_{k-1}) \in \mathbb{R}^{n\times k}$. The normalized Gram-Schmidt orthogonalization of B, denoted as* $\mathsf{NGS}(B) = (\mathsf{NGS}(b_0), \cdots, \mathsf{NGS}(b_{k-1}))$*, is defined for $i = 0, ..., k-1$ as $\mathsf{NGS}(b_i) := \mathsf{GS}(b_i)/\|\mathsf{GS}(b_i)\|_2$ where $\mathsf{GS}(b_i)$ is defined in Definition 6.*

The following lemma is helpful for bounding the length of GSO vectors.

Lemma 4 (Derived from Corollary 14 of [Mic12]). *Let $D = (d_0, ..., d_{k-1}) := B\cdot(B^T\cdot B)^{-1}$. Then we have $\|\mathsf{GS}(b_{k-1})\|_2 = 1/\|d_{k-1}\|_2$.*

GSO of circulant matrices. Let $C \in \mathbb{R}^{n \times n}$ be a real circulant matrix, defined as

$$
C := \begin{pmatrix}
c_0 & c_1 & c_2 & \cdots & c_{n-1} \\
c_{n-1} & c_0 & c_1 & \cdots & c_{n-2} \\
c_{n-2} & c_{n-1} & c_0 & \cdots & c_{n-3} \\
\cdots & \cdots & \cdots & \cdots & \cdots \\
c_1 & c_2 & c_3 & \cdots & c_0
\end{pmatrix}.
\tag{9}
$$

Fact 10. *The QFT basis is an eigenbasis of a circulant matrix, namely,*

$$
C = F_n^{-1} \cdot \Lambda \cdot F_n,
\tag{10}
$$

where $(F_n)_{i,j} := \frac{1}{\sqrt{n}} \cdot \omega_n^{ij}$, *for* $0 \le i,j \le n-1$; $\Lambda := \mathrm{diag}\,(\lambda_0, ..., \lambda_{n-1})$, *where* $\lambda_i := \sum_{j=0}^{n-1} c_j \cdot \omega_n^{ij}$. *In other words, the eigenvalues of* C *are the QFT of the first row of* C.

In our application, we need to compute the lower bound of the length of the kth column of $\mathsf{GS}\,(C)$, for some $1 \le k \le n$ such that the first k columns of C are linearly independent. Below we present a lemma for general parameter settings. For simplicity, the readers can assume we are interested in the range of parameters where n is a polynomial, and k is either equal to n or $n - c$ where c is a constant.

Lemma 5. *Let* $C = F_n^{-1} \cdot \Lambda \cdot F_n$ *be a real circulant matrix where* $\Lambda :=$ $\mathrm{diag}\,(\lambda_0, ..., \lambda_{n-1})$, $\lambda_i := \sum_{j=0}^{n-1} c_j \cdot \omega_n^{ij}$. *Suppose* $\lambda_0, ..., \lambda_{k-1}$ *are non-zero and* $\lambda_k, ..., \lambda_{n-1}$ *are zero. Then the length of the* k^{th} *column of* $\mathsf{GS}\,(C)$, *i.e.,* $\|\mathsf{GS}\,(C)_{k-1}\|_2$, *is lower-bounded by*

1. *If* $k = n$, *then* $\|\mathsf{GS}\,(C)_{n-1}\|_2 \ge \frac{1}{\sqrt{n}} \cdot \min_{i=0,...,n-1} |\lambda_i|$.
2. *If* $k < n$, *then* $\|\mathsf{GS}\,(C)_{k-1}\|_2 \ge \frac{\sqrt{n}}{k \cdot 2^{n-k}} \cdot \min_{i=0,...,k-1} |\lambda_i|$.

Please refer to the full version for the proof.

5   Quantum Algorithm for Solving the LWE State Problems

Recall in our mini result, every time a "measurement" (we do not physically implement the measurement) gives a non-zero result; it provides us with an inequality $\langle u, a_i \rangle \ne y_i$. The algorithm, therefore, collects enough inequalities and then runs Arora-Ge to learn the secret vector u. There are two bottlenecks in the previous algorithm: (1) we are only able to filter out one value for $\langle u, a_i \rangle$; (2) to run Arora-Ge, one needs to collect many samples (up to roughly n^{q-1}). Therefore, it is only possible to provide quantum polynomial-time algorithms for $\mathsf{S}|\mathsf{LWE}\rangle$, $\mathsf{C}|\mathsf{LWE}\rangle$, and SIS^∞ for a constantly large modulus q.

In this section, we generalize the filtering algorithm in a way that allows us to filter out $q - c$ many possible values of $\langle u, a_i \rangle$ for some constant c even when q is a polynomially large modulus. In the best possible case, the filtering algorithm can filter out $q - 1$ possibilities and get the exact value of $\langle u, a_i \rangle$. Therefore, to learn the secret vector $u \in \mathbb{Z}_q^n$, one can collect roughly n samples and run Gaussian elimination. However, the probability of filtering out $q-1$ or $q-c$ (for some constant c) values depends on the concrete f and is typically very small. We will precisely show when such a probability is non-negligible.

We now provide quantum algorithms for $\mathsf{C}|\mathsf{LWE}\rangle_{n,m,q,f}$ (cf. Definition 3) and $\mathsf{S}|\mathsf{LWE}\rangle_{n,m,q,f}$ (cf. Definition 4). Let us first present the algorithms for a general error amplitude f, then state corollaries for some functions f of special interest. Looking ahead, the results in the full version use a slight modification of the algorithms presented in this section. Namely, in this section we will only show algorithms for functions f which allow us to filter out $q - 1$ possible values then use Gaussian elimination, whereas the results in in the full version require us to deal with a function f that allows us to filter out $q-c$ possible values then use Arora-Ge.

5.1   Overview of the General Filtering Algorithm

Let q be a polynomially large modulus, f be an arbitrary noise amplitude. Define $|\psi_v\rangle := \sum_{e \in \mathbb{Z}_q} f(e)|v + e \bmod q\rangle$ for every $v \in \mathbb{Z}_q$. Following the basic notations and ideas in Sect. 3.2, let us now explain how to filter out two possible values for $(u^T A)_i$, say we are filtering out $(u^T A)_i = y_i$ and $(u^T A)_i = y_i + 1$ where y_i is a random value in $\mathbb{Z}_q$. To do so, let us define a basis $\{|\alpha_{i,j}\rangle\}_{j=0}^{q-1}$ where $|\alpha_{i,0}\rangle = |\psi_{y_i}\rangle$ and $|\alpha_{i,1}\rangle = \mathsf{NGS}\,(|\psi_{y_i+1}\rangle)$. The rest of the vectors in the basis are picked arbitrarily as long as they are orthogonal to $|\alpha_{i,0}\rangle$ and $|\alpha_{i,1}\rangle$.

Define $U_{y_i} := \sum_{j=0}^{q-1} |j\rangle\langle\alpha_{i,j}|$. Suppose we "measure" $U_{y_i}|\psi_{(u^T A)_i}\rangle$ and get an outcome in $\{0, 1, ..., q-1\}$:

1. If the outcome is 0, then $(u^T A)_i$ can be any values in $\mathbb{Z}_q$;
2. If the outcome is 1, then we are 100% sure that $(u^T A)_i \neq y_i$, since if $(u^T A)_i = y_i$, then the measurement outcome must be 0.
3. If the outcome is ≥ 2, then we are 100% sure that $(u^T A)_i$ does not equal to y_i or $y_i + 1$.

The idea can be further generalized by continuing to do normalized Gram-Schmidt orthogonalization. Suppose for a moment that $|\psi_{y_i+j}\rangle$, for $j = 0, ..., q-1$, are linearly independent. Then we define unitary matrices

$$U_{y_i} := \sum_{j=0}^{q-1} |j\rangle\langle\alpha_{i,j}|, \text{ where } |\alpha_{i,j}\rangle = \mathsf{NGS}\,(|\psi_{y_i+j}\rangle).$$

Following the previous logic, if we "measure" $U_{y_i}|\psi_{(u^T A)_i}\rangle$, only the outcome "$q - 1$" gives us a definitive answer of $(u^T A)_i$, that is, $(u^T A)_i = y_i + q - 1 \pmod q$.

The probability of filtering out q-1 values. It remains to understand the probability of getting the measurement outcome $q - 1$.

$$\Pr_{y_i \in \mathbb{Z}_q} [(u^T A)_i = y_i + q - 1 \pmod q \,\wedge\, q - 1 \leftarrow M_{\mathsf{st}} \circ U_{y_i}|\psi_{(u^T A)_i}\rangle]$$

$$= \frac{1}{q} \cdot \sum_{j \in \mathbb{Z}_q} |\langle\alpha_{i,q-1}|\psi_{y_i+j}\rangle|^2 = \frac{1}{q} \cdot |\langle\alpha_{i,q-1}|\psi_{y_i+q-1}\rangle|^2,$$

where the second equality follows from the fact that $|\alpha_{i,q-1}\rangle$ is defined to be orthogonal to all the states except $|\psi_{y_i+q-1}\rangle$. Furthermore,

$$|\langle \alpha_{i,q-1}|\psi_{y_i+q-1}\rangle| = \left|\mathsf{NGS}\left(|\psi_{y_i+q-1}\rangle\right)^\dagger |\psi_{y_i+q-1}\rangle\right| = \|\mathsf{GS}\left(|\psi_{y_i+q-1}\rangle\right)\|_2,$$

i.e., it is exactly the norm of the Gram-Schmidt of $|\psi_{y_i+q-1}\rangle$. This quantity has been shown in Lemma 5 to be related to the minimum of $\hat{f}$ over $\mathbb{Z}_q$, namely,

$$\|\mathsf{GS}\left(|\psi_{y_i+q-1}\rangle\right)\|_2 \geq \min_{x=0,\ldots,q-1} |\hat{f}(x)|.$$

Therefore, we are able to use the general filtering technique to achieve polynomial-time quantum algorithms for $\mathsf{S}|\mathsf{LWE}\rangle_{n,m,q,f}$ and $\mathsf{C}|\mathsf{LWE}\rangle_{n,m,q,f}$ where q is polynomially large and f is a function such that the minimum of $\hat{f}$ over $\mathbb{Z}_q$ is non-negligible.

5.2 Quantum Algorithm for Generating LWE States with General Error

Theorem 11. *Let q be a polynomially large modulus. Let $f : \mathbb{Z}_q \to \mathbb{R}$ be the amplitude for the error state such that the state $\sum_{e \in \mathbb{Z}_q} f(e)|e\rangle$ is efficiently constructible and $\eta := \min_{z \in \mathbb{Z}_q} |\hat{f}(z)|$ is non-negligible. Let $m \in \Omega\left(n \cdot q/\eta^2\right) \subseteq \mathrm{poly}(n)$, there exist polynomial-time quantum algorithms that solve $\mathsf{C}|\mathsf{LWE}\rangle_{n,m,q,f}$ and $\mathsf{S}|\mathsf{LWE}\rangle_{n,m,q,f}$.*

Proof. We will describe an algorithm for $\mathsf{C}|\mathsf{LWE}\rangle_{n,m,q,f}$. The algorithm for $\mathsf{S}|\mathsf{LWE}\rangle_{n,m,q,f}$ appears as a subroutine in the algorithm for $\mathsf{C}|\mathsf{LWE}\rangle_{n,m,q,f}$.

1. The algorithm first prepares the following state:

$$\bigotimes_{i=1}^{m} \left(\sum_{e_i \in \mathbb{Z}_q} f(e_i)|e_i\rangle\right) \otimes \sum_{u \in \mathbb{Z}_q^n} |u\rangle.$$

We abuse the notation of f to let $f(e) := \prod_{i=1}^{m} f(e_i)$ for $e := (e_1, \ldots, e_m)$. Then the state above can be written as $\sum_{e \in \mathbb{Z}_q^m} f(e)|e\rangle \otimes \sum_{u \in \mathbb{Z}_q^n} |u\rangle$.

2. It then adds $u^T A$ to the e registers in superposition, the state is:

$$\sum_{u \in \mathbb{Z}_q^n} \sum_{e \in \mathbb{Z}_q^m} f(e)|u^T A + e\rangle \otimes |u\rangle \tag{11}$$

Similarly, let us define

$$\text{for } v \in \mathbb{Z}_q, |\psi_v\rangle := \sum_{e \in \mathbb{Z}_q} f(e)|(v + e) \bmod q\rangle. \tag{12}$$

Therefore Eq. (11) can also be written as

$$\sum_{u \in \mathbb{Z}_q^n} \bigotimes_{i=1,\ldots,m} |\psi_{(u^T A)_i}\rangle \otimes |u\rangle. \tag{13}$$

3. Pick m uniformly random values $y_1, \ldots, y_m \in \mathbb{Z}_q$. Construct unitary matrices

$$\text{For } 1 \leq i \leq m, \quad U_i := \sum_{j=0}^{q-1} |j\rangle\langle\alpha_{i,j}|, \text{ where } |\alpha_{i,j}\rangle := \text{NGS}\left(|\psi_{y_i+j}\rangle\right). \tag{14}$$

4. For $i = 1, \ldots, m$, apply U_i to the ith register, we get

$$U_i|\psi_{(u^T A)_i}\rangle = U_i \left(\sum_{j=0}^{q-1} \langle\alpha_{i,j}|\psi_{(u^T A)_i}\rangle \cdot |\alpha_{i,j}\rangle \right)$$

$$= \left(\sum_{j=0}^{q-1} \langle\alpha_{i,j}|\psi_{(u^T A)_i}\rangle \cdot |j\rangle \right) =: \sum_{s_{u,i} \in \mathbb{Z}_q} w_{s_{u,i}}|s_{u,i}\rangle.$$

5. Then we apply the quantum unitary implementation of Gaussian elimination to the superposition $\sum_u \sum_{s_u \in \mathbb{Z}_q^m} w_{s_u}|s_u\rangle := \sum_u \bigotimes_{i=1}^m \sum_{s_{u,i} \in \mathbb{Z}_q} w_{s_{u,i}}|s_{u,i}\rangle$. The algorithm $D_{y_1,y_2,\cdots,y_m}$ is described in Algorithm 2. In Lemma 8, we prove our parameters guarantee that with overwhelming probability,
   (a) There exists a set Bad_u such that for all $s_u \in \text{Bad}_u$, when we apply $D_{y_1,y_2,\cdots,y_m}$ to s_u, it does not compute u correctly;
   (b) For an overwhelming choice of $y_1, \cdots, y_m$, for all u, $\sum_{s_u \in \text{Bad}_u} |w_{s_u}|^2 = O(q^n e^{-m} + q^{-n}) = \text{negl}(n)$. Here q^{-n} is the probability that the linear system is not full rank with $2n$ samples.

Algorithm 2. Learning u from $u^T A$

1: **procedure** $D_{y_1,y_2,\cdots,y_m}(\{s_{u,i}\}_{1 \leq i \leq m})$
2:     **for** each $i = 1, 2, \cdots, m$ **do**
3:         **if** If $s_{u,i} = q - 1$ (meaning that $(u^T A)_i = y_i + q - 1 \pmod{q}$) **then**
4:             Let a_i and $y_i - 1 \bmod q$ be one sample of the linear system
5:         **end if**
6:     **end for**
7:     With overwhelming probability, there are $\geq 2 \cdot n$ random samples (to make sure the linear system is full rank)
8:     Run the Gaussian elimination algorithm to learn u and return u
9: **end procedure**

Therefore, for an overwhelming fraction of $A, y_1, \cdots, y_m$, the resulting state is:

$$|\phi\rangle := q^{-n/2} \cdot D_{y_1, y_2, \cdots, y_m} \sum_{u \in \mathbb{Z}_q^n} \sum_{s_u \in \mathbb{Z}_q^m} w_{s_u} |s_u, u\rangle$$

$$= q^{-n/2} \sum_{u \in \mathbb{Z}_q^n} \left(\sum_{s_u \notin \mathrm{Bad}_u} w_{s_u} |s_u, 0\rangle + \sum_{s_u \in \mathrm{Bad}_u} w_{s_u} |s_u, D_{y_1, \cdots, y_m}(s_u)\rangle \right)$$

$$= q^{-n/2} \sum_{u \in \mathbb{Z}_q^n} \sum_{s_u} w_{s_u} |s_u, 0\rangle + \mathsf{negl}(n) |\mathsf{err}\rangle.$$

Here $\mathsf{negl}_u(n)$ returns a complex number whose norm is negligible in n, $|\mathsf{err}\rangle$ is some unit vector.

6. Finally, we just apply $\bigotimes_{i=1}^m U_i^{-1}$ to uncompute the projections and get

$$\bigotimes_{i=1}^m U_i^{-1} |\phi\rangle = \sum_{u \in \mathbb{Z}_q^n} \bigotimes_{i=1,\ldots,m} |\psi_{(u^T A)_i}\rangle \otimes |0\rangle + \mathsf{negl}(n) |\mathsf{err}'\rangle.$$

Thus, with overwhelming probability, we get a state close to $|\sum_{u \in \mathbb{Z}_q^n} \sum_{e \in \mathbb{Z}_q^m} f(e) |u^T A + e\rangle|$. It completes the description of our algorithm.

The Analysis. Let us begin with an explanation of the properties of the unitary matrices U_i defined in Eq. (14). Recall from Eq. (12) that $|\psi_v\rangle = \sum_{e \in \mathbb{Z}_q} f(e) |(v + e) \bmod q\rangle$.

Let $W_i := \sum_{j=0}^{q-1} |j\rangle\langle\psi_{y_i+j}|$. In other words, $W_i^T = (|\psi_{y_i}\rangle, \cdots, |\psi_{y_i+q-1}\rangle)$. Then $U_i^T = \mathsf{NGS}(W_i^T)$. We would like to show that the length of the GSO of $|\psi_{y_i+q-1}\rangle$, i.e., the length of the last column of $\mathsf{GS}(W_i^T)$, is non-negligible.

Lemma 6. $\|\mathsf{GS}(|\psi_{y_i+q-1}\rangle)\|_2 \geq \min_{z \in \mathbb{Z}_q} |\hat{f}(z)| = \eta.$

Proof. Note that W_i^T is a circulant matrix. The eigenvalues of W_i^T are $\{\sqrt{q} \cdot \hat{f}(z)\}_{z \in \mathbb{Z}_q}$ (see Fact 10). Therefore, by applying Lemma 5, we have $\|\mathsf{GS}(|\psi_{y_i+q-1}\rangle)\|_2 \geq \min_{z \in \mathbb{Z}_q} |\hat{f}(z)| = \eta.$ □

Next, we relate the GSO of $|\psi_{y_i+q-1}\rangle$ to the probability of getting desirable samples in Algorithm 2.

Lemma 7. *For any fixed* $x_1, \cdots, x_m \in \mathbb{Z}_q$,

$$\Pr_{y_1, \cdots, y_m \in \mathbb{Z}_q} \left[z \geq \Omega\left(m \cdot (\eta^2/q)\right) \wedge \forall i, s_i \leftarrow M_{\mathsf{st}} \circ U_{y_i} |\psi_{x_i}\rangle \right] \geq 1 - O(e^{-m}),$$

where z *is defined as the number of outcomes such that* $s_i = q - 1$ *among all* $s_1, \cdots, s_m$ *and* M_{st} *is a measurement operator in the computational basis.*

Proof. For $i = 1, ..., m$, we have

$$\Pr_{y_i}[y_i + q - 1 = x_i] \cdot \Pr\left[s_i = q - 1 \wedge s_i \leftarrow M_{\mathsf{st}} \circ U_{y_i}|\psi_{x_i}\rangle \mid y_i + q - 1 = x_i\right]$$

$$= \frac{1}{q} \cdot |\langle \alpha_{i,q-1}|\psi_{y_i+q-1}\rangle|^2 = \frac{1}{q} \cdot \|\mathsf{GS}\left(|\psi_{y_i+q-1}\rangle\right)\|_2^2 \geq \frac{\eta^2}{q}.$$

The lemma then follows Chernoff bound. $\qquad\square$

Lemma 8. *When* $m \in \Omega\left(n \cdot q/\eta^2\right) \subseteq \mathsf{poly}(n)$, *for an overwhelming fraction of all possible* $A, y_1, \cdots, y_m$, *we have: for all* u, $\sum_{s_u \in \mathsf{Bad}_u} |w_{s_u}|^2 \leq \mathsf{negl}(n)$.

Proof. It follows from Lemma 7 that when $m \in \Omega\left(n \cdot q/\eta^2\right)$, we have $\geq 2 \cdot n$ samples where $(u^T A)_i = y_i - 1 \pmod{q}$ with overwhelming probability. Thus, we can use Gaussian elimination to compute u. Therefore $\sum_{s_u \in \mathsf{Bad}_u} |w_{s_u}|^2 \leq \mathsf{negl}(n)$. $\qquad\square$

This completes the proof of Theorem 11. $\qquad\square$

5.3 Examples of Error Distributions of Special Interest

We give some examples of error amplitude f where $\min_{y \in \mathbb{Z}_q} |\hat{f}(y)|$ is non-negligible and q is polynomially large. The first example is where f is the bounded uniform distribution.

Corollary 4. *Let* q *be a polynomially large modulus. Let* $B \in \mathbb{Z}$ *such that* $0 < 2B+1 < q$ *and* $\gcd(2B+1, q) = 1$. *Let* $f : \mathbb{Z}_q \to \mathbb{R}$ *be* $f(x) := 1/\sqrt{2B+1}$ *where* $x \in [-B, B] \cap \mathbb{Z}$ *and* 0 *elsewhere. Let* $m \in \Omega\left(n \cdot q^4 \cdot (2B + 1)\right) \subseteq \mathsf{poly}(n)$, *there exist polynomial-time quantum algorithms that solve* $\mathsf{C|LWE}\rangle_{n,m,q,f}$ *and* $\mathsf{S|LWE}\rangle_{n,m,q,f}$.

Proof. The QFT of f is

$$\forall y \in \mathbb{Z}_q, \ \hat{f}(y) := \sqrt{\frac{1}{q \cdot (2B+1)}} \cdot \sum_{x=-B}^{B} \omega_q^{xy} = \sqrt{\frac{1}{q \cdot (2B+1)}} \cdot \frac{\sin\left(\frac{2\pi}{q} \cdot \frac{2B+1}{2} \cdot y\right)}{\sin\left(\frac{2\pi}{q} \cdot \frac{y}{2}\right)}.$$

(15)

Here we use the identity: $1 + 2\cos x + \cdots + 2\cos nx = \sin\left((n + \frac{1}{2})x\right)/\sin\left(\frac{x}{2}\right)$.

Note that when $y = 0$, $\hat{f}(y) = \sqrt{\frac{2B+1}{q}}$. When $y \in \{1, ..., q-1\}$, the denominator satisfies $0 < \sin\left(\frac{2\pi}{q} \cdot \frac{y}{2}\right) \leq 1$; since $\gcd(2B+1, q) = 1$, we have $\frac{(2B+1)y}{q} \notin \mathbb{Z}$ for any $y \in \{1, ..., q-1\}$, the numerator satisfies $\left|\sin\left(\frac{2\pi}{q} \cdot \frac{2B+1}{2} \cdot y\right)\right| \geq \left|\sin\left(\frac{\pi}{q}\right)\right| > \frac{1}{q}$.

Therefore $\eta = \min_{y \in \mathbb{Z}_q} |\hat{f}(y)| \geq \sqrt{\frac{1}{q \cdot (2B+1)}} \cdot \frac{1}{q}$. The corollary follows by plugging $\eta \geq \sqrt{\frac{1}{q \cdot (2B+1)}} \cdot \frac{1}{q}$ in Theorem 11. $\qquad\square$

Remark 3. When $\gcd(2B + 1, q) = v$ for some $v > 1$, we have $\frac{(2B+1)y}{q} \in \mathbb{Z}$ for $q/v - 1$ values of $y \in \{1, ..., q - 1\}$. Therefore $\hat{f}(y)$ defined in Eq. (15) is 0 on $q/v - 1$ values. It is not clear to us how to extend our algorithm to the case where $\gcd(2B + 1, q) > 1$.

Other examples of f where $\min_{y \in \mathbb{Z}_q} |\hat{f}(y)|$ is non-negligible and q is polynomially large include Laplace and super-Gaussian functions. Their q-DFT is easier to express by first taking the continuous Fourier transform (CFT) of f, denoted as g, then discretize to obtain the DFT. Namely, for $y \in \mathbb{Z}_q$, $\hat{f}(y) = \frac{\sum_{z \in y+q\mathbb{Z}} g(z/q)}{\sum_{z \in \mathbb{Z}} g(z/q)}$. Let $0 < B < q/n^c$ for some $c > 0$.

1. Laplace: $f(x) = e^{-|x/B|}$, the CFT of f is $g(y) \propto \frac{2}{1+4(\pi By)^2}$.
2. Super-Gaussian: For $0 < p < 2$, $f(x) = e^{-|x/B|^p}$, the CFT of f is asymptotic to $g(y) \propto -\frac{\pi^{-p-\frac{1}{2}}|By|^{-p-1}\Gamma(\frac{p+1}{2})}{\Gamma(-\frac{p}{2})}$ (see, for example, [MS19]).

Acknowledgement. We sincerely thank Gábor Ivanyos for telling us the results in [IPS18]. We would also like to thank Luowen Qian, Léo Ducas, and the anonymous reviewers for their helpful comments. Y.C. is supported by Tsinghua University start-up funding and Shanghai Qi Zhi Institute. Q.L. is supported by the Simons Institute for the Theory of Computing, through a Quantum Postdoctoral Fellowship. M.Z. is supported in part by NSF.

References

[AG11] Arora, S., Ge, R.: New algorithms for learning in presence of errors. In: Automata, Languages and Programming - 38th International Colloquium, ICALP 2011, Zurich, Switzerland, 4–8 July 2011, Proceedings, Part I, pp. 403–415 (2011)

[Ajt96] Ajtai, M.: Generating hard instances of lattice problems (extended abstract). In: STOC, pp. 99–108 (1996)

[BDK+18] Bos, J.W., et al.: CRYSTALS - kyber: A cca-secure module-lattice-based KEM. In: EuroS&P, pp. 353–367. IEEE (2018)

[BKSW18] Brakerski, Z., Kirshanova, E., Stehlé, D., Wen, W.: Learning with errors and extrapolated dihedral cosets. In: Abdalla, M., Dahab, R. (eds.) PKC 2018. LNCS, vol. 10770, pp. 702–727. Springer, Cham (2018). https://doi.org/10.1007/978-3-319-76581-5_24

[BS16] Biasse, J.F., Song, F.: Efficient quantum algorithms for computing class groups and solving the principal ideal problem in arbitrary degree number fields. In: Proceedings of the Twenty-Seventh Annual ACM-SIAM Symposium on Discrete Algorithms, pp. 893–902. SIAM (2016)

[BV11] Brakerski, Z., Vaikuntanathan, V.: Efficient fully homomorphic encryption from (standard) LWE. In: IEEE 52nd Annual Symposium on Foundations of Computer Science, FOCS 2011, Palm Springs, CA, USA, 22–25 October 2011, pp. 97–106 (2011)

[BV15] Brakerski, Z., Vaikuntanathan, V.: Constrained key-homomorphic PRFs from standard lattice assumptions. In: Dodis, Y., Nielsen, J.B. (eds.) TCC 2015. LNCS, vol. 9015, pp. 1–30. Springer, Heidelberg (2015). https://doi.org/10.1007/978-3-662-46497-7_1

[CDPR16] Cramer, R., Ducas, L., Peikert, C., Regev, O.: Recovering short generators of principal ideals in cyclotomic rings. In: Fischlin, M., Coron, J.-S. (eds.) EUROCRYPT 2016. LNCS, vol. 9666, pp. 559–585. Springer, Heidelberg (2016). https://doi.org/10.1007/978-3-662-49896-5_20

[CDW17] Cramer, R., Ducas, L., Wesolowski, B.: Short stickelberger class relations and application to ideal-SVP. In: Coron, J.-S., Nielsen, J.B. (eds.) EUROCRYPT 2017. LNCS, vol. 10210, pp. 324–348. Springer, Cham (2017). https://doi.org/10.1007/978-3-319-56620-7_12

[CGS14] Campbell, P., Groves, M., Shepherd, D.: Soliloquy: A cautionary tale (2014)

[CN97] Cai, J.Y., Nerurkar, A.: An improved worst-case to average-case connection for lattice problems. In: FOCS, pp. 468–477. IEEE Computer Society (1997)

[CvD07] Childs, A.M., Dam, W.V.: Quantum algorithm for a generalized hidden shift problem. In: SODA, pp. 1225–1232. SIAM (2007)

[DKL+18] Ducas, L.: Crystals-dilithium: a lattice-based digital signature scheme. IACR Trans. Cryptogr. Hardw. Embed. Syst. **2018**(1), 238–268 (2018)

[DKRV18] D'Anvers, J.-P., Karmakar, A., Sinha Roy, S., Vercauteren, F.: Saber: module-LWR based key exchange, CPA-secure encryption and CCA-secure KEM. In: Joux, A., Nitaj, A., Rachidi, T. (eds.) AFRICACRYPT 2018. LNCS, vol. 10831, pp. 282–305. Springer, Cham (2018). https://doi.org/10.1007/978-3-319-89339-6_16

[DM13] Döttling, N., Müller-Quade, J.: Lossy codes and a new variant of the learning-with-errors problem. In: Johansson, T., Nguyen, P.Q. (eds.) EUROCRYPT 2013. LNCS, vol. 7881, pp. 18–34. Springer, Heidelberg (2013). https://doi.org/10.1007/978-3-642-38348-9_2

[EHKS14] Eisenträger, K., Hallgren, S., Kitaev, A.Y., Song, F.: A quantum algorithm for computing the unit group of an arbitrary degree number field. In: STOC, pp. 293–302. ACM (2014)

[ES16] Eldar, L., Shor, P.W.: An efficient quantum algorithm for a variant of the closest lattice-vector problem (2016)

[FIM+03] Friedl, K., Ivanyos, G., Magniez, F., Santha, M., Sen, P.: Hidden translation and orbit coset in quantum computing. In: STOC, pp. 1–9. ACM (2003)

[GGH96] Goldreich, O., Goldwasser, S., Halevi, S.: Collision-free hashing from lattice problems. Electron. Colloq. Comput. Compl. (ECCC) **3**(42) (1996)

[GKZ19] Grilo, A.B., Kerenidis, I., Zijlstra, T.: Learning-with-errors problem is easy with quantum samples. Phys. Rev. A **99**(3), 032314 (2019)

[GPV08] Gentry, C., Peikert, C., Vaikuntanathan, V.: Trapdoors for hard lattices and new cryptographic constructions. In: STOC, pp. 197–206 (2008)

[GVW13] Gorbunov, S., Vaikuntanathan, V., Wee, H.: Attribute-based encryption for circuits. In: STOC, pp. 545–554. ACM (2013)

[IPS18] Ivanyos, G., Prakash, A., Santha, M.: On learning linear functions from subset and its applications in quantum computing. In: ESA, vol. 112 of LIPIcs, pp. 66:1–66:14. Schloss Dagstuhl - Leibniz-Zentrum für Informatik (2018)

[Kup05] Kuperberg, G.: A subexponential-time quantum algorithm for the dihedral hidden subgroup problem. SIAM J. Comput. **35**(1), 170–188 (2005)

[Mah18] Mahadev, U.: Classical homomorphic encryption for quantum circuits. In: FOCS, pp. 332–338. IEEE Computer Society (2018)

[Mic02] Micciancio, D.: Improved cryptographic hash functions with worst-case/average-case connection. In: STOC, pp. 609–618. ACM (2002)

[Mic12] Micciancio, D.: CSE 206A: Lattice Algorithms and Applications. Lecture 2: The dual lattice (2012)

[MP13] Micciancio, D., Peikert, C.: Hardness of SIS and LWE with small parameters. In: Canetti, R., Garay, J.A. (eds.) CRYPTO 2013. LNCS, vol. 8042, pp. 21–39. Springer, Heidelberg (2013). https://doi.org/10.1007/978-3-642-40041-4_2

[MR07] Micciancio, D., Regev, O.: Worst-case to average-case reductions based on Gaussian measure. SIAM J. Comput. **37**(1), 267–302 (2007)

[MS19] Miller, S.D., Stephens-Davidowitz, N.: Kissing numbers and transference theorems from generalized tail bounds. SIAM J. Disc. Math. **33**(3), 1313–1325 (2019)

[NC16] Nielsen, M.A., Chuang, I.L.: Quantum Computation and Quantum Information (10th Anniversary edition). Cambridge University Press, Cambridge (2016)

[Per88] Peres, A.: How to differentiate between non-orthogonal states. Phys. Lett. A **128**, 19–19 (1988)

[Reg02] Regev, O.: Quantum computation and lattice problems. In: FOCS, pp. 520–529. IEEE Computer Society (2002)

[Reg05] Regev, O.: On lattices, learning with errors, random linear codes, and cryptography. In: STOC, pp. 84–93. ACM (2005)

[SE94] Schnorr, C.-P., Euchner, M.: Lattice basis reduction: improved practical algorithms and solving subset sum problems. Math. Program. **66**(1), 181–199 (1994)

[SSTX09] Stehlé, D., Steinfeld, R., Tanaka, K., Xagawa, K.: Efficient public key encryption based on ideal lattices. In: Matsui, M. (ed.) ASIACRYPT 2009. LNCS, vol. 5912, pp. 617–635. Springer, Heidelberg (2009). https://doi.org/10.1007/978-3-642-10366-7_36

Anonymous, Robust Post-quantum Public Key Encryption

Paul Grubbs[1], Varun Maram[2(✉)] ⓘ, and Kenneth G. Paterson[2]

[1] University of Michigan, Ann Arbor, USA
paulgrub@umich.edu
[2] Department of Computer Science, ETH Zurich, Zurich, Switzerland
{vmaram,kenny.paterson}@inf.ethz.ch

Abstract. A core goal of the NIST PQC competition is to produce PKE schemes which, even if attacked with a large-scale quantum computer, maintain the security guarantees needed by applications. The main security focus in the NIST PQC context has been IND-CCA security, but other applications demand that PKE schemes provide *anonymity* (Bellare *et al.*, ASIACRYPT 2001), and *robustness* (Abdalla *et al.*, TCC 2010). Examples of such applications include anonymous cryptocurrencies, searchable encryption, and auction protocols. However, almost nothing is known about how to build post-quantum PKE schemes offering these security properties. In particular, the status of the NIST PQC candidates with respect to anonymity and robustness is unknown.

This paper initiates a systematic study of anonymity and robustness for post-quantum PKE schemes. Firstly, we identify implicit rejection as a crucial design choice shared by most post-quantum KEMs, show that implicit rejection renders prior results on anonymity and robustness for KEM-DEM PKEs inapplicable, and transfer prior results to the implicit-rejection setting where possible. Secondly, since they are widely used to build post-quantum PKEs, we examine how the Fujisaki-Okamoto (FO) transforms (Fujisaki and Okamoto, Journal of Cryptology 2013) confer robustness and enhance weak anonymity of a base PKE.

We then leverage our theoretical results to study the anonymity and robustness of three NIST KEM finalists—Saber, Kyber, and Classic McEliece—and one alternate, FrodoKEM. Overall, our findings for robustness are definitive: we provide positive robustness results for Saber, Kyber, and FrodoKEM, and a negative result for Classic McEliece. Our negative result stems from a striking property of KEM-DEM PKE schemes built with the Classic McEliece KEM: for any message m, we can construct a single hybrid ciphertext c which decrypts to the chosen m under *any* Classic McEliece private key.

Our findings for anonymity are more mixed: we identify barriers to proving anonymity for Saber, Kyber, and Classic McEliece. We also found that in the case of Saber and Kyber, these barriers lead to issues with their IND-CCA security claims. We have worked with the Saber and Kyber teams to fix these issues, but they remain unresolved. On the positive side, we were able to prove anonymity for FrodoKEM and a variant of Saber introduced by D'Anvers *et al.* (AFRICACRYPT 2018). Our analyses of these two schemes also identified technical gaps in their IND-CCA security claims, but we were able to fix them.

© International Association for Cryptologic Research 2022
O. Dunkelman and S. Dziembowski (Eds.): EUROCRYPT 2022, LNCS 13277, pp. 402–432, 2022.
https://doi.org/10.1007/978-3-031-07082-2_15

1   Introduction

The increasingly real threat of quantum computers breaking all widely-deployed public-key cryptography has driven research in new paradigms for building core public-key primitives like signatures, public-key encryption (PKE), and key encapsulation mechanisms (KEMs) from problems that are computationally intractable even for quantum computers. An umbrella term for this is *Post-Quantum Cryptography* (PQC). The US National Institute of Standards and Technology (NIST) is in the process of selecting new standards which will be used for decades to come. The process has reached its third round with four finalist candidates and five alternate candidates in the KEM/PKE category. The main security target of evaluation for these schemes until now has been IND-CCA security. This was appropriate as a starting point because it suffices for many important use cases. But we argue that the time has now come for a broader study of the candidates' fitness for emerging applications where security properties other than IND-CCA are required.

Two important security properties that go beyond IND-CCA security are *anonymity* (or key privacy) and *robustness*. Anonymity was first formalised in the public key setting by [8]. Roughly, a PKE scheme is anonymous if a ciphertext does not leak anything about which public key was used to create it; strong forms of anonymity equip the adversary with a decryption oracle. Anonymous PKE is a fundamental component of several deployed anonymity systems, most notably anonymous cryptocurrencies like Zcash [10]. It is also important in building anonymous broadcast encryption schemes [6,29], anonymous credential systems [12] and auction protocols [35]. Robustness for PKE, first formalised in [2], goes hand-in-hand with anonymity. Suppose a party equipped with a private key receives a ciphertext for an anonymous PKE scheme. In the absence of other information, how does a party decide that it is the intended receiver of that ciphertext? The standard approach is to perform trial decryption. Robustness provides an assurance that this process does not go wrong – that the receiver is not fooled into accepting a plaintext intended for someone else. Robustness is also important for maintaining consistency in searchable encryption [1] and ensuring auction bid correctness [35]. Various robustness notions for PKE were studied in [2], while stronger notions were introduced in [16]; the symmetric setting was treated in [15,17,21,28].

To date, there is almost no work that shows how to build anonymous, robust post-quantum PKE schemes. Nor is it known whether the NIST candidates meet these extended notions. The only directly relevant work is by Mohassel [32], who showed a number of foundational results on anonymity and robustness of hybrid PKEs built via the KEM-DEM paradigm ("DEM" being an abbreviation for "data encapsulation mechanism"). Our work is influenced by Mohassel's general approach; however, Mohassel only considers KEMs that are directly constructed from strongly-secure PKEs via sampling a random message from the PKE scheme's message space and then PKE-encrypting it. This makes the results of [32] inapplicable to NIST candidates, for a few reasons. First, the NIST candidates are all KEMs, not PKEs, so there is a basic syntactic mismatch. Second, the base PKEs used within the candidate KEMs are only weakly (e.g. OW-CPA) secure, but [32] relies on the starting PKE having (e.g.) IND-CCA security. Finally, [32] only analyzes explicit-rejection KEMs, for which decapsulation can fail, but all the NIST candidates except the alternate candidate HQC [31] are actually implicit-rejection KEMs that never output ⊥. This means, e.g., the NIST *finalist* KEMs cannot be even weakly robust, while the constructions of [32] all start from robust KEMs.

One of the negative results of [32] is that even if a KEM enjoys a strong anonymity property, the hybrid PKE scheme that results from applying the standard KEM-DEM construction may not be anonymous. This is concerning, since it indicates that if one only focuses on KEMs in the NIST competition, rather than the PKE schemes that will inevitably be built from them using the standard KEM-DEM approach, then there is no guarantee that desired security properties will actually carry over. Thus, one must dig into a KEM's internals if the target is to achieve anonymous hybrid PKE.

In fact, all the NIST candidates in the KEM/PKE category are constructed using variants of the Fujisaki-Okamoto (FO) transform [18–20]. The FO transform takes a weakly secure PKE scheme (e.g. one that is OW-CPA or IND-CPA secure) and elevates it to a KEM that is IND-CCA secure. The FO transform and variants of it have recently been heavily analysed, [24–26,34,37], in the Random Oracle Model (ROM) and the Quantum ROM (QROM) [11], but insofar as we are aware, only with a view to establishing IND-CCA security of the resulting KEMs. Only one prior work [23] studies the relationship between FO transforms and anonymity; it shows that the original FO transform enhances anonymity in the ROM. But this result does not tell us whether the modern FO variants used by the NIST finalists also enhance (or even preserve) robustness and anonymity properties; notably, the results of [23] are not in the QROM.

Anonymity and robustness for the KEM-DEM paradigm. Our first main contribution is a modular theory of anonymity and robustness for PKE schemes built via the KEM-DEM paradigm. This extends the work of [32] to general KEMs (instead of those built only from PKEs). An interesting aspect that emerges is a fundamental separation between our results for implicit- and explicit-rejection KEMs. At a high level, KEMs that perform implicit rejection do not in general transfer anonymity and robustness to PKEs obtained via the KEM-DEM paradigm from the KEM component, whilst KEMs that offer explicit rejection, and that also satisfy a mild robustness property, do. Our positive result for explicit rejection KEMs relies on a relatively weak anonymity notion for KEMs which we introduce here, wANO-CCA security. Our negative results for the implicit rejection case are proved through the construction of specific counterexamples and are surprisingly strong. For example, an implicit rejection KEM cannot be robust, but can achieve a strong form of collision freeness (SCFR-CCA, that we define here). This is in some sense the next best thing to robustness. We show that even this property is not sufficient, by exhibiting an implicit rejection KEM that is ANO-CCA, IND-CCA and SCFR-CCA secure, and a DEM that is AE (authenticated encryption) secure and satisfies a strong robustness property

(XROB, from [17]), but where the PKE scheme resulting from composing this KEM and DEM is not ANO-CCA secure.

Anonymity and robustness from FO transforms. Since all the NIST finalists are KEMs of the implicit rejection type and we have a strong negative result there, we must dig deeper if we wish to assure ourselves that anonymity and robustness will be obtained for PKEs built from those KEMs. This introduces our second main contribution, wherein we analyse how the FO transform (and its variants) lift anonymity and robustness properties from a starting weakly-secure PKE scheme, first to the strongly-secure KEM built by the FO transform, and then to the hybrid PKE scheme constructed using the KEM-DEM paradigm.

For explicit-rejection KEMs, we show that for a slight variant of the $HFO^{\perp}$ transform of [24], the base PKE's weak anonymity and robustness are enhanced to strong (ANO-CCA) anonymity and strong (SROB-CCA) robustness, as long as an intermediate deterministic PKE used in the transform is collision-free. For implicit-rejection KEMs, we show that the $FO^{\not\perp}$ transform of [24] similarly enhances anonymity and collision-freeness. The culmination of this analysis is showing that KEMs and PKEs built via FO-type transforms can bypass our negative result for implicit rejection KEMs.

Application to NIST candidates. We then apply our above generic analysis for implicit-rejection KEMs to specific schemes related to the NIST PQC competition which employ a transform close to $FO^{\not\perp}$. In particular, we focus on the NIST finalist Classic McEliece [3], a simplified version of the NIST finalist Saber [7] from [14] that we call "proto-Saber", and the NIST alternate candidate FrodoKEM [4]. The reason we consider proto-Saber instead of the actual Saber scheme is that the IND-CCA security claims made for Saber in its NIST third round specification [7] seem to have been taken from those of proto-Saber in [14] *without modification*. However, the actual technical specification of Saber in [7, Section 8] and the reference implementation of Saber differ from proto-Saber in crucial ways that impact on its formal security analysis. We return to this issue in more detail below and in Sect. 5.

For Classic McEliece, we show that the hybrid PKE resulting from applying the standard KEM-DEM construction is not strongly robust (in the sense defined in [2]). In fact, we can show that, for any plaintext m, it is possible to construct a single ciphertext c such that c always decrypts to m under *any* Classic McEliece private key. The construction of c does not even need the public key! We stress that this property does not indicate any problem with IND-CCA security of Classic McEliece, but it does expose its limitations as a general-purpose KEM for the broad set of applications that can be envisaged for NIST public key algorithms. Since our $FO^{\not\perp}$-related results on anonymity of KEMs and PKEs built from them depend on robustness properties, Classic McEliece's limitations in this regard present a barrier to establishing its anonymity using our techniques (but do not preclude a direct proof).

For proto-Saber, the news is better. We provide positive results on anonymity and robustness properties of its KEM and the hybrid PKE schemes derived from it. Towards these results, we have to adapt our analysis on $FO^{\cancel{\perp}}$ to the actual transform used by proto-Saber. In doing so, we were also able to obtain an explicit proof of IND-CCA security for proto-Saber in the QROM that matches the tightness claimed in [14]. This is relevant because despite claims to the contrary in [14], we find that even the IND-CCA security of proto-Saber cannot be directly proved using any of the known results concerning the $FO^{\cancel{\perp}}$ transform. This is due to low-level details of how proto-Saber applies hash functions to intermediate values in its internal computations. These details are crucial given the delicate nature of QROM proofs and invalidate the direct application of known results on "standard" FO transforms in the QROM.

FrodoKEM uses an FO-type transform that is *identical* to that of proto-Saber. Hence, our positive results on tight IND-CCA security, anonymity and robustness of proto-Saber also apply to FrodoKEM in a similar fashion.

Saber and Kyber [5] both implement the same transform, one which hashes even more intermediate values than proto-Saber does. This creates barriers in applying the proof strategies that we used for proto-Saber when trying to establish anonymity of Saber and Kyber. Interestingly, as we explain in detail, these extra hashes also act as barriers in proving even the IND-CCA security of these two finalists in the QROM with the bounds as claimed in their respective specifications. We consider this an important finding given the centrality of IND-CCA security as the design target in the NIST competition. On a positive note, we show that our robustness analysis of proto-Saber can be extended to Saber and Kyber, which implies that these two NIST finalists lead to strongly robust hybrid PKE schemes. Finally, we suggest small modifications to Saber and Kyber that would bring their FO-type transforms closer to that of proto-Saber and allow us to overcome the aforementioned problems.

Subsequent Work. The NIST finalist NTRU [13] uses altogether a different transform, namely $FO_m^{\cancel{\perp}}$ [24], that differs from $FO^{\cancel{\perp}}$ in a way which makes it difficult to extend our analysis of $FO^{\cancel{\perp}}$ to NTRU. However, in subsequent work to ours, Xagawa [39] has established the anonymity and robustness properties of NTRU by utilizing a stronger property of its base PKE scheme, namely the so-called *strong disjoint-simulatability.*

Paper organisation. Section 2 contains preliminary definitions. Section 3 contains our anonymity and robustness definitions for KEMs, and analysis of generic KEM-DEM composition. Section 4 contains our study of anonymity and robustness enhancement for FO-type transforms, and the security of hybrid PKE built from FO-type KEMs. Section 5 contains our study of the NIST candidate KEMs.

2   Preliminaries

In this section, we briefly define the preliminaries necessary for the main body. We begin with defining the syntax of primitives of interest.

Primitives. A key encapsulation mechanism (KEM) KEM = (KGen, Encap, Decap) is a tuple of algorithms. The randomized key generation algorithm KGen takes no input and outputs a pair (pk, sk) of a public encapsulation key pk and a private decapsulation key sk. The randomized encapsulation algorithm Encap takes as input the encapsulation key pk, and outputs a pair (C, k) where C is a ciphertext and k is a bit string. The determinstic decapsulation algorithm Decap takes as input the encapsulation key pk, the decapsulation key sk, and the ciphertext C. If decapsulation can output either a key k or an error symbol $\perp$, we call the KEM an *explicit-rejection* KEM. If decapsulation can only output a key k, we call the KEM an *implicit-rejection* KEM.

A public-key encryption (PKE) scheme PKE = (KGen, Enc, Dec) is a tuple of algorithms. The algorithm KGen is the same as above for KEMs. (It is conventional to call KGen's outputs the encryption/public and decryption/private key, respectively, instead of "encapsulation"/"decapsulation" keys.) The randomized encryption algorithm Enc takes as input the public key pk, and message m, and outputs a ciphertext C. Below, we will sometimes use a modified syntax for encryption, where instead of sampling internal randomness, the algorithm is deterministic and takes random coins as an additional input. Letting r be a string of random bits, we will write Enc(pk, m; r) to denote the output of Enc when run with randomness r. Finally, the deterministic decryption algorithm Dec takes as input the public key pk, the secret key sk, and a ciphertext C, and outputs a message m or an error symbol $\perp$.

We assume the reader is familiar with the syntax for authenticated encryption with associated data (AEAD or AE) schemes and message authentication codes (MACs), along with the *correctness* and γ-*spreadness* properties of PKE schemes and KEMs. We provide the corresponding formal definitions in the full version of this paper [22].

Associated to each algorithm that comprises a primitive above is one or more input spaces (e.g. sets of possible keys $\mathcal{K}$ and messages $\mathcal{M}$) and an output space (e.g. the set of possible ciphertexts $\mathcal{C}$). We assume each algorithm checks that each of inputs is in this set, and aborts if not. To reduce notational clutter, we will not make these input/output spaces explicit below, except where necessary.

The KEM-DEM framework. Composing a KEM and a data encapsulation mechanism (DEM) is a standard way to build PKE. Schemes built this way are often called "hybrid" PKE. For completeness, we describe the hybrid PKE built via KEM-DEM composition. Let KEM be a KEM, and DEM be an authenticated encryption scheme. (Below, we will use "DEM" and "AEAD" synonymously.) The hybrid PKE PKE^{hy} = (KGen, Enc, Dec) is built as follows. The algorithm PKE^{hy}.KGen is the same as KEM.KGen. The algorithm PKE^{hy}.Enc takes as input the encapsulation key pk and a message m. It first runs $(C_0, k) \leftarrow_\$ \mathsf{KEM.Encap}(pk)$, the computes $C_1 \leftarrow_\$ \mathsf{AEAD.Enc}(k, m)$ and outputs ciphertext (C_0, C_1). The algorithm PKE^{hy}.Dec first uses sk to decapsulate C_0 and get k or possibly an error symbol $\perp$. Unless decapsulation failed, the algorithm completes by running $\mathsf{AEAD.Dec}(k, C_1)$, outputting either m or an error symbol $\perp$.

The Fujisaki-Okamoto transform. Classical results of Fujisaki and Okamoto [18–20] show how to amplify (in the random oracle model, or ROM) the security of public-key encryption, from one-wayness (OW) or indistinguishability (IND) under chosen-plaintext attack (CPA) to indistinguishability under chosen-ciphertext attack (IND-CCA). In this work we will mostly be interested in modern variants of this so-called "FO transform" studied first by Hofheinz et al. [24] in the classical ROM and QROM; extensions in the QROM were then given by [26,34,37]. Details of these transforms can be found in Sect. 4.

2.1 Security Definitions

Next we state several standard security notions which we will use below. In this work we use the "concrete" security paradigm, which explicitly measures the success probability and resource usage of specific adversaries, which we specify using the code-based game-playing framework of Bellare and Rogaway [9]. We will not relate quantities of interest, such as runtime or oracle queries, to a security parameter. We define relevant security notions for PKE (upper box), AEAD and MAC (lower box) in Fig. 1.

PKE security notions are given for chosen-ciphertext attacks. All adversaries have access to a decryption oracle D that takes a ciphertext and (where relevant, i.e., in games with *two* key-pairs) a bit that selects which secret key to use. In ANO-CCA and IND-CCA games, the decryption oracle $D_{\mathcal{C}}$ disallows queries for the challenge ciphertext. For each PKE notion, the corresponding definition for chosen-plaintext attacks can be obtained by simply removing the decryption oracle. In INT-CTXT, the adversary has an encryption (resp., decryption) oracle that takes associated data and a message (resp., ciphertext); flag win is set to true if the adversary submits a query to its decryption oracle that returns non-$\perp$, but was not returned from an encryption query. In SUF-CMA, the oracle TagO's inputs and outputs are stored in the table $\mathbf{T}$ after each query. In otROR-CCA, the oracles $E_1, \$_1$ are one-time encryption and random-bits oracles, respectively. The many-time security definition ROR-CCA is identical to otROR-CCA, but without this restriction. As for PKE above, CPA variants can be obtained by removing decryption oracles.

For any game G in Fig. 1, we define an associated advantage measure for an adversary $\mathcal{A}$ and primitive P, denoted $\mathbf{Adv}_P^G(\mathcal{A})$, to be either $\Pr\left[G_P^{\mathcal{A}} \Rightarrow \text{true}\right]$ or the absolute difference between that quantity and $1/2$, if the game G is a bit-guessing game like IND-CCA.

3 Anonymity and Robustness of KEMs

In [32], Mohassel studied the anonymity and robustness of KEMs. However, all of his definitions and results apply only to the special case of KEMs that are constructed from PKE schemes in a restricted way, namely KEMs in which the encapsulation algorithm selects a random message for the PKE scheme and encrypts it using the PKE scheme's encryption algorithm. With this limitation,

SROB-CCA$_{\mathsf{PKE}}^{\mathcal{A}}$	WROB-CCA$_{\mathsf{PKE}}^{\mathcal{A}}$	ANO-CCA$_{\mathsf{PKE}}^{\mathcal{A}}$
$(\mathsf{pk}_0, \mathsf{sk}_0) \leftarrow_{\$} \mathsf{KGen}$	$(\mathsf{pk}_0, \mathsf{sk}_0) \leftarrow_{\$} \mathsf{KGen}$	$(\mathsf{pk}_0, \mathsf{sk}_0) \leftarrow_{\$} \mathsf{KGen}$
$(\mathsf{pk}_1, \mathsf{sk}_1) \leftarrow_{\$} \mathsf{KGen}$	$(\mathsf{pk}_1, \mathsf{sk}_1) \leftarrow_{\$} \mathsf{KGen}$	$(\mathsf{pk}_1, \mathsf{sk}_1) \leftarrow_{\$} \mathsf{KGen}$
$C \leftarrow_{\$} \mathcal{A}^D(\mathsf{pk}_0, \mathsf{pk}_1)$	$(m, b) \leftarrow_{\$} \mathcal{A}^D(\mathsf{pk}_0, \mathsf{pk}_1)$	$b \leftarrow_{\$} \{0, 1\}$
$m_0 \leftarrow \mathsf{Dec}(\mathsf{pk}_0, \mathsf{sk}_0, C)$	$C \leftarrow_{\$} \mathsf{Enc}(\mathsf{pk}_b, m)$	$(m, \mathsf{st}) \leftarrow_{\$} \mathcal{A}^D(\mathsf{pk}_0, \mathsf{pk}_1)$
$m_1 \leftarrow \mathsf{Dec}(\mathsf{pk}_1, \mathsf{sk}_1, C)$	$b' \leftarrow 1 - b$	$C \leftarrow_{\$} \mathsf{Enc}(\mathsf{pk}_b, m)$
return $m_0 \neq \bot \wedge m_1 \neq \bot$	$m_1 \leftarrow \mathsf{Dec}(\mathsf{pk}_{b'}, \mathsf{sk}_{b'}, C)$	$b' \leftarrow_{\$} \mathcal{A}^{D_{\not{C}}}(C, \mathsf{st})$
	return $m_1 \neq \bot$	**return** $b = b'$

SCFR-CCA$_{\mathsf{PKE}}^{\mathcal{A}}$	WCFR-CCA$_{\mathsf{PKE}}^{\mathcal{A}}$	IND-CCA$_{\mathsf{PKE}}^{\mathcal{A}}$
$(\mathsf{pk}_0, \mathsf{sk}_0) \leftarrow_{\$} \mathsf{KGen}$	$(\mathsf{pk}_0, \mathsf{sk}_0) \leftarrow_{\$} \mathsf{KGen}$	$(\mathsf{pk}, \mathsf{sk}) \leftarrow_{\$} \mathsf{KGen}$
$(\mathsf{pk}_1, \mathsf{sk}_1) \leftarrow_{\$} \mathsf{KGen}$	$(\mathsf{pk}_1, \mathsf{sk}_1) \leftarrow_{\$} \mathsf{KGen}$	$b \leftarrow_{\$} \{0, 1\}$
$C \leftarrow_{\$} \mathcal{A}^D(\mathsf{pk}_0, \mathsf{pk}_1)$	$(m, b) \leftarrow_{\$} \mathcal{A}^D(\mathsf{pk}_0, \mathsf{pk}_1)$	$(m_0, m_1, \mathsf{st}) \leftarrow_{\$} \mathcal{A}^D(\mathsf{pk})$
$m_0 \leftarrow \mathsf{Dec}(\mathsf{pk}_0, \mathsf{sk}_0, C)$	$C \leftarrow_{\$} \mathsf{Enc}(\mathsf{pk}_b, m)$	$C \leftarrow_{\$} \mathsf{Enc}(\mathsf{pk}, m_b)$
$m_1 \leftarrow \mathsf{Dec}(\mathsf{pk}_1, \mathsf{sk}_1, C)$	$b' \leftarrow 1 - b$	$b' \leftarrow_{\$} \mathcal{A}^{D_{\not{C}}}(C, \mathsf{st})$
return $m_0 = m_1 \neq \bot$	$m' \leftarrow \mathsf{Dec}(\mathsf{pk}_{b'}, \mathsf{sk}_{b'}, C)$	**return** $b = b'$
	return $m' = m \neq \bot$	

FROB$_{\mathsf{AEAD}}^{\mathcal{A}}$	XROB$_{\mathsf{AEAD}}^{\mathcal{A}}$	INT-CTXT$_{\mathsf{AEAD}}^{\mathcal{A}}$
$(C, \mathsf{AD}, \mathsf{k}_0, \mathsf{k}_1) \leftarrow_{\$} \mathcal{A}$	$(S_0, S_1) \leftarrow_{\$} \mathcal{A}$	$\mathsf{k} \leftarrow_{\$} \mathsf{KGen}$
$m_0 \leftarrow \mathsf{Dec}(\mathsf{k}_0, \mathsf{AD}, C)$	Parse $S_0 = (m_0, \mathsf{k}_0, R_0, \mathsf{AD}_0)$	$\mathsf{win} \leftarrow \mathsf{false}$
$m_1 \leftarrow \mathsf{Dec}(\mathsf{k}_1, \mathsf{AD}, C)$	Parse $S_1 = (\mathsf{k}_1, \mathsf{AD}_1, C_1)$	$\mathcal{A}^{E(\cdot, \cdot), D(\cdot, \cdot)}$
$b \leftarrow m_0 \neq \bot \wedge m_1 \neq \bot$	$C_0 \leftarrow \mathsf{Enc}(\mathsf{k}_0, m_0; R_0)$	**return** win
return $(b \wedge (\mathsf{k}_0 \neq \mathsf{k}_1))$	$m_1 \leftarrow \mathsf{Dec}(\mathsf{k}_1, \mathsf{AD}_1, C_1)$	
	$b \leftarrow m_0 \neq \bot \wedge m_1 \neq \bot$	SUF-CMA$_{\mathsf{MAC}}^{\mathcal{A}}$
otROR-CCA$_{\mathsf{AEAD}}^{\mathcal{A}}$	$b_k \leftarrow \mathsf{k}_0 \neq \mathsf{k}_1$	$\mathsf{k} \leftarrow_{\$} \mathsf{KGen}$
$\mathsf{k} \leftarrow_{\$} \mathsf{KGen}$	$b_c \leftarrow C_0 = C_1 \neq \bot$	$\mathbf{T} \leftarrow []$
$b \leftarrow_{\$} \{0, 1\}$	$b_a \leftarrow \mathsf{AD}_0 = \mathsf{AD}_1 \neq \bot$	$(m, T) \leftarrow \mathcal{A}^{\mathsf{TagO}(\cdot)}$
if $b = 0$ **then**	**return** $(b \wedge b_k \wedge b_c \wedge b_a)$	$b \leftarrow \mathsf{Vf}(\mathsf{k}, m, T)$
$\quad b' \leftarrow_{\$} \mathcal{A}^{E_1(\cdot, \cdot), D(\cdot, \cdot)}$		$b_t \leftarrow (m, T) \notin \mathbf{T}$
else $b' \leftarrow_{\$} \mathcal{A}^{\$_1(\cdot, \cdot), \bot(\cdot, \cdot)}$		**return** $b \wedge b_t$
return $b = b'$		

Fig. 1. Security games used in this paper w.r.t. PKE PKE = (KGen, Enc, Dec) (upper box), and AEAD AEAD = (KGen, Enc, Dec) and MAC = (KGen, Tag, Vf) (lower box). In all games associated with PKE above *except* IND-CCA, the decryption oracle D (and $D_{\not{C}}$ in ANO-CCA) also takes as input a *bit* that denotes which secret key (sk_0 or sk_1) to use to decrypt the queried ciphertext. Also, see Sect. 2.1 for more details.

Mohassel provided a number of interesting results (positive and negative) concerning the anonymity and robustness of KEMs and of PKEs constructed from them via the KEM-DEM framework.

In this section, we bridge the definitional gap left by Mohassel's work by first considering fully general definitions for KEM anonymity and robustness, and then revisiting his results on these properties in the context of the KEM-DEM framework. As we shall see, how much can be recovered depends in a critical way on the KEM's behaviour with respect to rejection of invalid encapsulations.

We first define ANO-CCA security of a KEM KEM = (KGen, Encap, Decap) via the security game between an adversary and a challenger, as described in Fig. 2. Note that the security game differs from the AI-ATK game defined for so-called *general encryption schemes* in [2], where in the latter, an adversary can have access to multiple public-keys (and some corresponding secret keys which will not result in a trivial win for the adversary). Since we are only considering PKE schemes and KEMs in this paper, it is not hard to show that the two security notions are equivalent up to a factor depending on the number of secret key queries an adversary could make (as already discussed in [2]).

An analogous ANO-CPA definition can be obtained simply by removing decapsulation queries in the above game. An adversary $\mathcal{A}$'s advantage in the ANO-{CPA,CCA} game is then defined to be:

$$\mathbf{Adv}_{\mathsf{KEM}}^{\mathrm{ANO-\{CPA,CCA\}}}(\mathcal{A}) = |\Pr[\mathsf{G}^{\mathcal{A}} = 1] - 1/2|$$

where $\mathsf{G}^{\mathcal{A}}$ refers to $\mathcal{A}$ playing in the appropriate version of the anonymity game,

In the context of KEM-DEM framework for constructing PKE schemes, we will find it sufficient to work with an even weaker notion of anonymity for KEMs, that we refer to as *weak* anonymity. Here, the security game above is modified by giving the adversary only C^* in response to its challenge query, instead of (C^*, k^*); see Fig. 2. We then refer to wANO-{CPA,CCA} security and define adversarial advantages as above.

We also define weak robustness (WROB) and strong robustness (SROB) security notions for general KEMs. The security games described in Fig. 2 define both notions via two different finalisation steps. Note that the security game for WROB has a subtle difference from the corresponding WROB-ATK game defined for general encryption schemes in [2] (in addition to the fact that, in the latter game, an adversary can have access to multiple public-keys). The difference is that in our notion, an adversary outputs a bit b that determines which of the two public-keys ($\mathsf{pk}_0, \mathsf{pk}_1$) will be used for encapsulation. This is required because the weak robustness notion is inherently *asymmetric* w.r.t. the two challenge public-keys, since one key is used for encapsulation (resp. encryption in case of PKE schemes) and the other for decapsulation (resp. decryption in case of PKE schemes).

Again, analogous WROB-CPA and SROB-CPA definitions can be obtained simply by removing decapsulation queries in the above games. The advantage of an adversary $\mathcal{A}$ in the {WROB,SROB}-{CPA,CCA} game is then defined as:

$$\mathbf{Adv}_{\mathsf{KEM}}^{\{\mathrm{WROB,SROB}\}-\{\mathrm{CPA,CCA}\}}(\mathcal{A}) = \Pr[\mathsf{G}^{\mathcal{A}} = 1]$$

ANO-CCA$_{\mathsf{KEM}}^{\mathcal{A}}$	wANO-CCA$_{\mathsf{KEM}}^{\mathcal{A}}$
$(\mathsf{pk}_0, \mathsf{sk}_0) \leftarrow_{\$} \mathsf{KGen}$	$(\mathsf{pk}_0, \mathsf{sk}_0) \leftarrow_{\$} \mathsf{KGen}$
$(\mathsf{pk}_1, \mathsf{sk}_1) \leftarrow_{\$} \mathsf{KGen}$	$(\mathsf{pk}_1, \mathsf{sk}_1) \leftarrow_{\$} \mathsf{KGen}$
$b \leftarrow_{\$} \{0, 1\}$	$b \leftarrow_{\$} \{0, 1\}$
$(C^*, k^*) \leftarrow_{\$} \mathsf{Encap}(\mathsf{pk}_b)$	$(C^*, k^*) \leftarrow_{\$} \mathsf{Encap}(\mathsf{pk}_b)$
$b' \leftarrow_{\$} \mathcal{A}^{D(\cdot,\cdot)}(\mathsf{pk}_0, \mathsf{pk}_1, (C^*, k^*))$	$b' \leftarrow_{\$} \mathcal{A}^{D(\cdot,\cdot)}(\mathsf{pk}_0, \mathsf{pk}_1, C^*)$
return $b = b'$	**return** $b = b'$

SROB-CCA$_{\mathsf{KEM}}^{\mathcal{A}}$	WROB-CCA$_{\mathsf{KEM}}^{\mathcal{A}}$
$(\mathsf{pk}_0, \mathsf{sk}_0) \leftarrow_{\$} \mathsf{KGen}$	$(\mathsf{pk}_0, \mathsf{sk}_0) \leftarrow_{\$} \mathsf{KGen}$
$(\mathsf{pk}_1, \mathsf{sk}_1) \leftarrow_{\$} \mathsf{KGen}$	$(\mathsf{pk}_1, \mathsf{sk}_1) \leftarrow_{\$} \mathsf{KGen}$
$C \leftarrow_{\$} \mathcal{A}^{D(\cdot,\cdot)}(\mathsf{pk}_0, \mathsf{pk}_1)$	$b \leftarrow_{\$} \mathcal{A}^{D(\cdot,\cdot)}(\mathsf{pk}_0, \mathsf{pk}_1)$
$k_0 \leftarrow \mathsf{Decap}(\mathsf{pk}_0, \mathsf{sk}_0, C)$	$(C, k_b) \leftarrow_{\$} \mathsf{Encap}(\mathsf{pk}_b)$
$k_1 \leftarrow \mathsf{Decap}(\mathsf{pk}_1, \mathsf{sk}_1, C)$	$k_{1-b} \leftarrow \mathsf{Decap}(\mathsf{pk}_{1-b}, \mathsf{sk}_{1-b}, C)$
return $k_0 \neq \bot$ AND $k_1 \neq \bot$	**return** $k_{1-b} \neq \bot$

SCFR-CCA$_{\mathsf{KEM}}^{\mathcal{A}}$	WCFR-CCA$_{\mathsf{KEM}}^{\mathcal{A}}$
$(\mathsf{pk}_0, \mathsf{sk}_0) \leftarrow_{\$} \mathsf{KGen}$	$(\mathsf{pk}_0, \mathsf{sk}_0) \leftarrow_{\$} \mathsf{KGen}$
$(\mathsf{pk}_1, \mathsf{sk}_1) \leftarrow_{\$} \mathsf{KGen}$	$(\mathsf{pk}_1, \mathsf{sk}_1) \leftarrow_{\$} \mathsf{KGen}$
$C \leftarrow_{\$} \mathcal{A}^{D(\cdot,\cdot)}(\mathsf{pk}_0, \mathsf{pk}_1)$	$b \leftarrow_{\$} \mathcal{A}^{D(\cdot,\cdot)}(\mathsf{pk}_0, \mathsf{pk}_1)$
$k_0 \leftarrow \mathsf{Decap}(\mathsf{pk}_0, \mathsf{sk}_0, C)$	$(C, k_b) \leftarrow_{\$} \mathsf{Encap}(\mathsf{pk}_b)$
$k_1 \leftarrow \mathsf{Decap}(\mathsf{pk}_1, \mathsf{sk}_1, C)$	$k_{1-b} \leftarrow \mathsf{Decap}(\mathsf{pk}_{1-b}, \mathsf{sk}_{1-b}, C)$
return $k_0 = k_1 \neq \bot$	**return** $k_b = k_{1-b} \neq \bot$

Fig. 2. KEM security notions for chosen-ciphertext attacks. All adversaries have access to a decryption oracle D that takes a ciphertext and (where relevant) a bit that selects which secret key to use. In ANO-CCA and wANO-CCA games, the decryption oracle disallows queries for the challenge ciphertext. For each notion, the corresponding definition for chosen-plaintext attacks can be obtained by simply removing the decryption oracle.

where $\mathsf{G}^{\mathcal{A}}$ refers to $\mathcal{A}$ playing in the appropriate version of the robustness game.

Note that these robustness definitions apply mainly for KEMs that have explicit rejection on decapsulation errors. KEMs that offer only implicit rejection can never satisfy even the WROB-CPA notion.

With these anonymity and robustness notions in hand, it is straightforward to extend the result of [32, Claim 3.3] concerning anonymity preservation from the specific case of KEMs constructed directly from PKEs to fully general KEMs (with a non-zero decapsulation error probability); in fact, we can also show the robustness of hybrid PKE schemes constructed from robust KEMs via the KEM-DEM framework. Namely, we have the following:

Theorem 1. *Let* $\mathsf{PKE}^{hy} = (\mathsf{KGen}, \mathsf{Enc}^{hy}, \mathsf{Dec}^{hy})$ *be a hybrid encryption scheme obtained by composing a KEM* $\mathsf{KEM} = (\mathsf{KGen}, \mathsf{Encap}, \mathsf{Decap})$ *with a one-time secure authenticated encryption scheme* $\mathsf{DEM} = (\mathsf{Enc}, \mathsf{Dec})$. *If KEM is* δ-*correct, then:*

1. *For any ANO-CCA adversary* $\mathcal{A}$ *against* PKE^{hy}, *there exist wANO-CCA adversary* $\mathcal{B}$, *IND-CCA adversary* $\mathcal{C}$ *and WROB-CPA adversary* $\mathcal{D}$ *against KEM, and INT-CTXT adversary* $\mathcal{E}$ *against DEM such that*

$$\mathbf{Adv}_{\mathsf{PKE}^{hy}}^{\mathrm{ANO\text{-}CCA}}(\mathcal{A}) \leq \mathbf{Adv}_{\mathsf{KEM}}^{\mathrm{wANO\text{-}CCA}}(\mathcal{B}) + 2\mathbf{Adv}_{\mathsf{KEM}}^{\mathrm{IND\text{-}CCA}}(\mathcal{C})$$
$$+ \mathbf{Adv}_{\mathsf{KEM}}^{\mathrm{WROB\text{-}CPA}}(\mathcal{D}) + \mathbf{Adv}_{\mathsf{DEM}}^{\mathrm{INT\text{-}CTXT}}(\mathcal{E}) + \delta.$$

The running times of $\mathcal{B}$, $\mathcal{C}$ *and* $\mathcal{E}$ *are the same as that of* $\mathcal{A}$. *The running time of* $\mathcal{D}$ *is independent (and less than that) of the running time of* $\mathcal{A}$.

2. *For any WROB-ATK (resp. SROB-ATK) adversary* $\mathcal{A}$ *against* PKE^{hy}, *there exists WROB-ATK (resp. SROB-ATK) adversary* $\mathcal{B}$ *against KEM such that*

$$\mathbf{Adv}_{\mathsf{PKE}^{hy}}^{\mathrm{WROB\text{-}ATK}}(\mathcal{A}) \leq \mathbf{Adv}_{\mathsf{KEM}}^{\mathrm{WROB\text{-}ATK}}(\mathcal{B}),$$
$$\mathbf{Adv}_{\mathsf{PKE}^{hy}}^{\mathrm{SROB\text{-}ATK}}(\mathcal{A}) \leq \mathbf{Adv}_{\mathsf{KEM}}^{\mathrm{SROB\text{-}ATK}}(\mathcal{B}),$$

where $\mathrm{ATK} \in \{\mathrm{CPA}, \mathrm{CCA}\}$ *and the running time of* $\mathcal{B}$ *is that of* $\mathcal{A}$.

Proof (sketch). The proof of Theorem 1.1 closely follows that of [32, Claim 3.3] in terms of the sequence of game-hops. Also for certain game-hops, we rely on security notions that are weaker than the corresponding notions considered in the proof of [32, Claim 3.3] (e.g., WROB-CPA, instead of WROB-CCA, security of the underlying KEM). The complete details of the proof can be found in the full version [22].

To sketch a proof for Theorem 1.2, note that an adversary $\mathcal{A}$ wins the WROB-ATK game w.r.t. PKE^{hy} if it returns a pair (m, b) such that $\mathsf{Dec}^{hy}(\mathsf{sk}_{1-b}, C) \neq \bot$ where $C(= (C_{\mathsf{KEM}}, C_{\mathsf{DEM}})) \leftarrow_{\$} \mathsf{Enc}^{hy}(\mathsf{pk}_b, m)$. Let $(C_{\mathsf{KEM}}, k_b) \leftarrow_{\$} \mathsf{Encap}(\mathsf{pk}_b)$ and $\mathsf{Decap}(\mathsf{sk}_{1-b}, C_{\mathsf{KEM}}) = k_{1-b}$. It is easy to see that $k_{1-b} \neq \bot$, since $\mathsf{Dec}^{hy}(\mathsf{sk}_{1-b}, C) \neq \bot$. This implies that we can return bit b to win the WROB-ATK game w.r.t. KEM. We can use a similar argument for the SROB-ATK case as well. The complete details can again be found in the full version [22].

Note that Theorem 1 is only meaningful for KEMs with explicit rejection, since for implicit rejection KEMs, the term $\mathbf{Adv}_{\mathsf{KEM}}^{\mathrm{WROB\text{-}ATK}}(\cdot)$ in the above security bounds can be large.

3.1 Generic Composition for Implicit Rejection KEMs

Robustness: We first consider what can be said about robustness for PKE schemes built from KEMs offering implicit rejection. We begin with a relaxed notion of robustness, namely *collision freeness* (as introduced for the specific case of KEMs obtained from PKEs in [32]). Informally, a scheme is said to be collision-free if a ciphertext always decrypts to two *different* messages under two different secret keys. We consider two variants, weak (WCFR) and strong collision freeness (SCFR). The security games defined in Fig. 2 define both notions via two different finalisation steps.

As usual, analogous WCFR-CPA and SCFR-CPA definitions can be obtained by removing decapsulation queries in the above games. Adversary A's advantage in the {WCFR,SCFR}-{CPA,CCA} game is defined to be:

$$\mathbf{Adv}_{\mathsf{KEM}}^{\{\mathrm{WCFR,SCFR}\}-\{\mathrm{CPA,CCA}\}}(\mathcal{A}) := \Pr[\mathsf{G}^{\mathcal{A}} = 1]$$

where $\mathsf{G}^{\mathcal{A}}$ refers to A playing in the appropriate version of the CFR game.

Now suppose we have a KEM that is SCFR-CCA (resp. WCFR-CCA) secure and a DEM that is FROB (resp. XROB) secure. (Recall that FROB and XROB are robustness notions for symmetric encryption schemes introduced in [17] and defined in Fig. 1) Then we can show that the hybrid PKE scheme obtained by composing these KEM and DEM schemes is SROB-CCA (resp. WROB-CCA) secure. More formally,

Theorem 2. *Let* $\mathsf{PKE}^{hy} = (\mathsf{KGen}, \mathsf{Enc}^{hy}, \mathsf{Dec}^{hy})$ *be a hybrid encryption scheme obtained by composing a KEM* $\mathsf{KEM} = (\mathsf{KGen}, \mathsf{Encap}, \mathsf{Decap})$ *with a DEM* $\mathsf{DEM} = (\mathsf{Enc}, \mathsf{Dec})$. *Then for any* SROB-CCA *(resp.* WROB-CCA*) adversary* $\mathcal{A}$ *against* PKE^{hy}, *there exist* SCFR-CCA *(resp.* WCFR-CCA*) adversary* $\mathcal{B}$ *against* KEM *and* FROB *(resp.* XROB*) adversary* $\mathcal{C}$ *against* DEM *such that*

$$\mathbf{Adv}_{\mathsf{PKE}^{hy}}^{\mathrm{SROB\text{-}CCA}}(\mathcal{A}) \leq \mathbf{Adv}_{\mathsf{KEM}}^{\mathrm{SCFR\text{-}CCA}}(\mathcal{B}) + \mathbf{Adv}_{\mathsf{DEM}}^{\mathrm{FROB}}(\mathcal{C}),$$
$$\mathbf{Adv}_{\mathsf{PKE}^{hy}}^{\mathrm{WROB\text{-}CCA}}(\mathcal{A}) \leq \mathbf{Adv}_{\mathsf{KEM}}^{\mathrm{WCFR\text{-}CCA}}(\mathcal{B}) + \mathbf{Adv}_{\mathsf{DEM}}^{\mathrm{XROB}}(\mathcal{C}),$$

where the running times of $\mathcal{B}$ *and* $\mathcal{C}$ *are the same as that of* $\mathcal{A}$.

Proof (sketch). Note that an adversary $\mathcal{A}$ wins the SROB-CCA game w.r.t. PKE^{hy} if it returns a ciphertext C ($= (C_{\mathsf{KEM}}, C_{\mathsf{DEM}})$) such that $\mathsf{Dec}^{hy}(sk_0, C) \neq \bot$ and $\mathsf{Dec}^{hy}(sk_1, C) \neq \bot$. Let $\mathsf{Decap}(sk_0, C_{\mathsf{KEM}}) = k_0$ and $\mathsf{Decap}(sk_1, C_{\mathsf{KEM}}) = k_1$. It is easy to see that $k_0 \neq \bot$ and $k_1 \neq \bot$. Now if $k_0 = k_1$, we can return C_{KEM} to win the SCFR-CCA game w.r.t. KEM. If $k_0 \neq k_1$, we can return $(C_{\mathsf{DEM}}, k_0, k_1)$ to win the FROB game w.r.t. DEM. We can do a similar case-distinction to argue about WROB-CCA security as well. The complete details of the proof can be found in the full version [22].

Note that Farshim et al. [17] provide efficient constructions of FROB- and XROB-secure AE schemes, meaning that the requirements for the above theorem can be easily met. At the same time, they showed that a symmetric AE scheme that achieves the standard ROR-CCA notion of security is also inherently robust, albeit w.r.t. some weaker notions compared to FROB. Namely, such ROR-CCA secure AE schemes were shown to satisfy the so-called *semi-full robustness* (SFROB) notion in [17]. The SFROB notion of robustness for symmetric AE schemes is a (potentially) weaker variant of FROB where, in the corresponding security game, the adversary does not get to choose any keys.

Instead, two keys are honestly generated and the adversary is given oracle access to encryption and decryption algorithms under both keys. The adversary is also given access to one of the keys, and the game is won (similar to that of FROB) if the adversary returns a ciphertext that decrypts correctly under both honestly generated keys.

The following theorem shows that a DEM that is only ROR-CCA secure – and that lacks the stronger robustness properties from [17] – is incapable of *generically* transforming strongly collision-free implicit rejection KEMs to strongly robust hybrid PKEs.

Theorem 3. *Suppose there exists a KEM that is simultaneously SCFR-CCA, IND-CCA and ANO-CCA secure. Suppose that there exists a SUF-CMA-secure MAC scheme and an ROR-CPA secure symmetric encryption scheme (such schemes can be built assuming only the existence of one-way functions). Suppose also that collision-resistant hash functions exist. Then there exists an implicit-rejection KEM that is SCFR-CCA, IND-CCA and ANO-CCA secure and a DEM that is ROR-CCA secure, such that the hybrid PKE scheme obtained from their composition is not SROB-CCA secure.*

Proof (sketch). Let $\mathsf{MAC} = (\mathsf{Tag}, \mathsf{Vf})$ be an SUF-CMA secure MAC. We construct $\overline{\mathsf{MAC}} = (\overline{\mathsf{Tag}}, \overline{\mathsf{Vf}})$ where the only difference from MAC is that we fix a "faulty" key $\overline{k}$ chosen uniformly at random from the original MAC key-space such that $\overline{\mathsf{Vf}}(\overline{k}, \cdot) = 1$. Note that $\overline{\mathsf{MAC}}$ is also SUF-CMA secure. So by composing $\overline{\mathsf{MAC}}$ with an ROR-CPA secure symmetric encryption scheme SE that *never* rejects invalid ciphertexts via the "Encrypt-then-MAC" construction, we get an AE-secure $\overline{\mathsf{DEM}}$. Now let $\mathsf{KEM} = (\mathsf{KGen}, \mathsf{Encap}, \mathsf{Decap})$ be a KEM that is SCFR-CCA, IND-CCA and ANO-CCA secure, and H be a collision-resistant hash function with its range being the key-space of SE. We construct $\overline{\mathsf{KEM}} = (\mathsf{KGen}, \mathsf{Encap}, \overline{\mathsf{Decap}})$ where the only difference from KEM is that the ciphertext space is augmented by a "special" bitstring $\overline{c}$ such that $\overline{\mathsf{Decap}}(\mathsf{sk}, \overline{c}) = H(\mathsf{pk})\|\overline{k}$, for any KEM key-pair $(\mathsf{pk}, \mathsf{sk})$. It is not hard to see that $\overline{\mathsf{KEM}}$ is also IND-CCA, ANO-CCA secure, and SCFR-CCA secure (relying on the collision-resistance of H). Now the composition of $\overline{\mathsf{KEM}}$ and $\overline{\mathsf{DEM}}$ will not result in an SROB-CCA secure hybrid PKE. Specifically, an adversary can return the ciphertext $(\overline{c}, c'\|\sigma')$, where $c'\|\sigma'$ is an arbitrary $\overline{\mathsf{DEM}}$ ciphertext, to win the corresponding SROB-CCA game with probability 1. Complete details of the proof can be found in the full version [22].

Anonymity: Now we turn to the question of what can be said about anonymity for PKE schemes built from KEMs offering implicit rejection. We prove a negative result that strengthens an analogous result of [32]. That result showed that there exist KEMs that are ANO-CCA (and IND-CCA) secure and XROB-secure authenticated encryption schemes, such that the hybrid PKE scheme resulting from their composition is *not* ANO-CCA secure. Thus anonymity is not preserved in the hybrid construction. However the KEM construction that was used to show this negative result in [32] is not SCFR-CCA secure, which might lead one to think that the strong collision freeness of implicit rejection KEMs might be sufficient to preserve anonymity. Here, we show this not to be true.

Theorem 4. *Suppose there exists a KEM that is simultaneously SROB-CCA, IND-CCA and ANO-CCA secure, a claw-free pair of permutations with domain and range being the encapsulated key-space of the KEM, and a collision-resistant hash function. Suppose also that there exists a DEM that is ROR-CCA and XROB-secure. Then there exists an implicit-rejection KEM that is SCFR-CCA, IND-CCA and ANO-CCA secure and a DEM that is ROR-CCA and XROB-secure, such that the resulting hybrid PKE is not ANO-CCA secure.*

Proof (sketch). Let KEM = (KGen, Encap, Decap) be a KEM that is IND-CCA, ANO-CCA and SROB-CCA secure. Let II be a collision-resistant hash function that maps the space of public-keys of KEM to its encapsulated key-space. We now construct $\overline{\mathsf{KEM}}$ = (KGen, $\overline{\mathsf{Encap}}$, $\overline{\mathsf{Decap}}$) as follows. For the public parameters of $\overline{\mathsf{KEM}}$, we first generate a pair of claw-free permutations with corresponding fixed public-key PK (see [11, Section 4.2] for a more formal definition) $f_1(\mathsf{PK}, \cdot)$ and $f_2(\mathsf{PK}, \cdot)$ with domain and range being the encapsulated key-space of KEM. Now $\overline{\mathsf{Encap}}(\mathsf{pk})$ returns $(C, \overline{k})$ where $(C, k) \leftarrow_{\$} \mathsf{Encap}(\mathsf{pk})$ and $\overline{k} := f_1(\mathsf{PK}, k)$. $\overline{\mathsf{Decap}}(\mathsf{sk}, C)$ returns $\overline{k}'$ where, for $k' \leftarrow \mathsf{Decap}(\mathsf{sk}, C)$, $\overline{k}' := f_1(\mathsf{PK}, k')$ if $k' \neq \bot$ and $\overline{k}' := f_2(\mathsf{PK}, II(\mathsf{pk}))$ if $k' = \bot$. Using straightforward reductions, it is not hard to show that $\overline{\mathsf{KEM}}$ is also IND-CCA and ANO-CCA secure. In addition, we can show that $\overline{\mathsf{KEM}}$ is SCFR-CCA secure by relying on the SROB-CCA security of KEM, collision-resistance of H and claw-freeness assumption w.r.t. $f_1(\mathsf{PK}, \cdot)$ and $f_2(\mathsf{PK}, \cdot)$.

Now let DEM = (Enc, Dec) be an ROR-CCA secure AEAD which is additionally XROB-secure. We now describe an adversary $\mathcal{A}$ against the ANO-CCA security of the hybrid PKE scheme w.r.t. the composition of $\overline{\mathsf{KEM}}$ and DEM. Upon receiving two public-keys pk_0 and pk_1 (along with the public-parameters $f_1(\mathsf{PK}, \cdot)$ and $f_2(\mathsf{PK}, \cdot)$), $\mathcal{A}$ selects an arbitrary message m and forwards m to the ANO-CCA challenger. It then receives the ciphertext $C = (C_{\mathsf{KEM}}, C_{\mathsf{DEM}})$ where $(C_{\mathsf{KEM}}, k) \leftarrow_{\$} \overline{\mathsf{Encap}}(\mathsf{pk}_b)$ and $C_{\mathsf{DEM}} \leftarrow_{\$} \mathsf{Enc}(k, m)$, for bit $b \leftarrow_{\$} \{0, 1\}$. Then, $\mathcal{A}$ asks for the decryption of ciphertext $C' = (C_{\mathsf{KEM}}, C'_{\mathsf{DEM}})$ w.r.t. sk_0 where $C'_{\mathsf{DEM}} = \mathsf{Enc}(\hat{k}, m)$ with $\hat{k} = f_2(\mathsf{PK}, H(\mathsf{pk}_0))$. If the response is $\bot$, then $\mathcal{A}$ outputs 0; else, it outputs 1. We use similar arguments as that of [32, Claim 3.1] to show that $\mathcal{A}$ succeeds with a high probability. Complete details of the proof can be found in the full version [22].

The consequence of the above theorem (and its counterexample) is that, for implicit rejection KEMs, we cannot hope to transfer anonymity properties of the KEM to those of the hybrid PKE scheme resulting from the standard KEM-DEM construction in a fully generic manner. To make further progress in this direction, then, we need to look more closely at specific KEM constructions.

Encap(pk)	Decap(sk, c)
1 : $m \leftarrow_{\$} \mathcal{M}$	1 : Parse $c = (c_1, c_2)$
2 : $c_1 \leftarrow \mathsf{Enc}(\mathsf{pk}, m; G(m))$	2 : $m' \leftarrow \mathsf{Dec}(\mathsf{sk}, c_1)$
3 : $c_2 \leftarrow H'(m)$	3 : $c_1' \leftarrow \mathsf{Enc}(\mathsf{pk}, m'; G(m'))$
4 : $\boxed{c_2 \leftarrow H'(m, c_1)}$	4 : **if** $c_1' = c_1 \wedge H'(m') = c_2$ **then**
5 : $c \leftarrow (c_1, c_2)$	5 : $\boxed{\textbf{if } c_1' = c_1 \wedge H'(m', c_1) = c_2 \textbf{ then}}$
6 : $k = H(m, c)$	6 : **return** $H(m', c)$
7 : **return** (c, k)	7 : **else return** $\perp$

Fig. 3. The KEM $\mathsf{HFO}^{\perp}[\mathsf{PKE}, G, H, H']$. Boxed code shows modifications to $\mathsf{HFO}^{\perp}[\mathsf{PKE}, G, H, H']$ required to obtain scheme $\mathsf{HFO}^{\perp'}[\mathsf{PKE}, G, H, H']$. Both constructed schemes reuse algorithm KGen from PKE.

4   Anonymity and Robustness of KEMs Obtained from Fujisaki-Okamoto Transforms in the QROM

Fujisaki and Okamoto [18–20] introduced generic transformations that turn weakly secure PKE schemes (e.g. OW-CPA or IND-CPA secure PKE schemes) into IND-CCA secure KEMs and PKE schemes. Several distinct transforms have emerged, each with slightly different flavours; we broadly follow the naming conventions in [24]. One main distinction is whether the constructed KEM offers implicit rejection ($\mathsf{FO}^{\not\perp}$) or explicit rejection ($\mathsf{QFO}_m^{\perp}$). As we have already seen, this distinction is important in considering robustness, and we divide our analysis of the FO transforms in the same way. Since all NIST PQC candidates in the KEM/PKE category except one alternate candidate offer implicit rejection, we mainly focus on the corresponding $\mathsf{FO}^{\not\perp}$ transform. Also, since we are mainly concerned with the post-quantum setting, our analysis that follows will be in the QROM.

4.1   KEMs with Explicit Rejection

Before we focus on the $\mathsf{FO}^{\not\perp}$ transform, we briefly discuss our results related to explicit-rejection KEMs. The paper [27] presents a variant of the Fujisaki-Okamato transform, namely $\mathsf{HFO}^{\perp}$, that results in IND-CCA secure KEMs in the QROM. Given a PKE scheme $\mathsf{PKE} = (\mathsf{KGen}, \mathsf{Enc}, \mathsf{Dec})$ (with message space $\mathcal{M}$) and hash functions G, H and H', the resulting $\mathsf{KEM}^{\perp} = \mathsf{HFO}^{\perp}[\mathsf{PKE}, G, H, H'] = (\mathsf{KGen}, \mathsf{Encap}, \mathsf{Decap})$ is described in Fig. 3.

KGen$'$	Encap(pk)	Decap(sk$'$, c)
1: (pk, sk) $\leftarrow$ KGen	1: $m \leftarrow_\$ \mathcal{M}$	1: Parse sk$'$ = (sk, s)
2: $s \leftarrow_\$ \mathcal{M}$	2: $r \leftarrow G(m)$	2: $m' \leftarrow$ Dec(sk, c)
3: sk$'$ = (sk, s)	3: $c \leftarrow$ Enc(pk, m; r)	3: $r' \leftarrow G(m')$
4: **return** (pk, sk$'$)	4: $k \leftarrow H(m, c)$	4: $c' \leftarrow$ Enc(pk, m'; r')
	5: **return** (c, k)	5: **if** $c' = c$ **then**
		6: **return** $H(m', c)$
		7: **else return** $H(s, c)$

Fig. 4. The KEM FO$^{\not\perp}$[PKE, G, H].

We introduce a slight variant of the above transform, namely HFO$^{\perp'}$, as shown in Fig. 3. The only change is that the c_2 component of the ciphertext–used for so-called *plaintext confirmation*–is derived as $c_2 \leftarrow H'(m, c_1)$ instead of as $c_2 \leftarrow H'(m)$. However, this seemingly minor change not only allows the HFO$^{\perp'}$ transform to result in IND-CCA secure KEMs, but also strongly anonymous (ANO-CCA secure) and robust (SROB-CCA secure) KEMs in the QROM. In the full version [22], we formally state and prove the corresponding theorems.

4.2 KEMs with Implicit Rejection

Given a PKE scheme PKE = (KGen, Enc, Dec) with message space $\mathcal{M}$ and hash functions G and H, the KEM KEM$^{\not\perp}$ = FO$^{\not\perp}$[PKE, G, H] is shown in Fig. 4. As described in [24], the FO$^{\not\perp}$ transform "implicitly" uses a modular transformation T that converts a OW-CPA/IND-CPA secure PKE scheme PKE into a *deterministic* PKE scheme PKE$_1$ = T [PKE, G] = (KGen, Enc$'$, Dec$'$) that is secure in the presence of so-called *plaintext-checking attacks*. The deterministic encryption Enc$'$(pk, m) returns c where $c \leftarrow$ Enc(pk, m; $G(m)$). The decryption Dec$'$(sk, c) first computes $m' \leftarrow$ Dec(sk, c) and then returns m' if the *re-encryption* check "Enc(pk, m'; $G(m')$) = c" succeeds; otherwise, $\perp$ is returned.

It was proved in [26] that the FO$^{\not\perp}$ transform lifts IND-CPA security of PKE to IND-CCA security of KEM$^{\not\perp}$ in the QROM. We provide some further enhancement results for FO$^{\not\perp}$. They demonstrate that, provided the starting PKE scheme PKE and the derived deterministic scheme PKE$_1$ satisfy some mild security assumptions on anonymity (wANO-CPA[1]) and collision-freeness (SCFR-CPA) respectively, then FO$^{\not\perp}$ confers strong anonymity (ANO-CCA) and collision-freeness (SCFR-CCA) to the final KEM$^{\not\perp}$ in the QROM.

---

[1] The wANO-CPA security notion for PKE is a weaker variant of ANO-CPA where, in the corresponding security game, the challenger encrypts a uniformly random *secret* message under either of the two honestly generated public-keys and *only* provides the resulting ciphertext to the adversary, along with the generated public-keys.

Theorem 5. *Suppose* $\mathsf{PKE} = (\mathsf{KGen}, \mathsf{Enc}, \mathsf{Dec})$ *is* δ-*correct and has message space* $\mathcal{M}$. *Then for any* ANO-CCA *adversary* $\mathcal{A}$ *against* $\mathsf{KEM}^{\not\perp} = \mathsf{FO}^{\not\perp}[\mathsf{PKE}, G, H]$ *issuing at most* q_G (*resp.* q_H) *queries[2] to the quantum random oracle* G (*resp.* H) *and at most* q_D *queries to the* (*classical*) *decapsulation oracles, there exist* wANO-CPA *adversary* $\mathcal{B}$ *and* OW-CPA *adversary* $\mathcal{C}$ *against* PKE, *and* SCFR-CPA *adversary* $\mathcal{D}$ *against* $\mathsf{PKE}_1 = \mathsf{T}[\mathsf{PKE}, G]$ *issuing at most* q_G *queries to* G, *such that:*

$$\mathbf{Adv}_{\mathsf{KEM}^{\not\perp}}^{\mathsf{ANO\text{-}CCA}}(\mathcal{A}) \leq \mathbf{Adv}_{\mathsf{PKE}}^{\mathsf{wANO\text{-}CPA}}(\mathcal{B}) + 2(q_G + q_H)\sqrt{\mathbf{Adv}_{\mathsf{PKE}}^{\mathsf{OW\text{-}CPA}}(\mathcal{C})}$$

$$+ \, q_D \cdot \mathbf{Adv}_{\mathsf{PKE}_1}^{\mathsf{SCFR\text{-}CPA}}(\mathcal{D}) + \frac{4q_H}{\sqrt{|\mathcal{M}|}} + 2q_G(q_D + 2)\sqrt{2\delta}\,.$$

Moreover, the running times of $\mathcal{B}$, $\mathcal{C}$ *and* $\mathcal{D}$ *are the same as that of* $\mathcal{A}$.

Proof (sketch). In a reduction from ANO-CCA security of $\mathsf{KEM}^{\not\perp}$ to wANO-CPA security of PKE, note that we need to simulate two different decapsulation oracles consistently without possessing the corresponding secret keys. Our approach is to generalize the simulation trick of [26,34] in the QROM from a single-key setting (in the context of IND-CCA security) to a two-key setting (ANO-CCA). Namely, given two public-keys pk_0, pk_1, note that the encapsulation algorithm for both of them uses a common key-derivation function (KDF) "$k = H(m, c)$" (see Fig. 4). So we associate this KDF with two *secret* random functions H_0 and H_1 as follows: given an input (m, c), if $c = \mathsf{Enc}(\mathsf{pk}_i, m; G(m))$ (i.e., c results likely from $\mathsf{Encap}(\mathsf{pk}_i)$), then replace the KDF with "$k = H_i(c)$". Note that in this case, we can simply simulate the decapsulation oracles as $\mathsf{Decap}(\mathsf{sk}_i, c) = H_i(c)$ without requiring the secret keys. Now to argue that this replacement of KDF is indistinguishable w.r.t. an adversary, we require the functions $\mathsf{Enc}(\mathsf{pk}_i, \cdot \, ; G(\cdot))$ to be injective. Thus, following [26], we first replace oracle G with G' where G' only returns "good" encryption randomness w.r.t. $(\mathsf{pk}_0, \mathsf{sk}_0)$ and $(\mathsf{pk}_1, \mathsf{sk}_1)$ – i.e., $\forall m$, $\mathsf{Dec}(sk_i, \mathsf{Enc}(\mathsf{pk}_i, m; G'(m))) = m$, for $i \in \{0, 1\}$. We again generalize the argument of [26] from a single-key setting to a two-key setting to show that this replacement of G is indistinguishable, relying on the δ-correctness of PKE.

However, note that we additionally have to account for pairs (m, c) which satisfy $\mathsf{Enc}(\mathsf{pk}_0, m; G'(m)) = \mathsf{Enc}(\mathsf{pk}_1, m; G'(m)) = c$; in this case, the reduction does not know which public-key was used to generate c during key-encapsulation. So we rely on SCFR-CPA security to argue that it is computationally hard for an adversary to ask for the (classical) decapsulation of such "peculiar" ciphertexts c. Such a c results in $\mathsf{Dec}(sk_0, c) = \mathsf{Dec}(sk_1, c) = m$, thereby breaking the SCFR-CPA security of $\mathsf{T}[\mathsf{PKE}, G']$, and hence, that of $\mathsf{PKE}_1 = \mathsf{T}[\mathsf{PKE}, G]$ (up to an additive loss). Complete details of the proof can be found in the full version [22]. Note that it is similar in structure to that of [26, Theorem 1] in terms of the

---

[2] Following [24,26], we make the convention that the number q_O of queries made by an adversary $\mathcal{A}$ to a random oracle O counts the total number of times O is executed in the corresponding security experiment; i.e., the number of $\mathcal{A}$'s explicit queries to O plus the number of implicit queries to O made by the experiment.

sequence of game-hops. But for the sake of completeness, we provide a self-contained proof.

To establish strong collision-freeness of the implicit-rejection KEMs constructed using $FO^{\not\perp}$, we require the following *claw-freeness* property of quantum random oracles.

Lemma 1 [39, Lemma 2.3]. *There is a universal constant α (< 648) such that the following holds: Let $\mathcal{X}_0$, $\mathcal{X}_1$ and $\mathcal{Y}$ be finite sets. Let $N_0 = |\mathcal{X}_0|$ and $N_1 = |\mathcal{X}_1|$, with $N_0 \leq N_1$. Let $H_0 : \mathcal{X}_0 \to \mathcal{Y}$ and $H_1 : \mathcal{X}_1 \to \mathcal{Y}$ be two random oracles.*

If an unbounded time quantum adversary $\mathcal{A}$ makes a query to H_0 and H_1 at most q times, then we have

$$\Pr[H_0(x_0) = H_1(x_1) : (x_0, x_1) \leftarrow \mathcal{A}^{H_0, H_1}] \leq \frac{\alpha(q + 1)^3}{|\mathcal{Y}|},$$

where all oracle accesses of $\mathcal{A}$ can be quantum.

For the following result, we in-fact need a weaker property than the one described in the above lemma; namely, it's hard for an adversary to return a value $x \in \mathcal{X}_0 \cap \mathcal{X}_1$ such that $H_0(x) = H_1(x)$. We leave the derivation of the corresponding upper-bound as an open problem.

Theorem 6. *Suppose $PKE = (KGen, Enc, Dec)$ is δ-correct. Then for any SCFR-CCA adversary $\mathcal{A}$ against $KEM^{\not\perp} = FO^{\not\perp}[PKE, G, H]$ issuing at most q_D queries to the (classical) decapsulation oracles, at most q_G (resp. q_H) queries to the quantum random oracle G (resp. H), there exists an SCFR-CPA adversary $\mathcal{B}$ against $PKE_1 = T[PKE, G]$ issuing at most q_G queries to G such that*

$$\mathbf{Adv}_{KEM^{\not\perp}}^{SCFR\text{-}CCA}(\mathcal{A}) \leq q_D \cdot \mathbf{Adv}_{PKE_1}^{SCFR\text{-}CPA}(\mathcal{B}) + \frac{\alpha(q_H + 1)^3}{|\mathcal{K}|}$$

$$+ \frac{4q_H}{\sqrt{|\mathcal{M}|}} + 2q_G(q_D + 2)\sqrt{2\delta}.$$

Here $\mathcal{K}$ denotes the encapsulated key-space of $KEM^{\not\perp}$ and α (< 648) is the constant from Lemma 1. The running time of $\mathcal{B}$ is the same as that of $\mathcal{A}$.

Proof (sketch). Here we reduce the SCFR-CCA security of $KEM^{\not\perp}$ to the hardness of claw-finding w.r.t. QROs. The proof is similar in structure to that of Theorem 5. Namely, we start with an SCFR-CCA adversary $\mathcal{A}$ and do a similar sequence of game-hops until the point where the decapsulation oracles don't require the corresponding secret keys – namely, $Decap(sk_i, c) = H_i(c)$ for (secret) random functions $H_0, H_1 : \overline{\mathcal{C}} \to \mathcal{K}$, where $\overline{\mathcal{C}}$ denotes the ciphertext space of $PKE/KEM^{\not\perp}$. Now $\mathcal{A}$ wins this modified SCFR-CCA game if it returns c such that $Decap(sk_0, c) = Decap(sk_1, c)$, or equivalently, $H_0(c) = H_1(c)$. Note that (c, c) is then a *claw* w.r.t. the pair of QROs (H_0, H_1). Hence, we can bound $\mathcal{A}$'s winning probability using Lemma 1. A complete proof can be found in the full version [22].

From Theorems 5 and 6, we see that by applying the $\mathsf{FO}^{\not\perp}$ transformation to weakly secure (i.e., OW-CPA) and weakly anonymous (i.e., wANO-CPA) PKE schemes, with an additional assumption of strong collision-freeness (against chosen plaintext attacks) of the deterministic version of the underlying PKE scheme ($\mathsf{PKE}_1 = \mathsf{T}[\mathsf{PKE}, G]$), not only do we obtain strongly secure KEMs (i.e., IND-CCA security) but also KEMs that are strongly anonymous (i.e., ANO-CCA) and are strongly collision-free against chosen ciphertext attacks (SCFR-CCA) in the QROM.

At the same time, we showed a negative result in Theorem 4. It essentially shows that starting from a KEM that is IND-CCA, ANO-CCA and SCFR-CCA secure does not *generically* result in a strongly anonymous (ANO-CCA) hybrid PKE scheme via the KEM-DEM composition. Nonetheless, we are able to show the following positive result for KEMs obtained via the $\mathsf{FO}^{\not\perp}$ transform. We only need a weak additional property of the underlying PKE scheme, namely that it be γ-spread.

Theorem 7. *Let* $\mathsf{PKE}^{hy} = (\mathsf{KGen}', \mathsf{Enc}^{hy}, \mathsf{Dec}^{hy})$ *be a hybrid encryption scheme obtained by composing* $\mathsf{KEM}^{\not\perp} = \mathsf{FO}^{\not\perp}[\mathsf{PKE}, G, H]$ *with a one-time authenticated encryption scheme* $\mathsf{DEM} = (\mathsf{Enc}^{sym}, \mathsf{Dec}^{sym})$. *Suppose* PKE *is* δ-*correct and* γ-*spread (with message space* $\mathcal{M}$*). Then for any ANO-CCA adversary* $\mathcal{A}$ *against* PKE^{hy} *issuing at most* q_G *(resp.* q_H*) queries to the quantum random oracle* G *(resp.* H*), there exist ANO-CCA adversary* $\mathcal{B}$ *and IND-CCA adversary* $\mathcal{C}$ *against* $\mathsf{KEM}^{\not\perp}$*, WCFR-CPA adversary* $\mathcal{D}$ *against* $\mathsf{PKE}_1 = \mathsf{T}[\mathsf{PKE}, G]$*, and INT-CTXT adversary* $\mathcal{E}$ *against* DEM *such that:*

$$\mathbf{Adv}_{\mathsf{PKE}^{hy}}^{\mathrm{ANO\text{-}CCA}}(\mathcal{A}) \leq \mathbf{Adv}_{\mathsf{KEM}^{\not\perp}}^{\mathrm{ANO\text{-}CCA}}(\mathcal{B}) + 2\mathbf{Adv}_{\mathsf{KEM}^{\not\perp}}^{\mathrm{IND\text{-}CCA}}(\mathcal{C}) + \mathbf{Adv}_{\mathsf{PKE}_1}^{\mathrm{WCFR\text{-}CPA}}(\mathcal{D})$$

$$+ 2\mathbf{Adv}_{\mathsf{DEM}}^{\mathrm{INT\text{-}CTXT}}(\mathcal{E}) + \frac{4q_H}{\sqrt{|\mathcal{M}|}} + 4q_G\sqrt{\delta} + 2^{-\gamma}.$$

Moreover, the running times of $\mathcal{B}$*,* $\mathcal{C}$ *and* $\mathcal{E}$ *are the same as that of* $\mathcal{A}$*. The running time of* $\mathcal{D}$ *is independent (and less than that) of the running time of* $\mathcal{A}$*.*

Proof (sketch). We use the proof of Theorem 1. Let $(\mathsf{pk}_0, \mathsf{sk}_0')$ and $(\mathsf{pk}_1, \mathsf{sk}_1')$ be two key-pairs generated in the ANO-CCA security game w.r.t. PKE^{hy}, and $b \leftarrow_{\$}\{0, 1\}$ be the challenge bit. Let $c^* = (c_1^*, c_2^*)$ be the challenge ciphertext given to an adversary $\mathcal{A}$; i.e., $(c_1^*, k^*) \leftarrow \mathsf{KEM}^{\not\perp}.\mathsf{Encap}(\mathsf{pk}_b)$ and $c_2^* \leftarrow \mathsf{Enc}^{sym}(m)$ where m is chosen by $\mathcal{A}$ upon first receiving $\mathsf{pk}_0, \mathsf{pk}_1$. In the proof of Theorem 1, we make some initial game-hops to modify the $\mathsf{Dec}^{hy}(\mathsf{sk}_{1-b}', \cdot)$ oracle such that if the query is of the form (c_1^*, c_2), the oracle returns $\perp$. There we rely on the WROB-CPA security of the underlying KEM to justify this modification. However, $\mathsf{KEM}^{\not\perp}$ is trivially not WROB-CPA secure. Nevertheless, we show that by relying on γ-spreadness of PKE, WCFR-CPA security of PKE_1 and INT-CTXT security of DEM, we can still make the above modification of the $\mathsf{Dec}^{hy}(\mathsf{sk}_{1-b}', \cdot)$ oracle. From that point on, we essentially use the same game-hops as in the proof of Theorem 1 in our reduction to ANO-CCA security of $\mathsf{KEM}^{\not\perp}$. Complete details can be found in the full version [22].

5 Anonymity and Robustness of NIST PQC Candidates

After analyzing the anonymity and robustness enhancing properties of the "standard" FO transforms in Sect. 4, we extend our analysis to the specific instantiations of these transforms used by Classic McEliece, proto-Saber (the simplified version of Saber in [14]) and FrodoKEM. We conclude this section by discussing some limitations of our techniques w.r.t. analyzing Saber and Kyber.

5.1 Classic McEliece

KGen$'$	Encap(pk)	Decap(sk$'$, (c, h))
1 : $(\mathsf{pk}, \mathsf{sk}) \leftarrow \mathsf{KGen}$	1 : $m \leftarrow_\$ \mathcal{M}$	1 : Parse sk$'$ = $(\mathsf{sk}, \mathsf{pk}, s)$
2 : $s \leftarrow_\$ \mathcal{M}$	2 : $c \leftarrow \mathsf{Enc}(\mathsf{pk}, m)$	2 : $m' \leftarrow \mathsf{Dec}(\mathsf{sk}, c)$
3 : $\mathsf{sk}' \leftarrow (\mathsf{sk}, \mathsf{pk}, s)$	3 : $h \leftarrow H_2(m)$	3 : $c' \leftarrow \mathsf{Enc}(\mathsf{pk}, m')$
4 : return $(\mathsf{pk}, \mathsf{sk}')$	4 : $k \leftarrow H_1(m, (c, h))$	4 : if $c' = c \wedge H_2(m') = h$ then
	5 : return $((c, h), k)$	5 : return $H_1(m', (c, h))$
		6 : else return $H_0(s, (c, h))$

Fig. 5. Classic McEliece uses a slight variant of the FO$^{\not\perp}$ transform that starts with deterministic PKE schemes. Here H_0 and H_1 are two different hash functions. The so-called "Dent hash" H_2 is used as an additional component in the KEM ciphertext [3].

Classic McEliece (CM) as defined in its third round NIST specification [3] applies a slight variant of the FO$^{\not\perp}$ transform to its starting deterministic PKE scheme (see Fig. 5). It can easily be shown that our generic transformation results on FO$^{\not\perp}$, namely Theorems 5 and 6, apply to the FO$^{\not\perp}$-like transformation used by CM, while accounting for the additional "Dent hash". Hence, the only thing that would remain to be analyzed is whether the base PKE scheme used by CM satisfies the pre-requisite security properties of Theorems 5 and 6, namely wANO-CPA and SCFR-CPA. As we show next, the base PKE scheme used by CM fails to be collision-free in a striking way that rules out the application of these results. This failure also propagates to PKE schemes built from the CM KEM via the standard KEM-DEM construction.

The base CM scheme: The base CM scheme is deterministic. To encrypt a message m, first encode m as a binary column vector e of some fixed length n and fixed Hamming weight t. Then compute ciphertext $c = He \in \mathbb{F}_2^n$ where H is an $(n-k) \times n$ matrix of the form $H = (I_{n-k} \,|\, T)$, where T is some $(n-k) \times k$ matrix whose value is unimportant below. Matrix H is the parity check matrix of an error correcting code whose error correcting capacity is at least t. Decryption is done by using the private key to rewrite matrix H in such a way that efficient decoding can be performed to recover e with perfect correctness. The base CM scheme is closely related to the Niederreiter variant of the McEliece PKE scheme.

Collision-freeness of the base CM scheme: Recall that we would require the base CM scheme to satisfy the SCFR-CPA property in order to make use of our generic results concerning the FO$^{\not\perp}$ transform. This property is crucial in the CPA $\rightarrow$ CCA security proofs where we have to simulate the decapsulation oracles under two different secret keys without access to the keys. As we will show now, the base CM scheme is not SCFR-CPA secure, nor even WCFR-CPA secure. In fact, we can go further and exhibit a strong robustness failure of the base CM scheme, and explain how it leads to robustness failures in the CM KEM and hybrid PKE schemes built from it.

Consider any weight t error vector e in which the t 1's in e are concentrated in the first $n - k$ bit positions of e (in all the parameter sets used in Classic McEliece, $n - k = mt \geq t$, for a positive integer m, so this is always possible). We call such an e *concentrated*. Note that any concentrated e can be written $e = \binom{e_{n-k}}{0_k}$ with e_{n-k} of length $n - k$ and 0_k being the vector of k zeros. Since encryption is done by computing $c = He$, and H is of the form $(I_{n-k} \,|\, T)$, it is easy to see that c is a fixed vector independent of the T part of H: namely, $He = e_{n-k}$ which depends only on the first $n - k$ bit positions of e.

Note that this property holds independent of the public key of the base CM scheme (which is effectively the matrix H). Thus there is a class of base CM messages (of size $\binom{n-k}{t}$) for which the resulting ciphertext c can be predicted as a function of the message *without even knowing the public key*. By correctness of the base CM scheme, such ciphertexts must decrypt to the selected message *under any base CM scheme private key*.

It is immediate that this property can be used to violate SCFR-CPA and WCFR-CPA security of the base CM scheme. This presents a significant barrier to the application of our general theorems for establishing robustness and anonymity of the full CM KEM.

Robustness of the CM KEM and Hybrid PKEs derived from it: The base CM scheme is used to construct the CM KEM according to procedure described in Fig. 5. This means that the CM KEM encapsulations are also of the form $c = (He, H_2(e))$ where $H_2(\cdot)$ is a hash function; meanwhile the encapsulated keys are set as $H_1(e, c)$ where $H_1(\cdot)$ is another hash function. The CM KEM performs implicit rejection, so one cannot hope for robustness. However, one might hope for some form of collision-freeness. Our analysis above shows that the CM KEM does not provide even this, since when e is concentrated, $c = (He, H_2(e))$ decapsulates to $H_1(e, c)$ under any CM private key.

Finally, one might ask about the robustness of PKE scheme built by combining the CM KEM with a DEM in the standard way. Again, such a PKE cannot be strongly collision free (and therefore not strongly robust either), since it is trivial using our observations to construct a hybrid PKE ciphertext that decrypts correctly under *any* CM private key to *any* fixed choice of message m (without even knowing the public key). To see this, simply consider hybrid ciphertexts of the form $(He, H_2(e), \text{AEAD.Enc}(K, m; r))$ where e is concentrated, $K = H_1(e, c)$ is the symmetric key encapsulated by the KEM part $c = (He, H_2(e))$ of the hybrid ciphertext, and r is some fixed randomness for the AEAD scheme. Such ciphertexts decrypt to the freely chosen message m under any CM private key.

Robustness could plausibly be conferred on this hybrid PKE scheme by including a hash of the public key in the key derivation step. However CM keys are large, so this would have a negative effect on performance. Robustness is *not* conferred in general by replacing the DEM with an AEAD scheme and including the hash of the public key in the associated data to create a "labelled DEM". This is easy to see by adapting the counter-example construction used in the proof of Theorem 3.

Further remarks on CM: The analysis above shows that we cannot hope to establish anonymity or robustness of the CM KEM or PKEs built from it via the standard KEM-DEM construction using the sequence of results in this paper. But this does not rule out more direct approaches to proving anonymity. For example, Persichetti [33] has analysed the anonymity of a scheme called HN (for "hybrid Niederreiter") that is rather close to the natural hybrid scheme one would obtain from CM. However, the analysis is in the ROM rather than the QROM. We are not aware of any further analysis of the anonymity properties of schemes that are close to CM and that might be easily adapted to CM.

In the context of the NIST PQC process, it remains an important open problem to establish anonymity of the CM scheme.

5.2   Proto-Saber

KGen$'$	Encap(pk)	Decap(sk$'$, c)
1 : $(pk, sk) \leftarrow$ KGen	1 : $m \leftarrow_{\$} \mathcal{M}$	1 : Parse sk$' = (sk, pk, F(pk), s)$
2 : $s \leftarrow_{\$} \mathcal{M}$	2 : $h \leftarrow F(pk)$	2 : $m' \leftarrow$ Dec(sk, c)
3 : $pk' \leftarrow (pk, F(pk))$	3 : $(\hat{k}, r) \leftarrow G(h, m)$	3 : $(\hat{k}', r') \leftarrow G(F(pk), m')$
4 : $sk' \leftarrow (sk, pk', s)$	4 : $c \leftarrow$ Enc(pk, m; r)	4 : $c' \leftarrow$ Enc(pk, m'; r')
5 : **return** (pk, sk')	5 : $k \leftarrow H(\hat{k}, c)$	5 : **if** $c' = c$ **then**
	6 : **return** (c, k)	6 : **return** $H(\hat{k}', c)$
		7 : **else return** $H(s, c)$

Fig. 6. pSaber uses a variant of the FO$^{\not\perp}$ transform. Here G, F and H are hash functions.

The scheme "proto-Saber" (pSaber for short) is a KEM that was introduced in [14] and which is included in the NIST third round specification document for

Saber [7]. Saber and pSaber use the same base PKE scheme but apply *different* FO-type transforms to obtain their respective KEMs. The QROM IND-CCA security claims for Saber [7, Theorem 6.5] seem to have been taken directly from those for pSaber [14, Theorem 6] without any modification. However, as we will explain below, there are issues with pSaber's IND-CCA security claims, and yet further issues for Saber's.

Now pSaber uses a transform that differs significantly from the standard FO$^{\not\perp}$ one (see Fig. 6). These significant deviations act as an obstacle to applying our generic results on anonymity and SCFR enhancement of FO$^{\not\perp}$ to pSaber. The nature of these deviations also led us to ask whether they also act as a barrier in applying the results of [26] to establish the IND-CCA security of pSaber, as claimed in [14]. We believe this to be the case, as we explain next.

IND-CCA security of pSaber in the QROM: We claim that the specific proof techniques used by [26], to obtain relatively tight IND-CCA security bounds for the standard FO$^{\not\perp}$ transform in the QROM, do not directly apply to pSaber's variant of the FO transform. An important trick used by [26] in their security proofs of FO$^{\not\perp}$ is to replace the computation of the key "$k \leftarrow H(m, c)$" with "$k \leftarrow H'(g(m))(= H'(c))$" for function $g(\cdot) = \mathsf{Enc}(\mathsf{pk}, \cdot; G(\cdot))$ and a secret random function $H'(\cdot)$; note that in this case, we simply have $\mathsf{Decap}(\mathsf{sk}, c) = H'(c)$ leading to an "efficient" simulation of the decapsulation oracle without using the secret key sk. To justify this replacement, the authors of [26] then argue about the injectivity of $g(\cdot)$, relying on the correctness of the underlying PKE scheme to establish this.

But in pSaber, the keys are computed as "$k \leftarrow H(\hat{k}, c)$" where the "pre-key" $\hat{k}$ is derived as a hash of the message m (to be specific, $(\hat{k}, r) \leftarrow G(F(\mathsf{pk}), m)$). So there is an extra *layer* of hashing between m and the computation of k. Hence, to use a similar trick as [26], we would require some additional injectivity arguments. Thus, strictly speaking, the proof techniques of [26] do not directly apply to pSaber.

Nevertheless, we are able to overcome the above barrier by adapting the analysis of FO$^{\not\perp}$ in [26] to obtain an explicit IND-CCA security proof for pSaber in the QROM, with the *same* tightness as claimed in [14]. The formal proof can be found in the full version [22]. We give a high-level overview of our approach below.

First, note that we can replace the step "$(\hat{k}, r) \leftarrow G(F(\mathsf{pk}), m)$" in pSaber's encapsulation by "$\hat{k} \leftarrow G_{\hat{k}}(m)$" and "$r \leftarrow G_r(m)$" for two fresh random oracles $G_{\hat{k}}, G_r : \{0,1\}^{256} \rightarrow \{0,1\}^{256}$. Now our key observation is that the extra layer of hashing "$G_{\hat{k}}(\cdot)$" between m and k is actually *length-preserving*, i.e., the hash function has the same domain and range. So following [24,37], we can replace the random oracle $G_{\hat{k}}(\cdot)$ with a random *polynomial* of degree $2q_G - 1$ over a finite field representation of $\{0,1\}^{256}$ (i.e., a $2q_G$-wise independent function). Here q_G is the number of queries made to oracle G in the IND-CCA security reduction for pSaber. Thanks to a result in [40], this change is perfectly indistinguishable to an adversary making at most q_G queries to $G_{\hat{k}}$. This will allow us to recover m from a corresponding pre-key value $\hat{k}$ by computing roots of the polynomial

$G_{\hat{k}}(x) - \hat{k}$. Hence we can *invert* this "nested" hashing of m in order to apply the trick of [26]. Namely, we can now replace the key derivation "$k \leftarrow H(\hat{k}, c)$" with "$k \leftarrow H'(g(m))(= H'(c))$" for function $g(\cdot) = \mathsf{Enc}(\mathsf{pk}, \cdot; G_r(\cdot))$, where in addition, m is a root of the polynomial $G_{\hat{k}}(x) - \hat{k}$.

Anonymity and Robustness of pSaber in the QROM: Our approach to repairing pSaber's IND-CCA proof also allows us to derive proofs of anonymity and SCFR enhancement for pSaber with similar tightness.

Now pSaber, and Saber, is a KEM whose claimed security relies on the hardness of the module learning-with-rounding problem, or mod-LWR for short (see [7,14] for a precise description of the assumption). In the following, we prove the ANO-CPA security of the base PKE scheme Saber.PKE that is used by pSaber, and also currently used by Saber (as per [7]). The result relies on the hardness of mod-LWR. The proof can be found in the full version [22]. The proof adapts the proof of [14, Theorem 3] showing IND-CPA security of Saber.PKE.

Theorem 8. *For any ANO-CPA adversary $\mathcal{A}$ against Saber.PKE, there exists a distinguisher $\mathcal{B}_1$ (resp., $\mathcal{B}_2$) between l (resp. $l + 1$) samples from a mod-LWR distribution from that of a uniform distribution, with corresponding parameters l, μ, q and p, such that*

$$\mathbf{Adv}_{\mathsf{Saber.PKE}}^{\mathsf{ANO\text{-}CPA}}(\mathcal{A}) \leq 2 \cdot \mathbf{Adv}_{l,l,\mu,q,p}^{\mathsf{mod\text{-}lwr}}(\mathcal{B}_1) + \mathbf{Adv}_{l+1,l,\mu,q,p}^{\mathsf{mod\text{-}lwr}}(\mathcal{B}_2).$$

Moreover, the running times of $\mathcal{B}_1$ and $\mathcal{B}_2$ are the same as that of $\mathcal{A}$.

Now we establish anonymity and strong collision-freeness of pSaber KEM, which we will denote as "pSaber.KEM" in the following to contrast the scheme with Saber.PKE. We use similar proof strategies that were used to show the same properties for FO$^{\not\perp}$ in Sect. 4 (Theorems 5 and 6). A major difference is that instead of relying on the SCFR-CPA security property of Saber.PKE (specifically, its deterministic version), we again rely on hardness of the *claw-finding* problem in a quantum setting (see Lemma 1).

In our next results, we show that the stronger properties of ANO-CCA and SCFR-CCA hold for pSaber.KEM. Below we define $\mathbf{Coll}_{\mathsf{Saber.PKE}}^{F}$ as the probability of the event "$F(\mathsf{pk}_0) = F(\mathsf{pk}_1)$" where pk_0 and pk_1 are two honestly-generated Saber.PKE public-keys. Given the space of Saber's public-keys is sufficiently large (of size greater than 2^{256}), if the hash function F is sufficiently collision-resistant, then $\mathbf{Coll}_{\mathsf{Saber.PKE}}^{F}$ can be considered to be negligible. The proofs of Theorems 9 and 10 can be found in the full version [22].

Theorem 9. *Given Saber.PKE $= (\mathsf{KGen}, \mathsf{Enc}, \mathsf{Dec})$ is δ-correct, for any ANO-CCA adversary $\mathcal{A}$ against pSaber.KEM $= (\mathsf{KGen'}, \mathsf{Encap}, \mathsf{Decap})$ issuing at most q_D classical queries to the decapsulation oracles, at most q_G (resp. q_H) quantum queries to the random oracle G (resp. H), there exist ANO-CPA adversary $\mathcal{B}$, OW-CPA adversary $\mathcal{C}$ against Saber.PKE and a distinguisher $\mathcal{B}_1$ between l samples from a mod-LWR distribution and a uniform distribution with corresponding* *parameters l, μ, q and p, such that*

$$\mathbf{Adv}_{\mathsf{pSaber.KEM}}^{\mathrm{ANO\text{-}CCA}}(\mathcal{A}) \leq \mathbf{Adv}_{\mathsf{Saber.PKE}}^{\mathrm{ANO\text{-}CPA}}(\mathcal{B}) + 2(q_G + q_H)\sqrt{\mathbf{Adv}_{\mathsf{Saber.PKE}}^{\mathrm{OW\text{-}CPA}}(\mathcal{C})}$$

$$+ \mathit{Coll}_{\mathsf{Saber.PKE}}^{F} + \frac{\alpha(q_G+1)^3}{2^{256}} + \mathbf{Adv}_{l,l,\mu,q,p}^{mod\text{-}lwr}(\mathcal{B}_1) + \frac{2}{2^{256}} + \frac{4q_H}{2^{128}} + 8q_G\sqrt{\delta}$$

Here α (< 648) is the constant from Lemma 1. The running times of $\mathcal{B}$ and $\mathcal{C}$ are the same as that of $\mathcal{A}$. The running time of $\mathcal{B}_1$ is independent (and less than that) of the running time of $\mathcal{A}$.

Theorem 10. *Given $\mathsf{Saber.PKE} = (\mathsf{KGen}, \mathsf{Enc}, \mathsf{Dec})$ is δ-correct, for any SCFR-CCA adversary $\mathcal{A}$ against $\mathsf{pSaber.KEM} = (\mathsf{KGen'}, \mathsf{Encap}, \mathsf{Decap})$ issuing at most q_D queries to the (classical) decapsulation oracles, at most q_G (resp. q_H) queries to the quantum random oracle G (resp. H), we have*

$$\mathbf{Adv}_{\mathsf{pSaber.KEM}}^{\mathrm{SCFR\text{-}CCA}}(\mathcal{A}) \leq \mathit{Coll}_{\mathsf{Saber.PKE}}^{F} + \frac{\alpha(q_G+1)^3}{2^{256}} + \frac{\alpha(q_H+1)^3}{2^{256}} + \frac{4q_H}{2^{128}}$$

Here α (< 648) is the constant from Lemma 1.

Regarding hybrid PKE schemes obtained from $\mathsf{pSaber.KEM}$ via the KEM-DEM composition, we additionally show that such PKE schemes satisfy the stronger ANO-CCA notion of anonymity, in a similar vein to Theorem 7 w.r.t. $\mathrm{FO}^{\not\perp}$-based KEMs. The proof can be found in the full version [22].

Theorem 11. *Let $\mathsf{pSaber.PKE}^{hy} = (\mathsf{KGen'}, \mathsf{Enc}^{hy}, \mathsf{Dec}^{hy})$ be a hybrid encryption scheme obtained by composing $\mathsf{pSaber.KEM} = (\mathsf{KGen'}, \mathsf{Encap}, \mathsf{Decap})$ with a one-time authenticated encryption scheme $\mathsf{DEM} = (\mathsf{Enc}^{sym}, \mathsf{Dec}^{sym})$. Given $\mathsf{Saber.PKE} = (\mathsf{KGen}, \mathsf{Enc}, \mathsf{Dec})$ is δ-correct, then for any ANO-CCA adversary $\mathcal{A}$ against $\mathsf{pSaber.PKE}^{hy}$ issuing at most q_G (resp. q_H) queries to the quantum random oracle G (resp. H), there exist ANO-CCA adversary $\mathcal{B}$, IND-CCA adversary $\mathcal{C}$ against $\mathsf{pSaber.KEM}$, INT-CTXT adversary $\mathcal{E}$ against DEM and distinguisher $\mathcal{B}_1$ between l samples from a mod-LWR distribution and a uniform distribution, with corresponding parameters l, μ, q and p, such that*

$$\mathbf{Adv}_{\mathsf{pSaber.PKE}^{hy}}^{\mathrm{ANO\text{-}CCA}}(\mathcal{A}) \leq \mathbf{Adv}_{\mathsf{pSaber.KEM}}^{\mathrm{ANO\text{-}CCA}}(\mathcal{B}) + 2\mathbf{Adv}_{\mathsf{pSaber.KEM}}^{\mathrm{IND\text{-}CCA}}(\mathcal{C}) + \mathit{Coll}_{\mathsf{Saber.PKE}}^{F}$$

$$+ 2\mathbf{Adv}_{\mathsf{DEM}}^{\mathrm{INT\text{-}CTXT}}(\mathcal{E}) + \mathbf{Adv}_{l,l,\mu,q,p}^{mod\text{-}lwr}(\mathcal{B}_1) + \frac{4q_H}{2^{128}} + 8q_G\sqrt{\delta} + \frac{1}{2^{256}}$$

and the running times of $\mathcal{B}$, $\mathcal{C}$ and $\mathcal{E}$ are the same as that of $\mathcal{A}$. The running time of $\mathcal{B}_1$ is independent (and less than that) of the running time of $\mathcal{A}$.

At the same time, from Theorems 2 and 10, we note that if the DEM component is also FROB secure, then the corresponding hybrid PKE scheme will be strongly robust (i.e., SROB-CCA secure). Hence, our above results give a complete picture of anonymity and robustness properties of pSaber as well as the hybrid PKE schemes derived from it.

5.3 FrodoKEM

FrodoKEM uses an *identical* FO-type transform, described as "FO$^{\not{L}\prime}$" in the specification document [4], as pSaber does (see Fig. 6) on its base PKE scheme "FrodoPKE". Hence, our positive results on tight IND-CCA security, anonymity and robustness of pSaber should also apply to FrodoKEM in a similar fashion; instead of relying on hardness of mod-LWR problem, we have to rely on hardness of the learning-with-errors (LWE) problem.

For example, when it comes to establishing anonymity of FrodoKEM, we only need to prove the ANO-CPA security of FrodoPKE and then rely on the "ANO-CPA $\rightarrow$ ANO-CCA" enhancement property of FO$^{\not{L}\prime}$ (LWE variant of Theorem 9). The ANO-CPA security of FrodoPKE can be shown in a similar manner as that of Saber.PKE (Theorem 8): namely, by adapting the IND-CPA security proof of FrodoPKE. To be more precise, it is shown in [4,30] w.r.t. FrodoPKE = (KGen, Enc, Dec) that given (pk, sk) $\leftarrow_s$KGen and *any* valid message m, the distribution (pk, Enc(pk, m)) is computationally indistinguishable from (pk, c^*) where c^* is a uniformly random ciphertext, relying on the LWE hardness assumption. Hence, in the ANO-CPA security game w.r.t. FrodoPKE, given two honestly-generated public-keys pk_0, pk_1 and a message m chosen by an adversary, it cannot distinguish the encryption of m under pk_0 from a uniformly random ciphertext that is independent of pk_0. Similarly, the adversary also cannot distinguish the uniformly random ciphertext from the encryption of m under pk_1. It follows that the adversary cannot distinguish between the encryptions of m under pk_0 and pk_1, thereby establishing the ANO-CPA security of FrodoPKE.

5.4 Saber and Kyber

It turns out that Saber and Kyber implement a transform that deviates *even further* from the FO$^{\not{L}}$ transform than pSaber does (see Fig. 7). Specifically, the keys in Saber are computed as "$k \leftarrow F(\hat{k}, F(c))$" where the "pre-key" $\hat{k}$ is derived as a hash of the message m (to be specific, $(\hat{k}, r) \leftarrow G(F(pk), m)$). Again there is an extra hashing step between m and the computation of k, as we have seen for pSaber. But at the same time, there is also a "nested" hashing of ciphertext in the key-derivation (i.e., Saber uses "$F(c)$" in place of just "c") as opposed to the standard "single" hashing in FO$^{\not{L}}$ and pSaber.

This "extra" hash of the ciphertext is a significant barrier to applying the techniques we used to prove anonymity of pSaber. It also acts as a barrier when trying to apply the generic proof techniques of [26] towards establishing the IND-CCA security of Saber in the QROM, with the *same* bounds as was claimed in its NIST third round specification [7]. At least for pSaber, as discussed above, we were able to account for the "nested" hashing of message because it was *length-preserving*. However, this is not the case for "$F(c)$" in Saber. We believe that an IND-CCA security reduction for Saber, along the lines of [26], in the QROM would need to rely on the collision-resistance of $F(\cdot)$ when modelled as a quantum random oracle. But a corresponding additive term is missing in the IND-CCA

KGen'	Encap(pk)	Decap(sk', c)
1 : (pk, sk) ← KGen	1 : $m \leftarrow_\$ \mathcal{M}$	1 : Parse sk' = (sk, pk, F(pk), s)
2 : $s \leftarrow_\$ \mathcal{M}$	2 : $m \leftarrow F(m)$	2 : $m' \leftarrow$ Dec(sk, c)
3 : pk' ← (pk, F(pk))	3 : $h \leftarrow F(pk)$	3 : $(\hat{k}', r') \leftarrow G(F(pk), m')$
4 : sk' ← (sk, pk', s)	4 : $(\hat{k}, r) \leftarrow G(h, m)$	4 : $c' \leftarrow$ Enc(pk, m'; r')
5 : **return** (pk, sk')	5 : $c \leftarrow$ Enc(pk, m; r)	5 : **if** $c' = c$ **then**
	6 : $k \leftarrow F(\hat{k}, F(c))$	6 : **return** $F(\hat{k}', F(c))$
	7 : **return** (c, k)	7 : **else return** $F(s, F(c))$

Fig. 7. Saber uses a variant of the FO$^{\not\perp}$ transform. Here G and F are hash functions [7].

security bounds claimed in the Saber specification. We have shared these observations with the Saber team. A representative of the team [38] accepted our findings on the IND-CCA security of pSaber. Regarding Saber, they maintain that the nested hash of ciphertext $F(c)$ should not pose a security problem for Saber as c is "deterministically derived from limited entropy". However, they do not know if this allows a security proof to go through in the QROM [38].

When it comes to robustness however, the news is better. Namely, we can apply similar proof strategies used to establish strong collision-freeness of FO$^{\not\perp}$-based KEMs (Theorem 6) and pSaber (Theorem 10) to show SCFR-CCA security of Saber in the QROM. The corresponding proof, presented in detail in the full version [22], on a high-level uses the fact that the hash of public-keys are included in Saber's key-derivation step (in contrast to Classic McEliece). This allows us to establish the SCFR-CCA security of Saber KEM by mainly relying on properties of quantum random oracles G and F, namely collision-resistance and claw-freeness.

Theorem 12. *For any SCFR-CCA adversary $\mathcal{A}$ against the scheme* Saber.KEM = (KGen', Encap, Decap) *issuing at most q_G (resp. q_F) queries to the quantum random oracle G (resp. F), we have*

$$\mathbf{Adv}_{\text{Saber.KEM}}^{\text{SCFR-CCA}}(\mathcal{A}) \leq \mathbf{Coll}_{\text{Saber.PKE}}^{F} + \frac{\alpha(q_G + 1)^3}{2^{256}} + \frac{4\alpha(q_F + 1)^3}{2^{256}} + \frac{4q_F}{2^{128}}$$

Here α (< 648) is the constant from Lemma 1.

Kyber uses an FO-type transform which is essentially the same as that of Saber (see Fig. 7). Hence, the issues we identified with Saber above w.r.t. IND-CCA security claims in the QROM as described in the specification document, as well as establishing anonymity of the scheme, apply to Kyber too. We have shared these observations with the Kyber team. At the 3rd NIST PQC Standardization Conference, a representative of the Kyber team [36] acknowledged that the nested hash of ciphertext $F(c)$ could make it "tricky" to prove the security of Kyber in the QROM, while removing this nested hash would overcome this issue.

But on the positive side, our result on strong collision-freeness (SCFR-CCA security) of Saber–namely, Theorem 12 above–also applies to Kyber in the same fashion, because of the similarity in their respective FO-type transforms. In other words, the current versions of Kyber and Saber also lead to strongly robust hybrid PKE schemes in the QROM.

In conclusion, we consider the *concrete* IND-CCA security–as claimed in [5, 7]–and anonymity (ANO-CCA security) of Saber and Kyber to remain open. We also suggest a modification to Saber and Kyber: namely, to apply the *same* FO-type transform as pSaber uses (as in Fig. 6) to the relevant base PKE scheme, thus replacing the "nested" hashing of ciphertext in key-derivation with single hashing. In doing so, not only would the two NIST finalists then enjoy the same provable IND-CCA security guarantees of $FO^{\not\perp}$-based KEMs in the QROM as established in the literature [26,34], but this would also allow our techniques establishing anonymity of pSaber to be extended to Saber and Kyber.[3]

6 Conclusions and Future Work

In this work, we initiated the study of anonymous and robust KEMs and PKE schemes in the post-quantum setting. We resolved several core technical questions, and showed that proto-Saber, a simplified version of Saber, and FrodoKEM can be used to build anonymous, robust hybrid PKE schemes. We also pointed out gaps in the current IND-CCA security analyses of Saber and Kyber. Both NIST finalists do lead to robust hybrid PKE from our analysis. Finally, we highlighted a surprising property of Classic McEliece (CM) showing that it does not lead to robust PKE schemes via the standard KEM-DEM construction.

Important questions remain about the anonymity and robustness of the NIST finalists and alternate candidates. For example, it is plausible that the anonymity of CM could be proven by a direct approach; the same applies for Saber and Kyber. Notable among the alternate schemes is SIKE, which uses radically different algebraic problems to build a KEM; extending our work to SIKE would be interesting. One broader question about post-quantum PKE which has not been widely studied is multi-receiver hybrid PKE (with or without anonymity/robustness). Such schemes would have applications in group-oriented end-to-end secure messaging.

Acknowledgements. It is our pleasure to thank the Classic McEliece, Kyber, Saber and FrodoKEM teams, along with Kathrin Hövelmanns and Keita Xagawa, for helpful discussions. We also thank the anonymous reviewers of Eurocrypt 2022 for their constructive comments and suggestions. Paterson's research was supported in part by a gift from VMware.

---

[3] For Kyber's anonymity, we would rely on the hardness of module learning-with-errors (mod-LWE) problem instead of mod-LWR, akin to our discussion on FrodoKEM; see Subsect. 5.3.

References

1. Abdalla, M., et al.: Searchable encryption revisited: consistency properties, relation to anonymous IBE, and extensions. In: Shoup, V. (ed.) CRYPTO 2005. LNCS, vol. 3621, pp. 205–222. Springer, Heidelberg (2005). https://doi.org/10.1007/11535218_13
2. Abdalla, M., Bellare, M., Neven, G.: Robust encryption. In: Micciancio, D. (ed.) TCC 2010. LNCS, vol. 5978, pp. 480–497. Springer, Heidelberg (2010). https://doi.org/10.1007/978-3-642-11799-2_28
3. Albrecht, M.R., et al.: Classic McEliece: NIST round 3 submission (2021)
4. Alkim, E., et al.: FrodoKEM: NIST round 3 submission (2021)
5. Avanzi, R., et al.: CRYSTALS-Kyber: NIST round 3 submission (2021)
6. Barth, A., Boneh, D., Waters, B.: Privacy in encrypted content distribution using private broadcast encryption. In: Di Crescenzo, G., Rubin, A. (eds.) FC 2006. LNCS, vol. 4107, pp. 52–64. Springer, Heidelberg (2006). https://doi.org/10.1007/11889663_4
7. Basso, A., et al.: Saber: NIST round 3 submission (2021)
8. Bellare, M., Boldyreva, A., Desai, A., Pointcheval, D.: Key-privacy in public-key encryption. In: Boyd, C. (ed.) ASIACRYPT 2001. LNCS, vol. 2248, pp. 566–582. Springer, Heidelberg (2001). https://doi.org/10.1007/3-540-45682-1_33
9. Bellare, M., Rogaway, P.: The security of triple encryption and a framework for code-based game-playing proofs. In: Vaudenay, S. (ed.) EUROCRYPT 2006. LNCS, vol. 4004, pp. 409–426. Springer, Heidelberg (2006). https://doi.org/10.1007/11761679_25
10. Ben-Sasson, E., et al.: Zerocash: decentralized anonymous payments from bitcoin. In: 2014 IEEE Symposium on Security and Privacy, pp. 459–474 (2014)
11. Boneh, D., Dagdelen, Ö., Fischlin, M., Lehmann, A., Schaffner, C., Zhandry, M.: Random oracles in a quantum world. In: Lee, D.H., Wang, X. (eds.) ASIACRYPT 2011. LNCS, vol. 7073, pp. 41–69. Springer, Heidelberg (2011). https://doi.org/10.1007/978-3-642-25385-0_3
12. Camenisch, J., Lysyanskaya, A.: An efficient system for non-transferable anonymous credentials with optional anonymity revocation. In: Pfitzmann, B. (ed.) EUROCRYPT 2001. LNCS, vol. 2045, pp. 93–118. Springer, Heidelberg (2001). https://doi.org/10.1007/3-540-44987-6_7
13. Chen, C., et al.: NTRU: NIST round 3 submission (2021)
14. D'Anvers, J.-P., Karmakar, A., Sinha Roy, S., Vercauteren, F.: Saber: module-LWR based key exchange, CPA-secure encryption and CCA-secure KEM. In: Joux, A., Nitaj, A., Rachidi, T. (eds.) AFRICACRYPT 2018. LNCS, vol. 10831, pp. 282–305. Springer, Cham (2018). https://doi.org/10.1007/978-3-319-89339-6_16
15. Dodis, Y., Grubbs, P., Ristenpart, T., Woodage, J.: Fast message franking: from invisible salamanders to encryptment. In: Shacham, H., Boldyreva, A. (eds.) CRYPTO 2018, Part I. LNCS, vol. 10991, pp. 155–186. Springer, Cham (2018). https://doi.org/10.1007/978-3-319-96884-1_6
16. Farshim, P., Libert, B., Paterson, K.G., Quaglia, E.A.: Robust encryption, revisited. In: Kurosawa, K., Hanaoka, G. (eds.) PKC 2013. LNCS, vol. 7778, pp. 352–368. Springer, Heidelberg (2013). https://doi.org/10.1007/978-3-642-36362-7_22
17. Farshim, P., Orlandi, C., Roşie, R.: Security of symmetric primitives under incorrect usage of keys. IACR Trans. Symm. Cryptol. **2017**(1), 449–473 (2017)
18. Fujisaki, E., Okamoto, T.: How to enhance the security of public-key encryption at minimum cost. In: Imai, H., Zheng, Y. (eds.) PKC 1999. LNCS, vol. 1560, pp. 53–68. Springer, Heidelberg (1999). https://doi.org/10.1007/3-540-49162-7_5

19. Fujisaki, E., Okamoto, T.: Secure integration of asymmetric and symmetric encryption schemes. In: Wiener, M. (ed.) CRYPTO 1999. LNCS, vol. 1666, pp. 537–554. Springer, Heidelberg (1999). https://doi.org/10.1007/3-540-48405-1_34
20. Fujisaki, E., Okamoto, T.: Secure integration of asymmetric and symmetric encryption schemes. J. Cryptol. **26**(1), 80–101 (2013)
21. Grubbs, P., Lu, J., Ristenpart, T.: Message franking via committing authenticated encryption. In: Katz, J., Shacham, H. (eds.) CRYPTO 2017, Part III. LNCS, vol. 10403, pp. 66–97. Springer, Cham (2017). https://doi.org/10.1007/978-3-319-63697-9_3
22. Grubbs, P., Maram, V., Paterson, K.G.: Anonymous, robust post-quantum public key encryption. Cryptology ePrint Archive, Report 2021/708 (2021). https://ia.cr/2021/708
23. Hayashi, R., Tanaka, K.: PA in the two-key setting and a generic conversion for encryption with anonymity. In: Batten, L.M., Safavi-Naini, R. (eds.) ACISP 2006. LNCS, vol. 4058, pp. 271–282. Springer, Heidelberg (2006). https://doi.org/10.1007/11780656_23
24. Hofheinz, D., Hövelmanns, K., Kiltz, E.: A modular analysis of the Fujisaki-Okamoto transformation. In: Kalai, Y., Reyzin, L. (eds.) TCC 2017, Part I. LNCS, vol. 10677, pp. 341–371. Springer, Cham (2017). https://doi.org/10.1007/978-3-319-70500-2_12
25. Hövelmanns, K., Kiltz, E., Schäge, S., Unruh, D.: Generic authenticated key exchange in the quantum random oracle model. In: Kiayias, A., Kohlweiss, M., Wallden, P., Zikas, V. (eds.) PKC 2020, Part II. LNCS, vol. 12111, pp. 389–422. Springer, Cham (2020). https://doi.org/10.1007/978-3-030-45388-6_14
26. Jiang, H., Zhang, Z., Chen, L., Wang, H., Ma, Z.: IND-CCA-secure key encapsulation mechanism in the quantum random oracle model, revisited. In: Shacham, H., Boldyreva, A. (eds.) CRYPTO 2018, Part III. LNCS, vol. 10993, pp. 96–125. Springer, Cham (2018). https://doi.org/10.1007/978-3-319-96878-0_4
27. Jiang, H., Zhang, Z., Ma, Z.: Key encapsulation mechanism with explicit rejection in the quantum random oracle model. In: Lin, D., Sako, K. (eds.) PKC 2019, Part II. LNCS, vol. 11443, pp. 618–645. Springer, Cham (2019). https://doi.org/10.1007/978-3-030-17259-6_21
28. Len, J., Grubbs, P., Ristenpart, T.: Partitioning oracle attacks. In: USENIX Security (2021)
29. Libert, B., Paterson, K.G., Quaglia, E.A.: Anonymous broadcast encryption: adaptive security and efficient constructions in the standard model. In: Fischlin, M., Buchmann, J., Manulis, M. (eds.) PKC 2012. LNCS, vol. 7293, pp. 206–224. Springer, Heidelberg (2012). https://doi.org/10.1007/978-3-642-30057-8_13
30. Lindner, R., Peikert, C.: Better key sizes (and attacks) for LWE-based encryption. In: Kiayias, A. (ed.) CT-RSA 2011. LNCS, vol. 6558, pp. 319–339. Springer, Heidelberg (2011). https://doi.org/10.1007/978-3-642-19074-2_21
31. Melchor, C.A., et al.: HQC: NIST round 3 submission (2021)
32. Mohassel, P.: A closer look at anonymity and robustness in encryption schemes. In: Abe, M. (ed.) ASIACRYPT 2010. LNCS, vol. 6477, pp. 501–518. Springer, Heidelberg (2010). https://doi.org/10.1007/978-3-642-17373-8_29
33. Persichetti, E.: Secure and anonymous hybrid encryption from coding theory. In: Gaborit, P. (ed.) PQCrypto 2013. LNCS, vol. 7932, pp. 174–187. Springer, Heidelberg (2013). https://doi.org/10.1007/978-3-642-38616-9_12

34. Saito, T., Xagawa, K., Yamakawa, T.: Tightly-secure key-encapsulation mechanism in the quantum random oracle model. In: Nielsen, J.B., Rijmen, V. (eds.) EURO-CRYPT 2018, Part III. LNCS, vol. 10822, pp. 520–551. Springer, Cham (2018). https://doi.org/10.1007/978-3-319-78372-7_17

35. Sako, K.: An auction protocol which hides bids of losers. In: Imai, H., Zheng, Y. (eds.) PKC 2000. LNCS, vol. 1751, pp. 422–432. Springer, Heidelberg (2000). https://doi.org/10.1007/978-3-540-46588-1_28

36. Schwabe, P.: Crystals-kyber round 3 presentation. In: 3rd NIST PQC Standardization Conference (2021)

37. Targhi, E.E., Unruh, D.: Post-quantum security of the Fujisaki-Okamoto and OAEP transforms. In: Hirt, M., Smith, A. (eds.) TCC 2016, Part II. LNCS, vol. 9986, pp. 192–216. Springer, Heidelberg (2016). https://doi.org/10.1007/978-3-662-53644-5_8

38. Vercauteren, F.: Private communication (2021)

39. Xagawa, K.: Ntru leads to anonymous, robust public-key encryption. Cryptology ePrint Archive, Report 2021/741 (2021). https://ia.cr/2021/741

40. Zhandry, M.: Secure identity-based encryption in the quantum random oracle model. In: Safavi-Naini, R., Canetti, R. (eds.) CRYPTO 2012. LNCS, vol. 7417, pp. 758–775. Springer, Heidelberg (2012). https://doi.org/10.1007/978-3-642-32009-5_44

McEliece Needs a Break – Solving McEliece-1284 and Quasi-Cyclic-2918 with Modern ISD

Andre Esser[1], Alexander May[2], and Floyd Zweydinger[2]([✉])

[1] Cryptography Research Center, Technology Innovation Institute, Abu Dhabi, UAE
andre.esser@tii.ae
[2] Ruhr University Bochum, Bochum, Germany
{alex.may,floyd.zweydinger}@rub.de

Abstract. With the recent shift to post-quantum algorithms it becomes increasingly important to provide precise bit-security estimates for code-based cryptography such as McEliece and quasi-cyclic schemes like BIKE and HQC. While there has been significant progress on information set decoding (ISD) algorithms within the last decade, it is still unclear to which extent this affects current cryptographic security estimates.

We provide the first concrete implementations for representation-based ISD, such as May-Meurer-Thomae (MMT) or Becker-Joux-May-Meurer (BJMM), that are parameter-optimized for the McEliece and quasi-cyclic setting. Although MMT and BJMM consume more memory than naive ISD algorithms like Prange, we demonstrate that these algorithms lead to significant speedups for practical cryptanalysis on medium-sized instances (around 60 bit). More concretely, we provide data for the record computations of McEliece-1223 and McEliece-1284 (old record: 1161), and for the quasi-cyclic setting up to code length 2918 (before: 1938).

Based on our record computations we extrapolate to the bit-security level of the proposed BIKE, HQC and McEliece parameters in NIST's standardization process. For BIKE/HQC, we also show how to transfer the Decoding-One-Out-of-Many (DOOM) technique to MMT/BJMM. Although we achieve significant DOOM speedups, our estimates confirm the bit-security levels of BIKE and HQC.

For the proposed McEliece round-3 192 bit and two out of three 256 bit parameter sets, however, our extrapolation indicates a security level overestimate by roughly 20 and 10 bits, respectively, i.e., the high-security McEliece instantiations may be a bit less secure than desired.

Keywords: MMT/BJMM decoding · Representation technique · McEliece

A. May—Funded by DFG under Germany's Excellence Strategy - EXC 2092 CASA - 390781972.
F. Zweydinger—Funded by BMBF under Industrial Blockchain - iBlockchain.

O. Dunkelman and S. Dziembowski (Eds.): EUROCRYPT 2022, LNCS 13277, pp. 433–457, 2022.
https://doi.org/10.1007/978-3-031-07082-2_16

1   Introduction

For building trust in cryptographic instantiations it is of utmost importance to provide a certain level of real-world cryptanalysis effort. Code-based cryptography is usually build on the difficulty of correcting errors in binary linear codes. Let C be a binary linear code of length n and dimension k, i.e., C is a k-dimensional subspace of $\mathbb{F}_2^n$. We denote by $H \in \mathbb{F}_2^{(n-k) \times n}$ a parity-check matrix of C, thus we have $H\mathbf{c} = \mathbf{0}$ for all $\mathbf{c} \in C$.

Let $\mathbf{x} = \mathbf{c} + \mathbf{e}$ be an erroneous codeword with error $\mathbf{e}$ of small known Hamming weight $\omega = \text{wt}(\mathbf{e})$. Let $\mathbf{s} := H\mathbf{x} = H\mathbf{e}$ denote the syndrome of $\mathbf{x}$. Then decoding $\mathbf{x}$ is equivalent to the recovery of the weight-ω error vector from $H\mathbf{e} = \mathbf{s}$.

Permutation-Dominated ISD – Prange. Let $P \in \mathbb{F}_2^{n \times n}$ be a permutation matrix. Then $(HP)(P^{-1}\mathbf{e}) = \bar{H}\bar{\mathbf{e}} = \mathbf{s}$ is another weight-ω decoding instance with permutated solution $\bar{\mathbf{e}} = P^{-1}\mathbf{e}$.

Assume that $\bar{\mathbf{e}} = (\mathbf{e}_1, \mathbf{e}_2)$ with $\mathbf{e}_2 = 0^k$. An application of Gaussian elimination $G \in \mathbb{F}_2^{(n-k) \times (n-k)}$ on the first $n - k$ columns of $\bar{H}$ yields

$$G\bar{H}\bar{\mathbf{e}} = (I_{n-k}H')\bar{\mathbf{e}} = \mathbf{e}_1 + H'\mathbf{e}_2 = \mathbf{e}_1 = G\mathbf{s}. \tag{1}$$

Thus, from $\text{wt}(G\mathbf{s}) = \omega$ we conclude that $\bar{\mathbf{e}} = (G\mathbf{s}, 0^k)$ and $\mathbf{e} = P\bar{\mathbf{e}}$.

In summary, if we apply the correct permutation P that sends all weight ω to the first $n - k$ coordinates, then we decode correctly in polynomial time. This is why the first $n - k$ coordinates are called an *information set*, and the above algorithm is called *information set decoding* (ISD). This ISD algorithm, due to Prange [18], is the main tool for estimating the security of code-based cryptography such as McEliece and BIKE/HQC.

We would like to stress that the complexity of Prange's algorithm is mainly dominated by finding a proper permutation P, which takes super-polynomial time for cryptographic instances. All other steps of the algorithm are polynomial time. This is why we call Prange a *permutation-dominated* ISD algorithm. A permutation-dominated ISD performs especially well for small weight errors $\mathbf{e}$ and large co-dimension $n - k$. More precisely, we have to find a permutation P that sends all weight ω to the size-$(n - k)$ information set, which happens with probability

$$\Pr[P \text{ good}] = \frac{\binom{n-k}{\omega}}{\binom{n}{\omega}} = \frac{(n - k)(n - k - 1) \ldots (n - k - \omega + 1)}{n(n - 1) \ldots (n - \omega + 1)}.$$

Let $\omega = o(n)$, and let us denote C's rate by $R = \frac{k}{n}$. Then Prange's permutation-based ISD takes up to polynomial factors expected running time

$$T = \frac{1}{\Pr[P \text{ good}]} \approx \left(\frac{1}{1 - R}\right)^{\omega}. \tag{2}$$

Modern Enumeration-Dominated ISD – MMT/BJMM. The core idea of all ISD improvements since Prange's algorithm is to allow for some weight

$p > 0$ outside the information set. Thus we allow in Eq. (1) that $\mathrm{wt}(\mathbf{e}_2) = p$, and have to *enumerate* $H'\mathbf{e}_2$. However, the cost of enumerating $H'\mathbf{e}_2$ may be well compensated by the larger success probability of a good permutation

$$\Pr[P \text{ good}] = \frac{\binom{n-k}{\omega-p}\binom{k}{p}}{\binom{n}{\omega}}.$$

Indeed, modern ISD algorithms like MMT [15] and BJMM [6] use the *representation technique* to heavily speed up enumeration. In the large weight regime $\omega = \Theta(n)$, parameter optimization of MMT/BJMM yields that these ISD algorithm do not only balance the cost of permutation and enumeration, but their enumeration is so efficient that it eventually almost completely dominates their runtime. This is why we call these algorithms *enumeration-dominated* ISD.

The large error regime $\omega = \Theta(n)$ is beneficial for MMT/BJMM, since for large-weight errors $\mathbf{e}$ it becomes hard to send all weight to the information set, and additionally a large-weight $\mathbf{e}$ introduces a large number of representations. From a cryptographic perspective however it remains unclear if MMT/BJMM also offer speedups for concrete cryptographic instances of interest.

Main question: How much improve modern enumeration-based ISD algorithms cryptanalysis of code-based crypto in practice (if at all)?

What makes this question especially hard to answer is that as opposed to permutation-based ISD, all enumeration-based ISD algorithms require a significant amount of memory. Thus, even if enumeration provides significant speedups it is unclear if it can compensate for the introduced memory access costs. As a consequence, the discussion of enumeration-based ISD in the NIST standardization process of McEliece already led to controversial debates [22,23]. We would like to stress that up to our work, all decoding records on decodingchallenge.org have been achieved either using Prange's permutation-based ISD, or Dumer's first generation enumeration-based ISD [10].

In the asymptotic setting, Canto-Torres and Sendrier [21] showed that all enumeration-dominated ISD approaches offer in the small-weight setting $\omega = o(n)$ only a speedup from T in Eq. (2) to $T^{1-o(1)}$, i.e., the speedup asymptotically vanishes. While this is good news for the overall soundness of our cryptographic constructions, it tells us very little about the concrete hardness of their instantiations.

Recently, Esser and Bellini [11] pursued a more practice-oriented approach by providing a concrete *code estimator*, analogous to the successfully applied *lattice estimators* [2]. Their code estimator also serves us as a basis for optimizing our ISD implementations. However, such an estimator certainly fails to model realistic memory access costs.

1.1 Our Contributions

Fast Enumeration-Dominated ISD Implementation. We provide the first efficient, freely available implementation of MMT/BJMM, i.e., a representation-based enumeration-dominated ISD. Our implementation uses depth 2 search-trees, which seems to provide best results for the cryptographic weight regime.

For the cryptographic instances that we attack we used weight $p = 4$ for McEliece with code length up to 1284, and $p = 3$ for BIKE/HQC. However, our benchmarking predicts that McEliece with code length larger than 1350 should be attacked with significantly larger weight $p = 8$. Our code is publicly available on GitHub.[1]

In comparison to other available implementations of (first-generation) enumeration-based ISD algorithms, our implementation performs significantly faster. Our experimental results demonstrate that in cryptanalytic practice even moderately small instances of McEliece can be attacked faster using modern enumeration-based ISD.

So far, our efforts to additionally speed up our enumeration-based ISD implementations with localilty-sensitive hashing (LSH) techniques [8,16] did not succeed. We discuss the reasons in Sect. 3.3.

Real-World Cryptanalysis of Medium-Sized Instances. For building trust in the bit-security level of cryptographic instances, it is crucial to solve medium-sized instances, e.g. with 60 bit security. This gives us stable data points from which we can more reliably extrapolate to high security levels. An example of good cryptanalysis practice is the break of RSA-768 [13] that allows us to precisely estimate the security of RSA-1024.

Before our work, for McEliece the record code length $n = 1161$ on decodingchallenge.org was reported by Narisada, Fukushima, Kiyomoto with an estimated bit-security level of 56.0. We add two new records McEliece-1223 and McEliece-1284 with estimated bit-security levels of 58.3 and 60.7, respectively. These record computations took us approximately 5 CPU years and 22 CPU years.

As a small technical ingredient to further speed up our new MMT/BJMM implementation, we show how to use the parity of ω to increase the information set size by 1, which saved us approximately 9% of the total running time.

For the quasi-cyclic setting we improved the previously best code length 1938 of Bossard [3] with 6400 CPU days to the five new records 2118, 2306, 2502, 2706, and 2918. The last has a bit-security level of 58.6, and took us (only) 1700 CPU days.

As a technical contribution for the quasi-cyclic setting, we show how to properly generalize the Decoding-One-Out-of-Many (DOOM) strategy to the setting of tree-based enumeration-dominated ISD algorithms. Implementing our DOOM strategy gave us roughly a $\sqrt{n-k}$ experimental speedup, where $n - k = n/2$ is the co-dimension in the quasi-cyclic setting. This coincides with our theoretical analysis, see Sect. 5.1.

Our real-world cryptanalysis shows that memory access certainly has to be taken into account when computing bit-security, but it might be less costly than suggested. More precisely, our ISD implementations support the so-called *logarithmic cost model*, where an algorithm with time T and memory M has cost $T \cdot \log_2 M$.

---

[1] https://github.com/FloydZ/decoding.

Solid Bit-Security Estimations for McEliece and BIKE/HQC. Based on our record computations and further extensive benchmarking for larger dimensions, we extrapolate to the proposed round-3 McEliece and BIKE/HQC instances. To this end, we also estimate via benchmarking the complexity of breaking AES-128 (NIST Category 1), AES-192 (Category 3) and AES-256 (Category 5) on our hardware.

For McEliece, we find that in the logarithmic cost model the Category 1 instance mceliece348864 achieves quite precisely the desired 128-bit security level, whereas the Category 3 instance (mceliece460896) and two out of three Category 5 instances (mceliece6688128 and mceliece6960119) fail to reach their security level by roughly 20 and 10 bit, even when restricting our attacks to a memory upper limit of $M \leq 2^{80}$. Hence, these instances seem to overestimate security.

For BIKE/HQC, our extrapolation shows that the proposed round-3 instances achieve their desired bit-security levels quite accurately.

Discussion of our Results. In our opinion, the appearance of a small security gap for McEliece and no security gap for BIKE/HQC is due to the different weight regimes. Whereas BIKE/HQC use small weight $\omega = \sqrt{n}$, McEliece relies on Goppa codes with relatively large weight $\omega = \Theta(n/\log n)$,

Both the BIKE/HQC and McEliece teams use the asymptotic formula from Eq. (2) to analyze their bit-security, which is the more accurate the smaller the weight ω. Hence, while in the BIKE/HQC setting the speedups that we achieve from enumeration-dominated ISD in practice are compensated by other polynomial factors (e.g. Gaussian elimination), in McEliece's (large) weight regime the speedups are so significant that they indeed lead to measurable security losses.

Comparison to Previous Security Estimates. Baldi et al. [4] and more recently Esser and Bellini [11] already provide concrete bit security estimates for code-based NIST candidates. Further, Esser and Bellini introduce new variations of the BJMM and MMT algorithm based on nearest neighbor search, which however did not result in practical gains for our implementation (see Sect. 3.3 for details).

Both works [4,11] take into account memory access costs. While [4] uses a logarithmic cost model, [11] considers three models (constant, logarithmic, and cube-root). As opposed to our work, [4,11] both solely rely on the computation of runtime formulas.

Our work extends and specifies these estimates in the following way. For the first time, we establish with our record computations solid experimental data points for the hardness of instances with roughly 60 bits security. Moreover, our implementation for the first time allows us to identify a proper memory access model that closely matches our experimental observations. Based on our data points, we extrapolate to NIST parameters of cryptographic relevance, using an estimator like [11] with the proper memory access model choice. This eventually allows for a much more reliable security estimate.

2 The MMT/BJMM Algorithm

Let us briefly recap the MMT and BJMM algorithm. From an algorithmic point of view both algorithms are the same. The benefit from BJMM over MMT comes from allowing a more fine-grained parameter selection. In our practical experiments, we mainly used the simpler MMT parameters. Therefore, we refer to our implementation as MMT in the simple parameter setting, and as BJMM in the fine-grained parameter setting.

Main Idea. Let $H\mathbf{e} = \mathbf{s}$ be our syndrome decoding instance with parity check matrix $H \in \mathbb{F}_2^{(n-k)\times n}$, unknown error $\mathbf{e} \in \mathbb{F}_2^n$ of known Hamming weight ω, and syndrome $\mathbf{s} \in \mathbb{F}_2^{n-k}$.

As usual in information set decoding, we use some permutation matrix $P \in \mathbb{F}_2^{n\times n}$ to send most of the weight ω to the information set. Let $\bar{H} = HP$ and $\bar{\mathbf{e}} = P^{-1}\mathbf{e}$. Then, obviously $\mathbf{s} = \bar{H}\bar{\mathbf{e}}$.

MMT/BJMM now computes the *semi-systematic form* as originally suggested by Dumer [10]. To this end, fix some parameter $\ell \leq n - k$. Let $\bar{\mathbf{e}} = (\mathbf{e}_1, \mathbf{e}_2) \in \mathbb{F}_2^{n-k-\ell} \times \mathbb{F}_2^{k+\ell}$, and assume for ease of exposition that the first $n - k - \ell$ columns of $\bar{H}$ form a full rank matrix. Then we can apply a Gaussian elimination $G \in \mathbb{F}_2^{(n-k)\times(n-k)}$ that yields

$$\bar{\mathbf{s}} := G\mathbf{s} = G\bar{H}\bar{\mathbf{e}} = \begin{pmatrix} I_{n-k-\ell} & H_1 \\ 0 & H_2 \end{pmatrix} = (\mathbf{e}_1 + H_1\mathbf{e}_2, H_2\mathbf{e}_2) \in \mathbb{F}_2^{n-k-\ell} \times \mathbb{F}_2^\ell. \quad (3)$$

Let $\bar{\mathbf{s}} = (\mathbf{s}_1, \mathbf{s}_2) \in \mathbb{F}_2^{n-k-\ell} \times \mathbb{F}_2^\ell$. From Eq. (3) we obtain the identity $\mathbf{s}_2 = H_2\mathbf{e}_2$. MMT/BJMM constructs $\mathbf{e}_2$ of weight p satisfying $\mathbf{s}_2 = H_2\mathbf{e}_2$. Notice that for the correct $\mathbf{e}_2$ we directly obtain from Eq. (3) that

$$\mathbf{e}_1 = \mathbf{s}_1 + H_1\mathbf{e}_2. \quad (4)$$

Since we know that $\mathrm{wt}(\mathbf{e}_1) = \omega - p$, MMT/BJMM checks for correctness of $\mathbf{e}_2$ via $\mathrm{wt}(\mathbf{s}_1 + H_1\mathbf{e}_2) \overset{?}{=} \omega - p$.

Tree-Based Recursive Construction of $\mathbf{e}_2$ *Using Representations.* For the tree-based construction of $\mathbf{e}_2$ the reader is advised to closely follow Fig. 1. Here, we assume at least some reader's familiarity with the representation technique, otherwise we refer to [12,15] for an introduction.

We write $\mathbf{e}_2$ as a sum $\mathbf{e}_2 = \mathbf{x}_1 + \mathbf{x}_2$ with $\mathbf{x}_1, \mathbf{x}_2 \in \mathbb{F}_2^{k+\ell}$ and $\mathrm{wt}(\mathbf{x}_1) = \mathrm{wt}(\mathbf{x}_2) = p_1$. In MMT we choose $p_1 = p/2$, whereas in BJMM we allow for $p_1 \geq p/2$ s.t. a certain amount of one-coordinates in $\mathbf{x}_1, \mathbf{x}_2$ has to cancel in their $\mathbb{F}_2$-sum.

The number of ways to represent the weight-p $\mathbf{e}_2$ as a sum of two weight-p_1 $\mathbf{x}_1, \mathbf{x}_2$, called the number of *representations*, is

$$R = \binom{p}{p/2}\binom{k+\ell-p}{p_1-p/2}.$$

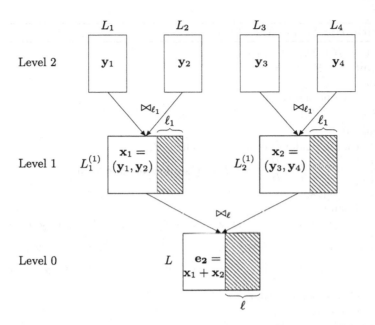

Fig. 1. Search tree of the MMT algorithm. Striped areas indicate matching of the last coordinates of $H\mathbf{x}_i$ or $H(\mathbf{x}_1 + \mathbf{x}_2)$ with some predefined values.

However, it suffices to construct $\mathbf{e}_2$ from a single representation $(\mathbf{x}_1, \mathbf{x}_2)$. Recall from Eq. (4) that we have

$$H_2\mathbf{x}_1 = H_2\mathbf{x}_2 + \mathbf{s}_2 \in \mathbb{F}_2^\ell.$$

Notice that we do not know the value of $H_2\mathbf{x}_1$. Let us define $\ell_1 := \lfloor \log_2(R) \rfloor$. Since there exist R representations $(\mathbf{x}_1, \mathbf{x}_2)$ of $\mathbf{e}_2$, we expect that for any fixed random target vector $\mathbf{t} \in \mathbb{F}_2^{\ell_1}$ and any projection $\pi : \mathbb{F}_2^\ell \to \mathbb{F}_2^{\ell_1}$ on ℓ_1 coordinates (e.g. the last ℓ_1 bits), there is on expectation at least one representation $(\mathbf{x}_1, \mathbf{x}_2)$ that satisfies

$$\pi(H_2\mathbf{x}_1) = \mathbf{t} = \pi(H_2\mathbf{x}_2 + \mathbf{s}_2).$$

We construct all $\mathbf{x}_1$ satisfying $\pi(H_2\mathbf{x}_1) = \mathbf{t}$ in a standard Meet-in-the-Middle fashion. To this end, we enumerate vectors of length $\frac{k+\ell}{2}$ and weight $p_2 := \frac{p_1}{2}$ in baselists L_1, L_2. Analogously, we find all $\mathbf{x}_2$ that satisfy $\pi(H_2\mathbf{x}_2 + \mathbf{s}_2)$ via a Meet-in-the-Middle from baselists L_3, L_4, see Fig. 1.

The resulting MMT/BJMM algorithm is described in Algorithm 1.

Runtime Analysis. For every permutation P, MMT/BJMM builds the search tree from Fig. 1. P has to send weight $\omega - p$ to the information set of size $n - k - \ell$ which happens with probability

$$q := \Pr[P \text{ good}] = \frac{\binom{n-k-\ell}{\omega-p}\binom{k+\ell}{p}}{\binom{n}{\omega}}. \tag{5}$$

Algorithm 1: MMT ALGORITHM

Input : $H \in \mathbb{F}_2^{(n-k)\times n}, \mathbf{s} \in \mathbb{F}_2^{n-k}, w \in \mathbb{N}$
Output: $\mathbf{e} \in \mathbb{F}_2^n, H\mathbf{e} = \mathbf{s}$

1 **begin**

2   Choose optimal ℓ, p, p_2

3   Set $\ell_1 = \lfloor \binom{p}{p/2}\binom{k+\ell-p}{p_1-p/2}\rfloor$ and $p_1 = 2p_2$

4   **repeat**

5   choose random permutation matrix P

6          $\bar{H} = \begin{pmatrix} I_{n-k-\ell} & H_1 \\ 0 & H_2 \end{pmatrix} = GHP$ in semi-systematic form

7          $\bar{\mathbf{s}} = (\mathbf{s}_1, \mathbf{s}_2) = G\mathbf{s}$

8   Compute
$$L_1 = L_3 = \{(\mathbf{y}_1, H_2\mathbf{y}_1) \mid \mathbf{y}_1 \in \mathbb{F}_2^{(k+\ell)/2} \times 0^{(k+\ell)/2}, \mathrm{wt}(\mathbf{y}_1) = p_2\}$$
$$L_2 = \{(\mathbf{y}_2, H_2\mathbf{y}_2) \mid \mathbf{y}_2 \in 0^{(k+\ell)/2} \times \mathbb{F}_2^{(k+\ell)/2}, \mathrm{wt}(\mathbf{y}_2) = p_2\}$$
$$L_4 = \{(\mathbf{y}_2, H_2\mathbf{y}_2 + \mathbf{s}_2) \mid \mathbf{y}_2 \in 0^{(k+\ell)/2} \times \mathbb{F}_2^{(k+\ell)/2}, \mathrm{wt}(\mathbf{y}_2) = p_2\}$$

9   Choose some random $t \in \mathbb{F}_2^{\ell_1}$

10   Compute
$$L_1^{(1)} = \{(\mathbf{x}_1, H_2\mathbf{x}_1) \mid \pi(H_2\mathbf{x}_1) = t, \mathbf{x}_1 = \mathbf{y}_1 + \mathbf{y}_2\} \text{ from } L_1, L_2$$
$$L_2^{(1)} = \{(\mathbf{x}_2, H_2\mathbf{x}_2 + \mathbf{s}_2) \mid \pi(H_2\mathbf{x}_2 + \mathbf{s}_2) = t, \mathbf{x}_2 = \mathbf{y}_1 + \mathbf{y}_2\} \text{ from } L_3, L_4$$

11   Compute $L = \{\mathbf{e}_2 \mid H_2\mathbf{e}_2 = \mathbf{s}_2, \mathbf{e}_2 = \mathbf{x}_1 + \mathbf{x}_2\}$ from $L_1^{(1)}, L_2^{(2)}$

12   **for** $\mathbf{e}_2 \in L$ **do**

13              $\mathbf{e}_1 = H_1\mathbf{e}_2 + \mathbf{s}_1$

14   **if** $\mathrm{wt}(\mathbf{e}_1) \leq \omega - p$ **then**

15   **return** $P^{-1}(\mathbf{e}_1, \mathbf{e}_2)$

16

17   **end**

18   **end**

19 **end**

The tree construction works in time T_{list}, which is roughly linear in the maximal list size in Fig. 1. Let $|L_i|$ denote the common list base size. Then it is not hard to see that the overall expected runtime can be bounded by

$$T = q^{-1} \cdot \tilde{\mathcal{O}}(T_{\mathrm{list}}), \text{ where } T_{\mathrm{list}} = \max\left\{|L_i|, \frac{|L_i|^2}{2^{\ell_1}}, \frac{|L_i|^4}{2^{\ell+\ell_1}}\right\}.$$

Part of the strength of our MMT/BJMM implementation in the subsequent section is to keep the polynomial factors hidden in the above $\tilde{\mathcal{O}}(\cdot)$-notion small, e.g. by using a suitable hash map data structure.

Locality-Sensitive Hashing (LSH). Most recent improvements to the ISD landscape [8,16] use nearest neighbor search techniques to speed-up the search-tree computation. We also included LSH techniques in our implementation. However for the so far benchmarked code dimensions, LSH did not (yet) lead to relevant speedups. See Sect. 3.3 for further discussion on LSH.

3 Implementing MMT/BJMM Efficiently

In Sect. 3.1 we introduce an elementary, but at least for McEliece practically effective decoding trick. We then detail our MMT/BJMM implementation in Sect. 3.2

3.1 Parity Bit Trick

Let us introduce a small technical trick to speed up ISD algorithms, whenever the weight of the error vector is known. Known error weight is the standard case in code-based cryptography. The trick is so elementary that we would be surprised if it was missed in literature so far, but we failed to find a reference, let alone some proper analysis.

Let $H\mathbf{e} = \mathbf{s}$ be our syndrome decoding instance, where ω is the known error weight of $\mathbf{e}$. Then certainly

$$\langle 1^n, \mathbf{e} \rangle = \omega \mod 2.$$

Thus, we can initially append to the parity-check matrix the row vector 1^n, and append to $\mathbf{s}$ the parity bit $\omega \mod 2$.

Notice that this *parity bit* trick increases the co-dimension by 1, and therefore also the size of the information set. For Prange's permutation-dominated ISD this results in a speedup of

$$\frac{\binom{n}{\omega}}{\binom{n-k}{\omega}} \cdot \frac{\binom{n-k+1}{\omega}}{\binom{n}{\omega}} = \frac{\binom{n-k+1}{\omega}}{\binom{n-k}{\omega}} .$$

The speedup for Prange with *parity bit* is the larger the smaller our co-dimension $n - k$ is. For McEliece with small co-dimension and our new record instance ($n = 1284, k = 1028, \omega = 24$) we obtain more than a 10% speedup, and for the proposed round-3 McEliece parameter sets it is in the range 8–9 %. If instead of Prange's algorithm we use the MMT/BJMM variant that performed best in our benchmarks then the speedup is still in practice a remarkable 9% for the $n = 1284$ instance, and 6–7% for the round-3 parameter sets.

For BIKE and HQC with large co-dimension $n - k = \frac{n}{2}$ and way bigger n, the speedup from the *parity bit* goes down to only 0.5–1%.

3.2 Implementation

Parameter Selection and Benchmarking. As seen in Sect. 3 and Algorithm 1, the MMT/BJMM algorithm—even when limited to depth 2 search trees—still has to be run with optimized parameters for the weights on all levels of the search tree, and an optimized ℓ. We used an adapted formula based on the syndrome decoding estimator tool by Esser and Bellini [11] that precisely reflects our implementation to obtain initial predictions for those parameters on concrete instances. We then refined the choice experimentally.

To this end, we measure the number of iterations per second our cluster is able to process for a specific parameter configuration. We then calculate the expected runtime to solve the instance as the number of expected permutations q^{-1} (from Eq. (5)) divided by the number of permutations per second. We then (brute-force) searched for an optimal configuration in a small interval around the initial prediction that minimizes the expected runtime.

For instances with McEliece code length $n \leq 1350$ we find optimality of the most simple non-trivial MMT weight configuration with weight $p_2 = 1$ for the baselists $L_1, \ldots, L_4$ on level 2, weight $p_1 = 2$ in level 1, and eventually weight $p = 4$ on level 0 in Fig. 1. We refer to the weight configuration $p_2 = 1$ in the baselists as the *low-memory* configuration. Recall that for $p_2 = 0$ MMT becomes Prange's algorithm, and therefore is a memory-less algorithm.

We call configurations with $p_2 \in \{2,3\}$ *high-memory* configurations. The choice $p_2 = 3$ already requires roughly 40 GB of memory. Increasing the weight to $p_2 = 4$ would increase the memory consumption by another factor of approximately 2^{11}.

Gaussian Elimination. For the Gaussian elimination step we use an open source version [1] of the *Method of the four Russians for Inversion* (M4RI), as already proposed by Bernstein et al. and Peters [7,17]. According to [5] the M4RI algorithm is preferable to other advanced algorithms like Strassen [20] up to matrices of dimension six-thousand. We extended the functionality of [1] to allow for performing a transformation to semi-systematic form, without fully inverting the given matrix. Even for small-memory configurations the permutation and Gaussian elimination step together only account for roughly 2–3% of our total computation time. Therefore we refrain from further optimizations of this step, as introduced in [7,17].

Search Tree Construction. To save memory, we implemented the search tree from Fig. 1 in a streaming fashion, as already suggested by Wagner in [25]. See Fig. 2 for an illustration showing that we have to store only two baselists and one intermediate list.

Our implementation exploits that $L_1 = L_3$, and L_2 and L_4 only differ by addition of s_2 to the label H_2y_2. To compute the join of L_1, L_2 to $L_1^{(1)}$ we hash list L_1 into a hashmap H_{L_1} using $\pi(H_2y_1)$ as an index. Then we search each label $\pi(H_2y_2)$ of list L_2 in H_{L_1}, and store all resulting matches in another hashmap $H_{L_1^{(1)}}$ using the remaining $\ell - \ell_1$ bits of label H_2x_2.

For the right half of the tree we reuse the hashmap H_{L_1} and the list L_2, to which we add s_2. The resulting matches from $L_2^{(1)}$ are directly processed on-the-fly with $H_{L_1^{(1)}}$, producing $e_2 \in L$. The candidates e_2 are again processed on the fly, and checked whether they lead to the correct counterpart e_1.

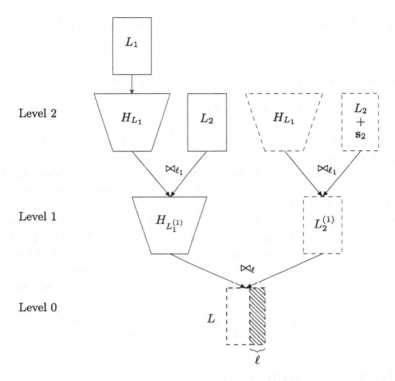

Fig. 2. Streaming implementation of the MMT/BJMM search tree in depth two using two physically stored lists and hashmaps. H_{L_1} and $H_{L_1^{(1)}}$ denote the hashmaps, while dashed lists and hashmaps are processed on the fly.

For speed optimization we worked with a single 64-bit register computation of our candidate solutions throughout all levels of the tree. Even eventually falsifying incorrect e_1 can be performed within 64 bit most of the time. For construction of the baselists L_1, L_2 we used a Gray-code type enumeration.

Parallelization of Low- and High-Memory Configuration. Recall that ISD algorithms consist of a permutation and an enumeration part. In the low-memory regime, we only perform a light enumeration with $p_2 = 1$. The algorithmic complexity is in this configuration dominated by the number of permutations. Therefore, we choose to fully parallelize permutations, i.e., each thread computes its own permutation, Gaussian elimination, and copy of the search tree.

In the high memory regime however, the number of permutations is drastically reduced at the cost of an increasing enumeration complexity. Therefore for the $p_2 = 2, 3$ configurations we choose to parallelize the search tree construction. To this end, we parallelize among N threads by splitting the baselist into N chunks of equal size. To prevent race conditions, every bucket of a hashmap is also split in N equally sized partitions, where only thread number i can insert into partition i.

3.3   Other Benchmarked Variants – Depth 3 and LSH

It is known that asymptotically, and in the high error regime, an increased search tree depth and the use of LSH techniques [8,16] both yield asymptotic improvements. We implemented these techniques, but for the following reasons we did not use them for our record computations.

The estimates for depth 2 and 3 complexities are rather close, not giving clear favor to depth 3. This explains why in practice the overhead of another tree level outweighs its benefits.

LSH allows to save on some permutations at the cost of an increased complexity of computing L from the level-one lists $L_1^{(1)}, L_2^{(2)}$. Accordingly, the LSH savings lie in the Gaussian elimination, the base list construction and the matching to level one. Our benchmarks reveal that these procedures together only account for 10–15% of the total running time in the low-memory setting. Moreover, LSH is not well compatible with our streaming design. Therefore, LSH did not yet provide speedups for our computations, but this will likely change for future record computations, see the discussion in Sect. 4.2.

4   McEliece Cryptanalysis

In this section we give our experimental results on McEliece instances. Besides giving background information on our two record computations, we discuss how good different memory cost models fit our experimental data.

Moreover, we show that MMT reaches its asymptotics *slowly from below*, which in turn implies that purely asymptotic estimates tend to overestimate bit security levels. We eloborate on how to properly estimate McEliece bit security levels in Sect. 7.

For our computations we used a cluster consisting of two nodes, each one equipped with 2 AMD EPYC 7742 processors and 2 TB of RAM. This amounts for a total of 256 physical cores, allowing for a parallelization via 512 threads.

4.1   Record Computations

Table 1 states the instance parameters of our records we achieved in the McEliece-like decoding category of decodingchallenge.org.

McEliece-1223. We benchmarked an optimal MMT parameter choice of $(\ell, \ell_1, p, p_2) = (17, 2, 4, 1)$. With this low-memory configuration our computing cluster processed $2^{33.32}$ permutations per day, which gives an expected computation time of 8.22 days, since in total we expect $2^{36.36}$ permutations from Eq. (5). We solved the instance in 2.45 days, only 30% of the expected running time.

Table 1. Parameters of the largest solved McEliece instances, needed wallclock time, CPU years and bit complexity estimate.

n	k	ω	Time (days)	CPU years	Bit complexity
1223	979	23	2.45	1.71	58.3
1284	1028	24	31.43	22.04	60.7

If we model the runtime as a geometrically distributed random variable with parameter $q = 2^{-36.36}$, then we succeed within 30% of the expectation with probability 26%.

McEliece-1284. Our benchmarks identified the same optimal parameter set $(\ell, \ell_1, p, p_2) = (17, 2, 4, 1)$ as for McEliece-1223. For this configuration our estimator formula yields an expected amount of $2^{38.49}$ permutations. We benchmarked a total performance of $2^{33.26}$ permutations per day, leading to an expected 37.47 days. We solved the challenge within 31.43 days which is about 84% of the expected running time, and happens with probability about 57%.

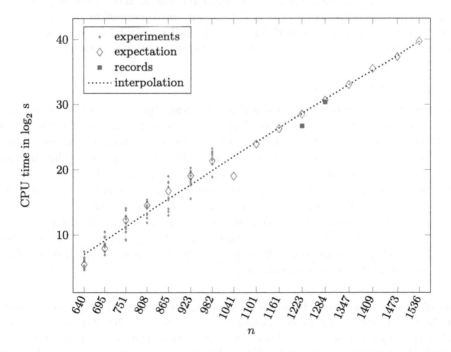

Fig. 3. Running time of experiments and records as well as interpolation for McEliece.

Experimental Results and Discussion. In Fig. 3, we plot our record computations as squares. Before we performed our record computations, we heavily tested our implementation with smaller instances $n < 1000$. As before, we computed the expected running time for every value of n, denoted as larger open diamonds in Fig. 3, via the quotient of expected permutations and permutations per second on our cluster. The small diamonds depict the actual data points which cluster around their expectation, as desired.

The runtime jumps from $n = 695$ to $n = 751$ and from $n = 982$ to $n = 1041$ can be explained by the instance generation method. For every choice of n the parameters k and ω are derived on decodingchallenge.org as (see [3]) $k = \lceil \frac{4n}{5} \rceil$ and $\omega = \left\lceil \frac{n}{5\lceil \log n \rceil} \right\rceil$.

For most consecutive instances ω increases by one, but for $n = 695$ to $n = 751$ there is an increase of 2, whereas for $n = 982$ to $n = 1041$ there is a decrease of 1. Besides these jumps, the instance generation closely follows the Classic McEliece strategy.

Comparison with Other Implementations. We also compare our implementation to those of Landais [14] and Vasseur [24]. These implementations were used to break the previous McEliece challenges, with the only exception of the $n = 1161$ computation by Narisada, Fukushima, and Kiyomoto that uses non-publicly available code. We find that our implementation performs 12.46 and 17.85 times faster on the McEliece-1284 challenge and 9.56 and 20.36 times faster on the McEliece-1223 instance than [14] and [24], respectively.

4.2 The Cost of Memory

Not very surprising, our experimental results show that large memory consumption leads to practical slowdown. This is in line with the conclusion of the McEliece team [9] that a constant memory access cost model, not accounting for any memory costs, underestimates security. However, this leaves the question how to properly penalize an algorithm with running time T for using memory M. Most prominent models use logarithmic, cube-root or square-root penalty factors, i.e. costs of $T \cdot \log M$, $T \cdot \sqrt[3]{M}$ or $T \cdot \sqrt{M}$, respectively.

In [11] it was shown that logarithmic costs do not heavily influence parameter selection of enumeration-based ISD algorithms, whereas cube-root costs let the MMT advantage deteriorate. Thus, it is crucial to evaluate which cost model most closely matches experimental data.

Break-Even Point for High-Memory Regime. Using our estimator formula we find that under cube-root memory access costs the point where the low-memory configuration $p_2 = 1$ becomes inferior lies around $n = 6000$, falling in the 256-bit security regime of McEliece. In contrast, the logarithmic cost model predicts the break even point at $n \geq 1161$.

By benchmarking the running time of our implementation in the range $n = 1101$ to 1536 for different choices of p_2, see Fig. 4, we experimentally find a

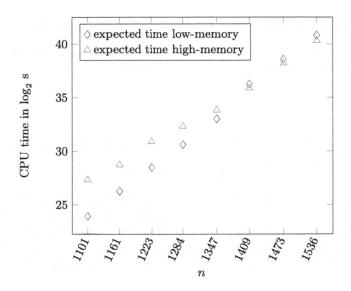

Fig. 4. Estimated running times for low- and high-memory configurations.

break even point at $n \approx 1400$. For $n \geq 1400$ the choice $p_2 = 3$ performs best. The configuration $p_2 = 2$ was experimentally always inferior to $p_2 = 1$ and $p_2 = 3$ (which is consistent with our estimation). The reason is that as opposed to $p_2 = 2$ the configuration $p_2 = 3$ does allow for a BJMM parameter selection with $p = 8 < 4p_2$, and also leads to a better balancing of list sizes in the search tree.

In conclusion, the experimentally benchmarked break-even point is way closer to the theoretical point of $n = 1161$ in the logarithmic cost model than to $n = 6000$ in the cube-root model. This already supports the use of logarithmic costs, especially when we take into account that many of our implementation details heavily reward the use of low-memory configurations, such as:

– *Large L3 Caches.* Our processors have an exceptionally large L3 cache of 256 MB that is capable of holding our complete lists in low-memory configurations.
– *Use of Hashmaps.* As indicated in Sect. 3.2, our parallelization is less effective e.g. for hashmaps in the large-memory regime.
– *Communication complexity.* As opposed to low-memory configurations the high-memory regime requires thread communication for parallelization.

4.3   McEliece Asymptotics: From Above and from Below

It was analyzed in [21], that asymptotically all ISD algorithms converge for McEliece instances to Pranges complexity bound

$$\left(1 - \frac{k}{n}\right)^{\omega}, \text{ see Eq. (2).}$$

Since we have rate $\frac{k}{n} = 0.8$ for the decodingchallenge.org parameters, we expect an asymptotic runtime of

$$T(n) = 2^{2.32 \frac{n}{\log n}}. \tag{6}$$

This asymptotic estimates supresses polynomial factors. Thus, in Prange's algorithm we have rather $2^{2.32(1 + o(1)) \frac{n}{\log n}}$, and the algorithm converges to Eq. (6) from *above*. For other advanced ISD algorithms the asymptotics suppresses polynomial runtime factors as well as second order improvements. Thus, they have runtime $2^{2.32(1 \pm o(1)) \frac{n}{\log n}}$, and it is unclear whether they converge from above or below.

Let us take the interpolation line from our data in Fig. 3, where we use for the runtime exponent the model function $f(n) = a \cdot \frac{n}{5 \log n} + b$. The interpolation yields

$$a = 2.17 \text{ and } b = -22.97,$$

where the negative b accounts for instances which can be solved in less than a second. The small slope a experimentally demonstrates that the convergence is clearly from *below*, even including realistic memory cost.

However, we still want to find the most realistic memory cost model. To this end, we used our estimator for all instances from Fig. 3 in the three different memory access models, constant, logarithmic and cube-root. The resulting bit complexities are illustrated in Fig. 5 in a range $n \in [640, 1536]$ for which in practice we have optimal $p_2 \leq 3$. For each model we computed the interpolation according to $f(n) = a \cdot \frac{n}{5 \log n} + b$. For a constant access cost we find $a = 2.04$, for a logarithmic $a = 2.13$, and for the cube-root model we find $a = 2.24$. Hence, again a logarithmic access cost most accurately models our experimental data.

Cryptographic Parameters. So far, we considered only instances with $n \leq 1536$. However, the current round 3 McEliece parameters reach up to code length $n = 8192$. Thus, we also used our estimator to check the slopes a in this cryptographic regime. We compared the ISD algorithms of Prange, Stern and our MMT/BJMM variant. For all algorithms we imposed logarithmic memory access costs $T \cdot \log M$ and considered the three cases of unlimited available memory, as well as 2^{80}-bit and 2^{60}-bit as memory limitation for M. The results for the exponent model $f(n) = a \cdot \frac{n}{5 \log n} + b$ are given in Table 2.

We observe that Prange does not quickly converge to Eq. (2) from above. For Stern and MMT however we are even in the most restrictive memory setting below the exponent from Eq. (2). This clearly indicates an overestimate of McEliece security using Eq. (2). We eloborate on this more qualitatively in Sect. 7.

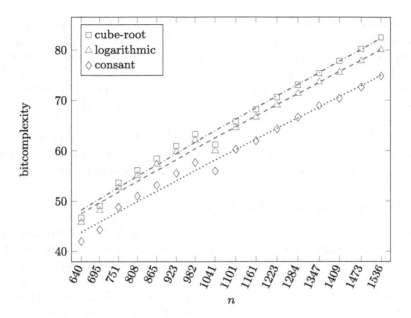

Fig. 5. Estimated bitcomplexities for different memory access cost models and corresponding interpolations.

Table 2. Slope of interpolation of bitcomplexities under logarithmic memory access costs considering instances with $n \leq 8192$ according to the model function $f(n) = a \cdot \frac{n}{5 \log n} + b$.

	Prange	Stern	MMT
Unlimited	2.438	2.297	2.075
$M \leq 2^{80}$	2.438	2.299	2.207
$M \leq 2^{60}$	2.438	2.308	2.287

5 The Quasi-Cyclic Setting: BIKE and HQC

The proposals of BIKE and HQC—both alternate finalists of the NIST PQC competition—use double circulant codes with code rate $\frac{1}{2}$, i.e., $n = 2k$. It has been shown by Sendrier [19] that these codes allow for a speedup of Stern's ISD algorithm by a factor of up to $\sqrt{k}$. The basic observation is that the cyclicity immediately introduces k instances of the syndrome decoding problem, where a solution to any of the k instances is a cyclic rotation of the original solution. Thus, this technique is widely known as *Decoding One Out of Many* (DOOM).

Let $H_1, H_2 \in \mathbb{F}_2^{k \times k}$ be two circulant matrices satisfying

$$\left(H_1 \; H_2\right)(e_1, e_2) = s$$

with $e_1, e_2 \in \mathbb{F}_2^k$. Let us denote by $\text{rot}_i(\mathbf{x})$ the cyclic left rotation of $\mathbf{x}$ by i positions. Then for any $i = 0, \ldots, k-1$ we have

$$\left(H_1 \; H_2\right)(\text{rot}_i(e_1), \text{rot}_i(e_2)) = \text{rot}_i(s) =: s_i.$$

This implies that a solution to any of the k instances $(H_1 H_2, \mathbf{s}_i, \omega)$ yields $(\mathbf{e}_1, \mathbf{e}_2)$.

Note that in the special case of $\mathbf{s} = \mathbf{0}$, thus, when actually searching for a small codeword the instances are all the same, meaning there simply exist k different solutions $\mathbf{e}$. In this case any ISD algorithm obtains a speedup of k.

For $\mathbf{s} \neq \mathbf{0}$ one usually assumes a speedup of $\sqrt{k}$ in the quasi-cyclic setting, referring to Sendrier's DOOM result [19]. However, [19] only analyzes Stern's algorithm.

In the following section we adapt the idea of Sendrier's DOOM to the MMT/BJMM algorithm in the specific setting of double circulant codes, achieving speedups slightly larger than $\sqrt{k}$ both in theory and practical experiments.

5.1   Decoding One Out of k (DOOM$_k$)

To obtain a speedup from the k instances we modify the search tree of our MMT/BJMM variant such that in every iteration all k syndromes are considered. To this end, similar to Sendrier, we first enlarge list L_4 (compare to Fig. 2) by exchanging every element $(\mathbf{x}, H\mathbf{x}) \in L_4$ by $(\mathbf{x}, H\mathbf{x} + \bar{\mathbf{s}}_i)$ for all $i = 1 \ldots k$, where $\bar{\mathbf{s}}_i := G\mathbf{s}_i$ denotes the i-th syndrome after the Gaussian elimination. This results in a list that is k times larger than L_4. To compensate for this increased list size we enumerate in L_4 initially only vectors of weight $p_2 - 1$ rather than p_2.

This simple change already allows for a speedup of our MMT/BJMM algorithm of order $\sqrt{k}$, as shown in the following lemma.

Lemma 1 (DOOM$_k$ speedup). *A syndrome decoding instance with double circulant parity-check matrix, code rate $\frac{k}{n} = \frac{1}{2}$ and error weight $\omega = \Theta(\sqrt{k})$ allows for a speedup of the MMT/BJMM algorithm by a factor of $\Omega(\sqrt{k})$.*

Proof. First note, that since list L_4 is duplicated for every syndrome $\mathbf{s}_i$ by the correctness of the original MMT algorithm our modification is able to retrieve any of the rotated solutions if permutation distributed the weight properly.

Let us first analyze the impact of our change on the size of the list L_4. The decrease of the weight of the vectors in L_4 from p_2 to $p_2 - 1$ decreases the size by a factor of

$$\delta_{\mathrm{L}} := \frac{\binom{(k+\ell)/2}{p_2}}{\binom{(k+\ell)/2}{p_2-1}} = \frac{\frac{k+\ell}{2} - p_2 + 1}{p_2} \approx \frac{k}{2 \cdot p_2},$$

since $\ell, p_2 \ll k$. Thus, together with the initial blowup by k for every syndrome we end up with a list that is roughly $2p_2$ times as large as the original list. Next let us study the effect on the probability of a random permutation distributing the error weight properly for anyone of the k error vector rotations, which is

$$\delta_P := \frac{\binom{n-k-\ell}{\omega-p+1}\binom{k+\ell}{p-1} \cdot k / \binom{n}{\omega}}{\binom{n-k-\ell}{\omega-p}\binom{k+\ell}{p} / \binom{n}{\omega}} = \frac{\binom{n-k-\ell}{\omega-p+1}\binom{k+\ell}{p-1} \cdot k}{\binom{n-k-\ell}{\omega-p}\binom{k+\ell}{p}}$$

$$= \frac{(k - \ell - \omega + p) \cdot p \cdot k}{(\omega - p + 1)(k + \ell - p + 1)} = \Omega(\sqrt{k}).$$

Table 3. Estimated DOOM_k speedups for Stern and MMT in the quasi-cyclic setting with double circulant codes ($n = 2k$).

| Instance | | $\log\left(\sqrt{k}\right)$ | Speedup | |
	k	ω		Stern	MMT
Challenge-1	451	30	4.41	4.88	4.96
Challenge-2	883	42	4.89	5.39	5.43
QC-2918	1459	54	5.26	5.77	5.77
BIKE-1	12323	134	6.79	7.58	7.47
BIKE-3	24659	199	7.29	8.00	7.55
BIKE-5	40973	264	7.66	8.32	8.06
HQC-1	17669	132	7.05	8.14	8.00
HQC-3	35851	200	7.56	8.55	8.39
HQC-5	57637	262	7.91	8.83	8.66

Here the denominator states the probability of a permutation inducing the correct weight distribution on any of the k syndromes, while the numerator is the probability of success in any iteration of the MMT algorithm (compare to Eq. (5)). Observe that the last equality follows from the fact, that $\omega = \Theta(\sqrt{k})$ and $p \ll \omega$ as well as $\ell \ll k$.

So far we showed, that our modification increases the list size of L_1 by a small factor of $2p_2$, while we enhance the probability of a good permutation for any of the given k instances by a factor of $\Omega(\sqrt{k})$. While in the case of Sterns' algorithm this is already enough to conclude that the overall speedup in this setting is $\Omega(\sqrt{k})$, as long as $p_2 \ll k$, for MMT/BJMM we also need to consider the reduced amount of representations. Note that the amount of representations decreases from an initial R to R_k, i.e., by a factor of

$$\delta_R := \frac{R_k}{R} = \frac{\binom{p-1}{p/2}\binom{k+\ell-p+1}{p_1-p/2}}{\binom{p}{p/2}\binom{k+\ell-p}{p_1-p/2}}$$
$$= \frac{(k+\ell-p+1)\cdot p/2}{(k+\ell-p/2-p_1+1)\cdot p} = \frac{(k+\ell-p+1)}{2(k+\ell-p+1-\varepsilon)} \approx \frac{1}{2},$$

Here $\varepsilon = p_1 - p/2$ is the amount of 1-entries added by BJMM to cancel out during addition, which is usually a small constant. Hence $\ell_1 := \log R$ in Algorithm 1 decreases by one. This in turn increases the time for computing the search-tree by a factor of at most two.

In summary, we obtain a speedup of $\delta_P = \Omega(\sqrt{k})$ on the probability while losing a factor of at most $\frac{\delta_L}{\delta_R} = 4p_2$ in the construction of the tree. Hence, for MMT/BJMM with $p_2 \ll \sqrt{k}$ this yields an overall speedup of $\Omega(\sqrt{k})$.   □

We included the $DOOM_k$ improvement in our estimator formulas for Stern as well as MMT. Table 3 shows the derived estimated speedups. As a result both algorithms Stern and MMT achieve comparable $DOOM_k$ speedups slightly larger than $\sqrt{k}$. Additionally, we performed practical experiments on the instances listed as *Challenge-1* and *Challenge-2* to verify the estimates. Therefore, we solved these instances with MMT with and without the $DOOM_k$ technique. Averaged over ten executions we find speedups of 4.99 and 5.40 respectively (closely matching 4.96 and 5.43 from Table 3).

6   Quasi-Cyclic Cryptanalysis

In the quasi-cyclic setting we obtained five new decoding records on decodingchallenge.org with our MMT implementation [3], see Table 4. Instances are defined on [3] for every w using parameters $n = w^2 + 2$ and $k = \frac{n}{2}$, closely following the BIKE and HQC design.

Table 4. Parameters of the largest solved BIKE/HQC instances, needed wallclock time, CPU years and bit complexity estimates.

n	k	w	Time (days)	CPU years	Bit complexity
2118	1059	46	0.08	0.05	50.5
2306	1153	48	0.22	0.15	52.5
2502	1459	50	0.30	0.21	54.6
2706	1353	52	1.18	0.83	56.6
2918	1459	54	3.33	2.33	58.6

QC-2918. The largest instance we were able to solve has parameters $(n, k, w) = (2918, 1459, 54)$, and took us 3.33 days on our cluster. The optimal identified parameter set is $(\ell, \ell_1, p, p_2) = (21, 1, 3, 1)$, for which we estimated $2^{31.9}$ permutations. We were able to perform $2^{29.31}$ permutations per day, resulting in an expected running time of 6.02 days. Our computation took only 55% of the expected time, which happens with probability 42%.

Interpolation. In Fig. 6 we give the expected running times that we obtained via benchmarking, both with (diamonds) and without (triangles) our $DOOM_k$ result from Sect. 5.1. Our five record computations are depicted as squares. All record computations where achieved in a runtime closely matching the expected values.

In the quasi-cyclic setting with rate $\frac{k}{n} = \frac{1}{2}$ and $w = \sqrt{n}$ Prange's runtime formula from Eq. (2) gives $2^{\sqrt{n}}$. An interpolation of our experimental data points using the model $f(n) = a\sqrt{n} + b$ yields a best fit for

$$f(n) = 1.01\sqrt{n} - 26.42. \tag{7}$$

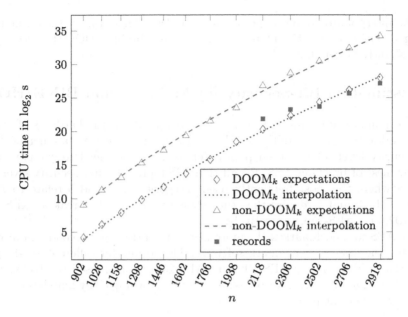

Fig. 6. Estimated running times and interpolations for low- and high-memory configurations.

The slope $a = 1.01$ shows how accurately our MMT implementation matches the asymptotics already for medium sized instances, i.e., our MMT advantage and the polynomial runtime factors almost cancel out.

Concrete vs Asymptotic. Similar to the McEliece setting in Sect. 4.3 and in Table 2, we also performed for BIKE/HQC an interpolation of estimated bit complexities in the logarithmic cost model using the algorithms of Prange, Stern and our MMT variant. We included instances up to code length $120,000$, reflecting the largest choice made by an HQC parameter set. As opposed to Sect. 4.3 we do not need additional memory limitations, since none of the optimal configurations exceeds 2^{60}-bit of memory.

The interpolation with $f(n) = a\sqrt{n} + b$ gave us slopes of 1.054, 1.019 and 1.017 for Prange, Stern and MMT, respectively, i.e., all slopes are slightly above the asymptotic prediction of $a = 1$. Thus, as opposed to the McEliece setting our MMT benefits are canceled by polynomial factors.

Verification of the DOOM$_k$ Speedup. From Fig. 6, we can also experimentally determine the speedup of our DOOM$_k$ technique inside MMT. Lemma 1 predicts a speedup of $\sqrt{k} = \sqrt{n/2}$. Let $f(n) = 1.01\sqrt{n} - 26.42$ as before, and in addition take the model $f(n) + c \cdot \frac{\log(n/2)}{2}$ for non-DOOM$_k$. The new model should fit with $c = 1$.

The interpolation of our experimental non-DOOM_k data, see the dashed line in Fig. 6, yields $c = 1.17$. Thus, in practice we obtain a DOOM_k speedup of $k^{0.58}$, slightly larger than $\sqrt{k}$.

7   Estimating Bit-Security for McEliece and BIKE/HQC

Based on our record computations, let us extrapolate to the hardness of breaking round-3 McEliece, BIKE and HQC. To provide precise statements about the security levels of proposed parameter sets, we also need to compare with the hardness of breaking AES. Recall that NIST provides five security level categories, where the most frequently used categories 1, 3, and 5 relate to AES. Category 1, 3, and 5 require that the scheme is as hard to break as AES-128, AES-192, and AES-256, respectively.

For AES we benchmarked the amount of encryptions per second on our cluster using the openssl benchmark software. The results for different key-lengths are listed in Table 5. For AES-192 and AES-256, we increased the blocklength from 128 to 256 bit, such that on expectation only a single key matches a known plaintext-ciphertext pair.

Table 5. Number of AES encryptions per second performed by our cluster.

	AES-128	AES-192	AES-256
10^9enc/sec	2.16	0.96	0.83

From Table 5 we extrapolate the running time to break AES-128, AES-192, and AES-256 on our hardware.

Extrapolation for McEliece and BIKE/HQC. Let us detail our extrapolation methodology. We take as starting points the real runtimes of $22.04 = 2^{4.46}$ CPU years for McEliece-1284 and 2.33 CPU years for QC-2918.

Then we estimate by which factor it is harder to break the round-3 instances, and eventually compare the resulting runtime to the hardness of breaking AES.

Let us give a numerical example for McEliece-4608. Assume that we take 2^{60}-bit memory limitation for M, and we are in the most realistic logarithmic memory cost model. In this setting our estimator (without LSH) gives for $n = 4608$ a bit complexity of 187.72, and for $n = 1284$ a bit complexity of 65.27. Thus, it is a factor of $2^{122.45}$ harder to break McEliece-4608 than to break our record McEliece-1284. Therefore, we conclude that a break of McEliece-4608 on our hardware would require $2^{4.46} \cdot 2^{122.45} = 2^{126.91}$ CPU years.

In contrast, from Table 5 we conclude that breaking AES-192 on our hardware requires $2^{145.24}$ CPU years. Thus, from our extrapolation McEliece-4608 is a factor of $2^{18.33}$ *easier to break* than AES-192. This is denoted by -18.33 in Table 6.

McEliece Slightly Overestimates Security. For completeness, we consider in Table 6 all three different memory-access cost models, constant, logarithmic and cube-root, even though we identified the *logarithmic* model as most realistic (compare to Sect. 4.2). Recall that in these models an algorithm with memory M suffers either no penalty (constant), a multiplicative factor of $\log M$ (logarithmic) or even a $\sqrt[3]{M}$ factor penalty (cube-root).

Moreover, we also provide memory limitations for the constant and logarithmic models. This is unnecessary in the cube-root model, in which no optimal parameter configuration exceeds a memory bit complexity of 60.

Table 6. Difference in bit complexity of breaking McEliece and corresponding AES instantiation under different memory access cost.

McEliece		Category 1 $n = 3488$	Category 3 $n = 4608$	Category 5a $n = 6688$	Category 5b $n = 6960$	Category 5c $n = 8192$
	Unlimited	0.09	−24.86	−23.18	−23.80	6.10
Constant	$M \le 2^{80}$	1.54	−21.52	−11.67	−10.87	23.37
	$M \le 2^{60}$	4.80	−19.12	− 3.86	− 3.80	32.70
	Unlimited	1.77	−23.11	−20.70	−21.29	8.84
Logarithmic	$M \le 2^{80}$	2.86	−20.41	−10.46	− 9.63	24.64
	$M \le 2^{60}$	5.55	−18.33	− 3.46	− 3.40	33.16
Cube-root		10.37	−12.27	0.82	1.38	38.22

Let T_{McEliece} denote the extrapolated McEliece runtime, and let T_{AES} be the extrapolated AES runtime in the respective security category. Then Table 6 provides the entries $\log_2(\frac{T_{\mathrm{McEliece}}}{T_{\mathrm{AES}}})$. Thus, a negative x-entry indicates that this McEliece instance is x bits easier to break than its desired security category.

Whereas the Category 1 instance McEliece-3488 meets its security level in all memory models, the Category 3 instance McEliece-4608 misses the desired level by roughly 20 bits for constant/logarithmic costs. Even for cube-root costs McEliece-4608 is still 12 bits below the required level.

The Category 5a and 5b McEliece instances are in the realistic logarithmic model with 2^{80}-bit memory also 10 bits below their desired security level, whereas the Category 5c McEliece instance is independent of the memory model above its security level.

BIKE/HQC Accurately Matches Security. In Table 7 we state our results for BIKE and HQC. As opposed to the McEliece setting we do not need memory limitations here, since none of the estimates exceeded 2^{60}-bit of memory.

Table 7. Difference in bit complexity of breaking BIKE/HQC and corresponding AES instantiation under different memory access cost.

BIKE / HQC			Category 1	Category 3	Category 5
	BIKE	Message	2.44	2.50	3.49
Constant		Key	3.88	2.13	5.87
	HQC		1.24	4.28	2.23
	BIKE	Message	2.86	3.04	4.10
Logarithmic		Key	4.42	3.11	6.74
	HQC		1.72	4.87	2.90
	BIKE	Message	4.47	5.20	6.68
Cube-root		Key	5.77	5.00	9.03
	HQC		3.62	7.34	5.75

Note that for BIKE we need to distinguish an attack on the key and an attack on a message. That is because recovering the secret key from the public key corresponds to finding a low-weight codeword, whereas recovering the message from a ciphertext corresponds to a syndrome decoding instance, where the syndrome is usually not the zero vector. Both settings allow for different speedups as outlined in Sect. 5.

We observe that the BIKE as well as the HQC instances precisely match their claimed security levels already in the conservative setting of constant memory access costs. Introducing memory penalties only leads to slight increases in the security margins.

References

1. Albrecht, M., Bard, G.: The M4RI Library. The M4RI Team (2021). http://m4ri.sagemath.org
2. Albrecht, M.R., Player, R., Scott, S.: On the concrete hardness of learning with errors. J. Math. Cryptol. **9**(3), 169–203 (2015)
3. Aragon, N., Lavauzelle, J., Lequesne, M.: decodingchallenge.org (2019). http://decodingchallenge.org
4. Baldi, M., Barenghi, A., Chiaraluce, F., Pelosi, G., Santini, P.: A finite regime analysis of information set decoding algorithms. Algorithms **12**(10), 209 (2019)
5. Bard, G.V.: Algorithms for Solving Linear and Polynomial Systems of Equations Over Finite Fields, with Applications to Cryptanalysis. University of Maryland, College Park (2007)
6. Becker, A., Joux, A., May, A., Meurer, A.: Decoding random binary linear codes in $2^{n/20}$: how $1 + 1 = 0$ improves information set decoding. In: Pointcheval, D., Johansson, T. (eds.) EUROCRYPT 2012. LNCS, vol. 7237, pp. 520–536. Springer, Heidelberg (2012). https://doi.org/10.1007/978-3-642-29011-4_31

7. Bernstein, D.J., Lange, T., Peters, C.: Attacking and defending the McEliece cryptosystem. In: Buchmann, J., Ding, J. (eds.) PQCrypto 2008. LNCS, vol. 5299, pp. 31–46. Springer, Heidelberg (2008). https://doi.org/10.1007/978-3-540-88403-3_3

8. Both, L., May, A.: Decoding linear codes with high error rate and its impact for LPN security. In: Lange, T., Steinwandt, R. (eds.) PQCrypto 2018. LNCS, vol. 10786, pp. 25–46. Springer, Cham (2018). https://doi.org/10.1007/978-3-319-79063-3_2

9. Chou, T., et al.: Classic McEliece: conservative code-based cryptography, 10 October 2020 (2020)

10. Dumer, I.: On minimum distance decoding of linear codes. In: Proceedings of the 5th Joint Soviet-Swedish International Workshop Information Theory, pp. 50–52 (1991)

11. Esser, A., Bellini, E.: Syndrome decoding estimator. IACR Cryptol. ePrint Arch. **2021**, 1243 (2021)

12. Howgrave-Graham, N., Joux, A.: New generic algorithms for hard knapsacks. In: Gilbert, H. (ed.) EUROCRYPT 2010. LNCS, vol. 6110, pp. 235–256. Springer, Heidelberg (2010). https://doi.org/10.1007/978-3-642-13190-5_12

13. Kleinjung, T., et al.: Factorization of a 768-bit RSA modulus. In: Rabin, T. (ed.) CRYPTO 2010. LNCS, vol. 6223, pp. 333–350. Springer, Heidelberg (2010). https://doi.org/10.1007/978-3-642-14623-7_18

14. Landais, G.: Code of Grégory Landais (2012). https://gforge.inria.fr/projects/collision-dec/

15. May, A., Meurer, A., Thomae, E.: Decoding random linear codes in $\tilde{O}(2^{0.054n})$. In: Lee, D.H., Wang, X. (eds.) ASIACRYPT 2011. LNCS, vol. 7073, pp. 107–124. Springer, Heidelberg (2011). https://doi.org/10.1007/978-3-642-25385-0_6

16. May, A., Ozerov, I.: On computing nearest neighbors with applications to decoding of binary linear codes. In: Oswald, E., Fischlin, M. (eds.) EUROCRYPT 2015, Part I. LNCS, vol. 9056, pp. 203–228. Springer, Heidelberg (2015). https://doi.org/10.1007/978-3-662-46800-5_9

17. Peters, C.: Information-set decoding for linear codes over F_q. In: Sendrier, N. (ed.) PQCrypto 2010. LNCS, vol. 6061, pp. 81–94. Springer, Heidelberg (2010). https://doi.org/10.1007/978-3-642-12929-2_7

18. Prange, E.: The use of information sets in decoding cyclic codes. IRE Trans. Inf. Theory **8**(5), 5–9 (1962)

19. Sendrier, Nicolas: Decoding one out of many. In: Yang, Bo-Yin. (ed.) PQCrypto 2011. LNCS, vol. 7071, pp. 51–67. Springer, Heidelberg (2011). https://doi.org/10.1007/978-3-642-25405-5_4

20. Strassen, V.: Gaussian elimination is not optimal. Numer. Math. **13**(4), 354–356 (1969)

21. Canto Torres, R., Sendrier, N.: Analysis of information set decoding for a sub-linear error weight. In: Takagi, T. (ed.) PQCrypto 2016. LNCS, vol. 9606, pp. 144–161. Springer, Cham (2016). https://doi.org/10.1007/978-3-319-29360-8_10

22. Various: PQC-forum: Round 3 official comment: classic McEliece (2021). https://groups.google.com/a/list.nist.gov/g/pqc-forum/c/EiwxGnfQgec

23. Various: PQC-forum: security strength categories for code based crypto (and trying out crypto stack exchange) (2021). https://groups.google.com/a/list.nist.gov/g/pqc-forum/c/6XbG66gI7v0

24. Vasseur, V.: Code of Valentin Vasseur (2020). https://gitlab.inria.fr/vvasseur/isd

25. Wagner, D.: A generic birthday problem. In: Yung, M. (ed.) CRYPTO 2002. LNCS, vol. 2442, pp. 288–304. Springer, Heidelberg (2002). https://doi.org/10.1007/3-540-45708-9_19

Post-Quantum Security
of the Even-Mansour Cipher

Gorjan Alagic[1]($\boxtimes$), Chen Bai[2]($\boxtimes$), Jonathan Katz[3]($\boxtimes$) (iD),
and Christian Majenz[4]($\boxtimes$) (iD)

[1] QuICS, University of Maryland, and NIST, College Park, USA
galagic@gmail.com
[2] Department of Electrical and Computer Engineering, University of Maryland,
College Park, USA
cbai1@terpmail.umd.edu
[3] Department of Computer Science, University of Maryland, College Park, USA
jkatz2@gmail.com
[4] Department of Applied Mathematics and Computer Science, Technical University
of Denmark, Kongens Lyngby, Denmark
christian.majenz@gmail.com

Abstract. The Even-Mansour cipher is a simple method for constructing a (keyed) pseudorandom permutation E from a public random permutation $P : \{0,1\}^n \rightarrow \{0,1\}^n$. It is secure against classical attacks,
with optimal attacks requiring q_E queries to E and q_P queries to P such
that $q_E \cdot q_P \approx 2^n$. If the attacker is given *quantum* access to both E
and P, however, the cipher is completely insecure, with attacks using
$q_E, q_P = O(n)$ queries known.

In any plausible real-world setting, however, a quantum attacker
would have only *classical* access to the keyed permutation E implemented
by honest parties, while retaining quantum access to P. Attacks in this
setting with $q_E \cdot q_P^2 \approx 2^n$ are known, showing that security degrades as
compared to the purely classical case, but leaving open the question as
to whether the Even-Mansour cipher can still be proven secure in that
natural, "post-quantum" setting.

We resolve this question, showing that any attack in that setting
requires $q_E \cdot q_P^2 + q_P \cdot q_E^2 \approx 2^n$. Our results apply to both the two-key and
single-key variants of Even-Mansour. Along the way, we establish sev-
eral generalizations of results from prior work on quantum-query lower
bounds that may be of independent interest.

1 Introduction

The Even-Mansour cipher [11] is a well-known approach for constructing a block
cipher E from a public random permutation $P : \{0,1\}^n \rightarrow \{0,1\}^n$. The cipher
$E : \{0,1\}^{2n} \times \{0,1\}^n \rightarrow \{0,1\}^n$ is defined as

$$E_{k_1,k_2}(x) = P(x \oplus k_1) \oplus k_2$$

where, at least in the original construction, k_1, k_2 are uniform and independent.
Security in the standard (classical) setting is well understood [9,11]: roughly, an

© International Association for Cryptologic Research 2022
O. Dunkelman and S. Dziembowski (Eds.): EUROCRYPT 2022, LNCS 13277, pp. 458–487, 2022.
https://doi.org/10.1007/978-3-031-07082-2_17

unbounded attacker with access to P and P^{-1} cannot distinguish whether it is interacting with E_{k_1,k_2} and $E^{-1}_{k_1,k_2}$ (for uniform k_1, k_2) or R and R^{-1} (for an independent, random permutation R) unless it makes $\approx 2^{n/2}$ queries to its oracles. The variant where k_1 is uniform and $k_2 = k_1$ has the same security [9]. These bounds are tight, and key-recovery attacks using $O(2^{n/2})$ queries are known [9,11].

Unfortunately, the Even-Mansour construction is insecure against a fully quantum attack in which the attacker is given *quantum* access to all its oracles [17,20]. In such a setting, the adversary can evaluate the unitary operators

$$U_P : |x\rangle|y\rangle \mapsto |x\rangle|y \oplus P(x)\rangle$$
$$U_{E_{k_1,k_2}} : |x\rangle|y\rangle \mapsto |x\rangle|y \oplus E_{k_1,k_2}(x)\rangle$$

(and the analogous unitaries for P^{-1} and $E^{-1}_{k_1,k_2}$) on any quantum state it prepares, and Simon's algorithm [22] can be applied to $E_{k_1,k_2} \oplus P$ to give a key-recovery attack using only $O(n)$ queries.

To place this seemingly devastating attack in context, it is worth recalling the original motivation for considering unitary oracles of the form above in quantum-query complexity: one can always transform a classical circuit for a function f into a reversible (and hence unitary) quantum circuit for U_f. In a cryptographic context, it is thus reasonable (indeed, necessary) to consider adversaries that use U_f whenever f is a function whose circuit they know. On the other hand, if the circuit for f is *not* known to the adversary, then there is no mechanism by which it can implement U_f on its own. In particular, if f involves a private key, then the only way an adversary could possibly obtain quantum access to f would be if there were an explicit interface granting such access. In most (if not all) real-world applications, however, the honest parties using the keyed function f would implement f using a classical computer. In fact, even if they were to implement f on a quantum computer, there is no reason for them to support anything but a classical interface to f. In such cases, an adversary would have no way to evaluate the unitary operator corresponding to f.

In most real-world applications of Even-Mansour, therefore, an attacker would have only *classical* access to the keyed permutation E_{k_1,k_2} and its inverse, while retaining quantum access to P and P^{-1}. In particular, this seems to be the "right" attack model for most applications of the resulting block cipher, e.g., for constructing a secure encryption scheme from the cipher using some mode of operation. The setting in which the attacker is given quantum access to public primitives but only classical access to keyed primitives is sometimes called the "Q1 setting" [5]; we will refer to it simply as the *post-quantum* setting.

Security of the Even-Mansour cipher in this setting is currently unclear. Kuwakado and Morii [20] show a key-recovery attack using the BHT collision-finding algorithm [7] that requires only $\approx 2^{n/3}$ oracle queries. Their attack uses exponential memory but this was improved in subsequent work [5,14], culminating in an attack using the same number of queries but with polynomial memory complexity. While these results demonstrate that the Even-Mansour construction is *quantitatively* less secure in the post-quantum setting than in the classical setting, they do not answer the *qualitative* question of whether the Even-Mansour construction remains secure as a block cipher in the post-quantum setting, or whether attacks using polynomially many queries might be possible.

In work concurrent with ours, Jaeger et al. [16] prove security of a forward-only variant of the Even-Mansour construction, as well as for the full Even-Mansour cipher against *non-adaptive* adversaries who make all their classical queries before any quantum queries. They explicitly leave open the question of proving adaptive security in the latter case.

1.1   Our Results

As our main result, we prove a lower bound showing that $\approx 2^{n/3}$ queries are *necessary* for attacking the Even-Mansour cipher in the post-quantum setting. In more detail, if q_P denotes the number of (quantum) queries to P, P^{-1} and q_E denotes the number of (classical) queries to $E_{k_1,k_2}, E_{k_1,k_2}^{-1}$, we show that any attack succeeding with constant probability requires either $q_P^2 \cdot q_E = \Omega(2^n)$ or $q_P \cdot q_E^2 = \Omega(2^n)$. (Equating q_P and q_E gives the claimed result.) Formally:

Theorem 1. *Let $\mathcal{A}$ be a quantum algorithm making q_E classical queries to its first oracle (including forward and inverse queries) and q_P quantum queries to its second oracle (including forward and inverse queries.) Then*

$$\left| \Pr_{k_1,k_2,P} \left[\mathcal{A}^{E_{k_1,k_2},P}(1^n) = 1 \right] - \Pr_{R,P} \left[\mathcal{A}^{R,P}(1^n) = 1 \right] \right|$$
$$\leq 10 \cdot 2^{-n/2} \cdot \left(q_E \sqrt{q_P} + q_P \sqrt{q_E} \right) ,$$

where P, R are uniform n-bit permutations, and the marginal distributions of $k_1, k_2 \in \{0,1\}^n$ are uniform.

The above applies, in particular, to the two-key and one-key variants of the cipher. A simplified version of the proof works also for the case where P is a random function, we consider the cipher $E_k(x) = P(x \oplus k)$ with k uniform, and $\mathcal{A}$ is given forward-only access to both P and E.

Real-world attackers are usually assumed to make far fewer queries to keyed, "online" primitives than to public, "offline" primitives. (Indeed, while an offline query is just a local computation, an online query requires, e.g., causing an honest user to encrypt a certain message.) In such a regime, where $q_E \ll q_P$, the bound on the adversary's advantage in Theorem 1 simplifies to $O(q_P \sqrt{q_E}/2^{n/2})$. In that case $q_P^2 q_E = \Omega(2^n)$ is necessary for constant success probability, which matches the BHT and offline Simon algorithms [5,20].[1]

Techniques and New Technical Results. Proving Theorem 1 required us to develop new techniques that we believe are interesting beyond our immediate application. We describe the main challenge and its resolution in what follows.

---

[1] While our bound is tight with respect to the number of queries, it is loose with regard to the attacker's advantage, as both the BHT and offline Simon algorithms achieve advantage $\Theta(q_P^2 q_E/2^n)$. Reducing this gap is an interesting open question.

As we have already discussed, in the setting of post-quantum security adversaries may have a combination of classical and quantum oracles. This is the case, in particular, when a post-quantum security notion that involves keyed oracles is analyzed in the quantum random oracle model (QROM), such as when analyzing the Fujisaki-Okamoto transform [4,8,13,19,23,26] or the Fiat-Shamir transform [12,18,24]. In general, dealing with a mix of quantum and classical oracles presents a problem: quantum-query lower bounds typically begin by "purifying" the adversary and postponing all measurements to the end of its execution, but this does not work if the adversary may decide what query to make to a classical oracle (or even whether to query that oracle at all) *based on the outcome* of an intermediate measurement. The works cited above address this problem in various ways, often by relaxing the problem and allowing quantum access to *all* oracles. This is not an option for us if we wish to prove security, because the Even-Mansour cipher is insecure when the adversary is given quantum access to all its oracles! In the concurrent work of Jaeger et al. [16], the authors overcome the above barrier for the forward-only Even-Mansour case using Zhandry's compressed oracle technique [26], which is not currently known to be applicable to inverse-accessible permutations.

Instead, we deal with the problem by dividing the execution of an algorithm that has classical access to some oracle O_c and quantum access to another oracle O_q into *stages*, where a stage corresponds to a period between classical queries to O_c. We then analyze the algorithm stage-by-stage. In doing so, however, we introduce another problem: the adversary may adaptively choose the number of queries to O_q in each stage based on outcomes of intermediate measurements. While it is possible to upper bound the number of queries to O_q in each stage by the number of queries made to O_q overall, this will (in general) result in a loose security bound. To avoid such a loss, we extend the "blinding lemma" of Alagic et al. [1] so that (in addition to some other generalizations) we obtain a bound in terms of the *expected* number of queries made by a distinguisher:

Lemma 1 (Arbitrary reprogramming, informal). *Consider the following experiment involving a distinguisher D making at most q queries in expectation.*

Phase 1: *D outputs a function F and a randomized algorithm B that specifies how to reprogram F.*
Phase 2: *Randomness r is sampled and $B(r)$ is run to reprogram F, giving F'. A uniform $b \in \{0,1\}$ is chosen, and D receives quantum oracle access to either F (if $b = 0$) or F' (if $b = 1$).*
Phase 3: *D loses access to its oracle, is given r, and outputs a bit b'.*

Then $|\Pr[D \text{ outputs } 1 \mid b = 0] - \Pr[D \text{ outputs } 1 \mid b = 1]| \leq 2q \cdot \sqrt{\epsilon}$, where ϵ is an upper bound on the probability that any given input is reprogrammed.

The name "arbitrary reprogramming" is motivated by the facts that F is arbitrary (and known), and the adversary can reprogram F arbitrarily—so long as some bound on the probability of reprogramming each individual input exists.

We also extend the "adaptive reprogramming lemma" of Grilo et al. [12] to the case of two-way-accessible, random permutations:

Lemma 2 (Resampling lemma for permutations, informal). *Consider the following experiment involving a distinguisher $\mathcal{D}$.*

Phase 1: $\mathcal{D}$ *makes at most q (forward or inverse) quantum queries to a uniform permutation $P : \{0,1\}^n \to \{0,1\}^n$.*

Phase 2: *A uniform $b \in \{0,1\}$ is chosen, and $\mathcal{D}$ is allowed to make arbitrarily many queries to an oracle that is either equal to P (if $b = 0$) or P' (if $b = 1$), where P' is obtained from P by swapping the output values at two uniform points (which are given to $\mathcal{D}$). Finally, $\mathcal{D}$ outputs a bit b'.*

Then $|\Pr[\mathcal{D} \text{ outputs } 1 \mid b = 0] - \Pr[\mathcal{D} \text{ outputs } 1 \mid b = 1]| \leq 4\sqrt{q} \cdot 2^{-n/2}$.

This is tight up to a constant factor (cf. [12, Theorem 7]). The name "resampling lemma" is motivated by the fact that here reprogramming is restricted to resampling output values from the *same* distribution used to initially sample outputs of P. While Lemma 1 allows for more general resampling, Lemma 2 gives a bound that is independent of the number of queries $\mathcal{D}$ makes after the reprogramming occurs.

Implications for a Variant of the Hidden Shift Problem. In the well-studied Hidden Shift problem [25], one is asked to find an unknown shift s by querying an oracle for a (typically injective) function f on a group G along with an oracle for the shifted function $f_s(x) = f(x \cdot s)$. If both oracles are classical, this problem has query complexity superpolynomial in $\log |G|$. If both oracles are quantum, then the query complexity is polynomial [10] but the algorithmic difficulty appears to depend critically on the structure of G (e.g., while $G = \mathbb{Z}_2^n$ is easy [22], $G = S_n$ appears to be intractable [2]).

The obvious connection between the Hidden Shift problem and security of Even-Mansour in general groups has been considered before [2,6,15]. In our case, it leads us to define two natural variants of the Hidden Shift problem:

1. "post-quantum" Hidden Shift: the oracle for f is quantum while the oracle for f_s is classical;
2. "two-sided" Hidden Shift: in place of f_s, use $f_{s_1,s_2}(x) = f(x \cdot s_1) \cdot s_2$; if f is a permutation, grant access to f^{-1} and f_{s_1,s_2}^{-1} as well.

These two variants can be considered jointly or separately and, for either variant, one can consider worst-case or average-case settings [2]. Our main result implies:

Theorem 2 (informal). *Solving the post-quantum Hidden Shift problem on any group G requires a number of queries that is superpolynomial in $\log |G|$. This holds for both the one-sided and two-sided versions of the problem, and for both the worst-case and the average-case settings.*

Theorem 2 follows from the proof of Theorem 1 via a few straightforward observations. First, an inspection of the proof shows that the particular structure of the underlying group (i.e., the XOR operation on $\{0,1\}^n$) is not relevant; the proof works identically for any group, simply replacing 2^n with $|G|$ in the bounds. The two-sided case of Theorem 2 then follows almost immediately: worst-case search is at least as hard as average-case search, and average-case search is at least as hard as average-case decision, which is precisely Theorem 1 (with the appropriate underlying group). Finally, as noted earlier, an appropriate analogue of Theorem 1 also holds in the "forward-only" case where $E_k(x) = P(x \oplus k)$ and P is a random function. This yields the one-sided case of Theorem 2.

1.2 Paper Organization

In Sect. 2 we state the technical lemmas needed for our main result. In Sect. 3 we prove Theorem 1, showing post-quantum security of the Even-Mansour cipher (both the two-key and one-key variants), based on the technical lemmas. In Sect. 4 we prove the technical lemmas themselves. Finally, in Appendix A, we give a proof of post-quantum security for the one-key, "forward-only" variant of Even-Mansour (also considered by Jaeger et al. [16]). While this is a relatively straightforward adaptation of the proof of our main result, it does not follow directly from it; moreover, it is substantially simpler and so may serve as a good warm-up for the reader before tackling our main result.

2 Reprogramming Lemmas

In this section we collect some technical lemmas that we will need for the proof of Theorem 1. We first discuss a particular extension of the "blinding lemma" of Alagic et al. [1, Theorem 11], which formalizes Lemma 1. We then state a generalization of the "reprogramming lemma" of Grilo et al. [12], which formalizes Lemma 2. The complete proofs of these technical results are given in Sect. 4.

We frequently consider adversaries with quantum access to some function $f : \{0,1\}^n \to \{0,1\}^m$. This means the adversary is given access to a black-box gate implementing the $(n + m)$-qubit unitary operator $|x\rangle|y\rangle \mapsto |x\rangle|y \oplus f(x)\rangle$.

2.1 Arbitrary Reprogramming

Consider a reprogramming experiment that proceeds as follows. First, a distinguisher $\mathcal{D}$ specifies an arbitrary function F along with a probabilistic algorithm $\mathcal{B}$ which describes how to reprogram F. Specifically, the output of $\mathcal{B}$ is a set of points B_1 at which F may be reprogrammed, along with the values the function should take at those potentially reprogrammed points. Then $\mathcal{D}$ is given quantum access to either F or the reprogrammed version of F, and its goal is to determine which is the case. When $\mathcal{D}$ is done making its oracle queries, it is also given the randomness that was used to run $\mathcal{B}$. Intuitively, the only way $\mathcal{D}$ can tell if its oracle has been reprogrammed is by querying with significant amplitude on some point in B_1. We bound $\mathcal{D}$'s advantage in terms of the probability that any particular value lies in the set B_1 defined by $\mathcal{B}$'s output.

By suitably modifying the proof of Alagic et al. [1, Theorem 11], one can show that the distinguishing probability of $\mathcal{D}$ in the scenario described above is at most $2q \cdot \sqrt{\epsilon}$, where q is an upper bound on the number of oracle queries and

ϵ is an upper bound on the probability that any given input x is reprogrammed (i.e., that $x \in B_1$). However, that result is only proved for distinguishers with a fixed upper bound on the number of queries they make. To obtain a tighter bound for our application, we need a version of the result for distinguishers that may *adaptively* choose how many queries they make based on outcomes of intermediate measurements. We recover the aforementioned bound in the case where we now let q denote the number of queries made by $\mathcal{D}$ *in expectation*.

For a function $F : \{0,1\}^m \to \{0,1\}^n$ and a set $B \subset \{0,1\}^m \times \{0,1\}^n$ such that each $x \in \{0,1\}^m$ is the first element of at most one tuple in B, define

$$F^{(B)}(x) := \begin{cases} y & \text{if } (x,y) \in B \\ F(x) & \text{otherwise.} \end{cases}$$

We prove the following in Sect. 4.1:

Lemma 3 (Formal version of Lemma 1). *Let $\mathcal{D}$ be a distinguisher in the following experiment:*

Phase 1: *$\mathcal{D}$ outputs descriptions of a function $F_0 = F : \{0,1\}^m \to \{0,1\}^n$ and a randomized algorithm $\mathcal{B}$ whose output is a set $B \subset \{0,1\}^m \times \{0,1\}^n$ where each $x \in \{0,1\}^m$ is the first element of at most one tuple in B. Let $B_1 = \{x \mid \exists y : (x,y) \in B\}$ and $\epsilon = \max_{x \in \{0,1\}^m} \{\Pr_{B \leftarrow \mathcal{B}}[x \in B_1]\}$.*
Phase 2: *$\mathcal{B}$ is run to obtain B. Let $F_1 = F^{(B)}$. A uniform bit b is chosen, and $\mathcal{D}$ is given quantum access to F_b.*
Phase 3: *$\mathcal{D}$ loses access to F_b, and receives the randomness r used to invoke $\mathcal{B}$ in phase 2. Then $\mathcal{D}$ outputs a guess b'.*

For any $\mathcal{D}$ making q queries in expectation when its oracle is F_0, it holds that

$$|\Pr[\mathcal{D} \text{ outputs } 1 \mid b = 1] - \Pr[\mathcal{D} \text{ outputs } 1 \mid b = 0]| \leq 2q \cdot \sqrt{\epsilon}.$$

2.2 Resampling

Here, we consider the following experiment: first, a distinguisher $\mathcal{D}$ is given quantum access to an oracle for a random function F; then, in the second stage, F may be "reprogrammed" so its value on a single, uniform point s is changed to an independent, uniform value. Because the distribution of $F(s)$ is the same both before and after any reprogramming, we refer to this as "resampling." The goal for $\mathcal{D}$ is to determine whether or not its oracle was resampled. Intuitively, the only way $\mathcal{D}$ can tell if this is the case—even if it is given s and unbounded access to the oracle in the second stage—is if $\mathcal{D}$ happened to put a large amplitude on s in some query to the oracle in the first stage. We now formalize this intuition.

We begin by establishing notation and recalling a result of Grilo et al. [12]. Given a function $F : \{0,1\}^m \to \{0,1\}^n$ and $s \in \{0,1\}^m$, $y \in \{0,1\}^n$, define the "reprogrammed" function $F_{s \mapsto y} : \{0,1\}^m \to \{0,1\}^n$ as

$$F_{s \mapsto y}(w) = \begin{cases} y & \text{if } w = s \\ F(w) & \text{otherwise.} \end{cases}$$

The following is a special case of [12, Prop. 1]:

Lemma 4 (Resampling for random functions). *Let $\mathcal{D}$ be a distinguisher in the following experiment:*

Phase 1: *A uniform $F : \{0,1\}^m \to \{0,1\}^n$ is chosen, and $\mathcal{D}$ is given quantum access to $F_0 = F$.*

Phase 2: *Uniform $s \in \{0,1\}^m$, $y \in \{0,1\}^n$ are chosen, and we let $F_1 = F_{s \mapsto y}$. A uniform bit b is chosen, and $\mathcal{D}$ is given s and quantum access to F_b. Then $\mathcal{D}$ outputs a guess b'.*

For any $\mathcal{D}$ making at most q queries to F_0 in phase 1, it holds that

$$|\Pr[\mathcal{D} \text{ outputs } 1 \mid b = 1] - \Pr[\mathcal{D} \text{ outputs } 1 \mid b = 0]| \leq 1.5\sqrt{q/2^m}.$$

We extend the above to the case of two-way accessible, random *permutations*. Now, a random permutation $P : \{0,1\}^n \to \{0,1\}^n$ is chosen in the first phase; in the second phase, P may be reprogrammed by swapping the outputs corresponding to two uniform inputs. For $a, b \in \{0,1\}^n$, let $\mathsf{swap}_{a,b} : \{0,1\}^n \to \{0,1\}^n$ be the permutation that maps $a \mapsto b$ and $b \mapsto a$ but is otherwise the identity. We prove the following in Sect. 4.2:

Lemma 5 (Formal version of Lemma 2). *Let $\mathcal{D}$ be a distinguisher in the following experiment:*

Phase 1: *A uniform permutation $P : \{0,1\}^n \to \{0,1\}^n$ is chosen, and $\mathcal{D}$ is given quantum access to $P_0 = P$ and $P_0^{-1} = P^{-1}$.*

Phase 2: *Uniform $s_0, s_1 \in \{0,1\}^n$ are chosen, and we let $P_1 = P \circ \mathsf{swap}_{s_0,s_1}$. Uniform $b \in \{0,1\}$ is chosen, and $\mathcal{D}$ is given s_0, s_1, and quantum access to P_b, P_b^{-1}. Then $\mathcal{D}$ outputs a guess b'.*

For any $\mathcal{D}$ making at most q queries (combined) to P_0, P_0^{-1} in the first phase, $|\Pr[\mathcal{D} \text{ outputs } 1 \mid b = 1] - \Pr[\mathcal{D} \text{ outputs } 1 \mid b = 0]| \leq 4\sqrt{q/2^n}.$

3   Post-Quantum Security of Even-Mansour

We now establish the post-quantum security of the Even-Mansour cipher based on the lemmas from the previous section. Recall that the Even-Mansour cipher is defined as $E_k(x) := P(x \oplus k_1) \oplus k_2$, where $P : \{0,1\}^n \to \{0,1\}^n$ is a public random permutation and $k = (k_1, k_2) \in \{0,1\}^{2n}$ is a key. Our proof assumes only that the marginal distributions of k_1 and k_2 are each uniform. This covers the original Even-Mansour cipher [11] where k is uniform over $\{0,1\}^{2n}$, as well as the one-key variant [9] where k_1 is uniform and then k_2 is set equal to k_1.

For E_k to be efficiently invertible, the permutation P must itself support efficient inversion; that is, the oracle for P must be accessible in both the forward and inverse directions. We thus consider adversaries $\mathcal{A}$ who can access both the cipher E_k and the permutation P in both the forward and inverse directions. The goal of $\mathcal{A}$ is to distinguish this world from the ideal world in which it interacts with independent random permutations R, P. In this section, it will be implicit in our notation that all oracles are two-way accessible.

In the following, we let $\mathcal{P}_n$ be the set of all permutations of $\{0,1\}^n$. We write $E_k[P]$ to denote the Even-Mansour cipher using permutation P and key k; we do this both to emphasize the dependence on P, and to enable references to Even-Mansour with a permutation other than P. Our main result is as follows:

Theorem 3 (Theorem 1, restated). *Let D be a distribution over $k = (k_1, k_2)$ such that the marginal distributions of k_1 and k_2 are each uniform, and let $\mathcal{A}$ be an adversary making q_E classical queries to its first oracle and q_P quantum queries to its second oracle. Then*

$$\left| \Pr_{\substack{k \leftarrow D \\ P \leftarrow \mathcal{P}_n}} \left[\mathcal{A}^{E_k[P],P}(1^n) = 1 \right] - \Pr_{R,P \leftarrow \mathcal{P}_n} \left[\mathcal{A}^{R,P}(1^n) = 1 \right] \right|$$

$$\leq 10 \cdot 2^{-n/2} \left(q_E \sqrt{q_P} + q_P \sqrt{q_E} \right).$$

Proof. Without loss of generality, we assume $\mathcal{A}$ never makes a redundant classical query; that is, once it learns an input/output pair (x, y) by making a query to its classical oracle, it never again submits the query x (respectively, y) to the forward (respectively, inverse) direction of that oracle.

We divide an execution of $\mathcal{A}$ into $q_E + 1$ stages $0, \ldots, q_E$, where the jth stage corresponds to the time between the jth and $(j+1)$st classical queries of $\mathcal{A}$. In particular, the 0th stage corresponds to the period of time before $\mathcal{A}$ makes its first classical query, and the q_Eth stage corresponds to the period of time after $\mathcal{A}$ makes its last classical query. We allow $\mathcal{A}$ to adaptively distribute its q_P quantum queries between these stages arbitrarily. We let $q_{P,j}$ denote the expected number of queries $\mathcal{A}$ makes in the jth stage in the ideal world $\mathcal{A}^{R,P}$; note that $\sum_{j=0}^{q_E} q_{P,j} = q_P$.

We denote the ith classical query of $\mathcal{A}$ by (x_i, y_i, b_i), where $b_i = 0$ means that $\mathcal{A}$ queried x_i in the forward direction and received response y_i, and $b_i = 1$ means that $\mathcal{A}$ queried y_i in the inverse direction and received response x_i. Let $T_j = \big((x_1, y_1, b_1), \ldots, (x_j, y_j, b_j) \big)$ be the ordered list describing the first j classical queries made by $\mathcal{A}$. We use "$\prod$" to denote sequential composition of operations, i.e., $\prod_{i=1}^n f_i = f_1 \circ \cdots \circ f_n$. (Note that order matters, since in general composition of operators is not commutative.) Recall that $\mathsf{swap}_{a,b}$ swaps a and b. Define:

$$\overrightarrow{S}_{T_j,P,k} \overset{\text{def}}{=} \prod_{i=1}^{j} \mathsf{swap}^{1-b_i}_{P(x_i \oplus k_1), y_i \oplus k_2}$$

$$\overrightarrow{Q}_{T_j,P,k} \overset{\text{def}}{=} \prod_{i=1}^{j} \mathsf{swap}^{1-b_i}_{x_i \oplus k_1, P^{-1}(y_i \oplus k_2)}$$

$$\overleftarrow{S}_{T_j,P,k} \overset{\text{def}}{=} \prod_{i=j}^{1} \mathsf{swap}^{b_i}_{P(x_i \oplus k_1), y_i \oplus k_2}$$

$$\overleftarrow{Q}_{T_j,P,k} \overset{\text{def}}{=} \prod_{i=j}^{1} \text{swap}_{x_i \oplus k_1, P^{-1}(y_i \oplus k_2)}^{b_i}$$

where, as usual, f^0 is the identity and $f^1 = f$. Finally, define

$$P_{T_j,k} \overset{\text{def}}{=} \overleftarrow{S}_{T_j,P,k} \circ P \circ \overrightarrow{Q}_{T_j,P,k}. \tag{1}$$

Since, for any P, x_1, y_1, x_2, y_2, it holds that

$$\text{swap}_{P(x_1),P(y_1)} \circ \text{swap}_{P(x_2),P(y_2)} \circ P = \text{swap}_{P(x_1),P(y_1)} \circ P \circ \text{swap}_{x_2,y_2}$$
$$= P \circ \text{swap}_{x_1,y_1} \circ \text{swap}_{x_2,y_2},$$

we also have

$$P_{T_j,k} = \overleftarrow{S}_{T_j,P,k} \circ \overrightarrow{S}_{T_j,P,k} \circ P = P \circ \overleftarrow{Q}_{T_j,P,k} \circ \overrightarrow{Q}_{T_j,P,k}. \tag{2}$$

Intuitively, when the $\{x_i\}$ are distinct and the $\{y_i\}$ are distinct, $P_{T_j,k}$ is a "small" modification of P for which $E_k[P_{T_j,k}](x_i) = y_i$ for all i. (Note, however, that this may fail to hold if there is an "internal collision," i.e., $P(x_i \oplus k_1) = y_j \oplus k_2$ for some $i \neq j$. But such collisions occur with low probability over choice of k_1, k_2.)

We now define a sequence of experiments $\mathbf{H}_j$, for $j = 0, \ldots, q_E$.

Experiment $\mathbf{H}_j$. Sample $R, P \leftarrow \mathcal{P}_n$ and $k \leftarrow D$. Then:

1. Run $\mathcal{A}$, answering its classical queries using R and its quantum queries using P, stopping immediately *before* its $(j+1)$st classical query. Let $T_j = ((x_1, y_1, b_1), \ldots, (x_j, y_j, b_j))$ be the ordered list of classical queries/answers.
2. For the remainder of the execution of $\mathcal{A}$, answer its classical queries using $E_k[P]$ and its quantum queries using $P_{T_j,k}$.

We can compactly represent $\mathbf{H}_j$ as the experiment in which $\mathcal{A}$'s queries are answered using the oracle sequence

$$\underbrace{P, R, P, \cdots, R, P}_{j \text{ classical queries}}, \underbrace{E_k[P], P_{T_j,k}, \cdots, E_k[P], P_{T_j,k}}_{q_E - j \text{ classical queries}}.$$

Each appearance of R or $E_k[P]$ indicates a single classical query. Each appearance of P or $P_{T_j,k}$ indicates a stage during which $\mathcal{A}$ makes multiple (quantum) queries to that oracle but no queries to its classical oracle. Observe that $\mathbf{H}_0$ corresponds to the execution of $\mathcal{A}$ in the real world, i.e., $\mathcal{A}^{E_k[P],P}$, and that $\mathbf{H}_{q_E}$ is the execution of $\mathcal{A}$ in the ideal world, i.e., $\mathcal{A}^{R,P}$.

For $j = 0, \ldots, q_E - 1$, we introduce additional experiments $\mathbf{H}'_j$:

Experiment $\mathbf{H}'_j$. Sample $R, P \leftarrow \mathcal{P}_n$ and $k \leftarrow D$. Then:

1. Run $\mathcal{A}$, answering its classical queries using R and its quantum queries using P, stopping immediately *after* its $(j+1)$st classical query. Let $T_{j+1} = ((x_1, y_1, b_1), \ldots, (x_{j+1}, y_{j+1}, b_{j+1}))$ be the ordered list indicating $\mathcal{A}$'s classical queries/answers.

2. For the remainder of the execution of $\mathcal{A}$, answer its classical queries using $E_k[P]$ and its quantum queries using $P_{T_{j+1},k}$.

Thus, $\mathbf{H}'_j$ corresponds to running $\mathcal{A}$ using the oracle sequence

$$\underbrace{P, R, P, \cdots, R, P,}_{j \text{ classical queries}} R, P_{T_{j+1},k}, \underbrace{E_k[P], P_{T_{j+1},k} \cdots, E_k[P], P_{T_{j+1},k}}_{q_E - j - 1 \text{ classical queries}} .$$

In Lemmas 6 and 7, we establish bounds on the distinguishability of $\mathbf{H}'_j$ and $\mathbf{H}_{j+1}$, as well as $\mathbf{H}_j$ and $\mathbf{H}'_j$. For $0 \leq j < q_E$ these give:

$$\left| \Pr[\mathcal{A}(\mathbf{H}'_j) = 1] - \Pr[\mathcal{A}(\mathbf{H}_{j+1}) = 1] \right| \leq 2 \cdot q_{P,j+1} \cdot \sqrt{\frac{2 \cdot (j+1)}{2^n}}.$$

$$\left| \Pr[\mathcal{A}(\mathbf{H}_j) = 1] - \Pr[\mathcal{A}(\mathbf{H}'_j) = 1] \right| \leq 8 \cdot \sqrt{\frac{q_P}{2^n}} + 2q_E \cdot 2^{-n}$$

Using the above, we have

$$\left| \Pr[\mathcal{A}(\mathbf{H}_0) = 1] - \Pr[\mathcal{A}(\mathbf{H}_{q_E}) = 1] \right|$$

$$\leq \sum_{j=0}^{q_E - 1} \left(8 \cdot \sqrt{\frac{q_P}{2^n}} + 2q_E \cdot 2^{-n} + 2 \cdot q_{P,j+1} \sqrt{\frac{2 \cdot (j+1)}{2^n}} \right)$$

$$\leq 2q_E^2 \cdot 2^{-n} + \sum_{j=0}^{q_E - 1} \left(8 \cdot \sqrt{\frac{q_P}{2^n}} + 2 \cdot q_{P,j+1} \sqrt{\frac{2q_E}{2^n}} \right)$$

$$\leq 2q_E^2 \cdot 2^{-n} + 2^{-n/2} \cdot \left(8q_E \sqrt{q_P} + 2 \cdot q_P \sqrt{2q_E} \right).$$

We now simplify the bound further. If $q_P = 0$, then E_k and R are perfectly indistinguishable and the theorem holds; thus, we may assume $q_P \geq 1$. We can also assume $q_E < 2^{n/2}$ since otherwise the bound is larger than 1. Under these assumptions, we have $q_E^2 \cdot 2^{-n} \leq q_E \cdot 2^{-n/2} \leq q_E \sqrt{q_P} \cdot 2^{-n/2}$ and so

$$2q_E^2 \cdot 2^{-n} + 2^{-n/2} \left(8q_E \sqrt{q_P} + 2q_P \sqrt{2q_E} \right)$$

$$\leq 2 \cdot q_E \sqrt{q_P} \cdot 2^{-n/2} + 2^{-n/2} \left(8q_E \sqrt{q_P} + 2q_P \sqrt{2q_E} \right)$$

$$\leq 10 \cdot 2^{-n/2} \left(q_E \sqrt{q_P} + q_P \sqrt{q_E} \right),$$

as claimed. $\square$

To complete the proof of Theorem 3, we now show that $\mathbf{H}'_j$ is indistinguishable from to $\mathbf{H}_{j+1}$ and $\mathbf{H}_j$ is indistinguishable from $\mathbf{H}'_j$.

Lemma 6. *For $j = 0, \ldots, q_E - 1$,*

$$\Pr[\mathcal{A}(\mathbf{H}'_j) = 1] - \Pr[\mathcal{A}(\mathbf{H}_{j+1}) = 1]| \leq 2 \cdot q_{P,j+1} \sqrt{2 \cdot (j+1)/2^n},$$

where $q_{P,j+1}$ is the expected number of queries $\mathcal{A}$ makes to P in the $(j+1)$st stage in the ideal world (i.e., in $\mathbf{H}_{q_E}$.)

Proof. Recall we can write the oracle sequences defined by $\mathbf{H}'_j$ and $\mathbf{H}_{j+1}$ as

$$\mathbf{H}'_j : \underbrace{P, R, P, \cdots, R, P, \quad R, P_{T_{j+1},k},}_{j \text{ classical queries}} \underbrace{E_k[P], P_{T_{j+1},k}, \cdots, E_k[P], P_{T_{j+1},k}}_{q_E - j - 1 \text{ classical queries}}$$

$$\mathbf{H}_{j+1} : \underbrace{P, R, P, \cdots, R, P, \quad R, P,}_{j \text{ classical queries}} \underbrace{E_k[P], P_{T_{j+1},k}, \cdots, E_k[P], P_{T_{j+1},k}}_{q_E - j - 1 \text{ classical queries}} .$$

Let $\mathcal{A}$ be a distinguisher between $\mathbf{H}'_j$ and $\mathbf{H}_{j+1}$. We construct from $\mathcal{A}$ a distinguisher $\mathcal{D}$ for the blinding experiment from Lemma 3:

Phase 1: $\mathcal{D}$ samples $P, R \leftarrow \mathcal{P}_n$. It then runs $\mathcal{A}$, answering its quantum queries using P and its classical queries using R, until after it responds to $\mathcal{A}$'s $(j + 1)$st classical query. Let $T_{j+1} = ((x_1, y_1, b_1), \ldots, (x_{j+1}, y_{j+1}, b_{j+1}))$ be the list of classical queries/answers. $\mathcal{D}$ defines $F(t, x) := P^t(x)$ for $t \in \{1, -1\}$. It also defines the following randomized algorithm $\mathcal{B}$: sample $k \leftarrow D$ and then compute the set B of input/output pairs to be reprogrammed so that $F^{(B)}(t, x) = P^t_{T_{j+1},k}(x)$ for all t, x.

Phase 2: $\mathcal{B}$ is run to generate B, and $\mathcal{D}$ is given quantum access to an oracle F_b. $\mathcal{D}$ resumes running $\mathcal{A}$, answering its quantum queries using $P^t = F_b(t, \cdot)$. Phase 2 ends when $\mathcal{A}$ makes its next (i.e., $(j + 2)$nd) classical query.

Phase 3: $\mathcal{D}$ is given the randomness used by $\mathcal{B}$ to generate k. It resumes running $\mathcal{A}$, answering its classical queries using $E_k[P]$ and its quantum queries using $P_{T_{j+1},k}$. Finally, it outputs whatever $\mathcal{A}$ outputs.

Observe that $\mathcal{D}$ is a valid distinguisher for the reprogramming experiment of Lemma 3. It is immediate that if $b = 0$ (i.e., $\mathcal{D}$'s oracle in phase 2 is $F_0 = F$), then $\mathcal{A}$'s output is identically distributed to its output in $\mathbf{H}_{j+1}$, whereas if $b = 1$ (i.e., $\mathcal{D}$'s oracle in phase 2 is $F_1 = F^{(B)}$), then $\mathcal{A}$'s output is identically distributed to its output in $\mathbf{H}'_j$. It follows that $|\Pr[\mathcal{A}(\mathbf{H}'_j) = 1] - \Pr[\mathcal{A}(\mathbf{H}_{j+1}) = 1]|$ is equal to the distinguishing advantage of $\mathcal{D}$ in the reprogramming experiment. To bound this quantity using Lemma 3, we bound the reprogramming probability ϵ and the expected number of queries made by $\mathcal{D}$ in phase 2 (when $F = F_0$.)

The reprogramming probability ϵ can be bounded using the definition of $P_{T_{j+1},k}$ and the fact that $F^{(B)}(t, x) = P^t_{T_{j+1},k}$. Fixing P and T_{j+1}, the probability that any given (t, x) is reprogrammed is at most the probability (over k) that it is in the set

$$\left\{(1, x_i \oplus k_1), (1, P^{-1}(y_i \oplus k_2)), (-1, P(x_i \oplus k_1)), (-1, y_i \oplus k_2)\right\}_{i=1}^{j+1} .$$

Taking a union bound and using the fact that the marginal distributions of k_1 and k_2 are each uniform, we get $\epsilon \leq 2(j + 1)/2^n$.

The expected number of queries made by $\mathcal{D}$ in Phase 2 when $F = F_0$ is equal to the expected number of queries made by $\mathcal{A}$ in its $(j + 1)$st stage in $\mathbf{H}_{j+1}$. Since $\mathbf{H}_{j+1}$ and $\mathbf{H}_{q_E}$ are identical until after the $(j + 1)$st stage is complete, this is precisely $q_{P,j+1}$. □

Lemma 7. *For* $j = 0, \ldots, q_E$,

$$|\Pr[\mathcal{A}(\mathbf{H}_j) = 1] - \Pr[\mathcal{A}(\mathbf{H}'_j) = 1]| \leq 8 \cdot \sqrt{\frac{q_P}{2^n}} + 2q_E \cdot 2^{-n}.$$

Proof. Recall that we can write the oracle sequences defined by $\mathbf{H}_j$ and $\mathbf{H}'_j$ as

$$\mathbf{H}_j: \underbrace{P, R, P, \cdots, R, P,}_{} \quad \underbrace{E_k[P], P_{T_j,k}, \quad E_k[P], P_{T_j,k} \quad, \cdots, E_k[P], P_{T_j,k}}_{}$$

$$\mathbf{H}'_j: \underbrace{P, R, P, \cdots, R, P,}_{j \text{ classical queries}} \quad R, \quad \underbrace{P_{T_{j+1},k}, \; E_k[P], P_{T_{j+1},k}, \cdots, E_k[P], P_{T_{j+1},k}}_{q_E-j-1 \text{ classical queries}}.$$

Let $\mathcal{A}$ be a distinguisher between $\mathbf{H}_j$ and $\mathbf{H}'_j$. We construct from $\mathcal{A}$ a distinguisher $\mathcal{D}$ for the reprogramming experiment of Lemma 5:

Phase 1: $\mathcal{D}$ is given quantum access to a permutation P. It samples $R \leftarrow \mathcal{P}_n$ and then runs $\mathcal{A}$, answering its quantum queries with P and its classical queries with R (in the appropriate directions), until $\mathcal{A}$ submits its $(j+1)$st classical query x_{j+1} in the forward direction[2] (i.e., $b_{j+1} = 0$). Let $T_j = ((x_1, y_1, b_1), \cdots, (x_j, y_j, b_j))$ be the list of classical queries/answers thus far.

Phase 2: Now $\mathcal{D}$ receives $s_0, s_1 \in \{0,1\}^n$ and quantum oracle access to a permutation P_b. Then $\mathcal{D}$ sets $k_1 := s_0 \oplus x_{j+1}$, chooses $k_2 \leftarrow D_{|k_1}$ (where this represents the conditional distribution on k_2 given k_1), and sets $k := (k_1, k_2)$. $\mathcal{D}$ continues running $\mathcal{A}$, answering its remaining classical queries (including the $(j+1)$st one) using $E_k[P_b]$, and its remaining quantum queries using

$$(P_b)_{T_j,k} = \overleftarrow{S}_{T_j,P_b,k} \circ \overrightarrow{S}_{T_j,P_b,k} \circ P_b.$$

Finally, $\mathcal{D}$ outputs whatever $\mathcal{A}$ outputs.

Note that although $\mathcal{D}$ makes additional queries to P_b in phase 2 (to determine $P_b(x_1 \oplus k_1), \ldots, P_b(x_j \oplus k_1)$), the bound of Lemma 5 only depends on the number of quantum queries $\mathcal{D}$ makes in phase 1, which is at most q_P.

We now analyze the execution of $\mathcal{D}$ in the two cases of the game of Lemma 5: $b = 0$ (no reprogramming) and $b = 1$ (reprogramming). In both cases, P and R are independent, uniform permutations, and $\mathcal{A}$ is run with quantum oracle P and classical oracle R until it makes its $(j+1)$st classical query; thus, through the end of phase 1, the above execution of $\mathcal{A}$ is consistent with both $\mathbf{H}_j$ and $\mathbf{H}'_j$.

At the start of phase 2, uniform $s_0, s_1 \in \{0,1\}^n$ are chosen. Since $\mathcal{D}$ sets $k_1 := s_0 \oplus x_{j+1}$, the distribution of k_1 is uniform and hence k is distributed according to D. The two cases ($b = 0$ and $b = 1$) now begin to diverge.

Case $b = 0$ (No Reprogramming). In this case, $\mathcal{A}$'s remaining classical queries (including its $(j+1)$st classical query) are answered using $E_k[P_0] = E_k[P]$, and its remaining quantum queries are answered using $(P_0)_{T_j,k} = P_{T_j,k}$. The output of $\mathcal{A}$ is thus distributed identically to its output in $\mathbf{H}_j$ in this case.

Case $b = 1$ (Reprogramming). In this case, we have

$$P_b = P_1 = P \circ \mathsf{swap}_{s_0,s_1} = \mathsf{swap}_{P(s_0),P(s_1)} \circ P = \mathsf{swap}_{P(x_{j+1}\oplus k_1),P(s_1)} \circ P. \quad (3)$$

---

[2] We assume for simplicity that this query is in the forward direction, but the case where it is in the inverse direction can be handled entirely symmetrically (using the fact that the marginal distribution of k_2 is uniform). The strings s_0 and s_1 are in that case replaced by $P_b(s_0)$ and $P_b(s_1)$. See Appendix B.2 for details.

The response to $\mathcal{A}$'s $(j+1)$st classical query is thus

$$y_{j+1} \stackrel{\text{def}}{=} E_k[P_1](x_{j+1}) = P_1(x_{j+1} \oplus k_1) \oplus k_2 = P_1(s_0) \oplus k_2 = P(s_1) \oplus k_2 . \quad (4)$$

The remaining classical queries of $\mathcal{A}$ are then answered using $E_k[P_1]$, while its remaining quantum queries are answered using $(P_1)_{T_j,k}$. If we let Expt_j refer to the experiment in which $\mathcal{D}$ executes $\mathcal{A}$ as a subroutine when $b = 1$, it follows from Lemma 5 that

$$\left| \Pr[\mathcal{A}(\mathbf{H}_j) = 1] - \Pr[\mathcal{A}(\mathsf{Expt}_j) = 1] \right| \leq 4\sqrt{q_P/2^n}. \quad (5)$$

We now define three events:

1. bad_1 is the event that $y_{j+1} \in \{y_1, \ldots, y_j\}$.
2. bad_2 is the event that $s_1 \oplus k_1 \in \{x_1, \ldots, x_j\}$.
3. bad_3 is the event that, in phase 2, $\mathcal{A}$ queries its classical oracle in the forward direction on $s_1 \oplus k_1$, or the inverse direction on $P(s_0) \oplus k_2$ (with result $s_1 \oplus k_1$).

Since $y_{j+1} = P(s_1) \oplus k_2$ is uniform (because k_2 is uniform and independent of P and s_1), it is immediate that $\Pr[\mathsf{bad}_1] \leq j/2^n$. Similarly, $s_1 \oplus k_1 = s_1 \oplus s_0 \oplus x_{j+1}$ is uniform, and so $\Pr[\mathsf{bad}_2] \leq j/2^n$. As for the last event, we have:

Claim. $\Pr[\mathsf{bad}_3] \leq (q_E - j)/2^n + 4\sqrt{q_P/2^n}$.

Proof. Consider the algorithm $\mathcal{D}'$ that behaves identically to $\mathcal{D}$ in phases 1 and 2, but then when $\mathcal{A}$ terminates outputs 1 iff event bad_3 occurred. When $b = 0$ (no reprogramming), the execution of $\mathcal{A}$ is independent of s_1, and so the probability that bad_3 occurs is at most $(q_E - j)/2^n$. Now observe that $\mathcal{D}'$ is a distinguisher for the reprogramming game of Lemma 5. The claim follows. $\qquad\square$

In Fig. 1, we show code for Expt_j and a related experiment Expt'_j. Note that Expt_j and Expt'_j are identical until either $\mathsf{bad}_1, \mathsf{bad}_2$, or bad_3 occur, and so by the fundamental lemma of game playing[3] [3] we have

$$\left| \Pr[\mathcal{A}(\mathsf{Expt}'_j) = 1] - \Pr[\mathcal{A}(\mathsf{Expt}_j) = 1] \right| \leq \Pr[\mathsf{bad}_1 \vee \mathsf{bad}_2 \vee \mathsf{bad}_3]$$
$$\leq 2q_E/2^n + 4\sqrt{q_P/2^n} . \quad (6)$$

We complete the proof by arguing that Expt'_j is identical to $\mathbf{H}'_j$:

1. In Expt'_j, the oracle Q used in line 12 is always equal to $P_{T_{j+1},k}$. When bad_1 or bad_2 occurs this is immediate (since then Q is set to $P_{T_{j+1},k}$ in line 11). But if bad_1 does not occur then Eq. (4) holds, and if bad_2 does not occur then for $i = 1, \ldots, j$ we have $x_i \oplus k_1 \neq s_0$ and $x_i \oplus k_1 \neq s_1$ (where the former

---

[3] This lemma is an information-theoretic result, and can be applied in our setting since everything we say in what follows holds even if $\mathcal{A}$ is given the entire function table for its quantum oracle Q in line 12.

---

1 $P, R \leftarrow \mathcal{P}_n$

2 Run $\mathcal{A}$ with quantum access to P and classical access to R, until $\mathcal{A}$ makes its $(j+1)$st classical query x_{j+1}; let T_j be as in the text

3 $s_0, s_1 \leftarrow \{0,1\}^n$, $P_1 := P \circ \mathrm{swap}_{s_0, s_1}$

4 $k_1 := s_0 \oplus x_{j+1}$, $k_2 \leftarrow D_{|k_1}$, $k := (k_1, k_2)$

5 $y_{j+1} := E_k[P_1](x_{j+1})$

6 $Q := (P_1)_{T_j, k}$

7 if $y_{j+1} \in \{y_1, \ldots, y_j\}$ then $\mathsf{bad}_1 := \mathrm{true}$, $\boxed{y_{j+1} \leftarrow \{0,1\}^n \setminus \{y_1, \ldots, y_j\}}$

8 Give y_{j+1} to $\mathcal{A}$ as the answer to its $(j+1)$st classical query

9 $T_{j+1} := ((x_1, y_1, b_1), \ldots, (x_{j+1}, y_{j+1}, b_{j+1}))$

10 if $s_1 \oplus k_1 \in \{x_1, \ldots, x_j\}$ then $\mathsf{bad}_2 := \mathrm{true}$

11 if $\mathsf{bad}_1 = \mathrm{true}$ or $\mathsf{bad}_2 = \mathrm{true}$ then $\boxed{Q := P_{T_{j+1}, k}}$

12 Continue running $\mathcal{A}$ with quantum access to Q and classical access to $\mathcal{O}/\mathcal{O}^{-1}$

---

13 $\underline{\mathcal{O}(x)}$

14 $y := E_k[P_1](x)$

15 if $x = s_1 \oplus k_1$ then

16 $\quad \mathsf{bad}_3 := \mathrm{true}$, $\boxed{y := E_k[P](x)}$

17 return y

18 $\underline{\mathcal{O}^{-1}(y)}$

19 $x := E_k^{-1}[P_1](y)$

20 if $x = s_1 \oplus k_1$ then

21 $\quad \mathsf{bad}_3 := \mathrm{true}$, $\boxed{x := E_k^{-1}[P](y)}$

22 return x

Fig. 1. Expt$'_j$ includes the boxed statements, whereas Expt$_j$ does not.

is because $x_{j+1} \oplus k_1 = s_0$ but $x_i \neq x_{j+1}$ by assumption, and the latter is by definition of bad_2). So $P_1(x_i \oplus k_1) = P(x_i \oplus k_1)$ for $i = 1, \ldots, j$, and thus

$$\overrightarrow{S}_{T_j, P_1, k} = \prod_{i=1}^{j} \mathrm{swap}_{P_1(x_i \oplus k_1), y_i \oplus k_2}^{1-b_i} = \prod_{i=1}^{j} \mathrm{swap}_{P(x_i \oplus k_1), y_i \oplus k_2}^{1-b_i} = \overrightarrow{S}_{T_j, P, k}$$

and

$$\overleftarrow{S}_{T_j, P_1, k} = \prod_{i=j}^{1} \mathrm{swap}_{P_1(x_i \oplus k_1), y_i \oplus k_2}^{b_i} = \prod_{i=j}^{1} \mathrm{swap}_{P(x_i \oplus k_1), y_i \oplus k_2}^{b_i} = \overleftarrow{S}_{T_j, P, k}.$$

Therefore

$$Q = (P_1)_{T_j, k} = \overleftarrow{S}_{T_j, P_1, k} \circ \overrightarrow{S}_{T_j, P_1, k} \circ P_1$$
$$= \overleftarrow{S}_{T_j, P, k} \circ \overrightarrow{S}_{T_j, P, k} \circ \mathrm{swap}_{P(x_{j+1} \oplus k_1), y_{j+1} \oplus k_2} \circ P$$
$$= \overleftarrow{S}_{T_{j+1}, P, k} \circ \overrightarrow{S}_{T_{j+1}, P, k} \circ P$$
$$= P_{T_{j+1}, k},$$

using Eqs. (3) and (4) and the fact that $b_{j+1} = 0$.

2. In Expt$'_j$, the value y_{j+1} is uniformly distributed in $\{0,1\}^n \setminus \{y_1, \ldots, y_j\}$. Indeed, we have already argued above that the value y_{j+1} computed in line 14

is uniform in $\{0,1\}^n$. But if that value lies in $\{y_1, \ldots, y_j\}$ (and so bad_1 occurs) then y_{j+1} is re-sampled uniformly from $\{0,1\}^n \setminus \{y_1, \ldots, y_j\}$ in line 7.

3. In Expt'_j, the response from oracle $\mathcal{O}(x)$ is always equal to $E_k[P](x)$. When bad_3 occurs this is immediate. But if bad_3 does not occur then $x \neq s_1 \oplus k_1$; we also know that $x \neq s_0 \oplus k_1 = x_{j+1}$ by assumption. But then $P_1(x \oplus k_1) = P(x \oplus k_1)$ and so $E_k[P_1](x) = E_k[P](x)$. A similar argument shows that the response from $\mathcal{O}^{-1}(y)$ is always $E_k^{-1}[P](y)$.

Syntactically rewriting Expt'_j using the above observations yields an experiment that is identical to $\mathbf{H}'_j$. (See Appendix B.1 for further details.) Lemma 7 thus follows from Eqs. (5) and (6). $\qquad\qquad\qquad\qquad\qquad\qquad\qquad\qquad\qquad\qquad\qquad\quad$ □

4 Proofs of the Technical Lemmas

In this section, we give the proofs of our technical lemmas: the "arbitrary reprogramming lemma" (Lemma 3) and the "resampling lemma" (Lemma 5).

4.1 Proof of the Arbitrary Reprogramming Lemma

Lemma 3 allows for distinguishers that choose the number of queries they make adaptively, e.g., depending on the oracle provided and the outcomes of any measurements, and the bound is in terms of the number of queries $\mathcal{D}$ makes *in expectation*. As discussed in Sect. 1.1, the ability to directly handle such adaptive distinguishers is necessary for our proof, and to our knowledge has not been addressed before. To formally reason about adaptive distinguishers, we model the intermediate operations of the distinguisher and the measurements it makes as *quantum channels*. With this as our goal, we first recall some necessary background and establish some notation.

Recall that a density matrix ρ is a positive semidefinite matrix with unit trace. A quantum channel—the most general transformation between density matrices allowed by quantum theory—is a completely positive, trace-preserving, linear map. The quantum channel corresponding to the unitary operation U is the map $\rho \mapsto U\rho U^\dagger$. Another type of quantum channel is a *pinching*, which corresponds to the operation of making a measurement. Specializing to the only kind of pinching needed in our proof, consider the measurement of a single-qubit register C given by the projectors $\{\Pi_0, \Pi_1\}$ with $\Pi_b = |b\rangle\langle b|_C$. This corresponds to the pinching $\mathcal{M}_C$ where

$$\mathcal{M}_C(\rho) = \Pi_0 \rho \Pi_0 + \Pi_1 \rho \Pi_1.$$

Observe that a pinching only produces the post-measurement state, and does not separately give the outcome (i.e., the result 0 or 1).

Consider a quantum algorithm $\mathcal{D}$ with access to an oracle $\mathcal{O}$ operating on registers X, Y (so $\mathcal{O}|x\rangle|y\rangle = |x\rangle|y \oplus \mathcal{O}(x)\rangle$). We define the unitary $c\mathcal{O}$ for the *controlled* version of $\mathcal{O}$, operating on registers C, X, and Y (with C a single-qubit register), as

$$c\mathcal{O}|c\rangle|x\rangle|y\rangle = |c\rangle|x\rangle|y \oplus c \cdot \mathcal{O}(x)\rangle.$$

With this in place, we may now view an execution of $\mathcal{D}^O$ as follows. The algorithm uses registers C, X, Y, and E. Let $q_{\max}$ be an upper bound on the number of queries $\mathcal{D}$ ever makes. Then $\mathcal{D}$ applies the quantum channel

$$(\Phi \circ c\mathcal{O} \circ \mathcal{M}_C)^{q_{\max}} \tag{7}$$

to some initial state $\rho = \rho_0^{(0)}$. That is, for each of $q_{\max}$ iterations, $\mathcal{D}$ applies to its current state the pinching $\mathcal{M}_C$ followed by the controlled oracle $c\mathcal{O}$ and then an arbitrary quantum channel Φ (that we take to be the same in all iterations without loss of generality[4]) operating on all its registers. Finally, $\mathcal{D}$ applies a measurement to produce its final output. If we let $\rho_{i-1}^{(0)}$ denote the intermediate state immediately before the pinching is applied in the ith iteration, then $p_{i-1} = \mathrm{Tr}\left[|1\rangle\langle 1|_C\, \rho_{i-1}^{(0)}\right]$ represents the probability that the oracle is applied (or, equivalently, that a query is made) in the ith iteration, and so $q = \sum_{i=1}^{q_{\max}} p_{i-1}$ is the expected number of queries made by $\mathcal{D}$ when interacting with oracle $\mathcal{O}$.

Proof of Lemma 3. An execution of $\mathcal{D}$ takes the form of Eq. (7) up to a final measurement. For some fixed value of the randomness r used to run $\mathcal{B}$, set $\Upsilon_b = \Phi \circ c\mathcal{O}_{F_b} \circ \mathcal{M}_C$, and define

$$\rho_k \stackrel{\text{def}}{=} \left(\Upsilon_1^{q_{\max}-k} \circ \Upsilon_0^k\right)(\rho),$$

so that ρ_k is the final state if the first k queries are answered using a (controlled) F_0 oracle and then the remaining $q_{\max} - k$ queries are answered using a (controlled) F_1 oracle. Furthermore, we define $\rho_i^{(0)} = \Upsilon_0^i(\rho)$. Note also that $\rho_{q_{\max}}$ (resp., ρ_0) is the final state of the algorithm when the F_0 oracle (resp., F_1 oracle) is used the entire time. We bound $\mathbb{E}_r\left[\delta\left(|r\rangle\langle r| \otimes \rho_{q_{\max}}, |r\rangle\langle r| \otimes \rho_0\right)\right]$, where $\delta(\cdot, \cdot)$ denotes the trace distance.

Define $\tilde{F}^{(B)}(x) = F(x) \oplus F^{(B)}(x)$, and note that $\tilde{F}^{(B)}(x) = 0^n$ for $x \notin B_1$. Since trace distance is non-increasing under quantum channels, for any r we have

$$\delta\left(|r\rangle\langle r| \otimes \rho_k, |r\rangle\langle r| \otimes \rho_{k-1}\right) \leq \delta\left(c\mathcal{O}_{F_0} \circ \mathcal{M}_C\left(\rho_{k-1}^{(0)}\right), c\mathcal{O}_{F_1} \circ \mathcal{M}_C\left(\rho_{k-1}^{(0)}\right)\right)$$

$$= \delta\left(\mathcal{M}_C\left(\rho_{k-1}^{(0)}\right), c\mathcal{O}_{\tilde{F}^{(B)}} \circ \mathcal{M}_C\left(\rho_{k-1}^{(0)}\right)\right).$$

By definition of a controlled oracle,

$$c\mathcal{O}_{\tilde{F}^{(B)}} \circ \mathcal{M}_C\left(\rho_{k-1}^{(0)}\right) = c\mathcal{O}_{\tilde{F}^{(B)}}\left(|1\rangle\langle 1|_C\, \rho_{k-1}^{(0)}\, |1\rangle\langle 1|_C\right) + |0\rangle\langle 0|_C\, \rho_{k-1}^{(0)}\, |0\rangle\langle 0|_C$$

$$= \mathcal{O}_{\tilde{F}^{(B)}}\left(|1\rangle\langle 1|_C\, \rho_{k-1}^{(0)}\, |1\rangle\langle 1|_C\right) + |0\rangle\langle 0|_C\, \rho_{k-1}^{(0)}\, |0\rangle\langle 0|_C,$$

and thus

$$\delta\left(\mathcal{M}_C\left(\rho_{k-1}^{(0)}\right), c\mathcal{O}_{\tilde{F}^{(B)}} \circ \mathcal{M}_C\left(\rho_{k-1}^{(0)}\right)\right)$$

$$= \delta\left(|1\rangle\langle 1|_C\, \rho_{k-1}^{(0)}\, |1\rangle\langle 1|_C, \mathcal{O}_{\tilde{F}^{(B)}}\left(|1\rangle\langle 1|_C\, \rho_{k-1}^{(0)}\, |1\rangle\langle 1|_C\right)\right)$$

$$= p_{k-1} \cdot \delta\left(\sigma_{k-1}, \mathcal{O}_{\tilde{F}^{(B)}}(\sigma_{k-1})\right)$$

---

[4] This can be done by having a register serve as a counter that is incremented with each application of Φ.

where, recall, $p_{k-1} = \text{Tr}\left[|1\rangle\langle 1|_C\, \rho_{k-1}^{(0)}\right]$ is the probability that a query is made in the kth iteration, and we define the normalized state $\sigma_{k-1} \overset{\text{def}}{=} \frac{|1\rangle\langle 1|_C\, \rho_{k-1}^{(0)}\, |1\rangle\langle 1|_C}{p_{k-1}}$. Therefore,

$$\mathbb{E}_r\left[\delta\left(|r\rangle\langle r| \otimes \rho_{q_{\max}},\; |r\rangle\langle r| \otimes \rho_0\right)\right]$$

$$\leq \sum_{k=1}^{q_{\max}} \mathbb{E}_B\left[\delta((|r\rangle\langle r| \otimes \rho_k,\; |r\rangle\langle r| \otimes \rho_{k-1})\right]$$

$$\leq \sum_{k=1}^{q_{\max}} p_{k-1} \cdot \mathbb{E}_B\left[\delta\left(\sigma_{k-1},\; \mathcal{O}_{\tilde{F}(B)}\left(\sigma_{k-1}\right)\right)\right]$$

$$\leq q \cdot \max_{\sigma} \mathbb{E}_B\left[\delta\left(\sigma,\; \mathcal{O}_{\tilde{F}(B)}\left(\sigma\right)\right)\right], \tag{8}$$

where we write $\mathbb{E}_B$ for the expectation over the set B output by $\mathcal{B}$ in place of $\mathbb{E}_r$.

Since σ can be purified to some state $|\psi\rangle$, and $\delta(|\psi\rangle, |\psi'\rangle) \leq \||\psi\rangle - |\psi'\rangle\|_2$ for pure states $|\psi\rangle, |\psi'\rangle$, we have

$$\max_{\sigma} \mathbb{E}_B\left[\delta\left(\sigma,\; \mathcal{O}_{\tilde{F}(B)}\left(\sigma\right)\right)\right] \leq \max_{|\psi\rangle} \mathbb{E}_B\left[\delta\left(|\psi\rangle,\; \mathcal{O}_{\tilde{F}(B)}|\psi\rangle\right)\right]$$

$$\leq \max_{|\psi\rangle} \mathbb{E}_B\left[\||\psi\rangle - \mathcal{O}_{\tilde{F}(B)}|\psi\rangle\|_2\right].$$

Because $\mathcal{O}_{\tilde{F}(B)}$ acts as the identity on $(\mathbb{I} - \Pi_{B_1})|\psi\rangle$ for any $|\psi\rangle$, we have

$$\mathbb{E}_B\left[\||\psi\rangle - \mathcal{O}_{\tilde{F}(B)}|\psi\rangle\|_2\right]$$
$$= \mathbb{E}_B\left[\|\Pi_{B_1}|\psi\rangle - \mathcal{O}_{\tilde{F}(B)}\Pi_{B_1}|\psi\rangle + (\mathbb{I} - \mathcal{O}_{\tilde{F}(B)})(\mathbb{I} - \Pi_{B_1})|\psi\rangle\|_2\right]$$
$$\leq \mathbb{E}_B\left[\|\Pi_{B_1}|\psi\rangle\|_2\right] + \mathbb{E}_B\left[\|\mathcal{O}_{\tilde{F}(B)}\Pi_{B_1}|\psi\rangle\|_2\right]$$
$$= 2 \cdot \mathbb{E}_B\left[\|\Pi_{B_1}|\psi\rangle\|_2\right]$$
$$\leq 2\sqrt{\mathbb{E}_B\left[\|\Pi_{B_1}|\psi\rangle\|_2^2\right]}, \tag{9}$$

using Jensen's inequality in the last step. Let $|\psi\rangle = \sum_{x\in\{0,1\}^m, y\in\{0,1\}^n} \alpha_{x,y}|x\rangle|y\rangle$ where $\||\psi\rangle\|_2^2 = \sum_{x,y} \alpha_{x,y}^2 = 1$. Then

$$\mathbb{E}_B\left[\|\Pi_{B_1}|\psi\rangle\|_2^2\right] = \mathbb{E}_B\left[\sum_{x,y:\, x\in B_1} \alpha_{x,y}^2\right]$$
$$= \sum_{x,y} \alpha_{x,y}^2 \cdot \Pr[x \in B_1] \leq \epsilon.$$

Together with Eqs. (8) and (9), this gives the desired result. $\qquad\square$

4.2   Proof of the Resampling Lemma

We begin by introducing a superposition-oracle technique based on the one by Zhandry [26], but different in that our oracle represents a two-way accessible, uniform permutation (rather than a uniform function). We also do not need to "compress" the oracle, as an inefficient representation suffices for our purposes.

For an arbitrary function $f : \{0,1\}^n \to \{0,1\}^n$, define the state

$$|f\rangle_F = \bigotimes_{x \in \{0,1\}^n} |f(x)\rangle_{F_x},$$

where F is the collection of registers $\{F_x\}_{x \in \{0,1\}^n}$. We represent an evaluation of f via an operator O whose action on the computational basis is given by

$$O_{XYF} |x\rangle_X |y\rangle_Y |f\rangle_F = \text{CNOT}^{\otimes n}_{F_x:Y} |x\rangle_X |y\rangle_Y |f\rangle_F = |x\rangle_X |y \oplus f(x)\rangle_Y |f\rangle_F,$$

where X, Y are n-qubit registers. Handling inverse queries to f is more difficult. We want to define an inverse operator O^{inv} such that, for any permutation π,

$$O^{\text{inv}}_{XYF} |\pi\rangle_F = \left(\sum_{x,y \in \{0,1\}^n} |y\rangle\langle y|_Y \otimes \mathsf{X}^x_X \otimes |y\rangle\langle y|_{F_x} \right) |\pi\rangle_F \tag{10}$$

(where X is the Pauli-X operator, and for $x \in \{0,1\}^n$ we let $\mathsf{X}^x := \mathsf{X}^{x_1} \otimes \mathsf{X}^{x_2} \otimes \ldots \otimes \mathsf{X}^{x_n}$ so that $\mathsf{X}^x |\hat{x}\rangle = |\hat{x} \oplus x\rangle$); then,

$$O^{\text{inv}}_{XYF} |x\rangle_X |y\rangle_Y |\pi\rangle_F = |x \oplus \pi^{-1}(y)\rangle_X |y\rangle_Y |\pi\rangle_F.$$

In order for O^{inv} to be a well-defined unitary operator, however, we must extend its definition to the entire space of functions. A convenient extension is given by the following action on arbitrary computational basis states:

$$O^{\text{inv}}_{XYF} = \prod_{x' \in \{0,1\}^n} \left(\mathsf{X}^{x'}_X \otimes |y\rangle\langle y|_{F_{x'}} + (\mathbb{1} - |y\rangle\langle y|)_{F_{x'}} \right),$$

so that

$$O^{\text{inv}}_{XYF} |x\rangle_X |y\rangle_Y |f\rangle_F = |x \oplus (\oplus_{x':f(x')=y} x')\rangle_X |y\rangle_Y |f\rangle_F.$$

In other words, the inverse operator XORs all preimages (under f) of the value in register Y into the contents of register X.

We may view a uniform permutation as a uniform superposition over all permutations in $\mathcal{P}_n$; i.e., we model a uniform permutation as the state

$$|\phi_0\rangle_F = (2^n!)^{-\frac{1}{2}} \sum_{\pi \in \mathcal{P}_n} |\pi\rangle_F.$$

The final state of any oracle algorithm $\mathcal{D}$ is identically distributed whether we (1) sample uniform $\pi \in \mathcal{P}_n$ and then run $\mathcal{D}$ with access to π and π^{-1}, or (2) run $\mathcal{D}$ with access to O and O^{inv} after initializing the F-registers to $|\phi_0\rangle_F$ (and, if desired, at the end of its execution, measure the F-registers to obtain π and the residual state of $\mathcal{D}$).

Our proof relies on the following lemma, which is a special case of the conclusion of implication $(\diamond')$ in [21]. (Here and in the following, we denote the complementary projector of a projector P by $\bar{P} \overset{\text{def}}{=} \mathbb{1} - P$.)

Lemma 8 (Gentle measurement lemma). *Let $|\psi\rangle$ be a quantum state and let $\{P_i\}_{i=1}^q$ be a collection of projectors with $\left\|\bar{P}_i|\psi\rangle\right\|_2^2 \le \epsilon_i$ for all i. Then*

$$1 - |\langle\psi| (P_q \cdots P_1) |\psi\rangle|^2 \le \sum_{i=1}^q \epsilon_i.$$

Proof of Lemma 5. We split the distinguisher $\mathcal{D}$ into two stages $\mathcal{D} = (\mathcal{D}_0, \mathcal{D}_1)$ corresponding to the first and second phases of the experiment in Lemma 5. As discussed above, we run the experiment using the superposition oracle $|\phi_0\rangle_F$ and then measure the F-registers at the end. Informally, our goal is to show that on average over the choice of reprogrammed positions s_0, s_1, the adversary-oracle state after $\mathcal{D}_0$ finishes is almost invariant under the reprogramming operation (i.e., the swap of registers F_{s_0} and F_{s_1}) unless $\mathcal{D}_0$ makes a large number of oracle queries. This will follow from Lemma 8 because, on average over the choice of s_0, s_1, any particular query of $\mathcal{D}_0$ (whether using O or O^{inv}) only involves F_{s_0} or F_{s_1} with negligible amplitude.

We begin by defining the projectors

$$\left(P_{s_0 s_1}\right)_X = \begin{cases} \mathbb{1} & s_0 = s_1 \\ \mathbb{1} - |s_0\rangle\langle s_0| - |s_1\rangle\langle s_1| & s_0 \ne s_1 \end{cases}$$

$$\left(P_{s_0 s_1}^{\text{inv}}\right)_{FY} = \begin{cases} \mathbb{1} & s_0 = s_1 \\ \sum_{y \in \{0,1\}^n} |y\rangle\langle y|_Y \otimes (\mathbb{1} - |y\rangle\langle y|)_{F_{s_0} F_{s_1}}^{\otimes 2} & s_0 \ne s_1. \end{cases}$$

It is straightforward to verify that for any s_0, s_1:

$$\left[\text{Swap}_{F_{s_0} F_{s_1}}, O_{XYF} \left(P_{s_0 s_1}\right)_X\right] = 0 \tag{11}$$

$$\left[\text{Swap}_{F_{s_0} F_{s_1}}, O_{XYF}^{\text{inv}} \left(P_{s_0 s_1}^{\text{inv}}\right)_{FY}\right] = 0, \tag{12}$$

where $[\cdot, \cdot]$ denotes the commutator operation, and Swap_{AB} is the swap operator (i.e., $\text{Swap}_{A,B}|x\rangle_A|x'\rangle_B = |x'\rangle_A|x\rangle_B$ if the target registers A, B are distinct, and the identity if A and B refer to the same register). In words, this means that if we project a forward query to inputs other than s_0, s_1, then swapping the outputs of a function at s_0 and s_1 before evaluating that function has no effect; the same holds if we project an inverse query (for some associated function f) to the set of output values that are not equal to $f(s_0)$ or $f(s_1)$.

Since $\bar{P}_{s_0 s_1} \overset{\text{def}}{=} \mathbb{1} - P_{s_0 s_1} \le |s_0\rangle\langle s_0| + |s_1\rangle\langle s_1|$ it follows that for any normalized state $|\psi\rangle_{XE}$ (where E is an arbitrary other register),

$$\underset{s_0, s_1}{\mathbb{E}} \left[\left\|\left(\bar{P}_{s_0 s_1}\right)_X |\psi\rangle_{XE}\right\|_2^2\right] \le \underset{s_0, s_1}{\mathbb{E}} \left[\langle\psi| \left(|s_0\rangle\langle s_0| + |s_1\rangle\langle s_1|\right) |\psi\rangle\right]$$

$$= 2 \cdot 2^{-n}. \tag{13}$$

We show a similar statement about $P_{s_0 s_1}^{\text{inv}}$. We can express a valid adversary/oracle state $|\psi\rangle_{YXEF}$ (that is thus only supported on the span of $\mathcal{P}_n$)

as

$$|\psi\rangle_{YXEF} = \sum_{x,y\in\{0,1\}^n} c_{xy}|y\rangle_Y|y\rangle_{F_x}|\psi_{xy}\rangle_{XEF_{x^c}}, \tag{14}$$

for some normalized quantum states $\{|\psi_{xy}\rangle\}_{x,y\in\{0,1\}^n}$, with $\sum_{x,y\in\{0,1\}^n}|c_{xy}|^2 = 1$ and $\langle y|_{F_{x'}}|\psi_{xy}\rangle_{XEF_{x^c}} = 0$ for all $x' \neq x$. If $s_0 = s_1$, then $\left\|(\bar{P}^{inv}_{s_0 s_1})_{YF}|\psi\rangle_{YXEF}\right\|_2^2 = 0 \leq 2 \cdot 2^{-n}$. It is thus immediate from Eq. (14) that

$$\mathop{\mathbb{E}}_{s_0,s_1}\left[\left\|(\bar{P}^{inv}_{s_0 s_1})_{YF}|\psi\rangle_{YXEF}\right\|_2^2\right] \leq 2 \cdot 2^{-n} \tag{15}$$

Without loss of generality, we assume $\mathcal{D}_0$ starts with initial state $|\psi_0\rangle = |\psi'_0\rangle|\phi_0\rangle$ (which we take to include the superposition oracle's initial state $|\phi_0\rangle$), computes the state

$$|\psi\rangle = U_{\mathcal{D}_0}|\psi_0\rangle = U_q O_q U_{q-1} O_{q-1} \cdots U_1 O_1 |\psi_0\rangle,$$

and outputs all its registers as a state register E. Here, each $O_i \in \{O, O^{inv}\}$ acts on registers XYF, and each U_j acts on registers XYE. To each choice of s_0, s_1 we assign a decomposition $|\psi\rangle = |\psi_{good}(s_0, s_1)\rangle + |\psi_{bad}(s_0, s_1)\rangle$ by defining

$$|\psi_{good}(s_0, s_1)\rangle = z \cdot U_q O_q P^q_{s_0 s_1} U_{q-1} O_{q-1} P^{q-1}_{s_0 s_1} \cdots U_1 O_1 P^1_{s_0 s_1} |\psi_0\rangle,$$

where $P^i_{s_0 s_1} = P_{s_0 s_1}$ if $O_i = O$, $P^i_{s_0 s_1} = P^{inv}_{s_0 s_1}$ if $O_i = O^{inv}$, and $z \in \mathbb{C}$ is such that $|z| = 1$ and $\langle\psi \mid \psi_{good}(s_0, s_1)\rangle \in \mathbb{R}_{\geq 0}$.

$$|\psi_{good}(s_0, s_1)\rangle = z \cdot U_{\mathcal{D}_0} Q^q_{s_0 s_1} \cdots Q^1_{s_0 s_1} |\psi_0\rangle,$$

with $Q^i_{s_0 s_1} = \tilde{U}^\dagger_i P^i_{s_0 s_1} \tilde{U}_i$ for $\tilde{U}_i = U_{i-1} O_{i-1} \ldots U_1 O_1$. Let

$$\epsilon_i(s_0, s_1) = \left\|\bar{Q}^i_{s_0 s_1}|\psi_0\rangle\right\|_2^2 = \left\|\bar{P}^i_{s_0 s_1} \tilde{U}_i|\psi_0\rangle\right\|_2^2.$$

Applying Lemma 8 yields

$$1 - |\langle\psi \mid \psi_{good}(s_0, s_1)\rangle|^2 \leq \sum_{i=1}^q \epsilon_i(s_0, s_1). \tag{16}$$

We will now analyze the impact of reprogramming the superposition oracle after $\mathcal{D}_0$ has finished. Recall that reprogramming swaps the values of the permutation at points s_0 and s_1, which is implemented in the superposition-oracle framework by applying $\mathsf{Swap}_{F_{s_0} F_{s_1}}$. Note that $\mathsf{Swap}_{F_{s_0} F_{s_1}}|\phi_0\rangle = |\phi_0\rangle$. As the adversary's internal unitaries U_i do not act on F, Eqs. (11) and (12) then imply that

$$\mathsf{Swap}_{F_{s_0} F_{s_1}}|\psi_{good}(s_0, s_1)\rangle = |\psi_{good}(s_0, s_1)\rangle.$$

The standard formula for the trace distance of pure states thus yields

$$\frac{1}{2}\left\||\psi\rangle\langle\psi| - \mathsf{Swap}_{F_{s_0} F_{s_1}}|\psi\rangle\langle\psi|\mathsf{Swap}_{F_{s_0} F_{s_1}}\right\|_1 = \sqrt{1 - \left|\langle\psi|\mathsf{Swap}_{F_{s_0} F_{s_1}}|\psi\rangle\right|^2}. \tag{17}$$

We further have

$$\left| \langle \psi | \mathsf{Swap}_{F_{s_0} F_{s_1}} | \psi \rangle \right| = \left| \langle \psi \mid \psi \rangle + \langle \psi_{\mathrm{bad}}(s_0, s_1) | \left(\mathsf{Swap}_{F_{s_0} F_{s_1}} - \mathbb{1} \right) | \psi_{\mathrm{bad}}(s_0, s_1) \rangle \right|$$
$$\geq 1 - 2 \| | \psi_{\mathrm{bad}}(s_0, s_1) \rangle \|_2^2 \tag{18}$$

using the triangle and Cauchy-Schwarz inequalities. Combining Eqs. (17) and (18) we obtain

$$\frac{1}{2} \left\| | \psi \rangle \langle \psi | - \mathsf{Swap}_{F_{s_0} F_{s_1}} | \psi \rangle \langle \psi | \mathsf{Swap}_{F_{s_0} F_{s_1}} \right\|_1 \leq 2 \cdot \| | \psi_{\mathrm{bad}}(s_0, s_1) \rangle \|_2.$$

But as $| \psi_{\mathrm{bad}}(s_0, s_1) \rangle = | \psi \rangle - | \psi_{\mathrm{good}}(s_0, s_1) \rangle$, we have

$$\| | \psi_{\mathrm{bad}}(s_0, s_1) \rangle \|_2^2 = 2 - 2 \cdot \mathrm{Re} \langle \psi \mid \psi_{\mathrm{good}}(s_0, s_1) \rangle$$
$$= 2 - 2 \cdot | \langle \psi \mid \psi_{\mathrm{good}}(s_0, s_1) \rangle |$$
$$\leq 2 \sum_{i=1}^{q} \epsilon_i(s_0, s_1).$$

Combining the last two equations we obtain

$$\frac{1}{2} \left\| | \psi \rangle \langle \psi | - \mathsf{Swap}_{F_{s_0} F_{s_1}} | \psi \rangle \langle \psi | \mathsf{Swap}_{F_{s_0} F_{s_1}} \right\|_1 \leq 2\sqrt{2} \sqrt{\sum_{i=1}^{q} \epsilon_i(s_0, s_1)}. \tag{19}$$

The remainder of the proof is the same as the analogous part of the proof of [12, Theorem 6]. $\mathcal{D}_1$'s task boils down to distinguishing the states $| \psi \rangle$ and $\mathsf{Swap}_{F_{s_0} F_{s_1}} | \psi \rangle$, for uniform s_0, s_1 that $\mathcal{D}_1$ receives as input, using the limited set of instructions allowed by the superposition oracle. We can therefore bound $\mathcal{D}$'s advantage by the maximum distinguishing advantage for these two states when using arbitrary quantum computation, averaged over the choice of s_0, s_1. Using the standard formula for this maximum distinguishing advantage we obtain

$$\Pr \left[\mathcal{D} \text{ outputs } b \right] - \frac{1}{2} \leq \frac{1}{4} \mathop{\mathbb{E}}_{s_0, s_1} \left[\left\| | \psi \rangle \langle \psi | - \mathsf{Swap}_{F_{s_0} F_{s_1}} | \psi \rangle \langle \psi | \mathsf{Swap}_{F_{s_0} F_{s_1}} \right\|_1 \right]$$
$$\leq \sqrt{2} \mathop{\mathbb{E}}_{s_0, s_1} \left[\sqrt{\sum_{i=1}^{q} \epsilon_i(s_0, s_1)} \right]$$
$$\leq \sqrt{2} \sqrt{\mathop{\mathbb{E}}_{s_0, s_1} \left[\sum_{i=1}^{q} \epsilon_i(s_0, s_1) \right]} \leq 2 \sqrt{\frac{q}{2^n}},$$

where the second inequality is Eq. (19), the third is Jensen's inequality, and the last is from Eqs. (13)–(16). This implies the lemma.   □

Acknowledgments. The authors thank Andrew Childs, Bibhusa Rawal, and Patrick Struck for useful discussions. Work of Jonathan Katz was supported in part by financial assistance award 70NANB19H126 from the U.S. Department of Commerce, National Institute of Standards and Technology. Work of Christian Majenz was funded by a NWO VENI grant (Project No. VI.Veni.192.159). Gorjan Alagic acknowledges support from the U.S. Army Research Office under Grant Number W911NF-20-1-0015, the U.S. Department of Energy under Award Number DE-SC0020312, and the AFOSR under Award Number FA9550-20-1-0108.

A   Security of Forward-Only Even-Mansour

In this section we consider a simpler case, where $E_k[F](x) := F(x \oplus k)$ for $F : \{0,1\}^n \to \{0,1\}^n$ a uniform *function* and k a uniform n-bit string. Here we restrict the adversary to forward queries only, i.e., the adversary has classical access to $E_k[F]$ and quantum access to F; note that $E_k^{-1}[F]$ and F^{-1} may not even be well-defined. This setting was also analyzed by Jaeger et al. [16] using different techniques.

We let $\mathcal{F}_n$ denote the set of all functions from $\{0,1\}^n$ to $\{0,1\}^n$.

Theorem 4. *Let $\mathcal{A}$ be a quantum algorithm making q_E classical queries to its first oracle and q_F quantum queries to its second oracle. Then*

$$\left| \Pr_{\substack{k \leftarrow \{0,1\}^n \\ F \leftarrow \mathcal{F}_n}} \left[\mathcal{A}^{E_k[F],F}(1^n) = 1 \right] - \Pr_{R,F \leftarrow \mathcal{F}_n} \left[\mathcal{A}^{R,F}(1^n) = 1 \right] \right|$$

$$\leq 2^{-n/2} \cdot \left(2q_E\sqrt{q_F} + 2q_F\sqrt{q_E} \right).$$

Proof. We make the same assumptions about $\mathcal{A}$ as in the initial paragraphs of the proof of Theorem 3. We also adopt analogous notation for the stages of $\mathcal{A}$, now using q_E, q_F, and $q_{F,j}$ as appropriate.

Given a function $F : \{0,1\}^n \to \{0,1\}^n$, a set T of pairs where any $x \in \{0,1\}^n$ is the first element of at most one pair in T, and a key $k \in \{0,1\}^n$, we define the function $F_{T,k} : \{0,1\}^n \to \{0,1\}^n$ as

$$F_{T,k}(x) := \begin{cases} y & \text{if } (x \oplus k, y) \in T \\ F(x) & \text{otherwise.} \end{cases}$$

Note that, in contrast to the analogous definition in Theorem 3, here the order of the tuples in T does not matter and so we may take it to be a set. Note also that we are redefining the notation $F_{T,k}$ from how it was used in Theorem 3; this notation applies to this appendix only.

We now define a sequence of experiments $\mathbf{H}_j$, for $j = 0, \ldots, q_E$:

Experiment $\mathbf{H}_j$. Sample $R, F \leftarrow \mathcal{F}_n$ and $k \leftarrow \{0,1\}^n$. Then:

1. Run $\mathcal{A}$, answering its classical queries using R and its quantum queries using F, stopping immediately before its $(j+1)$st classical query. Let $T_j = \{(x_1, y_1), \ldots, (x_j, y_j)\}$ be the set of all classical queries made by $\mathcal{A}$ thus far and their corresponding responses.

2. For the remainder of the execution of $\mathcal{A}$, answer its classical queries using $E_k[F]$ and its quantum queries using $F_{T_j,k}$.

We can represent $\mathbf{H}_j$ as the experiment in which $\mathcal{A}$'s queries are answered using the oracle sequence

$$\underbrace{F, R, F, \cdots, R, F}_{j \text{ classical queries}}, \underbrace{E_k[F], F_{T_j,k}, \cdots, E_k[F], F_{T_j,k}}_{q_E - j \text{ classical queries}} .$$

Note that $\mathbf{H}_0$ is exactly the real world (i.e., $\mathcal{A}^{E_k[F],F}$) and $\mathbf{H}_{q_E}$ is exactly the ideal world (i.e., $\mathcal{A}^{R,F}$.)

For $j = 0, \ldots, q_E - 1$, we define an additional experiment $\mathbf{H}'_j$:

Experiment $\mathbf{H}'_j$. Sample $R, F \leftarrow \mathcal{F}_n$ and $k \leftarrow \{0,1\}^n$. Then:

1. Run $\mathcal{A}$, answering its classical queries using R and its quantum queries using F, stopping immediately after its $(j+1)$st classical query. Let $T_{j+1} = ((x_1, y_1), \ldots, (x_{j+1}, y_{j+1}))$ be the set of all classical queries made by $\mathcal{A}$ thus far and their corresponding responses.
2. For the remainder of the execution of $\mathcal{A}$, answer its classical queries using $E_k[F]$ and its quantum queries using $F_{T_{j+1},k}$.

I.e., $\mathbf{H}'_j$ corresponds to answering $\mathcal{A}$'s queries using the oracle sequence

$$\underbrace{F, R, F, \cdots, R, F}_{j \text{ classical queries}}, R, F_{T_{j+1},k}, \underbrace{E_k[F], F_{T_{j+1},k} \cdots, E_k[F], F_{T_{j+1},k}}_{q_E - j - 1 \text{ classical queries}} .$$

We now show that $\mathbf{H}'_j$ is close to $\mathbf{H}_{j+1}$ and $\mathbf{H}_j$ is close to $\mathbf{H}'_j$ for $0 \leq j < q_E$.

Lemma 9. For $j = 0, \ldots, q_E - 1$,

$$|\Pr[\mathcal{A}(\mathbf{H}'_j) = 1] - \Pr[\mathcal{A}(\mathbf{H}_{j+1}) = 1]| \leq 2 \cdot q_{F,j+1} \sqrt{(j+1)/2^n}.$$

Proof. Given an adversary $\mathcal{A}$, we construct a distinguisher $\mathcal{D}$ for the "blinding game" of Lemma 3 that works as follows:

Phase 1: $\mathcal{D}$ samples $F, R \leftarrow \mathcal{F}_n$. It then runs $\mathcal{A}$, answering its quantum queries with F and its classical queries with R, until it replies to $\mathcal{A}$'s $(j+1)$st classical query. Let $T_{j+1} = \{(x_1, y_1), \ldots, (x_{j+1}, y_{j+1})\}$ be the set of classical queries/answers thus far. $\mathcal{D}$ defines algorithm $\mathcal{B}$ as follows: on randomness $k \in \{0,1\}^n$, output $B = \{(x_j \oplus k, y_j)\}_{j=1}^{j+1}$. Finally, $\mathcal{D}$ outputs F and $\mathcal{B}$.

Phase 2: $\mathcal{D}$ is given quantum access to a function F_b. It continues to run $\mathcal{A}$, answering its quantum queries with F_b until $\mathcal{A}$ makes its next classical query.

Phase 3: $\mathcal{D}$ is given the randomness k used to run $\mathcal{B}$. It continues running $\mathcal{A}$, answering its classical queries with $E_k[F]$ and its quantum queries with $F_{T_{j+1},k}$. Finally, $\mathcal{D}$ outputs whatever $\mathcal{A}$ outputs.

When $b = 0$ (so $F_b = F_0 = F$), then $\mathcal{A}$'s output is identically distributed to its output in $\mathbf{H}_{j+1}$. On the other hand, when $b = 1$ then $F_b = F_1 = F^{(B)} = F_{T_{j+1},k}$ and so $\mathcal{A}$'s output is identically distributed to its output in $\mathbf{H}'_j$. The expected number of queries made by $\mathcal{D}$ in phase 2 when $F = F_0$ is the expected number of queries made by $\mathcal{A}$ in stage $(j+1)$ in $\mathbf{H}_{j+1}$. Since $\mathbf{H}_{j+1}$ and $\mathbf{H}_{q_E}$ are identical until after the $(j+1)$st stage, this is precisely $q_{F,j+1}$. Because k is uniform, we can apply Lemma 3 with $\epsilon = (j+1)/2^n$. The lemma follows. $\qquad\square$

Lemma 10. *For $j = 0, \ldots, q_E$,*

$$|\Pr[\mathcal{A}(\mathbf{H}_j) = 1] - \Pr[\mathcal{A}(\mathbf{H}'_j) = 1]| \leq 1.5 \cdot \sqrt{q_F/2^n}\,.$$

Proof. From any adversary $\mathcal{A}$, we construct a distinguisher $\mathcal{D}$ for the game of Lemma 4. $\mathcal{D}$ works as follows:

Phase 1: $\mathcal{D}$ is given quantum access to a (random) function F. It samples $R \leftarrow \mathcal{F}_n$ and then runs $\mathcal{A}$, answering its quantum queries using F and its classical queries using R, until $\mathcal{A}$ submits its $(j+1)$st classical query x_{j+1}. At that point, let $T_j = \{(x_1, y_1), \ldots, (x_j, y_j)\}$ be the set of input/output pairs $\mathcal{A}$ has received from its classical oracle thus far.

Phase 2: $\mathcal{D}$ is given (uniform) $s \in \{0,1\}^n$ and quantum oracle access to a function F_b. Then $\mathcal{D}$ sets $k := s \oplus x_{j+1}$, and then continues running $\mathcal{A}$, answering its classical queries (including the $(j+1)$st) using $E_k[F_b]$ and its quantum queries using the function $(F_b)_{T_j,k}$, i.e.,

$$x \mapsto \begin{cases} y & \text{if } (x \oplus k, y) \in T_j \\ F_b(x) & \text{otherwise.} \end{cases}$$

Finally, $\mathcal{D}$ outputs whatever $\mathcal{A}$ outputs.

We analyze the execution of $\mathcal{D}$ in the two cases of the game of Lemma 4. In either case, the quantum queries of $\mathcal{A}$ in stages $0, \ldots, j$ are answered using a random function F, and $\mathcal{A}$'s first j classical queries are answered using an independent random function R. Note further that since s is uniform, so is k.

Case 1: $b = 0$. In this case, all the remaining classical queries of $\mathcal{A}$ (i.e., from the $(j+1)$st on) are answered using $E_k[F]$, and the remaining quantum queries of $\mathcal{A}$ are answered using $F_{T_j,k}$. The output of $\mathcal{A}$ is thus distributed identically to its output in $\mathbf{H}_j$ in this case.

Case 2: $b = 1$. Here, $F_b = F_1 = F_{s \to y}$ for a uniform y. Now, the response to the $(j+1)$st classical query of $\mathcal{A}$ is

$$E_k[F_b](x_{j+1}) = E_k[F_{s \to y}](x_{j+1}) = F_{s \to y}(k \oplus x_{j+1}) = F_{s \to y}(s) = y.$$

Since y is uniform and independent of anything else, and since $\mathcal{A}$ has never previously queried x_{j+1} to its classical oracle, this is equivalent to answering the first $j+1$ classical queries of $\mathcal{A}$ using a random function R. The remaining classical queries of $\mathcal{A}$ are also answered using $E_k[F_{s \mapsto y}]$. However, since

$E_k[F_{s\to y}](x) = E_k[F](x)$ for all $x \neq x_{j+1}$ and $\mathcal{A}$ never repeats the query x_{j+1}, this is equivalent to answering the remaining classical queries of $\mathcal{A}$ using $E_k[F]$.

The remaining quantum queries of $\mathcal{A}$ are answered with the function

$$x \mapsto \begin{cases} y' & \text{if } (x \oplus k, y') \in T_j \\ F_{s\to y}(x) & \text{otherwise.} \end{cases}$$

This, in turn, is precisely the function $F_{T_{j+1},k}$, where T_{j+1} is obtained by adding (x_{j+1}, y) to T_j (and thus consists of the first $j+1$ classical queries made by $\mathcal{A}$ and their corresponding responses). Thus, the output of $\mathcal{A}$ in this case is distributed identically to its output in $\mathbf{H}'_j$.

The number of quantum queries made by $\mathcal{D}$ in phase 1 is at most q_F. The claimed result thus follows from Lemma 4. ⊔⊓

Using Lemmas 9 and 10, and the fact that $\sum_{j=1}^{q_E} q_{F,j} = q_F$, we have

$$|\Pr[\mathcal{A}(\mathbf{H}_0) = 1] - \Pr[\mathcal{A}(\mathbf{H}_{q_E}) = 1]| \leq 1.5 q_E \sqrt{q_F/2^n} + 2 \sum_{j=1}^{q_E} q_{F,j} \sqrt{j/2^n}$$

$$\leq 1.5 q_E \sqrt{q_F/2^n} + 2\sqrt{q_E/2^n} \sum_{j=1}^{q_E} q_{F,j}$$

$$\leq 1.5 q_E \sqrt{q_F/2^n} + 2 q_F \sqrt{q_E/2^n},$$

as required. □

B   Further Details for the Proof of Lemma 7

B.1   Equivalence of Expt'_j and $\mathbf{H}'_j$

The code in the top portion of Fig. 2 is a syntactic rewriting of Expt'_j. (Flags that have no effect on the output of $\mathcal{A}$ are omitted.) In line 27, the computation of y_{j+1} has been expanded (note that $E_k[P_1](x_{j+1}) = P_1(s_0) \oplus k_2 = P(s_1) \oplus k_2$). In line 31, Q has been replaced with $P_{T_{j+1},k}$ and $\mathcal{O}$ has been replaced with $E_k[P]$ as justified in the proof of Lemma 7.

The code in the middle portion of Fig. 2 results from the following changes: first, rather than sampling uniform s_0 and then setting $k_1 := s_0 \oplus x_{j+1}$, the code now samples a uniform k_1. Similarly, rather than choosing uniform s_1 and then setting $y_{j+1} := P(s_1) \oplus k_2$, the code now samples a uniform y_{j+1} (note that P is a permutation, so $P(s_1)$ is uniform). Since neither s_0 nor s_1 is used anywhere else, each can now be omitted.

The code in the bottom portion of Fig. 2 simply chooses $k = (k_1, k_2)$ according to distribution D, and chooses uniform $y_{j+1} \in \{0,1\}^n \setminus \{y_1, \ldots, y_j\}$. It can be verified by inspection that this final experiment is equivalent to $\mathbf{H}'_j$.

---

23 $P, R \leftarrow \mathcal{P}_n$
24 Run $\mathcal{A}$ with quantum access to P and classical access to R, until $\mathcal{A}$ makes its
$(j+1)$st classical query x_{j+1}; let T_j be as in the text
25 $s_0, s_1 \leftarrow \{0,1\}^n$
26 $k_1 := s_0 \oplus x_{j+1}$, $k_2 \leftarrow D_{|k_1}$, $k := (k_1, k_2)$
27 $y_{j+1} := P(s_1) \oplus k_2$
28 if $y_{j+1} \in \{y_1, \ldots, y_j\}$ then $y_{j+1} \leftarrow \{0,1\}^n \setminus \{y_1, \ldots, y_j\}$
29 Give y_{j+1} to $\mathcal{A}$ as the answer to its $(j+1)$st classical query
30 $T_{j+1} := ((x_1, y_1, b_1), \ldots, (x_{j+1}, y_{j+1}, b_{j+1}))$
31 Continue running $\mathcal{A}$ with quantum access to $P_{T_{j+1}, k}$ and classical access
to $E_k[P]$

---

32 $P, R \leftarrow \mathcal{P}_n$
33 Run $\mathcal{A}$ with quantum access to P and classical access to R, until $\mathcal{A}$ makes its
$(j+1)$st classical query x_{j+1}; let T_j be as in the text
34 $k_1 \leftarrow \{0,1\}^n$, $k_2 \leftarrow D_{|k_1}$, $k := (k_1, k_2)$, $y_{j+1} \leftarrow \{0,1\}^n$
35 if $y_{j+1} \in \{y_1, \ldots, y_j\}$ then $y_{j+1} \leftarrow \{0,1\}^n \setminus \{y_1, \ldots, y_j\}$
36 Give y_{j+1} to $\mathcal{A}$ as the answer to its $(j+1)$st classical query
37 $T_{j+1} := ((x_1, y_1, b_1), \ldots, (x_{j+1}, y_{j+1}, b_{j+1}))$
38 Continue running $\mathcal{A}$ with quantum access to $P_{T_{j+1}, k}$ and classical access
to $E_k[P]$

---

39 $P, R \leftarrow \mathcal{P}_n$
40 Run $\mathcal{A}$ with quantum access to P and classical access to R, until $\mathcal{A}$ makes its
$(j+1)$st classical query x_{j+1}; let T_j be as in the text
41 $k \leftarrow D$, $y_{j+1} \leftarrow \{0,1\}^n \setminus \{y_1, \ldots, y_j\}$
42 Give y_{j+1} to $\mathcal{A}$ as the answer to its $(j+1)$st classical query
43 $T_{j+1} := ((x_1, y_1, b_1), \ldots, (x_{j+1}, y_{j+1}, b_{j+1}))$
44 Continue running $\mathcal{A}$ with quantum access to $P_{T_{j+1}, k}$ and classical access
to $E_k[P]$

Fig. 2. Syntactic rewritings of Expt'_j.

B.2   Handling an Inverse Query

In this section we discuss the case where the $(j+1)$st classical query of $\mathcal{A}$ is a
inverse query in the proof of Lemma 7. Phase 1 is exactly as described in the
proof of Lemma 7, though we now let y_{j+1} denote the $(j+1)$st classical query
made by $\mathcal{A}$, and now $b_{j+1} = 1$.

Phase 2: $\mathcal{D}$ receives $s_0, s_1 \in \{0,1\}^n$ and quantum oracle access to a permutation P_b. First, $\mathcal{D}$ sets $t_0 := P_b(s_0)$ and $t_1 := P_b(s_1)$. It then sets $k_2 := t_0 \oplus y_{j+1}$,
chooses $k_1 \leftarrow D_{|k_2}$ (where this represents the conditional distribution on
k_1 given k_2), and sets $k := (k_1, k_2)$. $\mathcal{D}$ continues running $\mathcal{A}$, answering its
remaining classical queries (including the $(j+1)$st one) using $E_k[P_b]$, and its
remaining quantum queries using

$$(P_b)_{T_j,k} = \overleftarrow{S}_{T_j,P_b,k} \circ \overrightarrow{S}_{T_j,P_b,k} \circ P_b = P_b \circ \overleftarrow{Q}_{T_j,P_b,k} \circ \overrightarrow{Q}_{T_j,P_b,k}.$$

Finally, $\mathcal{D}$ outputs whatever $\mathcal{A}$ outputs.

Note that t_0, t_1 are uniform, and so k is distributed according to D. Then:

Case $b = 0$ (No Reprogramming). In this case, $\mathcal{A}$'s remaining classical queries (including its $(j+1)$st classical query) are answered using $E_k[P_0] = E_k[P]$, and its remaining quantum queries are answered using $(P_0)_{T_j,k} = P_{T_j,k}$. The output of $\mathcal{A}$ is thus distributed identically to its output in $\mathbf{H}_j$ in this case.

Case $b = 1$ (Reprogramming). In this case, $k_2 = P_1(s_0) \oplus y_{j+1} = P(s_1) \oplus y_{j+1}$ and so

$$\begin{aligned} P_b^{-1} = P_1^{-1} = (P \circ \mathsf{swap}_{s_0,s_1})^{-1} &= (\mathsf{swap}_{P(s_0),P(s_1)} \circ P)^{-1} \\ &= P^{-1} \circ \mathsf{swap}_{P(s_0),P(s_1)} \\ &= P^{-1} \circ \mathsf{swap}_{P(s_0),y_{j+1} \oplus k_2}. \end{aligned}$$

The response to $\mathcal{A}$'s $(j+1)$st classical query is thus

$$x_{j+1} \overset{\text{def}}{=} E_k^{-1}[P_1](y_{j+1}) = P_1^{-1}(y_{j+1} \oplus k_2) \oplus k_1 = P_1^{-1}(P(s_1)) \oplus k_1 = s_0 \oplus k_1.$$

The remaining classical queries of $\mathcal{A}$ are then answered using $E_k[P_1]$, while its remaining quantum queries are answered using $(P_1)_{T_j,k}$.

Now we define the following three events:

1. bad_1 is the event that $x_{j+1} \in \{x_1, \ldots, x_j\}$.
2. bad_2 is the event that $P(s_0) \oplus k_2 \in \{y_1, \ldots, y_j\}$.
3. bad_3 is the event that, in phase 2, $\mathcal{A}$ queries its classical oracle in the forward direction on $s_1 \oplus k_1$, or the inverse direction on $P(s_0) \oplus k_2$.

Comparing the above to the proof of Lemma 7, we see (because P is a permutation) that the situation is entirely symmetric, and the analysis is therefore the same.

References

1. Alagic, G., Majenz, C., Russell, A., Song, F.: Quantum-access-secure message authentication via blind-unforgeability. In: Canteaut, A., Ishai, Y. (eds.) EUROCRYPT 2020, Part III. LNCS, vol. 12107, pp. 788–817. Springer, Cham (2020). https://doi.org/10.1007/978-3-030-45727-3_27
2. Alagic, G., Russell, A.: Quantum-secure symmetric-key cryptography based on hidden shifts. In: Coron, J.-S., Nielsen, J.B. (eds.) EUROCRYPT 2017, Part III. LNCS, vol. 10212, pp. 65–93. Springer, Cham (2017). https://doi.org/10.1007/978-3-319-56617-7_3
3. Bellare, M., Rogaway, P.: The security of triple encryption and a framework for code-based game-playing proofs. In: Vaudenay, S. (ed.) EUROCRYPT 2006. LNCS, vol. 4004, pp. 409–426. Springer, Heidelberg (2006). https://doi.org/10.1007/11761679_25. Full version available at https://eprint.iacr.org/2004/331

4. Bindel, N., Hamburg, M., Hövelmanns, K., Hülsing, A., Persichetti, E.: Tighter proofs of CCA security in the quantum random oracle model. In: Hofheinz, D., Rosen, A. (eds.) TCC 2019, Part II. LNCS, vol. 11892, pp. 61–90. Springer, Cham (2019). https://doi.org/10.1007/978-3-030-36033-7_3

5. Bonnetain, X., Hosoyamada, A., Naya-Plasencia, M., Sasaki, Yu., Schrottenloher, A.: Quantum attacks without superposition queries: the offline Simon's algorithm. In: Galbraith, S.D., Moriai, S. (eds.) ASIACRYPT 2019, Part I. LNCS, vol. 11921, pp. 552–583. Springer, Cham (2019). https://doi.org/10.1007/978-3-030-34578-5_20

6. Bonnetain, X., Naya-Plasencia, M.: Hidden shift quantum cryptanalysis and implications. In: Peyrin, T., Galbraith, S. (eds.) ASIACRYPT 2018, Part I. LNCS, vol. 11272, pp. 560–592. Springer, Cham (2018). https://doi.org/10.1007/978-3-030-03326-2_19

7. Brassard, G., Høyer, P., Tapp, A.: Quantum algorithm for the collision problem (1997). https://arxiv.org/abs/quant-ph/9705002

8. Don, J., Fehr, S., Majenz, C., Schaffner, C.: Online-extractability in the quantum random-oracle model. Cryptology ePrint Archive, Report 2021/280 (2021). https://eprint.iacr.org/2021/280

9. Dunkelman, O., Keller, N., Shamir, A.: Minimalism in cryptography: the even-mansour scheme revisited. In: Pointcheval, D., Johansson, T. (eds.) EUROCRYPT 2012. LNCS, vol. 7237, pp. 336–354. Springer, Heidelberg (2012). https://doi.org/10.1007/978-3-642-29011-4_21

10. Ettinger, M., Høyer, P., Knill, E.: The quantum query complexity of the hidden subgroup problem is polynomial. Inf. Process. Lett. **91**(1), 43–48 (2004)

11. Even, S., Mansour, Y.: A construction of a cipher from a single pseudorandom permutation. J. Cryptol. **10**(3), 151–161 (1997). https://doi.org/10.1007/s001459900025

12. Grilo, A.B., Hövelmanns, K., Hülsing, A., Majenz, C.: Tight adaptive reprogramming in the QROM. In: Tibouchi, M., Wang, H. (eds.) ASIACRYPT 2021, Part I. LNCS, vol. 13090, pp. 637–667. Springer, Cham (2021). https://doi.org/10.1007/978-3-030-92062-3_22. Available at https://eprint.iacr.org/2020/1361

13. Hofheinz, D., Hövelmanns, K., Kiltz, E.: A modular analysis of the Fujisaki-Okamoto transformation. In: Kalai, Y., Reyzin, L. (eds.) TCC 2017, Part I. LNCS, vol. 10677, pp. 341–371. Springer, Cham (2017). https://doi.org/10.1007/978-3-319-70500-2_12

14. Hosoyamada, A., Sasaki, Yu.: Cryptanalysis against symmetric-key schemes with online classical queries and offline quantum computations. In: Smart, N.P. (ed.) CT-RSA 2018. LNCS, vol. 10808, pp. 198–218. Springer, Cham (2018). https://doi.org/10.1007/978-3-319-76953-0_11

15. Hougaard, H.B.: How to generate pseudorandom permutations over other groups: Even-Mansour and Feistel revisited (2017). https://arxiv.org/abs/1707.01699

16. Jaeger, J., Song, F., Tessaro, S.: Quantum key-length extension. In: Nissim, K., Waters, B. (eds.) TCC 2021, Part I. LNCS, vol. 13042, pp. 209–239. Springer, Cham (2021). https://doi.org/10.1007/978-3-030-90459-3_8

17. Kaplan, M., Leurent, G., Leverrier, A., Naya-Plasencia, M.: Breaking symmetric cryptosystems using quantum period finding. In: Robshaw, M., Katz, J. (eds.) CRYPTO 2016, Part II. LNCS, vol. 9815, pp. 207–237. Springer, Heidelberg (2016). https://doi.org/10.1007/978-3-662-53008-5_8

18. Kiltz, E., Lyubashevsky, V., Schaffner, C.: A concrete treatment of Fiat-Shamir signatures in the quantum random-oracle model. In: Nielsen, J.B., Rijmen, V. (eds.) EUROCRYPT 2018, Part III. LNCS, vol. 10822, pp. 552–586. Springer, Cham (2018). https://doi.org/10.1007/978-3-319-78372-7_18

19. Kuchta, V., Sakzad, A., Stehlé, D., Steinfeld, R., Sun, S.-F.: Measure-rewind-measure: tighter quantum random oracle model proofs for one-way to hiding and CCA security. In: Canteaut, A., Ishai, Y. (eds.) EUROCRYPT 2020, Part III. LNCS, vol. 12107, pp. 703–728. Springer, Cham (2020). https://doi.org/10.1007/978-3-030-45727-3_24

20. Kuwakado, H., Morii, M.: Security on the quantum-type Even-Mansour cipher. In: Proceedings of the International Symposium on Information Theory and its Applications, pp. 312–316. IEEE Computer Society (2012)

21. O'Donnell, R., Venkateswaran, R.: The quantum union bound made easy (2021). https://arxiv.org/abs/2103.07827

22. Simon, D.R.: On the power of quantum computation. SIAM J. Comput. **26**(5), 1474–1483 (1997)

23. Targhi, E.E., Unruh, D.: Post-quantum security of the Fujisaki-Okamoto and OAEP transforms. In: Hirt, M., Smith, A. (eds.) TCC 2016, Part II. LNCS, vol. 9986, pp. 192–216. Springer, Heidelberg (2016). https://doi.org/10.1007/978-3-662-53644-5_8

24. Unruh, D.: Post-quantum security of Fiat-Shamir. In: Takagi, T., Peyrin, T. (eds.) ASIACRYPT 2017, Part I. LNCS, vol. 10624, pp. 65–95. Springer, Cham (2017). https://doi.org/10.1007/978-3-319-70694-8_3

25. van Dam, W., Hallgren, S., Ip, L.: Quantum algorithms for some hidden shift problems. SIAM J. Comput. **36**(3), 763–778 (2006)

26. Zhandry, M.: How to record quantum queries, and applications to quantum indifferentiability. In: Boldyreva, A., Micciancio, D. (eds.) CRYPTO 2019, Part II. LNCS, vol. 11693, pp. 239–268. Springer, Cham (2019). https://doi.org/10.1007/978-3-030-26951-7_9

Watermarking PRFs Against Quantum Adversaries

Fuyuki Kitagawa$^{(\boxtimes)}$ and Ryo Nishimaki$^{(\boxtimes)}$

NTT Corporation, Tokyo, Japan
{fuyuki.kitagawa.yh,ryo.nishimaki.zk}@hco.ntt.co.jp

Abstract. We initiate the study of software watermarking against quantum adversaries. A quantum adversary generates a *quantum state* as a pirate software that potentially removes an embedded message from a *classical* marked software. Extracting an embedded message from quantum pirate software is difficult since measurement could irreversibly alter the quantum state. In software watermarking against classical adversaries, a message extraction algorithm crucially uses the (input-output) behavior of a classical pirate software to extract an embedded message. Even if we instantiate existing watermarking PRFs with quantum-safe building blocks, it is not clear whether they are secure against quantum adversaries due to the quantum-specific property above. Thus, we need entirely new techniques to achieve software watermarking against quantum adversaries.

In this work, we define secure watermarking PRFs for quantum adversaries (unremovability against quantum adversaries). We also present two watermarking PRFs as follows.

- We construct a privately extractable watermarking PRF against quantum adversaries from the quantum hardness of the learning with errors (LWE) problem. The marking and extraction algorithms use a public parameter and a private extraction key, respectively. The watermarking PRF is unremovable even if adversaries have (the public parameter and) access to the extraction oracle, which returns a result of extraction for a queried quantum circuit.
- We construct a publicly extractable watermarking PRF against quantum adversaries from indistinguishability obfuscation (IO) and the quantum hardness of the LWE problem. The marking and extraction algorithms use a public parameter and a public extraction key, respectively. The watermarking PRF is unremovable even if adversaries have the extraction key (and the public parameter).

We develop a quantum extraction technique to extract information (a classical string) from a quantum state without destroying the state too much. We also introduce the notion of extraction-less watermarking PRFs as a crucial building block to achieve the results above by combining the tool with our quantum extraction technique.

O. Dunkelman and S. Dziembowski (Eds.): EUROCRYPT 2022, LNCS 13277, pp. 488–518, 2022.
https://doi.org/10.1007/978-3-031-07082-2_18

1   Introduction

1.1   Background

Software watermarking is a cryptographic primitive that achieves a digital analog of watermarking. A marking algorithm of software watermarking can embed an arbitrary message (bit string) into a computer software modeled as a circuit. A marked software almost preserves the functionality of the original software. An extraction algorithm of software watermarking can extract the embedded message from a marked software. Secure software watermarking should guarantee that no adversary can remove the embedded message without significantly destroying the functionality of the original software (called unremovability).

Barak et al. [BGI+12] initiate the study of software watermarking and present the first definition of cryptographically secure software watermarking. Hopper et al. [HMW07] also study the definition of cryptographically secure watermarking for perceptual objects. However, both works do not present a secure concrete scheme. A few works study secure constructions of watermarking for cryptographic primitives [NSS99, YF11, Nis13, Nis19], but they consider only restricted removal strategies. Cohen et al. [CHN+18] present stronger definitions for software watermarking and the first secure watermarking schemes for cryptographic primitives *against arbitrary removal strategies*. After the celebrated work, watermarking for cryptographic primitives have been extensively studied [BLW17, KW21, QWZ18, KW19, YAL+19, GKM+19, YAYX20, Nis20].

Primary applications of watermarking are identifying ownership of objects and tracing users that distribute illegal copies. Watermarking for cryptographic primitives also has another exciting application. Aaronson et al. [ALL+21] and Kitagawa et al. [KNY21] concurrently and independently find that we can construct secure software leasing schemes by combining watermarking with quantum cryptography.[1] Secure software leasing [AL21] is a quantum cryptographic primitive that prevents users from generating authenticated pirated copies of leased software.[2] Since watermarking has such an exciting application in quantum cryptography and quantum computers might be an imminent threat to cryptography due to rapid progress in research on quantum computing, it is natural and fascinating to study secure software watermarking in the quantum setting.

In quantum cryptography, building blocks must be quantum-safe such as lattice-based cryptography [Reg09]. However, even if we replace building blocks of existing cryptographic primitives/protocols with quantum-safe ones, we do not necessarily obtain quantum-safe cryptographic primitives/protocols [BDF+11, ARU14]. We sometimes need new proof techniques which are different from classical ones due to quantum specific properties such as no-cloning and superposition access [Wat09, Zha12b, Zha12a, Unr12, Zha19, CMSZ21]. Even worse, we must consider entirely different security models in some settings.

---

[1] Precisely speaking, Aaronson et al. achieve copy-detection schemes [ALL+21], which are essentially the same as secure software leasing schemes.

[2] Leased software must be a quantum state since classical bit strings can be easily copied.

Zhandry [Zha20] studies traitor tracing [CFN94] in the quantum setting as such an example. In quantum traitor tracing, an adversary can output a *quantum state* as a pirate decoder. Zhandry shows that we need new techniques for achieving quantum traitor tracing because running a quantum pirate decoder to extract information may irreversibly alter the state due to measurement.

Zhandry [Zha20] refers to software watermarking as a cryptographic primitive that has a similar issue to quantum traitor tracing. However, his work focuses only on traitor tracing and does not study software watermarking against quantum adversaries. If we use software watermarking in the quantum setting, an adversary can output a *quantum state* as a pirate circuit where an embedded message might be removed. However, previous works consider a setting where an adversary outputs a *classical* pirate circuit. It is not clear whether watermarking schemes based on quantum-safe cryptography are secure against quantum adversaries because we need an entirely new extraction algorithm to extract an embedded message from a *quantum* pirate circuit. Thus, the main question in this study is:

Can we achieve secure watermarking for cryptographic primitives against quantum adversaries?

We affirmatively answer this question in this work.

1.2 Our Result

Our main contributions are two-fold. One is the definitional work. We define watermarking for pseudorandom functions (PRFs) against quantum adversaries, where adversaries output a quantum state as a pirate circuit that distinguishes a PRF from a random function.[3] The other one is constructing the first secure watermarking PRFs against quantum adversaries. We present two watermarking PRFs as follows.

- We construct a privately extractable watermarking PRF against quantum adversaries from the quantum hardness of the learning with errors (LWE) problem. This watermarking PRF is secure in the presence of the extraction oracle and supports public marking. That is, the marking and extraction algorithms use a public parameter and secret extraction key, respectively. The watermarking PRF is unremovable even if adversaries have access to the extraction oracle, which returns a result of extraction for a queried quantum circuit.
- We construct a publicly extractable watermarking PRF against quantum adversaries from indistinguishability obfuscation (IO) and the quantum hardness of the LWE problem. This watermarking PRF also supports public marking. That is, the marking and extraction algorithms use a public parameter

---

[3] This definitional choice comes from the definition of traceable PRFs [GKWW21]. See Sect. 1.3 and the full version for the detail.

and a public extraction key, respectively. The watermarking PRF is unremovable (we do not need to consider the mark and extraction oracles since it supports public marking and public extraction).

The former and latter PRFs satisfy weak pseudorandomness and standard (strong) pseudorandomness even against a watermarking authority, respectively.

We develop a quantum extraction algorithm to achieve the results above. Zhandry [Zha20] presents a useful technique for extracting information from quantum states without destroying them too much. However, we cannot simply apply his technique to the watermarking setting. Embedded information (arbitrary string) is chosen from an exponentially large set in the watermarking setting. On the other hand, in the traitor tracing setting, we embed a user index, which could be chosen from a polynomially large set, in a decryption key. Zhandry's technique is tailored to traitor tracing based on private linear broadcast encryption (PLBE) [BSW06] where user information is chosen from a polynomially large set with linear structure. Thus, we extend Zhandry's technique [Zha20] to extract information chosen from an exponentially large set. We also introduce the notion of extraction-less watermarking as a crucial tool to achieve watermarking against quantum adversaries. This tool is a suitable building block for our quantum extraction technique in our watermarking extraction algorithm. These are our technical contributions. See Sect. 1.3 for the detail.

Although this paper focuses on watermarking PRFs against quantum adversaries, it is easy to extend our definitions to watermarking public-key encryption (PKE) against quantum adversaries. In particular, our construction technique easily yields watermarking PKE (where a decryption circuit is marked) schemes. However, we do not provide the detail of watermarking PKE in this paper. We will provide them in the full version.

1.3   Technical Overview

Syntax of Watermarking PRF. We first review the syntax of watermarking PRF used in this work. A watermarking PRF scheme consists of five algorithms (Setup, Gen, Eval, Mark, $\mathcal{E}\!x\!tract$).[4] Setup outputs a public parameter pp and an extraction key xk. Gen is given pp and outputs a PRF key prfk and a public tag τ. Eval is the PRF evaluation algorithm that takes as an input prfk and x in the domain and outputs y. By using Mark, we can generate a marked evaluation circuit that has embedded message m $\in \{0,1\}^{\ell_m}$ and can be used to evaluate Eval(prfk, x') for almost all x'. Finally, $\mathcal{E}\!x\!tract$ is the extraction algorithm supposed to extract the embedded message from a pirated quantum evaluation circuit generated from the marked evaluation circuit. By default, in this work, we consider the public marking setting, where anyone can execute Mark. Thus, Mark takes pp as an input. On the other hand, we consider both the private extraction and the public extraction settings. Thus, the extraction key xk used

---

[4] In this paper, standard math font stands for classical algorithms, and calligraphic font stands for quantum algorithms.

by *Extract* is kept secret by an authority in the private extraction setting and made public in the public extraction setting.

In this work, we allow *Extract* to take the public tag τ generated with the original PRF key corresponding to the pirate circuit. In reality, we execute *Extract* for a software when a user claims that the software is illegally generated by using her/his PRF key. Thus, it is natural to expect we can use a user's public tag for extraction. Moreover, pirate circuits are distinguishers, not predictors in this work. As discussed by Goyal et al. [GKWW21], security against pirate distinguishers is much preferable compared to security against pirate predictors considered in many previous works on watermarking. In this case, it seems that such additional information fed to *Extract* is unavoidable. For a more detailed discussion on the syntax, see the discussion in Sect. 3.1.

It is also natural to focus on distinguishers breaking weak pseudorandomness of PRFs when we consider pirate distinguishers instead of pirate predictors. Goyal et al. [GKWW21] already discussed this point. Thus, we focus on watermarking weak PRF in this work.

Definition of Unremovability Aagainst Quantum Adversaries. We say that a watermarking PRF scheme satisfies unremovability if given a marked evaluation circuit $\widetilde{C}$ that has an embedded message m, any adversary cannot generate a circuit such that it is a "good enough circuit", but the extraction algorithm fails to output m. In this work, we basically follow the notion of "good enough circuit" defined by Goyal et al. [GKWW21] as stated above. Let D be the following distribution for a PRF Eval(prfk, $\cdot$) : Dom $\to$ Ran.

D:Generate $b \leftarrow \{0,1\}$, $x \leftarrow$ Dom, and $y_0 \leftarrow$ Ran. Compute $y_1 \leftarrow$ Eval(prfk, x).
　　Output (b, x, y_b).

A circuit is defined as good enough circuit with respect to Eval(prfk, $\cdot$) if given (x, y_b) output by D, it can correctly guess b with probability significantly greater than $1/2$. In other words, a circuit is defined as good enough if the circuit breaks weak PRF security.

Below, for a distribution D' whose output is of the form (b, x, y), let $\mathcal{M}_{D'} = (\boldsymbol{M}_{D',0}, \boldsymbol{M}_{D',1})$ be binary positive operator valued measures (POVMs) that represents generating random (b, x, y) from D' and testing if a quantum circuit can guess b from (x, y). Then, for a quantum state $|\psi\rangle$, the overall distinguishing advantage of it for the above distribution D is $\langle\psi| \boldsymbol{M}_{D,0} |\psi\rangle$. Thus, a natural adaptation of the above notion of goodness for quantum circuits might be to define a quantum state $|\psi\rangle$ as good if $\langle\psi| \boldsymbol{M}_{D,0} |\psi\rangle$ is significantly greater than $1/2$. However, this notion of goodness for quantum circuits is not really meaningful. The biggest issue is that it does not consider the stateful nature of quantum programs.

This issue was previously addressed by Zhandry [Zha20] in the context of traitor tracing against quantum adversaries. In the context of classical traitor tracing or watermarking, we can assume that a pirate circuit is stateless, or can be rewound to its original state. This assumption is reasonable. If we have the software description of the pirate circuit, such a rewinding is trivial. Even if we have a hardware box in which a pirate circuit is built, it seems that such a rewinding is possible by hard reboot or cutting power. On the other hand, in the context of quantum watermarking, we have to consider that a pirate circuit is inherently stateful since it is described as a quantum state. Operations to a quantum state can alter the state, and in general, it is impossible to rewind the state into its original state. Regarding the definition of good quantum circuits above, if we can somehow compute the average success probability $\langle \psi | \, M_{D,0} \, | \psi \rangle$ of the quantum state $| \psi \rangle$, the process can change or destroy the quantum state $| \psi \rangle$. Namely, even if we once confirm that the quantum state $| \psi \rangle$ is good by computing $\langle \psi | \, M_{D,0} \, | \psi \rangle$, we cannot know the success probability of the quantum state even right after the computation. Clearly, the above notion of goodness is not the right notion, and we need one that captures the stateful nature of quantum programs.

In the work on traitor tracing against quantum adversaries, Zhandry [Zha20] proposed a notion of goodness for quantum programs that solves the above issue. We adopt it. For the above POVMs $\mathcal{M}_D$, let $\mathcal{M}'_D$ be the projective measurement $\{P_p\}_{p \in [0,1]}$ that projects a state onto the eigenspaces of $M_{D,0}$, where each p is an eigenvalue of $M_{D,0}$. $\mathcal{M}'_D$ is called projective implementation of $\mathcal{M}_D$ and denoted as $\mathsf{ProjImp}(\mathcal{M}_D)$. Zhandry showed that the following process has the same output distribution as $\mathcal{M}_D$:

1. Apply the projective measurement $\mathcal{M}'_D = \mathsf{ProjImp}(\mathcal{M}_D)$ and obtain p.
2. Output 0 with probability p and output 1 with probability $1 - p$.

Intuitively, $\mathcal{M}'_D$ project a state to an eigenvector of $M_{D,0}$ with eigenvalue p, which can be seen as a quantum state with success probability p. Using $\mathcal{M}'_D$, Zhandry defined that a quantum circuit is Live if the outcome of the measurement $\mathcal{M}'_D$ is significantly greater than $1/2$. The notion of Live is a natural extension of the classical goodness since it collapses to the classical goodness for a classical decoder. Moreover, we can ensure that a quantum state that is tested as Live still has a high success probability. On the other hand, the above notion of goodness cannot say anything about the post-tested quantum state's success probability even if the test is passed. In this work, we use the notion of Live quantum circuits as the notion of good quantum circuits.

Difficulty of Quantum Watermarking PRF. From the above discussion, our goal is to construct a watermarking PRF scheme that guarantees that we can extract the embedded message correctly if a pirated quantum circuit is Live. In watermarking PRF schemes, we usually extract an embedded message by applying several tests on success probability to a pirate circuit. When a pirate circuit is a quantum state, the set of tests that we can apply is highly limited compared to a classical circuit due to the stateful nature of quantum states.

One set of tests we can apply without destroying the quantum state is $\mathsf{ProjImp}(\mathcal{M}_{D'})$ for distributions D' that are indistinguishable from D from the view of the pirate circuit.[5] We denote this set as $\{\mathsf{ProjImp}(\mathcal{M}_{D'}) \mid D' \overset{c}{\approx} D\}$. Zhandry showed that if distributions D_1 and D_2 are indistinguishable, the outcome of $\mathsf{ProjImp}(\mathcal{M}_{D_1})$ is close to that of $\mathsf{ProjImp}(\mathcal{M}_{D_2})$. By combining this property with the projective property of projective implementations, as long as the initial quantum state is Live and we apply only tests contained in $\{\mathsf{ProjImp}(\mathcal{M}_{D'}) \mid D' \overset{c}{\approx} D\}$, the quantum state remains Live. On the other hand, if we apply a test outside of $\{\mathsf{ProjImp}(\mathcal{M}_{D'}) \mid D' \overset{c}{\approx} D\}$, the quantum state might be irreversibly altered. This fact is a problem since the set $\{\mathsf{ProjImp}(\mathcal{M}_{D'}) \mid D' \overset{c}{\approx} D\}$ only is not sufficient to implement the existing widely used construction method for watermarking PRF schemes.

To see this, we briefly review the method. In watermarking PRF schemes, the number of possible embedded messages is super-polynomial, and thus we basically need to extract an embedded message in a bit-by-bit manner. In the method, such a bit-by-bit extraction is done as follows. For every $i \in [\ell_\mathsf{m}]$, we define two distributions $S_{i,0}$ and $S_{i,1}$ whose output is of the form (b, x, y) as D above. Then, we design a marked circuit with embedded message $\mathsf{m} \in \{0,1\}^{\ell_\mathsf{m}}$ so that it can be used to guess b from (x, y) with probability significantly greater than $1/2$ only for $S_{i,0}$ (resp. $S_{i,1}$) if $\mathsf{m}[i] = 0$ (resp. $\mathsf{m}[i] = 1$). The extraction algorithm can extract i-th bit of the message $\mathsf{m}[i]$ by checking for which distributions of $S_{i,0}$ and $S_{i,1}$ a pirate circuit has a high distinguishing advantage.

As stated above, we cannot use this standard method to extract a message from quantum pirate circuits. The reason is that $S_{i,0}$ and $S_{i,1}$ are typically distinguishable. This implies that at least either one of $\mathsf{ProjImp}(\mathcal{M}_{S_{i,0}})$ or $\mathsf{ProjImp}(\mathcal{M}_{S_{i,1}})$ is not contained in $\{\mathsf{ProjImp}(\mathcal{M}_{D'}) \mid D' \overset{c}{\approx} D\}$. Since the test outside of $\{\mathsf{ProjImp}(\mathcal{M}_{D'}) \mid D' \overset{c}{\approx} D\}$ might destroy the quantum state, we might not be able to perform the process for all i, and fail to extract the entire bits of the embedded message.

It seems that to perform the bit-by-bit extraction for a quantum state, we need to extend the set of applicable tests and come up with a new extraction method.

Our Solution: Use of Reverse Projective Property. We find that as another applicable set of tests, we have $\mathsf{ProjImp}(\mathcal{M}_{D'})$ for distributions D' that are indistinguishable from D^{rev}, where D^{rev} is the following distribution.

D^{rev}: Generate $b \leftarrow \{0,1\}$, $x \leftarrow \mathsf{Dom}$, and $y_0 \leftarrow \mathsf{Ran}$. Compute $y_1 \leftarrow \mathsf{Eval}(\mathsf{prfk}, x)$. Output $(1 \oplus b, x, y_b)$.

We denote the set as $\{\mathsf{ProjImp}(\mathcal{M}_{D'}) \mid D' \overset{c}{\approx} D^{\mathrm{rev}}\}$. D^{rev} is the distribution the first bit of whose output is flipped from that of D. Then, $\mathcal{M}_{D^{\mathrm{rev}}}$ can be seen as POVMs that represents generating random (b, x, y_b) from D and testing if a quantum circuit *cannot* guess b from (x, y_b). Thus, we see that $\mathcal{M}_{D^{\mathrm{rev}}} = (\boldsymbol{M}_{D,1}, \boldsymbol{M}_{D,0})$. Recall that $\mathcal{M}_D = (\boldsymbol{M}_{D,0}, \boldsymbol{M}_{D,1})$.

---

[5] In the actual extraction process, we use an approximation of projective implementation introduced by Zhandry [Zha20] since applying a projective implementation is inefficient. In this overview, we ignore this issue for simplicity.

Let $D_1 \in \{\mathsf{ProjImp}(\mathcal{M}_{D'}) \mid D' \overset{c}{\approx} D\}$ and D_1^{rev} be the distribution that generates $(b, x, y) \leftarrow D_1$ and outputs $(1 \oplus b, x, y)$. D_1^{rev} is a distribution contained in $\{\mathsf{ProjImp}(\mathcal{M}_{D'}) \mid D' \overset{c}{\approx} D^{\mathrm{rev}}\}$. Similarly to the relation between D and D^{rev}, if $\mathcal{M}_{D_1} = (\boldsymbol{M}_{D_1,0}, \boldsymbol{M}_{D_1,1})$, we have $\mathcal{M}_{D_1^{\mathrm{rev}}} = (\boldsymbol{M}_{D_1^{\mathrm{rev}},1}, \boldsymbol{M}_{D_1^{\mathrm{rev}},0})$. Since $\boldsymbol{M}_{D_1,0} + \boldsymbol{M}_{D_1,1} = \boldsymbol{I}$, $\boldsymbol{M}_{D_1,0}$ and $\boldsymbol{M}_{D_1,1}$ share the same set of eigenvectors, and if a vector is an eigenvector of $\boldsymbol{M}_{D_1,0}$ with eigenvalue p, then it is also an eigenvector of $\boldsymbol{M}_{D_1,1}$ with eigenvalue $1 - p$. Thus, if apply $\mathsf{ProjImp}(\mathcal{M}_{D_1})$ and $\mathsf{ProjImp}(\mathcal{M}_{D_1^{\mathrm{rev}}})$ successively to a quantum state and obtain the outcomes $\widetilde{p}_1$ and $\widetilde{p}_1'$, it holds that $\widetilde{p}_1' = 1 - \widetilde{p}_1$. We call this property the reverse projective property of the projective implementation.

Combining projective and reverse projective properties and the outcome closeness for indistinguishable distributions of the projective implementation, we see that the following key fact holds.

Key fact: As long as the initial quantum state is Live and we apply tests contained in $\{\mathsf{ProjImp}(\mathcal{M}_{D'}) \mid D' \overset{c}{\approx} D\}$ or $\{\mathsf{ProjImp}(\mathcal{M}_{D'}) \mid D' \overset{c}{\approx} D^{\mathrm{rev}}\}$, the quantum state remains Live. Moreover, if the outcome of applying $\mathsf{ProjImp}(\mathcal{M}_D)$ to the initial state is p, we get the outcome close to p every time we apply a test in $\{\mathsf{ProjImp}(\mathcal{M}_{D'}) \mid D' \overset{c}{\approx} D\}$, and we get the outcome close to $1 - p$ every time we apply a test in $\{\mathsf{ProjImp}(\mathcal{M}_{D'}) \mid D' \overset{c}{\approx} D^{\mathrm{rev}}\}$.

In this work, we perform bit-by-bit extraction of embedded messages by using the above key fact of the projective implementation. To this end, we introduce the new notion of extraction-less watermarking PRF as an intermediate primitive.

Via Extraction-Less Watermarking PRF. An extraction-less watermarking PRF scheme has almost the same syntax as a watermarking PRF scheme, except that it does not have an extraction algorithm $\mathcal{E}xtract$ and instead has a simulation algorithm Sim. Sim is given the extraction key xk, the public tag τ, and an index $i \in [\ell_m]$, and outputs a tuple of the form (γ, x, y). Sim simulates outputs of D or D^{rev} for a pirate circuit depending on the message embedded to the marked circuit corresponding to the pirate circuit. More concretely, we require that from the view of the pirate circuit generated from a marked circuit with embedded message $\mathsf{m} \in \{0,1\}^{\ell_m}$, outputs of Sim are indistinguishable from those of D if $\mathsf{m}[i] = 0$ and are indistinguishable from those of D^{rev} if $\mathsf{m}[i] = 1$ for every $i \in [\ell_m]$. We call this security notion simulatability for mark-dependent distributions (SIM-MDD security).

By using an extraction-less watermarking PRF scheme ELWMPRF, we construct a watermarking PRF scheme WMPRF against quantum adversaries as follows. We use Setup, Gen, Eval, Mark of ELWMPRF as Setup, Gen, Eval, Mark of WMPRF, respectively. We explain how to construct the extraction algorithm $\mathcal{E}xtract$ of WMPRF using Sim of ELWMPRF. For every $i \in [\ell_m]$, we define $D_{\tau,i}$ as the distribution that outputs randomly generated $(\gamma, x, y) \leftarrow \mathsf{Sim}(\mathsf{xk}, \tau, i)$. Given xk, τ, and a quantum state $|\psi\rangle$, $\mathcal{E}xtract$ extracts the embedded message in the bit-by-bit manner by repeating the following process for every $i \in [\ell_m]$.

- Apply $\mathsf{ProjImp}(\mathcal{M}_{D_{\tau,i}})$ to $|\psi_{i-1}\rangle$ and obtain the outcome $\widetilde{p}_i$, where $|\psi_0\rangle = |\psi\rangle$ and $|\psi_{i-1}\rangle$ is the state after the $(i-1)$-th loop for every $i \in [\ell_\mathsf{m}]$.
- Set $\mathsf{m}'_i = 0$ if $\widetilde{p}_i > 1/2$ and otherwise $\mathsf{m}'_i = 1$.

The extracted message is set to $\mathsf{m}'_1 \| \cdots \| \mathsf{m}'_{\ell_\mathsf{m}}$.

We show that the above construction satisfies unremovability. Suppose an adversary is given marked circuit $\widetilde{C} \leftarrow \mathsf{Mark}(\mathsf{pp}, \mathsf{prfk}, \mathsf{m})$ and generates a quantum state $|\psi\rangle$, where $(\mathsf{pp}, \mathsf{xk}) \leftarrow \mathsf{Setup}(1^\lambda)$ and $(\mathsf{prfk}, \tau) \leftarrow \mathsf{Gen}(\mathsf{pp})$. Suppose also that $|\psi\rangle$ is Live. This assumption means that the outcome p of applying $\mathsf{ProjImp}(\mathcal{M}_D)$ to $|\psi\rangle$ is $1/2 + \epsilon$, where ϵ is an inverse polynomial. For every $i \in [\ell_\mathsf{m}]$, from the SIM-MDD security of ELWMPRF, $D_{\tau,i}$ is indistinguishable from D if $\mathsf{m}[i] = 0$ and is indistinguishable from D^rev if $\mathsf{m}[i] = 1$. This means that $D_{\tau,i} \in \{\mathsf{ProjImp}(\mathcal{M}_{D'}) \mid D' \overset{\mathsf{c}}{\approx} D\}$ if $\mathsf{m}[i] = 0$ and $D_{\tau,i} \in \{\mathsf{ProjImp}(\mathcal{M}_{D'}) \mid D' \overset{\mathsf{c}}{\approx} D^\mathsf{rev}\}$ if $\mathsf{m}[i] = 1$. Then, from the above key fact of the projective implementation, it holds that $\widetilde{p}_i$ is close to $1/2 + \epsilon > 1/2$ if $\mathsf{m}[i] = 0$ and is close to $1/2 - \epsilon < 1/2$ if $\mathsf{m}[i] = 1$. Therefore, we see that $\mathcal{E}xtract$ correctly extract m from $|\psi\rangle$. This means that WMPRF satisfies unremovability.

The above definition, construction, and security analysis are simplified and ignore many subtleties. The most significant point is that we use approximated projective implementations introduced by Zhandry [Zha20] instead of projective implementations in the actual construction since applying a projective implementation is an inefficient process. Moreover, though the outcomes of (approximate) projective implementations for indistinguishable distributions are close, in the actual analysis, we have to take into account that the outcomes gradually change every time we apply an (approximate) projective implementation. These issues can be solved by doing careful parameter settings.

Comparison with the Work by Zhandry [Zha20]. Some readers familiar with Zhandry's work [Zha20] might think that our technique contradicts the lesson from Zhandry's work since it essentially says that once we find a large gap in success probabilities, the tested quantum pirate circuit might self-destruct. However, this is not the case. What Zhandry's work really showed is the following. Once a quantum pirate circuit itself detects that there is a large gap in success probabilities, it might self-destruct. Even if an extractor finds a large gap in success probabilities, if the tested quantum pirate circuit itself cannot detect the large gap, the pirate circuit cannot self-destruct. In Zhandry's work, whenever an extractor finds a large gap, the tested pirate circuit also detects the large gap. In our work, the tested pirate circuit cannot detect a large gap throughout the extraction process while an extractor can find it.

The reason why a pirate circuit cannot detect a large gap in our scheme even if an extractor can find it is as follows. Recall that in the above extraction process of our scheme based on an extraction-less watermarking PRF scheme, we apply $\mathsf{ProjImp}(\mathcal{M}_{D_{\tau,i}})$ to the tested pirate circuit for every $i \in [\ell_\mathsf{m}]$. Each $D_{\tau,i}$ outputs a tuple of the form (b, x, y) and is indistinguishable from D or D^rev depending on the embedded message. In the process, we apply $\mathsf{ProjImp}(\mathcal{M}_{D_{\tau,i}})$ for every $i \in [\ell_\mathsf{m}]$, and we get the success probability p if $D_{\tau,i}$ is indistinguishable from D

and we get $1 - p$ if $D_{\tau,i}$ is indistinguishable from D^{rev}. The tested pirate circuit needs to know which of D or D^{rev} is indistinguishable from the distribution $D_{\tau,i}$ behind the projective implementation to know which of p or $1 - p$ is the result of an application of a projective implementation. However, this is impossible. The tested pirate circuit receives only (x, y) part of $D_{\tau,i}$'s output and not b part. (Recall that the task of the pirate circuit is to guess b from (x, y).) The only difference between D and D^{rev} is that the first-bit b is flipped. Thus, if the b part is dropped, $D_{\tau,i}$ is, in fact, indistinguishable from both D and D^{rev}. As a result, the pirate program cannot know which of p or $1 - p$ is the result of an application of a projective implementation. In other words, the pirate circuit cannot detect a large gap in our extraction process.

Instantiating Extraction-Less Watermarking PRF. In the rest of this overview, we will explain how to realize extraction-less watermarking PRF.

We consider the following two settings similar to the ordinary watermarking PRF. Recall that we consider the public marking setting by default.

Private-Simulatable: In this setting, the extraction key xk fed into Sim is kept secret. We require that SIM-MDD security hold under the existence of the simulation oracle that is given a public tag τ' and an index $i' \in [\ell_m]$ and returns $\text{Sim}(\text{xk}, \tau', i')$. An extraction-less watermarking PRF scheme in this setting yields a watermarking PRF scheme against quantum adversaries in private-extractable setting where unremovability holds for adversaries who can access the extraction oracle.

Public-Simulatable: In this setting, the extraction key xk is publicly available. An extraction-less watermarking PRF scheme in this setting yields a watermarking PRF scheme against quantum adversaries in the public-extractable setting.

We provide a construction in the first setting using private constrained PRF based on the hardness of the LWE assumption. Also, we provide a construction in the second setting based on IO and the hardness of the LWE assumption.

To give a high-level idea behind the above constructions, in this overview, we show how to construct a public-simulatable extraction-less watermarking PRF in the token-based setting [CHN+18]. In the token-based setting, we treat a marked circuit $\widetilde{C} \leftarrow \text{Mark}(\text{pp}, \text{prfk}, m)$ as a tamper-proof hardware token that an adversary can only access in a black-box way.

Before showing the actual construction, we explain the high-level idea. Recall that SIM-MDD security requires that an adversary $\mathcal{A}$ who is given $\widetilde{C} \leftarrow \text{Mark}(\text{pp}, \text{prfk}, m)$ cannot distinguish $(\gamma^*, x^*, y^*) \leftarrow \text{Sim}(\text{xk}, \tau, i^*)$ from an output of D if $m[i^*] = 0$ and from that of D^{rev} if $m[i^*] = 1$. This is the same as requiring that $\mathcal{A}$ cannot distinguish $(\gamma^*, x^*, y^*) \leftarrow \text{Sim}(\text{xk}, \tau, i^*)$ from that of the following distribution D_{real,i^*}. We can check that D_{real,i^*} is identical with D if $m[i^*] = 0$ and with D^{rev} if $m[i^*] = 1$.

D_{real,i^*}:Generate $\gamma \leftarrow \{0, 1\}$ and $x \leftarrow \text{Dom}$. Then, if $\gamma = m[i^*]$, generate $y \leftarrow$ Ran, and otherwise, compute $y \leftarrow \text{Eval}(\text{prfk}, x)$. Output (γ, x, y).

Essentially, the only attack that $\mathcal{A}$ can perform is to feed x^* contained in the given tuple (γ^*, x^*, y^*) to $\widetilde{C}$ and compares the result $\widetilde{C}(x^*)$ with y^*, if we ensure that γ^*, x^* are pseudorandom. In order to make the construction immune to this attack, letting $\widetilde{C} \leftarrow \mathsf{Mark}(\mathsf{pp}, \mathsf{prfk}, \mathsf{m})$ and $(\gamma^*, x^*, y^*) \leftarrow \mathsf{Sim}(\mathsf{xk}, \tau, i^*)$, we have to design Sim and $\widetilde{C}$ so that

- If $\gamma = \mathsf{m}[i^*]$, $\widetilde{C}(x^*)$ outputs a value different from y^*.
- If $\gamma \neq \mathsf{m}[i^*]$, $\widetilde{C}(x^*)$ outputs y^*.

We achieve these conditions as follows. First, we set (γ^*, x^*, y^*) output by $\mathsf{Sim}(\mathsf{xk}, \tau, i^*)$ so that γ^* and y^* is random values and x^* is an encryption of $y^* \| i^* \| \gamma^*$ by a public-key encryption scheme with pseudorandom ciphertext property, where the encryption key pk is included in τ. Then, we set $\widetilde{C}$ as a token such that it has the message m and the decryption key sk corresponding to pk hardwired, and it outputs y^* if the input is decryptable and $\gamma^* \neq \mathsf{m}[i^*]$ holds for the decrypted $y^* \| i^* \| \gamma^*$, and otherwise behaves as $\mathsf{Eval}(\mathsf{prfk}, \cdot)$. The actual construction is as follows.

Let PRF be a PRF family consisting of functions $\{\mathsf{F}_{\mathsf{prfk}}(\cdot) : \{0,1\}^n \rightarrow \{0,1\}^\lambda | \mathsf{prfk}\}$, where λ is the security parameter and n is sufficiently large. Let $\mathsf{PKE} = (\mathsf{KG}, \mathsf{E}, \mathsf{D})$ be a CCA secure public-key encryption scheme satisfying pseudorandom ciphertext property. Using these ingredients, We construct an extraction-less watermarking PRF scheme $\mathsf{ELWMPRF} = (\mathsf{Setup}, \mathsf{Gen}, \mathsf{Eval}, \mathsf{Mark}, \mathsf{Sim})$ as follows.

$\mathsf{Setup}(1^\lambda)$: In this construction, $\mathsf{pp} := \bot$ and $\mathsf{xk} := \bot$.
$\mathsf{Gen}(\mathsf{pp})$: It generates a fresh PRF key prfk of PRF and a key pair $(\mathsf{pk}, \mathsf{sk}) \leftarrow \mathsf{KG}(1^\lambda)$. The PRF key is $(\mathsf{prfk}, \mathsf{sk})$ and the corresponding public tag is pk.
$\mathsf{Eval}((\mathsf{prfk}, \mathsf{sk}), x)$: It simply outputs $\mathsf{F}_{\mathsf{prfk}}(x)$.
$\mathsf{Mark}(\mathsf{pp}, (\mathsf{prfk}, \mathsf{sk}), \mathsf{m})$: It generates the following taken $\widetilde{C}[\mathsf{prfk}, \mathsf{sk}, \mathsf{m}]$.

Hard-Coded Constants: $\mathsf{prfk}, \mathsf{sk}, \mathsf{m}$.
Input: $x \in \{0,1\}^n$.

1. Try to decrypt $y \| i \| \gamma \leftarrow \mathsf{D}(\mathsf{sk}, x)$ with $y \in \{0,1\}^\lambda$, $i \in [\ell_\mathsf{m}]$, and $\gamma \in \{0,1\}$.
2. If decryption succeeds, output y if $\gamma \neq \mathsf{m}[i]$ and $\mathsf{F}_{\mathsf{prfk}}(x)$ otherwise.
3. Otherwise, output $\mathsf{F}_{\mathsf{prfk}}(x)$.

$\mathsf{Sim}(\mathsf{xk}, \tau, i)$: It first generates $\gamma \leftarrow \{0,1\}$ and $y \leftarrow \{0,1\}^\lambda$. Then, it parses $\tau := \mathsf{pk}$ and generates $x \leftarrow \mathsf{E}(\mathsf{pk}, y \| i \| \gamma)$. Finally, it outputs (γ, x, y).

We check that $\mathsf{ELWMPRF}$ satisfies SIM-MDD security. For simplicity, we fix the message $\mathsf{m} \in [\ell_\mathsf{m}]$ embedded into the challenge PRF key. Then, for any adversary $\mathcal{A}$ and $i^* \in [\ell_\mathsf{m}]$, SIM-MDD security requires that given $\widetilde{C}[\mathsf{prfk}, \mathsf{sk}, \mathsf{m}] \leftarrow \mathsf{Mark}(\mathsf{mk}, \mathsf{prfk}, \mathsf{m})$ and $\tau = \mathsf{pk}$, $\mathcal{A}$ cannot distinguish $(\gamma^*, x^* = \mathsf{E}(\mathsf{pk}, y^* \| i^* \| \gamma^*), y^*) \leftarrow \mathsf{Sim}(\mathsf{xk}, \tau, i^*)$ from an output of D if $\mathsf{m}[i^*] = 0$ and is indistinguishable from D^{rev} if $\mathsf{m}[i^*] = 1$.

We consider the case of $\mathsf{m}[i^*] = 0$. We can finish the security analysis by considering the following sequence of mutually indistinguishable hybrid games, where $\mathcal{A}$ is given $(\gamma^*, x^* = \mathsf{E}(\mathsf{pk}, y^*\|i^*\|\gamma^*), y^*) \leftarrow \mathsf{Sim}(\mathsf{xk}, \tau, i^*)$ in the first game, and on the other hand, is given $(\gamma^*, x^*, y^*) \leftarrow D$ in the last game. We first change the game so that x^* is generated as a uniformly random value instead of $x^* \leftarrow \mathsf{E}(\mathsf{pk}, y^*\|i^*\|\gamma^*)$ by using the pseudorandom ciphertext property under CCA of PKE. This is possible since the CCA oracle can simulate access to the marked token $\widetilde{C}[\mathsf{prfk}, \mathsf{sk}, \mathsf{m}]$ by $\mathcal{A}$. Then, we further change the security game so that if $\gamma^* = 1$, y^* is generated as $\mathsf{F}_{\mathsf{prfk}}(x^*)$ instead of a uniformly random value by using the pseudorandomness of PRF. Note that if $\gamma^* = 0$, y^* remains uniformly at random. We see that if $\gamma^* = 1$, the token $\widetilde{C}[\mathsf{prfk}, \mathsf{sk}, \mathsf{m}]$ never evaluate $\mathsf{F}_{\mathsf{prfk}}(x^*)$ since $\mathsf{m}[i^*] \neq \gamma^*$. Thus, this change is possible. We see that now the distribution of (γ^*, x^*, y^*) is exactly the same as that output by D. Similarly, in the case of $\mathsf{m}[i^*] = 1$, we can show that an output of $\mathsf{Sim}(\mathsf{xk}, \tau, i^*)$ is indistinguishable from that output by D^{rev}. The only difference is that in the final step, we change the security game so that y^* is generated as $\mathsf{F}_{\mathsf{prfk}}(x^*)$ if $\gamma^* = 0$.

In the actual public-simulatable construction, we implement this idea using iO and puncturable encryption [CHN+18] instead of token and CCA secure public-key encryption. Also, in the actual secret-simulatable construction, we basically follow the same idea using private constrained PRF and secret-key encryption.

1.4 Organization

Due to the space limitation, we omit preliminaries including notations, basics on quantum informations, and definitions of standard cryptographic tools. We also omit most security proofs. See the full version of this paper for omitted contents. In Sect. 2, we introduce some notions of quantum measurements. In Sect. 3, we define watermarking PRF against quantum adversaries. In Sect. 4, we define extraction-less watermarking PRF. In Sect. 5, we show we can realize watermarking PRF against quantum adversaries from extraction-less watermarking PRF. In Sect. 6, we provide an instantiation of extraction-less watermarking PRF with private simulation based on the LWE assumption. In Sect. 7, we provide an instantiation of extraction-less watermarking PRF with public simulation based on IO and the LWE assumption.

2 Measurement Implementation

Definition 2.1 (Projective Implementation). *Let:*

- $\mathcal{P} = (\boldsymbol{P}, \boldsymbol{I} - \boldsymbol{P})$ *be a binary outcome POVM*
- D *be a finite set of distributions over outcomes* $\{0, 1\}$
- $\mathcal{E} = \{\boldsymbol{E}_D\}_{D \in \mathcal{D}}$ *be a projective measurement with index set* $\mathcal{D}$.

We define the following measurement.

1. *Measure under the projective measurement* $\mathcal{E}$ *and obtain a distribution* D *over* $\{0, 1\}$.
2. *Output a bit sampled from the distribution* D.

We say this measurement is a projective implementation of $\mathcal{P}$, *denoted by* ProjImp($\mathcal{P}$) *if it is equivalent to* $\mathcal{P}$.

Theorem 2.1 ([Zha20, Lemma 1]). *Any binary outcome POVM* $\mathcal{P} = (\boldsymbol{P}, \boldsymbol{I} - \boldsymbol{P})$ *has a projective implementation* ProjImp($\mathcal{P}$).

Definition 2.2 (Shift Distance). *For two distributions* D_0, D_1, *the shift distance with parameter* ϵ, *denoted by* $\Delta^\epsilon_{\text{Shift}}(D_0, D_1)$, *is the smallest quantity* δ *such that for all* $x \in \mathbb{R}$:

$$\Pr[D_0 \le x] \le \Pr[D_1 \le x + \epsilon] + \delta, \qquad \Pr[D_0 \ge x] \le \Pr[D_1 \ge x - \epsilon] + \delta,$$
$$\Pr[D_1 \le x] \le \Pr[D_0 \le x + \epsilon] + \delta, \qquad \Pr[D_1 \ge x] \le \Pr[D_0 \ge x - \epsilon] + \delta.$$

For two real-valued measurements $\mathcal{M}$ *and* $\mathcal{N}$ *over the same quantum system, the shift distance between* $\mathcal{M}$ *and* $\mathcal{N}$ *with parameter* ϵ *is*

$$\Delta^\epsilon_{\text{Shift}}(\mathcal{M}, \mathcal{N}) := \sup_{|\psi\rangle} \Delta^\epsilon_{\text{Shift}}(\mathcal{M}(|\psi\rangle), \mathcal{N}(|\psi\rangle)).$$

Definition 2.3 ((ϵ, δ)-**Almost Projective** [Zha20]). *A real-valued quantum measurement* $\mathcal{M} = \{\boldsymbol{M}_i\}_{i \in \mathcal{I}}$ *is* (ϵ, δ)-*almost projective if the following holds. For any quantum state* $|\psi\rangle$, *we apply* $\mathcal{M}$ *twice in a row to* $|\psi\rangle$ *and obtain measurement outcomes* x *and* y, *respectively. Then,* $\Pr[|x - y| \le \epsilon] \ge 1 - \delta$.

Theorem 2.2 ([Zha20, Theorem 2]). *Let* D *be any probability distribution and* $\mathcal{P}$ *be a collection of projective measurements. For any* $0 < \epsilon, \delta < 1$, *there exists an algorithm of measurement* $\mathcal{API}^{\epsilon,\delta}_{\mathcal{P},D}$ *that satisfies the following.*

- $\Delta^\epsilon_{\text{Shift}}(\mathcal{API}^{\epsilon,\delta}_{\mathcal{P},D}, \text{ProjImp}(\mathcal{P}_D)) \le \delta$.
- $\mathcal{API}^{\epsilon,\delta}_{\mathcal{P},D}$ *is* (ϵ, δ)-*almost projective.*
- *The expected running time of* $\mathcal{API}^{\epsilon,\delta}_{\mathcal{P},D}$ *is* $T_{\mathcal{P},D} \cdot \text{poly}(1/\epsilon, \log(1/\delta))$ *where* $T_{\mathcal{P},D}$ *is the combined running time of* D, *the procedure mapping* $i \to (\boldsymbol{P}_i, \boldsymbol{I} - \boldsymbol{P}_i)$, *and the running time of measurement* $(\boldsymbol{P}_i, \boldsymbol{I} - \boldsymbol{P}_i)$.

Theorem 2.3 ([Zha20, Corollary 1]). *Let* q *be an efficiently constructible, potentially mixed state, and* D_0, D_1 *efficiently sampleable distributions. If* D_0 *and* D_1 *are computationally indistinguishable, for any inverse polynomial* ϵ *and any function* δ, *we have* $\Delta^{3\epsilon}_{\text{Shift}}(\mathcal{API}^{\epsilon,\delta}_{\mathcal{P},D_0}, \mathcal{API}^{\epsilon,\delta}_{\mathcal{P},D_1}) \le 2\delta + \text{negl}(\lambda)$.

Note that the indistinguishability of D_0 and D_1 needs to hold against distinguishers who can construct q in the theorem above. However, this fact is not explicitly stated in [Zha20]. We need to care about this condition if we need secret information to construct q, and the secret information is also needed to sample an output from D_0 or D_1. We handle such a situation when analyzing the unremovability of our privately extractable watermarking PRF. In that situation, we need a secret extraction key to construct q and sample an output from D_0 and D_1.

We also define the notion of the reverse almost projective property of API.

Definition 2.4 $((\epsilon, \delta)$-Reverse Almost Projective). *Let* $\mathcal{P} = \{(\Pi_i, \boldsymbol{I} - \Pi_i)\}_i$ *be a collection of binary outcome projective measurements. Let D be a distribution. We also let* $\mathcal{P}^{\mathtt{rev}} = \{(\boldsymbol{I} - \Pi_i, \Pi_i)\}_i$. *We say* $\mathcal{API}$ *is* (ϵ, δ)-*reverse almost projective if the following holds. For any quantum state* $|\psi\rangle$, *we apply* $\mathcal{API}^{\epsilon,\delta}_{\mathcal{P},D}$ *and* $\mathcal{API}^{\epsilon,\delta}_{\mathcal{P}^{\mathtt{rev}},D}$ *in a row to* $|\psi\rangle$ *and obtain measurement outcomes x and y, respectively. Then,* $\Pr[|(1 - x) - y| \le \epsilon] \ge 1 - \delta$.

We show that the measurement algorithm $\mathcal{API}^{\epsilon,\delta}_{\mathcal{P},D}$ in Theorem 2.2 also satisfies Definition 2.4. See the full version for the proof.

3 Definition of Quantum Watermarking

We introduce definitions for watermarking PRFs against quantum adversaries in this section.

3.1 Syntax and Pseudorandomness

Definition 3.1 (Watermarking PRF). *A watermarking PRF* WMPRF *for the message space* $\mathcal{M} := \{0, 1\}^{\ell_m}$ *with domain* Dom *and range* Ran *is a tuple of five algorithms* (Setup, Gen, Eval, Mark, Extract).

Setup$(1^\lambda) \to$ (pp, xk): *The setup algorithm takes as input the security parameter and outputs a public parameter* pp *and an extraction key* xk.

Gen(pp) $\to$ (prfk, τ): *The key generation algorithm takes as input the public parameter* pp *and outputs a PRF key* prfk *and a public tag* τ.

Eval(prfk, x) $\to y$: *The evaluation algorithm takes as input a PRF key* prfk *and an input $x \in$* Dom *and outputs $y \in$* Ran.

Mark(pp, prfk, m) $\to \widetilde{C}$: *The mark algorithm takes as input the public parameter* pp, *a PRF key* prfk, *and a message* m $\in \{0, 1\}^{\ell_m}$, *and outputs a marked evaluation circuit* $\widetilde{C}$.

Extract(xk, τ, C', ϵ) $\to$ m′: *The extraction algorithm takes as input an extraction key* xk, *a tag* τ, *a quantum circuit with classical inputs and outputs* $C' = (q, \boldsymbol{U})$, *and a parameter* ϵ, *and outputs* m′ *where* m′ $\in \{0, 1\}^{\ell_m} \cup$ {unmarked}.

Evaluation Correctness: *For any message* m $\in \{0, 1\}^{\ell_m}$, *it holds that*

$$\Pr\left[\widetilde{C}(x) = \mathsf{Eval}(\mathsf{prfk}, x) \,\middle|\, \begin{array}{l} (\mathsf{pp}, \mathsf{xk}) \leftarrow \mathsf{Setup}(1^\lambda) \\ (\mathsf{prfk}, \tau) \leftarrow \mathsf{Gen}(\mathsf{pp}) \\ \widetilde{C} \leftarrow \mathsf{Mark}(\mathsf{pp}, \mathsf{prfk}, \mathsf{m}) \\ x \leftarrow \mathsf{Dom} \end{array} \right] \ge 1 - \mathsf{negl}(\lambda).$$

Remark 3.1 (On Extraction Correctness). Usually, a watermarking PRF scheme is required to satisfy extraction correctness that ensures that we can correctly extract the embedded mark from an honestly marked circuit. However, as observed by Quach et al. [QWZ18], if we require the extraction correctness to hold for a randomly chosen PRF key, it is implied by unremovability defined below. Note that the unremovability defined below considers a distinguisher as a pirate circuit. However, it implies the extraction correctness since we can easily transform an honestly marked circuit into a successful distinguisher. Thus, we do not explicitly require a watermarking PRF scheme to satisfy extraction correctness in this work.

Remark 3.2 (On Public Marking). We consider only watermarking PRFs with public marking as in Definition 3.1 since we can achieve public marking by default. The reason is as follows. Suppose that we generate pp, xk, and a marking key mk at the setup. When we generate a PRF key and a public tag at Gen, we can first generate $(\mathsf{pp}', \mathsf{xk}', \mathsf{mk}') \leftarrow \mathsf{Setup}(1^\lambda)$ from scratch (ignoring the original $(\mathsf{pp}, \mathsf{xk}, \mathsf{mk})$) and set a PRF key $\widehat{\mathsf{prfk}} := (\mathsf{prfk}', \mathsf{mk}')$ and a public tag $\widehat{\tau} := (\mathsf{pp}', \mathsf{xk}', \tau')$ where $(\mathsf{prfk}', \tau') \leftarrow \mathsf{Gen}(\mathsf{pp}')$. That is, anyone can generate a marked circuit from $\widehat{\mathsf{prfk}} = (\mathsf{prfk}', \mathsf{mk}')$ by $\mathsf{Mark}(\mathsf{mk}', \mathsf{prfk}', m)$. Therefore, we consider public marking by default in our model.

Discussion on Syntax. Definition 3.1 is a natural quantum variant of classical watermarking PRFs except that the key generation algorithm outputs a public tag τ, and the extraction algorithm uses it. Such a public tag is not used in previous works on watermarking PRFs [CHN+18, KW21, QWZ18, KW19, YAL+19]. A public tag should not harm watermarking PRF security. We justify using τ as follows.

First, we need to obtain many pairs of input and output to extract an embedded message from a marked PRF in almost all known (classical) watermarking constructions [CHN+18, BLW17, KW21, QWZ18, KW19, YAL+19, GKM+19, Nis20]. This is because we must check whether a tested PRF circuit outputs particular values for particular inputs which *depends on the target PRF* (such particular inputs are known as marked points). Suppose marked points are fixed and do not depend on a PRF that will be marked. In that case, an adversary can easily remove an embedded message by destroying functionalities at the fixed marked points that could be revealed via a (non-target) marked PRF that an adversary generated. Recall that we consider the public marking setting. The attack was already observed by Cohen et al. [CHN+18].

Second, we consider a stronger adversary model than that in most previous works as the definition of traceable PRFs by Goyal et al. [GKWW21]. An adversary outputs a distinguisher-based pirate circuit in our security definition rather than a pirate circuit that computes an entire output of a PRF. This is a refined and realistic model, as Goyal et al. [GKWW21] argued. In this model, we cannot obtain a valid input-output pair from a pirate circuit anymore. Such a pair is typical information related to a target PRF. Goyal et al. resolve this issue by introducing a tracing key that is generated from a target PRF. Note that parameters of watermarking (pp and xk) should *not* be generated from a PRF since we consider many different PRF keys in the watermarking PRF setting.

Thus, if we would like to achieve an extraction algorithm and the stronger security notion simultaneously, an extraction algorithm should somehow take information related to a target PRF as input to correctly extract an embedded message. In the weaker adversary model, an extraction algorithm can easily obtain many valid input and output pairs by running a tested circuit many times. However, in the stronger distinguisher-based pirate circuit model, a pirate circuit outputs a single decision bit.

To resolve this issue, we introduce public tags. We think it is natural to have information related to the original PRF key in an extraction algorithm. In reality, we check a circuit when a user claims that her/his PRF key (PRF evaluation circuit) is illegally used. Thus, it is natural to expect we can use a user's public tag for extraction. This setting resembles watermarking for public-key cryptographic primitives, where a user public key is available in an extraction algorithm. In addition, public tags do not harm PRF security in our constructions. It is unclear whether we can achieve unremovability in the stronger distinguisher-based model without any syntax change (even in the classical setting).[6]

Extended Pseudorandomness. We consider extended weak pseudorandomness, where weak pseudorandomness holds even if the adversary generates pp. This notion is the counterpart of extended pseudorandomness by Quach et al. [QWZ18], where pseudorandomness holds in the presence of the extraction oracle. However, our pseudorandomness holds even against an authority unlike extended pseudorandomness by Quach et al. since we allow adversaries to generate a public parameter.

Definition 3.2 (Extended Weak Pseudorandomness against Authority). *To define extended weak pseudorandomness for watermarking PRFs, we define the game* $\mathsf{Exp}^{\mathsf{ext\text{-}wprf}}_{\mathcal{A},\mathsf{WMPRF}}(\lambda)$ *as follows.*

1. $\mathcal{A}$ *first sends* pp *to the challenger.*
2. *The challenger generates* $(\mathsf{prfk}, \tau) \leftarrow \mathsf{Gen}(\mathsf{pp})$ *and sends* τ *to* $\mathcal{A}$.
3. *The challenger chooses* coin $\leftarrow \{0,1\}$. $\mathcal{A}$ *can access to the following oracles.*
   O_{wprf}: *When this is invoked (no input), it returns* (a,b) *where* $a \leftarrow$ Dom *and* $b := \mathsf{Eval}(\mathsf{prfk}, a)$.
   O_{chall}: *When this is invoked (no input), it returns:*
   - (a,b) *where* $a \leftarrow$ Dom *and* $b := \mathsf{Eval}(\mathsf{prfk}, a)$ *if* coin $= 0$,
   - (a,b) *where* $a \leftarrow$ Dom *and* $b \leftarrow$ Ran *if* coin $= 1$.
   This oracle is invoked only once.
4. *When* $\mathcal{A}$ *terminates with output* coin′, *the challenger outputs 1 if* coin $=$ coin′ *and 0 otherwise.*

---

[6] Even if we consider the weaker adversary model, the same issue appears in the quantum setting in the end. If we run a quantum circuit for an input and measure the output, the measurement could irreversibly alter the quantum state and we lost the functionality of the original quantum state. That is, there is no guarantee that we can correctly check whether a tested quantum circuit is marked or not *after* we obtain a single valid pair of input and output by running the circuit. However, as we explained above, we want to obtain information related to a target PRF for extraction. Thus, we need a public tag in the syntax in either case.

We say that WMPRF *is extended weak pseudorandom if for every QPT* $\mathcal{A}$, *we have*

$$\mathsf{Adv}^{\mathsf{ext\text{-}wprf}}_{\mathcal{A},\mathsf{WMPRF}}(\lambda) = 2 \left| \Pr\left[\mathsf{Exp}^{\mathsf{ext\text{-}wprf}}_{\mathcal{A},\mathsf{WMPRF}}(\lambda) = 1 \right] - \frac{1}{2} \right| = \mathsf{negl}(\lambda).$$

3.2   Unremovability Against Quantum Adversaries

We define unremovability for watermarking PRFs against quantum adversaries. We first define quantum program with classical inputs and outputs and then define unremovability.

Definition 3.3 (Quantum Program with Classical Inputs and Outputs [ALL+21]). *A quantum program with classical inputs is a pair of quantum state q and unitaries $\{\boldsymbol{U}_x\}_{x \in [N]}$ where $[N]$ is the domain, such that the state of the program evaluated on input x is equal to $\boldsymbol{U}_x q \boldsymbol{U}_x^\dagger$. We measure the first register of $\boldsymbol{U}_x q \boldsymbol{U}_x^\dagger$ to obtain an output. We say that $\{\boldsymbol{U}_x\}_{x \in [N]}$ has a compact classical description $\boldsymbol{U}$ when applying $\boldsymbol{U}_x$ can be efficiently computed given $\boldsymbol{U}$ and x.*

Definition 3.4 (Unremovability for private extraction). *We consider the public marking and secret extraction setting here. Let $\epsilon \geq 0$. We define the game $\mathsf{Expt}^{\mathsf{nrmv}}_{\mathcal{A},\mathsf{WMPRF}}(\lambda, \epsilon)$ as follows.*

1. *The challenger generates* $(\mathsf{pp}, \mathsf{xk}) \leftarrow \mathsf{Setup}(1^\lambda)$ *and gives* pp *to the adversary $\mathcal{A}$. $\mathcal{A}$ send $\mathsf{m} \in \{0,1\}^{\ell_m}$ to the challenger. The challenger generates $(\mathsf{prfk}, \tau) \leftarrow \mathsf{Gen}(\mathsf{pp})$, computes $\widetilde{C} \leftarrow \mathsf{Mark}(\mathsf{pp}, \mathsf{prfk}, \mathsf{m})$, and sends τ and $\widetilde{C}$ to $\mathcal{A}$.*
2. *$\mathcal{A}$ can access to the following oracle.*
   O_{ext}: *On input τ' and a quantum circuit C, it returns $\mathsf{Extract}(\mathsf{xk}, C, \tau', \epsilon)$.*
3. *Finally, the adversary outputs a "pirate" quantum circuit $C_{\mathbb{Q}} = (q, \boldsymbol{U})$, where $C_{\mathbb{Q}}$ is a quantum program with classical inputs and outputs whose first register (i.e., output register) is $\mathbb{C}^2$ and $\boldsymbol{U}$ is a compact classical description of $\{\boldsymbol{U}_{x,y}\}_{x \in \mathsf{Dom}, y \in \mathsf{Ran}}$.*

Let D be the following distribution.

D: *Generate $b \leftarrow \{0,1\}$, $x \leftarrow \mathsf{Dom}$, and $y_0 \leftarrow \mathsf{Ran}$. Compute $y_1 \leftarrow \mathsf{Eval}(\mathsf{prfk}, x)$. Output (b, x, y_b).*

We also let $\mathcal{P} = (\boldsymbol{P}_{b,x,y}, \boldsymbol{Q}_{b,x,y})_{b,x,y}$ be a collection of binary outcome projective measurements, where

$$\boldsymbol{P}_{b,x,y} = \boldsymbol{U}_{x,y}^\dagger |b\rangle \langle b| \boldsymbol{U}_{x,y} \quad \text{and} \quad \boldsymbol{Q}_{b,x,y} = \boldsymbol{I} - \boldsymbol{P}_{b,x,y}.$$

Moreover, we let $\mathcal{M}_D = (\boldsymbol{P}_D, \boldsymbol{Q}_D)$ be binary outcome POVMs, where

$$\boldsymbol{P}_D = \sum_{r \in \mathcal{R}} \frac{1}{|\mathcal{R}|} \boldsymbol{P}_{D(r)} \quad \text{and} \quad \boldsymbol{Q}_D = \boldsymbol{I} - \boldsymbol{P}_D.$$

Live: *When applying the measurement $\mathsf{ProjImp}(\mathcal{M}_D)$ to q, we obtain a value p such that $p \geq \frac{1}{2} + \epsilon$.*

GoodExt: *When Computing* $\mathsf{m'} \leftarrow \mathit{Extract}(\mathsf{xk}, C_{\clubsuit}, \tau, \epsilon)$, *it holds that* $\mathsf{m'} \neq$ unmarked.

BadExt: *When Computing* $\mathsf{m'} \leftarrow \mathit{Extract}(\mathsf{xk}, C_{\clubsuit}, \tau, \epsilon)$, *it holds that* $\mathsf{m'} \notin$ {m, unmarked}.

We say that WMPRF *satisfies unremovability if for every* $\epsilon > 0$ *and QPT* $\mathcal{A}$, *we have*

$$\Pr[\mathsf{BadExt}] \leq \mathsf{negl}(\lambda) \qquad and \qquad \Pr[\mathsf{GoodExt}] \geq \Pr[\mathsf{Live}] - \mathsf{negl}(\lambda).$$

Intuitively, $(\boldsymbol{P}_{b,x,y}, \boldsymbol{Q}_{b,x,y})$ is a projective measurement that feeds (x, y) to $C_{\clubsuit}$ and checks whether the outcome is b or not (and then uncomputes). Then, $\mathcal{M}_D$ can be seen as POVMs that results in 0 with the probability that $C_{\clubsuit}$ can correctly guess b from (x, y_b) for (b, x, y_b) generated randomly from D.

Remark 3.3 (On Attack Model). We check whether $C_{\clubsuit}$ correctly distinguishes a real PRF value from a random value or not by applying $\mathsf{ProjImp}(\mathcal{M}_D)$ to q. This attack model follows the refined and more realistic attack model by Goyal et al. [GKWW21]. The adversary outputs a pirate circuit that computes an entire PRF value in all previous works except their work.

The distinguisher-based pirate circuit model is compatible with the (quantum) pirate decoder model of traitor tracing. Thus, our attack model also follows the attack model of quantum traitor tracing (the black box projection model) by Zhandry [Zha20, Sect. 4.2].[7]

As in the traitor tracing setting [Zha20], $\mathsf{ProjImp}(\mathcal{M}_D)$ is inefficient in general. We can handle this issue as Zhandry did. We will use an approximate version of $\mathsf{ProjImp}(\mathcal{M}_D)$ to achieve an efficient reduction. In addition, we cannot apply both $\mathsf{ProjImp}(\mathcal{M}_D)$ and $\mathit{Extract}$ to $C_{\clubsuit}$ simultaneously. However, the condition $\Pr[\mathsf{GoodExt}] \geq \Pr[\mathsf{Live}] - \mathsf{negl}(\lambda)$ claims that an embedded mark cannot be removed as long as the pirate circuit is alive. This fits the spirit of watermarking. See Zhandry's paper [Zha20, Sect. 4] for more discussion on the models.

Remark 3.4 (On Selective Message). As we see in Definition 3.4, we consider the selective setting for private extraction case, where $\mathcal{A}$ must send the target message m to the challenger before $\mathcal{A}$ accesses to the oracle O_{ext} and after pp is given. This is the same setting as that by Quach et al. [QWZ18]. We can consider the fully adaptive setting, where $\mathcal{A}$ can send the target message m after it accesses to the oracle O_{ext}, as Kim and Wu [KW19]. However, our privately extractable watermarking PRF satisfies only selective security. Thus, we write only the selective variant for the private extraction case.

Definition 3.5 (Unremovability for Public Extraction). *This is the same as Definition 3.4 except we use the game* $\mathsf{Exp}^{\mathsf{pub\text{-}ext\text{-}nrmv}}_{\mathcal{A},\mathsf{WMPRF}}(\lambda, \epsilon)$ *defined in the same way as* $\mathsf{Expt}^{\mathsf{nrmv}}_{\mathcal{A},\mathsf{WMPRF}}(\lambda, \epsilon)$ *except the following differences.*

---

[7] In the watermarking setting, an extraction algorithm can take the description of a pirate circuit as input (corresponding to the software decoder model [Zha20, Sect. 4.2]), unlike the black-box tracing model of traitor tracing. However, we use a pirate circuit in the black box way for our extraction algorithms. Thus, we follow the black box projection model by Zhandry [Zha20].

- *In item 1, $\mathcal{A}$ is given* xk *together with* pp.
- *Item 2 is removed.*

4   Definition of Extraction-Less Watermarking

We introduce the notion of extraction-less watermarking PRF as an intermediate primitive towards watermarking PRFs secure against quantum adversaries.

4.1   Syntax and Pseudorandomness

Definition 4.1 (Extraction-Less Watermarking PRF). *An extraction-less watermarking PRF* WMPRF *for the message space* $\{0,1\}^{\ell_m}$ *with domain* Dom *and range* Ran *is a tuple of five algorithms* (Setup, Gen, Eval, Mark, Sim), *where the first four algorithms have the same input/output behavior as those defined in Definition 3.1 and* Sim *has the following input/output behavior.*

Sim(xk, τ, i) $\rightarrow (\gamma, x, y)$: *The simulation algorithm* Sim *takes as input the extraction key* xk, *a tag* τ, *and an index* i, *and outputs a tuple* (γ, x, y).

Evaluation Correctness: *It is defined in exactly the same way as the evaluation correctness for watermarking PRF defined in Definition 3.1.*

Extended Pseudorandomness. Extended pseudorandomness for extraction-less watermarking PRF is defined in exactly the same way as that for watermarking PRF, that is Definition 3.2.

4.2   Simulatability for Mark-Dependent Distributions (SIM-MDD Security)

We introduce the security notion for extraction-less watermarking PRF that we call simulatability for mark-dependent distributions. Let D and D^{rev} be the following distributions.

D: Generate $b \leftarrow \{0,1\}$, $x \leftarrow$ Dom, and $y_0 \leftarrow$ Ran. Compute $y_1 \leftarrow$ Eval(prfk, x). Output (b, x, y_b).
D^{rev}: Generate $(b, x, y) \leftarrow D$. Output $(1 \oplus b, x, y)$.

Namely, D is the distribution that outputs a random value if the first bit $b = 0$ and a PRF evaluation if the first bit $b = 1$, and D^{rev} is its opposite (i.e., a PRF evaluation if $b = 0$ and a random value if $b = 1$). SIM-MDD security is a security notion that guarantees that an adversary given $\widetilde{C} \leftarrow$ Mark(mk, prfk, m) cannot distinguish an output of Sim(xk, τ, i) from that of D if m[i] = 0 and from that of D^{rev} if m[i] = 1.

Definition 4.2 (SIM-MDD Security with Private Simulation). *To define SIM-MDD security with private simulation, we define the game* $\mathsf{Expt}^{\mathsf{sim\text{-}mdd}}_{i^*, \mathcal{A}, \mathsf{WMPRF}}(\lambda)$ *as follows, where* $i^* \in [\ell_m]$.

1. *The challenger generates* $(pp, xk) \leftarrow \mathsf{Setup}(1^\lambda)$ *and sends* pp *to* $\mathcal{A}$. $\mathcal{A}$ *sends* $m \in \{0,1\}^{\ell_m}$ *to the challenger. The challenger generates* $(\mathsf{prfk}, \tau) \leftarrow \mathsf{Gen}(pp)$ *and computes* $\widetilde{C} \leftarrow \mathsf{Mark}(mk, \mathsf{prfk}, m)$. *The challenger sends* τ *and* $\widetilde{C}$ *to* $\mathcal{A}$.
2. $\mathcal{A}$ *can access to the following oracle.*
   O_{sim}: *On input* τ' *and* $i' \in [\ell_m]$, *it returns* $\mathsf{Sim}(xk, \tau', i')$.
3. *Let* D_{real,i^*} *be the following distribution. Note that* D_{real,i^*} *is identical with* D *if* $m[i^*] = 0$ *and with* D^{rev} *if* $m[i^*] = 1$.
   D_{real,i^*}: *Generate* $\gamma \leftarrow \{0,1\}$ *and* $x \leftarrow \mathsf{Dom}$. *Then, if* $\gamma = m[i^*]$, *generate* $y \leftarrow \mathsf{Ran}$, *and otherwise, compute* $y \leftarrow \mathsf{Eval}(\mathsf{prfk}, x)$. *Output* (γ, x, y).
   The challenger generates $\mathsf{coin} \leftarrow \{0,1\}$. *If* $\mathsf{coin} = 0$, *the challenger samples* $(\gamma, x, y) \leftarrow D_{\mathsf{real},i^*}$. *If* $\mathsf{coin} = 1$, *the challenger generates* $(\gamma, x, y) \leftarrow \mathsf{Sim}(xk, \tau, i^*)$. *The challenger sends* (γ, x, y) *to* $\mathcal{A}$.
4. *When* $\mathcal{A}$ *terminates with output* coin', *the challenger outputs* 1 *if* $\mathsf{coin} = \mathsf{coin}'$ *and* 0 *otherwise.*

Note that $\mathcal{A}$ *is not allowed to access to* O_{sim} *after* $\mathcal{A}$ *is given* (γ, x, y).

We say that WMPRF *is SIM-MDD secure if for every* $i^* \in [\ell_m]$ *and QPT* $\mathcal{A}$, *we have*

$$\mathsf{Adv}^{\mathsf{sim\text{-}mdd}}_{i^*, \mathcal{A}, \mathsf{WMPRF}}(\lambda) = 2 \left| \Pr\left[\mathsf{Expt}^{\mathsf{sim\text{-}mdd}}_{i^*, \mathcal{A}, \mathsf{WMPRF}}(\lambda) = 1 \right] - \frac{1}{2} \right| = \mathsf{negl}(\lambda).$$

We consider the selective setting above as unremovability for private extraction in Definition 3.4 since we use SIM-MDD security with private simulation to achieve unremovability for private simulation.

Remark 4.1 (On Multi Challenge Security). We can prove that the above definition implies the multi-challenge variant where polynomially many outputs of $\mathsf{Sim}(xk, \tau, i^*)$ are required to be indistinguishable from those of D_{real,i^*}. This is done by hybrid arguments where outputs of $\mathsf{Sim}(xk, \tau, i^*)$ are simulated using O_{sim} and those of D_{real,i^*} are simulated using $\widetilde{C}$. To apply Theorem 2.3, we need the multi challenge variant. However, we consider the single challenge variant due to the implication above. A similar remark is applied to the variants of SIM-MDD security introduced below.

SIM-MDD Security with Private Simulation Under the $\mathcal{API}$ Oracle. Let the $\mathcal{API}$ oracle be an oracle that is given $(\epsilon, \delta, \tau', i')$ and a quantum state q, and returns the result of $\mathcal{API}^{\epsilon,\delta}_{\mathcal{P}, D_{\tau',i'}}(q)$ and the post measurement state, where $\mathcal{P}$ is defined in the same way as that in Definition 3.4 and $D_{\tau',i'}$ be the distribution that outputs randomly generated $(\gamma, x, y) \leftarrow \mathsf{Sim}(xk, \tau', i')$. The $\mathcal{API}$ oracle cannot be simulated using the simulation oracle O_{sim} since we need superposition of outputs of Sim to compute $\mathcal{API}^{\epsilon,\delta}_{\mathcal{P}, D_{\tau',i'}}(q)$. When constructing watermarking PRFs with private simulation from extraction-less watermarking PRFs, the underlying extraction-less watermarking PRF scheme needs to satisfy SIM-MDD security with private simulation under the $\mathcal{API}$ oracle that we call QSIM-MDD security with private simulation. The reason is as follows. In the security analysis of the construction, the indistinguishability guarantee provided by SIM-MDD security needs to hold for an adversary against the resulting watermarking scheme who can access the extraction oracle. This means that it also needs to hold for an adversary who can access the $\mathcal{API}$ oracle since $\mathcal{API}$ is repeatedly invoked in the extraction algorithm of the resulting scheme.

Fortunately, as we will see, we can generically convert an extraction-less watermarking PRF scheme satisfying SIM-MDD security with private simulation into one satisfying QSIM-MDD security with private simulation, using QPRFs. Thus, when realizing an extraction-less watermarking PRF scheme as an intermediate step towards privately extractable watermarking PRFs, we can concentrate on realizing one satisfying SIM-MDD security with private simulation.

Remark 4.2. There is a similar issue in the traitor tracing setting. If PLBE is a secret-key based one, we need a counterpart of QSIM-MDD in secret-key based PLBE to achieve traitor tracing with a secret tracing algorithm against quantum adversaries by using Zhandry's framework [Zha20]. Note that Zhandry focuses on public-key based PLBE in his work [Zha20].

Definition 4.3 (QSIM-MDD Security with Private Simulation). *Let* $\mathsf{D}_{\tau,i}$ *be a distribution defined as follows.*

$\mathsf{D}_{\tau,i}$: *Output* $(\gamma, x, y) \leftarrow \mathsf{Sim}(\mathsf{xk}, \tau, i)$.

Then, we define the game $\mathsf{Exp}^{\mathsf{q\text{-}sim\text{-}mdd}}_{i^*, \mathcal{A}, \mathsf{WMPRF}}(\lambda)$ *in the same way as* $\mathsf{Exp}^{\mathsf{sim\text{-}mdd}}_{i^*, \mathcal{A}, \mathsf{WMPRF}}(\lambda)$ *except that in addition to* O_{sim}, $\mathcal{A}$ *can access to the following oracle in the step 2.*

O_{api}: *On input* $(\epsilon, \delta, \tau', i')$ *and a quantum state* q, *it returns the result of* $\mathcal{API}^{\epsilon, \delta}_{\mathcal{P}, \mathsf{D}_{\tau', i'}}(q)$ *and the post measurement state, where* $\mathcal{P}$ *is defined in the same way as that in Definition 3.4.*

We say that WMPRF *is QSIM-MDD secure with private simulation if for every* $i^* \in [\ell_{\mathsf{m}}]$ *and QPT* $\mathcal{A}$, *we have*

$$\mathsf{Adv}^{\mathsf{q\text{-}sim\text{-}mdd}}_{i^*, \mathcal{A}, \mathsf{WMPRF}}(\lambda) = 2 \left| \Pr\left[\mathsf{Exp}^{\mathsf{q\text{-}sim\text{-}mdd}}_{i^*, \mathcal{A}, \mathsf{WMPRF}}(\lambda) = 1 \right] - \frac{1}{2} \right| = \mathsf{negl}(\lambda).$$

We have the following theorem.

Theorem 4.1. *Assume there exists an extraction-less watermarking PRF scheme satisfying SIM-MDD security with private simulation and a QPRF. Then, there exists an extraction-less watermarking PRF scheme satisfying QSIM-MDD security with private simulation.*

We prove this theorem in the full version.

Definition 4.4 (SIM-MDD Security with Public Simulation). *We define the game* $\mathsf{Exp}^{\mathsf{sim\text{-}mdd\text{-}pub}}_{i^*, \mathcal{A}, \mathsf{WMPRF}}(\lambda)$ *in the same way as* $\mathsf{Expt}^{\mathsf{sim\text{-}mdd}}_{i^*, \mathcal{A}, \mathsf{WMPRF}}(\lambda)$ *except the following differences, where* $i^* \in [\ell_{\mathsf{m}}]$.

- *In item 1, $\mathcal{A}$ is given* xk *together with* pp.
- *Item 2 is removed.*

We say that WMPRF *satisfies SIM-MDD security with public simulation if for every* $i^* \in [\ell_m]$ *and QPT* $\mathcal{A}$, *we have*

$$\mathsf{Adv}^{\mathsf{sim-mdd-pub}}_{i^*,\mathcal{A},\mathsf{WMPRF}}(\lambda) = 2\left|\Pr\left[\mathsf{Exp}^{\mathsf{sim-mdd-pub}}_{i^*,\mathcal{A},\mathsf{WMPRF}}(\lambda) = 1\right] - \frac{1}{2}\right| = \mathsf{negl}(\lambda).$$

5   Watermarking PRF from Extraction-Less Watermarking PRF

We show how to construct watermarking PRF secure against quantum adversaries from extraction-less watermarking PRF.

Let ELWMPRF = (Setup, Gen, Eval, Mark, Sim) be an extraction-less watermarking PRF scheme whose message space is $\{0,1\}^{\ell_m+1}$. We construct a watermarking PRF scheme WMPRF = (WM.Setup, WM.Gen, WM.Eval, WM.Mark, $\mathcal{E}xtract$) whose message space is $\{0,1\}^{\ell_m}$ as follows. We use Setup, Gen, and Eval as WM.Setup, WM.Gen, and WM.Eval, respectively. Thus, the domain and range of WMPRF are the same as those of ELWMPRF. Also, we construct WM.Mark and $\mathcal{E}xtract$ as follows.

WM.Mark(pp, prfk, m):
  - Output $\widetilde{C} \leftarrow \mathsf{Mark}(\mathsf{pp}, \mathsf{prfk}, \mathsf{m}\|0)$.

$\mathcal{E}xtract(\mathsf{xk}, C, \tau, \epsilon)$:
  - Let $\epsilon' = \epsilon/4(\ell_m + 1)$ and $\delta' = 2^{-\lambda}$.
  - Parse $(q, U) \leftarrow C$.
  - Let $\mathcal{P}$ be defined in the same way as that in Definition 3.4 and $D_{\tau,i}$ be the following distribution for every $i \in [\ell_m + 1]$.
    $D_{\tau,i}$: Output $(\gamma, x, y) \leftarrow \mathsf{Sim}(\mathsf{xk}, \tau, i)$.
  - Compute $\widetilde{p}_{\ell_m+1} \leftarrow \mathcal{API}^{\epsilon',\delta'}_{\mathcal{P},D_{\tau,\ell_m+1}}(q)$. If $\widetilde{p}_{\ell_m+1} < \frac{1}{2}+\epsilon-4\epsilon'$, return unmarked. Otherwise, letting q_0 be the post-measurement state, go to the next step.
  - For all $i \in [\ell_m]$, do the following.
    1. Compute $\widetilde{p}_i \leftarrow \mathcal{API}^{\epsilon',\delta'}_{\mathcal{P},D_{\tau,i}}(q_{i-1})$. Let q_i be the post-measurement state.
    2. If $\widetilde{p}_i > \frac{1}{2} + \epsilon - 4(i+1)\epsilon'$, set $\mathsf{m}'_i = 0$. If $\widetilde{p}_i < \frac{1}{2} - \epsilon + 4(i+1)\epsilon'$, set $\mathsf{m}'_i = 1$. Otherwise, exit the loop and output $\mathsf{m}' = 0^{\ell_m}$.
  - Output $\mathsf{m}' = \mathsf{m}'_1\|\cdots\|\mathsf{m}'_{\ell_m}$.

We have the following theorems.

Theorem 5.1. *If* ELWMPRF *satisfies extended weak pseudorandomness against authority, then so does* WMPRF.

Theorem 5.2. *If* ELWMPRF *is an extraction-less watermarking PRF that satisfies QSIM-MDD security,* WMPRF *is a privately extractable watermarking PRF.*

Theorem 5.3. *If* ELWMPRF *is an extraction-less watermarking PRF that satisfies SIM-MDD security with public simulation,* WMPRF *is a publicly extractable watermarking PRF.*

It is clear that Theorem 5.1 holds since the evaluation algorithm of WMPRF is the same as that of ELWMPRF and extended weak pseudorandomness is insensitive to how the marking and extraction algorithms are defined. Thus, we omit a formal proof.

The proofs of Theorem 5.2 and 5.3 are almost the same. Thus, we only provide the proof for the former, and omit the proof for the latter.

Proof of Theorem 5.2. Let $\epsilon > 0$. Let $\mathcal{A}$ be a QPT adversary attacking the unremovability of WMPRF. The description of $\mathsf{Expt}^{\mathsf{nrmv}}_{\mathcal{A},\mathsf{WMPRF}}(\lambda, \epsilon)$ is as follows.

1. The challenger generates $(\mathsf{pp}, \mathsf{xk}) \leftarrow \mathsf{Setup}(1^\lambda)$ and gives pp to the adversary $\mathcal{A}$. $\mathcal{A}$ sends $\mathsf{m} \in \{0,1\}^{\ell_m}$ to the challenger. The challenger generates $(\mathsf{prfk}, \tau) \leftarrow \mathsf{Gen}(\mathsf{pp})$, computes $\widetilde{C} \leftarrow \mathsf{Mark}(\mathsf{pp}, \mathsf{prfk}, \mathsf{m}\|0)$, and sends $\widetilde{C}$ to $\mathcal{A}$.
2. $\mathcal{A}$ can access to the following oracle.
   O_{ext}.On input τ' and a quantum circuit C, it returns $\mathcal{E}\!\mathit{xtract}(\mathsf{xk}, C, \tau', \epsilon)$.
3. Finally, the adversary outputs a quantum circuit $C_{\mathcal{g}} = (q, U)$.

We define D, $\mathcal{P}$, $\mathcal{M}_D$, and the three events Live, GoodExt, and BadExt in the same way as Definition 3.4.

The proof of $\Pr[\mathsf{GoodExt}] \geq \Pr[\mathsf{Live}] - \mathsf{negl}(\lambda)$. $\mathcal{E}\!\mathit{xtract}$ outputs unmarked if and only if $\widetilde{p}_{\ell+1} < \frac{1}{2} + \epsilon - 4\epsilon'$, that is we have $\Pr[\mathsf{GoodExt}] = \Pr[\widetilde{p}_{\ell+1} \geq \frac{1}{2} + \epsilon - 4\epsilon']$. Let p the probability obtained by applying $\mathsf{ProjImp}(\mathcal{M}_D)$ to q. Then, we have $\Pr[\mathsf{Live}] = \Pr[p \geq \frac{1}{2} + \epsilon]$. Let $\widetilde{p}$ be the outcome obtained if we apply $\mathcal{API}^{\epsilon',\delta'}_{\mathcal{P},D}$ to q. From the property of $\mathcal{API}$, we have

$$\Pr[\mathsf{Live}] = \Pr\left[p \geq \frac{1}{2} + \epsilon\right] \leq \Pr\left[\widetilde{p} \geq \frac{1}{2} + \epsilon - \epsilon'\right] + \mathsf{negl}(\lambda).$$

D and D_{τ,ℓ_m+1} are computationally indistinguishable from the QSIM-MDD security of ELWMPRF since outputs of $\mathsf{Sim}(\mathsf{xk}, \tau, i)$ is indistinguishable from those of D if $\mathsf{m}[i] = 0$. This indistinguishability holds even under the existence of O_{api}. Then, from Theorem 2.3, we have

$$\Pr\left[\widetilde{p} \geq \frac{1}{2} + \epsilon - \epsilon'\right] \leq \Pr\left[\widetilde{p}_{\ell+1} \geq \frac{1}{2} + \epsilon - 4\epsilon'\right] + \mathsf{negl}(\lambda) = \Pr[\mathsf{GoodExt}] + \mathsf{negl}(\lambda).$$

By combining the above two equations, we obtain $\Pr[\mathsf{GoodExt}] \geq \Pr[\mathsf{Live}] - \mathsf{negl}(\lambda)$.

The reason D and $D_{\tau,\ell+1}$ need to be computationally indistinguishable under the existence of O_{api} to apply Theorem 2.3 is as follows. In this application of Theorem 2.3, the quantum state appeared in the statement of it is set as q contained in the quantum circuit C output by $\mathcal{A}$. Then, Theorem 2.3 (implicitly) requires that D and $D_{\tau,\ell+1}$ be indistinguishable for distinguishers who can construct q. To construct q, we need to execute $\mathcal{A}$ who can access to O_{ext} in which $\mathcal{API}$ is repeatedly executed. This is the reason D and $D_{\tau,\ell+1}$ need to be indistinguishable under the existence of O_{api}.

The proof of $\Pr[\mathsf{BadExt}] \leq \mathsf{negl}(\lambda)$. We define the event BadExt_i as follows for every $i \in [\ell_{\mathsf{m}}]$.

BadExt_i:When Running $\mathcal{E}xtract(\mathsf{xk}, C_{\mathbf{g}}, \tau^*, \epsilon)$,, the following conditions hold.
- $\widetilde{p}_{\ell+1} \geq \frac{1}{2} + \epsilon - 4\epsilon'$ holds.
- $\mathsf{m}'_j = \mathsf{m}_j$ holds for every $j \in [i-1]$.
- $\mathcal{E}xtract$ exits the i-th loop or $\mathsf{m}'_i \neq \mathsf{m}_i$ holds.

Then, we have $\Pr[\mathsf{BadExt}] \leq \sum_{i \in [\ell]} \Pr[\mathsf{BadExt}_i]$. Below, we estimate $\Pr[\mathsf{BadExt}_i]$.

We first consider the case of $\mathsf{m}_{i-1} = 0$ and $\mathsf{m}_i = 0$. Assume $\mathsf{m}'_{i-1} = \mathsf{m}_{i-1} = 0$ holds. Then, we have $\widetilde{p}_{i-1} > \frac{1}{2} + \epsilon - 4i\epsilon'$. Let $\widetilde{p}'_{i-1} \leftarrow \mathcal{API}^{\epsilon',\delta'}_{\mathcal{P},D_{\tau,i-1}}(q_{i-1})$. From, the almost-projective property of $\mathcal{API}$, we have

$$\Pr\left[\widetilde{p}'_{i-1} > \frac{1}{2} + \epsilon - 4i\epsilon' - \epsilon'\right] \geq 1 - \delta'.$$

When $\mathsf{m}_{i-1} = 0$ and $\mathsf{m}_i = 0$, $D_{\tau,i-1}$ and $D_{\tau,i}$ are computationally indistinguishable since both of them are computationally indistinguishable from D by the QSIM-MDD security of ELWMPRF. This indistinguishability holds under the existence of O_{api}. Thus, from Theorem 2.3, we have

$$1 - \delta' \leq \Pr\left[\widetilde{p}'_{i-1} > \frac{1}{2} + \epsilon - (4i+1)\epsilon'\right] \leq \Pr\left[\widetilde{p}_i > \frac{1}{2} + \epsilon - 4(i+1)\epsilon'\right] + \mathsf{negl}(\lambda).$$

This means that $\Pr[\mathsf{BadExt}_i] = \mathsf{negl}(\lambda)$ in this case. Note that the reason the indistinguishability of $D_{\tau,i-1}$ and $D_{\tau,i}$ needs to hold under O_{api} is that Theorem 2.3 requires it hold for distinguishers who can construct q_{i-1}.

Next, we consider the case of $\mathsf{m}_{i-1} = 0$ and $\mathsf{m}_i = 1$. Assume $\mathsf{m}'_{i-1} = \mathsf{m}_{i-1} = 0$ holds. Then, we have $\widetilde{p}_{i-1} > \frac{1}{2} + \epsilon - 4i\epsilon'$. We then define an additional distribution $D^{\mathsf{rev}}_{\tau,i}$ as follows.

$D^{\mathsf{rev}}_{\tau,i}$: Generate $(\gamma, x, y) \leftarrow \mathsf{Sim}(\mathsf{xk}, \tau, i)$. Output $(1 \oplus \gamma, x, y)$.

That is, the first bit of the output is flipped from $D_{\tau,i}$. Then, for any random coin r, we have $(\mathbf{P}_{D^{\mathsf{rev}}_{\tau,i}(r)}, \mathbf{Q}_{D^{\mathsf{rev}}_{\tau,i}(r)}) = (\mathbf{Q}_{D_{\tau,i}(r)}, \mathbf{P}_{D_{\tau,i}(r)})$. This is because we have $\mathbf{Q}_{b,x,y} = \mathbf{I} - \mathbf{P}_{b,x,y} = \mathbf{P}_{1\oplus b,x,y}$ for any tuple (b, x, y). Therefore, $\mathcal{API}^{\epsilon',\delta'}_{\mathcal{P},D^{\mathsf{rev}}_{\tau,i-1}}$ is exactly the same process as $\mathcal{API}^{\epsilon',\delta'}_{\mathcal{P}^{\mathsf{rev}},D_{\tau,i-1}}$. Let $\widetilde{p}'_{i-1} \leftarrow \mathcal{API}^{\epsilon',\delta'}_{\mathcal{P},D^{\mathsf{rev}}_{\tau,i-1}}(q_{i-1})$. From, the reverse-almost-projective property of $\mathcal{API}$, we have

$$\Pr\left[\widetilde{p}'_{i-1} < \frac{1}{2} - \epsilon + 4i\epsilon' + \epsilon'\right] \geq 1 - \delta'.$$

When $\mathsf{m}_{i-1} = 0$ and $\mathsf{m}_i = 1$, $D^{\mathsf{rev}}_{\tau,i-1}$ and $D_{\tau,i}$ are computationally indistinguishable since both of them are computationally indistinguishable from the following distribution D^{rev} by the QSIM-MDD security of ELWMPRF.

$D^{\mathtt{rev}}$: Generate $(\gamma, x, y) \leftarrow D$. Output $(1 \oplus \gamma, x, y)$.

This indistinguishability holds under the existence of $O_{\mathtt{api}}$. Thus, from Theorem 2.3, we have

$$1 - \delta' \leq \Pr\left[\widetilde{p}'_{i-1} < \frac{1}{2} - \epsilon + (4i+1)\epsilon'\right] \leq \Pr\left[\widetilde{p}_i < \frac{1}{2} - \epsilon + 4(i+1)\epsilon'\right] + \mathsf{negl}(\lambda).$$

This means that $\Pr[\mathsf{BadExt}_i] = \mathsf{negl}(\lambda)$ also in this case. Note that the reason the indistinguishability of $D^{\mathtt{rev}}_{\tau, i-1}$ and $D_{\tau, i}$ needs to hold under $O_{\mathtt{api}}$ is that Theorem 2.3 requires it hold for distinguishers who can construct q_{i-1}.

Similarly, we can prove that $\Pr[\mathsf{BadExt}_i] = \mathsf{negl}(\lambda)$ holds in the case of $(\mathsf{m}_{i-1}, \mathsf{m}_i) = (1, 0)$ and $(\mathsf{m}_{i-1}, \mathsf{m}_i) = (1, 1)$.

Overall, we see that $\Pr[\mathsf{BadExt}] = \mathsf{negl}(\lambda)$ holds in all cases.   ∎

6   Extraction-Less Watermarking PRF from LWE

We present an extraction-less watermarking PRF, denoted by $\mathsf{PRF}_{\mathsf{cprf}}$, whose message space is $\{0,1\}^{\ell_{\mathsf{m}}}$ with domain $\{0,1\}^{\ell_{\mathsf{in}}}$ and range $\{0,1\}^{\ell_{\mathsf{out}}}$. We use the following tools, which can be instantiated with the QLWE assumption:

- Private CPRF CPRF = (CPRF.Setup, CPRF.Eval, CPRF.Constrain, CPRF. CEval). For ease of notation, we denote CPRF evaluation circuit CPRF.Eval $(\mathsf{msk}, \cdot)$ and constrained evaluation circuits CPRF.CEval$(\mathsf{sk}_f, \cdot)$ by G : $\{0,1\}^{\ell_{\mathsf{in}}} \to \{0,1\}^{\ell_{\mathsf{out}}}$ and $\mathsf{G}_{\notin \mathcal{V}} : \{0,1\}^{\ell_{\mathsf{in}}} \to \{0,1\}^{\ell_{\mathsf{out}}}$, respectively, where $x \in \mathcal{V}$ iff $f(x) = 1$.
- SKE scheme SKE = (SKE.Gen, SKE.Enc, SKE.Dec). The plaintext space and ciphertext space of SKE are $\{0,1\}^{\ell_{\mathsf{ske}}}$ and $\{0,1\}^{\ell_{\mathsf{in}}}$, respectively, where $\ell_{\mathsf{ske}} = \log \ell_{\mathsf{m}} + 1$.
- PKE scheme PKE = (Gen, Enc, Dec). The plaintext space of PKE is $\{0,1\}^{2\lambda}$.

Construction Overview. We already explained the high-level idea for how to realize extraction-less watermarking PRFs in Sect. 1.3. However, the construction of $\mathsf{PRF}_{\mathsf{cprf}}$ requires some additional efforts. Thus, before providing the actual construction, we provide a high-level overview of $\mathsf{PRF}_{\mathsf{cprf}}$.

Recall that letting $\widetilde{C} \leftarrow \mathsf{Mark}(\mathsf{pp}, \mathsf{prfk}, \mathsf{m})$ and $(\gamma^*, x^*, y^*) \leftarrow \mathsf{Sim}(\mathsf{xk}, \tau, i^*)$, we have to design Sim and $\widetilde{C}$ so that

- If $\gamma = \mathsf{m}[i^*]$, $\widetilde{C}(x^*)$ outputs a value different from y^*.
- If $\gamma \neq \mathsf{m}[i^*]$, $\widetilde{C}(x^*)$ outputs y^*.

In the token-based construction idea, we achieve these conditions by setting x^* as an encryption of $y^* \| i^* \| \gamma^*$ and designing $\widetilde{C}$ as a token such that it outputs y^* if the input is decryptable and $\gamma^* \neq \mathsf{m}[i^*]$ holds for the decrypted value $y^* \| i^* \| \gamma^*$, and otherwise behaves as the original evaluation circuit. However, in $\mathsf{PRF}_{\mathsf{cprf}}$, we use a constrained evaluation circuit of CPRF as $\widetilde{C}$, and thus we cannot program output values for specific inputs. Intuitively, it seems that Sim needs to use the original PRF key prfk to achieve the above two conditions.

To solve the issue, we adopt the idea used by Quach et al. [QWZ18]. In $\mathsf{PRF_{cprf}}$, the setup algorithm Setup generates $(\mathsf{pk}, \mathsf{sk}) \leftarrow \mathsf{Gen}(1^\lambda)$ of PKE, and sets $\mathsf{pp} = \mathsf{pk}$ and $\mathsf{xk} = \mathsf{sk}$. Then, the PRF key generation algorithm is given pk, generates $\mathsf{G} \leftarrow \mathsf{CPRF.Setup}(1^\lambda, 1^\kappa)$ along with $\mathsf{ske.k} \leftarrow \mathsf{SKE.Gen}(1^\lambda)$, and sets the public tag τ as an encryption of $(\mathsf{G}, \mathsf{ske.k})$ under pk. The evaluation algorithm of $\mathsf{PRF_{cprf}}$ is simply that of CPRF.

Now, we explain how to design Sim and $\widetilde{C} \leftarrow \mathsf{Mark}(\mathsf{pp}, \mathsf{prfk}, m)$ to satisfy the above two conditions. Given $\mathsf{xk} = \mathsf{sk}$, $\tau = \mathsf{Enc}(\mathsf{pk}, \mathsf{prfk})$ and i, Sim is able to extract $\mathsf{prfk} = (\mathsf{G}, \mathsf{ske.k})$. Then, Sim generates $\gamma \leftarrow \{0, 1\}$ and sets $x \leftarrow \mathsf{SKE.Enc}(\mathsf{ske.k}, i\|\gamma)$ and $y \leftarrow \mathsf{G}(x)$. We set $\widetilde{C}$ as a constrained version of G for a circuit D that outputs 1 if the input x is decryptable by $\mathsf{ske.k}$ and $\gamma = m[i]$ holds for decrypted value $i\|\gamma$, and otherwise outputs 0. For an input x, the constrained version of G outputs the correct output $\mathsf{G}(x)$ if and only if $D(x) = 0$. We can check that $\mathsf{PRF_{cprf}}$ satisfies the above two conditions.

The above construction does not satisfy extended weak pseudorandomness against authority since the authority can extract the original CPRF key G by $\mathsf{xk} = \mathsf{sk}$. However, this problem can be fixed by constraining G. We see that Sim needs to evaluate G for valid ciphertexts of SKE. Thus, to implement the above mechanism, it is sufficient to set the public tag τ as an encryption of $\mathsf{ske.k}$ and a constrained version of G for a circuit D_{auth} that output 0 if and only if the input is decryptable by $\mathsf{ske.k}$. Then, the authority can only extract such a constrained key. By requiring sparseness for SKE, the constrained key cannot be used to break the pseudorandomness of $\mathsf{PRF_{cprf}}$ for random inputs. This means that $\mathsf{PRF_{cprf}}$ satisfies extended weak pseudorandomness against an authority. Note that we only need a single-key CPRF for $\mathsf{PRF_{cprf}}$ since either a user or the authority (not both) is a malicious entity in security games.

The description of $\mathsf{PRF_{cprf}}$ is as follows.

$\mathsf{Setup}(1^\lambda)$:
- Generate $(\mathsf{pk}, \mathsf{sk}) \leftarrow \mathsf{Gen}(1^\lambda)$.
- Output $(\mathsf{pp}, \mathsf{xk}) := (\mathsf{pk}, \mathsf{sk})$.

$\mathsf{Gen}(\mathsf{pp})$:
- Parse $\mathsf{pp} = \mathsf{pk}$.
- Generate $\mathsf{G} \leftarrow \mathsf{CPRF.Setup}(1^\lambda, 1^\kappa)$. In our construction, κ is the size of circuit $D[\mathsf{ske.k}, m]$ described in Fig. 2, which depends on ℓ_m (and λ).
- Generate $\mathsf{ske.k} \leftarrow \mathsf{SKE.Gen}(1^\lambda)$.
- Construct a circuit $D_{\mathsf{auth}}[\mathsf{ske.k}]$ described in Fig. 1.
- Compute $\mathsf{G}_{\notin \mathcal{V}_{\mathsf{auth}}} := \mathsf{CPRF.Constrain}(\mathsf{G}, D_{\mathsf{auth}}[\mathsf{ske.k}])$, where $\mathcal{V}_{\mathsf{auth}} \subset \{0, 1\}^{\ell_{\mathsf{in}}}$ is a set such that $x \in \mathcal{V}_{\mathsf{auth}}$ iff $D_{\mathsf{auth}}[\mathsf{ske.k}](x) = 1$.
- Output $\mathsf{prfk} := (\mathsf{G}, \mathsf{ske.k})$ and $\tau \leftarrow \mathsf{Enc}(\mathsf{pk}, (\mathsf{G}_{\notin \mathcal{V}_{\mathsf{auth}}}, \mathsf{ske.k}))$.

$\mathsf{Eval}(\mathsf{prfk}, x \in \{0, 1\}^{\ell_{\mathsf{in}}})$: Recall that G is a keyed CPRF evaluation circuit.
- Parse $\mathsf{prfk} = (\mathsf{G}, \mathsf{ske.k})$.
- Output $y := \mathsf{G}(x)$.

$\mathsf{Mark}(\mathsf{pp}, \mathsf{prfk}, m)$:

- Parse $pp = pk$ and $prfk = (G, ske.k)$.
- Construct a circuit $D[ske.k, m]$ described in Fig. 2.
- Compute $G_{\notin \mathcal{V}} \leftarrow$ CPRF.Constrain$(G, D[ske.k, m])$, where $\mathcal{V} \subset \{0,1\}^{\ell_{in}}$ is a set such that $x \in \mathcal{V}$ iff $D[ske.k, m](x) = 1$.
- Output $\widetilde{C} = G_{\notin \mathcal{V}}$.

Sim(xk, τ, i):

- Parse $xk = sk$.
- Compute $(G_{\notin \mathcal{V}_{auth}}, ske.k) \leftarrow$ Dec(sk, τ).
- Choose $\gamma \leftarrow \{0,1\}$.
- Compute $x \leftarrow$ SKE.Enc$(ske.k, i\|\gamma)$ and $y \leftarrow G_{\notin \mathcal{V}_{auth}}(x)$.
- Output (γ, x, y).

Circuit $D_{auth}[ske.k]$

Constants: An SKE key ske.k, and a message m.

Input: A string $x \in \{0,1\}^n$.

1. Compute $d \leftarrow$ SKE.Dec$(ske.k, x)$.
2. Output 0 if $d \neq \perp$ and 1 otherwise.

Fig. 1. The description of D_{auth}

Circuit $D[ske.k, m]$

Constants: An SKE key ske.k, and a message m.

Input: A string $x \in \{0,1\}^n$.

1. Compute $d \leftarrow$ SKE.Dec$(ske.k, x)$.
2. If $d \neq \perp$, do the following
   (a) Parse $d = i\|\gamma$, where $i \in [\ell_m]$ and $\gamma \in \{0,1\}$.
   (b) If $\gamma = m[i]$, output 1. Otherwise, output 0.
3. Otherwise output 0.

Fig. 2. The description of D

The evaluation correctness of $\mathsf{PRF_{cprf}}$ follows from the sparseness of SKE and the correctness of CPRF. For the security of $\mathsf{PRF_{cprf}}$, we have the following theorems.

Theorem 6.1. SKE *is a secure SKE scheme with pseudorandom ciphertext,* CPRF *is a selectively single-key private CPRF,* PKE *is a CCA secure PKE scheme, then* $\mathsf{PRF_{cprf}}$ *is an extraction-less watermarking PRF satisfying SIM-MDD security.*

Theorem 6.2. *If* CPRF *is a selective single-key private CPRF,* $\mathsf{PRF_{cprf}}$ *satisfies extended weak pseudorandomness.*

We prove Theorems 6.1 and 6.2 in the full version.

7   Extraction-Less Watermarking PRF with Public Simulation from IO

We construct an extraction-less watermarking PRF satisfying SIM-MDD security with public simulation. In the construction, we use puncturable encryption (PE) [CHN+18]. We provide the definition of PE in the full version.

We describe our extraction-less watermarking PRF $\mathsf{PRF_{io}}$ for message space $\{0,1\}^{\ell_m}$ with domain $\{0,1\}^{\ell_{in}}$ and range $\{0,1\}^{\ell_{out}}$ below. We use the following tools:

- PPRF $\mathsf{PRF} = \mathsf{PRF}.(\mathsf{Gen}, \mathsf{Eval}, \mathsf{Puncture})$. We denote a PRF evaluation circuit $\mathsf{PRF.Eval_{prfk}}(\cdot)$ by $\mathsf{F} : \{0,1\}^{\ell_{in}} \rightarrow \{0,1\}^{\ell_{out}}$, a PRF evaluation circuit with punctured key $\mathsf{PRF.Eval_{prfk_{\neq x}}}(\cdot)$ by $\mathsf{F}_{\neq x}$ (that is, we omit prfk and simply write $\mathsf{F}(\cdot)$ instead of $\mathsf{F_{prfk}}(\cdot)$) for ease of notations.
- PE scheme $\mathsf{PE} = \mathsf{PE}.(\mathsf{Gen}, \mathsf{Puncture}, \mathsf{Enc}, \mathsf{Dec})$. The plaintext and ciphertext space of PE are $\{0,1\}^{\ell_{pt}}$ and $\{0,1\}^{\ell_{ct}}$, respectively, where $\ell_{pt} = \ell + \log \ell_m + 1$ and $\ell_{in} := \ell_{ct}$ ($\ell_{ct} = \mathrm{poly}(\ell, \log \ell_m)$).
- Indistinguishability obfuscator $i\mathcal{O}$.
- PRG $\mathsf{PRG} : \{0,1\}^{\ell} \rightarrow \{0,1\}^{\ell_{out}}$.

$\mathsf{Setup}(1^\lambda)$:
  - Output $(\mathsf{pp}, \mathsf{xk}) := (\bot, \bot)$.
$\mathsf{Gen}(\mathsf{pp})$:
  - Parse $\mathsf{pp} = \bot$.
  - Compute $\mathsf{F} \leftarrow \mathsf{PRF.Gen}(1^\lambda)$.
  - Generate $(\mathsf{pe.ek}, \mathsf{pe.dk}) \leftarrow \mathsf{PE.Gen}(1^\lambda)$.
  - Output $\mathsf{prfk} := (\mathsf{F}, \mathsf{pe.dk})$ and $\tau := \mathsf{pe.ek}$.
$\mathsf{Eval}(\mathsf{prfk}, x \in \{0,1\}^{\ell_{in}})$:
  - Parse $\mathsf{prfk} = (\mathsf{F}, \mathsf{pe.dk})$.
  - Compute and output $y \leftarrow \mathsf{F}(x)$.
$\mathsf{Mark}(\mathsf{pp}, \mathsf{prfk}, \mathsf{m} \in \{0,1\}^{\ell_m})$:
  - Parse $\mathsf{pp} = \bot$ and $\mathsf{prfk} = (\mathsf{F}, \mathsf{pe.dk})$.
  - Construct a circuit $D[\mathsf{F}, \mathsf{pe.dk}, \mathsf{m}]$ described in Fig. 3.
  - Compute and output $\widetilde{C} := i\mathcal{O}(D[\mathsf{F}, \mathsf{pe.dk}, \mathsf{m}])$.
$\mathsf{Sim}(\mathsf{xk}, \tau, i)$:
  - Parse $\mathsf{xk} = \bot$ and $\tau = \mathsf{pe.ek}$.
  - Choose $\gamma \leftarrow \{0,1\}$ and $s \leftarrow \{0,1\}^{\ell}$.
  - Compute $y := \mathsf{PRG}(s)$.
  - Compute $x \leftarrow \mathsf{PE.Enc}(\mathsf{pe.ek}, s\|i\|\gamma)$.
  - Output (γ, x, y)

The size of the circuit D is appropriately padded to be the maximum size of all modified circuits, which will appear in the security proof.

Circuit $D[\mathsf{F}, \mathsf{pe.dk}, \mathsf{m}]$

Constants: A PRF F, a PE decryption key $\mathsf{pe.dk}$, and a message m.

Input: A string $x \in \{0,1\}^{\ell_{\mathsf{in}}}$.

1. Compute $d \leftarrow \mathsf{PE.Dec}(\mathsf{pe.dk}, x)$.
2. If $d \neq \perp$, do the following
   (a) Parse $d = s\|i\|\gamma$, where $s \in \{0,1\}^{\ell}$, $i \in [\ell_{\mathsf{m}}]$, and $\gamma \in \{0,1\}$.
   (b) If $\mathsf{m}[i] \neq \gamma$, output $\mathsf{PRG}(s)$. Otherwise, output $\mathsf{F}(x)$.
3. Otherwise, output $\mathsf{F}(x)$.

Fig. 3. The description of D

The evaluation correctness of $\mathsf{PRF}_{\mathsf{io}}$ immediately follows from the sparseness of PE and the functionality of $i\mathcal{O}$.[8] $\mathsf{PRF}_{\mathsf{io}}$ trivially satisfies pseudorandomness (against an authority) since Setup outputs nothing, τ is a public key $\mathsf{pe.ek}$, and Eval is independent of $(\mathsf{pe.ek}, \mathsf{pe.dk})$ ($\mathsf{pe.dk}$ is not used in Eval). Moreover, we have the following theorem.

Theorem 7.1. *If* PRF *is a secure PPRF,* PRG *is a secure PRG,* PE *is a secure PE with strong ciphertext pseudorandomness, and* $i\mathcal{O}$ *is a secure IO, then* $\mathsf{PRF}_{\mathsf{io}}$ *is an extraction-less watermarking PRF satisfying SIM-MDD security with public simulation.*

We prove Theorem 7.1 in the full version.

References

[AL21] Ananth, P., La Placa, R.L.: Secure software leasing. In EUROCRYPT 2021, Part II, pp. 501–530 (2021)

[ALL+21] Aaronson, S., Liu, J., Liu, Q., Zhandry, M., Zhang, R.: New approaches for quantum copy-protection. In: CRYPTO 2021, Part I, pp. 526–555. Virtual Event (2021)

[ARU14] Ambainis, A., Rosmanis, A., Unruh, D.: Quantum attacks on classical proof systems: the hardness of quantum rewinding. In: 55th FOCS, pp. 474–483 (2014)

[BDF+11] Boneh, D., Dagdelen, Ö., Fischlin, M., Lehmann, A., Schaffner, C., Zhandry, M.: Random oracles in a quantum world. In: ASIACRYPT, pp. 41–69 (2011)

[BGI+12] Barak, B., et al.: On the (IM) possibility of obfuscating programs. J. ACM **59**(2), 6:1–6:48 (2012)

[BLW17] Boneh, D., Lewi, K., Wu, D.J.: Constraining pseudorandom functions privately. In: PKC 2017, Part II, pp. 494–524 (2017)

---

[8] In fact, $\mathsf{PRF}_{\mathsf{io}}$ satisfies a stronger evaluation correctness than one written in Definition 4.1. The evaluation correctness holds even for any PRF key prfk and input $x \in \mathsf{Dom}$ like the statistical correctness by Cohen et al. [CHN+18].

[BSW06]   Boneh, D., Sahai, A., Waters, B.: Fully collusion resistant traitor tracing with short Ciphertexts and private keys. In: EUROCRYPT 2006, pp. 573–592 (2006)

[CFN94]   Chor, B., Fiat, A., Naor, M.: Tracing traitors. In: CRYPTO 1994, pp. 257–270 (1994)

[CHN+18] Cohen, A., Holmgren, J., Nishimaki, R., Vaikuntanathan, V., Wichs, D.: Watermarking cryptographic capabilities. SIAM J. Comput. 47(6), 2157–2202 (2018)

[CMSZ21] Chiesa, A., Ma, F., Spooner, N., Zhandry, M.: Post-quantum succinct arguments: breaking the quantum rewinding barrier. In: FOCS 2021 (2021)

[GKM+19] Goyal, R., Kim, S., Manohar, N., Waters, B., Wu, D.J.: Watermarking public-key cryptographic primitives. In: CRYPTO 2019, Part III, pp. 367–398 (2019)

[GKWW21] Goyal, R., Kim, S., Waters, B., Wu, D.J.: Beyond software watermarking: traitor-tracing for pseudorandom functions. In: Asiacrypt 2021, LNCS, Springer Cham (2021). https://doi.org/10.1007/978-3-030-92062-3

[HMW07]   Hopper, N., Molnar, D., Wagner, D.: From weak to strong watermarking. In: TCC 2007, pp. 362–382 (2007)

[KNY21]   Kitagawa, F., Nishimaki, R., Yamakawa, T.: Secure software leasing from standard assumptions. In: Nissim, K., Waters, B. (eds.) TCC 2021. LNCS, vol. 13042, pp. 31–61. Springer, Cham (2021). https://doi.org/10.1007/978-3-030-90459-3_2

[KW19]   Kim, S., Wu, D.J.: Watermarking PRFs from lattices: stronger security via extractable PRFs. In: CRYPTO 2019, Part III, pp. 335–366 (2019)

[KW21]   Kim, S., Wu, D.J.: Watermarking cryptographic functionalities from standard lattice assumptions. J. Cryptol. 34(3), 28 (2021)

[Nis13]   Nishimaki, R.: How to watermark cryptographic functions. In: EUROCRYPT 2013, pp. 111–125 (2013)

[Nis19]   Nishimaki, R.: How to watermark cryptographic functions by bilinear maps. IEICE Trans. 102 A(1):99–113 (2019)

[Nis20]   Nishimaki, R.: Equipping public-key cryptographic primitives with watermarking (or: a hole is to watermark). In: TCC 2020, Part I, pp. 179–209 (2020)

[NSS99]   Naccache, D., Shamir, A., Stern, J.P.: How to copyright a function? In: PKC 1999, pp. 188–196 (1999)

[QWZ18]   Quach, W., Wichs, D., Zirdelis, G.: Watermarking PRFs under standard assumptions: public marking and security with extraction queries. In: TCC 2018, Part II, pp. 669–698 (2018)

[Reg09]   Regev, O.: On lattices, learning with errors, random linear codes, and cryptography. J. ACM 56(6), 34:1–34:40 (2009)

[Unr12]   Unruh, D.: Quantum proofs of knowledge. In: EUROCRYPT 2012, pp. 135–152 (2012)

[Wat09]   Watrous, J.: Zero-knowledge against quantum attacks. SIAM J. Comput. 39(1), 25–58 (2009)

[YAL+19] Yang, R., Au, M.H., Lai, J., Xu, Q., Yu, Z.: Collusion resistant watermarking schemes for cryptographic functionalities. In: ASIACRYPT 2019, Part I, pp. 371–398 (2019)

[YAYX20] Yang, R., Au, M.H., Yu, Z., Xu, Q.: Collusion resistant watermarkable PRFs from standard assumptions. In: CRYPTO 2020, Part I, pp. 590–620 (2020)

[YF11] Yoshida, M., Fujiwara, T.: Toward digital watermarking for cryptographic data. IEICE Trans. **94-A**(1):270–272 (2011)

[Zha12a] Zhandry, M.: How to construct quantum random functions. In: 53rd FOCS, pp. 679–687 (2012)

[Zha12b] Zhandry, M.: Secure identity-based encryption in the quantum random oracle model. In: CRYPTO 2012, pp. 758–775 (2012)

[Zha19] Zhandry, M.: How to record quantum queries, and applications to quantum indifferentiability. In: CRYPTO 2019, Part II, pp. 239–268 (2019)

[Zha20] Zhandry, M.: Schrödinger's pirate: how to trace a quantum decoder. In: TCC 2020, Part III, pp. 61–91 (2020)

Non-malleable Commitments Against Quantum Attacks

Nir Bitansky[1]([⊠]), Huijia Lin[2], and Omri Shmueli[1]

[1] Tel Aviv University, Tel Aviv, Israel
{nirbitan,omrishmueli}@tau.ac.il
[2] Washington University, Seattle, WA, USA
rachel@cs.washington.edu

Abstract. We construct, under standard hardness assumptions, the first non-malleable commitments secure against quantum attacks. Our commitments are statistically binding and satisfy the standard notion of *non-malleability with respect to commitment*. We obtain a $\log^\star(\lambda)$-round classical protocol, assuming the existence of post-quantum one-way functions.

Previously, non-malleable commitments with quantum security were only known against a restricted class of adversaries known as *synchronizing adversaries*. At the heart of our results is a new general technique that allows to modularly obtain non-malleable commitments from any extractable commitment protocol, obliviously of the underlying extraction strategy (black-box or non-black-box) or round complexity. The transformation may also be of interest in the classical setting.

1 Introduction

Commitments are one of the most basic cryptographic primitives. They enable a sender to commit to a string to be *opened* at a later stage. As long as the commitment is not opened, it is *hiding*—efficient receivers learn nothing about the committed value. Furthermore, the commitment is *statistically binding*—with overwhelming probability, the commitment can be opened to a single, information-theoretically determined value in the commitment phase. While these basic security guarantees go a long way in terms of applications, they do not always suffice. In particular, they do not prevent a *man-in-the-middle* adversary from receiving a commitment to a given value v from one party and trying to send to another party a commitment to a related value, say $v-1$ (without knowing the committed value v at all).

Such attacks are called "mauling attacks" and in some settings could be devastating. For instance, consider the scenario where a city opens a bidding process for the construction of a new city hall. Companies are instructed to commit to their proposed bid using a commitment scheme, and these commitments are opened at the end of the bidding period. If the scheme is "malleable", company A may manage to underbid company B, by covertly mauling B's commitment to create their

O. Dunkelman and S. Dziembowski (Eds.): EUROCRYPT 2022, LNCS 13277, pp. 519–550, 2022.
https://doi.org/10.1007/978-3-031-07082-2_19

own commitment to a lower bid. More generally, ensuring independence of private values is vital in many applications of commitments, such as coin tossing, federated learning, and collaborative computation over private data.

In their seminal work, Dolev, Dwork and Naor introduced the concept of *non-malleable commitments* to protect against mauling attacks [DDN03]. They guarantee that the value $\tilde{v}$ a man-in-the-middle adversary commits to is computationally independent of the value v in the commitment it receives (unless the man-in-the-middle simply "copies", by relaying messages between the honest sender and receiver it interacts with, in which case $\tilde{v} = v$). From its onset, the study of non-malleable cryptography has put stress on achieving solutions without any reliance on trusted parties or any form of trusted setup, and solutions that hold when honest parties may not even be aware of the existence of a man-in-the-middle, and the way it manipulates the messages they send over time. The latter is particularly important in applications where the man-in-the-middle acts "in the dark". For instance, in the aforementioned example, company A may not be aware of the competing company B.

Since their conception, non-malleable commitments have indeed proved to be a useful and versatile building block for ensuring independence of values. They have been used in coin-tossing protocols, secure multiparty computation protocols, non-malleable proof systems (zero-knowledge, witness indistinguishability, multi-prover interactive proofs), and more. Techniques developed for non-malleable commitments are also useful for building non-malleable codes, non-malleable extractors (and two source extractors), and non-malleable time-lock puzzles. The work of [DDN03] constructed the first non-malleable commitments against classical adversaries based on one-way functions. Since then, a plethora of constructions have been proposed achieving different, sometimes optimal, tradeoffs between round-complexity, efficiency, and underlying assumptions (c.f. [Bar02, PR05a, PPV08, LPV09, PW10, Wee10, Goy11, GLOV12, COSV16, GPR16a, GKS16, Khu17, KS17, LPS17, BL18, KK19, GR19, GKLW20]).

Non-Malleability Against Quantum Adversaries. In contrast to the comprehensive understanding of non-malleability in the classical setting, our understanding of non-malleability against quantum adversaries is very much lacking. The threat of quantum attacks has prompted the development of post-quantum cryptography, and yet despite its important role in cryptography, post-quantum non-malleability has yet to catch up. In this work, we construct, under standard assumptions, the first non-malleable commitments with post-quantum security, namely, the hiding and non-malleability properties hold even against efficient quantum adversaries (and binding continues to be information theoretic).

Prior to our work, post-quantum non-malleable commitments were not known under any assumption. Partial progress was made by Agrawal, Bartusek, Goyal, Khurana, and Malavolta [ABG+20] who, assuming super-polynomial quantum hardness of Learning With Errors, construct post-quantum non-malleable commitments against a restricted class of adversaries known as *synchronizing adversaries*. A synchronizing adversary is limited as follows: When acting as a man-in-the-middle between a sender and a receiver, it is bound to synchronize its interactions with the honest parties; namely, when it receives the i-th message from the sender, it immediately sends the i-th message to the receiver and vice versa. Such synchronicity may often not exist for example due to network's asynchronicity, lack of synchronized clocks, or concurrent executions where parties are unaware of the existence of other executions. Enforcing synchronizing behaviour in general requires a trusted setup (like a broadcast channel) and coordination among parties to enforce message ordering.

The gold standard of non-malleability (since its introduction in [DDN03]) requires handling general, *non-synchronizing* adversaries, who can arbitrarily schedule messages in the two interactions (without awareness of the sender and receiver). In this work, for the first time, we achieve this gold standard non-malleability in the post-quantum setting. As we shall explain later on, the challenge stems from the fact that classical techniques previously used to obtain non-malleability against non-synchronizing adversaries (e.g., as robust extraction [LP09], simulation extractability [PR05a, PR05b] and so on) do not generally apply in the quantum setting. This is due to basic quantum phenomena such as *unclonability* [WZ82] and *state disturbance* [FP96].

Our Results in More Detail. We construct statistically binding non-malleable commitments against quantum non-synchronizing adversaries, assuming post-quantum one-way functions. Our main result is a modular construction of post-quantum non-malleable commitments from post-quantum extractable commitments. The latter is a statistically binding commitment protocol that is extractable in the following sense: There exists an efficient quantum extractor-simulator, which given the code of any quantum sender, can simulate the arbitrary output of the sender up to, while extracting the committed value. The construction, in fact, only requires ε-extractability, meaning that the extractor-simulator obtains an additional *simulation accuracy parameter* $1^{1/\varepsilon}$, and the simulation only guarantees ε-indistinguishability

Theorem 1 (Informal). *Assuming k-round post-quantum ε-extractable commitments, there exist $k^{O(1)} \cdot \log^* \lambda$-round post-quantum non-malleable commitments, where λ is the security parameter.*

By default, when we say "post-quantum" we mean protocols that can be executed by classical parties, but which are secure against quantum adversaries. In particular, starting from a post-quantum classical ε-extractable commitment, we obtain a post-quantum classical non-malleable commitment. Constant-round ε-extractable commitments were constructed by Chia et al. [CCLY21] based on post-quantum one-way functions. Hence, we get the following corollary.

Corollary 1. *Assuming there exist post-quantum one-way functions, there exist $O(\log^* \lambda)$-round post-quantum non-malleable commitments.*

2 Technical Overview

We now give an overview of the main ideas behind our construction. Following the convention in the non-malleability literature, we refer to the interaction between Sen and $\mathcal{A}$ as the left interaction/commitment, and that between Rec and $\mathcal{A}$ the right interaction/commitment. Similarly, we refer to v, tg (and $\tilde{v}$, $\tilde{\text{tg}}$) as the left (and right) committed values or tag.

2.1   Understanding the Challenges

Before presenting our base commitments, we explain the main challenges that arise in the quantum setting. First, we recall a basic approach toward proving non-malleability in the classical setting *via extraction*. Here the basic idea is to provide a reduction that given a MIM adversary $\mathcal{A}$, can efficiently extract the value $\tilde{v}$ that $\mathcal{A}$ commits to on the right. Accordingly, if the MIM $\mathcal{A}$ manages to maul the commitment to v on the left and commit to a related value $\tilde{v}$ on the right, the reduction will gain information about v, and be able to break the *hiding* of the commitment.

The Difficulty in MIM Extraction. Extractable commitments allow for efficient extraction from adversarial senders in *the stand-alone setting*. Such extraction is traditionally done by either means of rewinding, or more generally using the sender's code. In the MIM setting, where $\mathcal{A}$ acts as a sender on the right, while acting as a receiver on the left, extraction from $\mathcal{A}$ is much more challenging. The problem is that the interaction of $\mathcal{A}$ with the receiver Rec on the right may occur concurrently to its interaction with the sender Sen on the left. This means that a reduction attempting to rewind $\mathcal{A}$ to extract the right committed value, may effectively also need to rewind the sender Sen on the left. (This may happen for example if, when the reduction rewinds $\mathcal{A}$ and sends $\mathcal{A}$ a new message, $\mathcal{A}$ also sends a new message in the left commitment and expects a reply from Sen before proceeding in the right commitment.) In such a case, extraction does not generally work—the "actual" sender of the right commitment is essentially the MIM $\mathcal{A}$ *combined with the sender* Sen *on the left*. However, the reduction does not posses the code of Sen, specifically, it does not posses its randomness. The challenge is to perform such extraction without access to the secret randomness of the sender on the left, and thus without compromising the hiding of the left commitment.

Indeed, classical non-malleable commitments tend to require more than *plain extractable commitments*. A long array of works (c.f., [DDN03, PR05b, PR05a, LP09, PW10, LP11, Goy11]) design various *safe extraction techniques*, which guarantee extraction on the right without compromising hiding of the left committed value. These safe-extraction techniques rely on properties of specific protocols and extraction strategies, rather than general (stand-alone) extractable commitments. For instance, the protocols of [DDN03, LP09, LP11, Goy11, GPR16a] rely on three-message witness-indistinguishable protocols satisfying an extraction guarantee known as *special soundness*, whereas the protocols in [PR05b, PR05a] rely on the specific structure of Barak's non-black-box zero knowledge protocol.

The Quantum Barrier. The (safe) extraction techniques used to obtain non malleability in the classical setting fail in the quantum setting. For once, rewinding does not generally work. We cannot record the adversary's quantum state between rewinding attempts due to the no-cloning theorem [WZ82]. Also, we cannot simply measure between rewindings, as this disturbs that the adversary's state [FP96]. In this case, even if we do extract, we may not be able to faithfully simulate the adversary's output state in the protocol[1]. Similarly, non-black-box techniques do not generally apply. For instance, it is unclear how to apply Barak's non-black-box simulation technique [Bar02], due to the lack of *universal arguments* [BG08] for quantum computations (this is just to mention one difficulty in using Barak's strategy in the quantum setting).

The difficulty of applying classical proof techniques in the setting of quantum adversaries is indeed a well known phenomena, and in some settings, quantum proof techniques have been successfully developed to circumvent this difficulty. Perhaps the most famous example of this is in the context of zero-knowledge simulation. Here Watrous [Wat09] shows that in certain settings quantum rewinding is possible and used it to obtain zero-knowledge protocols. Several other rewinding techniques enable extraction, but disturb the adversary's state in the process [Unr12, CCY20, CMSZ21]. Alternatively, several recent works [AP19, BS20, ABG+20] obtain constant round zero-knowledge via non-black-box quantum techniques, using quantum FHE (and assuming LWE). While post-quantum extractable commitments do exist, they do not satisfy the specific properties that the classical safe-extraction techniques require.

Given the above state of affairs, in this work, we aim to construct post-quantum non-malleable commitments modularly based on *any* post-quantum extractable (or ε-extractable) commitment. The equivalence between extractability and non-malleability is interesting on its own from a theoretical perspective. It turns out that doing so is challenging, and requires designing completely new safe-extraction techniques that work with general quantum extractable commitments, which we explain next.

For the sake of simplicity, and toward highlighting the main new ideas in this work, we ignore the difference between fully-extractable and ε-extractable commitments through the rest of this overview. We note that the transition from full extractable commitments to ε-extractable ones is quite direct and is based on the common knowledge that ε-simulation is sufficient when aiming to achieve indistinguishability-based definitions. Indeed, the definition of non-malleability is an indistinguishability-based definition, and accordingly showing ε-indistinguishability for any inverse polynomial ε is sufficient. In this case, the simulators invoked in the reduction are all still polynomial-time.

The Synchronizing Setting. As observed in [ABG+20], if restricted to synchronizing adversaries, such a modular construction exists using ideas from early works [CR87, DDN03]: When committing under a tag $\mathsf{tg} \in [\tau]$ for $\tau \leq \lambda$, in every round $i \neq \mathsf{tg}$ send an empty message, and in round tg, send an extractable commitment to the value v. Indeed, in the synchronizing setting, a commitment on the left under tag tg would never interleave with the commitment on the right under tag

---

[1] Recall that non-malleability requires that the joint distribution of the output state of the adversary and the committed value are indistinguishable regardless of the committed value on the left. Hence the reduction needs to extract the committed value without disturbing the state of the quantum adversary.

$\tilde{\mathsf{tg}} \neq \mathsf{tg}$. Thus, safe-extraction opportunities come for free, circumventing the real challenge in achieving non-malleability. It is not hard to see, however, that in the non-synchronizing setting, this approach would completely fail as the adversary can always align the extractable commitment on the right with that on the left. The work of [ABG+20] further constructed constant-round non-malleable commitments for a super-constant number of tags, based on mildly super-polynomial security of quantum FHE and LWE. The non-malleabilty of the new protocol, however, still relies on the synchronization of the left and right commitments.

2.2   Leveraging Extractable Com in Non-synchronizing Setting

We design a base protocol for a constant number of tags that, using *any* (post-quantum) extractable commitment scheme. The protocol guarantees extraction on the right while preserving hiding on the left, even against a quantum non-synchronizing MIM adversary. In this overview, we explain our base commitments in three steps:

- First, we introduce our basic idea in the simplified *one-sided* non-malleability setting where the MIM is restricted to choose a smaller tag on the right than the tag on the left, $\tilde{\mathsf{tg}} < \mathsf{tg}$.
- Then, we extend the basic idea to the general setting where the MIM may also choose a right tag that is larger $\tilde{\mathsf{tg}} > \mathsf{tg}$. We illustrate the main ideas here under the simplifying assumption of a certain honest behavior of the adversary.
- Finally, we show how to remove the simplifying assumption on the adversary.

Step 1: One-sided Non-malleability Let us first consider a MIM adversary that given a commitment on the left under tag tg, produces a commitment on the right under a smaller tag $\tilde{\mathsf{tg}} < \mathsf{tg}$. In our commitment, the sender first secret shares the value v to be committed into shares $u_1, \ldots, u_n$. It then sequentially sends extractable commitments to each of the shares $u_1, \ldots, u_n$ – we refer to the entire batch of these sequential extractable commitments as a *block-commitment to v*. The binding and hiding of this protocol follow directly from those of the underlying extractable commitment. We focus on non-malleability.

To achieve non-malleability, the number of shares n is chosen as a function of the tag tg. The goal is to guarantee that in every execution where the tag $\tilde{\mathsf{tg}}$ on the right is smaller than the tag tg on the left, there will exist, on the *left*, a commitment to one of the shares u_i that is *free* in the sense that it does not interleave with the interaction on the right; namely, during the commitment to u_i on the left, no message is sent in the right execution (see Fig. 1). Before explaining how freeness is achieved, let us explain how we use it to establish non-malleability.

Extracting While Preserving Hiding and First-Message Binding. To argue non-malleability, we show that we can efficiently extract *all* shares $\tilde{u}_1, \ldots, \tilde{u}_{\tilde{n}}$ on the right, while preserving the hiding of the free share u_i on the left, and by the security of secret sharing, also the hiding of the committed value v.

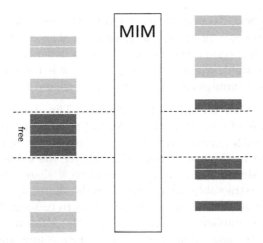

Fig. 1. Freeness Example. Each share commitment has 4 messages and there are $n = 3$ shares on the left, and $\tilde{n} = 2$ shares on the right. The second commitment on the left is free. Note that it splits the second commitment on the right.

Freeness guarantees that almost all commitments on the right do not interleave with the commitment to u_i on the left, more precisely, a single commitment on the right could be "split" by the commitment to u_i on the left (as in Fig. 1), which prevents extraction of that right split commitment. To deal with this, we rely on extractable commitments that are *first-message binding*; namely their first sender message fixes the value of the commitment. This gives rise to a simple extraction strategy: for any commitment on the right, where the first sender's message is sent before the free commitment (on the left), we can extract the corresponding share *non-uniformly*; for the commitments where the first sender's message occurs afterwards, we use the efficient extractor. Accordingly, we get a non-uniform reduction to the hiding of the free extractable commitment on the left.

We observe that any extractable commitment can be made first-message binding without any additional assumptions, and while increasing round complexity by at most a constant factor. For simplicity we describe how to achieve this assuming also non-interactive commitments.[2] We append to the original extractable commitment a first message where the sender sends a non-interactive commitment to the committed value and add at the end a zero-knowledge argument that this commitment is consistent with the commitment in the original extractable commitment. Extractability follows from the extractability of the original scheme and soundness of the argument, whereas hiding follows from that of the original scheme and the zero knowledge property. We note that (post-quantum) zero-knowledge arguments follow from (post-quantum) extractable commitments with a constant round complexity overhead (see e.g. [BS20]), and the same holds for ε-zero-knowledge and ε-extractable commitments, respectively.

---

[2] In the body, we observe that Naor commitments [Nao91], which can be obtained from (post-quantum) one-way functions, and thus also from any commitment, are in fact sufficient.

Guaranteeing Freeness. To achieve the required freeness property, it suffices to guarantee that whenever $\tilde{\mathsf{tg}} < \mathsf{tg}$, the number of shares $n(\mathsf{tg})$ (and hence the number of extractable commitments) on the left is larger than the total number of messages on the right, which is $k \cdot n(\tilde{\mathsf{tg}})$, where k is the number of messages in each extractable commitment. Accordingly, we choose $n(\mathsf{tg}) = (k+1)^{\mathsf{tg}}$.

Step 2: Dealing with General Adversaries. The above commitment does not prevent mauling of commitments under tag tg to commitments under tags $\tilde{\mathsf{tg}} > \mathsf{tg}$. To deal with general adversaries, we invoke the above idea again in reverse order. That is, the sender now secret shares the value v twice independently: once to n shares $u_1, \ldots, u_n$, and again to $\bar{n}$ shares $\bar{u}_1, \ldots, \bar{u}_{\bar{n}}$. It then sequentially sends extractable commitments to the shares $u_1, \ldots, u_n, \bar{u}_1, \ldots, \bar{u}_{\bar{n}}$, that is, sending two sequential block-commitments to v. To understand the basic idea, we assume for simplicity, in this step, that the MIM attacker always commits to shares of the same value $\tilde{v}$ in the two block-commitments on the right (in Step 3, we will remove this assumption using zero-knowledge arguments).

Our goal now is to set the number of shares $n(\cdot), \bar{n}(\cdot)$, based on the tags, to guarantee that there exists a block-commitment on the right with respect to which there exist two extractable commitments to shares u_i and $\bar{u}_{\bar{i}}$ on the left (one from each left block-commitment) that are *free*. This means we can extract every share from that right block-commitment, while keeping the shares u_i and $\bar{u}_{\bar{i}}$, and hence the left committed value, hidden. We say that the corresponding block-commitment on the right is *ideally scheduled* (see Fig. 2).

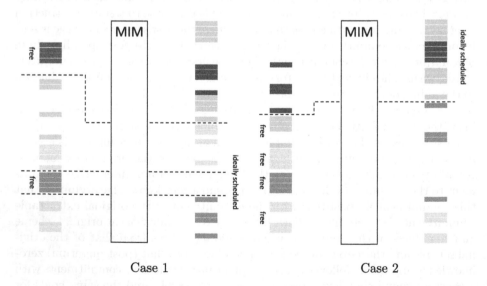

Fig. 2. Examples of an ideally scheduled block of shares (on the right). The first block of share commitments is colored in (light/dark) blue and the second in (light/dark) yellow. We mark the commitments on the left that are free with respect to the ideally scheduled block. (Color figure online)

Once we establish the existence of an ideally scheduled block, we can prove non-malleability using a non-uniform reduction to the hiding of the extractable commitments to u_i and $\bar{u}_{\bar{\imath}}$ similar to the one we used in the first step. Since we are only able to extract from one of the two block-commitments on the right, it is important that both commit to the same value $\tilde{v}$, and thus our reduction would work, regardless of which one of the two it is able to extract from. Before we explain how to enforce this using ZK in Step 3, we explain how the existence of an ideally scheduled block is established.

Guaranteeing an Ideally Scheduled Block-Commitment. We prove that by setting the parameters $n, \bar{n}$ appropriately, an ideally scheduled block of shares always exists. For this purpose we generalize the combinatorial argument from before. Concretely, we set $n, \bar{n}$ to guarantee that:

1. *Either,* the number of shares $n = n(\mathsf{tg})$ in the first left block-commitment is larger than the total number of messages $k \cdot n(\tilde{\mathsf{tg}})$ in the first right block-commitment,
2. *Or,* the number of shares $\bar{n} = \bar{n}(\mathsf{tg})$ in the second left block-commitment is larger than the total number of messages $k \cdot \bar{n}(\tilde{\mathsf{tg}})$ in the second right block-commitment.

In addition, we require that $n, \bar{n}$ are both at least 2. These conditions can be satisfied for example by setting $n = (k+1)^{\mathsf{tg}}, \bar{n} = (k+1)^{\tau-\mathsf{tg}} + 1$, where τ is the total number of tags (namely, $\mathsf{tg} \in [\tau]$).

To see why the above is sufficient, let us assume for instance that Condition 2 of the two above conditions holds (at this point, both are treated symmetrically). We consider two cases:

- **Case 1 (depicted in Fig. 2a):** the commitment to share u_1 (i.e., the first share of the first block-commitment) on the left ends before the second block-commitment starts on the right. In this case, the commitment to u_1 on the left is free with respect to the second block-commitment on the right. Furthermore, since Condition 2 holds, (by the argument in Step 1,) there also exists a commitment to a share $\bar{u}_i$ (in the second block-commitment) on the left that is also free with respect to the second block-commitment on the right. Accordingly, the second block-commitment on the right is ideally scheduled.
- **Case 2 (depicted in Fig. 2b):** the commitment to share u_1 on the left ends after the second block of share commitments starts on the right. In this case, the commitments to shares $u_2, \ldots, u_n, \bar{u}_1, \ldots, \bar{u}_{\bar{n}}$ on the left are all free with respect to the first block-commitment on the right, and thus it is ideally scheduled. (We use the fact that $n \geq 2$, to deduce that a free share u_2 indeed exists.)

Step 3: Use ZK to Ensure Consistency of Right Block-Commitments. Recall that in the last step, we made the simplifying assumption that the MIM adversary always commits to the same value $\tilde{v}$ in the two right block-commitments. The expected approach to removing this assumption, would be to require that the sender gives a (post-quantum) zero-knowledge argument that such consistency indeed holds.

While the soundness of the argument guarantees the required consistency on the right, the addition of a zero knowledge proof brings about new challenges in the reduction of non-malleability to hiding on the left, due to non-synchronizing advesaries. Indeed, in the proof of non-malleability, before using the hiding of the extractable commitments on the left, we must use the zero knowledge property on the left to argue that the proof does not compromise the hidden shares. The problem is that the zero-knowledge argument on the left might interleave with our ideally scheduled block-commitment on the right, and thus with our extraction procedure. For instance, if the extractor wants to rewind the MIM, it might have to rewind the zero knowledge prover on the left, which is not possible. More generally, there could be a circular dependency: The zero-knowledge simulation needs to be applied to the verifier's code which depends on the extractor's code; however, extraction needs to be applied to the sender's code which depends on the simulator's code.

To circumvent this difficulty, we would like to guarantee that an ideally scheduled block-commitment would also be free of the zero knowledge messages on the left, namely, during its execution, no zero knowledge messages should be sent in the left execution (see Fig. 3). Indeed, if this is the case, then we can apply the zero knowledge simulator to the verifier that when needed runs the extractor on the right *in its head*. Note that since the right block-commitment is free from zero knowledge messages on the left, the code of the extractor, and induced verifier, is independent of the simulator's code, breaking the circularity.

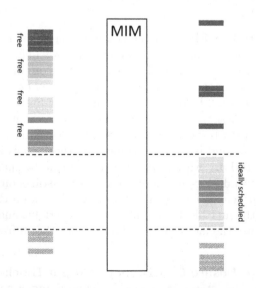

Fig. 3. The zero knowledge argument on the left is colored in green. The ideally scheduled block of shares on the right is required to be free of any zero knowledge messages (as well as satisfy the same conditions as before). (Color figure online)

Guaranteeing (the Stronger Form of) Ideal Scheduling. To achieve the stronger form of ideal scheduling, we augment the protocol yet again. Specifically, we repeat sequentially for $\ell + 1$ times the second block-commitment to shares $\bar{u}_1, \ldots, \bar{u}_{\bar{n}}$, where ℓ is the number of rounds in the zero knowledge protocol. We now require that there is a block-commitment I among the $\ell + 2$ right block-commitments (one of $u_1, \ldots, u_n$, and $\ell + 1$ of $\bar{u}_1, \ldots, \bar{u}_{\bar{n}}$) that is ideally scheduled in the following stronger sense:

1. There exist shares u_i and $\bar{u}_{\bar{\imath}}$ such that *all* commitments to these shares (one to u_i and $\ell + 1$ ones to $\bar{u}_i$) on the left, are free of the I'th right block-commitment.
2. The I'th right block-commitment is free of the zero knowledge argument on the left.

We provide a more involved combinatorial argument (and choice of parameters $n, \bar{n}$) showing that an ideally scheduled right block-commitment I always exists. Concretely, we set $n, \bar{n}$ to guarantee that:

1. *Either*, the number of shares $n = n(\mathsf{tg})$ in the first left block-commitment as well as the number of shares $\bar{n} = \bar{n}(\mathsf{tg})$ in each of the left block-commitments $2, \ldots, \ell + 2$ are *both* larger than the total number of messages $k \cdot n(\tilde{\mathsf{tg}})$ in the first right block-commitment.
2. *Or*, the number of shares $\bar{n} = \bar{n}(\mathsf{tg})$ in each of the left block-commitments $2, \ldots, \ell + 2$ is larger than the total number of messages $k \cdot \bar{n}(\tilde{\mathsf{tg}})$ in each of the right block-commitments $2, \ldots, \ell + 2$.

Again, we also require that $n, \bar{n}$ are both at least 2. The above conditions can be satisfied for example by setting $n = (k + 1)^{\mathsf{tg}}, \bar{n} = (k + 1)^{2\tau - \mathsf{tg}} + 1$, where τ is the total number of tags. The above two conditions can no longer be treated symmetrically as before. We explain separately, how each one of them implies the existence of an ideally scheduled block on the right (in the stronger sense defined above).

- **Case 1 (applies for either one of the two conditions):** the first block-commitment on the right ends after the knowledge argument on the left had started. In this case, block commitments $2, \ldots, \ell + 2$ on the right do not interleave with any of the block commitments on the left. Thus, we only need to establish that one of them does not interleave with the zero knowledge argument on the left. This follows from the fact that there are $\ell + 1$ of them, but only ℓ messages in the zero knowledge argument.
- **Case 2:** Condition 1 holds, but Case 1 above does not hold. First, since Case 1 does not hold, the first right block commitment does not interleave the zero knowledge argument on the left (which only starts after this block commitments ends). Accordingly, it is left to establish that there exist share commitments u_i in left block commitment 1 and $\bar{u}_{\bar{\imath}}$ in each of the left block commitments $2, \ldots, \ell + 2$ that are free with respect to the first right block commitment. This is where we use Condition 1—since the number of messages in this right block is strictly smaller than the number of shares $n, \bar{n}$ in each left block, the required free share commitments are guaranteed to exist.

- **Case 3 (applies for either one of the two conditions):** the commitment to share u_1 on the left ends after the second block of share commitments starts on the right. In this case, the commitments to shares $u_2, \ldots, u_n, \bar{u}_1, \ldots, \bar{u}_{\bar{n}}$, as well as the zero knowledge argument on the left are all free with respect to the first block-commitment on the right, and thus it is ideally scheduled. (This case is similar to the simplified case depicted in Fig. 2a.)
- **Case 4:** Condition 2 holds, but Case 3 above does not hold. First, since Case 3 does not hold, all the right block commitments $2, \ldots, \ell + 2$ do not interleave with the commitment to share u_1 in the first left block commitment. Furthermore, one of these right blocks $\mathsf{blk} \in \{2, \ldots, \ell + 2\}$ does not interleave with the zero knowledge argument on the left (which consists of ℓ messages). To deduce that blk is ideally schedule, it is left to show that there is a free share $\bar{u}_{\tilde{i}}$ in each of the left blocks $2, \ldots, \ell + 2$. Here we invoke Condition 2— the number of messages in blk is strictly smaller than the number of shares $\bar{n}$ in each of the left blocks $2, \ldots, \ell + 2$, the required free share commitments are again guaranteed to exist.

2.3 Tag Amplification

We now briefly overview the tag amplification process, which takes a non-malleable commitment $\langle \mathsf{Sen}, \mathsf{Rec} \rangle$ for $t \in [3, O(\log \lambda)]$ bit tags and transforms it into $\langle \widehat{\mathsf{Sen}}, \widehat{\mathsf{Rec}} \rangle$ for $T = 2^{t-1}$ bit tags. The amplification procedure is an adaptation of existing procedures from the literature mostly similar to [KS17, ABG+20] which in turn is based on that of [DDN03]; however, unlike the first of the two, it relies on polynomial hardness assumptions, and avoids complexity leveraging, and unlike the second, it works against non-synchronizing adversaries and not only synchronizing ones.

The basic way that previous amplification schemes work is as follows: to commit to a value v, under a tag $\hat{\mathsf{tg}} \in \{0,1\}^T$ for $T = 2^{t-1}$, we consider $t - 1$ tags of the form $\mathsf{tg}_i = (i, \hat{\mathsf{tg}}[i]) \in \{0,1\}^t$ corresponding to the base scheme (here $\hat{\mathsf{tg}}[i]$ is the i-th bit of $\hat{\mathsf{tg}}$). The committer then sends $t - 1$ commitments to the value v in parallel under each one of the tags tg_i, using the base protocol $\langle \mathsf{Sen}, \mathsf{Rec} \rangle$. Finally, a proof that all $t - 1$ commitments are consistent is added.

The basic idea behind the transformation is that if all the commitments are consistent, then in order to maul a commitment to value v under tag $\hat{\mathsf{tg}}$ to a commitment to a related value $\tilde{v}$ under tag $\hat{\mathsf{tg}}' \neq \hat{\mathsf{tg}}$, the MIM must create a commitment to $\tilde{v}$ using the base protocol under tag $\mathsf{tg}_i' = (i, \hat{\mathsf{tg}}'[i])$ for every $i \in [t-1]$, by potentially mauling from some of the left commitments to v under tags $\{\mathsf{tg}_i = (i, \hat{\mathsf{tg}}[i])\}_{i \in [t-1]}$. However, the fact that $\hat{\mathsf{tg}} \neq \hat{\mathsf{tg}}'$ means that they differ on at least one bit, that is, $\hat{\mathsf{tg}}[j] \neq \hat{\mathsf{tg}}'[j]$ for some j. Thus, tag $\mathsf{tg}_j' = (j, \hat{\mathsf{tg}}'[j])$ on the right is different from all the tags $\{\mathsf{tg}_i = (i, \hat{\mathsf{tg}}[i])\}_{j \in [t-1]}$ on the left. By the non-malleability of the base protocol, the value committed to under tag $\mathsf{tg}_j' = (j, \hat{\mathsf{tg}}'[j])$ on the right must be independent of the value v committed under tags $\{\mathsf{tg}_i = (i, \hat{\mathsf{tg}}[i])\}$ on the left. Given additionally that the values committed to in all base commitments on the right are the same, the non-malleability of $\langle \widehat{\mathsf{Sen}}, \widehat{\mathsf{Rec}} \rangle$ with respect to $\hat{\mathsf{tg}}, \hat{\mathsf{tg}}'$ then follows.

In the setting of synchronizing MIM adversaries the above intuition can be formalized as expected, when the proof of consistency is instantiated with a zero-knowledge argument. In the more general setting of non-synchronizing adversaries, things become more subtle. Specifically, if the zero knowledge argument on the left interleaves with the non-malleable commitments on the right, then it is not clear how to leverage the non-malleability of the base protocol $\langle \mathsf{Sen}, \mathsf{Rec} \rangle$. (More specifically, we need to apply zero-knowledge simulation on the code of the verifier, which however might depend on the honest receiver Rec's code. Then, we can no longer reduce to the non-malleability of the base protocol.)

To overcome this difficulty, we rely on the Feige-Lapidot-Shamir trapdoor paradigm [FLS99]. The first receiver message in our protocol sets up a trapdoor (a solution to a hard problem), and the final proof of consistency is a witness indistinguishable (WI) proof that either: (1) the $t - 1$ commitments are consistent, or (2) the sender "knows" the trapdoor (where formally knowledge is enforced using an extractable commitment). The idea behind the FLS paradigm is that the trapdoor cannot be obtained by a sender running the protocol, and thus the validity of assertion (1) is guaranteed on right. In contrast, we would like to ensure that the reduction of non-malleability to hiding on the left would be able to obtain the trapdoor and use it in order to simulate the WI proof.

We can show that the reduction can indeed do this, but only provided certain scheduling conditions. Specifically, the trapdoor on the left should be set up before the non-malleable commitment on the right occurs. In this case, we can non-uniformly obtain the witness. To deal with the other case, we augment the protocol yet again, adding a plain non-interactive commitment to the committed value v between the trapdoor set up phase and the non-malleable commitment phase. In case the non-malleable commitment on the right starts before the trapdoor set up on the left, then in particular the plain commitment on the right occurs before any commitment was made on the left. In this case, we have a direct reduction from non-malleability to hiding, which non-uniformly obtains the value of the plain commitment on the right (this is akin to our earlier use of "first-message binding"). We refer the reader to Fig. 5 for the amplification scheme and Sect. 5 for the proof.

Robustness. One challenge in the proof above is that even in the case that we can obtain the trapdoor witness on the left, it is not immediate that non-malleability holds when the commitments on the right interleave with the proof. For this, we require that the base non-malleable commitment satisfies an extra property known as r-robustness [LP12]. This property essentially says that the committed value on the right can be extracted without rewinding an arbitrary r-message protocol (the WI proof in our case) executed concurrently. This allows to switch the witness used in the WI on the left, and argue that the right committed value stays the same after the switch.

We show that our base protocol (described in Sect. 2.2) is indeed robust for an appropriate choice of parameters. We further show that the tag amplification transformation described here, preserves r-robustness.

Two-Sided Extraction via Watrous' Rewinding Lemma. One challenge in our analysis of both the base protocol and the tag amplification procedure is that the adversary's scheduling of messages is *adaptive*. In particular, even though the protocol's design guarantees that executions always contain certain *extraction opportunities*, we do not know ahead of time when they will occur. This is not a problem in the classical setting, where one can typically run first the so called main thread to identify the extraction opportunities and then rewind back to extract. However, such rewinding in the quantum setting might disturb the adversary's state.

The analysis of our base scheme circumvents this difficulty by showing a reduction to adversaries that commit ahead of time to the timing of the so called extraction opportunities. This reduction strongly relies on the fact that the definition of non-malleability is an indistinguishability-based definition. In contrast, r-robustness is a simulation based definition—it requires a simulator that given the code of the MIM adversary can extract on the right, while interacting with an r-message protocol on the left. Let us briefly explain the difficulty in this setting.

To achieve r-robustness, we make sure there are more than r extraction opportunities on the right. Consider a simplified scenario where the MIM gives $r + 1$ extractable commitments, and we want to extract from the "free" extractable commitment that does not interleave with any of the r left messages—we refer to this as *non-interleaving extraction*. The difficulty is that the simulator does not know which extractable commitment would be "free". If the simulator starts an extractable commitment without applying the extractor, it might miss the sole extraction opportunity. On the other hand, if it always applies the extractor, extraction may halt when the adversary expects a message on the left, and the simulator should give up extraction but still faithfully simulate the left and right interactions from here. To resolve this conundrum, we need the extractor of an extractable commitment protocol to be able to interchangeably simulate two types of interactions, ones that will eventually constitute an extraction opportunity and ones that will turn out not to be extractable due to the adversary's scheduling.

Toward this, we prove a *two-sided simulation lemma* for extractable commitments. This lemma shows that we can always enhance the extractor so that in case the sender in the commitment prematurely aborts, not only can we simulate the sender's state at that point, *but also the state of the receiver* (in case of abort, extraction is not required); otherwise, the extractor simulates the sender's state and extracts the committed value as usual (without simulating the state of the receiver). Using this two-sided extractor we can deal with cases where a commitment on the right turns out not to be extractable due to scheduled messages on the left by viewing this event as a premature abort, and then using the simulated state of the receiver to faithfully continue the interaction (without extracting).

The proof of the lemma is inspired by [BS20] and uses the fact that up to the point of abort a real execution and an execution simulated by the extractor are indistinguishable. Our two-sided extractor first tosses a random coin to decide whether to simulate with extraction or to honestly simulate the receiver anticipating an abort; if the guess failed, it tries again (the expected number of trials is negligibly close to two). While this works smoothly in the classical setting, in the quantum setting it should be done with care, as rewinding without state disturbance is typically a problem. In this specific setting, however, we meet the conditions of Watrous' *quantum rewinding lemma* [Wat09]—our extractor is guaranteed to succeed with probability close to $1/2$, obliviously of the quantum internal state of the adversarial sender.

3   Preliminaries

We rely on standard notions of classical Turing machines and Boolean circuits:

- A PPT algorithm is a probabilistic polynomial-time Turing machine.
- For a PPT algorithm M, we denote by $M(x; r)$ the output of M on input x and random coins r. For such an algorithm and any input x, we write $m \in M(x)$ to denote the fact that m is in the support of $M(x; \cdot)$.

We follow standard notions from quantum computation.

- A QPTalgorithm is a quantum polynomial-time Turing machine.
- An interactive algorithm M, in a two-party setting, has input divided into two registers and output divided into two registers. For the input, one register I_m is for an input message from the other party, and a second register I_a is an auxiliary input that acts as an inner state of the party. For the output, one register O_m is for a message to be sent to the other party, and another register O_a is again for auxiliary output that acts again as an inner state. For a quantum interactive algorithm M, both input and output registers are quantum.

The Adversarial Model. Throughout, efficient adversaries are modeled as quantum circuits with non-uniform quantum advice (i.e. quantum auxiliary input). Formally, *a polynomial-size adversary* $\mathcal{A} = \{\mathcal{A}_\lambda, \rho_\lambda\}_{\lambda \in \mathbb{N}}$, consists of a polynomial-size non-uniform sequence of quantum circuits $\{\mathcal{A}_\lambda\}_{\lambda \in \mathbb{N}}$, and a sequence of polynomial-size mixed quantum states $\{\rho_\lambda\}_{\lambda \in \mathbb{N}}$.

For an interactive quantum adversary in a classical protocol, it can be assumed without loss of generality that its output message register is always measured in the computational basis at the end of computation. This assumption is indeed without the loss of generality, because whenever a quantum state is sent through a classical channel then qubits decohere and are effectively measured in the computational basis.

3.1   Indistinguishability in the Quantum Setting

- Let $f : \mathbb{N} \to [0, 1]$ be a function.
  - f is negligible if for every constant $c \in \mathbb{N}$ there exists $N \in \mathbb{N}$ such that for all $n > N$, $f(n) < n^{-c}$.
  - f is noticeable if there exists $c \in \mathbb{N}, N \in \mathbb{N}$ such that for every $n \geq N$, $f(n) \geq n^{-c}$.

- f is overwhelming if it is of the form $1 - \mu(n)$, for a negligible function μ.
- We may consider random variables over bit strings or over quantum states. This will be clear from the context.
- For two random variables X and Y supported on quantum states, quantum distinguisher circuit D with, quantum auxiliary input ρ, and $\mu \in [0,1]$, we write $X \approx_{\mathsf{D},\rho,\mu} Y$ if

$$|\Pr[\mathsf{D}(X; \rho) = 1] - \Pr[\mathsf{D}(Y; \rho) = 1]| \leq \mu.$$

- Two ensembles of random variables $\mathcal{X} = \{X_i\}_{\lambda \in \mathbb{N}, i \in I_\lambda}$, $\mathcal{Y} = \{Y_i\}_{\lambda \in \mathbb{N}, i \in I_\lambda}$ over the same set of indices $I = \cup_{\lambda \in \mathbb{N}} I_\lambda$ are said to be *computationally indistinguishable*, denoted by $\mathcal{X} \approx_c \mathcal{Y}$, if for every polynomial-size quantum distinguisher $\mathsf{D} = \{\mathsf{D}_\lambda, \rho_\lambda\}_{\lambda \in \mathbb{N}}$ there exists a negligible function $\mu(\cdot)$ such that for all $\lambda \in \mathbb{N}, i \in I_\lambda$,

$$X_i \approx_{\mathsf{D}_\lambda, \rho_\lambda, \mu(\lambda)} Y_i \ .$$

For a (non-negligible) function $\varepsilon(\lambda) \in [0,1]$, the ensembles $\mathcal{X}, \mathcal{Y}$ are ε-indistinguishable if the above requirement is replaced with

$$X_i \approx_{\mathsf{D}_\lambda, \rho_\lambda, \varepsilon(\lambda) + \mu(\lambda)} Y_i \ .$$

- The trace distance between two distributions X, Y supported over quantum states, denoted $\mathrm{TD}(X, Y)$, is a generalization of statistical distance to the quantum setting and represents the maximal distinguishing advantage between two distributions supported over quantum states, by unbounded quantum algorithms. We thus say that ensembles $\mathcal{X} = \{X_i\}_{\lambda \in \mathbb{N}, i \in I_\lambda}$, $\mathcal{Y} = \{Y_i\}_{\lambda \in \mathbb{N}, i \in I_\lambda}$, supported over quantum states, are statistically indistinguishable (and write $\mathcal{X} \approx_s \mathcal{Y}$), if there exists a negligible function $\mu(\cdot)$ such that for all $\lambda \in \mathbb{N}, i \in I_\lambda$,

$$\mathrm{TD}\,(X_i, Y_i) \leq \mu(\lambda) \ .$$

Standard Tools. Due to the lack of space, some of the basic definitions such as Witness Indistinguishability, Zero Knowledge, and Commitments, are omitted and can be found in the full version of the paper.

3.2   Non-malleable Commitments

Standard commitment schemes are defined in the full version of the paper Let $\langle \mathsf{Sen}, \mathsf{Rec} \rangle$ be a commitment scheme. In an interaction between a malicious sender Sen^* and honest receiver Rec, we say that Sen^* is *non-aborting* if the Rec accepts (i.e., outputs 1) at the end of the commitment stage. Let $\mathsf{open}_{\langle \mathsf{Sen}, \mathsf{Rec} \rangle}(c, v, d)$ be the function for verifying decommitments of $\langle \mathsf{Sen}, \mathsf{Rec} \rangle$. Define the following value function:

$$\mathsf{val}(c) = \begin{cases} v & \text{if } \exists \text{ unique } v \text{ s.t. } \exists d, \ \mathsf{open}_{\langle \mathsf{Sen}, \mathsf{Rec} \rangle}(c, v, d) = 1 \\ \bot & \text{otherwise} \end{cases}$$

A commitment c is *valid* if $\mathsf{val}(c) \neq \bot$, and otherwise *invalid*.

Tag-Based Commitment Scheme. Following [DDN03,PR05b], we consider *tag-based commitment schemes* where, in addition to the security parameter, the sender and the receiver also receive a "tag"—a.k.a. the identity—tg as common input.

We recall the definition of non-malleability from [LPV08], adapted to quantum polynomial-size man-in-the-middle adversaries.

Let $\langle \mathsf{Sen}, \mathsf{Rec} \rangle$ be a tag-based commitment scheme, and let $\lambda \in \mathbb{N}$ be a security parameter. Consider a man-in-the-middle (MIM) adversary $\mathcal{A}$ that participates in one left and one right interactions simultaneously. In the left interactions the MIM adversary $\mathcal{A}$, on auxiliary quantum state ρ, interacts with Sen, receiving commitments to value v, using a tag $\mathsf{tg} \in [T]$ of its choice. In the right interactions $\mathcal{A}$ interacts with Rec attempting to commit to a related value $\tilde{v}$, again using a tag $\tilde{\mathsf{tg}}$ of length t of its choice. If the right commitment is invalid, or $\tilde{\mathsf{tg}} = \mathsf{tg}$, set $\tilde{v}_i = \bot$—i.e., choosing the same tags in the left and right interactions is considered invalid. Let $\mathsf{mim}_{\langle \mathsf{Sen}, \mathsf{Rec} \rangle}(\mathcal{A}, \rho, v)$ denote a random variable that describes the value $\tilde{v}$ along with the quantum output of $\mathcal{A}(\rho)$ at the end of the interaction where Sen commits to v on the left.

Definition 1. *A commitment scheme* $\langle \mathsf{Sen}, \mathsf{Rec} \rangle$ *is said to be* non-malleable *if for every quantum polynomial-size man-in-the-middle adversary* $A = \{A_\lambda, \rho_\lambda\}_{\lambda \in \mathbb{N}}$ *and a polynomial* $\ell : \mathbb{N} \to \mathbb{N}$,

$$\left\{ \mathsf{mim}_{\langle \mathsf{Sen}, \mathsf{Rec} \rangle}(A_\lambda, \rho_\lambda, v) \right\}_{\lambda, v, v'} \approx_c \left\{ \mathsf{mim}_{\langle \mathsf{Sen}, \mathsf{Rec} \rangle}(A_\lambda, \rho_\lambda, v') \right\}_{\lambda, v, v'} ,$$

where $\lambda \in \mathbb{N}$ *is the security parameter and* $v, v' \in \{0, 1\}^{\ell(\lambda)}$ *are two committed values by the honest sender.*

Generally, the distributions in the MIM experiment include a quantum algorithm with a quantum auxiliary state. A standard strengthening of indistinguishability definitions for distributions of the above-mentioned type is to let the distinguisher prepare an entangled register, which is entangled with the register that contains the auxiliary state of the quantum algorithm in the distribution. In our specific case of MIM distributions the stronger definition (defined below) is equivalent as we prove next.

Definition 2 (Stronger Definition of Non-malleability). *A commitment scheme* $\langle \mathsf{Sen}, \mathsf{Rec} \rangle$ *is said to be* non-malleable *(with respect to entanglement) if for every quantum polynomial-size man-in-the-middle adversary* $A = \{A_\lambda\}_{\lambda \in \mathbb{N}}$ *that can obtain a quantum auxiliary state, a polynomial-size quantum state* $\sigma = \{\sigma_\lambda\}_{\lambda \in \mathbb{N}}$ *of size at least what A obtains, and a polynomial* $\ell : \mathbb{N} \to \mathbb{N}$,

$$\left\{ \mathsf{mim}_{\langle \mathsf{Sen}, \mathsf{Rec} \rangle}(A_\lambda, \sigma_{1,\lambda}, v), \sigma_{2,\lambda} \right\}_{\lambda, v, v'} \approx_c \left\{ \mathsf{mim}_{\langle \mathsf{Sen}, \mathsf{Rec} \rangle}(A_\lambda, \sigma_{1,\lambda}, v'), \sigma_{2,\lambda} \right\}_{\lambda, v, v'} ,$$

where $\lambda \in \mathbb{N}$ *is the security parameter,* $v, v' \in \{0, 1\}^{\ell(\lambda)}$ *are two committed values by the honest sender and* σ_1 *is the first register of the state* σ *such that it is in the size of the auxiliary state for A and* σ_2 *is the rest of the state.*

Claim. Any commitment scheme $\langle \mathsf{Sen}, \mathsf{Rec} \rangle$ satisfying security Definition 1 also satisfy security Definition 2.

Proof. Assume $\langle \mathsf{Sen}, \mathsf{Rec} \rangle$ is secure with respect to Definition 1 and assume toward contradiction that it is not secure with respect to Definition 2. Let $A = \{A_\lambda\}_{\lambda \in \mathbb{N}}$ a MIM adversary and let $D = \{D_\lambda, \sigma_\lambda\}$ a distinguisher that distinguishes between,

$$\left\{\mathsf{mim}_{\langle \mathsf{Sen}, \mathsf{Rec}\rangle}(A_\lambda, \sigma_{1,\lambda}, v), \sigma_{2,\lambda}\right\}_{\lambda, v, v'} \quad, \quad \left\{\mathsf{mim}_{\langle \mathsf{Sen}, \mathsf{Rec}\rangle}(A_\lambda, \sigma_{1,\lambda}, v'), \sigma_{2,\lambda}\right\}_{\lambda, v, v'} \quad,$$

for some v, v'. Consider A' a new MIM adversary: A' has quantum auxiliary state σ. The MIM execution of A' is to run A with auxiliary state σ_1, and keep the rest of σ, which we denote by σ_2, untouched on the side. D can thus distinguish between the distributions

$$\left\{\mathsf{mim}_{\langle \mathsf{Sen}, \mathsf{Rec}\rangle}(A'_\lambda, \sigma_\lambda, v)\right\}_{\lambda, v, v'} \quad, \quad \left\{\mathsf{mim}_{\langle \mathsf{Sen}, \mathsf{Rec}\rangle}(A'_\lambda, \sigma_\lambda, v')\right\}_{\lambda, v, v'} \quad,$$

in contradiction to the security of $\langle \mathsf{Sen}, \mathsf{Rec} \rangle$ with respect to Definition 1.

3.3   Committed Value Oracle

Let $\langle \mathsf{Sen}, \mathsf{Rec} \rangle$ be a (possibly tag-based) commitment scheme. A sequential committed-value oracle $\mathcal{O}^\infty[\langle \mathsf{Sen}, \mathsf{Rec}\rangle]$ of $\langle \mathsf{Sen}, \mathsf{Rec} \rangle$ acts as follows in interaction with a sender Sen^*: it interacts with Sen^* in many *sequential* sessions; in each session,

- it participates with Sen^* in the commit phase of $\langle \mathsf{Sen}, \mathsf{Rec} \rangle$ as the honest receiver Rec (using a tag chosen adaptively by Sen^*), obtaining a commitment c, and
- if Sen^* is *non-aborting* in the commit phase and sends request break, it returns $\mathsf{val}(c)$.

The single-session oracle $\mathcal{O}^1[\langle \mathsf{Sen}, \mathsf{Rec}\rangle]$ is similar to $\mathcal{O}^\infty$, except that it interacts with the adversary in a single session.

Throughout, when the commitment scheme is clear from the context, we write $\mathcal{O}^\infty$, $\mathcal{O}^1$ for simplicity.

3.4   Extractable Commitments

We define the standard notion of post-quantum extractable commitments (and ε-extractable) along with several enhancements of this notion. These enhancements of extractable commitments are for both the ε-extractable and (fully) extractable versions.

Definition 3. *Let* $\langle \mathsf{ExCom.Sen}, \mathsf{ExCom.Rec} \rangle$ *be a (possibly tag-based) commitment scheme and* $\mathcal{O}^1$ *its (single-session) committed value oracle. We say that* $\langle \mathsf{ExCom.Sen}, \mathsf{ExCom.Rec} \rangle$ *is* ε-*extractable if there exists a QPT simulator* Sim^1, *such that, for every quantum polynomial-size sender* $\mathsf{Sen}^* = \{\mathsf{Sen}^*_\lambda, \rho_\lambda\}_{\lambda \in \mathbb{N}}$ *and function* $\varepsilon(\lambda) \in [0, 1]$,

– *For every quantum polynomial-time distinguisher* $D^* = \{D^*_\lambda, \rho_\lambda\}_{\lambda \in \mathbb{N}}$,

$$\left\{ \mathsf{OUT}_{\mathsf{Sen}^*_\lambda} \left(\mathsf{Sen}^{*\mathcal{O}^1}_\lambda (\rho_\lambda) \right) \right\}_{\lambda \in \mathbb{N}} \approx_\varepsilon \left\{ \mathsf{Sim}^1(\mathsf{Sen}^*_\lambda, \rho_\lambda, 1^{1/\varepsilon}) \right\}_{\lambda \in \mathbb{N}} .$$

We say the scheme is (fully) extractable if there is a QPT *simulator* Sim^1, *such that, for every quantum polynomial-size sender* $\mathsf{Sen}^* = \{\mathsf{Sen}^*_\lambda, \rho_\lambda\}_{\lambda \in \mathbb{N}}$,

$$\left\{ \mathsf{OUT}_{\mathsf{Sen}^*_\lambda} \left(\mathsf{Sen}^{*\mathcal{O}^1}_\lambda (\rho_\lambda) \right) \right\}_{\lambda \in \mathbb{N}} \approx_c \left\{ \mathsf{Sim}^1(\mathsf{Sen}^*_\lambda, \rho_\lambda) \right\}_{\lambda \in \mathbb{N}} .$$

Sequential Extraction. We analogously define sequential extractability.

Definition 4. *Let* $\langle \mathsf{ExCom.Sen}, \mathsf{ExCom.Rec} \rangle$ *be a (possibly tag-based) commitment scheme and* $\mathcal{O}^\infty$ *its sequential committed value oracle. We say that* $\langle \mathsf{ExCom.Sen}, \mathsf{ExCom.Rec} \rangle$ *is sequentially extractable if there exists a* QPT *simulator* Sim^∞, *such that, for every quantum polynomial-size sender* $\mathsf{Sen}^* = \{\mathsf{Sen}^*_\lambda, \rho_\lambda\}_{\lambda \in \mathbb{N}}$,

$$\left\{ \mathsf{OUT}_{\mathsf{Sen}^*_\lambda} \left(\mathsf{Sen}^{*\mathcal{O}^\infty}_\lambda (\rho_\lambda) \right) \right\}_{\lambda \in \mathbb{N}} \approx_c \{ \mathsf{Sim}^\infty(\mathsf{Sen}^*_\lambda, \rho_\lambda) \}_{\lambda \in \mathbb{N}} .$$

Sequential ε-*extractability is defined analogously when considering* ε-*indistinguishability instead of (plain) computational indistinguishability.*

Constructions of post-quantum extractable commitments with have been known for a while either in polynomially many rounds assuming post-quantum oblivious transfer [HSS15,LN11] or in constant rounds assuming Learning with Errors in quantum fully homomorphic encryption [BS20]. More recently Chia et al. [CCLY21] constructed post-quantum ε-extractable commitments with in constant rounds, assuming the existence of post-quantum one-way functions. (Lombardi, Ma, and Spooner [LMS21] also construct such commitments, but relying super-polynomial hardness of the one-way functions.)

These constructions address the single-session oracle. However, a standard proof shows that sequential extraction follows.

Lemma 1. *Any extractable commitment is sequentially extractable. This applies also for* ε-*extractability.*

r-Robustness. The work of [LP12] introduced the notion of r-robustness w.r.t. committed value oracle, following similar notions of r-*robustness* introduced in [CLP16,LP09]. We here recall their definition, adapted to working with quantum polynomial-size adversaries. Let $\langle \mathsf{Sen}, \mathsf{Rec} \rangle$ be a (possibly tag-based) commitment scheme. Consider a man-in-the-middle adversary that participates in an *arbitrary* left interaction with a *limited number r of rounds*, while having access to the committed value oracle $\mathcal{O}^\infty[\langle \mathsf{Sen}, \mathsf{Rec} \rangle]$. Roughly speaking, $\langle \mathsf{Sen}, \mathsf{Rec} \rangle$ is r-robust if the output of $\mathcal{A}$ in any r-round interaction, with access to the oracle $\mathcal{O}^\infty[\langle \mathsf{Sen}, \mathsf{Rec} \rangle]$, can be simulated without the oracle. In other words, having access to the oracle does not help the adversary in breaking the security in any r-round protocol much.

Definition 5 (r-robust extraction). *Let* $\langle \mathsf{Sen}, \mathsf{Rec} \rangle$ *be a (possibly tag-based) commitment scheme. We say that* $\langle \mathsf{Sen}, \mathsf{Rec} \rangle$ *is* r-*robust w.r.t. the committed-value oracle, if there exists a QPT simulator* Sim_r, *such that, for every QPT adversary* $\mathcal{A} = \{\mathcal{A}_\lambda, \rho_\lambda\}_{\lambda \in \mathbb{N}}$, *the following holds:*

- *Simulation: For every PPT* r-*round machine* B,

$$\left\{ \mathsf{OUT}_{\mathcal{A}_\lambda} \langle B(z, 1^\lambda), A_\lambda^{\mathcal{O}^\infty[\langle \mathsf{Sen}, \mathsf{Rec} \rangle]}(\rho_\lambda) \rangle \right\}_{\lambda \in \mathbb{N}, z \in \{0,1\}^*}$$
$$\approx_c \left\{ \mathsf{OUT}_{\mathsf{Sim}} \langle B(z, 1^\lambda), \mathsf{Sim}_r(\mathcal{A}_\lambda, \rho_\lambda) \rangle \right\}_{\lambda \in \mathbb{N}, z \in \{0,1\}^*} .$$

(ε, r)-*robustness is defined analogously when considering* ε-*indistinguishability instead of (plain) computational indistinguishability.*

First-Message Binding. We define an additional property of extractable commitments which will come in handy later in the construction of post-quantum non-malleable commitments. The property, which we call first-message binding, asserts that the first message of the sender determines the committed value. Additionally, if the first message in the extractable commitment protocol is a receiver message, then the extractor simulates it honestly, in particular, independently of the malicious sender's circuit.

Definition 6. *Let* $\langle \mathsf{ExCom.Sen}, \mathsf{ExCom.Rec} \rangle$ *be an extractable commitment scheme. We say that the scheme has first-message binding if:*

1. *With overwhelming probability over the choice of the honest receiver randomness, the first sender message in the protocol fixes the committed value.*
2. *If the first message in the protocol is a receiver message, in a simulated session, the extractor* $\mathsf{ExCom.Ext}$ *samples this message by invoking the honest receiver (independently of the malicious sender circuit).*

We observe that every extractable commitment can easily be turned into an extractable commitment with first-message binding. A proof sketch is provided in supplemental material.

Lemma 2. *Let* $\langle \mathsf{ExCom.Sen}, \mathsf{ExCom.Rec} \rangle$ *be an extractable commitment scheme. Then there exists an extractable commitment scheme* $\langle \mathsf{Sen}, \mathsf{Rec} \rangle$ *with first-message binding. Furthermore, the sequential extractor* Sim^∞ *for the scheme also satisfies Property 2 in the above definition. The same also holds for* ε-*extractability.*

3.5 Two-Sided Extraction

In this section, we state a *two-sided extraction lemma* for any extractable commitment. We then use it to prove a *non-interleaving extraction lemma*, which we later rely on.

Two-Sided Extractor. We define the following variant $\mathcal{O}^1_\perp$ of the committed value oracle $\mathcal{O}^1$. Recall that $\mathcal{O}^1$ participates in a session of the commit phase of $\langle \mathsf{ExCom.Sen}, \mathsf{ExCom.Rec} \rangle$ with Sen^*, acting as the honest receiver $\mathsf{ExCom.Rec}$. If Sen^* is non-aborting in the commit phase and requests break, $\mathcal{O}^1$ returns the value $\mathsf{val}(c)$ committed in the produced commitment c.

$\mathcal{O}^1_\perp$ does the same, except that in the case that Sen^* aborts, it sends back the internal state of the honest receiver $\mathsf{ExCom.Rec}$ in that session. That is,

$$\mathcal{O}^1_\perp \text{ returns} \begin{cases} \text{internal state of } \mathsf{ExCom.Rec} & \text{if } \mathsf{Sen}^* \text{ aborts} \\ \mathsf{val}(c) & \text{if } \mathsf{Sen}^* \text{ is non-aborting in } c \text{ and requests break} \\ \text{nothing} & \text{otherwise} \end{cases}$$

In the full version of this work, we prove that every extractable commitment satisfies such *two-sided extractability*.

Claim. Let $\langle \mathsf{ExCom.Sen}, \mathsf{ExCom.Rec} \rangle$ be an extractable commitment scheme and $\mathcal{O}^1_\perp$ its enhanced committed value oracle. There exists a QPT simulator $\mathsf{Sim}^1_\perp$, such that, for every quantum polynomial-size sender $\mathsf{Sen}^* = \{\mathsf{Sen}^*_\lambda, \rho_\lambda\}_{\lambda \in \mathbb{N}}$, the following two ensembles are computationally indistinguishable,

$$\left\{ \mathsf{OUT}_{\mathsf{Sen}^*_\lambda} \left(\mathsf{Sen}^{*\mathcal{O}^1_\perp}_\lambda (\rho_\lambda) \right) \right\}_{\lambda \in \mathbb{N}} \approx_c \left\{ \mathsf{Sim}^1_\perp (\mathsf{Sen}^*_\lambda, \rho_\lambda) \right\}_{\lambda \in \mathbb{N}}.$$

The same also holds for ε-extractability.

ε-Extractability vs Full Extractability. To simplify notation, the technical sections in this extended abstract are based on fully extractability (and corresponding indistinguishability) rather than full extractability. As mentioned in the introduction, the transition between the two is quite direct. In more detail, our final goal is to achieve an indistinguishability-based definition of non-malleability. The proof toward that is based on a fixed polynomial number $h(\lambda) = \mathrm{poly}(\lambda)$ of hybrid distributions that depends only on the security parameter. Thus when relying on indistinguishability between a simulated execution and a real execution, the corresponding indistinguishability between hybrids is only ε indistinguishability. Accordingly, for any polynomial $p(\lambda)$, to overall obtain $1/p(\lambda)$ indistinguishability, we can set $\varepsilon = 1/(h(\lambda) \cdot p(\lambda))$. All corresponding simulators still run in polynomial time, and hence all intermediate reductions still hold.

4   Post-quantum Non-malleable Commitment for Few Tags

In this section, we present our construction of a classical post-quantum non-malleable commitment protocol with at most a logarithmic number of tags τ. It makes use of A quantumly-extractable classical commitment scheme (ExCom.Sen, ExCom.Rec) with first-message binding, and a post-quantum classical zero-knowledge argument (P, V). We describe the protocol in Fig. 4.

Using post-quantum ε-extractable commitments with k rounds one can obtain post-quantum ε-zero-knowledge arguments with $k + O(1)$ rounds [Ros04, BS20]. It follows that the number of rounds in Protocol 4 is $k^{O(\tau)}$. Statistical binding of the commitment scheme follows readily from the statistical binding of the extractable commitment scheme. Hiding of any commitment scheme follows directly from non-malleability, so it remains for us to show that our commitment protocol is non-malleable. Later, we also show that our commitment scheme satisfies r-robustness, a property of the commitment protocol which we use in our tag amplification scheme in Sect. 5.

Proposition 1. *The protocol in Fig. 4 is non malleable.*

4.1   Ideally-Scheduled Block Commitments

Before turning to prove Proposition 1, we state and prove a combinatorial claim regarding the structure of executions. We first fix relevant terminology for addressing different parts of the protocol.

Block Commitments. For $m, N \in \mathbb{N}$, a block commitment of length N and sub-block length m for a string $s = s_1, s_2, \ldots, s_N \in \{0,1\}^{m \times N}$ (such that $\forall i \in s_i \in \{0,1\}^m$) consists of N sequential extractable commitment to each of the strings $s_1, \ldots, s_N$ in their respective order. In particular, note that in Phase 1 of our Protocol 4, the sender gives one block commitment of length n with sub-block length $|v|$ to $\mathbf{u} = (u_1, \ldots, u_n)$ and $\ell + 1$ block commitments to $\bar{\mathbf{u}} = (\bar{u}_1, \ldots, \bar{u}_{\bar{n}})$, each of length $\bar{n}$ and sub-block length $|v|$.

Ideally Scheduled Block Commitments. Consider a two-sided MIM execution of Protocol 4; that is, the MIM adversary $\mathcal{A}$ interacts with Sen on the left and Rec on the right.

We call an execution of a block commitment on the left *free* on index i with respect to a given block commitment on the right, if interaction during the i-th extractable commitment in that block commitment does not interleave with the interaction during the given right block commitment. We call an execution of a block commitment on the right free if it does not interleave with the interaction during Phase 2 of the protocol on the left.

An execution I of a block commitment on the right is *ideally scheduled* if all of the above hold:

- It is free (with respect to the second phase on the left).

Protocol 6

Parameters: λ is the security parameter. r is the robustness parameter. k is the total number of messages in the extractable commitment protocol. $\tau \leq O(\log_k(\lambda))$ is the number of tags. ℓ is the maximum between (1) the robustness parameter r, and (2) the total number of messages in the zero knowledge argument system.

Common input: Security parameter $\lambda \in \mathbb{N}$, robustness parameter $r \leq \text{poly}(\lambda)$, an identification tag $\mathbf{tg} \in [\tau]$ for the sender.

Sender private input: A value $v \in \{0,1\}^*$ to commit to.

Phase 1: Commitments to Secret Shares of Value:

- Let $n := (k+1)^{\mathbf{tg}}$ and $\bar{n} := (k+1)^{2\tau - \mathbf{tg}}$.
- Sen secret-shares the value v twice, first into n shares and second into $\bar{n}$ shares: $\mathbf{u} = (u_1, \ldots, u_n)$ and $\bar{\mathbf{u}} = (\bar{u}_1, \ldots, \bar{u}_{\bar{n}})$, respectively.
- Sen provides extractable commitments to the two sequences of shares:
  1. An extractable commitment to u_i, for every $i \in [n]$, sequentially, one after the other.
  2. An extractable commitment to $\bar{u}_i$, for every $i \in [\bar{n}]$, sequentially, one after the other. This sequential commitment to $\bar{\mathbf{u}}$ is repeated $\ell + 1$ times, sequentially.

Phase 2: Zero-knowledge Argument of Consistency: The protocol ends with Sen giving a ZK argument that its generated transcript is consistent; namely, there exists private input and randomness for the honest sender inducing the transcript.

Decommitment. If the interaction ends in an accepting proof, the decommitment information includes the shares $u_1, \ldots, u_n$ along with the decommitment information for each of their corresponding extractable commitments. The decommitment verification algorithm checks that the shares yield the value v and then runs the decommitment verification algorithm of the extractable commitment on each of the shares and its decommitment information. If the ZK argument is not accepting, or the sender prematurely aborts, the verification algorithm rejects, regardless of the decommitment information given.

Fig. 4. A τ-tag post-quantum non-malleable commitment $(\mathsf{Sen}, \mathsf{Rec})$.

- There is some index $i \in [n]$ such that the block commitment to $\mathbf{u}$ on the left is free on index i with respect to I.
- There is some index $j \in [\bar{n}]$ such that *all* $\ell + 1$ block commitments to $\bar{\mathbf{u}}$ on the left are free on *the same* index j with respect to I.

In case, the MIM adversary aborts, we assume w.l.o.g it keeps sending messages $\perp$ according to some schedule, so that the above notion is always defined. The proof of the following claim is provided in the full version of this work.

Claim. In every MIM execution of Protocol 4 with tag tg on the left and tag $\tilde{\mathsf{tg}}$ on the right, if $\mathsf{tg} \neq \tilde{\mathsf{tg}}$, there is an ideally scheduled execution of a block commitment on the right.

4.2   Adversaries with Predetermined Ideal Schedule

Before proving Proposition 1, we prove a lemma that basically says that we can restrict attention to MIM adversaries that always announce ahead of time the structure of the ideal schedule. This lemma will later simplify our proof of Proposition 1.

In what follows, let N be a bound on the size of $n := (k+1)^{\mathsf{tg}}, \bar{n} := (k+1)^{2\tau - \mathsf{tg}}$, for every possible tg. We consider *configurations* of the form

$$ C = (i, c, \bar{c}, w) \in [\ell + 2] \times [N] \times [N] \times \{\mathsf{IP}_2, \mathsf{P}_2\mathsf{I}\} \ . $$

We say that a given MIM execution is consistent with such a configuration C if:

- The i-th block commitment on the right is the first ideally scheduled block.
- The commitment to u_c (in the first block) on the left is free with respect to the ideally scheduled block i.
- The commitment to $\bar{u}_{\bar{c}}$ in every one of the blocks $2, \ldots, \ell + 2$ on the left is free with respect to the ideally scheduled block i.
- If the first ideally scheduled block i on the right ends before Phase 2 on the left begins, $w = \mathsf{IP}_2$. Otherwise (Phase 2 on the left begins before the first ideally scheduled block i has ended), $w = \mathsf{P}_2\mathsf{I}$. Note that in case $w = \mathsf{P}_2\mathsf{I}$, due to the fact that block i on the right is ideally scheduled and in particular is continuous with respect to Phase 2 on the left, we can also say that block i on the right *begins* after Phase 2 on the left has started (rather than say that it only ends after the beginning of Phase 2 on the left).

Note that the number of possible configurations is bounded by $\Delta := (\ell + 2) \times N \times N \times 2 = \mathrm{poly}(\lambda)$.

Definition 7 (MIM with predetermined ideal schedule). *A MIM QPT adversary $\mathcal{A} = \{\mathcal{A}_\lambda, \rho_\lambda\}_\lambda$ has a predetermined ideal schedule $C = \{C_\lambda\}_\lambda$, if any execution in which $\mathcal{A}_\lambda$ participates is consistent with configuration C_λ.*

Lemma 3. *If the protocol in Fig. 4 is secure against MIM QPT adversaries with predetermined ideal schedule, then it is also secure against arbitrary MIM QPT adversaries.*

Proof. Given an arbitrary MIM QPT $\mathcal{A}$ and QPT distinguisher D that break non-malleability for some values v, v' with advantage δ, we construct an MIM QPT adversary with predetermined schedule, which breaks the scheme with probability δ/Δ.

Consider an adversary $\mathcal{A}'$ that first samples uniformly at random a configuration $C \leftarrow [\ell + 2] \times [N] \times [N] \times \{\text{IP}_2, \text{P}_2\text{I}\}$. It then emulates $\mathcal{A}$, and if at any point the execution is about to become inconsistent with C, $\mathcal{A}'$ stops emulating $\mathcal{A}$, completes the execution consistently with C, and eventually outputs $\perp$. If the emulation of $\mathcal{A}$ is completed consistently with C, $\mathcal{A}'$ outputs the same as $\mathcal{A}$.

Then, since every execution has an ideally scheduled block (Claim 4.1), $\mathcal{A}'$ breaks non-malleability with probability exactly δ/Δ (with respect to the same distinguisher D and v, v'). Finally, by an averaging argument, we fix the choice of $\mathcal{A}'$ for a configuration to be the configuration C that maximizes D's distinguishing advantage. We obtain a corresponding MIM with predetermined ideal schedule with the same advantage δ/Δ.

4.3 Proof of Proposition 1

We prove the Proposition by a hybrid argument, specifically, we show that the MIM experiment output distribution for any value v on the left is indistinguishable from an experiment independent of v. Following Lemma 3, we restrict attention to a MIM adversary with a predetermined ideal schedule $C = (i, c, \bar{c}, w)$.

$\mathcal{H}_0$: **The original MIM experiment output.** This includes the output of the MIM adversary in the experiment and the committed value on the right.

$\mathcal{H}_1$: **Inefficient extraction from ideally-scheduled block.** In this hybrid, instead of the committed value $\tilde{v}$ on the right, we consider the value $\tilde{v}_1$ reconstructed from the shares of the ideally scheduled block i on the right. If the value of any of the commitments to these shares is $\perp$, we set $\tilde{v}_1 = \perp$. $\mathcal{H}_0$ and $\mathcal{H}_1$ are statistically indistinguishable following the from the soundness of the ZK argument that $\mathcal{A}$ gives to the receiver on the right in Phase 2.

$\mathcal{H}_2$: **Alternative description via oracle extraction.** In this hybrid we consider an augmented adversary $\mathcal{A}_2^{\mathcal{O}^\infty}$, which is given access to the sequential committed-value oracle $\mathcal{O}^\infty = \mathcal{O}^\infty[\text{ExCom.Sen}, \text{ExCom.Rec}]$ and acts as follows:

- $\mathcal{A}_2$ emulates $\mathcal{A}$. On the left, $\mathcal{A}_2$ relays all messages between $\mathcal{A}$ and the sender. On the right,
  - During the ideally scheduled block i, $\mathcal{A}_2$ interacts with its oracle $\mathcal{O}^\infty$, in every extractable commitment. Recall that $\mathcal{O}^\infty$ acts as the honest receiver, and answers break requests with the corresponding committed value. $\mathcal{A}_2$ submits such a break request after each of the commitments and stores the received share value.
  - In any other (than i) block in Phase 1, $\mathcal{A}_2$ internally emulates the receiver on the right.
  - In Phase 2, $\mathcal{A}_2$ internally emulates the zero knowledge verifier on the right.

- Eventually, $\mathcal{A}_2$ outputs the output of $\mathcal{A}$ as well as the value $\tilde{v}_1$ reconstructed from the ideal block shares obtained from the oracle $\mathcal{O}^\infty$.

The output of this hybrid is the output of $\mathcal{A}_2$. It follows directly from the construction of $\mathcal{A}_2^{\mathcal{O}^\infty}$ and the definition of $\mathcal{O}^\infty$ that $\mathcal{H}_1 \equiv \mathcal{H}_2$.

$\mathcal{H}_3$: **Efficient extraction on the right when** $w = \mathtt{P_2I}$. This hybrid, differs from the previous hybrid only if $w = \mathtt{P_2I}$; namely, Phase 2 on the left begins before the ideally scheduled block commitment i on the right had started. In such executions, for the ideally scheduled block commitment i, we perform sequential extraction to obtain the corresponding shares.

In more detail, let ψ be the (quantum) state of $\mathcal{A}_2$ when it initiates the ideally scheduled block i on the right, and let $\bar{\mathcal{A}}_2^{\mathcal{O}^\infty}$ be the adversary that starting from ψ, emulates $\mathcal{A}_2^{\mathcal{O}^\infty}$ during block i and outputs its state at the end (Note that since block i is ideally scheduled and also starts after Phase 2 on the left, it follows that $\bar{\mathcal{A}}_2$ does not perform *any* interaction on the left during the right block i).

In $\mathcal{H}_3$, we consider another augmented adversary $\mathcal{A}_3$ that acts like $\mathcal{A}_2$, only that instead of executing $\bar{\mathcal{A}}_2^{\mathcal{O}^\infty}$ during block i, it invokes the sequentially-extracting simulator $\mathsf{Sim}^\infty(\bar{\mathcal{A}}_2, \psi)$, given by Lemma 1, which eliminates the use of the commitment oracle $\mathcal{O}^\infty$. Computational indistinguishability of $\mathcal{H}_2$ and $\mathcal{H}_3$ follows directly from the sequential extraction guarantee (Lemma 1).

$\mathcal{H}_4$: **Simulating the ZK argument on the left.** In this hybrid, the ZK argument on the left is generated by the zero knowledge simulator.

Specifically, let ψ be the state of $\mathcal{A}_3$ when the zero-knowledge argument is initiated on the left. We consider the zero-knowledge verifier V^* that starting from ψ emulates $\mathcal{A}_3$ in the rest of the interaction while forwarding its messages on the left to the zero-knowledge prover, and eventually outputs the same. In particular, if $w = \mathtt{P_2I}$ then the code of V^* includes the code of the simulator Sim^∞, which is applied to $(\bar{\mathcal{A}}_2, \psi)$ as part of the execution of $\mathcal{A}_3$. Note that in both cases $w = \mathtt{IP_2}$ and $w = \mathtt{P_2I}$, once Phase 2 on the left starts, $\mathcal{A}_3$ no longer makes oracle calls to $\mathcal{O}^\infty$, so the code of V^* is fully specified and executes in polynomial time.

In $\mathcal{H}_4$, we consider an augmented adversary $\mathcal{A}_4$ that acts as $\mathcal{A}_3$, only that when Phase 2 starts on the left, instead of executing V^* and interacting on the left with the zero knowledge prover, $\mathcal{A}_4$ runs the zero knowledge simulator $\mathsf{Sim}(\mathsf{V}^*, \psi)$, and outputs the same.

$\mathcal{H}_3 \approx_c \mathcal{H}_4$. This is because by construction, the output of V^* is identically distributed to the output of $\mathcal{H}_3$. Computational indistinguishability of $\mathcal{H}_3$ and $\mathcal{H}_4$ now follows from the zero knowledge simulation guarantee (we note that any use of the inefficient oracle $\mathcal{O}^\infty$, in case $w = \mathtt{IP_2}$, occurs before Phase 2 on the left, and can thus be non-uniformly fixed).

$\mathcal{H}_5$ and $\mathcal{H}_6$: **Interchangeably, changing left committed values and efficient extraction threshold.** As a preliminary high-level explanation to the next step, at this point in our hybrid distributions, we consider the $1 + (\ell + 1)$ block commitments given to the MIM adversary on the left, and in each block, we'll switch a commitment for a secret share (of v), to a commitment for a string of zeros. For this, we will need to use the computational hiding property of the extractable commitments. The point, however, is to be able to use the hiding of the extractable commitments while still being able to *efficiently* extract the value $\tilde{v}_1$ from the right interaction with the MIM adversary[3].

Formally, we next define two sequences of hybrids $\mathcal{H}_{5,j}$ and $\mathcal{H}_{6,j}$ (for $j \in [\ell + 3]$) that augment one another interchangeably:

$$\mathcal{H}_4 = \mathcal{H}_{5,\ell+3} \to \mathcal{H}_{6,\ell+2} \to \mathcal{H}_{5,\ell+2} \to \cdots \to \mathcal{H}_{5,2} \to \mathcal{H}_{6,1} \to \mathcal{H}_{5,1} \ .$$

In what follows, recall that $\mathcal{A}_4$ in $\mathcal{H}_4$ is following a predetermined ideal schedule $C = (i, c, \bar{c}, w)$.

$\mathcal{H}_{5,j}$, for $j = \ell+3, \ldots, 1$: **Swapping one more free commitment to zeros.** In this hybrid, we simulate the most bottom free commitment on the left. Formally:

- $\mathcal{H}_{5,\ell+3}$ is defined as $\mathcal{H}_4$.
- For $j \leq \ell+2$, $\mathcal{H}_{5,j}$ is defined exactly as $\mathcal{H}_{6,j}$, except that the left extractable commitment c_j (to share u_c or $\bar{u}_{\bar{c}}$) in the left block j is replaced with a commitment to $0^{|v|}$.

$\mathcal{H}_{6,j}$, for $j = \ell+2, \ldots, 1$: **Raising the threshold for efficient extraction.** Recall $\mathcal{A}_4$ in $\mathcal{H}_4$ interacts with the sender in Phase 1 on the left and in case $w = \mathtt{IP}_2$, namely, the ideally scheduled block on the right ends before Phase 2 on the left begins, $\mathcal{A}_4$ interacts with the sequential commitment oracle $\mathcal{O}^\infty$ on the right during block i. For a left block index $j \in [\ell + 2]$, we denote by c_j the corresponding free extractable commitment; namely, $c_j = c$ if $j = 1$, and $c_j = \bar{c}$ if $j \geq 2$.

Informally, in hybrid $\mathcal{H}_{6,j}$, we move to simulating the oracle $\mathcal{O}^\infty$ in any right extractable commitment that starts after the free left commitment c_j. Formally, $\mathcal{H}_{6,j}$ is different from $\mathcal{H}_{5,j+1}$ only if $w = \mathtt{IP}_2$. In this case, we consider an augmented adversary $\mathcal{A}_{6,j}$ defined as follows for $j \in [\ell + 2]$:

- $\mathcal{A}_{6,j}$ acts as $\mathcal{A}_{6,j+1}^{\mathcal{O}^\infty}$ until the first right extractable commitment (in the ideally scheduled right block i) in which the first sender message is sent after the free left commitment c_j.
- $\mathcal{A}_{6,j}$ simulates the remaining calls to $\mathcal{O}^\infty$ as follows:
  - Let ψ be the state of $\mathcal{A}_{6,j+1}^{\mathcal{O}^\infty}$ at the abovementioned point, just before the right extractable commitment begins.

---

[3] Recall that currently, if $w = \mathtt{IP}_2$, we extract $\tilde{v}_1$ inefficiently using the sequential committed-value oracle $\mathcal{O}^\infty = \mathcal{O}^\infty[\mathsf{ExCom.Sen}, \mathsf{ExCom.Rec}]$. If $w = \mathtt{P}_2\mathtt{I}$ we don't have this problem, as the ideally scheduled right block commitment i starts after the beginning of Phase 2 on the left.

- Let $\bar{\mathcal{A}}^{\mathcal{O}^\infty}_{6,j+1}$ be the adversary that starting from ψ emulates $\mathcal{A}^{\mathcal{O}^\infty}_{6,j+1}$ in the following right extractable commitments, up to those that are already simulated, while internally emulating the sender in any left commitment.
  - $\mathcal{A}_{6,j}$ invokes the sequentially-extracting simulator $\mathsf{Sim}^\infty(\bar{\mathcal{A}}_{6,j+1}, \psi)$ to remove the use $\mathcal{O}^\infty$.
- $\mathcal{A}_{6,j}$ then completes the execution as $\mathcal{A}_{6,j+1}$ and outputs the same.

In the full version of this work, we prove the following claim, which concludes Proposition 1,

Claim. 1) The output of $\mathcal{H}_{5,1}$ is independent of the committed value v. 2) $\forall j \in [\ell+2] : \mathcal{H}_{5,j+1} \approx_c \mathcal{H}_{6,j}$. 3) $\forall j \in [\ell+2] : \mathcal{H}_{6,j} \approx_c \mathcal{H}_{5,j}$.

Due to space limits, we prove that our protocol is robust in the full version of this work.

5   Tag Amplification

In this section, we present a tag amplification transformation that converts a non-malleable commitment scheme $\langle \mathsf{Sen}, \mathsf{Rec} \rangle$ for $t \in [3, O(\log(\lambda))]$ bit tags into a non-malleable commitment scheme $\langle \widehat{\mathsf{Sen}}, \widehat{\mathsf{Rec}} \rangle$ for $T = 2^{t-1}$ bit tags. The transformation can be applied iteratively to amplify the number of tags from constant to exponential in the security parameter λ,

The transformation uses the following ingredients: 1) A post-quantum secure one-way function f. 2) Naor's 2-message statistically binding commitment [Nao91] instantiated with a post-quantum secure pseudo-random generator, which in turn can be based on post-quantum one-way functions. The receiver of Naor's protocol is public coin and sends a random string a as the first message, the sender then responds with $c = \mathsf{Com}_a(m; d)$ depending on a; the decommitment is simply sender's private random coins. The receiver can reuse a across many commitments sent to it, and we can effectively use the second message of Naor's commitments as a non-interactive commitment. 3) A post-quantum secure ε-extractable commitment scheme ECom. Let k_1 be the number of rounds in this commitment scheme. 4) A post-quantum secure WI protocol which can be based on any post-quantum one-way functions. Let k_2 be the number of rounds of WI. 5) A non-malleable commitment scheme $\langle \mathsf{Sen}, \mathsf{Rec} \rangle$ for $t \geq 3$ bit tags that is also r-robust for $r = k_1 + k_2$. Let n be the length of messages the scheme can commit to. The transformed non-malleable commitment $\langle \widehat{\mathsf{Sen}}, \widehat{\mathsf{Rec}} \rangle$ for $T = 2^{t-1}$ tags is presented in Fig. 5.

In the full version of this work, we show that $\langle \widehat{\mathsf{Sen}}, \widehat{\mathsf{Rec}} \rangle$ is statistically binding, r-robust and post-quantum non-malleable as well as the detailed analysis of the complexity growth and security loss.

Protocol 7

Common Input: Security parameter $\lambda \in \mathbb{N}$ and a tag $\hat{\text{tg}} \in \{0,1\}^T$ for the sender, where $T = 2^{t-1}$.

$\widehat{\text{Sen}}$**'s private input:** A message $m \in \{0,1\}^n$ to commit to.

1. **Trapdoor Setup:** $\widehat{\text{Rec}}$ sends two random images $y_1 = f(u_1)$ and $y_2 = f(u_2)$ of the one-way function f, where $u_1 \leftarrow \{0,1\}^\lambda$, $u_2 \leftarrow \{0,1\}^\lambda$. $\widehat{\text{Rec}}$ proves using WI that either y_1 or y_2 is in the image of f for λ-bit inputs. We refer to u_1 and u_2 as the trapdoors.

2. **Initial Commitment:** $\widehat{\text{Rec}}$ sends the first message a of Naor's commitment. $\widehat{\text{Sen}}$ commits to m using Naor's commitment $c = \text{Com}_a(m; d)$ w.r.t. receiver's message a, using random coins d.

3. $\langle \text{Sen}, \text{Rec} \rangle$ **commitments:** For every bit $\hat{\text{tg}}_i$ in the $T = 2^{t-1}$ bit tag $\hat{\text{tg}}$, define tag $\text{tg}_i = (i, \hat{\text{tg}}_i)$, which has exactly t bits.
   For every $i \in [T]$, $\widehat{\text{Sen}}$ commits to m using $\langle \text{Sen}, \text{Rec} \rangle$ and tag tg_i; let c_i denote the produced commitment and d_i the decommitment. All commitments are sent in parallel.

4. **Proof of Consistency:** $\widehat{\text{Sen}}$ first commits to 0^λ using the extractable commitment scheme ECom. Let c_e denote the produced commitment. $\widehat{\text{Sen}}$ proves using WI that either $c, c_1 \cdots, c_T$ are all valid commitments to m, or c_e commits to a preimage of y_1 or y_2. Formally, it proves that the statement $X = (a, c, c_1, \cdots, c_T, c_e, y_1, y_2)$ belongs to the language $\mathcal{L}$ defined by the following witness relation:

   $$\mathcal{R}_\mathcal{L}(X, W = (m, d, d_1, \cdots, d_T, d_e, u)) = 1 \text{ iff}$$
   $$\textit{Either} \quad c = \text{Com}_a(m; d) \, \wedge \, \forall i \in [T], \, \text{open}_{\langle \text{Sen}, \text{Rec} \rangle}(c_i, m, d_i) = 1 \, ,$$
   $$\textit{Or} \quad \text{open}_{\text{ECom}}(c_e, u, d_e) = 1 \text{ and } (y_1 = f(u) \text{ or } y_2 = f(u))$$

5. **Receiver's Decision:** $\widehat{\text{Rec}}$ accepts the commitment iff the proof of consistency is accepting.

6. **Decommitment:** $\widehat{\text{Sen}}$ outputs decommitment d. The decommitment is accepted if $c = \text{Com}_a(m; d)$.

Fig. 5. Post-quantum tag amplification.

Acknowledgements. Nir Bitansky is a Member of the Check Point Institute of Information Security, supported by ISF grants 18/484 and 19/2137, by Len Blavatnik and the Blavatnik Family Foundation, by the Blavatnik Interdisciplinary Cyber Research Center at Tel Aviv University, and by the European Union Horizon 2020 Research and Innovation Program via ERC Project REACT (Grant 756482). Huijia is supported by NSF grant CNS-1936825 (CAREER), CNS-2026774, a Hellman Fellowship, a JP Morgan AI Research Award, a Simons Collaboration grant on the Theory of Algorithmic Fairness. Omri Shmueli is supported by a Clore Fellowship, ISF grants 18/484 and 19/2137, by Len

Blavatnik and the Blavatnik Family Foundation, and by the European Union Horizon 2020 Research and Innovation Program via ERC Project REACT (Grant 756482). The authors are grateful to Fang Song for valuable discussions.

References

ABG+20. Agarwal, A., Bartusek, J., Goyal, V., Khurana, D., Malavolta, G.: Post-quantum multi-party computation in constant rounds. CoRR, abs/2005. 12904 (2020)

AP19. Ananth, P., La Placa, R.L.: Secure quantum extraction protocols. IACR Cryptol. ePrint Arch. **2019**, 1323 (2019)

Bar02. Barak, B.: Constant-round coin-tossing with a man in the middle or realizing the shared random string model, pp. 345–355 (2002)

BG08. Barak, B., Goldreich, O.: Universal arguments and their applications. SIAM J. Comput. **38**(5), 1661–1694 (2008)

BL18. Bitansky, N., Lin, H.: One-message zero knowledge and non-malleable commitments. In: Beimel, A., Dziembowski, S. (eds.) TCC 2018, Part I. LNCS, vol. 11239, pp. 209–234. Springer, Cham (2018). https://doi.org/10.1007/978-3-030-03807-6_8

BS20. Bitansky, N., Shmueli, O.: Post-quantum zero knowledge in constant rounds. In: Makarychev, K., Makarychev, Y., Tulsiani, M., Kamath, G., Chuzhoy, J. (eds.) Proceedings of the 52nd Annual ACM SIGACT Symposium on Theory of Computing, STOC 2020, Chicago, IL, USA, 22–26 June 2020, pp. 269–279. ACM (2020)

CCLY21. Chia, N.-H., Chung, K.-M., Liang, X., Yamakawa, T.: Post-quantum simulatable extraction with minimal assumptions: black-box and constant-round. arXiv preprint arXiv:2111.08665 (2021)

CCY20. Chia, N.-H., Chung, K.-M., Yamakawa, T.: Black-box approach to post-quantum zero-knowledge in constant round. arXiv preprint arXiv:2011.02670 (2020)

CLP16. Canetti, R., Lin, H., Pass, R.: Adaptive hardness and composable security in the plain model from standard assumptions. SIAM J. Comput. **45**(5), 1793–1834 (2016)

CMSZ21. Chiesa, A., Ma, F., Spooner, N., Zhandry, M.: Post-quantum succinct arguments. arXiv preprint arXiv:2103.08140 (2021)

COSV16. Ciampi, M., Ostrovsky, R., Siniscalchi, L., Visconti, I.: Concurrent non-malleable commitments (and more) in 3 rounds. In: Robshaw, M., Katz, J. (eds.) CRYPTO 2016. LNCS, vol. 9816, pp. 270–299. Springer, Heidelberg (2016). https://doi.org/10.1007/978-3-662-53015-3_10

CR87. Chor, B., Rabin, M.O.: Achieving independence in logarithmic number of rounds. In: Proceedings of the Sixth Annual ACM Symposium on Principles of Distributed Computing, Vancouver, British Columbia, Canada, 10–12 August 1987, pp. 260–268 (1987)

DDN03. Dolev, D., Dwork, C., Naor, M.: Nonmalleable cryptography. SIAM Rev. **45**(4), 727–784 (2003)

FLS99. Feige, U., Lapidot, D., Shamir, A.: Multiple noninteractive zero knowledge proofs under general assumptions. SIAM J. Comput. **29**(1), 1–28 (1999)

FP96. Fuchs, C.A., Peres, A.: Quantum-state disturbance versus information gain: uncertainty relations for quantum information. Phys. Rev. A **53**, 2038–2045 (1996)

GKLW20. Garg, R., Khurana, D., Lu, G., Waters, B.: Black-box non-interactive non-malleable commitments. Cryptology ePrint Archive, Report 2020/1197 (2020). https://eprint.iacr.org/2020/1197

GKS16. Goyal, V., Khurana, D., Sahai, A.: Breaking the three round barrier for non-malleable commitments, pp. 21–30 (2016)

GLOV12. Goyal, V., Lee, C.-K., Ostrovsky, R., Visconti, I.: Constructing non-malleable commitments: a black-box approach, pp. 51–60 (2012)

Goy11. Goyal, V.: Constant round non-malleable protocols using one way functions, pp. 695–704 (2011)

GPR16a. Goyal, V., Pandey, O., Richelson, S.: Textbook non-malleable commitments. In: Proceedings of the 48th Annual ACM SIGACT Symposium on Theory of Computing, STOC 2016, Cambridge, MA, USA, 18–21 June 2016, pp. 1128–1141 (2016)

GR19. Goyal, V., Richelson, S.: Non-malleable commitments using Goldreich-Levin list decoding. In: 60th IEEE Annual Symposium on Foundations of Computer Science, FOCS 2019, Baltimore, Maryland, USA, 9–12 November 2019, pp. 686–699 (2019)

HSS15. Hallgren, S., Smith, A., Song, F.: Classical cryptographic protocols in a quantum world. Int. J. Quant. Inf. **13**(04), 1550028 (2015). Preliminary version appeared in IACR Crypto 2011

Khu17. Khurana, D.: Round optimal concurrent non-malleability from polynomial hardness. In: Kalai, Y., Reyzin, L. (eds.) TCC 2017, Part II. LNCS, vol. 10678, pp. 139–171. Springer, Cham (2017). https://doi.org/10.1007/978-3-319-70503-3_5

KK19. Kalai, Y.T., Khurana, D.: Non-interactive non-malleability from quantum supremacy. In: Boldyreva, A., Micciancio, D. (eds.) CRYPTO 2019. LNCS, vol. 11694, pp. 552–582. Springer, Cham (2019). https://doi.org/10.1007/978-3-030-26954-8_18

KS17. Khurana, D., Sahai, A.: How to achieve non-malleability in one or two rounds. In: 58th IEEE Annual Symposium on Foundations of Computer Science, FOCS 2017, Berkeley, CA, USA, 15–17 October 2017, pp. 564–575 (2017)

LMS21. Lombardi, A., Ma, F., Spooner, N.: Post-quantum zero knowledge, revisited (or: How to do quantum rewinding undetectably). arXiv preprint arXiv:2111.12257 (2021)

LN11. Lunemann, C., Nielsen, J.B.: Fully simulatable quantum-secure coin-flipping and applications. In: Nitaj, A., Pointcheval, D. (eds.) AFRICACRYPT 2011. LNCS, vol. 6737, pp. 21–40. Springer, Heidelberg (2011). https://doi.org/10.1007/978-3-642-21969-6_2

LP09. Lin, H., Pass, R.: Non-malleability amplification, pp. 189–198 (2009)

LP11. Lin, H., Pass, R.: Constant-round non-malleable commitments from any one-way function, pp. 705–714 (2011)

LP12. Lin, H., Pass, R.: Black-box constructions of composable protocols without set-up. In: Safavi-Naini, R., Canetti, R. (eds.) CRYPTO 2012. LNCS, vol. 7417, pp. 461–478. Springer, Heidelberg (2012). https://doi.org/10.1007/978-3-642-32009-5_27

LPS17. Lin, H., Pass, R., Soni, P.: Two-round and non-interactive concurrent non-malleable commitments from time-lock puzzles, pp. 576–587 (2017)

LPV08. Lin, H., Pass, R., Venkitasubramaniam, M.: Concurrent non-malleable commitments from any one-way function. In: Canetti, R. (ed.) TCC 2008. LNCS, vol. 4948, pp. 571–588. Springer, Heidelberg (2008). https://doi.org/10.1007/978-3-540-78524-8_31

LPV09. Lin, H., Pass, R., Venkitasubramaniam, M.: A unified framework for concurrent security: universal composability from stand-alone non-malleability. In: Mitzenmacher, M. (ed.) Proceedings of the 41st Annual ACM Symposium on Theory of Computing, STOC 2009, Bethesda, MD, USA, May 31–June 2 2009, pp. 179–188. ACM (2009)

Nao91. Naor, M.: Bit commitment using pseudorandomness. J. Cryptol. 4(2), 151–158 (1991). https://doi.org/10.1007/BF00196774

PPV08. Pandey, O., Pass, R., Vaikuntanathan, V.: Adaptive one-way functions and applications. In: Wagner, D. (ed.) CRYPTO 2008. LNCS, vol. 5157, pp. 57–74. Springer, Heidelberg (2008). https://doi.org/10.1007/978-3-540-85174-5_4

PR05a. Pass, R., Rosen, A.: Concurrent non-malleable commitments, pp. 563–572 (2005)

PR05b. Pass, R., Rosen, A.: New and improved constructions of non-malleable cryptographic protocols, pp. 533–542 (2005)

PW10. Pass, R., Wee, H.: Constant-round non-malleable commitments from subexponential one-way functions. In: Gilbert, H. (ed.) EUROCRYPT 2010. LNCS, vol. 6110, pp. 638–655. Springer, Heidelberg (2010). https://doi.org/10.1007/978-3-642-13190-5_32

Ros04. Rosen, A.: A note on constant-round zero-knowledge proofs for NP. In: Naor, M. (ed.) TCC 2004. LNCS, vol. 2951, pp. 191–202. Springer, Heidelberg (2004). https://doi.org/10.1007/978-3-540-24638-1_11

Unr12. Unruh, D.: Quantum proofs of knowledge. In: Pointcheval, D., Johansson, T. (eds.) EUROCRYPT 2012. LNCS, vol. 7237, pp. 135–152. Springer, Heidelberg (2012). https://doi.org/10.1007/978-3-642-29011-4_10

Wat09. Watrous, J.: Zero-knowledge against quantum attacks. SIAM J. Comput. 39(1), 25–58 (2009)

Wee10. Wee, H.: Efficient chosen-ciphertext security via extractable hash proofs. In: Rabin, T. (ed.) CRYPTO 2010. LNCS, vol. 6223, pp. 314–332. Springer, Heidelberg (2010). https://doi.org/10.1007/978-3-642-14623-7_17

WZ82. Wootters, W.K., Zurek, W.H.: A single quantum cannot be cloned. Nature 299, 802–803 (1982)

Anonymity of NIST PQC Round 3 KEMs

Keita Xagawa[(✉)]

NTT Social Informatics Laboratories, Tokyo, Japan
keita.xagawa.zv@hco.ntt.co.jp

Abstract. This paper investigates *anonymity* of all NIST PQC Round 3 KEMs: Classic McEliece, Kyber, NTRU, Saber, BIKE, FrodoKEM, HQC, NTRU Prime (Streamlined NTRU Prime and NTRU LPRime), and SIKE. We show the following results:

- NTRU is anonymous in the quantum random oracle model (QROM) if the underlying deterministic PKE is strongly disjoint-simulatable. NTRU is collision-free in the QROM. A hybrid PKE scheme constructed from NTRU as KEM and appropriate DEM is anonymous and robust. (Similar results for BIKE, FrodoKEM, HQC, NTRU LPRime, and SIKE hold except one of three parameter sets of HQC.)
- Classic McEliece is anonymous in the QROM if the underlying PKE is strongly disjoint-simulatable and a hybrid PKE scheme constructed from it as KEM and appropriate DEM is anonymous.
- Grubbs, Maram, and Paterson pointed out that Kyber and Saber have a gap in the current IND-CCA security proof in the QROM (EUROCRYPT 2022). We found that Streamlined NTRU Prime has another technical obstacle for the IND-CCA security proof in the QROM.

Those answer the open problem to investigate the anonymity and robustness of NIST PQC Round 3 KEMs posed by Grubbs, Maram, and Paterson (EUROCRYPT 2022).

We use strong disjoint-simulatability of the underlying PKE of KEM and strong pseudorandomness and smoothness/sparseness of KEM as the main tools, which will be of independent interest.

Keywords: Anonymity · Robustness · Post-quantum cryptography · NIST PQC standardization · KEM · PKE · Quantum random model

1 Introduction

Public-key encryption (PKE) allows us to send a message to a receiver confidentially if the receiver's public key is available. However, a ciphertext of PKE may reveal the receiver's public key, and the recipient of the ciphertext will be identified. This causes trouble in some applications, and researchers study the anonymity of PKE. Roughly speaking, PKE is said to be *anonymous* [7] if a ciphertext hides the receiver's information. Anonymous primitive is often used in the context of privacy-enhancing technologies.

© International Association for Cryptologic Research 2022
O. Dunkelman and S. Dziembowski (Eds.): EUROCRYPT 2022, LNCS 13277, pp. 551–581, 2022.
https://doi.org/10.1007/978-3-031-07082-2_20

A ciphertext of anonymous PKE indicates (computationally) no information of a receiver. Thus, when a receiver receives a ciphertext, it should decrypt the ciphertext into a message and verify the message in order to check if the ciphertext is sent to the receiver or not. There may be a ciphertext from which two (or more) recipients can obtain messages in this situation, and this causes trouble in some applications, e.g., auction protocols [40]. Intuitively speaking, PKE is said to be *robust* [2] if only the intended receiver can obtain a meaningful message from a ciphertext.

Both anonymity and robustness are important and useful properties beyond the standard IND-CCA security. Anonymous PKE is an important building primitive for anonymous credential systems [13], auction protocols [40], (weakly) anonymous authenticated key exchange [12,20,21,43], and so on. Robust PKE has an application for searchable encryption [1] and auction [40].

Previous Works on Anonymity and Robustness of KEM and Hybrid PKE: Mohassel [36] studied the anonymity and robustness of a special KEM/DEM framework, a hybrid PKE with KEM that is implemented by a PKE with random plaintext. He showed that even if anonymous KEM and DEM sometimes fail to lead to an anonymous hybrid PKE by constructing a counterexample.

Grubbs, Maram, and Paterson [24] discussed anonymity and robustness of *post-quantum* KEM schemes and KEM/DEM framework in the quantum random oracle model (QROM). They also studied the anonymity and robustness of the hybrid PKE based on KEM with implicit rejection. On the variants of the Fujisaki-Okamoto (FO) transform [22,23], they showed that anonymity and collision-freeness of KEMs obtained by the FO transform with implicit rejection and its variant[1], and they lead to anonymous, robust hybrid PKEs from appropriate assumptions. They also showed anonymity and robustness of KEM obtained by a variant of the FO transform with explicit rejection and key-confirmation hash[2] and showed that it leads to anonymous, robust hybrid PKE from appropriate assumptions.

They examined NIST PQC Standardization finalists (Classic McEliece [5], Kyber [42], NTRU [14], and Saber [18]). They showed the following results:

- Classic McEliece: They found that Classic McEliece is not collision-free. Since their anonymity proof in [24, Theorem 5] strongly depends on the collision-freeness of the underlying PKE, we cannot apply their anonymity proof to Classic McEliece. They also showed that the hybrid PKE fails to achieve robustness since Classic McEliece is not collision-free.
- Kyber: They found that Kyber's anonymity (and even IND-CCA security) has two technical obstacles ('pre-key' and 'nested random oracles') in the QROM.
- NTRU: NTRU's anonymity has another technical obstacle: Their proof technique requires the computation of a key of KEM involving a message and a

---

[1] A variant of the FO transform with implicit rejection using 'pre-key' technique. They wrote "a variant of the FO$^{\not\perp}$ transform" in their paper.

[2] They modify 'key-confirmation hash' to involve a ciphertext on input.

ciphertext, but, in NTRU, the computation of a key of NTRU involves only a message. The robustness of the hybrid PKE with NTRU is unclear.
- Saber: They insisted they show Saber's anonymity and IND-CCA security and the robustness of the hybrid PKE with Saber in the QROM, because they considered that Saber employs the FO transform with 'pre-key'. Unfortunately, Saber in [18] also uses both 'pre-key' and 'nested random oracles' as Kyber, and their proofs cannot be applied to Saber. See their slides [25]. (Fortunately, FrodoKEM can be shown anonymous and lead to anonymous, robust hybrid PKE, because FrodoKEM employs the FO transform with 'pre-key'.)

Unfortunately, we do not know whether all four finalists are anonymous or not, although the much effort of Grubbs et al. and their clean and modular framework. Grubbs et al. left several open problems: One of them is the anonymity and robustness of NTRU; the other important one is the anonymity of Classic McEliece.

1.1 Our Contribution

We investigate anonymity and robustness of *all* NIST PQC Round 3 KEM candidates and obtain Table 1. This answers the open problems posed by Grubbs et al.

In order to investigate anonymity, we first study strong pseudorandomness of PKE/KEM instead of studying anonymity directly. To show strong pseudorandomness of the hybrid PKE, we study strong pseudorandomness and introduce smoothness and sparseness of KEM. We then show such properties of KEM obtained by the variants of the FO transform if the underlying deterministic PKE is strongly disjoint-simulatable. We finally study the properties of NIST PQC Round 3 KEM candidates. See the details in the following.

Anonymity through Strong Pseudorandomness, Sparseness, and Smoothness: Our starting point is *strong pseudorandomness* instead of anonymity. We say PKE/KEM/DEM is *strongly pseudorandom* if its ciphertext is indistinguishable from a random string chosen by a simulator on input the security parameter.[3] It is easy to show that strong pseudorandomness implies anonymity.

Using this notion, we attempt to follow the IND-CCA security proof of the KEM/DEM framework [16], that is, we try to show that the hybrid PKE from strongly pseudorandom KEM/DEM is also strongly pseudorandom, which implies that the hybrid PKE is anonymous. If we directly try to prove anonymity against chosen-ciphertext attacks (the ANON-CCA security) of the hybrid PKE, then we will need to simulate *two* decryption oracles as Grubbs et al. Considering pseudorandomness allows us to treat a *single* key and oracle and simplifies the security proof. Unfortunately, we face another obstacle in the security proof when considering pseudorandomness.

To resolve the obstacle, we define *sparseness* of KEM with explicit rejection and *smoothness* of KEM with implicit rejection: We say KEM with explicit

---

[3] If the simulator can depend on an encryption key, then we just say pseudorandom.

Table 1. Summary of anonymity and robustness of NIST PQC Round 3 KEM candidates (finalists and alternate candidates) and the hybrid PKEs using them. In the first row, IND = Indistinguishability, SPR = Strong Pseudorandomness, ANO = Anonymity, CF = Collision Freeness, and ROB = Robustness under chosen-ciphertext attacks in the QROM. Y = Yes, N = No, ? = Unknown. The underline implies our new findings.

Name	KEM					Hybrid PKE	
	IND	SPR	ANO	CF	ROB	ANO	ROB
Classic McEliece [5]	Y	$\underline{Y}$	$\underline{Y}$	N	N	$\underline{Y}$	N
Kyber [42]	?	?	?	?	N	?	?
NTRU [14]	Y	$\underline{Y}$	$\underline{Y}$	$\underline{Y}$	N	$\underline{Y}$	$\underline{Y}$
Saber [18]	?	?	?	?	N	?	?
BIKE [6]	Y	$\underline{Y}$	$\underline{Y}$	$\underline{Y}$	N	$\underline{Y}$	$\underline{Y}$
FrodoKEM [37]	Y	Y	Y	Y	N	Y	Y
HQC-128/192 [4]	Y	$\underline{Y}$	$\underline{Y}$	$\underline{Y}$	$\underline{Y}$	$\underline{Y}$	$\underline{Y}$
HQC-256 [4]	Y	$\underline{N}$	$\underline{N}$	$\underline{Y}$	$\underline{Y}$	$\underline{N}$	$\underline{Y}$
Streamlined NTRU Prime [10]	$\underline{?}$	?	?	?	N	?	?
NTRU LPRime [10]	Y	$\underline{Y}$	$\underline{Y}$	$\underline{Y}$	N	$\underline{Y}$	$\underline{Y}$
SIKE [30]	Y	$\underline{Y}$	$\underline{Y}$	$\underline{Y}$	N	$\underline{Y}$	$\underline{Y}$

rejection is *sparse* if a ciphertext c chosen by a simulator is decapsulated into $\perp$ with overwhelming probability. We say KEM with implicit rejection is *smooth* if, given a ciphertext c chosen by a simulator, any efficient adversary cannot distinguish a random key from a decapsulated key. This definition imitates the smoothness of the hash proof system [16]. Those notions help us to prove the pseudorandomness of the hybrid PKE.

Pseudorandomness, Smoothness, and Collision-freeness of the FO Variants: In order to treat the case for Classic McEliece and NTRU, in which the underlying PKE is deterministic, we treat SXY [39], variants of U [26], and variants of HU [32]. Modifying the IND-CCA security proofs of them, we show that the obtained KEM is strongly pseudorandom and smooth if the underlying PKE is strongly disjoint-simulatable [39]. We also show that the obtained KEM is collision-free if the underlying deterministic PKE is collision-free. We finally note that our reductions are *tight* as a bonus.

Grubbs et al. [24] discussed a barrier to show anonymity of NTRU (and Classic McEliece implicitly), which stems from the design choice $K = H(\mu)$ instead of $K = H(\mu, c)$. In addition, their proof technique requires the underlying PKE to be collision-free. Since the underlying PKE of Classic McEliece lacks collision freeness, they left the proof of anonymity of Classic McEliece as an open problem. Both barriers stem from the fact that we need to simulate *two* decapsulation oracles in the proof of ANON-CCA-security. We avoid those technical barriers by using a stronger notion, strong pseudorandomness against chosen-ciphertext attacks (SPR-CCA security); in the proof of SPR-CCA-security, we only need to simulate a *single* decapsulation oracle.

Application to NIST PQC Round-3 KEM Candidates: Using the above techniques, we solve open problems posed by Grubbs et al. and extend the study of finalists and alternative candidates of NIST PQC Round 3 KEMs as depicted in Table 1.

We found the following properties (we omit the detail of the assumptions):

- Classic McEliece is anonymous and the hybrid PKE using it is anonymous, which is in the full version.
- NTRU is anonymous and collision-free. The hybrid PKE using it is anonymous and robust. See Sect. 5. Similar results for BIKE, HQC (HQC-128 and HQC-196)[4], NTRU LPRime, and SIKE hold, which are in the full version.
- We found that Streamlined NTRU Prime has another technical obstacle for anonymity: the key and key-confirmation hash involves 'pre-key' problem.[5] While this is not a big problem for the IND-CCA security in the ROM, we fail to show the IND-CCA security in the QROM. We will discuss it in detail in the full version.

Remark 1. Bernstein [9] suggests to use *quantum indifferentiability* of the domain extension of quantum random oracles in [49, Section 5]. While we did not check the detail, this quantum indifferentiability would solve the problems on 'pre-key' of Kyber, Saber, and Streamlined NTRU Prime.

Open Problems: We leave showing anonymity and the IND-CCA security of Kyber, Saber, and Streamlined NTRU Prime in the QROM as an important open problem as Grubbs et al. posed.

Organization: Section 2 reviews the QROM, definitions of primitives, and the results of Grubbs et al. [24]. In addition, it also shows strong pseudorandomness implies anonymity. Section 3 studies the strong pseudorandomness of the KEM/DEM framework. Section 4 studies SXY's security properties. Section 5 examines the anonymity and robustness of NTRU. Due to the space limit, we omit a lot of contents from the conference version.

Appendix Highlights: The full version contains the missing proofs. Moreover, its appendices contain the properties of the variants of the FO transform (T, variants of U, and variants of HU) and examine the other NIST PQC Round-3 KEM candidates, Classic McEliece, Kyber, Saber, BIKE, FrodoKEM, HQC, NTRU Prime (Streamlined NTRU Prime and NTRU LPRime), and SIKE, as summarized in Table 1.

---

[4] HQC-256 is not anonymous because the parity of the ciphertext leaks the parity of the encapsulation key. See the full version for the detail.

[5] The key and key-confirmation value on a plaintext μ and an encapsulation key ek is computed as $K = \mathsf{H}(k, c_0, c_1)$ and $h = \mathsf{F}(k, \mathsf{Hash}(ek))$, where $k = \mathsf{H}_3(\mu)$ and (c_0, c_1) is a main body of a ciphertext.

2 Preliminaries

Notations: A security parameter is denoted by κ. We use the standard O-notations. DPT, PPT, and QPT stand for a deterministic polynomial time, probabilistic polynomial time, and quantum polynomial time, respectively. A function $f(\kappa)$ is said to be *negligible* if $f(\kappa) = \kappa^{-\omega(1)}$. We denote a set of negligible functions by $\mathsf{negl}(\kappa)$. For a distribution χ, we often write "$x \leftarrow \chi$," which indicates that we take a sample x according to χ. For a finite set S, $U(S)$ denotes the uniform distribution over S. We often write "$x \leftarrow S$" instead of "$x \leftarrow U(S)$." For a set S and a deterministic algorithm A, $\mathsf{A}(S)$ denotes the set $\{\mathsf{A}(x) \mid x \in S\}$. If inp is a string, then "out $\leftarrow \mathsf{A}(\text{inp})$" denotes the output of algorithm A when run on input inp. If A is deterministic, then out is a fixed value and we write "out $:= \mathsf{A}(\text{inp})$." We also use the notation "out $:= \mathsf{A}(\text{inp}; r)$" to make the randomness r explicit.

For a statement P (e.g., $r \in [0,1]$), we define $\mathsf{boole}(P) = 1$ if P is satisfied and 0 otherwise.

For two finite sets $\mathcal{X}$ and $\mathcal{Y}$, $\mathcal{F}(\mathcal{X}, \mathcal{Y})$ denotes a set of all mapping from $\mathcal{X}$ to $\mathcal{Y}$.

Lemma 1 (Generic distinguishing problem with bounded probabilities [29, Lemma 2.9], adapted). *Let $\mathcal{X}$ be a finite set. Let $\delta \in [0,1]$. Let $\mathsf{F}\colon \mathcal{X} \to \{0,1\}$ be the following function: for each $x \in \mathcal{X}$, $\mathsf{F}(x) = 1$ with probability $\delta_x \le \delta$ and $\mathsf{F}(x) = 0$ else. Let $\mathsf{Z}\colon \mathcal{X} \to \{0,1\}$ be the zero function, that is, $\mathsf{Z}(x) = 0$ for all x. If an unbounded-time quantum adversary $\mathcal{A}$ makes a query to F or Z at most Q times, then we have*

$$\left| \Pr[b \leftarrow \mathcal{A}^{\mathsf{F}(\cdot)}() : b = 1] - \Pr[b \leftarrow \mathcal{A}^{\mathsf{Z}(\cdot)}() : b = 1] \right| \le 8(Q+1)^2 \delta.$$

where all oracle accesses of $\mathcal{A}$ can be quantum.

Quantum Random Oracle Model: Roughly speaking, the quantum random oracle model (QROM) is an idealized model where a hash function is modeled as a publicly and quantumly accessible random oracle. In this paper, we model a quantum oracle O as a mapping $|x\rangle|y\rangle \mapsto |x\rangle|y \oplus O(x)\rangle$, where $x \in \{0,1\}^n$, $y \in \{0,1\}^m$, and $O\colon \{0,1\}^n \to \{0,1\}^m$. See [11] for a more detailed description of the model.

Lemma 2 (QRO is PRF). *Let ℓ be a positive integer. Let $\mathcal{X}$ and $\mathcal{Y}$ be finite sets. Let $\mathsf{H}_{\mathsf{prf}}\colon \{0,1\}^\ell \times \mathcal{X} \to \mathcal{Y}$ and $\mathsf{H}_q\colon \mathcal{X} \to \mathcal{Y}$ be two independent random oracles. If an unbounded-time quantum adversary $\mathcal{A}$ makes queries to the random oracles at most Q times, then we have*

$$\left| \begin{array}{l} \Pr[s \leftarrow \mathcal{M}, b \leftarrow \mathcal{A}^{\mathsf{H}_{\mathsf{prf}}(\cdot,\cdot), \mathsf{H}_{\mathsf{prf}}(s,\cdot)}() : b = 1] \\ \quad - \Pr[b \leftarrow \mathcal{A}^{\mathsf{H}_{\mathsf{prf}}(\cdot,\cdot), \mathsf{H}_q(\cdot)}() : b = 1] \end{array} \right| \le 2Q \cdot 2^{-\ell/2}$$

where all oracle accesses of $\mathcal{A}$ can be quantum.

See [39] and [31] for the proof.

Lemma 3 (QRO is collision-resistant [48, Theorem 3.1]). *There is a universal constant C such that the following holds: Let $\mathcal{X}$ and $\mathcal{Y}$ be finite sets. Let $\mathsf{H} \colon \mathcal{X} \to \mathcal{Y}$ be a random oracle. If an unbounded time quantum adversary $\mathcal{A}$ makes queries to H at most Q times, then we have*

$$\Pr_{\mathsf{H}, \mathcal{A}}[(x, x') \leftarrow \mathcal{A}^{\mathsf{H}(\cdot)} : x \neq x' \wedge \mathsf{H}(x) = \mathsf{H}(x')] \leq C(Q + 1)^3 / |\mathcal{Y}|,$$

where all oracle accesses of $\mathcal{A}$ can be quantum.

Remark 2. We implicitly assume that $|\mathcal{X}| = \Omega(|\mathcal{Y}|)$, because of the birthday bound.

Lemma 4 (QRO is claw-free). *There is a universal constant C such that the following holds: Let $\mathcal{X}_0$, $\mathcal{X}_1$, and $\mathcal{Y}$ be finite sets. Let $N_0 = |\mathcal{X}_0|$ and $N_1 = |\mathcal{X}_1|$. Without loss of generality, we assume $N_0 \leq N_1$. Let $\mathsf{H}_0 \colon \mathcal{X}_0 \to \mathcal{Y}$ and $\mathsf{H}_1 \colon \mathcal{X}_1 \to \mathcal{Y}$ be two random oracles. If an unbounded time quantum adversary $\mathcal{A}$ makes queries to H_0 and H_1 at most Q_0 and Q_1 times, then we have*

$$\Pr[(x_0, x_1) \leftarrow \mathcal{A}^{\mathsf{H}_0(\cdot), \mathsf{H}_1(\cdot)} : \mathsf{H}_0(x_0) = \mathsf{H}_1(x_1)] \leq C(Q_0 + Q_1 + 1)^3 / |\mathcal{Y}|,$$

where all oracle accesses of $\mathcal{A}$ can be quantum.

We omit the security proof, which is due to Hosoyamada [28]. See the full version.

2.1 Public-Key Encryption (PKE)

The model for PKE schemes is summarized as follows:

Definition 1. *A PKE scheme* PKE *consists of the following triple of PPT algorithms* (Gen, Enc, Dec).

- Gen$(1^\kappa; r_g) \to (ek, dk)$: *a key-generation algorithm that on input 1^κ, where κ is the security parameter, and randomness $r_g \in \mathcal{R}_{\mathsf{Gen}}$, outputs a pair of keys (ek, dk). ek and dk are called the encryption key and decryption key, respectively.*
- Enc$(ek, \mu; r_e) \to c$: *an encryption algorithm that takes as input encryption key ek, message $\mu \in \mathcal{M}$, and randomness $r_e \in \mathcal{R}_{\mathsf{Enc}}$, and outputs ciphertext $c \in \mathcal{C}$.*
- Dec$(dk, c) \to \mu/\bot$: *a decryption algorithm that takes as input decryption key dk and ciphertext c and outputs message $\mu \in \mathcal{M}$ or a rejection symbol $\bot \notin \mathcal{M}$.*

We review δ-correctness in Hofheinz, Hövelmanns, and Kiltz [26].

Definition 2 (δ-Correctness). *Let $\delta = \delta(\kappa)$. We say* PKE $=$ (Gen, Enc, Dec) *is δ-correct if*

$$\mathrm{Exp}_{(ek, dk) \leftarrow \mathsf{Gen}(1^\kappa)}\left[\max_{\mu \in \mathcal{M}} \Pr[c \leftarrow \mathsf{Enc}(ek, \mu) : \mathsf{Dec}(dk, c) \neq \mu]\right] \leq \delta.$$

In particular, we say that PKE is perfectly correct *if $\delta = 0$.*

We also define a key pair's accuracy.

Definition 3 (Accuracy [47]). *We say that a key pair* (ek, dk) *is accurate if for any* $\mu \in \mathcal{M}$, $\Pr_{c \leftarrow \mathsf{Enc}(ek,\mu)}[\mathsf{Dec}(dk, c) = \mu] = 1$. *If a key pair is not accurate, then we call it* inaccurate. *We note that if* PKE *is deterministic, then* $\Pr_{(ek,dk) \leftarrow \mathsf{Gen}(1^{\kappa})}[(ek, dk) \text{ is accurate}] \leq \delta$.

Security Notions: We define pseudorandomness under chosen-ciphertext attacks (PR-CCA) and its strong version (SPR-CCA) with simulator $\mathcal{S}$ as a generalization of IND\$-CCA-security in [27,46]. We also review anonymity (ANON-CCA) [7] and robustness (SROB-CCA) [36]. We additionally define extended collision-freeness (XCFR), in which any efficient adversary cannot find a colliding ciphertext even if the adversary is given two decryption keys. Due to the space limit, we omit the definitions of the standard security notions (OW-CPA, IND-CPA, OW-CCA, and IND-CCA) [8,38], weak robustness (WROB-CCA) and collision-freeness (WCFR-CCA and SCFR-CCA) [36].

Definition 4 (Security notions for PKE). *Let* PKE $= (\mathsf{Gen}, \mathsf{Enc}, \mathsf{Dec})$ *be a PKE scheme. Let* $\mathcal{D}_{\mathcal{M}}$ *be a distribution over the message space* $\mathcal{M}$.

For any $\mathcal{A}$ *and* goal-atk $\in \{\mathrm{pr\text{-}cca}, \mathrm{anon\text{-}cca}\}$, *we define its* goal-atk *advantage against* PKE *as follows:*

$$\mathsf{Adv}^{\text{goal-atk}}_{\mathsf{PKE}[,\mathcal{S}],\mathcal{A}}(\kappa) := \left| 2\Pr[\mathsf{Expt}^{\text{goal-atk}}_{\mathsf{PKE}[,\mathcal{S}],\mathcal{A}}(\kappa) = 1] - 1 \right|,$$

where $\mathsf{Expt}^{\text{goal-atk}}_{\mathsf{PKE}[,\mathcal{S}],\mathcal{A}}(\kappa)$ *is an experiment described in Fig. 1 and* $\mathcal{S}$ *is a PPT simulator.*

For any $\mathcal{A}$ *and* goal-atk $\in \{\mathrm{srob\text{-}cca}, \mathrm{xcfr}\}$, *we define its* goal-atk *advantage against* PKE *as follows:*

$$\mathsf{Adv}^{\text{goal-atk}}_{\mathsf{PKE}[,\mathcal{D}_{\mathcal{M}}],\mathcal{A}}(\kappa) := \Pr[\mathsf{Expt}^{\text{goal-atk}}_{\mathsf{PKE}[,\mathcal{D}_{\mathcal{M}}],\mathcal{A}}(\kappa) = 1],$$

where $\mathsf{Expt}^{\text{goal-atk}}_{\mathsf{PKE}[,\mathcal{D}_{\mathcal{M}}],\mathcal{A}}(\kappa)$ *is an experiment described in Fig. 1.*

For GOAL-ATK $\in \{\mathrm{PR\text{-}CCA}, \mathrm{ANON\text{-}CCA}, \mathrm{SROB\text{-}CCA}, \mathrm{XCFR}\}$, *we say that* PKE *is* GOAL-ATK*-secure if* $\mathsf{Adv}^{\text{goal-atk}}_{\mathsf{PKE}[,\mathcal{D}_{\mathcal{M}},\mathcal{S}],\mathcal{A}}(\kappa)$ *is negligible for any QPT adversary* $\mathcal{A}$. *We also say that* PKE *is* SPR-CCA*-secure if it is* PR-CCA*-secure, and its simulator ignores* ek. *We also say that* PKE *is* GOAL-CPA*-secure if it is* GOAL-CCA*-secure even without the decryption oracle.*

We observe that strong pseudorandomness of PKE/KEM immediately implies anonymity of PKE/KEM, which may be folklore. We give the proof in the full version for completeness.

Theorem 1. *If* PKE/KEM *is* SPR-CCA*-secure, then it is* ANON-CCA*-secure.*

Disjoint Simulatability: We review disjoint simulatability defined in [39].

$\mathrm{Expt}_{\mathsf{PKE},\mathcal{S},\mathcal{A}}^{\mathrm{pr\text{-}cca}}(\kappa)$	$\mathrm{Expt}_{\mathsf{PKE},\mathcal{A}}^{\mathrm{anon\text{-}cca}}(\kappa)$	$\mathrm{DEC}_a(c)$
$b \leftarrow \{0,1\}$	$b \leftarrow \{0,1\}$	if $c = a$, return $\perp$
$(ek, dk) \leftarrow \mathsf{Gen}(1^\kappa)$	$(ek_0, dk_0) \leftarrow \mathsf{Gen}(1^\kappa)$	$\mu := \mathsf{Dec}(dk, c)$
$(\mu, state) \leftarrow \mathcal{A}_1^{\mathrm{DEC}_\perp(\cdot)}(ek)$	$(ek_1, dk_1) \leftarrow \mathsf{Gen}(1^\kappa)$	return μ
$c_0^* \leftarrow \mathsf{Enc}(ek, \mu)$	$(\mu, state) \leftarrow \mathcal{A}_1^{\mathrm{DEC}_\perp(\cdot,\cdot)}(ek_0, ek_1)$	
$c_1^* \leftarrow \mathcal{S}(1^\kappa, ek)$	$c^* \leftarrow \mathsf{Enc}(ek_b, \mu)$	$\mathrm{DEC}_a(\mathrm{id}, c)$
$b' \leftarrow \mathcal{A}_2^{\mathrm{DEC}_{c_b^*}(\cdot)}(c_b^*, state)$	$b' \leftarrow \mathcal{A}_2^{\mathrm{DEC}_{c^*}(\cdot,\cdot)}(c^*, state)$	if $c = a$, return $\perp$
return boole$(b = b')$	return boole$(b = b')$	$\mu := \mathsf{Dec}(dk_{id}, c)$
		return μ

$\mathrm{Expt}_{\mathsf{PKE},\mathcal{A}}^{\mathrm{srob\text{-}cca}}(\kappa)$	$\mathrm{Expt}_{\mathsf{PKE},\mathcal{A}}^{\mathrm{xcfr}}(\kappa)$	$\mathrm{Expt}_{\mathsf{PKE},\mathcal{D}_\mathcal{M},\mathcal{S},\mathcal{A}}^{\mathrm{ds\text{-}ind}}(\kappa)$
$(ek_0, dk_0) \leftarrow \mathsf{Gen}(1^\kappa)$	$(ek_0, dk_0) \leftarrow \mathsf{Gen}(1^\kappa)$	$(ek, dk) \leftarrow \mathsf{Gen}(1^\kappa)$
$(ek_1, dk_1) \leftarrow \mathsf{Gen}(1^\kappa)$	$(ek_1, dk_1) \leftarrow \mathsf{Gen}(1^\kappa)$	$\mu* \leftarrow \mathcal{D}_\mathcal{M}$
$c \leftarrow \mathcal{A}^{\mathrm{DEC}_\perp(\cdot,\cdot)}(ek_0, ek_1)$	$c \leftarrow \mathcal{A}(ek_0, dk_0, ek_1, dk_1)$	$c_0^* := \mathsf{Enc}(ek, \mu^*)$
$\mu_0 \leftarrow \mathsf{Dec}(dk_0, c)$	$\mu_0 \leftarrow \mathsf{Dec}(dk_0, c)$	$c_1^* \leftarrow \mathcal{S}(1^\kappa, ek)$
$\mu_1 \leftarrow \mathsf{Dec}(dk_1, c)$	$\mu_1 \leftarrow \mathsf{Dec}(dk_1, c)$	$b' \leftarrow \mathcal{A}(ek, c_b^*)$
return boole$(\mu_0 \neq \perp \wedge \mu_1 \neq \perp)$	return boole$(\mu_0 = \mu_1 \neq \perp)$	return boole$(b = b')$

Fig. 1. Games for PKE schemes

Definition 5 (Disjoint simulatability [39]). *Let $\mathcal{D}_\mathcal{M}$ denote an efficiently sampleable distribution on a set $\mathcal{M}$. A deterministic PKE scheme $\mathsf{PKE} = (\mathsf{Gen}, \mathsf{Enc}, \mathsf{Dec})$ with plaintext and ciphertext spaces $\mathcal{M}$ and $\mathcal{C}$ is $\mathcal{D}_\mathcal{M}$-disjoint-simulatable if there exists a PPT algorithm $\mathcal{S}$ that satisfies the followings:*

– *(Statistical disjointness:)*

$$\mathsf{Disj}_{\mathsf{PKE},\mathcal{S}}(\kappa) := \max_{(ek, dk) \in \mathsf{Gen}(1^\kappa; \mathcal{R}_{\mathsf{Gen}})} \Pr[c \leftarrow \mathcal{S}(1^\kappa, ek) : c \in \mathsf{Enc}(ek, \mathcal{M})]$$

is negligible.
– *(Ciphertext-indistinguishability:) For any QPT adversary $\mathcal{A}$, its ds-ind advantage $\mathsf{Adv}_{\mathsf{PKE},\mathcal{D}_\mathcal{M},\mathcal{S},\mathcal{A}}^{\mathrm{ds\text{-}ind}}(\kappa)$ is negligible: The advantage is defined as*

$$\mathsf{Adv}_{\mathsf{PKE},\mathcal{D}_\mathcal{M},\mathcal{S},\mathcal{A}}^{\mathrm{ds\text{-}ind}}(\kappa) := \left| 2 \Pr[\mathrm{Expt}_{\mathsf{PKE},\mathcal{D}_\mathcal{M},\mathcal{S},\mathcal{A}}^{\mathrm{ds\text{-}ind}}(\kappa) = 1] - 1 \right|,$$

where $\mathrm{Expt}_{\mathsf{PKE},\mathcal{D}_\mathcal{M},\mathcal{S},\mathcal{A}}^{\mathrm{ds\text{-}ind}}(\kappa)$ is an experiment described in Fig. 1 and $\mathcal{S}$ is a PPT simulator.

Liu and Wang gave a slightly modified version of statistical disjointness in [33]. As they noted, their definition below is enough to show the security proof:

$$\mathsf{Disj}_{\mathsf{PKE},\mathcal{S}}(\kappa) := \Pr[(ek, dk) \leftarrow \mathsf{Gen}(1^\kappa), c \leftarrow \mathcal{S}(1^\kappa, ek) : c \in \mathsf{Enc}(ek, \mathcal{M})]$$

Definition 6 (strong disjoint-simulatability). *We call PKE has strong disjoint-simulatability if $\mathcal{S}$ ignores ek.*

Remark 3. We note that a deterministic PKE scheme produced by TPunc [39] or Punc [29] is not *strongly* disjoint-simulatable, because their simulator outputs a random ciphertext $\mathsf{Enc}(ek, \hat{\mu})$ of a special plaintext $\hat{\mu}$.

2.2   Key Encapsulation Mechanism (KEM)

The model for KEM schemes is summarized as follows:

Definition 7. *A KEM scheme* KEM *consists of the following triple of polynomial-time algorithms* $(\overline{\mathsf{Gen}}, \overline{\mathsf{Enc}}, \overline{\mathsf{Dec}})$:

- $\overline{\mathsf{Gen}}(1^{\kappa}) \rightarrow (ek, dk)$: *a key-generation algorithm that on input* 1^{κ}, *where* κ *is the security parameter, outputs a pair of keys* (ek, dk). *ek and dk are called the encapsulation key and decapsulation key, respectively.*
- $\overline{\mathsf{Enc}}(ek) \rightarrow (c, K)$: *an encapsulation algorithm that takes as input encapsulation key ek and outputs ciphertext* $c \in \mathcal{C}$ *and key* $K \in \mathcal{K}$.
- $\overline{\mathsf{Dec}}(dk, c) \rightarrow K/\bot$: *a decapsulation algorithm that takes as input decapsulation key dk and ciphertext c and outputs key K or a rejection symbol* $\bot \notin \mathcal{K}$.

Definition 8 (δ-Correctness). *Let* $\delta = \delta(\kappa)$. *We say that* $\mathsf{KEM} = (\overline{\mathsf{Gen}}, \overline{\mathsf{Enc}}, \overline{\mathsf{Dec}})$ *is* δ-*correct if*

$$\Pr[(ek, dk) \leftarrow \overline{\mathsf{Gen}}(1^{\kappa}), (c, K) \leftarrow \overline{\mathsf{Enc}}(ek) : \overline{\mathsf{Dec}}(dk, c) \neq K] \leq \delta(\kappa).$$

In particular, we say that KEM *is* perfectly correct *if* $\delta = 0$.

Security: We define pseudorandomness under chosen-ciphertext attacks (PR-CCA) and its strong version (SPR-CCA) with simulator $\mathcal{S}$ as a generalization of IND\$-CCA-security in [27,46]. We also review anonymity (ANON-CCA), robustness (SROB-CCA), and collision-freeness (SCFR-CCA) [24]. We also define *smoothness* under chosen-ciphertext attacks (denoted by SMT-CCA) by following smoothness of hash proof system [16]. Due to the space limit, we omit the definitions of the standard security notions (OW-CPA, IND-CPA, OW-CCA, and IND-CCA) and weak robustness (WROB-CCA) and weak collision-freeness (WCFR-CCA) [24].

Definition 9 (Security notions for KEM). *Let* $\mathsf{KEM} = (\overline{\mathsf{Gen}}, \overline{\mathsf{Enc}}, \overline{\mathsf{Dec}})$ *be a KEM scheme.*

For any $\mathcal{A}$ *and* goal-atk $\in \{$pr-cca, anon-cca, smt-cca$\}$, *we define its* goal-atk *advantage against* KEM *as follows:*

$$\mathsf{Adv}^{\text{goal-atk}}_{\mathsf{KEM}[,\mathcal{S}],\mathcal{A}}(\kappa) := \left| 2 \Pr[\mathsf{Expt}^{\text{goal-atk}}_{\mathsf{KEM}[,\mathcal{S}],\mathcal{A}}(\kappa) = 1] - 1 \right|,$$

where $\mathsf{Expt}^{\text{goal-atk}}_{\mathsf{KEM}[,\mathcal{S}],\mathcal{A}}(\kappa)$ *is an experiment described in Fig. 1 and* $\mathcal{S}$ *is a PPT simulator.*

For any $\mathcal{A}$ *and* goal-atk $\in$ {srob-cca, scfr-cca}, *we define its* goal-atk *advantage against* KEM *as follows:*

$$\mathsf{Adv}^{\text{goal-atk}}_{\mathsf{KEM},\mathcal{A}}(\kappa) := \Pr[\mathsf{Expt}^{\text{goal-atk}}_{\mathsf{KEM},\mathcal{A}}(\kappa) = 1],$$

where $\mathsf{Expt}^{\text{goal-atk}}_{\mathsf{KEM},\mathcal{A}}(\kappa)$ *is an experiment described in Fig. 1.*

For GOAL-ATK $\in$ {PR-CCA, ANON-CCA, SMT-CCA, SROB-CCA, SCFR-CCA}, *we say that* KEM *is* GOAL-ATK-*secure if* $\mathsf{Adv}^{\text{goal-atk}}_{\mathsf{KEM}[,\mathcal{S}],\mathcal{A}}(\kappa)$ *is negligible for any QPT adversary* $\mathcal{A}$. *We say that* KEM *is* SPR-CCA-*secure or* SSMT-CCA-*secure if it is* PR-CCA-*secure or* SMT-CCA-*secure and its simulator ignores* ek, *respectively. We say that* KEM *is* wANON-CCA-*secure if it is* ANON-CCA-*secure where the input to the adversary is* (ek_0, ek_1, c^*). *We also say that* KEM *is* GOAL-CPA-*secure if it is* GOAL-CCA-*secure even without the decapsulation oracle.*

We additionally define ϵ-sparseness for KEM with explicit rejection (Fig. 2).

$\mathsf{Expt}^{\text{pr-cca}}_{\mathsf{KEM},\mathcal{S},\mathcal{A}}(\kappa)$	$\mathsf{Expt}^{\text{anon-cca}}_{\mathsf{KEM},\mathcal{A}}(\kappa)$	$\mathrm{DEC}_a(c)$
$b \leftarrow \{0,1\}$	$b \leftarrow \{0,1\}$	if $c = a$, return $\perp$
$(ek, dk) \leftarrow \overline{\mathsf{Gen}}(1^\kappa)$	$(ek_0, dk_0) \leftarrow \overline{\mathsf{Gen}}(1^\kappa)$	$K := \overline{\mathsf{Dec}}(dk, c)$
$(c_0^*, K_0^*) \leftarrow \overline{\mathsf{Enc}}(ek);$	$(ek_1, dk_1) \leftarrow \overline{\mathsf{Gen}}(1^\kappa)$	**return** K
$(c_1^*, K_1^*) \leftarrow \mathcal{S}(1^\kappa, ek) \times \mathcal{K}$	$(c^*, K^*) \leftarrow \overline{\mathsf{Enc}}(ek);$	$\mathrm{DEC}_a(\mathrm{id}, c)$
$b' \leftarrow \mathcal{A}^{\mathrm{DEC}_{c_b^*}(\cdot)}(ek, c_b^*, K_b^*)$	$b' \leftarrow \mathcal{A}^{\mathrm{DEC}_{c^*}(\cdot,\cdot)}(ek_0, ek_1, c^*, K^*)$	if $c = a$, return $\perp$
return boole($b = b'$)	**return** boole($b = b'$)	$K := \overline{\mathsf{Dec}}(dk_{\mathrm{id}}, c)$
		return K

$\mathsf{Expt}^{\text{smt-cca}}_{\mathsf{KEM},\mathcal{S},\mathcal{A}}(\kappa)$	$\mathsf{Expt}^{\text{scfr-cca}}_{\mathsf{KEM},\mathcal{A}}(\kappa)$	$\mathsf{Expt}^{\text{srob-cca}}_{\mathsf{KEM},\mathcal{A}}(\kappa)$
$b \leftarrow \{0,1\}$	$(ek_0, dk_0) \leftarrow \overline{\mathsf{Gen}}(1^\kappa)$	$(ek_0, dk_0) \leftarrow \overline{\mathsf{Gen}}(1^\kappa)$
$(ek, dk) \leftarrow \overline{\mathsf{Gen}}(1^\kappa)$	$(ek_1, dk_1) \leftarrow \overline{\mathsf{Gen}}(1^\kappa)$	$(ek_1, dk_1) \leftarrow \overline{\mathsf{Gen}}(1^\kappa)$
$(c^*, K_0^*) \leftarrow \mathcal{S}(1^\kappa, ek) \times \mathcal{K}$	$c \leftarrow \mathcal{A}^{\mathrm{DEC}\perp(\cdot,\cdot)}(ek_0, ek_1)$	$c \leftarrow \mathcal{A}^{\mathrm{DEC}\perp(\cdot,\cdot)}(ek_0, ek_1)$
$K_1^* \leftarrow \overline{\mathsf{Dec}}(dk, c^*)$	$K_0 \leftarrow \overline{\mathsf{Dec}}(dk_0, c)$	$K_0 \leftarrow \overline{\mathsf{Dec}}(dk_0, c)$
$b' \leftarrow \mathcal{A}^{\mathrm{DEC}_{c^*}(\cdot)}(ek, c^*, K_b^*)$	$K_1 \leftarrow \overline{\mathsf{Dec}}(dk_1, c)$	$K_1 \leftarrow \overline{\mathsf{Dec}}(dk_1, c)$
return boole($b = b'$)	**return** boole($K_0 = K_1 \neq \perp$)	**return** boole($K_0 \neq \perp \wedge K_1 \neq \perp$)

Fig. 2. Games for KEM schemes

Definition 10. *Let* $\mathcal{S}$ *be a simulator for the* PR-CCA *security. We say that* KEM *is* ϵ-*sparse if*

$$\Pr[(ek, dk) \leftarrow \overline{\mathsf{Gen}}(1^\kappa), c^* \leftarrow \mathcal{S}(1^\kappa, ek) : \overline{\mathsf{Dec}}(dk, c) \neq \perp] \leq \epsilon.$$

2.3 Data Encapsulation Mechanism (DEM)

The model for DEM schemes is summarized as follows:

Definition 11. *A DEM scheme* DEM *consists of the following triple of polynomial-time algorithms* (E, D) *with key space* $\mathcal{K}$ *and message space* $\mathcal{M}$:

- $E(K, \mu) \rightarrow d$: *an encapsulation algorithm that takes as input key K and data μ and outputs ciphertext d.*
- $D(K, d) \rightarrow m/\perp$: *a decapsulation algorithm that takes as input key K and ciphertext d and outputs data μ or a rejection symbol $\perp \notin \mathcal{M}$.*

Definition 12 (Correctness). *We say* DEM $= (E, D)$ *has perfect correctness if for any $K \in \mathcal{K}$ and any $\mu \in \mathcal{M}$, we have*

$$\Pr[d \leftarrow E(K, \mu) : D(K, d) = \mu] = 1.$$

Security: We review pseudorandomness under chosen-ciphertext attacks (PR-CCA) and pseudorandomness under one-time chosen-ciphertext attacks (PR-OTCCA). We also review integrity of ciphertext (INT-CTXT). Robustness of DEM (FROB) are taken from Farshim, Orlandi, and Roşi [19]. Due to the space limit, we omit the definitions of the standard security notion IND-CCA and robustness (XROB) [19] (Fig. 3).

$\mathrm{Expt}_{\mathsf{DEM},\mathcal{A}}^{\mathrm{pr\text{-}cca}}(\kappa)$	$\mathrm{Expt}_{\mathsf{DEM},\mathcal{A}}^{\mathrm{pr\text{-}otcca}}(\kappa)$	$\mathrm{ENC}(\mu)$
$b \leftarrow \{0,1\}$	$b \leftarrow \{0,1\}$	$d \leftarrow E(K, \mu)$
$K \leftarrow \mathcal{K}$	$K \leftarrow \mathcal{K}$	**return** d
$(\mu, state) \leftarrow \mathcal{A}^{\mathrm{ENC}(\cdot), \mathrm{DEC}_\perp(\cdot)}(1^\kappa)$	$(\mu, state) \leftarrow \mathcal{A}(1^\kappa)$	
$d_0^* \leftarrow E(K, \mu)$	$d_0^* \leftarrow E(K, \mu)$	$\mathrm{DEC}_a(d)$
$d_1^* \leftarrow U(\mathcal{C}_{|\mu|})$	$d_1^* \leftarrow U(\mathcal{C}_{|\mu|})$	**if** $d = a$
$b' \leftarrow \mathcal{A}^{\mathrm{ENC}(\cdot), \mathrm{DEC}_{d_b^*}(\cdot)}(d_b^*, state)$	$b' \leftarrow \mathcal{A}^{\mathrm{DEC}_{d_b^*}(\cdot)}(d_b^*, state)$	**then return** $\perp$
return $\mathsf{boole}(b = b')$	**return** $\mathsf{boole}(b = b')$	$\mu \leftarrow D(K, d)$
		return μ

$\mathrm{Expt}_{\mathsf{DEM},\mathcal{A}}^{\mathrm{int\text{-}ctxt}}(\kappa)$	$\mathrm{ENC2}(\mu)$	$\mathrm{Expt}_{\mathsf{DEM},\mathcal{A}}^{\mathrm{frob}}(\kappa)$
$K \leftarrow \mathcal{K}$	$d \leftarrow E(K, \mu)$	$(d, k_0, k_1) \leftarrow \mathcal{A}(1^\kappa)$
$w \leftarrow \perp$	$L \leftarrow L \cup \{d\}$	$\mu_0 \leftarrow D(k_0, d)$
$L \leftarrow \emptyset$	**return** d	$\mu_1 \leftarrow D(k_1, d)$
$\mathcal{A}^{\mathrm{ENC2}(\cdot), \mathrm{DEC2}(\cdot)}(1^\kappa)$		$b \leftarrow \mathsf{boole}(\mu_0 \neq \perp \wedge \mu_1 \neq \perp)$
return w	$\mathrm{DEC2}(d)$	$b_k \leftarrow \mathsf{boole}(k_0 \neq k_1)$
	$\mu \leftarrow D(K, d)$	**return** $\mathsf{boole}(b \wedge b_k)$
	if $\mu \neq \perp$ and $d \notin L$	
	then $w := \top$	
	return μ	

Fig. 3. Games for DEM schemes

Definition 13 (Security notions for DEM). *Let* DEM $= (E, D)$ *be a DEM scheme whose key space is $\mathcal{K}$. For $\mu \in \mathcal{M}$, let $\mathcal{C}_{|\mu|}$ be a ciphertext space defined by the length of message μ.*

For any $\mathcal{A}$ and goal-atk $\in \{\text{pr-cca}, \text{pr-otcca}\}$, *we define its* goal-atk *advantage against* DEM *as follows:*

$$\mathsf{Adv}_{\mathsf{DEM},\mathcal{A}}^{\text{goal-atk}}(\kappa) := \left| 2 \Pr[\mathsf{Expt}_{\mathsf{DEM},\mathcal{A}}^{\text{goal-atk}}(\kappa) = 1] - 1 \right|,$$

where $\mathsf{Expt}_{\mathsf{DEM},\mathcal{A}}^{\text{goal-atk}}(\kappa)$ *is an experiment described in Fig. 1.*

For any $\mathcal{A}$ and goal-atk $\in \{\text{int-ctxt}, \text{frob}\}$, *we define its* goal-atk *advantage against* DEM *as follows:*

$$\mathsf{Adv}_{\mathsf{DEM},\mathcal{A}}^{\text{goal-atk}}(\kappa) := \Pr[\mathsf{Expt}_{\mathsf{DEM},\mathcal{A}}^{\text{goal-atk}}(\kappa) = 1],$$

where $\mathsf{Expt}_{\mathsf{DEM},\mathcal{A}}^{\text{goal-atk}}(\kappa)$ *is an experiment described in Fig. 1.*

For GOAL-ATK $\in \{\text{PR-CCA}, \text{PR-oTCCA}, \text{INT-CTXT}, \text{FROB}\}$, *we say that* DEM *is* GOAL-ATK-*secure if* $\mathsf{Adv}_{\mathsf{DEM},\mathcal{A}}^{\text{goal-atk}}(\kappa)$ *is negligible for any QPT adversary $\mathcal{A}$.*

2.4 Review of Grubbs, Maram, and Paterson [24]

Grubbs et al. studied KEM's anonymity and hybrid PKE's anonymity and robustness by extending the results of Mohassel [36]. We use $\mathsf{KEM}^{\perp}$ and $\mathsf{KEM}^{\not\perp}$ to indicate KEM with explicit rejection and implicit rejection, respectively. For KEM with explicit rejection, they showed the following theorem which generalizes Mohassel's theorem [36]:

Theorem 2 ([24, Theorem 1]). *Let* $\mathsf{PKE}_{\mathsf{hy}} = \mathsf{Hyb}[\mathsf{KEM}^{\perp}, \mathsf{DEM}]$, *a hybrid PKE scheme obtained by composing* $\mathsf{KEM}^{\perp}$ *and* DEM. *(See Fig. 4.)*

1. *If* $\mathsf{KEM}^{\perp}$ *is* wANON-CPA-*secure,* IND-CCA-*secure,* WROB-CCA-*secure, and δ-correct and* DEM *is* INT-CTXT-*secure, then* $\mathsf{PKE}_{\mathsf{hy}}$ *is* ANON-CCA-*secure.*

2. *If* $\mathsf{KEM}^{\perp}$ *is* SROB-CCA-*secure (and* WROB-CCA-*secure), then* $\mathsf{PKE}_{\mathsf{hy}}$ *is* SROB-CCA-*secure (and* WROB-CCA-*secure), respectively.*

Grubbs et al. [24] then treat KEM with implicit rejection, which is used in all NIST PQC Round 3 KEM candidates except HQC. Their results are related to the FO transform with implicit rejection, which is decomposed into two transforms, T and $\mathsf{U}^{\not\perp}$: T transforms a probabilistic PKE scheme PKE into a deterministic PKE scheme PKE_1 with a random oracle G; $\mathsf{U}^{\not\perp}$ transforms a deterministic PKE scheme PKE_1 into a probabilistic KEM KEM with a random oracle H. Roughly speaking, they showed the following two theorems on robustness and anonymity of hybrid PKE from KEM with implicit rejection:

Theorem 3 (Robustness of $\mathsf{PKE}_{\mathsf{hy}}$ [24, Theorem 2]). *Let* $\mathsf{PKE}_{\mathsf{hy}} = \mathsf{Hyb}[\mathsf{KEM}^{\not\perp}, \mathsf{DEM}]$. *If* $\mathsf{KEM}^{\not\perp}$ *is* SCFR-CCA-*secure (and* WCFR-CCA-*secure) and* DEM *is* FROB-*secure (and* XROB-*secure), then* $\mathsf{PKE}_{\mathsf{hy}}$ *is* SROB-CCA-*secure (and* WROB-CCA-*secure), respectively.*

Theorem 4 (Anonymity of $\mathsf{PKE_{hy}}$ using $\mathsf{FO}^{\not\perp}$ [24, Theorem 7]). *Let* $\mathsf{PKE_{hy}} = \mathsf{Hyb}[\mathsf{KEM}^{\not\perp}, \mathsf{DEM}]$. *If* PKE *is* δ-*correct, and* γ-*spreading,* $\mathsf{PKE_1} = \mathsf{T}[\mathsf{PKE}, \mathsf{G}]$ *is* WCFR-CPA-*secure,* $\mathsf{KEM}^{\not\perp} = \mathsf{FO}^{\not\perp}[\mathsf{PKE}, \mathsf{G}, \mathsf{H}]$ *is* ANON-CCA-*secure and* IND-CCA-*secure,* DEM *is* INT-CTXT-*secure, then* $\mathsf{PKE_{hy}}$ *is* ANON-CCA-*secure.*

They also showed that the following theorem:

Theorem 5 (Anonymity of $\mathsf{KEM}^{\not\perp}$ using $\mathsf{FO}^{\not\perp}$ [24, Theorem 5]). *If* PKE *is* wANON-CPA-*secure,* OW-CPA-*secure, and* δ-*correct, and* $\mathsf{PKE_1} = \mathsf{T}[\mathsf{PKE}, \mathsf{G}]$ *is* SCFR-CPA-*secure, then a KEM scheme* $\mathsf{KEM} = \mathsf{FO}^{\not\perp}[\mathsf{PKE}, \mathsf{G}, \mathsf{H}]$ *is* ANON-CCA-*secure.*

Grubbs et al. reduced from the wANON-CPA-security of PKE to the ANON-CCA-security of KEM. We note that there are two decapsulation oracles in the security game of the ANON-CCA-security of KEM. Thus, they need to simulate *both* decapsulation oracles without secrets. Jiang et al. [31] used the simulation trick that replaces $\mathsf{H}(\mu, c)$ with $\mathsf{H}_q(\mathsf{Enc}(ek, \mu))$ if $c = \mathsf{Enc}(ek, \mu)$ and $\mathsf{H}'_q(\mu, c)$ else, which helps the simulation of the decapsulation oracle without secrets in the QROM. Grubbs et al. extended this trick to simulate *two* decapsulation oracles by replacing $\mathsf{H}(\mu, c)$ with $\mathsf{H}_{q,i}(\mathsf{Enc}(ek_i, \mu))$ if $c = \mathsf{Enc}(ek_i, \mu)$ and $\mathsf{H}'_q(\mu, c)$ else. Notice that this extended simulation heavily depends on the fact that H takes μ and c and the SCFR-CCA-security of $\mathsf{PKE_1}$. If the random oracle takes μ only, their trick fails the simulation.

3   Strong Pseudorandomness of Hybrid PKE

The hybrid PKE $\mathsf{PKE_{hy}} = (\mathsf{Gen_{hy}}, \mathsf{Enc_{hy}}, \mathsf{Dec_{hy}})$ constructed from $\mathsf{KEM} = (\overline{\mathsf{Gen}}, \overline{\mathsf{Enc}}, \overline{\mathsf{Dec}})$ and $\mathsf{DEM} = (\mathsf{E}, \mathsf{D})$ is summarized as in Fig. 4

$\mathsf{Gen_{hy}}(1^\kappa)$	$\mathsf{Enc_{hy}}(ek, \mu)$	$\mathsf{Dec_{hy}}(dk, ct = (c, d))$
$(ek, dk) \leftarrow \overline{\mathsf{Gen}}(1^\kappa)$	$(c, K) \leftarrow \overline{\mathsf{Enc}}(ek)$	$K' \leftarrow \overline{\mathsf{Dec}}(dk, c)$
return (ek, dk)	$d \leftarrow \mathsf{E}(K, \mu)$	**if** $K' = \perp$ **then return** $\perp$
	return $ct := (c, d)$	$\mu' \leftarrow \mathsf{D}(K', d)$
		if $\mu' = \perp$ **then return** $\perp$
		return μ'

Fig. 4. $\mathsf{PKE_{hy}} = \mathsf{Hyb}[\mathsf{KEM}, \mathsf{DEM}]$

We show the following two theorems on strong pseudorandomness and anonymity of a hybrid PKE:

Theorem 6 (Case for KEM with Explicit Rejection). *Let* $\mathsf{PKE_{hy}} =$
$(\mathsf{Gen_{hy}}, \mathsf{Enc_{hy}}, \mathsf{Dec_{hy}})$ *be a hybrid encryption scheme obtained by composing a*
KEM scheme $\mathsf{KEM}^{\perp} = (\overline{\mathsf{Gen}}, \overline{\mathsf{Enc}}, \overline{\mathsf{Dec}})$ *and a DEM scheme* $\mathsf{DEM} = (\mathsf{E}, \mathsf{D})$ *that*
share key space $\mathcal{K}$. *If* $\mathsf{KEM}^{\perp}$ *is* SPR-CCA*-secure,* δ*-correct with negligible* δ, *and*
ϵ*-sparse and* DEM *is* PR-OTCCA*-secure and* INT-CTXT*-secure, then* $\mathsf{PKE_{hy}}$
is SPR-CCA*-secure (and* ANON-CCA*-secure).*

Theorem 7 (Case for KEM with Implicit Rejection). *Let* $\mathsf{PKE_{hy}} =$
$(\mathsf{Gen_{hy}}, \mathsf{Enc_{hy}}, \mathsf{Dec_{hy}})$ *be a hybrid encryption scheme obtained by composing a*
KEM scheme $\mathsf{KEM}^{\not\perp} = (\overline{\mathsf{Gen}}, \overline{\mathsf{Enc}}, \overline{\mathsf{Dec}})$ *and a DEM scheme* $\mathsf{DEM} = (\mathsf{E}, \mathsf{D})$
that share key space $\mathcal{K}$. *If* $\mathsf{KEM}^{\not\perp}$ *is* SPR-CCA*-secure,* SSMT-CCA*-secure,*
and δ*-correct with negligible* δ *and* DEM *is* PR-OTCCA*-secure, then* $\mathsf{PKE_{hy}}$ *is*
SPR-CCA*-secure (and* ANON-CCA*-secure).*

We here prove Theorem 7 and give the proof of Theorem 6 in the full version.

3.1   Proof of Theorem 7

Let us consider Game_i for $i = 0, \ldots, 6$. We summarize the games in Table 2. Let
S_i denote the event that the adversary outputs $b' = 1$ in Game_i.

Let $\mathcal{S}$ be the simulator for the SPR-CCA security of $\mathsf{KEM}^{\not\perp}$. We define
$\mathcal{S}_{\mathsf{hy}}(1^\kappa, |\mu^*|) := \mathcal{S}(1^\kappa) \times U(\mathcal{C}_{|\mu^*|})$ be the simulator for the SPR-CCA security of
$\mathsf{PKE_{hy}}$.

The security proof is similar to the security proof of the IND-CCA secu-
rity of KEM/DEM [17] for $\mathsf{Game}_0, \ldots, \mathsf{Game}_4$. We need to take care of pseudorandom ciphertexts when moving from Game_4 to Game_5 and require the
SSMT-CCA security of $\mathsf{KEM}^{\not\perp}$.

Table 2. Summary of Games for the Proof of Theorem 7

Game	c^* and K^*	d^*	Decryption	Justification
Game_0	$\overline{\mathsf{Enc}}(ek)$	$\mathsf{E}(K^*, \mu^*)$		
Game_1	$\overline{\mathsf{Enc}}(ek)$ at first	$\mathsf{E}(K^*, \mu^*)$		conceptual change
Game_2	$\overline{\mathsf{Enc}}(ek)$ at first	$\mathsf{E}(K^*, \mu^*)$	use K^* if $c = c^*$	δ-correctness of $\mathsf{KEM}^{\not\perp}$
Game_3	$\mathcal{S}(1^\kappa) \times U(\mathcal{K})$ at first	$\mathsf{E}(K^*, \mu^*)$	use K^* if $c = c^*$	SPR-CCA security of $\mathsf{KEM}^{\not\perp}$
Game_4	$\mathcal{S}(1^\kappa) \times U(\mathcal{K})$ at first	$U(\mathcal{C}_{|\mu^*|})$	use K^* if $c = c^*$	SPR-OTCCA security of DEM
Game_5	$\mathcal{S}(1^\kappa) \times U(\mathcal{K})$ at first	$U(\mathcal{C}_{|\mu^*|})$		SSMT-CCA security of $\mathsf{KEM}^{\not\perp}$
Game_6	$\mathcal{S}(1^\kappa) \times U(\mathcal{K})$	$U(\mathcal{C}_{|\mu^*|})$		conceptual change

Game_0: This is the original game $\mathsf{Expt}^{\text{spr-cca}}_{\mathsf{PKE_{hy}}, \mathcal{S}_{\mathsf{hy}}, \mathcal{A}}(\kappa)$ with $b = 0$. Given μ^*, the
challenge ciphertext is computed as follows:

$$(c^*, K^*) \leftarrow \overline{\mathsf{Enc}}(ek); d^* \leftarrow \mathsf{E}(K^*, \mu^*); \text{ return } ct^* = (c^*, d^*).$$

We have
$$\Pr[S_0] = 1 - \Pr[\mathsf{Expt}^{\text{spr-cca}}_{\mathsf{PKE}_{\text{hy}}, \mathcal{S}_{\text{hy}}, \mathcal{A}}(\kappa) = 1 \mid b = 0].$$

Game_1: In this game, c_0^* and K_0^* are generated before invoking $\mathcal{A}$ with ek. This change is just conceptual, and we have

$$\Pr[S_0] = \Pr[S_1].$$

Game_2: In this game, the decryption oracle uses K^* if $c = c^*$ instead of $K = \overline{\mathsf{Dec}}(dk, c^*)$. Game_1 and Game_2 differ if correctly generated ciphertext c^* with K^* is decapsulated into different $K \neq K^*$ or $\bot$, which violates the correctness and occurs with probability at most δ. Hence, the difference of Game_1 and Game_2 is bounded by δ, and we have

$$|\Pr[S_1] - \Pr[S_2]| \leq \delta.$$

We note that this corresponds to the event $\mathsf{BadKeyPair}$ in [17].

Game_3: In this game, the challenger uses random (c^*, K^*) and uses K^* in DEM. The challenge ciphertext is generated as follows:

$$(c^*, K^*) \leftarrow \mathcal{S}(1^\kappa) \times U(\mathcal{K}); d^+ \leftarrow \mathsf{E}(K^*, \mu^*); \text{ return } ct^* = (c^*, d^+).$$

The difference is bounded by SPR-CCA security of $\mathsf{KEM}^{\not\perp}$: There is an adversary $\mathcal{A}_{23}$ whose running time is approximately the same as that of $\mathcal{A}$ satisfying

$$|\Pr[S_2] - \Pr[S_3]| \leq \mathsf{Adv}^{\text{spr-cca}}_{\mathsf{KEM}^{\not\perp}, \mathcal{S}, \mathcal{A}_{23}}(\kappa).$$

We omit the detail of $\mathcal{A}_{23}$ since it is straightforward.

Game_4: In this game, the challenger uses random d^*. The challenge ciphertext is generated as follows:

$$(c^*, K^*) \leftarrow \mathcal{S}(1^\kappa) \times \mathcal{K}; d^* \leftarrow U(\mathcal{C}_{|\mu^*|}); \text{ return } ct^* = (c^*, d^*).$$

The difference is bounded by SPR-OTCCA security of DEM: There is an adversary $\mathcal{A}_{34}$ whose running time is approximately the same as that of $\mathcal{A}$ satisfying

$$|\Pr[S_3] - \Pr[S_4]| \leq \mathsf{Adv}^{\text{spr-otcca}}_{\mathsf{DEM}, \mathcal{A}_{34}}(\kappa).$$

We omit the detail of $\mathcal{A}_{34}$ since it is straightforward.

Game_5: We replace the decryption oracle defined as follows: If given $ct = (c^*, d)$, the decryption oracle uses $K = \overline{\mathsf{Dec}}(dk, c^*)$ instead of K^*.

The difference is bounded by SSMT-CCA security of $\mathsf{KEM}^{\not\perp}$: There is an adversary $\mathcal{A}_{45}$ whose running time is approximately the same as that of $\mathcal{A}$ satisfying

$$|\Pr[S_4] - \Pr[S_5]| \leq \mathsf{Adv}^{\text{ssmt-cca}}_{\mathsf{KEM}^{\not\perp}, \mathcal{S}, \mathcal{A}_{45}}(\kappa).$$

We omit the detail of $\mathcal{A}_{45}$ since it is straightforward.

$Game_6$: We finally change the timing of the generation of (c^*, K^*). This change is just conceptual, and we have

$$\Pr[S_5] = \Pr[S_6].$$

Notice that this is the original game $\mathsf{Expt}^{\text{spr-cca}}_{\mathsf{PKE}_{\text{hy}}, \mathcal{S}_{\text{hy}}, \mathcal{A}}(\kappa)$ with $b = 1$, thus, we have

$$\Pr[S_6] = \Pr[\mathsf{Expt}^{\text{spr-cca}}_{\mathsf{PKE}_{\text{hy}}, \mathcal{S}_{\text{hy}}, \mathcal{A}}(\kappa) = 1 \mid b = 1].$$

Summing the (in)equalities, we obtain the bound in the statement as follows:

$$\mathsf{Adv}^{\text{spr-cca}}_{\mathsf{PKE}_{\text{hy}}, \mathcal{S}_{\text{hy}}, \mathcal{A}}(\kappa) = |\Pr[S_0] - \Pr[S_6]| \leq \sum_i |\Pr[S_i] - \Pr[S_{i+1}]|$$

$$\leq \delta + \mathsf{Adv}^{\text{spr-cca}}_{\mathsf{KEM}^{\measuredangle}, \mathcal{S}, \mathcal{A}_{23}}(\kappa) + \mathsf{Adv}^{\text{spr-otcca}}_{\mathsf{DEM}, \mathcal{A}_{34}}(\kappa) + \mathsf{Adv}^{\text{ssint-cca}}_{\mathsf{KEM}^{\measuredangle}, \mathcal{S}, \mathcal{A}_{45}}(\kappa).$$

$\square$

4   Properties of SXY

Let us review SXY [39] as known as $\mathsf{U}^{\measuredangle}_m$ with explicit re-encryption check [26].

Let $\mathsf{PKE} = (\mathsf{Gen}, \mathsf{Enc}, \mathsf{Dec})$ be a deterministic PKE scheme. Let $\mathcal{M}$, $\mathcal{C}$, and $\mathcal{K}$ be a plaintext, ciphertext, and key space of PKE, respectively. Let $\mathsf{H} \colon \mathcal{M} \to \mathcal{K}$ and $\mathsf{H}_{\text{prf}} \colon \{0, 1\}^{\ell} \times \mathcal{C} \to \mathcal{K}$ be hash functions modeled by random oracles. $\mathsf{KEM} = (\overline{\mathsf{Gen}}, \overline{\mathsf{Enc}}, \overline{\mathsf{Dec}}) = \mathsf{SXY}[\mathsf{PKE}, \mathsf{H}, \mathsf{H}_{\text{prf}}]$ is defined as in Fig. 5.

$\overline{\mathsf{Gen}}(1^{\kappa})$	$\overline{\mathsf{Enc}}(ek)$	$\overline{\mathsf{Dec}}(\overline{dk}, c)$, where $\overline{dk} = (dk, ek, s)$
$(ek, dk) \leftarrow \mathsf{Gen}(1^{\kappa})$	$\mu \leftarrow \mathcal{D}_{\mathcal{M}}$	$\mu' \leftarrow \mathsf{Dec}(dk, c)$
$s \leftarrow \{0, 1\}^{\ell}$	$c := \mathsf{Enc}(ek, \mu)$	if $\mu' = \bot$ or $c \neq \mathsf{Enc}(ek, \mu')$
$\overline{dk} := (dk, ek, s)$	$K := \mathsf{H}(\mu)$	$\quad$ then return $K := \mathsf{H}_{\text{prf}}(s, c)$
return $(ek, \overline{dk})$	return (c, K)	else return $K := \mathsf{H}(\mu')$

Fig. 5. KEM $= \mathsf{SXY}[\mathsf{PKE}, \mathsf{H}, \mathsf{H}_{\text{prf}}]$

Table 3. Summary of games for the proof of Theorem 8

Game	H	c^*	K^*	Decapsulation valid c	invalid c	Justification
$Game_0$	$\mathsf{H}(\cdot)$	$\mathsf{Enc}(ek, \mu^*)$	$\mathsf{H}(\mu^*)$	$\mathsf{H}(\mu)$	$\mathsf{H}_{\text{prf}}(s, c)$	
$Game_1$	$\mathsf{H}(\cdot)$	$\mathsf{Enc}(ek, \mu^*)$	$\mathsf{H}(\mu^*)$	$\mathsf{H}(\mu)$	$\mathsf{H}_q(c)$	Lemma 2
$Game_{1.5}$	$\mathsf{H}'_q(\mathsf{Enc}(ek, \cdot))$	$\mathsf{Enc}(ek, \mu^*)$	$\mathsf{H}(\mu^*)$	$\mathsf{H}(\mu)$	$\mathsf{H}_q(c)$	key's accuracy
$Game_2$	$\mathsf{H}_q(\mathsf{Enc}(ek, \cdot))$	$\mathsf{Enc}(ek, \mu^*)$	$\mathsf{H}(\mu^*)$	$\mathsf{H}(\mu)$	$\mathsf{H}_q(c)$	key's accuracy
$Game_3$	$\mathsf{H}_q(\mathsf{Enc}(ek, \cdot))$	$\mathsf{Enc}(ek, \mu^*)$	$\mathsf{H}_q(c^*)$	$\mathsf{H}_q(c)$	$\mathsf{H}_q(c)$	key's accuracy
$Game_4$	$\mathsf{H}_q(\mathsf{Enc}(ek, \cdot))$	$\mathcal{S}(1^{\kappa})$	$\mathsf{H}_q(c^*)$	$\mathsf{H}_q(c)$	$\mathsf{H}_q(c)$	ciphertext indistinguishability
$Game_5$	$\mathsf{H}_q(\mathsf{Enc}(ek, \cdot))$	$\mathcal{S}(1^{\kappa})$	$U(\mathcal{K})$	$\mathsf{H}_q(c)$	$\mathsf{H}_q(c)$	statistical disjointness
$Game_6$	$\mathsf{H}_q(\mathsf{Enc}(ek, \cdot))$	$\mathcal{S}(1^{\kappa})$	$U(\mathcal{K})$	$\mathsf{H}(\mu)$	$\mathsf{H}_q(c)$	key's accuracy
$Game_{6.5}$	$\mathsf{H}'_q(\mathsf{Enc}(ek, \cdot))$	$\mathcal{S}(1^{\kappa})$	$U(\mathcal{K})$	$\mathsf{H}(\mu)$	$\mathsf{H}_q(c)$	key's accuracy
$Game_7$	$\mathsf{H}(\cdot)$	$\mathcal{S}(1^{\kappa})$	$U(\mathcal{K})$	$\mathsf{H}(\mu)$	$\mathsf{H}_q(c)$	key's accuracy
$Game_8$	$\mathsf{H}(\cdot)$	$\mathcal{S}(1^{\kappa})$	$U(\mathcal{K})$	$\mathsf{H}(\mu)$	$\mathsf{H}_{\text{prf}}(s, c)$	Lemma 2

4.1 SPR-CCA Security

We first show that KEM is strongly pseudorandom if the underlying PKE is strongly disjoint-simulatable.

Theorem 8. *Suppose that a ciphertext space C of PKE depends on the public parameter only. If PKE is strongly disjoint-simulatable and δ-correct with negligible δ, then KEM = SXY[PKE, H, H_{prf}] is SPR-CCA-secure.*

Correctly speaking, the bound of the advantage differ if PKE is derandomized by T. See the full version for the detail.

Proof of Theorem 8: We use the game-hopping proof. We consider Game_i for $i = 0, \ldots, 8$. We summarize the games in Table 3. Let S_i denote the event that the adversary outputs $b' = 1$ in game Game_i. Let Acc be an event that a key pair (ek, dk) is accurate. Let $\overline{\mathsf{Acc}}$ denote the event that a key pair (ek, dk) is inaccurate. We note that we have $\Pr[\overline{\mathsf{Acc}}] \leq \delta$ since PKE is deterministic. We extend the security proof for IND-CCA security of SXY in [33, 39, 47].

Game_0: This game is the original game $\mathsf{Expt}_{\mathsf{KEM},\mathcal{A}}^{\mathrm{spr\text{-}cca}}(\kappa)$ with $b = 0$. Thus, we have

$$\Pr[S_0] = 1 - \Pr[\mathsf{Expt}_{\mathsf{KEM},\mathcal{A}}^{\mathrm{spr\text{-}cca}}(\kappa) = 1 \mid b = 0].$$

Game_1: This game is the same as Game_0 except that $\mathsf{H}_{\mathsf{prf}}(s, c)$ in the decapsulation oracle is replace with $\mathsf{H}_q(c)$ where $\mathsf{H}_q \colon C \to \mathcal{K}$ is another random oracle. We remark that $\mathcal{A}$ cannot access H_q directly.

As in [47, Lemmas 4.1], from Lemma 2 we have the bound

$$|\Pr[S_0] - \Pr[S_1]| \leq 2(q_{\mathsf{H}_{\mathsf{prf}}} + q_{\mathrm{DEC}}) \cdot 2^{-\ell/2},$$

where $q_{\mathsf{H}_{\mathsf{prf}}}$ and q_{DEC} denote the number of queries to $\mathsf{H}_{\mathsf{prf}}$ and DEC the adversary makes, respectively.

In addition, according to Lemma 8, for any $p \geq 0$, we have

$$|\Pr[S_1] - p| \leq |\Pr[S_1 \wedge \mathsf{Acc}] - p| + \delta.$$

$\mathsf{Game}_{1.5}$: This game is the same as Game_1 except that the random oracle $\mathsf{H}(\cdot)$ is simulated by $\mathsf{H}'_q(\mathsf{Enc}(ek, \cdot))$ where $\mathsf{H}'_q \colon C \to \mathcal{K}$ is yet another random oracle. We remark that the decapsulation oracle and the generation of K^* also use $\mathsf{H}'_q(\mathsf{Enc}(ek, \cdot))$ as $\mathsf{H}(\cdot)$.

If the key pair (ek, dk) is accurate, then $g(\mu) := \mathsf{Enc}(ek, \mu)$ is *injective*. Thus, if the key pair is accurate, then $\mathsf{H}'_q \circ g \colon \mathcal{M} \to \mathcal{K}$ is a random function and the two games Game_1 and $\mathsf{Game}_{1.5}$ are equivalent Thus, we have

$$\Pr[S_1 \wedge \mathsf{Acc}] = \Pr[S_{1.5} \wedge \mathsf{Acc}].$$

Game_2: This game is the same as $\mathsf{Game}_{1.5}$ except that the random oracle H is simulated by $\mathsf{H}_q \circ g$ instead of $\mathsf{H}'_q \circ g$.

A ciphertext c is said to be *valid* if we have $\mathsf{Enc}(ek, \mathsf{Dec}(dk, c)) = c$ and *invalid* otherwise.

Notice that, in $\mathsf{Game}_{1.5}$, H_q is used for *invalid* ciphertext, and an adversary cannot access a value of H_q for a valid ciphertext. In addition, in $\mathsf{Game}_{1.5}$, an adversary can access a value of H'_q on input a valid ciphertext and cannot access a value of H'_q on input an invalid ciphertext if the key pair is accurate. Thus, there is no difference between $\mathsf{Game}_{1.5}$ and Game_2 if the key pair is accurate and we have

$$\Pr[S_{1.5} \wedge \mathsf{Acc}] = \Pr[S_2 \wedge \mathsf{Acc}].$$

Game_3: This game is the same as Game_2 except that K^* is set as $\mathsf{H}_q(c^*)$ and the decapsulation oracle always returns $\mathsf{H}_q(c)$ as long as $c \neq c^*$.

If the key pair is accurate, for a valid ciphertext c and its decrypted result μ, we have $\mathsf{H}(\mu) = \mathsf{H}_q(\mathsf{Enc}(ek, \mu)) = \mathsf{H}_q(c)$. Thus, the two games Game_2 and Game_3 are equivalent and we have

$$\Pr[S_2 \wedge \mathsf{Acc}] = \Pr[S_3 \wedge \mathsf{Acc}].$$

According to Lemma 8, for any $p \geq 0$, we have

$$|\Pr[S_3 \wedge \mathsf{Acc}] - p| \leq |\Pr[S_3] - p| + \delta.$$

Game_4: This game is the same as Game_3 except that c^* is generated by $\mathcal{S}(1^\kappa)$.

The difference between two games Game_3 and Game_4 is bounded by the advantage of ciphertext indistinguishability in disjoint simulatability as in [47, Lemma 4.7]. The reduction algorithm is obtained straightforwardly, and we omit it. We have

$$|\Pr[S_3] - \Pr[S_4]| \leq \mathsf{Adv}^{\text{ds-ind}}_{\mathsf{PKE}, \mathcal{D}_\mathcal{M}, \mathcal{S}, \mathcal{A}_{34}}(\kappa).$$

Game_5: This game is the same as Game_4 except that $K^* \leftarrow \mathcal{K}$ instead of $K^* \leftarrow \mathsf{H}_q(c^*)$.

In Game_4, if $c^* \leftarrow \mathcal{S}(1^\kappa)$ is not in $\mathsf{Enc}(ek, \mathcal{M})$, then the adversary has no information about $K^* = \mathsf{H}_q(c^*)$ and thus, K^* looks uniformly at random. Hence, the difference between two games Game_4 and Game_5 is bounded by the statistical disjointness in disjoint simulatability as in [47, Lemma 4.8]. We have

$$|\Pr[S_4] - \Pr[S_5]| \leq \mathsf{Disj}_{\mathsf{PKE}, \mathcal{S}}(\kappa).$$

According to Lemma 8, for any $p \geq 0$, we have

$$|\Pr[S_5] - p| \leq |\Pr[S_5 \wedge \mathsf{Acc}] - p| + \delta.$$

Game_6: This game is the same as Game_5 except that the decapsulation oracle is reset as DEC. Similar to the case for Game_2 and Game_3, if a key pair is accurate, the two games Game_5 and Game_6 are equivalent as in the proof of [47, Lemma 4.5]. We have

$$\Pr[S_5 \wedge \mathsf{Acc}] = \Pr[S_6 \wedge \mathsf{Acc}].$$

$\mathsf{Game}_{6.5}$: This game is the same as Game_6 except that the random oracle H is simulated by $\mathsf{H}'_q \circ g$ where $\mathsf{H}'_q : \mathcal{C} \to \mathcal{K}$ is yet another random oracle as in $\mathsf{Game}_{1.2}$ instead of $\mathsf{H}_q \circ g$. If a key pair is accurate, then two games Game_6 and $\mathsf{Game}_{6.5}$ are equal to each other as the two games $\mathsf{Game}_{1.5}$ and Game_2 are equal to each other. We have

$$\Pr[S_6 \wedge \mathsf{Acc}] = \Pr[S_{6.5} \wedge \mathsf{Acc}].$$

Game_7: This game is the same as $\mathsf{Game}_{6.5}$ except that the random oracle $\mathsf{H}(\cdot)$ is set as the original. If a key pair is accurate, then the two games $\mathsf{Game}_{6.5}$ and Game_7 are equal to each other as the two games $\mathsf{Game}_{1.5}$ and Game_1 are equal to each other. We have

$$\Pr[S_{6.5} \wedge \mathsf{Acc}] = \Pr[S_7 \wedge \mathsf{Acc}].$$

According to Lemma 8, for any $p \geq 0$, we have

$$|\Pr[S_7 \wedge \mathsf{Acc}] - p| \leq |\Pr[S_7] - p| + \delta.$$

Game_8: This game is the same as Game_7 except that $\mathsf{H}_q(c)$ in the decapsulation oracle is replaced by $\mathsf{H}_{\mathsf{prf}}(s, c)$.

As we discussed the difference between the two games Game_0 and Game_1, from Lemma 2 we have the bound

$$|\Pr[S_7] - \Pr[S_8]| \leq 2(q_{\mathsf{H}_{\mathsf{prf}}} + q_{\mathrm{DEC}}) \cdot 2^{-\ell/2}.$$

We note that this game is the original game $\mathsf{Expt}^{\mathsf{spr\text{-}cca}}_{\mathsf{KEM},\mathcal{A}}(\kappa)$ with $b = 1$. Thus, we have

$$\Pr[S_8] = \Pr[\mathsf{Expt}^{\mathsf{spr\text{-}cca}}_{\mathsf{KEM},\mathcal{A}}(\kappa) = 1 \mid b = 1].$$

Summing those (in)equalities, we obtain the following bound:

$$\mathsf{Adv}^{\mathsf{spr\text{-}cca}}_{\mathsf{KEM},\mathcal{A}}(\kappa) = |\Pr[S_0] - \Pr[S_8]| \leq \sum_{i=0}^{7} |\Pr[S_i] - \Pr[S_{i+1}]|$$
$$\leq \mathsf{Adv}^{\mathsf{ds\text{-}ind}}_{\mathsf{PKE},\mathcal{D}_\mathcal{M},\mathcal{S},\mathcal{A}_{34}}(\kappa) + \mathsf{Disj}_{\mathsf{PKE},\mathcal{S}}(\kappa)$$
$$+ 4(q_{\mathsf{H}_{\mathsf{prf}}} + q_{\mathrm{DEC}}) \cdot 2^{-\ell/2} + 4\delta.$$

Table 4. Summary of games for the proof of Theorem 9: '$\mathcal{S}(1^\kappa) \setminus \mathsf{Enc}(ek, \mathcal{M})$' implies that the challenger generates $c^* \leftarrow \mathcal{S}(1^\kappa)$ and returns $\perp$ if $c^* \in \mathsf{Enc}(ek, \mathcal{M})$.

			Decapsulation		
Game	c^*	K^*	valid c	invalid c	Justification
Game$_0$	$\mathcal{S}(1^\kappa)$	random	$\mathsf{H}(\mu)$	$\mathsf{H}_{\mathsf{prf}}(s, c)$	
Game$_1$	$\mathcal{S}(1^\kappa) \setminus \mathsf{Enc}(ek, \mathcal{M})$	random	$\mathsf{H}(\mu)$	$\mathsf{H}_{\mathsf{prf}}(s, c)$	statistical disjointness
Game$_2$	$\mathcal{S}(1^\kappa) \setminus \mathsf{Enc}(ek, \mathcal{M})$	random	$\mathsf{H}(\mu)$	$\mathsf{H}_q(c)$	Lemma 2
Game$_3$	$\mathcal{S}(1^\kappa) \setminus \mathsf{Enc}(ek, \mathcal{M})$	$\mathsf{H}_q(c^*)$	$\mathsf{H}(\mu)$	$\mathsf{H}_q(c)$	$\mathsf{H}_q(c^*)$ is hidden
Game$_4$	$\mathcal{S}(1^\kappa) \setminus \mathsf{Enc}(ek, \mathcal{M})$	$\mathsf{H}_{\mathsf{prf}}(s, c^*)$	$\mathsf{H}(\mu)$	$\mathsf{H}_{\mathsf{prf}}(s, c)$	Lemma 2
Game$_5$	$\mathcal{S}(1^\kappa) \setminus \mathsf{Enc}(ek, \mathcal{M})$	$\overline{\mathsf{Dec}}(dk, c^*)$	$\mathsf{H}(\mu)$	$\mathsf{H}_{\mathsf{prf}}(s, c)$	re-encryption check
Game$_6$	$\mathcal{S}(1^\kappa)$	$\overline{\mathsf{Dec}}(dk, c^*)$	$\mathsf{H}(\mu)$	$\mathsf{H}_{\mathsf{prf}}(s, c)$	statistical disjointness

4.2 SSMT-CCA Security

Theorem 9. *Suppose that a ciphertext space $\mathcal{C}$ of* PKE *depends on the public parameter only. If* PKE *is strongly disjoint-simulatable, then* KEM $=$ SXY[PKE, H, $\mathsf{H}_{\mathsf{prf}}$] *is SSMT-CCA-secure.*

Formally speaking, for any adversary $\mathcal{A}$ against SSMT-CCA security of KEM *issuing at most $q_{\mathsf{H}_{\mathsf{prf}}}$ and q_{DEC} queries to $\mathsf{H}_{\mathsf{prf}}$ and DEC, we have*

$$\mathsf{Adv}^{\mathsf{ssmt\text{-}cca}}_{\mathsf{KEM}, \mathcal{S}, \mathcal{A}}(\kappa) \leq 2\mathsf{Disj}_{\mathsf{PKE}, \mathcal{S}}(\kappa) + 4(q_{\mathsf{H}_{\mathsf{prf}}} + q_{\mathrm{DEC}}) \cdot 2^{-\ell/2}.$$

We note that this security proof is unrelated to PKE is deterministic PKE or one derandomized by T.

Proof: We use the game-hopping proof. We consider Game$_i$ for $i = 0, \ldots, 6$. We summarize those games in Table 4. Let S_i denote the event that the adversary outputs $b' = 1$ in game Game$_i$.

Game$_0$: This game is the original game $\mathsf{Expt}^{\mathsf{ssmt\text{-}cca}}_{\mathsf{KEM}, \mathcal{S}, \mathcal{A}}(\kappa)$ with $b = 0$. The challenge is generated as $c^* \leftarrow \mathcal{S}(1^\kappa)$ and $K_0^* \leftarrow \mathcal{K}$. We have

$$\Pr[S_0] = 1 - \Pr[\mathsf{Expt}^{\mathsf{ssmt\text{-}cca}}_{\mathsf{KEM}, \mathcal{S}, \mathcal{A}}(\kappa) = 1 \mid b = 0].$$

Game$_1$: In this game, the challenge ciphertext is set as $\perp$ if c^* is in $\mathsf{Enc}(ek, \mathcal{M})$. Since the difference between two games Game$_0$ and Game$_1$ is bounded by statistical disjointness, we have

$$|\Pr[S_0] - \Pr[S_1]| \leq \mathsf{Disj}_{\mathsf{PKE}, \mathcal{S}}(\kappa).$$

Game$_2$: This game is the same as Game$_1$ except that $\mathsf{H}_{\mathsf{prf}}(s, c)$ in the decapsulation oracle is replace with $\mathsf{H}_q(c)$ where $\mathsf{H}_q : \mathcal{C} \to \mathcal{K}$ is another random oracle.

As in [47, Lemmas 4.1], from Lemma 2 we have the bound

$$|\Pr[S_1] - \Pr[S_2]| \leq 2(q_{\mathsf{H}_{\mathsf{prf}}} + q_{\mathrm{DEC}}) \cdot 2^{-\ell/2}.$$

Game$_3$: This game is the same as Game$_2$ except that K^* is set as $\mathsf{H}_q(c^*)$ instead of chosen randomly. Since c^* is always outside of $\mathsf{Enc}(ek, \mathcal{M})$, $\mathcal{A}$ cannot obtain any information about $\mathsf{H}_q(c^*)$. Hence, the two games Game$_2$ and Game$_3$ are equivalent and we have

$$\Pr[S_2] = \Pr[S_3].$$

Game$_4$: This game is the same as Game$_3$ except that $\mathsf{H}_q(\cdot)$ is replaced by $\mathsf{H}_{\mathsf{prf}}(s, \cdot)$. As in [47, Lemmas 4.1], from Lemma 2 we have the bound

$$|\Pr[S_3] - \Pr[S_4]| \leq 2(q_{\mathsf{H}_{\mathsf{prf}}} + q_{\mathrm{DEC}}) \cdot 2^{-\ell/2}.$$

Game$_5$: This game is the same as Game$_4$ except that K^* is set as $\overline{\mathsf{Dec}}(dk, c^*)$ instead of $\mathsf{H}_{\mathsf{prf}}(s, c^*)$. Recall that c^* is always in *outside* of $\mathsf{Enc}(ek, \mathcal{M})$. Thus, we always have $\mathsf{Dec}(c^*) = \bot$ or $\mathsf{Enc}(ek, \mathsf{Dec}(c^*)) \neq c^*$ and, thus, $K^* = \mathsf{H}_{\mathsf{prf}}(s, c^*)$ in Game$_5$. Hence, the two games are equivalent and we have

$$\Pr[S_4] = \Pr[S_5].$$

Game$_6$: We finally replace the way to compute c^*: In this game, the ciphertext is chosen by $\mathcal{S}(1^\kappa)$ as in Game$_0$. Again, since the difference between two games Game$_5$ and Game$_6$ is bounded by statistical disjointness, we have

$$|\Pr[S_5] - \Pr[S_6]| \leq \mathsf{Disj}_{\mathsf{PKE}, \mathcal{S}}(\kappa).$$

Moreover, this game Game$_6$ is the original game $\mathsf{Expt}^{\mathsf{ssmt\text{-}cca}}_{\mathsf{KEM}, \mathcal{S}, \mathcal{A}}(\kappa)$ with $b = 1$ and we have

$$\Pr[S_6] = \Pr[\mathsf{Expt}^{\mathsf{ssmt\text{-}cca}}_{\mathsf{KEM}, \mathcal{S}, \mathcal{A}}(\kappa) = 1 \mid b = 1].$$

Summing those (in)equalities, we obtain Theorem 9:

$$\mathsf{Adv}^{\mathsf{ssmt\text{-}cca}}_{\mathsf{KEM}, \mathcal{S}, \mathcal{A}}(\kappa) = |\Pr[S_0] - \Pr[S_6]|$$
$$\leq 2\mathsf{Disj}_{\mathsf{PKE}, \mathcal{S}}(\kappa) + 4(q_{\mathsf{H}_{\mathsf{prf}}} + q_{\mathrm{DEC}}) \cdot 2^{-\ell/2}.$$

4.3   SCFR-CCA Security

Theorem 10. *If* PKE *is XCFR-secure or SCFR-CCA-secure, then* KEM $=$ SXY[PKE, H, $\mathsf{H}_{\mathsf{prf}}$] *is SCFR-CCA-secure in the QROM.*

Proof. Suppose that an adversary against KEM's SCFR-CCA security outputs a ciphertext c which is decapsulated into $K \neq \bot$ by both $\overline{dk}_0$ and $\overline{dk}_1$, that is, $K = \overline{\mathsf{Dec}}(\overline{dk}_0, c) = \overline{\mathsf{Dec}}(\overline{dk}_1, c) \neq \bot$. For $i \in \{0, 1\}$, we define μ'_i as an internal decryption result under dk_i, that is, $\mu'_i = \mathsf{Dec}(dk_i, c)$. For $i \in \{0, 1\}$, we also define $\mu_i := \mu'_i$ if $c = \mathsf{Enc}(ek_i, \mu'_i)$ and $\mu_i := \bot$ otherwise.

We have five cases classified as follows:

- Case 1 ($\mu_0 = \mu_1 \neq \bot$): This $\mu_0 = \mu_1 \neq \bot$ violates the XCFR security (or the SCFR-CCA security) of the underlying PKE and it is easy to make a reduction.

- Case 2 ($\bot \neq \mu_0 \neq \mu_1 \neq \bot$): In this case, the decapsulation algorithm outputs $K = \mathsf{H}(\mu_0) = \mathsf{H}(\mu_1)$. Thus, we succeed to find a collision for H, which is negligible for any QPT adversary (Lemma 3).
- Case 3 ($\mu_0 = \bot$ and $\mu_1 \neq \bot$): In this case, the decapsulation algorithm outputs $K = \mathsf{H}_{\mathsf{prf}}(s_0, c) = \mathsf{H}(\mu_1)$ and we find a claw $((s_0, c), \mu_1)$ of $\mathsf{H}_{\mathsf{prf}}$ and H. The probability that we find such claw is negligible for any QPT adversary (Lemma 4).
- Case 4 ($\mu_0 \neq \bot$ and $\mu_1 = \bot$): In this case, the decapsulation algorithm outputs $K = \mathsf{H}(\mu_0) = \mathsf{H}_{\mathsf{prf}}(s_1, c)$ and we find a claw $(\mu_0, (s_1, c))$ of H and $\mathsf{H}_{\mathsf{prf}}$. The probability that we find such claw is negligible for any QPT adversary (Lemma 4).
- Case 5 (The other cases): In this case, we find a collision $((s_0, c), (s_1, c))$ of $\mathsf{H}_{\mathsf{prf}}$, which is indeed collision if $s_0 \neq s_1$ which occurs with probability at lease $1 - 1/2^\ell$. The probability that we find such collision is negligible for any QPT adversary (Lemma 3).

We conclude that the advantage of the adversary is negligible in any case.   □

5   NTRU

We briefly review NTRU [14] in Subsect. 5.1, discuss the security properties of the underlying PKE, NTRU-DPKE, in Subsect. 5.2, and discuss the security properties of NTRU in Subsect. 5.3. We want to show that, under appropriate assumptions, NTRU is ANON-CCA-secure in the QROM, and NTRU leads to ANON-CCA-secure and SROB-CCA-secure hybrid PKE in the QROM. In order to do so, we show that the underlying NTRU-DPKE of NTRU is strongly disjoint-simulatable under the modified DSPR and PLWE assumptions and XCFR-secure in Subsect. 5.2. Since NTRU is obtained by applying SXY to NTRU-DPKE, the former implies that NTRU is SPR-CCA-secure and SSMT-CCA-secure in the QROM under those assumptions and the latter implies that NTRU is SCFR-CCA-secure in the QROM. Those three properties lead to the anonymity of NTRU and hybrid PKE in the QROM as we wanted.

5.1   Review of NTRU

Preliminaries: Φ_1 denotes the polynomial $x-1$ and Φ_n denotes $(x^n - 1)/(x - 1) = x^{n-1} + x^{n-2} + \cdots + 1$. We have $x^n - 1 = \Phi_1 \Phi_n$. R, $R/3$, and R/q denotes $\mathbb{Z}[x]/(\Phi_1 \Phi_n)$, $\mathbb{Z}[x]/(3, \Phi_1 \Phi_n)$, and $\mathbb{Z}[x]/(q, \Phi_1 \Phi_n)$, respectively. S, $S/3$, and S/q denotes $\mathbb{Z}[x]/(\Phi_n)$, $\mathbb{Z}[x]/(3, \Phi_n)$, and $\mathbb{Z}[x]/(q, \Phi_n)$, respectively.

We say a polynomial *ternary* if its coefficients are in $\{-1, 0, +1\}$. $\underline{\mathsf{S3}}(a)$ returns a canonical $S/3$-representative of $z \in \mathbb{Z}[x]$, that is, $b \in \mathbb{Z}[x]$ of degree at most $n-2$ with ternary coefficients in $\{-1, 0, +1\}$ such that $a \equiv b \pmod{(3, \Phi_n)}$. Let $\mathcal{T}$ be a set of non-zero ternary polynomials of degree at most $n - 2$, that is, $\mathcal{T} = \{a = \sum_{i=0}^{n-2} a_i x^i : a \neq 0 \wedge a_i \in \{-1, 0, +1\}\}$. We say a ternary polynomial $v = \sum_i v_i x^i$ has the *non-negative correlation* property if

$\sum_i v_i v_{i+1} \geq 0$. $\mathcal{T}_+$ is a set of non-zero ternary polynomials of degree at most $n - 2$ with *non-negative correlation* property. $\mathcal{T}(d)$ is a set of non-zero balanced ternary polynomials of degree at most $n - 2$ with Hamming weight d, that is, $\{a \in \mathcal{T} : |\{a_i : a_i = 1\}| = |\{a_i : a_i = -1\}| = d/2\}$.

The following lemma is due to Schanck [41]. (See, e.g., [14] for this design choice.)

Gen(1^κ)	Enc($h, (r, m) \in \mathcal{L}_r \times \mathcal{L}_m$)	Dec($(f, f_p, h_q), c$)
$(f, g) \leftarrow$ Sample_fg()	$\mu' := \text{Lift}(m)$	if $c \not\equiv 0 \bmod (q, \Phi_1)$
$f_q := (1/f) \in S/q$	$c := (h \cdot r + \mu') \in R/q$	then return $(0, 0, 1)$
$h := (3 \cdot g \cdot f_q) \in R/q$	return c	$a := (c \cdot f) \in R/q$
$h_q := (1/h) \in S/q$		$m := (a \cdot f_p) \in S/3$
$f_p := (1/f) \in S/3$		$\mu' := \text{Lift}(m)$
$ek := h, dk := (f, f_p, h_q)$		$r := ((c - \mu') \cdot h_q) \in S/q$
return (ek, dk)		if $(r, m) \in \mathcal{L}_r \times \mathcal{L}_m$
		then return $(r, m, 0)$
		else return $(0, 0, 1)$

Fig. 6. NTRU-DPKE

Lemma 5. *Suppose that* $(n, q) = (509, 2048)$, $(677, 2048)$, $(821, 4096)$, *or* $(701, 8192)$, *which are the parameter sets in NTRU. If* $r \in \mathcal{T}$, *then* r *has an inverse in* S/q.

Proof. Φ_n is irreducible over $\mathbb{F}_2$ if and only if n is prime and 2 is primitive element in $\mathbb{F}_n^\times$ (See e.g., Cohen et al. [15]). The conditions are satisfied for all $n = 509$, 677, 701, and 821. Hence, $\mathbb{Z}[x]/(2, \Phi_n)$ is a finite field and every polynomial r in $\mathcal{T}$ has an inverse in $\mathbb{Z}[x]/(2, \Phi_n)$. Such r is also invertible in $S/q = \mathbb{Z}[x]/(q, \Phi_n)$ with $q = 2^k$ for some k and, indeed, one can find it using the Newton method or the Hensel lifting. $\square$

NTRU: NTRU involves four subsets $\mathcal{L}_f, \mathcal{L}_g, \mathcal{L}_r, \mathcal{L}_m$ of R. It uses $\text{Lift}(m)$: $\mathcal{L}_m \rightarrow R$. NTRU has two types of parameter sets, NTRU-HPS and NTRU-HRSS, specified as later.

- NTRU-HPS: The parameters are defined as follows: $\mathcal{L}_f = \mathcal{T}, \mathcal{L}_g = \mathcal{T}(q/8 - 2), \mathcal{L}_r = \mathcal{T}, \mathcal{L}_m = \mathcal{T}(q/8 - 2)$, and $\text{Lift}(m) = m$.
- NTRU-HRSS: The parameters are defined as follows: $\mathcal{L}_f = \mathcal{T}_+, \mathcal{L}_g = \{\Phi_1 \cdot v \mid v \in \mathcal{T}_+\}, \mathcal{L}_r = \mathcal{T}, \mathcal{L}_m = \mathcal{T}$, and $\text{Lift}(m) = \Phi_1 \cdot \underline{\text{S3}}(m/\Phi_1)$.

It uses Sample_fg() to sample f and g from $\mathcal{L}_f$ and $\mathcal{L}_g$. NTRU also uses Sample_rm() to sample r and m from $\mathcal{L}_r$ and $\mathcal{L}_m$.

The underlying DPKE of NTRU, which we call NTRU-DPKE, is defined as Fig. 6. We note that, for an encryption key h, we have $h \equiv 0 \pmod{(q, \Phi_1)}$, h is invertible in S/q, and $hr + m \equiv 0 \pmod{(q, \Phi_1)}$. (See [14, Section 2.3].)

NTRU then apply SXY to NTRU-DPKE in order to obtain IND-CCA-secure KEM as in Fig. 7, where $\mathsf{H} = \mathsf{SHA3\text{-}256}$ and $\mathsf{H_{prf}} = \mathsf{SHA3\text{-}256}$. Since the lengths of their input space differ, we can treat them as different random oracles.

Rigidity: NTRU uses SXY, while its KEM version (Fig. 7) seems to lack the re-encryption check. We note that NTRU implicitly checks $hr + \mathsf{Lift}(m) = c$ by checking if $(r, m) \in \mathcal{L}_r \times \mathcal{L}_m$ in NTRU-DPKE (Fig. 6). See [14] for the details.

$\overline{\mathsf{Gen}}(1^\kappa)$	$\overline{\mathsf{Enc}}(ek = h)$	$\overline{\mathsf{Dec}}(\overline{dk} = (dk, s), c)$
$(ek, dk) \leftarrow \mathsf{Gen}(1^\kappa)$	$\mathrm{coins} \leftarrow \{0,1\}^{256}$	$(r, m, \mathsf{fail}) := \mathsf{Dec}(dk, c)$
$s \leftarrow \{0,1\}^{256}$	$(r, m) \leftarrow \mathsf{Sample\_rm}(\mathrm{coins})$	$k_1 := \mathsf{H}(r, m)$
$\overline{dk} := (dk, s)$	$c := \mathsf{Enc}(h, (r, m))$	$k_2 := \mathsf{H_{prf}}(s, c)$
$\mathbf{return}\ (ek, \overline{dk})$	$K := \mathsf{H}(r, m)$	$\mathbf{if}\ \mathsf{fail} = 0\ \mathbf{then\ return}\ k_1$
	$\mathbf{return}\ (c, K)$	$\mathbf{else\ return}\ k_2$

Fig. 7. NTRU

5.2 Properties of NTRU-DPKE

We show that NTRU-DPKE is strongly disjoint-simulatable and XCFR-secure.

We have known that the generalized NTRU PKE is pseudorandom [44] and disjointly simulatable [39] if the decisional small polynomial ratio (DSPR) assumption [34] and the polynomial learning with errors (PLWE) assumption [35,45] hold. See [39, Section 3.3 of the ePrint version.].

Let us adapt their arguments to NTRU-DPKE. We modify the DSPR and the PLWE assumptions as follows:

Definition 14. *Fix the parameter set. Define $R' := \{c \in R/q : c \equiv 0 \pmod{(q, \Phi_1)}\}$, which is efficiently sampleable.*

- *The modified DSPR assumption: It is computationally hard to distinguish $h := 3 \cdot g \cdot f_q \pmod{q, \Phi_1 \Phi_n}$ from h', where $(f, g) \leftarrow \mathsf{Sample\_fg}()$, $f_q \leftarrow (1/f) \bmod (q, \Phi_n)$, and $h' \leftarrow R'$.*
- *The modified PLWE assumption: It is computationally hard to distinguish $(h, hr + \mathsf{Lift}(m) \pmod{q, \Phi_1 \Phi_n})$ from (h, c') with $h, c' \leftarrow R'$ and $(r, m) \leftarrow \mathsf{Sample\_rm}()$.*

We can show NTRU-DPKE is strongly disjoint-simulatable under those two assumptions:

Lemma 6. *Suppose that the modified DSPR and PLWE assumptions hold. Then, NTRU-DPKE is strongly disjoint-simulatable with a simulator $\mathcal{S}$ that outputs a random polynomial chosen from R'.*

Proof. The proof for ciphertext-indistinguishability is obtained by modifying the proof in [39]. We want to show that $(h, c = hr + \mathsf{Lift}(m) \bmod (q, \Phi_1\Phi_n)) \approx_c (h, c')$, where $h = 3gf_q \bmod (q, \Phi_1\Phi_n)$ and $f_q = (1/f) \bmod (q, \Phi_n)$ with $(f, g) \leftarrow \mathsf{Sample\_fg}()$, $(r, m) \leftarrow \mathsf{Sample\_rm}()$, and $c' \leftarrow R'$.

- We first replace h with $h' \leftarrow R'$, which is justified by the modified DSPR assumption.
- We next replace $c = h'r + \mathsf{Lift}(m) \bmod (q, \Phi_1\Phi_n)$ with $c' \leftarrow R'$, which is justified by the modified PLWE assumption.
- We then go backward by replacing random h' with h, which is is justified by the modified DSPR assumption again.

Statistical disjointness follows from the fact that $|R'| = q^{n-1} \gg 3^{2n} = |\mathcal{T} \times \mathcal{T}| \geq |\mathcal{L}_m \times \mathcal{L}_r| \geq |\mathsf{Enc}(h, \mathcal{L}_m \times \mathcal{L}_r)|$. Since R' is independent of an encryption key h, NTRU-DPKE is strong disjoint-simulatability. □

We next show the XCFR security of NTRU-DPKE.

Lemma 7. *NTRU-DPKE is XCFR-secure.*

Proof. Suppose that the adversary wins with its output c on input ek_0, dk_0, ek_1, and dk_1, where $ek_i = h_i$ for $i \in \{0, 1\}$. Let us define $\mu_0 = \mathsf{Dec}(dk_0, c)$ and $\mu_1 = \mathsf{Dec}(dk_1, c)$.

If the adversary wins, we can assume $\mu_0 = \mu_1 = (r, m, 0) \in \mathcal{L}_r \times \mathcal{L}_m \times \{0, 1\}$. Otherwise, that is, if $\mu_0 = \mu_1 = (0, 0, 1)$, then the output is treated as $\perp$ and the adversary loses.

Moreover, because of the check in the decryption, we have $c \equiv h_0 \cdot r + \mathsf{Lift}(m) \equiv h_1 \cdot r + \mathsf{Lift}(m) \pmod{q, \Phi_1\Phi_n}$, which implies $r(h_0 - h_1) \equiv 0 \pmod{(q, \Phi_n)}$. On the other hand, according to Lemma 5, for any $r \in \mathcal{L}_r = \mathcal{T}$, we have $r \neq 0 \in S/q$ In addition, we have $h_0 \equiv h_1 \in S/q$ with negligible probability. Thus, all but negligible choices of h_0 and h_1, any $r \in \mathcal{L}_r = \mathcal{T}$ results in $r(h_0 - h_1) \not\equiv 0 \pmod{(q, \Phi_n)}$ and $h_0 \cdot r + \mathsf{Lift}(m) \not\equiv h_1 \cdot r + \mathsf{Lift}(m) \pmod{q, \Phi_1\Phi_n}$. Hence, the probability that the adversary wins is negligible, concluding the proof. □

5.3 Properties of NTRU

Combining NTRU-DPKE's strong disjoint-simulatability and XCFR security with previous theorems on SXY, we obtain the following theorems.

Theorem 11. *Suppose that the modified DSPR and PLWE assumptions hold. Then, NTRU is SPR-CCA-secure and SSMT-CCA-secure in the QROM.*

Proof. Under the modified DSPR and PLWE assumptions, NTRU-DPKE is strongly disjoint-simulatable (Lemma 6). In addition, NTRU-DPKE is perfectly correct. Applying Theorem 8 and Theorem 9, we obtain the theorem. □

Theorem 12. *NTRU is SCFR-CCA-secure in the QROM.*

Proof. NTRU-DPKE is XCFR-secure (Lemma 7). Applying Theorem 10, we have that NTRU is SCFR-CCA-secure in the QROM. □

Theorem 13. *Under the modified DSPR and PLWE assumptions, NTRU is ANON-CCA-secure in the QROM.*

Proof. Due to Theorem 11, under the modified DSPR and PLWE assumptions, NTRU is SPR-CCA-secure in the QROM. Thus, applying Theorem 1, we have that, under those assumptions, NTRU is ANON-CCA-secure in the QROM. □

Theorem 14. *Under the modified DSPR and PLWE assumptions, NTRU leads to ANON-CCA-secure and SROB-CCA-secure hybrid PKE in the QROM, combined with SPR-oTCCA-secure and FROB-secure DEM.*

Proof. Due to Theorem 11, under the modified DSPR and PLWE assumptions, NTRU is SPR-CCA-secure and SSMT-CCA-secure in the QROM. Moreover, NTRU is perfectly correct. Thus, combining NTRU with SPR-oTCCA-secure DEM, we obtain a SPR-CCA-secure hybrid PKE in the QROM (Theorem 7). Moreover, NTRU is SCFR-CCA-secure in the QROM (Theorem 12). Thus, if DEM is FROB-secure, then the hybrid PKE is SROB-CCA-secure (Theorem 3). □

Acknowledgement. The author is grateful to John Schanck for insightful comments and suggestions on NTRU, Akinori Hosoyamada and Takashi Yamakawa for insightful comments and discussion on quantum random oracles. The author would like to thank Daniel J. Bernstein for insightful comments and discussion on the indifferentiability of the quantum random oracles. The author would like to thank anonymous reviewers for their valuable comments and suggestions on this paper.

A   Missing Lemma

Lemma 8. *Let* A *and* B *denote events. Suppose that we have* $\Pr[A] \leq \delta$. *For any* $p \geq 0$, *we have*

$$|\Pr[B] - p| \leq |\Pr[B \wedge \neg A] - p| + \delta \quad and \quad |\Pr[B \wedge \neg A] - p| \leq |\Pr[B] - p| + \delta.$$

Proof. Those bounds are obtained by using the triangle inequality. We have

$$|\Pr[B] - p| = |\Pr[B \wedge A] + \Pr[B \wedge \neg A] - p| \leq \Pr[B \wedge A] + |\Pr[B \wedge \neg A] - p|$$
$$\leq \Pr[A] + |\Pr[B \wedge \neg A] - p| \leq |\Pr[B \wedge \neg A] - p| + \delta$$

and

$$|\Pr[B \wedge \neg A] - p| = |\Pr[B \wedge \neg A] + \Pr[B \wedge A] - \Pr[B \wedge A] - p|$$
$$= |\Pr[B] - p - \Pr[B \wedge A]| \leq |\Pr[B] - p| + \Pr[B \wedge A]$$
$$\leq |\Pr[B] - p| + \Pr[A] \leq |\Pr[B] - p| + \delta$$

as we wanted. □

References

1. Abdalla, M., et al.: Searchable encryption revisited: consistency properties, relation to anonymous IBE, and extensions. In: Shoup, V. (ed.) CRYPTO 2005. LNCS, vol. 3621, pp. 205–222. Springer, Heidelberg (2005). https://doi.org/10.1007/11535218_13
2. Abdalla, M., Bellare, M., Neven, G.: Robust encryption. In: Micciancio, D. (ed.) TCC 2010. LNCS, vol. 5978, pp. 480–497. Springer, Heidelberg (2010). https://doi.org/10.1007/978-3-642-11799-2_28
3. Abe, M. (ed.): ASIACRYPT 2010. LNCS, vol. 6477. Springer, Heidelberg (2010). https://doi.org/10.1007/978-3-642-17373-8
4. Aguilar Melchor, C., et al.: HQC. Technical report, National Institute of Standards and Technology (2020). https://csrc.nist.gov/projects/post-quantum-cryptography/round-3-submissions
5. Albrecht, M.R., et al.: Classic McEliece. Technical report, National Institute of Standards and Technology (2020). https://csrc.nist.gov/projects/post-quantum-cryptography/round-3-submissions
6. Aragon, N., et al.: BIKE. Technical report, National Institute of Standards and Technology (2020). https://csrc.nist.gov/projects/post-quantum-cryptography/round-3-submissions
7. Bellare, M., Boldyreva, A., Desai, A., Pointcheval, D.: Key-privacy in public-key encryption. In: Boyd, C. (ed.) ASIACRYPT 2001. LNCS, vol. 2248, pp. 566–582. Springer, Heidelberg (2001). https://doi.org/10.1007/3-540-45682-1_33
8. Bellare, M., Desai, A., Pointcheval, D., Rogaway, P.: Relations among notions of security for public-key encryption schemes. In: Krawczyk, H. (ed.) CRYPTO 1998. LNCS, vol. 1462, pp. 26–45. Springer, Heidelberg (1998). https://doi.org/10.1007/BFb0055718
9. Bernstein, D.J.: Personal communication (October 2021)
10. Bernstein, D.J., et al.: NTRU Prime. Technical report, National Institute of Standards and Technology (2020). https://csrc.nist.gov/projects/post-quantum-cryptography/round-3-submissions
11. Boneh, D., Dagdelen, Ö., Fischlin, M., Lehmann, A., Schaffner, C., Zhandry, M.: Random oracles in a quantum world. In: Lee, D.H., Wang, X. (eds.) ASIACRYPT 2011. LNCS, vol. 7073, pp. 41–69. Springer, Heidelberg (2011). https://doi.org/10.1007/978-3-642-25385-0_3
12. Boyd, C., Cliff, Y., González Nieto, J.M., Paterson, K.G.: One-round key exchange in the standard model. Int. J. Appl. Cryptogr. 1(3), 181–199 (2009). https://doi.org/10.1504/IJACT.2009.023466
13. Camenisch, J., Lysyanskaya, A.: An efficient system for non-transferable anonymous credentials with optional anonymity revocation. In: Pfitzmann, B. (ed.) EUROCRYPT 2001. LNCS, vol. 2045, pp. 93–118. Springer, Heidelberg (2001). https://doi.org/10.1007/3-540-44987-6_7
14. Chen, C., et al.: NTRU. Technical report, National Institute of Standards and Technology (2020). https://csrc.nist.gov/projects/post-quantum-cryptography/round-3-submissions
15. Cohen, H., et al.: Handbook of elliptic and hyperelliptic curve cryptography (2005)
16. Cramer, R., Shoup, V.: Universal hash proofs and a paradigm for adaptive chosen ciphertext secure public-key encryption. In: Knudsen, L.R. (ed.) EUROCRYPT 2002. LNCS, vol. 2332, pp. 45–64. Springer, Heidelberg (2002). https://doi.org/10.1007/3-540-46035-7_4

17. Cramer, R., Shoup, V.: Design and analysis of practical public-key encryption schemes secure against adaptive chosen ciphertext attack. SIAM J. Comput. **33**(1), 167–226 (2003)
18. D'Anvers, J.P., et al.: SABER. Technical report, National Institute of Standards and Technology (2020). https://csrc.nist.gov/projects/post-quantum-cryptography/round-3-submissions
19. Farshim, P., Orlandi, C., Roşie, R.: Security of symmetric primitives under incorrect usage of keys. IACR Trans. Symmetric Cryptol. **2017**(1), 449–473 (2017). https://doi.org/10.13154/tosc.v2017.i1.449-473
20. Fujioka, A., Suzuki, K., Xagawa, K., Yoneyama, K.: Practical and post-quantum authenticated key exchange from one-way secure key encapsulation mechanism. In: Chen, K., Xie, Q., Qiu, W., Li, N., Tzeng, W.G. (eds.) ASIACCS 2013, pp. 83–94. ACM Press (May 2013)
21. Fujioka, A., Suzuki, K., Xagawa, K., Yoneyama, K.: Strongly secure authenticated key exchange from factoring, codes, and lattices. Des. Codes Cryptogr. **76**(3), 469–504 (2015). https://doi.org/10.1007/s10623-014-9972-2
22. Fujisaki, E., Okamoto, T.: Secure integration of asymmetric and symmetric encryption schemes. In: Wiener, M. (ed.) CRYPTO 1999. LNCS, vol. 1666, pp. 537–554. Springer, Heidelberg (1999). https://doi.org/10.1007/3-540-48405-1_34
23. Fujisaki, E., Okamoto, T.: Secure integration of asymmetric and symmetric encryption schemes. J. Cryptol. **26**(1), 80–101 (2011). https://doi.org/10.1007/s00145-011-9114-1
24. Grubbs, P., Maram, V., Paterson, K.G.: Anonymous, robust post-quantum public key encryption. Cryptology ePrint Archive, Report 2021/708 (2021). https://eprint.iacr.org/2021/708. To appear in EUROCRYPT 2022
25. Grubbs, P., Maram, V., Paterson, K.G.: Anonymous, robust post-quantum public key encryption (presentation slides). In: Proceedings of the Third NIST PQC Standardization Conference (2021). https://csrc.nist.gov/Presentations/2021/anonymous-robust-post-quantum-public-key-encryptio
26. Hofheinz, D., Hövelmanns, K., Kiltz, E.: A modular analysis of the Fujisaki-Okamoto transformation. In: Kalai, Y., Reyzin, L. (eds.) TCC 2017, Part I. LNCS, vol. 10677, pp. 341–371. Springer, Cham (2017). https://doi.org/10.1007/978-3-319-70500-2_12
27. Hopper, N.: On steganographic chosen covertext security. In: Caires, L., Italiano, G.F., Monteiro, L., Palamidessi, C., Yung, M. (eds.) ICALP 2005. LNCS, vol. 3580, pp. 311–323. Springer, Heidelberg (2005). https://doi.org/10.1007/11523468_26
28. Hosoyamada, A.: Personal communication (June 2021)
29. Hövelmanns, K., Kiltz, E., Schäge, S., Unruh, D.: Generic authenticated key exchange in the quantum random oracle model. In: Kiayias, A., Kohlweiss, M., Wallden, P., Zikas, V. (eds.) PKC 2020, Part II. LNCS, vol. 12111, pp. 389–422. Springer, Cham (2020). https://doi.org/10.1007/978-3-030-45388-6_14
30. Jao, D., et al.: SIKE. Technical report, National Institute of Standards and Technology (2020). https://csrc.nist.gov/projects/post-quantum-cryptography/round-3-submissions
31. Jiang, H., Zhang, Z., Chen, L., Wang, H., Ma, Z.: IND-CCA-secure key encapsulation mechanism in the quantum random oracle model, revisited. In: Shacham, H., Boldyreva, A. (eds.) CRYPTO 2018, Part III. LNCS, vol. 10993, pp. 96–125. Springer, Cham (2018). https://doi.org/10.1007/978-3-319-96878-0_4

32. Jiang, H., Zhang, Z., Ma, Z.: Key encapsulation mechanism with explicit rejection in the quantum random oracle model. In: Lin, D., Sako, K. (eds.) PKC 2019, Part II. LNCS, vol. 11443, pp. 618–645. Springer, Cham (2019). https://doi.org/10. 1007/978-3-030-17259-6_21

33. Liu, X., Wang, M.: QCCA-secure generic key encapsulation mechanism with tighter security in the quantum random oracle model. In: Garay, J.A. (ed.) PKC 2021, Part I. LNCS, vol. 12710, pp. 3–26. Springer, Cham (2021). https://doi.org/10.1007/ 978-3-030-75245-3_1

34. López-Alt, A., Tromer, E., Vaikuntanathan, V.: On-the-fly multiparty computation on the cloud via multikey fully homomorphic encryption. In: Karloff, H.J., Pitassi, T. (eds.) 44th ACM STOC, pp. 1219–1234. ACM Press (May 2012). https://doi. org/10.1145/2213977.2214086

35. Lyubashevsky, V., Peikert, C., Regev, O.: On ideal lattices and learning with errors over rings. In: Gilbert, H. (ed.) EUROCRYPT 2010. LNCS, vol. 6110, pp. 1–23. Springer, Heidelberg (2010). https://doi.org/10.1007/978-3-642-13190-5_1

36. Mohassel, P.: A closer look at anonymity and robustness in encryption schemes. In: Abe [3], pp. 501–518

37. Naehrig, M., et al.: FrodoKEM. Technical report, National Institute of Standards and Technology (2020). https://csrc.nist.gov/projects/post-quantum-cryptography/round-3-submissions

38. Rackoff, C., Simon, D.R.: Non-interactive zero-knowledge proof of knowledge and chosen ciphertext attack. In: Feigenbaum, J. (ed.) CRYPTO 1991. LNCS, vol. 576, pp. 433–444. Springer, Heidelberg (1992). https://doi.org/10.1007/3-540-46766-1_35

39. Saito, T., Xagawa, K., Yamakawa, T.: Tightly-secure key-encapsulation mechanism in the quantum random oracle model. In: Nielsen, J.B., Rijmen, V. (eds.) EUROCRYPT 2018, Part III. LNCS, vol. 10822, pp. 520–551. Springer, Cham (2018). https://doi.org/10.1007/978-3-319-78372-7_17

40. Sako, K.: An auction protocol which hides bids of losers. In: Imai, H., Zheng, Y. (eds.) PKC 2000. LNCS, vol. 1751, pp. 422–432. Springer, Heidelberg (2000). https://doi.org/10.1007/978-3-540-46588-1_28

41. Schanck, J.: Personal communication (June 2021)

42. Schwabe, P., et al.: CRYSTALS-KYBER. Technical report, National Institute of Standards and Technology (2020). https://csrc.nist.gov/projects/post-quantum-cryptography/round-3-submissions

43. Schwabe, P., Stebila, D., Wiggers, T.: Post-quantum TLS without handshake signatures. In: Ligatti, J., Ou, X., Katz, J., Vigna, G. (eds.) ACM CCS 2020, pp. 1461–1480. ACM Press (November 2020). https://doi.org/10.1145/3372297.3423350

44. Stehlé, D., Steinfeld, R.: Faster fully homomorphic encryption. In: Abe [3], pp. 377–394

45. Stehlé, D., Steinfeld, R., Tanaka, K., Xagawa, K.: Efficient public key encryption based on ideal lattices. In: Matsui, M. (ed.) ASIACRYPT 2009. LNCS, vol. 5912, pp. 617–635. Springer, Heidelberg (2009). https://doi.org/10.1007/978-3-642-10366-7_36

46. von Ahn, L., Hopper, N.J.: Public-key steganography. In: Cachin, C., Camenisch, J.L. (eds.) EUROCRYPT 2004. LNCS, vol. 3027, pp. 323–341. Springer, Heidelberg (2004). https://doi.org/10.1007/978-3-540-24676-3_20

47. Xagawa, K., Yamakawa, T.: (Tightly) QCCA-secure key-encapsulation mechanism in the quantum random oracle model. In: Ding, J., Steinwandt, R. (eds.) PQCrypto 2019. LNCS, vol. 11505, pp. 249–268. Springer, Cham (2019). https://doi.org/10.1007/978-3-030-25510-7_14

48. Zhandry, M.: A note on the quantum collision and set equality problems. Quantum Inf. Comput. **15**(7–8), 557–567 (2015)

49. Zhandry, M.: How to record quantum queries, and applications to quantum indifferentiability. In: Boldyreva, A., Micciancio, D. (eds.) CRYPTO 2019, Part II. LNCS, vol. 11693, pp. 239–268. Springer, Cham (2019). https://doi.org/10.1007/978-3-030-26951-7_9

Practical Post-Quantum Signature Schemes from Isomorphism Problems of Trilinear Forms

Gang Tang[1], Dung Hoang Duong[2], Antoine Joux[3], Thomas Plantard[4], Youming Qiao[1]([✉]), and Willy Susilo[2]

[1] Centre for Quantum Software and Information, School of Computer Science, Faculty of Engineering and Information Technology, University of Technology Sydney, Ultimo, NSW, Australia
gang.tang-1@student.uts.edu.au, Youming.Qiao@uts.edu.au

[2] Institute of Cybersecurity and Cryptology, School of Computing and Information Technology, University of Wollongong, Northfields Avenue, Wollongong, NSW 2522, Australia
{hduong,wsusilo}@uow.edu.au

[3] CISPA Helmholtz Center for Information Security, Saarbrücken, Germany
joux@cispa.de

[4] Emerging Technology Research Group, PayPal, San Jose, USA
tplantard@paypal.com

Abstract. In this paper, we propose a practical signature scheme based on the alternating trilinear form equivalence problem. Our scheme is inspired by the Goldreich-Micali-Wigderson's zero-knowledge protocol for graph isomorphism, and can be served as an alternative candidate for the NIST's post-quantum digital signatures.

First, we present theoretical evidences to support its security, especially in the post-quantum cryptography context. The evidences are drawn from several research lines, including hidden subgroup problems, multivariate cryptography, cryptography based on group actions, the quantum random oracle model, and recent advances on isomorphism problems for algebraic structures in algorithms and complexity.

Second, we demonstrate its potential for practical uses. Based on algorithm studies, we propose concrete parameter choices, and then implement a prototype. One concrete scheme achieves 128 bit security with public key size ≈ 4100 bytes, signature size ≈ 6800 bytes, and running times (key generation, sign, verify) ≈ 0.8 ms on a common laptop computer.

1 Introduction

Since the 1990s, several researchers observed the digital signature scheme obtained from the zero-knowledge proof protocol for graph isomorphism (GI) [41] by Goldreich, Micali and Wigderson (GMW), via the Fiat-Shamir transformation [39]. However, this scheme based on GI is not secure, as GI has long been considered as easy to solve in practice [62,63], not to mention Babai's

© International Association for Cryptologic Research 2022
O. Dunkelman and S. Dziembowski (Eds.): EUROCRYPT 2022, LNCS 13277, pp. 582–612, 2022.
https://doi.org/10.1007/978-3-031-07082-2_21

quasipolynomial-time algorithm [6]. Still, this design pattern can be easily adapted to accommodate other isomorphism problems, and has been studied in multivariate cryptography and isogeny-based cryptography.

In multivariate cryptography, Patarin [71] first proposed to use polynomial isomorphism (PI) to replace graph isomorphism in the GMW identification protocol. Depending on the degrees and the number of polynomials involved, PI is actually a family of problems. The most studied cases include cubic forms and systems of quadratic polynomials. For systems of quadratic polynomials, there are also subcases such as homogeneous vs inhomogeneous (as explained in Example 3 of Sect. 4.2). Some problems, such as the isomorphism of quadratic polynomials with one secret, turn out to be easy [15,37,51]. The other proposal of Patarin in [71], namely utilizing hidden field equations, turns out to be more fruitful, as witnessed by the celebrated Rainbow scheme by Ding and Schmidt [28] which makes to the third round of the NIST call for proposals on post-quantum cryptography [3].

In isogeny-based cryptography, Couveignes [25] first proposed the use of class group actions on elliptic curves in cryptography. He adapted the GMW identification protocol to this action. Stolbunov [80] suggested to apply the Fiat-Shamir transformation to this identification protocol to get a signature scheme. However, the use of ordinary elliptic curves has issues including the subexponential-time quantum algorithm [23] and the slow performance. The attention then turned to *supersingular* elliptic curves [54], which lead Castryck, Lange, Martindale, Panne and Renes to propose the so-called CSIDH scheme based on a group action deduced from rational endomorphisms [22]. Since their work, there has been considerable progress on this signature scheme recently [11,31,38]. However, signature protocols based on class group actions met with several technical difficulties, such as computing the group action efficiently. Indeed, this was one key motivation to develop the SeaSign [38] and the CSI-FiSh [11] schemes. While these works come close to yield an efficient secure protocol based on class group actions, recent works [13,72] indicate that these parameters originally proposed in [22] do not achieve the claimed security level in the face of quantum attacks, leading to re-evaluations of those protocols; see [4] for more details.

These quantum attacks reaffirm the importance of quantum algorithms in post-quantum cryptography. Indeed, these attacks are based on careful analyses and clever uses of the quantum algorithms [13,72] for the dihedral Hidden Subgroup Problem (HSP) [57,58,74] and for the elliptic curve isogeny problem [23]. The Hidden Subgroup Problem (HSP) is one of the most prominent family of problems in quantum computation. HSP and the related hidden shift problem are of particular relevance to post-quantum cryptography. Generalizing Shor's quantum algorithms for integer factoring and discrete logarithm [79], they can also accommodate certain lattice problems [74] (the HSP for dihedral groups) and isogeny problems [23] (the abelian hidden shift problem).

In this paper, we consider the *alternating trilinear form equivalence* (ATFE) problem, defined as follows. Let $\mathbb{F}_q$ be the finite field of order q. A trilinear form $\phi : \mathbb{F}_q^n \times \mathbb{F}_q^n \times \mathbb{F}_q^n \to \mathbb{F}_q$ is *alternating*, if ϕ evaluates to 0 whenever two arguments are the same. Let A be an invertible matrix of size $n \times n$ over $\mathbb{F}_q$. Then A sends ϕ to another alternating trilinear form $\phi \circ A$, defined as $(\phi \circ A)(u, v, w) := \phi(A^\mathrm{t}(u), A^\mathrm{t}(v), A^\mathrm{t}(w))$. The ATFE problem then asks, given two alternating trilinear forms $\phi, \psi : \mathbb{F}_q^n \times \mathbb{F}_q^n \times \mathbb{F}_q^n \to \mathbb{F}_q$, whether there exists an invertible matrix A such that $\phi = \psi \circ A$.

ATFE can be formulated as an HSP instance over $\mathrm{GL}(n, q)$, the general linear group of degree n over $\mathbb{F}_q$. The research on HSP suggests that for $\mathrm{GL}(n, q)$ and symmetric groups, current quantum algorithm techniques cannot provide further speedup compared to classical algorithms [43,48,67]. This was termed by Moore, Russell, and Vazirani as "the strongest such insights we have about the limits of quantum algorithms" [68]. As far as we know, this insight had not been used to *directly* support the security of any practical post-quantum cryptosystems. In this paper, we will, for the first time, utilize this insight to investigate the practical use of ATFE in post-quantum cryptography.

Remark 1. Our use of HSP to support ATFE in post-quantum cryptography follows the use of HSP to support lattices in post-quantum cryptography. That is, by [74], certain lattice problems reduce to HSP over dihedral groups. However, to the best of our knowledge, it is not known that the HSP over dihedral groups reduces to lattice problems. Similarly, here ATFE can be formulated as a HSP over general linear groups, but the reverse direction is not known.

1.1   Theoretical Preparations

Theoretical evidences for using ATFE in cryptography, besides HSP, are based on works from several research lines. Detailed discussions on the complexity, cryptography, and algorithm aspects of ATFE can be found in Sects. 4 and 5. Here we present a brief summary illustrating some key ideas.

Recent advances in complexity theory [44,46] and algorithms [18,46,59] reveal a much clearer picture on the complexity of isomorphism problems of algebraic structures. In [46], it is shown that ATFE is complete for the *Tensor Isomorphism complexity class* (TI) [44]. This puts ATFE into a family of problems which have been studied in various areas including cryptography, machine learning, computer algebra, and quantum information. These problems are known to be difficult to solve *in practice*, a sharp contrast to graph isomorphism and code equivalence, which, despite being notoriously difficult for algorithms with rigorous worst-case analyses, allow for effective heuristic algorithms in practice [63,77].

The TI-completeness notion is useful in connecting ATFE with many algorithmic problems. However, as the reductions produce instances which are quite structured, from the algorithmic viewpoint it is most useful for worst-case analysis. For cryptographic uses of ATFE, average-case hardness or even stronger criteria are required. This is where *cryptography based on group actions* comes into the theme. Using group actions in cryptography has been studied by Brassard and Yung [17], Couveignes [25], and more recently in two papers [4,53], among others. In Sect. 4.2, we present evidence for ATFE to satisfy the one-way [17] and pseudorandom [53] assumptions, which generalize the discrete logarithm hardness assumption and the Decisional Diffie-Hellman assumption, respectively.

To use ATFE in cryptography requires to pin down the algorithm for ATFE with the best time complexity. At first sight, ATFE seems little studied before. Fortunately, the Tensor Isomorphism-completeness of ATFE allows us to tap into years of research from multivariate cryptography, computational group theory, and theoretical computer science. This is because ATFE is polynomial-time equivalent to the cubic form isomorphism problem (CFI; see Definition 7), the quadratic form map isomorphism problem (QFMI; see Definition 8), and the class-2 p-group isomorphism problem (pGpI; see Definition 9). There is a large body of works in multivariate cryptography tackling CFI and QFMI, and in computational group theory and theoretical computer science tackling pGpI. The research in these communities produce non-trivial algorithms, utilizing tools and algorithmic ideas such as Gröbner basis, individualization and refinement, birthday paradox, and the min-rank attack. Still, these problems remain difficult to solve in practice.

1.2 Our Contribution

In this paper, we propose and study a digital signature scheme based on the ATFE problem through the following steps.

1. We carefully study the hardness of ATFE and provide theoretical evidences for using ATFE in cryptography based on works from several research lines including hidden subgroup problems, multivariate cryptography, cryptography based on group actions, security proofs for cryptographic protocols in the quantum oracle model, and recent advances on isomorphism problems from algorithms and complexity.
2. We propose a post-quantum signature scheme based on the ATFE problem. Our scheme is inspired by the GMW zero-knowledge interaction protocol [41] for graph isomorphism. Our scheme is proven to be secure in the Random Oracle Model (ROM) based on the hardness of the ATFE problem.
3. We also provide some discussion and support for proving our schemes' security in the quantum random oracle model (QROM) based on [29,60]; see Sect. 3.2.
4. In Sect. 5, we go over many relevant algorithms from the study of CFI, QFMI, and pGpI and combine them with certain experiment studies on alternating trilinear forms, to pin down the best algorithm for ATFE to our best knowledge.
5. Based on the algorithmic study in Sect. 5, we propose criteria for setting the parameters of these schemes to achieve a fixed security level in Sect. 6.1. Further concrete instantiations lead to concrete schemes whose public key and signature sizes are reported in Table 1.
6. We implement a prototype of the basic scheme as in Table 1 using C, and report its preformance in Table 2. For more details see Sect. 6.2.

Table 1. Output parameters for four concrete schemes based on ATFE for the 128-bit security. The sizes are measured in bytes.

	Public key	Private key	Signature
Concrete Scheme 1	6384	6156	5018
Concrete Scheme 2	8160	6800	5542
Concrete Scheme 3	4080	3400	6816
Concrete Scheme 4	10560	7744	6309

7. Borrowing ideas from isogeny-based cryptography [11,38], we also observe a variant of this scheme with Merkle trees, which helps to reduce the public key size. This will be reported in the full version of the paper.

Table 2. Running times (in microsecond, μs, averaged over 10^5 runs) for Concrete Schemes 1 to 4 on Linux 5.11.0-37-generic with Intel Core i7-8565U CPU (1.80 GHz).

	Set-Up	Sign	Verify
Concrete Scheme 1	285.9	471.7	416.5
Concrete Scheme 2	383.1	660.0	578.9
Concrete Scheme 3	190.7	795.4	708.8
Concrete Scheme 4	514.0	861.1	765.2

From the above, we belive that the main message is that this digital signature is potential for practical uses. In Sect. 1.3, we provide a comparison of our signature scheme with those are in the third round of NIST's Post-quantum Standardization process, and it shows that our scheme is comparable to those practical ones in terms of key sizes and running time. We also expect that our implementation can be further improved and optimized, that we will leave as a future work. This scheme is also simple in both terms of conceptual and implementation viewpoints.

Our digital signature scheme can be served as an alternative candidate for post-quantum signatures. This also aligns to the recent announcement of NIST [69] at PQCrypto 2021 on calling for a general-purpose digital signature scheme which is not based on structured lattices, which are currently the most promising candidates of post-quantum signature standardization [3].

1.3 Comparison with 3rd Round NIST's Post-quantum Signature Schemes

Post-quantum cryptography has seen tremendous growth in the past few years. The National Institute of Standards and Technology (NIST) initiated the selection of proposals on post-quantum cryptographic algorithms for potential standardisation in November 2016, and the selection process came to the third round in mid 2020 [3]. There are three finalist proposals for signature schemes in the third round, namely Dilithium [7], Falcon [40], and Rainbow [78]. Dilithium and Falcon are based on lattice problems, and Rainbow is based on multivariate polynomials. Besides these schemes, the progress on isogeny-based signature schemes has been impressive in the past few years [11,27,38], and the SQISign scheme [27] probably comes closest to be practical.

We briefly review the public key and signature sizes of these schemes at NIST security level I or II, according to their latest specifications. The public key and signature sizes of Dilithium are 1312 bytes and 2420 bytes. The public key and signature sizes of Falcon-512 are 897 bytes and 666 bytes. Rainbow's signature size is small (528 *bits*), but it requires relatively large public key size ($\approx$ 58,800 bytes). The recently proposed SQISign achieves 204-byte signature size and 64-byte public key size. The running times of Dilithium, Falcon and Rainbow are very fast. As it would probably not be very instructive to list specific running times, we just mention that the running times of these schemes (sign and verify) are mostly within the range between 0.1 ms and 1 ms on a common laptop computer. On the other hand, the SQISign requires 2500 ms for signing and 50 ms for verification.

Based on the above observations, we believe that the parameters and running times of concrete schemes as shown in Tables 1 and 2 fall into the range for practical uses, when compared with the most promising schemes. Of course, Dilithium and Falcon take the lead in terms of these parameters. However, we offer as well a new direction with a *different* security basis and still a strong theoretical support.

1.4 On Interactions with Other Research Lines

From discussions above, this work has connections to many works from several research lines. We now provide some remarks to clarify the situations for readers with different backgrounds.

For experts on multivariate cryptography, we wish to deliver the message that Patarin's signature scheme based on polynomial isomorphism [71] could be practical if we are careful about the parameter choices, and replacing polynomial isomorphism with alternating trilinear form equivalence. Indeed, this scheme of Patarin was thought to be not practical, because the original parameters proposed were quickly broken [15,16,37]. Furthermore, some variants such as isomorphism of quadratic polynomials with one secret were shown to be easily solvable [10,14,15,51]. One main reason is that in the 2000's, signatures of say 3000 bytes would be considered as too large. Now in post-quantum cryptography, signatures of 5000 bytes are acceptable at least at the brainstorming stage. (For example, Dilithium produces signatures of 2420 bytes and SPHINCS+ [52], an alternate candidate in NIST round 3 [3], produces signatures of 7856 bytes.) With this in mind, it is actually reasonable to use cubic form isomorphism (CFI) to experiment with various parameters, assuming that the best algorithm runs in time say $q^n \cdot \mathrm{poly}(n, \log q)$ [15]. Utilizing ATFE has one advantage over CFI, as alternating trilinear forms require less storage than cubic forms ($\binom{n}{3}$ vs $\binom{n+2}{3}$), which results in better public key sizes.

For experts on isogeny-based cryptography, especially those who are familiar with SeaSign [38] and CSI-FiSh [11], s/he would quickly recognise that our scheme has the same structure. The key difference lies in using a different action. The class group action as in CSIDH [22] has smaller group and set element representations, but is more difficult to compute. The group action here (general linear groups acting on alternating trilinear forms) is easy to compute but the group and set elements are of larger sizes, resulting in larger public key and signature sizes.

Organization of the Paper. In Sect. 2, we describe the alternating trilinear form equivalence problem (ATFE) and several variants. We describe the proposed schemes in Sect. 3, prove its security in the Random Oracle Model, and discuss its security in the Quantum Random Oracle Model (QROM). In Sect. 4, we discuss on the complexity and cryptography aspects of ATFE. In Sect. 5, we present a detailed study of algorithms for ATFE. In Sect. 6, we propose concrete parameters, describe our implementation, and report on its performance.

2 Preliminaries

2.1 Defining ATFE and Variants

Our proposed signature protocol relies on the assumed hardness of the *alternating trilinear form equivalence* (ATFE) problem over finite fields. To define this problem we need some preparations.

Alternating Trilinear forms with a Natural Group Action. Let $\mathbb{F}_q$ be the finite field of order q. A trilinear form $\phi : \mathbb{F}_q^n \times \mathbb{F}_q^n \times \mathbb{F}_q^n \to \mathbb{F}_q$ is *alternating*, if ϕ evaluates to 0 whenever two arguments are the same. Let $\mathrm{ATF}(n, q)$ be the set of all alternating trilinear forms defined over $\mathbb{F}_q^n$. The general linear group $\mathrm{GL}(n, q)$ of degree n over $\mathbb{F}_q$ naturally acts on $\mathrm{ATF}(n, q)$ as follows: $A \in \mathrm{GL}(n, q)$ sends ϕ to $\phi \circ A$, defined as $(\phi \circ A)(u, v, w) := \phi(A^{\mathrm{t}}(u), A^{\mathrm{t}}(v), A^{\mathrm{t}}(w))$. This action defines an equivalence relation $\sim$ on $\mathrm{ATF}(n, q)$, namely $\phi \sim \psi$ if and only if there exists $A \in \mathrm{GL}(n, q)$, such that $\phi = \psi \circ A$.

Algorithmic Representations. It is well-known that an alternating trilinear form $\phi : \mathbb{F}_q^n \times \mathbb{F}_q^n \times \mathbb{F}_q^n \to \mathbb{F}_q$ can be represented as $\sum_{1 \leq i < j < k \leq n} c_{i,j,k} e_i^* \wedge e_j^* \wedge e_k^*$, where $c_{i,j,k} \in \mathbb{F}_q$, e_i is the ith standard basis vector, e_i^* is the linear form sending $u = (u_1, \ldots, u_n)^{\mathrm{t}} \in \mathbb{F}_q^n$ to u_i, and $\wedge$ denotes the wedge (or exterior) product. Indeed, we can view $e_i^* \wedge e_j^* \wedge e_k^*$ as an alternating trilinear form, sending (u, v, w), where $u = (u_1, \ldots, u_n)^{\mathrm{t}}$, $v = (v_1, \ldots, v_n)^{\mathrm{t}}$, $w = (w_1, \ldots, w_n)^{\mathrm{t}}$ are in $\mathbb{F}_q^n$, to

$$\det \begin{bmatrix} u_i & v_i & w_i \\ u_j & v_j & w_j \\ u_k & v_k & w_k \end{bmatrix}.$$

Therefore, in algorithms we can store the alternating trilinear form ϕ as $(c_{i,j,k} : 1 \leq i < j < k \leq n)$, $c_{i,j,k} \in \mathbb{F}_q$, which requires $\binom{n}{3} \cdot \lceil \log q \rceil$ many bits.

The action of $\mathrm{GL}(n,q)$ on $\mathrm{ATF}(n,q)$ can be represented concretely as follows. Let $A = (a_{i,j}) \in \mathrm{GL}(n,q)$. It sends $e_i^* \wedge e_j^* \wedge e_k^*$ to $\sum_{1 \leq r < s < t \leq n} d_{r,s,t} e_r^* \wedge e_s^* \wedge e_t^*$,

where $d_{r,s,t} = \det \begin{bmatrix} a_{i,r} & a_{i,s} & a_{i,t} \\ a_{j,r} & a_{j,s} & a_{j,t} \\ a_{k,r} & a_{k,s} & a_{k,t} \end{bmatrix}$. For general $\phi \in \mathrm{ATF}(n,q)$, the action of A can be obtained by linearly extending this action to each term $e_i^* \wedge e_j^* \wedge e_k^*$.

Formal Statements of the Algorithmic Problems. We can now formally state the alternating trilinear form equivalence problem.

Definition 1. *The decision version of the alternating trilinear form equivalence problem (ATFE) is the following.*

Input *Two alternating trilinear forms* $\phi, \psi : \mathbb{F}_q^n \times \mathbb{F}_q^n \times \mathbb{F}_q^n \to \mathbb{F}_q$.
Output *"Yes" if there exists* $A \in \mathrm{GL}(n,q)$ *such that* $\phi = \psi \circ A$. *"No" otherwise.*

Definition 2. *The promised search version of the alternating trilinear form equivalence problem (psATFE) is the following.*

Input *Two alternating trilinear forms* $\phi, \psi : \mathbb{F}_q^n \times \mathbb{F}_q^n \times \mathbb{F}_q^n \to \mathbb{F}_q$, *with the promise that* $\phi \sim \psi$.
Output *Some* $A \in \mathrm{GL}(n,q)$ *such that* $\phi = \psi \circ A$.

Definition 3. *The promised search version of the alternating trilinear form equivalence problem with m-instances (m-psATFE) is the following.*

Input m *alternating trilinear forms* $\phi_1, \ldots, \phi_m : \mathbb{F}_q^n \times \mathbb{F}_q^n \times \mathbb{F}_q^n \to \mathbb{F}_q$, *with the promise that* $\phi_i \sim \phi_j$ *for any* $i, j \in [m]$.
Output *Some* $A \in \mathrm{GL}(n,q)$ *and* $i, j \in [m]$, $i \neq j$, *such that* $\phi_i = \phi_j \circ A$.

Remark 2. It is not known whether the search version of ATFE reduces to the decision version in polynomial time. In [45], it was shown that for some related problems, such as the quadratic form map isomorphism (cf. Definition 8), search to decision can be done in time $q^{O(n)}$ (improving from $q^{n^2} \cdot \mathrm{poly}(n, \log q)$). So it is expected that for ATFE, a search to decision reduction can be achieved in time $q^{O(n)}$. However, a polynomial-time search to decision reduction seems difficult.

On the one hand, m-psATFE generalises the original version. On the other hand, it is easy to get a non-tight reduction from m-psATFE to the original version of psATFE. So we believe that m-psATFE is of the same difficulty as psATFE.

2.2 Digital Signatures

Definition 4. *A signature scheme consists of a triplet of polynomial-time (possible probabilistic) algorithms* (KEYGEN, SIGN, VERIFY) *such that for every pair of outputs* $(\mathrm{PK}, \mathrm{SK}) \leftarrow \mathrm{KEYGEN}(1^\lambda)$ *and any n-bit message* μ, *we have*

$$\mathrm{VERIFY}(\mathrm{PK}, \mu, \mathrm{SIGN}(\mathrm{SK}, \mu)) = 1$$

holds true, except with negligible probability (in λ).

A signature is said to be secure if it is impossible for an attacker to forge a valid signature. Explicitly, the standard definition of security for digital signature schemes are given in the game between the challenger $\mathcal{C}$ and an adversary $\mathcal{A}$ as the following.

- The challenger $\mathcal{C}$ generates $(\text{PK}, \text{SK}) \leftarrow \text{KEYGEN}(1^\lambda)$ and gives PK to $\mathcal{A}$.
- $\mathcal{A}$ is allowed to make the following queries at maximum Q times. For $i = 1, \cdots, Q$:
  - $\mathcal{A}$ chooses a message μ_i and sends to $\mathcal{C}$
  - $\mathcal{C}$ computes $\sigma_i \leftarrow \text{SIGN}(\text{SK}, \mu_i)$ and sends σ_i to $\mathcal{A}$.
- $\mathcal{A}$ outputs a forgery (μ^*, σ^*)
- $\mathcal{A}$ wins if $\text{VERIFY}(\text{PK}, \mu^*, \sigma^*) = 1$ and $\mu^* \notin \{\mu_1, \cdots, \mu_Q\}$.

We say that a signature scheme is Existentially UnForgeable under adaptive Chosen Message Attacks (EUF-CMA) if no probabilistic polynomial-time adversary $\mathcal{A}$ wins the game above with non-negligible probability $\lambda^{-\mathcal{O}(1)}$.

3   Signature Schemes Based on ATFE

Our scheme is inspired by the zero-knowledge protocol for graph isomorphisms by Goldreich, Micali and Wigderson (GMW) [41]. As a high level, we will incorporate the ATFE to obtain a generalized GMW-like scheme and then apply the Fiat-Shamir transformation [39] to obtain a signature scheme. This basic scheme is described in Sect. 3.1. We emphasize that one may think it is straightforward to just replace the graph isomorphisms in GMW to ATFE, which is exactly the route we go, but the technical details are involved; see Sect. 3.1 for the detail. In the full version of this paper, we will introduce a variant of the basic scheme in Sect. 3.1 by utilizing Merkle tree techniques that have been employed in many constructions including some isogeny-based signatures [11,38].

3.1   The Basic Scheme

The original GMW protocol [41] has two graphs as input. For the purpose of using it in identification and signature, it is useful to generalize this to more than two graphs, as already observed by several researchers including Patarin [71] and De Feo and Galbraith [38].

We present this slightly generalized scheme based on ATFE in Algorithms 1, 2, and 3. It involves four parameters: $n \in \mathbb{N}$ and a prime power q to specify $\text{ATF}(n, q)$, the round number r, and the number of alternating trilinear forms in the public key $C = 2^c$. Note that we use $C = 2^c$ to simplify the analysis; in fact any number C would do.

Note that by randomly sampling $\phi \in \text{ATF}(n, q)$, we sample independently randomly $\binom{n}{3}$ field elements from $\mathbb{F}_q$. By randomly sampling $A \in \text{ATF}(n, q)$, we can sample a random matrix from $M(n, q)$ until we get an invertible one, or use the method described in Sect. 6.2.

Algorithm 1: Key generation.

Input: The variable number $n \in \mathbb{N}$, a prime power q, the alternating trilinear
form number $C = 2^c$.

Output: Public key: C alternating trilinear forms $\phi_i \in \mathrm{ATF}(n, q)$ such that
$\phi_i \sim \phi_j$ for any $i, j \in [C]$.
Private key: C matrices $A_1, \ldots, A_C$, such that $\phi_i \circ A_i = \phi_C$.

1 Randomly sample an alternating trilinear form $\phi_C : \mathbb{F}_q^n \times \mathbb{F}_q^n \times \mathbb{F}_q^n \to \mathbb{F}_q$.
2 Randomly sample $C - 1$ invertible matrices, $A_1, \ldots, A_{C-1} \in \mathrm{GL}(n, q)$.
3 For every $i \in [C - 1]$, $\phi_i \leftarrow \phi_C \circ A_i$.
4 For every $i \in [C - 1]$, $A_i \leftarrow A_i^{-1}$.
5 $A_C \leftarrow I_n$.
6 **return** *Public key:* $\phi_1, \phi_2, \ldots, \phi_C$. *Private Key:* $A_1, \ldots, A_C$.

Algorithm 2: Signing procedure.

Input: The public key $\phi_1, \ldots, \phi_C \in \mathrm{ATF}(n, q)$. The private key
$A_1, \ldots, A_C \in \mathrm{GL}(n, q)$. $r \in \mathbb{N}$, $C = 2^c$. The message M. A hash function
$H : \{0, 1\}^* \to \{0, 1\}^\ell$, with the promise that $\lfloor \ell/c \rfloor \geq r$.

Output: The signature S on M.

1 **for** $i \in [r]$ **do**
2 $\quad$ Randomly sample $B_i \in \mathrm{GL}(n, q)$.
3 $\quad$ $\psi_i \leftarrow \phi_C \circ B_i$.
4 **end**
5 Compute $L = H(\mathrm{M}|\psi_1| \ldots |\psi_r) \in \{0, 1\}^\ell$.
$\quad$ /* For the next step we need $\lfloor \ell/c \rfloor \geq r$. $\qquad\qquad\qquad\qquad$ */
6 Slice L into $\lfloor \ell/c \rfloor$ bit strings in $\{0, 1\}^c$, and set $b_1, \ldots, b_r \in [C]$ to be the integer
represented by the first r bit strings.
7 **for** $i \in [r]$ **do**
8 $\quad$ $D_i \leftarrow A_{b_i} B_i$; $\qquad\qquad\qquad\qquad$ // Note that $\phi_{h_i} \circ D_i = \psi_i$.
9 **end**
10 **return** $S = (b_1, \ldots, b_r, D_1, \ldots, D_r)$.

It is straightforward to verify the correctness of the scheme. We now analyze
its security. It is well-known that the Goldreich-Micali-Wigderson (GMW) protocol satisfies completeness, special soundness, and special honest-verifier zero
knowledge properties. These allow us to prove the security of the digital signature
scheme as follows.

Theorem 1. *The basic signature scheme described above is EUF-CMA secure in
the Random Oracle Model (ROM) under the hardness of the m-psATFE problem.*

Proof. We proceed the proof by contradiction. Assume that there exists an
adversary $\mathcal{A}$ that having maximum Q queries to the hash function H, which
is modelled as random oracle, can break the EUF-CMA security, as described in
Sect. 2.2, of the signature scheme. We will build an algorithm $\mathcal{B}$ that solves the
ATFE with non-negligible probability using $\mathcal{A}$. The proof follows the standard
one in Fiat-Shamir-type signature, we present it here for completeness.

Algorithm 3: Verification procedure.

Input: The public key $\phi_1, \ldots, \phi_C \in \mathrm{ATF}(n, q)$. The signature
$S = (b_1, \ldots, b_r, D_1, \ldots, D_r)$, $b_i \in [C]$, $D_i \in \mathrm{GL}(n, q)$. The message M.
The A hash function $H : \{0,1\}^* \to \{0,1\}^\ell$, with the promise that
$\lfloor \ell/c \rfloor \geq r$.

Output: "Yes" if S is a valid signature for M. "No" otherwise.

1 **for** $i \in [r]$ **do**
2   Compute $\psi_i = \phi_{b_i} \circ D_i$.
3 **end**
4 Compute $L' = H(\mathrm{M}|\psi_1|\ldots|\psi_r) \in \{0,1\}^\ell$.
    /* For the next step we need $\lfloor \ell/c \rfloor \geq r$.   */
5 Slice L' into $\lfloor \ell/c \rfloor$ bit strings in $\{0,1\}^c$, and set $b'_1, \ldots, b'_r \in [C]$ to be the integer
   represented by the first r bit strings.
6 **if** *for every* $i \in [r]$, $b_i = b'_i$ **then**
7   **return** *Yes*
8 **else**
9   **return** *No*
10

At the beginning, $\mathcal{B}$ is given an instance of the C-psATFE problem, that are
C alternative trilinear forms $\phi_1, \ldots, \phi_C : \mathbb{F}_q^n \times \mathbb{F}_q^n \times \mathbb{F}_q^n \to \mathbb{F}_q$ such that $\phi_i \sim \phi_j$
for any $i, j \in [C]$. The goal of $\mathcal{B}$ is to find $i \neq j$ and some $A \in \mathrm{GL}(n, q)$ such
that $\phi_i = \phi_j \circ A$.

Let $L_1, \ldots, L_Q$ be random elements in $\{0,1\}^l$, which $\mathcal{B}$ will use to answer hash
queries from the adversary $\mathcal{A}$, and let R be an entry from the set of possible ran-
dom tapes of adversary $\mathcal{A}$. The algorithm $\mathcal{B}$ will take $(R, \phi_1, \ldots, \phi_C, L_1, \ldots, L_Q)$
as input. When $\mathcal{A}$ makes a signing query on the message M, then $\mathcal{B}$ executes
the following steps:

- Take the next hash query value input to $\mathcal{B}$, and let this be L_j for $j \in [Q]$.
- Slice L_j into $\lfloor l/c \rfloor$ bit strings in $\{0,1\}^c$ and let $b_{j1}, \ldots, b_{jr} \in [C]$ be the integer
  represented by the first r bit strings of L_j.
- For $i \in [r]$, choose randomly $D_i \leftarrow \mathrm{GL}(n, q)$ and set $\psi_i := \phi_{b_{ji}} \circ D_i$.
- Define $L_j := H(M|\psi_1|\ldots|\psi_r)$. If this value has already been defined then we
  pick another values of D_i's.
- Return a signature $(b_{j1}, \ldots, b_{jr}, D_1, \ldots, D_r)$ to the adversary $\mathcal{A}$.

One can easily see that the distribution of the signature generated by $\mathcal{B}$ is statistically closed to that generated by the signing algorithm in Algorithm 2. In this
case, the adversary $\mathcal{A}$ can verify the signature as in the verification procedure
in Algorithm 3.

Assume now that $\mathcal{A}$ outputs a valid forgery $(b_1^*, \ldots, b_j^*, D_1^*, \ldots, D_r^*)$ for a
message M^*. We let L^* be the corresponding hash query of the adversary, i.e.,
L^* is defined by $H(M^*|\psi_1^*|\cdots|\psi_r^*)$ by the algorithm $\mathcal{B}$. We let $(\psi_1^*, \cdots, \psi_r^*)$
be the associated commitments computed from $(b_1^*, \ldots, b_j^*, D_1^*, \ldots, D_r^*)$, i.e.,
$\psi_i^* = \phi_{b_i^*} \circ D_i^*$ for $i \in [r]$. Now the challenger $\mathcal{B}$ runs $\mathcal{A}$ a second time using

the same randomness R as before. By the General Forking Lemma [12], $\mathcal{A}$ will output another forgery $(b'_1, \ldots, b'_j, D'_1, \ldots, D'_r)$ with associated commitments $(\psi'_1, \cdots, \psi'_r)$ for the same message M^* such that $\psi^*_i = \psi'_i$ for $i = 1, \cdots, r$ and $L^* \neq L'$, where L' is programmed to be $H(M^*|\psi'_1|\cdots|\psi'_r)$. Since $L^* \neq L'$, then there exist $i \in [r]$ such that $b^*_i \neq b'_i$. Now $\mathcal{B}$ outputs $A := D^*_i (D'_i)^{-1}$ as an answer for the given C-psATFE instance.

In fact, we have $\phi_{b^*_i} \circ A = \phi_{b^*_i} \circ D^*_i (D'_i)^{-1} = \psi^*_i \circ (D'_i)^{-1} = \psi'_i \circ (D'_i)^{-1} = \phi_{b'_i}$. Hence $\mathcal{B}$ already finds an invertible matrix $A \in \mathrm{GL}(n, q)$ and two indices $b^*_i \neq b'_i$ such that $\phi_{b^*_i} \circ A = \phi_{b'_i}$. This completes the proof.   □

3.2   Security in Quantum Oracle Model (QROM)

Recently, the security of the Fiat-Shamir transformation in the quantum random oracle model (QROM) was established in [29,60]. Using these works, we follow the route of arguments in [11] to provide evidences – but not a rigorous proof – to support the security of our scheme in QROM. Indeed, to prove QROM security for concrete schemes based on Fiat-Shamir transformations is not trivial even based on [29,60]. For example, the QROM security of Dilithium, one finalist in the NIST call for proposals, is only proved assuming some conjecture [7].

In order to utilize [29,60], a key is to establish the collapsing property [60] or the quantum computational unique response property [29] of the GMW protocol for ATFE. This property is a generalization of the computational unique response property. In the context of the GMW protocol for ATFE, this property essentially asks, given $\phi, \psi \in \mathrm{ATF}(n, q)$ such that $\phi \sim \psi$, to produce different $A, B \in \mathrm{GL}(n, q)$ such that $\phi = \psi \circ A = \psi \circ B$, if there exist such A and B. Then note that AB^{-1} is a non-trivial automorphism of ψ. This then leads us to ask the following.

Definition 5 (Alternating trilinear form automorphism, ATFA). *Given a random $\phi \in \mathrm{ATF}(n, q)$, decide if the automorphism group $\mathrm{Aut}(\phi) = \{A \in \mathrm{GL}(n, q) : \phi \circ A = \phi\}$ is trivial, and if not, compute a non-trivial automorphism.*

The same problem for graph isomorphism, known as the graph automorphism problem, has received considerable attention [56]. From the worst-case analysis viewpoint, it was considered a difficult problem before Babai's breakthrough on graph isomorphism [6]. For random graphs, it is well-known that most graphs have the trivial automorphism group [32,82] as long as the number of edges is between $[cn, \binom{n}{2} - cn]$ for some constant c.

ATFA seems a difficult problem. The algorithm in [46] actually shows that for most $\phi \in \mathrm{ATF}(n, q)$, $|\mathrm{Aut}(\phi)| \leq q^{O(n)}$, but it runs in time $q^{O(n)}$. In [24,50,65], alternating trilinear forms in $\mathrm{ATF}(7, q)$ and $\mathrm{ATF}(8, q)$ over finite fields of characteristic not 3 are classified, and the automorphism groups are computed. To use such information, we will need to solve the ATFE problem for the alternating trilinear form at hand, and one of the canonical forms presented in [65]. As ATFE is considered as difficult (see Sect. 4.1), the classification information seems not very helpful, and this is only available for $n = 7$ or 8.

We believe it an interesting direction to explore ATFA further, and whether it is possible to prove formally the security of our protocol assuming that ATFA is hard, perhaps using the weakly collapsing property in [60].

4   Complexity and Cryptography Aspects of **ATFE**

4.1   **ATFE** in Complexity Theory

In Sect. 1.1, we mentioned the recent introduction of the Tensor Isomorphism-complete class (TI) in [44], which captures many isomorphism problems arising from multivariate crytography, machine learning, quantum information, and computer algebra. In [46], ATFE was proved to be TI-complete. Among those TI-complete problems, the following algorithmic problems are of particular relevance to our discussion.

Definition 6. *The 3-tensor isomorphism problem (3TI) is the following.*

Input *Two 3-way arrays* $D = (d_{i,j,k}), E = (e_{i,j,k})$, *where* $d_{i,j,k}, e_{i,j,k} \in \mathbb{F}_q$ *and* $i, j, k \in [n]$.
Output *"Yes" if there exist* $A = (a_{i,r}), B = (b_{j,s}), C = (c_{k,t}) \in \mathrm{GL}(n, q)$, *such that* $D = (A, B, C) \star E$, *where* $(A, B, C) \star E := F = (f_{i,j,k})$, $f_{i,j,k} = \sum_{r,s,t \in [n]} a_{i,r} b_{j,s} c_{k,t} e_{r,s,t}$. *"No" otherwise.*

3TI appears in quantum information, characterising equivalence classes of tripartite states under stochastic local operation and classical communication (SLOCC) [44].

Definition 7. *The cubic form isomorphism problem (CFI) is the following.*

Input *Two cubic forms (homogeneous degree-3 polynomials)* $f, g \in \mathbb{F}_q[x_1, \ldots, x_n]$.
Output *"Yes" if there exists* $A = (a_{i,j}) \in \mathrm{GL}(n, q)$, *such that* $f = A \star g$, *where the action of* A *on* g *is by sending* x_i *to* $\sum_{j \in [n]} a_{i,j} x_j$. *"No" otherwise.*

CFI has been studied in multivariate cryptography [15] and theoretical computer science [1,2].

Definition 8. *The quadratic form map isomorphism problem (QFMI) is the following.*

Input *Two tuples of quadratic forms* $\mathbf{f} = (f_1, \ldots, f_m)$, $\mathbf{g} = (g_1, \ldots, g_m)$, *where* $f_i, g_j \in \mathbb{F}_q[x_1, \ldots, x_n]$ *are quadratic forms (homogeneous degree-2 polynomials).*
Output *"Yes" if there exist* $A = (a_{i,j}) \in \mathrm{GL}(n, q)$, $B = (b_{i,j}) \in \mathrm{GL}(n, q)$, *such that* $\forall i \in [m]$, $f'_i = A \star g_i$, *where* $f'_i = \sum_{j \in [m]} b_{i,j} f_j$, *and the action of* A *on* g_i *is by sending* x_i *to* $\sum_{j \in [n]} a_{i,j} x_j$. *"No" otherwise.*

QFMI has been studied in multivariate cryptography. It was first raised by Patarin [71] and has been studied in several works including [10,16,37]. Several variants of this problem have also been studied, such as replacing quadratic forms with quadratic polynomials (from homogeneous to possibly inhomogeneous), or restricting B to be the identity matrix (also known as the one secret version of the problem).

Definition 9. *The class-2 and exponent-p p-group isomorphism problem (pGpl) is the following.*

Input *Two sets of matrices $A = \{A_1, \ldots, A_m\}, B = \{B_1, \ldots, B_m\} \in \mathrm{GL}(n, p)$, with the promise that A (resp. B) generates a p-group G (resp. H) of class 2 and exponent p.*
Output *"Yes" if G and H are isomorphic (as abstract groups). "No" otherwise.*

pGpl has long been known to be one bottleneck case of the group isomorphism problem, which asks whether two finite groups are isomorphic. It is studied in both computational group theory [19,70,81] and theoretical computer science [18,44,59].

The following theorem is important for our understanding of ATFE.

Theorem 2 ([44,46]). *The following problems are equivalent under polynomial-time reductions: ATFE, 3TI, CFI, QFMI, and pGpl.*

Theorem 2 allows us to tap into research areas such as multivariate cryptography, computational group theory, and theoretical computer science, to understand the complexity of ATFE. In particular, we have seen that CFI and QFMI are known to be difficult in multivariate cryptography, and pGpl is known to be difficult in computational group theory. This gives us confidence in the worst-case hardness of ATFE. However, for cryptographic uses, ATFE needs to be difficult in the average-case sense. This is addressed in the next subsection.

4.2 ATFE and Cryptography Based on Group Actions

Let G be a group and S a set. A group action is a function $\alpha : G \times S \to S$ satisfying certain axioms. For the purpose of this article we don't need to spell out these axioms; instead, it is enough to realize that the functions underlying isomorphism problems are all group actions.

Cryptography based on group actions, as a framework, has been studied by Brassard and Yung [17], Couveignes [25], and more recently in two papers [4,53]. We review this framework and explain the roles of the discrete logarithm problem and ATFE in this framework.

In [17], Brassard and Yung defined the group action α to be *one-way*, if there exists $s \in S$, such that $\alpha_s : G \to S$, defined as $\alpha_s(g) = \alpha(g, s)$, is a one-way function. In [53], this is slightly relaxed to α_s is a one-way function for a random $s \in S$. The following example, known at least since [25], shows how to interpret the discrete logarithm problem as a problem about group action.

Example 1. To illustrate the notion of one-way group actions, let us consider an important group action in cryptography. Let C_p be the cyclic group of order p, and let $\text{Aut}(C_p)$ be the automorphism group of C_p. Note that $G = \text{Aut}(C_p) \cong \mathbb{Z}_p^*$, the multiplicative group of units in $\mathbb{Z}_p$. Then given $a \in \mathbb{Z}_p^*$ and $g \in C_p$, a sends g to g^a. Let $S = C_p \setminus \{\text{id}\}$ where id is the identity element, and let $\alpha : \text{Aut}(C_p) \times S \to S$ be the group action just defined. Then α is one-way, if and only if α_g is one-way for some $g \in S$, if and only if the discrete logarithm problem (with a fixed generator) is one-way.

Clearly, the action underlying ATFE being one-way in the relaxed sense is equivalent to saying that the problem of solving psATFE is hard on average.

In [25], Couveignes studied what he called hard homogeneous spaces, which is in fact also a group action with certain properties. In particular, he defined the parallelization problem for a group action α as follows. Given $s_1, t_1, s_2 \in S$ with the promise that there exists $g \in G$ such that $\alpha(g, s_1) = t_1$, compute $\alpha(g, s_2)$. For the group action defining discrete logarithm as in Example 1, its parallelization problem is hard on average is equivalent to the Computational Diffie-Hellman assumption.

Recently, the notion pseudorandom group actions was independently introduced in [53] and [4].[1] Briefly speaking, a group action $\alpha : G \times S \to S$ is pseudorandom, if efficient algorithms cannot distinguish the following two distributions. The first distribution is the random distribution, namely $(s, t) \in S \times S$ where $s, t \in_R S$. The second distribution is the pseudorandom distribution, namely $(s, t) \in S \times S$ where $s \in_R S$, and $t = \alpha(g, s)$ where $g \in_R G$. In [53], it was observed that this assumption generalizes the Decisional Diffie-Hellman assumption. We reproduce this example here.

Example 2. Let C_p, $G = \text{Aut}(C_p)$, and $S = C_p \setminus \{\text{id}\}$ be from Example 2. Note that the action of G on C_p is transitive, i.e. for any $g, h \in S$, there exists $a \in G$ such that $g^a = h$. In particular, for a fixed $g \in S$, when a is uniformly sampled from G, g^a is uniformly sampled from S. Let G act on $S \times S$ diagonally, i.e. $a \in G$ sends (g, h) to (g^a, h^a). Then the random distribution (of this diagonal action) is $((g, h), (g', h')) = ((g, g^a), (g^b, g^c))$ where $g \in_R S$, $a, b, c \in_R G$. The pseudorandom distribution is $((g, h), (g^b, h^b)) = ((g, g^a), (g^b, g^{ab}))$ where $g \in_R S$ and $a, b \in_R G$. Distinguishing these two distributions is then exactly the Decisional Diffie-Hellman problem.

We give an example suggesting that the pseudorandom group action is a useful criterion for cryptographic uses in the context of multivariate cryptography as follows.

Example 3. Consider the quadratic form map isomorphism problem (QFMI) from Definition 8, where $\text{GL}(n, q) \times \text{GL}(m, q)$ acts on tuples of quadratic forms $\mathbf{f} = (f_1, \ldots, f_m) \in \mathbb{F}_q[x_1, \ldots, x_n]$. Consider the following two variations. First, we relax f_i to be quadratic polynomials, that is, f_i's are allowed to have linear and constant terms. Call this Variant 1 of QFMI. Second, we relax f_i's to be

---

[1] In [4] this is called weak pseudorandom group actions.

quadratic polynomials with constant terms being 0, that is, f_i's are allowed to have linear terms but no constant terms. Call this Variant 2 of QFMI.

The experience in multivariate cryptography (cf. Bouillaguet's thesis [14]) suggests that Variant 2 is easier than Variant 1, which is in turn easier than QFMI itself. From the pseudorandom group action viewpoint, Variant 1 is clearly not pseudorandom, as the constant terms are not changed under the group action. Variant 2 is also not pseudorandom: in the setting $m = n$ (the most studied situation), the rank of the n linear forms from f_i's is an invariant under the group action, which can be computed easily to distinguish the random and pseudorandom distributions. (Note that over $\mathbb{F}_q$, the rank of n linear forms in n variables is not full with probability $\geq 1/q^{\Theta(1)}$.)

It is clear that the pseudorandom assumption is stronger than the one-way assumption and the assumption that solving paralleization is hard. In [4,53], pseudorandom group actions are shown to have applications ranging from pseudorandom functions, to signature, and to oblivious transfer. The candidate pseudorandom group actions are the 3-tensor action as in Definition 6 (proposed in [53]) and the class group action underlying CSIDH [22] (proposed in [4]). Note that certain technical modifications are required to address some computational issues in the class group action underlying CSIDH. Furthermore, certain applications of pseudorandom group actions in [4] require the group to be commutative.

The main conjecture in this article is the following.

Conjecture 1. The group action underlying ATFE is pseudorandom.

To prove ATFE to be pseudorandom (even based on certain assumptions) seems difficult. Instead, as customary for this type of question, we provide certain arguments to support Conjecture 1.

- Several researchers have noted that the mathematics of alternating trilinear forms is "much harder" [5], or "much more complicated (and interesting)" [30], especially when compared to alternating bilinear forms. For example, in general one cannot expect to classify alternating trilinear forms when n is large enough.
- A basic approach to refute an action from being pseudorandom is to identify easy-to-compute isomorphism invariants, which are quantities unchanged by the group action. Such isomorphism invariants are also expected to be non-trivial for random instances. For example, rank is an isomorphism invariant for the action of $\mathrm{GL}(n,q) \times \mathrm{GL}(n,q)$ on $M(n,q)$ by left and right multiplications. It is non-trivial because at least $1/q^{\Theta(1)}$ fraction of $M(n,q)$ are of non-full rank.
  As far as we known, for 3TI, CFI, QFMI, and pGpl, ATFE, despite having been studied in several areas for decades, no such isomorphism invariants are found. For example, tensor rank is certainly an isomorphism invariant for 3TI, but it is NP-hard [49], and most tensors are of full-rank, which makes it not useful for breaking the pseudorandom assumption.
- There are some non-trivial attack strategies in [53] supporting 3TI to be pseudorandom, including utilizing supergroups and invariant theory. These

attack strategies works for certain settings (such as unitary groups and special linear groups), but do not work with general linear groups. Such arguments can be used to support Conjecture 1 as well.

5   Algorithms for ATFE

In this section we study algorithms for ATFE, which are crucial to pin down the parameter choices of our signature scheme. Based on these, we state the best algorithm for ATFE, based on the current literature, runs in time

$$O\big(q^{2/3 \cdot n} \cdot n^{2 \cdot \omega} \cdot \log_2(q)\big), \tag{1}$$

where ω is the matrix multiplication exponent. This is based on the heuristic (but still analysable) algorithm to be explained below.

Let us first list known algorithms with rigorous analyses for ATFE. It should be noted that current algorithms actually solve the search version of ATFE, so the following applies to psATFE as well.

- The brute-force algorithm for ATFE enumerates $A \in \mathrm{GL}(n, q)$ and then verifies if $\phi = \psi \circ A$. This runs in time $q^{n^2} \cdot \mathrm{poly}(n, \log q)$.
- Worst-case algorithms: One can adapt the dynamic programming method in [59] to obtain an algorithm for ATFE in time $q^{\frac{1}{4}n^2 + O(n)}$.
- Average-case algorithms: An average-case algorithm for ATFE needs to solve the problem for inputs of the form ϕ, ψ for most $\phi \in \mathrm{ATF}(n, q)$ and arbitrary $\psi \in \mathrm{ATF}(n, q)$. In [46], an average-case algorithm for ATFE in time $q^{O(n)}$ was presented, which works for all but $\frac{1}{q^{\Omega(n)}}$ fraction of $\phi \in \mathrm{ATF}(n, q)$.[2] However, the constant hidden in the big O is at least 4 [46, arXiv version, Appendix C], therefore it is still not useful in practice.
- Quantum algorithms: as described in Sect. 1, known research on the hidden subgroup problem over general linear groups has mostly produced negative evidences. This may partly explain why there seems no non-trivial quantum algorithms in this setting, unlike the dihedral hidden subgroup problem. Still, it may be possible to use Grover search [47] to help speeding up some procedures useful for solving ATFE; see Remark 5.

From the above, we see that average-case algorithms are known to run in time $q^{O(n)}$. For practical purposes, however, it is desirable to obtain an algorithm in time $q^n \cdot \mathrm{poly}(n, \log q)$. The main purpose of this section is to explore ways of developing *heuristic* algorithms in time $q^{2/3 \cdot n} \cdot \mathrm{poly}(n, \log q)$. This seems to be a previously uncharted territory of heuristic algorithms for ATFE, but, thanks to Theorem 2, we can borrow ideas and experiences from multivariate cryptography and computational group theory. Conversely, any progress on ATFE should help with making progress on CFI and pGpI that have withstood attacks for decades.

---

[2] In [46] an algorithm in such time was presented for CFI, but its algorithmic idea can be readily applied to ATFE.

5.1   A Useful Isomorphism Invariant

To start with, we introduce the following notion which will be important for discussions on heuristic algorithms.

Definition 10. *Let $\phi \in \mathrm{ATF}(n, q)$. For $u \in \mathbb{F}_q^n$, let $\phi_u : \mathbb{F}_q^n \times \mathbb{F}_q^n \to \mathbb{F}_q$ be the alternating bilinear form defined by $\phi_u(v, w) = \phi(u, v, w)$.*

The rank of ϕ_u as an alternating trilinear form is an important invariant under isomorphism. That is, if $\phi = \psi \circ A$, then A must sends $u \in \mathbb{F}_q^n$ with $\mathrm{rk}(\phi_u) = r$ to some $v \in \mathbb{F}_q^n$ with $\mathrm{rk}(\psi_v) = r$. Also note that the rank of an alternating trilinear form must be an even number.

Given $\phi \in \mathrm{ATF}(n, q)$ and $r \in \mathbb{N}$, let $R_{\phi,r} := \{u \in \mathbb{F}_q^n : \mathrm{rk}(\phi_u) = r\}$. The sizes of $R_{\phi,r}$, $r \in \mathbb{N}$, form an important isomorphism invariant of ϕ. At present, there seems little research into the sizes of R_ϕ. So we run experiments to get an idea for small n and q. Our experiment results are summarized in Table 3.

Table 3. Experiment results on rank statistics. The first columns are of the form $(n, q)_a$, where a denotes the number of experiments run. The results are averaged over these many experiments. All these experiments produce ϕ with $R_{\phi,0} = \{0\}$.

	2	4	6	8	10
$(7, 5)_{100}$	5.76	16218.24	61900	N/A	N/A
$(8, 5)_1$	0	2064	388020	N/A	N/A
$(8, 7)_1$	0	17100	5747700	N/A	N/A
$(9, 2)_{100}$	0.01	9.77	281.62	291.60	N/A
$(9, 3)_{100}$	0	30	7064.24	12587.76	N/A
$(9, 5)_1$	0	216	409908	154300	N/A
$(10, 3)_{100}$	0	0.96	2451.74	56595.3	N/A
$(12, 3)_1$	0	0	10	25312	50918

Remark 3. Some interesting observations can be made regarding Table 3. For odd $n = 2k + 1$ and random $\phi \in \mathrm{ATF}(n, q)$, it seems that $|R_{\phi,2(k-1)}|$ is slightly larger than q^{n-1}, and $|R_{\phi,2(k-2)}|$ is slightly larger than q^{n-6}. For even $n = 2k$ and random $\phi \in \mathrm{ATF}(n, q)$, it seems that $|R_{\phi,2(k-2)}|$ is slightly larger than q^{n-3}, and $|R_{\phi,2(k-3)}|$ is slightly larger than q^{n-10}. It would be interesting to formally prove certain properties of rank statistics for random $\phi \in \mathrm{ATF}(n, q)$.

Remark 4. Rank statistics has been used to tackle pGpl in [18]. Following the approach in [18], one can design a heuristic algorithm in time $q^n \cdot \mathrm{poly}(n, \log q)$. However, that approach requires to enumerate all low rank matrices, which seems to prohibit from getting an algorithm in time $q^{cn} \cdot \mathrm{poly}(n, \log q)$, $c < 1$.

5.2   The Heuristic Algorithm with Running Time in Eq. (1)

We now describe the heuristic algorithm in time $O\bigl(q^{2/3 \cdot n} \cdot n^{2 \cdot \omega} \cdot \log_2(q)\bigr)$. This algorithm closely follows the algorithm for QFMI in [16] based on the Gröbner basis method.

Setting Up the Equations. One approach to set up a system of polynomials to solve ATFE is as follows. Let $\phi, \psi \in \mathrm{ATF}(n, q)$. We set up two $n \times n$ variable matrices X and Y, and impose that $XY = I$, where I is the identity matrix. (So X and Y are inverses to each other.) This gives us n^2 quadratic equations. Then instead of setting up equations in the form $\phi(X(u), X(v), X(w)) = \psi(u, v, w)$, we set it as

$$\phi(X(u), X(v), w) = \psi(u, v, Y(w)). \tag{2}$$

This helps us to get quadratic equations instead of cubic ones. This gives us $\binom{n}{3}$ equations. In total, we have $\binom{n}{3} + n^2$ quadratic equations in $2n^2$ variables.

The Direct Gröbner Basis Method: Experimental Results. To directly solve the above system of polynomial equations seems difficult. This echoes the experiences in directly solving QFMI and CFI by the Gröbner basis method in [14–16]. For example, in [14, Chap. 16] it was reported that for CFI, Gröbner basis attacks succeeded for $n = 6$ (in about $400\,\mathrm{s}$) and $n = 7$ (in about $17000\,\mathrm{s}$), but failed for $n = 8$.

We experimented with this direct attack for ATFE on a workstation[3] using Maple [61]. We carried out successful computations for $n = 6$ and $q = 5$ in about $700\,\mathrm{s}$, but could not achieve a successful one for $n = 7$ and $q = 5$ (using several monomial orders and both the quadratic and cubic methods): our experiments suggested that the memory usage went beyond 87 GB.

Maybe surprisingly, the Gröbner basis attack can be improved by adding more, seemingly redundant equations to the system. More precisely, we add equations to encode $YX = I$ on top of $XY = I$, and complete $\phi(X(u), X(v), w) = \psi(u, v, Y(w))$ with equations encoding $\phi(X(u), v, w) = \psi(u, Y(v), Y(w))$, $\phi(u, v, w) = \psi(Y(u), Y(v), Y(w))$, and $\phi(X(u), X(v), X(w)) = \psi(u, v, w)$. On top of this, we fix a subset of the variables and randomly assign values to them, before calling the Gröbner basis algorithm. This is in the spirit of hybrid Gröbner basis algorithms and also exploit the fact that many solutions may exist, especially in small dimension. This leads to a very fast attack on $n = 7$ and permits breaking $n = 8$. However, $n = 9$ remains out of range of this improvement.

Since the behaviours of Gröbner basis algorithms in our case on small sizes seemed not uniform, we didn't extrapolate the time needed by Gröbner basis attacks. Instead, we performed a theoretical anlysis as follows.

The Direct Gröbner Basis Method: Theoretical Asymptotic Analyses. From the theoretical analysis side, while a rigorous analysis of the Gröbner basis algorithm is notoriously difficult, it is possible to give some estimates based on certain assumptions.[4] Following the approach in [14, 16], we can give an upper bound on the regularity for these equations, *assuming* that these polynomials form a semi-regular sequence and using the results of Bardet et al. [8, 9].

---

[3] Processor: 2.6 GHz 18-core Intel(R) Xeon(R) Gold 6132; Memory 87 GB.
[4] We would like to thank Charles Bouillaguet for his help with understanding these methods here.

Let $(f_1, \ldots, f_m)$, $f_i \in \mathbb{F}[x_1, \ldots, x_n]$, be a sequence of polynomials. Generalising the classical notion of regular sequences of polynomials (for $m = n$), Bardet and Faugère introduced the notion of semi-regular sequences of polynomials (for $m > n$), and Bardet et al. studied the degree of regularities of the ideal spanned by these polynomials in [8,9]. An asymptotic estimate on the degree of regularity for semi-regular sequences of $m = \alpha N$ *quadratic* polynomials in N variables, α a constant, is given in [9] as

$$N\left(\alpha - \frac{1}{2} - \sqrt{\alpha(\alpha-1)}\right) - \frac{a_1}{2(\alpha(\alpha-1))^{1/6}} \cdot N^{1/3} - \left(2 - \frac{2\alpha-1}{4\sqrt{\alpha(\alpha-1)}}\right) + O(1/N^{1/3}),$$

$$(3)$$

where $a_1 \approx -2.33811$.

To apply Eq. (3) to ATFE, we need to *assume* that (i) the equations form a semi-regular sequence, and (ii) Eq. (3) applies to the setting when α is not necessarily a constant. These were assumed for QFMI and CFI in [14,16], and we assume so here as well. By Eq. (2), we have $\binom{n}{3} + n^2$ quadratic equations in $2n^2$ variables. Using Eq. (3) (with $\alpha = \frac{n}{12} + \frac{1}{4} + \frac{1}{6n}$ and $N = 2n^2$), we obtain that the degree of regularity is asymptotically $3n$. Therefore the F5 algorithm of Faugère [33] is expected to perform

$$O(N^{\omega \cdot 3n}) = O(2^{6\omega \cdot n \cdot \log_2(n)})$$

$$(4)$$

many arithmetic operations.

We would like to emphasize that the above estimation is heuristic, and only gives an upper bound. So while it is useful as a guidance, it is necessary to perform experiments.

The XL Method: Theoretical Asymptotic Analyses. Another approach of solving system of polynomial equations is the eXtended Linearisation (XL) method [21]. The XL method with a sparse matrix (such as Wiedemann) solver was proposed in [83] as an alternative to F4/F5 [33]. For the purpose of theoretical analyses here, the sparse matrix solver could improve the matrix multiplication exponent ω to 2 in Eq. (4). In particular, this implies that we need to take into account n^{12} in determining the underlying finite field order q. Because of this, for the sake of security, we will use 2 instead of ω in the choice of parameters (cf. Sect. 6.1). It will be interesting to experiment with XL for solving the polynomial equation system in Eq. (2), and we leave this in a future work.

Gröbner Basis Attack with Partial Information. To make progress, we can set the first row of the variable matrix X to be known, which amounts to say that the image of e_1 under X is known. This also gives a linear constraint on the columns of Y. We then essentially solve a system of polynomials in $2(n^2 - n)$ many variables. Such ideas have been used to solve CFI in [15].

We experiment with the improved Gröbner basis method with guessing one row (but without fixing a subset of variables and randomly assigning values to them). It turns out that, in this setting, the maximum degrees for the Gröbner basis computation to succeed are 3 for n up to 13. Furthermore, we can even use results from the Gröbner basis computation at degree 2 to solve the system. We take these as evidence that the Gröbner basis with partial information runs much faster than the method without partial information, and make the following assumption.

Assumption 1. Suppose $\phi, \psi \in \text{ATF}(n, q)$ such that $\phi = \psi \circ A$. Suppose the first column of A is known. Then the Gröbner basis computation reveals the rest entries of A in time $O(n^{2 \cdot \omega} \cdot \log(q))$.

Assumption 1 is consistent with the discoveries in [37] that the inhomogeneous version of QFMI can be solved by the Gröbner basis method in time $O(n^9)$, and in [15] that CFI can be solved with the Gröbner basis method with partial information in time $O(n^6)$.

Making Use of the Birthday Paradox. We now combine Assumption 1 with birthday paradox, following the idea in [16][5]. The key idea is to make use of those u whose ϕ_u has low rank.

Let us describe the idea in a concrete setting. Let $\phi, \psi \in \text{ATF}(n, q)$. For $u \in \mathbb{F}_q^n$, ϕ_u is the bilinear form defined in Definition 10, and *assume* that there exists $r \in \mathbb{N}$, such that $|R_{\phi,r}| \approx q^{2n/3}$. Then we sample $q^{n/3}$ vectors, say $S \subseteq R_{\phi,r}$ and $T \subseteq R_{\psi,r}$ respectively, in time $O(q^{2n/3})$. By the birthday paradox, there exist $u \in S$ and $v \in T$, such that $Au = v$ with constant probability. Knowing the image of A on one vector should help with recovering the whole A by using e.g. the Gröbner basis attack with partial information.

Note that the above relies on the assumption[6] that there exists r such that $|R_{\phi,r}| \approx q^{2n/3}$. For other parameters this method still gives improvement but, because it needs to balance sampling vectors to get S and T and the use of birtday paradox, so $q^{2/3 \cdot n}$ is the best it can achieve.

Combining Assumption 1 with the above, we have a heuristic algorithm in time $O(q^{2/3 \cdot n} \cdot n^{2 \cdot \omega} \cdot \log_2(q))$.

5.3   Attacks Based on Min-Rank

Several attacks on the hidden field equation proposal [71] rely on solving the min-rank problem: given matrices $A_0, A_1, \ldots, A_m \in M(n, q)$, let $\mathcal{A} = \{A_0 + \sum_{i=1}^n \alpha_i A_i : \alpha_i \in \mathbb{F}_q\}$ be the affine subspace of $M(n, q)$. The min-rank problem asks to compute a matrix of minimum rank in $\mathcal{A}$. It is NP-complete [20], but several non-trivial algorithms have been developed for this problem.

---

[5] There is another algorithm in [16] with time complexity $q^{n/2} \cdot \text{poly}(n, \log q)$, but it was designed for characteristic 2 fields, which we do not use for concrete instantiations in Sect. 6.1.

[6] By Table 3, for $n = 10$ which will be used to instantiate our scheme in Sect. 6.1, we see that $|R_{\phi,6}| \approx q^7$, where $7 \approx 20/3$. On the other hand for odd n there is no such r.

The min-rank problem is of relevance to **ATFE** because of the rank statistics in Sect. 5.1. To make the connection more obvious, we review the well-known connection between alternating trilinear forms and 3-way arrays.

Definition 11. *Given $\phi \in \text{ATF}(n,q)$, written as $\phi = \sum_{1 \leq i < j < k \leq n} a_{i,j,k} e_i^* \wedge e_j^* \wedge e_k^*$ (cf. Sect. 2.1), we define a 3-way array $(b_{r,s,t})_{r,s,t \in [n]}$, $b_{r,s,t} \in \mathbb{F}_q$, by setting $b_{r,s,t} = \phi(e_r, e_s, e_t)$. Then for $t \in [n]$, construct a matrix $B_t = (b_{r,s,t})_{r,s \in [n]}$. Let $u = (u_1, \ldots, u_n)^t \in \mathbb{F}_q^n$. Then it is easy to verify that $\text{rk}(\phi_u) = \text{rk}(\sum_{i=1}^n u_i B_i)$.*

As we have seen in Sect. 5.2, the rank statistics is useful for algorithmic purposes. In particular, in the algorithm in Sect. 5.2, it is useful to get some $u \in \mathbb{F}_q^n$ of such that ϕ_u is of minimum rank among non-zero vectors. Note though that for isomorphism testing purposes, just one such u seems not quite helpful. Instead, we need a large fraction, if not all, of the u whose ϕ_u is of minimum rank in order to create a collision.

So we examine some algorithms for the min-rank problem and their potential consequences on **ATFE**. Note that the instance of the min-rank problem relevant to us is the following: given $A_1, \ldots, A_n \in M(n,q)$ be n matrices, and $\mathcal{A}$ be the linear subspace of $M(n,q)$ spanned by A_i's. The problem is to find a non-zero matrix $A \in \mathcal{A}$ of rank $\leq r$.

The Kernel Attack. In [42], the kernel method on the min-rank problem was proposed. In our context, because we have n matrices of size $n \times n$, this method works as follows. Let $A \in \mathcal{A}$ be of rank $\leq r$. Suppose $v \in \mathbb{F}_q^n$ is in the kernel of A. Then construct $(\sum_{i \in [n]} x_i A_i) v = \mathbf{0}$, which consists of n linear equations in the variables $x_1, \ldots, x_n$. It can be expected that the solution space is of 1-dimensional, and any non-zero solution gives rise to λA for some nonzero $\lambda \in \mathbb{F}_q$. So the problem is to sample a non-zero vector in $\ker(A)$. Since $|\ker(A)| = q^{n-r}$ we expect to get one after q^r many samplings.

To adapt the above to our setting incurs an extra cost. Recall the matrices B_i's in Definition 11, constructed from an alternating trilinear form $\phi \in \Lambda(n,q)$. Let $\mathcal{B}$ be the space of matrices spanned by B_i's. Suppose for some $B = \sum_{i \in [n]} u_i B_i \in \mathcal{B}$, we have $\text{rk}(B) = r$. For $v \in \ker(B)$, set up the equations $(\sum_{i \in [n]} x_i B_i) v = \mathbf{0}$, and let S be the solution space. So S contains $u = (u_1, \ldots, u_n)$ as promised, but S also contains v due to the alternating property. In other words, $\dim(S)$ is at least 2, and we need to go through all the lines in $\dim(S)$. This adds a multiplicative factor of q to the original sampling.

To use the above in solving **ATFE**, we can combine the above with the birthday paradox idea from [16] as follows. Let $\phi, \psi \in \text{ATF}(n,q)$ be the input to **ATFE**. Suppose $\min\{\text{rk}(\phi_u) : u \in \mathbb{F}_q^n\} = \min\{\text{rk}(\psi_u) : u \in \mathbb{F}_q^n\}$, which should holds with high probability. Let r be this minimum rank and it is known to us (by carrying out experiments from Table 3). Suppose $R_{\phi,r}$ and $R_{\psi,r}$ (defined in Sect. 5.1) are of size $\approx s$, which can also be determined before hand using experiments. By birthday paradox, to create a collision it is enough to sampling $\sqrt{s}$ many $u \in \mathbb{F}_q^n$ from $R_{\phi,r}$ and $R_{\psi,r}$, respectively. Each sampling requires $q^r \cdot q$ many operations, so total sampling needs $q^{r+1} \cdot \sqrt{s}$ many operations. After that we get a collision (i.e. u and v such that $Au = v$ for some A sending ϕ to ψ)

with constant probability by trying over $\sqrt{s} \cdot \sqrt{s} = s$ many possibilities. Because of Assumption 1, the rest can be solved in polynomial time.

From the above we see that the main multiplicative factors are $q^{r+1} \cdot \sqrt{s}$ and s. From Table 3 and Remark 3, when $n = 9$, we seem to have $r = 4$ and $s = q^3$ in this case. So $q^{r+1} \cdot \sqrt{s}$ becomes $q^{6.5} > q^{2/3 \cdot n}$. Combining with Assumption 1, the running time of the algorithm is not competitive with $O(q^{2/3 \cdot n} \cdot n^{2 \cdot \omega} \cdot \log_2(q))$.

Remark 5. The Grover search should be helpful in the above setting. Note that it is easy to formulate searching a (non-zero) matrix of minimum rank as a marked search problem. Using the terminologies above, the multi-target Grover search can return a matrix of rank r (minimum rank) in quantum time $\sqrt{\frac{q^n}{s}}$. Therefore getting $\sqrt{s}$-many min-rank matrices requires quantum time $q^{n/2}$. This is better than q^{r+1} when $n \le 2(r+1)$.

We also studied attacks based on the Kipnis-Shamir relinearisation attack [55] and that with the Gröbner basis method [34–36]. These will be reported in the full version of this paper.

6   Implementation Results

6.1   Parameter Choices

The following analysis on parameters with respect to a fixed security level is modelled after CSI-FiSh [11]. We present here the choice of parameters for the basic scheme in Sect. 3.1.

To achieve the security level as λ bits, there are four parameters to determine: n and q as in $\mathsf{ATF}(n, q)$, the round number r, and the number of alternating trilinear forms generated in each round which is $C = 2^c$. Some key criteria are as follows.

– First, by Eq. (1) from the algorithmic study of ATFE, we use

$$\frac{2}{3} \cdot n \cdot \log_2(q) + 2\omega \cdot \log_2(n) + \log_2(\log_2(q)) \ge \lambda. \tag{5}$$

to estimate the bit complexity for solving ATFE. Here ω is the matrix multiplication exponent, and we take $\omega = 2$ for the sake of added security.
– As discussed in [11], as customary it is reasonable to assume that the probability of a successful attack is at most $Q \times E$, where Q is the number of hash function evaluations and E is the soundness error of the zero-knowledge Goldreich-Micali-Wigderson protocol. Therefore we require $C^{-r} \le 2^{-\lambda}$, leading to

$$r \cdot c \ge \lambda. \tag{6}$$

It is possible to improve this a little bit by "slowing down" the hash function as indicated in [11], but we shall not explore this here.

- The scheme implies that the public key, private key, and signature sizes in terms of bytes are as follows.

$$\text{PubKeySize} = \quad 2^c \cdot \binom{n}{3} \cdot \lceil \log_2(q) \rceil / 8, \qquad (7)$$

$$\text{PriKeySize} = \quad 2^c \cdot n^2 \cdot \lceil \log_2(q) \rceil / 8, \qquad (8)$$

$$\text{SigSize} = \quad r \cdot (c + n^2 \cdot \lceil \log_2(q) \rceil) / 8. \qquad (9)$$

We list our reasons for parameter choices.

The Choice of n. As the public key size grows in n^3, we wish to keep n as small as possible. By the attack methods described in Sect. 5, the only attack method that is insensitive to q is the Gröbner basis attack. So we need to set up n such that the Gröbner basis attack fails.

The practical experiments with Gröbner basis as reported in Sect. 5.2 indicate setting $n \geq 9$. This is partly due to an important distinction between $n = 8$ and $n = 9$. That is, when $n = 8$, the dimension of ATF$(8, q)$ (56) is less than the dimension of GL$(8, q)$ (64). This weakness disappears at $n = 9$, when the dimension of ATF$(9, q)$ (84) exceeds the dimension of GL$(9, q)$ (81). Because of these, we choose n to be 9, 10, and 11 as first test beds.

The Choice of q. Since the only thing that matters in our analysis about q is its size, it seems reasonable to set q to be a prime for simpler and hopefully faster implementation.

The Choice of r and c. It seems reasonable to set r and $C = 2^c$ to be roughly the same. This is because C controls the public key size and r controls the signature size. Making r and C close helps to achieve the best performance regarding the sum of public key and signature sizes. We also need to ensure that $q^{2/3} \leq n^{12}$ so that $q^{2/3n} \leq n^{12n}$ by the Gröbner basis method analysis.

Based on the above, we provide two sets of parameter choices for the basic scheme as follows. Note that we include both $n = 8$ and $n = 9$, as odd and even numbers seem to demonstrate different behaviours regarding the rank statistics (Table 3), which in turn affects the attack methods.

6.2   A Prototype Implementation

In this section, we provide a prototype implementation of the basic scheme using C to evaluate its practical efficiency. We first explain some optimizations we have performed on our prototype. We then propose some concrete parameter sets and report the running times of our implementation.

1. First, to efficiently generate random invertible matrix A_i over $\mathbb{F}_q$, we generate each time two random matrices $L_i \in \mathbb{F}_q^{n,n}$ and $U_i \in \mathbb{F}_q^{n,n}$ such that
   - $L_{i,j} \overset{\$}{\leftarrow} \mathbb{F}_q$ if $i > j$, $L_{i,j} = 0$ if $i < j$ and $L_{i,i} = 1$,

– $U_{i,j} \xleftarrow{\$} \mathbb{F}_q$ if $i < j, U_{i,j} = 0$ if $i > j$ and $U_{i,i} \xleftarrow{\$} \mathbb{F}_q^*$.

Consequently, we can efficiently compute $A_i = L_i U_i$. The LU decomposition guarantees a bijection between the set of the invertible matrices in $\mathbb{F}_q$ and the $q^{n(n-1)}(q-1)^n$ possible combinations of L_i and U_i. It allows us to avoid determinant computation as well as re-sampling in case A_i is a singular matrix.

2. Secondly, we use a dedicated technique to perform modular reduction. Operating on matrices and tensors require multiple computations of a sum of products of elements over $\mathbb{F}_q$. To perform those inner products efficiently, we will start by computing the sum of products in $\mathbb{Z}$ and then performing a modular reduction, which we employ the algorithm proposed recently by Plantard in [73]. It allows us to efficiently reduce the resulting inner product, which is smaller than nq^2, to a number smaller than q by in just 2 multiplications, 2 bit-shifts and one addition; see [73] for more detail. In such situation, this choice is outperforming the usage of Pseudo-Mersenne number [26] as well as Montgomery reduction [66]. However, it requires two specific corrections:

   – the result is $\leq q$ not $< q$. This slight redundancy needs to be corrected at the final stage of computations; and
   – the modular arithmetic uses a Montgomery-like representation, i.e., in our computations, $x \bmod q$ will be represented by $x \cdot (-2^{64}) \bmod q$. However, the computation output do not need to be in such representation. Furthermore, to pick random elements in $\mathbb{F}_q$ or $\mathbb{F}_q^*$, one can assume those elements being already in such representation. Nevertheless, when initializing the identity matrix we will simply initiate 1 in the diagonal directly to $-2^{64} \bmod q$.

Our experience suggests that the main overhead lies at the computation of the group action. The procedure described in Sect. 2.1 requires $O(n^6)$ many operations. To bring this down we can first turn alternating trilinear forms into 3-way arrays as in Definition 11, and then perform $3n$ many matrix multiplications. This results in a procedure with $O(n^4)$ many operations. The alternating structure helps to reduce the constant hidden in the big O notation.

Remark 6. For modular arithmetics, we also implemented the Montgomery classic method [66], the reduction modulo a Pseudo-Mersenne method [26], as well as Seiler's method [76]. Our experiments suggested that, while there were no significant differences among these four methods, the method we use in this paper following [73] is the most efficient, as shown in Table 4.

Some Concrete Proposals. Based on the above analysis, we propose some concrete instantiations in Tables 5. For timing, we performed 10^5 tests for each function and computed the average. Our tests were performed on a Linux 5.11.0-37-generic with Intel Core i7-8565U CPU (1.80 GHz) and compiled with g++10.3.0 with "-Ofast -flto -fwhole-program -march=native" options.

Table 4. The timings for four modular arithmetic methods for Option 2 in Table 5. The results were averaged over 10^5 tests for each method.

Method	Set-Up	Sign	Verify
[73]	383.1	660.0	578.9
[66]	414.1	678.8	616.1
[26]	412.8	682.8	598.8
[76]	425.0	692.7	609.1

Table 5. Proposed concrete instantiations of the proposed scheme.

	Parameters					Size in Byte			Time in μs		
	n	q	r	c	λ	Public key	Private key	Signature	Set-Up	Sign	Verify
Option 1	9	524287	26	5	128	6384	6156	5018	285.9	471.7	416.5
Option 2	10	131071	26	5	128	8160	6800	5542	383.1	660.0	578.9
Option 3	10	131071	32	4	128	4080	3400	6816	190.7	795.4	708.8
Option 4	11	65521	26	5	128	10560	7744	6309	514.0	861.1	765.2

Acknowledgement. We thank the reviewers for their careful reading and several questions and suggestions. Y.Q. was partly supported by the Australian Research Council Discovery Projects DP200100950. D.H.D. and W.S. were partly supported by the Australian Research Council Linkage Projects LP190100984. A.J. was supported by the European Union's H2020 Programme under grant agreement number ERC-669891.

References

1. Agrawal, M., Saxena, N.: Automorphisms of finite rings and applications to complexity of problems. In: Diekert, V., Durand, B. (eds.) STACS 2005. LNCS, vol. 3404, pp. 1–17. Springer, Heidelberg (2005). https://doi.org/10.1007/978-3-540-31856-9_1

2. Agrawal, M., Saxena, N.: Equivalence of f-algebras and cubic forms. In: Durand, B., Thomas, W. (eds.) STACS 2006. LNCS, vol. 3884, pp. 115–126. Springer, Heidelberg (2006). https://doi.org/10.1007/11672142_8

3. Alagic, G., et al.: Status report on the second round of the NIST post-quantum cryptography standardization process. Technical report, National Institute of Standards and Technology (2020)

4. Alamati, N., De Feo, L., Montgomery, H., Patranabis, S.: Cryptographic group actions and applications. In: Moriai, S., Wang, H. (eds.) ASIACRYPT 2020. LNCS, vol. 12492, pp. 411–439. Springer, Cham (2020). https://doi.org/10.1007/978-3-030-64834-3_14

5. Atkinson, M.D.: Alternating trilinear forms and groups of exponent 6. J. Aust. Math. Soc. **16**(1), 111–128 (1973)

6. Babai, L.: Graph isomorphism in quasipolynomial time [extended abstract]. In: STOC 2016, pp. 684–697 (2016)
7. Bai, S., et al.: Crystals-dilithium: algorithm specifications and supporting documentation (version 3.1) (2021). https://pq-crystals.org/dilithium/data/dilithium-specification-round3-20210208.pdf
8. Bardet, M.: Étude des systèmes algébriques surdéterminés. Applications aux codes correcteurs et à la cryptographie. PhD thesis, Université Pierre et Marie Curie-Paris VI (2004)
9. Bardet, M., Faugère, J.C., Salvy, B., Yang, B.Y.: Asymptotic behaviour of the degree of regularity of semi-regular polynomial systems. In: Proceedings of the MEGA, vol. 5 (2005)
10. Berthomieu, J., Faugère, J.-C., Perret, L.: Polynomial-time algorithms for quadratic isomorphism of polynomials: the regular case. J. Complex. **31**(4), 590–616 (2015)
11. Beullens, W., Kleinjung, T., Vercauteren, F.: CSI-FiSh: efficient isogeny based signatures through class group computations. In: Galbraith, S.D., Moriai, S. (eds.) ASIACRYPT 2019. LNCS, vol. 11921, pp. 227–247. Springer, Cham (2019). https://doi.org/10.1007/978-3-030-34578-5_9
12. Bellare, M., Neven, G.: Multi-signatures in the plain public-Key model and a general forking lemma. In: CCS 2006, pp. 390–399 (2016)
13. Bonnetain, X., Schrottenloher, A.: Quantum security analysis of CSIDH. In: Canteaut, A., Ishai, Y. (eds.) EUROCRYPT 2020. LNCS, vol. 12106, pp. 493–522. Springer, Cham (2020). https://doi.org/10.1007/978-3-030-45724-2_17
14. Bouillaguet, C.: Etudes d'hypotheses algorithmiques et attaques de primitives cryptographiques. PhD thesis, PhD thesis, Université Paris-Diderot-École Normale Supérieure (2011)
15. Bouillaguet, C., Faugère, J.-C., Fouque, P.-A., Perret, L.: Practical cryptanalysis of the identification scheme based on the isomorphism of polynomial with one secret problem. In: Catalano, D., Fazio, N., Gennaro, R., Nicolosi, A. (eds.) PKC 2011. LNCS, vol. 6571, pp. 473–493. Springer, Heidelberg (2011). https://doi.org/10.1007/978-3-642-19379-8_29
16. Bouillaguet, C., Fouque, P.-A., Véber, A.: Graph-theoretic algorithms for the "isomorphism of polynomials" problem. In: Johansson, T., Nguyen, P.Q. (eds.) EUROCRYPT 2013. LNCS, vol. 7881, pp. 211–227. Springer, Heidelberg (2013). https://doi.org/10.1007/978-3-642-38348-9_13
17. Brassard, G., Yung, M.: One-way group actions. In: Menezes, A.J., Vanstone, S.A. (eds.) CRYPTO 1990. LNCS, vol. 537, pp. 94–107. Springer, Heidelberg (1991). https://doi.org/10.1007/3-540-38424-3_7
18. Brooksbank, P.A., Li, Y., Qiao, Y., Wilson, J.B.: Improved algorithms for alternating matrix space isometry: from theory to practice. In: 28th ESA 2020, pp. 26:1–26:15 (2020)
19. Brooksbank, P.A., Maglione, J., Wilson, J.B.: A fast isomorphism test for groups whose Lie algebra has genus 2. J. Algebra **473**, 545–590 (2017)
20. Buss, J.F., Frandsen, G.S., Shallit, J.O.: The computational complexity of some problems of linear algebra. J. Comput. Syst. Sci. **58**(3), 572–596 (1999)
21. Courtois, N., Klimov, A., Patarin, J., Shamir, A.: Efficient algorithms for solving overdefined systems of multivariate polynomial equations. In: Preneel, B. (ed.) EUROCRYPT 2000. LNCS, vol. 1807, pp. 392–407. Springer, Heidelberg (2000). https://doi.org/10.1007/3-540-45539-6_27

22. Castryck, W., Lange, T., Martindale, C., Panny, L., Renes, J.: CSIDH: an efficient post-quantum commutative group action. In: Peyrin, T., Galbraith, S. (eds.) ASIACRYPT 2018. LNCS, vol. 11274, pp. 395–427. Springer, Cham (2018). https://doi.org/10.1007/978-3-030-03332-3_15

23. Childs, A., Jao, D., Soukharev, V.: Constructing elliptic curve isogenies in quantum subexponential time. J. Math. Cryptol. **8**(1), 1–29 (2014)

24. Cohen, A.M., Helminck, A.G.: Trilinear alternating forms on a vector space of dimension 7. Commun. Algebra **16**(1), 1–25 (1988)

25. Couveignes, J.M.: Hard homogeneous spaces. IACR Cryptology ePrint Archive (2006)

26. Crandall, R.E.: Method and apparatus for public key exchange in a cryptographic system. U.S. Patent number 5159632 (1992)

27. De Feo, L., Kohel, D., Leroux, A., Petit, C., Wesolowski, B.: SQISign: compact post-quantum signatures from quaternions and isogenies. In: Moriai, S., Wang, H. (eds.) ASIACRYPT 2020. LNCS, vol. 12491, pp. 64–93. Springer, Cham (2020). https://doi.org/10.1007/978-3-030-64837-4_3

28. Ding, J., Schmidt, D.: Rainbow, a new multivariable polynomial signature scheme. In: Ioannidis, J., Keromytis, A., Yung, M. (eds.) ACNS 2005. LNCS, vol. 3531, pp. 164–175. Springer, Heidelberg (2005). https://doi.org/10.1007/11496137_12

29. Don, J., Fehr, S., Majenz, C., Schaffner, C.: Security of the fiat-shamir transformation in the quantum random-oracle model. In: Boldyreva, A., Micciancio, D. (eds.) CRYPTO 2019. LNCS, vol. 11693, pp. 356–383. Springer, Cham (2019). https://doi.org/10.1007/978-3-030-26951-7_13

30. Draisma, J., Shaw, R.: Some noteworthy alternating trilinear forms. J. Geom. **105**(1), 167–176 (2013). https://doi.org/10.1007/s00022-013-0202-2

31. El Kaafarani, A., Katsumata, S., Pintore, F.: Lossy CSI-FiSh: efficient signature scheme with tight reduction to decisional CSIDH-512. In: Kiayias, A., Kohlweiss, M., Wallden, P., Zikas, V. (eds.) PKC 2020. LNCS, vol. 12111, pp. 157–186. Springer, Cham (2020). https://doi.org/10.1007/978-3-030-45388-6_6

32. Erdős, P., Rényi, A.: Asymmetric graphs. Acta Math. Hung. **14**(3–4), 295–315 (1963)

33. Faugère, J.-C.: A new efficient algorithm for computing gröbner bases without reduction to zero (F5). In: Proceedings of the 2002 International Symposium on Symbolic and Algebraic Computation, pp. 75–83 (2002)

34. Faugere, J.-C., El Din, M.S., Spaenlehauer, P.-J.: Computing loci of rank defects of linear matrices using gröbner bases and applications to cryptology. In: ISSAC 2010, pp. 257–264 (2010)

35. Faugere, J.-C., El Din, M.S., Spaenlehauer, P.-J.: On the complexity of the generalized minrank problem. J. Symb. Comput. **55**, 30–58 (2013)

36. Faugère, J.-C., Levy-dit-Vehel, F., Perret, L.: Cryptanalysis of MinRank. In: Wagner, D. (ed.) CRYPTO 2008. LNCS, vol. 5157, pp. 280–296. Springer, Heidelberg (2008). https://doi.org/10.1007/978-3-540-85174-5_16

37. Faugère, J.-C., Perret, L.: Polynomial equivalence problems: algorithmic and theoretical aspects. In: Vaudenay, S. (ed.) EUROCRYPT 2006. LNCS, vol. 4004, pp. 30–47. Springer, Heidelberg (2006). https://doi.org/10.1007/11761679_3

38. De Feo, L., Galbraith, S.D.: SeaSign: compact isogeny signatures from class group actions. In: Ishai, Y., Rijmen, V. (eds.) EUROCRYPT 2019. LNCS, vol. 11478, pp. 759–789. Springer, Cham (2019). https://doi.org/10.1007/978-3-030-17659-4_26

39. Fiat, A., Shamir, A.: How to prove yourself: practical solutions to identification and signature problems. In: Odlyzko, A.M. (ed.) CRYPTO 1986. LNCS, vol. 263, pp. 186–194. Springer, Heidelberg (1987). https://doi.org/10.1007/3-540-47721-7_12

40. Fouque, P.-A., et al.: Falcon: fast-fourier lattice-based compact signatures over NTRU (specification v1.2) (2020). https://falcon-sign.info/falcon.pdf
41. Goldreich, O., Micali, S., Wigderson, A.: Proofs that yield nothing but their validity for all languages in NP have zero-knowledge proof systems. J. ACM **38**(3), 691–729 (1991)
42. Goubin, L., Courtois, N.T.: Cryptanalysis of the TTM cryptosystem. In: Okamoto, T. (ed.) ASIACRYPT 2000. LNCS, vol. 1976, pp. 44–57. Springer, Heidelberg (2000). https://doi.org/10.1007/3-540-44448-3_4
43. Grigni, M., Schulman, L.J., Vazirani, M., Vazirani, U.V.: Quantum mechanical algorithms for the nonabelian hidden subgroup problem. Comb. **24**(1), 137–154 (2004)
44. Grochow, J.A., Qiao, Y.: On the complexity of isomorphism problems for tensors, groups, and polynomials I: tensor isomorphism-completeness. In: ITCS 2021, pp. 31:1–31:19 (2021)
45. Grochow, J.A., Qiao, Y.: On p-group isomorphism: search-to-decision, counting-to-decision, and nilpotency class reductions via tensors. In: CCC 2021, pp. 16:1–16:38 (2021)
46. Grochow, J.A., Qiao, Y., Tang, G.: Average-case algorithms for testing isomorphism of polynomials, algebras, and multilinear forms. In: STACS 2021, pp. 38:1–38:17 (2021)
47. Grover, L.K.: A fast quantum mechanical algorithm for database search. In Proceedings of the Twenty-eighth Annual ACM Symposium on Theory of Computing, pp. 212–219 (1996)
48. Hallgren, S., Moore, C., Rötteler, M., Russell, A., Sen, P.: Limitations of quantum coset states for graph isomorphism. J. ACM **57**(6):34:1–34:33 (2010)
49. Håstad, J.: Tensor rank is NP-complete. J. Algorithms **11**(4), 644–654 (1990)
50. Hora, J., Pudlák, P.: Classification of 8-dimensional trilinear alternating forms over gf (2). Commun. Algebra **43**(8), 3459–3471 (2015)
51. Ivanyos, G., Qiao, Y.: Algorithms based on *-algebras, and their applications to isomorphism of polynomials with one secret, group isomorphism, and polynomial identity testing. SIAM J. Comput. **48**(3), 926–963 (2019)
52. Beullens, W., et al.: SPHINCS+: submission to the NIST post-quantum project, vol. 3 (2020). https://sphincs.org/data/sphincs+-round3-specification.pdf
53. Ji, Z., Qiao, Y., Song, F., Yun, A.: General linear group action on tensors: a candidate for post-quantum cryptography. In: Hofheinz, D., Rosen, A. (eds.) TCC 2019. LNCS, vol. 11891, pp. 251–281. Springer, Cham (2019). https://doi.org/10.1007/978-3-030-36030-6_11
54. Jao, D., De Feo, L.: Towards quantum-resistant cryptosystems from supersingular elliptic curve isogenies. In: Yang, B.-Y. (ed.) PQCrypto 2011. LNCS, vol. 7071, pp. 19–34. Springer, Heidelberg (2011). https://doi.org/10.1007/978-3-642-25405-5_2
55. Kipnis, A., Shamir, A.: Cryptanalysis of the HFE public key cryptosystem by relinearization. In: Wiener, M. (ed.) CRYPTO 1999. LNCS, vol. 1666, pp. 19–30. Springer, Heidelberg (1999). https://doi.org/10.1007/3-540-48405-1_2
56. Köbler, J., Schöning, U., Torán, J.: The graph isomorphism problem. Basel Birkhäuser (1993)
57. Kuperberg, G.: A subexponential-time quantum algorithm for the dihedral hidden subgroup problem. SIAM J. Comput. **35**(1), 170–188 (2005)
58. Kuperberg, G.: Another subexponential-time quantum algorithm for the dihedral hidden subgroup problem. In: TQC 2013, pp. 20–34 (2013)

59. Li, Y., Qiao, Y.: Linear algebraic analogues of the graph isomorphism problem and the Erdős-Rényi model. In: FOCS 2017, pp. 463–474. IEEE Computer Society (2017)

60. Liu, Q., Zhandry, M.: Revisiting post-quantum Fiat-Shamir. In: Boldyreva, A., Micciancio, D. (eds.) CRYPTO 2019. LNCS, vol. 11693, pp. 326–355. Springer, Cham (2019). https://doi.org/10.1007/978-3-030-26951-7_12

61. Waterloo, Ontario: Maplesoft, a division of Waterloo Maple Inc., Maple (2020.2) (2020)

62. McKay, B.D.: Practical graph isomorphism. Congr. Numer. **30**, 45–87 (1980)

63. McKay, B.D., Piperno, A.: Practical graph isomorphism II. J. Symb. Comput. **60**, 94–112 (2014)

64. Merkle, R.C.: A certified digital signature. In: Brassard, G. (ed.) CRYPTO 1989. LNCS, vol. 435, pp. 218–238. Springer, New York (1990). https://doi.org/10.1007/0-387-34805-0_21

65. Midoune, N., Noui, L.: Trilinear alternating forms on a vector space of dimension 8 over a finite field. Linear Multilinear Algebra **61**(1), 15–21 (2013)

66. Montgomery, P.L.: Modular multiplication without trial division. Math. Comput. **44**, 519–521 (1985)

67. Moore, C., Russell, A., Schulman, L.J.: The symmetric group defies strong fourier sampling. SIAM J. Comput. **37**(6), 1842–1864 (2008)

68. Moore, C., Russell, A., Vazirani, U.: A classical one-way function to confound quantum adversaries. arXiv preprint quant-ph/0701115 (2007)

69. Moody, D.: The Homestretch: the beginning of the end of the NIST PQC 3rd Round, PQCrypto (2021). https://pqcrypto2021.kr/download/program/2.2_PQCrypto2021.pdf

70. O'Brien, E.A.: Isomorphism testing for p-groups. J. Symb. Comput. **17**(2), 133–147 (1994)

71. Patarin, J.: hidden fields equations (HFE) and isomorphisms of polynomials (IP): two new families of asymmetric algorithms. In: Maurer, U. (ed.) EUROCRYPT 1996. LNCS, vol. 1070, pp. 33–48. Springer, Heidelberg (1996). https://doi.org/10.1007/3-540-68339-9_4

72. Peikert, C.: He gives C-sieves on the CSIDH. In: Canteaut, A., Ishai, Y. (eds.) EUROCRYPT 2020. LNCS, vol. 12106, pp. 463–492. Springer, Cham (2020). https://doi.org/10.1007/978-3-030-45724-2_16

73. Plantard, T.: Efficient word size modular arithmetic. IEEE Trans. Emerg. Top. Comput. **9**(3), 1506–1518 (2021)

74. Regev, O.: Quantum computation and lattice problems. SIAM J. Comput. **33**(3), 738–760 (2004)

75. Schulman, L.J.: Cryptography from tensor problems. IACR Cryptol. ePrint Arch. **2012**, 244 (2012)

76. Seiler, G.: Faster AVX2 optimized NTT multiplication for Ring-LWE lattice cryptography. IACR Cryptol. ePrint Arch. **2018**, 039 (2018)

77. Sendrier, N.: Finding the permutation between equivalent linear codes: the support splitting algorithm. IEEE Trans. Inf. Theory **46**(4), 1193–1203 (2000)

78. Chen, M.S., et al.: Rainbow signature: one of the three nist post-quantum signature finalists (2021). https://www.pqcrainbow.org/

79. Shor, P.W.: Polynomial-time algorithms for prime factorization and discrete logarithms on a quantum computer. SIAM J. Comput. **26**(5), 1484–1509 (1997)

80. Stolbunov, A.: Cryptographic schemes based on isogenies. PhD thesis, Norwegian University of Science and Technology (2012)

81. Wilson, J.B.: Decomposing p-groups via Jordan algebras. J. Algebra **322**(8), 2642–2679 (2009)
82. Wright, E.M.: Graphs on unlabelled nodes with a given number of edges. Acta Math. **126**(1), 1–9 (1971)
83. Yeh, J.Y.-C., Cheng, C.-M., Yang, B.-Y.: Operating degrees for XL vs. F4/F5 for generic $\mathcal{MQ}$ with number of equations linear in that of variables. In: Fischlin, M., Katzenbeisser, S. (eds.) Number Theory and Cryptography. LNCS, vol. 8260, pp. 19–33. Springer, Heidelberg (2013). https://doi.org/10.1007/978-3-642-42001-6_3

On IND-qCCA Security in the ROM
and Its Applications

CPA Security Is Sufficient for TLS 1.3

Loïs Huguenin-Dumittan[✉] and Serge Vaudenay

EPFL, Lausanne, Switzerland
{lois.huguenin-dumittan,serge.vaudenay}@epfl.ch

Abstract. Bounded IND-CCA security (IND-qCCA) is a notion similar
to the traditional IND-CCA security, except the adversary is restricted
to a constant number q of decryption/decapsulation queries. We show in
this work that IND-qCCA is easily obtained from any passively secure
PKE in the (Q)ROM. That is, simply adding a confirmation hash or
computing the key as the hash of the plaintext and ciphertext holds
an IND-qCCA KEM. In particular, there is no need for derandomization or re-encryption as in the Fujisaki-Okamoto (FO) transform [15].
This makes the decapsulation process of such IND-qCCA KEM much
more efficient than its FO-derived counterpart. In addition, IND-qCCA
KEMs could be used in the recently proposed KEMTLS protocol [29] that
requires IND-1CCA ephemeral key-exchange mechanisms, or in TLS 1.3.
Then, using similar proof techniques, we show that CPA-secure KEMs
are sufficient for the TLS 1.3 handshake to be secure, solving an open
problem in the ROM. In turn, this implies that the PRF-ODH assumption used to prove the security of TLS 1.3 is not necessary and can be
replaced by the CDH assumption in the ROM. We also highlight and
briefly discuss several use cases of IND-1CCA KEMs in protocols and
ratcheting primitives.

1 Introduction

As the NIST standardization process for post-quantum (PQ) public-key cryptography progresses, studying how these new PQ schemes could be integrated
into existing protocols has become a hot topic. In particular, the newly adopted
TLS 1.3 in its standard form is already "PQ-obsolete" in the sense that only
traditional Diffie-Hellman (DH) key-exchange is supported. Indeed, as most PQ
schemes come into the form of *Key-Encapsulation Mechanisms* (KEMs) and not
Key-Exchange (KEX) such as DH, TLS 1.3 needs modifications to be quantum-
resistant.

Several implementations of PQ TLS 1.3 have already been experimented, the
most well-known one surely being the OQS-OpenSSL project [1]. This library
implements a TLS handshake that supports KEMs and *hybrid cryptography* (i.e.
the final shared secret is a combination of a DH secret and a KEM secret/key).

© International Association for Cryptologic Research 2022
O. Dunkelman and S. Dziembowski (Eds.): EUROCRYPT 2022, LNCS 13277, pp. 613–642, 2022.
https://doi.org/10.1007/978-3-031-07082-2_22

The changes compared to the standard version of the TLS 1.3 handshake are minimal. That is, the client (resp. server) DH share is replaced by a public-key (resp. a ciphertext encapsulated under the public-key), and the shared secret is the key encapsulated in the ciphertext. Several works have analysed the performance and implementation challenges of OQS-OpenSSL (e.g. [9,25]).

More recently, based on the observation that (PQ) KEM public-keys/ciphertexts are usually more compact than (PQ) public-keys/signatures, Schwabe et al. [29] proposed KEMTLS as a variant of the TLS 1.3 handshake. The main difference between both protocols is that KEMTLS uses a KEM for (implicit) server authentication instead of a signature. This reduces the overall bandwidth of the handshake and the computation time on the server-side. Thus, two KEMs are used in KEMTLS: one for establishing an ephemeral shared secret and the other one to authenticate the server. While the latter needs to be IND-CCA secure as it uses long-term keys, the authors showed that IND-1CCA security is sufficient for the former KEM for the whole handshake to be secure. That is, the KEM needs to be secure against an adversary that can make a *unique* decapsulation query. Similarly, in the security proof of TLS 1.3 handshake by Dowling et al. [12], DH key-exchange can be replaced by an IND-1CCA KEM and the proof would still go through.

However, in KEMTLS or PQ implementations of TLS 1.3 (e.g. [1]), the ephemeral KEMs are implemented with IND-CCA KEMs, which are usually obtained by applying the Fujisaki-Okamoto (FO) transform or a variant (e.g. [15,19]) on an OW/IND-CPA public-key encryption scheme (PKE). The FO construction re-encrypts the decrypted plaintext during decapsulation, making it an expensive operation. This motivates the present work, which studies whether IND-1CCA KEM can be obtained from CPA-secure PKEs through a more efficient transform than FO (in the ROM). We reply by the affirmative by showing that IND-1CCA KEMs with much faster decapsulation than FO-derived IND-CCA KEM can be obtained from any CPA-secure PKE. Using similar tools, we also study the security of the PQ TLS 1.3 handshake when the KEM used for key exchange is only CPA-secure.

Our Contributions

We show how to build an efficient IND-qCCA KEM (i.e. the adversary can only make q decapsulation queries) from any OW-CPA PKE in the ROM. The bound has a loose factor of 2^q, making it insecure or impractical for large q. However, such construction is sufficient to build an efficient IND-1CCA KEM from any OW-CPA public-key encryption scheme. The transform simply sends a confirmation hash along the ciphertext encrypting the seed. In addition, we prove the security of this construction in the QROM as well.

Such a transform might be useful in several applications such as the KEMTLS protocol [29] mentioned above, PQ variants of TLS 1.3 or ratcheting, as discussed in Sect. 5.

Similarly, we show that deriving the key as $K := H(m, \mathsf{ct})$, where m is the seed encrypted in the ciphertext ct, holds an IND-qCCA KEM in the ROM. The bound is worse compared to the first transform, having a $\approx q_H^{2q}$ factor, where q_H is the number of queries an adversary can make to the random oracle H. The intuition is that any decapsulation query that returns $H(m, \mathsf{ct})$ with $\mathsf{ct} \neq \mathsf{ct}^*$ does not help much the adversary to recover the real key $H(m^*, \mathsf{ct}^*)$ due to the independence of RO values. However, each query to the decapsulation oracle still leaks a little information (such as equality between decrypted values), leading to the $\approx q_H^{2q}$ factor.

Compared to the FO transform and its variants, our CPA-to-qCCA transforms offer several advantages. The main one is a significant speed boost in decapsulation, as there is no need for re-encryption. Depending on the cost of encryption of the underlying scheme, the difference can be large. For instance, removing the re-encryption check in the optimized version of the isogeny-based scheme SIKE [21] cuts by more than 50% the decapsulation time (32235377 vs 73282449 cycles for SIKEp434_compressed on Ubuntu 21.04 with 2.8GHz Intel Core i7-1165G7). Another interesting feature of our transform is that we do not need to de-randomize the encryption (i.e. computing the random coins for encapsulation as the hash of the message/seed), removing the need for an additional random oracle.

We then consider the PQ TLS 1.3 handshake as it is implemented in OQS-OpenSSL [1]. Based on the observation that the key-schedule computes the keys as key-derivation functions (KDFs) applied on the shared secret and (the hash of) the transcript so far (including the ciphertext), we prove that if the KEM is OW-CPA secure, then the handshake is secure in the MultiStage model of Dowling et al. [12]. The proof is inspired by the proof of security of our second transform. Note that this result holds in the ROM (the KDFs/hash function are assumed to be ROs) and the security bound is very much "non-tight". Still, this shows that CPA-secure KEMs are sufficient for the TLS 1.3 handshake to be secure, solving an open problem raised by several authors (e.g. [12,25]). Then, since one can consider DH as a KEM, this implies that TLS 1.3 is secure as long as the *computational Diffie-Hellman* (CDH) problem is hard, showing that the PRF-ODH assumption used in the original proof [12] is not necessary (in the ROM). We note that this last result can also be derived from the fact that DH as used in TLS 1.3 is a IND-1CCA KEM in the ROM, assuming that CDH is hard. We prove this in the full version of the paper [20].

Finally, in Sect. 5, we discuss possible use cases of IND-qCCA in the context of communication protocols and ratcheting primitives. In particular, we note that IND-1CCA security is sufficient in many recent applications as the trend is to move to forward secure schemes, which discard key pairs after one use.

Remark on IND-CPA vs IND-1CCA

We note that plain IND-CPA PQ schemes are often not IND-1CCA. In particular, it is stated in Sect. 4.3 of the KEMTLS paper [30]:

> "We leave as an open question to what extent non-FO-protected post-quantum KEMs may be secure against a single decapsulation query, but at this point IND-CCA is the safe choice."

The answer to this question obviously depends on how the "non-FO protected" IND-CPA PKE is used as a KEM. However, if it used in the trivial way (i.e. $m \leftarrow_\$ \mathcal{M}$, $K := H(m)$, $\mathsf{ct} := \mathsf{enc}(\mathsf{pk}, m)$), the resulting KEM can usually be broken with 1 query for most of the PQ schemes. The adversary receives $K^*, \mathsf{ct}^* := \mathsf{enc}(\mathsf{pk}, m^*)$, queries $\mathsf{ct}^* + \delta$ and gets back $H(m^*)$ with high probability, if δ is "small". Then, it can just compare whether $H(m^*) = K^*$ or not and break IND-1CCA security. The reaction attacks (e.g. [13]) requiring thousands of queries mentioned in the same paper [30] are key-recovery attacks, not distinguishing attacks. The simple distinguishing adversary given above actually gives a good intuition of why adding a confirmation hash $H'(m, \mathsf{ct})$ along the ciphertext as in our first transform holds a IND-qCCA KEM. In order to submit a valid decapsulation query, the adversary must compute $H'(m, \mathsf{ct})$ with $\mathsf{ct} \neq \mathsf{ct}^*$. Hence, the adversary itself needs to query $H'(m, \mathsf{ct})$ beforehand, thus it knows m and the decapsulation query is (nearly) useless.

Related Work

The notion of bounded IND-CCA (i.e. IND-qCCA) has been studied in several works. Cramer et al. [8] defined IND-qCCA and showed that one can build an IND-qCCA PKE from any CPA-secure PKE in a black-box manner in the standard model, using one-time signatures. While this construction is valid in the standard model and ours in the ROM only, their reduction is inefficient compared to FO transforms, which we aim to improve. Following their work, Peirera et al. [26] built a more efficient IND-qCCA PKE based on the CDH assumption, and Yamakawa et al. [32] proposed other constructions based on the factoring and bilinear CDH assumptions. As far as we know, we are the first to note that a IND-qCCA KEM can be obtained from any CPA-secure PKE through a very simple and efficient transform in the ROM.

Starting from the original Fujisaki-Okamoto transform [14,15], many works have been dedicated to building variants of FO with tighter security bounds in the QROM (e.g. [4,19,23,28]). While these are CPA-to-CCA transforms, ours guarantee qCCA security only but at a lesser computational cost.

Dowling et al. [12] proved the security of the standard TLS 1.3 handshake in the MultiStage security model. We extend their result by showing that TLS 1.3 security still holds if the DH KEX is replaced by a CPA-secure KEM (in the ROM). In turn, this also implies that the CDH assumption is sufficient for proving the security of the original TLS 1.3, which was based on the PRF-ODH assumption so far. In two more recent works, Diemert et al. [11] and Davis et al. [10] aimed at proving a tighter security bound for TLS 1.3. Their proofs are valid in the ROM and are based on the Strong Diffie-Hellman (SDH) assumption. Our result on TLS 1.3 is complementary to theirs in the sense that we prove that TLS security holds under a weaker assumption but with a looser security bound.

Brendel et al. [5] studied the PRF-ODH assumption. In particular, they showed that PRF-ODH is hard if the SDH assumption holds in the ROM. The PRF-ODH notion considered in their work is generic as the adversary can query two types of "decapsulation" oracles multiple times. On the other hand, if we restrict ourselves to the notion where the adversary can make a unique query (which is sufficient for TLS 1.3 security), we show in the full version of the paper [20] that CDH hardness is sufficient for PRF-ODH (with one query) to hold.

Finally, following the KEMTLS paper [29], several recent works used the notion of IND-1CCA KEM to build secure protocols (e.g. [6,18,31]), showing the growing importance of such a notion.

2 Preliminaries

2.1 Notation

For $\mathcal{A}$ a randomized algorithm, we write $b \leftarrow_\$ \mathcal{A}$ to indicate b is set to the value output by $\mathcal{A}$. Similarly, if Ψ (resp. $\mathcal{X}$) is a distribution (resp. a set), then $x \leftarrow_\$ \Psi$ (resp. $x \leftarrow_\$ \mathcal{X}$) means that x is sampled uniformly at random from Ψ (resp. $\mathcal{X}$). We denote by 1_P the indicator function which returns 1 if the predicate P is fulfilled and 0 otherwise. We write $[n]$ the set $\{1, \ldots, n\}$. For $\mathcal{A}$ an algorithm, we write $\mathcal{A} \Rightarrow b$ to denote the event $\mathcal{A}$ *outputs* b. Finally, in a game, we write **abort** to mean that the algorithm is stopped.

2.2 Public-Key Encryption Scheme

A Public-Key Encryption (PKE) scheme is defined as follows.

Definition 1 (Public-Key Encryption). *A Public-Key Encryption scheme over a domain $\mathcal{M}$ is composed of three algorithms* gen, enc, dec:

- $(\mathsf{pk}, \mathsf{sk}) \leftarrow_\$ \mathsf{gen}(1^\lambda)$: *The key generation algorithm takes the security parameter as input and outputs the public key* pk *and the secret key* sk.
- $\mathsf{ct} \leftarrow_\$ \mathsf{enc}(\mathsf{pk}, \mathsf{pt})$: *The encryption algorithm takes as inputs the public key* pk *and a plaintext* pt $\in \mathcal{M}$ *and it outputs a ciphertext* ct.
- $\mathsf{pt}' \leftarrow \mathsf{dec}(\mathsf{sk}, \mathsf{ct})$: *The decryption procedure takes as inputs the secret key* sk *and the ciphertext* ct $\in \mathcal{C}$ *and it outputs a plaintext* pt' $\in \mathcal{M} \cup \{\bot\}$.

The gen *and* enc *are probabilistic algorithms that can be made deterministic by adding random coins as inputs. The decryption procedure is deterministic.*

Correctness. We say a PKE scheme is δ correct if for any ppt adversary $\mathcal{A}$ playing the game CORR defined in Fig. 1, we have

$$\Pr[\mathrm{CORR}_{\mathsf{PKE}}(\mathcal{A}) \Rightarrow 1] \leq \delta(\lambda)$$

where λ is the security parameter, we omit it from now on for the sake of simplicity.

$$\underline{\text{CORR}_{\text{PKE}}(\mathcal{A})}$$

$(\text{pk}, \text{sk}) \leftarrow_\$ \text{gen}(1^\lambda)$
$\text{pt} \leftarrow \mathcal{A}(\text{pk}, \text{sk})$
$\text{ct} \leftarrow_\$ \text{enc}(\text{pk}, \text{pt})$
$\textbf{return } 1_{\text{dec}(\text{sk}, \text{ct}) \neq \text{pt}}$

Fig. 1. Correctness game.

$$\underline{\text{OW-ATK}_{\text{PKE}}(\mathcal{A})} \qquad \textbf{Oracle } \mathcal{O}^{\text{PCO}}(\text{pt}, \text{ct})$$

ATK	CPA	PCA
$\mathcal{O}^{\text{ATK}}$	$\perp$	$\mathcal{O}^{\text{PCO}}$

$(\text{pk}, \text{sk}) \leftarrow_\$ \text{gen}(1^\lambda)$ $\text{pt}' \leftarrow \text{dec}(\text{sk}, \text{ct})$
$\text{pt}^* \leftarrow_\$ \mathcal{M}$ $\textbf{return } 1_{\text{pt}' = \text{pt}}$
$\text{ct}^* \leftarrow \text{enc}(\text{pk}, \text{pt}^*)$
$\text{pt}' \leftarrow \mathcal{A}^{\mathcal{O}^{\text{ATK}}}(\text{pk}, \text{ct}^*)$
$\textbf{return } 1_{\text{pt}' = \text{pt}^*}$

Fig. 2. One-Wayness games.

Plaintext Checking. We recall the notions of One-Wayness under Chosen Plaintext Attacks (OW-CPA) and Plaintext-Checking Attacks (OW-PCA).

Definition 2 (One-Wayness and Plaintext Checking). *Let $\mathcal{M}$ be a finite message space, PKE a PKE scheme over $\mathcal{M}$ and we consider the games defined on the left in Fig. 2 with the different oracles as defined in the table on the right of Fig. 2. Then, PKE is OW-ATK, for ATK $\in \{\text{CPA}, \text{PCA}\}$, if for any ppt adversary $\mathcal{A}$ we have*

$$\text{Adv}_{\text{PKE}}^{\text{ow-atk}}(\mathcal{A}) = \Pr\left[\text{OW-ATK}_{\text{PKE}}(\mathcal{A}) \Rightarrow 1\right] = \text{negl}(\lambda)$$

where $\Pr\left[\text{OW-ATK}_{\text{PKE}}(\mathcal{A}) \Rightarrow 1\right]$ is the probability that the adversary wins the OW-ATK game.

2.3 Key Encapsulation Mechanism (KEM)

A Key Encapsulation Mechanism is defined as follows.

Definition 3 (Key Encapsulation Mechanism). *A KEM over $\mathcal{K}$ is a tuple of three algorithms* gen, encaps, decaps:

- $(\text{pk}, \text{sk}) \leftarrow_\$ \text{gen}(1^\lambda)$: *The key generation algorithm takes as inputs the security parameter and it outputs the public key* pk *and the secret key* sk.
- $\text{ct}, K \leftarrow_\$ \text{encaps}(\text{pk})$: *The encapsulation algorithm takes as inputs the public key* pk *and it outputs a ciphertext* $\text{ct} \in \mathcal{C}$ *and a key* $K \in \mathcal{K}$.
- $K' \leftarrow \text{decaps}(\text{sk}, \text{ct})$: *The decapsulation procedure takes as inputs the secret key* sk *and the ciphertext* $\text{ct} \in \mathcal{C}$ *and it outputs a key* K. *If the KEM allows explicit rejection, the output is a key* $K \in \mathcal{K}$ *or the rejection symbol* $\perp$. *If the rejection is implicit, the output is always a key* $K \in \mathcal{K}$.

IND-(q)CCA$_{\mathsf{KEM}}(\mathcal{A})$	Oracle $\mathcal{O}^{\mathsf{Dec}}(\mathsf{ct})$
$(\mathsf{pk}, \mathsf{sk}) \leftarrow_\$ \mathsf{gen}(1^\lambda)$	if $\mathsf{ct} = \mathsf{ct}^*$: return $\bot$
$b \leftarrow_\$ \{0, 1\}$	if more than q queries : return $\bot \mathbin{/\!/}$ If IND-qCCA
$\mathsf{ct}^*, K_0 \leftarrow_\$ \mathsf{encaps}(\mathsf{pk})$	$K' \leftarrow \mathsf{decaps}(\mathsf{sk}, \mathsf{ct})$
$K_1 \leftarrow_\$ \mathcal{K}$	return K'
$b' \leftarrow \mathcal{A}^{\mathcal{O}^{\mathsf{Dec}}}(\mathsf{pk}, \mathsf{ct}^*, K_b)$	
return $1_{b'=b}$	

Fig. 3. Indistinguishability games.

The gen *and* encaps *are probabilistic algorithms. The randomness can be made explicit by adding random coins as inputs. The decapsulation function is deterministic.*

Indistinguishability Security. KEM indistinguishability is defined as follows.

Definition 4 (KEM Indistinguishability). *We consider the games defined in Fig. 3. Let $\mathcal{K}$ be a finite key space. A KEM scheme over $\mathcal{K}$* KEM $=$ (gen, encaps, decaps) *is* IND-CCA *(resp.* IND-qCCA*) if for any ppt adversary $\mathcal{A}$ (resp. any ppt $\mathcal{A}$ limited to q decapsulation queries) we have*

$$\mathsf{Adv}_{\mathsf{KEM}}^{\mathsf{ind}\text{-}(\mathsf{q})\mathsf{cca}}(\mathcal{A}) = \left| \Pr\left[\mathrm{IND} - (\mathrm{q})\mathrm{CCA}_{\mathsf{KEM}}(\mathcal{A}) \Rightarrow 1\right] - \frac{1}{2} \right| = \mathsf{negl}(\lambda)$$

where $\Pr[\mathrm{IND} - (\mathrm{q})\mathrm{CCA}_{\mathsf{KEM}}(\mathcal{A}) \Rightarrow 1]$ *is the probability that $\mathcal{A}$ wins the* IND-$(q)CCA_{\mathsf{KEM}}(\mathcal{A})$ *game defined in Fig. 3.*

We can also define OW-CPA for KEMs, which is similar to the equivalent notion for PKE.

Definition 5 (KEM OW-CPA). *A KEM scheme* KEM $=$ (gen, encaps, decaps) *is* OW-CPA *if for any ppt adversary $\mathcal{A}$ we have*

$$\mathsf{Adv}_{\mathsf{KEM}}^{\mathsf{ow}\text{-}\mathsf{cpa}}(\mathcal{A}) = \Pr\left[\mathcal{A}(\mathsf{pk}, \mathsf{ct}^*) \Rightarrow K : (\mathsf{pk}, \mathsf{sk}) \leftarrow_\$ \mathsf{gen}(1^\lambda); (K, \mathsf{ct}^*) \leftarrow_\$ \mathsf{encaps}(\mathsf{pk})\right]$$
$$= \mathsf{negl}(\lambda) \, ,$$

where the probability is taken over the randomness of the public-key generation, encapsulation and the adversary $\mathcal{A}$.

gen()	encaps(pk)	decaps(sk, ct)
$(\mathsf{pk}, \mathsf{sk}) \leftarrow\!\!\$\ \mathsf{gen}^p()$	$\sigma \leftarrow\!\!\$\ \mathcal{M}$	$(\mathsf{ct}_0', \mathsf{tag}') \leftarrow \mathsf{ct}$
return $(\mathsf{pk}, \mathsf{sk})$	$\mathsf{ct}_0 \leftarrow\!\!\$\ \mathsf{enc}^p(\mathsf{pk}, \sigma)$	$\sigma' \leftarrow \mathsf{dec}^p(\mathsf{sk}, \mathsf{ct}_0')$
	$\mathsf{tag} \leftarrow H'(\sigma, \mathsf{ct}_0)$	**if** $H'(\sigma', \mathsf{ct}_0') \neq \mathsf{tag}'$:
	$K \leftarrow H(\sigma)$	**return** $\perp$
	return $K, (\mathsf{ct}_0, \mathsf{tag})$	**return** $H(\sigma')$

Fig. 4. $\mathsf{T_{CH}}$ transform.

3   OW-CPA to IND-qCCA Transforms

We first prove the following simple lemma.

Lemma 1. *Let* PKE *be a PKE. Then, for any ppt OW-PCA adversary $\mathcal{A}$ making at most q queries to the PCO oracle, there exists a OW-CPA adversary $\mathcal{B}$ s.t.*

$$\mathsf{Adv}_{\mathsf{PKE}}^{\mathrm{ow-pca}}(\mathcal{A}) \leq 2^q \cdot \mathsf{Adv}_{\mathsf{PKE}}^{\mathrm{ow-cpa}}(\mathcal{B}).$$

Proof. We can simply see that the PCO oracle returns 1 bit of information, thus PKE loses at most q bits of security when a PCO oracle is available. More formally, given $\mathcal{A}$, one can build $\mathcal{B}$ as follows. It passes its input to $\mathcal{A}$ and simulates the PCO oracle by sampling a response at random in $\{0, 1\}$. Then, it returns the response of $\mathcal{A}$. Its probability of success is $\mathsf{Adv}_{\mathsf{PKE}}^{\mathrm{ow-cpa}}(\mathcal{B}) \geq \frac{1}{2^q}\mathsf{Adv}_{\mathsf{PKE}}^{\mathrm{ow-pca}}(\mathcal{A})$, as the probability the q responses are correct is $\frac{1}{2^q}$. □

We consider the transform $\mathsf{T_{CH}}$ given in Fig. 4. This construction takes a PKE PKE $= (\mathsf{gen}^p, \mathsf{enc}^p, \mathsf{dec}^p)$ and outputs a KEM $(\mathsf{gen}, \mathsf{encaps}, \mathsf{decaps})$. Note that $\mathsf{T_{CH}}$ is basically the REACT transform [24] without the asymmetric part (to get a KEM instead of a PKE).

We now show that the resulting KEM is IND-qCCA assuming the underlying PKE is OW-PCA.

Theorem 1. *We consider two random oracles $H, H' : \{0, 1\}^* \mapsto \{0, 1\}^n$. Let* KEM *be the KEM resulting from applying the $\mathsf{T_{CH}}$ transform to a δ-correct* PKE. *Then, for any IND-qCCA adversary $\mathcal{A}$ that makes at most q_H (resp. $q_{H'}$) queries to H (resp. H'), there exists a OW-PCA adversary $\mathcal{B}$ s.t.*

$$\mathsf{Adv}_{\mathsf{KEM}}^{\mathrm{ind-qcca}}(\mathcal{A}) \leq \frac{(q + q_{H'} + 1)^2}{2^n} + \delta + \frac{q}{2^n} + (q_H + q_{H'}) \cdot \mathsf{Adv}_{\mathsf{PKE}}^{\mathrm{ow-pca}}(\mathcal{B}) \ ,$$

where $\mathcal{B}$ makes at most q queries to its plaintext-checking oracle. In addition, if PKE *is a deterministic encryption scheme, the bound becomes*

$$\mathsf{Adv}_{\mathsf{KEM}}^{\mathrm{ind-qcca}}(\mathcal{A}) \leq \frac{(q + q_{H'} + 1)^2}{2^n} + \delta + \frac{q}{2^n} + \mathsf{Adv}_{\mathsf{PKE}}^{\mathrm{ow-pca}}(\mathcal{B}) \ .$$

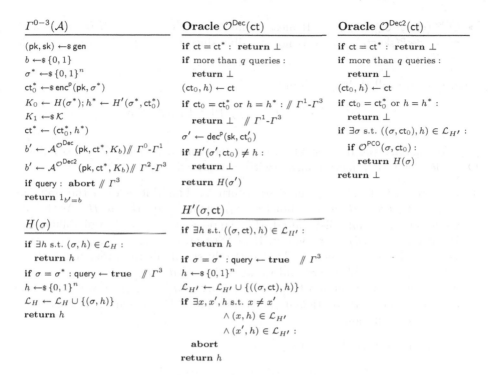

Fig. 5. Sequence of games for the proof of Theorem 1. $\mathcal{O}^{PCO}$ is defined as in the OW-PCA game (see Fig. 2).

Proof. We proceed by game hopping, the sequence of games is presented in Fig. 5. Let $\mathcal{L}_H$ (resp. $\mathcal{L}_{H'}$) be the list of queries (x, h) made to the RO H (resp. H') s.t. $H(x) = h$ (resp. $H'(x) = h$). In addition, let the challenge ciphertext be $ct^* = (ct_0^*, h^*)$, and σ^* be s.t. $enc^P(pk, \sigma^*) = ct_0^*$. We start with game Γ^0 which is the IND-qCCA game, except we abort if the adversary finds a collision on H' (i.e. $H'(x) = H'(x')$ for $x \neq x'$ and $(x, h), (x', h) \in \mathcal{L}_{H'}$). This happens with prob. at most $\frac{(q+q_{H'}+1)^2}{2^n}$ and we have

$$\left| \Pr\left[\text{IND} - \text{qCCA}_{KEM}(\mathcal{A}) \Rightarrow 1 \right] - \Pr[\Gamma^0(\mathcal{A}) \Rightarrow 1] \right| \leq \frac{(q + q_{H'} + 1)^2}{2^n} .$$

$\underline{\Gamma^1}$: The decapsulation oracle is modified s.t. it returns $\perp$ whenever ct_0^* or h^* is queried (note that both cannot be submitted at the same time). This game is the same as Γ^0 except if the oracle in Γ^0 does not return $\perp$ on such queries. Let bad be this event. We split this into two cases:

- $\mathcal{O}^{Dec}(ct_0^*, h \neq h^*) \neq \perp$. This happens only if

$$H'(dec(sk, ct_0^*), ct_0^*) = h \neq h^* = H'(\sigma^*, ct_0^*).$$

In turn, this implies that $dec(sk, ct_0^*) \neq \sigma^*$ and thus it is a correctness error. Such an error happens at most with probability δ.

- $\mathcal{O}^{\mathsf{Dec}}(\mathsf{ct}_0 \neq \mathsf{ct}_0^*, h^*) \neq \bot$. It means that $h^* = H'(\sigma^*, \mathsf{ct}_0^*) = H'(\sigma', \mathsf{ct}_0)$, with $\sigma' \leftarrow \mathsf{dec}^\mathsf{P}(\mathsf{sk}, \mathsf{ct}_0)$, which is not possible since $\mathsf{ct}_0 \neq \mathsf{ct}_0^*$ and we assume no collision occurs.

Therefore, overall $\Pr[\mathsf{bad}] \leq \delta$ and

$$|\Pr[\Gamma^0 \Rightarrow 1] - \Pr[\Gamma^1 \Rightarrow 1]| \leq \Pr[\mathsf{bad}] \leq \delta.$$

$\underline{\Gamma^2}$: We modify the decapsulation oracle into another oracle $\mathcal{O}^{\mathsf{Dec}'}$ as follows. On a decapsulation query (ct_0, h) (with $\sigma' \leftarrow \mathsf{dec}(\mathsf{sk}, \mathsf{ct}_0)$):

1. If there is no $((*, \mathsf{ct}_0), h)$ in $\mathcal{L}_{H'}$: return $\bot$. This differs from the previous game only if $h = H'(\sigma', \mathsf{ct}_0)$ but (σ', ct_0) was never queried to H'. As the RO values are uniformly distributed, this happens at most with probability $\frac{1}{2^n}$.
2. If $((\sigma, \mathsf{ct}_0), h) \in \mathcal{L}_{H'}$ for some σ: If $\mathcal{O}^{\mathsf{PCO}}(\sigma, \mathsf{ct}_0) := 1_{\mathsf{dec}(\mathsf{sk},\mathsf{ct}_0)=\sigma} = 1$, return $H(\sigma)$. Otherwise, return $\bot$. This perfectly simulates the previous oracle as $\mathcal{O}^{\mathsf{PCO}}(\sigma, \mathsf{ct}_0) = 1$ iff $\sigma = \sigma'$ and we know $h = H(\sigma = \sigma', \mathsf{ct}_0)$.
   Note that there is at most one σ s.t. $((\sigma, \mathsf{ct}_0), h) \in \mathcal{L}_{H'}$ as we assume no collision occurs. In particular, it means that $\mathcal{O}^{\mathsf{PCO}}$ is called at most once every decapsulation query.

Therefore, by a union bound we get

$$|\Pr[\Gamma^1 \Rightarrow 1] - \Pr[\Gamma^2 \Rightarrow 1]| \leq \frac{q}{2^n}.$$

$\underline{\Gamma^3}$: Finally, we abort whenever $\mathcal{A}$ queries σ^* to H or $(\sigma^*, \cdot)$ to H'. Let this event be query. Note that $\mathcal{A}$ could also learn the value of $H(\sigma^*)$ through a query to $\mathcal{O}^{\mathsf{Dec2}}$. However, the latter oracle would return $H(\sigma^*)$ only if $\mathcal{A}$ queried $H'(\sigma^*, \cdot)$ before (thus triggering query).

Then, we can build a OW-PCA adversary $\mathcal{B}$ (shown in Fig. 6) that perfectly simulates $\mathcal{A}$'s view as long as query does not happen. More precisely, $\mathcal{B}$ can simulate the decapsulation oracle using its PCO oracle. Then, on input $(\mathsf{pk}, \mathsf{ct}_0^*)$, $\mathcal{B}$ runs $\mathcal{A}(\mathsf{pk}, (\mathsf{ct}_0^*, h^*), K^*)$, where h^* and K^* are picked at random. Unless query occurs, $\mathcal{A}$ cannot distinguish between these random h^*, K^* and the real ones. Finally, if query occurs, $\mathcal{B}$ can recover σ^* with probability $\frac{1}{q_H + q_{H'}}$ by sampling a random σ from $S = \{\sigma : (\sigma, *) \in \mathcal{L}_H^{\mathcal{A}} \vee ((\sigma, *), *) \in \mathcal{L}_{H'}\}$, where $\mathcal{L}_H^{\mathcal{A}}$ is the set of queries to H made by $\mathcal{A}$. Thus,

$$|\Pr[\Gamma^2 \Rightarrow 1] - \Pr[\Gamma^3 \Rightarrow 1]| \leq \Pr[\mathsf{query}] \leq (q_H + q_{H'}) \cdot \mathsf{Adv}_{\mathsf{PKE}}^{\mathsf{ow-pca}}(\mathcal{B})$$

where $\mathcal{B}$ makes q query to the PCO oracle. Note that if PKE is deterministic, $\mathcal{B}$ can check whether $\mathsf{enc}(\mathsf{pk}, \sigma) = \mathsf{ct}_0^*$ for all $\sigma \in S$ to find σ^*. This fails only if there exists $\sigma' \neq \sigma^*$ s.t. $\mathsf{enc}(\mathsf{pk}, \sigma') = \mathsf{ct}_0^*$. In turn this implies that there exists $\sigma \in S \cup \{\sigma^*\}$ that would break the correctness, but such an event is already covered by the previous δ factor. In this case, we obtain

$$|\Pr[\Gamma^2 \Rightarrow 1] - \Pr[\Gamma^3 \Rightarrow 1]| \leq \Pr[\mathsf{query}] \leq \mathsf{Adv}_{\mathsf{PKE}}^{\mathsf{ow-pca}}(\mathcal{B}).$$

$\mathcal{B}^{\mathcal{O}^{\mathsf{PCO}}}(\mathsf{pk}, \mathsf{ct}^*)$	**Oracle** $\mathcal{O}^{\mathsf{Dec2}}(\mathsf{ct})$

$\mathcal{B}^{\mathcal{O}^{\mathsf{PCO}}}(\mathsf{pk}, \mathsf{ct}^*)$
init $\mathcal{L}_H, \mathcal{L}_{H'} \leftarrow \emptyset$
$h^* \leftarrow_\$ \{0,1\}^n$
$K^* \leftarrow_\$ \{0,1\}^n$
simulate H, H' for $\mathcal{A}$ with lazy sampling:
run $\mathcal{A}^{H,H',\mathcal{O}^{\mathsf{Dec2}}}(\mathsf{pk}, (\mathsf{ct}^*, h^*), K^*)$
$\sigma' \leftarrow_\$ \{\sigma : \sigma \in \mathcal{L}_H^{\mathcal{A}} \vee (\sigma, *) \in \mathcal{L}_{H'}\}$
return σ'

Oracle $\mathcal{O}^{\mathsf{Dec2}}(\mathsf{ct})$
if more than q queries :
return $\bot$
$(\mathsf{ct}_0, h) \leftarrow \mathsf{ct}$
if $\mathsf{ct}_0 = \mathsf{ct}_0^*$ or $h = h^*$:
return $\bot$
if $\exists \sigma$ s.t. $((\sigma, \mathsf{ct}), h) \in \mathcal{L}_{H'}$:
if $\mathcal{O}^{\mathsf{PCO}}(\sigma, \mathsf{ct}_0)$: **return** $H(\sigma)$
return $\bot$

Fig. 6. $\mathcal{B}$ adversary for the proof of Theorem 1.

Finally, since $\mathcal{A}$ cannot query σ^* to H anymore, it cannot distinguish between a random key and $H(\sigma^*)$. Hence, $\Pr[\Gamma^3 \Rightarrow 1] = \frac{1}{2}$. Collecting the probabilities holds the result. $\qquad \square$

Corollary 1. *We consider two random oracles* $H, H' : \{0,1\}^* \mapsto \{0,1\}^n$. *Let* KEM *be the KEM resulting from applying the* T_{CH} *transform to a* δ-*correct* PKE. *Then, for any IND-qCCA adversary* $\mathcal{A}$ *that makes at most* q_H *(resp.* $q_{H'}$*) queries to* H *(resp.* H'*), there exists a OW-CPA adversary* $\mathcal{B}$ *s.t.*

$$\mathsf{Adv}_{\mathsf{KEM}}^{\mathsf{ind-qcca}}(\mathcal{A}) \leq \frac{(q + q_{H'})^2}{2^n} + \delta + \frac{q}{2^n} + (q_H + q_{H'} + q)2^q \cdot \mathsf{Adv}_{\mathsf{PKE}}^{\mathsf{ow-cpa}}(\mathcal{B}) \ .$$

If PKE *is deterministic, we get*

$$\mathsf{Adv}_{\mathsf{KEM}}^{\mathsf{ind-qcca}}(\mathcal{A}) \leq \frac{(q + q_{H'})^2}{2^n} + \delta + \frac{q}{2^n} + 2^q \cdot \mathsf{Adv}_{\mathsf{PKE}}^{\mathsf{ow-cpa}}(\mathcal{B}).$$

In particular, in the case of IND-1CCA (i.e. $q = 1$), if the underlying PKE is OW-CPA the KEM obtained from the T_{CH} transform is IND-1CCA with a security loss of ≈ 1 bit compared to the OW-CPA advantage (if we omit the other negligible terms). Finally, we note that as q is a constant that does not depend on the security parameter (e.g. n) of the PKE, if the OW-CPA advantage of the PKE is negligible, so is the KEM IND-qCCA one. However, in practice, we would need to take n very large to guarantee security for more than a few queries.

gen()	encaps(pk)	decaps(sk, ct)
$(\mathsf{pk}, \mathsf{sk}) \leftarrow\!\!\$\ \mathsf{gen}^{\mathsf{P}}()$	$\sigma \leftarrow\!\!\$\ \mathcal{M}$	$\sigma' \leftarrow \mathsf{dec}^{\mathsf{P}}(\mathsf{sk}, \mathsf{ct})$
return $(\mathsf{pk}, \mathsf{sk})$	$\mathsf{ct} \leftarrow\!\!\$\ \mathsf{enc}^{\mathsf{P}}(\mathsf{pk}, \sigma)$	if $\sigma' = \bot$: return $\bot$
	$K \leftarrow H(\sigma, \mathsf{ct})$	return $H(\sigma', \mathsf{ct})$
	return K, ct	

Fig. 7. $\mathsf{T_H}$ transform.

3.1 Security in the QROM

We also show that the $\mathsf{T_{CH}}$ transform is secure in the Quantum Random Oracle Model (QROM) by proving that Theorem 1 holds in the QROM.

Theorem 2. *We consider two quantum random oracles $H, H' : \{0,1\}^* \mapsto \{0,1\}^n$. Let KEM be the KEM resulting from applying the $\mathsf{T_{CH}}$ transform to a PKE. Then, for any IND-qCCA adversary $\mathcal{A}$ that makes at most q_H (resp. $q_{H'}$) quantum queries to H (resp. H'), there exists a OW-PCA adversary $\mathcal{B}$ s.t.*

$$\mathsf{Adv}^{\mathrm{ind-qcca}}_{\mathsf{KEM}}(\mathcal{A}) \leq \delta + 2(2q_{H'} + q_H + q) \cdot \sqrt{(2(2q_{H'} + q))^q \cdot \mathsf{Adv}^{\mathrm{ow-pca}}_{\mathsf{PKE}}(\mathcal{B})}$$

where $\mathcal{B}$ makes at most q queries to its plaintext-checking oracle.

Proof. Due to space constraint, we defer the proof to the full version of the paper [20]. □

Corollary 2. *We consider two quantum random oracles $H, H' : \{0,1\}^* \mapsto \{0,1\}^n$. Let KEM be the KEM resulting from applying the $\mathsf{T_{CH}}$ transform to a δ-correct PKE. Then, for any IND-qCCA adversary $\mathcal{A}$ that makes at most q_H (resp. $q_{H'}$) queries to H (resp. H'), there exists a OW-CPA adversary $\mathcal{B}$ s.t.*

$$\mathsf{Adv}^{\mathrm{ind-qcca}}_{\mathsf{KEM}}(\mathcal{A}) \leq \delta + 2(2q_{H'} + q_H + q) \cdot 2^q \sqrt{((2q_{H'} + q))^q \cdot \mathsf{Adv}^{\mathrm{ow-pca}}_{\mathsf{PKE}}(\mathcal{B})}.$$

3.2 Hashing the Plaintext and Ciphertext

One can also wonder what is the leakage of the decapsulation oracle in the ROM, when the key is simply the hash of the seed and the plaintext. That is, we consider the simple PKE to KEM transform given in Fig. 7, which we call $\mathsf{T_H}$. Note that this is the same transform as the one called $\mathsf{U}^{\perp}$ in [19]. We now show that if q is small (logarithmic in the security parameter), then $\mathsf{T_H}$ holds a secure IND-qCCA scheme in the ROM, given that the underlying PKE is OW-CPA.

Theorem 3. *We consider a random oracle $H : \{0,1\}^* \mapsto \{0,1\}^n$. Let KEM be the KEM resulting from applying the $\mathsf{T_H}$ transform to a PKE PKE (which never queries H). Then, for any IND-qCCA adversary $\mathcal{A}$ that makes at most q_H queries to H, there exists a OW-CPA adversary $\mathcal{B}$ s.t.*

$$\mathsf{Adv}^{\mathrm{ind-qcca}}_{\mathsf{KEM}}(\mathcal{A}) \leq q_H \cdot ((q_H + 1)(q_H + 2))^q \cdot \mathsf{Adv}^{\mathrm{ow-cpa}}_{\mathsf{PKE}}(\mathcal{B}).$$

$$\mathcal{O}^i(\mathcal{L}_H, \mathsf{ct})$$

---

sort $\mathcal{L}_H$ according to query order :

$\mathcal{L}_H = ((\sigma_i, \mathsf{ct}_i), K_i)_{i \in \{1, \ldots, |\mathcal{L}_H|\}}$

$\sigma' \leftarrow \mathsf{dec}^p(\mathsf{sk}, \mathsf{ct})$

if $\sigma' = \bot$: return $\bot_d$

for $i \in \{1, \ldots, |\mathcal{L}_H|\}$:

    if $\mathsf{ct}_i = \mathsf{ct}$ and $\sigma' = \sigma_i$:

        return i

return $\bot$

Fig. 8. $\mathcal{O}^i$ oracle for the proof of Theorem 3.

If PKE *is deterministic, we get*

$$\mathsf{Adv}_{\mathsf{KEM}}^{\mathsf{ind-qcca}}(\mathcal{A}) \leq \delta + ((q_H + 1)(q_H + 2))^q \cdot \mathsf{Adv}_{\mathsf{PKE}}^{\mathsf{ow-cpa}}(\mathcal{B}).$$

Proof. We start by defining an oracle $\mathcal{O}^i(\mathcal{L}_H, \mathsf{ct})$ (see Fig. 8). This oracle returns the index i s.t. $((\sigma_i, \mathsf{ct}_i), K_i) \in \mathcal{L}_H$ (we first sort $\mathcal{L}_H$ according to some fixed order) and $\mathsf{ct}_i = \mathsf{ct}$ and $\mathsf{dec}^p(\mathsf{sk}, \mathsf{ct}_i) = \sigma_i$. If such a i does not exist and $\mathsf{dec}^p(\mathsf{sk}, \mathsf{ct}_i) = \bot$ it returns $\bot_d$, otherwise it returns $\bot$.

Now we show how to simulate the IND-qCCA decapsulation oracle in the ROM, using $\mathcal{O}^i$ and $\mathcal{O}^{\mathsf{PCO}}$ only. The original (resp. modified) oracles $\mathcal{O}^{\mathsf{Dec}}$ and H (resp. $\mathcal{O}^{\mathsf{Dec}'}$ and H') are on the left (resp. right) in Fig. 9. We now prove that any IND-qCCA adversary cannot distinguish between the real and modified oracles.

First, we show that the outputs of the ROs H and H' on any query (σ, ct) have the same distribution, given the adversary's view. We break this into four subcases:

- (σ, ct) was queried before to H (resp. H'): In this case, both H and H' return the value h returned on the previous similar query. Thus, we assume from now on that every RO query made by the adversary is unique.
- ct was never queried to the decapsulation oracle before: In this case, both H and H' return a random value h and store the query/response in $\mathcal{L}_H$.
- ct was queried to the decapsulation oracle before: In both cases (original and modified oracles) one can see that if the decryption of ct either fails or $\sigma' = \mathsf{dec}^p(\mathsf{sk}, \mathsf{ct})$ is different from σ, then the output of the decapsulation oracle is independent of $H(\sigma, \mathsf{ct})$ (and $H'(\sigma, \mathsf{ct})$). In both cases, the ROs sample a fresh value (H' will do so because $\mathcal{O}^{\mathsf{PCO}}(\sigma, \mathsf{ct})$ will output 0 in this case, as $\sigma \neq \sigma'$ or the ciphertext is not valid). Now, if ct decrypts to σ, the original decapsulation oracle outputs $H(\sigma, \mathsf{ct})$. In the modified game, the decapsulation oracle outputs a random K. Indeed, as we assume (σ, ct) was never queried to H, $\mathcal{O}^i(\mathcal{L}_H, \mathsf{ct})$ outputs $\bot$. Then, the modified RO will output the same K, as $\mathcal{O}^{\mathsf{PCO}}(\sigma, \mathsf{ct})$ will verify. In both cases, the ROs output the same value as the decapsulation oracle.

Oracle $\mathcal{O}^{\mathsf{Dec}}(\mathsf{ct})$	**Oracle** $\mathcal{O}^{\mathsf{Dec}'}(\mathsf{ct})$

if $\mathsf{ct} = \mathsf{ct}^*$: **return** $\perp$
 if more than q queries :
    return $\perp$
 $\sigma' \leftarrow \mathsf{dec}^{\mathsf{P}}(\mathsf{sk}, \mathsf{ct})$
 if $\sigma' = \perp$: **return** $\perp$
 return $H(\sigma', \mathsf{ct})$
	if $\mathsf{ct} = \mathsf{ct}^*$: **return** $\perp$
	 if more than q queries : **return** $\perp$
	 if $\exists K$ s.t. $(\mathsf{ct}, K) \in \mathcal{L}_K$:
	    return K
	 $i \leftarrow \mathcal{O}^{\mathsf{i}}(\mathcal{L}_H, \mathsf{ct})$
	 if $i = \perp_d$: **return** $\perp$
	 if $i \neq \perp$:
	    $((\sigma_i, \mathsf{ct}_i), K_i) \leftarrow \mathcal{L}_H[i]$
	    return K_i // return i-th valued returned by H'
	 $K \leftarrow_\$ \{0,1\}$
	 $\mathcal{L}_K \leftarrow \mathcal{L}_K \cup \{(\mathsf{ct}, K)\}$
	 return K

$\underline{H(\sigma, \mathsf{ct})}$	$\underline{H'(\sigma, \mathsf{ct})}$

if $\exists h$ s.t. $((\sigma, \mathsf{ct}), h) \in \mathcal{L}_H$:
    return h
 $h \leftarrow_\$ \{0,1\}^n$
 $\mathcal{L}_H \leftarrow \mathcal{L}_H \cup \{((\sigma, \mathsf{ct}), h)\}$
 return h
	if $\exists h$ s.t. $((\sigma, \mathsf{ct}), h) \in \mathcal{L}_H$:
	    return h
	 if $\exists K$ s.t. $(\mathsf{ct}, K) \in \mathcal{L}_K$:
	    if $\mathcal{O}^{\mathsf{PCO}}(\sigma, \mathsf{ct})$:
	      $\mathcal{L}_H \leftarrow \mathcal{L}_H \cup \{((\sigma, \mathsf{ct}), K)\}$
	      return K
	 $h \leftarrow_\$ \{0,1\}^n$
	 $\mathcal{L}_H \leftarrow \mathcal{L}_H \cup \{((\sigma, \mathsf{ct}), h)\}$
	 return h

Fig. 9. Original and modified oracles for the proof of Theorem 3.

We now show that the decapsulation oracles $\mathcal{O}^{\mathsf{Dec}}$ and $\mathcal{O}^{\mathsf{Dec}'}$ are indistinguishable. Let ct be the queried ciphertext and $\sigma = \mathsf{dec}^{\mathsf{P}}(\mathsf{sk}, \mathsf{ct})$.

- $\mathsf{ct} = \mathsf{ct}^*$: both oracles return $\perp$.
- $\sigma = \perp$: Both oracles return $\perp$, as $\mathcal{O}^{\mathsf{i}}(\mathcal{L}_H, \mathsf{ct})$ returns $\perp_d$.
- $H(\sigma, \mathsf{ct})$ (resp. $H'(\sigma, \mathsf{ct})$) was never queried. Both oracles return a random value if ct was never queried, or a consistent value if it was. It is straightforward to see this is the case in the original oracle. In the modified oracle, as $H'(\sigma, \mathsf{ct})$ was never queried, we have $\mathcal{O}^{\mathsf{i}}(\mathcal{L}_H, \mathsf{ct})$ that returns $\perp$. Thus, the decapsulation oracle returns a random K if ct was not queried or a consistent K if it was.
- $H(\sigma, \mathsf{ct})$ (resp. $H'(\sigma, \mathsf{ct})$) was queried and it output K. Both oracles return K. In the modified decapsulation oracle, $\mathcal{O}^{\mathsf{i}}(\mathcal{L}_H, \mathsf{ct})$ will output a valid i s.t. $H'(\sigma_i, \mathsf{ct}) = h_i$ and h_i is returned. Thus, the answer is consistent with the RO.

Now we can prove the theorem by game hopping as before. We define Γ^0 as the original IND-qCCA game.

$\mathcal{B}(\mathsf{pk}, \mathsf{ct}^*)$

init $\mathcal{L}_H, \mathcal{L}_K \leftarrow \emptyset$
init $\mathcal{L}_q \leftarrow []$
$K^* \leftarrow_\$ \mathcal{K}$
run $\mathcal{A}^{H'', \mathcal{O}^{\mathsf{Dec}''}}(\mathsf{pk}, \mathsf{ct}^*, K^*)$
sample random query (σ', ct') made to H''
return σ'

$H''(\sigma, \mathsf{ct})$

$i_q \leftarrow$ query number
if $\exists h$ s.t. $((\sigma, \mathsf{ct}), h) \in \mathcal{L}_H$:
    return h
if $\exists K$ s.t. $(\mathsf{ct}, K) \in \mathcal{L}_K$:
    if $\mathcal{L}_q[\mathsf{ct}] = i_q$:
        $\mathcal{L}_H \leftarrow \mathcal{L}_H \cup \{((\sigma, \mathsf{ct}), K)\}$
        return K
$h \leftarrow_\$ \{0, 1\}^n$
$\mathcal{L}_H \leftarrow \mathcal{L}_H \cup \{((\sigma, \mathsf{ct}), h)\}$
return h

Oracle $\mathcal{O}^{\mathsf{Dec}''}(\mathsf{ct})$

if $\mathsf{ct} = \mathsf{ct}^*$: return $\perp$
if more than q queries : return $\perp$
if $\exists K$ s.t. $(\mathsf{ct}, K) \in \mathcal{L}_K$:
    return K
$i \leftarrow_\$ \{1, \ldots, q_H, \perp, \perp_d\}$
if $i = \perp_d$: return $\perp$
if $i \neq \perp$:
    $(\mathsf{ct}_i, K_i) \leftarrow \mathcal{L}_H[i]$
    return K_i // return i-th valued returned by H''
$K \leftarrow_\$ \{0, 1\}$
$\mathcal{L}_K \leftarrow \mathcal{L}_K \cup \{(\mathsf{ct}, K)\}$
$\mathcal{L}_q[\mathsf{ct}] \leftarrow_\$ \{0, \ldots, q_H\}$
return K

Fig. 10. $\mathcal{B}$ adversary for the proof of Theorem 3.

$\underline{\Gamma^1}$: We modify the original IND-qCCA game into another game Γ^1 where the random/decapsulation oracles are the modified ones (i.e. H' and $\mathcal{O}^{\mathsf{Dec}'}$) described above. As shown, both games are indistinguishable and thus

$$|\Pr[\Gamma^0 \Rightarrow 1] - \Pr[\Gamma^1 \Rightarrow 1]| = 0.$$

$\underline{\Gamma^2}$: We replace the challenge key by a random one, as in the previous proof. Then, similarly, the real key is indistinguishable from a random one unless $H(\sigma^*, \mathsf{ct}^*)$ is queried. We define this event as query and

$$|\Pr[\Gamma^1 \Rightarrow 1] - \Pr[\Gamma^2 \Rightarrow 1]| \leq \Pr[\mathsf{query}].$$

We can upper bound this probability by the advantage of a OW-CPA adversary $\mathcal{B}$ against PKE. That is, given a IND-qCCA adversary playing game Γ^2, we build an adversary $\mathcal{B}$ as shown in Fig. 10. One can see that if $\mathcal{B}$ was simulating $\mathcal{A}$ with the H' and $\mathcal{O}^{\mathsf{Dec}'}$ oracles (instead of its own oracles H'' and $\mathcal{O}^{\mathsf{Dec}''}$), the simulation would be perfect as long as query did not occur. Then, whenever query would happen, $\mathcal{B}$ would recover σ^* with prob. $\frac{1}{q_H}$. Now $\mathcal{B}$ does not simulate the modified oracles perfectly but instead makes some guessing in its own oracles H'' and $\mathcal{O}^{\mathsf{Dec}''}$:

- $\mathcal{O}^{\mathsf{Dec}''}$: In line 5, i is picked at random instead of being the returned value of the $\mathcal{O}^i$ oracle. On each query the simulation is perfect with prob. $1/(q_H + 2)$ and overall with probability $\frac{1}{(q_H+2)^q}$, as there are at most q queries to this oracle. In line 11, we associate a random index to each ct s.t. $(\mathsf{ct}, *) \in \mathcal{L}_K$.

- H'': In line 5, when $(ct, *) \in \mathcal{L}_K$, instead of querying the plaintext-checking oracle we check whether the corresponding sampled index $\mathcal{L}_q[ct]$ is equal to the query number. If it is, we reply with K s.t. $(ct, K) \in \mathcal{L}_K$ otherwise we proceed as before (i.e. as in H'). Let's assume w.l.o.g that each query to H'' is unique. For each ct s.t. $(ct, *) \in \mathcal{L}_K$, there can be at most one query (σ, ct) s.t. $\mathcal{O}^{PCO}(\sigma, ct)$ returns 1 (it is when σ is the decryption of ct). Here, $\mathcal{B}$ guesses beforehand which query it is (or if no such query will be made) and gets the correct answer with prob. $\frac{1}{q_H+1}$. Note that $\mathcal{B}$ needs to make one guess per query to $\mathcal{O}^{Dec''}$ (not per query to H''). Overall, the probability H'' simulates correctly H' is $\frac{1}{(q_H+1)^q}$.

From this we can deduce that $\mathcal{B}$ correctly simulates Γ^2 with probability $\frac{1}{((q_H+1)(q_H+2))^q}$ and wins the OW-CPA game with prob. at least $\frac{1}{q_H} \cdot \Pr[\text{query}]$. Hence,

$$|\Pr[\Gamma^1 \Rightarrow 1] - \Pr[\Gamma^2 \Rightarrow 1]| \leq \Pr[\text{query}] \leq q_H \cdot ((q_H+1)(q_H+2))^q \cdot \mathsf{Adv}_{PKE}^{ow-cpa}(\mathcal{B}).$$

Note that when PKE is deterministic, in order to recover σ^*, $\mathcal{B}$ can check which σ' queried is s.t. $\mathsf{enc}(pk^*, \sigma') = ct^*$ instead of guessing. This works as long as the challenge seed σ^* and queried seeds are correct. If that is not the case, one can build an adversary that wins the correctness game defined in Fig. 1. Note that this adversary knows which will be the correct seed as it is given sk and the PKE is deterministic. As the correctness advantage is upper bounded by δ, we obtain that for deterministic PKEs the last inequality becomes

$$|\Pr[\Gamma^1 \Rightarrow 1] - \Pr[\Gamma^2 \Rightarrow 1]| \leq \Pr[\text{query}] \leq \delta + ((q_H+1)(q_H+2))^q \cdot \mathsf{Adv}_{PKE}^{ow-cpa}(\mathcal{B}).$$

Finally, in game Γ^2, the challenge key is always random and thus $\Pr[\Gamma^2 \Rightarrow 1] = \frac{1}{2}$. Collecting the probabilities holds the result. □

4   CPA-security Is Sufficient for TLS 1.3 in the ROM

We show in this section that a CPA-secure KEM is sufficient for the handshake in TLS 1.3 to be secure in the ROM. The security bound is very loose, but this still solves an interesting open problem. TLS 1.3 only supports DH key-exchange but it can be trivially modified to support KEMs as done in several PQ variants of TLS (e.g. [1,7]). That is, the client runs $(sk, pk) \leftarrow_\$ \mathsf{gen}$ and sends pk as its share (instead of g^x). Then, the server runs $K, ct \leftarrow_\$ \mathsf{encaps}$ and sends ct as its secret share (instead of g^y). Finally, the client runs $K \leftarrow \mathsf{decaps}(sk, ct)$ and the shared secret is set to K. By abuse of language, we refer to this modified protocol as TLS 1.3 in what follows. An overview of this modified handshake is given in Fig. 14.

$\text{IND-1CCA-MAC}_{\text{KEM}}(\mathcal{A})$

$b \leftarrow\!\!\text{\$}\ \{0,1\}$

$(\text{pk}, \text{sk}) \leftarrow\!\!\text{\$}\ \text{gen}()$

$\text{ct}^*, K^* \leftarrow\!\!\text{\$}\ \text{encaps}(\text{pk})$

$n^* \leftarrow\!\!\text{\$}\ \{0,1\}^n$

$\text{HS}^* \leftarrow G(K^*)$

$\text{CHTS}_0 \leftarrow H_1(\text{HS}^*, H_T(\text{ct}^*, n^*))$

$\text{SHTS}_0 \leftarrow H_2(\text{HS}^*, H_T(\text{ct}^*, n^*))$

$\text{dHS}_0 \leftarrow H_3(\text{HS}^*)$

$(\text{CHTS}_1, \text{SHTS}_1, \text{dHS}_1) \leftarrow\!\!\text{\$}\ \{0,1\}^{3n}$

$b' \leftarrow \mathcal{A}^{\mathcal{O}^{\text{Dec}}, \mathcal{O}^{\text{Dec}}_{\text{MAC}}}(\text{pk}, \text{ct}^*, n^*, (\text{CHTS}_b, \text{SHTS}_b, \text{dHS}_b))$

$\text{return } 1_{b'=b}$

Oracle $\mathcal{O}^{\text{Dec}}((\text{ct}, n))$

if more than 1 query : **return** $\perp$

if $(\text{ct}, n) = (\text{ct}^*, n^*)$: **return** $\perp$

$K' \leftarrow \text{decaps}(\text{sk}, \text{ct})$

if $K' = \perp$: **return** $\perp$

$\text{HS}' \leftarrow G(K')$

$\text{CHTS} \leftarrow H_1(\text{HS}', H_T(\text{ct}, n))$

$\text{SHTS} \leftarrow H_2(\text{HS}', H_T(\text{ct}, n))$

$\text{tk}_\text{c} \leftarrow H_D(\text{CHTS}); \text{tk}_\text{s} \leftarrow H_D(\text{SHTS})$

return $(\text{tk}_\text{c}, \text{tk}_\text{s})$

Oracle $\mathcal{O}^{\text{Dec}}_{\text{MAC}}(\text{ct}, n, \text{tag}, \text{txt})$

if more than 1 query : **return** $\perp$

if $(\text{ct}, n) = (\text{ct}^*, n^*)$: **return** $\perp$

$K' \leftarrow \text{decaps}(\text{sk}, \text{ct})$

$\text{HS}' \leftarrow G(K'); \text{SHTS} \leftarrow H_2(\text{HS}', H_T(\text{ct}, n))$

$\text{fk}_S \leftarrow H_4(\text{SHTS})$

if $\text{MAC.Vrf}(\text{fk}_S, \text{txt}, \text{tag}) = \textbf{true}$:

$\quad$ **return** HS'

return $\perp$

Fig. 11. IND-1CCA-MAC game.

4.1   IND-1CCA-MAC

In order to show that a CPA-secure KEM is sufficient for TLS 1.3 to be secure, we first introduce an intermediary notion of security for KEMs, called IND-1CCA-MAC. This security definition has no application and will serve only as a useful intermediary building block for the proof.

Definition 6 (IND-1CCA-MAC). *We consider the games defined in Fig. 11. Let $\mathcal{K}$ be the key space, G, H_1, H_2, H_3, H_4 and H_D be key-derivation functions with images in $\{0,1\}^n$, H_T be a hash function with images in $\{0,1\}^n$, and MAC a MAC scheme. A KEM scheme $\text{KEM} = (\text{gen}, \text{encaps}, \text{decaps})$ is IND-1CCA-MAC if for any ppt adversary $\mathcal{A}$ we have*

$$\text{Adv}^{\text{ind-1cca-mac}}_{KEM}(\mathcal{A}) := \left| \Pr\left[\text{IND} - 1\text{CCA} - \text{MAC}_{\text{KEM}}(\mathcal{A}) \Rightarrow 1 \right] - \frac{1}{2} \right| = \text{negl}(\lambda)$$

where $\Pr\left[\text{IND} - 1\text{CCA} - \text{MAC}^b_{\text{KEM}}(\mathcal{A}) \Rightarrow 1 \right]$ *is the probability that $\mathcal{A}$ wins the IND-1CCA-MAC$^b_{\text{KEM}}(\mathcal{A})$ game defined in Fig. 11.*

In this game, the adversary receives a challenge ciphertext encapsulating a key K, a nonce n^*, and either three secrets $(\text{CHTS}_b, \text{SHTS}_b, \text{dHS}_b)$ derived from K through a key schedule, or three random secrets. Jumping ahead, these three values are computed (nearly) in the same as way as their identically named counterparts in the modified TLS 1.3 protocol. The adversary has also access to two oracles that it can query *at most once*. The first is simply a decapsulation oracle that applies a key schedule (similar to TLS's) on the decapsulated key and returns two secrets tk_c and tk_s. The second oracle takes a ciphertext (which must be different than the challenge ciphertext), a tag, and some data. Then, the ciphertext is decrypted to recover a secret HS' that is passed through a key schedule to get a MAC key fk_S. Finally, the oracle checks whether tag is a valid MAC on the data with the key fk_S. If this is the case it returns HS', otherwise it returns an error $\perp$. Informally, this last oracle outputs the root secret HS if the adversary can forge a valid tag corresponding to the tuple (ct, n). In the TLS proof, this will be used to argue that if a participant can send a valid tag, it should know the root secret HS.

4.2   OW-CPA Implies IND-1CCA-MAC

First, we briefly define the notion of MAC unforgeability we will need.

Definition 7 (MAC EUF-0T). *Let* $\mathsf{MAC} = (\mathsf{MAC.Vrf}, \mathsf{MAC.Tag})$ *be a message authentication code scheme (MAC). We say* MAC *is EUF-0T if for any ppt adversary* $\mathcal{A}$,

$$\mathsf{Adv}_{\mathsf{MAC}}^{\mathsf{euf-0t}}(\mathcal{A}) := \Pr[\mathsf{MAC.Vrf}(K, M, T) = 1 : (M, T) \leftarrow_{\$} \mathcal{A}; K \leftarrow_{\$} \mathcal{K}]$$

is negligible in the security parameter, where the probability is taken over the sampling of the key and the randomness of the adversary.

We now prove that any OW-CPA KEM is also IND-1CCA-MAC secure in the ROM if the MAC used is EUF-0T secure. More precisely, the KDFs G, H_1, H_2, H_3, H_4 and H_D, and the hash function H_T in the IND-1CCA-MAC games are assumed to be ROs.

Theorem 4. *Let* $\mathsf{KEM} = (\mathsf{gen}, \mathsf{encaps}, \mathsf{decaps})$ *be a KEM. Let the KDFs and the hash function in the IND-1CCA-MAC game be modelled as random oracles. Then, for any ppt adversary* $\mathcal{A}$ *making at most* $q_G, q_{H_1}, q_{H_2}, q_{H_3}, q_{H_4} q_{H_D}, q_{H_T}$ *queries to* $G, H_1, H_2, H_3, H_4, H_D, H_T$ *respectively, there exists a OW-CPA adversary* $\mathcal{B}$ *s.t.*

$$\mathsf{Adv}_{\mathsf{KEM}}^{\mathsf{ind-1cca-mac}}(\mathcal{A}) \leq \mathsf{Adv}_{\mathsf{MAC}}^{\mathsf{euf-0t}}(\mathcal{B}) + \frac{3q_{H_1} + 4q_{H_2} + q_{H_3} + q_{H_4} + q_{H_D} + 1}{2^n}$$

$$+ \frac{(q_{H_T} + 4)^2}{2^n} + q_G(q_{H_1} + 2)^2(q_{H_2} + 2)^3 \cdot \mathsf{Adv}_{\mathsf{KEM}}^{\mathsf{ow-cpa}}(\mathcal{C}),$$

where $\mathcal{B}$ *has approximately the same running time as* $\mathcal{A}$.

Proof. The first step of the proof is very similar to the proof of Theorem 3. Indeed, one can see that the decapsulation oracle outputs secrets that are computed as (a function of) $H_i(HS, H_T(ct, n))$, where H_i and H_T are ROs. Note that

$\Gamma_{\mathsf{KEM}}^{0\text{-}6}(\mathcal{A})$

$b \leftarrow_\$ \{0,1\}$

$(\mathsf{pk}, \mathsf{sk}) \leftarrow_\$ \mathsf{gen}()$

$\mathsf{ct}^*, K^* \leftarrow_\$ \mathsf{encaps}(\mathsf{pk})$

$n^* \leftarrow_\$ \{0,1\}^n$

$\mathsf{HS}^* \leftarrow G(K^*)$

$\mathsf{CHTS}_0 \leftarrow H_1(\mathsf{HS}^*, H_T(\mathsf{ct}^*, n^*))$

$\mathsf{SHTS}_0 \leftarrow H_2(\mathsf{HS}^*, H_T(\mathsf{ct}^*, n^*))$

$\mathsf{dHS}_0 \leftarrow H_3(\mathsf{HS}^*)$

$(\mathsf{CHTS}_1, \mathsf{SHTS}_1, \mathsf{dHS}_1) \leftarrow_\$ \{0,1\}^{3n}$

$b' \leftarrow \mathcal{A}^{\mathcal{O}^{\mathsf{Dec}}, \mathcal{O}^{\mathsf{Dec}}_{\mathsf{MAC}}, H_1, H_2}(\mathsf{pk}, \mathsf{ct}^*, n^*,$

$\qquad (\mathsf{CHTS}_b, \mathsf{SHTS}_b, \mathsf{dHS}_b)) /\!/ \; \Gamma^0\text{-}\Gamma^3$

$b' \leftarrow \mathcal{A}^{\mathcal{O}^{\mathsf{Dec}'}, \mathcal{O}^{\mathsf{Dec}}_{\mathsf{MAC}}, H'_1, H'_2}(\mathsf{pk}, \mathsf{ct}^*, n^*,$

$\qquad (\mathsf{CHTS}_b, \mathsf{SHTS}_b, \mathsf{dHS}_b)) /\!/ \; \Gamma^4\text{-}$

if collision on H_T : **abort** $/\!/ \; \Gamma^1$-

if $\mathcal{A}$ queries $H_i(\mathsf{HS}^*, H_T(\mathsf{ct}^*, n^*))$, $i \in [2]$ or $H_3(\mathsf{HS}^*)$:

$\quad$ **abort** $/\!/ \; \Gamma^6$

$\quad$ if $\mathcal{A}$ did not query $G(K^*)$: **abort** $/\!/ \; \Gamma^5$

return $1_{b'=b}$

Oracle $\mathcal{O}^{\mathsf{Dec}}_{\mathsf{MAC}}(\mathsf{ct}, n, \mathsf{tag}, \mathsf{txt})$

if more than 1 query : **return** $\perp$

if $(\mathsf{ct}, n) = (\mathsf{ct}^*, n^*)$: **return** $\perp$

$K' \leftarrow \mathsf{decaps}(\mathsf{sk}, \mathsf{ct})$

$\mathsf{HS}' \leftarrow G(K'); \mathsf{SHTS} \leftarrow H_2(\mathsf{HS}', H_T(\mathsf{ct}, n))$

$\mathsf{fk}_S \leftarrow H_4(\mathsf{SHTS})$

if $\mathsf{SHTS} = \mathsf{SHTS}_b$: $/\!/ \; \Gamma^2$-

$\quad$ **abort** $/\!/ \; \Gamma^2$-

if $\mathsf{MAC.Vrf}(\mathsf{fk}_S, \mathsf{txt}, \mathsf{tag}) = \mathbf{true}$:

$\quad$ if $\mathcal{A}$ did not query $H_4(\mathsf{SHTS})$: $/\!/ \; \Gamma^2$-

$\qquad$ **abort** $/\!/ \; \Gamma^2$-

$\quad$ if $\mathcal{A}$ did not query $H_2(\mathsf{HS}', H_T(\mathsf{ct}, n))$: $/\!/ \; \Gamma^3$-

$\qquad$ **abort** $/\!/ \; \Gamma^3$-

$\quad$ **return** HS'

return $\perp$

$H_j(\mathsf{HS}, y), \; j \in \{1, 2\}$

if $\nexists (\mathsf{ct}, n)$ s.t. $((\mathsf{ct}, n), y) \in \mathcal{L}_{H_T}$: $/\!/ \; \Gamma^1$-

$\quad h \leftarrow_\$ \{0,1\}^n$; **return** $h /\!/ \; \Gamma^1$-

usual lazy sampling

Fig. 12. Games for the proof of Theorem 4. The adversary has access to all the other ROs G, H_3, H_4 and H_D, even if it is not explicited in the games. H'_1, H'_2 and $\mathcal{O}^{\mathsf{Dec}'}$ are defined in Fig. 13.

the only difference is that H_T is applied on (ct, n). However, as H_T is a RO, this difference will not matter much in the proof. Hence, as in Theorem 3, one can program the ROs s.t. the decapsulation oracle $\mathcal{O}^{\mathsf{Dec}}$ can be simulated without the secret key. In a second step, we show that the adversary can also simulate the $\mathcal{O}^{\mathsf{Dec}}_{\mathsf{MAC}}$ oracle with good probability. More precisely, let HS be the secret corresponding to the submitted ciphertext ct. Then, either $H_2(\mathsf{HS}, H_T(\mathsf{ct}, n))$ has been queried by the adversary or it is very unlikely that $\mathcal{A}$ knows the MAC key fk_S. In the first case we can recover HS from the list of queries, and in the second we can return $\perp$ as most likely the MAC verification will fail.

We proceed with a sequence of games, which are given in detail in Fig. 12.

$\underline{\Gamma^0}$: This is the original IND-1CCA-MAC game. From now on, we assume w.l.o.g. that each query to ROs are unique (i.e. they never repeat).

$\underline{\Gamma^1}$: We modify the previous game as follows. First, we abort if a collision on H_T occurs in the game. As there are at most $q_{H_T} + 4$ queries to H_T in the game, a collision occurs with prob. less than $\frac{(q_{H_T}+4)^2}{2^n}$. Then, on adversary's queries $H_j(\mathsf{HS}, y)$, $j \in \{1, 2\}$, if $H_T(\mathsf{ct}, n) = y$ was never queried by $\mathcal{A}$ for some (ct, n), we mark y as *unpaired* and return a random value. The only way it differs from the previous game, is if a query $H_j(\mathsf{HS}, y)$ for an *unpaired* y is performed by the game (i.e. not by the adversary), either before or after y was marked as *unpaired*. Now, the $\mathcal{A}$ does not get any information about values $H_T(\mathsf{ct}, n)$ from the game (or oracles), except a few values $H_j(\mathsf{HS}, H_T(\mathsf{ct}, n))$ (or values that depends on these), for some HS. Note that these values completely "hide" the result of the H_T query, as H_j is a RO. Hence, the best strategy for $\mathcal{A}$ to query $H_j(\mathsf{HS}, y)$ s.t. y is *unpaired* but is queried by the game at some point, is to try random values for y. As the game makes at most 2 queries to H_1 (one in the challenge part and one in the decapsulation oracle) and 3 queries to H_2 (one in the challenge part and one in each oracle), the probability that a random unpaired y is s.t. y was the result of a H_T query by the game at some point, is at most $\frac{2}{2^n}$ for a H_1 call, and $\frac{3}{2^n}$ for a H_2 call. Overall, we have

$$|\Pr[\Gamma^0 \Rightarrow 1] - \Pr[\Gamma^1 \Rightarrow 1]| \leq \frac{2q_{H_1} + 3q_{H_2}}{2^n}.$$

We note that this step ensures that on a query $H_j(\mathsf{HS}, y)$, one can recover a unique tuple (ct, n) s.t. $H_T(\mathsf{ct}, n) = y$, or a random value is returned.

$\underline{\Gamma^2}$: We modify the original game s.t. we abort whenever the MAC verification succeeds on the query $\mathcal{O}_{\mathsf{MAC}}^{\mathsf{Dec}}(\mathsf{ct}, n, \mathsf{tag}, \mathsf{txt})$ but $\mathsf{fk}_S := H_4(\mathsf{SHTS})$ was never queried, where $\mathsf{SHTS} := H_2(G(K), H_T(\mathsf{ct}, n))$ and $K := \mathsf{decaps}(\mathsf{sk}, \mathsf{ct})$. If that is the case, it means the MAC key $\mathsf{fk}_S := H_4(\mathsf{SHTS})$ is indistinguishable from a random value for $\mathcal{A}$, but it managed to forge a valid tag. Thus, one can build an adversary $\mathcal{B}$ that breaks MAC unforgeability. More formally, $\mathcal{B}$ samples a pair of keys $(\mathsf{sk}, \mathsf{pk}) \leftarrow_\$ \mathsf{gen}$, generates a valid input for $\mathcal{A}$ and simulates the decryption oracle with the secret key. Then, when $\mathcal{A}$ submits $(\mathsf{ct}, n, \mathsf{tag}, \mathsf{txt})$ to $\mathcal{O}_{\mathsf{MAC}}^{\mathsf{Dec}}$, $\mathcal{B}$ outputs $(\mathsf{txt}, \mathsf{tag})$ as a forgery. We also abort if the value SHTS computed in the oracle is s.t. $\mathsf{SHTS} = \mathsf{SHTS}_b$. As there are no collision on H_T and $(\mathsf{ct}, n) \neq (\mathsf{ct}^*, n^*)$, this happens with probability at most $\frac{1}{2^n}$. Then, we have

$$|\Pr[\Gamma^1 \Rightarrow 1] - \Pr[\Gamma^2 \Rightarrow 1]| \leq \mathsf{Adv}_{\mathsf{MAC}}^{\mathsf{euf-0t}}(\mathcal{B}) + \frac{1}{2^n}.$$

$\underline{\Gamma^3}$: We abort whenever the MAC verification succeeds on the query $\mathcal{O}_{\mathsf{MAC}}^{\mathsf{Dec}}(\mathsf{ct}, n, \mathsf{tag}, \mathsf{txt})$ but $H_2(G(K), H_T(\mathsf{ct}, n))$ was never queried, where $K := \mathsf{decaps}(\mathsf{sk}, \mathsf{ct})$. By the previous game, it means that the adversary queried $\mathsf{SHTS} := H_2(G(K), H_T(\mathsf{ct}, n))$ to H_4 without having queried $H_2(G(K), H_T(\mathsf{ct}, n))$ beforehand. If we analyse what information $\mathcal{A}$ has about $\mathsf{SHTS} \neq \mathsf{SHTS}_b$ if it did not query $H_2(G(K), H_T(\mathsf{ct}, n))$, we see that the only potential "leakage" is from a decapsulation query that returns $\mathsf{tk}_s := H_D(\mathsf{SHTS})$, where H_D is a RO perfectly hiding SHTS.

Thus, the best strategy for $\mathcal{A}$ to find SHTS without querying H_2 is to query random values $x \in \{0,1\}^n$ to H_D or H_4 until it finds x s.t. $H_D(x) = \mathsf{tk}_s$ or $H_4(x) = \mathsf{fk}_S$. This happens with probability at most $\frac{q_{H_D} + q_{H_4}}{2^n}$. Hence, we have

$$|\Pr[\Gamma^2 \Rightarrow 1] - \Pr[\Gamma^3 \Rightarrow 1]| \leq \frac{q_{H_D} + q_{H_4}}{2^n}.$$

Oracle $\mathcal{O}^{\mathsf{Dec}'}(\mathsf{ct}, n)$	$H_j'(\mathsf{HS}, y),\ j \in \{1, 2\}$
if $(\mathsf{ct}, n) = (\mathsf{ct}^*, n^*)$: **return** $\perp$	**if** $\nexists(\mathsf{ct}, n)$ s.t. $((\mathsf{ct}, n), y) \in \mathcal{L}_{H_T}$:
if more than 1 query : **return** $\perp$	$\quad h \leftarrow_{\$} \{0, 1\}^n$; **return** h
$q_1 \leftarrow_{\$} \{0, \ldots, q_{H_1}\}$	set (ct, n) s.t. $((\mathsf{ct}, n), y) \in \mathcal{L}_{H_T}$
$q_2 \leftarrow_{\$} \{0, \ldots, q_{H_2}\}$	**if** $\mathcal{L}_K^j = (\mathsf{ct}, n, h)$ for some h :
$i \leftarrow \mathcal{O}^i(\mathcal{L}_{H_1}, \mathsf{ct}, n)$	$\quad$ **if** $\mathsf{HS} = G(\mathsf{decaps}(\mathsf{sk}, \mathsf{ct}))$:
if $i = \perp_d$: **return** $\perp$	$\qquad \mathcal{L}_{H_j} \leftarrow \mathcal{L}_{H_j} \cup \{((\mathsf{HS}, \mathsf{ct}, n), h)\}$
if $i \neq \perp$:	$\quad$ **return** h
$/\!/$ get i-th valued returned by H_1	$h \leftarrow_{\$} \{0, 1\}^n$
$\quad ((\mathsf{HS}_i, \mathsf{ct}_i, n_i), h_i) \leftarrow \mathcal{L}_{H_1}[i]$	$\mathcal{L}_{H_j} \leftarrow \mathcal{L}_{H_j} \cup \{((\mathsf{HS}, \mathsf{ct}, n), h)\}$
$\quad \mathsf{CHTS} \leftarrow h_i$	**return** h
else :	
$\quad \mathsf{CHTS} \leftarrow_{\$} \{0, 1\}$	
$\mathcal{L}_K^1 \leftarrow (\mathsf{ct}, n, \mathsf{CHTS})$	$\mathcal{O}_G^i(\mathcal{L}, n, \mathsf{ct})$
$i \leftarrow \mathcal{O}^i(\mathcal{L}_{H_2}, \mathsf{ct}, n)$	sort $\mathcal{L}$ according to query order :
if $i \neq \perp$:	$\mathcal{L} = ((\mathsf{HS}_i, \mathsf{ct}_i, n_i), h_i)_{i \in \{1, \ldots, |\mathcal{L}_H|\}}$
$/\!/$ get i-th valued returned by H_2	$K' \leftarrow \mathsf{decaps}(\mathsf{sk}, \mathsf{ct})$
$\quad ((\mathsf{HS}_i, \mathsf{ct}_i, n_i), h_i) \leftarrow \mathcal{L}_{H_2}[i]$	**if** $K' = \perp$: **return** $\perp_d$
$\quad \mathsf{SHTS} \leftarrow h_i$	$\mathsf{HS}' \leftarrow G(K')$
else :	**for** $i \in \{1, \ldots, |\mathcal{L}|\}$:
$\quad \mathsf{SHTS} \leftarrow_{\$} \{0, 1\}$	$\quad$ **if** $(\mathsf{ct}_i, n_i) = (\mathsf{ct}, n)$ **and** $\mathsf{HS}' = \mathsf{HS}_i$:
$\mathcal{L}_K^2 \leftarrow (\mathsf{ct}, n, \mathsf{SHTS})$	$\qquad$ **return** i
return $(H_D(\mathsf{CHTS}), H_D(\mathsf{SHTS}))$	**return** $\perp$

Fig. 13. Simulation of decapsulation and random oracles with sub-oracle $\mathcal{O}_G^i$ for the proof of Theorem 4. Note that as we assume that each query to H_j is unique, H_j' does not check whether a query was previously made.

Γ^4 : We program both ROs H_1 and H_2 s.t. we can perfectly simulate the decapsulation oracle with an oracle $\mathcal{O}_G^i$. This follows exactly the idea of the proof of Theorem 3. First, we introduce an oracle $\mathcal{O}_G^i$ in Fig. 13 that takes a list of RO queries, a nonce n and a ciphertext ct, checks whether $(G(K), H_T(\mathsf{ct}, n))$ (where K is the key encapsulated in ct) was ever queried and if that is the case, the index of the corresponding query. This is exactly the same as the oracle $\mathcal{O}^i$ in the proof of Theorem 3, except we query the decapsulated K to the RO G and there is the additional nonce. Then, we can program the ROs H_j, $j \in \{1, 2\}$ and simulate the (1-time) decapsulation oracle as shown in Fig. 13.

The simulation works nearly as in the proof of Theorem 3. Let ct be the unique decapsulation query, $K := \mathsf{decaps}(\mathsf{sk}, \mathsf{ct})$ and $\mathsf{HS} := G(K)$. For $j \in [2]$, the simulated decapsulation oracle checks whether $(G(K), H_T(\mathsf{ct}, n))$ was already queried to H_j using $\mathcal{O}_G^i$, if that is the case it recovers the corresponding value, otherwise it means $H_j(\mathsf{HS}, H_T(\mathsf{ct}, n))$ was never queried by the adversary *nor* the challenger, as $(\mathsf{ct}, n) \neq (\mathsf{ct}^*, n^*)$. Thus it samples the hash value at random, queries it to H_D and returns it to the adversary.

The simulation of H_j is such that it is consistent with the values returned by the simulated decapsulation oracle. First, if $H_j(\mathsf{HS}, y)$ is queried s.t. y is *unpaired*, we can simply return a random value, this is consistent with the game. Then, if y is not *unpaired*, one can recover the unique (as there are no collision) tuple (ct, n) s.t. $y = H_T(\mathsf{ct}, n)$. We consider from now on only queries with y s.t. $H_T(\mathsf{ct}, n) = y$ for some (ct, n). On a query $H_j(\mathsf{HS}, H_T(\mathsf{ct}, n))$, if (ct, n) was already queried to the decapsulation oracle, then $h := H_j(\mathsf{HS}, \mathsf{ct}, n)$ was set by $\mathcal{O}^{\mathsf{Dec}'}$ iff $\mathsf{HS} = G(K)$, where $K := \mathsf{decaps}(\mathsf{sk}, \mathsf{ct})$. Hence, we return the same K if $G(\mathsf{decaps}(\mathsf{sk}, \mathsf{ct})) = \mathsf{HS}$. Otherwise we sample a random value and return it. Note that this is the only place where the secret key sk is used anymore (except implicitly in the $\mathcal{O}_G^i$ oracle). The simulation is perfect and therefore we have

$$|\Pr[\Gamma^3 \Rightarrow 1] - \Pr[\Gamma^4 \Rightarrow 1]| = 0.$$

$\underline{\Gamma^5}$: In game Γ^5, we abort whenever the adversary did not query $G(K^*)$ (which is equal to HS^*) but it queried $H_1(\mathsf{HS}^*, H_T(\mathsf{ct}^*, n^*))$, $H_2(\mathsf{HS}^*, H_T(\mathsf{ct}^*, n^*))$ or $H_3(\mathsf{HS}^*)$. Note that the (modified) decryption oracle never queries $H_1(\mathsf{HS}^*, H_T(\mathsf{ct}^*, n^*))$, $H_2(\mathsf{HS}^*, H_T(\mathsf{ct}^*, n^*))$ or $H_3(\mathsf{HS}^*)$. In addition, the challenge values given to $\mathcal{A}$ are either perfectly random or completely hide HS^*. Thus, the probability that $\mathcal{A}$ queries HS^* to H_1, H_2 or H_3 is upper bounded by $\frac{q_{H_1} + q_{H_2} + q_{H_3}}{2^n}$ and hence we have

$$|\Pr[\Gamma^4 \Rightarrow 1] - \Pr[\Gamma^5 \Rightarrow 1]| \le \frac{q_{H_1} + q_{H_2} + q_{H_3}}{2^n} .$$

$\underline{\Gamma^6}$: Finally, in game Γ^6 we abort whenever $H_1(\mathsf{HS}^*, H_T(\mathsf{ct}^*, n^*))$, $H_2(\mathsf{HS}^*, H_T(\mathsf{ct}^*, n^*))$ or $H_3(\mathsf{HS}^*)$ is queried by the adversary. Let query be this event. By the previous game, it means that K^* was queried to G before query happens. Finally, as in the previous proofs, we can upper bound $\Pr[\mathsf{query}]$ by the advantage of a OW-CPA adversary times a constant. The challenge keys $(\mathsf{CHTS}_b, \mathsf{SHTS}_b, \mathsf{dHS}_b)$ are sampled at random in the reduction, as long query does not happen both the real and random cases are perfectly indistinguishable. The only challenge for such a OW-CPA adversary $\mathcal{C}$ is to simulate the oracles without having access to the secret key. It proceeds as follows (see the full version of the paper [20] for a complete and detailed presentation of $\mathcal{C}$).

- $\mathcal{O}_{\mathsf{MAC}}^{\mathsf{Dec}''}$: This oracle returns something else than $\bot$ iff $(\mathsf{HS}, H_T(\mathsf{ct}, n))$ was queried to H_2, where $\mathsf{HS} := G(K)$ and $K := \mathsf{decaps}(\mathsf{sk}, \mathsf{ct})$. Hence, one can simply pick a random value $r \leftarrow_\$ \{0, \ldots, q_{H_2}\}$ and guess whether $\mathcal{O}_{\mathsf{MAC}}^{\mathsf{Dec}}(\mathsf{ct})$ fails (if $r = 0$) or succeeds and HS is in the r-th query made to H_2. In the latter case, one can recover HS in the r-th query and return it. Overall the simulation works with probability $\frac{1}{q_{H_2}+1}$.

- $\mathcal{O}^{\mathsf{Dec}''}$: In this oracle, the secret-key is used only in the $\mathcal{O}_G^i$ sub-oracle. A reply of $\mathcal{O}_G^i$ is in the set $\{\bot, \bot_d, 1, \ldots, q_{H_j}\}$ for $j \in [2]$. Thus, one can guess the correct reply by sampling a random value in that set, which gives a success probability of $\frac{1}{(q_{H_j}+2)}$. Overall, there are at most 2 calls to $\mathcal{O}_G^i$ (one for $j = 1$

and $j = 2$) and therefore the probability that the simulation is successful is $\frac{1}{(q_{H_1}+2)(q_{H_2}+2)}$.

- H_j'', $j \in [2]$: The only time the secret key is used is when there is a query $(\mathsf{HS}, H_T(\mathsf{ct}, n))$ s.t. (ct, n) was already queried to $\mathcal{O}^{\mathsf{Dec}'}$ (i.e. $\mathcal{L}_K^j = (\mathsf{ct}, n, h)$ for some h). In this case h is returned iff $G(\mathsf{decaps}(\mathsf{sk}, \mathsf{ct})) = \mathsf{HS}$ (let's call this Condition (1)). Recalling that queries to H_j never repeat by assumption, there will be at most one query $H_j''(\mathsf{HS}, H_T(\mathsf{ct}, n))$ s.t. (ct, n) was queried to the decapsulation oracle and Condition (1) is fulfilled. Hence, one can simulate H_j by sampling an index $q_j \in \{0, \ldots, q_{H_j}\}$ and returning h (if it exists) in the q_j-th query or never in case $q_j = 0$. This successfully simulates H_j with prob. $\frac{1}{(q_{H_j}+1)}$. Overall, the probability that both H_1 and H_2 are simulated correctly is $\frac{1}{(q_{H_1}+1)(q_{H_2}+1)}$.

The other ROs can be simulated perfectly by $\mathcal{C}$ using lazy sampling. Collecting the probabilities holds that $\mathcal{C}$ simulates perfectly $\mathcal{A}$'s view in game Γ^6 (as long as query does not occur) with probability

$$p = \frac{1}{(q_{H_2}+1)^2(q_{H_1}+2)(q_{H_2}+2)(q_{H_1}+1)}.$$

Then if query happens, K^* will be in the list of queries made by $\mathcal{A}$ to G. The adversary can guess which one it is and succeeds with probability $\frac{1}{q_G}$. Hence, we have

$$|\Pr[\Gamma^5 \Rightarrow 1] - \Pr[\Gamma^6 \Rightarrow 1]| \leq \Pr[\mathsf{query}] \leq q_G(q_{H_1}+2)^2(q_{H_2}+2)^3 \cdot \mathsf{Adv}_{\mathsf{KEM}}^{\mathrm{ow-cpa}}(\mathcal{C}).$$

Finally, in game Γ^6, as $H_1(\mathsf{HS}^*, \mathsf{ct}^*, n^*)$, $H_2(\mathsf{HS}^*, \mathsf{ct}^*, n^*)$ or $H_3(\mathsf{HS}^*)$ cannot be queried anymore, the challenge keys are perfectly indistinguishable from random for the adversary. Hence,

$$\Pr[\Gamma^6 \Rightarrow 1] = \frac{1}{2}.$$

Collecting the probabilities holds the result. $\square$

4.3 Security of TLS 1.3 with IND-1CCA-MAC KEM

We can now use the (slightly modified) notion IND-1CCA-MAC KEM to prove the security of the TLS 1.3 handshake in the multi-stage security model of Günther [17]. We provide a brief reminder of the notion of MultiStage security in the full version of the paper [20]. The security of (the original) TLS 1.3 handshake was proven by Dowling et al. [12] and we refer the reader to their work for a complete analysis of the handshake. We will simply show that IND-1CCA-MAC KEMs, thus OW-CPA KEMs (if the MAC is secure), can be used in place of the original snPRF-ODH assumption for DH key-exchange.

First, we show the relevant part of the (full 1-RTT) handshake of TLS 1.3 in Fig. 14. One can see that the key schedule is nearly identical to the ones used in the IND-1CCA-MAC game. Note that several simplifications have been made and several steps irrelevant to our proofs are missing. In particular, we do not see the derivation of the finals keys, which all depend on the secret dHS. As we will show, the intermediary secrets (CHTS, SHTS, dHS) are secure (i.e. indistinguishable from random for a Multi-Stage adversary), thus all subsequent keys will be secure as well, assuming the KDFs are secure. Finally, we write $\mathsf{HKDF.Exp}_i(\mathsf{HS}, T_2)$ for $\mathsf{HKDF.Exp}(\mathsf{HS}, \mathsf{label}_i, T_2)$, where label_i is some string. As we consider the KDFs $\mathsf{HKDF.Ext}$ and $\mathsf{HKDF.Exp}$ to be ROs, this denotes the fact that the label implements oracle separation.

The security of the modified 1-RTT TLS 1.3 handshake is stated in the following theorem.

Theorem 5. *Let* $\mathsf{HKDF.Ext}$, $\mathsf{HKDF.TK}$ *and* $\mathsf{HKDF.Exp}_j$, $j \in \{0,4,5,6\}$ *(the KDFs in TLS 1.3) be random oracles. Let* Hash *(the hash function used to compute the hashed transcripts* T_i*) be a RO, and* Sig *the signature scheme used for server authentication (not shown in Fig. 14). For any Multi-Stage ppt adversary* $\mathcal{A}$ *there exist ppt adversaries* $\{\mathcal{B}_i\}_{i \in [6]}$ *s.t.*

$$\mathsf{Adv}^{\mathrm{multi\text{-}stage}}_{\mathrm{TLS1.3-1RTT}}(\mathcal{A}) \leq 6t_s \Bigg(\mathsf{Adv}^{\mathrm{coll}}_H(\mathcal{B}_1) + t_u \mathsf{Adv}^{\mathrm{euf-cma}}_{\mathsf{Sig}}(\mathcal{B}_2)$$

$$+ t_s \Big(\mathsf{Adv}^{\mathrm{ind-1cca-mac}}_{\mathsf{KEM}}(\mathcal{B}_3) + 2 \cdot \mathsf{Adv}^{\mathrm{prf}}_{\mathsf{HKDF.Exp}}(\mathcal{B}_4)$$

$$+ \mathsf{Adv}^{\mathrm{prf}}_{\mathsf{HKDF.Ext}}(\mathcal{B}_5) + \mathsf{Adv}^{\mathrm{prf}}_{\mathsf{HKDF.Exp}}(\mathcal{B}_6) \Big) \Bigg).$$

where t_s *(resp.* t_u*) is the maximal number of sessions (resp. users). Note that for the sake of the comparison with the original bound, we keep several PRF advantages and the collision advantage in the bound, even though they could be replaced by negligible terms, as the KDFs and* Hash *are ROs.*

Proof sketch. Due to space constraint, we defer the proof to the full version of the paper [20]. However, as hinted above, the idea of the proof is simply to replace the snPRF-ODH step of the original proof by using our IND-1CCA-MAC. Note that while the snPRF-ODH assumption is used to replace the root secret HS by a random one, we will be able to replace the values (CHTS, SHTS, dHS) by random ones in one step, due to the structure of the IND-1CCA-MAC definition. From a high-level point of view, the proof goes through because CHTS and SHTS are computed similarly as in the T_H transform (i.e. the secrets are the hashed seed and ciphertext) and thus resist to 1 adversarial decapsulation query. Then, dHS is used only once a MAC has been verified, which implies that an adversary relaying a correct tag should already know the root key HS.   □

Similarly, one can prove the security of the modified TLS 1.3 PSK-(EC)DHE 0-RTT handshake. Note that in our case the key-exchange will be done with KEMs, but we keep the "-(EC)DHE" in the name for consistency with the original protocol. We state this in the following informal theorem.

TLS 1.3 with KEM Handhsake

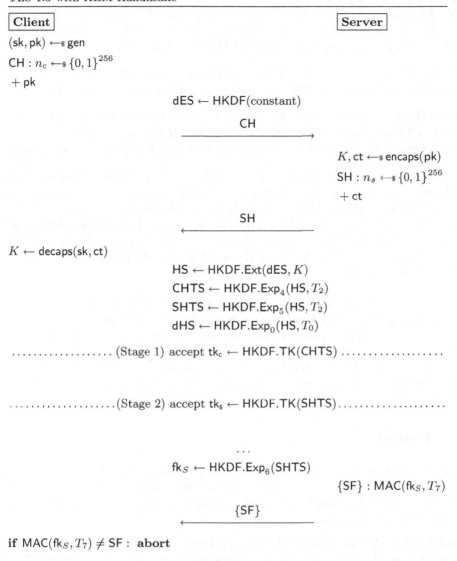

Fig. 14. TLS 1.3 handshake with KEM. $\{\ldots\}$ indicates an encrypted message with $\mathrm{tk_S}$, T_i is the hash of the transcript up to message i. For simplicity, the CH (resp. SH) message captures both the *ClientHello* and *ClientKeyShare* (resp. *ServerHello* and *ServerKeyShare*). Only the relevant steps for the proof are shown. Keys in the remaining stages (3-6, not shown) are all derived from dHS.

Theorem 6. *The modified TLS 1.3 handshake in the pre-shared key (optional) 0-RTT mode with key-exchange (i.e. TLS 1.3 PSK-(EC)-DHE 0-RTT) is secure in the MultiStage model if the underlying KEM is OW-CPA (and signature, MAC, etc. are secure), in the sense of Dowling et al. [12].*

Proof. The only step in the original proof involving the KEMs can be dealt with a similar reduction from IND-1CCA-MAC as in the proof of Theorem 5.   □

Corollary 3. *The original TLS 1.3 handshake is MultiStage secure in the ROM if the CDH problem is hard (and the signature, MAC, etc. are secure). Stronger assumptions used in previous proofs (e.g. PRF-ODH [12]) are not necessary.*

Proof. This simply follows from the fact that DH can be described as a KEM $(\mathsf{sk}, \mathsf{pk}) := (x, g^x)$, $(K, \mathsf{ct}) := (\mathsf{pk}^y, g^y)$ and $\mathsf{decaps}(\mathsf{sk}, \mathsf{ct}) := \mathsf{ct}^x$. Integrating this KEM in our modified TLS 1.3 handshake exactly holds the standard TLS 1.3 handshake. Finally, this KEM is OW-CPA as long as the CDH problem is hard, thus by Theorems 4 and 5, the handshake is secure. One can also directly show that DH as used in TLS 1.3 is a IND-1CCA KEM. We provide such a proof in the full version [20].   □

Remarks. Note that due to non-tightness of the bound in Theorem 4, the overall bound for TLS security is very much non-tight. This is clearly not sufficient to guarantee security in practice, and we leave as an interesting open question the improvement of the bounds. In addition, we leave security in the QROM as future work. As we extensively use the programming property of ROs, new QROM techniques such as the *compressed oracles* by Zhandry [33] might be of use in such a proof.

5   Impact

The transforms introduced in Sect. 3 produce IND-qCCA KEMs without any derandomization and re-encryption steps. Thus, using IND-1CCA ephemeral KEMs obtained through these transforms could speed up the decapsulation process in several protocols.

KEMTLS. As discussed in the introduction, improving the KEMTLS protocol [29] was the main motivation of this work. In particular, a more efficient decapsulation in the ephemeral KEM would decrease overall latency and computation on the client-side. In particular, this could be of interest for less powerful clients like IoT devices, which would not need to perform re-encryption. Overall, the efficiency gain in practice would obviously depend on the ephemeral KEM used, as encryption is expensive in some schemes while it is not in others. For instance, using KEMTLS with a modified version of SIKE (i.e. obtained through our transform instead of the FO one) would reduce probably significantly the handshake latency and computation cost on the client-side.

The same remarks apply to the very recent variants of KEMTLS with pre-distributed keys proposed by Günther et al. [18] and Schwabe et al. [31].

Note also that following a similar proof as the one in Sect. 4, we conjecture that one should be able to prove that CPA-security of the ephemeral KEM should suffice for KEMTLS to be secure in the ROM (but at the expense of a non-tight security bound, as in the TLS case).

TLS 1.3. TLS 1.3 only supports ephemeral DH as a key-exchange. In turn, in the original security proof [12], the snPRF-ODH assumption is used for the key-exchange security. The snPRF-ODH assumption can be seen as a variant of the hashed Diffie-Hellman assumption with a 1-time "decapsulation" oracle. More precisely, an adversary is given (g, g^u, g^v) and either $y_0 := \mathsf{PRF}(g^{uv}, \mathsf{ad}^*)$ or a random y_1, where ad^* is some auxiliary data chosen by the adversary. Then, the adversary must distinguish between y_0 and y_1 with the help of *one* query to an oracle $\mathcal{O}((x, \mathsf{ad}) \neq (g^u, \mathsf{ad}^*)) := \mathsf{PRF}(x^v, \mathsf{ad})$.

One can notice that snPRF-ODH security is very close to IND-1CCA security transposed to DH key-exchange. Actually, one can show that IND-1CCA KEM is sufficient for the PQ TLS 1.3 handshake to hold. Indeed, instead of using our IND-1CCA-MAC assumption in the proof, one can use the decapsulation oracle of the IND-1CCA adversary to recover the key if needed. One can check the transition between games $B.1$ and $B.2$ in the proof of KEMTLS security [29] for more details.

Therefore, using IND-1CCA KEMs in the PQ TLS 1.3 handshake seems a sound idea, as in this case the security bound will offer better guarantees than with a OW-CPA KEM. In addition, the handshake would be faster using IND-1CCA KEMs generated by our transforms instead of the slower IND-CCA KEMs derived with FO.

Finally, by Corollary 3, we now know that the snPRF-ODH assumption is not necessary in the ROM for TLS 1.3 to be secure (even though the security bound is very much non-tight), but CDH is sufficient. Alternatively, as shown in the full version [20], DII as used in TLS 1.3 is actually an IND-1CCA KEM ($\approx$ snPRF-ODH) in the ROM if CDH holds. This gives a tighter security bound compared to Corollary 3.

Ratcheting. IND-1CCA security is also a property used (often implicitly) in several works on ratcheting. For instance, Jost et al. [22] build a *healable and key-updating public-key encryption* scheme based on a *one time* IND-CCA2 PKE (with authenticated data). The latter primitive can easily be made out of an IND-1CCA KEM using KEM/DEM techniques. Another paper by Poettering et al. [27] introduces a construction of *unidirectional ratcheted key exchange* (URKE) that is based (implicitly) on IND-1CCA KEMs, as noticed by Balli et al. [2].

In another recent paper, Brendel et al. [6] propose an alternative to the Signal handshake based on KEMs and designated verifier signature schemes. They first define a core protocol that uses two KEMs in the same vein as KEMTLS: one with long-term keys for implicit authentication of one of the parties and another one with ephemeral keys for guaranteeing forward security. Again, the latter one requires only IND-1CCA security for the handshake to be secure. Similarly, in the full Signal-like handshake built upon the core protocol (called SPQR), three KEMs are used and one requires only IND-1CCA security.

Concerns Over Key-reuse. The main security risk of using an IND-1CCA KEM instead of its IND-CCA counterpart is the vulnerability to key-reuse/misuse attacks. Indeed, if a system/protocol is misimplemented s.t. the IND-1CCA KEM is used with a "static" public key instead of an ephemeral one, an adversary might be able to recover the secret key after several decryption queries. In KEMTLS, this risk is mitigated by the use of an IND-CCA KEM in addition to the ephemeral one (which can be IND-1CCA). In particular, the final shared key is derived from shares of both KEMs. Thus, even if the public-key meant to be ephemeral is reused, the final shared key should remain "secure" (but forward security would be lost).

In other systems (e.g. TLS 1.3), the risk of key recovery after a few reuses could be mitigated by using hybrid cryptography. For instance, a very efficient IND-CCA KEM could be combined with an IND-1CCA one. That would improve the overall security and resistance against key-reuse attacks at a small cost (see e.g. Giacon et al. [16] or Bindel et al. [3] for KEM combiners). Finally, we stress again that if ephemeral keys were misimplemented as static ones in these systems, the forward security property would be lost.

Conclusion. Ratcheting and several recent protocols (e.g. TLS 1.3) are aiming at forward security, which often implies generating a new pair of public/secret keys for each message exchanged. Informally, in many settings this means that an adversary requesting a decryption will be able to do so only once for a given key pair. Thus, IND-1CCA security of the underlying encryption/encapsulation primitive might be sufficient to guarantee the security of such systems.

Acknowledgment. We thank Daniel Collins for pointing out possible use-cases of IND-1CCA KEMs in ratcheting and the anonymous reviewers for their helpful comments. Loïs Huguenin-Dumittan is supported by a grant (project № 192364) of the Swiss National Science Foundation (SNSF).

References

1. OQS OpenSSL (June 2021). https://github.com/open-quantum-safe/openssl
2. Balli, F., Rösler, P., Vaudenay, S.: Determining the core primitive for optimally secure ratcheting. In: Moriai, S., Wang, H. (eds.) ASIACRYPT 2020. LNCS, vol. 12493, pp. 621–650. Springer, Cham (2020). https://doi.org/10.1007/978-3-030-64840-4_21
3. Bindel, N., Brendel, J., Fischlin, M., Goncalves, B., Stebila, D.: Hybrid key encapsulation mechanisms and authenticated key exchange. In: Ding, J., Steinwandt, R. (eds.) PQCrypto 2019. LNCS, vol. 11505, pp. 206–226. Springer, Cham (2019). https://doi.org/10.1007/978-3-030-25510-7_12
4. Bindel, N., Hamburg, M., Hövelmanns, K., Hülsing, A., Persichetti, E.: Tighter proofs of CCA security in the quantum random oracle model. In: Hofheinz, D., Rosen, A. (eds.) TCC 2019. LNCS, vol. 11892, pp. 61–90. Springer, Cham (2019). https://doi.org/10.1007/978-3-030-36033-7_3

5. Brendel, J., Fischlin, M., Günther, F., Janson, C.: PRF-ODH: Relations, instantiations, and impossibility results. Cryptology ePrint Archive, Report 2017/517 (2017). https://ia.cr/2017/517
6. Brendel, J., Fiedler, R., Günther, F., Janson, C., Stebila, D.: Post-quantum asynchronous deniable key exchange and the signal handshake. Cryptology ePrint Archive, Report 2021/769 (2021). https://eprint.iacr.org/2021/769
7. Celi, S., et al.: Implementing and measuring KEMTLS. Cryptology ePrint Archive, Report 2021/1019 (2021). https://ia.cr/2021/1019
8. Cramer, R., et al.: Bounded CCA2-secure encryption. In: Kurosawa, K. (ed.) ASIACRYPT 2007. LNCS, vol. 4833, pp. 502–518. Springer, Heidelberg (2007). https://doi.org/10.1007/978-3-540-76900-2_31
9. Crockett, E., Paquin, C., Stebila, D.: Prototyping post-quantum and hybrid key exchange and authentication in TLS and SSH. IACR Cryptol. ePrint Arch. **2019**, 858 (2019)
10. Davis, H., Günther, F.: Tighter proofs for the SIGMA and TLS 1.3 key exchange protocols. In: Sako, K., Tippenhauer, N.O. (eds.) ACNS 2021. LNCS, vol. 12727, pp. 448–479. Springer, Cham (2021). https://doi.org/10.1007/978-3-030-78375-4_18
11. Diemert, D., Jager, T.: On the tight security of TLS 1.3: theoretically sound cryptographic parameters for real-world deployments. J. Cryptol. **34**(3), 1–57 (2021)
12. Dowling, B., Fischlin, M., Günther, F., Stebila, D.: A cryptographic analysis of the TLS 1.3 handshake protocol. J. Cryptol. **34** (2020)
13. Fluhrer, S.: Cryptanalysis of ring-LWE based key exchange with key share reuse. Cryptology ePrint Archive, Report 2016/085 (2016). https://eprint.iacr.org/2016/085
14. Fujisaki, E., Okamoto, T.: Secure integration of asymmetric and symmetric encryption schemes. In: Wiener, M. (ed.) CRYPTO 1999. LNCS, vol. 1666, pp. 537–554. Springer, Heidelberg (1999). https://doi.org/10.1007/3-540-48405-1_34
15. Fujisaki, E., Okamoto, T.: Secure integration of asymmetric and symmetric encryption schemes. J. Cryptol. **26**(1), 80–101 (2013). https://doi.org/10.1007/s00145-011-9114-1
16. Giacon, F., Heuer, F., Poettering, B.: KEM Combiners. Cryptology ePrint Archive, Report 2018/024 (2018). https://eprint.iacr.org/2018/024
17. Günther, F.: Modeling advanced security aspects of key exchange and secure channel protocols (2018)
18. Günther, F., Towa, P.: KEMTLS with delayed forward identity protection in (almost) a single round trip. Cryptology ePrint Archive, Report 2021/725 (2021). https://eprint.iacr.org/2021/725
19. Hofheinz, D., Hövelmanns, K., Kiltz, E.: A modular analysis of the Fujisaki-Okamoto transformation. In: Kalai, Y., Reyzin, L. (eds.) TCC 2017. LNCS, vol. 10677, pp. 341–371. Springer, Cham (2017). https://doi.org/10.1007/978-3-319-70500-2_12
20. Huguenin-Dumittan, L., Vaudenay, S.: A note on IND-qCCA security in the ROM and its applications: CPA security is sufficient for TLS 1.3. Cryptology ePrint Archive, Report 2021/844 (2021). https://ia.cr/2021/844
21. Jao, D., et al.: SIKE (2020). https://csrc.nist.gov/Projects/post-quantum-cryptography/round-3-submissions
22. Jost, D., Maurer, U., Mularczyk, M.: Efficient ratcheting: almost-optimal guarantees for secure messaging. In: Ishai, Y., Rijmen, V. (eds.) EUROCRYPT 2019. LNCS, vol. 11476, pp. 159–188. Springer, Cham (2019). https://doi.org/10.1007/978-3-030-17653-2_6

23. Kuchta, V., Sakzad, A., Stehlé, D., Steinfeld, R., Sun, S.-F.: Measure-rewind-measure: tighter quantum random oracle model proofs for One-Way to hiding and CCA security. In: Canteaut, A., Ishai, Y. (eds.) EUROCRYPT 2020. LNCS, vol. 12107, pp. 703–728. Springer, Cham (2020). https://doi.org/10.1007/978-3-030-45727-3_24

24. Okamoto, T., Pointcheval, D.: REACT: rapid enhanced-security asymmetric cryptosystem transform. In: Naccache, D. (ed.) CT-RSA 2001. LNCS, vol. 2020, pp. 159–174. Springer, Heidelberg (2000). https://doi.org/10.1007/3-540-45353-9_13

25. Paquin, C., Stebila, D., Tamvada, G.: Benchmarking post-quantum cryptography in TLS. Cryptology ePrint Archive, Report 2019/1447 (2019). https://eprint.iacr.org/2019/1447

26. Pereira, M., Dowsley, R., Hanaoka, G., Nascimento, A.C.A.: Public key encryption schemes with bounded CCA security and optimal ciphertext length based on the CDH assumption. In: Burmester, M., Tsudik, G., Magliveras, S., Ilić, I. (eds.) ISC 2010. LNCS, vol. 6531, pp. 299–306. Springer, Heidelberg (2011). https://doi.org/10.1007/978-3-642-18178-8_26

27. Poettering, B., Rösler, P.: Towards bidirectional ratcheted key exchange. In: Shacham, H., Boldyreva, A. (eds.) CRYPTO 2018. LNCS, vol. 10991, pp. 3–32. Springer, Cham (2018). https://doi.org/10.1007/978-3-319-96884-1_1

28. Saito, T., Xagawa, K., Yamakawa, T.: Tightly-secure key-encapsulation mechanism in the quantum random oracle model. In: Nielsen, J.B., Rijmen, V. (eds.) EUROCRYPT 2018. LNCS, vol. 10822, pp. 520–551. Springer, Cham (2018). https://doi.org/10.1007/978-3-319-78372-7_17

29. Schwabe, P., Stebila, D., Wiggers, T.: Post-quantum TLS without handshake signatures. In: Proceedings of the 2020 ACM SIGSAC Conference on Computer and Communications Security, pp. 1461–1480 (2020)

30. Schwabe, P., Stebila, D., Wiggers, T.: Post-quantum TLS without handshake signatures. Cryptology ePrint Archive, Report 2020/534 (2020). https://eprint.iacr.org/2020/534

31. Schwabe, P., Stebila, D., Wiggers, T.: More efficient post-quantum KEMTLS with pre-distributed public keys. Cryptology ePrint Archive, Report 2021/779 (2021). https://eprint.iacr.org/2021/779

32. Yamakawa, T., Yamada, S., Matsuda, T., Hanaoka, G., Kunihiro, N.: Reducing public key sizes in bounded CCA-secure KEMs with optimal ciphertext length. In: Desmedt, Y. (ed.) ISC 2013. LNCS, vol. 7807, pp. 100–109. Springer, Cham (2015). https://doi.org/10.1007/978-3-319-27659-5_7

33. Zhandry, M.: How to record quantum queries, and applications to quantum indifferentiability. In: Boldyreva, A., Micciancio, D. (eds.) CRYPTO 2019. LNCS, vol. 11693, pp. 239–268. Springer, Cham (2019). https://doi.org/10.1007/978-3-030-26951-7_9

On the Lattice Isomorphism Problem, Quadratic Forms, Remarkable Lattices, and Cryptography

Léo Ducas[1,2] and Wessel van Woerden[1(✉)]

[1] CWI, Cryptology Group, Amsterdam, The Netherlands
wvw@cwi.nl
[2] Mathematical Institute, Leiden University, Leiden, The Netherlands

Abstract. A natural and recurring idea in the knapsack/lattice cryptography literature is to start from a lattice with remarkable decoding capability as your private key, and hide it somehow to make a public key. This is also how the code-based encryption scheme of McEliece (1978) proceeds.

This idea has never worked out very well for lattices: ad-hoc approaches have been proposed, but they have been subject to ad-hoc attacks, using tricks beyond lattice reduction algorithms. On the other hand the framework offered by the Short Integer Solution (SIS) and Learning With Errors (LWE) problems, while convenient and well founded, remains frustrating from a coding perspective: the underlying decoding algorithms are rather trivial, with poor decoding performance.

In this work, we provide generic realizations of this natural idea (independently of the chosen remarkable lattice) by basing cryptography on the lattice isomorphism problem (LIP). More specifically, we provide:

- a worst-case to average-case reduction for search-LIP and distinguish-LIP within an isomorphism class, by extending techniques of Haviv and Regev (SODA 2014).
- a zero-knowledge proof of knowledge (ZKPoK) of an isomorphism. This implies an identification scheme based on search-LIP.
- a key encapsulation mechanism (KEM) scheme and a hash-then-sign signature scheme, both based on distinguish-LIP.

The purpose of this approach is for remarkable lattices to improve the security and performance of lattice-based cryptography. For example, decoding within poly-logarithmic factor from Minkowski's bound in a remarkable lattice would lead to a KEM resisting lattice attacks down to poly-logarithmic approximation factor, provided that the dual lattice is also close to Minkowski's bound. Recent works have indeed reached such decoders for certain lattices (Chor-Rivest, Barnes-Sloan), but these do not perfectly fit our need as their duals have poor minimal distance.

1 Introduction

At repeated occasions [8, 22, 24, 33, 45], and over more than 30 years, it has been attempted to adapt the public-key encryption scheme of McEliece [25] from codes

© International Association for Cryptologic Research 2022
O. Dunkelman and S. Dziembowski (Eds.): EUROCRYPT 2022, LNCS 13277, pp. 643–673, 2022.
https://doi.org/10.1007/978-3-031-07082-2_23

to lattices. More specifically, these works attempted to construct particularly good lattices with efficient decoding algorithms, to use it as a secret-key, and to give a bad description of a similar lattice as the corresponding public-key. For example, it was analysed in [11] that the Chor-Rivest cryptosystem [8] was implicitly relying on a family of lattices for which it is possible to efficiently decode errors up to a radius within a factor of $O(\log n)$ from optimal (Minkowski bound). For comparison, the decoding algorithm underlying schemes based on the Learning with Error problem [39] (LWE) fall short from the Minkowski bound by polynomial factors; they essentially reduce decoding to the case of the trivial lattice $\mathbb{Z}^n$.

This McEliece-like approach has unfortunately not been very popular lately. Perhaps it has suffered from the failure of the Merkle-Hellman Knapsack-based cryptosystem [26,43] more than it should have. Indeed, from the "knapsack-era", only the Merkle-Hellman cryptosystem and its variants were completely devastated by a polynomial-time attack [32]. In contrast, the best known attack against the scheme of Chor and Rivest [8,24] remains sub-exponential in the dimension n; what may be concerning is that those attacks are not pure lattice reduction attacks. For both versions of this scheme, the canonical coordinates are partially brute-forced during the best attack. Lapiha [20] found that an Information Set Decoding attack was possible against the variant of Li *et al.* [24]. Brickell's attack against the original scheme also relies on guessing over a few canonical coordinates, inside of an arithmetic attack [8, Sec. VII.5].

However, we note that these attacks are enabled by the fact that these schemes only re-randomize the lattice by applying a permutation of the coordinates.[1] Such permutations are isometries, i.e. lattice isomorphism, but those are not the only ones... The isometry group $\mathcal{O}_n(\mathbb{R})$ acting on lattices is much larger than the one acting on codes, and applying a random isometry from this larger group should convincingly thwart those code-style attacks: the canonical coordinate system becomes irrelevant.

All these remarks point toward the Lattice Isomorphism Problem (LIP) as a potential theoretical platform for finally getting this natural approach properly formalized, and hopefully, truely "lattice-based" in the cryptanalytic sense: the best known attack should be based on generic lattice reduction algorithms such as LLL [21] and BKZ [40]. The current state of the art on LIP supports this hypothesis: all known algorithms [17,37,38,44] rely on finding short vectors. This is the case even for algorithms specialized to the trivial lattice $\mathbb{Z}^n$ [46]. However, experimental studies [6] show that the basis randomization step requires care.

While instantiating LIP with $\mathbb{Z}^n$ may already give rise to secure cryptosystems, the end goal of this work is to enable lattice-based cryptosystems that

---

[1] This permutation is in fact implicit, hidden in the ordering of the evaluation points used to define the lattice. Furthermore, both in these lattice schemes and in subsequent versions of the McEliece, one may also discard some the evaluation points to randomize the lattice/code itself beyond isometry. In this article, we will not consider this extra randomization.

could be even more secure than those based on LWE and SIS, by instantiating the constructed schemes with remarkably decodable lattices.

1.1 Contributions

We propose a formal and convenient framework for LIP-based cryptography, from which we build an identification scheme based on search-LIP (sLIP), a (passively secure) Key Encapsulation Mechanism (KEM) based on distinguish-LIP (ΔLIP), as well as signature scheme also based on ΔLIP. In more details:

- We first discuss the LIP problem, recall the quadratic form formalism (Sect. 2.2), and rephrase the LIP problem in terms of quadratic forms to conveniently avoid real numbers. Then, thanks to Gaussian Sampling [12,34], we define an average-case distribution for LIP and establish a worst-case to average-case reduction within an isomorphism class (Sect. 3). This addresses the concerns raised by Blanks and Miller [6], and formalizes their heuristic countermeasure.
- The above cryptographic foundations are directly inspired by the Zero-Knowledge proof of lattice non-isomorphism of Haviv and Regev [16]. We further extend on their techniques by proposing a Zero-Knowledge proof of knowledge (ZKPoK) of a lattice isomorphism (Sect. 4). This directly implies an identification scheme based on sLIP.
- We propose a KEM scheme (Sect. 5) and a hash-then-sign signature scheme (Sect. 6), both based on ΔLIP. Perhaps surprisingly, and unlike the original scheme of McEliece for codes, we circumvent the additional assumption that decoding a certain class of random lattices would be hard. This is done via a lossyness argument [36] for the KEM, and a dual argument for the signature scheme.
- We review the state of the art for solving LIP (Sect. 7). In particular we note that all known algorithms go through lattice reduction, and we quantify the required approximation factor.
- We discuss natural instantiations for each scheme (Sect. 8) from any remarkable lattice. This section handles the construction of the auxiliary lattice appearing in ΔLIP for the lossyness arguments to get through.

1.2 Potential Advantages

The KEM. To instantiate our KEM, consider a lattice L (w.l.o.g. of volume 1) such that:

- the minimal distance is within a factor f from Minkowski's bound: $\lambda_1(L) \geqslant \Omega(\sqrt{n}/f)$,
- there exists an efficient algorithm that can decode errors in L up to radius ρ within a factor f' from Minkowski's bound: $\rho \geqslant \Omega(\sqrt{n}/f').$[2]

---

[2] Note that uniqueness of decoding implies $f' \geqslant 2f$.

– the dual minimal distance is within a factor f^* from Minkowski's bound: $\lambda_1(L^*) \geqslant \Omega(\sqrt{n}/f^*)$.

Then, our instantiated KEM appears to resist lattice attack down to an approximation factor $O(\max(f, f^*) \cdot f^* \cdot f')$. More specifically, it's security is based on ΔLIP for two lattices whose primals and duals are all within a factor $O(\max(f, f^*) \cdot f^* \cdot f')$ from Minkowski's bound.

The trivial lattice $\mathbb{Z}^n$ gives all three factors f, f', f^* of the order $\Theta(\sqrt{n})$. The Barnes-Wall [28] lattice improves all three factors down to $\Theta(\sqrt[4]{n})$.

The endgame would be to instantiate with lattices for which all three factors would be very small. In particular, one would naturally turn to recent work on decoding the Chor-Rivest lattices [8,11,20,24] and the Barnes-Sloane lattices [31] giving $f = \text{polylog}(n)$ and $f' = \text{polylog}(n)$, but unfortunately their dual are not that good: $f^* \geqslant \Theta(\sqrt{n})$. Indeed, all these constructions are integer lattices $L \subset \mathbb{Z}^n$ with single exponential volume $\det(L) = c^n$: their dual L^* have a Minkowski's bound of $\Theta(\sqrt{n}/\det(L)^{1/n}) = \Theta(\sqrt{n})$, but contain all of $\mathbb{Z}^n \subset L^*$, including vectors of norm 1.

Note nevertheless that there is no geometric impossibility to the existence of the desired remarkably decodable lattice: random lattices have $f = O(1)$ and $f^* = O(1)$; so decoding is possible down to $f' = O(1)$ but the best known algorithm is conjectured to take exponential time.

The Signature Scheme. The same principle also applies to our signature scheme, but this time with respect to Gaussian sampling rather than decoding: lattices with tight sampling (and large dual minimal distance) would lead to a scheme resisting attacks down to very small approximation factors. Alas, even ignoring the constraint on the dual lattice, we do not know of any lattice much better than $\mathbb{Z}^n$ for efficient gaussian sampling. Yet, instantiated with $\mathbb{Z}^n$ our scheme still has an interesting feature: not having to deal with any Gram-Schmidt or Cholesky matrices over the reals. This may be a worthy practical advantage over current hash-then-sign signature schemes [12].

The Identification Scheme. Because sLIP seems super-exponentially hard in the dimension for well chosen lattices (large kissing number), it might be secure to instantiate our ZKPoK with a rather small lattice dimension, maybe down to about a hundred. Yet, this is more a theoretical curiosity than a practical advantage—the protocol still needs soundness amplification, and each round requires exchanging $\tilde{O}(n^2)$ bits.

1.3   Open Questions

A KEM with polylog-Approximation Factor Security. Is there any family of lattices that can be efficiently decoded within a polylog factor from Minkowski's bound such as [8,11,20,24,31], but whose dual would also have an equally large minimal distance?

Tight Gaussian Sampling for Signatures. Is there any family of lattices L (of volume 1) in which one can efficiently sample Gaussian with small parameter $\sigma < o(\sqrt{n})$, if not $\sigma = \text{polylog}(n)$ (with exponential smoothing $\sigma > \eta_{2^{-n}}(L)$)? And if so, do they and their dual have a large minimal distance? Note that quantumly, this question is related to the previous one via the reduction of Regev [39]: decoding in the primal for a large radius gives Gaussian sampling in the dual for a small width. But a classical algorithm would be much preferable.

Concrete Instantiation with Simple Lattices. Instantiated with $\mathbb{Z}^n$, our signature scheme has the advantage of not requiring any Gram-Schmidt or Cholesky decomposition, contrary to existing hash-then-sign signature schemes; and may therefore be of practical interest. It could also be reasonable to instantiate our KEM with the lattice of Barnes and Wall, thanks to the decoder of Micciancio and Nicolesi [28].

Module-LIP. At last, it also seems natural to explore structured variants of LIP, where both the lattice and the isometry should be structured. We note that for any ideal lattice in complex-multiplication number fields, a classical polynomial time algorithm is known [13,23]. Could the module variant be secure? Can our constructions gain a linear factor on key sizes from this variant? And are there remarkably decodable lattices that are also ideals in certain number fields? The repeated-difference lattices (a.k.a. Craig's lattices [9]) are indeed ideal lattices in cyclotomic number field with large minimal distances, but a polynomial decoding algorithm for them remains to be discovered.

2 Preliminaries

2.1 Notation

Vectors x are denoted in bold and should be interpreted as column vectors. For a matrix B with columns $b_1, \ldots, b_n$ we denote its Gram-Schmidt orthogonalisation by B^* with columns $b_1^*, \ldots, b_n^*$, and we denote the matrix norm by $\|B\| := \max_i \|b_i\|_2$. We denote $\mathbb{T}_q$ the discretized torus $\mathbb{T}_q := (\frac{1}{q}\mathbb{Z})/\mathbb{Z}$ and identify it with its set of reduced representatives $\{0, \frac{1}{q}, \ldots, \frac{q-1}{q}\}$. The statistical distance between two random variable X and Y will be denoted $\Delta(X, Y)$.

2.2 Lattice Isomorphism and Quadratic Forms

Abstractly, the set of (full-rank, n-dimensional) lattices can be thought as the homogeneous space[3] $\mathcal{GL}_n(\mathbb{R})/\mathcal{GL}_n(\mathbb{Z})$: a lattice $L = \mathcal{L}(B) := B \cdot \mathbb{Z}^n$ is generated by the columns of a basis $B \in \mathcal{GL}_n(\mathbb{R})$, and two basis $B, B' \in \mathcal{GL}_n(\mathbb{R})$ generate the same lattice if and only if there exists a unimodular matrix $U \in \mathcal{GL}_n(\mathbb{Z})$ such that $B' = BU$.

---

[3] This footnote should read as the quotient of a *set* by the action of group, and not a group quotient. Indeed $\mathcal{GL}_n(\mathbb{Z})$ is *not* a normal subgroup of $\mathcal{GL}_n(\mathbb{R})$ for $n > 1$.

Two lattices are *isomorphic* if there exists an orthonormal transformation $O \in \mathcal{O}_n(\mathbb{R})$ sending one to the other. Finding this transformation, if it exists, is known as the Lattice Isomorphism Problem (LIP).

Definition 2.1 (LIP, lattice version). *Given two isomorphic lattices $\mathcal{L}, \mathcal{L}' \subset \mathbb{R}^n$ find an orthonormal transformation $O \in \mathcal{O}_n(\mathbb{R})$ such that $\mathcal{L}' = O \cdot \mathcal{L}$.*

Algorithmically lattices $\mathcal{L} = \mathcal{L}(B), \mathcal{L}' = \mathcal{L}(B')$ are represented by bases $B, B' \in \mathcal{GL}_n(\mathbb{R})$, and if $\mathcal{L}' = O \cdot \mathcal{L}$, then OB is a basis of $\mathcal{L}'$. If $OB = B'$, then we can easily compute $O := B'B^{-1}$, however in general OB will only be equal to B' up to some unimodular transformation. More specifically when $\mathcal{L} = \mathcal{L}(B)$, and $\mathcal{L}' = \mathcal{L}(B')$ for some lattice bases $B, B' \in \mathcal{GL}_n(\mathbb{R})$ the Lattice Isomorphism Problem asks to find an orthonormal $O \in \mathcal{O}_n(\mathbb{R})$ *and* a unimodular $U \in \mathcal{GL}_n(\mathbb{Z})$ such that $B' = OBU$. The presence of both the orthonormal and the unimodular transformation is what makes LIP a hard problem. In other words, reconstructing (or even testing) equivalence in either quotient $\mathcal{GL}_n(\mathbb{R})/\mathcal{GL}_n(\mathbb{Z})$ or $\mathcal{O}_n(\mathbb{R})\backslash\mathcal{GL}_n(\mathbb{R})$ is easy, doing so in the double quotient $\mathcal{O}_n(\mathbb{R})\backslash\mathcal{GL}_n(\mathbb{R})/\mathcal{GL}_n(\mathbb{Z})$ appears to be hard.

The real-valued coordinates of the basis and orthonormal transformation can be inconvenient and inefficient to work with. We can alleviate some of these concerns by moving to the (equivalent) quadratic form setting, where instead of a basis B we focus on the Gram matrix $Q = B^t B$.

Quadratic Forms and Integral Equivalence. The idea of the Quadratic Form point of view on LIP is to consider the quotient in the opposite order than in the lattice point of view: first on the left by $\mathcal{O}_n(\mathbb{R})$ and then only on the right by $\mathcal{GL}_n(\mathbb{Z})$.

We define a *quadratic form* as a positive definite real symmetric matrix. A quadratic form can be thought as a basis modulo rotation; they realize the quotient $\mathcal{O}_n(\mathbb{R})\backslash\mathcal{GL}_n(\mathbb{R})$. More precisely, consider the surjective Gram map $\gamma : \mathcal{GL}_n(\mathbb{R}) \to \mathcal{S}_n^{>0}(\mathbb{R})$ sending a lattice basis B to the quadratic form $Q = B^t B$. Note that the preimages of $\gamma(B)$ are precisely the OB for $O \in \mathcal{O}_n(\mathbb{R})$.

For a lattice basis B the Gram matrix $Q = B^t B$ naturally gives a quadratic form. Additionally every quadratic form Q induces a unique upper-triangular lattice basis B_Q such that $Q = B_Q^t B_Q$ (Cholesky decomposition). In the quadratic form setting lattice vectors $Bx \in \mathbb{R}^n$ are represented by their integral basis coefficients $x \in \mathbb{Z}^n$. The inner product with respect to a quadratic form is naturally given by $\langle x, y \rangle_Q := x^t Q y$, and the norm by $\|x\|_Q^2 := x^t Q x$. Note that this perfectly coincides with the geometry between the original lattice vectors. We denote the ball of radius r by $\mathcal{B}_Q(r) := \{x \in \mathbb{R}^n : \|x\|_Q \leq r\}$. Translating the lattice definition, one get the *first minimum* $\lambda_1(Q)$ defined by

$$\lambda_1(Q) := \min_{x \in \mathbb{Z}^n \backslash \{0\}} \|x\|_Q,$$

and more generally the i-th minimal distance $\lambda_i(Q)$ defined as the smallest $r > 0$ such that $\{x \in \mathbb{Z}^n \mid \|x\|_Q \leq r\}$ spans a space of dimension at least i.

In this realization $\mathcal{S}_n^{>0}(\mathbb{R})$ of the quotient $\mathcal{O}_n(\mathbb{R})\backslash\mathcal{GL}_n(\mathbb{R})$, the action of $U \in \mathcal{GL}_n(\mathbb{Z})$ is given by $Q \mapsto U^t QU$. We may now rephrase LIP for two lattice bases B and B'. Note that if $B' = OBU$, then for $Q := B^t B$ we have:

$$Q' := (B')^t B' = U^t B^t O^t OBU = U^t B^t BU = U^t QU,$$

and we call Q and Q' equivalent if such a unimodular $U \in \mathcal{GL}_n(\mathbb{Z})$ exists, and denote the equivalence class by $[Q]$, moving the real-valued orthonormal transform $O \in \mathcal{O}_n(\mathbb{R})$ out of the picture. Additionally many remarkable lattices attain a rational-valued Gram matrix Q, removing the need for real-valued or approximate arithmetic. Later in this work we will restrict ourselves to integer-valued quadratic forms.

Weaker Equivalence (Genus). The study of integral equivalence of quadratic forms is classically approached via weaker notions, namely, equivalence over larger rings [9, Chapter 15, Sec 4]. In particular, we shall consider the rational equivalence class $[Q]_\mathbb{Q}$ of all $U^t QU$ for $U \in \mathcal{GL}_n(\mathbb{Q})$, as well as the p-adic integer equivalence class $[Q]_{\mathbb{Z}_p}$ of all $U^t QU$ for $U \in \mathcal{GL}_n(\mathbb{Z}_p)$. These equivalences are coarser than integral equivalence: $[Q] = [Q'] \Rightarrow [Q]_\mathbb{Q} = [Q']_\mathbb{Q}$ and $[Q]_{\mathbb{Z}_p} = [Q']_{\mathbb{Z}_p}$. These data $([Q]_\mathbb{Q}, ([Q]_{\mathbb{Z}_p})_p)$ about a quadratic form are called the *genus* of the quadratic form.

One could also consider equivalence over the reals $\mathbb{R}$, or over the p-adic rationals $\mathbb{Q}_p$. By a local-global principle (Minkowski-Hasse Theorem [42, Thm. 9, pp. 44]) these data are redundant with the rational class $[Q]_\mathbb{Q}$.

The Lattice Isomorphism Problem, Quadratic Form Formulation. The Lattice Isomorphism Problem can now be restated. We start by properly defining the worst-case problems, in both a search and distinguishing variant.

Definition 2.2 (wc-sLIP^Q). *For a quadratic form $Q \in \mathcal{S}_n^{>0}$ the problem wc-sLIP^Q is, given any quadratic form $Q' \in [Q]$, to find a unimodular $U \in \mathcal{GL}_n(\mathbb{Z})$ such that $Q' = U^t QU$.*

Note that the problem is equivalent to the original LIP problem as we can still extract an orthonormal transformation by computing $O = B'(BU)^{-1}$. Moreover, the automorphism group $\mathrm{Aut}(Q) := \{V \in \mathcal{GL}_n(\mathbb{Z}) : V^t QV = Q\}$ is finite, and for any solution $U \in \mathcal{GL}_n(\mathbb{Z})$ to wc-sLIP^Q such that $Q' = U^t QU$, the full set of solutions is given by $\{VU : V \in \mathrm{Aut}(Q)\}$.

We also consider a *distinguishing* variant of LIP, denoted wc-ΔLIP. It is not to be confused with the *decisional* version of LIP (which we will refer to as dLIP).[4]

---

[4] In dLIP^{Q_0} one is given an arbitrary Q' and must decide whether Q' belongs to $[Q_0]$. The distinguishing version is potentially easier in that Q' is promised to belong to either $[Q_0]$ or $[Q_1]$ for some known fixed $[Q_1]$.

Definition 2.3 (wc-ΔLIP^{Q_0,Q_1}). *For two quadratic forms $Q_0, Q_1 \in \mathcal{S}_n^{>0}$ the problem wc-ΔLIP^{Q_0,Q_1} is, given any quadratic form $Q' \in [Q_b]$ where $b \in \{0,1\}$ is a uniform random bit, to find b.*

Because (part of) the genus is efficiently computable (see Sect. 7), we will make sure that $[Q_0]_R = [Q_1]_R$ for all relevant ring extensions $R \in \{\mathbb{Q}, \mathbb{R}, \mathbb{Q}_p, \mathbb{Z}_p\}$.

Hardness Statements. When we discuss the hardness of LIP problems, we will implicitly assume that we are not talking of a single quadratic form Q (or of a single pair (Q_0, Q_1) for ΔLIP), but of a family $(Q_n)_n$ (or a family of pairs $(Q_{0,n}, Q_{1,n})_n$ for ΔLIP) where n ranges over an infinite set of positive integer.

2.3 Discrete Gaussians and Sampling

Discrete Gaussian sampling has been fundamental to the development of lattice based cryptography, by allowing to return short or nearby lattice vectors without leaking information about the secret key [12]. We rephrase the relevant definitions and propositions in the quadratic form language.

Distribution. For any quadratic form $Q \in \mathcal{S}_n^{>0}$ we define the Gaussian function on $\mathbb{R}^n$ with parameter $s > 0$ and center $c \in \mathbb{R}^n$ by

$$\forall x \in \mathbb{R}^n, \rho_{Q,s,c}(x) := \exp(-\pi \|x - c\|_Q^2 / s^2).$$

The discrete Gaussian distribution is obtained by restricting the continuous Gaussian distribution to a discrete lattice. In the quadratic form setting the discrete lattice will always be $\mathbb{Z}^n$, but with the geometry induced by the quadratic form. For any quadratic form $Q \in \mathcal{S}_n^{>0}$ we define the discrete Gaussian distribution $\mathcal{D}_{Q,s,c}$ with center $c \in \mathbb{R}^n$ and parameter $s > 0$ by

$$\Pr_{X \sim \mathcal{D}_{Q,s,c}}[X = x] := \frac{\rho_{Q,s,c}(x)}{\rho_{Q,s,c}(\mathbb{Z}^n)} \text{ if } x \in \mathbb{Z}^n, \text{and } 0 \text{ otherwise.}$$

If the center c is not denoted we have $c = 0$. An important property of the discrete gaussian distribution is the smoothing parameter, i.e. how much gaussian noise $s > 0$ is needed to 'smooth out' the discrete structure.

Definition 2.4 (Smoothing Parameter). *For a quadratic form $Q \in \mathcal{S}_n^{>0}$ and $\epsilon > 0$ we define the smoothing parameter $\eta_\epsilon(Q)$ as the minimal $s > 0$ such that $\rho_{Q^{-1}, 1/s}(\mathbb{Z}^n) \leqslant 1 + \epsilon$.*

The smoothing parameter is a central quantity for gaussians over lattice, for example it permits to control the variations of $\rho_{Q,s,c}(\mathbb{Z}^n)$ is over all centers c.

Lemma 2.5 ([29]). *For any quadratic form $Q \in \mathcal{S}_n^{>0}$, $\epsilon > 0$, center $c \in \mathbb{R}^n$ and parameter $s > \eta_\epsilon(Q)$ we have:*

$$(1 - \epsilon)\frac{s^n}{\sqrt{\det(Q)}} \leqslant \rho_{Q,s,c}(\mathbb{Z}^n) \leqslant (1 + \epsilon)\frac{s^n}{\sqrt{\det(Q)}}.$$

Note that the smoothing parameter $\eta_\epsilon(Q)$ is an invariant property of the similarity class $[Q]$, and so we might also denote $\eta_\epsilon([Q])$ for a similarity class. While computing or even approximating the exact smoothing parameter is hard, we can obtain sufficient bounds via the dual form.

Lemma 2.6 (Smoothing bound [29]). *For any quadratic form $Q \in S_n^{>0}$ we have $\eta_{2^{-n}}(Q) \leqslant \sqrt{n}/\lambda_1(Q^{-1})$ and $\eta_\epsilon(Q) \leqslant \|B_Q^*\| \cdot \sqrt{\ln(2n(1 + 1/\epsilon))/\pi}$ for $\epsilon > 0$.*

Above the smoothing parameter the discrete gaussian distribution is in some sense 'well behaved' and we have the following tailbound that one would expect from a Gaussian distribution.

Lemma 2.7 (Tailbound [30, Lemma 4.4]). *For any quadratic form $Q \in S_n^{>0}$, $\epsilon \in (0, 1)$, center $c \in \mathbb{R}^n$ and parameter $s \geqslant \eta_\epsilon(Q)$, we have*

$$\Pr_{x \sim \mathcal{D}_{Q,s,c}} [\|x - c\|_Q > s\sqrt{n}] \leqslant \frac{1 + \epsilon}{1 - \epsilon} \cdot 2^{-n}.$$

A constant factor above the smoothing parameter we can furthermore lower bound the min-entropy of the distribution.

Lemma 2.8 (Min-entropy [35]). *For any quadratic form $Q \in S_n^{>0}$, positive $\epsilon > 0$, center $c \in \mathbb{R}^n$, parameter $s \geqslant 2\eta_\epsilon(Q)$, and for every $x \in \mathbb{Z}^n$, we have*

$$\Pr_{X \sim \mathcal{D}_{Q,s,c}} [X = x] \leqslant \frac{1 + \epsilon}{1 - \epsilon} \cdot 2^{-n}.$$

Gaussian Sampling. While the discrete Gaussian distribution already is an important theoretical tool, for many practical purposes we want to actually sample (close to) the distribution in an efficient manner. In their breakthrough work Gentry et al. [12] showed that Klein's [19] randomized Babai's nearest plane algorithm does exactly that. Given a lattice basis one can sample statistically close to the discrete Gaussian distribution with parameters depending on the shortness of the (Gram-Schmidt) basis; a better reduced basis allows for a lower Gaussian width s. To simplify later proofs we use an exact sampling algorithm by Brakerski et al. [7].

Lemma 2.9 (Discrete Sampling [7, Lemma 2.3]). *There is a polynomial-time algorithm **DiscreteSample**(Q, s, c) that given a quadratic form $Q \in S_n^{>0}$, center $c \in \mathbb{R}^n$, and a parameter $s \geqslant \|B_Q^*\| \cdot \sqrt{\ln(2n + 4)/\pi}$, returns a sample distributed as $\mathcal{D}_{Q,s,c}$.*

2.4   Randomness Extractors

A randomness extractor allows, using a publicly known random seed, to convert a non-uniform randomness source X with high min-entropy $H_\infty(X) := -\log_2(\max_x \Pr[X = x])$ to a near-uniform random variable [3,15].[5]

Definition 2.10 (Extractor). *An efficient function* $\mathcal{E} : \mathcal{X} \times \{0,1\}^z \to \{0,1\}^v$ *is an* (m, ϵ)-*extractor, if, for all random variable* X *distributed over* $\mathcal{X}$ *and* $H_\infty(X) \geqslant m$, *it holds that*

$$\Delta\left((Z, \mathcal{E}(X, Z)), (Z, V)\right) \leqslant \epsilon$$

where the seed $Z \leftarrow \mathcal{U}(\{0,1\}^z)$ *and* $V \leftarrow \mathcal{U}(\{0,1\}^v)$ *are drawn uniformly at random, and independently of* X.

When instantiating our scheme, we will rely on the existence of an (m, ϵ)-extractor with parameters $m = \Theta(v)$ and $\epsilon = 2^{-\Theta(m)}$.

3   LIP and Self-reducibility

In this section we lay the foundation for using the Lattice Isomorphism Problem in cryptography. We present an average-case distribution for any quadratic form equivalence class, show how to sample from it, and conclude with a worst-case to average-case reduction. Note that the worst-case to average-case reduction is realized *within* an equivalence class.

3.1   An Average-Case Distribution

First we define our average-case distribution within an equivalence class $[Q]$, which can be seen as an extension of the techniques used by Haviv and Regev [17] to show that LIP lies in SZK. While in their work they use a discrete Gaussian sampler [12] to sample a generating set of the lattice, we extend this by a linear algebra step that returns a canonically distributed lattice basis—or in our case a quadratic form.

A posteriori, this algorithm appears very similar to the heuristic approach of [6], but the use of Gaussian sampling formally guarantees that the output distribution solely depends on the lattice and not on the specific input basis—or in our case, depends only on the class of the input quadratic form.

First we consider the linear algebra step, that given a quadratic form and short linearly independent vectors, returns a well reduced equivalent form.

Lemma 3.1 (Adapted from [27, Lemma 7.1]). *There is a polynomial time algorithm* $(R, U) \leftarrow$ **Extract**(Q, Y) *that on input a quadratic form* Q, *and linearly independent vectors* $Y = (\boldsymbol{y}_1, \ldots, \boldsymbol{y}_n) \in \mathbb{Z}^{n \times n}$, *outputs a transformation* $U \in \mathcal{GL}_n(\mathbb{Z})$ *and a quadratic form* $R = U^t Q U$ *equivalent to* Q *such that* $\|B_R^*\| \leqslant \max_i \|\boldsymbol{y}_i\|_Q$.

---

[5] For our application, we do not need to relax the source to only have average min-entropy, and therefore work with the simpler worst-case version.

Proof. First let $U \in \mathcal{GL}_n(\mathbb{Z})$ be the unique transformation such that $T = U^{-1}Y$ is the canonical upper-diagonal Hermite Normal Form of Y. Let $R = U^t Q U$ and note that R is equivalent to Q. Denote the column vectors of U by $u_1, \ldots, u_n$. Because T is upper triangular and in Hermite Normal Form we have $y_i = \sum_{j=1}^i T_{j,i} u_j$, where $T_{j,j} \geqslant 1$. In particular we have that $\mathrm{span}(y_1, \ldots, y_k) = \mathrm{span}(u_1, \ldots, u_k)$. Let y_i^* and u_i^* be the i-th Gram-Schmidt vector of Y and U respectively w.r.t. Q. Note that $y_i^* = T_{i,i} \cdot u_i^*$, and thus $\|u_i^*\|_Q = \|y_i^*\|_Q / T_{i,i} \leqslant \|y_i^*\|_Q \leqslant \|y_i\|_Q$. We conclude by $\|B_R^*\| = \max_i \|u_i^*\|_Q \leqslant \max_i \|y_i\|_Q$. $\qquad\square$

For our final distribution to be well defined we need that the extracted quadratic form only depends on the geometry of the input vectors, and not on the particular representative Q.

Lemma 3.2 (Independence of representative). *Let* $y_1, \ldots, y_n \in \mathbb{Z}^n$ *be linearly independent. If* $(R, U) \leftarrow \mathbf{Extract}(Q, Y)$, *and for some unimodular* $V \in \mathcal{GL}_n(\mathbb{Z})$ *we have* $(R', U') \leftarrow \mathbf{Extract}(V^t Q V, V^{-1} Y)$, *then* $R' = R$, *and* $U' = V^{-1} \cdot U$.

Proof. From the canonicity of the Hermite Normal Form we immediately obtain that $(U')^{-1} V^{-1} Y = T = U^{-1} Y$, and thus $U' = V^{-1} \cdot U$. It follows that $R' = (V^{-1} \cdot U)^t V^t Q V (V^{-1} \cdot U) = U^t Q U = R$. $\qquad\square$

Now we can formally define our average-case distribution for a parameter $s > 0$.

Definition 3.3. *Given a quadratic form equivalence class* $[Q] \subset \mathcal{S}_n^{>0}$ *we define the Gaussian form distribution* $\mathcal{D}_s([Q])$ *over* $[Q]$ *with parameter* $s > 0$ *algorithmically as follows:*

1. *Fix a representative* $Q \in [Q]$.
2. *Sample n vectors* $(y_1, \ldots, y_n) =: Y$ *from* $\mathcal{D}_{Q,s}$. *Repeat until linearly independent.*
3. $(R, U) \leftarrow \mathbf{Extract}(Q, Y)$.
4. *Return R.*

By Lemma 3.2 the output is independent of the chosen representative and thus the distribution is well-defined.

Given the algorithmic definition of $\mathcal{D}_s([Q])$, an actual efficient sampling algorithm follows with only a few adaptations. Firstly, we need to efficiently sample from $\mathcal{D}_{Q,s}$ which puts some constraints on the parameter s depending on the reducedness of the representative Q. Secondly the probability that n sampled vectors are linearly independent can be quite small, instead we sample vectors one by one and only add them to our set Y if they are independent. Still we require the additional constraint $s \geqslant \lambda_n(Q)$ to show that this succeeds with a polynomial amount of samples.

Lemma 3.4. *For any quadratic form* $Q \in \mathcal{S}_n^{>0}(\mathbb{Z})$, *and parameter*

$$s \geqslant \max\{\lambda_n(Q), \|B_Q^*\| \cdot \sqrt{\ln(2n+4)/\pi}\},$$

Algorithm 1: Sampling from $\mathcal{D}_s([Q])$.

Data: A quadratic form $Q \in \mathcal{S}_n^{>0}(\mathbb{Z}^n)$, and a parameter
    $s \geqslant \max\{\lambda_n(Q), \|B_Q^*\| \cdot \sqrt{\ln(2n+4)/\pi}\}$.
Result: Sample $R = U^t QU$ from $\mathcal{D}_s([Q])$, with a transformation $U \in \mathcal{GL}_n(\mathbb{Z})$.
$Y \leftarrow \varnothing$;
while $|Y| < n$ **do**
  $\quad x \leftarrow \mathcal{D}_{Q,s}$;   // Using Lemma 2.9
  $\quad$**if** $x \notin \mathrm{span}(Y)$ **then**
  $\quad\quad |$ Append x to Y;
  $\quad$**end**
end
$(R, U) \leftarrow \mathbf{Extract}(Q, Y)$;

Algorithm 1 runs in expected polynomial time and returns (R, U) where R is a sample from $\mathcal{D}_s([Q])$, and a unimodular $U \in \mathcal{GL}_n(\mathbb{Z})$ such that $R = U^t QU$. Furthermore, the isomorphism U is uniform over the set of isomorphisms from Q to R.

Proof. By Lemmas 2.9 and 3.1 every step in Algorithm 1 runs in polynomial time. What remains is to show that the number of iterations is polynomially bounded. Let the random variable K be the number of samples before we find n independent ones. If $|Y| < n$, then because $s \geqslant \lambda_n(Q)$ we have by [17, Lemma 5.1] that every newly sampled vector $x \leftarrow \mathcal{D}_{Q,s}$ is not in the span of Y with constant probability at least $C := 1 - (1 + e^{-\pi})^{-1} > 0$. So K is bounded from above by a negative binomial distribution for n successes with success probability C, which implies that $\mathbb{E}[K] \leqslant \frac{n}{C}$, and in particular that $\Pr[K > n^2] \leqslant e^{-\Omega(n^2)}$. When the while loop succeeds the set Y is distributed as n vectors sampled from $\mathcal{D}_{Q,s}$ under the linear independence condition, following exactly Definition 3.3.

Suppose that the algorithm runs and finishes with a final spanning set Y, and returning $(R, U) \leftarrow \mathbf{Extract}(Q, Y)$. For any automorphism $V \in \mathrm{Aut}(Q)$, i.e. such that $V^t QV = Q$, it would have been just as likely that the final spanning set equalled VY, because the samples from $\mathcal{D}_{Q,s}$ only depend on the norm of the vectors w.r.t. Q. Then by Lemma 3.2 we have:

$$\mathbf{Extract}(Q, VY) = \mathbf{Extract}((V^{-1})^t QV^{-1}, VY) = (R, VU),$$

and thus the algorithm would have returned VU with the same probability as U, which makes the returned transformation uniform over the set of isomorphisms $\{VU : V \in \mathrm{Aut}(Q)\}$ from Q to R. $\square$

For (exponentially) large parameters s we can always efficiently sample from the average-case distribution by first LLL-reducing the representative.

Lemma 3.5. *Given any quadratic form $Q \in \mathcal{S}_n^{>0}(\mathbb{Z})$ we can sample from $\mathcal{D}_s([Q])$ in polynomial time for $s \geqslant 2^{\Theta(n)} \cdot \lambda_n([Q])$.*

Proof. Run the LLL algorithm on Q to obtain a representative $Q' \in [Q]$ for which $\|B_{Q'}^*\| \leqslant 2^{\Theta(n)} \cdot \lambda_n([Q])$. Then apply Lemma 3.4. $\square$

Lemma 3.6. *For any quadratic form $Q \in \mathcal{S}_n^{>0}$, parameter $\epsilon \in (0,1)$, and $s \geqslant \max\{\lambda_n(Q), \eta_\epsilon(Q)\}$, we have*

$$\Pr_{Q' \sim \mathcal{D}_s([Q])}[\|B_{Q'}^*\| > s\sqrt{n}] \leqslant \frac{1+\epsilon}{1-\epsilon} \cdot 25n \cdot 2^{-n}.$$

Proof. Given linearly independent vectors $Y = \{y_1, \ldots, y_n\} \in \mathbb{Z}^n$ the extractor returns a quadratic form Q' such that $\|B_{Q'}^*\| \leqslant \max_i \|y_i\|_Q$ and thus we can just focus on the norms $\|y_i\|_Q$. Let the random variable K be the number of samples $x_1, \ldots, x_K \leftarrow \mathcal{D}_{Q,s}$ before we find n independent ones. By Lemma 2.7 we have $\|x_i\| > s\sqrt{n}$ with probability at most $(1+\epsilon)/(1-\epsilon) \cdot 2^{-n}$. By the proof of Lemma 3.4 we have $\mathbb{E}[K] \leqslant \frac{n}{C} \leqslant 25n$, and by a union bound we conclude:

$$\Pr\left[\max_i \|y_i\|_Q > s\sqrt{n}\right] = \sum_{k=n}^{\infty} \Pr[K = k] \Pr\left[\max_{1 \leqslant i \leqslant k} \|x_i\|_Q > s\sqrt{n}\right]$$

$$\leqslant \underbrace{\sum_{k=n}^{\infty} \Pr[K = k] \cdot k}_{\mathbb{E}[K]} \cdot \frac{1+\epsilon}{1-\epsilon} \cdot 2^{-n} \leqslant \frac{n}{C} \cdot \frac{1+\epsilon}{1-\epsilon} \cdot 2^{-n}.$$

$\square$

3.2 Average Case LIP

The above definition of a distribution over a class which is efficiently sampleable from any representative of that class leads us to a natural average-case version of both version of LIP. It is parametrized by a width parameter $s > 0$.

Definition 3.7 (ac-sLIP$_s^Q$). *For a quadratic form $Q \in \mathcal{S}_n^{>0}$ and $s > 0$ the problem ac-sLIP$_s^Q$ is, given a quadratic form sampled as $Q' \leftarrow \mathcal{D}_s([Q])$, to find a unimodular $U \in \mathcal{GL}_n(\mathbb{Z})$ such that $Q' = U^t Q U$.*

Definition 3.8 (ac-ΔLIP$_s^{Q_0,Q_1}$). *For two quadratic forms $Q_0, Q_1 \in \mathcal{S}_n^{>0}$ and $s > 0$ the problem ac-ΔLIP$_s^{Q_0,Q_1}$ is, given a quadratic form sampled as $Q' \leftarrow \mathcal{D}_s([Q_b])$ where $b \in \{0,1\}$ is a uniform random bit, to find b.*

Trivially the average-case variants can be reduced to their respective worst-case variants. In the following section we show that the reverse is also true.

3.3 A Worst-Case to Average-Case Reduction

In general lattice problems become easier when given a short basis; and harder when given a long basis. Similarly one would expect that ac-sLIP$_s^Q$ and ac-ΔLIP$_s^{Q_0,Q_1}$ become harder when the parameter $s > 0$ increases. In fact when s is large enough the average-case problem becomes at least as hard as any worst-case instance; making the average-case and worst-case problems equivalent.

Lemma 3.9 (ac-sLIP$_s^Q \geqslant$ wc-sLIP^Q **for large** s). *Given an oracle that solves ac-sLIP$_s^Q$ for some $s \geqslant 2^{\Theta(n)} \cdot \lambda_n(Q)$ in time T_0 with probability $\epsilon > 0$, we can solve wc-sLIP^Q with probability at least ϵ in time $T = T_0 + poly(n, \log s)$.*

Proof. Given any $Q' \in [Q]$, apply Lemma 3.5 to sample $Q'' \leftarrow \mathcal{D}_s([Q])$ for some $s \geqslant 2^{O(n)} \cdot \lambda_n([Q])$, together with a U'' such that $Q'' = U''^t Q' U''$. Note that $\mathcal{D}_s([Q]) = \mathcal{D}_s([Q'])$; we can therefore apply our ac-sLIP$_s^Q$-oracle to Q'' and obtain $U \in \mathcal{GL}_n(\mathbb{Z})$ such that $Q'' = U^t Q U$. Now for $U' := U U''^{-1} \in \mathcal{GL}_n(\mathbb{Z})$ we have:

$$U'^t Q U' = (U''^{-1})^t U^t Q U U''^{-1} = (U''^{-1})^t Q'' U''^{-1} = Q'.$$

So given an ac-sLIP$_s^Q$-oracle we can solve wc-sLIP^Q.   □

To allow for more efficient schemes we would like to decrease the parameter $s > 0$ in the worst-case to average-case reduction. We can do so at the cost of stronger lattice reduction than LLL.

Lemma 3.10. *Given an oracle that solves ac-sLIP$_s^Q$ for some $s \geqslant \lambda_n(Q)$ in time T_0 with probability $\epsilon > 0$, we can solve wc-sLIP^Q with probability at least $\frac{1}{2}$ in time*

$$T = \frac{1}{\epsilon}(T_0 + poly(n, \log s)) + C\left(n, \frac{s}{\lambda_n(Q) \cdot \sqrt{\ln(2n+4)/\pi}}\right),$$

where $C(n, f)$ is the cost of solving the Shortest Independent Vector Problem (SIVP, [39]) within an approximation factor of f.

Proof. The f-approx-SIVP oracle returns n linearly independent vectors of norm at most $f \cdot \lambda_n(Q)$, and thus using Lemma 3.1 we can construct an equivalent form $Q' \in [Q]$ with $\|B_{Q'}^*\| \leqslant f \cdot \lambda_n(Q)$. For $f := s/(\lambda_n(Q) \cdot \sqrt{\ln(2n+4)/\pi})$ we obtain that $s \geqslant \|B_{Q'}^*\| \cdot \sqrt{\ln(2n+4)/\pi}$, and thus we can sample efficiently from $\mathcal{D}_s([Q])$. The rest of the proofs follows similar to that of Lemma 3.9. Additionally the reduction succeeds with some probability $\epsilon > 0$, so we need to repeat it $\frac{1}{\epsilon}$ times to obtain a success probability of at least $\frac{1}{2}$. Note that each additional sample can be computed in polynomial time from the same representative Q'. □

Remark 3.11. Note that the overhead is entirely additive, in particular it does not suffer from the $\frac{1}{\epsilon}$ amplification. So, while the reduction is not polynomial time, concretely, one can afford huge overheads; for example an overhead of 2^{100} would barely affect a underlying hardness of 2^{128} as $2^{128} - 2^{100} = 2^{127.999\ldots}$. This situation is quite different from the usual inefficient reductions found in the literature, where the overhead is multiplicative.

In Lemma 3.10, the SIVP oracle can be instantiated by a variant of the BKZ algorithm [40]. With a sub-linear blocksize of $\beta := n/\log(n)$ we could decrease s to a quasi-polynomial factor $\exp(\log^2(n)) \cdot \lambda_n(Q)$, with only a sub-exponential additive cost to the reduction. For security based on exponential hardness (e.g. $T_0/\epsilon = \exp(\Omega(n))$) this would still be meaningful, while maintaining a poly-logarithmic bitlength for the integer entries of the manipulated matrices.

Going down to polynomial factors $s = \text{poly}(n) \cdot \lambda_n(Q)$ (and hence single logarithmic integer bitlength) would require a linear blocksize $\beta := \Theta(n)$, and an exponential cost 2^{cn}. For small constants $c > 0$ such that cn is smaller than the security parameter the reduction would still be meaningful. However for provable algorithms this constant c is rather large, and the gap between provable [1] and heuristic results [4] is significant. As we want to keep our reduction non-heuristic in this initial work, we will leave this regime for further research.

Using a similar strategy, one can also establish a worst-case to average-case reduction for ΔLIP. Note that, because it is a distinguishing problem, the advantage amplification now requires $O(1/\alpha^2)$ calls to the average-case oracle.

Lemma 3.12 (ac-ΔLIP$_s^{Q_0,Q_1} \geqslant$ wc-ΔLIP^{Q_0,Q_1} **for large** s**).** *Given an oracle that solves* ac-ΔLIP$_s^{Q_0,Q_1}$ *for some* $s \geqslant 2^{\Theta(n)} \cdot \max\{\lambda_n(Q_0), \lambda_n(Q_1)\}$ *in time* T_0 *with advantage* $\alpha > 0$*, we can solve* wc-ΔLIP^{Q_0,Q_1} *with advantage* α *in time* $T + \text{poly}(n, \log s)$*.*

Lemma 3.13. *Given an oracle that solves* ac-ΔLIP$_s^{Q_0,Q_1}$ *in time* T_0 *for some* $s \geqslant \max\{\lambda_n(Q_0), \lambda_n(Q_1)\}$ *with advantage* $\alpha > 0$*, we can solve* wc-ΔLIP^{Q_0,Q_1} *with advantage at least* $\frac{1}{4}$ *in time*

$$T = \frac{1}{\alpha^2}(T_0 + \text{poly}(n, \log s)) + C\left(n, \frac{s}{\max\{\lambda_n(Q_0), \lambda_n(Q_1)\} \cdot \sqrt{\ln(2n+4)/\pi}}\right),$$

where $C(n, f)$ *is the cost of solving the Shortest Independent Vector Problem (SIVP, [39]) within an approximation factor of* f*.*

4   Zero Knowledge Proof of Knowledge

At high level, the protocol of Haviv and Regev [17], as well as ours, is very similar to protocols for other types of isomorphisms, in particular protocols for graph ismorphism [14] and for code isomorphism [5].

A notable difference however, is that both these protocols [5,14] relied on the action of a finite group (permutations), allowing to show zero-knowledgness by uniformity of the distribution over an orbit. In our case, the group acting $\mathcal{GL}_n(\mathbb{Z})$ is not finite, and not even compact, admitting no such uniform distribution. It is perhaps surprising to see that uniformity is in fact not required.

4.1   The Σ-Protocol

Efficiency and Completeness. For efficiency of Σ we have to check that Algorithm 1 runs in polynomial time, and indeed by Lemma 3.4 this is the case because

$$s \geqslant \max\left\{\lambda_n([Q_0]), \|B_{Q_0}^*\| \cdot \sqrt{\ln(2n+4)/\pi}\right\}.$$

Zero Knowledge Proof of Knowledge Σ

Consider two equivalent public quadratic forms $Q_0, Q_1 \in \mathcal{S}_n^{>0}(\mathbb{Z})$ and a secret unimodular $U \in \mathcal{GL}_n(\mathbb{Z})$ such that $Q_1 = U^t Q_0 U$. Given the public parameter

$$s \geqslant \max\left\{ \lambda_n([Q_0]), \max\left\{ \|B_{Q_0}^*\|, \|B_{Q_1}^*\| \right\} \cdot \sqrt{\ln(2n+4)/\pi} \right\},$$

we define the following protocol Σ that gives a zero-knowledge proof of knowledge of an isomorphism between Q_0 and Q_1:

Prover		Verifier
Sample $Q' \leftarrow \mathcal{D}_s([Q_0])$ by Alg. 1, together with V s.t. $Q' = V^t Q_0 V$		
	$\xrightarrow{\quad Q' \quad}$	Sample $c \leftarrow \mathcal{U}(\{0,1\})$
Compute $W = U^{-c} \cdot V$	$\xleftarrow{\quad c \quad}$	
	$\xrightarrow{\quad W \quad}$	Check if $W \in \mathcal{GL}_n(\mathbb{Z})$, and $Q' = W^t Q_c W$.

For the verification we have that $W \in \mathcal{GL}_n(\mathbb{Z})$ if and only if W is integral and $\det(W) = \pm 1$, both of which are easy to check in polynomial time.

For the completeness of Σ note that when the prover executes the protocol honestly we have $W := U^{-c} \cdot V \in \mathcal{GL}_n(\mathbb{Z})$ because U and V are both unimodular by definition. Additionally we have

$$Q' = V^t Q_0 V = \underbrace{(V^t(U^{-c})^t)}_{W^t} \underbrace{((U^c)^t Q_0 U^c)}_{Q_c} \underbrace{(U^{-c} V)}_{W} = W^t Q_c W,$$

and thus the verifier accepts.

Special Soundness. Suppose we have two accepting conversations $(Q', 0, W_0)$ and $(Q', 1, W_1)$ of Σ where the first message is identical. The acceptance implies that $W_0, W_1 \in \mathcal{GL}_n(\mathbb{Z})$ and $W_0^t Q_0 W_0 = Q' = W_1^t Q_1 W_1$, and thus $U' := W_0 W_1^{-1} \in \mathcal{GL}_n(\mathbb{Z})$ gives an isomorphism from Q_0 to Q_1 as

$$U'^t Q_0 U' = (W_1^{-1})^t (W_0^t Q_0 W_0) W_1^{-1} = (W_1^{-1})^t (W_1^t Q_1 W_1) W_1^{-1} = Q_1.$$

We conclude that Σ has the special soundness property.

Special Honest-Verifier Zero-Knowledge. We create a simulator that given the public input Q_0, Q_1 outputs an accepting conversation with the same probability distribution as between an honest prover and verifier. Note that the first message Q' is always distributed as $\mathcal{D}_s([Q_0])$, the challenge c as $\mathcal{U}(\{0,1\})$, and V is uniform over the set of isomorphisms from Q_0 to Q' by Lemma 3.4. Because U is an isomorphism from Q_0 to Q_1 we have, given the challenge c, that $W = U^{-c} \cdot V$ is uniform over the set of isomorphisms from Q_c to Q'.

To simulate this we first sample the uniformly random challenge $c \leftarrow \mathcal{U}(\{0,1\})$. If $c = 0$ we can proceed the same as in Σ itself, e.g. sample

$Q' \leftarrow \mathcal{D}_s([Q_0])$ using Algorithm 1, together with a V such that $Q' = V^t Q_0 V$, and set $W := V$. The final conversation $(Q', 0, W)$ is accepting and follows by construction the same distribution as during an honest execution conditioned on challenge $c = 0$.

If $c = 1$ we use the fact that $[Q_0] = [Q_1]$, and that we can use Algorithm 1 with representative Q_1 as input instead of Q_0. So again we obtain $Q' \leftarrow \mathcal{D}_s([Q_1]) = \mathcal{D}_s([Q_0])$ following the same distribution, but now together with a unimodular $W \in \mathcal{GL}_n(\mathbb{Z})$ such that $Q' = W^t Q_1 W$. The conversation $(Q', 1, W)$ is accepting by construction, and Q' follows the same distribution $\mathcal{D}_s([Q_0])$. Additionally by Lemma 3.4 the transformation W is indeed uniform over the set of isomorphisms from Q_1 to Q'.

We conclude that Σ has the special honest-verifier zero-knowledge property.

4.2   Identification Scheme

The Zero Knowledge Proof of Knowledge in the previous section is worst-case in the sense that given any two equivalent forms $Q_0, Q_1 \in \mathcal{S}_n^{>0}(\mathbb{Z})$ and a secret isomorphism $U \in \mathcal{GL}_n(\mathbb{Z})$ from Q_0 to Q_1 we can show knowledge of such an isomorphism. However to turn this Σ-protocol into an Identification Scheme (see e.g. [10]) we need to define a distribution of $U \in \mathcal{GL}_n(\mathbb{Z})$ (or alternatively of Q_1 w.r.t Q_0). Finding an isomorphism between Q_0 and Q_1 is at most as hard as solving either ac-sLIP$_s^{Q_0}$ or ac-sLIP$_s^{Q_1}$ for parameter s as in Σ. Therefore a natural choice is to have Q_1 distributed according to $\mathcal{D}_{s'}([Q_0])$ for some parameter $s' \geqslant \max\{\lambda_n([Q_0]), \|B_{Q_0}^*\| \cdot \sqrt{\ln(2n+4)/\pi}\}$, which we can efficiently sample from using Algorithm 1. The security of our identification scheme is then solely based on the hardness of ac-sLIP$_{s'}^{Q_0}$.

5   Key Encapsulation Mechanism

In this section we construct a Key Encapsulation Mechanism (KEM) with a security proof based on the hardness of ΔLIP. In short we will need a quadratic form S along with an efficient decoder up to some radius $\rho < \lambda_1(S)/2$. The public key will consist of a long equivalent form $P := U^t S U \leftarrow \mathcal{D}_s([S])$, while the unimodular transformation U will be the secret key. Knowledge of the transformation U allows to decode w.r.t. P via S; without any loss in decoding performance. The key will be a random error e of norm $\|e\|_P \leqslant \rho$, and it can be encapsulated as the syndrome $\overline{e} := e \mod \mathbb{Z}^n \in [0, 1)^n$. The receiver with knowledge of the secret transformation U can recover e by decoding via S. The correctness follows from the fact that the decoding is unique due to $\rho < \lambda_1(S)/2$.

For the security we assume that it is (computationally) hard to differentiate between $P \leftarrow \mathcal{D}_s([S])$ and some random sample $R \leftarrow \mathcal{D}_s([Q])$ from a special class $[Q]$, a class corresponding to a lattice admitting a dense sublattice. This assumption allows us to replace P by R, which completely breaks the uniqueness of the decoding. That is, the syndrome $\overline{e}$ has many (say $\exp \Omega(\lambda)$) nearby points w.r.t. R, and retrieving the exact original point becomes statistically hard.

Key Encapsulation Scheme

Let $\rho < \lambda_1(S)/2$ and let $S \in \mathcal{S}_n^{>0}(\mathbb{Z})$ be a quadratic form with an efficient decoder **Decode** with decoding radius ρ. Let $\mathcal{E} : \frac{1}{q}\mathbb{Z}^n \times \{0,1\}^z \to \{0,1\}^\ell$ be a $(\ell, \text{negl}(n))$-extractor for some $\ell = \Theta(n)$. Given the public parameters

$$s \geqslant \max\{\lambda_n(S), \|B_S^*\| \cdot \sqrt{\ln(2n+4)/\pi}\}, \text{ and}$$

$$q := \left\lceil \frac{s \cdot n}{\rho} \cdot \sqrt{\ln(2n+4)/\pi} \right\rceil,$$

we define the KEM $\mathcal{K} := (\textbf{Gen}, \textbf{Encaps}, \textbf{Decaps})$ as follows:

- $(pk, sk) \leftarrow \textbf{Gen}(1^n)$: on input 1^n do:
  1. Sample $P \leftarrow \mathcal{D}_s([S])$ using Alg. 1, together with U such that $P = U^t S U$.
  2. Output $(pk, sk) = (P, U)$.
- $(c, k) \leftarrow \textbf{Encaps}(pk)$: on input 1^n and a public key $P = pk$ do:
  1. Sample $e \leftarrow \frac{1}{q}\mathcal{D}_{P, q\rho/\sqrt{n}} \in \frac{1}{q}\mathbb{Z}^n$ using Lemma 2.9.
  2. Compute $c \leftarrow e \bmod \mathbb{Z}^n$ s.t. $c \in \mathbb{T}_q^n = \{0, \frac{1}{q}, \ldots, \frac{q-1}{q}\}^n$.
  3. Sample a random extractor seed $Z \leftarrow \{0, 1\}^z$.
  4. Compute $k \leftarrow \mathcal{E}(e, Z)$.
  5. Output (c, k) where $c := (c, Z)$.
- $k \leftarrow \textbf{Decaps}(sk, c)$: on input $c = (c, Z)$ and a secret key $U := sk$ do:
  1. Compute $y \leftarrow \textbf{Decode}(S, Uc)$ s.t. $\|y - Uc\|_S \leqslant \rho$, output $\perp$ on failure.
  2. Compute $k \leftarrow \mathcal{E}(c - U^{-1}y, Z)$.
  3. Output k.

Efficiency and Correctness. We consider the efficiency and correctness of the KEM $\mathcal{K} := (\textbf{Gen}, \textbf{Encaps}, \textbf{Decaps})$ instantiated with quadratic form $S \in \mathcal{S}_n^{>0}(\mathbb{Z})$ and public parameter

$$s \geqslant \max\{\lambda_n(S), \|B_S^*\| \cdot \sqrt{\ln(2n+4)/\pi}\}.$$

By the above constraint on s, Algorithm 1 will run in polynomial-time by Lemma 3.4. Furthermore by Lemma 3.6 we have with overwhelming probability that

$$q\rho/\sqrt{n} \geqslant s\sqrt{n} \cdot \sqrt{\ln(2n+4)/\pi} \geqslant \|B_P^*\| \cdot \sqrt{\ln(2n+4)/\pi},$$

and thus we can efficiently sample from $\mathcal{D}_{P, q\rho/\sqrt{n}}$ by Lemma 2.9.

For correctness note that in the key encapsulation algorithm the sampled error e has norm at most $\|e\|_P \leqslant \rho$ except with negligible probability by Lemma 2.7, and we denote the encapsulated key by $k := \mathcal{E}(e, Z)$, where Z denotes the randomness extractor's seed. Because $\rho < \lambda_1(S)/2$ the vector $x := c - e \in \mathbb{Z}^n$ is the unique closest vector to c with respect to P, which makes Ux the unique closest vector to Uc with respect to $S = (U^{-1})^t P U^{-1}$. In the decapsulation the decoder computes the unique vector y at distance at most ρ from Uc, which implies that $y = Ux$. So indeed the output $k' := \mathcal{E}(c - U^{-1}y, Z) = \mathcal{E}(c - x, Z) = \mathcal{E}(e, Z) = k$ equals the encapsulated key with overwhelming probability.

CPA Security. To show that our KEM is CPA-secure we fall back to a lossy trap-door argument a la [36]. Under the hardness of decisional LIP we can replace our unique ρ-decodable quadratic form by one that is far from uniquely decodable. For the latter it is enough to have a dense sublattice.

Lemma 5.1. *Let $Q \in \mathcal{S}_n^{>0}(\mathbb{Z})$ be a quadratic form with a rank r sublattice $D\mathbb{Z}^r \subset \mathbb{Z}^n$. For positive $\epsilon > 0$, center $c \in \mathbb{R}^n$, parameter $s := \rho/\sqrt{n} \geq 2\eta_\epsilon([D^t QD])$, and for every $x \in \mathbb{Z}^n$ we have*

$$\Pr_{X \sim \mathcal{D}_{Q,s,c}}[X = x] \leq \frac{1 + \epsilon}{1 - \epsilon} \cdot 2^{-r}.$$

Proof. Let $y := x - c \in \mathbb{R}^n$, and decompose $y =: y_D + y_{D^\perp}$ where $y_D \in \text{span}(D\mathbb{Z}^r)$, and $y_{D^\perp}$ is orthogonal to y_D w.r.t Q. Then we have

$$\Pr_{X \sim \mathcal{D}_{Q,s,c}}[X = x] = \frac{\rho_{Q,s,c}(x)}{\rho_{Q,s,c}(\mathbb{Z}^n)} = \frac{\rho_{Q,s}(y)}{\rho_{Q,s}(y + \mathbb{Z}^n)} \leq \frac{\rho_{Q,s}(y)}{\rho_{Q,s}(y + D\mathbb{Z}^r)}$$

$$= \frac{\rho_{Q,s}(y_{D^\perp}) \cdot \rho_{Q,s}(y_D)}{\rho_{Q,s}(y_{D^\perp}) \cdot \rho_{Q,s}(y_D + D\mathbb{Z}^r)} = \frac{\rho_{Q,s}(y_D)}{\rho_{Q,s}(y_D + D\mathbb{Z}^r)}.$$

Note that we can write $y_D = Dz$ for some $z \in \mathbb{R}^r$, then the above equals $\Pr_{X \sim \mathcal{D}_{D^t QD, s, z}}[X = 0]$, which by Lemma 2.8 is bounded by $\frac{1+\epsilon}{1-\epsilon} \cdot 2^{-r}$. □

Theorem 5.2. *We consider the KEM $\mathcal{K} := (\textbf{Gen}, \textbf{Encaps}, \textbf{Decaps})$ instantiated with quadratic form $S \in \mathcal{S}_n^{>0}(\mathbb{Z})$, decoding radius ρ, and public key parameter $s > 0$. Let $Q \in \mathcal{S}_n^{>0}(\mathbb{Z})$ be a quadratic form with a dense rank $r = \Theta(n)$ sublattice $D\mathbb{Z}^r \subset \mathbb{Z}^n$, in particular such that $\eta_{\frac{1}{2}}(D^t QD) \leq \rho/(2\sqrt{n})$. Then $\mathcal{K}$ is CPA-secure if ac-$\Delta\text{LIP}_s^{S,Q}$ is hard.*

Proof. Let $\mathcal{A}$ be a probabilistic polynomial-time adversary. We present two games $\textbf{Game}_1$ and $\textbf{Game}_2$, where $\textbf{Game}_1$ is the regular CPA-security game with the original scheme, and $\textbf{Game}_2$ is almost identical but with the only change that the public key is drawn from $\mathcal{D}_s([Q])$ instead of $\mathcal{D}_s([S])$. By the hardness of ac-$\Delta\text{LIP}_s^{S,Q}$ the two games are computationally indistinguishable, and due to the dense sublattice we can conclude that winning $\textbf{Game}_2$ with a non-negligible advantage is statistically impossible.

Let the key-size $\ell = \Theta(n)$ be such that $\ell \leq r - \log_2(3)$. The original KEM CPA game $\textbf{Game}_1$ is as follows [18]:

- $\textbf{Gen}(1^n)$ is run to obtain a public key $pk = P$. Then $\textbf{Encaps}(pk)$ is run to generate (c, k) with $k \in \{0, 1\}^\ell$.
- A uniform bit $b \in \{0, 1\}$ is chosen. If $b = 0$, set $\hat{k} := k$, if $b = 1$, choose a uniform $\hat{k} \in \{0, 1\}^\ell$.
- Given $(pk, c = (c, Z), \hat{k})$ the adversary $\mathcal{A}$ wins the experiment if b is guessed correctly.

The only difference between $\textbf{Game}_1$ and $\textbf{Game}_2$ is that in $\textbf{Game}_2$ we sample the public key P from $\mathcal{D}_s([Q])$ instead of $\mathcal{D}_s([S])$. Note that $\textbf{Game}_1$ and $\textbf{Game}_2$

both only use public information and thus by the hardness of ac-$\Delta\text{LIP}_s^{S,Q}$ the two are computationally indistinguishable by $\mathcal{A}$.

Now we take a look at **Game$_2$**. Consider the output $(c = (\boldsymbol{c}, Z), k) \leftarrow$ **Encaps**(pk) where $pk := Q' \in [Q]$. For any fixed $\boldsymbol{c}$ we have by construction that $k := \mathcal{E}(\boldsymbol{e}, Z)$, where $\boldsymbol{e} \leftarrow \frac{1}{q}\mathcal{D}_{Q',q\rho/\sqrt{n}}$ under the condition that $\boldsymbol{e} = \boldsymbol{c} \bmod \mathbb{Z}^n$. Equivalently we could say that $\boldsymbol{e} \leftarrow \boldsymbol{c} - \mathcal{D}_{Q',\rho/\sqrt{n},\boldsymbol{c}}$, then by Lemma 5.1 we know that $\boldsymbol{e}$ has a min-entropy of at least $r - \log_2(3) \geqslant l$, and thus $k := \mathcal{E}(\boldsymbol{e}, Z) \in \{0,1\}^\ell$ is negligibly close to uniform independent of $\boldsymbol{c}$. So in **Game$_2$** we have that $\hat{k}$ is negligibly close to uniform, independent of $\boldsymbol{c}$ and the choice of $b \in \{0,1\}$, making it impossible for $\mathcal{A}$ to guess b with non-negligible advantage. $\square$

6   Signature Scheme

Similar to the Key Encapsulation Mechanism we propose in this section a *hash-then-sign* signature scheme based on ΔLIP. The main requirement is a quadratic form S along with an efficient discrete Gaussian sampling algorithm of smallish width $\rho/\sqrt{n} \geqslant \eta_{2-\Theta(n)}(S)$.

Again the public key will consist of some lesser reduced form $P := U^t S U \leftarrow \mathcal{D}_s([S])$ equivalent to S, where the unimodular transformation U is the secret key. To sign a message we use a full domain hash to obtain a uniform coset $\boldsymbol{t} + \mathbb{Z}^n$, the signature then consists of a nearby vector $\boldsymbol{\sigma} \leftarrow \mathcal{D}_{P,\rho/\sqrt{n},\boldsymbol{t}}$ w.r.t. the form P. The nearby vector is obtained via S by the secret transformation U.

The security assumption is similar, but in some way dual to that of the KEM. Again assume that it is computationally hard to differentiate between P and some special class of forms $[Q]$; however in this case Q must admit a sparse projection (equivalently, their dual should contain a dense lattice). The sparsity implies that a uniformly random target $\boldsymbol{t}$ does not have a nearby vector with overwhelming probability, making the signage vacuously hard.

Correctness. For correctness we mainly have to check that the returned signature $\boldsymbol{\sigma} \in \mathbb{Z}^n$ is indeed close to $\boldsymbol{t} := \mathcal{H}(m)$ w.r.t P. Because $P = U^t S U$ we have:

$$\|\boldsymbol{\sigma} - \boldsymbol{t}\|_P = \|U(\boldsymbol{\sigma} - \boldsymbol{t})\|_S = \|\boldsymbol{\sigma}' - U\boldsymbol{t}\|_S,$$

and by Lemma 2.7 we have with overwhelming probability that $\|\boldsymbol{\sigma} - \boldsymbol{t}\|_P = \|\boldsymbol{\sigma}' - U\boldsymbol{t}\|_S \leqslant \rho/\sqrt{n} \cdot \sqrt{n} = \rho$, concluding the correctness.

Security. For the security proof we first consider a class of quadratic forms for which the signage is vacuously hard, e.g. for a random target $\boldsymbol{t} \in \mathbb{R}^n/\mathbb{Z}^n$ there exists no nearby vector.

Lemma 6.1. *Let $Q \in \mathcal{S}_n^{>0}(\mathbb{Z})$ be a quadratic form with a dense rank k sublattice $D\mathbb{Z}^k \subset \mathbb{Z}^n$, in particular such that $\rho/\sqrt{k} \leqslant 1/(\sqrt{8\pi e} \cdot \det(D^t QD)^{1/2k})$. Then for the dual form Q^{-1} we have*

$$\Pr_{\boldsymbol{t} \sim \mathcal{U}([0,1]^n)}[|(\boldsymbol{t} + \mathcal{B}_{Q^{-1},\rho}^n) \cap \mathbb{Z}^n| \geqslant 1] \leqslant 2^{-k}.$$

Signature Scheme

Let $S \in \mathcal{S}_n^{>0}(\mathbb{Z})$ be a quadratic form together with a sampling algorithm **DiscreteSample** that allows to sample statistically close to $\mathcal{D}_{P,\rho/\sqrt{n}}(t + \mathbb{Z}^n)$ for some parameter $\rho/\sqrt{n} \geqslant \eta_{2-\Theta(n)}([S])$ and any target $t \in \mathbb{T}_q^n$. Let $\mathcal{H} : \mathcal{M} \to \mathbb{T}_q^n$ be a full domain hash function (modeled as a random oracle). Given the public parameters

$$s \geqslant \max\{\lambda_n(S), \|B_S^*\| \cdot \sqrt{\ln(2n+4)/\pi}\}, \text{ and}$$

$$q := \left\lceil \frac{s \cdot n}{\rho} \cdot \sqrt{\ln(2n+4)/\pi} \right\rceil,$$

we define the signature scheme $\mathcal{S} := (\mathbf{Gen}, \mathbf{Sign}, \mathbf{Verify})$ as follows:

- $(pk, sk) \leftarrow \mathbf{Gen}(1^n)$: on input 1^n do:
  1. Sample $P \leftarrow \mathcal{D}_s([S])$ using Alg. 1, together with U s.t. $P = U^t S U$.
  2. Output $(pk, sk) = (P, U) \in \mathcal{S}_n^{>0}(\mathbb{Z}) \times \mathcal{GL}_n(\mathbb{Z})$.
- $\sigma \leftarrow \mathbf{Sign}(sk, m)$: on input a message m and a secret key $U := sk$ do:
  1. Compute $t \leftarrow \mathcal{H}(m)$.
  2. Sample $\sigma' \leftarrow \mathcal{D}_{S,\rho/\sqrt{n},Ut}$ using **DiscreteSample**.
  3. Compute $\sigma \leftarrow U^{-1}\sigma'$.
  4. Output $\sigma \in \mathbb{Z}^n$.
- $b := \mathbf{Verify}(pk, m, \sigma)$: on input a public key $P = pk$, a message m and a signature σ do:
  1. Compute $t \leftarrow \mathcal{H}(m)$.
  2. If $\sigma \in \mathbb{Z}^n$, and $\|t - \sigma\|_P \leqslant \rho$, output $b = 1$.
  3. Otherwise, output $b = 0$.

Proof. Let $V := \mathrm{span}(D) \subset \mathbb{R}^n$ such that the orthogonal projection w.r.t. Q^{-1} of $\mathbb{Z}^n$ onto V defines a projected lattice $C\mathbb{Z}^k := \pi_{Q^{-1},V}(\mathbb{Z}^n)$ of rank k, with $\det(C^t Q^{-1} C) \geqslant 1/\det(D^t Q D)$. Because a projection is non-increasing in length we have

$$\Pr_{t \sim \mathcal{U}(\mathbb{R}^n/\mathbb{Z}^n)}[|(t + \mathcal{B}_{Q^{-1},\rho}^n) \cap \mathbb{Z}^n| \geqslant 1] \leqslant \Pr_{t \sim \mathcal{U}(\mathbb{R}^k/\mathbb{Z}^k)}[|(t + \mathcal{B}_{C^t Q^{-1} C,\rho}^k) \cap \mathbb{Z}^n| \geqslant 1] = (*).$$

Then using Markov's inequality we can bound the above by

$$(*) \leqslant \mathbb{E}_{t \sim \mathcal{U}(\mathbb{R}^k/\mathbb{Z}^k)}[|(t + \mathcal{B}_{C^t Q^{-1} C,\rho}^k) \cap \mathbb{Z}^n|] = \frac{\mathrm{Vol}_{C^t Q^{-1} C}(\mathcal{B}_{C^t Q^{-1} C,\rho}^k)}{\mathrm{Vol}_{C^t Q^{-1} C}(\mathbb{R}^k/\mathbb{Z}^k)}$$

$$\leqslant \frac{(2\pi e/k)^{k/2} \cdot \rho^k}{\sqrt{\det(C^t Q^{-1} C)}} \leqslant 2^{-k}. \qquad \square$$

Theorem 6.2. *We consider the signature scheme* $\mathcal{S} := (\mathbf{Gen}, \mathbf{Sign}, \mathbf{Verify})$ *instantiated with quadratic form* $S \in \mathcal{S}_n^{>0}(\mathbb{Z})$, *sampling parameter* ρ, *and public key parameter* $s > 0$. *Let* $Q \in \mathcal{S}_n^{>0}(\mathbb{Z})$ *be a quadratic form with a dense rank* $k = \Theta(n)$ *sublattice* $D\mathbb{Z}^k \subset \mathbb{Z}^n$, *in particular such that* $2\rho/\sqrt{k} \leqslant (\sqrt{8\pi e} \cdot \det(D^t Q D^t)^{1/k})^{-1}$. *Then* $\mathcal{S}$ *is EUF-CMA secure if* ac-$\Delta\mathrm{LIP}_s^{S,Q^{-1}}$ *is hard.*

Proof. Let $\mathcal{A}$ be a probabilistic polynomial-time adversary. We present three games $\mathbf{Game_1}, \mathbf{Game_2}, \mathbf{Game_3}$ where $\mathbf{Game_1}$ is the regular EUF-CMA game with the original scheme, $\mathbf{Game_2}$ reprograms the random oracle to generate valid signatures without knowledge of the secret key, and $\mathbf{Game_3}$ samples the public key from $[Q^{-1}]$ instead of $[S]$. By a standard smoothness argument the adversary's view of $\mathbf{Game_1}$ and $\mathbf{Game_2}$ is statistically indistinguishable, and $\mathbf{Game_2}$ and $\mathbf{Game_3}$ are indistinguishable by the hardness of ac-$\Delta\mathrm{LIP}_s^{S,Q^{-1}}$. Then we conclude by Lemma 6.1 that the problem of forging a signature in $\mathbf{Game_3}$ is statistically hard. The original EUF-CMA game $\mathbf{Game_1}$ is as follows [18]:

- $\mathbf{Gen}(1^n)$ is run to obtain keys $(pk = P, sk = U)$.
- Adversary $\mathcal{A}$ is given $pk = P$ and access to an oracle $\mathbf{Sign}(sk, \cdot)$. The adversary then outputs $(m, \boldsymbol{\sigma})$ where m was not queried before to the oracle.
- $\mathcal{A}$ succeeds if and only if $\mathbf{Verify}(pk, m, \boldsymbol{\sigma}) = 1$.

To show that our signature scheme $\mathcal{S}$ is EUF-CMA secure we have to show that $\mathbf{Game_1}$ succeeds only with negligible probability. We assume that the adversary queries the oracle on $l = \mathrm{poly}(n)$ distinct[6] message $m_1, \ldots, m_l$. In $\mathbf{Game_1}$ the secret key is used to obtain a valid signature $(m_i, \boldsymbol{\sigma}_i)$ where $\boldsymbol{\sigma}_i \leftarrow \mathcal{D}_{P,\rho/\sqrt{n}, \mathcal{H}(m_i)}$. In $\mathbf{Game_2}$ instead we first sample a random error $\boldsymbol{e}_i \leftarrow \frac{1}{q} \cdot \mathcal{D}_{P, q\rho/\sqrt{n}}$. By Lemma 3.6 we have $q\rho/\sqrt{n} \geqslant \|B_P^*\| \cdot \sqrt{\ln(2n+4)/\pi}$ with overwhelming probability, and thus by Lemma 2.9 we can do the sampling without using the secret key. Then we reprogram the random oracle such that $\mathcal{H}(m_i) := \boldsymbol{t}_i = \boldsymbol{e} \bmod \mathbb{Z}^n \in \mathbb{T}_q$, and return the signature pair $(m_i, \boldsymbol{\sigma}_i := \boldsymbol{t}_i - \boldsymbol{e}_i)$. Note that the probability that $\boldsymbol{t}_i$ equals any target $\boldsymbol{t} \in \mathbb{T}_q^n$ is proportional to $\rho_{P,\rho/\sqrt{n}, \boldsymbol{t}}(\mathbb{Z}^n)$. So $\boldsymbol{t}_i$ is close to uniform by Lemma 2.5 because $\rho/\sqrt{n} \geqslant \eta_{2^{-\Theta(n)}}([S]) = \eta_{2^{-\Theta(n)}}([P])$, and thus the random oracle is still simulated correctly. Additionally the conditional probability of $\boldsymbol{\sigma}_i$ conditioned on $\boldsymbol{t}_i$ is exactly the same as in $\mathbf{Game_1}$, so we can conclude that $\mathbf{Game_1}$ and $\mathbf{Game_2}$ are statistically indistinguishable from the adversary's point of view.

The only difference between $\mathbf{Game_2}$ and $\mathbf{Game_3}$ is that in $\mathbf{Game_3}$ we sample the public key P from $\mathcal{D}_s([Q^{-1}])$ instead of $\mathcal{D}_s([S])$. Note that $\mathbf{Game_2}$ and $\mathbf{Game_3}$ both only use public information and thus by the hardness of ac-$\Delta\mathrm{LIP}_s^{S,Q^{-1}}$ the two are computationally indistinguishable.

To conclude note that for any message m we obtain a random target $\boldsymbol{t} := \mathcal{H}(m) \in \mathbb{T}_q^n$. Let $\boldsymbol{e}'$ be uniform over the Babai nearest plane region defined by P, then $\|\boldsymbol{e}'\|_P \leqslant \frac{\sqrt{n}}{2}\|B_P^*\|$, and $\boldsymbol{t}' := \boldsymbol{t} + \frac{1}{q}\boldsymbol{e}'$ is uniform over $\mathbb{R}^n/\mathbb{Z}^n$. By Lemma 6.1 the uniformly random target $\boldsymbol{t}'$ lies at distance at least 2ρ from $\mathbb{Z}^n$ w.r.t. P with overwhelming probability. So for $\boldsymbol{t}$ we have with overwhelming probability that:

$$\mathrm{dist}_P(\boldsymbol{t}, \mathbb{Z}^n) \geqslant \mathrm{dist}_P(\boldsymbol{t}', \mathbb{Z}^n) - \left\|\frac{1}{q}\boldsymbol{e}'\right\|_P \geqslant 2\rho - \frac{\sqrt{n} \cdot \|B_P^*\|}{2q}$$

$$\geqslant 2\rho - \rho/(2\sqrt{\ln(2n+4)/\pi}) > \rho.$$

Therefore it is statistically impossible for the adversary to return a valid signature for m, and thus to win $\mathbf{Game_3}$. □

---

[6] This can be enforced by salting messages or by derandomization.

7   Cryptanalysis of LIP

Equivalent quadratic forms $Q, Q' := U^t Q U$ (for some $U \in \mathcal{GL}_n(\mathbb{Z})$) share many common properties, and these invariants can be used to decide that two quadratic forms cannot be equivalent, or can guide the search for an isomorphism.

7.1   Invariants

Arithmetic Invariants. Firstly we have $\det(U) = \pm 1$, and thus for two equivalent quadratic forms we have $\det(Q') = \det(U^t) \det(Q) \det(U) = \det(Q)$. Secondly because U and U^{-1} are both integral, the quantity $\gcd(Q) = \gcd\{Q_{ij} : 1 \leqslant i, j \leqslant n\}$ is also an invariant.

A third and less obvious invariant is the parity of the quadratic form. The notion is standard for unimodular lattices: it is called even if all norms are even, and odd otherwise. More generally, writing $\|x\|_Q = \sum_i Q_{ii} x_i^2 + 2\sum_{i<j} x_j Q_{ij} x_i$ one gets that $\gcd\{\|x\|_Q : x \in \mathbb{Z}^n\} \in \{1, 2\} \cdot \gcd(Q)$. We call this factor $\mathrm{par}(Q) \in \{1, 2\}$ the parity of Q. It is also efficiently computable by noting that $\mathrm{par}(Q) = \gcd(\{Q_{ii} : 1 \leqslant i \leqslant n\} \cup \{2\gcd(Q)\}) / \gcd(Q)$.

Further arithmetic invariants are induced by R-equivalence of quadratic forms for extensions $R \supset \mathbb{Z}$. The invariants for $\mathbb{Q}$-equivalence can be decomposed via a local-global principle, namely the Hasse-Minkowski theorem [42, Thm. 9, pp. 44]. Together with the discriminant, these invariants are complete (they entirely determine quadratic forms up to $\mathbb{Q}$-equivalence), and they can be computed efficiently. They consists of the signature, and the Cassel-Hasse invariant at each prime p. The Sylvester signature ($\mathbb{R}$-equivalence) is always $(n, 0)$ in our case as we are only considering positive quadratic forms. The Cassel-Hasse invariant ($\mathbb{Q}_p$-invariance) for a prime p is given for a diagonal matrix $D = \mathrm{diag}(d_1, \ldots, d_n)$ by

$$h_p = \prod_{i<j} (d_i, d_j)_p \tag{1}$$

where $(\cdot, \cdot)_p$ denotes the Hilbert Symbol at p. Using LDL^t decomposition (Cholesky decomposition over the rationals), one can efficiently compute Hasse invariant for any positive quadratic form.

Similarly, there are also invariants induced by p-adic equivalence of quadratic forms: $Q' = V^t Q V$ for $V \in \mathcal{GL}_n(\mathbb{Z}_p)$, see [9, Chap. 15, Sec 4.1].

All these arithmetic invariants provide a fingerprint

$$\mathrm{ari}(Q) = (\det(Q), \gcd(Q), \mathrm{par}(Q), [Q]_{\mathbb{Q}}, ([Q]_{\mathbb{Z}_p})_p) \tag{2}$$

and they appear to all be efficiently computable, but are essentially only useful to answer the ΔLIP problem in the negative. When instantiating ΔLIP, we should therefore make sure that these fingerprint matches.

The Hull. In the literature for linear code equivalence a relevant notion is that of the efficiently computable hull $C \cap C^\perp$ of a code $C \subset \mathbb{F}_q^n$. Properties such as the rank of the hull are invariant under equivalence, and a small rank even allows to efficiently find the isometry [41]. For a lattice $\mathcal{L}$ and its dual $\mathcal{L}^*$ we could define the hull as $\mathcal{L} \cap \mathcal{L}^*$. However, for integral lattices (or more generally if the associated quadratic form is integral) we always have $\mathcal{L} \subset \mathcal{L}^*$ and thus the hull $\mathcal{L} \cap \mathcal{L}^* = \mathcal{L}$ does not present us with new information. We could generalize definition to consider $\mathcal{L} \cap (k \cdot \mathcal{L}^*)$ for rational $k \in \mathbb{Q}_{\neq 0}$, and although we do not see a direct threat for our instantiation (in Sect. 8) from this, we do encourage more research into the geometric properties of the resulting lattices.

Geometric Invariant. The defining and most important property of a unimodular transformation $U \in \mathcal{GL}_n(\mathbb{Z})$ is that it gives a bijection $\mathbb{Z}^n \to \mathbb{Z}^n$ by $\boldsymbol{x} \mapsto U\boldsymbol{x}$ (or $\boldsymbol{x} \mapsto U^{-1}\boldsymbol{x}$). With respect to the quadratic forms $Q, Q' := U^t Q U$ this even gives an isometry (from Q' to Q) as

$$\langle \boldsymbol{x}, \boldsymbol{y} \rangle_{Q'} = \boldsymbol{x}^t Q' \boldsymbol{y} = \boldsymbol{x}^t U^t Q U \boldsymbol{y} = \langle U\boldsymbol{x}, U\boldsymbol{y} \rangle_Q \text{ for } \boldsymbol{x}, \boldsymbol{y} \in \mathbb{R}^n.$$

This isometry results in several natural geometric invariants related to the norms and inner products of integral vectors. We have already seen some, namely the first minimum $\lambda_1(Q)$ and the i-th minimum $\lambda_i(Q)$. Further geometric invariants can be defined, such as the kissing number $\kappa(Q) = |\text{Min}(Q)|$ where

$$\text{Min}(Q) := \{\boldsymbol{x} \in \mathbb{Z}^n : \|\boldsymbol{x}\|_Q = \lambda_1(Q)\},$$

and more generally the (formal) Theta-series $\Theta_Q(q) = \sum_{\ell \geq 0} N_\ell q^\ell$ associated to Q, where $N_\ell = | \{\boldsymbol{x} \in \mathbb{Z}^n : \|\boldsymbol{x}\|_Q = \ell\} |$.

All these geometric invariant appears to involve finding or even enumerating short vectors; in particular they are plausibly hard to compute.

7.2   Algorithms for Distinguish-LIP and Hardness Conjecture

In Sect. 8, we will use ΔLIP with quadratic forms with different minimal distances $\lambda_1(Q_0) < \lambda_1(Q_1)$. However we will be careful to ensure that their arithmetic invariant match $\text{ari}(Q_0) = \text{ari}(Q_1)$ to not make the problem trivial.

Approximate-SVP Oracle. An f-approx-SVP oracle applied to a form Q finds a short vector of length at most $f \cdot \lambda_1(Q)$. So ΔLIP is no harder than f-approx-SVP for $f = \lambda_1(Q_1)/\lambda_1(Q_0)$ in any of those lattices.

Unusual-SVP via Lattice Reduction. However even when the gap between $\lambda_1(Q_0)$ and $\lambda_1(Q_1)$ is small, the minimal vectors may individually still be unusually short, which make them significantly easier to find than in a random lattice. This is usually formalized via the f-unique-SVP problem, but many instances of interest do not have such a gap between λ_1 and λ_2; in fact $\mathbb{Z}^n$, Barnes-Wall and Barnes-Sloane lattices all have $\lambda_1 = \lambda_2 = \cdots = \lambda_n$. But practical and heuristic studies have showed that uniqueness is not that relevant to lattice attacks [2]. We therefore introduce yet another lattice problem, called *unusual-SVP* to discuss such instances. A formal complexity reduction between unusual-SVP and unique-SVP matching or approaching the heuristic state of the art appears to be a valuable research objective, but is beyond the scope of the present article.

We define f-unusual-SVP: find a minimal vector under the promise that $\lambda_1(Q) \leqslant \mathrm{gh}(Q)/f$, where the Gaussian Heuristic $\mathrm{gh}(Q)$ is a heuristic estimate for $\lambda_1(Q)$ given by:

$$\mathrm{gh}(Q) := \det(Q)^{1/2n} \cdot \frac{1}{\sqrt{\pi}} \cdot \Gamma(1 + n/2)^{1/n} \approx \det(Q)^{1/2n} \cdot \sqrt{\frac{n}{2\pi e}}.$$

State of the art lattice reduction techniques find these unusually short vector more easily than longer vectors with length around $\mathrm{gh}(Q)$, and (heuristically) the hardness is directly driven by the ratio $f = \mathrm{gh}(Q)/\lambda_1(Q)$ [2]. Given a form $Q' \in [Q_0] \cup [Q_1]$ we parametrize the lattice reduction algorithm to find a unusual short vector with length $\min\{\lambda_1(Q_0), \lambda_1(Q_1)\}$, then depending on success we learn that either $Q' \in [Q_0]$ or $Q' \in [Q_1]$.

An Approach of Szydlo. Additionally there is one heuristic algorithm in the literature [46] for ΔLIP, that applies to lattices obtained by mild sparsification of the orthogonal lattice $\mathbb{Z}^n$. This algorithm proceeds by sampling vectors of length $O(\sqrt{n})$ and then decides via a statistical test: the Theta-series appears sufficiently different at such low lengths to distinguish the two lattices. Remarkably, the parameters for state of the art lattice reduction algorithms parametrized to solve $O(\sqrt{n})$-approx-SVP for (mild sparsifications of) $\mathbb{Z}^n$, match those to solve $\mathrm{gh}(\mathbb{Z}^n)/\lambda_1(\mathbb{Z}^n) = O(\sqrt{n})$-unusual-SVP; instead of finding approximate vectors we immediately find the shortest vectors. Again we see that the ratio $\mathrm{gh}(Q)/\lambda_1(Q)$ is what seems to matter.

Conclusion. To conclude, let us also note that any of the above attack can also be run over the dual. To state a hardness conjecture capturing these attacks we define the primal-dual gap to the Gaussian Heuristic as:

$$\mathrm{gap}(Q) = \max\left\{\frac{\mathrm{gh}(Q)}{\lambda_1(Q)}, \frac{\mathrm{gh}(Q^{-1})}{\lambda_1(Q^{-1})}\right\}.$$

Note that this quantity might be slightly lower than 1 (but no lower than $1/2$ by Minkowski bound): there might exist excellent lattice packings beating the Gaussian Heuristic. We will be assuming[7] $\mathrm{gap}(Q_i) \geqslant 1$, which implies that $\lambda_1(Q_i)/\lambda_1(Q_{1-i}) \leqslant \mathrm{gap}(Q_i)$, therefore also capturing the first approach.

In all the attacks above, one first searches for vector no larger than $f \cdot \lambda_1(Q_i)$ w.r.t. Q_i for $f = \mathrm{gap}(Q_i)$, hence the following conjecture.

---

[7] That is, we cowardly shy away from making hardness conjecture on such exceptionally dense lattice packings. Such a regime has never been considered in practical cryptanalysis and would deserve specific attention. We suspect that SVP in such lattices to be even harder than in random lattices.

Conjecture 7.1 (Hardness of ΔLIP (Strong)). For any class of quadratic forms $[Q_0], [Q_1]$ of dimension n, with $\mathrm{ari}([Q_0]) = \mathrm{ari}([Q_1])$, $1 \leqslant \mathrm{gap}([Q_i]) \leqslant f$, the best attack against wc-ΔLIP^{Q_0,Q_1} requires solving f-approx-SVP in the worst-case from either $[Q_0]$ or $[Q_1]$.

This conjecture is meant to offer a comparison point with existing lattice-based cryptography in terms of the approximating factor. Beyond contradicting this assumption, we also invite cryptanalysis effort toward concrete comparison of f-approx-SVP on those instances to SIS and LWE with the same approximation factor f. If one only wishes to argue exponential security in n of the schemes proposed in this paper, a sufficient conjecture is the following.

Conjecture 7.2 (Hardness of ΔLIP (Mild)). For any class of quadratic forms $[Q_0], [Q_1]$ of dimension n, with $\mathrm{ari}([Q_0]) = \mathrm{ari}([Q_1])$, $\mathrm{gap}([Q_i]) \leqslant \mathrm{poly}(n)$, wc-$\Delta$LIP^{Q_0,Q_1} is $2^{\Theta(n)}$-hard.

Note that the conjecture above are "best-case" over the choice of the isomorphism class, and worst-case over the representation of the class (however note that we have a worst-case to average-case reduction over that representation). That is, even though we may only want to use ΔLIP for specific choices of isomorphism classes, we gladly invite cryptanalysis effort on ΔLIP on any choice of isomorphism classes.

7.3 Algorithms for Search-LIP and Challenges

While the above invariants allow to semi-decide LIP, the search version requires more effort; though all methods known to us at least require the enumeration of short primal or dual vectors. In the extended version of this work[8] we discuss these methods in more detail.

8 Instantiating ΔLIP Pairs from Remarkable Lattices

To instantiate our schemes, we do not only need a lattice with efficient decoding or sampling; we also need a second lattice with a specific property to instantiate the ΔLIP problem and argue security. This section deals with how the ΔLIP pair is constructed from a single remarkable lattice.

8.1 Key Encapsulation Mechanism

To instantiate our KEM we need two quadratic forms: a form S along with an efficient decoder that can decode up to some distance $\rho < \lambda_1(Q)/2$, and a form Q with a dense rank k sublattice $D \cdot \mathbb{Z}^k \subset \mathbb{Z}^n$ such that $\eta_{\frac{1}{2}}(D^t Q D) \leqslant \rho/(2\sqrt{n})$. For simplicity of notation we move to the lattice point of view.

We assume to have an n-dimensional lattice Λ for which $\mathrm{gap}(\Lambda) \leqslant f = f(n)$, and for which we can decode up to $\rho = \Theta(1/f) \cdot \mathrm{gh}(\Lambda) < \lambda_1(\Lambda)/2$. We

---

[8] The full version of this work is available at https://eprint.iacr.org/2021/1332.

consider a general construction leading to a $2n$-dimensional primary lattice Λ_S and secondary lattice Λ_Q with gap bounded by $O(f^3)$ and such that Λ_Q has a dense enough sublattice to instantiate our KEM.

Note that due to the bounded gap of Λ we have by Lemma 2.6 that

$$\eta_{\frac{1}{2}}(\Lambda) \leqslant \eta_{2-n}(\Lambda) \leqslant \frac{\sqrt{n}}{\lambda_1(\Lambda^*)} \leqslant \frac{\sqrt{n} \cdot f}{\mathrm{gh}(\Lambda^*)} = \Theta(f \cdot \det(\Lambda)^{1/n}).$$

Now let $g = \Theta(f^2)$ be a positive integer and consider the lattices:

$$\Lambda_S := g \cdot \Lambda \oplus (g+1) \cdot \Lambda, \text{ and } \Lambda_Q := \Lambda \oplus g(g+1)\Lambda,$$

where by construction Λ_Q has a dense sublattice Λ. Note that we can still decode Λ_S up to radius $\rho' := g \cdot \rho - \Theta(g/f) \cdot \mathrm{gh}(\Lambda)$.

Invariants Match. Both lattices have determinant $g^n(g+1)^n \det(\Lambda)^2$. Due to the coprimality of g and $g+1$ we still have $\gcd(\Lambda_S) = \gcd(\Lambda_Q) = \gcd(\Lambda)$, and similarly for the parity. It remains to check rational equivalence and p-adic equivalence for all primes p. Let R denote a quadratic form representing Λ. Up to integral equivalence, we have:

$$S := \begin{pmatrix} g^2 R & 0 \\ 0 & (g+1)^2 R \end{pmatrix} \qquad Q := \begin{pmatrix} R & 0 \\ 0 & g^2(g+1)^2 R \end{pmatrix}.$$

Let I_n be the $n \times n$ identity matrix and consider the transformations:

$$U_1 := \begin{pmatrix} g^{-1} I_n & 0 \\ 0 & g I_n \end{pmatrix} \qquad U_2 := \begin{pmatrix} 0 & (g+1) I_n \\ (g+1)^{-1} I_n & 0 \end{pmatrix}$$

Then $Q = U_1^t S U_1$ over $\mathbb{Q}$: this implies $[S]_{\mathbb{Q}} = [Q]_{\mathbb{Q}}$. For any prime p we have that either $\gcd(g, p) = 1$ or $\gcd(g+1, p) = 1$ (or both). So either g or $(g+1)$ is invertible over the p-adic integers $\mathbb{Z}_p$, and thus either $U_1 \in \mathcal{GL}_d(\mathbb{Z}_p)$ exists and $Q = U_1^t S U_1$ over $\mathbb{Z}_p$ or $U_2 \in \mathcal{GL}_d(\mathbb{Z}_p)$ exists and $Q = U_2^t S U_2$ over $\mathbb{Z}_p$. In either case, we have established $[S]_{\mathbb{Z}_p} = [Q]_{\mathbb{Z}_p}$, which concludes the comparison of arithmetic invariants: $\mathrm{ari}(S) = \mathrm{ari}(Q)$.

Dense Sublattice. We now check the requirements for Theorem 5.2, namely that $\eta_{\frac{1}{2}}(\Lambda) \leqslant \rho'/(2\sqrt{2n})$. Given that $\eta_{\frac{1}{2}}(\Lambda) \leqslant \Theta(f \cdot \mathrm{gh}(\Lambda)/\sqrt{n})$, it is sufficient if

$$\Theta(f \cdot \mathrm{gh}(\Lambda)/\sqrt{n}) \leqslant \rho'/(2\sqrt{2n}) = \Theta(g/f) \cdot \mathrm{gh}(\Lambda)/\sqrt{n},$$

and thus we can conclude that some $g = \Theta(f^2)$ indeed suffices.

Following the conclusions from the cryptanalysis in Sect. 7.2 and more specifically Conjecture 7.1, we take a look at the primal-dual gap for Λ_S and Λ_Q. We have that $\mathrm{gap}(\Lambda_S) = \Theta(\mathrm{gap}(\Lambda)) \leqslant O(f)$, and $\mathrm{gap}(\Lambda_Q) = \Theta(g \cdot \mathrm{gap}(\Lambda)) \leqslant O(f^3)$. Note that following the same computation above but for a primal gap of f, dual gap of f^*, and a decoding gap of $f' \geqslant 2f$ we would have $g = \Theta(f^* \cdot f')$ and obtain a final primal-dual gap of $O(\max(f, f^*) \cdot f^* \cdot f')$.

8.2 Signature Scheme

Our signature scheme can be instantiated with any lattice for which we can sample efficiently at small Gaussian widths, following a similar ΔLIP pair as above. Namely, we assume to have a lattice Λ with gap$(\Lambda) \leqslant f$ and such that we can sample efficiently with parameter $\rho/\sqrt{n} = \Theta(\eta_{2^{-\Theta(n)}}(\Lambda))$ close to the smoothing bound. Similarly to the KEM we set $\Lambda_S := g \cdot \Lambda \oplus (g+1) \cdot \Lambda$, and $\Lambda_{Q^{-1}} = \Lambda \oplus g(g+1) \cdot \Lambda$ for some integer $g \geqslant 1$. In particular, as in the KEM, we do have ari$(S) =$ ari(Q^{-1}).

Then for the dual we have $\Lambda_Q = \Lambda^* \oplus \frac{1}{g(g+1)}\Lambda^*$, with $\frac{1}{g(g+1)}\Lambda^*$ as a dense sublattice. The constraint of Theorem 6.2 boils down to the inequality $\Theta(g \cdot f \cdot \det(\Lambda)^{1/n}) \leqslant \Theta(g^2 \det(\Lambda)^{1/n})$, and thus some $g = \Theta(f)$ suffices. The final primal-dual gap of Λ_S and $\Lambda_{Q^{-1}}$ is then bounded by $O(f^2)$.

The simplest lattice for which we have very efficient samplers is of course the integer lattice $\mathbb{Z}^n$, leading to a gap of $O(n)$ via the above construction. Instantiating our scheme with this lattice would lead to an interesting signature scheme where there is no need to compute any Cholesky decomposition, even for signing, and that could be fully implemented with efficient integer arithmetic.

We refer to our last open question (Sect. 1.3) regarding lattices with a tighter Gaussian sampler, in order to obtain a signature scheme with a better underlying approximation factor.

Getting Down to $O(f)$. The general constructions presented turn a good decodable or sampleable lattice Λ with gap f into a primary and secondary lattice with gap $O(f^3)$ and $O(f^2)$ to instantiate our KEM and signature scheme respectively. We suggest here that these losses might be an artifact of the security proof.

Suppose we can generate a random lattice Λ_Q such that ari$(\Lambda_Q) =$ ari(Λ); without the arithmetic constraint we would have with overwhelming probability that gap$(\Lambda_Q) = O(1)$ (but even $O(f)$ would suffice). Let's assume that the constraint does not affect this gap. Then similar to the scheme of McEliece, by adding the extra security assumption that it is hard to decode in Λ_Q (or hard to sample for the signature scheme), we could remove the lossyness argument from the security proof and directly instantiate our schemes with the pair (Λ, Λ_Q), leading to a gap of $O(f)$.

Acknowledgments. The authors would like to express their gratitude to Jelle Don, Chris Peikert, Alice Pellet-Mary, Damien Stehlé and Benjamin Wesolowski for relevant discussions and their precious feedback. Special thanks go to Aron van Baarsen for bringing the genus to our attention, and to Thomas Debris-Alazard and Alain Couvreur for bringing the hull to our attention.

The research of L. Ducas was supported by the European Union's H2020 Programme under PROMETHEUS project (grant 780701) and the ERC-StG-ARTICULATE project (no. 947821). W. van Woerden is funded by the ERC-ADG-ALGSTRONGCRYPTO project (no. 740972).

References

1. Aggarwal, D., Dadush, D., Regev, O., Stephens-Davidowitz, N.: Solving the shortest vector problem in 2^n time using discrete Gaussian sampling. In: Proceedings of the Forty-Seventh Annual ACM Symposium on Theory of Computing, pp. 733–742 (2015)
2. Albrecht, M., Ducas, L.: Lattice attacks on NTRU and LWE: a history of refinements. Cryptology ePrint Archive Report 2021/799 (2021). https://ia.cr/2021/799
3. Barak, B., et al.: Leftover hash lemma, revisited. In: Rogaway, P. (ed.) CRYPTO 2011. LNCS, vol. 6841, pp. 1–20. Springer, Heidelberg (2011). https://doi.org/10.1007/978-3-642-22792-9_1
4. Becker, A., Ducas, L., Gama, N., Laarhoven, T.: New directions in nearest neighbor searching with applications to lattice sieving. In: Proceedings of the Twenty-Seventh Annual ACM-SIAM Symposium on Discrete Algorithms, pp. 10–24. SIAM (2016)
5. Biasse, J.-F., Micheli, G., Persichetti, E., Santini, P.: LESS is more: code-based signatures without syndromes. In: Nitaj, A., Youssef, A. (eds.) AFRICACRYPT 2020. LNCS, vol. 12174, pp. 45–65. Springer, Cham (2020). https://doi.org/10.1007/978-3-030-51938-4_3
6. Blanks, T.L., Miller, S.D.: Generating cryptographically-strong random lattice bases and recognizing rotations of $\mathbb{Z}^n$. CoRR (2021)
7. Brakerski, Z., Langlois, A., Peikert, C., Regev, O., Stehlé, D.: Classical hardness of learning with errors. In: STOC, pp. 575–584 (2013)
8. Chor, B., Rivest, R.L.: A knapsack-type public key cryptosystem based on arithmetic in finite fields. IEEE Trans. Inf. Theory **34**(5), 901–909 (1988)
9. Conway, J.H., Sloane, N.J.A.: Sphere Packings, Lattices and Groups, vol. 290. Springer, Heidelberg (2013)
10. Damgård, I.: On σ-protocols. Lecture Notes, University of Aarhus, Department for Computer Science (2002)
11. Ducas, L., Pierrot, C.: Polynomial time bounded distance decoding near Minkowski's bound in discrete logarithm lattices. Des. Codes Crypt. **87**(8), 1737–1748 (2019). https://doi.org/10.1007/s10623-018-0573-3
12. Gentry, C., Peikert, C., Vaikuntanathan, V.: Trapdoors for hard lattices and new cryptographic constructions. In: STOC, pp. 197–206 (2008)
13. Gentry, C., Szydlo, M.: Cryptanalysis of the revised NTRU signature scheme. In: Knudsen, L.R. (ed.) EUROCRYPT 2002. LNCS, vol. 2332, pp. 299–320. Springer, Heidelberg (2002). https://doi.org/10.1007/3-540-46035-7_20
14. Goldreich, O., Micali, S., Wigderson, A.: Proofs that yield nothing but their validity or all languages in NP have zero-knowledge proof systems. J. ACM (JACM) **38**(3), 690–728 (1991)
15. Håstad, J., Impagliazzo, R., Levin, L.A., Luby, M.: A pseudorandom generator from any one-way function. SIAM J. Comput. **28**(4), 1364–1396 (1999)
16. Haviv, I., Regev, O.: Hardness of the covering radius problem on lattices. In: IEEE Conference on Computational Complexity, pp. 145–158 (2006)
17. Haviv, I., Regev, O.: On the lattice isomorphism problem. In: Proceedings of the Twenty-Fifth Annual ACM-SIAM Symposium on Discrete Algorithms, pp. 391–404. SIAM (2014)
18. Katz, J., Lindell, Y.: Introduction to Modern Cryptography. CRC Press, Boca Raton (2020)

19. Klein, P.N.: Finding the closest lattice vector when it's unusually close. In: SODA, pp. 937–941 (2000)
20. Lapiha, O.: Comparing lattice families for bounded distance decoding near Minkowski's bound. Cryptology ePrint Archive Report 2021/1052 (2021). https://ia.cr/2021/1052
21. Lenstra, A.K., Lenstra, H.W., Jr., Lovász, L.: Factoring polynomials with rational coefficients. Math. Ann. **261**(4), 515–534 (1982)
22. Lenstra, H.W.: On the Chor-Rivest knapsack cryptosystem. J. Cryptol. **3**(3), 149–155 (1991). https://doi.org/10.1007/BF00196908
23. Lenstra, H.W., Silverberg, A.: Revisiting the Gentry-Szydlo algorithm. In: Garay, J.A., Gennaro, R. (eds.) CRYPTO 2014. LNCS, vol. 8616, pp. 280–296. Springer, Heidelberg (2014). https://doi.org/10.1007/978-3-662-44371-2_16
24. Li, Z., Ling, S., Xing, C., Yeo, S.L.: On the bounded distance decoding problem for lattices constructed and their cryptographic applications. IEEE Trans. Inf. Theory **66**(4), 2588–2598 (2020)
25. McEliece, R.J.: A public-key cryptosystem based on algebraic coding theory. Coding Thv **4244**, 114–116 (1978)
26. Merkle, R., Hellman, M.: Hiding information and signatures in trapdoor knapsacks. IEEE Trans. Inf. Theory **24**(5), 525–530 (1978)
27. Micciancio, D., Goldwasser, S.: Complexity of Lattice Problems: A Cryptographic Perspective. The Kluwer International Series in Engineering and Computer Science, vol. 671. Kluwer Academic Publishers, Boston (2002)
28. Micciancio, D., Nicolosi, A.: Efficient bounded distance decoders for Barnes-Wall lattices. In: 2008 IEEE International Symposium on Information Theory, pp. 2484–2488. IEEE (2008)
29. Micciancio, D., Regev, O.: Worst-case to average-case reductions based on gaussian measures. SIAM J. Comput. **37**(1), 267–302 (2007). https://doi.org/10.1137/S0097539705447360
30. Micciancio, D., Regev, O.: Worst-case to average-case reductions based on Gaussian measures. SIAM J. Comput. **37**(1), 267–302 (2007). Preliminary version in FOCS 2004
31. Mook, E., Peikert, C.: Lattice (list) decoding near Minkowski's inequality. IEEE Trans. Inf. Theory **68**(2), 863–870 (2022)
32. Odlyzko, A.M.: The rise and fall of knapsack cryptosystems. In: Pomerance, C. (ed.) Cryptology and Computational Number Theory. Proceedings of Symposia in Applied Mathematics, vol. 42, pp. 75–88 (1990)
33. Okamoto, T., Tanaka, K., Uchiyama, S.: Quantum public-key cryptosystems. In: Bellare, M. (ed.) CRYPTO 2000. LNCS, vol. 1880, pp. 147–165. Springer, Heidelberg (2000). https://doi.org/10.1007/3-540-44598-6_9
34. Peikert, C.: An efficient and parallel Gaussian sampler for lattices. In: Rabin, T. (ed.) CRYPTO 2010. LNCS, vol. 6223, pp. 80–97. Springer, Heidelberg (2010). https://doi.org/10.1007/978-3-642-14623-7_5
35. Peikert, C., Rosen, A.: Efficient collision-resistant hashing from worst-case assumptions on cyclic lattices. In: Halevi, S., Rabin, T. (eds.) TCC 2006. LNCS, vol. 3876, pp. 145–166. Springer, Heidelberg (2006). https://doi.org/10.1007/11681878_8
36. Peikert, C., Waters, B.: Lossy trapdoor functions and their applications. SIAM J. Comput. **40**(6), 1803–1844 (2011)
37. Plesken, W., Pohst, M.: Constructing integral lattices with prescribed minimum. I. Math. Comput. **45**(171), 209–221 (1985)
38. Plesken, W., Souvignier, B.: Computing isometries of lattices. J. Symb. Comput. **24**(3–4), 327–334 (1997)

39. Regev, O.: On lattices, learning with errors, random linear codes, and cryptography. J. ACM **56**(6), 1–40 (2009). Preliminary version in STOC 2005
40. Schnorr, C.P.: A hierarchy of polynomial time lattice basis reduction algorithms. Theor. Comput. Sci. **53**, 201–224 (1987)
41. Sendrier, N.: Finding the permutation between equivalent linear codes: the support splitting algorithm. IEEE Trans. Inf. Theory **46**(4), 1193–1203 (2000)
42. Serre, J.P.: A Course in Arithmetic, vol. 7. Springer, Heidelberg (2012)
43. Shamir, A.: A polynomial time algorithm for breaking the basic Merkle-Hellman cryptosystem. In: 23rd Annual Symposium on Foundations of Computer Science (SFCS 1982), pp. 145–152. IEEE (1982)
44. Sikiric, M.D., Haensch, A., Voight, J., van Woerden, W.P.: A canonical form for positive definite matrices. In: ANTS XIV, p. 179 (2020)
45. Solé, P., Charnes, C., Martin, B.: A lattice-based McEliece scheme for encryption and signature. Electron. Notes Discrete Math. **6**, 402–411 (2001)
46. Szydlo, M.: Hypercubic lattice reduction and analysis of GGH and NTRU signatures. In: Biham, E. (ed.) EUROCRYPT 2003. LNCS, vol. 2656, pp. 433–448. Springer, Heidelberg (2003). https://doi.org/10.1007/3-540-39200-9_27

Information-Theoretic Security

Online-Extractability in the Quantum Random-Oracle Model

Jelle Don[1(✉)], Serge Fehr[1,2], Christian Majenz[3], and Christian Schaffner[4,5]

[1] Centrum Wiskunde and Informatica (CWI), Amsterdam, Netherlands
{jelle.don,serge.fehr}@cwi.nl
[2] Mathematical Institute, Leiden University, Leiden, Netherlands
[3] Cyber Security Section, Department of Applied Mathematics and Computer Science, Technical University of Denmark, Kgs. Lyngby, Denmark
chmaj@dtu.dk
[4] Informatics Institute, University of Amsterdam, Amsterdam, Netherlands
c.schaffner@uva.nl
[5] QuSoft, Amsterdam, Netherlands

Abstract. We show the following generic result: When a quantum query algorithm in the quantum random-oracle model outputs a classical value t that is promised to be in some tight relation with $H(x)$ for some x, then x can be efficiently extracted with almost certainty. The extraction is by means of a suitable simulation of the random oracle and works *online*, meaning that it is *straightline*, i.e., without rewinding, and *on-the-fly*, i.e., during the protocol execution and (almost) without disturbing it.

The technical core of our result is a new commutator bound that bounds the operator norm of the commutator of the unitary operator that describes the evolution of the compressed oracle (which is used to simulate the random oracle above) and of the measurement that extracts x.

We show two applications of our generic online extractability result. We show *tight* online extractability of commit-and-open Σ-protocols in the quantum setting, and we offer the first complete post-quantum security proof of the *textbook* Fujisaki-Okamoto transformation, i.e., without adjustments to facilitate the proof, including concrete security bounds.

1 Introduction

Background. *Extractability* plays an important role in cryptography. In an extractable protocol, an algorithm $\mathcal{A}$ sends messages that depend on some secret s, and while the secret remains private in an honest run of the protocol, an *extractor* can learn s via some form of enhanced access to $\mathcal{A}$. The probably most prominent example is that of zero-knowledge *proofs* (or *arguments*) *of knowledge*, for which, by definition, there must exist an extractor that manages to extract a witness from any successful prover. Another example are *extractable commitments*, which have a wide range of applications. Hash-based extractable commitments are extremely simple to construct and prove secure in the random-oracle

---

Full version available at https://eprint.iacr.org/2021/280.

O. Dunkelman and S. Dziembowski (Eds.): EUROCRYPT 2022, LNCS 13277, pp. 677–706, 2022.
https://doi.org/10.1007/978-3-031-07082-2_24

model (ROM) [22]. Indeed, when the considered hash function H is modelled as a random oracle, the hash input x for the commitment $c = H(x)$, where $x = s \| r$ consists of the actual secret s and randomness r, can be extracted simply by finding a query x to the random oracle that yielded c as an output.

The general notion of extractability comes in different flavors. The most well-known example is extraction by *rewinding*. Here, the extractor is allowed to run A several times, on the same private input and using different randomness. This is the notion usually considered in the context of proofs/arguments of knowledge. In some contexts, extraction via rewinding access is not possible. For example, the UC security model prohibits the simulator to rewind the adversary. In other occasions, rewinding may be possible but not desirable due to a loss of efficiency, which stems from having to run A multiple times. In comparison, so-called *straightline* extraction works with a single ordinary run of A, without rewinding. Instead, the extractor is then assumed to know some trapdoor information, or it is given enhanced control over some part of the setting. For instance, in the above construction of an extractable commitment, the extractor is given "read access" to A's random-oracle queries.

Another binary criterion is whether the extraction takes place *on-the-fly*, i.e., during the run of the protocol, or *after-the-fact*, i.e., at the end of the execution. For instance, in the context of proving CCA security for an encryption scheme, to simulate decryption queries without knowing the secret key, it is necessary to extract the plaintext for a queried ciphertext on-the-fly; otherwise, the attacker may abort and not produce the output for which the reduction is waiting.

The extractability of our running example of an extractable commitment in the ROM is *both*, straightline and on-the-fly; we refer to this combination as *online* extraction. This notion is what we are aiming for: online extractability of (general) hash-based commitments, but now with *post-quantum security*.

For post-quantum security, the ROM needs to be replaced by the *quantum random-oracle model* (QROM) [4] to reflect the fact that attackers can implement hash functions on a quantum computer. Here, adversaries have quantum superposition access to the random oracle. Many ROM techniques fail in the QROM due to fundamental features of quantum information, such as the so-called *no-cloning principle*. In particular, it is impossible to maintain a query transcript (a fact sometimes referred to as the *recording barrier*), and so one cannot simply "search for a query x to the random oracle", as was exploited for the (classical) RO-security of the extractable-commitment example.

A promising step in the right direction is the compressed-oracle technique, recently developed by Zhandry [27]. This technique enables to maintain *some sort* of a query transcript, but now in the form of a quantum state. This state can be inspected via quantum measurements, offering the possibility to learn some information about the interaction history of the random oracle. However, since quantum measurements disturb the state to which they are applied, and this disturbance is often hard to control, this inspection of the query transcript can *per-se*, i.e., without additional argumentation, only be done at the end of the execution (see the Related Work paragraph for more on this).

Our Resultss. Our main contribution is the following generic extractability result in the QROM: We consider an arbitrary quantum query algorithm $\mathcal{A}$ in the QROM, which announces during its execution some classical value t that is supposed to be equal to $f(x, H(x))$ for some x. Here, f is an arbitrary fixed function, subject to that it must tie t sufficiently to x and $H(x)$, e.g., there must not be too many y's with $f(x, y) = t$; a canonical example is the function $f(x, y) = y$ so that t is supposed to be $t = H(x)$. In general, it is helpful to think of $t = f(x, H(x))$ as a commitment to x. We then show that x can be *efficiently extracted* with almost certainty. The extraction works *online* and is by means of a simulator $\mathcal{S}$ that simulates the quantum random oracle, but which additionally offers an *extraction interface* that produces a guess $\hat{x}$ for x when queried with t. The simulation is statistically indistiguishable from the real quantum random oracle, and $\hat{x}$ is such that whenever $\mathcal{A}$ outputs x with $f(x, H(x)) = t$ at some later point, $\hat{x} = x$ holds except with negligible probability, while $\hat{x} = \emptyset$ (some special symbol) indicates that $\mathcal{A}$ will not be able to output such an x.

The simulator $\mathcal{S}$ simulates the random oracle using Zhandry's compressed-oracle technique, and extraction is done via a suitable measurement of the compressed oracle's internal register. The technical core of our result is a new bound for the operator norm $\|[O, M]\|$ of the commutator of O, the unitary operator that describes the evolution of the compressed oracle, and of M, the extraction measurement. This bound allows us to show that the extraction measurement only negligibly disturbs the behavior of the compressed oracle, and so can indeed be performed *on-the-fly*. At first glance, our technical result has some resemblance with Lemma 39 in [27], which also features an almost-commutativity property, and, indeed, with Lemma 3 we use (a reformulated version of) Lemma 39 in [27] as a first step in our proof. However, the challenging part of the main proof consists of lifting the almost-commutativity property of the "local" projectors Π^x from Lemma 3 to the "global" measurement M.

We emphasize that even though the existence of the simulator with its extraction interface is proven using the compressed-oracle technique, our presentation is in terms of a black-box simulator $\mathcal{S}$ with certain interfaces and with certain promises on its behavior, abstracting away all the (mainly internal) quantum workings. This makes our generic result applicable (e.g. for the applications discussed below) without the need to understand the underlying quantum aspects.

A first concrete application of our generic result is in the context of so-called commit-and-open Σ-protocols. These are (typically honest-verifier zero-knowledge) interactive proofs of a special form, where the prover first announces a list of commitments and is then asked to open a subset of them, chosen at random by the verifier. We show that, when implementing the commitments with a typical hash-based commitment scheme (like committing to s by $H(s\|r)$ with a random r), such Σ-protocols allow for *online* extraction of a witness in the QROM, with a *smaller security loss* than witness extraction via rewinding.

Equipped with our extractable RO-simulator $\mathcal{S}$, the idea for the above online extraction is very simple: we simulate the random oracle using $\mathcal{S}$ and use its extraction interface to extract the prover's commitments from the first message of the Σ-protocol. As we work out in detail, this procedure gives rise to an online witness extractor that has a polynomial additive overhead in running time compared to the considered prover, and that outputs a valid witness with a probability that is *linear* in the difference of the prover's success probability and the trivial cheating probability, up to an additive error . Using rewinding techniques, on the other hand, incurs a *square-root* loss in success probability classically and a *cube-root* loss quantumly for special-sound Σ-protocols, and typically an even worse loss in case of weaker soundness guarantees, like a k-th-root loss classically and a $(2k+1)$-th-root loss quantumly for k-sound protocols.

Our second application is a security reduction for the Fujisaki-Okamoto (FO) transformation. We offer the first complete post-quantum security proof of the *textbook* FO transformation [13], with concrete security bounds. Most of the prior post-quantum security proofs had to adjust the transformation to facilitate the proof (like [16]); those security proofs either consider a FO variant that employs an *implicit-rejection* routine, or have to resort to an additional "key confirmation" hash [24] that is appended to the ciphertex, thus increasing the ciphertext size. The *unmodified* FO transformation was analyzed in [27] and [18]; however, as we explain in detail in Appendix A of the full version, the given post-quantum security proofs are incomplete, both having the same gap.

Beyond its theoretical relevance of showing that no adjustment is necessary, the security of the original unmodified FO transformation with explicit rejection in particular ensures that the conservative variant with implicit rejection remains secure even when the decapsulation algorithm is not implemented carefully enough and admits a side-channel attack that reveals information on whether the submitted ciphertext is valid or not.

The core idea of our proof for the textbook FO transformation is to use the extractability of the RO-simulator to handle the decryption queries. Indeed, letting $f(x, y)$ be the encryption $Enc_{pk}(x; y)$ of the message x under the randomness y, a "commitment" $t = f(x, H(x))$ is then the encryption of x under the derandomized scheme, and so the extraction interface recovers x.

Related Work. The compressed-oracle technique has proven to be a powerful tool for lifting classical ROM proofs to the QROM setting. Examples are [10, 19] for quantum query complexity lower bounds and [15] for space-time trade-off bounds, [9] for the security of succinct arguments, [1] for quantum-access security, and [3] for a new "double-sided" O2H lemma in the context of the FO transformation. In these cases, the argument exploits the possibility to extract information on the interaction history of the algorithm $\mathcal{A}$ and the (compressed) oracle *after-the-fact*, i.e., at the very end of the run.

In addition, some tools have been developed that allow measuring (the internal state of) the compressed oracle *on-the-fly*, which then causes the state, and thus the behavior of the oracle, to change. In some cases, the disturbance is significant yet asymptotically good enough for the considered application, causing "only" a polynomial blow-up of a negligible error term, as, e.g., in [20] for proving the security of the Fiat-Shamir transformation. In other cases [11,27], it is shown for some limited settings that certain measurements do not render the simulation of the random oracle distinguishable (except for negligible advantage). The indifferentiability result in [11], for example, only uses measurements that have an almost certain outcome.

In particular, [27] contains a security reduction for the FO transformation that implicitly uses a measurement similar to the one we analyze in Sect. 3, but without analyzing the disturbance it causes. We discuss this in more detail in Appendix A of the full version. The same gap exists in follow-up work by Katsumata et al. [18], who follow the FO proof outline from [27].

2 Preliminaries

For Sects. 3 and 4 (only), we assume some familiarity with the mathematics of quantum information as well as with the compressed-oracle technique of [27]. Below, we summarize the concepts that will be of particular importance. For a function or algorithm f, we write $\text{Time}[f]$ to denote the time complexity of (an algorithm computing) f.

2.1 Mathematical Preliminaries

Let $\mathcal{H}$ be a finite-dimensional complex Hilbert space. We use the standard bra-ket notation for the vectors in $\mathcal{H}$ and its dual space. We write $\||\varphi\rangle\|$ for the (Euclidean) norm $\||\varphi\rangle\| = \sqrt{\langle\varphi|\varphi\rangle}$ of $|\varphi\rangle \in \mathcal{H}$. Furthermore, for an operator $A \in \mathcal{L}(\mathcal{H})$, we denote by $\|A\|$ its *operator norm*, i.e., $\|A\| = \max_{|\psi\rangle} \|A|\psi\rangle\|$, where the max is over all $|\psi\rangle \in \mathcal{H}$ with norm 1. We assume the reader to be familiar with basic properties of these norms, like triangle inequality, $\||\varphi\rangle\langle\psi|\|\| = \||\varphi\rangle\|\||\psi\rangle\|$, $\|A|\varphi\rangle\| \leq \|A\|\||\varphi\rangle\|$, $\|AB\| \leq \|A\|\|B\|$, etc. Less well known may be the inequality[1]

$$\||\varphi\rangle\langle\psi| - |\psi\rangle\langle\varphi|\| \leq \||\varphi\rangle\|\||\psi\rangle\| \,. \tag{1}$$

Another basic yet important property that we will exploit is the following.

Lemma 1. *Let A and B be operators in $\mathcal{L}(\mathcal{H})$ with $A^\dagger B = 0$ and $AB^\dagger = 0$. Then, $\|A + B\| \leq \max\{\|A\|, \|B\|\}$.*

Exploiting that $\|A \otimes B\| = \|A\|\|B\|$, the following is a direct consequence.

Corollary 1. *If $A = \sum_x |x\rangle\langle x| \otimes A^x$ then $\|A\| \leq \max_x \|A^x\|$.*

Definition 1. *For $A, B \in \mathcal{L}(\mathcal{H})$, the* commutator *is $[A, B] := AB - BA$.*

Some obvious properties of the commutator are:

$$[B, A] = -[A, B] = [A, \mathbb{1} - B]\,, \quad [A \otimes \mathbb{1}, B \otimes C] = [A, B] \otimes C \tag{2}$$
$$\text{and} \quad [AB, C] = A[B, C] + [A, C]B\,. \tag{3}$$

---

[1] It is immediate for normalized $|\phi\rangle$ and $|\psi\rangle$ when expanding both vectors in an orthonormal basis containing $|\varphi\rangle$ and $\frac{|\psi\rangle - \langle\varphi|\psi\rangle|\varphi\rangle}{\sqrt{1 - |\langle\varphi|\psi\rangle|^2}}$, and the general case then follows by homogeneity of the norms.

Combining the right equality in (2) with basic properties of the operator norm, if $\|C\| \leq 1$, e.g., if C is a unitary of a projection, we have

$$\|[A \otimes \mathbb{1}, B \otimes C]\| = \|[A, B]\| \|C\| \leq \|[A, B]\| . \tag{4}$$

It is common in quantum information science to write A_X to emphasize that the operator A acts on *register* X, i.e., on a Hilbert space $\mathcal{H}_X$ that is labeled by the X. It is then understood that when applied to registers X and Y, say, A_X acts as A on register X and as identity $\mathbb{1}$ on register Y, i.e., A_X is identified with $A_X \otimes \mathbb{1}_Y$. Property (4) would then e.g. be written as $\|[A_X, B_X \otimes C_Y]\| \leq \|[A_X, B_X]\|$. In this work, we will write or not write these subscripts emphasizing the register(s) at our convenience; typically we write them when the argument crucially depends on the registers, and we may omit them otherwise.

Another important matrix norm is the *trace norm*, $\|A\|_1 = \operatorname{tr}\left[\sqrt{A^\dagger A}\right]$. For density matrices ρ and σ, the *trace distance* is defined as $\delta(\rho, \sigma) = \frac{1}{2}\|\rho - \sigma\|_1$. By equation (9.110) in [21], for any norm-1 vectors $|\varphi\rangle$ and $|\psi\rangle$,

$$\delta(|\varphi\rangle\langle\varphi|, |\psi\rangle\langle\psi|) \leq \||\varphi\rangle - |\psi\rangle\| . \tag{5}$$

For probability distributions p and q, we write $\delta(p, q)$ for the *total variational distance*; this is justified as $\|\rho_0 - \rho_1\|_1 = \delta(p_0, q_1)$ for $\rho_i = \sum_x p_i(x)|x\rangle\langle x|$, $i = 0, 1$. In case of a hybrid classical-quantum state, consisting of a randomized classical value x that follows a distribution p and of a quantum register W with a state ρ_W^x that depends on x, we write $[x, W] = \sum_x p(x)|x\rangle\langle x| \otimes \rho_W^x$.[2] When the distribution p and the density operators ρ_W^x are implicitly given by a game (or experiment) $\mathcal{G}$ then we may write $[x, W]_{\mathcal{G}}$, in particular when considering and comparing different such games. For instance, we write $\delta\big([x, W]_{\mathcal{G}}, [x, W]_{\mathcal{G}'}\big)$ for the trace distance of the respective density matrices in game $\mathcal{G}$ and in game $\mathcal{G}'$.

2.2   The (Compressed) Random Oracle

The (Quantum) Random-Oracle Model. In the *random-oracle model*, a cryptographic hash function $H : \mathcal{X} \to \mathcal{Y}$ is treated as an oracle RO that the adversary needs to query on $x \in \mathcal{X}$ to learn $H(x)$. The random oracle answers these queries by means of a uniformly random function $H : \mathcal{X} \to \mathcal{Y}$. For concreteness, we restrict here to $\mathcal{Y} = \{0, 1\}^n$; on the other hand, we do not further specify the domain $\mathcal{X}$ except that we assume it to have an efficiently computable order, so one may well think of $\mathcal{X}$ as $\mathcal{X} = \{1, \ldots, M\}$ for some positive $M \in \mathbb{Z}$ or as bit strings of bounded size. We then often write $RO(x)$ instead of $H(x)$ to emphasize that $H(x)$ is obtained by querying the random oracle and/or to emphasize the randomized nature of H. In the *quantum* random oracle model (QROM), a quantum algorithm $\mathcal{A}$ may make *superposition queries* to RO, meaning that the oracle acts as unitary $|x\rangle|y\rangle \mapsto |x\rangle|y \oplus H(x)\rangle$. The QROM still admits *classical*

---

[2] In this equality and at other occasions, we use the same letter, here x, for the considered *random variable* as well as for a *particular value*.

queries, which are queries with the query register set to $|x\rangle|0\rangle$ for some x, and the second register is subsequently measured to obtain the classical output y.

The Compressed Oracle. We recall here (some version of) the *compressed oracle*, as introduced in [27], which offers a powerful tool for QROM proofs. For this purpose, we consider the multi-register $D = (D_x)_{x \in \mathcal{X}}$, where the state space of D_x is given by $\mathcal{H}_{D_x} = \mathbb{C}[\{0,1\}^n \cup \{\perp\}]$, meaning that it is spanned by an orthonormal set of vectors $|y\rangle$ labelled by $y \in \{0,1\}^n \cup \{\perp\}$. The initial state is set to be $|\perp\rangle_D := \bigotimes_x |\perp\rangle_{D_x}$. Consider the unitary F defined by

$$F|\perp\rangle = |\phi_0\rangle, \quad F|\phi_0\rangle = |\perp\rangle \quad \text{and} \quad F|\phi_y\rangle = |\phi_y\rangle \; \forall y \in \{0,1\}^n \setminus \{0^n\},$$

where $|\phi_y\rangle := H|y\rangle$ with H the Hadamard transform on $\mathbb{C}[\{0,1\}^n] = (\mathbb{C}^2)^{\otimes n}$. Exploiting the relation $|y\rangle = 2^{-n/2} \sum_\eta (-1)^{\eta \cdot y} |\phi_\eta\rangle$, we see that

$$F|y\rangle = |y\rangle + 2^{-n/2} (|\perp\rangle - |\phi_0\rangle). \tag{6}$$

When the oracle is queried, a unitary O_{XYD}, acting on the query registers X and Y and the oracle register D, is applied, given by

$$O_{XYD} = \sum_x |x\rangle\langle x|_X \otimes O^x_{YD_x} \quad \text{with} \quad O^x_{YD_x} = F_{D_x} \text{CNOT}_{YD_x} F_{D_x}, \tag{7}$$

where $\text{CNOT}|y\rangle|y_x\rangle = |y \oplus y_x\rangle|y_x\rangle$ for $y, y_x \in \{0,1\}^n$, and $\text{CNOT}|y\rangle|\perp\rangle = |y\rangle|\perp\rangle$. As long as no other operations are applied to the state of D, the compressed oracle exactly simulates the quantum random oracle. Also, the support of the state of D_x then remains orthogonal to $|\phi_0\rangle$ for all x. However, these properties may change when, e.g., measurements are performed on D. The oracle may then behave differently than the quantum random oracle, and the state of D may have a non-trivial overlap with $|\phi_0\rangle$. Note that, by the convention on CNOT to act trivially for control registers in state $|\perp\rangle$, it holds that $O^x_{YD_x}|y\rangle|\phi_0\rangle = |y\rangle|\phi_0\rangle$.

We briefly discuss the behavior of the compressed oracle under a *classical* query, i.e., a query with the XY-register in state $|x\rangle|0\rangle$ for some x, and where the Y-register is then measured after the application of O_{XYD}. If D_x is in state ρ then a classical query on x will give response h with probability $\text{tr}(|h\rangle\langle h|F\rho F)$ — unless ρ has nontrivial overlap with $|\phi_0\rangle$ and $h = 0$, in which a classical query on x will give response 0 with probability $\text{tr}(|0\rangle\langle 0|F\rho F) + \text{tr}(|\perp\rangle\langle\perp|F\rho F)$. The latter is an artifact of CNOT defined to act trivially on $|y\rangle|\perp\rangle$, which has the effect that $|\phi_0\rangle$ is treated like $F|0\rangle$. We note that, for any $h \in \mathcal{Y}$ and $\rho = |h\rangle\langle h|$,

$$\text{tr}(|h\rangle\langle h|F\rho F) = |\langle h|F|h\rangle|^2 = \left|\langle h|\left(|h\rangle + 2^{-n/2}(|\perp\rangle - |\phi_0\rangle)\right)\right|^2$$

$$= \left|1 - 2^{-n/2}\langle h|\phi_0\rangle\right|^2 = \left|1 - 2^{-n}\right|^2 \geq 1 - 2 \cdot 2^{-n}. \tag{8}$$

Vice-versa, after a classical query on x with response h, the state of D_x is $F|h\rangle$ — unless, the state of D_x prior to the query had a nontrivial overlap with $|\phi_0\rangle$ and $h = 0$, then the state after the query is supported by $F|0\rangle$ and $F|\perp\rangle = |\phi_0\rangle$.

Efficient Representation of the Compressed Oracle. Following [27], one can make the (above variant of the) compressed oracle efficient. Indeed, by applying the standard classical sparse encoding to quantum states with the right choice of basis, one can *efficiently* maintain the state D, compute the unitary O_{XYD}, and extract information from D. More details are given in Appendix B of the full version. For simplicity, we mostly use the inefficient variant in this paper.

3   Main Technical Result: A Commutator Bound

3.1   Setup and the Technical Statement

Throughout this section, we consider an arbitrary but fixed relation $R \subset \mathcal{X} \times \{0,1\}^n$. A crucial parameter of the relation R is the number of y's that fulfill the relation together with x, maximized over all possible $x \in \mathcal{X}$:

$$\Gamma_R := \max_{x \in \mathcal{X}} \left| \{ y \in \{0,1\}^n | (x,y) \in R \} \right| . \tag{9}$$

Given the relation R, we consider the following projectors:

$$\Pi_{D_x}^x := \sum_{\substack{y \text{ s.t.} \\ (x,y) \in R}} |y\rangle\langle y|_{D_x} \quad \text{and} \quad \Pi_D^{\emptyset} := \mathbb{1}_D - \sum_{x \in \mathcal{X}} \Pi_{D_x}^x = \bigotimes_{x \in \mathcal{X}} \bar{\Pi}_{D_x}^x \tag{10}$$

with $\bar{\Pi}_{D_x}^x := \mathbb{1}_{D_x} - \Pi_{D_x}^x$. Informally, $\Pi_{D_x}^x$ checks whether register D_x contains a value $y \neq \perp$ such that $(x,y) \in R$. We then define the measurement $\mathcal{M} = \mathcal{M}^R$ to be given by the projectors

$$\Sigma^x := \bigotimes_{x' < x} \bar{\Pi}_{D_{x'}}^{x'} \otimes \Pi_{D_x}^x \quad \text{and} \quad \Sigma^{\emptyset} := \mathbb{1} - \sum_{x'} \Sigma^{x'} = \bigotimes_{x'} \bar{\Pi}_{D_{x'}}^{x'} = \Pi^{\emptyset} \tag{11}$$

where x ranges over all $x \in \mathcal{X}$. Informally, a measurement outcome x means that register D_x is the first that contains a value y such that $(x,y) \in R$; outcome $\emptyset$ means that no register contains such a value. For technical reasons, we consider the *purified* measurement $M_{DP} = M_{DP}^R \in \mathcal{L}(\mathcal{H}_D \otimes \mathcal{H}_R)$ given by the unitary[3]

$$M_{DP} := \sum_{x \in \mathcal{X} \cup \{\emptyset\}} \Sigma^x \otimes \mathsf{X}^x : |\varphi\rangle_D |w\rangle_P \mapsto \sum_{x \in \mathcal{X} \cup \{\emptyset\}} \Sigma^x |\varphi\rangle_D |w+x\rangle_P . \tag{12}$$

The following main technical result is a bound on the norm of $[O_{XYD}, M_{DP}]$.

Theorem 1. *For any relation $R \subset \mathcal{X} \times \{0,1\}^n$ and Γ_R as defined in Eq. (9), the purified measurement M_{DP} defined in Eq. (12) almost commutes with the oracle unitary O_{XYD}:*

$$\| [O_{XYD}, M_{DP}] \| \leq 8 \cdot 2^{-n/2} \sqrt{2\Gamma_R} .$$

---

[3] Both in X^x and in $w+x$ we understand $x \in \mathcal{X} \cup \{\emptyset\}$ to be encoded as an element in $\mathbb{Z}/(|\mathcal{X}|+1)\mathbb{Z}$, $\dim(\mathcal{H}_P) = d := |\mathcal{X}| + 1$, and $\mathsf{X} \in \mathcal{L}(\mathcal{H}_P)$ is the generalized Pauli of order d that maps $|w\rangle$ to $|w+1\rangle$.

We note that Lemma 8 in [9] (with the subsequent discussion there) also provides a bound on a commutator involving O_{XYD}; however, there are various differences that make the two bounds incomparable. E.g., we consider a specific *measurement* whereas Lemma 8 in [9] is for a rather general *projector*. See further down for a comparison with Lemma 39 in [27].

Corollary 2. *For any state vector* $|\psi\rangle \in \mathcal{H}_{WXYDP}$, *with W an arbitrary additional register,* $|\psi'\rangle := O_{XYD}M_{DP}|\psi\rangle$ *and* $|\psi''\rangle := M_{DP}O_{XYD}|\psi\rangle$ *satisfy*

$$\delta\big(|\psi'\rangle\langle\psi'|, |\psi''\rangle\langle\psi''|\big) \leq 8 \cdot 2^{-n/2}\sqrt{2\Gamma_R}\,.$$

The same holds for mixed states $\rho' := O_{XYD}M_{DP}\rho M_{DP}^{\dagger}O_{XYD}^{\dagger}$ *and* $\rho'' := M_{DP}O_{XYD}\rho O_{XYD}^{\dagger}M_{DP}^{\dagger}$.

Proof. By elementary properties and applying Theorem 1, we have that

$$\big\||\psi'\rangle - |\psi''\rangle\big\| \leq \big\|[O_{XYD}, M_{DP}]\big\| \leq 8 \cdot 2^{-n/2}\sqrt{2\Gamma_R}\,,$$

and the claim on the trace distance then follows from (5). The claim for mixed states follows from purification. $\qquad\square$

3.2   The Proof

We prove the Theorem 1 by means of the following two lemmas.

Lemma 2. *Let F and $O_{YD_x}^x$ be the unitaries introduced in Sect. 2.2, and let $\Pi_{D_x}^x$ and $\Pi_D^\emptyset$ be as in (10). Set $\Gamma_x := \big|\{y \in \{0,1\}^n \,|\, (x,y) \in R\}\big|$. Then*

$$\big\|[F_{D_x}, \Pi_{D_x}^x]\big\| \leq 2^{-n/2}\sqrt{2\Gamma_x}\,, \qquad \text{as well as}$$

$$\big\|[O_{YD_x}^x, \Pi_{D_x}^x]\big\| \leq 2 \cdot 2^{-n/2}\sqrt{2\Gamma_x} \quad \text{and} \quad \big\|[O_{YD_x}^x, \Pi_D^\emptyset]\big\| \leq 2 \cdot 2^{-n/2}\sqrt{2\Gamma_x}\,.$$

The bound on $\|[F, \Pi^x]\|$ can be considered a compact reformulation of Lemma 39 in [27]. We state it here in this form, and (re-)prove it in Appendix C of the full version, for convenience and completeness. The conceptually new and technically challenging ingredient to the proof of Theorem 1 is Lemma 3 below.[4]

Lemma 3. *The purified measurement M_{DP} defined in Eq. (12) satisfies*

$$\big\|[F_{D_x}, M_{DP}]\big\| \leq 3\big\|[F_{D_x}, \Pi_D^x]\big\| + \big\|[F_{D_x}, \Pi_D^\emptyset]\big\| \qquad \qquad \text{and}$$

$$\big\|[O_{YD_x}^x, M_{DP}]\big\| \leq 3\big\|[O_{YD_x}^x, \Pi_D^x]\big\| + \big\|[O_{YD_x}^x, \Pi_D^\emptyset]\big\|\,.$$

---

[4] The challenging aspect of Lemma 3 is that M_{DP} is made up of an exponential number of projectors Π^x, and thus the obvious approach of using triangle inequality leads to an exponential blow-up of the error term.

Proof. We do the proof for the second claim. The first is proven exactly the same way: the sole property we exploit from $O^x_{YD_x}$ is that it acts only on the D_x register within D, which holds for F_{D_x} as well. Let

$$\bar{\Delta}^\xi := \bigotimes_{\xi' < \xi} \bar{\Pi}^{\xi'}_{D_{\xi'}},$$

be the projection that accepts if no register $D_{\xi'}$ with $\xi' < \xi$ contains a value y' with $(\xi', y') \in R$, and let Δ^ξ be the complement. We then have, using that Π^ξ and $\bar{\Delta}^\xi$ act on disjoint registers,

$$\Sigma^\xi = \bar{\Delta}^\xi \otimes \Pi^\xi = \Pi^\xi \bar{\Delta}^\xi = \bar{\Delta}^\xi \Pi^\xi. \tag{13}$$

We also observe that, with respect to the Loewner order, $\bar{\Delta}^{\xi'} \geq \bar{\Delta}^\xi$ for $\xi' < \xi$. Taking it as understood that $O^x_{YD_x}$ acts on registers Y and D_x, we can write

$$[O^x, M_{DP}] = \sum_\xi [O^x, \Sigma^\xi] \otimes \mathsf{X}^\xi + [O^x, \Sigma^\emptyset] \otimes \mathsf{X}^\emptyset. \tag{14}$$

Exploiting basic properties of the operator norm and recalling that $\Sigma^\emptyset = \Pi^\emptyset_D$, we see that the norm of the last term is bounded by $\|[O^x, \Sigma^\emptyset]\| = \|[O^x, \Pi^\emptyset]\|$.

To deal with the sum in (14), we use $\mathbb{1} = \Delta^\xi + \bar{\Delta}^\xi$ to further decompose

$$[O^x, \Sigma^\xi] = \bar{\Delta}^\xi [O^x, \Sigma^\xi] \bar{\Delta}^\xi + \bar{\Delta}^\xi O^x, \Sigma^\xi] \Delta^\xi + \Delta^\xi [O^x, \Sigma^\xi] \bar{\Delta}^\xi + \Delta^\xi [O^x, \Sigma^\xi] \Delta^\xi. \tag{15}$$

We now analyze the four different terms. For the first one, using (13) we see that

$$\bar{\Delta}^\xi [O^x, \Sigma^\xi] \bar{\Delta}^\xi = \bar{\Delta}^\xi (O^x \Sigma^\xi - \Sigma^\xi O^x) \bar{\Delta}^\xi = \bar{\Delta}^\xi O^x \Pi^\xi \bar{\Delta}^\xi - \bar{\Delta}^\xi \Pi^\xi O^x \bar{\Delta}^\xi = \bar{\Delta}^\xi [O^x, \Pi^\xi] \bar{\Delta}^\xi,$$

which vanishes for $\xi \neq x$, since then O^x and Π^ξ act on different registers and thus commute. For $\xi = x$, its norm is upper bounded by $\|[O^x, \Pi^x]\|$.

We now consider the second term; the third one can be treated the same way by symmetry, and the fourth one vanishes, as will become clear immediately from below. Using (13) and $\bar{\Delta}^\xi \Delta^\xi = 0$, so that $\bar{\Delta}^\xi \Sigma^\xi = 0$, we have

$$\bar{\Delta}^\xi [O^x, \Sigma^\xi] \Delta^\xi = \bar{\Delta}^\xi (O^x \Sigma^\xi - \Sigma^\xi O^x) \Delta^\xi = \Sigma^\xi O^x \Delta^\xi =: N_\xi. \tag{16}$$

Looking at (14), we want to control the norm of the sum $N := \sum_\xi N_\xi \otimes \mathsf{X}^\xi$. To this end, we show that N_ξ and $N_{\xi'}$ have orthogonal images and orthogonal support, i.e., $N^\dagger_{\xi'} N_\xi = 0 = N_{\xi'} N^\dagger_\xi$, for all $\xi \neq \xi'$. We first observe that if $x \geq \xi$ then O^x commutes with Δ^ξ, since they act on different registers then, and thus

$$N_\xi = \Sigma^\xi O^x \Delta^\xi = \Sigma^\xi \Delta^\xi O^x = \Pi^\xi \bar{\Delta}^\xi \Delta^\xi O^x = 0,$$

exploiting once more that $\bar{\Delta}^\xi \Delta^\xi = 0$. Therefore, we only need to consider $N_\xi, N_{\xi'}$ for $\xi, \xi' > x$ (see Fig. 1 top left), where we may assume $\xi > \xi'$. For the orthogonality of the images, we observe that

$$\Pi^{\xi'} \bar{\Delta}^\xi = 0 \tag{17}$$

by definition of $\bar\Delta^\xi$ as a tensor product with $\bar\Pi^{\xi'}$ being one of the components. Therefore,

$$(\Sigma^{\xi'})^\dagger \Sigma^\xi = \Sigma^{\xi'} \Sigma^\xi = \bar\Delta^{\xi'} \Pi^{\xi'} \bar\Delta^\xi \Pi^\xi = 0,$$

and $N_{\xi'}^\dagger N_\xi = 0$ follows directly (see also Fig. 1 top right). For the orthogonality of the supports, we recall that $\bar\Delta^{\xi'} \geq \bar\Delta^\xi$, and thus $\Delta^{\xi'} \leq \Delta^\xi$, from which it follows that $\Delta^\xi \Delta^{\xi'} = \Delta^{\xi'}$. $N_{\xi'} N_\xi^\dagger = 0$ then follows by exploiting (17) again (see Fig. 1 bottom).

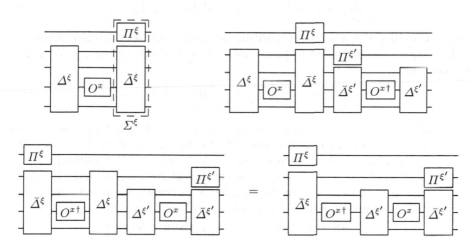

Fig. 1. Operators N_ξ (top left), $N_{\xi'}^\dagger N_\xi$ (top right), and $N_{\xi'} N_\xi^\dagger$ (bottom), for $x < \xi' < \xi$.

These orthogonality properties for the images and supports of the N_ξ immediately extend to $N_\xi \otimes \mathsf{X}^\xi$, so we have

$$\|N\| \leq \max_{\xi > x} \|N_\xi \otimes \mathsf{X}^\xi\| \leq \max_{\xi > x} \|N_\xi\|$$

by Lemma 1. Recall from (16) that $N_\xi = \bar\Delta^\xi [\Sigma^\xi, O^x] \Delta^\xi$. Furthermore, we exploit that, by definition, Σ^ξ is in tensor-product form and O^x acts trivially on all components in this tensor product except for the component $\bar\Pi^x$, so that $[\Sigma^\xi, O^x] = [\bar\Pi^x, O^x]$ by property (4). Thus, $\|N_\xi\| \leq \|[\Sigma^\xi, O^x]\| = \|[\bar\Pi^x, O^x]\| = \|[\Pi^x, O^x]\|$. Using the triangle inequality with respect to the sum versus the last term in (14), and another triangle inequality with respect to the decomposition (15), we obtain the claimed inequality. $\qquad\square$

The proof of Theorem 1 is now an easy consequence.

Proof (of Theorem 1). Since O_{XYD} is a control unitary $O_{XYD} = \sum_x |x\rangle\langle x| \otimes O_{YD_x}^x$, controlled by $|x\rangle$), while M_{DP} does not act on register X, it follows that

$$\|[O_{XYD}, M_{DP}]\| \leq \max_x \|[O_{YD_x}^x, M_{DP}]\|.$$

The claim now follows by combining Lemma 3 with Lemma 2. $\qquad\square$

3.3 A First Immediate Application

As an immediate application of the commutator bound of Theorem 1, we can easily derive the following generic query-complexity bound for finding x with $(x, H(x)) \in R$ and Γ_R as defined in Eq. (9). Applied to $R = \mathcal{X} \times \{0^n\}$, where $\Gamma_R = 1$, we recover the famous lower bound for search in a random function.

Proposition 1. *For any algorithm $\mathcal{A}$ that makes q queries to the random oracle RO,*

$$\Pr_{x \leftarrow \mathcal{A}^{RO}} [(x, RO(x)) \in R] \leq 152(q+1)^2 \Gamma_R / 2^n . \tag{18}$$

Proof. Consider the modified algorithm $\mathcal{A}'$ that runs $\mathcal{A}$ to obtain output x, makes a query to obtain $RO(x)$ and outputs $(x, RO(x))$. By Lemma 5 in [27], we have that[5]

$$\sqrt{\Pr_{x \leftarrow \mathcal{A}'^H} [(x, RO(x)) \in R]} \leq \sqrt{\Pr_{x' \leftarrow G^R} [x' \neq \emptyset]} + 2^{-n/2}, \tag{19}$$

where G^R is the following procedure/game: (1) run $\mathcal{A}'$ using the compressed oracle, and (2) apply the measurement $\mathcal{M}^R$ to obtain $x' \in \mathcal{X} \cup \{\emptyset\}$, which is the same as preparing a register P, applying $M_{DP} = M_{DP}^R$, and measuring P.

In other words, writing $|\psi\rangle_{WXY}$ for the initial state of $\mathcal{A}'$ and V_{WXY} for the unitary applied between any two queries of $\mathcal{A}'$ (which we may assume to be fixed), and setting $U_{WXYD} := V_{WXY} O_{XYD}$, $\Pi_P := \mathbb{1}_P - |\emptyset\rangle\langle\emptyset|_P$ and $|\Psi\rangle := |\psi\rangle_{WXY} \otimes |\perp\rangle_D^{\otimes |\mathcal{X}|} \otimes |0\rangle_P$, we have, omitting register subscripts,

$$\sqrt{\Pr[x' \neq \emptyset]} = \left\| \Pi M U^{q+1} |\Psi\rangle \right\|$$
$$\leq \sum_{i=1}^{q+1} \left\| \Pi U^{i-1} [M, U] U^{q+1-i} |\Psi\rangle \right\| + \left\| \Pi U^{q+1} M |\Psi\rangle \right\|$$
$$\leq (q+1) \left\| [M_{DP}, O_{XYD}] \right\| + \left\| \Pi_P M_{DP} |\Psi\rangle \right\|$$
$$= (q+1) \left\| [M_{DP}, O_{XYD}] \right\| \leq 8 \cdot 2^{-n/2} (q+1) \sqrt{2\Gamma_R} ,$$

where the last equation exploits that $\Pi_P M_{DP}$ applied to $|\perp\rangle_D^{\otimes |\mathcal{X}|} \otimes |0\rangle_P$ vanishes, and the final inequality is by Theorem 1. Observing $(8\sqrt{2}+1)^2 = 129 + 16\sqrt{2} \approx 151.6$ finishes the proof. □

4 Extraction of Random-Oracle Based Commitments

Throughout this Sect. 4, let $f : \mathcal{X} \times \mathcal{Y} \to \mathcal{T}$ be an arbitrary fixed function with $\mathcal{Y} = \{0, 1\}^n$. For a hash function $H : \mathcal{X} \to \mathcal{Y}$, which will then be modelled as a random oracle RO, we will think and sometimes speak of $f(x, H(x))$ as a *commitment* of x (though we do not require it to be a commitment scheme in the strict sense). Typical examples are $f(x, y) = y$ and $f(x, y) = \mathsf{Enc}_{pk}(x; y)$, where the latter is the encryption of x under public key pk with randomness y.

---

[5] Lemma 5 in [27] applies to an algorithm $\mathcal{A}$ that outputs both x and what is supposed to be its hash value; this is why we need to do this additional query.

4.1 Informal Problem Description

Consider a query algorithm $\mathcal{A}^{RO}$ in the random oracle model, which, during the course of its run, announces some $t \in \mathcal{T}$. This t is supposed to be $t = f(x, RO(x))$ for some x, and, indeed, $\mathcal{A}^{RO}$ may possibly reveal x later on. Intuitively, for the required relation between x and t to hold, we expect that $\mathcal{A}^{RO}$ *first* has to query RO on x and only *then* can output t; thus, one may hope to be able to extract x from RO *early on*, i.e., at the time $\mathcal{A}^{RO}$ announces t.

This is clearly true when $\mathcal{A}$ is restricted to classical queries, simply by checking all the queries made so far. This observation was first made and utilized by Pass [22] and only requires looking at the query transcript (it can be done in the *non-programmable* ROM). As the extractor does not change the course of the experiment, it works on-the-fly.

In the setting considered here, $\mathcal{A}^{RO}$ may query the random oracle in *superposition* over various choices of x, making it impossible to maintain a classical query transcript. On the positive side, since the output t is required to be classical, $\mathcal{A}^{RO}$ has to perform a measurement before announcing t, enforcing such a superposition to collapse.[6] We show here that early extraction of x is indeed possible in this quantum setting as well.

Note that if the goal is to extract *the same* x as $\mathcal{A}$ will (potentially) output, which is what we aim for, then we must naturally assume that it is hard for $\mathcal{A}$ to find $x \neq x'$ that are both consistent with the same t, i.e., we must assume the commitment to be binding. Formally, we will think of $\Gamma(f)$ and $\Gamma'(f)$, defined as follows, to be small compared to 2^n. When f is fixed, we simply write Γ and Γ'.

Definition 2. *For* $f : \mathcal{X} \times \{0,1\}^n \to \mathcal{T}$, *let* $\Gamma(f) := \max_{x,t} |\{y \mid f(x,y) = t\}|$ *and* $\Gamma'(f) := \max_{x \neq x', y'} |\{y \mid f(x,y) = f(x',y')\}|$.

For the example $f(x,y) = y$, we have $\Gamma(f) = 1 = \Gamma'(f)$. For the example $f(x,y) = \mathsf{Enc}_{pk}(x; y)$, they both depend on the choice of the encryption scheme but typically are small, e.g. $\Gamma(f) = 1$ if Enc is injective as a function of the randomness y and $\Gamma'(f) = 0$ if there are no decryption errors.

4.2 The Extractable RO-Simulator $\mathcal{S}$

Towards formalizing the above goal, we introduce a simulator $\mathcal{S}$ that replaces RO and tries to extract x early on, right after $\mathcal{A}$ announces t. In more detail, $\mathcal{S}$ acts as a black-box oracle with two interfaces, the *RO-interface* $\mathcal{S}.RO$ providing access to the simulated random oracle, and the *extraction interface* $\mathcal{S}.E$ providing the functionality to extract x early on (see Fig. 3, left). In principle, both interfaces can be accessed quantumly, i.e., in superposition over different classical inputs, but in our applications we only use classical access to $\mathcal{S}.E$. We stress that $\mathcal{S}$ is per-se *stateful* and thus may change its behavior from query to query.

Formally, the considered simulator $\mathcal{S}$ is defined to work as follows. It simulates the random oracle and answers queries to $\mathcal{S}.RO$ by means of the compressed

---

[6] We can also think of this measurement being done by the interface that receives t.

oracle. For the $\mathcal{S}.E$ interface, upon a classical input $t \in \mathcal{T}$, $\mathcal{S}$ applies the measurement $\mathcal{M}^t := \mathcal{M}^{R_t}$ from (11) for the relation $R_t := \{(x,y) \mid f(x,y) = t\}$ to obtain $\hat{x} \in \mathcal{X} \cup \{\emptyset\}$, which it then outputs (see Fig. 2). In case of a *quantum* query to $\mathcal{S}.E$, the above is performed coherently: given the query registers TP, the unitary $\sum_t |t\rangle\langle t|_T \otimes M_{DP}^{R_t}$ is applied to TPD, and TP is then returned.

The extractable RO-oracle $\mathcal{S}$:

Initialization: $\mathcal{S}$ prepares its internal register D to be in state $|\bot\rangle_D := \bigotimes_x |\bot\rangle_{D_x}$.

$\mathcal{S}.RO$-query: Upon a (quantum) RO-query, with query registers XY, $\mathcal{S}$ applies O_{XYD} to registers XYD.

$\mathcal{S}.E$-query: Upon a classical extraction-query with input t, $\mathcal{S}$ applies $\mathcal{M}^t$ to D and returns the outcome $\hat{x}$.

Fig. 2. The (inefficient version of) simulator $\mathcal{S}$, restricted to classical extraction queries.

As described here, the simulator $\mathcal{S}$ is inefficient, having to maintain an exponential number of qubits; however, using the sparse representation of the internal state D, as discussed in Appendix B of the full version, $\mathcal{S}$ can well be made efficient without affecting its query-behavior (see Theorem 2 for details).

The following statement captures the core properties of $\mathcal{S}$. We refer to two subsequent queries as being *independent* if they can in principle be performed in either order, i.e., if the input to one query does not depend on the output of the other. More formally, e.g., two $\mathcal{S}.RO$ queries are independent if they can be captured by first preparing the two in-/output registers XY and $X'Y'$, and then doing the two respective queries with XY and $X'Y'$. The commutativity claim then means that the order does not matter. Furthermore, whenever we speak of a *classical* query (to $\mathcal{S}.RO$ or to $\mathcal{S}.E$), we consider the obvious classical variant of the considered query, with a classical input and a classical response. Finally, the almost commutativity claims are in terms of the trace distance of the (possibly quantum) output of any algorithm interacting with $\mathcal{S}$ arbitrarily and doing the two considered independent queries in one or the other order.

Theorem 2. *The extractable RO-simulator $\mathcal{S}$ constructed above, with interfaces $\mathcal{S}.RO$ and $\mathcal{S}.E$, satisfies the following properties.*

1. *If $\mathcal{S}.E$ is unused, $\mathcal{S}$ is perfectly indistinguishable from the random oracle RO.*
2.a *Any two subsequent independent queries to $\mathcal{S}.RO$ commute. Thus, two subsequent classical $\mathcal{S}.RO$-queries with the same input x give identical responses.*
2.b *Any two subsequent independent queries to $\mathcal{S}.E$ commute. Thus, two subsequent classical $\mathcal{S}.E$-queries with the same input t give identical responses.*
2.c *Any two subsequent independent queries to $\mathcal{S}.E$ and $\mathcal{S}.RO$ ε-almost-commute with $\varepsilon = 8\sqrt{2\Gamma(f)/2^n}$.*

3.a Any classical query $S.RO(x)$ is idempotent.[7]
3.b Any classical query $S.E(t)$ is idempotent.
4.a If $\hat{x} = S.E(t)$ and $\hat{h} = S.RO(\hat{x})$ are two subsequent classical queries then

$$\Pr[f(\hat{x}, \hat{h}) \neq t \wedge \hat{x} \neq \emptyset] \leq \Pr[f(\hat{x}, \hat{h}) \neq t \mid \hat{x} \neq \emptyset] \leq 2 \cdot 2^{-n} \Gamma(f) \qquad (20)$$

4.b If $h = S.RO(x)$ and $\hat{x} = S.E(f(x, h))$ are two subsequent classical queries such that no prior query to $S.E$ has been made, then

$$\Pr[\hat{x} = \emptyset] \leq 2 \cdot 2^{-n}. \qquad (21)$$

Furthermore, the total runtime of S, when implemented using the sparse representation of the compressed oracle described in Sect. 2.2, is bounded as

$$T_S = O\big(q_{RO} \cdot q_E \cdot \mathrm{Time}[f] + q_{RO}^2\big),$$

where q_E and q_{RO} are the number of queries to $S.E$ and $S.RO$, respectively .

Proof. All the properties follow rather directly by construction of S. Indeed, without $S.E$-queries, S is simply the compressed oracle, known to be perfectly indistinguishable from the random oracle, confirming 1. Property 2.a follows because the unitaries O_{XYD} and $O_{X'Y'D}$, acting on the same register D but on distinct query registers, are both controlled unitaries with control register D, conjugated by a fixed unitary $(F^{\otimes|\mathcal{X}|})$. They thus commute. For 2.b, the claim follows because the unitaries M_{DP}^t and $M_{DP'}^{t'}$ commute, as they are both controlled unitaries with control register D. 2.c is a direct consequence of our main technical result Theorem 1 (in the form of Corollary 2). 3.a follows because a classical $S.RO$ query with input x acts as a projective measurement on register D_x, which is, as any projective measurement, idempotent. Thus, so is the measurement $\mathcal{M}^t$, confirming 3.b.

To prove 4.a, consider the state $\rho_{D_{\hat{x}}}$ of register $D_{\hat{x}}$ after the measurement $\mathcal{M}^t$ that is performed by the extraction query $\hat{x} = S.E(t)$, assuming $\hat{x} \neq \emptyset$. Let $|\psi\rangle$ be a purification of $\rho_{D_{\hat{x}}}$. By definition of $\mathcal{M}^t$, it holds that $\Pi_{D_{\hat{x}}}^{\hat{x}} |\psi\rangle = |\psi\rangle$. Then, understanding that all operators act on register $D_{\hat{x}}$, by definition of $\bar{\Pi}^{\hat{x}}$ the probability of interest is bounded as[8]

$$\Pr[f(\hat{x}, \hat{h}) \neq t \mid \hat{x} \neq \emptyset] \leq \left\| \bar{\Pi}^{\hat{x}} F |\psi\rangle \right\|^2 = \left\| \bar{\Pi}^{\hat{x}} F \Pi^{\hat{x}} |\psi\rangle \right\|^2 \leq \left\| \bar{\Pi}^{\hat{x}} F \Pi^{\hat{x}} \right\|^2$$
$$\leq \left\| [F, \Pi^{\hat{x}}] \right\|^2,$$

where the last inequality exploits that $\bar{\Pi}^{\hat{x}} \Pi^{\hat{x}} = 0$. The claim now follows from Lemma 2.

For 4.b, we first observe that, given that there were no prior extraction queries, the state of D_x before the $h = S.RO(x)$ query has no overlap with

---

[7] I.e., applying it twice has the same effect on the state of S as applying it once.
[8] The first inequality is an artefact of the $|\perp\rangle\langle\perp|$-term in $\bar{\Pi}^{\hat{x}}$ contributing to the probability of $\hat{h} = 0$, as discussed in Sect. 2.2.

$|\phi_0\rangle$, and thus the state after the query is $F|h\rangle$ (see the discussion above Equation (8)). For the purpose of the argument, instead of applying the measurement $\mathcal{M}^{f(x,h)}$ to answer the $\mathcal{S}.E(f(x,h))$ query, we may equivalently consider a measurement in the basis $\{|\mathbf{y}\rangle\}$, and then set $\hat{x}$ to be the smallest element $\mathcal{X}$ so that $f(\hat{x}, y_{\hat{x}}) = t := f(x,h)$, with $\hat{x} = \emptyset$ if no such element exists. Then,

$$\Pr[\hat{x} \neq \emptyset] = \Pr[\exists \xi : f(\xi, y_\xi) = t] \geq \Pr[f(x, y_x) = t]$$
$$\geq \Pr[y_x = h] = |\langle h|F|h\rangle|^2 \geq 1 - 2 \cdot 2^{-n}$$

where the last two (in)equalities are by Eq. (8).

$\square$

4.3   Two More Properties of $\mathcal{S}$

On top of the above basic features of our extractable RO-simulator $\mathcal{S}$, we show the following two additional, more technical, properties, which in essence capture that the extraction interface cannot be used to bypass query hardness results.

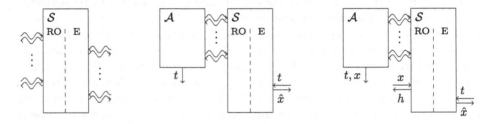

Fig. 3. The extractable RO-simulator $\mathcal{S}$, with its $\mathcal{S}.RO$ and $\mathcal{S}.E$ interfaces, distinguished here by queries from the left and right (left), and the games considered in Proposition 2 (middle) and 3 (right) for $\ell = 1$. Waved arrows denote quantum queries, straight arrows denote classical queries.

The first property is easiest to understand in the context of the example $f(x, y) = y$, where $\mathcal{S}.E(t)$ tries to extract a hash-preimage of t, and where the relations R and R' in Proposition 2 below then coincide. In this case, recall from Proposition 1 that, informally, if Γ_R is small then it is hard to find $x \in \mathcal{X}$ so that $t := RO(x)$ satisfies $(x, t) \in R$. The statement below ensures that this hardness cannot be bypassed by first selecting a "good" hash value t and then trying to extract a preimage by means of $\mathcal{S}.E$ (Fig. 3, middle).

Proposition 2. *Let $R' \subseteq \mathcal{X} \times \mathcal{T}$ be a relation. Consider a query algorithm $\mathcal{A}$ that makes q queries to the $\mathcal{S}.RO$ interface of $\mathcal{S}$ but no query to $\mathcal{S}.E$, outputting some $\mathbf{t} \in \mathcal{T}^\ell$. For each i, let $\hat{x}_i$ then be obtained by making an additional query to $\mathcal{S}.E$ on input t_i (see Fig. 3, middle). Then*

$$\Pr_{\substack{\mathbf{t} \leftarrow \mathcal{A}^{\mathcal{S}.RO} \\ \hat{x}_i \leftarrow \mathcal{S}.E(t_i)}} [\exists i : (\hat{x}_i, t_i) \in R'] \leq 128 \cdot q^2 \Gamma_R / 2^n ,$$

where $R \subseteq \mathcal{X} \times \mathcal{Y}$ is the relation $(x, y) \in R \Leftrightarrow (x, f(x, y)) \in R'$ and Γ_R as in (9).

Proof. The considered experiment is like the experiment G^R in the proof of Proposition 1, the only difference being that in G^R the measurement $\mathcal{M}^R$ is applied to register D to obtain x' (see Fig. 4, middle), while here we have ℓ measurements $\mathcal{M}^{t_i}$ that are applied to obtain $\hat{x}_i$ (see Fig. 4, left). Since all measurements are defined by means of projections that are diagonal in the same basis $\{|\mathbf{y}\rangle\}$ with $|\mathbf{y}\rangle$ ranging over $\mathbf{y} \in (\mathcal{Y} \cup \{\bot\})^{\mathcal{X}}$, we may equivalently measure D in that basis to obtain $\mathbf{y}$ (see Fig. 4, right), and let $\hat{x}_i$ be minimal so that $f(\hat{x}_i, y_{\hat{x}_i}) = t_i$ (and $\hat{x}_i = \emptyset$ if no such value exists), and let x' be minimal so that $(x', y_{x'}) \in R$ (and $x' = \emptyset$ if no such value exists). By the respective definitions of $\mathcal{M}_i^t$ and $\mathcal{M}^R$, both pairs of random variables $(\hat{\mathbf{x}}, \mathbf{t})$ and $(x', \mathbf{t})$ then have the same distributions as in the respective original two games. But now, we can consider their joint distribution and argue that

$$\Pr[\exists i : (\hat{x}_i, t_i) \in R'] = \Pr[\exists i : (\hat{x}_i, f(\hat{x}_i, y_{\hat{x}_i})) \in R']$$
$$= \Pr[\exists i : (\hat{x}_i, y_{\hat{x}_i}) \in R] \leq \Pr[\exists x : (x, y_x) \in R] = \Pr[x' \neq \emptyset].$$

The bound on $\Pr[x' \neq \emptyset]$ from the proof of Proposition 1 concludes the proof. $\square$

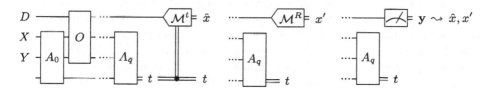

Fig. 4. Quantum circuit diagrams of the experiments in the proof of Proposition 2 for $\ell = 1$.

In a somewhat similar spirit, the following ensures that if it is hard in the QROM to find x and x' with $f(x, RO(x)) = f(x', RO(x'))$ then this hardness cannot be bypassed by, say, first choosing x, querying $h = \mathcal{S}.RO(x)$, computing $t := f(x, h)$, and then extracting $\hat{x} := \mathcal{S}.E(t)$. The latter will most likely give $\hat{x} = x$, except, intuitively, if $\mathcal{S}.RO$ has additionally been queried on a colliding x'.

Proposition 3. *Consider a query algorithm A that makes q queries to $\mathcal{S}.RO$ but no query to $\mathcal{S}.E$, outputting some $t \in \mathcal{T}$ and $x \in \mathcal{X}$. Let h then be obtained by making an additional query to $\mathcal{S}.RO$ on input x, and $\hat{x}$ by making an additional query to $\mathcal{S}.E$ on input t (see Fig. 3, right). Then*

$$\Pr_{\substack{t, x \leftarrow A^{\mathcal{S}.RO} \\ h \leftarrow \mathcal{S}.RO(x) \\ \hat{x} \leftarrow \mathcal{S}.E(t)}} [\hat{x} \neq x \wedge f(x, h) = t] \leq \frac{40e^2(q+2)^3 \Gamma'(f) + 2}{2^n}.$$

More generally, if $\mathcal{A}$ outputs ℓ-tuples $\mathbf{t} \in \mathcal{T}^\ell$ and $\mathbf{x} \in \mathcal{X}^\ell$, and $\mathbf{h} \in \mathcal{Y}^\ell$ is obtained by querying $\mathcal{S}.RO$ component-wise on $\mathbf{x}$, and $\hat{\mathbf{x}} \in (\mathcal{X} \cup \{\emptyset\})^\ell$ by querying $\mathcal{S}.E$ component-wise on $\mathbf{t}$, then

$$\Pr_{\substack{\mathbf{t},\mathbf{x} \leftarrow \mathcal{A}^{\mathcal{S}.RO} \\ \mathbf{h} \leftarrow \mathcal{S}.RO(\mathbf{x}) \\ \hat{\mathbf{x}} \leftarrow \mathcal{S}.E(\mathbf{t})}} [\exists i : \hat{x}_i \neq x_i \wedge f(x_i, h_i) = t] \leq \frac{40e^2(q + \ell + 1)^3 \Gamma'(f) + 2}{2^n}.$$

The proof is similar in spirit to the proof of Proposition 2, but relying on the hardness of collision finding rather than on (the proof of) Proposition 1, and so is moved to Appendix C in the full version.

Remark 1. The claim of Proposition 3 stays true when the queries $\mathcal{S}.RO(x_i)$ are not performed as *additional* queries *after* the run of $\mathcal{A}$ but are explicitly *among* the q queries that are performed by $\mathcal{A}$ *during* its run. Indeed we observe that the proof does not exploit that these queries are performed at the end, which additionally shows that in this case the ℓ-term on the right hand side of the bound vanishes, i.e., scales as $(q + 1)^3$ rather than as $(q + \ell + 1)^3$.

4.4 Early Extraction

We consider here the following concrete setting. Let $\mathcal{A}$ be a two-round query algorithm, interacting with the random oracle RO and behaving as follows. At the end of the first round, $\mathcal{A}^{RO}$ outputs some $t \in \mathcal{T}$, and at the end of the second round, it outputs some $x \in \mathcal{X}$ that is supposed to satisfy $f(x, RO(x)) = t$; on top, $\mathcal{A}^{RO}$ may have some additional (possibly quantum) output W.

We now show how the extractable RO-simulator $\mathcal{S}$ provides the means to extract x early on, i.e., right after $\mathcal{A}$ has announced t. To formalize this claim, we consider the following experiment, which we denote by $G_{\mathcal{S}}^{\mathcal{A}}$. The RO-interface $\mathcal{S}.RO$ of $\mathcal{S}$ is used to answer all the oracle queries made by $\mathcal{A}$. In addition, as soon as $\mathcal{A}$ outputs t, the interface $\mathcal{S}.E$ is queried on t to obtain $\hat{x} \in \mathcal{X} \cup \{\emptyset\}$, and after $\mathcal{A}$ has finished, $\mathcal{S}.RO$ is queried on $\mathcal{A}$'s final output x to generate h.

Informally, we want that $\mathcal{A}$ does not notice any difference when RO is replaced by $\mathcal{S}.RO$, and that $\hat{x} = x$ whenever $f(x, h) = t$, while $\hat{x} = \emptyset$ implies that $\mathcal{A}$ will fail to output x with $f(x, h) = t$. This situation is captured by the following statement.

Corollary 3. *The extractable RO-simulator $\mathcal{S}$ is such that the following holds. For any $\mathcal{A}$ that outputs t after q_1 queries and $x \in \mathcal{X}$ and W after an additional q_2 queries, setting $q = q_1 + q_2$, it holds that*

$$\delta\big([t, x, RO(x), W]_{\mathcal{A}^{RO}}, [t, x, h, W]_{G_{\mathcal{S}}^{\mathcal{A}}}\big) \leq 8(q_2 + 1)\sqrt{2\Gamma/2^n} \qquad and$$

$$\Pr_{G_{\mathcal{S}}^{\mathcal{A}}}[x \neq \hat{x} \wedge f(x, h) = t] \leq 8(q_2 + 1)\sqrt{2\Gamma/2^n} + \frac{40e^2(q + 2)^3 \Gamma'(f) + 2}{2^n},$$

Proof. The first claim follows because the trace distance vanishes when $\mathcal{S}.E(t)$ is performed at the very end, after the $\mathcal{S}.RO(x)$-query, in combination with the (almost-)commutativity of the two interfaces (Theorem 2, 2.a to 2.c). Similarly, the second claim follows from Proposition 3 when considering the $\mathcal{S}.E(t)$ query to be performed at the very end, in combination with the (almost-)commutativity of the interfaces again. □

The statements above extend easily to *multi*-round algorithms $\mathcal{A}^{RO}$ that output $t_1, \ldots, t_\ell$ in (possibly) different rounds, and $x_1, \ldots, x_\ell \in \mathcal{X}$ and some (possibly quantum) output W at the end of the run. We then extend the definition of $G_{\mathcal{S}}^{\mathcal{A}}$ in the obvious way: $\mathcal{S}.E$ is queried on each output t_i to produce $\hat{x}_i$, and at the end of the run $\mathcal{S}.RO$ is queried on each of the final outputs $x_1, \ldots, x_\ell$ of $\mathcal{A}$ to obtain $\mathbf{h} = (h_1, \ldots, h_\ell) \in \mathcal{Y}^\ell$. As a minor extension, we allow some of the x_i to be $\bot$, i.e., $\mathcal{A}^{RO}$ may decide to not output certain x_i's; the $\mathcal{S}.RO$ query on x_i is then not done and h_i is set to $\bot$ instead, and we declare that $RO(\bot) = \bot$ and $f(\bot, h_i) \neq t_i$. To allow for a compact notation, we write $RO(\mathbf{x}) = (RO(x_1), \ldots, RO(x_\ell))$ for $\mathbf{x} = (x_1, \ldots, x_\ell)$.

Corollary 4. *The extractable RO-simulator $\mathcal{S}$ is such that the following holds. For any $\mathcal{A}$ that makes q queries in total, it holds that*

$$\delta\big([\mathbf{t}, \mathbf{x}, RO(\mathbf{x}), W]_{\mathcal{A}^{RO}}, [\mathbf{t}, \mathbf{x}, \mathbf{h}, W]_{G_{\mathcal{S}}^{\mathcal{A}}}\big) \leq 8\ell(q + \ell)\sqrt{2\Gamma/2^n} \qquad and$$

$$\Pr_{G_{\mathcal{S}}^{\mathcal{A}}}\big[\exists i : x_i \neq \hat{x}_i \wedge f(x_i, h_i) = t_i\big] \leq 8\ell(q+1)\sqrt{2\Gamma/2^n} + \frac{40e^2(q+\ell+1)^3\Gamma'(f)+2}{2^n}.$$

5   Extractability of Commit-and-Open Σ-protocols

5.1   Commit-and-Open Σ-protocols

We assume the reader to be familiar with the concept of an interactive proof for a language $\mathcal{L}$ or a relation R, and specifically with the notion of a Σ-protocol.

Here, we consider the notion of a *commit-and-open* Σ-protocol, which is as follows. The prover begins by sending commitments $a_1, \ldots, a_\ell$ to the prover, computed as $a_i = H(x_i)$ for $x_1, \ldots, x_\ell \in \mathcal{X}$, where $H : \mathcal{X} \to \{0,1\}^n$ is a hash function. Here, x_i can either be the actual message m_i to be committed, or m_i concatenated with randomness. The verifier answers by sending a challenge c, which is a subset $c \subseteq [\ell] = \{1, \ldots, \ell\}$, picked uniformly at random from a challenge set $C \subseteq 2^{[\ell]}$, upon which the prover sends the response $z = (x_i)_{i \in c}$. Finally, the verifier checks whether $H(x_i) = a_i$ for every $i \in c$, computes an additional verification predicate $V(c, z)$ and outputs 1 if both check out, 0 otherwise. Such (usually zero-knowledge) protocols have been known since the concept of zero-knowledge proofs was developed [5,14].

Commit-and-open Σ-protocols are (classically) extractable in a straightforward manner as soon as a witness can be computed from sufficiently many of the x_i's: rewind the prover a few times until it has opened every commitment

a_i at least once.[9] There is, however, an alternative (classical) *online* extractor if the hash function H is modelled as a random oracle: simply look at the query transcript of the prover to find preimages of the commitments $a_1, ..., a_\ell$. As the challenge is chosen independently, the extractability and collision resistance of the commitments implies that for a prover with a high success probability, the ℓ extractions succeed simultaneously with good probability. This is roughly how the proof of online extractability of the ZK proof system for graph 3-coloring by Goldreich et al. [14], instantiated with random-oracle based commitments, works that was announced in [22] and shown in [23] (Proposition 5).

Equipped with our extractable RO-simulator S, we can mimic the above in the quantum setting. Indeed, the only change is that the look-ups in the transcript are replaced with the additional interface of the simulator S. Corollary 4 can then be used to prove the success of extraction using essentially the same extractor as in the classical case.

5.2   Notions of Special Soundness

The property that allows such an extraction is most conveniently expressed in terms of special soundness and its variants. Because there are, next to special and k-soundness, a number of additional variants in the literature (e.g. in the context of Picnic2/Picnic3 [17] or MQDSS [8]), we begin by formulating a generalized notion of special soundness that captures in a broad sense that a witness can be computed from correct responses to "*sufficiently many*" challenges.[10] While the notions introduced below can be formulated for arbitrary public-coin interactive proof systems, we present them here tailored to commit-and-open Σ-protocols. In [26], Wikström considers a similar notion of general special soundness (but then for arbitrary multi-round public-coin interactive proof systems); however, the formalism in [26] is more restrictive in that it requires the set system we call $\mathfrak{S}_{\min}$ below to form the set of bases of a matroid. As a consequence, the r-fold parallel repetition of a k-sound protocol is for instance not captured by the formalism suggested by Wikström.

In the remainder, Π is thus assumed to be an arbitrary commit-and-open Σ-protocol for a relation R with associated language $\mathcal{L}$, and C is the challenge space of Π. Furthermore, we consider a non-empty, monotone increasing set $\mathfrak{S}$ of subsets $S \subseteq C$, i.e., such that $S \in \mathfrak{S} \wedge S \subseteq S' \Rightarrow S' \in \mathfrak{S}$, and we let $\mathfrak{S}_{\min} := \{S \in \mathfrak{S} \mid S_\circ \subsetneq S \Rightarrow S_\circ \notin \mathfrak{S}\}$ consist of the minimal sets in $\mathfrak{S}$.

Definition 3. Π *is called* $\mathfrak{S}$*-sound if there exists an efficient algorithm* $\mathcal{E}_{\mathfrak{S}}(I, x_1, \ldots, x_\ell, S)$ *that takes as input an instance* $I \in \mathcal{L}$*, strings* $x_1, \ldots, x_\ell \in \mathcal{X}$ *and a set* $S \in \mathfrak{S}_{\min}$*, and outputs a witness for* I *whenever* $V(c, (x_i)_{i \in c}) = 1$ *for all* $c \in S$*, and outputs* $\perp$ *otherwise.*[11]

---

[9] Naturally, we can assume $[\ell] = \bigcup_{c \in C} c$.

[10] Using the language from secret sharing, we consider an arbitrary access structure $\mathfrak{S}$, while the k-soundness case corresponds to a threshold access structure.

[11] The restriction for S to be in $\mathfrak{S}_{\min}$, rather than in $\mathfrak{S}$, is only to avoid an exponentially sized input. When C is constant in size, we may admit any $S \in \mathfrak{S}$.

Note that there is no correctness requirement on the x_i's with $i \notin \bigcup_{c \in S} c$; thus, those x_i's may just as well be set to be empty strings.

This property generalizes k-soundness, which is recovered for $\mathfrak{S} = \mathfrak{T}_k := \{S \subseteq C \mid |S| \geq k\}$, but it also captures more general notions. For instance, the r-fold parallel repetition of a k-sound protocol is not k-sound anymore, but it is $\mathfrak{T}_k^{\vee r}$-sound with $\mathfrak{T}_k^{\vee r}$ consisting of those subsets of challenge-sequences $(c_1, \ldots, c_r) \in C^r$ for which the restriction to at least one of the positions is a set in $\mathfrak{T}_k$. This obviously generalizes to the parallel repetition of an arbitrary $\mathfrak{S}$-sound protocol, with the parallel repetition then being $\mathfrak{S}^{\vee r}$-sound with

$$\mathfrak{S}^{\vee r} := \{S \subseteq C^r \mid \exists i : S_i \in \mathfrak{S}\},$$

where $S_i := \{c \in C \mid \exists (c_1, \ldots, c_r) \in S : c_i = c\}$ is the i-th *marginal* of S.

For our result to apply, we need a strengthening of the above soundness condition where $\mathcal{E}_\mathfrak{S}$ has to find the set S himself. This is clearly the case for $\mathfrak{S}$-sound protocols that have a *constant sized* challenge space C, but also for the parallel repetition of $\mathfrak{S}$-sound protocols with a constant sized challenge space. Formally, we require the following strengthened notion of $\mathfrak{S}$-sound protocols.

Definition 4. *Π is called $\mathfrak{S}$-sound* if there exists an efficient algorithm $\mathcal{E}_\mathfrak{S}^*(I, x_1, \ldots, x_\ell)$ that takes as input an instance $I \in \mathcal{L}$ and strings $x_1, \ldots, x_\ell \in \mathcal{X}$, and outputs a witness for I whenever there exists $S \in \mathfrak{S}$ with $V(c, (x_i)_{i \in c}) = 1$ for all $c \in S$, and outputs $\bot$ otherwise.*

$\mathfrak{S}$-sound Σ-protocols may — and often do — have the property that a dishonest prover can pick any set $\hat{S} = \{\hat{c}_1, \ldots, \hat{c}_m\} \notin \mathfrak{S}$ of challenges $\hat{c}_i \in C$ and then prepare $\hat{x}_1, \ldots, \hat{x}_\ell$ in such a way that $V(c, (\hat{x}_i)_{i \in c}) = 1$ if $c \in \hat{S}$, i.e., after having committed to $\hat{x}_1, \ldots, \hat{x}_\ell$ the prover can successfully answer challenge c if $c \in \hat{S}$. We call this a *trivial* attack. The following captures the largest success probability of such a trivial attack, maximized over the choice of $\hat{S}$:

$$p_{triv}^{\mathfrak{S}} := \frac{1}{|C|} \max_{\hat{S} \notin \mathfrak{S}} |\hat{S}|. \tag{22}$$

When there is no danger of confusion, we omit the superscript $\mathfrak{S}$. Looking ahead, our result will show that for any prover that does better than the trivial attack by a non-negligible amount, online extraction is possible. For special sound commit-and-open Σ-protocols, $p_{triv} = 1/|C|$, and for k-sound protocols, $p_{triv} = (k-1)/|C|$. Furthermore, our definition of $\mathfrak{S}$-soundness allows a straightforward parallel repetition lemma on the combinatorial level providing an expression for p_{triv} of parallel-repeated commit-and-open Σ-protocols (the proof is an easy computation).

Lemma 4. *Let Π be $\mathfrak{S}$-sound. Then $p_{triv}^{\mathfrak{S}^{\vee r}} = \left(p_{triv}^{\mathfrak{S}}\right)^r$.*

5.3 Online Extractability in the QROM

We are now ready to define our extractor and prove that it succeeds. Equipped with the results from the previous section, the intuition is very simple. Given a (possibly dishonest) prover $\mathcal{P}$, running the considered Σ-protocol in the QROM, we use the simulator $\mathcal{S}$ to answer $\mathcal{P}$'s queries to the random oracle but also to extract the commitments $a_1, \ldots, a_\ell$, and if the extracted $\hat{x}_1, \ldots, \hat{x}_\ell$ satisfy the verification predicate V for sufficiently many challenges, we can compute a witness by applying $\mathcal{E}_{\mathfrak{S}}^*$.

The following relates the success probability of this extraction procedure to the success probability of the (possibly dishonest) prover.

Theorem 3. *Let Π be an $\mathfrak{S}$-sound* commit-and-open Σ-protocol where the first message consists of ℓ commitments. Then it admits an online extractor $\mathcal{E}$ in the QROM that succeeds with probability*

$$\Pr[\mathcal{E} \text{ succeeds}] \geq \frac{1}{1 - p_{triv}} \left(\Pr[\mathcal{P}^{RO} \text{ succeeds}] - p_{triv} - \varepsilon \right) \quad \text{where} \quad (23)$$

$$\varepsilon = 8\sqrt{2}\,\ell(2q + \ell + 1)/\sqrt{2^n} + \frac{40e^2(q + \ell + 1)^3\Gamma'(f) + 2}{2^n}$$

and p_{triv} is defined in Eq. (22). For $q \geq \ell + 1$, the bound simplifies to

$$\varepsilon \leq 34\ell q/\sqrt{2^n} + 2365q^3/2^n .$$

Furthermore, the running time of $\mathcal{E}$ is bounded as $T_{\mathcal{E}} = T_{\mathcal{P}_1} + T_{\mathcal{E}_{\mathfrak{S}}^*} + O(q_1^2)$, where $T_{\mathcal{P}_1}$ and $T_{\mathcal{E}_{\mathfrak{S}}^*}$ are the respective runtimes of $\mathcal{P}_1$ and $\mathcal{E}_{\mathfrak{S}}^*$.

Recall that $p_{triv} = (k-1)/|C|$ for k-soundness, giving a corresponding bound. We note that the bound (23) is tight, and the additive term ε has a matching attack for some schemes, see Section 5.4 of the full version.

Proof. We begin by describing the extractor $\mathcal{E}$. First, using $\mathcal{S}.RO$ to answer $\mathcal{P}$'s queries, $\mathcal{E}$ runs the prover $\mathcal{P}$ until it announces $a_1, \ldots, a_\ell$, and then it uses $\mathcal{S}.E$ to extract $\hat{x}_1, \ldots, \hat{x}_\ell$. I.e., $\mathcal{E}$ acts as $\mathcal{S}$ in Corollary 4 for the function $f(x, h) = h$ and runs the game $G_{\mathfrak{S}}^{\mathcal{P}}$ to the point where $\mathcal{S}.E$ outputs $\hat{x}_1, \ldots, \hat{x}_\ell$ on input $a_1, \ldots, a_\ell$. As a matter of fact, for the purpose of the analysis, we assume that $G_{\mathfrak{S}}^{\mathcal{P}}$ is run until the end, with the challenge c chosen uniformly at random, and where $\mathcal{P}$ then outputs x_i for all $i \in c$ (and $\perp$ for $i \notin c$) at the end of $G_{\mathfrak{S}}^{\mathcal{P}}$; we also declare that $\mathcal{P}$ additionally outputs c and $a_1, \ldots, a_\ell$ at the end. Then, upon having obtained $\hat{x}_1, \ldots, \hat{x}_\ell$, the extractor $\mathcal{E}$ runs $\mathcal{E}_{\mathfrak{S}}^*$ on $\hat{x}_1, \ldots, \hat{x}_\ell$ to try to compute a witness. By definition, this succeeds if $\hat{S} := \{\hat{c} \in C \mid V(\hat{c}, (\hat{x}_i)_{i \in \hat{c}}) = 1\}$ is in $\mathfrak{S}$.

It remains to relate the success probability of $\mathcal{E}$ to that of the prover $\mathcal{P}^{RO}$. By the first statement of Corollary 4, writing $\mathbf{x}_c = (x_i)_{i \in c}$, $RO(\mathbf{x}_c) = (RO(x_i))_{i \in c}$, $\mathbf{a}_c = (a_i)_{i \in c}$, etc., we have, writing $V(c, \mathbf{x}_c)$ instead of $V(c, \mathbf{x}_c) = 1$ for brevity,

$$\Pr[\mathcal{P}^{RO} \text{ succeeds}] = \Pr_{\mathcal{P}^{RO}}[V(c, \mathbf{x}_c) \wedge RO(\mathbf{x}_c) = \mathbf{a}_c]$$
$$\leq \Pr_{G_{\mathfrak{S}}^{\mathcal{P}}}[V(c, \mathbf{x}_c) \wedge \mathbf{h}_c = \mathbf{a}_c] + \delta_1 \quad (24)$$

with $\delta_1 = 8\sqrt{2}\,\ell(q+\ell)/\sqrt{2^n}$. Omitting the subscript $G_{\mathcal{S}}^{\mathcal{P}}$ now,

$$\Pr[V(c, \mathbf{x}_c) \wedge \mathbf{h}_c = \mathbf{a}_c]$$
$$\leq \Pr[V(c, \mathbf{x}_c) \wedge \mathbf{h}_c = \mathbf{a}_c \wedge \mathbf{x}_c = \hat{\mathbf{x}}_c] + \Pr[\mathbf{h}_c = \mathbf{a}_c \wedge \mathbf{x}_c \neq \hat{\mathbf{x}}_c]$$
$$\leq \Pr[V(c, \hat{\mathbf{x}}_c)] + \Pr[\exists\, j \in c : x_j \neq \hat{x}_j \wedge h_j = a_j] \leq \Pr[V(c, \hat{\mathbf{x}}_c)] + \delta_2 \qquad (25)$$

with $\delta_2 = 8\sqrt{2}\,\ell(q+1)/\sqrt{2^n} + \frac{40e^2(q+\ell+1)^3\Gamma'(f)+2}{2^n}$, where the last inequality is by the second statement of Corollary 4, noting that, by choice of f, the event $h_j = a_j$ is equal to $f(x_j, h_j) = a_j$. Recalling the definition of $\hat{S}$,

$$\Pr[V(c, \hat{\mathbf{x}}_c) = 1] = \Pr[c \in \hat{S}] \leq \Pr[\hat{S} \in \mathfrak{S}] + \Pr[c \in \hat{S}\,|\,\hat{S} \notin \mathfrak{S}]\Pr[\hat{S} \notin \mathfrak{S}] \qquad (26)$$
$$\leq \Pr[\mathcal{E}\text{ succeeds}] + p_{triv}(1 - \Pr[\mathcal{E}\text{ succeeds}]).$$

The last inequality holds as c is chosen at random independent of the $\hat{x}_i$, and hence independent of the event $\hat{S} \notin \mathfrak{S}$. Combining (24), (25) and (26), we obtain

$$\Pr[\mathcal{P}^{RO}\text{ succeeds}] \leq \Pr[\mathcal{E}\text{ succeeds}] + p_{triv}(1 - \Pr[\mathcal{E}\text{ succeeds}]) + \delta_1 + \delta_2$$

and solving for $\Pr[\mathcal{E}\text{ succeeds}]$ gives the claimed bound. $\qquad\square$

Application to Fiat Shamir Signatures. In Appendix E of the full version, we discuss the impact on Fiat Shamir signatures, in particular on the round-3 signature candidate Picnic [7] in the NIST standardization process for post-quantum cryptographic schemes . In short, a crucial part in the chain of arguments to prove security of Fiat Shamir signatures is to prove that the underlying Σ-protocol is a proof of knowledge. For post-quantum security, so far this step relied on Unruh's rewinding lemma, which leads (after suitable generalization), to a $(2k+1)$-th root loss for a k-sound protocols. For commit-and-open Σ-protocols, Theorem 3 can replace Unruhs rewinding lemma when working in the QROM, making this step in the chain of arguments tight up to unavoidable additive errors.

As an example, Theorem 3 implies a sizeable improvement over the current best QROM security proof of Picnic2 [6,7,17]. Indeed, Unruh's rewinding lemma implies a 6-th root loss for the variant of special soundness the underlying Σ-protocol possesses [12], while Theorem 3 is tight.

6 QROM-Security of Textbook Fujisaki-Okamoto

6.1 The Fujisaki-Okamoto Transformation

The Fujisaki-Okamoto (FO) transform [13] is a general method to turn any public-key encryption scheme secure against *chosen-plaintext attacks* (CPA) into a key-encapsulation mechanism (KEM) that is secure against *chosen-ciphertext attacks* (CCA). We can start either from a scheme with one-way security (OW-CPA) or from one with indistinguishability (IND-CPA), and in both cases obtain an IND-CCA secure KEM. We recall that a KEM establishes a shared key, which can then be used for symmetric encryption.

We include the (standard) formal definitions of a public-key encryption scheme and of a KEM in Appendix F of the full version, and we recall the notions of δ-correctness and γ-spreadness there. In addition, we define a relaxed version of the latter property, *weak γ-spreadness* (see Definition F.4), where the ciphertexts are only required to have high min-entropy when averaged over key generation[12]. The security games for OW-CPA security of a public-key encryption scheme and for IND-CCA security of a KEM are given in Sect. 6.1 of the full version. The formal specification of the FO transformation, mapping a public-key encryption scheme PKE = (Gen, Enc, Dec) and two suitable hash functions H and G (which will then be modeled as random oracles) into a key encapsulation mechanism FO[PKE, H, G] = (Gen, Encaps, Decaps), is given in Fig. 5.

Gen	Encaps(pk)	Decaps$_{sk}(c)$
1: $(sk, pk) \leftarrow$ Gen	3: $m \xleftarrow{\$} \mathcal{M}$	5: $m := \mathsf{Dec}_{sk}(c)$
2: **return** (sk, pk)	4: $c \leftarrow \mathsf{Enc}_{pk}(m; H(m))$	6: **if** $m = \bot$ or $\mathsf{Enc}_{pk}(m; H(m)) \neq c$
	5: $K := G(m)$	**return** $\bot$
	6: **return** (K, c)	7: **else return** $K := G(m)$

Fig. 5. The KEM FO[PKE, H, G], obtained by applying the FO transformation to PKE.

6.2 Post-quantum Security of FO in the QROM

Our main contribution here is a new security proof for the FO transformation in the QROM. In contrast to most previous works on the topic, our result applies to the *standard* FO transformation, without any adjustments. Next to being CPA secure, we require the underlying public-key encryption scheme to be so that ciphertexts have a lower-bounded amount of min-entropy (resulting from the encryption randomness), captured by the mentioned spreadness property. This seems unavoidable for the FO transformation with explicit rejection and without any adjustment, like an additional key confirmation hash (as e.g. in [24]).

Theorem 4. *Let* PKE *be a δ-correct public-key encryption scheme satisfying weak γ-spreadness. Let $\mathcal{A}$ be any* IND-CCA *adversary against* FO[PKE, H, G], *making $q_D \geq 1$ queries to the decapsulation oracle* DECAPS *and q_H and q_G queries to $H : \mathcal{M} \to \mathcal{R}$ and $G : \mathcal{M} \to \mathcal{K}$, respectively, where H and G are modeled as random oracles. Let $q := q_H + q_G + 2q_D$. Then, there exists a* OW-CPA *adversary $\mathcal{B}$ against* PKE *with*

$$\mathsf{ADV}[\mathcal{A}]_{\mathsf{KEM}}^{\mathsf{IND\text{-}CCA}} \leq 2q\sqrt{\mathsf{ADV}_{\mathsf{PKE}}^{\mathsf{OW\text{-}CPA}}[\mathcal{B}]} + 24q^2\sqrt{\delta} + 24q\sqrt{qq_D} \cdot 2^{-\gamma/4}.$$

Furthermore, $\mathcal{B}$ has a running time $T_{\mathcal{B}} \leq T_{\mathcal{A}} + O(q_H \cdot q_D \cdot \mathsf{Time}[\mathsf{Enc}] + q^2)$.

---

[12] This seems relevant e.g. for lattice-based schemes, where the ciphertext has little (or even no) entropy for certain very unlikely choices of the key (like being all 0).

We start with a proof outline, which is simplified in that it treats FO[PKE, H, G] as an encryption scheme rather than as a KEM. We will transform the adversary $\mathcal{A}$ of the IND-CCA game into a OW-CPA adversary against the PKE in a number of steps. There are two main challenges to overcome. (1) We need to switch from the *deterministic* challenge ciphertext $c^* = \mathsf{Enc}_{pk}(m^*; H(m^*))$ that $\mathcal{A}$ attacks to a *randomized* challenge ciphertext $c^* = \mathsf{Enc}_{pk}(m^*; r^*)$ that $\mathcal{B}$ attacks. We do this by re-programming $H(m^*)$ to a random value right after the computation of c^*, which is equivalent to keeping H but choosing a random r^* for computing c^*. For reasons that we explain later, we do this switch from H to its re-programmed variant, denoted $H^\diamond$, in two steps, where the first step (from **Game 0** to **1**) will be "for free", and the second step (from **Game 1** to **2**) is argued using the O2H lemma ([25], we use the version given in [2], Theorem 3). (2) We need to answer decryption queries without knowing the secret key. At this point our extractable RO-simulator steps in. We replace $H^\diamond$, modelled as a random oracle, by $\mathcal{S}$, and we use its extraction interface to extract m from any correctly formed encryption $c = \mathsf{Enc}_{pk}(m; H^\diamond(m))$ and to identify incorrect ciphertexts.

One subtle issue in the argument above is the following. The O2H lemma ensures that we can find m^* by measuring one of the queries to the random oracle. However, given that also the decryption oracle makes queries to the random oracle (for performing the re-encryption check), it could be the case that one of those decryption queries is the one selected by the O2H extractor. This situation is problematic since, once we switch to $\mathcal{S}$ to deal with the decryption queries, some of these queries will be dropped (namely when $\mathcal{S}.E(c) = \emptyset$). This is problematic because, per-se, we cannot exclude that this is the one query that will give us m^*. We avoid this problem by our two-step approach for switching from H to $H^\diamond$, which ensures that the only ciphertext c that would bring us in the above unfortunate situation is the actual (randomized) *challenge ciphertext* $c^* = \mathsf{Enc}_{pk}(m^*; r^*)$, which is forbidden by the specification of the security game.

Proof (of Theorem 4). **Games 0** to **8** below gradually turn $\mathcal{A}$ into $\mathcal{B}$ (in the full version we provide pseudocode for the hybrids that compactly illustrates the change from hybrid to hybrid.). We analyze the sequence of hybrids for a fixed key pair (sk, pk). For a key pair (sk, pk), let $\mathsf{ADV}_{sk}[\mathsf{A}]_{\mathrm{KEM}}^{\mathrm{IND\text{-}CCA}}$ be A's advantage, δ_{sk} the maximum decryption error probability and g_{sk} the maximum probability of any ciphertext, so that $\mathbb{E}[\delta_{sk}] \leq \delta$ and $\mathbb{E}[g_{sk}] \leq 2^{-\gamma}$, with the expectation over $(sk, pk) \leftarrow \mathsf{Gen}$.[13]

Game 0 is the IND-CCA game for KEMs, except that we provide G and H via arandom oracle F, by setting $H(x) := F(0||x)$ and $G(x) := F(1||x)$.[14] When convenient, we still refer to $F(0||\cdot)$ as H and $F(1||\cdot)$ as G. This change does not

---

[13] We can assume without loss of generality that pk is included in sk.

[14] These assignments seem to suggest that $\mathcal{R} = \mathcal{K}$, which may not be the case. Indeed, we understand here that $F : \mathcal{M} \to \{0,1\}^n$ with n large enough, and $F(0||x)$ and $F(1||x)$ are then cut down to the right size.

affect the view of the adversary nor the outcome of the game; therefore,

$$\Pr[b = b' \text{ in } \textbf{Game 0}] = 1/2 + \mathsf{ADV}_{sk}[\mathsf{A}]_{\mathrm{KEM}}^{\mathrm{IND\text{-}CCA}}.$$

In **Game 1**, we introduce a new oracle $F^\diamond$ by setting $F^\diamond(0\|m^*) := r^\diamond$ and $F^\diamond(1\|m^*) := k^\diamond$ for uniformly random $r^\diamond \in \mathcal{R}$ and $k^\diamond \in \mathcal{K}$, while letting $F^\diamond(b\|m) := F(b\|m)$ for $m \neq m^*$ and $b \in \{0,1\}$. We note that while the *joint* behavior of $F^\diamond$ and F depends on the choice of the challenge message m^*, each one individually is a purely random function, i.e., a random oracle. In line with F, we write $H^\diamond$ for $F^\diamond(0\|\cdot)$ and $G^\diamond$ for $F^\diamond(1\|\cdot)$ when convenient.

Using these definitions, **Game 1** is obtained from **Game 0** via the following modifications. After m^* and c^* have been produced and before $\mathcal{A}$ is executed, we compute $c^\diamond := \mathsf{Enc}_{pk}(m^*; r^\diamond) = \mathsf{Enc}_{pk}(m^*; H^\diamond(m^*))$, making a query to $H^\diamond$ to obtain $r^\diamond$. Furthermore, for every decapsulation query by $\mathcal{A}$, we let DECAPS use $H^\diamond$ and $G^\diamond$ instead of H and G for checking correctness of the queried ciphertexts c_i and for computing the key K_i, *except* when $c_i = c^\diamond$ (which we may assume to happen at most once), in which case DECAPS still uses H and G. We claim that

$$\Pr[b = b' \text{ in } \textbf{Game 1}] = \Pr[b = b' \text{ in } \textbf{Game 0}] = \frac{1}{2} + \mathsf{ADV}_{sk}[\mathsf{A}]_{\mathrm{KEM}}^{\mathrm{IND\text{-}CCA}}.$$

Indeed, for any decryption query c_i, we either have $\mathsf{Dec}_{sk}(c_i) =: m_i \neq m^*$ and thus $F^\diamond(b\|m_i) = F(b\|m_i)$, or else $m_i = m^*$; in the latter case we then either have $c_i = c^\diamond$, where nothing changes by definition of the game, or else $\mathsf{Enc}_{pk}(m^*; H(m^*)) = c^* \neq c_i \neq c^\diamond = \mathsf{Enc}_{pk}(m^*; H^\diamond(m^*))$, and hence the re-encryption check fails and $K_i := \bot$ in either case, without querying G or $G^\diamond$. Therefore, the input-output behavior of Decaps is not affected.

In **Game 2**, all oracle calls by Decaps (also for $c_i = c^\diamond$) and all calls by $\mathcal{A}$ are now to $F^\diamond$. Only the challenge ciphertext $c^* = \mathsf{Enc}_{pk}(m^*; H(m^*))$ is still computed using H, and thus with randomness $r^* = H(m^*)$ that is random and independent of m^* and $F^\diamond$. Hence, looking ahead, we can think of c^* as the input to the OW-CPA game that the to-be-constructed attacker $\mathcal{B}$ will attack. Similarly, $K_0^* = G(m^*)$ is random and independent of m^* and $F^\diamond$, exactly as K_1^* is, which means that $\mathcal{A}$ can only win with probability $\frac{1}{2}$.

By the O2H lemma ([2], Theorem 3), the difference between the respective probabilities of $\mathcal{A}$ guessing b in **Game 1** and **2** gives a lower bound on the success probability of a particular procedure to find an input on which F and $F^\diamond$ differ, and thus to find m^*. Formally,

$$2(q_H + q_G + 2)\sqrt{\Pr[m' = m^* \text{ in } \textbf{Game 3}]}$$
$$\geq |\Pr[b' = b \text{ in } \textbf{Game 1}] - \Pr[b' = b \text{ in } \textbf{Game 2}]|$$
$$= \frac{1}{2} + \mathsf{ADV}_{sk}[\mathsf{A}]_{\mathrm{KEM}}^{\mathrm{IND\text{-}CCA}} - \frac{1}{2} = \mathsf{ADV}_{sk}[\mathsf{A}]_{\mathrm{KEM}}^{\mathrm{IND\text{-}CCA}}$$

where **Game 3** is identical to **Game 2** above, except that we introduce and consider a new variable m' (with the goal that $m' = m^*$), obtained as follows.

Either one of the $q_H + q_G$ queries from $\mathcal{A}$ to $H^\diamond$ and $G^\diamond$ is measured, or one of the two respective queries from DECAPS to $H^\diamond$ and $G^\diamond$ upon a possible decryption query $c^\diamond$ is measured, and, in either case, m' is set to be the corresponding measurement outcome. The choice of which of these $q_H + q_G + 2$ queries to measure is done uniformly at random.[15]

We note that, since we are concerned with the measurement outcome m' only, it is irrelevant whether the game stops right after the measurement, or it continues until $\mathcal{A}$ outputs b'. Also, rather than actually measuring DECAPS' classical query to $H^\diamond$ or $G^\diamond$ upon decryption query $c_i = c^\diamond$ (if instructed to do so), we can equivalently set $m' := m_i = \mathsf{Dec}_{sk}(c^\diamond)$.

For **Game 4**, we consider the function $f : \mathcal{M} \times \mathcal{R} \to \mathcal{C}$, $(m, r) \mapsto \mathsf{Enc}_{pk}(m; r)$, and we replace the random oracle $H^\diamond$ with the extractable RO-simulator $\mathcal{S}$ from Theorem 2. Furthermore, *at the very end* of the game, we invoke the extractor interface $\mathcal{S}.E$ to compute $\hat{m}_i := \mathcal{S}.E(c_i)$ for each c_i that A queried to DECAPS in the course of its run. By the first statement of Theorem 2, given that the $\mathcal{S}.E$ queries take place only *after* the run of $\mathcal{A}$,

$$\Pr[m' = m^* \text{ in } \textbf{Game 4}] = \Pr[m' = m^* \text{ in } \textbf{Game 3}].$$

Applying Proposition 2 for $R' := \{(m, c) : \mathsf{Dec}_{sk}(c) \neq m\}$, we get that the event $P^\dagger := \left[\forall i : \hat{m}_i = m_i \vee \hat{m}_i = \emptyset \right]$ holds except with probability $\varepsilon_1 := 128(q_H + q_D)^2 \Gamma_R / |\mathcal{R}|$ for Γ_R as in Proposition 2, which here means that $\Gamma_R / |\mathcal{R}| = \delta_{sk}$. Thus

$$\Pr[m' = m^* \wedge P^\dagger \text{ in } \textbf{Game 4}] \geq \Pr[m' = m^* \text{ in } \textbf{Game 4}] - \varepsilon_1.$$

In **Game 5**, we query $\mathcal{S}.E(c_i)$ *at runtime*, that is, as part of the DECAPS procedure upon input c_i, right after $\mathcal{S}.RO(m)$ has been invoked as part of the re-encryption check. Since $\mathcal{S}.RO(m)$ and $\mathcal{S}.E(c_i)$ now constitute two subsequent classical queries, it follows from the contraposition of 4.b of Theorem 2 that except with probability $2 \cdot 2^{-n}$, $\hat{m}_i = \emptyset$ implies $\mathsf{Enc}_{pk}(m_i; \mathcal{S}.RO(m_i)) \neq c_i$. Applying the union bound, we find that $P^\dagger$ implies $P := \left[\forall i : \hat{m}_i = m_i \vee (\hat{m}_i = \emptyset \wedge \mathsf{Enc}_{pk}(m_i; \mathcal{S}.RO(m_i)) \neq c_i) \right]$ except with probability $q_D \cdot 2 \cdot 2^{-n}$. Furthermore, By 2.c of that same Theorem 2, each swap of a $\mathcal{S}.RO$ with a $\mathcal{S}.E$ query affects the final probability by at most $8\sqrt{2\Gamma(f)/|\mathcal{R}|} = 8\sqrt{2g_{sk}}$. Thus, setting $\varepsilon_2 := 2q_D \cdot \left((q_H + q_D) \cdot 4\sqrt{2g_{sk}} + 2^{-n}\right)$,

$$\Pr[m' = m^* \wedge P \text{ in } \textbf{Game 5}] \geq \Pr[m' = m^* \wedge P^\dagger \text{ in } \textbf{Game 4}] - \varepsilon_2$$

In **Game 6**, DECAPS uses $\hat{m}_i$ instead of m_i to compute K_i. That is, it sets $K_i := \perp$ if $\hat{m}_i = \emptyset$ and $K_i := G^\diamond(\hat{m}_i)$ otherwise. Also, if instructed to output $m' := m_i$ where $c_i = c^\diamond$, then the output is set to $m' := \hat{m}_i$ instead. In all cases, DECAPS still queries $\mathcal{S}.RO(m_i)$, so that the interaction pattern between DECAPS and $\mathcal{S}.RO$ remains as in **Game 5**. Here, we note that if the event $P_i := \left[\hat{m}_i = \right.$

---

[15] If this choice instructs to measure DECAPS's query to $H^\diamond$ or to $G^\diamond$ for the decryption query $c^\diamond$, but there is no decryption query $c_i = c^\diamond$, $m' := \perp$ is output instead.

$m_i \vee (\hat{m}_i = \emptyset \wedge \mathsf{Enc}_{pk}(m_i; \mathcal{S}.RO(m_i)) \neq c_i)]$ holds for a given i then the above change will not affect DECAPS' response K_i, and thus neither the probability of P_{i+1}. Therefore, by induction, $\Pr[P \text{ in } \textbf{Game 6}] = \Pr[P \text{ in } \textbf{Game 5}]$, and since conditioned on the event P the two games are identical, we have

$$\Pr[m' = m^* \wedge P \text{ in } \textbf{Game 6}] = \Pr[m' = m^* \wedge P \text{ in } \textbf{Game 5}].$$

In **Game 7**, instead of obtaining m' by measuring a random query of $\mathcal{A}$ to either $\mathcal{S}.RO$ or G, or outputting $\hat{m}_i$ with $c_i = c^\circ$, here m' is obtained by measuring a random query of $\mathcal{A}$ to either $\mathcal{S}.RO$ or G, or outputting $\hat{m}_i$ for a *random* $i \in \{1, \ldots, q_D\}$, where the first cases is chosen with probability $(q_H + q_G)/(q_H + q_G + 2q_D)$, and the second otherwise. As conditioned on choosing the first case, or the second one with $i = i_\diamond$, **Game 7** equals **Game 6**, we have

$$\Pr[m' = m^* \text{ in } \textbf{Game 7}] \geq \frac{q_H + q_G + 2}{q_H + q_G + 2q_D} \cdot \Pr[m' = m^* \text{ in } \textbf{Game 6}].$$

In **Game 8**, we observe that the response to the query $\mathcal{S}.RO(m^*)$, introduced in **Game 1** to compute c°, and the responses to the queries that DECAPS makes to $\mathcal{S}.RO$ on input m_i do not affect the game anymore, so we can drop these queries, or, equivalently, move them to the end of the game's execution. Invoking 2.c of Theorem 2 again and setting $\varepsilon_3 = (q_D + 1) \cdot q_H \cdot 8\sqrt{2g_{sk}}$, we get

$$\Pr[m' = m^* \text{ in } \textbf{Game 8}] \geq \Pr[m' = m^* \text{ in } \textbf{Game 7}] - \varepsilon_3,$$

We now see that **Game 8** works without knowledge of the secret key sk, and thus constitutes a OW-CPA attacker $\mathcal{B}$ against PKE, which takes as input a public key pk and an encryption c^* of a random message $m^* \in \mathcal{M}$, and outputs m^* with the given probability, i.e., $\mathsf{ADV}_{sk}[\mathsf{B}]^{\mathsf{OW\text{-}CPA}}_{\mathsf{PKE}} \geq \Pr[m' = m^* \text{ in } \textbf{Game 8}]$. We note that the oracle G° can be simulated using standard techniques. Backtracking all the above (in)equalities and setting $\varepsilon_{23} := \varepsilon_2 + \varepsilon_3$, $q_{HG} := q_H + q_G$ etc. and $q := q_H + q_G + 2q_D$, we get the following bounds,

$$\mathsf{ADV}_{sk}[\mathcal{A}]^{\mathsf{IND\text{-}CCA}}_{\mathsf{KEM}} \leq 2(q_{HG} + 2)\sqrt{\frac{q_{HG} + 2q_D}{q_{HG} + 2}\left(\mathsf{ADV}_{sk}[\mathsf{B}]^{\mathsf{OW\text{-}CPA}}_{\mathsf{PKE}} + \varepsilon_3\right) + \varepsilon_1 + \varepsilon_2}$$

$$\leq 2(q_{HG} + 2q_D)\sqrt{\mathsf{ADV}_{sk}[\mathsf{B}]^{\mathsf{OW\text{-}CPA}}_{\mathsf{PKE}} + \varepsilon_{23}} + 2(q_{HG} + 2)\sqrt{\varepsilon_1}$$

$$\leq 2q\left(\sqrt{\mathsf{ADV}_{sk}[\mathsf{B}]^{\mathsf{OW\text{-}CPA}}_{\mathsf{PKE}}} + \sqrt{\varepsilon_{23}} + \sqrt{\varepsilon_1}\right) \tag{27}$$

and

$$\sqrt{\varepsilon_{23}} = \sqrt{2q_D \cdot \left(4((q_H + q_D) + (q_D + 1)q_H)\sqrt{2g_{sk}} + 2^{-n}\right)}$$

$$\leq 6\sqrt{q_H q_D} \cdot \left(g_{sk}^{1/4} + 2^{-n/2}\right) \leq 12\sqrt{q q_D} \cdot g_{sk}^{1/4}, \tag{28}$$

where we have used that $2^{-n} \leq g_{sk} \leq 1$ in the last line. Taking the expectation over $(sk, pk) \leftarrow \mathsf{Gen}$, applying Jensen's inequality and using $q_H + q_D \leq q$ once more, we get the claimed bound. Finally, we note that the runtime of $\mathcal{B}$ is given by $T_{\mathcal{B}} = T_{\mathcal{A}} + T_{\text{DECAPS}} + T_G + T_{\mathcal{S}}$, where apart from its oracle queries DECAPS runs in time linear in q_D, and by Theorem 2 $\mathcal{S}$ and G can be simulated in time $T_{\mathcal{S}} = O\big(q_{RO} \cdot q_E \cdot \text{Time}[f] + q_{RO}^2\big) = O\big(q_H \cdot q_D \cdot \text{Time}[\text{Enc}] + q^2\big)$. $\qquad\square$

Acknowledgements. The authors thank Andreas Hülsing and Kathrin Hövelmanns for helpful discussions, and Eike Kiltz and anonymous referees for helpful comments on an earlier version of this article. JD was funded by ERC-ADG project 740972 (ALGSTRONGCRYPTO). SF was partly supported by the EU Horizon 2020 Research and Innovation Program Grant 780701 (PROMETHEUS). CM was funded by a NWO VENI grant (Project No. VI.Veni.192.159). CS was supported by a NWO VIDI grant (Project No. 639.022.519).

References

1. Alagic, G., Majenz, C., Russell, A., Song, F.: Quantum-access-secure message authentication via blind-unforgeability. In: Canteaut, A., Ishai, Y. (eds.) EURO-CRYPT 2020. LNCS, vol. 12107, pp. 788–817. Springer, Cham (2020). https://doi.org/10.1007/978-3-030-45727-3_27

2. Ambainis, A., Hamburg, M., Unruh, D.: Quantum security proofs using semi-classical oracles. In: Boldyreva, A., Micciancio, D. (eds.) CRYPTO 2019. LNCS, vol. 11693, pp. 269–295. Springer, Cham (2019). https://doi.org/10.1007/978-3-030-26951-7_10

3. Bindel, N., Hamburg, M., Hövelmanns, K., Hülsing, A., Persichetti, E.: Tighter proofs of CCA security in the quantum random oracle model. In: Hofheinz, D., Rosen, A. (eds.) TCC 2019. LNCS, vol. 11892, pp. 61–90. Springer, Cham (2019). https://doi.org/10.1007/978-3-030-36033-7_3

4. Boneh, D., Dagdelen, Ö., Fischlin, M., Lehmann, A., Schaffner, C., Zhandry, M.: Random oracles in a quantum world. In: Lee, D.H., Wang, X. (eds.) ASIACRYPT 2011. LNCS, vol. 7073, pp. 41–69. Springer, Heidelberg (2011). https://doi.org/10.1007/978-3-642-25385-0_3

5. Brassard, G., Chaum, D., Crépeau, C.: Minimum disclosure proofs of knowledge. J. Comput. Syst. Sci. **37**(2), 156–189 (1988)

6. Chase, M., et al.: The picnic signature scheme, design document v2.1 (2019)

7. Chase, M., et al.: Post-quantum zero-knowledge and signatures from symmetric-key primitives. In: Proceedings of the 2017 ACM SIGSAC Conference on Computer and Communications Security, CCS 2017, pp. 1825–1842, ACM, New York (2017)

8. Chen, M.-S., Hülsing, A., Rijneveld, J., Samardjiska, S., Schwabe, P.: From 5-pass $\mathcal{MQ}$-based identification to $\mathcal{MQ}$-based signatures. In: Cheon, J.H., Takagi, T. (eds.) ASIACRYPT 2016. LNCS, vol. 10032, pp. 135–165. Springer, Heidelberg (2016). https://doi.org/10.1007/978-3-662-53890-6_5

9. Chiesa, A., Manohar, P., Spooner, N.: Succinct arguments in the quantum random oracle model. In: Hofheinz, D., Rosen, A. (eds.) Theory of Cryptography. pp, pp. 1–29. Springer, Cham (2019). https://doi.org/10.1007/978-3-642-54242-8

10. Chung, K.-M., Fehr, S., Huang, Y.-H., Liao, T.-N.: On the compressed-oracle technique, and post-quantum security of proofs of sequential work. Cryptology ePrint Archive, Report 2020/1305 (2020). https://eprint.iacr.org/2020/1305

11. Czajkowski, J., Majenz, C., Schaffner, C., Zur, S.: Quantum lazy sampling and game-playing proofs for quantum indifferentiability. Cryptology ePrint Archive, Report 2019/428 (2019). https://eprint.iacr.org/2019/428

12. Don, J., Fehr, S., Majenz, C., Schaffner, C.: Security of the Fiat-Shamir transformation in the quantum random-oracle model. In: Boldyreva, A., Micciancio, D. (eds.) CRYPTO 2019. LNCS, vol. 11693, pp. 356–383. Springer, Cham (2019). https://doi.org/10.1007/978-3-030-26951-7_13

13. Fujisaki, E., Okamoto, T.: How to enhance the security of public-key encryption at minimum cost. In: Imai, H., Zheng, Y. (eds.) PKC 1999. LNCS, vol. 1560, pp. 53–68. Springer, Heidelberg (1999). https://doi.org/10.1007/3-540-49162-7_5

14. Goldreich, O., Micali, S., Wigderson, A.: Proofs that yield nothing but their validity or all languages in NP have zero-knowledge proof systems. J. ACM **38**(3), 690–728 (1991)

15. Hamoudi, Y., Magniez, F.: Quantum time-space tradeoff for finding multiple collision pairs (2020)

16. Hofheinz, D., Hövelmanns, K., Kiltz, E.: A modular analysis of the Fujisaki-Okamoto transformation. In: Kalai, Y., Reyzin, L. (eds.) Theory of Cryptography, pp. 341–371. Springer, Cham (2017). https://doi.org/10.1007/978-3-642-54242-8

17. Kales, D., Zaverucha, G.: Improving the performance of the picnic signature scheme. In: IACR Transactions on Cryptographic Hardware and Embedded Systems, pp. 154–188 (2020)

18. Katsumata, S., Kwiatkowski, K., Pintore, F., Prest, T.: Scalable ciphertext compression techniques for post-quantum KEMs and their applications. In: Moriai, S., Wang, H. (eds.) ASIACRYPT 2020. LNCS, vol. 12491, pp. 289–320. Springer, Cham (2020). https://doi.org/10.1007/978-3-030-64837-4_10

19. Liu, Q., Zhandry, M.: On finding quantum multi-collisions. In: Ishai, Y., Rijmen, V. (eds.) EUROCRYPT 2019. LNCS, vol. 11478, pp. 189–218. Springer, Cham (2019). https://doi.org/10.1007/978-3-030-17659-4_7

20. Liu, Q., Zhandry, M.: Revisiting post-quantum Fiat-Shamir. In: Boldyreva, A., Micciancio, D. (eds.) CRYPTO 2019. LNCS, vol. 11693, pp. 326–355. Springer, Cham (2019). https://doi.org/10.1007/978-3-030-26951-7_12

21. Nielsen, M.A., Chuang, I.L.: Quantum Computation and Quantum Information: 10th Anniversary Edition, 10th edn. Cambridge University Press, New York (2011)

22. Pass, R.: On deniability in the common reference string and random oracle model. In: Boneh, D. (ed.) CRYPTO 2003. LNCS, vol. 2729, pp. 316–337. Springer, Heidelberg (2003). https://doi.org/10.1007/978-3-540-45146-4_19

23. Pass, R.: Alternative variants of zero-knowledge proofs. PhD thesis, KTH Stockholm (2004)

24. Targhi, E.E., Unruh, D.: Post-quantum security of the Fujisaki-Okamoto and OAEP Transforms. In: Hirt, M., Smith, A. (eds.) TCC 2016. LNCS, vol. 9986, pp. 192–216. Springer, Heidelberg (2016). https://doi.org/10.1007/978-3-662-53644-5_8

25. Unruh, D.: Revocable quantum timed-release encryption. In: Nguyen, P.Q., Oswald, E. (eds.) EUROCRYPT 2014. LNCS, vol. 8441, pp. 129–146. Springer, Heidelberg (2014). https://doi.org/10.1007/978-3-642-55220-5_8

26. Wikström, D.: Special soundness revisited. Cryptology ePrint Archive, Report 2018/1157 (2018). https://ia.cr/2018/1157

27. Zhandry, M.: How to record quantum queries, and applications to quantum indifferentiability. In: Boldyreva, A., Micciancio, D. (eds.) CRYPTO 2019. LNCS, vol. 11693, pp. 239–268. Springer, Cham (2019). https://doi.org/10.1007/978-3-030-26951-7_9

Constant-Round Blind Classical Verification of Quantum Sampling

Kai-Min Chung[1]($\boxtimes$)(iD), Yi Lee[2](iD), Han-Hsuan Lin[3](iD), and Xiaodi Wu[2,4](iD)

[1] Institute of Information Science, Academia Sinica, Taipei, Taiwan
kmchung@iis.sinica.edu.tw
[2] Department of Computer Science, University of Maryland, College Park, USA
ylee1228@umd.edu, xwu@cs.umd.edu
[3] Department of Computer Science, National Tsing Hua University, Hsinchu, Taiwan
linhh@cs.nthu.edu.tw
[4] Joint Center for Quantum Information and Computer Science,
University of Maryland, College Park, USA

Abstract. In a recent breakthrough, Mahadev constructed a classical verification of quantum computation (CVQC) protocol for a classical client to delegate decision problems in BQP to an untrusted quantum prover under computational assumptions. In this work, we explore further the feasibility of CVQC with the more general *sampling* problems in BQP and with the desirable *blindness* property. We contribute affirmative solutions to both as follows.

- Motivated by the sampling nature of many quantum applications (e.g., quantum algorithms for machine learning and quantum supremacy tasks), we initiate the study of CVQC for *quantum sampling problems* (denoted by SampBQP). More precisely, in a CVQC protocol for a SampBQP problem, the prover and the verifier are given an input $x \in \{0,1\}^n$ and a quantum circuit C, and the goal of the classical client is to learn a sample from the output $z \leftarrow C(x)$ up to a small error, from its interaction with an untrusted prover. We demonstrate its feasibility by constructing a four-message CVQC protocol for SampBQP based on the quantum *Learning With Errors* assumption.
- The *blindness* of CVQC protocols refers to a property of the protocol where the prover learns nothing, and hence is blind, about the client's input. It is a highly desirable property that has been intensively studied for the delegation of quantum computation. We provide a simple yet powerful *generic* compiler that transforms any CVQC protocol to a blind one while preserving its completeness and soundness errors as well as the number of rounds.

Applying our compiler to (a parallel repetition of) Mahadev's CVQC protocol for BQP and our CVQC protocol for SampBQP yields the first *constant-round* blind CVQC protocol for BQP and SampBQP respectively, with negligible and inverse polynomial soundness errors respectively, and negligible completeness errors.

Keywords: Classical delegation of quantum computation · Blind quantum computation · Quantum sampling problems

O. Dunkelman and S. Dziembowski (Eds.): EUROCRYPT 2022, LNCS 13277, pp. 707–736, 2022.
https://doi.org/10.1007/978-3-031-07082-2_25

1   Introduction

Can quantum computation, with potential computational advantages that are intractable for classical computers, be efficiently verified by classical means? This problem has been a major open problems in quantum complexity theory and delegation of quantum computation [1]. A complexity-theoretic formulation of this problem by Gottesman in 2004 [1] asks about the possibility for an efficient classical verifier (a BPP machine) to verify the output of an efficient quantum prover (a BQP machine). In the absence of techniques for directly tackling this question, earlier feasibility results on this problem have been focusing on two weaker formulations. The first type of feasibility results (e.g., [4,13,21,22]) considers the case where the verifier is equipped with limited quantum power. The second type of feasibility results (e.g., [18,23,25,35]) considers a BPP verifier interacting with at least two entangled, non-communicating quantum provers.

Recently, the problem is resolved by a breakthrough result of Mahadev [30], who constructed the first Classical Verification of Quantum Computation (CVQC) protocol for BQP, where an efficient classical (BPP) verifier can interact with an efficient quantum (BQP) prover to verify any BQP language. Soundness of Mahadev's protocol is based on a widely recognized computational assumption that the learning with errors (LWE) problem [34] is hard for BQP machines. The technique invented therein has inspired many subsequent developments of CVQC protocols with improved parameters and functionality. For example, Mahadev's protocol has a large constant soundness error. The works of [7,15] use parallel repetition to achieve a negligible soundness error. As another example, the work of [24] extends Mahadev's techniques in an involved way to obtain a CVQC protocol with an additional blindness property.

In this work, we make two more contributions to this exciting line of research. First, we observe that the literature has mostly restricted the attention to delegation of *decision* problems (i.e., BQP). Motivated by the intrinsic randomness of quantum computation and the sampling nature of many quantum applications, we initiate the study of CVQC for quantum *sampling* problems. Second, we further investigate the desirable *blindness* property and construct the first *constant-round* blind CVQC protocols. We elaborate on our contributions in Sect. 1.1 and 1.2, respectively.

1.1   CVQC for Quantum Sampling Problems

We initiate the study of CVQC for quantum sampling problem, which we believe is highly desirable and natural for delegation of quantum computation. Due to the intrinsic randomness of quantum mechanics, the output from a quantum computation is randomized and described by a distribution. Thus, if a classical verifier want to utilize the full power of a quantum machine, the ability to get a verifiable sample from the quantum circuit's output distribution is desirable. On a more concrete level, quantum algorithms like Shor's algorithm [37] has a significant quantum sampling component, and the recent quantum supremacy proposals (e.g., [3,8,36]) are built around sampling tasks, suggesting the importance of sampling in quantum computation.

It is worth noting that the difficulty of extending the delegation of decision problem to the delegation of sampling problems is quantum-specific. This is because there is a simple reduction from the delegation of *classical* sampling problems to decision ones: the verifier can sample and fix the random seed of the computation, which makes the computation deterministic. Then, the verifier can delegate the output of the computation bit-by-bit as decision problems. However, this derandomization trick does not work in the quantum setting due to its intrinsic randomness.

Our Contribution. As the first step to formalize CVQC for quantum sampling problems, we consider the complexity class SampBQP introduced by Aaronson [2] as a natural class to capture efficiently computable quantum sampling problems. SampBQP consists of sampling problems $(D_x)_{x \in \{0,1\}^*}$ that can be approximately sampled by a BQP machine with a desired inverse polynomial error (See Sect. 2 for the formal definition). We consider CVQC for a SampBQP problem $(D_x)_{x \in \{0,1\}^*}$ where a classical BPP verifier delegates the computation of a sample $z \leftarrow D_x$ for some input x to a quantum BQP prover. Completeness requires that when the prover is honest, the verifier should accept with high probability and learn a correct sample $z \leftarrow D_x$. For soundness, intuitively, the verifier should not accept and output a sample with incorrect distribution when interacting with a malicious prover. We formalize the soundness by a strong *simulation-based* definition, (Definition 3), where we require that the joint distribution (d, z) of the decision bit $d \in \{\mathsf{Acc}, \mathsf{Rej}\}$ and the output z (which is $\perp$ when $d = \mathsf{Rej}$) is ϵ-close (in either statistical or computational sense) to an "ideal distribution" (d, z_{ideal}), where z_{ideal} is sampled from the desired distribution D_x when $d = \mathsf{Acc}$ and set to $\perp$ when $d = \mathsf{Rej}$.[1]

As our main result, we construct a constant-round CVQC protocol for SampBQP, based on the quantum LWE (QLWE) assumption that the learning-with-errors problem is hard for BQP machines.

Theorem 1 (informal). *Assuming the QLWE assumption, there exists a four-message CVQC protocol for all sampling problems in* SampBQP *with computational soundness and negligible completeness error.*

We note that since the definition of SampBQP allows an inverse polynomial error, our CVQC protocol also implicitly allows an arbitrary small inverse polynomial error in soundness (see Sect. 2 for the formal definition). Achieving negligible soundness error for delegating sampling problems is an intriguing open question; see Sect. 1.3 for further discussions.

The construction of our CVQC protocol follows the blueprint of Mahadev's construction [30]. However, there are several obstacles we need to overcome along the way. To explains the obstacles and our ideas, we first present a high-level overview of Mahadev's protocol.

---

[1] This simulation-based formulation is analogous to the standard composable security definition for QKD.

Overview of Mahadev's Protocol. Following [30], we define QPIP_τ as classes of interactive proof systems between an (almost) classical verifier and a quantum prover, where the classical verifier has limited quantum computational capability, formalized as possessing τ-qubit quantum memory. A formal definition is given in our full version [17].

At a high-level, the heart of Mahadev's protocol is a measurement protocol Π_{Measure} that can compile an one-round QPIP_1 protocol (with special properties) to a QPIP_0 protocol. Note that in a QPIP_1 protocol, the verifier with one-qubit memory can only measure the prover's quantum message qubit by qubit. Informally, the measurement protocol Π_{Measure} allows a BQP prover to "commit to" a quantum state ρ and a classical verifier to choose an X or Z measurement to apply to each qubit of ρ such that the verifier can learn the resulting measurement outcome.

Thus, if an (one-round) QPIP_1 verifier only applies X or Z measurement to the prover's quantum message, we can use the measurement protocol Π_{Measure} to turn the QPIP_1 protocol into a QPIP_0 protocol in a natural way. One additional requirement here is that the verifier's measurement choices need to be determined at the beginning (i.e., cannot depend adaptively on the intermediate measurement outcome).

Furthermore, in Π_{Measure}, the verifier chooses to run a "*testing*" round or a "*Hadamard*" round with 1/2 probability, respectively. Informally, the testing round is used to "test" the commitment of ρ, and the Hadamard round is used to learn the measurement outcome. (See Protocol 1 for further details about the measurement protocol Π_{Measure}.) Another limitation here is that in the testing round, the verifier only "test" the commitment without learning any measurement result.

In [30], Mahadev's CVQC protocol for BQP is constructed by applying her measurement protocol to the one-round QPIP_1 protocol of [21,32], which has the desired properties that the verifier only performs non-adaptive X/Z measurement to the prover's quantum message. The fact that the verifier does not learn the measurement outcome in the testing round is not an issue here since the verifier can simply accept when the test is passed (at the cost of a constant soundness error).

Overview of Our Construction. Following the blueprint of Mahadev's construction, our construction proceeds in the following two steps: 1. construct a QPIP_1 protocol for $\mathsf{SampBQP}$ with required special property, and 2. compile the QPIP_1 protocol using Π_{Measure} to get the desired QPIP_0 protocol. The first step can be done by combining existing techniques from different contexts, whereas the second step is the main technical challenge. At a high-level, the reason is the above-mentioned issue that the verifier does not learn the measurement outcome in the testing round. While this is not a problem for decision problems, for sampling problems, the verifier needs to produce an output sample when accepts, but there seems to be no way to produce the output for the verifier without learning the measurement outcome. We discuss both steps in turn as follows.

⋄ *Construct a* QPIP$_1$ *protocol for* SampBQP *with required special property:*
Interestingly, while the notion of delegation for quantum sampling problem is
not explicitly formalized in their work, Hayashi and Morimae [26] constructed
an one-round QPIP$_1$ protocol that can delegate quantum sampling problem and
achieve our notion of completeness and soundness[2]. Furthermore, their protocol
has information-theoretic security and additionally achieve the blindness property. However, in their protocol, the computation is performed by the verifier
using measurement-based quantum computation (MBQC)[3], and hence the verifier needs to perform adaptive measurement choices. Therefore, we cannot rely
on their QPIP$_1$ protocol for SampBQP.

Instead, we construct the desired QPIP$_1$ protocol for SampBQP by generalizing the approach of local Hamiltonian reduction used in [21,32] to verify
SampBQP. Doing so requires the combination of several existing techniques from
different context with some new ideas. For example, to handle SampBQP, we
need to prove lower bound on the spectral gap of the reduced local Hamiltonian
instance, which is reminiscent to the simulation of quantum circuits by adiabatic quantum computation [5]. To achieve soundness, we use cut-and-choose
and analyze it using de Finetti theorem in a way similar to [26,38]. See Sect. 3
and our full version [17] for detailed discussions.

⋄ *Compile the* QPIP$_1$ *protocol using* Π_{Measure}: We now discuss how to use
Mahadev's measurement protocol to compile the above QPIP$_1$ protocol for
SampBQP to a QPIP$_0$ protocol. As mentioned, a major issue we need to address
in Mahadev's original construction is that when the verifier V chooses to run a
testing round, V does not learn an output sample when it accepts.

Specifically, let Π_{int} be an "intermediate" QPIP$_0$ protocol obtained by applying Mahadev's compilation to the above QPIP$_1$ protocol. In such a protocol, when
the verifier V chooses to run the Hadamard round, it could learn a measurement
outcome from the measurement protocol and be able to run the QPIP$_1$ verifier
to generate a decision and an output sample when accepts. However, when V
chooses to run the testing round, it only decides to accept/reject without being
able to output a sample.

A natural idea to fix the issue is to execute multiple copies of Π_{int} in parallel[4], and to choose a random copy to run the Hadamard round to generate an
output sample and use all the remaining copies to run the testing round. The
verifier accepts only when all executions accept and outputs the sample from
the Hadamard round. We call this protocol Π_{Final}.

Clearly from the construction, the verifier now can output a sample when it
decides to accept, and output a correct sample when interacting with an honest

---

[2] They did not prove our notion of soundness for their construction, but it is not hard
to prove its soundness based on their analysis.

[3] In more detail, the prover of their protocol is required to send multiple copies of the
graph states to the verifier (qubit by qubit). The verifier tests the received supposedly
graph states using cut-and-choose and perform the computation using MBQC.

[4] It is also reasonable to consider sequential repetition, but we consider parallel repetition for its advantage of preserving the round complexity.

prover (completeness). The challenge is to show that Π_{Final} is computationally sound. Since we are now in the computational setting, we cannot use the quantum de Finetti theorem as above which only holds in the information-theoretical setting. Furthermore, parallel repetition for computationally sound protocols are typically difficult to analyze, and known to not always work for protocols with four or more messages even in the classical setting [10, 33].

Parallel repetition of Mahadev's protocol for BQP has been analyzed before in [7, 15]. However, the situation here is different. For BQP, the verifier simply chooses to run the Hadamard and testing rounds independently for each repetition. In contrast, our Π_{Final} runs the Hadamard round in one repetition and runs the testing rounds in the rest. The reason is that in SampBQP, as well as generically in sampling problems, there is no known approach to combine multiple samples to generate one sample with reduced error, i.e., there is no generic error reduction method for the sampling problem. In contrast, the error reduction for decision problems can be done with the majority vote. As a result, while the soundness error decreases exponentially for BQP, as we see below (and also in the above $QPIP_1$ protocols), for SampBQP, m-fold repetition only decreases the error to $\text{poly}(1/m)$.

To analyze the soundness of Π_{Final}, we use the *partition lemma* developed in [15] to analyze the prover's behavior while executing copies of Π_{Measure}.[5] Intuitively, the partition lemma says that for any cheating prover and for each copy $i \in [m]$, there exist two efficient "projectors"[6] $G_{0,i}$ and $G_{1,i}$ in the prover's internal space with $G_{0,i} + G_{1,i} \approx Id$. $G_{0,i}$ and $G_{1,i}$ splits up the prover's residual internal state after sending back his first message. $G_{0,i}$ intuitively represents the subspace where the prover does not knows the answer to the testing round on the i-th copy, while $G_{1,i}$ represents the subspace where the prover does. Note that the prover is using a single internal space for all copies, and every $G_{0,i}$ and every $G_{1,i}$ is acting on this single internal space. By using this partition lemma iteratively, we can decompose the prover's internal state $|\psi\rangle$ into sum of subnormalized states. First we apply it to the first copy, writing $|\psi\rangle = G_{0,1}|\psi\rangle + G_{1,1}|\psi\rangle \equiv |\psi_0\rangle + |\psi_1\rangle$. The component $|\psi_0\rangle$ would then get rejected as long as the first copy is chosen as a testing round, which occurs with pretty high probability. More precisely, the output corresponding to $|\psi_0\rangle$ is $1/m$-close to the ideal distribution that just rejects all the time. On the other hand, $|\psi_1\rangle$ is now binding on the first copy; we now similarly apply the partition lemma of the second copy to $|\psi_1\rangle$. We write $|\psi_1\rangle = G_{0,2}|\psi_1\rangle + G_{1,2}|\psi_1\rangle \equiv |\psi_{10}\rangle + |\psi_{11}\rangle$, and apply the same argument about $|\psi_{10}\rangle$ and $|\psi_{11}\rangle$. We then continue to decompose $|\psi_{11}\rangle = |\psi_{110}\rangle + |\psi_{111}\rangle$ and so on, until we reach the last copy and obtain $|\psi_{1\dots m}\rangle$. Intuitively, all the $|\psi_{1\dots 10}\rangle$ terms will be rejected with high probability, while the $|\psi_{1^m}\rangle$ term represents the "good" component where the prover knows the answer to every testing round and therefore has high accept probabil-

---

[5] The analysis of [7] is more tailored to the decision problems setting, and it is unclear how to extend it to sampling problems where there are multiple bits of output.

[6] Actually they are not projectors, but for the simplicity of this discussion let's assume they are.

ity. Therefore, $|\psi_{1^m}\rangle$ also satisfies some binding property, so the verifier should obtain a measurement result of some state on the Hadamard round copy, and the soundness of the QPIP_1 protocol Π_{Samp} follows.

However, the intuition that $|\psi_{1^m}\rangle$ is binding to every Hadamard round is incorrect. As $G_{1,i}$ does not commute with $G_{1,j}$, $|\psi_{1^m}\rangle$ is unfortunately only binding for the m-th copy. To solve this problem, we start with a pointwise argument and fix the Hadamard round on the i-th copy where $|\psi_{1^i}\rangle$ is binding, and show that the corresponding output is $O(\||\psi_{1^{i-1}0}\rangle\|)$-close to ideal. We can later average out this error over the different choices of i, since not all $\||\psi_{1^{i-1}0}\rangle\|$ can be large at the same time. Another way to see this issue is to notice that we are partitioning a quantum state, not probability events, so there are some inconsistencies between our intuition and calculation. Indeed, the error we get in the end is $O(\sqrt{1/m})$ instead of the $O(1/m)$ we expected.

The intuitive analysis outlined above glosses over many technical details, and we substantiate this outline with full details in Sect. 4.

1.2   Blind CVQC Protocols

Another desirable property of CVQC protocols is *blindness*, which means that the prover does not learn any information about the private input for the delegated computation.[7] In the relaxed setting where the verifier has a limited quantum capability, Hayashi and Morimae [26] constructed a blind QPIP_1 protocol for delegating quantum computation with information-theoretic security that also handles sampling problems. However, for purely classical verifiers, blind CVQC protocols seem much more difficult to construct. This goal is recently achieved by the seminal work of Gheorghiu and Vidick [24], who constructed the first blind CVQC protocol for BQP by constructing a composable remote state preparation protocol and combining it with the verifiable blind quantum computation protocol of Fitzsimons and Kashefi [22]. However, their protocol has polynomially many rounds and requires a rather involved analysis. Before our work, it is an open question whether constant-round blind CVQC protocol for BQP is achievable.

Our Contribution. Somewhat surprisingly, we provide a simple yet powerful *generic* compiler that transforms any CVQC protocol to a blind one while preserving completeness, soundness, as well as its round complexity. Our compiler relies on quantum fully homomorphic encryption (QFHE) schemes with certain "classical-friendly" properties, which is satisfied by both constructions of Mahadev [29] and Brakerski [12].

Theorem 2 (informal). *Assuming the QLWE assumption[8], there exists a protocol compiler that transforms any CVQC protocol Π to a CVQC protocol Π_{blind}*

---

[7] In literature, the definition of blindness may also require to additionally hide the computation. We note the two notions are equivalent from a feasibility point of view by a standard transformation (see our full version [17]).

[8] By using Brakerski's QFHE, we only need to rely on the QLWE assumption with polynomial modulus in this theorem.

that achieves blindness while preserves its round complexity, completeness, and soundness.

Applying our blindness compiler to the parallel repetition of Mahadev's protocol from [7,15], we obtain the first constant-round blind CVQC protocol for BQP with negligible completeness and soundness error, resolving the aforementioned open question.

Theorem 3 (informal). *Under the QLWE assumption, there exists a blind, four-message CVQC protocol for all languages in* BQP *with negligible completeness and soundness errors.*

We can also apply our compiler to our CVQC protocol for SampBQP to additionally achieve blindness.

Theorem 4 (informal). *Under the QLWE assumption, there exists a blind, four-message CVQC protocol for all sampling problems in* SampBQP *with computational soundness and negligible completeness error.*

Techniques. At a high-level, the idea is simple: we run the original protocol under a QFHE with the QFHE key generated by the verifier. Intuitively, this allows the prover to compute his next message under encryption without learning verifier's message, and hence achieves blindness while preserving the properties of the original protocol. One subtlety with this approach is the fact that the verifier is classical while the QFHE cipher text could contain quantum data. In order to make the classical verifier work in this construction, the ciphertext and the encryption/decryption algorithm need to be classical when the underlying message is classical. Fortunately, such "classical-friendly" property is satisfied by the construction of [12,29].

A more subtle issue is to preserve the soundness. In particular, compiled protocols with a single application of QFHE might (1) leak information about the circuit evaluated by the verifier through its outputted QFHE ciphertexts (i.e., no *circuit privacy*); or (2) fail to simulate original protocols upon receiving invalid ciphertexts from the prover. We address these issues by letting the verifier switch to a fresh new key for each round of the protocol. Details are given in Sect. 5.

1.3   Related and Followup Works and Discussions

As mentioned, while we are the first to explicitly investigate delegation of quantum sampling problems, Hayashi and Morimae [26] constructed an one-round blind QPIP$_1$ protocol that can be used to delegate SampBQP and achieve our notion of information-theoretical security. Like our SampBQP protocol, their protocol has an arbitrarily small inverse polynomial soundness error instead of negligible soundness error. Also as mentioned, Gheorghiu and Vidick [24] constructed the first blind CVQC protocol for BQP by constructing a composable remote state preparation protocol and combining it with the verifiable blind quantum computation protocol of Fitzsimons and Kashefi [22]. However, their protocol has polynomially many rounds and requires a rather involved analysis.

It is also worth noting that several existing constructions in the relaxed models (e.g., verifiable blind computation [22]) can be generalized to delegate SampBQP in a natural way, but it seems challenging to analyze the soundness of the generalized protocol. Furthermore, it is unlikely that these generalized protocols can achieve negligible soundness error for SampBQP. The reason is that in all these constructions, some form of cut and choose are used to achieve soundness. For sampling problems, as mentioned, there seems to be no generic way to combine multiple samples for error reduction, so the verifier needs to choose one sample to output in the cut and choose. In this case, an adversarial prover may choose to cheat on a random copy in the cut and choose and succeed in cheating with an inverse polynomial probability.

On the other hand, while the definition of SampBQP in [2,3] allows an inverse polynomial error, there seems to be no fundamental barriers to achieve negligible error. It is conceivable that negligible error can be achieved using quantum error correction. Negligible security error is also achievable in the related settings of secure multi-party quantum computation [19,20] and verifiable quantum FHE [6] based on verifiable quantum secret sharing or quantum authentication codes[9]. However, both primitives require computing and communicating quantum encodings and are not applicable in the context of CVQC and $QPIP_1$. An intriguing open problem is whether it is possible to achieve negligible soundness error with classical communication while delegating a quantum sampling problem.

In a recent work, Bartusek [9] used the technique we developed for delegation of SampBQP to construct secure quantum computation protocols with classical communication for pseudo-deterministic quantum functionalities.

Organization. For preliminary technical background, see our full version [17]. Our simulation-based definition of CVQC for SampBQP is discussed in Sect. 2. Our main technical contributions are explained in Sect. 3 (a construction of $QPIP_1$ protocol for SampBQP), Sect. 4 (the construction of $QPIP_0$ protocol for SampBQP based on the above $QPIP_1$ protocol), and Sect. 5 (a generic compiler to upgrade $QPIP_0$ protocols with blindness).

2   Delegation of Quantum Sampling Problems

In this section, we formally introduce the task of delegation for quantum sampling problems. We start by recalling the complexity class SampBQP defined by Aaronson [2,3], which captures the class of sampling problems that are approximately solvable by polynomial-time quantum algorithms.

Definition 1 (Sampling Problem). *A* sampling problem *is a collection of probability distributions* $(D_x)_{x \in \{0,1\}^*}$, *one for each input string* $x \in \{0,1\}^n$, *where* D_x *is a distribution over* $\{0,1\}^{m(n)}$ *for some fixed polynomial* m.

---

[9] The security definitions are not comparable, but it seems plausible that the techniques can be used to achieve negligible soundness error for sampling problems.

Definition 2 (SampBQP). SampBQP *is the class of sampling problems* $(D_x)_{x\in\{0,1\}^*}$ *that can be (approximately) sampled by polynomial-size uniform quantum circuits. Namely, there exists a Turing machine M such that for every $n \in \mathbb{N}$ and $\epsilon \in (0,1)$, $M(1^n, 1^{1/\epsilon})$ outputs a quantum circuit C in* $\mathrm{poly}(n, 1/\epsilon)$ *time such that for every $x \in \{0,1\}^n$, the output of $C(x)$ (measured in standard basis) is ϵ-close to D_x in the total variation distance.*

Note that in the above definition, there is an accuracy parameter ϵ and the quantum sampling algorithm only requires to output a sample that is ϵ-close to the correct distribution in time $\mathrm{poly}(n, 1/\epsilon)$. [2,3] discussed multiple reasons for allowing the inverse polynomial error, such as to take into account the inherent noise in conceivable physical realizations of quantum computer. On the other hand, it is also meaningful to require negligible error. As discussed, it is an intriguing open question to delegate quantum sampling problem with negligible error.

We next define what it means for a QPIP$_\tau$ protocol[10] to solve a SampBQP problem $(D_x)_{x\in\{0,1\}^*}$. Since sampling problems come with an accuracy parameter ϵ, we let the prover P and the verifier V receive the input x and $1^{1/\epsilon}$ as common inputs. Completeness is straightforward to define, which requires that when the prover P is honest, the verifier V should accept with high probability and output a sample z distributed close to D_x on input x. Defining soundness is more subtle. Intuitively, it requires that the verifier V should never be "cheated" to accept and output an incorrect sample even when interacting with a malicious prover. We formalize this by a strong simulation-based definition, where we require that the joint distribution of the decision bit $d \in \{\mathsf{Acc}, \mathsf{Rej}\}$ and the output z (which is $\perp$ when $d = \mathsf{Rej}$) is ϵ-close (in either statistical or computational sense) to an "ideal distribution" (d, z_{ideal}), where z_{ideal} is sampled from D_x when $d = \mathsf{Acc}$ and set to $\perp$ when $d = \mathsf{Rej}$. Since the protocol receives the accuracy parameter $1^{1/\epsilon}$ as input to specify the allowed error, we do not need to introduce an additional soundness error parameter in the definition.

Definition 3. *Let $\Pi = (P, V)$ be a QPIP$_\tau$ protocol. We say it is a protocol for the* SampBQP *instance $(D_x)_{x\in\{0,1\}^*}$ with completeness error $c(\cdot)$ and statistical (resp., computational) soundness if the following holds:*

- *On public inputs 1^λ, $1^{1/\epsilon}$, and $x \in \{0,1\}^{\mathrm{poly}(\lambda)}$, V outputs (d, z) where $d \in \{\mathsf{Acc}, \mathsf{Rej}\}$. If $d = \mathsf{Acc}$ then $z \in \{0,1\}^{m(|x|)}$ where m is given in Definition 1, otherwise $z = \perp$.*
- *(Completeness): For all accuracy parameters $\epsilon(\lambda) = \frac{1}{\mathrm{poly}(\lambda)}$, security parameters $\lambda \in \mathbb{N}$, and $x \in \{0,1\}^{\mathrm{poly}(\lambda)}$, let $(d, z) \leftarrow (P, V)(1^\lambda, 1^{1/\epsilon}, x)$, then $d = \mathsf{Rej}$ with probability at most $c(\lambda)$.*
- *(Statistical soundness): For all cheating provers P^*, accuracy parameters $\epsilon(\lambda) = \frac{1}{\mathrm{poly}(\lambda)}$, sufficiently large $\lambda \in \mathbb{N}$, and $x \in \{0,1\}^{\mathrm{poly}(\lambda)}$, consider the following experiment:*

---

[10] See our full version [17] for a formal definition of QPIP$_\tau$.

- Let $(d, z) \leftarrow (P^*, V)(1^\lambda, 1^{1/\epsilon}, x)$.
- Define z_{ideal} by

$$\begin{cases} z_{ideal} = \perp & \text{if } d = \mathsf{Rej} \\ z_{ideal} \leftarrow D_x & \text{if } d = \mathsf{Acc} \end{cases}$$

It holds that $\|(d, z) - (d, z_{ideal})\|_{\mathrm{TV}} \leq \epsilon$.

– (Computational soundness): For all cheating BQP provers P^*, BQP distinguishers D, accuracy parameters $\epsilon(\lambda) = \frac{1}{\text{poly}(\lambda)}$, sufficiently large $\lambda \in \mathbb{N}$, and all $x \in \{0, 1\}^{\text{poly}(\lambda)}$, let us define d, z, z_{ideal} by the same experiment as above. It holds that (d, z) is ϵ-computationally indistinguishable to (d, z_{ideal}) over λ.

As in the case of BQP, we are particularly interested in the case that $\tau = 0$, i.e., when the verifier V is classical. In this case, we say that $\varPi$ is a CVQC protocol for the $\mathsf{SampBQP}$ problem $(D_x)_{x \in \{0,1\}^*}$.

3   Construction of the QPIP_1 Protocol for $\mathsf{SampBQP}$

As we mentioned in this introduction, we will employ the circuit *history* state in the original construction of the Local Hamiltonian problem [28] to encode the circuit information for $\mathsf{SampBQP}$. However, there are distinct requirements between certifying the computation for BQP and $\mathsf{SampBQP}$ based on the history state. For any quantum circuit C on input x, the original construction for certifying BQP[11] consists of local Hamiltonian $H_{in}, H_{clock}, H_{prop}, H_{out}$ where H_{in} is used to certify the initial input x, H_{clock} to certify the validness of the clock register, H_{prop} to certify the gate-by-gate evolution according to the circuit description, and H_{out} to certify the final output. In particular, the corresponding history state is in the ground space of H_{in}, H_{clock}, and H_{prop}. Note that BQP is a decision problem and its outcome $(0/1)$ can be easily encoded into the energy H_{out} on the single output qubit. As a result, the outcome of BQP can simply be encoded by the *ground energy* of $H_{in} + H_{clock} + H_{prop} + H_{out}$.

To deal with $\mathsf{SampBQP}$, we will still employ H_{in}, H_{clock}, and H_{prop} to certify the circuit's input, the clock register, and gate-by-gate evolution. However, in $\mathsf{SampBQP}$, we care about the entire final state of the circuit, rather than the energy on the output qubit. Our approach to certify the entire final state (which is encoded inside the history state) is to make sure that the history state is the unique ground state of $H_{in} + H_{clock} + H_{prop}$ and all other orthogonal states will have much higher energies. Namely, we need to construct some $H'_{in} + H'_{clock} + H'_{prop}$ with the history state as the unique ground state and with a large *spectral* gap between the ground energy and excited energies. It is hence guaranteed that any state with close-to-ground energy must also be close to the history state. We remark that this is a different requirement from most local Hamiltonian constructions that focus on the ground energy. We achieve so by

---

[11] The original construction is for the purpose of certifying problems in QMA. We consider its simple restriction to problems inside BQP.

using the *perturbation* technique developed in [27] for reducing the locality of Hamiltonian. Another example of local Hamiltonian construction with a focus on the spectral gap can be found in [5], where the purpose is to simulate quantum circuits by adiabatic quantum computation.

We need two more twists for our purpose. First, as we will eventually measure the final state in order to obtain classical samples, we need that the final state occupies a large fraction of the history state. We can simply add dummy identity gates. Second, as we are only able to perform X or Z measurement by techniques from [30], we need to construct X-Z only local Hamiltonians. Indeed, this has been shown possible in, e.g., [11], which serves as the starting point of our construction.

We present the formal construction of our QPIP_1 protocol Π_{Samp} for SampBQP in our full version [17]. The soundness and completeness of Π_{Samp} is stated in the following theorem, whose proof is also deferred to [17].

Theorem 5. Π_{Samp} *is a* QPIP_1 *protocol for the* SampBQP *problem* $(D_x)_{x\in\{0,1\}^*}$ *with negligible completeness error and is statistically sound[12] where the verifier only needs to do non-adaptive* X/Z *measurements.*

4   SampBQP Delegation Protocol for Fully Classical Client

In this section, we create a delegation protocol for SampBQP with fully classical clients by adapting the approach taken in [30]. In [30], Mahadev designed a protocol Π_{Measure} (Protocol 1) that allows a BQP prover to "commit a state" for a classical verifier to choose a X or Z measurement and obtain corresponding measurement results. Composing it with the QPIP_1 protocol for BQP from [21] results in a QPIP_0 protocol for BQP. In this work, we will compose Π_{Measure} with our QPIP_1 protocol Π_{Samp} for SampBQP in order to obtain a QPIP_0 protocol for SampBQP.

A direct composition of Π_{Samp} and Π_{Measure}, however, results in Π_{int} (Protocol 2) which does not provide reasonable completeness or accuracy guarantees. As we will see, this is due to Π_{Measure} itself having peculiar and weak guarantees: the client doesn't always obtain measurement outcomes even if the server were honest. When that happens under the BQP context, the verifier can simply accept the prover at the cost of some soundness error; under our SampBQP context, however, we must run many copies of Π_{int} in parallel so the verifier can generate its outputs from some copy. We will spend the majority of this section analyzing the soundness of this parallel repetition.

4.1   Mahadev's Measurement Protocol

Π_{Measure} is a 4-round protocol between a verifier (which corresponds to our client) and a prover (which corresponds to our server). The verifier (secretly) chooses a string h specifying the measurements he wants to make, and generates keys pk, sk from h. It sends pk to the prover. The prover "commits" to a state ρ of

---

[12] The soundness and completeness of a SampBQP protocol is defined in Definition 3.

its choice using pk and replies with its commitment y. The verifier must then choose between two options: do a *testing round* or a *Hadamard round*. In a testing round the verifier can catch cheating provers, and in a Hadamard round the verifier receives some measurement outcome. He sends his choice to the prover, and the prover replies accordingly. If the verifier chose testing round, he checks the prover's reply against the previous commitment, and rejects if he sees an inconsistency. If the verifier chose Hadamard round, he calculates $M_{XZ}(\rho, h)$ based on the reply. We now formally describe the interface of Π_{Measure} while omitting the implementation details.

Protocol 1 Mahadev's measurement protocol $\Pi_{\mathsf{Measure}} = (P_{\mathsf{Measure}}, V_{\mathsf{Measure}})$

Inputs:

- Common input: Security parameter 1^λ where $\lambda \in \mathbb{N}$.
- Prover's input: a state $\rho \in \mathcal{B}^{\otimes n}$ for the verifier to measure.
- Verifier's input: the measurement basis choice $h \in \{0,1\}^n$.

Protocol:

1. The verifier generates a public and secret key pair $(pk, sk) \leftarrow V_{\mathsf{Measure},1}(1^\lambda, h)$. It sends pk to the prover.
2. The prover generates $(y, \sigma) \leftarrow P_{\mathsf{Measure},2}(pk, \rho)$. y is a classical "commitment", and σ is some internal state. He sends y to the verifier.
3. The verifier samples $c \xleftarrow{\$} \{0,1\}$ uniformly at random and sends it to the prover. $c = 0$ indicates a *testing round*, while $c = 1$ indicates a *Hadamard round*.
4. The prover generates a classical string $a \leftarrow P_{\mathsf{Measure},4}(pk, c, \sigma)$ and sends it back to the verifier.
5. If it is a testing round ($c = 0$), then the verifier generates and outputs $o \leftarrow V_{\mathsf{Measure},T}(pk, y, a)$ where $o \in \{\mathsf{Acc}, \mathsf{Rej}\}$. If it is a Hadamard round ($c = 1$), then the verifier generates and outputs $v \leftarrow V_{\mathsf{Measure},H}(sk, h, y, a)$.

Π_{Measure} has negligible completeness errors, i.e. if both the prover and verifier are honest, the verifier accepts with overwhelming probability and his output on Hadamard round is computationally indistinguishable from $M_{XZ}(\rho, h)$. As for soundness, it gives the following *binding property* against cheating provers: if a prover would always succeed on the testing round, then there exists some ρ so that for any h the verifier obtains $M_{XZ}(\rho, h)$ if he had chosen the Hadamard round.

Lemma 1 (binding property of Π_{Measure}; special case of Claim 7.1 in [30]). *Let P^*_{Measure} be a BQP cheating prover for Π_{Measure} and λ be the security parameter. Let $1 - p_{h,T}$ be the probability that the verifier accepts P^*_{Measure} in the* *testing round on basis choice h.*[13] *Under the QLWE assumption, there exists some ρ^* so that for all verifier's input $h \in \{0,1\}^n$, the verifier's outputs on the Hadamard round is $\sqrt{p_{h,T}} + \text{negl}(n)$-computationally indistinguishable from $M_{XZ}(\rho^*, h)$.*

We now combine Π_{Measure} with our QPIP$_1$ Protocol for SampBQP, $\Pi_{\text{Samp}} = (P_{\text{Samp}}, V_{\text{Samp}})$, to get a corresponding QPIP$_0$ protocol Π_{int}. Recall that in Π_{Samp} the verifier takes X and Z measurements on the prover's message. In Π_{int} we let the verifier use Π_{Measure} to learn those measurement outcomes instead.

Protocol 2 Intermediate QPIP$_0$ protocol Π_{int} for the SampBQP problem $(D_x)_{x \in \{0,1\}^*}$

Inputs:

- Security parameter 1^λ where $\lambda \in \mathbb{N}$
- Error parameter $\epsilon \in (0,1)$
- Classical input $x \in \{0,1\}^n$ to the SampBQP instance

Protocol:

1. The verifier chooses a XZ-measurement h in the same way as in Π_{Samp}.
2. The prover prepares ρ in the same way as in Π_{Samp}.
3. The verifier and prover run $(P_{\text{Measure}}(\rho), V_{\text{Measure}}(h))(1^\lambda)$.
   (a) The verifier samples $(pk, sk) \leftarrow V_{\text{int},1}(1^\lambda, h)$ and sends pk to the prover, where $V_{\text{int},1}$ is the same as $V_{\text{Measure},1}$ of Protocol 1.
   (b) The prover runs $(y, \sigma) \leftarrow P_{\text{int},2}(pk, \rho)$ and sends y to the verifier, where $P_{\text{int},2}$ is the same as $P_{\text{Measure},2}$. Here we allow the prover to abort by sending $y = \perp$, which does not benefit cheating provers but simplifies our analysis of parallel repetition later.
   (c) The verifier samples $c \xleftarrow{\$} \{0,1\}$ and sends it to the prover.
   (d) The prover replies $a \leftarrow P_{\text{int},4}(pk, c, \sigma)$.
   (e) If it is a testing round, the verifier accepts or rejects based on the outcome of Π_{Measure}. If it is a Hadamard round, the verifier obtains v.
4. If it's a Hadamard round, the verifier finishes the verification step of Π_{Samp} by generating and outputting (d, z)

There are several problems with using Π_{int} as a SampBQP protocol. First, since the verifier doesn't get a sample if he had chosen the testing round in Step 3c, the protocol has completeness error at least $1/2$. Moreover, since Π_{Measure} does not check anything on the Hadamard round, a cheating prover can give up passing the testing round and breaks the commitment on the Hadamard round,

---

[13] Compared to Claim 7.1 of [30], we don't have a $p_{h,H}$ term here. This is because on rejecting a Hadamard round, the verifier can output a uniformly random string, and that is same as the result of measuring h on the totally mixed state.

with only a constant $1/2$ probability of being caught. However, we can show that Π_{int} has a binding property similar to $\Pi_{Measure}$: if a cheating prover P^*_{int} passes the testing round with overwhelming probability whenever it doesn't abort on the second message, then the corresponding output $(d, z) \leftarrow (P^*_{int}, V_{int})$ is close to (d, z_{ideal}). Recall the ideal output is

$$\begin{cases} z_{ideal} = \bot & \text{if } d = \text{Rej} \\ z_{ideal} \leftarrow D_x & \text{if } d = \text{Acc.} \end{cases}$$

This binding property is formalized in Theorem 6. Intuitively, the proof of Theorem 6 combines the binding property of Protocol 2 (Lemma 1) and Π_{Samp}'s soundness (Theorem 5). There is a technical issue that Protocol 2 allows the prover to abort while Protocol 1 does not. This issue is solved by constructing another BQP prover P^* for every cheating prover P^*_{int}. Specifically, P^* uses P^*_{int}'s strategy when it doesn't abort, otherwise honestly chooses the totally mixed state for the verifier to measure.

Theorem 6 (binding property of Π_{int}). *Let P^*_{int} be a cheating* BQP *prover for Π_{int} and λ be the security parameter. Suppose that $\Pr[d = \text{Acc} \mid y \neq \bot, c = 0]$ is overwhelming, under the QLWE assumption, then the verifier's output in the Hadamard round is $O(\epsilon)$-computationally indistinguishable from (d, z_{ideal}).*

Proof (Theorem 6). We first introduce the *dummy strategy* for $\Pi_{Measure}$, where the prover chooses ρ as the maximally mixed state and executes the rest of the protocol honestly. It is straightforward to verify that this prover would be accepted in the testing round with probability $1 - \text{negl}(\lambda)$, but has negligible probability passing the verification after the Hadamard round.

Now we construct a cheating BQP prover for Protocol 2, P^*, that does the same thing as P^*_{int} except at Step 3, where the prover and verifier runs Protocol 1. P^* does the following in Step 3: for the second message, run $(y, \sigma) \leftarrow P^*_{int,2}(pk, \rho)$. If $y \neq \bot$, then reply y; else, run the corresponding step of the dummy strategy and reply with its results. For the fourth message, if $y \neq \bot$, run and reply with $a \leftarrow P^*_{int,4}(pk, c, \sigma)$; else, continue the dummy strategy.

In the following we fix an x. Let the distribution on h specified in Step 1 of the protocol be $p_x(h)$. Define $P^*_{sub}(x)$ as P^*'s response in Step 3. Note that we can view $P^*_{sub}(x)$ as a prover strategy for Protocol 1. By construction $P^*_{sub}(x)$ passes testing round with overwhelming probability over $p_x(h)$, i.e. $\sum_h p_x(h) p_{h,T} = \text{negl}(\lambda)$, where $p_{h,T}$ is P^*'s probability of getting accepted by the prover on the testing round on basis choice h. By Lemma 1 and Cauchy's inequality, there exists some ρ such that $\sum_h p_x(h) \|v_h - M_{XZ}(\rho, h)\|_c = \text{negl}(\lambda)$, where we use $\|A - B\|_c = \alpha$ to denote that A is α-computational indistinguishable to B. Therefore $v = \sum_h p_x(h) v_h$ is computationally indistinguishable to $\sum_h p_x(h) M_{XZ}(\rho, h)$. Combining it with Π_{Samp}'s soundness (Theorem 5), we see that $(d', z') \leftarrow (P^*, V_{int})(1^\lambda, 1^{1/\epsilon}, x)$ is ϵ-computationally indistinguishable to (d', z'_{ideal}).

Now we relate (d', z') back to (d, z). First, conditioned on that P^*_{int} aborts, since dummy strategy will be rejected with overwhelming probability in Hadamard round, we have (d', z') is computationally indistinguishable to $(\mathsf{Rej}, \perp) = (d, z)$. On the other hand, conditioned on P_{int}^* not aborting, clearly $(d, z) = (d', z')$. So (d, z) is computationally indistinguishable to (d', z'), which in turn is $O(\epsilon)$-computationally indistinguishable to (d', z'_{ideal}). Since $\|d - d'\|_{tr} = O(\epsilon)$, (d, z_{ideal}) is $O(\epsilon)$-computationally indistinguishable to (d', z'_{ideal}). Combining everything, we conclude that (d, z) is $O(\epsilon)$-computationally indistinguishable to (d, z_{ideal}).

4.2   QPIP$_0$ Protocol for SampBQP

We now introduce our QPIP$_0$ protocol Π_{Final} for SampBQP. It is essentially a m-fold parallel repetition of Π_{int}, from which we uniformly randomly pick one copy to run Hadamard round to get our samples and run testing round on all other $m-1$ copies. Intuitively, if the server wants to cheat by sending something not binding on some copy, he will be caught when that copy is a testing round, which is with probability $1-1/m$. This over-simplified analysis does not take into account that the server might create entanglement between the copies. Therefore, a more technically involved analysis is required.

In the description of our protocol below, we describe Π_{int} and Π_{Measure} in details in order to introduce notations that we need in our analysis.

Protocol 3 QPIP$_0$ protocol Π_{Final} for the SampBQP problem $(D_x)_{x \in \{0,1\}^*}$

Inputs:

- Security parameter 1^λ for $\lambda \in \mathbb{N}$.
- Accuracy parameter $1^{1/\epsilon}$ for the SampBQP problem.
- Input $x \in \{0, 1\}^{\mathrm{poly}(\lambda)}$ for the SampBQP instance.

Ingredient: Let $m = O(1/\epsilon^2)$ be the number of parallel repetitions to run.

Protocol:

1. The verifier generates m independent copies of basis choices $\boldsymbol{h} = (h_1, \ldots, h_m)$, where each copy is generated as in Step 1 of Π_{int}.
2. The prover prepares $\rho^{\otimes m}$; each copy of ρ is prepared as in Step 2 of Π_{int}.
3. The verifier generates m key pairs for Π_{Measure}, $\boldsymbol{pk} = (pk_1, \ldots, pk_m)$ and $\boldsymbol{sk} = (sk_1, \ldots, sk_m)$, as in Step 1 of Π_{Measure}. It sends $\boldsymbol{pk}$ to the prover.
4. The prover generates $\boldsymbol{y} = (y_1, \ldots, y_m)$ and σ as in Step 2 of Π_{Measure}. It sends $\boldsymbol{y}$ to the verifier.
5. The verifier samples $r \xleftarrow{\$} [m]$ which is the copy to run Hadamard round for. For $1 \leq i \leq m$, if $i \neq r$ then set $c_i \leftarrow 0$, else set $c_i \leftarrow 1$. It sends $\boldsymbol{c} = (c_1, \ldots, c_m)$ to the prover.
6. The prover generates $\boldsymbol{a}$ as in Step 4 of Π_{Measure}, and sends it back to the verifier.

7. The verifier computes the outcome for each round as in Step 4 of Π_{int}. If any of the testing round copies are rejected, the verifier outputs $(\text{Rej}, \perp)$. Else, it outputs the result from the Hadamard round copy.

By inspection, Π_{Final} is a QPIP_0 protocol for SampBQP with negligible completeness error. To show that it is computationally sound, we first use the partition lemma from [15].

Intuitively, the partition lemma says that for any cheating prover and for each copy $i \in [m]$, there exist two efficient "projectors"[14] $G_{0,i}$ and $G_{1,i}$ in the prover's internal space with $G_{0,i} + G_{1,i} \approx Id$. $G_{0,i}$ and $G_{1,i}$ splits up the prover's residual internal state after sending back his first message. $G_{0,i}$ intuitively represents the subspace where the prover does not knows the answer to the testing round on the i-th copy, while $G_{1,i}$ represents the subspace where the prover does. Note that the prover is using a single internal space for all copies, and every $G_{0,i}$ and every $G_{1,i}$ is acting on this single internal space. By using this partition lemma iteratively, we can decompose the prover's internal state $|\psi\rangle$ into sum of subnormalized states. First we apply it to the first copy, writing $|\psi\rangle = G_{0,1}|\psi\rangle + G_{1,1}|\psi\rangle \equiv |\psi_0\rangle + |\psi_1\rangle$. The component $|\psi_0\rangle$ would then get rejected as long as the first copy is chosen as a testing round, which occurs with pretty high probability. More precisely, the output corresponding to $|\psi_0\rangle$ is $1/m$-close to the ideal distribution that just rejects all the time. On the other hand, $|\psi_1\rangle$ is now binding on the first copy; we now similarly apply the partition lemma of the second copy to $|\psi_1\rangle$. We write $|\psi_1\rangle = G_{0,2}|\psi_1\rangle + G_{1,2}|\psi_1\rangle \equiv |\psi_{10}\rangle + |\psi_{11}\rangle$, and apply the same argument about $|\psi_{10}\rangle$ and $|\psi_{11}\rangle$. We then continue to decompose $|\psi_{11}\rangle = |\psi_{110}\rangle + |\psi_{111}\rangle$ and so on, until we reach the last copy and obtain $|\psi_{1^m}\rangle$. Intuitively, the $|\psi_{1^m}\rangle$ term represents the "good" component where the prover knows the answer to every testing round and therefore has high accept probability. Therefore, $|\psi_{1^m}\rangle$ also satisfies some binding property, so the verifier should obtain a measurement result of some state on the Hadamard round copy, and the analysis from the QPIP_1 protocol Π_{Samp} follows.

However, the intuition that $|\psi_{1^m}\rangle$ is binding to every Hadamard round is incorrect. As $G_{1,i}$ does not commute with $G_{1,j}$, $|\psi_{1^m}\rangle$ is unfortunately only binding for the m-th copy. To solve this problem, we start with a pointwise argument and fix the Hadamard round on the i-th copy where $|\psi_{1^i}\rangle$ is binding, and show that the corresponding output is $O(\||\psi_{1^{i-1}0}\rangle\|)$-close to ideal. We can later average out this error over the different choices of i, since not all $\||\psi_{1^{i-1}0}\rangle\|$ can be large at the same time. Another way to see this issue is to notice that we are partitioning a quantum state, not probability events, so there are some inconsistencies between our intuition and calculation. Indeed, the error we get in the end is $O(\sqrt{1/m})$ instead of the $O(1/m)$ we expected.

Also a careful reader might have noticed that the prover's space don't always decompose cleanly into parts that the verifier either rejects or accepts with high probability, as there might be some states that is accepted with mediocre proba-

---
[14] Actually they are not projectors, but for the simplicity of this discussion let's assume they are.

bility. As in [15], we solve this by splitting the space into parts that are accepted with probability higher or lower than a small threshold γ and applying Marriott-Watrous [31] amplification to boost the accept probability if it is bigger than γ, getting a corresponding amplified prover action Ext. However, states with accept probability really close to the threshold γ can not be classified, so we average over randomly chosen γ to have $G_{0,i} + G_{1,i} \approx Id$. Now we give a formal description of the partition lemma.

Lemma 2 (partition lemma; revision of Lemma 3.5 of [15][15]). *Let λ be the security parameter, and $\gamma_0 \in [0,1]$ and $T \in \mathbb{N}$ be parameters that will be related to the randomly-chosen threshold γ. Let (U_0, U) be a prover's strategy in a m-fold parallel repetition of Π_{Measure}[16], where U_0 is how the prover generates $\mathbf{y}$ on the second message, and U is how the prover generates $\mathbf{a}$ on the fourth message. Let $H_{\mathbf{X},\mathbf{Z}}$ be the Hilbert space of the prover's internal calculation. Denote the string $0^{i-1}10^{m-i} \in \{0,1\}^m$ as e_i, which corresponds to doing Hadamard round on the i-th copy and testing round on all others.*

For all $i \in [m]$, $\gamma \in \left\{ \frac{\gamma_0}{T}, \frac{2\gamma_0}{T}, \ldots, \frac{T\gamma_0}{T} \right\}$, there exist two $\mathrm{poly}(1/\gamma_0, T, \lambda)$-time quantum circuit with post selection[17] $G_{0,i,\gamma}$ and $G_{1,i,\gamma}$ such that for all (possibly sub-normalized) quantum states $|\psi\rangle_{\mathbf{X},\mathbf{Z}} \in H_{\mathbf{X},\mathbf{Z}}$, properties 1 2 3 4, to be described later, are satisfied. Before we describe the properties, we introduce the following notations:

$$|\psi_{0,i,\gamma}\rangle_{\mathbf{X},\mathbf{Z}} := G_{0,i,\gamma}|\psi\rangle_{\mathbf{X},\mathbf{Z}}, \tag{4.1}$$

$$|\psi_{1,i,\gamma}\rangle_{\mathbf{X},\mathbf{Z}} := G_{1,i,\gamma}|\psi\rangle_{\mathbf{X},\mathbf{Z}}, \tag{4.2}$$

$$|\psi_{err,i,\gamma}\rangle_{\mathbf{X},\mathbf{Z}} := |\psi\rangle_{\mathbf{X},\mathbf{Z}} - |\psi_{0,i,\gamma}\rangle_{\mathbf{X},\mathbf{Z}} - |\psi_{1,i,\gamma}\rangle_{\mathbf{X},\mathbf{Z}}. \tag{4.3}$$

Note that $G_{0,i,\gamma}$ and $G_{1,i,\gamma}$ has failure probabilities, and this is reflected by the fact that $|\psi_{0,i,\gamma}\rangle_{\mathbf{X},\mathbf{Z}}$ and $|\psi_{1,i,\gamma}\rangle_{\mathbf{X},\mathbf{Z}}$ are sub-normalized. $G_{0,i,\gamma}$ and $G_{1,i,\gamma}$ depend on (U_0, U) and $\mathbf{pk}, \mathbf{y}$.

The following properties are satisfied for all $i \in [m]$:

---

[15] G_0 and G_1 of this version are created from doing G of [15] and post-selecting on the ph, th, in register being 0^t01 or 0^t11 then discard ph, th, in. Property 1 corresponds to Property 1. Property 2 corresponds to Property 4, with 2^{m-1} changes to $m-1$ because we only have m possible choices of $\mathbf{c}$. Property 3 corresponds to Property 5. Property 4 comes from the fact that G_0 and G_1 are post-selections of orthogonal results of the same G.

[16] A m-fold parallel repetition of Π_{Measure} is running step 3 4 5 6 of Protocol 3 with verifier input $\mathbf{h}$ and prover input $\rho^{\otimes n}$, followed by an output step where the verifier rejects if any of the $m-1$ testing round copies is rejected, otherwise outputs the result of the Hadamard round copy.

[17] A quantum circuit with post selection is composed of unitary gates followed by a post selection on some measurement outcome on ancilla qubits, so it produces a sub-normalized state, where the amplitude square of the output state is the probability of post selection.

1.

$$\mathop{\mathbb{E}}_{\gamma} \||\psi_{err,i,\gamma}\rangle_{\mathbf{X},\mathbf{Z}}\|^2 \leq \frac{6}{T} + \mathrm{negl}(\lambda),$$

where the averaged is over uniformly sampled γ. This also implies

$$\mathop{\mathbb{E}}_{\gamma} \||\psi_{err,i,\gamma}\rangle_{\mathbf{X},\mathbf{Z}}\| \leq \sqrt{\frac{6}{T}} + \mathrm{negl}(\lambda) \tag{4.4}$$

by Cauchy's inequality.

2. For all $\mathbf{pk}$, $\mathbf{y}$, γ, and $j \neq i$, we have

$$\left\| P_{acc,i} \circ U \frac{|e_j\rangle_{\mathbf{C}} |\psi_{0,i,\gamma}\rangle_{\mathbf{X},\mathbf{Z}}}{\||\psi_{0,i,\gamma}\rangle_{\mathbf{X},\mathbf{Z}}\|} \right\|^2 \leq (m-1)\gamma_0 + \mathrm{negl}(\lambda), \tag{4.5}$$

where $P_{acc,i}$ are projector to the states that i-th testing round accepts with pk_i, y_i, including the last measurement the prover did before sending $\mathbf{a}$. This means that $|\psi_{0,i,\gamma}\rangle$ is rejected by the i-th testing round with high probability.

3. For all $\mathbf{pk}$, $\mathbf{y}$, γ, and $j \neq i$, there exists an efficient quantum algorithm Ext_i such that

$$\left\| P_{acc,i} \circ \mathsf{Ext}_i \left(\frac{|e_j\rangle_{\mathbf{C}} |\psi_{1,i,\gamma}\rangle_{\mathbf{X},\mathbf{Z}}}{\||\psi_{1,i,\gamma}\rangle_{\mathbf{X},\mathbf{Z}}\|} \right) \right\|^2 = 1 - \mathrm{negl}(\lambda). \tag{4.6}$$

This will imply that $|\psi_{1,i,\gamma}\rangle$ is binding to the i-th Hadamard round.

4. For all γ,

$$\||\psi_{0,i,\gamma}\rangle_{\mathbf{X},\mathbf{Z}}\|^2 + \||\psi_{1,i,\gamma}\rangle_{\mathbf{X},\mathbf{Z}}\|^2 \leq \||\psi\rangle_{\mathbf{X},\mathbf{Z}}\|^2. \tag{4.7}$$

Note that in property 3, we are using Ext_i instead of U because we use amplitude amplification to boost the success probability.

We now decompose the prover's internal state by using Lemma 2 iteratively. Let $|\psi\rangle$ be the state the prover holds before he receives $\mathbf{c}$; we denote the corresponding Hilbert space as $H_{\mathbf{X},\mathbf{Z}}$. For all $k \in [m]$, $d \in \{0,1\}^k$, $\gamma = (\gamma_1, \ldots, \gamma_k)$ where each $\gamma_j \in \{\frac{\gamma_0}{T}, \frac{2\gamma_0}{T}, \ldots, \frac{T\gamma_0}{T}\}$, and $|\psi\rangle \in H_{\mathbf{X},\mathbf{Z}}$, define

$$|\psi_{d,\gamma}\rangle := G_{d_k,k,\gamma_k} \ldots G_{d_2,2,\gamma_2} G_{d_1,1,\gamma_1} |\psi\rangle.$$

For all $i \in [m]$, we then decompose $|\psi\rangle$ into

$$|\psi\rangle = \sum_{j=0}^{i-1} |\psi_{1^j 0,\gamma}\rangle + |\psi_{1^i,\gamma}\rangle + \sum_{j=1}^{i} |\psi_{err,j,\gamma}\rangle \tag{4.8}$$

by using Equations (4.1) to (4.3) repeatedly, where $|\psi_{err,i,\gamma}\rangle$ denotes the error state from decomposing $|\psi_{1^{i-1},\gamma}\rangle$.

We denote the projector in $H_{\mathbf{X},\mathbf{Z}}$ corresponding to outputting string z when doing Hadamard on i-th copy as $P_{acc,-i,z}$. Note that $P_{acc,-i,z}$ also depends on $\mathbf{pk}, \mathbf{y}$, and (sk_i, h_i) since it includes the measurement the prover did before sending a, verifier's checking on $(m-1)$ copies of testing rounds, and the verifier's final computation from (sk_i, h_i, y_i, a_i). $P_{acc,-i,z}$ is a projector because it only involves the standard basis measurements to get a and classical postprocessing of the verifiers. Also note that $P_{acc,-i,z}P_{acc,-i,z'} = 0$ for all $z \neq z'$, and $\sum_z P_{acc,-i,z} = \Pi_{j \neq i} P_{acc,j} \leq Id$.

We denote the string $0^{i-1}10^{m-i} \in \{0,1\}^m$ as e_i. The output string corresponding to $|\psi\rangle \in H_{\mathbf{X},\mathbf{Z}}$ when $c = e_i$ is then

$$z_i := \mathop{\mathbb{E}}_{pk,y} \sum_z \left\| P_{acc,-i,z} U |e_i, \psi\rangle \right\|^2 |z\rangle\langle z|, \tag{4.9}$$

where $|e_i, \psi\rangle = |e_i\rangle_{\mathbf{C}} |\psi\rangle_{\mathbf{X},\mathbf{Z}}$ and U is the unitary the prover applies on the last round. Note that we have averaged over pk, y where as previously everything has fixed pk and y.

By Property 2 of Lemma 2, it clearly follows that

Corollary 1 *For all* $\gamma \in \{\frac{\gamma_0}{T}, \frac{2\gamma_0}{T}, \ldots, \frac{T\gamma_0}{T}\}$, *and all* $i, j \in [m]$ *such that* $j < i-1$, *we have*

$$\left\| \sum_z P_{acc,-i,z} U |e_i, \psi_{1^j 0, \gamma}\rangle \right\|^2 \leq (m-1)\gamma_0 + \mathrm{negl}(n).$$

Now we define

$$z_{good,i} = \mathop{\mathbb{E}}_{\gamma,pk,y} \sum_z \left\| P_{acc,-i,z} U |e_i, \psi_{1^{i-1}1, \gamma}\rangle \right\|^2 |z\rangle\langle z| \tag{4.10}$$

as the output corresponding to a component that would pass the i-th testing rounds. We will show that it is $O(\||\psi_{1^{i-1}0}\rangle\|)$-close to z_i. Before doing so, we present a technical lemma.

Lemma 3. *For any state* $|\psi\rangle$, $|\phi\rangle$ *and projectors* $\{P_z\}$ *such that* $P_z P_{z'} = 0$ *for all* $z \neq z'$, *we have*

$$\sum_z |\langle\psi|P_z|\phi\rangle| \leq \sqrt{\left\|\sum_z P_z|\psi\rangle\right\|^2} \sqrt{\left\|\sum_z P_z|\phi\rangle\right\|^2}.$$

Proof.

$$\sum_z |\langle\psi|P_z|\phi\rangle| = \sum_z |\langle\psi|P_z P_z|\phi\rangle| \leq \sum_z \|\langle\psi|P_z\| \, \|P_z|\phi\rangle\|$$

$$\leq \sqrt{\sum_z \|P_z|\psi\rangle\|^2} \sqrt{\sum_z \|P_z|\phi\rangle\|^2}$$

$$\leq \sqrt{\left\|\sum_z P_z|\psi\rangle\right\|^2} \sqrt{\left\|\sum_z P_z|\phi\rangle\right\|^2},$$

where we used Cauchy's inequality on the first two inequalities and $P_z P_{z'} = 0$ on the last one.

Corollary 2 *For any state $|\psi\rangle$, $|\phi\rangle$ and projectors $\{P_z\}$ such that $\sum_z P_z \leq Id$ and $P_z P_{z'} = 0$ for all $z \neq z'$, we have*

$$\sum_z |\langle\psi|P_z|\phi\rangle| \leq \|\psi\| \, \|\phi\| .$$

Now we can estimate z_i using $z_{good,i}$, with errors on the orders of $\||\psi_{1^{i-1}0}\rangle\|$. This error might not be small in general, but we can average it out later by considering uniformly random $i \in [m]$. The analysis is tedious but straightforward; we simply expand z_i and bound the terms that are not $z_{good,i}$.

Lemma 4.

$$\operatorname{tr}|z_i - z_{good,i}| \leq \mathop{\mathbb{E}}_{pk,y,\gamma}\left[\||\psi_{1^{i-1}0,\gamma}\rangle\|^2 + 2\,\||\psi_{1^{i-1}0,\gamma}\rangle\|\right]$$

$$+ O\left(\frac{m^2}{\sqrt{T}} + m\sqrt{(m-1)\gamma_0}\right).$$

Proof (Lemma 4). We take expectation of Eq. (4.8) over γ

$$|\psi\rangle = \mathop{\mathbb{E}}_{\gamma}\left[\sum_{j=0}^{i-1}|\psi_{1^j0,\gamma}\rangle + |\psi_{1^i,\gamma}\rangle + \sum_{j=1}^{i}|\psi_{err,j,\gamma}\rangle\right],$$

and expand z_i from Eq. (4.9) as

$$z_i = z_{good,i} + \mathop{\mathbb{E}}_{pk,y,\gamma}\sum_z\left[\sum_{k=0}^{i-1}\langle\psi_{1^k0,\gamma}|U^\dagger P_{acc,-i,z}U\sum_{j=0}^{i-1}|\psi_{1^j0,\gamma}\rangle\right.$$

$$+ \sum_{k=0}^{i-1}\langle\psi_{1^k0,\gamma}|U^\dagger P_{acc,-i,z}U|\psi_{1^i,\gamma}\rangle + \sum_{k=0}^{i-1}\langle\psi_{1^k0,\gamma}|U^\dagger P_{acc,-i,z}U\sum_{j=1}^{i}|\psi_{err,j,\gamma}\rangle$$

$$+ \langle\psi_{1^i,\gamma}|U^\dagger P_{acc,-i,z}U\sum_{j=0}^{i-1}|\psi_{1^j0,\gamma}\rangle + \langle\psi_{1^i,\gamma}|U^\dagger P_{acc,-i,z}U\sum_{j=1}^{i}|\psi_{err,j,\gamma}\rangle$$

$$+ \sum_{k=1}^{i}\langle\psi_{err,k,\gamma}|U^\dagger P_{acc,-i,z}U\sum_{j=0}^{i-1}|\psi_{1^j0,\gamma}\rangle + \sum_{k=1}^{i}\langle\psi_{err,k,\gamma}|U^\dagger P_{acc,-i,z}U|\psi_{1^i,\gamma}\rangle$$

$$\left.+ \sum_{k=1}^{i}\langle\psi_{err,k,\gamma}|U^\dagger P_{acc,-i,z}U\sum_{j=1}^{i}|\psi_{err,j,\gamma}\rangle\right]|z\rangle\langle z|,$$

where we omitted writing out e_i. Therefore we have

$$
\mathrm{tr}|z_i - z_{good,i}| \leq \mathop{\mathbb{E}}_{pk,y,\gamma} \sum_z \left[\sum_{k=0}^{i-1}\sum_{j=0}^{i-1} \left| \langle \psi_{1^k 0,\gamma}| U^\dagger P_{acc,-i,z} U |\psi_{1^j 0,\gamma}\rangle \right| \right.
$$

$$
+ 2\sum_{k=0}^{i-1} \left| \langle \psi_{1^k 0,\gamma}| U^\dagger P_{acc,-i,z} U |\psi_{1^i,\gamma}\rangle \right| + 2\sum_{k=0}^{i-1}\sum_{j=1}^{i} \left| \langle \psi_{1^k 0,\gamma}| U^\dagger P_{acc,-i,z} U |\psi_{err,j,\gamma}\rangle \right|
$$

$$
\left. + 2\sum_{j=1}^{i} \left| \langle \psi_{1^i,\gamma}| U^\dagger P_{acc,-i,z} U |\psi_{err,j,\gamma}\rangle \right| + \sum_{k=1}^{i}\sum_{j=1}^{i} \left| \langle \psi_{err,k,\gamma}| U^\dagger P_{acc,-i,z} U |\psi_{err,j,\gamma}\rangle \right| \right]
$$

by the triangle inequality. The last three error terms sum to $O\left(\frac{m^2}{\sqrt{T}}\right)$ by Corollary 2 and property 1 of Lemma 2. As for the first two terms, by Lemma 3 and Corollary 1, we see that

$$
\sum_z \sum_{k=0}^{i-1}\sum_{j=0}^{i-1} \left| \langle \psi_{1^k 0,\gamma}| U^\dagger P_{acc,-i,z} U |\psi_{1^j 0,\gamma}\rangle \right|
$$

$$
\leq \sum_z \left| \langle \psi_{1^{i-1}0,\gamma}| U^\dagger P_{acc,-i,z} U |\psi_{1^{i-1}0,\gamma}\rangle \right| + O\left(m^2(m-1)\gamma_0\right)
$$

$$
\leq \left\| |\psi_{1^{i-1}0,\gamma}\rangle \right\|^2 + O\left(m^2(m-1)\gamma_0\right)
$$

and similarly

$$
\sum_z \sum_{k=0}^{i-1} \left| \langle \psi_{1^k 0,\gamma}| U^\dagger P_{acc,-i,z} U |\psi_{1^i,\gamma}\rangle \right|
$$

$$
\leq \sum_z \left| \langle \psi_{1^{i-1}0,\gamma}| U^\dagger P_{acc,-i,z} U |\psi_{1^i,\gamma}\rangle \right| + O\left(m\sqrt{(m-1)\gamma_0}\right)
$$

$$
\leq \left\| |\psi_{1^i,\gamma}\rangle \right\| + O\left(m\sqrt{(m-1)\gamma_0}\right).
$$

Now let z_{true}, as a mixed state, be the correct sample of the SampBQP instance D_x, and let $z_{ideal,i} = \mathrm{tr}(z_{good,i})z_{true}$. We show that $z_{ideal,i}$ is close to $z_{good,i}$.

Lemma 5. $z_{good,i}$ *is $O(\epsilon)$-computationally indistinguishable to $z_{ideal,i}$, where $\epsilon \in \mathbb{R}$ is the accuracy parameter picked earlier in Π_{Final}.*

Proof (Lemma 5). For every $i \in [m]$ and every prover strategy (U_0, U) for Π_{Final}, consider the following composite strategy, $\Pi_{\mathsf{comp},i}$, as a prover for Π_{int}. Note that a prover only interacts with the verifier in Step 3 of Π_{int} where Π_{Measure} is run, so we describe a prover's action in terms of the four rounds of communication in Π_{Measure}.

$\Pi_{\mathsf{comp},i}$ tries to run U_0 by taking the verifier's input as the input to the i-th copy of Π_{Measure} in Π_{Final} and simulating other $m-1$ copies by himself.

The prover then picks a uniformly random γ and tries to generate $|\psi_{1^{i-1}1,\gamma}\rangle$ by applying $G_{i,1,\gamma}G_{i-1,1,\gamma}\cdots G_{2,1,\gamma}G_{1,1,\gamma}$. This can be efficiently done because of Lemma 2 and our choice of γ_0 and T in Theorem 7. If the prover fails to generate $|\psi_{1^{i-1}1,\gamma}\rangle$, he throws out everything and aborts by sending $\perp$ back. On the fourth round, If it's a testing round the prover reply with the i-th register of $\mathsf{Ext}_i\left(\frac{|e_j\rangle_{\mathbf{C}}|\psi_{1,i,\gamma}\rangle_{\mathbf{x},\mathbf{z}}}{\||\psi_1\rangle_{\mathbf{x},\mathbf{z}}\|}\right)$, where Ext_i is specified in property 3 of Lemma 2. If it's the Hadamard round the prover runs U and checks whether every copy except the i-th copy would be accepted. If all $m-1$ copies are accepted, he replies with the i-th copy, otherwise reply $\perp$.

Denote the result we would get in the Hadamard round by $z_{composite,i}$. By construction, when $G_{i,1,\gamma}\ldots G_{1,1,\gamma}$ succeeded, the corresponding output would be $z_{good,i}$. Also note that this is the only case where the verifier won't reject, so $z_{composite,i} = z_{good,i}$.

In the testing round, by property 3 of Lemma 2, the above strategy is accepted with probability $1 - \mathrm{negl}(n)$ when the prover didn't abort. Since the prover's strategy is also efficient, by Theorem 6, $z_{composite,i}$ is $O(\epsilon)$-computationally indistinguishable to $z_{ideal,i}$.

Now we try to put together all $i \in [m]$. First let

$$z = \frac{1}{m}\sum_i z_i = \frac{1}{m}\sum_i\sum_z |z\rangle\langle z| \cdot \langle e_i,\psi|U^\dagger P_{acc,-i,z}U|e_i,\psi\rangle,$$

which is the output distribution of Π_{Final}. We also define the following accordingly:

$$z_{good} := \frac{1}{m}\sum_i z_{good,i},$$

$$z_{ideal} := \frac{1}{m}\sum_i z_{ideal,i}.$$

Notice that z_{ideal} is some ideal output distribution, which might not have the same accept probability as z.

Theorem 7. *Under the* QLWE *assumption,* Π_{Final} *is a protocol for the* SampBQP *problem* $(D_x)_{x\in\{0,1\}^*}$ *with negligible completeness error and is computationally sound.*[18]

Proof. Completeness is trivial. In the following we prove the soundness.
By Property 4 of Lemma 2, we have

$$\||\psi\rangle\|^2 \geq \||\psi_{0,\gamma}\rangle\|^2 + \||\psi_{1,\gamma}\rangle\|^2$$
$$\geq \||\psi_{0,\gamma}\rangle\|^2 + \||\psi_{10,\gamma}\rangle\|^2 + \||\psi_{11,\gamma}\rangle\|^2$$
$$\geq \||\psi_{0,\gamma}\rangle\|^2 + \||\psi_{10,\gamma}\rangle\|^2 + \cdots + \||\psi_{1^{m-1}0,\gamma}\rangle\|^2 + \||\psi_{1^m,\gamma}\rangle\|^2. \quad (4.11)$$

---

[18] The soundness and completeness of a SampBQP protocol is defined in Definition 3.

We have

$$
\begin{aligned}
\mathrm{tr}|z - z_{good}| = \mathrm{tr}\left|\frac{1}{m}\sum_i (z_i - z_{good,i})\right| &\leq \frac{1}{m}\sum_i \mathrm{tr}|(z_i - z_{good,i})| \\
&\leq \frac{1}{m}\sum_i \left[\operatorname*{\mathbb{E}}_{pk,y,\gamma}\left[\left\||\psi_{1^{i-1}0,\gamma}\rangle\right\|^2 + 2\left\||\psi_{1^{i-1}0,\gamma}\rangle\right\|\right]\right. \\
&\qquad \left. + O\left(\frac{m^2}{\sqrt{T}} + m\sqrt{(m-1)\gamma_0}\right)\right] \\
&\leq \frac{1}{m} + 2\frac{1}{\sqrt{m}} + O\left(\frac{m^2}{\sqrt{T}} + m\sqrt{(m-1)\gamma_0}\right) \\
&= O\left(\frac{1}{\sqrt{m}} + \frac{m^2}{\sqrt{T}} + m\sqrt{(m-1)\gamma_0}\right), \quad\quad (4.12)
\end{aligned}
$$

where we used triangle inequality on the first inequality, Lemma 4 on the next one, Eq. 4.11 and Cauchy's inequality on the last one. Set $m = O(1/\epsilon^2), T = O(1/\epsilon^2), \gamma_0 = \epsilon^8$. Combining Lemma 5 and Eq. (4.12) by triangle inequality, we have z is $O(\epsilon)$-computationally indistinguishable to z_{ideal}. Therefore, (d, z) $O(\epsilon)$-computationally indistinguishable to (d, z_{ideal}).

Theorem 1 follows as a corollary.

5   Generic Blindness Protocol Compiler for QPIP$_0$

In this section, we present a generic protocol compiler that compiles any QPIP$_0$ protocol $\Pi = (P, V)$ (with an arbitrary number of rounds) to a protocol $\Pi_{\text{blind}} = (P_{\text{blind}}, V_{\text{blind}})$ that achieve blindness while preserving the completeness, soundness, and round complexity. At a high-level, the idea is simple: we simply run the original protocol under a quantum homomorphic encryption QHE with the verifier's key. Intuitively, this allows the prover to compute his next message under encryption without learning the underlying verifier's message, and hence achieves blindness while preserving the properties of the original protocol.

However, several issues need to be taking care to make the idea work. First, since the verifier is classical, we need the quantum homomorphic encryption scheme QHE to be *classical friendly* as defined in our full version [17]. Namely, the key generation algorithm and the encryption algorithm for classical messages should be classical, and when the underlying message is classical, the ciphertext (potentially from homomorphic evaluation) and the decryption algorithm should be classical as well. Fortunately, the quantum homomorphic encryption scheme of Mahadev [29] and Brakerski [12] are classical friendly. Moreover, Brakerski's scheme requires a weaker QLWE assumption, where the modulus is polynomial instead of super-polynomial.

A more subtle issue is to preserve the soundness. Intuitively, the soundness holds since the execution of Π_{blind} simulates the execution of Π, and hence the soundness of Π implies the soundness of Π_{blind}. However, to see the subtle issue, let us consider the following naive compiler that uses a single key: In Π_{blind}, the verifier V initially generates a pair QHE key (pk, sk), sends pk and encrypted input QHE.Enc(pk, x) to P. Then they run Π under encryption with this key, where both of them use homomorphic evaluation to compute their next message.

There are two reasons that the compiled protocol Π_{blind} may not be sound (or even not blind). First, in general, the QHE scheme may not have *circuit privacy*; namely, the homomorphic evaluation may leak information about the circuit being evaluated. Since the verifier computes his next message using homomorphic evaluation, a cheating prover P^*_{blind} seeing the homomorphically evaluated ciphertext of the verifier's message may learn information about the verifier's next message circuit, which may contain information about the secret input x or help P^*_{blind} to break the soundness. Second, P^*_{blind} may send invalid ciphertexts to V, so the execution of Π_{blind} may not simulate a valid execution of Π.

To resolve the issue, we let the verifier switch to a fresh new key for each round of the protocol.[19] For example, when the prover P_{blind} returns the ciphertext of his first message, the verifier V_{blind} decrypts the ciphertext, computes his next message (in the clear), and then encrypt it using a fresh key pk' and sends it to P_{blind}. Note that a fresh key pair is necessary here to ensure blindness, as decrypting uses information from the secret key. Since the verifier V_{blind} only sends fresh ciphertexts to P_{blind}, this avoids the issue of circuit privacy. Additionally, to allow P_{blind} to homomorphically evaluate its next message, V_{blind} needs to encrypt the previous secret key sk under the new public key pk' and send it along with pk' to P_{blind}. This allows the prover to homomorphically convert ciphertexts under key pk to ciphertexts under key pk'. By doing so, we show that for any cheating prover P^*_{blind}, the interaction $(P^*_{\text{blind}}, V_{\text{blind}})$ indeed simulates a valid interaction of (P^*, V) for some cheating P^*, and hence the soundness of Π implies the soundness of the compiled protocol. Finally, for the issue of the prover sending invalid ciphertexts, we note that this is not an issue if the decryption never fails, which can be achieved by simply let the decryption algorithm output a default dummy message (e.g., 0) when it fails.

We note that the idea of running the protocol under homomorphic encryptions is used in [16] in a classical setting, but for a different purpose of making the protocol "computationally simulatable" in their context.

We proceed to present our compiler. We start by introducing the notation of a QPIP$_0$ protocol Π as follows.

---

[19] An alternative strategy is to assume circuit privacy of QHE. This seems to require many additional properties such as *malicious* circuit privacy with efficient simulation and extraction when QHE.Keygen is honest and secret key is available, multi-hop evaluation, and classical QHE.Eval on classical ciphertexts and circuits. While existing constructions such as [14] achieves some of these properties, we are unsure if any construction satisfies all of these requirements.

Protocol 4 QPIP$_0$ protocol $\Pi = (P, V)(x)$ where only the verifier receives outputs

---

Common inputs[20]:

- Security parameter 1^λ where $\lambda \in \mathbb{N}$
- A classical input $x \in \{0, 1\}^{\text{poly}(\lambda)}$

Protocol:

1. V generates $(v_1, st_{V,1}) \leftarrow \mathcal{V}_1(1^\lambda, x)$ and sends v_1 to the prover.
2. P generates $(p_1, st_{P,1}) \leftarrow \mathcal{P}_1(1^\lambda, v_1, x)$ and sends p_1 to the verifier.
3. for $t = 2, \ldots, T$:
   (a) V generates $(v_t, st_{V,t}) \leftarrow \mathcal{V}_t(p_{t-1}, st_{V,t-1})$ and sends v_t to the prover.
   (b) P generates $(p_t, st_{P,t}) \leftarrow \mathcal{P}_t(v_t, st_{P,t-1})$ and sends p_t to the verifier.
4. V computes its output $o \leftarrow \mathcal{V}_{out}(p_T, st_{V,T})$.

We compile the above protocol to achieve blindness as follows. For notation, when there are many sets of QHE keys in play at the same time, we use $\widehat{x}^{(i)}$ to denote x encrypted under pk_i.

Protocol 5 Blind QPIP$_0$ protocol $\Pi_{\text{blind}} = (P_{\text{blind}}, V_{\text{blind}}(x))$ corresponding to Π_0

Inputs:

- Common input: Security parameter 1^λ where $\lambda \in \mathbb{N}$
- Verifier's input: $x \in \{0, 1\}^{\text{poly}(\lambda)}$

Ingredients:

- Let L be the maximum circuit depth of $\mathcal{P}_t$.

Protocol:

1. V_{blind} generates $(v_1, st_{V,1}) \leftarrow \mathcal{V}_1(1^\lambda, x)$. Then it generates $(pk_1, sk_1) \leftarrow$ QHE.Keygen$(1^\lambda, 1^L)$, and encrypts $\widehat{x}^{(1)} \leftarrow$ QHE.Enc(pk_1, x) and $\widehat{v}_1^{(1)} \leftarrow$ QHE.Enc(pk_1, v_1). It sends pk_1, $\widehat{x}^{(1)}$, and $\widehat{v}_1^{(1)}$ to the prover.
2. P_{blind} generates $(\widehat{p}_1^{(1)}, \widehat{st}_{P,1}^{(1)}) \leftarrow \mathcal{P}_{\text{blind},1}(1^\lambda, \widehat{v}_1^{(1)}, \widehat{x}^{(1)})$ by evaluating $(\widehat{p}_1^{(1)}, \widehat{st}_{P,1}^{(1)}) \leftarrow$ QHE.Eval$(pk, \mathcal{P}_1,$ QHE.Enc$(pk_1, 1^\lambda), \widehat{v}_1^{(1)}, \widehat{x}^{(1)})$. It sends $\widehat{p}_1^{(1)}$ to the verifier.
3. for $t = 2, \ldots, T$:

---

[20] For the sake of simplicity, we omit accuracy parameter ϵ where it exists

(a) V_{blind} decrypts the prover's last message by $p_{t-1} \leftarrow \mathsf{QHE.Dec}$ $(sk_{t-1}, \widehat{p}_{t-1}^{(t-1)})$, then generates $(v_t, st_{V,t}) \leftarrow V_t(p_{t-1}, st_{V,t-1})$. Then it generates $(pk_t, sk_t) \leftarrow \mathsf{QHE.Keygen}(1^\lambda, 1^L)$, and produces encryptions $\widehat{v}_t^{(t)} \leftarrow \mathsf{QHE.Enc}(pk_t, v_t)$ and $\widehat{sk}_{t-1}^{(t)} \leftarrow \mathsf{QHE.Enc}(pk_t, sk_{t-1})$. It sends pk_t, $\widehat{v}_t^{(t)}$, and $\widehat{sk}_{t-1}^{(t)}$ to the prover.

(b) P_{blind} generates $(\widehat{p}_t^{(t)}, \widehat{st}_{P,t}^{(t)}) \leftarrow P_{\mathsf{blind},t}(\widehat{v}_t^{(t)}, \widehat{sk}_{t-1}^{(t)}, \widehat{st}_{P,t-1}^{(t-1)})$ by first switching its encryption key; that is, it encrypts its state under the new key by $\widehat{st}_{P,t-1}^{(t-1,t)} \leftarrow \mathsf{QHE.Enc}(pk_t, \widehat{st}_{P,t-1}^{(t-1)}))$, then homomorphically decrypts the old encryption by $\widehat{st}_{P,t-1}^{(t)} \leftarrow \mathsf{QHE.Eval}(pk_t, \mathsf{QHE.Dec}, \ \widehat{sk}_{t-1}^{(t)}, \widehat{st}_{P,t-1}^{(t-1,t)})$. Then it applies the next-message function homomorphically, generating $(\widehat{p}_t^{(t)}, \widehat{st}_{P,t}^{(t)}) \leftarrow \mathsf{QHE.Eval}(pk_t, P_t, \widehat{v}_t^{(t)}, \widehat{st}_{P,t-1}^{(t)})$. It sends $\widehat{p}_t^{(t)}$ back to the verifier.

4. V_{blind} decrypts the prover's final message by $p_T \leftarrow \mathsf{QHE.Dec}(sk_T, \widehat{p}_T^{(T)})$. It then computes its output $o \leftarrow V_{out}(p_T, st_{V,T})$.

By the correctness of QHE, the completeness error of Π_{blind} is negligibly close to that of Π. In particular, note that the level parameter L is sufficient for the honest prover which has a bounded complexity. For the soundness property, we show the following lemma, which implies that Π_{blind} preserves the soundness of Π_0.

Theorem 8. *For all cheating BQP provers P_{blind}^*, there exists a cheating BQP prover P^* s.t. for all λ and inputs $x \in \{0,1\}^{\mathrm{poly}(\lambda)}$, the output distributions of $(P_{\mathsf{blind}}^*, V_{\mathsf{blind}}(x))$ and $(P^*, V)(x)$ are identical.*

Proof. We define P^* as follows.

For the first rounds, it generates $(pk_1, sk_1) \leftarrow \mathsf{QHE.Keygen}(1^\lambda, 1^L)$, then produces the encryptions $\widehat{x}^{(1)} \leftarrow \mathsf{QHE.Enc}(pk_1, x)$ and $\widehat{v}_1^{(1)} \leftarrow \mathsf{QHE.Enc}(pk_1, v_1)$. It then runs $(\widehat{p}_1^{(1)}, \widehat{st}_{P,1}^{(1)}) \leftarrow P_{\mathsf{blind},1}(1^\lambda, \widehat{v}_1^{(1)}, \widehat{x}^{(1)})$. Finally, it decrypts $p_1 \leftarrow \mathsf{QHE.Dec}(sk_1, \widehat{p}_1^{(1)})$ and sends it back to the verifier, and keeps $\widehat{st}_{P,1}^{(1)}$ and sk_1.

For the other rounds, it generates $(pk_t, sk_t) \leftarrow \mathsf{QHE.Keygen}(1^\lambda, 1^L)$, and produces ciphertexts $\widehat{v}_t^{(t)} \leftarrow \mathsf{QHE.Enc}(pk_t, v_t))$ and $\widehat{sk}_{t-1}^{(t)} \leftarrow \mathsf{QHE.Enc}(pk_t, sk_{t-1})$. It then runs $(\widehat{p}_t^{(t)}, \widehat{st}_{P,t}^{(t)}) \leftarrow P_{\mathsf{blind},t}(\widehat{v}_t^{(t)}, \ \widehat{sk}_{t-1}^{(t)}, \widehat{st}_{P,t-1}^{(t-1)})$. Finally, it decrypts $p_t \leftarrow \mathsf{QHE.Dec}(sk_t, \widehat{p}_1^{(1)})$ and sends it back to the verifier, and keeps $\widehat{st}_{P,t}^{(t)}$ and sk_t.

By construction, the experiments $(P_{\mathsf{blind}}^*, V_{\mathsf{blind}}(x))$ and $(P^*, V)(x)$ are identical.

Finally, we show the blindness of Π_{blind} through a standard hybrid argument where the sk_i's are "erased" one by one, starting from sk_T. Once sk_1 is eventually erased, $\mathsf{QHE.Enc}(pk_1, x)$ and $\mathsf{QHE.Enc}(pk_1, 0)$ become indistinguishable due to the IND-CPA security of $\mathsf{QHE.Enc}$. We now fill in the details.

Theorem 9. *Under the QLWE assumption with polynomial modulus, Π_{blind} is blind.*

Proof. We show that for all cheating BQP provers P^*, $\lambda \in \mathbb{N}$, $x \in \{0,1\}^n$, P^* cannot distinguish $(P^*, V_{\mathsf{blind}}(x))(1^\lambda)$ from $(P^*, V_{\mathsf{blind}}(0^n))(1^\lambda)$ with noticeable probability in λ. We use a hybrid argument; let $\mathrm{Hyb}_{T+1}^x = (P^*, V_{\mathsf{blind}}(x))(1^\lambda)$ and $\mathrm{Hyb}_{T+1}^0 = (P^*, V_{\mathsf{blind}}(0^n))(1^\lambda)$. For $2 \leq t < T + 1$, define Hyb_t^x to be the same as Hyb_{t+1}^x, except when V_{blind} should send $\widehat{v}_t^{(t)}$ and $\widehat{sk}_{t-1}^{(t)}$, it instead sends encryptions of 0 under pk_t. We define Hyb_1^x to be the same as Hyb_2^x except the verifier sends encryptions of 0 under pk_1 in place of $\widehat{x}^{(1)}$ and $\widehat{v}_1^{(1)}$. We define Hyb_1^0 similarly. Note that Hyb_1^x and Hyb_1^0 are identical.

For all t, from the perspective of the prover, as it receives no information on sk_t, Hyb_{t+1}^x is computationally indistinguishable from Hyb_t^x due to the CPA security of QHE under pk_t. By a standard hybrid argument, we observe that Hyb_1^x is computationally indistinguishable with Hyb_{T+1}^x. We use the same argument for the computational indistinguishability between Hyb_1^0 and Hyb_{T+1}^0. We conclude that P^* cannot distinguish between Hyb_{T+1}^x and Hyb_{T+1}^0, therefore Π_{blind} is blind.

Applying our compiler to the parallel repetition of Mahadev's protocol for BQP from [7,15] and our QPIP_0 protocol Π_{Final} from Protocol 3 for SampBQP yields the first constant-round blind QPIP_0 protocol for BQP and SampBQP, respectively.

Theorem 10. *Under the QLWE assumption, there exists a blind, four-message QPIP_0 protocol for all languages in BQP with negligible completeness and soundness errors.*

Theorem 11. *Under the QLWE assumption, there exists a blind, four-message QPIP_0 protocol for all sampling problems in SampBQP with negligible completeness error and computational soundness.*

Acknowledgments. The authors would like to thank Tomoyuki Morimae for his valuable feedback that helped improve the paper and for pointing out the related works [26,38]. We are also thankful to anonymous reviewers for various useful comments.

Kai-Min Chung is partially supported by the 2019 Academia Sinica Career Development Award under Grant no. 23-17, and MOST QC project under Grant no. MOST 108-2627-E-002-001. This work was done while Yi Lee was affiliated to Academia Sinica and to National Taiwan University. Part of this work was done while Han-Hsuan Lin was supported by Scott Aaronson's Vannevar Bush Faculty Fellowship from the US Department of Defense. Partially funded by MOST Grant no. 110-2222-E-007-002-MY3. Xiaodi Wu is partially supported by the U.S. National Science Foundation grant CCF-1755800, CCF-1816695, and CCF-1942837 (CAREER).

References

1. Aaronson, S.: The aaronson \$25.00 prize. http://www.scottaaronson.com/blog/?p=284
2. Aaronson, S.: The equivalence of sampling and searching. Theory Comput. Syst. **55**(2), 281–298 (2013)
3. Aaronson, S., Arkhipov, A.: The computational complexity of linear optics. In: Proceedings of the Forty-Third Annual ACM Symposium on Theory of Computing, STOC 2011, New York, NY, USA, pp. 333–342. Association for Computing Machinery (2011)
4. Aharonov, D., Ben-Or, M., Eban, E., Mahadev, U.: Interactive proofs for quantum computations. arXiv:1704.04487 (2017)
5. Aharonov, D., Van Dam, W., Kempe, J., Landau, Z., Lloyd, S., Regev, O.: Adiabatic quantum computation is equivalent to standard quantum computation. SIAM Rev. **50**(4), 755–787 (2008)
6. Alagic, G., Dulek, Y., Schaffner, C., Speelman, F.: Quantum fully homomorphic encryption with verification (2017)
7. Alagic, G., Childs, A.M., Grilo, A.B., Hung, S.-H.: Non-interactive classical verification of quantum computation. In: Pass, R., Pietrzak, K. (eds.) TCC 2020. LNCS, vol. 12552, pp. 153–180. Springer, Cham (2020). https://doi.org/10.1007/978-3-030-64381-2_6
8. Arute, F., Arya, K., Babbush, R., et al.: Quantum supremacy using a programmable superconducting processor. Nature **574**(7779), 505–510 (2019)
9. Bartusek, J.: Secure quantum computation with classical communication (2021)
10. Bellare, M., Impagliazzo, R., Naor, M.: Does parallel repetition lower the error in computationally sound protocols? In: 38th Annual Symposium on Foundations of Computer Science, FOCS 1997, Miami Beach, Florida, USA, 19–22 October 1997, pp. 374–383 (1997)
11. Biamonte, J.D., Love, P.J.: Realizable Hamiltonians for universal adiabatic quantum computers. Phys. Rev. A **78**, 012352 (2008)
12. Brakerski, Z.: Quantum FHE (almost) as secure as classical. In: Shacham, H., Boldyreva, A. (eds.) CRYPTO 2018. LNCS, vol. 10993, pp. 67–95. Springer, Cham (2018). https://doi.org/10.1007/978-3-319-96878-0_3
13. Broadbent, A., Fitzsimons, J., Kashefi, E.: Universal blind quantum computation. In: 2009 50th Annual IEEE Symposium on Foundations of Computer Science, pp. 517–526 (2009)
14. Chardouvelis, O., Döttling, N., Malavolta, G.: Rate-1 quantum fully homomorphic encryption. In: Nissim, K., Waters, B. (eds.) TCC 2021. LNCS, vol. 13042, pp. 149–176. Springer, Cham (2021). https://doi.org/10.1007/978-3-030-90459-3_6
15. Chia, N.-H., Chung, K.-M., Yamakawa, T.: Classical verification of quantum computations with efficient verifier. In: Pass, R., Pietrzak, K. (eds.) TCC 2020. LNCS, vol. 12552, pp. 181–206. Springer, Cham (2020). https://doi.org/10.1007/978-3-030-64381-2_7
16. Chung, K.-M.: Efficient parallel repetition theorems with applications to security amplification. PhD thesis, Harvard University (2011)
17. Chung, K.-M., Lee, Y., Lin, H.-H., Wu, X.: Constant-round blind classical verification of quantum sampling (2021)
18. Coladangelo, A., Grilo, A.B., Jeffery, S., Vidick, T.: Verifier-on-a-leash: new schemes for verifiable delegated quantum computation, with quasilinear resources. In: Ishai, Y., Rijmen, V. (eds.) EUROCRYPT 2019. LNCS, vol. 11478, pp. 247–277. Springer, Cham (2019). https://doi.org/10.1007/978-3-030-17659-4_9

19. Crépeau, C., Gottesman, D., Smith, A.: Secure multi-party quantum computation. In: Proceedings of the Thirty-Fourth Annual ACM Symposium on Theory of Computing - STOC 2002. ACM Press (2002)
20. Dupuis, F., Nielsen, J.B., Salvail, L.: Actively secure two-party evaluation of any quantum operation. In: Safavi-Naini, R., Canetti, R. (eds.) CRYPTO 2012. LNCS, vol. 7417, pp. 794–811. Springer, Heidelberg (2012). https://doi.org/10.1007/978-3-642-32009-5_46
21. Fitzsimons, J.F., Hajdušek, M., Morimae, T.: Post hoc verification of quantum computation. Phys. Rev. Lett. **120**, 040501 (2018)
22. Fitzsimons, J.F., Kashefi, E.: Unconditionally verifiable blind quantum computation. Phys. Rev. A **96**, 012303 (2017)
23. Gheorghiu, A., Kashefi, E., Wallden, P.: Robustness and device independence of verifiable blind quantum computing. New J. Phys. **17**(8), 083040 (2015)
24. Gheorghiu, A., Vidick, T.: Computationally-secure and composable remote state preparation. In: FOCS, pp. 1024–1033 (2019)
25. Hajdušek, M., Pérez-Delgado, C.A., Fitzsimons, J.F.: Device-independent verifiable blind quantum computation. arXiv e-prints, arXiv:1502.02563, February 2015
26. Hayashi, M., Morimae, T.: Verifiable measurement-only blind quantum computing with stabilizer testing. Phys. Rev. Lett. **115**(22), 220502 (2015)
27. Kempe, J., Kitaev, A., Regev, O.: The complexity of the local Hamiltonian problem. SIAM J. Comput. **35**(5), 1070–1097 (2006)
28. Kitaev, A.Y., Shen, A., Vyalyi, M.N.: Classical and Quantum Computation. Graduate Studies in Mathematics. American Mathematical Society (2002)
29. Mahadev, U.: Classical homomorphic encryption for quantum circuits. In: 2018 IEEE 59th Annual Symposium on Foundations of Computer Science (FOCS) (2018)
30. Mahadev, U.: Classical verification of quantum computations. In: 2018 IEEE 59th Annual Symposium on Foundations of Computer Science (FOCS) (2018)
31. Marriott, C., Watrous, J.: Quantum Arthur-Merlin games. Comput. Complex. **14**(2), 122–152 (2005). https://doi.org/10.1007/s00037-005-0194-x
32. Morimae, T., Nagaj, D., Schuch, N.: Quantum proofs can be verified using only single-qubit measurements. Phys. Rev. A **93**, 022326 (2016)
33. Pietrzak, K., Wikström, D.: Parallel repetition of computationally sound protocols revisited. J. Cryptol. **25**(1), 116–135 (2012)
34. Regev, O.: On lattices, learning with errors, random linear codes, and cryptography. J. ACM **56**(6), 34:1–34:40 (2009)
35. Reichardt, B.W., Unger, F., Vazirani, U.: Classical command of quantum systems. Nature **496**(7746), 456 (2013)
36. Shepherd, D., Bremner, M.J.: Temporally unstructured quantum computation. Proc. R. Soc. A. **465**, 1413–1439 (2009)
37. Shor, P.W.: Algorithms for quantum computation: discrete logarithms and factoring. In: Proceedings 35th Annual Symposium on Foundations of Computer Science, pp. 124–134 (1994)
38. Takeuchi, Y., Morimae, T.: Verification of many-qubit states. Phys. Rev. X **8**(2), 021060 (2018)

Authentication in the Bounded Storage Model

Yevgeniy Dodis[1], Willy Quach[2(✉)], and Daniel Wichs[3]

[1] NYU, New York, USA
dodis@cs.nyu.edu
[2] Northeastern University, Boston, USA
quach.w@northeastern.edu
[3] Northeastern and NTT Research, Boston, USA
wichs@ccs.neu.edu

Abstract. We consider the streaming variant of the Bounded Storage Model (BSM), where the honest parties can stream large amounts of data to each other, while only maintaining a small memory of size n. The adversary also operates as a streaming algorithm, but has a much larger memory size $m \gg n$. The goal is to construct unconditionally secure cryptographic schemes in the BSM, and prior works did so for symmetric-key encryption, key agreement, oblivious transfer and multi-party computation. In this work, we construct *message authentication and signatures* in the BSM.

First, we consider the symmetric-key setting, where Alice and Bob share a small secret key. Alice can authenticate arbitrarily many messages to Bob by streaming long authentication tags of size $k \gg m$, while ensuring that the tags can be generated and verified using only n bits of memory. We show a solution using local extractors (Vadhan; JoC '04), which allows for up to exponentially large adversarial memory $m = 2^{O(n)}$, and has tags of size $k = O(m)$.

Second, we consider the same setting as above, but now additionally require each individual tag to be small, of size $k \leq n$. We show a solution is still possible when the adversary's memory is $m = O(n^2)$, which is optimal. Our solution relies on a space lower bound for leaning parities (Raz; FOCS '16).

Third, we consider the public-key signature setting. A signer Alice initially streams a long verification key over an authentic channel, while only keeping a short signing key in her memory. A verifier Bob receives the streamed verification key and generates a short verification digest that he keeps in his memory. Later, Alice can sign arbitrarily many messages using her signing key by streaming large signatures to Bob, who can verify them using his verification digest. We show a solution for

Y. Dodis—Partially supported by gifts from VMware Labs and Google, and NSF grants 1619158, 1319051, 1314568.
W. Quach—Part of this work was done during an internship at NTT Research.
D. Wichs—Partially supported by NSF grants CNS-1413964, CNS-1750795 and the Alfred P. Sloan Research Fellowship.

O. Dunkelman and S. Dziembowski (Eds.): EUROCRYPT 2022, LNCS 13277, pp. 737–766, 2022.
https://doi.org/10.1007/978-3-031-07082-2_26

$m = O(n^2)$, which we show to be optimal. Our solution relies on a novel entropy lemma, of independent interest. We show that, if a sequence of blocks has sufficiently high min-entropy, then a large fraction of individual blocks must have high min-entropy. Naive versions of this lemma are false, but we show how to patch it to make it hold.

1   Introduction

It is well known that there are strong restrictions on what cryptography can achieve without imposing any limits on the adversary's resources. In particular, Shannon showed that Alice and Bob cannot communicate secretly over an insecure channel, unless they share a secret key that is at least as large as the total size of the messages exchanged. Similarly, Alice and Bob cannot ensure the authenticity of their communication over an insecure channel, unless they share a secret key that is at least as large at the total number of messages exchanged. In either case, no security is possible in the public-key setting, when Alice and Bob have no shared secrets to begin with. Traditionally, cryptography has focused on overcoming the above limitations by restricting the adversary Eve to run in polynomial time. Unfortunately, the security of such schemes relies on unproven computational hardness assumptions, and at the very least, requires that $P \neq NP$.

The *Bounded Storage Model (BSM)* [23] offers an alternative by bounding the attacker's space instead of her run time. The goal is to construct unconditionally secure cryptographic schemes in the BSM, without relying on any unproven assumptions. A long series of prior works [1–5, 9, 10, 12, 14, 16, 21, 22, 25–27] showed how to achieve symmetric-key encryption, key agreement, oblivious transfer and multiparty computation in the BSM. In this work, we show how to achieve (symmetric-key) message authentication and (public-key) signatures in the BSM. We first begin by describing the BSM and survey what was done in prior work. We then turn to the problem of authentication in the BSM, and describe our results.

The Bounded Storage Model (BSM). In the bounded storage model (BSM), we restrict the storage capacity rather than the run-time of the adversary. Two distinct variants of the BSM exist in the literature, and we follow the terminology of [9] to distinguish between them.

The default variant for this work will be the *streaming* BSM [9,14,25]. In the streaming BSM, parties are modeled as streaming processes, that can send and receive large amounts of data between them by processing it one bit at a time, while only maintaining a small amount of memory. We denote the memory bound for the honest parties by n and the memory bound for the adversary by m. Typically, we assume the adversary has much higher resources than the honest parties, namely $m \gg n$. Although the honest parties only have a small amount of memory, they can stream large amounts of communication $k \gg m$, so as to overwhelm the memory capacity of the adversary and prevent it from storing the communication between them in its entirety. Still, the honest parties are restricted to remembering even less about the exchanged communication than the adversary can remember! Surprisingly, as we will see, this suffices to construct many powerful cryptographic primitives in the BSM.

We contrast the streaming BSM with an earlier variant, referred to as the *traditional BSM* [23]. In the traditional BSM, a trusted third party (potentially, some natural process) broadcasts a long uniformly random string $X \in \{0,1\}^k$ referred to as a *randomizer string*. The honest parties can store a subset of n physical locations of X, while the adversary can store any m bis of information about X. After that, the string X disappears, and the adversary gets unrestricted additional memory.

Most cryptographic schemes in the traditional BSM naturally translate to the streaming BSM by having one of the parties generate and stream the randomizer string X. However, looking forward, this will not be the case when it comes to authentication. The traditional BSM guarantees that the honest parties all get access to the same trusted randomizer string X, while in the streaming model, the adversary can tamper with any value X sent by one honest party to another. This makes the authentication problem in the streaming BSM more natural, but potentially harder than in the traditional BSM, since the latter already implicitly assumes a mechanism for authenticating X.

On the other hand, the traditional BSM has additional features that we don't require in the streaming BSM: (a) in the traditional BSM, there is only one long randomizer string X used in each cryptographic operation, whereas in the streaming BSM, the parties can stream many long messages, (b) in the traditional BSM, the long string X is uniformly random, while in the streaming BSM, the streamed messages can have arbitrary structure, (c) in the traditional BSM, the honest parties can only access a small subset of locations in X, while in the streaming BSM, the parties read the entire communication while maintaining small local memory, (d) in the traditional BSM, the adversary is only limited to remembering m bits of information about X and gets unlimited memory otherwise, while in the streaming BSM, the adversary observes communication in a streaming manner and is limited to m bits of memory overall. While some of our schemes do achieve some of these additional features, we view this as being of secondary importance, and focus on the streaming BSM as our default model.

Prior Work in the BSM. The seminal work of Maurer [23] introduced the traditional BSM. A series of papers [1,6,10,22,23,27] showed how to achieve symmetric-key encryption in the traditional BSM, where the honest parties share a short secret key that they can use to encrypt arbitrarily many messages (i.e., CPA security). Each encryption relies on a fresh randomizer string X. The main technical tool in all these works was nicely abstracted in the work of Vadhan [27] as a locally computable (seeded) extractor, which can extract randomness from a long string X by only reading a few locations of X. Overall, these works show that symmetric-key encryption is possible even if the adversarial memory $m = 2^{O(n)}$ can be up to exponentially larger than honest user memory n, as long as the ciphertext size (in which we include the size of the randomizer string) can be sufficiently large $k = O(m)$.[1] In particular, if we also want the ciphertext size to be polynomial, then we have to restrict the adversarial memory $m = \text{poly}(n)$ to be some arbitrarily large polynomial.

The works of [2–5,16] showed that it is also possible to achieve public key agreement, oblivious transfer, and general multi-party computation with arbitrary corruptions thresholds in the traditional BSM when $m = O(n^2)$, and this was shown to be optimal by [11].

All of the above results in the traditional BSM also carry over to the streaming BSM, by having one of the honest parties generate the randomizer string X. However, it turns out that one can often do better in the streaming BSM. The work of Raz [25] proved memory lower bounds for learning parity, and used these to construct novel symmetric-key encryption in the streaming BSM with small ciphertexts of size $< n$, and with $m = O(n^2)$, which is tight. In particular, each individual ciphertext is small enough that it can even fully fit in honest user memory, but the adversary does not have enough memory to remember too many ciphertexts. Follow-up works [12,21,26] generalized this result and showed that, for up to exponentially large $m = 2^{O(n)}$, one can achieve ciphertext size $O(m/n)$, improving by a factor of n over the prior results in the traditional BSM.[2] The work of [14] studied key agreement and oblivious transfer in the streaming BSM, and showed how to use Raz's lower-bound to construct new protocols that improve over the prior works in the traditional BSM by removing any correctness error and mildly reducing the number of rounds and the communication cost, while still requiring that the adversarial memory is bounded by $m = O(n^2)$. The recent work of [9] noticed that the lower bound of $m = O(n^2)$ from [11] does not hold in the streaming BSM, and showed how to achieve key agreement, oblivious transfer, and general multiparty computation in the streaming BSM, even when the adversarial memory $m = 2^{O(n)}$ can be up to exponentially larger than honest user memory n, at the cost of growing the round and communication complexities polynomially with m.

The work of [6] also considered symmetric-key authentication in the traditional BSM, where parties have a short shared secret key and can use it to authenticate a large number of messages, by using a fresh (authentic) randomizer string X to authenticate each message. The construction is very simple – it uses a local extractor to extract a fresh secret key for a one-time message-authentication code (1-time MAC) from X, and then uses the 1-time MAC with this key to authenticate the message. Unfortunately, unlike all the previous results in the traditional BSM, this solution cannot immediately be ported to the streaming BSM: if one of the parties generates X and streams it, then the adversary can tamper with it. Indeed, this would result in a completely insecure scheme in the streaming BSM.

---

[1] Throughout the introduction, we ignore polynomial factors in the security parameter.

[2] The above bound is for 1-bit messages and is optimal; if the adversary can store $> n$ ciphertexts under an n-bit key, then she can learn something about the encrypted messages via the Shannon lower bound.

1.1   Our Results

In this work, we study the problem of message authentication and signatures in the streaming BSM. We study three variants of the problem, as outlined below.

Symmetric-Key Authentication. We start with the symmetric-key setting, where Alice and Bob share a short secret key sk, that they store in their n-bit memory. To authenticate a message μ, Alice streams a long authentication tag σ to Bob who verifies the stream and either accepts or rejects.[3] Even though the tag size $k = |\sigma|$ can be very large, namely $k \gg m$, we ensure that generating and verifying the tag can be done in a streaming manner using only n bits of memory. Our goal is to achieve unconditional security, where Alice and Bob can authenticate an arbitrarily large polynomial (or even sub-exponential) number of messages in this manner using their short secret key. We consider a streaming attacker Eve with m bits of memory. Eve sits on the channel between Alice and Bob, and can observe and modify all communication between them, subject only to keeping at most m bits of memory throughout this process. She performs a chosen-message attack, where she can adaptively choose many messages and observe the authentication tags honestly sent from Alice to Bob. Moreover, she can modify each of the messages and tags in transit and can observe whether Bob accepts or rejects. (We view the process of receiving and modifying the tags as a streaming algorithm, where Eve receives each tag as an input stream and produces a modified tag as an output stream. The streams need not be synchronized and Eve can wait to receive many/all of the bits of the input stream before outputting the first bit in the output stream.) Eve wins if she causes Bob to accept some arbitrary message that Alice did not authenticate.

We show how to solve this problem with up to exponentially large adversarial memory $m = 2^{O(n)}$ and tags of size $k = O(m)$. In particular, this means that if we also want the scheme to also be polynomially efficient (i.e., have polynomial-size tags), then we have to restrict the adversarial memory $m = \text{poly}(n)$ to be some arbitrarily large polynomial. We refer to Theorem 2 for a formal statement with parameters.

Symmetric-Key Authentication with Short Tags. Next, we consider the same problem as previously, but now also require that each individual tag σ is "short", of size $< n$. Moreover, each tag can be fully generated, stored and verified by the honest parties in n bits of memory, without needing to operate in the streaming model. We show how to solve this problem for $m = O(n^2)$, which is optimal.[4] This result relies on Raz's space lower bounds for learning parity [25]. We refer to Theorem 4 for a formal statement with parameters.

---

[3] We typically think of the messages μ as small relative to n, m. However, all of our results also extend to support long messages that Alice and Bob receive in a streaming manner.

[4] Optimality follows from the standard authentication lower bound; if an adversary has enough memory to store n tags (generated using an n bit key) then it has enough information to forge tags of new messages.

Public-Key Signatures. Lastly, we consider the public-key signature setting, where the honest parties do not have any shared secrets to begin with. As in the standard signature setting, we have an initialization stage where Alice generates a public verification key vk and a secret signing key sk, and she broadcasts her verification key vk to other honest users over a public but authentic channel. In the BSM, we allow the verification key vk to be large, of size $> m$, and Alice generates and broadcasts vk in a streaming manner while maintaining n bits of memory, which also bounds the size of the secret signing key sk that Alice retains in memory at the end of the initialization stage. An arbitrary verifier Bob receives and processes the streamed verification key vk using n bits of memory, and derives a short *verification digest* vd, which he keeps in his memory at the end of the initialization stage. Later, Alice can use her signing key sk to sign arbitrarily many messages by streaming large signatures over a fully insecure channel, and Bob can verify the streamed signatures using his verification digest vd. The adversary Eve has m bits of memory. During the initialization stage, Eve can observe (but not modify) the streamed verification key vk. Afterwards, Eve performs a chosen-message attack, where she can adaptively choose many messages and observe the signatures sent from Alice to Bob. Moreover, she can modify each of the messages and signatures in transit and can observe whether Bob accepts or rejects. Eve wins if she can cause Bob to accept some arbitrary message that Alice did not sign.

We give a solution to the above problem when $m = O(n^2)$, which we show to be optimal. The size of the verification key and each of the signatures is $O(m)$. Our proof of security relies on a new "block entropy lemma", which we view as a result of independent interest, and discuss below.

Block Entropy Lemma. Consider a random variable $X = (X_1, \ldots, X_k) \in (\{0,1\}^b)^k$ consisting of k blocks of b bits each. Assume that X has a high min-entropy rate with $\mathbf{H}_\infty(X) \geq \alpha \cdot (kb)$ for some parameter α. We would intuitively like to say that this must imply that a large α_1-fraction of the blocks X_i must individually have a high min-entropy rates $\mathbf{H}_\infty(X_i) \geq \alpha_2 \cdot b$. For example, if $\alpha = \Omega(1)$, then we may intuitively hope that the above should hold with some $\alpha_1 = \alpha_2 = \Omega(1)$.

Indeed, if we were to consider Shannon entropy instead of min-entropy, then $\mathbf{H}(X) \leq \sum_i \mathbf{H}(X_i)$, and therefore the above holds with (e.g.,) $\alpha_1 = \alpha_2 = \alpha/2$. Unfortunately, when it comes to min-entropy, such statements are false for any reasonable parameters. As an example, consider the distribution on X where we choose a random index $i^* \leftarrow [k]$, set $X_{i^*} = 0^b$, and for all other indices $i \neq i^*$ we choose $X_i \leftarrow \{0,1\}^b$ uniformly at random. Then $\mathbf{H}_\infty(X) \geq (k-1) \cdot b$, but for each individual index $i \in [k]$, we have $\mathbf{H}_\infty(X_i) \leq \log(k)$ since $\Pr[X_i = 0^b] \geq 1/k$.

While the above example shows that the statement is false in its basic form, it also highlights a potential way to augment the statement to make it hold while preserving its intuitive meaning. The example shows that for every fixed index i chosen a-priori, X_i may have low min-entropy. However, we may be able to find a large set of good indices i after seeing X (e.g., to avoid $i = i^*$ in the previous example), such that each such X_i has high min-entropy even if we reveal that i

is in this good set. We formalize this by showing that for any $\alpha_1 \approx \alpha_2 \approx \alpha/2$, with overwhelming probability over $x \leftarrow X$ there is a large set of "good' indices $\mathcal{I}(x)$ of size $|\mathcal{I}(x)| \geq \alpha_1 \cdot k$, such that the min-entropy of the i'th block is high if we condition on $i \in \mathcal{I}(X)$ begin a good index: $\mathbf{H}_\infty(X_i | i \in \mathcal{I}(X)) \geq \alpha_2 \cdot k$.

Our block-entropy lemma is somewhat related to previous lemmas of [24, 27] showing that, if we (pseudo-)randomly sample a sufficiently large subset of locations $S \subseteq [k]$, then $X_S = \{X_i : i \in S\}$ has a high entropy rate, close to the entropy rate of X. However, these previous lemmas do not allow us to say anything about the entropy rates of individual blocks X_i. Our lemma is also somewhat related to a lemma of [9], which shows that many individual *bits* of X have some non-trivial entropy. However, that lemma does not give good parameters when extended to blocks, and indeed, the natural attempt at extending it leads to a false statement as discussed above.

1.2   Our Techniques

We now discuss the high-level technical ideas behind each of our results. To keep things simple, we will avoid getting bogged down with parameter details. Instead, we use "short/small" to denote values of size $< n$ that can fit in honest user memory, and "long/big" to denote values of size $> m$ that cannot even fit in adversary memory.

Symmetric-Key Authentication. Our basic result for symmetric-key authentication is fairly simple. We rely on two building blocks:

- A (strong) local extractor Ext that takes as input a long source x and a small random seed, and produces a small output $\mathsf{Ext}(x; \mathsf{seed})$ by only reading a small subset of the locations in x, where the locations are determined by seed [27]. In particular, it can be computed by reading x in a streaming manner using small memory. The extracted output is statistically close to uniform even given seed, as long as x has sufficiently high entropy.
- A streaming one-time message-authentication code $\sigma = \mathsf{MAC}_{\mathsf{sk}}(\mu)$ that allows us to authenticate a single long message μ using a small secret key sk, by reading μ in a streaming manner. The authentication tag is also small. This can be constructed easily using polynomial evaluation.

We use these building blocks to construct a symmetric-key authentication scheme in the BSM.

- The small shared secret key $\mathsf{sk} = (\hat{\mathsf{sk}}, \mathsf{seed})$ consists of key $\hat{\mathsf{sk}}$ for the streaming one-time MAC and seed for an extractor.
- To authenticate a message μ, Alice then streams a long random string x to Bob, and as she does so, also computes $r = \mathsf{Ext}(x; \mathsf{seed})$ and $\hat{\sigma} = \mathsf{MAC}(\hat{\mathsf{sk}}, (x\|\mu))$ in a streaming manner using small memory. She then appends the short value $\psi = r \oplus \hat{\sigma}$ as the final component of the long tag $\sigma = (x, \psi)$

- To verify the tag $\sigma = (x, \psi)$ for message μ, Bob computes $r = \mathsf{Ext}(x; \mathsf{seed})$ and $\hat{\sigma} = \mathsf{MAC}(\hat{\mathsf{sk}}, (x, \mu))$ in a streaming manner using small memory. He then checks if $\psi = r \oplus \hat{\sigma}$ and, if so, accepts if $\hat{\sigma}$ is a valid tag for message $(x \| \mu)$ under MAC (using secret $\hat{\mathsf{sk}}$, and where the verification procedure is also performed in a streaming manner), and rejects otherwise.

In essence, Alice is "encrypting" the one-time MAC tags using a symmetric-key encryption in the BSM, and then uses a one-time MAC to also authenticate the BSM encryption randomness. Intuitively, the encryption ensures that even if the adversary sees many encrypted tags, she doesn't learn much about the secret key of the one-time MAC. However, formalizing this is somewhat subtle.

Consider an adversary Eve to first passively observes q honestly generated tags $\sigma_1, \ldots, \sigma_q$ from Alice in a streaming manner, while maintaining m bits of memory. Then Eve gets unlimited memory and observes an additional $(q+1)$'st tag σ and outputs σ'. She wins if Bob accepts σ' and $\sigma' \neq \sigma$. In our proof, we first switch the values ψ_i inside the q tags σ_i to uniformly random. We rely on the security of the strong local extractor to argue that the change is indistinguishable, *even* if we later reveal the entire secret key $\mathsf{sk} = (\mathsf{seed}, \hat{\mathsf{sk}})$ and can therefore check if the adversary wins the game. Once we make this change, the one-time MAC key $\hat{\mathsf{sk}}$ is only used to generate the $(q+1)$'st tag $\sigma = (x, \psi)$ for message μ and verify $\sigma' = (x', \psi')$ for message μ'. Therefore, we can rely on the security of the one-time MAC to argue that if $(\mu', \sigma') \neq (\mu, \sigma)$ then Bob rejects with overwhelming probability.

On a quick glance, it may seem that we could have applied the one-time MAC to just μ instead of the pair (x, μ), and still argued that Eve cannot cause Bob to accept any $\sigma' = (\mu', x', \psi')$ where $\mu' \neq \mu$, which should suffice. However, this turns out to be false and the scheme would be completely insecure with this modification. In particular, Eve would be able to learn something about the secret key by modifying the tags from Alice to Bob while keeping the message intact and seeing whether or not he accepts. For example, each time Alice generates a tag $\sigma_i = (\mu_i, x_i, \psi_i)$, Eve could flip a bit of x_i and see if Bob accepts or rejects. This would eventually reveal the set of locations in x read by $\mathsf{Ext}(x; \mathsf{seed})$. Once Eve learns this set, extractor security is lost, and indeed Eve can fully recover sk and break the scheme. In our proof, by showing that Eve cannot cause Bob to accept any $\sigma' \neq \sigma$, even for the same message μ, we ensure that verification queries are useless. Our formal argument is more involved, and requires to carefully answer verification queries using low memory: our reduction cannot even store an entire tag.

Overall, we can get security against adversaries with memory of size m where honest users only need memory of size $n = O(\log m)$ and where tags are of size $O(m)$. We refer to Sect. 5 for more details.

Symmetric-Key Authentication with Short Tags. Next, we turn to the same problem as in the previous paragraph, but additionally require that the authentication tags are small, of size $< n$. Furthermore, they can be fully generated, stored, and verified inside honest user memory, without relying on the streaming model. Since the secret key is also small, of size $< n$, if an adversary can simultaneously remember n tags, then it can break security via the classical authentication lower bound. Therefore, the above setting necessitates bounding the adversary's memory to $m = O(n^2)$.

Constructing this type of authentication scheme implies some sort of space lower bound on learning. In particular, the adversary observes many outputs of the (potentially randomized) authentication function with a secret key sk, but if its memory is bounded, it does not learn the function sufficiently well to authenticate new messages. Unlike the previous setting where each function output individually was long and could not be stored in memory, in this setting each output is short, but the adversary cannot store too many outputs. Lower bounds in this setting are highly non-trivial, and the first lower bound of this form was shown only recently in the celebrated work of Raz [25], and subsequently extended by [12,21,26]. In particular, Raz proved a space lower bound for learning random parities. Here, we choose a uniformly random $\mathbf{x} \leftarrow \mathbb{F}_2^n$. The adversary can get many samples $(\mathbf{a}_i, b_i)$ where $\mathbf{a}_i \leftarrow \mathbb{F}_2^n$ and $b_i = \langle \mathbf{x}, \mathbf{a}_i \rangle$. If the adversary has $> n^2$ bits of memory and can remember $> n$ samples in full, then it can perform Gaussian elimination and recover $\mathbf{x}$. The work of Raz shows that, if the adversary's memory is sufficiently smaller than n^2 (and the number of samples is smaller than exponential), then the adversary cannot recover $\mathbf{x}$ or even distinguish the samples from uniformly random values.

Abstracting the above, we can think of Raz's result as showing that the inner-product function $f_{\mathbf{x}}(\mathbf{a}) = \langle \mathbf{x}, \mathbf{a} \rangle$ is a "weak pseudorandom function" (weak PRF) in the BSM, in the sense that an adversary with sufficiently small memory cannot distinguish the outputs of the function on random inputs $\mathbf{a}_i$ from uniformly random values. Unfortunately, it is not a-priori clear how to use a weak PRF in the BSM to solve the message authentication problem in the BSM. Indeed, even in the computational setting, we do not know of any "nice" construction of computational message authentication codes from a generic weak PRF (beyond just using the weak PRF to construct a PRG and applying [13] to go from a PRG to a PRF, but this approach does not translate to the BSM). Instead, we rely on the specifics of the inner product function, rather than just generically relying on it being a weak PRF in the BSM. Notice that the inner-product function is essentially the same as Learning Parity with Noise (LPN), just without noise! Moreover, there is a long body of work tying to construct simple/efficient message authentication schemes from LPN [7,17,19,20]. In particular, the work of [7] abstracts out many of these ideas and shows how to construct message-authentication directly from any *key-homomorphic weak PRF*. We show that the same tricks there happen to carry over nicely to the BSM, and allow us to construct a message-authentication scheme with the desired parameters, by relying on the fact that the inner-product function is essentially a key-homomorphic weak PRF in the BSM via Raz's lower bound. Interestingly, we crucially rely on the linearity of the inner-product function in this construction, and do not know how to adapt subsequent space lower bounds for other functions (e.g., low-degree polynomials) [12] to get analogous results using them. Still, adapting the work of [7] to the bounded memory setting requires a great deal of care to ensure that all the reductions use small memory. We refer to Sect. 6 for more details.

Public-Key Signatures. In the public-key setting, we start with an initialization stage during which Alice streams a long verification key vk over an authentic channel. At the end of the initialization stage, Alice keeps a short signing key sk, while a verifier Bob keeps a short verification digest vd.

We first observe that if Alice and Bob could interact back-and-forth with each other during the initialization stage, we could solve the problem trivially by having them run a key-agreement protocol in the BSM [3,9,14], at the end of which they would have a shared secret key. Later, they could use the secret key to authenticate messages via a symmetric-key authentication schemes in the BSM that we constructed earlier. However, all such key-agreement protocols require at least two back-and-forth rounds of interaction, while in our case we only allow one-way communication from Alice to Bob.[5] Unfortunately, it is easy to see that key agreement in one round is impossible, since nothing differentiates an honest Bob from the attacker Eve – if Bob knows Alice's key, so can Eve.

Nevertheless, we show that a variant of key agreement that we call *set key agreement* is possible in one round! In a set key agreement scheme, Alice streams a long message vk and outputs a set of keys sk $= (\mathsf{sk}_1, \ldots, \mathsf{sk}_q)$, while Bob observes the stream and outputs some subset of Alice's keys vd $= (T, (\mathsf{sk}_i)_{i \in T})$ for $T \subseteq [q]$. Security requires that there is some shared key sk_t for $t \in T$, meaning that the key is known to both Alice and Bob, such that sk_t looks uniformly random even given Eve's view of the protocol and all the other keys sk_j for $j \in [q], j \neq t$. The index t of this "good" shared key is a random variable that depends on the entire protocol execution and on Eve's view, and it is therefore not known to Alice or Bob.

We construct such set key agreement when the adversarial memory is sufficiently small $m = O(n^2)$, as follows. Alice streams a random string $x = (x_1, \ldots, x_k)$ consisting of k blocks $x_i \in \{0,1\}^b$, where b is very small (depending only on the security parameter). Alice chooses a small random subset $S_A \subseteq [k]$ of size $|S_A| = q$ and remember the blocks $x_i : i \in S_A$. Similarly, Bob chooses a small random subset $S_B \subseteq [k]$ of size $|S_B| = q$ and remember the blocks $x_i : i \in S_B$. We choose $k = O(m)$ and $q = O(\sqrt{m})$ carefully to ensure that Alice/Bob only use $n = \widetilde{O}(\sqrt{m})$ bits of memory and that with high probability their sets have non-trivial intersection $|S_A \cap S_B|$ of roughly security parameter size. After Alice finishes streaming x, she then also streams her set $S_A = \{i_1, \ldots, i_q\}$ along with q extractor seeds seed_j, and sets her keys to be the extracted values $\mathsf{sk}_j = \mathsf{Ext}(x_{i_j}, \mathsf{seed}_j)$ for $j \in [q]$. Bob computes the set $T = \{j : i_j \in S_B\}$ and sets $\mathsf{sk}_j = \mathsf{Ext}(x_{i_j}; \mathsf{seed}_j)$ for $j \in T$. We argue that

---

[5] We view this as a crucial component of our model. Alice can broadcast her verification key to the world, obliviously of who is listening and who will want to very her signed messages in the future. There may potentially even be a large number of different verifiers and Alice should not need to know about them or interact with them.

security holds as long as Eve's memory is $\leq k/2$. Eve needs to decide what to remember about x before she learns anything about S_A, S_B. We will use our new block entropy lemma to argue that there is a large fraction of locations i, such that the individual blocks x_i have high min-entropy conditioned on what Eve remembered about x, and therefore it is likely that some such location $i^* = i_t$ appears in $S_A \cap S_B$. The corresponding key $\mathsf{sk}_t = \mathsf{Ext}(x_{i_t}; \mathsf{seed}_t)$ will then be the "good key" which looks uniform given Eve's view. As discussed in our description of the block entropy lemma, the set of locations i such that x_i has high min-entropy is not fixed, but rather a random variable that depends on x and on Eve's view. Therefore, also the index t of the "good key" is such a random variable.

Once we have a set key agreement protocol, it is easy to build a signature scheme on top of it. To sign each message μ, Alice uses each of the secret keys sk_i for $i \in [q]$ as a key for a symmetric-key authentication scheme in the BSM (from our first result), and sequentially authenticate the message μ using each of the q keys individually. The verifier Bob verifies the authentication tags corresponding to the indices $j \in T$. To argue security, we rely on the security of the symmetric-key authentication scheme in the location t corresponding to the "good" secret key. Note that, in the set key agreement protocol, we needed to choose $q = O(\sqrt{m})$ large to ensure that that S_A and S_B have a large overlap. This means that each of the keys sk_i needs to be very small, since Alice's storage is $n = q|\mathsf{sk}_i|$. However, this is not a problem since the symmetric-key authentication scheme in the BSM allowed us to make the keys as small as $O(\log m)$.[6]

We also give a lower bound to show that this type of public-key signatures in the BSM are impossible when $m > n^2$. We rely on a technical lemma due to Dziembowski and Maurer [11]. Translated to our context, the lemma addresses the scenario where Alice streams a long verification key vk to Bob, after which she stores some n bit state sk and Bob stores some n bit state vd. The lemma says that there is some small value $E(\mathsf{vk})$ of size $m < n^2$ that Eve can store about vk, such that, conditioned on $E(\mathsf{vk})$, the values sk and vd are statistically close to being independent. In particular, this means that if Eve samples a fresh sk' conditioned on $E(\mathsf{vk})$, then she can sign messages using sk' and Bob will accept the signatures with high probability. We refer to Sect. 7 for more details.

Block Entropy Lemma. Lastly, we give some intuition behind our block entropy lemma. We show that, for every fixed $x \in (\{0,1\}^b)^k$ there is some set $\mathcal{I}(x)$ such that, if X has sufficiently high entropy $\mathbf{H}_\infty(X) \geq \alpha \cdot (bk)$, then:

- With overwhelming probability over $x \leftarrow X$, we have $|\mathcal{I}(x)| \geq \alpha_1 \cdot k$
- For all x and $i \in \mathcal{I}(x)$: $\mathbf{H}_\infty(X_i | X_1 = x_1, \ldots, X_{i-1} = x_{i-1}, i \in \mathcal{I}(X)) \geq \alpha_2 \cdot b$.

where the above holds for any α_1 and $\alpha_2 = \alpha - \alpha_1 - \lambda/b$, where λ is the security parameter (see Lemma 4 for a formal statement). We start by observing that

---

[6] This is also why we need to rely on the symmetric-key authentication scheme with long tags from our first result, rather than the one with short tags from our second result – in the latter, the secret keys would be of size $O(\sqrt{m})$ and hence Alice/Bob would need memory of size $O(m)$ exceeding that of Eve.

the definition of min-entropy guarantees that for any x:

$$2^{-\alpha kb} \geq \Pr[X = x] = \prod_{i=1}^{k} \underbrace{\Pr[X_i = x_i | X_1 = x_1, \ldots, X_{i-1} = x_{i-1}]}_{2^{-e_i}} = 2^{-\sum_{i=1}^{k} e_i}.$$

By a simple averaging argument, there is an α_1 fraction of "good" indices $i \in \mathcal{I}(x) \subseteq [k]$ for which $e_i \geq (\alpha - \alpha_1) \cdot b$. But the fact that $\Pr[X_i = x_i | X_1 = x_1, \ldots, X_{i-1} = x_{i-1}]$ is small does not guarantee that $\mathbf{H}_\infty(X_i | X_1 = x_1, \ldots, X_{i-1} = x_{i-1})$ is large, since the concrete outcome x_i that we got may not have been the maximally likely one. However, let us additionally condition on the event that $i \in \mathcal{I}(X)$ is a good index. We show that, for each i, either (I) the conditional min-entropy is high $\mathbf{H}_\infty(X_i \mid X_1 = x_1, \ldots, X_{i-1} = x_{i-1}, i \in \mathcal{I}(X)) \geq \alpha - \alpha_1 - \lambda/b$ or (II) the probability $\Pr[i \in \mathcal{I}(X) | X_1 = x_1, \ldots, X_{i-1} = x_{i-1}] \leq 2^{-\lambda}$ is low. By removing indices i for which (II) holds from $\mathcal{I}(x)$, we get our lemma. For a random $x \leftarrow X$, the probability that any index was removed is negligible.

2   Preliminaries

Notation. When X is a distribution, or a random variable following this distribution, we let $x \leftarrow X$ denote the process of sampling x according to the distribution X. If X is a set, we let $x \leftarrow X$ denote sampling x uniformly at random from X. We use the notation $[k] = \{1, \ldots, k\}$. If $x \in \{0,1\}^k$ and $i \in [k]$ then we let $x[i]$ denote the i'th bit of x. If $s \subseteq [k]$, we let $x[s]$ denote the list of values $x[i]$ for $i \in s$.

We refer to the full version for more definitions and facts about information theory, including the local extractors of [27], which we call BSM-extractors in this work. We will use the following construction of BSM-extractors.

Theorem 1 ([27]). *For any* $m \geq \ell, \lambda$, *there is a* (n, m, ε)-*BSM extractor* $\mathsf{BSMExt} : \{0,1\}^k \times \{0,1\}^d \to \{0,1\}^\ell$ *with* $n = O(\ell + \lambda + \log m)$, $\varepsilon = 2^{-\Omega(\lambda)}$, $k = O(m + \lambda \log(\lambda))$, $d = O(\log m + \lambda)$.

We will use the following lemmas.

Lemma 1 ([8]). *For any random variables* X, Y, *for every* $\varepsilon > 0$ *we have*

$$\Pr_{y \leftarrow Y}[\mathbf{H}_\infty(X|Y = y) \geq \mathbf{H}_\infty(X|Y) - \log(1/\varepsilon)] \geq 1 - \varepsilon.$$

Lemma 2 ([8]). *For any random variables* X, Y, Z *where* Y *is supported over a set of size* T *we have* $\mathbf{H}_\infty(X|Y, Z) \leq \mathbf{H}_\infty(X|Z) - \log T$.

Lemma 3 ([4,15]). *Let* k *be an integer, and* S_A, $S_B \subset [k]$ *be two uniformly and independently sampled subset of* $[k]$ *of size* q *where* $q \geq 2\sqrt{\lambda \cdot k}$. *Then*

$$\Pr[|S_A \cap S_B| < \lambda] < e^{-\lambda/4}.$$

3 Definitions

In this section, we define message authentication codes (MACs) in Sect. 3.1 and signatures in Sect. 3.2 in the BSM. We discuss how we model honest parties and adversaries in these settings.

3.1 Message Authentication Codes

A message-authentication code (MAC) over a message space $\mathcal{M}$ is a tuple of algorithms (KeyGen, MAC, Verify) with the following syntax:

- KeyGen(1^λ) $\to$ sk: on input a security parameter λ, output a key sk.
- MAC(sk, μ): on input a key sk and a message $\mu \in \mathcal{M}$, output a tag σ.
- Verify(sk, μ, σ): on input a key sk, a message $\mu \in \mathcal{M}$ and a tag σ, output a bit b.

We define the following properties.

Definition 1 (Correctness). *We say that a MAC is* correct *if for all message $\mu \in \mathcal{M}$:*

$$\Pr[\mathsf{Verify}(\mathsf{sk}, \mu, \sigma) = 1 : \mathsf{sk} \leftarrow \mathsf{KeyGen}(1^\lambda), \sigma \leftarrow \mathsf{MAC}(\mathsf{sk}, \mu)] \geq 1 - \mathrm{negl}(\lambda).$$

Definition 2 (Streaming MAC). *For an integer n, we say that a MAC is a* streaming *MAC with memory n if MAC and Verify can respectively be computed by streaming algorithms with memory n, given streaming access to μ and (μ, σ) respectively, and if KeyGen can be computed (in place) with memory n. In particular, MAC keys sk have size at most n.*

Definition 3 ((Selective) unforgeability under chosen message (and verification) attacks). *For an algorithm Adv, consider the following experiment:*

Experiment $\mathsf{Exp}^{\mathsf{uf\text{-}cmva}}(1^\lambda, \mathsf{Adv})$:

1. *Sample* sk $\leftarrow$ KeyGen(1^λ).
2. *Compute* $(\mu^*, \sigma^*) \leftarrow \mathsf{Adv}^{\mathsf{MAC}(\mathsf{sk}, \cdot), \mathsf{Verify}(\mathsf{sk}, \cdot, \cdot)}$.
3. *Output 1 if* Verify(sk, μ^*, σ^*) $= 1$ *output 0 otherwise.*

We say that an adversary Adv is admissible *if Adv did not query MAC(sk, $\cdot$) on input μ^*. In the following, all the adversaries are assumed admissible.*

We say that a MAC is $(\varepsilon, \mathcal{A})$-unforgeable under chosen message and chosen verification queries attacks (uf-cmva) against a class $\mathcal{A}$ of adversaries, if for all adversary Adv $\in \mathcal{A}$:

$$\Pr[\mathsf{Exp}^{\mathsf{uf\text{-}cmva}}(1^\lambda, \mathsf{Adv}) = 1] \leq \varepsilon.$$

We simply say that a MAC is $\mathcal{A}$-uf-cmva-secure if it is $(\varepsilon, \mathcal{A})$-uf-cmva-secure for some $\varepsilon = \mathrm{negl}(\lambda)$.

We alternatively say that a MAC is $(\varepsilon, \mathcal{A})$-selectively unforgeable under chosen message and chosen verification queries attack (suf-cmva) if any adversary Adv $\in \mathcal{A}$ that declare μ^* before the beginning of experiment makes the associated experiment output 1 with probability at most ε.

Next, we say that a MAC is $(\varepsilon, \mathcal{A})$-(selectively) unforgeable under chosen message attacks ((s)uf-cma) if any adversary Adv $\in \mathcal{A}$ that only make tagging queries MAC(sk, ·) makes the associated experiment output 1 with probability at most ε.

Last, we say that a MAC is $\mathcal{A}$-((s)uf-cm(v)a) if it is $(\varepsilon, \mathcal{A})$-((s)uf-cm(v)a) for some $\varepsilon = \mathrm{negl}(\lambda)$.

Definition 4 (Indistinguishability under chosen message attacks). *We say that a MAC satisfies $(\varepsilon, \mathcal{A})$-indistinguishability under chosen-message attacks (ind-cma) if for all Adv $\in \mathcal{A}$:*

$$\left| \Pr[\mathsf{Adv}^{\mathsf{MAC}(\mathsf{sk},\cdot)} = 1] - \Pr[\mathsf{Adv}^{\mathsf{MAC}(\mathsf{sk},0)} = 1] \right| \leq \varepsilon$$

where the probabilities are over the randomness of sk $\leftarrow$ KeyGen(1^λ).
We say that a MAC is $\mathcal{A}$-ind-cma if it is $(\varepsilon, \mathcal{A})$-ind-cma for some $\varepsilon = \mathrm{negl}(\lambda)$.

Next, we define the class of adversaries we consider in this work.

Definition 5 (Streaming Adversaries for MACs). *We say that an adversary Adv in any of the security experiments above is streaming with memory m if it is a streaming algorithm that accesses oracles MAC and Verify (whenever applicable) in a streaming manner using memory at most m. Namely, it provides the inputs to oracles MAC and Verify as streams of bits and receives the outputs of MAC as streams. The calls to MAC and Verify are not required to be synchronous: for instance Adv can start a oracle call to Verify while streaming the input to MAC or receiving a tag in a streaming manner.*

We add the restriction that there is at most one current call to MAC and at most one current call to Verify at any given point in time during the experiment, namely, the calls to MAC are done in a sequential manner, and similarly for Verify. For technical reasons, we only allow any given oracle call to Verify to be concurrent with at most one call to MAC: we disallow a single verification query to span several tagging queries.

We will usually refer to Q (resp. Q_T, Q_V) as the number of total (resp. tagging, verification) queries made by Adv.

The class of adversaries above notably covers man-in-the-middle adversaries who have the ability alter a tag being currently streamed, and observe either the output of the verifier, or use it as a final forgery.

We argue that the restriction to the concurrency of oracle calls above is reasonable. Notably, in a setting where an authenticator streams tags to a single verifier and where a man-in-the-middle possibly tampers the communication between them, we believe it is reasonable to assume that the verifier only authenticates one streamed tag at a time. In such a setting, adversaries would satisfy the conditions of Definition 5.

Remark 1 (Adversaries with Unbounded Temporary Memory). In the traditional BSM, adversaries have access to unbounded temporary memory as long as they eventually compress the information given to them down to some bounded amount m. We can similarly define a class of adversaries stronger than Definition 5, who, given a streamed tag output by $\mathsf{MAC}(\mathsf{sk}, \cdot)$, can process any (blocks of) streamed bits using unbounded temporary memory as long as they compress their state down to some m-bit state before the next bit (or block) is streamed. In particular, such adversaries can compute bounded-size non-uniform advice on their own, before any query is made.

We will use the following MAC secure against unbounded adversaries, as long as only one tag is given out. We refer to the full version for a construction and a proof.

Claim 1 (One-Time Information-Theoretic MACs). *Let $\mathcal{A}$ be the set of (potentially unbounded) algorithm that make at most 1 tagging query and at most Q_V verification queries. Then for all integer k and constant $c > 0$, there exists a streaming MAC with memory $n = O(\lambda + \log k)$ and message space $\{0,1\}^k$ which is $(k \cdot Q_V / 2^{c\lambda}, \mathcal{A})$-uf-cmva-secure. Furthermore, the MAC produces tags of size n.*

3.2 Signatures

A *streaming* signature scheme over a message space $\mathcal{M}$ is a tuple of algorithms $(\mathsf{KeyGen}, \mathsf{Sign}, \mathsf{Verify})$ with the following syntax:

- $\mathsf{KeyGen}(1^\lambda) \to (\mathsf{vk}, \mathsf{sk})$: on input a security parameter λ, stream a verification key vk and store signing key sk.
- $\mathsf{KeyReceive}(1^\lambda, \mathsf{vk})$: on input a security parameter λ and a streamed verification key vk, output a verification state vd.
- $\mathsf{Sign}(\mathsf{sk}, \mu)$: on input a signing key sk and a (potentially streamed) message $\mu \in \mathcal{M}$, output a (potentially streamed) signature σ.
- $\mathsf{Verify}(\mathsf{vd}, \mu, \sigma)$: on input a verification state vd, a (potentially streamed) message $\mu \in \mathcal{M}$ and a (potentially streamed) signature σ, output a bit $b \in \{0, 1\}$.

Definition 6 (Correctness). *We say that a signature scheme is correct if for all message $\mu \in \mathcal{M}$:*

$$\Pr[\mathsf{Verify}(\mathsf{vd}, \mu, \sigma) = 1] \geq 1 - \mathrm{negl}(\lambda),$$

where $\mathsf{sk} \leftarrow \mathsf{KeyGen}(1^\lambda), \mathsf{vd} \leftarrow \mathsf{KeyReceive}(1^\lambda, \mathsf{vk}), \sigma \leftarrow \mathsf{Sign}(\mathsf{sk}, \mu)$.

Definition 7 (Streaming Signature). *For an integer n, we say that a streaming signature scheme has memory n if KeyGen, $\mathsf{KeyReceive}$, Sign and Verify can respectively be computed by streaming algorithms with memory n, given streaming access to μ and (μ, z) respectively. We additionally require that sk and vd have size at most n.*

Definition 8 (Unforgeability under chosen message attacks). *For an algorithm* Adv, *consider the following experiment:*

Experiment $\mathsf{Exp}^{\mathsf{uf}\text{-}\mathsf{cmva}}(1^\lambda, \mathsf{Adv})$:

1. *Sample* $(\mathsf{vk}, \mathsf{sk}) \leftarrow \mathsf{KeyGen}(1^\lambda)$, $\mathsf{vd} \leftarrow \mathsf{KeyReceive}(1^\lambda, \mathsf{vk})$, *and compute* $\mathsf{view}_{\mathsf{Adv}} \leftarrow \mathsf{Adv}(\mathsf{vk})$.
2. *Compute* $(\mu^*, \sigma^*) \leftarrow \mathsf{Adv}^{\mathsf{Sign}(\mathsf{sk}, \cdot), \mathsf{Verify}(\mathsf{vd}, \cdot, \cdot)}(\mathsf{view}_{\mathsf{Adv}})$.
3. *Output* 1 *if* $\mathsf{Verify}(\mathsf{vd}, \mu^*, \sigma^*) = 1$ *output* 0 *otherwise.*

We say that an adversary Adv *is* admissible *if* Adv *did not query* Sign(sk, ·) *on input* μ^*. *In the following, all the adversaries are assumed admissible.*

We say that a signature scheme is $(\varepsilon, \mathcal{A})$-*unforgeable under chosen message attacks* (uf-cma) *against a class* $\mathcal{A}$ *of adversaries, if for all adversary* Adv $\in \mathcal{A}$:

$$\Pr[\mathsf{Exp}^{\mathsf{uf}\text{-}\mathsf{cmva}}(1^\lambda, \mathsf{Adv}) = 1] \le \varepsilon.$$

We simply say that a signature scheme is $\mathcal{A}$-uf-cma-*secure if it is* $(\varepsilon, \mathcal{A})$-uf-cmva-*secure for some* $\varepsilon = \mathrm{negl}(\lambda)$.

We define variants of unforgeability, namely selective and/or without verification queries (((s)uf-cm(v)a)-*security), in a similar way than in Sect. 3.1.*

We consider a similar class of streaming adversaries for signatures, as in Definition 5.

Definition 9 (Streaming Adversaries for Signatures). *We say that an adversary* Adv *in any of the security experiments above is* streaming with memory m *if it is a streaming algorithm that accesses oracles* KeyGen, MAC *and* Verify *(whenever applicable) in a streaming manner using memory at most* m. *Namely, such adversaries first observe the stream* vk *produced by* KeyGen *(but not* sk*). Then, it provides the inputs to oracles* Sign *and* Verify *as streams of bits and receives the outputs of* Sign *as streams. The calls to* Sign *and* Verify *are not required to be synchronous: for instance* Adv *can start a oracle call to* Verify *while streaming an input to* Sign *or receiving a tag in a streaming manner. We add the restriction that there are at most one concurrent call to* Sign *and at most one concurrent call to* Verify *at any given point in time during the experiment, and any give oracle call to* Verify *can be concurrent with at most one call to* Sign.

We will refer to Q *(resp.* Q_S, Q_V*) as the number of total (resp. signing, verification) queries made by* Adv.

As in Remark 1, one can consider adversaries with temporary unbounded memory for signatures.

4   Block Entropy Lemma

In this section, we describe and prove our block entropy lemma (Lemma 4), which we will use to build signature schemes in the streaming BSM Sect. 7. In the full version, we state a corollary that might be of independent interest.

Lemma 4. *Let* $X = (X_1, \ldots, X_k) \in \{0,1\}^{kb}$ *be a random variable with blocks* $X_i \in \{0,1\}^b$, *such that* $\mathbf{H}_\infty(X) \geq \alpha \cdot (kb)$ *for some* $\alpha > 0$. *Then, there are some parameters* $\alpha_1, \alpha_2, \varepsilon$ *instantiated below and some set* $\mathsf{BAD} \subseteq \{0,1\}^{kb}$ *such that the following holds:*

1. $\Pr[X \in \mathsf{BAD}] \leq \varepsilon$.
2. *For all* $x = (x_1, \ldots, x_k)$ *there is a set* $\mathcal{I}(x) \subseteq [k]$ *such that:*
    (a) if $x \notin \mathsf{BAD}$ *then* $|\mathcal{I}(x)| \geq \alpha_1 \cdot k$,
    (b) for all $i \in \mathcal{I}(x)$: $\mathbf{H}_\infty(X_i \mid X_1 = x_1, \ldots, X_{i-1} = x_{i-1}, i \in \mathcal{I}(X)) \geq \alpha_2 \cdot b$.
    Furthermore, the values $x_1, \ldots, x_i$ *fully determine whether or not* $i \in \mathcal{I}(x)$.

The parameters $\alpha_1, \alpha_2, \varepsilon$ *can be set according to either of the following two options:*

(i) *For any* $\alpha_1 > 0, \gamma > 0$, *we can set* $\alpha_2 = (\alpha - \alpha_1 - \log(1/\gamma)/b), \varepsilon = k \cdot \gamma$.
    For example, for any $\rho > 0$, *we can set* $\alpha_1 = \alpha_2 = \alpha/2 - \rho$ *and* $\varepsilon = k \cdot 2^{-2\rho b}$.
(ii) *For any* $\beta > 0, \gamma > 0, \delta \in [0,1]$, *we can set:* $\alpha_1 = \beta - (1 + \delta)\gamma, \alpha_2 = (\alpha - \beta - \log(1/\gamma)/b), \varepsilon = \exp\left(-\frac{\delta^2}{3}\gamma k\right)$. *For example, for any* $\rho > 0$ *such that* $b \geq \log(1/(2\rho))/(2\rho)$, *we can set:* $\alpha_1 = \alpha_2 = \alpha/2 - \rho$ *and* $\varepsilon = e^{-\frac{2}{3}\rho k}$.

We refer to the full version for a proof for getting parameter choice (ii) in Lemma 4; parameter choice (i) will suffice in our applications.

Proof. Fix any $x = (x_1, \ldots, x_k)$. Then, by the definition of min-entropy, we have:

$$2^{-\alpha \cdot (kb)} \geq \Pr[X = x] = \prod_{i=1}^{k} \underbrace{\Pr[X_i = x_i | X_1 = x_1, \ldots, X_{i-1} = x_{i-1}]}_{\stackrel{\text{def}}{=} 2^{-e_i}} = 2^{-\sum_{i=1}^{k} e_i}.$$

Let $\beta > 0$ be some parameter and define the set $\mathbf{H}(x) \subseteq [k]$ via $\mathbf{H}(x) := \{i : e_i \geq (\alpha - \beta)b\}$. Intuitively, these are the indices i where the i'th block takes on a low probability value x_i conditioned on previous blocks, and therefore the indices where we should expect to find entropy. Note that $x_1, \ldots, x_i$ fully determines whether $i \in \mathbf{H}(x)$. By an averaging argument, it must be the case that $|\mathbf{H}(x)| \geq \beta \cdot k$.

Now, let us consider the random variable $\mathbf{H}(X)$. We claim that for every $i \in [k]$ and every $\gamma > 0$, at least *one* of the following two conditions must hold:

(I) Either $\Pr[i \in \mathbf{H}(X) \mid X_1 = x_1, \ldots, X_{i-1} = x_{i-1}] \leq \gamma$,
(II) or $\mathbf{H}_\infty(X_i \mid X_1 = x_1, \ldots, X_{i-1} = x_{i-1}, i \in \mathbf{H}(X)) \geq (\alpha - \beta) \cdot b - \log(\gamma)$.

Intuitively, the above says that if we condition on any choice of the first $i - 1$ blocks then either (I) it is unlikely for the i'th block to take on any value whose a-priori probability is too small, or (II) the i'th block has high entropy even if we condition on it taking some such value. In particular, if (I) does not hold, then

$$\max_z \Pr[X_i = z | X_1 = x_1, \ldots, X_{i-1} = x_{i-1}, i \in \mathbf{H}(X)]$$
$$= \max_z \frac{\Pr[X_i = z \wedge i \in \mathbf{H}(X) | X_1 = x_1, \ldots, X_{i-1} = x_{i-1}]}{\Pr[i \in \mathbf{H}(x) | X_1 = x_1, \ldots, X_{i-1} = x_{i-1}]}$$
$$\leq \max_{z \in \mathcal{Z}_i(x)} \frac{\Pr[X_i = z | X_1 = x_1, \ldots, X_{i-1} = x_{i-1}]}{\gamma}$$
$$\text{where } \mathcal{Z}_i(x) = \{z \ : \ \Pr[X_i = z | X_1 = x_1, \ldots, X_{i-1} = x_{i-1}] \leq 2^{-(\alpha-\beta)\cdot b}\}$$
$$\leq \frac{2^{-(\alpha-\beta)\cdot b}}{\gamma}$$

The second inequality follows by noting that $i \in \mathbf{H}(X) \Leftrightarrow X_i \in \mathcal{Z}_i(x)$ whenever $X_1 = x_1, \ldots, X_{i-1} = x_{i-1}$.

Now define $\mathcal{A}(x) = \{i \ : \ \Pr[i \in \mathbf{H}(X) \mid X_1 = x_1, \ldots, X_{i-1} = x_{i-1}] \leq \gamma\}$, which corresponds to the indices i for which case (I) holds. Let $\mathcal{I}(x) = \mathbf{H}(x) \setminus \mathcal{A}(x)$, which corresponds to the set of indices for which case (II) holds *and* they are in $\mathbf{H}(x)$. Then, for any $i \in \mathcal{I}(x)$:

$$\mathbf{H}_\infty(X_i \mid X_1 = x_1, \ldots, X_{i-1} = x_{i-1}, i \in \mathcal{I}(X))$$
$$= \mathbf{H}_\infty(X_i \mid X_1 = x_1, \ldots, X_{i-1} = x_{i-1}, i \in \mathbf{H}(X)) \geq (\alpha - \beta)b - \log(1/\gamma),$$

where the second first equality follows from the fact that $x_1, \ldots, x_{i-1}$ fully determine whether $i \in \mathcal{A}(x)$, and the second inequality follows from the definition of condition (II). This proves part 2.(b) of the lemma with $\alpha_2 = (\alpha - \beta - \log(1/\gamma)/b)$.

We first prove the lemma for the first parameter choice (i). Define BAD = $\{x \ : \ |\mathcal{I}(x)| < \beta \cdot k\}$. Clearly this ensures that part 2.(a) of the lemma is satisfied with $\alpha_1 = \beta$. Therefore, we are left to prove part 1 of the lemma. Note that $\mathcal{I}(X) = \mathbf{H}(X) \setminus \mathcal{A}(X)$ and $|\mathbf{H}(x)| \geq \beta k$. Intuitively, the only way we can have $X \in$ BAD is if there is some index i where the i'th block X_i was unlikely to take on any low-probability value conditioned on the prior blocks, but it did so anyway, and this is unlikely to occur. Formally

$$Pr[X \in \mathsf{BAD}] = \Pr[|\mathcal{I}(X)| < \beta k]$$
$$\leq \Pr[|\mathbf{H}(X) \cap \mathcal{A}(X)| \geq 1]]$$
$$\leq \sum_i \Pr[i \in H(X) \cap \mathcal{A}(X)]$$
$$\leq \sum_i \max_{\{(x_1, \ldots, x_{i-1}) \ : i \in \mathcal{A}(x)\}} \Pr[i \in H(X) \mid X_1 = x_1, \ldots, X_{i-1} = x_{i-1}]$$
$$\leq k \cdot \gamma.$$

The second line follows from the fact that $\mathcal{I}(X) = \mathbf{H}(X) \setminus \mathcal{A}(X)$ and $|\mathbf{H}(x)| \geq \beta k$ fopr all x. The second to last inequality follows by noting that $(x_1, \ldots, x_{i-1})$ fully determine whether $i \in \mathcal{A}(x)$, and the last inequality follows by noting that the definition of $\mathcal{A}(x)$ guarantees that for any $x_1, \ldots, x_{i-1}$ for which $i \in \mathcal{A}(x)$ we have $\Pr[i \in \mathbf{H}(X) \; : \; X_1 = x_1, \ldots, X_{i-1} = x_{i-1}] \leq \gamma$. Therefore this proves part 1 of the lemma with $\varepsilon = k \cdot \gamma$.   □

5 MAC with Long Tags

In this section, we build a streaming MAC in the streaming BSM where the size of tags grow with the memory bound of the adversary. More precisely, we prove the following theorem:

Theorem 2. *For all integers m, λ, there exists a streaming MAC with memory $n = O(\lambda + \mathrm{polylog}(m, \lambda)))$ (Definition 2) which can authenticate messages of length up to 2^λ, and which is $(2^{-\lambda}, \mathcal{A})$-uf-cmva-secure (Definition 3), where $\mathcal{A}$ is the set of streaming adversaries with memory m that make a total number of at most $Q = 2^\lambda$ oracle queries in the unforgeability experiment (Definition 5). Furthermore the (streamed) tags are of size $O(m + \lambda \log \lambda)$.*

5.1 Construction

Construction. Let $|\mu|$ be a parameter. Let n, m be integers such that $n \geq \Omega(\lambda + \mathrm{polylog}(m, \lambda, |\mu|))$. Let $\mathsf{Ext} : \{0,1\}^k \times \{0,1\}^d \rightarrow \{0,1\}^\ell$ be a $(n, m, 2^{-\Omega(\lambda)})$-BSM extractor (Theorem 1), where $\ell = O(\lambda + \log(k + |\mu|))$; and suppose $m \geq \ell$, and $k \geq m/2 + 2\lambda$ while $k = O(m + \lambda \log \lambda)$.

Let $c \geq 3$ be a constant. Let $(\mathsf{KeyGen}, \mathsf{MAC}, \mathsf{Verify})$ be a one-time, information-theoretic deterministic MAC with message space $\{0,1\}^{k+|\mu|}$ that can be evaluated in a streaming manner using memory $O(\lambda + \log(k + |\mu|))$ and tag size at most ℓ, which is $\frac{(k+|\mu|)Q_V}{2^{c\lambda}}$-secure against adversaries that make at most one tagging query and Q_V verification queries (which exists by Claim 1). We define the following algorithms:

- $\overline{\mathsf{KeyGen}}(1^\lambda)$: Sample a seed $\mathsf{seed} \leftarrow \{0,1\}^k$ for Ext and a key sk for the one-time MAC. Output:
$$\overline{\mathsf{sk}} = (\mathsf{sk}, \mathsf{seed}).$$

- $\overline{\mathsf{MAC}}(\mathsf{sk}, \mu)$: On input $\mu \leftarrow \{0,1\}^{|\mu|}$ and $\overline{\mathsf{sk}} = (\mathsf{sk}, \mathsf{seed})$, sample $x \leftarrow \{0,1\}^k$ and output:
$$\overline{\sigma} = (x, \quad \mathsf{Ext}(x, \mathsf{seed}) \oplus \mathsf{MAC}(\mathsf{sk}, (x \| \mu))).$$

  We consider here that x is generated and output in a streaming manner, while $\mathsf{Ext}(x; \mathsf{seed})$ and $\mathsf{MAC}(\mathsf{sk}, (x \| \mu))$ are computed in a streaming manner.
- $\overline{\mathsf{Verify}}(\mu, \mathsf{sk}, \sigma)$: on a streamed input $(\mu, \overline{\sigma} = (x, \psi))$, compute
$$\sigma := \psi \oplus \mathsf{Ext}(x; \mathsf{seed}),$$

  and output $\mathsf{Verify}(\mathsf{sk}, \sigma)$.

Claim 2 (Correctness). *Suppose* $(\mathsf{KeyGen}, \mathsf{MAC}, \mathsf{Verify})$ *is correct. Then* $(\overline{\mathsf{KeyGen}}, \overline{\mathsf{MAC}}, \overline{\mathsf{Verify}})$ *is correct.*

Claim 3 (Efficiency). $\overline{\mathsf{KeyGen}}$ *can be computed (in place) with memory* $O(n)$, *and* MAC *and* Verify *can be computed in a streaming manner using memory* $O(n)$.

Proof. Computing KeyGen, as well as the size of $\overline{\mathsf{sk}}$ follow directly by Theorem 1 and Claim 1, which gives a (one-time, information-theoretic) MAC with tag size $O(\lambda + \log(k + |\mu|))$ where keys can be sampled efficiently. Instantiating Ext with $k = O(m + \lambda \log \lambda)$ and $n \geq \Omega(\lambda + \log(k + |\mu|)) = \Omega(\lambda + \mathrm{polylog}(m, \lambda, |\mu|))$ gives the claim.

As for computing MAC and Verify in a streaming manner, given seed and $\overline{\mathsf{sk}}$, one can sample and output x in a streaming manner. Then one can compute both $\mathsf{Ext}(x, \mathsf{seed})$ and $\mathsf{MAC}(\mathsf{sk}, (x, \mu))$ given x as a streaming input, using memory $O(n)$. ☐

Theorem 3 (Security). *Let* $\mathcal{A}$ *be the set of streaming adversaries running in space* $m/2$ *and that make at most* Q *oracle queries in the* uf-cmva *experiment (Definition 5). Let* $\varepsilon \leq Q_T Q_V 2^{m/2 - k} + (Q_T + Q_V) 2^{-\Omega(\lambda)} + Q_V \cdot (k + |\mu|)/2^{c\lambda}$. *Then* $(\overline{\mathsf{KeyGen}}, \overline{\mathsf{MAC}}, \overline{\mathsf{Verify}})$ *is* $(\varepsilon, \mathcal{A})$-uf-cmva-*secure.*

We refer to the full version for a proof.

Setting $\ell = O(\lambda + \log(k + |\mu|))$, $m = 2^{(c-1)\lambda}$ where $c \geq 3$, and $k \geq m/2 + 2\lambda$ while $k = O(m + \lambda \log \lambda)$, and $|\mu| = 2^{\lambda}$ yields 2.

Remark 2 (Security against Adversaries with Temporary Unbounded Memory). The construction above is in fact secure against adversaries that have temporary unbounded memory. Namely, on input a streamed tag (x, ψ), they are allowed to use temporary unbounded memory to process x, as long as they compress their state down to some size m memory before ψ is received. BSM-extractor security still applies, as x has sufficient min-entropy, and verification queries can then be handled using a similarly strong reduction. In particular the construction is secure even given non-uniform advice of size at most m.

6   MAC with Short Tags

In this section, we build a streaming MAC in the streaming BSM where the size of tags does *not* grow with the memory bound of the adversary. In particular, honest parties can store entire tags. More precisely, we prove the following theorem:

Theorem 4 (MAC with Short Tags). *For all* m, λ *there exists a streaming MAC with memory* $n = O(\lambda \sqrt{m} + \lambda^2)$ *(Definition 2) which can authenticate messages of length up to* $2^{O(n)}$, *which is* $(2^{-\lambda}, \mathcal{A})$-uf-cmva-*secure (Definition 3), where* $\mathcal{A}$ *is the set of streaming adversaries with memory* m *that make at most* $Q = 2^{\lambda}$ *oracle queries in the unforgeability experiment (Definition 5) and that do not query the verification oracle on any input provided by the tagging oracle. Furthermore the resulting MAC has tags of size* $O(n)$.

Our main tool is the following result from [25].

Theorem 5 ([25]). *Let $k \geq 1$ be an integer. There exist constants $C, \alpha > 0$ such that the following holds. Let Adv be an algorithm which takes as input a stream $(\mathbf{a}_1, b_1), \ldots, (\mathbf{a}_Q, b_Q)$, where $\mathbf{a}_i \in \{0,1\}^k$, $\mathbf{s} \leftarrow \{0,1\}^k$ and $b_i = \langle \mathbf{a}_i, \mathbf{s} \rangle \in \mathbb{Z}_2$ and $Q \leq 2^{\alpha k}$, and outputs a vector $\mathbf{s}' \in \mathbb{Z}_2^k$. Suppose that Adv uses at most Ck^2 memory. Then $\Pr[\mathbf{s}' = \mathbf{s}] \leq O(2^{-\alpha k})$.*

Futhermore the same conclusion holds if Adv is given access to unbounded temporary memory between receiving elements $(\mathbf{a}, b)$, as long as its state is compressed down to Ck^2 bits whenever an element $(\mathbf{a}, b)$ is received. We refer to such adversaries as adversaries with memory Ck^2 and unbounded temporary memory (Remark 1).

We build our scheme as follows. We first give a construction of a MAC with small tags, with small message space and no verification queries which additionally satisfies message-hiding (Definition 4). We then show that any such MAC can be compiled to handle larger messages. The next step is to show that previously issued tagging queries can be efficiently recognized using a low amount of memory, independent of the number of queries made. Last, we show how to ensure security even given verification queries. We refer to the full version for more details.

7   Public-Key Signatures

In this section, we show how to build signature schemes in the streaming BSM. More precisely, we prove the following:

Theorem 6. *For all m, λ, there exists a streaming signature scheme with memory $n = \widetilde{O}(\lambda^3 + \sqrt{m\lambda})$ (Definition 7) which can authenticate messages of length up to 2^λ, and which is $(2^{-\Omega(\lambda)}, \mathcal{A})$-uf-cmva-secure (Definition 8) where $\mathcal{A}$ is the set of streaming adversaries with memory m that make a total number of at most $Q = 2^\lambda$ oracle queries in the unforgeability experiment (Definition 9). Furthermore, (streamed) signatures have size $\widetilde{O}(m + \lambda^{3/2})$.*

To do so, we first present a *set key-agreeement protocol* in Sect. 7.1, using our block entropy lemma Lemma 4 as our main technical tool. Then we show how to upgrade such a protocol to a signature scheme in Sect. 7.2. Last, we show that the quadratic gap between the adversary's memory bound and the honest users is optimal (up to poly(λ) factors), in Sect. 7.3 (Theorem 8).

7.1   Set Key-Agreement Protocol

Given any parameters m, λ and ℓ, we define additional parameters: $b = 8\lambda(\ell + 2)$, $k = \max(\lceil 4m/b \rceil + 4, 64\lambda)$, $q = \lceil 2\sqrt{k\lambda} \rceil$, which guarantees $k \geq 2m/b + 2q$. Let Ext $: \{0,1\}^b \times \{0,1\}^d \rightarrow \{0,1\}^\ell$ be a $(\ell + 2\lambda, 2^{-\lambda})$-seeded extractor with some seed-length d, that can be computed using $O(b)$ space ([18]). Consider the following "set key agreement" protocol between Alice and Bob, with one round of communication from Alice to Bob.

- $\overline{\text{KeyGen}}$: Alice stream a value $\text{vk} = (x = (x_1, \ldots, x_k), \mathcal{S}_A, (\text{seed}_1, \ldots, \text{seed}_q))$ generated as follows.
  - She chooses a uniformly random subset $\mathcal{S}_A \subseteq [k]$ of size $|\mathcal{S}_A| = q$ and stores it in memory as an ordered tuple $\mathcal{S}_A = (i_1^A, \ldots, i_q^A)$.
  - She streams a uniformly random value $x = (x_1, \ldots, x_k) \leftarrow (\{0,1\}^b)^k$ and additionally stores the values $x_{\mathcal{S}_A} = (x_{i_1^A}, \ldots, x_{i_q^A})$ in memory.
  - She streams her set $\mathcal{S}_A$.
  - She chooses q random extractor seeds $\text{seed}_j \leftarrow \{0,1\}^d$ and computes $\text{sk}_j = \text{Ext}(x[i_j^A]; \text{seed}_j)$ for $j \in [q]$. She sends $(\text{seed}_1, \ldots, \text{seed}_q)$ and stores $\text{sk} = (\text{sk}_1, \ldots, \text{sk}_q)$ in memory.

  Her final outputs consists of the secret key $\text{sk} = (\text{sk}_1, \ldots, \text{sk}_q) \in (\{0,1\}^\ell)^q$ stored in memory.

- $\overline{\text{KeyReceive}}$:
  Bob processes the stream $\text{vk} = (x = (x_1, \ldots, x_k), \mathcal{S}_A, (\text{seed}_1, \ldots, \text{seed}_q))$ as follows:
  - He chooses a uniformly random subset $\mathcal{S}_B \subseteq [k]$ of size $|\mathcal{S}_B| = q$ and stores it in memory.
  - As he receives the stream x, he additionally stores $x_{\mathcal{S}_B}$ in memory.
  - When he receives $\mathcal{S}_A = (i_1^A, \ldots, i_q^A)$ he stores it in memory.
  - When he receives $(\text{seed}_1, \ldots, \text{seed}_q)$ he computes $\mathcal{T} = \{j \in [q] : i_j^A \in \mathcal{S}_B\}$. For each $j \in \mathcal{T}$ he computes $\text{sk}_j = \text{Ext}(x_{i_j^A}; \text{seed}_j)$. He stores the value $(\mathcal{T}, \text{sk}_{\mathcal{T}} = (\text{sk}_j)_{j \in \mathcal{T}})$ in memory.

  Bob's final outputs consists of $\text{vd} = (\mathcal{T}, \text{sk}_{\mathcal{T}} = (\text{sk}_j)_{j \in \mathcal{T}})$ stored in memory.

Lemma 5. *The procedures* $\overline{\text{KeyGen}}$ *and* $\overline{\text{KeyReceive}}$ *can be computed by streaming algorithms with memory* $\widetilde{O}(bq) = \widetilde{O}(\lambda^2 \ell + \lambda \sqrt{\ell \cdot \lambda})$. *Furthermore* sk *and* vd *have size* $\widetilde{O}(q \cdot \ell) = \widetilde{O}(\sqrt{m\ell} + \lambda \ell)$.

Lemma 6 (Set Key-Agreement Lemma). *Let Eve be a streaming attacker with m bits of memory, who observes the stream* vk *and outputs* view_{Eve} *in the above protocol. Let* $\text{sk} = (\text{sk}_1, \ldots, \text{sk}_q)$ *be Alice's output and let* $\text{vd} = (\mathcal{T}, \text{sk}_{\mathcal{T}})$ *be Bob's output in the protocol. Then there is some index $t \in \mathcal{T} \cup \{\bot\}$ defined as a random variable depending on the entire protocol execution and the view of Eve, and some $\varepsilon = 2^{-\Omega(\lambda)}$ such that:*

$$(\text{view}_{Eve}, \mathcal{T}, t, \text{sk}_{-t} = (\text{sk}_j : j \in [q] \setminus \{t\}), \text{sk}_t)$$
$$\approx_\varepsilon (\text{view}_{Eve}, \mathcal{T}, t, \text{sk}_{-t} = (\text{sk}_j : j \in [q] \setminus \{t\}), u)$$

where $u \leftarrow \{0,1\}^\ell$ is random and independent of all other values, and we define $\text{sk}_t := \bot$ *if $t = \bot$.*

Proof. At the end of the protocol execution, we select the index t as follows:

1. If $|\mathcal{S}_A \cap \mathcal{S}_B| < \lambda$ then set $t = \bot$. (We refer to this event as $\bot_0$.)
2. Choose a uniformly random $\mathcal{V} \subseteq \mathcal{S}_A \cap \mathcal{S}_B$ such that $|\mathcal{V}| = \lambda$. Let $\mathcal{W} = \mathcal{S}_A \setminus \mathcal{V}$.
3. Let view_{Eve}^0 denote the view of Eve immediately after processing the x component of the stream but before receiving $\mathcal{S}_A$.

4. Let $\mathsf{aux} = (\mathsf{view}_{Eve}^0, \mathcal{W}, x_{\mathcal{W}})$, and let AUX be a random variable corresponding to aux. Let $X = (U_{kb}|\mathsf{AUX} = \mathsf{aux})$ be the random variable corresponding to choosing $x \leftarrow (\{0,1\}^b)^k$ from the uniform distribution, conditioned on $\mathsf{AUX} = \mathsf{aux}$. If, for the given value of aux, we have $\mathbf{H}_\infty(X) < kb/2$ then set $t = \bot$. (We refer to this event as $\bot_1$.)

5. Let the sets $\mathsf{BAD} \subseteq (\{0,1\}^b)^k$ and $\mathcal{I}(x) \subseteq [k]$ be the sets from Lemma 4 defined with respect to the distribution X with $\alpha = 1/2$, $\alpha_1 = \alpha_2 = 1/8$. Let x be the value sent during the protocol execution.
If $\mathcal{I}(x) \cap \mathcal{V} = \emptyset$ then set $t = \bot$. (We refer to this event as $\bot_2$.)

6. Let i^* be the smallest value in $\mathcal{I}(x) \cap \mathcal{V} \subseteq \mathcal{S}_A = \{i_1^A, \ldots, i_q^A\}$ and let t^* be the value such $i_{t^*}^A = i^*$. Set $t = t^*$.

We show a sequence of hybrid distributions that are statistically close.

Hybrid 0. This is the distribution on the left-hand side of the Lemma

$$(\mathsf{view}_{Eve}, \mathcal{T}, t, \mathsf{sk}_{-t} = (\mathsf{sk}_j \; : \; j \in [q] \setminus \{t\}), \mathsf{sk}_t)$$

Hybrid 1. We now change how we select the sets $\mathcal{S}_A, \mathcal{S}_B, \mathcal{V}, \mathcal{W}$.

In hybrid 0, $\mathcal{S}_A, \mathcal{S}_B \subseteq [k]$ are chosen uniformly at random with $|\mathcal{S}_A| = |\mathcal{S}_B| = q$. Then, if $|\mathcal{S}_A \cap \mathcal{S}_B| > \lambda$, we choose $\mathcal{V} \subseteq \mathcal{S}_A \cap \mathcal{S}_B$ of size $|\mathcal{V}| = \lambda$ uniformly at random and define $\mathcal{W} = \mathcal{S}_A \setminus \mathcal{V}$.

In hybrid 1, we instead choose $\mathcal{W} \subseteq [k]$ of size $|\mathcal{W}| = q - \lambda$ uniformly at random. Then we select $\mathcal{V} \subseteq [k] \setminus \mathcal{W}$ of size $|\mathcal{V}| = \lambda$ uniformly at random. We define $\mathcal{S}_A = \mathcal{V} \cup \mathcal{W}$. Then we choose $\mathcal{S}_B \subseteq [k]$ of size $|\mathcal{S}_B| = q$ uniformly at randomly subject to $\mathcal{V} \subseteq [k]$.

Note that the above change ensures that, in hybrid 1, $\mathcal{V} \subseteq \mathcal{S}_A \cap \mathcal{S}_B$ with $|\mathcal{V}| = \lambda$, and therefore the event $\bot_0$ never occurs.

Hybrids 1 is distributed identically to hybrid 0 if we condition on $\bot_0$ not occurring in hybrid 0. Therefore the statistical distance between the hybrids is bounded by the probability that $\bot_0$ occurs, meaning that $|\mathcal{S}_A \cap \mathcal{S}_B| < \lambda$, in hybrid 0. This is bounded by $\varepsilon_1 \leq 2^{-\lambda/4} = 2^{-\Omega(\lambda)}$ by Lemma 3 as $q \geq 2\sqrt{k\lambda}$.

Hybrid 2. In hybrid 1, if the event $\bot_1$ occurs (i.e., aux is such hat $\mathbf{H}_\infty(X) < kb/2$) then we set $t = \bot$ and $\mathsf{sk}_t = \bot$. In hybrid 2, if $\bot_1$ occurs then we set $t = \bot$ and choose $\mathsf{sk}_t \leftarrow \{0,1\}^\ell$ uniformly at random.

Hybrids 1 and 2 are distributed identically as long as $\bot_1$ does not occur, and so the statisticaly distance between them is bounded by the probability that $\mathbf{H}_\infty(X) < kb/2$. Note that $X = (U_{kb}|\mathsf{AUX} = \mathsf{aux})$. Furthermore, we have:

$$\mathbf{H}_\infty(U_{kb}|\mathsf{AUX}) \geq \mathbf{H}_\infty(U_{kb}|\mathcal{W}) - m - (q - \lambda) \cdot b \geq kb - m - (q - \lambda) \cdot b \geq kb/2 + \lambda,$$

where the first inequality follows from Lemma 2 since $\mathsf{aux} = (\mathsf{view}_{Eve}^0, \mathcal{W}, x_{\mathcal{W}})$ where $|\mathsf{view}_{Eve}^0| = m$ and $|x_{\mathcal{W}}| = (q - \lambda) \cdot b$, and the second inequality follows since $\mathcal{W}$ is chosen independently of $x \leftarrow U_{kb}$ and hence does not reduce entropy. Therefore, by Lemma 1:

$$\Pr_{\mathsf{aux} \leftarrow \mathsf{AUX}} [\underbrace{\mathbf{H}_\infty(U_{kb}|\mathsf{AUX} = \mathsf{aux})}_{\mathbf{H}_\infty(X)} < kb/2] \leq 2^{-\lambda},$$

and so the statistical distance between the hybrids is $\varepsilon_2 \leq 2^{-\lambda}$.

Hybrid 3. In hybrid 3, if $\perp_1$ does not occur and $x \in \mathsf{BAD}$, then we define $t = \perp$ and choose $\mathsf{sk}_t \leftarrow \{0,1\}^\ell$ uniformly at random. We refer to this event as $\perp_{1.5}$.

Hybrids 1 and 2 are distributed identically unless: $\perp_1$ does not occur and $x \in \mathsf{BAD}$. But, if we fix any aux for which $\perp_1$ does not occur, then by Lemma 4 we can bound the probability that $x \in \mathsf{BAD}$ by $k \cdot 2^{-b/4} = 2^{-\Omega(\lambda)}$. Therefore, the statistical distance between the hybrids is $\varepsilon_3 \leq 2^{-\Omega(\lambda)}$.

Hybrid 4. In hybrid 3, if $\perp_1$ and $\perp_{1.5}$ don't occur but $|\mathcal{I}(x) \cap \mathcal{V}| = \emptyset$ then we set $t = \perp$ and $\mathsf{sk}_t = \perp$. In hybrid 4, if $\perp_1$ and $\perp_{1.5}$ don't occur but $|\mathcal{I}(x) \cap \mathcal{V}| = \emptyset$, then we set $t = \perp$ and choose $\mathsf{sk}_t \leftarrow \{0,1\}^\ell$ uniformly at random.

Hybrids 3 and 4 are distributed identically unless: $\perp_1$ and $\perp_{1.5}$ don't occur but $|\mathcal{I}(x) \cap \mathcal{V}| = \emptyset$. Let us fix any aux, x such that $\perp_1, \perp_{1.5}$ do not occur. This also fixes $\mathcal{I}(x)$. Furthermore, by Lemma 4, we have $|\mathcal{I}(x)| \geq k/8$. Moreover, $I(x) \subseteq [k] \setminus \mathcal{W}$ since, for $i \in \mathcal{W}$, the values X_i are completely fixed by aux and hence have entropy 0. On the other hand $\mathcal{V}$ is uniformly random over $[k] \setminus \mathcal{W}$ with $|\mathcal{V}| = \lambda$, and independent of $\mathcal{I}(x)$. Therefore the probability that $\mathcal{V} \cap \mathcal{I}(x) = \emptyset$ is bounded by $\varepsilon_4 \leq (7/8)^\lambda = 2^{-\Omega(\lambda)}$, which also bounds the statistical distance between these hybrids.

Hybrid 5. We undo the change introduced in hybrid 3. That is, we no longer check if $x \in \mathsf{BAD}$ and take any special action if it is.

Hybrids 4 and 5 are statistically close for the same reason hybrids 2 and 3 are statistically close, with distance $\varepsilon_5 \leq 2^{-\Omega(\lambda)}$.

Hybrid 6. In hybrid 6, we now always choose $\mathsf{sk}_t \leftarrow \{0,1\}^\ell$ uniformly random.

We argue that hybrids 5 and 6 are statistically close by the security of the extractor. Let us fix and condition on any choice of values

$$(\mathsf{aux} = (\mathsf{view}_{Eve}^0, \mathcal{W}, x_{\mathcal{W}}), \mathcal{V}, \mathcal{S}_B, i^*, x_1, \ldots, x_{i^*-1}, (\mathsf{seed}_j)_{j \in [q] \setminus t^*})$$

chosen during the experiment, subject to $\perp_1, \perp_2$ not occurring. We define i^* as being the smallest value in $\mathcal{V} \cap \mathcal{I}(x)$ and t^* is defined as the value such $i_{t^*}^A = i^*$, which is fixed once i^* and $\mathcal{S}_A = \mathcal{V} \cup \mathcal{W} = \{i_1^A, \ldots, i_q^A\}$ are fixed. The above values also fix $\mathsf{sk}_{\mathcal{W}} := (\mathsf{sk}_j = \mathsf{Ext}(x_{i_j^A}; \mathsf{seed}_j))_{i_j^A \in \mathcal{W}}$.

If either $\perp_1$ occurs or $\perp_2$ occurs then the hybrids are identical, and therefore it suffices to only show that they are statistically close for any fixed choice of the values as above for which $\perp_1, \perp_2$ do not occur.

Note that, by Lemma 4, fixing $x_1, \ldots, x_{i^*-1}$ also fixes whether $i \in \mathcal{I}(x)$ for all $i \leq i^*$ and therefore, once we fix all of the above, conditioning on i^* being the smallest value in $\mathcal{V} \cap \mathcal{I}(x)$ is equivalent to just conditioning on $i^* \in \mathcal{I}(x)$. Therefore, the distribution of X_{i^*} (i.e., the i^* block of x) conditioned on the above is equivalent to $(X_{i^*}|X_1 = x_1, \ldots, X_{i^*-1} = x_{i_1^*}, i^* \in \mathcal{I}(x))$, and By Lemma 4, it has min-entropy $\mathbf{H}_\infty(X_{i^*}) \geq b/8$.[7]

---

[7] For the rest, of the argument we will condition on all the fixed values implicitly and will not write this conditioning explicitly.

Let $\mathsf{SK}_{\mathcal{V}-} := (\mathsf{SK}_j = \mathsf{Ext}(X_{i_j^A}; \mathsf{seed}_j))_{i_j^A \in \mathcal{V} \setminus \{i^*\}}$. Then

$$\mathbf{H}_\infty(X_{i^*} | \mathsf{SK}_{\mathcal{V}}^-) \geq \mathbf{H}_\infty(X_{i^*}) - (\lambda - 1) \cdot \ell \geq b/8 - (\lambda - 1) \cdot \ell \geq \ell + 2\lambda.$$

Let SEED_{t^*} to be a random variable for seed_{t^*}. Then

$$(\mathsf{SK}_{t^*} = \mathsf{Ext}(X_{i^*}; \mathsf{SEED}_{t^*}), \mathsf{SEED}_{t^*}, \mathsf{SK}_{\mathcal{V}-}) \approx_{\varepsilon_6} (U_\ell, \mathsf{SEED}_{t^*}, \mathsf{SK}_{\mathcal{V}-})$$

where $\varepsilon_6 \leq 2^{-\lambda}$, by the security of the extractor.

Now observe that, conditioned on the fixed values, the outputs of hybrid 5 and 6 are completely defined given the additional values $\mathsf{SEED}_{t^*}, \mathsf{SK}_{\mathcal{V}-}$ and either $\mathsf{SK}_{t^*} = \mathsf{Ext}(X_{i^*}; \mathsf{SEED}_{t^*})$ in hybrid 5 or U_ℓ in hybrid 6. In particular, everything else in the hybrid is defines as follows:

- $\mathcal{T}, t$ are completely determined by the fixed values $\mathcal{S}_A = \mathcal{V} \cup \mathcal{W} = \{i_1^A, \ldots, i_q^A\}, \mathcal{S}_B, i^*$.
- view_{Eve} is defined in terms of $\mathsf{view}_{Eve}^0, \mathcal{S}_A, \mathcal{S}_B, (\mathsf{seed}_j)_{j \in [q] \setminus t^*}, \mathsf{SEED}_{t^*}$.
- sk_{-t} consists of $\mathsf{SK}_{\mathcal{V}-}$ and $\mathsf{sk}_{\mathcal{W}} := (\mathsf{sk}_j = \mathsf{Ext}(x_{i_j^A}, \mathsf{seed}_j)_{i_j^A \in \mathcal{W}}$, where the latter only depends on the fixed values $\mathcal{W}, x_{\mathcal{W}}, (\mathsf{seed}_j)_{j \in [q] \setminus t^*}$.
- And the last component in the hybrid is SK_{t^*} in hybrid 5 and U_ℓ in hybrid 6.

Therefore, the statistical distance between the hybrids is bounded by $\varepsilon_6 \leq 2^{-\lambda}$.

Hybrid 7. Undo the change from Hybrid 1 and select $\mathcal{S}_A, \mathcal{S}_B, \mathcal{V}, \mathcal{W}$ as in Hybrid 0.

Hybrids 6 and 7 are statistically close for the same reason hybrids 0 and 1 are statistically close, with distance $\varepsilon_7 \leq 2^{-\Omega(\lambda)}$.

This hybrid is equivalent to the right-hand side distribution of the Lemma.

$$(\mathsf{view}_{Eve}, \mathcal{T}, t, \mathsf{sk}_{-t} = (\mathsf{sk}_j \; : \; j \in [q] \setminus \{t\}), u)$$

where $u \leftarrow \{0,1\}^\ell$ is random and independent of all other values.

Combining the above hybrids, the Lemma holds with $\varepsilon \leq \sum_{i=1}^{7} \varepsilon_i = 2^{-\Omega(\lambda)}$.

□

7.2   From Set Key Agreement to Signatures

Construction. Let $\ell, m, |\mu|$ be parameters. Let $\mathcal{A} = \mathcal{A}(O(m), Q)$ be any class of *non-uniform* streaming algorithms such that there exists a constant C' such that algorithms in $\mathcal{A}$ run with memory at most $C'm$ making at most Q oracle calls (Definition 5). Let (KeyGen, MAC, Verify) be a streaming MAC with memory ℓ and message space $\{0,1\}^{|\mu|}$ satisfying $(\varepsilon, \mathcal{A})$-uf-cmva-security (Definition 3) for some $\varepsilon > 0$, such that signing keys (of size at most ℓ) are uniformly random.

Let b, k, q, be the parameters instantiated in Sect. 7.1, and let $\mathsf{Ext} : \{0,1\}^b \times \{0,1\}^d \to \{0,1\}^\ell$ be a $(\ell + 2\lambda, 2^{-\lambda})$-seeded extractor.

We define a streaming signature scheme $(\overline{\mathsf{KeyGen}}, \overline{\mathsf{KeyReceive}}, \overline{\mathsf{Sign}}, \overline{\mathsf{Verify}})$ as follows.

- $\overline{\mathsf{KeyGen}}(1^\lambda)$: stream vk and store sk $= (\mathsf{sk}_1, \ldots, \mathsf{sk}_q)$, as defined in Sect. 7.1.
- $\overline{\mathsf{KeyReceive}}(1^\lambda, \mathsf{vk})$: on input a streamed verification key vk, store vd $= (\mathcal{T}, \mathsf{sk}_{\mathcal{T}} = (\mathsf{sk}_j)_{j \in \mathcal{T}})$ as specified in Sect. 7.1.
- $\overline{\mathsf{Sign}}(\mathsf{sk}, \mu)$: on input a (potentially streamed) message μ, compute and output (potentially in a streaming manner):

$$\sigma = \{\sigma_j = \mathsf{MAC}(\mathsf{sk}_j, \mu)\}_{j \in [q]}.$$

- $\overline{\mathsf{Verify}}(\mathsf{vd}, \mu, \sigma)$: on input vd $= (\mathcal{T}, \{\mathsf{sk}_j\}_{j \in \mathcal{T}})$, a (potentially streamed) message μ, and a (potentially streamed) signature $\sigma = \{\sigma_j\}_{j \in \mathcal{T}}$, output

$$\bigwedge_{i \in \mathcal{T}} \mathsf{Verify}(\mathsf{sk}_j, \mu, \sigma_j),$$

with the convention that it outputs 1 if $\mathcal{T} = \emptyset$.

Claim 4 (Correctness). *Suppose* $(\mathsf{KeyGen}, \mathsf{MAC}, \mathsf{Verify})$ *is correct. Then* $(\overline{\mathsf{KeyGen}}, \overline{\mathsf{MAC}}, \overline{\mathsf{Verify}})$ *is correct.*

Claim 5 (Efficiency). *Suppose* $(\mathsf{KeyGen}, \mathsf{MAC}, \mathsf{Verify})$ *be a streaming MAC with memory* ℓ *(Definition 2). Then* $\overline{\mathsf{KeyGen}}$ *and* $\overline{\mathsf{KeyReceive}}$ *can be computed by streaming algorithms with memory* $\widetilde{O}(\lambda^2 \ell + \lambda\sqrt{\ell \cdot \lambda})$, *and* sk *and* vd *have size* $\widetilde{O}(\sqrt{m\ell} + \lambda\ell)$. $\overline{\mathsf{Sign}}$ *and* $\overline{\mathsf{Verify}}$ *can be computed by streaming algorithms with memory* $O(\sqrt{m\ell} + \lambda\ell)$.

Theorem 7 (Security). *Let* $\mathcal{A}_{MAC} = \mathcal{A}(O(m), Q)$ *be any class of non-uniform*[8] *streaming algorithms such that there exists a constant* C' *such that algorithms in* $\mathcal{A}_{MAC}$ *run with memory at most* $C'm$ *making at most* Q *oracle calls (Definition 5), and* $\mathcal{A}_{Sig}$ *be its signature counterpart (Definition 9). Suppose* $(\mathsf{KeyGen}, \mathsf{MAC}, \mathsf{Verify})$ *is* $(\varepsilon, \mathcal{A}_{MAC})$-uf-cmva-*secure (Definition 3). Then* $(\overline{\mathsf{KeyGen}}, \overline{\mathsf{KeyReceive}}, \overline{\mathsf{Sign}}, \overline{\mathsf{Verify}})$ *is* $(2\varepsilon, \mathcal{A}_{Sig})$-uf-cmva-*secure (Definition 8).*

Proof. Let $\mathsf{Adv} \in \mathcal{A}_{MAC}$ be a streaming adversary with memory m for the uf-cmva experiment for $(\overline{\mathsf{KeyGen}}, \overline{\mathsf{MAC}}, \overline{\mathsf{Verify}})$. Consider the following hybrid experiments.

Hybrid H_0. This corresponds to the uf-cmva experiment $\mathsf{Exp}^{\mathsf{uf\text{-}cmva}}(1^\lambda, \mathsf{Adv})$.

Hybrid H_1. We change how $\overline{\mathsf{KeyReceive}}$ in Step 1 of $\mathsf{Exp}^{\mathsf{uf\text{-}cmva}}(1^\lambda, \mathsf{Adv})$ is computed. vd is now computed as $(\mathcal{T}, \mathsf{sk}_{-t}, u)$ where $u \leftarrow \{0, 1\}^\ell$. In other words, the secret key sk_t is replaced by uniformly random, where t is given by Lemma 6.

Lemma 7. *Suppose* b, k, q *are instantiated as in Sect. 7.1. Then the advantage of* Adv *decreases by at most* ε *between* H_0 *and* H_1:

$$\left| \Pr\left[\mathsf{Exp}_{H_1}^{\mathsf{uf\text{-}cmva}}(1^\lambda, \mathsf{Adv}) = 1 \right] - \Pr\left[\mathsf{Exp}_{H_0}^{\mathsf{uf\text{-}cmva}}(1^\lambda, \mathsf{Adv}) = 1 \right] \right| \leq \varepsilon,$$

where, for $b \in \{0, 1\}$, $\mathsf{Exp}_{H_b}^{\mathsf{uf\text{-}cmva}}$ *denotes the* uf-cmva *experiment in Hybrid* H_b.

---

[8] Looking ahead, this will not affect our final result, because our base MAC is secure against non-uniform adversaries.

Proof. Denote by view_{Eve} the state of Adv after Step 1 of $\mathrm{Exp}^{\mathsf{uf\text{-}cmva}}(1^\lambda, \mathsf{Adv})$. Let $\mathsf{sk} = (\mathsf{sk}_j)_{j\in[q]}$ and let $\mathsf{vd} = (\mathcal{T}, (\mathsf{sk}_j)_{\mathcal{T}})$ be the respective outputs of $\overline{\mathsf{KeyGen}}$ and $\overline{\mathsf{KeyReceive}}$ in Step 1.

The lemma follows as the output of $\mathrm{Exp}^{\mathsf{uf\text{-}cmva}}(1^\lambda, \mathsf{Adv})$ can be computed using $(\mathrm{view}_{Eve}, \mathcal{T}, t, \mathsf{sk}_{-t} = (\mathsf{sk}_j)_{j\neq t}, \mathsf{sk}_t)$ alone (with the convention that $\mathsf{Verify}(\bot, \mu, \sigma) = 1$ for all μ, σ.). Namely, run Adv starting from Step 2 with state view_{Eve}. Signing queries are answered using the knowledge of sk_{-t}, sk_t and t. Verification queries as well as the final forgery are answered using the knowledge of $\mathsf{sk}_{\mathcal{T}\setminus\{t\}}$, $\mathcal{T}$, sk_t and t.

By Lemma 6:

$$(\mathrm{view}_{Eve}, \mathcal{T}, t, \mathsf{sk}_{-t} = (\mathsf{sk}_j)_{j\neq t}, \mathsf{sk}_t) \approx_c (\mathrm{view}_{Eve}, \mathcal{T}, t, \mathsf{sk}_{-t} = (\mathsf{sk}_j)_{j\neq t}, u).$$

Now, computing the output of $\mathrm{Exp}^{\mathsf{uf\text{-}cmva}}(1^\lambda, \mathsf{Adv})$ using $\big(\mathrm{view}_{Eve}, \mathcal{T}, t, \mathsf{sk}_{-t} = (\mathsf{sk}_j)_{j\neq t}, \mathsf{sk}_t\big)$ corresponds to $\mathrm{Exp}^{\mathsf{uf\text{-}cmva}}_{H_0}(1^\lambda, \mathsf{Adv})$, and using $(\mathrm{view}_{Eve}, \mathcal{T}, t, \mathsf{sk}_{-t} = (\mathsf{sk}_j)_{j\neq t}, u)$ corresponds to $\mathrm{Exp}^{\mathsf{uf\text{-}cmva}}_{H_1}(1^\lambda, \mathsf{Adv})$, and the lemma follows. □

Lemma 8. *Suppose* $(\mathsf{KeyGen}, \mathsf{MAC}, \mathsf{Verify})$ *is* $(\varepsilon, \mathcal{A})$-*uf-cmva-secure. Then*

$$\Pr[\mathrm{Exp}^{\mathsf{uf\text{-}cmva}}_{H_1}(1^\lambda, \mathsf{Adv}) = 1] \leq \varepsilon.$$

Proof. Let Adv be an adversary for $(\overline{\mathsf{KeyGen}}, \overline{\mathsf{KeyReceive}}, \overline{\mathsf{Sign}}, \overline{\mathsf{Verify}})$ with memory m having advantage ε' in $\mathrm{Exp}^{\mathsf{uf\text{-}cmva}}_{H_1}$. We build a (non-uniform) adversary against the uf-cmva-security of $(\mathsf{KeyGen}, \mathsf{MAC}, \mathsf{Verify})$ with memory $m + O(q\ell)$ and advantage ε' as follows.

Our reduction computes $\overline{\mathsf{KeyGen}}$, streams vk to Adv and stores a secret key $(\mathsf{sk}_i)_{i\in[q]}$. It computes $\mathsf{vd} = (\mathcal{T}, \mathsf{sk}_{\mathcal{T}})$. It receives the (inefficiently computable) index t defined in Lemma 6 as non-uniform advice: note that t only depends on the execution of the set key agreement and the resulting view of the adversary, and is therefore independent of the unforgeability experiment for $(\mathsf{KeyGen}, \mathsf{MAC}, \mathsf{Verify})$.

To answer signing queries on message μ, the reduction computes for all $j \in [q], j \neq t$: $\sigma_j = \mathsf{Sign}(\mathsf{sk}_j, \mu)$, and makes a signing query μ to the MAC oracle (which implicitly uses $\mathsf{MAC.sk} = \mathsf{sk}_t$), thus obtaining σ_t. It forwards $(\sigma_j)_{j\in[q]}$ to Adv (using its knowledge of t).

To answer verification queries with message μ and signature $\sigma = (\sigma_j)_{j\in[q]}$, the reduction computes for all $j \in \mathcal{T}, j \neq t$: $b_j \leftarrow \mathsf{Verify}(\mathsf{sk}_j, \mu, \sigma_j)$ and makes a verification query with input (μ, σ_j) to Verify oracle, obtaining a bit b_t. It outputs $\bigwedge_{j\in\mathcal{T}} b_j$. The final output of the experiment is computed identically.

Our reduction runs in memory $m + q\ell$, makes the same number of queries Q as Adv, and succeeds if Adv successfully produces a forgery. Therefore its advantage is at least ε' which is at most ε by uf-cmva-security of $(\overline{\mathsf{KeyGen}}, \overline{\mathsf{KeyReceive}}, \overline{\mathsf{Sign}}, \overline{\mathsf{Verify}})$. □

Overall, the advantage of Adv in the uf-cmva experiment for $(\overline{\mathsf{KeyGen}}, \overline{\mathsf{MAC}}, \overline{\mathsf{Verify}})$ is at most

$$\Pr[\mathsf{Exp}_{H_0}^{\mathsf{uf\text{-}cmva}}(1^\lambda, \mathsf{Adv}) = 1] \le 2\varepsilon.$$

$\square$

We instantiate $(\mathsf{KeyGen}, \mathsf{MAC}, \mathsf{Verify})$ with our construction in Sect. 5, which has uniformly random MAC keys, using $|\mu| = 2^\lambda$. Recall that this construction is secure against non-uniform adversaries (and in fact, adversaries with unbounded temporary memory, see Remark 2). Setting $\ell = O(\lambda + \mathrm{polylog}(m, \lambda))$, gives $n = \widetilde{O}(\lambda^3 + \sqrt{m\lambda})$. Combined with the following observation with $\tau = m$, we obtain Theorem 6.

Remark 3 (Optimizing the Communication Cost). The signatures for our scheme consist of $[q]$ independent copies of $\mathsf{MAC}(\mathsf{sk}_j, \mu)$, $j \in [q]$, where MAC is our base MAC. Using our scheme from Sect. 5, and noting that (1) security only relies on security of a single of the copies, and (2) tags of the form (x, ψ) can be computed given x and sk, we can instead compute our signatures as $(x, (\psi_j)_{j \in [q]})$, namely reusing the x part across the different copies of the base MAC, while preserving correctness and security. This makes our signatures of size $\widetilde{O}(\tau + q\lambda)$, where τ is the size of the tags from MAC.

Remark 4 (Weaker Notions of Security). Our construction constructs a uf-cmva-secure signature scheme starting from any uf-cmva-secure MAC. We note that this extends to weaker notions of security, namely starting from a (selectively-)unforgeable MAC with signing (and verification) queries, one obtains a signature scheme satisfying the same notion of security.

7.3   Lower Bound for Signatures

We show here that any streaming signature with memory n, namely, where all the procedures can be run in a streaming manner with memory n, can only be secure against streaming adversaries with memory $m = O(n^2)$.

Theorem 8. *Suppose* $(\mathsf{KeyGen}, \mathsf{KeyReceive}, \mathsf{Sign}, \mathsf{Verify})$ *is a streaming signature with memory* n *(Definition 7). Let* $\mathcal{A} = \mathcal{A}(m)$ *be the set of streaming adversaries running with memory* m *(Definition 9). Suppose that* $(\mathsf{KeyGen}, \mathsf{KeyReceive}, \mathsf{Sign}, \mathsf{Verify})$ *is* $(\varepsilon, \mathcal{A})$-suf-cma-*secure (Definition 8). Then* $m = O(n^2)$.

Theorem 8 holds even for weakly secure schemes, where adversaries are not even allowed to make any oracle queries in the unforgeability experiment. We refer to the full version for a proof, which uses similar ideas to the lower bounds from [9,11].

References

1. Aumann, Y., Ding, Y.Z., Rabin, M.O.: Everlasting security in the bounded storage model. IEEE Trans. Inf. Theory **48**(6), 1668–1680 (2002)
2. Cachin, C., Crépeau, C., Marcil, J.: Oblivious transfer with a memory-bounded receiver. In: 39th FOCS, pp. 493–502. IEEE Computer Society Press, November 1998
3. Cachin, C., Maurer, U.: Unconditional security against memory-bounded adversaries. In: Kaliski, B.S. (ed.) CRYPTO 1997. LNCS, vol. 1294, pp. 292–306. Springer, Heidelberg (1997). https://doi.org/10.1007/BFb0052243
4. Ding, Y.Z.: Oblivious transfer in the bounded storage model. In: Kilian, J. (ed.) CRYPTO 2001. LNCS, vol. 2139, pp. 155–170. Springer, Heidelberg (2001). https://doi.org/10.1007/3-540-44647-8_9
5. Ding, Y.Z., Harnik, D., Rosen, A., Shaltiel, R.: Constant-round oblivious transfer in the bounded storage model. J. Cryptol. **20**(2), 165–202 (2007)
6. Ding, Y.Z., Rabin, M.O.: Hyper-encryption and everlasting security. In: Proceedings of the 19th Annual Symposium on Theoretical Aspects of Computer Science. STACS 2002, pp. 1–26, Berlin, Heidelberg, Springer-Verlag (2002). https://doi.org/10.1007/3-540-45841-7_1
7. Dodis, Y., Kiltz, E., Pietrzak, K., Wichs, D.: Message authentication, revisited. In: Pointcheval, D., Johansson, T. (eds.) EUROCRYPT 2012. LNCS, vol. 7237, pp. 355–374. Springer, Heidelberg (2012). https://doi.org/10.1007/978-3-642-29011-4_22
8. Dodis, Y., Ostrovsky, R., Reyzin, L., Smith, A.D.: Fuzzy extractors: how to generate strong keys from biometrics and other noisy data. SIAM J. Comput. **38**(1), 97–139 (2008)
9. Dodis, Y., Quach, W., Wichs, D.: Speak much, remember little: cryptography in the bounded storage model, revisited. Cryptology ePrint Archive, Report 2021/1270 (2021). https://ia.cr/2021/1270
10. Dziembowski, S., Maurer, U.M.: Tight security proofs for the bounded-storage model. In: 34th ACM STOC, pp. 341–350. ACM Press, May 2002
11. Dziembowski, S., Maurer, U.: On generating the initial key in the bounded-storage model. In: Cachin, C., Camenisch, J.L. (eds.) EUROCRYPT 2004. LNCS, vol. 3027, pp. 126–137. Springer, Heidelberg (2004). https://doi.org/10.1007/978-3-540-24676-3_8
12. Garg, S., Raz, R., Tal, A.: Extractor-based time-space lower bounds for learning. In: Diakonikolas, I., Kempe, D., Henzinger, M. (eds.) 50th ACM STOC, pp. 990–1002. ACM Press, June 2018
13. Goldreich, O., Goldwasser, S., Micali, S.: On the cryptographic applications of random functions. In: Blakley, G.R., Chaum, D. (eds.) CRYPTO 1984, vol. 196 of LNCS, pp. 276–288. Springer, Heidelberg, August 1984
14. Guan, J., Zhandary, M.: Simple schemes in the bounded storage model. In: Ishai, Y., Rijmen, V. (eds.) EUROCRYPT 2019. LNCS, vol. 11478, pp. 500–524. Springer, Cham (2019). https://doi.org/10.1007/978-3-030-17659-4_17
15. Hoeffding, W.: Probability inequalities for sums of bounded random variables. J. Am. stat. Assoc. **58**(301), 13–30 (1963)
16. Hong, D., Chang, K.-Y., Ryu, H.: Efficient oblivious transfer in the bounded-storage model. In: Zheng, Y. (ed.) ASIACRYPT 2002. LNCS, vol. 2501, pp. 143–159. Springer, Heidelberg (2002). https://doi.org/10.1007/3-540-36178-2_9

17. Hopper, N.J., Blum, M.: Secure human identification protocols. In: Boyd, C. (ed.) ASIACRYPT 2001. LNCS, vol. 2248, pp. 52–66. Springer, Heidelberg (2001). https://doi.org/10.1007/3-540-45682-1_4

18. Impagliazzo, R., Levin, L.A., Luby, M.: Pseudo-random generation from one-way functions. In: Proceedings of the Twenty-First Annual ACM Symposium on Theory of Computing, STOC 1989, pp. 12–24, New York, NY, USA. Association for Computing Machinery (1989)

19. Juels, A., Weis, S.A.: Authenticating pervasive devices with human protocols. In: Shoup, V. (ed.) CRYPTO 2005. LNCS, vol. 3621, pp. 293–308. Springer, Heidelberg (2005). https://doi.org/10.1007/11535218_18

20. Kiltz, E., Pietrzak, K., Cash, D., Jain, A., Venturi, D.: Efficient authentication from hard learning problems. In: Paterson, K.G. (ed.) EUROCRYPT 2011. LNCS, vol. 6632, pp. 7–26. Springer, Heidelberg (2011). https://doi.org/10.1007/978-3-642-20465-4_3

21. Kol, G., Raz, R., Tal, A.: Time-space hardness of learning sparse parities. In: Hatami, H., McKenzie, P., King, V., (eds.) 49th ACM STOC, pp. 1067–1080. ACM Press, June 2017

22. Lu, C.-J.: Hyper-encryption against space-bounded adversaries from on-line strong extractors. In: Yung, M. (ed.) CRYPTO 2002. LNCS, vol. 2442, pp. 257–271. Springer, Heidelberg (2002). https://doi.org/10.1007/3-540-45708-9_17

23. Maurer, U.M.: Conditionally-perfect secrecy and a provably-secure randomized cipher. J. Cryptol. 5(1), 53–66 (1992). https://doi.org/10.1007/BF00191321

24. Nisan, N., Zuckerman, D.: Randomness is linear in space. J. Comput. Syst. Sci. 52(1), 43–52 (1996)

25. Raz, R.: Fast learning requires good memory: a time-space lower bound for parity learning. In: Dinur, I. (ed.) 57th FOCS, pp. 266–275. IEEE Computer Society Press, October 2016

26. Raz, R.: A time-space lower bound for a large class of learning problems. In: Umans, C. (ed.) 58th FOCS, pp. 732–742. IEEE Computer Society Press, October 2017

27. Vadhan, S.P.: Constructing locally computable extractors and cryptosystems in the bounded-storage model. J. Cryptol. 17(1), 43–77 (2004)

Secure Non-interactive Simulation: Feasibility and Rate

Hamidreza Amini Khorasgani, Hemanta K. Maji, and Hai H. Nguyen[✉]

Department of Computer Science, Purdue University, West Lafayette, USA
{haminikh,hmaji,nguye245}@purdue.edu

Abstract. A natural solution to increase the efficiency of secure computation will be to non-interactively and securely transform diverse inexpensive-to-generate correlated randomness, like, joint samples from noise sources, into correlations useful for secure computation protocols. Motivated by this general application for secure computation, our work introduces the notion of *secure non-interactive simulation* (SNIS). Parties receive samples of correlated randomness, and they, without any interaction, securely convert them into samples from another correlated randomness.

Our work presents a simulation-based security definition for SNIS and initiates the study of the feasibility and efficiency of SNIS. We also study SNIS among fundamental correlated randomnesses like random samples from the binary symmetric and binary erasure channels, represented by BSS and BES, respectively. We show the impossibility of interconversion between BSS and BES samples.

Next, we prove that a SNIS of a BES(ε') sample (a BES with noise characteristic ε') from BES(ε) is feasible if and only if $(1 - \varepsilon') = (1 - \varepsilon)^k$, for some $k \in \mathbb{N}$. In this context, we prove that all SNIS constructions must be linear. Furthermore, if $(1 - \varepsilon') = (1 - \varepsilon)^k$, then the rate of simulating multiple independent BES(ε') samples is at most $1/k$, which is also achievable using (block) linear constructions.

Finally, we show that a SNIS of a BSS(ε') sample from BSS(ε) samples is feasible if and only if $(1 - 2\varepsilon') = (1 - 2\varepsilon)^k$, for some $k \in \mathbb{N}$. Interestingly, there are linear as well as non-linear SNIS constructions. When $(1 - 2\varepsilon') = (1 - 2\varepsilon)^k$, we prove that the rate of a *perfectly secure* SNIS is at most $1/k$, which is achievable using linear and non-linear constructions.

Our technical approach algebraizes the definition of SNIS and proceeds via Fourier analysis. Our work develops general analysis methodologies for Boolean functions, explicitly incorporating cryptographic

H. Amini Khorasgani, H.K. Maji, H.H. Nguyen—The research effort is supported in part by an NSF CRII Award CNS–1566499, NSF SMALL Awards CNS–1618822 and CNS–2055605, the IARPA HECTOR project, MITRE Innovation Program Academic Cybersecurity Research Awards (2019–2020, 2020–2021), a Ross-Lynn Research Scholars Grant, a Purdue Research Foundation (PRF) Award, and The Center for Science of Information, an NSF Science and Technology Center, Cooperative Agreement CCF–0939370.

O. Dunkelman and S. Dziembowski (Eds.): EUROCRYPT 2022, LNCS 13277, pp. 767–796, 2022.
https://doi.org/10.1007/978-3-031-07082-2_27

security constraints. Our work also proves strong forms of *statistical-to-perfect security* transformations: one can error-correct a statistically secure SNIS to make it perfectly secure. We show a connection of our research with *homogeneous Boolean functions* and *distance-invariant codes*, which may be of independent interest.

1   Introduction

Secure multi-party computation [26,52] (MPC) allows mutually distrusting parties to compute securely over their private data. MPC protocols often offload most cryptographically and computationally intensive components to an offline procedure [8,17,38,45]. The objective of this offline procedure is to output secure samples from highly structured correlated randomness, for example, Beaver triples [4]. The offline procedure relies on public-key cryptography to achieve this objective and, consequently, is computation and communication intensive.

On the other hand, there are diverse inexpensive-to-generate correlated randomness, like, joint samples from noise sources, that can also facilitate secure computation via interactive protocols [30]. A natural approach to increase the efficiency of this offline phase will be to non-interactively and securely transform such correlated randomness into correlations useful for secure computation while incurring low computational overhead. Motivated by this general application for secure computation, our work introduces the notion of *secure non-interactive simulation* (SNIS).

In SNIS, parties receive samples of correlated randomness, and they, without any interaction, securely convert them into samples from another correlated randomness. Section 1.1 defines this cryptographic primitive. SNIS is an information-theoretic analog of *pseudorandom correlation generators* (PCG) introduced by Boyle et al. [11,12]. PCG is a *silent* local computation that transforms the input correlated private randomness into samples from a target correlation without any interaction. Boyle et al. [11,12] construct this primitive based on various hardness of computation assumptions and illustrate their applications to increasing the efficiency of the preprocessing step of MPC protocols. SNIS shall convert diverse forms of correlated randomness sources into samples of a specific target correlation that is useful for the online phase of an MPC protocol with information-theoretic security.

SNIS is an extension of *non-interactive simulation of joint distribution* [18,21, 24,25,27,28,49,50] (NIS) and *non-interactive correlation distillation* [9,13,40,41, 51] (NICD) from information theory. In NIS, the emphasis is on the correctness of simulation, and cryptographic security is not a concern. Consequently, erasing information from parties' views, for example, is permissible in NIS, which may not be cryptographically secure. NICD specifically aims to establish shared keys securely; however, shared keys alone do not suffice for general secure computation [23,35,36]. The objective of SNIS extends to securely simulating more general correlated randomness as well, referred to as the *complete correlations* [30], which are necessary for general secure computation. One can also interpret SNIS as the non-interactive version of *one-way secure computation* [2,22] (OWSC) – secure computations where only one party sends messages.

Our work presents a simulation-based security definition for SNIS and initiates the study of the feasibility and efficiency of SNIS. Any hardness of computation results from NIS and OWSC automatically transfer to SNIS. This work initiates the study of tight feasibility and rate characterization in SNIS and considers the inter-conversion among fundamental correlated randomnesses like random samples from the binary symmetric and binary erasure channels. In this context, our work reveals strong forms of statistical-to-perfect security transformations where one can error-correct a statistically secure SNIS (with sufficiently small insecurity) to transform it into a perfect SNIS. In particular, there is a dichotomy: either (1) a perfect SNIS exists, or (2) every SNIS is constant insecure. For example, there are perfect rate-achieving SNIS; however, surpassing the maximum rate by how-so-ever small quantity immediately incurs constant-insecurity.

Our technical approach algebraizes the definition of SNIS and proceeds via Fourier analysis. A central contribution of our work is the development of general analysis methodologies for Boolean functions that explicitly incorporate the cryptographic security constraints. Our research uncovers fascinating new connections of SNIS with *homogeneous Boolean functions* and *distance-invariant codes*, which may be of independent interest (refer to Sect. 2.6).

Paper Organization. Section 1.1 presents the SNIS model. Section 2 summarizes our contributions, connections to other research areas (Sect. 2.6). All our results consider SNIS with *randomized reductions* and *statistical security* (except Theorem 6, which considers only perfect security). Section 3 introduces the technical background for our proofs. Section 4, Sect. 5, and Sect. 6 present the technical outline and details of our proofs. A full version of this paper is available at [29].

Independent Work. Independently, motivated by studying *cryptographic complexity* [6,7,33,37,44], Agarwal, Narayanan, Pathak, Prabhakaran, Prabhakaran, and Rehan [1] introduced SNIS as *secure non-interactive reduction*. They use spectral techniques to analyze this primitive. Determining tight rate of SNIS reductions and results pertaining to editing statistical reductions into perfect ones are beyond the scope of their work.

1.1 Definition: Secure Non-interactive Simulation

Let (X, Y) be a joint distribution over the sample space $(\mathcal{X}, \mathcal{Y})$, and (U, V) be a joint distribution over the sample space $(\mathcal{U}, \mathcal{V})$.[1] The intuitive definition of *secure non-interactive simulation of joint distributions* (SNIS) closely follows the presentation in Fig. 1 (with parameter $m = 1$). Sample $(x^n, y^n) \xleftarrow{\$} (X, Y)^{\otimes n}$, i.e.,

---

[1] As is typical in this line of work in cryptography and information theory, the joint distributions (U, V) and (X, Y) assign probabilities to samples that are either 0 or at least a positive constant.

draw n independent samples from the distribution (X, Y). Alice gets $x^n \in \mathcal{X}^n$, and Bob gets $y^n \in \mathcal{Y}^n$. Alice has private randomness $r_A \xleftarrow{\$} R_A$ and Bob has, independent, private randomness $r_B \xleftarrow{\$} R_B$, where R_A, R_B are random variables over the sample spaces $\mathcal{R}_A$ and $\mathcal{R}_B$, respectively. Suppose $f_n \colon \mathcal{X}^n \times \mathcal{R}_A \to \mathcal{U}$ and $g_n \colon \mathcal{Y}^n \times \mathcal{R}_B \to \mathcal{V}$ are the (possibly randomized) *reduction functions* for Alice and Bob, respectively. Alice computes $u' = f_n(x^n, r_A)$ and Bob computes $v' = g_n(y^n, r_B)$.

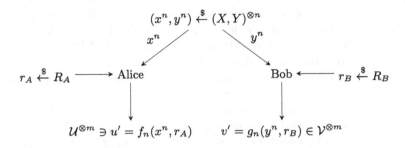

Fig. 1. Model for secure non-interactive simulation: SNIS.

For the ease of presentation, this section only considers deterministic reduction functions, i.e., there is no R_A and R_B. All formal definitions and results in this work consider randomized reductions.

We say that (U, V) *reduces to* $(X, Y)^{\otimes n}$ *via reduction functions* f_n, g_n *with insecurity* $\nu(n)$ (represented by, $(U, V) \sqsubseteq_{f_n, g_n}^{\nu(n)} (X, Y)^{\otimes n}$) if the following three conditions are satisfied.

1. *Correctness.* The distribution of the samples (u', v') is $\nu(n)$-close to the distribution (U, V) in the statistical distance.
2. *Security against corrupt Alice.* Consider any (u, v) in the support of the distribution (U, V). The distribution of x^n, conditioned on $u' = u$ and $v' = v$, is $\nu(n)$-close to being independent of v.[2]
3. *Security against corrupt Bob.* Consider any (u, v) in the support of the distribution (U, V). The distribution of y^n, conditioned on the fact that $u' = u$ and $v' = v$, is $\nu(n)$-close to being independent of u.

To discuss rate, consider SNIS of the form $(U, V)^{\otimes m(n)} \sqsubseteq_{f_n, g_n}^{\nu(n)} (X, Y)^{\otimes n}$. Here, the reduction functions output $m(n)$-independent samples from the distribution (U, V). Fixing (X, Y) and (U, V), our objective is to characterize the maximum achievable *production rate* $m(n)/n$ over all possible reductions (a standard single-letter characterization). Finally, $R(\ (U, V), (X, Y)\ )$ represents the maximum achievable $m(n)/n$, as $n \to \infty$, when considering all SNIS of (U, V) from (X, Y).

---

[2] The conditional distribution $(A|B = b)$ is ν-close to being independent of b if there exists a distribution A^* such that $(A|B = b)$ is ν-close to A^* in the statistical distance, for all $b \in \mathrm{Supp}(B)$.

When n is clear from the context, then, instead of x^n and f_n, we shall only write x and f for brevity.

Remark 1 (Adversarial model). Since we consider non-interactive protocols without private inputs, semi-honest and malicious security (with abort) are equivalent. So, for the simplicity, the presentation considers (statistical) security against semi-honest adversaries, that is, parties follow the protocol but are curious to find more information.

Remark 2 (Reasoning for providing private coins). In the cryptographic context, complete joint distributions [30] (X, Y) are the primary resources that one uses frugally. So, to define the rate with respect to the cryptographically expensive resource (namely, samples from the distribution $(X, Y)^{\otimes n}$), our definition of SNIS considers randomized reductions and provides private independent random coins as a free resource. If private coins are not free, they can be incorporated into the setup by considering the input joint distribution to be $(X, Y)^{\otimes n} \otimes \text{Coins}$.

2 Our Contribution

Rabin and Crépeau [14, 47, 48] and Crépeau and Kilian [15, 16], respectively, proved that erasure and binary symmetric channels suffice for general secure computation. These elegant sources of noise provide an uncluttered access to abstracting the primary hurdles in achieving security. In a similar vein, to initiate the study of the feasibility and rate of SNIS, this paper considers samples from the following two families of distributions.

1. *Binary symmetric source.* X and Y are uniformly random bits $\{+1, -1\}$ such that $X \neq Y$ with probability $\varepsilon \in (0, 1/2)$. We represent this joint distribution by $\mathsf{BSS}(\varepsilon)$.
2. *Binary erasure source.* X is a uniformly random bit $\{+1, -1\}$, and $Y = X$ with probability $(1 - \varepsilon)$, where $\varepsilon \in (0, 1)$; otherwise, $Y = 0$. We represent this joint distribution by $\mathsf{BES}(\varepsilon)$ (Fig. 2).

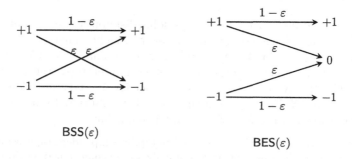

Fig. 2. Binary Symmetric Source (BSS) and Binary Erasure Source (BES) with noise characteristic ε.

Comparison Models. In information theory, *non-interactive simulation of joint distributions* (NIS) is a similar notion of simulating joint distributions [18,21, 24,25,27,28,49,50]. However, NIS only considers correctness (not security). On the other hand, there is also research on performing secure computation using one-way messages, a.k.a., *one-way secure computation* (OWSC) [2,22] – only one party sends messages to the other party. Table 1 compares our feasibility results to results in NIS and OWSC.

Remark 3. Non-interactive correlation distillation [9,13,40,41,51] is a special case of SNIS where (U, V) is restricted to shared coin, i.e., $\mathsf{BSS}(0)$ or $\mathsf{BES}(0)$ samples. This model has strong impossibility results and comparison with this model is not particularly insightful.

2.1 SNIS Composition and Projection

The following composition and projection results follow from the simulation-based definition of SNIS.

1. *Parallel Composition.* Let P, P', Q, and Q' be joint distributions. If ν-SNIS of P from Q and ν'-SNIS of P' from Q' exist, then a $(\nu + \nu')$-SNIS of $(P\|P')$ from $(Q\|Q')$ exists. The distribution $(P\|P')$ generates samples from both the joint distributions P and P', and $(Q\|Q')$ generates samples from both the joint distributions Q and Q'.
2. *Sequential Composition.* Let P, Q, and R be joint distributions. If ν-SNIS of P from Q and ν'-SNIS of Q from R exist, then a $(\nu + \nu')$-SNIS of P from R exists.
3. *Projection.* Let P, Q, and R be joint distributions. If a ν-SNIS of $(P\|Q)$ from R exists, then a ν-SNIS of P from R also exists.

These composition and projection theorems shall assist in proving our feasibility and rate results.

2.2 Derandomization

There are a few flavors of derandomization results (for reductions) that are useful for different contexts like feasibility/rate results with perfect/statistical security.

For Feasibility Results. Let (X, Y) be a joint distribution such that the distribution $(X|Y)$ has average conditional min-entropy [20]. Then, Alice can extract (statistically) secure coins from a sufficiently large number of (X, Y) samples.[3] Analogously, if $(Y|X)$ has average conditional min-entropy, then Bob can also construct statistically secure coins using other (X, Y) samples. Complete joint distributions [30] (X, Y) have both these average conditional min-entropy properties.[4] Consequently, the following result is immediate.

---

[3] Alice can perform a random walk on an appropriate expander graph using her samples to get one random bit that is statistically secure conditioned on Bob's samples.

[4] A joint distribution (X, Y) is *complete* if there exists samples $x_0, x_1 \in \mathrm{Supp}(X)$ and $y_0, y_1 \in \mathrm{Supp}(Y)$ such that

Proposition 1 (Derandomization: Feasibility results). *Let (X, Y) be a complete joint distribution. Consider a randomized SNIS $(U, V) \sqsubseteq^{\nu}_{f,g} (X, Y)^{\otimes n}$ with n_A and n_B Alice and Bob private randomness complexities, respectively. Then, there exists a deterministic SNIS $(U, V) \sqsubseteq^{\nu'}_{f',g'} (X, Y)^{\otimes n'}$ such that (for large-enough $k \in \mathbb{N}$)*

$$n' = k \cdot n_A + k \cdot n_B + n, \text{ and}$$
$$\nu' = (n_A + n_B) \cdot \exp(-\Theta k) + \nu.$$

The reduction function f' uses the first kn_A samples to extract n_A private bits for Alice, each with $\exp(-\Theta k)$ statistical security. The reduction function g' uses the next kn_B samples to extract n_B private bits for Bob. Finally, the reduction functions (f', g') restricted to the last n samples are identical to (f, g). This proposition effectively rules out the usefulness of independent private randomness in SNIS for feasibility results.

For Rate Results with Perfect Security. To study rate of SNIS, one needs a *sample-preserving* derandomization. However, in the context of perfect security, such a result is immediate for complete joint distribution (U, V). Intuitively, one can fix Alice's local randomness to an arbitrary value, and Bob's local randomness to an arbitrary value. Then, the reduction functions (with these fixed random tapes) continue to be a perfectly secure SNIS.

Proposition 2 (Derandomization: Sample-preserving & Perfect security). *Let (U, V) be a complete joint distribution. For any randomized SNIS $(U, V) \sqsubseteq^{0}_{f,g} (X, Y)^{\otimes n}$, there is a deterministic SNIS $(U, V) \sqsubseteq^{0}_{f',g'} (X, Y)^{\otimes n}$.*

The deterministic reduction functions f', g' are the randomized reductions f, g with their random tapes arbitrarily fixed.

For Rate Results with Statistical Security. For a statistical SNIS, we prove a sample-preserving derandomization result of the following form.

Theorem 1 (Derandomization: Sample-preserving & Statistical security). *Fix (X, Y) and a complete joint distribution (U, V). There is a positive constant c such that the following holds. Consider a randomized SNIS $(U, V) \sqsubseteq^{\nu}_{f,g} (X, Y)^{\otimes n}$. Then, there is a deterministic SNIS $(U, V) \sqsubseteq^{\nu'}_{f',g'} (X, Y)^{\otimes n}$ such that (a) $\nu' = c \cdot \nu^{1/4}$, (b) the reduction function f is ν'-close to the reduction function f', and (c) the reduction function g is ν'-close to the reduction function g'.*

1. $\Pr[X = x_0, Y = y_0], \Pr[X = x_1, Y = y_0], \Pr[X = x_1, Y = y_1] > 0$, and
2. $\Pr[X = x_0, Y = y_0] \cdot \Pr[X = x_1, Y = y_1] \neq \Pr[X = x_0, Y = y_1] \cdot \Pr[X = x_1, Y = y_0]$.

Multiple samples of a complete distributions can be used to (interactively) implement oblivious transfer [30], the atomic primitive for secure computation. The joint distribution $\mathsf{BES}(\varepsilon)$, for $\varepsilon \in (0, 1)$, and $\mathsf{BSS}(\varepsilon)$, for $\varepsilon \in (0, 1/2)$, are complete distributions. However, $\mathsf{BSS}(0) = \mathsf{BES}(0)$, $\mathsf{BES}(1)$, and $\mathsf{BSS}(1/2)$ are *not* complete distributions.

This theorem also yields Proposition 2 as a corollary.

The *closeness* of a randomized and a deterministic function is defined as follows. The function f, for example, has domain $\mathcal{X}^n \times \mathcal{R}_A$. Extend the domain of the deterministic function f' from $\mathcal{X}^n$ to $\mathcal{X}^n \times \mathcal{R}_A$. The two functions are ν'-close if their outputs differ for (at most) ν' fraction of the inputs.

The constant c in the theorem depends on the joint distributions (X, Y) and (U, V); however, it is independent of n. So, one can, for example, meaningfully derandomize the statistically secure SNIS $\mathsf{BES}(\varepsilon')^{\otimes 2} \sqsubseteq^{\nu} \mathsf{BES}(\varepsilon)^{\otimes n}$ by considering $(U, V) = \mathsf{BES}(\varepsilon')^{\otimes 2}$ and $(X, Y) = \mathsf{BES}(\varepsilon)$. However, it may not be possible to meaningfully derandomize the statistically secure SNIS $\mathsf{BES}(\varepsilon')^{\otimes m(n)} \sqsubseteq^{\nu(n)} \mathsf{BES}(\varepsilon)^{\otimes n}$ by considering $(U, V) = \mathsf{BES}(\varepsilon')^{\otimes m(n)}$ and $(X, Y) = \mathsf{BES}(\varepsilon)$. Because the value of c depends on n (via its dependence on $m(n)$), and the resulting insecurity bound $c \cdot \nu(n)^{1/4}$ may be meaningless (it may be greater than one). This discussion highlights a subtlety in proving the rate result in Theorem 4.

2.3   BSS from BES Samples

Table 1. Comparison of feasible parameters for OWSC, SNIS, and NIS involving reductions between BES and BSS families. A "$\supseteq S$" entry indicates that the feasible set is a superset of the set S. Therefore, a "$\supseteq \emptyset$" entry indicates that no characterization of the feasible set is known. Similarly, a "$\subseteq S$" entry indicates that the feasible set is a subset of the set S.

Input joint distribution	Output joint distribution	Feasible set of ε'		
		OWSC [22]	SNIS (our work)	NIS [53]
$\mathsf{BES}(\varepsilon)$	$\mathsf{BES}(\varepsilon')$	$(0, 1)$	$\left\{ 1 - (1-\varepsilon)^k : \ k \in \mathbb{N} \right\}$	$[\varepsilon, 1)$
	$\mathsf{BSS}(\varepsilon')$	$\supseteq \emptyset$	$\emptyset$	$\supseteq [\varepsilon/2, 1/2)$ $\subseteq \left[\frac{1-\sqrt{1-\varepsilon}}{2}, 1/2 \right)$
$\mathsf{BSS}(\varepsilon)$	$\mathsf{BES}(\varepsilon')$	$\emptyset$	$\emptyset$	$\emptyset$
	$\mathsf{BSS}(\varepsilon')$	$\supseteq \left\{ \frac{1-(1-2\varepsilon)^k}{2} : k \in \mathbb{N} \right\}$	$\left\{ \frac{1-(1-2\varepsilon)^k}{2} : k \in \mathbb{N} \right\}$	$[\varepsilon, 1/2)$

It is impossible to have a SNIS of $\mathsf{BES}(\varepsilon')$ from any number of $\mathsf{BSS}(\varepsilon)$ samples, for any $n \in \mathbb{N}$, $\varepsilon \in (0, 1/2)$, and $\varepsilon' \in (0, 1)$, because this reduction is already impossible in NIS and OWSC. *Reverse-hypercontractivity* [3,5,10,18,28,40–42] is a typical technical tool in NIS to show such impossibility results. Consider the feasibility of $(U, V) \sqsubseteq \mathsf{BSS}(\varepsilon)^{\otimes n}$. Reverse-hypercontractivity states that if there are two samples u and v such that $\Pr[U = u] > 0$ and $\Pr[V = v] > 0$, then $\Pr[U = u, V = v] > 0$. Therefore, for example, *correctly* constructing BES samples and random oblivious transfer samples are impossible, let alone securely.

The following result considers the reverse direction.

Theorem 2 (Infeasibility: BSS from BES). *Fix noise parameters $\varepsilon \in (0, 1)$ and $\varepsilon' \in (0, 1/2)$. There is a positive constant $c = c(\varepsilon, \varepsilon')$ such that $\mathsf{BSS}(\varepsilon') \sqsubseteq^{\nu} \mathsf{BES}(\varepsilon)^{\otimes n}$, for any $n \in \mathbb{N}$, implies that $\nu \geqslant c$.*

Section 4 proves this theorem. This impossibility result remains open in NIS and OWSC. However, using the properties of security, we even rule out SNIS that are constant-insecure. In particular, one cannot use a larger number of $\mathsf{BES}(\varepsilon)$ samples to arbitrarily reduce the insecurity.

2.4   BES from BES Samples

Next, we consider the inter-conversion among binary erasure sources with different erasure probabilities. At the outset, let us begin with an example of perfectly secure SNIS of $\mathsf{BES}(\varepsilon')$ from $\mathsf{BES}(\varepsilon)^{\otimes k}$, where $(1 - \varepsilon') = (1 - \varepsilon)^k$ for some $k \in \mathbb{N}$. Alice's reduction function $f \colon \{\pm 1\}^k \to \{\pm 1\}$ is defined by $f(x) = x_1 \cdot x_2 \cdots x_k$, a linear function. Bob's reduction function $g \colon \{\pm 1, 0\}^k \to \{\pm 1, 0\}$ is defined by $g(y) = y_1 \cdot y_2 \cdots y_k$. Observe that $g(y) = 0$ if and only if there is $i \in \{1, \dots, k\}$ such that $y_i = 0$. Such reductions (or their negations) shall be referred to as *k-linear* functions. One can verify that this reduction is a perfect SNIS.

Feasibility. We prove that, essentially, k-linear functions are the only reductions possible among BES samples.

Theorem 3 (Feasibility: BES-BES). *Fix erasure probabilities $\varepsilon, \varepsilon' \in (0, 1)$.*

1. *If $(1 - \varepsilon') \neq (1 - \varepsilon)^k$, for all $k \in \mathbb{N}$: There is a positive constant $c = c(\varepsilon, \varepsilon')$ such that $\mathsf{BES}(\varepsilon') \sqsubseteq^\nu \mathsf{BES}(\varepsilon)^{\otimes n}$, for any $n \in \mathbb{N}$, implies that $\nu \geqslant c$.*
2. *If $(1 - \varepsilon') = (1 - \varepsilon)^k$, for some $k \in \mathbb{N}$: There are positive constants $c = c(\varepsilon, \varepsilon')$ and $d = d(\varepsilon, \varepsilon')$ such that the following result holds. If $\mathsf{BES}(\varepsilon') \sqsubseteq^\nu_{f,g} \mathsf{BES}(\varepsilon)^{\otimes n}$, for any $n \in \mathbb{N}$, and $\nu \leqslant c$, then f is ν^d-close to a reduction function f^*, and g is ν^d-close to a reduction function g^* such that $\mathsf{BES}(\varepsilon') \sqsubseteq^0_{f^*,g^*} \mathsf{BES}(\varepsilon)^{\otimes n}$. Furthermore, f^* is a k-linear function.*

We remark that the "$\nu^{\ominus 1}$-closeness" in the theorem above can be replaced by "$\Theta\sqrt{\nu}$-closeness;" however, we forego this optimization as it does not change the qualitative nature of our results. This theorem intuitively states the following.

1. If $(1 - \varepsilon') \notin \{(1 - \varepsilon), (1 - \varepsilon)^2, (1 - \varepsilon)^3, \dots\}$, then any SNIS of $\mathsf{BES}(\varepsilon')$ from $\mathsf{BES}(\varepsilon)$ must be constant-insecure.
2. If $(1 - \varepsilon') = (1 - \varepsilon)^k$ and reduction functions f, g implement a SNIS of $\mathsf{BES}(\varepsilon')$ from $\mathsf{BES}(\varepsilon)$ with sufficient small insecurity, then the reduction functions f and g can be error-corrected (at most ν^d-fraction of its inputs) to create reduction functions f^*, g^*, respectively, such that the new SNIS is a perfectly secure. Furthermore, the function $f^*(x) = \pm x_{i_1} \cdot x_{i_2} \cdots x_{i_k}$, for distinct $i_1, i_2, \dots, i_k \in \{1, \dots, n\}$. This result, intuitively, is a strong form of *statistical-to-perfect transformation*: reductions implementing SNIS with sufficiently small insecurity can be error-corrected into perfectly secure SNIS reductions. Furthermore, the lower the insecurity, the lesser amount of error-correction shall be needed.

In the context of OWSC, one can achieve erasure probability ε' that is either lower or higher than the erasure probability ε. For SNIS, however, we show that $\varepsilon' \geqslant \varepsilon$ is necessary. Interestingly, our linear SNIS construction is identical in spirit to the OWSC protocol, as presented in [22] when $(1-\varepsilon') \in \{(1-\varepsilon), (1-\varepsilon)^2, \ldots\}$. However, all other values of ε' are feasible *only* for OWSC [22]; not for SNIS.

Typically, NIS literature's impossibility results rely on leveraging the reverse hypercontractivity theorem [27,28,43]. However, this approach encounters a significant hurdle for samples from the binary erasure channel [27]. The addition of the security constraint in our setting helps overcome this hurdle.

Rate of Statistical SNIS. Observe that if $(1 - \varepsilon') = (1 - \varepsilon)^k$, for $k \in \mathbb{N}$, then a block-linear reduction achieves $1/k$-rate via a perfectly secure SNIS. Our rate result states that these reductions are, essentially, the only rate-achieving constructions. For rate results, we consider (possibly, randomized) reduction functions $\boldsymbol{f}\colon \{\pm 1\}^n \to \{\pm 1\}^m$ and $\boldsymbol{g}\colon \{\pm 1, 0\}^n \to \{\pm 1, 0\}^m$. We interpret these reductions as the concatenation of m reductions. For example, $\boldsymbol{f} = \left(f^{(1)}, f^{(2)}, \ldots, f^{(m)}\right)$ such that $f^{(i)}\colon \{\pm 1\}^n \to \{\pm 1\}$, for each $i \in \{1, 2, \ldots, m\}$. We refer to the function $f^{(i)}$ as the *i-th component of $\boldsymbol{f}$*.

Theorem 4 (Rate: BES-BES). *Let $\varepsilon, \varepsilon' \in (0,1)$ be erasure probabilities such that $(1-\varepsilon') = (1-\varepsilon)^k$, for some $k \in \mathbb{N}$. There are positive constants $c = c(\varepsilon, \varepsilon')$ and $d = d(\varepsilon, \varepsilon')$ such that the following result holds. Suppose $\mathsf{BES}(\varepsilon')^{\otimes m} \sqsubseteq_{\boldsymbol{f}, \boldsymbol{g}}^{\nu} \mathsf{BES}(\varepsilon)^{\otimes n}$, for some $m, n \in \mathbb{N}$, and $\nu \leqslant c$. Then, there are deterministic reduction functions $\boldsymbol{f}^*$ and $\boldsymbol{g}^*$ such that the following conditions are satisfied.*

1. *$f^{(i)}$ is ν^d-close to $f^{*(i)}$, for $i \in \{1, \ldots, m\}$,*
2. *$g^{(i)}$ is ν^d-close to $g^{*(i)}$, for $i \in \{1, \ldots, m\}$,*
3. *Each $f^{*(i)}$ is k-linear with disjoint support, for $i \in \{1, \ldots, m\}$, and*
4. *$mk \leqslant n$, i.e., $R(\mathsf{BES}(\varepsilon'), \mathsf{BES}(\varepsilon)) \leqslant 1/k$.*

A block-linear construction achieves the rate as well. We emphasize that the reductions $\boldsymbol{f}$ and $\boldsymbol{g}$ are possibly randomized. Note that this theorem *does not* claim that the reduction function $\boldsymbol{f}$ is close to $\boldsymbol{f}^*$.

Section 5 outlines the proof of Theorem 3 and Theorem 4.

2.5 BSS from BSS Samples

Finally, we consider the inter-conversion among binary symmetric samples with different noise characteristics. Observe that if $(1 - 2\varepsilon') = (1 - 2\varepsilon)^k$, for some $k \in \mathbb{N}$, then the following reduction functions $f, g\colon \{\pm 1\}^k \to \{\pm 1\}$ implement a perfectly secure SNIS of $\mathsf{BSS}(\varepsilon')$ from $\mathsf{BSS}(\varepsilon)^{\otimes k}$: $f(x) = x_1 \cdot x_2 \cdots x_k$ and $g(y) = y_1 \cdot y_2 \cdots y_k$. One can verify that this is a perfectly secure SNIS. However, surprisingly, unlike BES inter-conversions, linear functions are not the *only* secure reductions in BSS inter-conversions. For $k \geqslant 2$, consider the following non-linear reductions $f_{2k}^{(1)}, g_{2k}^{(1)}\colon \{\pm 1\}^{2k} \to \{\pm 1\}$, $g_{2k}^{(1)} = f_{2k}^{(1)}$ where $f_{2k}^{(1)}(x) = \frac{(x_1 - x_2)}{2} \cdot \prod_{i=3}^{k+1} x_i + \frac{(x_1 + x_2)}{2} \cdot \prod_{i=k+2}^{2k} x_i$. In fact, any *$k$-homogeneous* Boolean reduction function f and $g = f$ define a perfectly secure SNIS.

Although these non-linear constructions individually have worse efficiency than the linear constructions, they can achieve *rate* $1/k$, similar to the block-linear constructions. For example, consider another pair of reduction functions $f_{2k}^{(2)}, g_{2k}^{(2)} : \{\pm 1\}^{2k} \to \{\pm 1\}$, $g_{2k}^{(2)} = f_{2k}^{(2)}$ where $f_{2k}^{(2)}(x) = \frac{(x_1 - x_2)}{2} \cdot \prod_{i=k+2}^{2k} x_i - \frac{(x_1 + x_2)}{2} \cdot \prod_{i=3}^{k+1} x_i$. Now, interestingly, the two reductions $f_{2k}^{(1)} \| f_{2k}^{(2)}$ and $g_{2k}^{(1)} \| g_{2k}^{(2)}$ realize $\mathsf{BSS}(\varepsilon')^{\otimes 2} \sqsubseteq^0 \mathsf{BSS}(\varepsilon)^{\otimes 2k}$ at rate $1/k$.

Feasibility. With this discussion as background, we mention our feasibility result.

Theorem 5 (Feasibility: BSS-BSS). *Fix noise characteristics $\varepsilon, \varepsilon' \in (0, 1/2)$.*

1. *If $(1 - 2\varepsilon') \neq (1 - 2\varepsilon)^k$, for all $k \in \mathbb{N}$: There is a positive constant $c = c(\varepsilon, \varepsilon')$ such that $\mathsf{BSS}(\varepsilon') \sqsubseteq^\nu \mathsf{BSS}(\varepsilon)^{\otimes n}$, for any $n \in \mathbb{N}$, implies that $\nu \geqslant c$.*
2. *If $(1 - 2\varepsilon') = (1 - 2\varepsilon)^k$, for some $k \in \mathbb{N}$: There are positive constants $c = c(\varepsilon, \varepsilon')$ and $d = d(\varepsilon, \varepsilon')$ such that the following result holds. If $\mathsf{BSS}(\varepsilon') \sqsubseteq_{f,g}^\nu \mathsf{BSS}(\varepsilon)^{\otimes n}$, for any $n \in \mathbb{N}$, and $\nu \leqslant c$, then f is ν^d-close to a reduction function f^* and g is ν^d-close to a reduction function g^* such that $\mathsf{BSS}(\varepsilon') \sqsubseteq_{f^*,g^*}^0 \mathsf{BSS}(\varepsilon)^{\otimes n}$. Furthermore, $f^* = g^*$ is a k-homogeneous Boolean function.*

Similar to the theorem for binary erasure sources, this theorem also states a strong form of a statistical-to-perfect transformation. In the binary symmetric source case, the perfect reduction need not be a linear function; it may be a k-homogeneous Boolean function. Incidentally, as a consequence of the Kindler-Safra junta theorem [31, 32] (refer to Imported Theorem 1), the k-homogeneous Boolean functions implicitly are also juntas. This junta property shall be crucial in our proofs to show that the simulation error cannot be driven arbitrarily low by using larger number of input samples.

Note that one cannot increase the reliability of the binary symmetric source, which is identical to the result in [22]. However, unlike [22], we also rule out the possibility of SNIS for any $(1 - 2\varepsilon') \notin \{(1 - 2\varepsilon), (1 - 2\varepsilon)^2, \dots\}$. For such ε', any non-interactive simulation is *constant-insecure*.

Rate for Perfect SNIS. Unlike, the rate result for BES samples, we only prove a rate result for perfectly secure SNIS for BSS samples. We leave the rate result for statistically-secure SNIS as a fascinating open problem.

Theorem 6 (Perfect Security Rate: BSS-BSS). *Let $\varepsilon, \varepsilon' \in (0, 1/2)$ be noise characteristics such that $(1 - 2\varepsilon') = (1 - 2\varepsilon)^k$, for some $k \in \mathbb{N}$. If $\mathsf{BSS}(\varepsilon')^{\otimes m} \sqsubseteq_{f,g}^0 \mathsf{BSS}(\varepsilon)^{\otimes n}$, for some $m, n \in \mathbb{N}$, then $g = f$, each component of f is a k-homogeneous Boolean function, and $mk \leqslant n$, i.e., $R(\mathsf{BSS}(\varepsilon'), \mathsf{BSS}(\varepsilon)) \leqslant 1/k$.*

We emphasize that the components of the reduction f need not have disjoint input supports (as illustrated by the example above where we construct 2 output samples from $2k$ input samples using non-linear functions with identical input support). Both linear and non-linear rate-achieving perfect SNIS exist.

Section 6 outlines the proof of Theorem 5 and Theorem 6.

2.6   Technical Contribution and Connections

Homogeneous Boolean Functions. A Boolean function $f\colon \{\pm 1\}^n \to \{\pm 1\}$ is k-homogeneous if its Fourier weight is entirely on degree-k (multi-)linear terms. For example, $f(x) = x_1 \cdots x_k$ is a k-homogeneous function and is *linear* as well (because its entire Fourier weight is concentrated on one character). Refer to the functions $f_{2k}^{(1)}, f_{2k}^{(2)}$ in Sect. 2.5 for examples of *non-linear* k-homogeneous functions. The algebraization of security in Claim 13 implies the following result.

Proposition 3. $\mathsf{BSS}(\varepsilon') \sqsubseteq_{f,g}^0 \mathsf{BSS}(\varepsilon)^{\otimes n}$ *if and only if* $g = f$, f *is a k-homogeneous Boolean function, and* $(1 - 2\varepsilon') = (1 - 2\varepsilon)^k$.

In fact, we show a stronger result. If the reduction in the proposition above realizes a SNIS with sufficiently small insecurity, then the reduction can be error-corrected to obtain a perfect reduction (see Theorem 5).

This proposition presents a new application for the study of homogeneous Boolean functions. The characterization of k-homogeneous Boolean functions is not well-understood. For example, the Kindler-Safra junta theorem [31, 32] implies that such functions are juntas as well. A better understanding of the analytical properties of these functions shall help resolve the rate of statistical SNIS among BSS samples.

Distance-Invariant Codes. For a reduction function $f\colon \{\pm 1\}^n \to \{\pm 1\}$, one can equivalently identify it by the following code

$$\{\pm 1\}^n \supseteq C(f, +1) = \{x\colon f(x) = +1\}.$$

Analogously, the code $C(f, -1)$ is the complement of the set $C(f, +1)$.

A code $C \subseteq \{\pm 1\}^n$ is *distance-invariant* [34] if the number of codewords $A_i(c)$ at distance $i \in \{0, 1, \dots, n\}$ from a codeword $c \in C$ is independent of c. For example, linear codes are distance-invariant. There are non-linear distance-invariant codes as well. For example, when $k = 2$, the function $f_{2k}^{(1)}$ in Sect. 2.5 yields the following code.

$$\{\pm 1\}^{2k} \supseteq C(f_{2k}^{(1)}, +1) = \left\{ \begin{matrix} 1111, & 11{-}11, & 1{-}11{-}1, & -1{-}11{-}1, & -1{-}1{-}1{-}1 \\ & 1{-}111, & -11{-}11, & -11{-}1{-}1, & \end{matrix} \right\}.$$

The codewords are sorted based on their distance from the codeword 1111 (i.e., their Hamming weight). Observe that every codeword $c \in C(f_{2k}^{(1)}, +1)$ has 2 codewords at distance 1, 2, and 3; and 1 codeword at distance 0 and 4. That is, the *distance enumerator* $A(c, Z) := \sum_{i=1}^{2k} A_i(c) Z^i = 1 + 2Z + 2Z^2 + 2Z^3 + Z^4$, for any codeword $c \in C(f_{2k}^{(1)}, +1)$.

In fact, the code $C(f_{2k}^{(1)}, -1)$ is also distance-invariant (codewords are sorted by weight below) and has an *identical distance enumerator*.

$$\{\pm 1\}^{2k} \supseteq C(f_{2k}^{(1)}, -1) = \left\{ \begin{matrix} -1111, & -1{-}111, & 1{-}1{-}1{-}1, \\ 111{-}1, & -111{-}1, & -1{-}1{-}11, \\ & 1{-}1{-}11, & \\ & 11{-}1{-}1, & \end{matrix} \right\}.$$

Each codeword $c \in C(f_{2k}^{(1)}, -1)$ has 2 codewords at distance 1, 2, and 3; and 1 codeword at distance 0 and 4. These properties are no coincidence.

Proposition 4. BSS$(\varepsilon') \sqsubseteq_{f,g}^0$ BSS(ε), *for some* $\varepsilon, \varepsilon' \in (0, 1/2)$, *if and only if (a)* $f = g$, *and (b) the distance enumerators for any codeword in* $C(f, +1)$ *and* $C(f, -1)$ *are identical.*

Therefore, if distance-invariant codes $C(f, +1)$ and $C(f, -1)$ have identical distance enumerator then f is homogeneous.

3 Preliminaries

We denote $[n]$ as the set $\{1, 2, \ldots n\}$. For two functions $f, g \colon \Omega \to \mathbb{R}$, the equation $f = g$ means that $f(x) = g(x)$ for every $x \in \Omega$. We use $\mathcal{X}, \mathcal{Y}, \mathcal{U}, \mathcal{V}$, or Ω to denote the sample spaces. We also use (X, Y) to denote the joint distribution over $(\mathcal{X}, \mathcal{Y})$ with probability mass function π, and π_x, π_y to denote the marginal probability distributions of X and Y, respectively. For $x \in \mathcal{X}^n$, we represent $x_i \in \mathcal{X}$ as the i-th coordinate of x.

Statistical Distance. The statistical distance (total variation distance) between two distributions P and Q over a finite sample space Ω is defined as SD $(P, Q) = \frac{1}{2} \sum_{x \in \Omega} |P(x) - Q(x)|$.

Norms. We use $L^2(\Omega, \mu)$ to denote the real inner product space of functions $f \colon \Omega \to \mathbb{R}$ with inner product $\langle f, g \rangle_\mu = \mathbb{E}_{x \sim \mu} [f(x) \cdot g(x)]$. The p-norm of a function $f \in L^2(\Omega, \mu)$ is defined as $\|f\|_p := [\mathbb{E}_{x \sim \mu} |f(x)|^p]^{1/p}$.

3.1 Introductory Fourier Analysis over Boolean Hypercube

We recall some background in Fourier analysis that will be useful for our analysis (see [46] for more details). Let $f, g \colon \{\pm 1\}^n \to \mathbb{R}$ be two real-valued functions. We define the inner product of two functions as following.

$$\langle f, g \rangle = \frac{1}{2^n} \sum_{x \in \{\pm 1\}^n} f(x) \cdot g(x) = \mathbb{E}_x [f(x) \cdot g(x)]$$

A function is *Boolean* if its range is $\{\pm 1\}$. For each $S \subseteq [n]$, the characteristic function $\chi_S(x) = \prod_{i \in S} x_i$ is a *linear* function. The set of all χ_S forms an orthonormal basis for the space of all real-valued functions on $\{\pm 1\}^n$. For any $S \subseteq [n]$, the *Fourier coefficient* of f at S is defined as $\widehat{f}(S) = \langle f, \chi_S \rangle$. Any function f can be uniquely expressed as $f = \sum_{S \subseteq [n]} \widehat{f}(S) \chi_S$ which is called *multi-linear Fourier expansion* of f. The *Fourier weight* of f on a set $S \subseteq [n]$ is defined to be $\widehat{f}(S)^2$, and the Fourier weight of f at degree k is $\mathsf{W}^k[f] := \sum_{S : |S| = k} \widehat{f}(S)^2$. Similarly, the Fourier weight of f on all degrees except k is $\mathsf{W}^{\neq k}[f] := \sum_{S : |S| \neq k} \widehat{f}(S)^2$ and the Fourier weight of f on all degrees greater than k is $\mathsf{W}^{>k}[f] := \sum_{S:|S|>k} \widehat{f}(S)^2$. Parseval's Identity says that $\|f\|_2^2 = \sum_{S \subseteq [n]} \widehat{f}(S)^2$. In particular, if f is Boolean, it implies that $\sum_{S \subseteq [n]} \widehat{f}(S)^2 = 1$.

Next, we summarize the basic Fourier analysis of Boolean function with *restriction* on the sub-cubes. Let J and $\bar{J}$ be a partition of the set $[n]$. Let $f_{J|z} : \{\pm 1\}^J \to \mathbb{R}$ denote the restriction of f to J when the coordinates in $\bar{J}$ are fixed to $z \in \{\pm 1\}^{|\bar{J}|}$. Let $\widehat{f_{J|z}}(S)$ be the Fourier coefficient of the function $f_{J|z}$ corresponding to the set $S \subseteq J$. Then, when we assume that $z \in \{\pm 1\}^{|\bar{J}|}$ is chosen uniformly at random, we have

$$\mathbb{E}_z[\widehat{f_{J|z}}(S)] = \widehat{f}(S) \tag{1}$$

$$\mathbb{E}_z[\widehat{f_{J|z}}(S)^2] = \sum_{T \subseteq \bar{J}} \widehat{f}(S \cup T)^2 \tag{2}$$

For any $y \in \{\pm 1, 0\}^n$, we define $J_y := \{i \in [n]: y_i = 0\}$, $\bar{J}_y := [n] \backslash J_y$, and we also define z_y as the concatenation of all non-zero symbols of y. For example, if $y = (1, 0, -1, 0)$, then $J_y = \{2, 4\}$, $\bar{J}_y = \{1, 3\}$ and $z_y = (1, -1)$.

Degree of a Function. The *degree* of a function $f : \{\pm 1\}^n \to \mathbb{R}$ is the degree of its multilinear expansion, i.e., $\max\{|S| : \widehat{f}(S) \neq 0\}$.

Homogeneous Functions. A function $f : \{\pm 1\}^n \to \mathbb{R}$ is *k-homogeneous* if every term in the multi-linear expansion of f has degree k.

Junta Functions. A function $f : \{\pm 1\}^n \to \mathbb{R}$ is *d-junta* if the output of the function f depends on at most d inputs, where d is usually a constant independent of n.

Linear Functions. A function f is *linear* if $f = \pm \chi_S$ for some $S \subseteq [n]$.

3.2 Noise and Markov Operators

Noise Operator. Let $\rho \in [0, 1]$ be the parameter determining the noise. For each fixed bit string $x \in \{\pm 1\}^n$, we write $y \xleftarrow{\$} N_\rho(x)$ to denote that the random string y is drawn as follows: for each $i \in [n]$, independently, y_i is equal to x_i with probability ρ and it is chosen uniformly at random with probability $1 - \rho$. The *noise operator* with parameter $\rho \in [0, 1]$ is the linear operator T_ρ that takes as input a function $f : \{\pm 1\}^n \to \mathbb{R}$ and outputs the function $\mathsf{T}_\rho f : \{\pm 1\}^n \to \mathbb{R}$ defined as $\mathsf{T}_\rho f(x) = \mathbb{E}_{y \sim N_\rho(x)}[f(y)]$.

Markov Operator [39]**.** Let (X, Y) be a finite distribution over $(\mathcal{X}, \mathcal{Y})$ with probability distribution π. The *Markov operator* associated with this distribution, denoted by T, maps a function $g \in L^2(\mathcal{Y}, \pi_y)$ to a function $\mathsf{T}g \in L^2(\mathcal{X}, \pi_x)$ by $(\mathsf{T}g)(x) := \mathbb{E}[g(Y) \mid X = x]$, where (X, Y) is distributed according to π. Furthermore, we define the *adjoint operator* of T, denoted as $\overline{\mathsf{T}}$, maps a function $f \in L^2(\mathcal{X}, \pi_x)$ to a function $\overline{\mathsf{T}}f \in L^2(\mathcal{Y}, \pi_y)$ by $(\overline{\mathsf{T}}f)(y) = \mathbb{E}[f(X) \mid Y = y]$.

Example 1. For $\mathsf{BSS}(\varepsilon)$, both marginal distributions π_x and π_y are the uniform distribution over $\{\pm 1\}$. Both the Markov operator T and its adjoint $\overline{\mathsf{T}}$ associated with $\mathsf{BSS}(\varepsilon)$ are identical to the noise operator T_ρ, where $\rho = 1 - 2\varepsilon$.

Example 2. For $\mathsf{BES}(\varepsilon)$, the marginal distribution π_x is the uniform distribution over $\{\pm 1\}$, and π_y satisfies $\pi_y(+1) = \pi_y(-1) = (1-\varepsilon)/2$ and $\pi_y(0) = \varepsilon$. For any functions $f \in L^2(\{\pm 1\}, \pi_x)$ and $g \in L^2(\{\pm 1, 0\}, \pi_y)$, the Markov operator and its adjoint associated with $\mathsf{BES}(\varepsilon)$ are as follows.

$$(\mathsf{T}g)(x) = (1 - \varepsilon) \cdot g(x) + \varepsilon \cdot g(0) \text{ for every } x \in \{\pm 1\}$$

$$(\overline{\mathsf{T}}f)(y) = \begin{cases} f(y) & \text{if } y \in \{\pm 1\} \\ 1/2 \cdot f(1) + 1/2 \cdot f(-1) & \text{if } y = 0 \end{cases}$$

3.3 Imported Theorems

This section present results that are useful for our proofs. We use the following version of Kindler-Safra junta theorem (Theorem 1.1 in [19]).

Imported Theorem 1 (Kindler-Safra Junta Theorem [31,32]). *Fix* $d \geqslant 0$. *There exists* $\varepsilon_0 = \varepsilon_0(d)$ *and constant* C *such that for every* $\varepsilon < \varepsilon_0$, *if* $f : \{\pm 1\}^n \to \{\pm 1\}$ *satisfies* $\mathsf{W}^{>d}[f] = \varepsilon$ *then there exists a* C^d-*junta and degree* d *function* $\tilde{f} : \{\pm 1\}^n \to \{\pm 1\}$ *such that* $\left\| f - \tilde{f} \right\|_2^2 \leqslant (\varepsilon + C^d \varepsilon^{5/4})$.

This theorem says that any Boolean function whose Fourier spectrum is concentrated on low degree multi-linear terms is close to a low degree Boolean Junta.

Lemma 1 (Exercise 1.11 Chapter 1 [46]). *Suppose that* $f : \{\pm 1\}^n \to \{\pm 1\}$ *has degree* $d \geqslant 1$. *Then, for every* $S \subseteq [n]$, *the Fourier coefficient* $\widehat{f}(S)$ *is an integer multiple of* $2/2^d$.

This lemma states that a bounded-degree function's spectrum is coarse-grained.

4 Technical Overview: BSS from BES Samples

We outline the proof of Theorem 2 below.

Infeasibility Outline. Consider a randomized SNIS $\mathsf{BSS}(\varepsilon') \sqsubseteq_{f,g}^\nu \mathsf{BES}(\varepsilon)^{\otimes n}$, where $\varepsilon \in (0,1)$ and $\varepsilon' \in (0, 1/2)$. Using Proposition 1 (the derandomization result for feasibility results), we can, without loss of generality, assume that f and g are deterministic functions. Therefore, we have $f : \{\pm 1\}^n \to \{\pm 1\}$ and $g : \{\pm 1, 0\}^n \to \{\pm 1\}$. Define $\rho = (1 - \varepsilon)$ and $\rho' = (1 - 2\varepsilon')$.

Step 1: Algebraization of Security. The simulation-based definition of SNIS of BSS from BES samples can be algebraized as follows.

Claim 1 (BSS-BES Algebraization of Security). *For any $\varepsilon \in (0,1)$ and $\varepsilon' \in (0,1/2)$, the following statements hold.*

1. *If $\mathsf{BSS}(\varepsilon') \sqsubseteq^{\nu}_{f,g} \mathsf{BES}(\varepsilon)^{\otimes n}$, then $\mathbb{E}[f] \leqslant \nu$, $\mathbb{E}[g] \leqslant \nu$, $\left\|\overline{\mathsf{T}}f - \rho'g\right\|_1 \leqslant 4\nu$, and $\left\|\mathsf{T}g - \rho'f\right\|_1 \leqslant 4\nu$.*
2. *If $\mathbb{E}[f] \leqslant \nu$, $\mathbb{E}[g] \leqslant \nu$, $\left\|\overline{\mathsf{T}}f - \rho'g\right\|_1 \leqslant \nu$, and $\left\|\mathsf{T}g - \rho'f\right\|_1 \leqslant \nu$, then $\mathsf{BSS}(\varepsilon') \sqsubseteq^{2\nu}_{f,g} \mathsf{BES}(\varepsilon)^{\otimes n}$.*

Recall that T and $\overline{\mathsf{T}}$ are the Markov and the adjoint Markov operators associated with the $\mathsf{BES}^{\otimes n}$ joint distribution. This claim shows the qualitative equivalence of the simulation-based security definition and the algebraized definition (they incur only a multiplicative constant loss in insecurity during interconversion). Furthermore, this claim preserves perfect security.

Step 2: Approximate Eigenvector Problem. Let us focus on the reduction function $f: \{\pm 1\}^n \to \{\pm 1\}$. Composing the two constraints (a) $\left\|\overline{\mathsf{T}}f - \rho'g\right\|_1 \leqslant 4\nu$, and (b) $\left\|\mathsf{T}g - \rho'f\right\|_1 \leqslant 4\nu$, we get that $\left\|\mathsf{T}\overline{\mathsf{T}}f - \rho'^2 f\right\|_1 \leqslant 8\nu$. This property is an eigenvector problem for the $\mathsf{T}\overline{\mathsf{T}} = \mathsf{T}_\rho$ operator.

Claim 2 ("Noisy Close-to-Scaling" Constraint). *If $\mathsf{BSS}(\varepsilon') \sqsubseteq^{\nu}_{f,g} \mathsf{BES}(\varepsilon)^{\otimes n}$, then it holds that $\left\|\mathsf{T}\overline{\mathsf{T}}f - \rho'^2 f\right\|_1 = \left\|\mathsf{T}_\rho f - \rho'^2 f\right\|_1 \leqslant 8\nu$.*

Step 3: Homogeneous Property. Recall that T_ρ operator scales $\widehat{f}(S)$ proportional to $\rho^{|S|}$. If $\rho'^2 \notin \{\rho, \rho^2, \rho^3, \dots\}$, then $\mathsf{T}_\rho f$ cannot be close to $\rho'^2 f$. In this case, when f is Boolean, there shall always be a constant gap between $\mathsf{T}_\rho f$ and $\rho'^2 f$. That is, ν is at least a constant. The proof is done.

On the other hand, suppose $\rho'^2 = \rho^k$, for some $k \in \mathbb{N}$. In this case, any weight on $\widehat{f}(S)$ such that $|S| \neq k$ contributes to the gap between $\mathsf{T}_\rho f$ and $\rho'^2 f$. Consequently, most of the Fourier-weight of f must be on the degree-k (multi-)linear terms. The following claim formalizes this argument.

Claim 3 (Properties of Reduction Functions). *Suppose $\left\|\mathsf{T}_\rho f - \rho^k f\right\|_1 \leqslant \delta$, then there exists $D = D(k)$ such that the following statements hold.*

1. *The function f is $\frac{2\delta}{(1-\rho)\rho^{2k}}$-close to k-homogeneous.*
2. *There exists a Boolean k-homogeneous D-junta function $\tilde{f}: \{\pm 1\}^n \to \{\pm 1\}$ such that $\left\|f - \tilde{f}\right\|_2^2 \leqslant \sigma + D\sigma^{5/4}$, where $\sigma = \frac{2}{(1-\rho)^2 \rho^{2k}} \cdot \delta$.*

The result that (the Boolean) f is close to a Boolean junta function is a consequence of Kindler-Safra junta theorem [31,32] (refer to Imported Theorem 1) and this property of f shall be crucial for our strong statistical-to-perfect transformation. Due to the qualitative equivalence of simulation-based and algebraic definition of security, if f, g witness a secure SNIS with ν insecurity, then

$\tilde{f}, g$ witness a secure SNIS with comparable insecurity (say, $\mathsf{poly}(\nu)$-insecurity). Henceforth, we shall use the k-homogeneous D-junta (Boolean) reduction function $\tilde{f}$ instead of the reduction f. The proof of the entire argument presented in this step relies on Theorem 8 and Theorem 9.

Step 4: Infeasibility. This step is the continuation of the case that $\rho'^2 = \rho^k$, for $k \in \mathbb{N}$. In this step, we shall use the properties of the reduction function $g \colon \{\pm 1, 0\}^n \to \{\pm 1\}$ and security to conclude that the reduction must be constant-insecure.

Theorem 7 (Insecurity Lower Bound). *Let $\overline{\mathsf{T}}$ be the adjoint Markov operator associated with the joint distribution $\mathsf{BES}(\varepsilon)^{\otimes n}$. Suppose $h \colon \{\pm 1\}^n \to \{\pm 1\}$ is a Boolean k-homogeneous D-junta function, and $g \colon \{\pm 1, 0\}^n \to \{\pm 1\}$ be any arbitrary function. Then $\left\| \overline{\mathsf{T}} h - \rho' g \right\|_1 \geqslant \rho' \cdot \min \left(\left(\frac{1-\varepsilon}{2} \right)^D , \varepsilon^D \right).$*

Observe that without the junta property of h, we would not have obtained a constant lower bound to the insecurity. Section 4.2 proves this theorem.

4.1 Our Technical Results

This section presents our technical results that are crucial to the proofs of the feasibility and rate results (for not only SNIS of BSS from BES but also SNIS of BES from BES and BSS from BSS). The following theorem basically solves the "approximate eigenvector problem". Intuitively, it says that if the noisy version of a Boolean function is sufficiently-close to a scaling of that function, then (1) the scaling factor must be an eigenvalue of the noise operator and (2) the Fourier spectrum of that function is concentrated on some particular degree, i.e., it is close to a homogeneous (not necessarily Boolean) function.

Theorem 8 (Constant Insecurity or Close to Homogeneous). *Fix parameters $\rho, \rho' \in (0, 1)$. Let $f \colon \{\pm 1\}^n \to \{\pm 1\}$ be a Boolean function, and let $\delta = \left\| \mathsf{T}_\rho f - \rho' f \right\|_1$. Then, the following statement hold.*

1. *If $\rho^{t+1} < \rho' < \rho^t$ for some $t \in [n]$, then $\delta \geqslant \frac{1}{2} \min((\rho' - \rho^t)^2, (\rho' - \rho^{t+1})^2)$.*
2. *If $\rho' = \rho^k$ for some $k \in [n]$, then $\mathsf{W}^k[f] \geqslant 1 - \frac{2}{(1-\rho)^2 \rho'^2} \cdot \delta$.*

Proof. Since $|(\mathsf{T}_\rho f)(x)| \leqslant 1$ and $f(x) \in \{\pm 1\}$ for every x, we have

$$|(\mathsf{T}_\rho f)(x) - \rho' \cdot f(x)| \leqslant 1 + \rho' \leqslant 2 \text{ for every } x.$$

This implies that

$$\left\| (\mathsf{T}_\rho f)(x) - \rho' f \right\|_2^2 = \mathbb{E}_x \left[(\mathsf{T}_\rho f)(x) - \rho' \cdot f(x) \right]^2 \leqslant 2 \mathbb{E}_x |(\mathsf{T}_\rho f)(x) - \rho' \cdot f(x)| \leqslant 2\delta.$$

Case 1: If $\rho^{t+1} < \rho' < \rho^t$ for some $t \in [n]$, then $\delta = \left\| (\mathsf{T}_\rho f)(x) - \rho' f \right\|_1$ is bounded from below by

$$\frac{1}{2} \left\| (\mathsf{T}_\rho f)(x) - \rho' f \right\|_2^2 = \frac{1}{2} \sum_{S \subseteq [n]} (\rho^{|S|} - \rho')^2 \widehat{f}(S)^2 \geqslant \frac{1}{2} \min((\rho' - \rho^t)^2, (\rho' - \rho^{t+1})^2).$$

Case 2: $\rho' = \rho^k$ for some $k \in \mathbb{N}$. Observe that $|\rho^{|S|} - \rho'| \geqslant |\rho^{k+1} - \rho^k|$ for any $|S| \neq k$. Therefore, we have

$$\sum_{|S| \neq k} (\rho^{k+1} - \rho^k)^2 \widehat{f}(S)^2 \leqslant \sum_{|S| \neq k} (\rho^{|S|} - \rho^k)^2 \widehat{f}(S)^2 = \left\| (\mathsf{T}_\rho f)(x) - \rho^k f \right\|_2^2 \leqslant 2\delta.$$

This implies that $\mathsf{W}^{\neq k}[f] = \sum_{S \,:\, |S| \neq k} \widehat{f}(S)^2 \leqslant \frac{2\delta}{\rho^{2k}(1-\rho)^2}$, as desired.

Next, we show that if a noisy version of a Boolean function is close to that function scaled by an eigenvalue of the noise operator, then the function is close to a homogeneous junta Boolean function.

Theorem 9 (Close to Homogeneous and Junta). *Let $\rho \in (0,1)$ and $k \in \mathbb{N}$. There exist constants $D = D(k) > 0$, $\delta_0 = \delta_0(\rho, k) > 0$ such that the following statement holds. For any $\delta < \delta_0$, if the function $f \colon \{\pm 1\}^n \to \{\pm 1\}$ satisfies $\left\| \mathsf{T}_\rho f - \rho^k f \right\|_1 = \delta$, then there exists a k-homogeneous D-junta function*

$$\tilde{f} \colon \{\pm 1\}^n \to \{\pm 1\} \text{ such that } \left\| f - \tilde{f} \right\|_2^2 \leqslant \sigma + D\sigma^{5/4}, \text{ where } \sigma = \frac{2}{(1-\rho)^2 \rho^{2k}} \cdot \delta.$$

We use the Kindler-Safra junta theorem (Imported Theorem 1) and the following claim to prove this theorem.

Claim 4. *Let $f, \tilde{f} \colon \{\pm 1\}^n \to \{\pm 1\}$ be two Boolean functions. Suppose $\mathsf{W}^k[f] \geqslant 1 - \delta$ and $\left\| f - \tilde{f} \right\|_2 \leqslant \gamma$. Then it holds that $\mathsf{W}^k[\tilde{f}] \geqslant 1 - \delta - 2\gamma$.*

Basically, the claim tells us that if a Boolean function $\tilde{f}$ is close to another Boolean function that is also close to a homogeneous (not necessarily Boolean) function, then $\tilde{f}$ is also close to a homogeneous function.

Proof (of Theorem 9). Applying Theorem 8 for the reduction function f satisfying $\left\| \mathsf{T}_\rho f - \rho^k f \right\|_1 \leqslant \delta$ yields $\mathsf{W}^{\neq k}[f] = 1 - \mathsf{W}^k[f] \leqslant \frac{2}{(1-\rho)^2 \rho^{2k}} \cdot \delta$. Let $\varepsilon_0 = \varepsilon_0(k)$ be the constant achieved by applying Imported Theorem 1. Let $\delta_1 = \frac{(1-\rho)^2 \rho^{2k}}{2} \cdot \varepsilon_0$. Note that δ_1 depends only on k and $\delta_1 \leqslant \varepsilon_0$. This implies that, for any $\delta < \delta_1$, we have $\mathsf{W}^{\neq k}[f] \leqslant \varepsilon_0$. Invoking Imported Theorem 1, there exists a C^k-junta and degree k function $\tilde{f} \colon \{\pm 1\}^n \to \{\pm 1\}$ such that $\left\| f - \tilde{f} \right\|_2^2 \leqslant \sigma + C^k \sigma^{5/4}$, where $\sigma = \frac{2}{(1-\rho)^2 \rho^{2k}} \cdot \delta$. Next, we show that $\tilde{f}$ is k-homogeneous, i.e., $\mathsf{W}^k[\tilde{f}] = 1$. By Claim 4, we have $\mathsf{W}^k[\tilde{f}] \geqslant 1 - \sigma - 2\sqrt{\sigma + C^k \sigma^{5/4}}$. We choose δ_2 to be a constant such that $\sigma + 2\sqrt{\sigma + C^k \sigma^{5/4}} < \frac{1}{2^{2(k-1)}}$ for every $\delta < \delta_2$. Note that δ_2 depends only on ρ and k. If $\mathsf{W}^k[\tilde{f}] \neq 1$, it follows from Lemma 1 that $\mathsf{W}^{=k}[\tilde{f}]$ is far from 1, in other words, $\mathsf{W}^k[\tilde{f}] \leqslant 1 - 1/2^{2(k-1)} < 1 - \sigma - 2\sqrt{\sigma + C^k \sigma^{5/4}}$, which is a contradiction. So it must be the case that $\mathsf{W}^k[\tilde{f}] = 1$ when $\delta \leqslant \delta_2$. Choosing $\delta_0 = \min(\delta_1, \delta_2)$ completes the proof.

Finally, the following result says that two low-degree Boolean functions cannot be too close. We use the granularity property of low-degree Boolean function (see Lemma 1) to prove this lemma.

Lemma 2 (Low-degree Boolean Functions are Far). *If $h, \ell \colon \{\pm 1\}^n \to \{\pm 1\}$ are distinct Boolean functions of degree (at most) d, then $\|h - \ell\|_2 \geqslant 2/2^d$.*

Proof. Since h and ℓ are two distinct functions, there exists a $S^* \subseteq [n]$ such that $\widehat{h}(S^*) \neq \widehat{\ell}(S^*)$. Invoking Lemma 1 for low degree functions h and ℓ yields that the Fourier coefficients of h and ℓ are integer multiple of $1/2^{d-1}$. This implies that $\left|\widehat{h}(S^*) - \widehat{\ell}(S^*)\right| \geqslant 1/2^{d-1}$. Therefore, we have

$$\|h - \ell\|_2^2 = \sum_{S \subseteq [n]} (\widehat{h}(S) - \widehat{\ell}(S))^2 \geqslant (\widehat{h}(S^*) - \widehat{\ell}(S^*))^2 \geqslant 1/2^{2(d-1)},$$

which completes the proof.

As a consequence, we have the following corollary.

Corollary 1. *Fix noise parameter $\rho \in (0, 1)$. Suppose $h, \ell \colon \{\pm 1\}^n \to \{\pm 1\}$ are two distinct d-homogeneous Boolean functions. Then, $\left\|\mathsf{T}_\rho h - \rho^d \ell\right\|_2 \geqslant 2\rho^d/2^d$.*

4.2 Proof of Theorem 7

First, we state some claims that are needed for the proof of Theorem 7. Recall that $J_y := \{i \in [n] : y_i = 0\}$ and z_y denotes the concatenation of all non-zero symbols of y as defined in Sect. 3.2.

Claim 5 (Connection with Restriction of Functions). *Let $\overline{\mathsf{T}}$ be the adjoint Markov operator of $\mathsf{BES}(\varepsilon)^{\otimes n}$, and let $f \colon \{\pm 1\}^n \to \{\pm 1\}$. Then, for every $y \in \{\pm 1, 0\}^n$, it holds that $(\overline{\mathsf{T}}f)(y) = \widehat{f}_{J_y | z_y}(\emptyset)$.*

Proof. Since the distribution of (X, Y) is $\mathsf{BES}(\varepsilon)$, for any $i \in [n]$ that $y_i = 1$, $\Pr[X_i = 1 | Y_i = y_i = 1] = 1$ and for any $i \in [n]$ that $y_i = -1$, $\Pr[X_i = -1 | Y_i = y_i = -1] = 1$; while for any $i \in [n]$ that $y_i = 0$, $\Pr[X_i = 1 | Y_i = y_i = 0] = \Pr[X_i = -1 | Y_i = y_i = 0] = 1/2$. This implies that conditioned on non-zero symbols of y, i.e., z_y, the conditional distribution over the corresponding symbols of x is deterministic while over the rest of symbols is uniform. Therefore, we have

$$\begin{aligned}
(\overline{\mathsf{T}}f)(y) &= \mathbb{E}[f(X)|Y = y] &&\text{(Definition of adjoint operator)} \\
&= \mathbb{E}[f(X)|J_y, z_y] &&(J_y, z_y \text{ implies } y) \\
&= \mathbb{E}[f_{J_y | z_y}(X)] &&\text{(Definition of restriction function)} \\
&= \widehat{f}_{J_y | z_y}(\emptyset).
\end{aligned}$$

Claim 6 (Fourier Property of Homogeneous Functions). *Let f be a Boolean k-homogeneous function. Then, for every $y \in \{\pm 1, 0\}^n$ satisfying $|\bar{J}_y| < k$, it holds that $\widehat{f}_{J_y | z_y}(\emptyset) = 0$.*

Proof. First, note that $\widehat{f}(S) = 0$ for every $|S| \neq k$. This together with Eq. (2) implies that, for every $y \in \{\pm 1, 0\}^n$ satisfying $|\bar{J}_y| < k$,

$$\underset{z_y}{\mathbb{E}}\left[\widehat{f}_{J_y|z_y}(\emptyset)^2\right] = \sum_{T \subseteq \bar{J}_y} \widehat{f}(T)^2 = 0.$$

Therefore, it must hold that $\widehat{f}_{J_y|z_y}(\emptyset) = 0$ as desired.

Now, we are ready to prove the main theorem.

Proof (of Theorem 7). We say that a node $y \in \{\pm 1, 0\}^n$ is "bad" if it incurs a large simulation error, in other words, $|(\overline{T}h)(y^*) - \rho' g(y^*)|$ is large. First, we show that there exists a "bad" $y^* \in \{\pm 1, 0\}^n$. Let $y^* \in \{\pm 1, 0\}^n$ be such that $|\bar{J}_{y^*}| < k$. It follows from Claim 5 and Claim 6 that $(\overline{T}h)(y^*) = \widehat{h}_{J_{y^*}|z_{y^*}}(\emptyset) = 0$. Now, since the $g(y^*) \in \{\pm 1\}$, we have $|(\overline{T}h)(y^*) - \rho' g(y^*)| = \rho'$. Next, we construct a large set $\mathcal{S}(y^*)$ such that every $y \in \mathcal{S}(y^*)$ is bad. Let I denote the set of the D coordinates that (might) have influence on the output of h. Since h is a D-junta function, every coordinate in $\bar{I} = [n] \backslash I$ does not have any influence on the output of the function. We construct a set of bad nodes as follow.

$$\mathcal{S}(y^*) := \{y \in \{\pm 1, 0\}^n : y_I = y_I^*\}$$

Here, y_I denotes the concatenation of all y_i where $i \in I$. It follows from the junta property of h that $(\overline{T}h)(y) = (\overline{T}h)(y^*) = (\overline{T}_I h)(y_I)$ for every $y \in \mathcal{S}(y^*)$, where $\overline{T}_I$ denotes the adjoint Markov operator associated with $\mathsf{BES}(\varepsilon)^{\otimes|I|}$. So it holds that $|(\overline{T}h)(y) - \rho' g(y)| = \rho'$ for every $y \in \mathcal{S}(y^*)$. Note that $|\mathcal{S}(y^*)| = 3^{n-D}$. Thus, we have

$$\|\overline{T}h - \rho' g\|_1 = \underset{y}{\mathbb{E}}\left|(\overline{T}h)(y) - \rho' g(y)\right| \qquad \text{(by definition)}$$

$$\geqslant \sum_{y \in \mathcal{S}(y^*)} \Pr[Y = y] \cdot \left|(\overline{T}h)(y) - \rho' g(y)\right|$$

$$= \sum_{y \in \mathcal{S}(y^*)} \Pr[Y = y] \cdot \rho' \qquad \text{(identity transformation)}$$

$$= \rho' \cdot \Pr[Y_I = y_I^*] \qquad \text{(identity transformation)}$$

$$= \rho' \cdot \left(\frac{1-\varepsilon}{2}\right)^{D-t} \cdot \varepsilon^t \qquad (t \text{ is the number of zeros in } y_I^*)$$

$$\geqslant \rho' \cdot \min\left(\left(\frac{1-\varepsilon}{2}\right)^D, \varepsilon^D\right).$$

5   Technical Overview: BES from BES Samples

First, we outline the proof of Theorem 3 below, then Theorem 4.

Feasibility Outline. Consider a randomized SNIS $\mathsf{BES}(\varepsilon') \sqsubseteq_{f,g}^\nu \mathsf{BES}(\varepsilon)^{\otimes n}$, where $\varepsilon, \varepsilon' \in (0, 1)$. Using Proposition 1, we can, without loss of generality, assume that f and g are deterministic functions. Therefore, we have $f \colon \{\pm 1\}^n \to \{\pm 1\}$ and $g \colon \{\pm 1, 0\}^n \to \{\pm 1, 0\}$. Define $\rho = (1 - \varepsilon)$ and $\rho' = (1 - \varepsilon')$.

Step 1: Algebraization of Security. We show that simulation-based SNIS definition is qualitatively equivalent to the algebraized definition of SNIS.

Claim 7 (BES-BES Algebraization of Security). *For any $\varepsilon, \varepsilon' \in (0,1)$, the following statements hold.*

1. *If $\mathsf{BES}(\varepsilon') \sqsubseteq_{f,g}^{\nu} \mathsf{BES}(\varepsilon)^{\otimes n}$, then $\mathbb{E}[f] \leqslant \nu$, $\mathbb{E}[g] \leqslant \nu$, $\left\|\overline{\mathsf{T}}f - g\right\|_1 \leqslant 4\nu$, and $\left\|\mathsf{T}g - \rho'f\right\|_1 \leqslant 4\nu$.*
2. *If $\mathbb{E}[f] \leqslant \nu$, $\mathbb{E}[g] \leqslant \nu$, $\left\|\overline{\mathsf{T}}f - g\right\|_1 \leqslant \nu$, and $\left\|\mathsf{T}g - \rho'f\right\|_1 \leqslant \nu$, then $\mathsf{BES}(\varepsilon') \sqsubseteq_{f,g}^{2\nu} \mathsf{BES}(\varepsilon)^{\otimes n}$.*

Step 2: Approximate Eigenvector Problem. Focusing on the reduction function and the guarantees (a) $\left\|\overline{\mathsf{T}}f - g\right\|_1 \leqslant 4\nu$, and (b) $\left\|\mathsf{T}g - \rho'f\right\|_1 \leqslant 4\nu$, we obtain the following result.

Claim 8 ("Noisy Close-to-Scaling" Constraint). *If $\mathsf{BES}(\varepsilon') \sqsubseteq_{f,g}^{\nu}$ $\mathsf{BES}(\varepsilon)^{\otimes n}$, then it holds that $\left\|\mathsf{T}\overline{\mathsf{T}}f - \rho'f\right\|_1 = \left\|\mathsf{T}_\rho f - \rho'f\right\|_1 \leqslant 8\nu$.*

Step 3: Homogeneous Property. There are two cases to consider. If $\rho' \notin \{\rho, \rho^2, \dots\}$, then the reduction is constant insecure (and the proof is done). However, if $\rho' = \rho^k$, for some $k \in \mathbb{N}$, then the reduction function must be close to a k-homogeneous D-junta Boolean function f^* (using Claim 3). We remark that if security is perfect then f is identical to f^*. Intuitively, the set of all possible junta functions has constant size and f can be *error-corrected* to the unique closest f^*.

Step 4: Only Linear Functions. Now it remains to prove that f^* is linear.

Theorem 10 (Must be Linear). *Let T be the adjoint Markov operator associated with the joint distribution $\mathsf{BES}(\varepsilon)^{\otimes n}$. Suppose $h: \{\pm 1\}^n \to \{\pm 1\}$ is a Boolean k-homogeneous D-junta function, and $g: \{\pm 1, 0\}^n \to \{\pm 1, 0\}$ be any arbitrary function. There is a constant $c = c(\varepsilon, D, k)$ such that if $\left\|\mathsf{T}h - g\right\|_1 \leqslant c$, then h must be a linear function.*

Section 5.1 proves this theorem. The proof proceeds by considering an appropriate martingale of the Fourier-coefficients of the restrictions of the reduction function.

It is instructive to compare this theorem with Theorem 7, where we proved that any reduction is constant-insecure. In the theorem here, our objective is to characterize h such that $\left\|\mathsf{T}h - g\right\|_1$ is small. In Theorem 7, the constraint was $\left\|\mathsf{T}h - \rho'g\right\|_1$ instead, where $\rho' \in (0,1)$. This additional ρ' factor made every reduction function constant-insecure.

Once we conclude that f is close to a k-linear f^*, we can argue that g is also close to g^* such that f^*, g^* witness a perfect SNIS of $\mathsf{BES}(\varepsilon')$ from $\mathsf{BES}(\varepsilon)$ samples. The following claim formalizes this reasoning.

Claim 9. *Suppose* $\mathsf{BES}(\varepsilon') \sqsubseteq_{f,g}^{\nu} \mathsf{BES}(\varepsilon)^{\otimes n}$, *where* $(1 - \varepsilon') = (1 - \varepsilon)^k$ *for some* $k \in \mathbb{N}$. *Suppose also that* $h\colon \{\pm 1\}^n \to \{\pm 1\}$ *is a* k-*linear character* χ_S *for some* $S \subseteq [n]$ *and* $\|f - h\|_1 \leqslant \delta$. *Let* $\ell\colon \{\pm 1, 0\}^n \to \{\pm 1, 0\}^n$ *be defined as* $\ell(y) = \prod_{i \in S} y_i$. *Then, it holds that* $\mathsf{BES}(\varepsilon') \sqsubseteq_{h,\ell}^0 \mathsf{BES}(\varepsilon)^{\otimes n}$ *and* $\|g - \ell\|_1 \leqslant 4\nu + \delta$.

Finally, we emphasize that if $\nu = 0$, then f and g are identical to f^* and g^*.

Outline: Rate of Statistical SNIS. The discussion below is the outline for the proof of Theorem 4. Fix erasure probabilities $\varepsilon, \varepsilon' \in (0, 1)$. Consider a randomized SNIS $\mathsf{BES}(\varepsilon')^{\otimes m} \sqsubseteq_{f,g}^{\nu} \mathsf{BES}(\varepsilon)^{\otimes n}$. We require a sample-preserving derandomization (for statistical SNIS) to prove the rate result. However, we cannot directly derandomize this SNIS using Theorem 1 (refer to the discussion following Theorem 1). Consequently, we have to follow a different strategy.

Let $f^{(i)}, g^{(i)}$ represent the i-th component of the reductions $\boldsymbol{f}, \boldsymbol{g}$, where $i \in \{1, \dots, m\}$. Let $f^{(i)} \| f^{(j)}$, for $1 \leqslant i < j \leqslant m$, represent the pair of components $f^{(i)}$ and $f^{(j)}$. Similarly, define $g^{(i)} \| g^{(j)}$. Observe that $\mathsf{BES}(\varepsilon')^{\otimes 2} \sqsubseteq_{f^{(i)} \| f^{(j)}, g^{(i)} \| g^{(j)}}^{\nu} \mathsf{BES}(\varepsilon)^{\otimes n}$ (by projecting on the i-th and j-th output samples). We can derandomize this construction using Theorem 1 (our sample-preserving derandomization for statistical SNIS). So, we get deterministic reduction function $\widetilde{f}^{(i)} \| \widetilde{f}^{(j)}$ that is close to $f^{(i)} \| f^{(j)}$ and deterministic $\widetilde{g}^{(i)} \| \widetilde{g}^{(j)}$ that is close to $g^{(i)} \| g^{(j)}$ such that $\mathsf{BES}(\varepsilon')^{\otimes 2} \sqsubseteq_{\widetilde{f}^{(i)} \| \widetilde{f}^{(j)}, \widetilde{g}^{(i)} \| \widetilde{g}^{(j)}}^{\nu'} \mathsf{BES}(\varepsilon)^{\otimes n}$, where $\nu' = \Theta\nu^{1/4}$.

We show that there are deterministic functions $f^{*(i)}$ and $f^{*(j)}$ such that $f^{*(i)}$ is close to $\widetilde{f}^{(i)}$ (which is in turn close to $f^{(i)}$) and $f^{*(j)}$ is close to $\widetilde{f}^{(j)}$ (which is in turn close to $f^{(j)}$). Furthermore, there are reduction functions $g^{*(i)}$ and $g^{*(j)}$ such that $\mathsf{BES}(\varepsilon')^{\otimes 2} \sqsubseteq_{f^{*(i)} \| f^{*(j)}, g^{*(i)} \| g^{*(j)}}^0 \mathsf{BES}(\varepsilon)^{\otimes n}$. We emphasize that $f^{*(i)}$ is independent of the choice of $j \in \{1, \dots, m\}$.

At this point, we can conclude that $f^{*(i)}$ and $f^{*(j)}$ are both k-linear (because reductions for perfect BES-from-BES SNIS are linear). We can use a linear construction to obtain one sample of $\mathsf{BES}(\varepsilon'')$ from $\mathsf{BES}(\varepsilon')^{\otimes 2}$ with perfect security, where $(1 - \varepsilon'') = (1 - \varepsilon')^2$. We compose these two constructions to obtain a perfectly secure SNIS of $\mathsf{BES}(\varepsilon'')$ from $\mathsf{BES}(\varepsilon)^n$, where $(1 - \varepsilon'') = (1 - \varepsilon')^2 = (1 - \varepsilon)^{2k}$. So, the reduction of the composed SNIS must be $2k$-linear; i.e., $f^{*(i)} \cdot f^{*(j)}$ is $2k$-linear. We conclude that $f^{*(i)}$ and $f^{*(j)}$ are k-linear such that they do not share any input variables.

So, we have $f^{*(1)}, \dots, f^{*(m)} \colon \{\pm 1\}^n \to \{\pm 1\}$ such that each function is k-linear with pairwise disjoint inputs. Therefore, $mk \leqslant n$. This entire reasoning describes the proof of Claim 10.

Claim 10. *Let* $\varepsilon, \varepsilon' \in (0, 1)$ *be erasure probabilities satisfying* $(1 - \varepsilon') = (1 - \varepsilon)^k$, *for some* $k \in \mathbb{N}$. *There is a constant* $c = c(\varepsilon, \varepsilon')$ *such that the following holds. Suppose* $\mathsf{BES}(\varepsilon')^{\otimes m} \sqsubseteq_{f,g}^{\nu} \mathsf{BES}(\varepsilon)^{\otimes n}$ *for some* $\nu \leqslant c$. *For each pair* $1 \leqslant i < j \leqslant m$, *let* $\widetilde{f}_{ij}^{(i)} \| \widetilde{f}_{ij}^{(j)}$ *and* $\widetilde{g}_{ij}^{(i)} \| \widetilde{g}_{ij}^{(j)}$ *be the deterministic functions obtained by derandomizing the SNIS of* $\mathsf{BES}(\varepsilon')^{\otimes 2} \sqsubseteq_{f^{(i)} \| f^{(j)}, g^{(i)} \| g^{(j)}}^{\nu} \mathsf{BES}(\varepsilon)^{\otimes n}$ *using Theorem 1. Let* $f_{ij}^{*(i)}$ *and* $f_{ij}^{*(j)}$ *be* k-*linear Boolean functions that are close to* $\widetilde{f}_{ij}^{(i)}$ *and* $\widetilde{f}_{ij}^{(i)}$, *respectively. It holds that*

1. $f_{ij}^{*\,(i)} = f_{ij'}^{*\,(i)}$ for any distinct triple $i, j, j' \in \{1, 2, \ldots, m\}$. For any $j \neq i$, represent $f^{*\,(i)} := f_{ij}^{*\,(i)}$.

2. There exists a unique $g^* = (g^{*\,(1)}, g^{*\,(2)}, \ldots, g^{*\,(m)})$ such that, for any $1 \leqslant i < j \leqslant m$,

$$\mathsf{BES}(\varepsilon')^{\otimes 2} \sqsubseteq^0_{f^{*\,(i)} \| f^{*\,(j)}, \, g^{*\,(i)} \| g^{*\,(j)}} \mathsf{BES}(\varepsilon)^{\otimes n}.$$

3. Furthermore, for distinct $i, j \in \{1, \ldots, m\}$, the input support of $f^{*\,(i)}$ and the support of $f^{*\,(j)}$ are disjoint. Consequently, $mk \leqslant n$.

5.1   Proof of Theorem 10

The following claim is crucial to the proof of the theorem.

Claim 11. *Let* $h \colon \{\pm 1\}^n \to \{\pm 1\}$ *be a k-homogeneous Boolean function such that* $\left| \widehat{h}_{J|z}(\emptyset) \right| = 1$ *for some* $J \subseteq [n]$ *satisfying* $|\bar{J}| = k$, *and for some* $z \in \{\pm 1\}^{|\bar{J}|}$. *Then h is the linear character function* $\chi_{\bar{J}}$ *or* $-\chi_{\bar{J}}$.

Remark 4. This claim still holds even if we replace the k-homogeneous constraint by $\mathsf{W}^{<k}[h] = 0$.

Intuitively, it says that if there is a size-k restriction of a k-homogeneous Boolean function f such that the restriction function is the constant function 1, then the function f must be a linear function. We provide proof using the Martingale structure of restriction function (implied by Eqs. 1) as follows.

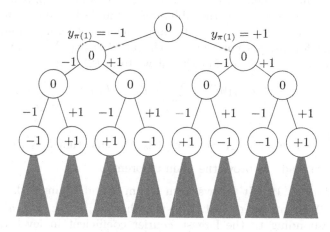

Fig. 3. The representation of a binary tree $\mathcal{T}_\pi$ of depth n with respect to a permutation π, and $k = 3$. Any edge between depth d and depth $d + 1$ denotes $y_{\pi(d)} \in \{\pm 1\}$. We assign the value $\alpha_\emptyset = \widehat{h}(\emptyset) = \mathbb{E}[h(X)]$ to the root and the value $\alpha_v = \widehat{h}_{J_v|v}(\emptyset) \in [-1, 1]$ to the node v. The value of any node is the average of the values of its children. The constraint $\mathsf{W}^{<k}[h] = 0$ implies that the value of any node at depth $< k$ is 0. If some node at depth k has a non-zero value then h must be χ_S or $-\chi_S$ where $S = \{\pi(i)\}_{i=1}^k$.

Proof. First, let us introduce some notation. Corresponding to each permutation $\pi \colon [n] \to [n]$, we define a binary tree T_π of depth n (refer to Fig. 3) such that each edge between a node and its left child is labeled by -1 and other edges are labeled by 1. This allows us to address each node v at depth $t \in [n]$ with a string $v = v_1 v_2 \ldots v_t$ of length $|v| = t$ which is the string of labels assigned to the edges of the path from root to that node. We assign to a node $v = v_1 v_2 \ldots v_t$, the value $\alpha_v := \widehat{h}_{J_v | z}(\emptyset)$ where $z = v$ and $J_v = [n] \backslash \bar{J}_v$ where $\bar{J}_v = \{\pi(1), \pi(2), \ldots, \pi(t)\}$.

Martingale Property. According to Claim 5, $\alpha_v = \mathbb{E}[h(X)|Y = y]$ where y is the unique string for which $z_y = v, J_y = J_v$ i.e. $y_{\pi(1)} = v_1, \ldots, y_{\pi(t)} = v_t$ and $y_j = 0$ whenever $j \notin \{\pi(1), \ldots, \pi(t)\}$ (J_y, z_y are defined in Claim 5). Therefore, $\alpha_v = \frac{\alpha_u + \alpha_w}{2}$ whenever nodes u, w are children of v in the tree T_π, i.e. the values α_v (for all v) assigned to the nodes of T_π forms a Martingale.

Since $\mathsf{W}^{<k}[h] = 0$, for each $T \subseteq [n]$ of size $|T| < k$, $\widehat{h}(T) = 0$. Therefore, it follows from (2) that for each $\bar{J}_1$ of size $k - 1$, and for any π that $\bar{J}_1 = \{\pi(j)\}_{j=1}^{k-1}$ the following holds

$$\mathbb{E}_{v \in T_\pi : |v| = k-1} [\alpha_v^2] = \mathbb{E}[\widehat{h}_{J_1|v}(\emptyset)^2] = \sum_{T \subseteq \bar{J}_1} \widehat{h}(T)^2 = 0$$

$$\implies \alpha_v = 0 \quad \forall v \in T_\pi : |v| \leqslant k - 1 \qquad \text{(Due to Martingale property)}$$

Without of loss of generality, we assume that $\widehat{h}_{J|z}(\emptyset) = 1$. This means that for some π and some node u of length $|u| = k$, we have $\alpha_u = 1$. Let v represent the parent of u in T_π, then since $|v| = k - 1$, $\alpha_v = 0$, and by applying Martingale property, $\alpha_w = -1$ where w is the sibling of v. Similarly, we can show that the sibling of w in any other tree is 1. By applying this argument iteratively, one can argue that for any permutation π such that $\bar{J} = \{\pi(i)\}_{i=1}^k$, any $v \in T_\pi$ that $|v| = k$, we have $\alpha_v^2 = 1$. Therefore, it follows from (2) that:

$$1 = \mathbb{E}_{v \in T_\pi : |v| = k} [\alpha_v^2] = \mathbb{E}[\widehat{h}_{J|v}(\emptyset)^2] = \sum_{T \subseteq \bar{J}} \widehat{h}(T)^2 = \widehat{h}(\bar{J})^2 + \sum_{\substack{T \subseteq \bar{J} \\ |T| < k}} \widehat{h}(T)^2 = \widehat{h}(\bar{J})^2$$

which implies that $\widehat{h}(\bar{J}) = \pm 1$. So it must be the case that $h = \chi_{\bar{J}}$ or $h = -\chi_{\bar{J}}$.

Now we are ready to prove the main theorem.

Proof (of Theorem 10). It follows from Claim 5 and Claim 6 that $(\overline{T}h)(y) = \widehat{h}_{J_y|z_y}(\emptyset) = 0$ for any $y \in \{\pm 1, 0\}^n$ such that $|\bar{J}_y| < k$. Let y^* be the filtration corresponding to the largest Fourier coefficient in level k, i.e., $y^* = \operatorname{argmax}_{y : |\bar{J}_y| = k} |\widehat{h}_{J_y|z_y}(\emptyset)|$. First, observe that $\widehat{h}_{J_{y^*}|z_{y^*}}(\emptyset)$ must be non-zero because otherwise h is the constant function 0.

Next, we claim that $|\widehat{h}_{J_{y^*}|z_{y^*}}(\emptyset)| = 1$ if c is sufficiently small, which is chosen later. For the sake of contradiction, suppose it is not. We will show that

$$|(\overline{T}h)(y^*) - g(y^*)| = |\widehat{h}_{J_{y^*}|z_{y^*}}(\emptyset) - g(y^*)| \geqslant 1/2^{k-1}. \qquad (3)$$

Observe that the Boolean function $h_{J_y|z_y}$ has degree at most k since it is a restriction of a degree-k Boolean function. According to Lemma 1, $\widehat{h}_{J_{y^*}|z_{y^*}}(\emptyset)$ is an integer multiple of $1/2^{k-1}$. Since it is not equal to 0 or ± 1, it holds that $1/2^{k-1} \leqslant \left|\widehat{h}_{J_{y^*}|z_{y^*}}(\emptyset)\right| \leqslant 1 - 1/2^{k-1}$. Note that $g(y^*) \in \{\pm 1, 0\}$. Therefore, the inequality (3) must hold. Using the same idea as in the proof of Theorem 7 yields

$$\left\|\overline{T}h - g\right\|_1 \geqslant \frac{1}{2^{k-1}} \cdot \min\left(\left(\frac{1-\varepsilon}{2}\right)^D, \varepsilon^D\right).$$

Now, choose $c < \frac{1}{2^{k-1}} \cdot \min\left(\left(\frac{1-\varepsilon}{2}\right)^D, \varepsilon^D\right)$, then we have reach a contradiction. Thus, it must be the case that $\left|\widehat{h}_{J_{y^*}|z_{y^*}}(\emptyset)\right| = 1$. Applying Claim 11 for the k-homogeneous Boolean function h implies that h is a linear function.

5.2 Proof of the Rate Result

This section provides a proof of Theorem 4. It suffices to prove Claim 10. The following results are needed for the proof.

Claim 12. Let $f^{(1)}, f^{(2)}, h^{(1)}, h^{(2)} \colon \{\pm 1\}^n \to \{\pm 1\}$ be Boolean functions such that $\left\|f^{(1)} - h^{(1)}\right\|_1 \leqslant \delta_1$ and $\left\|f^{(2)} - h^{(2)}\right\|_1 \leqslant \delta_2$. Then, it holds that

$$\left\|f^{(1)} \cdot f^{(2)} - h^{(1)} \cdot h^{(2)}\right\|_1 \leqslant \delta_1 + \delta_2.$$

Proposition 5. $\mathsf{BES}(\varepsilon') \sqsubseteq^0_{f,g} \mathsf{BES}(\varepsilon)^{\otimes n}$ if and only if (1) $(1 - \varepsilon') = (1 - \varepsilon)^k$, for some $k \in \mathbb{N}$, (2) f is a linear Boolean function $\sigma \cdot \chi_S$ for some size-k subset S of $[n]$, and (3) $g(y) = \sigma \cdot \prod_{i \in S} y_i$, where $\sigma \in \{\pm 1\}$.

Proof (of Claim 10). The notation $f \approx \widetilde{f}$ means that f and $\widetilde{f}$ are close in which the closeness is always $\mathsf{poly}(\nu)$. The notation $\mathsf{poly}(\nu)$ is always means that the constant in the polynomial is zero and all other coefficients depend only on $\varepsilon, \varepsilon'$. Let $1 \leqslant i < j \leqslant m$. Recall that $\widetilde{f}^{(i)}_{ij} \| \widetilde{f}^{(j)}_{ij}$ and $\widetilde{g}^{(i)}_{ij} \| \widetilde{g}^{(j)}_{ij}$ is the deterministic functions obtained by derandomizing the SNIS $\mathsf{BES}(\varepsilon')^{\otimes 2} \sqsubseteq^\nu_{f^{(i)} \| f^{(j)}, g^{(i)} \| g^{(j)}} \mathsf{BES}(\varepsilon)^{\otimes n}$. By Theorem 1, $\widetilde{f}^{(i)}_{ij}$ is close to $f^{(j)}$ and $\widetilde{f}^{(j)}_{ij}$ is close to $f^{(j)}$. By the feasibility result, $\widetilde{f}^{(i)}_{ij}$ is close to some k-linear function $f^{*\,(i)}_{ij}$. The relation between these function can be summarized as $f^{*\,(i)}_{ij} \approx \widetilde{f}^{(i)}_{ij} \approx f^{(i)}$.

Next, for any $j' \neq j$, a similar argument also yields $f^{*\,(i)}_{ij'} \approx \widetilde{f}^{(i)}_{ij'} \approx f^{(i)}$. By a simple application of triangle inequalities, it holds that $f^{*\,(i)}_{ij} \approx f^{*\,(i)}_{ij'}$. Now, using the fact that both $f^{*\,(i)}_{ij}$ and $f^{*\,(i)}_{ij'}$ are k-linear functions, we can conclude that they must be the same when ν is chosen sufficiently small because if they are different they are constant far apart (the constant is at least 1). Therefore, it holds that $f^{*\,(i)}_{ij} = f^{*\,(i)}_{ij'}$ for every distinct triple $i, j, j' \in [m]$. According to

Proposition 5, there is a unique $g_{ij}^{*\,(i)}$ such that $\mathsf{BES}(\varepsilon') \sqsubseteq^0_{f_{ij}^{*\,(i)}, g_{ij}^{*\,(i)}} \mathsf{BES}(\varepsilon)^{\otimes n}$.
By Claim 9, $g_{ij}^{*\,(i)}$ is close to $\widetilde{g}_{ij}^{(i)}$, which is also close to $g^{(i)}$. With a similar argument, one conclude that $g_{ij}^{*\,(i)} = g_{ij'}^{*\,(i)}$ for every distinct triple $i, j, j' \in [m]$.

Represent $f^{*\,(i)} := f_{ij}^{*\,(i)}$ and $g^{*\,(i)} := g_{ij}^{*\,(i)}$ for any $j \neq i$. By sequential composition, we have $\mathsf{BES}(\varepsilon'') \sqsubseteq^\nu_{\widetilde{f}_{ij}^{(i)} \cdot \widetilde{f}_{ij}^{(j)},\, \widetilde{g}_{ij}^{(i)} \cdot \widetilde{g}_{ij}^{(i)}} \mathsf{BES}(\varepsilon)^{\otimes n}$ where $(1-\varepsilon'') = (1-\varepsilon')^2 = (1-\varepsilon)^{2k}$. Note that $f^{*\,(i)} \approx \widetilde{f}_{ij}^{(i)}$ and $f^{*\,(j)} \approx \widetilde{f}_{ij}^{(j)}$. Therefore, it follows from Claim 12 that $f^{*\,(i)} \cdot f^{*\,(j)} \approx \widetilde{f}_{ij}^{(i)} \cdot \widetilde{f}_{ij}^{(j)}$. Similarly, $g^{*\,(i)} \cdot g^{*\,(j)} \approx \widetilde{g}_{ij}^{(i)} \cdot \widetilde{g}_{ij}^{(j)}$. By triangle inequality, we have $\mathsf{BES}(\varepsilon'') \sqsubseteq^{\mathsf{poly}(\nu)}_{f^{*\,(i)} \cdot f^{*\,(j)},\, g^{*\,(i)} \cdot g^{*\,(j)}} \mathsf{BES}(\varepsilon)^{\otimes n}$. This implies that $f^{*\,(i)} \cdot f^{*\,(j)}$ is $\mathsf{poly}(\lambda)(\nu)$-close to a $2k$-homogeneous function. Next, we argue that, in fact, $\mathsf{BES}(\varepsilon'') \sqsubseteq^0_{f^{*\,(i)} \cdot f^{*\,(j)},\, g^{*\,(i)} \cdot g^{*\,(j)}} \mathsf{BES}(\varepsilon)^{\otimes n}$, and the input supports of $f^{*\,(i)}$ and $f^{*\,(j)}$ are disjoint. For the sake of contradiction suppose that the input supports of $f^{*\,(i)}$ intersects the input supports of $f^{*\,(j)}$. Then $f^{*\,(i)} \cdot f^{*\,(j)}$ is a $< 2k$-linear function that is a contradiction with the requirement that it is close to a $2k$-homogeneous function. Therefore, it must hold that the input supports of $f^{*\,(i)}$ and $f^{*\,(j)}$ are disjoint for every distinct i, j. Note that the domain of $f^{*\,(i)}$ is still $\{\pm 1\}^n$ for every $i \in [m]$. Consequently, we have $mk \leqslant n$.

6   Technical Overview: BSS from BSS Samples

We outline the proof of Theorem 5 and Theorem 6 below.

Feasibility Outline. Consider a randomized SNIS $\mathsf{BSS}(\varepsilon') \sqsubseteq^\nu_{f,g} \mathsf{BSS}(\varepsilon)^{\otimes n}$, where $\varepsilon, \varepsilon' \in (0,1)$. Using Proposition 1, we can, without loss of generality, assume that f and g are deterministic functions. Therefore, we have $f \colon \{\pm 1\}^n \to \{\pm 1\}$ and $g \colon \{\pm 1\}^n \to \{\pm 1\}$. Define $\rho = (1 - 2\varepsilon)$ and $\rho' = (1 - 2\varepsilon')$.

Step 1: Algebraization of security. We show that simulation-based SNIS definition is qualitatively equivalent to the algebraized definition of SNIS.

Claim 13 (BSS-BSS Algebraization of Security). *For any $\varepsilon, \varepsilon' \in (0, 1/2)$, the following statements hold.*

1. *If* $\mathsf{BSS}(\varepsilon') \sqsubseteq^\nu_{f,g} \mathsf{BSS}(\varepsilon)^{\otimes n}$, *then* $\mathbb{E}[f] \leqslant \nu$, $\mathbb{E}[g] \leqslant \nu$, $\|\mathsf{T}_\rho f - \rho' g\|_1 \leqslant 4\nu$, *and* $\|\mathsf{T}_\rho g - \rho' f\|_1 \leqslant 4\nu$.
2. *If* $\mathbb{E}[f] \leqslant \nu$, $\mathbb{E}[g] \leqslant \nu$, $\|\mathsf{T}_\rho f - \rho' g\|_1 \leqslant \nu$, *and* $\|\mathsf{T}_\rho g - \rho' f\|_1 \leqslant \nu$, *then* $\mathsf{BSS}(\varepsilon') \sqsubseteq^{2\nu}_{f,g} \mathsf{BSS}(\varepsilon)^{\otimes n}$.

We remark that the Markov and the adjoint Markov operators associated with $\mathsf{BSS}(\varepsilon)^{\otimes n}$ are both identical to the noise operator T_ρ.

Step 2: Approximate eigenvector problem. Focusing on the reduction function and the guarantees (a) $\|\overline{\mathsf{T}} f - g\|_1 \leqslant 4\nu$, and (b) $\|\mathsf{T} g - \rho' f\|_1 \leqslant 4\nu$, we obtain the following result.

Claim 14 ("Noisy Close-to-Scaling" Constraint). *If* $\mathsf{BSS}(\varepsilon') \sqsubseteq^\nu_{f,g}$ $\mathsf{BSS}(\varepsilon)^{\otimes n}$, *then it holds that* $\left\|\mathsf{T}_\rho \mathsf{T}_\rho f - \rho'^2 f\right\|_1 = \left\|\mathsf{T}_{\rho^2} f - \rho'^2 f\right\|_1 \leqslant 8\nu$.

Step 3: Homogeneous property. There are two cases to consider. If $\rho' \notin \{\rho, \rho^2, \ldots\}$, then the reduction is constant insecure. However, if $\rho' = \rho^k$, then the reduction function must be close to a k-homogeneous D-junta Boolean function f^* (using Claim 3). Observe that when $\nu = 0$, then $f = g$ is a k-homogeneous function. In fact, any k-homogeneous Boolean function $f = g$ satisfies the algebraic security definition of SNIS perfectly when $\rho' = \rho^k$. Section 2.6 shows that such functions are related to special types of distance-invariant codes. Once we conclude that f is close to a k-homogeneous f^*, we can argue that g is also close to $g^* := f^*$ and that f^*, g^* witness a perfect SNIS of $\mathsf{BSS}(\varepsilon')$ from $\mathsf{BSS}(\varepsilon)$ samples. The following claim formalizes the argument.

Claim 15 *Suppose* $\mathsf{BSS}(\varepsilon') \sqsubseteq_{f,g}^{\nu} \mathsf{BSS}(\varepsilon)^{\otimes n}$*, where* $(1 - 2\varepsilon') = (1 - 2\varepsilon)^k$ *for some* $k \in \mathbb{N}$*, and* $h \colon \{\pm 1\}^n \to \{\pm 1\}$ *is a k-homogeneous Boolean function satisfying* $\|f - h\|_1 \leqslant \delta$*. Then, it holds that* $\mathsf{BSS}(\varepsilon') \sqsubseteq_{h,h}^{0} \mathsf{BSS}(\varepsilon)^{\otimes n}$ *and* $\|g - h\|_1 \leqslant 4\nu + \delta$*.*

Rate Outline. For reduction among BSS samples, we only prove a rate result for *perfect* SNIS. Consider a randomized SNIS $\mathsf{BSS}(\varepsilon')^{\otimes m} \sqsubseteq_{f,g}^{0} \mathsf{BSS}(\varepsilon)^{\otimes n}$, where $(1 - 2\varepsilon') = (1 - 2\varepsilon)^k$ and $k \in \mathbb{N}$. By Proposition 2 (the sample-preserving derandomization for perfect SNIS), we can assume, without loss of generality, that f, g are deterministic. For $(1 - 2\varepsilon'') = (1 - 2\varepsilon')^m$, there is a (deterministic) linear construction realizing $\mathsf{BSS}(\varepsilon'') \sqsubseteq_{f',g'}^{0} \mathsf{BSS}(\varepsilon')^{\otimes m}$. By the sequential composition of these two SNIS, we get a new SNIS $\mathsf{BSS}(\varepsilon'') \sqsubseteq^{0} \mathsf{BSS}(\varepsilon)^{\otimes n}$, where $(1 - 2\varepsilon'') = (1 - 2\varepsilon')^m = (1 - 2\varepsilon)^{mk}$. The reduction functions of this new SNIS must be mk-homogeneous; consequently, $mk \leqslant n$.

References

1. Agarwal, P., Narayanan, V., Pathak, S., Prabhakaran, M., Prabhakaran, V., Rehan, M.A.: Secure non-interactive reduction and spectral analysis of correlations. To appear at EUROCRYPT 2022 (2022)
2. Agrawal, S., et al.: Cryptography from one-way communication: on completeness of finite channels. In: Moriai, S., Wang, H. (eds.) ASIACRYPT 2020, Part III. LNCS, vol. 12493, pp. 653–685. Springer, Cham (2020). https://doi.org/10.1007/978-3-030-64840-4_22
3. Ahlswede, R., Gács, P.: Spreading of sets in product spaces and hypercontraction of the Markov operator. Ann. Probab. **4**, 925–939 (1976)
4. Beaver, D.: Efficient multiparty protocols using circuit randomization. In: Feigenbaum, J. (ed.) CRYPTO 1991. LNCS, vol. 576, pp. 420–432. Springer, Heidelberg (1992). https://doi.org/10.1007/3-540-46766-1_34
5. Beigi, S., Gohari, A.: On the duality of additivity and tensorization. In: 2015 IEEE International Symposium on Information Theory (ISIT), pp. 2381–2385. IEEE (2015)
6. Beimel, A., Ishai, Y., Kumaresan, R., Kushilevitz, E.: On the cryptographic complexity of the worst functions. In: Lindell, Y. (ed.) TCC 2014. LNCS, vol. 8349, pp. 317–342. Springer, Heidelberg (2014). https://doi.org/10.1007/978-3-642-54242-8_14

7. Beimel, A., Malkin, T.: A quantitative approach to reductions in secure computation. In: Naor, M. (ed.) TCC 2004. LNCS, vol. 2951, pp. 238–257. Springer, Heidelberg (2004). https://doi.org/10.1007/978-3-540-24638-1_14

8. Ben-David, A., Nisan, N., Pinkas, B.: FairplayMP: a system for secure multi-party computation. In: Ning, P., Syverson, P.F., Jha, S. (eds.) ACM CCS 2008, pp. 257–266. ACM Press (October 2008)

9. Bogdanov, A., Mossel, E.: On extracting common random bits from correlated sources. IEEE Trans. Inf. Theory **57**(10), 6351–6355 (2011)

10. Borell, C.: Positivity improving operators and hypercontractivity. Mathematische Zeitschrift **180**(3), 225–234 (1982)

11. Boyle, E., Couteau, G., Gilboa, N., Ishai, Y., Kohl, L., Scholl, P.: Efficient pseudorandom correlation generators: silent OT extension and more. In: Boldyreva, A., Micciancio, D. (eds.) CRYPTO 2019, Part III. LNCS, vol. 11694, pp. 489–518. Springer, Cham (2019). https://doi.org/10.1007/978-3-030-26954-8_16

12. Boyle, E., Couteau, G., Gilboa, N., Ishai, Y., Kohl, L., Scholl, P.: Efficient pseudorandom correlation generators from Ring-LPN. In: Micciancio, D., Ristenpart, T. (eds.) CRYPTO 2020, Part II. LNCS, vol. 12171, pp. 387–416. Springer, Cham (2020). https://doi.org/10.1007/978-3-030-56880-1_14

13. Chan, S.O., Mossel, E., Neeman, J.: On extracting common random bits from correlated sources on large alphabets. IEEE Trans. Inf. Theory **60**(3), 1630–1637 (2014)

14. Crépeau, C.: Equivalence between two flavours of oblivious transfers. In: Pomerance, C. (ed.) CRYPTO 1987. LNCS, vol. 293, pp. 350–354. Springer, Heidelberg (1988). https://doi.org/10.1007/3-540-48184-2_30

15. Crépeau, C., Kilian, J.: Achieving oblivious transfer using weakened security assumptions (extended abstract). In: 29th FOCS, pp. 42–52. IEEE Computer Society Press (October 1988)

16. Crépeau, C., Kilian, J.: Weakening security assumptions and oblivious transfer. In: Goldwasser, S. (ed.) CRYPTO 1988. LNCS, vol. 403, pp. 2–7. Springer, New York (1990). https://doi.org/10.1007/0-387-34799-2_1

17. Damgård, I., Pastro, V., Smart, N., Zakarias, S.: Multiparty computation from somewhat homomorphic encryption. In: Safavi-Naini, R., Canetti, R. (eds.) CRYPTO 2012. LNCS, vol. 7417, pp. 643–662. Springer, Heidelberg (2012). https://doi.org/10.1007/978-3-642-32009-5_38

18. De, A., Mossel, E., Neeman, J.: Non interactive simulation of correlated distributions is decidable. In: Czumaj, A. (ed.) 29th SODA, pp. 2728–2746. ACM-SIAM (January 2018)

19. Dinur, I., Filmus, Y., Harsha, P.: Low degree almost Boolean functions are sparse juntas. Electron. Colloquium Comput. Complex. **24**, 180 (2017)

20. Dodis, Y., Ostrovsky, R., Reyzin, L., Smith, A.D.: Fuzzy extractors: how to generate strong keys from biometrics and other noisy data. SIAM J. Comput. **38**(1), 97–139 (2008)

21. Gács, P., Körner, J.: Common information is far less than mutual information. Probl. Control Inf. Theory **2**(2), 149–162 (1973)

22. Garg, S., Ishai, Y., Kushilevitz, E., Ostrovsky, R., Sahai, A.: Cryptography with one-way communication. In: Gennaro, R., Robshaw, M. (eds.) CRYPTO 2015, Part II. LNCS, vol. 9216, pp. 191–208. Springer, Heidelberg (2015). https://doi.org/10.1007/978-3-662-48000-7_10

23. Gertner, Y., Kannan, S., Malkin, T., Reingold, O., Viswanathan, M.: The relationship between public key encryption and oblivious transfer. In: 41st FOCS, pp. 325–335. IEEE Computer Society Press (November 2000)

24. Ghazi, B., Kamath, P., Raghavendra, P.: Dimension reduction for polynomials over Gaussian space and applications. In: Servedio, R.A. (ed.) 33rd Computational Complexity Conference, CCC 2018, June 22–24, 2018, San Diego, CA, USA, volume 102 of LIPIcs, pp. 28: 1–28: 37. Schloss Dagstuhl - Leibniz Center for "u r Computer Science (2018)

25. Ghazi, B., Kamath, P., Sudan, M.: Decidability of non-interactive simulation of joint distributions. In: Dinur, I. (ed.) 57th FOCS, pp. 545–554. IEEE Computer Society Press (October 2016)

26. Goldreich, O., Micali, S., Wigderson, A.: How to play any mental game or a completeness theorem for protocols with honest majority. In: Aho, A. (ed.) 19th ACM STOC, pp. 218–229. ACM Press (May 1987)

27. Kamath, S., Anantharam, V.: Non-interactive simulation of joint distributions: the hirschfeld-gebelein-rényi maximal correlation and the hypercontractivity ribbon. In: 2012 50th Annual Allerton Conference on Communication, Control, and Computing (Allerton), pp. 1057–1064. IEEE (2012)

28. Kamath, S., Anantharam, V.: On non-interactive simulation of joint distributions. IEEE Trans. Inf. Theory **62**(6), 3419–3435 (2016)

29. Khorasgani, H.A., Maji, H.K., Nguyen, H.H.: Secure non-interactive simulation: feasibility & rate. Cryptology ePrint Archive, Report 2020/252 (2020). https://ia.cr/2020/252

30. Kilian, J.: More general completeness theorems for secure two-party computation. In: 32nd ACM STOC, pp. 316–324. ACM Press (May 2000)

31. Kindler, G.: Property Testing PCP. Ph.D. thesis, Tel-Aviv University (2002)

32. Kindler, G., Safra, S.: Noise-resistant Boolean functions are juntas. preprint (2002)

33. Kraschewski, D., Maji, H.K., Prabhakaran, M., Sahai, A.: A full characterization of completeness for two-party randomized function evaluation. In: Nguyen, P.Q., Oswald, E. (eds.) EUROCRYPT 2014. LNCS, vol. 8441, pp. 659–676. Springer, Heidelberg (2014). https://doi.org/10.1007/978-3-642-55220-5_36

34. MacWilliams, F.J., Sloane, N.J.A.: The Theory of Error Correcting Codes, vol. 16. Elsevier, Amsterdam (1977)

35. Mahmoody, M., Maji, H.K., Prabhakaran, M.: Limits of random oracles in secure computation. In: Naor, M. (ed.) ITCS 2014, pp. 23–34. ACM (January 2014)

36. Mahmoody, M., Maji, H.K., Prabhakaran, M.: On the power of public-key encryption in secure computation. In: Lindell, Y. (ed.) TCC 2014. LNCS, vol. 8349, pp. 240–264. Springer, Heidelberg (2014). https://doi.org/10.1007/978-3-642-54242-8_11

37. Maji, H.K., Prabhakaran, M., Rosulek, M.: Complexity of multi-party computation functionalities. In: Prabhakaran, M., Sahai, A. (eds.) Secure Multi-Party Computation, volume 10 of Cryptology and Information Security Series, pp. 249–283. IOS Press (2013)

38. Malkhi, D., Nisan, N., Pinkas, B., Sella, Y.: Fairplay - secure two-party computation system. In: Blaze, M. (ed.) USENIX Security 2004, pp. 287–302. USENIX Association (August 2004)

39. Mossel, E.: Gaussian bounds for noise correlation of functions and tight analysis of long codes. In: 49th FOCS, pp. 156–165. IEEE Computer Society Press (October 2008)

40. Mossel, E., O'Donnell, R.: Coin flipping from a cosmic source: on error correction of truly random bits. Random Struct. Algorithms **26**(4), 418–436 (2005)

41. Mossel, E., O'Donnell, R., Regev, O., Steif, J.E., Sudakov, B.: Non-interactive correlation distillation, inhomogeneous Markov chains, and the reverse Bonami-Beckner inequality. Israel J. Math. **154**(1), 299–336 (2006)

42. Mossel, E., Oleszkiewicz, K., Sen, A.: On reverse hypercontractivity. Geom. Funct. Anal. **23**(3), 1062–1097 (2013)

43. Nair, C., Wang, Y.N.: Reverse hypercontractivity region for the binary erasure channel. In: 2017 IEEE International Symposium on Information Theory (ISIT), pp. 938–942. IEEE (2017)

44. Narayanan, V., Prabhakaran, M., Prabhakaran, V.M.: Zero-communication reductions. In: Pass, R., Pietrzak, K. (eds.) TCC 2020, Part III. LNCS, vol. 12552, pp. 274–304. Springer, Cham (2020). https://doi.org/10.1007/978-3-030-64381-2_10

45. Nielsen, J.B., Nordholt, P.S., Orlandi, C., Burra, S.S.: A new approach to practical active-secure two-party computation. In: Safavi-Naini, R., Canetti, R. (eds.) CRYPTO 2012. LNCS, vol. 7417, pp. 681–700. Springer, Heidelberg (2012). https://doi.org/10.1007/978-3-642-32009-5_40

46. O'Donnell, R.: Analysis of Boolean Functions. Cambridge University Press, Cambridge (2014)

47. Rabin, M.O.: How to exchange secrets by oblivious transfer. Technical Memo TR-81 (1981)

48. Rabin, M.O.: How to exchange secrets with oblivious transfer. Cryptology ePrint Archive, Report 2005/187 (2005). https://eprint.iacr.org/2005/187

49. Witsenhausen, H.S.: On sequences of pairs of dependent random variables. SIAM J. Appl. Math. **28**(1), 100–113 (1975)

50. Wyner, A.: The common information of two dependent random variables. IEEE Trans. Inf. Theory **21**(2), 163–179 (1975)

51. Yang, K.: On the (im)possibility of non-interactive correlation distillation. In: Farach-Colton, M. (ed.) LATIN 2004. LNCS, vol. 2976, pp. 222–231. Springer, Heidelberg (2004). https://doi.org/10.1007/978-3-540-24698-5_26

52. Yao, A.C.-C.: Protocols for secure computations (extended abstract). In: 23rd FOCS, pp. 160–164. IEEE Computer Society Press (November 1982)

53. Yin, Z., Park, Y.: Hypercontractivity, maximal correlation and non-interactive simulation (2014)

Secure Non-interactive Reduction and Spectral Analysis of Correlations

Pratyush Agarwal[1](✉), Varun Narayanan[2](✉), Shreya Pathak[1], Manoj Prabhakaran[1], Vinod M. Prabhakaran[3]®, and Mohammad Ali Rehan[1]

[1] Indian Institute of Technology Bombay, Mumbai, India
{pratyush,shreyapathak,mp,alirehan}@cse.iitb.ac.in
[2] Technion, Haifa, Israel
varunnkv@gmail.com
[3] Tata Institute of Fundamental Research, Mumbai, India
vinodmp@tifr.res.in

Abstract. Correlated pairs of random variables are a central concept in information-theoretically secure cryptography. Secure reductions between different correlations have been studied, and completeness results are known. Further, the complexity of such reductions is intimately connected with circuit complexity and efficiency of locally decodable codes. As such, making progress on these complexity questions faces strong barriers. Motivated by this, in this work, we study a restricted form of secure reductions—namely, Secure *Non Interactive* Reductions (SNIR)—which is still closely related to the original problem, and establish several fundamental results and relevant techniques for it.

We uncover striking connections between SNIR and linear algebraic properties of correlations. Specifically, we define the spectrum of a correlation, and show that a target correlation has a SNIR to a source correlation only if the spectrum of the latter contains the entire spectrum of the former. We also establish a "mirroring lemma" that shows an unexpected symmetry between the two parties in a SNIR, when viewed through the lens of spectral analysis. We also use cryptographic insights and elementary linear algebraic analysis to fully characterize the role of common randomness as well as local randomness in SNIRs. We employ these results to resolve several fundamental questions about SNIRs, and to define future directions.

V. Narayanan—Supported by the Department of Atomic Energy, India project RTI4001, ERC Project NTSC (742754) and ISF Grants 1709/14 & 2774/20.
M. Prabhakaran—Supported by a Ramanujan Fellowship and Joint Indo-Israel Project DST/INT/ISR/P-16/2017 of Dept. of Science and Technology, India.
V. M. Prabhakaran—Supported by the Department of Atomic Energy, India project RTI4001, and Science & Engineering Research Board, India project MTR/2020/000308.

O. Dunkelman and S. Dziembowski (Eds.): EUROCRYPT 2022, LNCS 13277, pp. 797–827, 2022.
https://doi.org/10.1007/978-3-031-07082-2_28

1   Introduction

Correlated pairs of random variables—or correlations, for short—are central to information-theoretic cryptography. In particular, 2-party function evaluation can be *securely reduced* to sampling from such a correlation, with information-theoretic security, against passive or active corruption [16,17,20,24]. Among other things, such a reduction defines an important *cryptographic complexity* measure of a function [6,7,25–27] – namely, the number of samples of a correlation that need to be used in a secure 2-party computation protocol for the function[1]. Proving lower bounds for cryptographic complexity is a difficult problem, thanks to its implications to circuit complexity and locally decodable codes; even the existence of functions with super-linear cryptographic complexity remains open. As such, it is prudent to approach cryptographic complexity gently, through simplified problems and models. Taking a cue from circuit complexity, where simpler circuit models like AC^0 have served as a platform for developing new ideas and sophisticated techniques, here we consider a simplified model of secure *non-interactive* reductions (SNIR). Note that, without communication, it is impossible to *compute* non-trivial functions which take inputs from both parties;[2] hence we only consider the problem of *sampling* from a target correlation. In a non-interactive reduction of a target correlation D to a source correlation C, two parties receive correlated randomness from the source C; then they carry out a local computation (possibly randomized) and produce their outputs, which are to be jointly distributed according to D. The security requirement, informally, requires that a party should learn nothing more about the other party's output than is revealed by its own *output*, irrespective of what it receives from the source correlation.

Apart from being a simpler model to analyze, SNIR in fact isolates one of two components of an interactive secure reduction. A secure reduction can be viewed as consisting of two parts: Firstly, an interaction phase transforms the views of the two parties arbitrarily, subject only to the constraints of protocols (there is no element of security here); secondly, a local derivation step is used to transform the views resulting from this interaction to the outputs. The security condition solely applies to this second local derivation step. Thus the feasibility of an (interactive) secure reduction from D to C splits into the question of whether there exists a correlation C' such that (i) C' is the distribution of the views at the end of an interaction between the parties starting with C, and (ii) D has a SNIR to C'.

SNIR is also a natural and strictly stronger variant of a well-studied model in information-theory, namely, (non-secure) non-interactive reduction – or *non-interactive simulation* as it is more commonly known – which has attracted a

---

[1] The choice of the exact correlation is not crucial and can be replaced by any finite complete functionality, without altering the complexity beyond constant factors [25].

[2] There does exist an alternate model of *Zero Communication Reductions* which allows non-interactive function computation conditioned on a predicate [27]. But here we consider the standard model of secure 2-party computation, except for the restriction of being non-interactive.

significant amount of research in both information-theory and computer science literature [4,13,15,21,29–31].

Our Contributions. We introduce a spectral analysis toolkit for (statistically) secure non-interactive reductions (SNIR), and use it to resolve several fundamental questions about SNIR.

As part of the toolkit, we derive the following results. The results refer to the *spectrum of a correlation,* Λ_C which we define as the multi-set of singular values of the *correlation operator* associated with the correlation C (see Sect. 2.2). Also they deal with "non-redundant" correlations (since, as we shall see, redundancies – which can be introduced or removed using local operations – do not have any effect on the existence of SNIRs).

Suppose there is a statistical SNIR, that reduces a non-redundant correlation D to a correlation C with ϵ error, then:

- D has a statistical SNIR to C using *deterministic* protocols (Lemma 7).
- $\Lambda_D \subseteq \Lambda_{C^{\otimes \ell}}$ for some $\ell \in \mathbb{N}$ (Theorem 4).
- the "spectral representation" of the SNIR satisfies a symmetry property, that we term *mirroring* (Theorem 5).

Furthermore, if D does not have a statistical SNIR to C, then it has no statistical SNIR to C even when both parties have access to unlimited common randomness (Theorem 6).

These general results can in turn be used to derive a variety of results. In particular, we show that there is *no complete correlation* for SNIR (Theorem 7). We also obtain a full characterization of all the parameter changes that are possible via SNIR for two correlation classes of interest, namely *doubly symmetric binary correlation* BSC (Theorem 8) and *binary erasure correlation* BEC (Theorem 9). For OLE correlations over finite fields, we obtain a necessary condition for SNIR (Theorem 10). We also derive results (Theorem 11 and Theorem 12) implied by impossibility results in the one-way secure computation model [14], that BEC and *oblivious transfer correlation* do not have a SNIR to BSC; we remark that the proof in [14], based on isoperimetric inequalities, yields a quantitatively weaker form that leaves open the possibility of inverse-polynomial security.

Finally, we also relate SNIR to secure (interactive) reductions of a correlation D to another C. Recall from the discussion earlier that a secure interactive protocol for D includes a SNIR from D to the view of the two parties at the end of the interaction. In fact, a stronger statement is possible: We show that when a correlation involves common information (as is the case with the view after interaction, which includes the transcript – and possibly more – as common information), then D should have a SNIR to one of the correlations obtained from C conditioned on a value for the common information. (Lemma 4 and Lemma 12). This motivates a challenging (non-cryptographic) problem of characterizing the spectrum of correlations that can be obtained as the view of an interaction starting with a given correlation C. We leave this as an open problem.

Related Work. As mentioned above, (interactive) secure reductions and non-interactive (non-secure) reductions have both been widely studied. In an independent, concurrent work Khorasgani et al. [22,23] also studied SNIRs. While these works also followed a linear-algebraic approach, their motivations and results were different. In particular, their results were mostly restricted to studying specific simple target correlations—the binary symmetric and binary erasure correlations—which admitted the use of Fourier analysis of boolean functions. In contrast, driven by the connections to circuit complexity lower bounds, we derive results that apply to arbitrary target correlations, including those which may have a high circuit complexity. On the other hand, for the simpler target correlations, [22,23] consider more fine-grained questions related to the rate of reduction, and the decidability of reduction to other correlations. We do not address these problems. Boyle et al. [9,10] introduced *pseudorandom correlation generators* which achieve the same objective against computationally bounded adversaries.

While perhaps not explicitly studied previously, the notions of a correlation operator and the spectrum of a correlation that are defined in this work have been implicitly present in spectral graph theory (by representing a correlation as a bipartite graph). An important element of the spectrum of a correlation was defined as maximal correlation by [30] for proving a seminal result of (non-secure) interactive reductions; in [2], it was observed that this proof can be cast in the language of spectral graph theory.

2   Technical Overview

Here we present an overview of the tools that we develop to derive impossibility results for SNIRs. Our starting point is a linear-algebraic formulation of a SNIR. For this, a distribution over $\mathcal{X} \times \mathcal{Y}$ is represented by a $|\mathcal{X}| \times |\mathcal{Y}|$ matrix whose entry with row indexed by $x \in \mathcal{X}$ and column indexed by $y \in \mathcal{Y}$ is simply the probability $\Pr[(x, y)]$ of Alice getting x and Bob getting y. In the following, we consider a SNIR from a *target* correlation represented by a matrix $D \in \mathbb{R}^{m_D \times n_D}$ to a *source* correlation represented by a matrix $C \in \mathbb{R}^{m_C \times n_C}$. Restricting here to the case of perfect security, a SNIR translates to a pair of stochastic "protocol" matrices (A, B) representing Alice and Bob's actions (mapping a symbol from the source to a symbol in the target), and a pair of "simulation" matrices (U, V) such that

$$A^\mathsf{T} C B = D \qquad A^\mathsf{T} C = D V \qquad C B = U^\mathsf{T} D. \tag{1}$$

The first identity is a straightforward linear algebraic interpretation of the correctness of the protocol, while the next two capture the security against a corrupt Bob and a corrupt Alice, respectively, as linear algebraic constraints. These identities are proved in Theorem 3, more generally, for statistical SNIR. As we would be interested in allowing access to arbitrarily many copies of a given correlation C_0, one should interpret C as the tensor power $C_0^{\otimes \ell}$ for an arbitrarily large integer ℓ. (However, w.l.o.g. we may consider D to be a single copy of the correlation we are interested in obtaining. As such, when considering statistical security, we shall use the $O_D(\cdot)$ notation to indicate an upper bound that hides a factor that is a function of D alone.)

Once viewed linear algebraically, we start obtaining consequences, which may not be evident *a priori*, through a series of steps that combine cryptographic intuition with linear algebraic manipulation. For ease of exposition, first we describe these steps for a *perfect* SNIR where many of the delicate technicalities disappear. We shall also sometimes focus on the case when the *marginal distributions* of Alice's and Bob's side of the correlations are uniform.

2.1   Restricting to Non-redundant Correlations

Suppose two distinct symbols x_1, x_2 that Alice can obtain from D are such that conditioned on either, the distribution of the symbol obtained by Bob is the same. In this case, we may as well merge these two symbols into a single symbol, on obtaining which, Alice can probabilistically interpret it as x_1 or x_2 locally. We refer to the presence of such symbols, for either party, as *redundancy*. It is easily verified that for the purposes of secure sampling, every correlation is equivalent to a non-redundant correlation (obtained by merging groups of redundant symbols).

To understand the implications of having a SNIR from a non-redundant D to C, consider the following: Suppose Alice and Bob are given samples from D; then Alice outputs the value she got, but Bob locally samples an output based on the value he got as below.

- Bob's goal is that the joint distribution of what the two parties output should still correspond to D. The existence of a SNIR provides a way for Bob to do this: He first feeds the output from D to the *simulator* (V), to obtain a simulated view – i.e., his side of an output from C. The simulation guarantees that the joint distribution of Alice's output and Bob's view are as in a real execution of the protocol; now Bob applies his protocol (B) to the outcome of the simulation, to obtain his altered output.
- On the other hand, non-redundancy of D should imply – intuitively – that the only mapping Bob can use is the identity mapping.

Linear algebraically, the first statement corresponds to $DVB = A^\mathsf{T}CB = D$, and the latter is the assertion (which needs a proof) that, if D is non-redundant, then for any stochastic matrix X, $DX = D \Rightarrow X = I$. Taken together, this gives

$$VB = I, \qquad UA = I, \qquad (2)$$

where the second identity follows from the same argument with Alice's and Bob's roles reversed. Thus, the protocol must in fact invert the simulation. This is possible only if the protocol is *deterministic*, as applying a randomized strategy to the output of a process (namely, the simulation) cannot guarantee that the output will match the input to simulation. That is, the protocol (on each party's side) could be viewed as simply a partition of the alphabet of C, with symbols in each part being mapped to a different symbol in the alphabet of D. This tells us further that the simulation should simply distribute each D symbol back to C symbols according to their relative probabilities. When the marginal distribution for Alice (resp., Bob) from the correlations D and C are both uniform, this simplifies to

$$U = \frac{n_D}{n_C} A^{\mathsf{T}} \qquad \left(\text{resp., } V = \frac{m_D}{m_C} B^{\mathsf{T}} \right). \qquad (3)$$

An Eigenvalue Condition. Our first result is a necessary condition for SNIR in terms of the eigenvalues of matrices associated with the two correlations. Here, we first discuss the case of uniform marginal distributions and perfect security, followed by the important extensions to the general case.

Theorem 1 (Informal). *A uniform-marginal correlation with matrix $D \in \mathbb{R}^{m_D \times n_D}$ has an SNIR to a uniform-marginal correlation with matrix $C \in \mathbb{R}^{m_C \times n_C}$ only if all the eigenvalues of $m_D n_D D D^{\mathsf{T}}$ are also eigenvalues of $m_C n_C C C^{\mathsf{T}}$.*

Given our observations above, we have a short derivation of this result in the special case of uniform marginals. Using the two security conditions in (1) and the two equations in (3), we have

$$m_C n_C A^{\mathsf{T}} C C^{\mathsf{T}} = m_C n_C (DV) C^{\mathsf{T}} = m_D n_C D B^{\mathsf{T}} C^{\mathsf{T}}$$
$$= m_D n_C D (D^{\mathsf{T}} U) = m_D n_D D D^{\mathsf{T}} A^{\mathsf{T}}.$$

Now, suppose λ is an eigenvalue of the symmetric matrix $m_D n_D D D^{\mathsf{T}}$, with a corresponding eigenvector v. Then

$$(v^{\mathsf{T}} A^{\mathsf{T}}) \cdot m_C n_C \cdot C C^{\mathsf{T}} = v^{\mathsf{T}} (m_D n_D \cdot D D^{\mathsf{T}}) A^{\mathsf{T}} = \lambda v^{\mathsf{T}} A^{\mathsf{T}}.$$

Hence we conclude that λ is an eigenvalue of $m_C n_C \cdot C C^{\mathsf{T}}$ as well (with eigenvector Av).

2.2   Beyond Uniform Marginals: The Correlation Operator

So far, we represented a correlation of $\mathcal{X} \times \mathcal{Y}$ as a matrix M, with rows indexed by Alice's alphabet $\mathcal{X}$ and columns indexed by Bob's alphabet $\mathcal{Y}$, with $M_{x,y} = \Pr[(x, y)]$. However, when the marginal distributions of this correlation are not uniform, the above linear-algebraic arguments do not go through. This leads us to an alternate representation of a correlation in the form of what we call the **correlation operator**. It is a linear transformation defined by the matrix $\widetilde{M}$ as follows:[3]

$$\widetilde{M}_{x,y} = \frac{M_{x,y}}{\sqrt{a_x b_y}} \text{ where } a_x = \sum_{y' \in \mathcal{Y}} M_{x,y'} \text{ and } b_y = \sum_{x' \in \mathcal{X}} M_{x',y}.$$

---

[3] Here we use the convention that symbols with 0 probability are omitted from the alphabets $\mathcal{X}$ and $\mathcal{Y}$, so that all the marginal probabilities a_x and b_y are strictly positive.

A correlation operator transforms a $|\mathcal{Y}|$-dimensional (column) vector with entries of the form $q_y/\sqrt{b_y}$ into a $|\mathcal{X}|$-dimensional vector with entries of the form $p_x/\sqrt{a_x}$, where p denotes the conditional distribution of Alice's symbol according to M when Bob's symbol is conditioned to be according to q (i.e., $p_x = \sum_y q_y \Pr[x|y] = \sum_y q_y M_{x,y}/b_y$). The transpose of this operator carries out a similar transformation in the reverse direction. Here, note that the correlation operator operates on vectors with "normalized probabilities" in their respective vector spaces; the probabilities over $\mathcal{X}$ (resp. $\mathcal{Y}$) lie on the plane tangential to the unit sphere, touching it at $\sqrt{a}$ (resp. $\sqrt{b}$), since $\langle p/\sqrt{a}, \sqrt{a} \rangle = 1$ (and, $\langle q/\sqrt{b}, \sqrt{b} \rangle = 1$). The marginal distributions a and b themselves are represented by unit vectors ($\sqrt{a}$ and $\sqrt{b}$).

Clearly, the correlation operator and the marginal distributions together completely specify the correlation. But in fact, as the geometric interpretation above may suggest, the correlation operator encodes the marginal distribution as well.[4] Indeed, as we shall see, the direction in which the transformation is non-shrinking corresponds to the marginals in the respective vector spaces (unit vectors $\sqrt{a}, \sqrt{b}$); the action of the transformation on the vector space orthogonal to the marginal encodes the dependence component of the correlation.

Singular Value Decomposition (SVD). SVD provides us with a powerful tool to analyze the linear-algebraic properties of a correlation operator. Given an $m \times n$ distribution matrix M, we apply SVD to its correlation operator, to get

$$\widetilde{M} = \mathbf{\Psi}_M^\mathsf{T} \mathbf{\Sigma}_M \mathbf{\Phi}_M$$

where $\mathbf{\Sigma}_M$ is an $m \times n$ dimensional non-negative diagonal matrix, $\mathbf{\Psi}_M$ and $\mathbf{\Phi}_M$ are orthogonal matrices of dimensions $m \times m$ and $n \times n$, respectively (i.e., $\mathbf{\Psi}_M^{-1} = \mathbf{\Psi}_M^\mathsf{T}$ and $\mathbf{\Phi}_M^{-1} = \mathbf{\Phi}_M^\mathsf{T}$). It would be convenient to define *the spectrum* of M, $\mathbf{\Lambda}_M$ as the *multi-set* of singular values of $\widetilde{M}$ (i.e., the non-zero entries in $\mathbf{\Sigma}_M$).

Correlation Operator and Normalized Laplacian. A natural representation of a correlation M is in the form of a weighted bipartite graph G_M, with Alice's and Bob's alphabets forming the two vertex sets, and symbols x and y connected by an edge of weight $M_{x,y}$. (By our convention of omitting 0-probability symbols, there are no isolated vertices in G_M.) This representation allows one to use spectral graph theory to explore the correlation M. Indeed, the correlation operator $\widetilde{M}$ is closely related to the "Normalized Laplacian" $\mathcal{L}(G_M)$ of the bipartite graph described above. Specifically, from the definitions it follows

---

[4] There is a caveat: if the correlation involves common information – i.e., if it is over pairs that can be written as $((x,c),(y,c))$ where c indicates a piece of information available to both parties – then, the distribution of the common random variable itself is not captured by the correlation operator. But as we shall see, this component of the distribution can indeed be ignored when studying the feasibility of SNIRs.

that

$$\mathcal{L}(G_M) = I - \begin{bmatrix} & \widetilde{M} \\ \widetilde{M}^\mathsf{T} & \end{bmatrix}$$

Lemma 1. *For any correlation* $M \in \mathbb{R}^{m \times n}$, *the multi-set of eigenvalues of* $\mathcal{L}(G_M)$ *is given by* $\{1 \pm \sigma \mid \sigma \in \Lambda_M\} \cup \{\underbrace{1, \cdots, 1}_{\substack{m+n-2|\Lambda_M| \\ \text{times}}}\}$.

A formal proof of the lemma is deferred to the full version [1].

Using this connection, the basic properties of the spectrum of a correlation follow from well-known results in spectral graph theory [11]. In particular, we see that all the elements in the spectrum Λ_M lie in the range $[0, 1]$, and the largest one equals 1. The multiplicity of 1 in Λ_M is one, unless the correlation M involves non-trivial common information (i.e., multiple connected components in the bipartite graph G_M). This singular value corresponds to the transformations between unit vectors, $\sqrt{a}^\mathsf{T} \widetilde{M} = \sqrt{b}^\mathsf{T}$ and $\widetilde{M} \sqrt{b} = \sqrt{a}$. The second largest singular value, which indicates an upper bound on the extent to which M is not a product distribution of the marginals, has in fact been identified and used previously as *maximal correlation* by Witsenhausen in a seminal work that initiated the study of (non-secure) non-interactive reductions [30].

2.3 Spectral Protocols

Now we return to the question of generalizing Theorem 1 to correlations C and D whose marginals need not be uniform. A "spectral view" of SNIR, in terms of the correlation operators $\widetilde{C}$ and $\widetilde{D}$, and the spectra Λ_C and Λ_D provides us with just the right tools.

Given a SNIR (A, B) from D to C, we consider the singular value decompositions $\widetilde{C} = \Psi_C^\mathsf{T} \Sigma_C \Phi_C$ and $\widetilde{D} = \Psi_D^\mathsf{T} \Sigma_D \Phi_D$. Then, we can show that the linear algebraic conditions for correctness and privacy, originally formulated in the "probability domain," yields analogous conditions in the "spectral domain," where the protocols (A, B) are represented by their spectral counterparts, $(\widehat{A}, \widehat{B})$, defined as follows:

$$\widehat{A} = \Psi_C \, \Delta_{C^\mathsf{T}}^{1/2} \, A \, \Delta_{D^\mathsf{T}}^{-1/2} \, \Psi_D^\mathsf{T}, \qquad \widehat{B} = \Phi_C \, \Delta_C^{1/2} \, B \, \Delta_D^{-1/2} \, \Phi_D^\mathsf{T}.$$

Here, the notation Δ_M denotes a diagonal matrix with the vector $\mathbf{1}^\mathsf{T} M$ along its diagonal; note that $\widetilde{M} = \Delta_{M^\mathsf{T}}^{-1/2} M \Delta_M^{-1/2}$. The following lemma summarizes the properties of a SNIR, viewed in the spectral domain.

Lemma 2. *If* (A, B) *is a perfect SNIR from a non-redundant correlation* D *to a correlation* C, *then*

$$\widehat{A}^\mathsf{T} \Sigma_C \widehat{B} = \Sigma_D \quad \widehat{A}^\mathsf{T} \Sigma_C = \Sigma_D \widehat{B}^\mathsf{T} \quad \Sigma_C \widehat{B} = \widehat{A} \Sigma_D \quad \widehat{A}^\mathsf{T} \widehat{A} = I, \qquad \widehat{B}^\mathsf{T} \widehat{B} = I. \tag{4}$$

The lemma is formally proved in the full version [1]. The condition $\widehat{A}^\mathsf{T} \mathbf{\Sigma}_C \widehat{B} = \mathbf{\Sigma}_D$ is obtained by simply rearranging the linear algebraic conditions for correctness and privacy in the "probability domain" and using the definitions of $\widehat{A}, \widehat{B}, \mathbf{\Sigma}_C$ and $\mathbf{\Sigma}_D$. (It is also implied by the other equations.) To show that $\widehat{A}^\mathsf{T}\widehat{A}$ and $\widehat{B}^\mathsf{T}\widehat{B}$ are identity, we exploit the conditions $UA = I$ and $VB = I$, respectively, from (2). For the remaining two "privacy" conditions we use the generalization of (3) to the case of non-uniform marginals.

$$U = \mathbf{\Delta}_{D^\mathsf{T}}^{-1} A^\mathsf{T} \mathbf{\Delta}_{C^\mathsf{T}}, \qquad V = \mathbf{\Delta}_D^{-1} B^\mathsf{T} \mathbf{\Delta}_C. \qquad (5)$$

Compared to (1), the condition (4) in the "spectral domain" involves the diagonal matrices $\mathbf{\Sigma}_C$ and $\mathbf{\Sigma}_D$ instead of C and D. Further, it is devoid of simulators (U, V), which are replaced by $(\widehat{A}^\mathsf{T}, \widehat{B}^\mathsf{T})$. Further, $\widehat{A}$ and $\widehat{B}$ have orthonormal columns, rather than being stochastic and deterministic.

Spectral Criterion. The spectral formulation of the conditions for SNIR in Lemma 2 lead us to the following generalization of Theorem 1.

Theorem 2 (Informal). *A non-redundant correlation D has a perfect SNIR to C only if $\mathbf{\Lambda}_D \subseteq \mathbf{\Lambda}_C$ (as multi-sets).*

This result follows from the conditions in Lemma 2. Specifically, using the second and third conditions from (4), we have

$$\widehat{A}^\mathsf{T} \mathbf{\Sigma}_C \mathbf{\Sigma}_C^\mathsf{T} = \mathbf{\Sigma}_D \widehat{B}^\mathsf{T} \mathbf{\Sigma}_C^\mathsf{T} = \mathbf{\Sigma}_D \mathbf{\Sigma}_D^\mathsf{T} \widehat{A}^\mathsf{T}.$$

Since $\mathbf{\Sigma}_D$ is a diagonal matrix, for $j \in [m_D]$, $\boldsymbol{\xi}_j^\mathsf{T} \mathbf{\Sigma}_D \mathbf{\Sigma}_D^\mathsf{T} = (\mathbf{\Sigma}_D)_{j,j}^2 \boldsymbol{\xi}_j^\mathsf{T}$. Hence, premultiplying the above expression by $\boldsymbol{\xi}_j^\mathsf{T}$, we get

$$(\widehat{A}_{.,j})^\mathsf{T} \mathbf{\Sigma}_C \mathbf{\Sigma}_C^\mathsf{T} = (\mathbf{\Sigma}_D)_{j,j}^2 (\widehat{A}_{.,j})^\mathsf{T}.$$

Note that $\mathbf{\Sigma}_C \mathbf{\Sigma}_C^\mathsf{T}$ is a diagonal matrix, and in the LHS of the above equation, each coordinate of $\widehat{A}_{.,j}$ is scaled by the corresponding element in the diagonal, whereas in the RHS, all coordinates are scaled by the same scalar value. Hence, for every i such that $\widehat{A}_{i,j} > 0$, we require $(\mathbf{\Sigma}_C)_{i,i} = (\mathbf{\Sigma}_D)_{j,j}$. Since $\widehat{A}^\mathsf{T}\widehat{A} = I$ and, consequently, $\|\widehat{A}_{.,j}\| = 1$, there must be at least one $i \in [m_C]$ with $\widehat{A}_{i,j} > 0$. Thus, there exists $i \in [m_C]$ such that $(\mathbf{\Sigma}_C)_{i,i} = (\mathbf{\Sigma}_D)_{j,j}$. In fact, we can further argue that if a singular value appears multiple times in $\mathbf{\Sigma}_D$ it should appear at least as many times in $\mathbf{\Sigma}_C$. For $\lambda > 0$, let $S_\lambda = \{j \in [m_D] \mid (\mathbf{\Sigma}_D)_{j,j} = \lambda\}$, and $T_\lambda = \{i \in [m_C] \mid (\mathbf{\Sigma}_C)_{i,i} = \lambda\}$. Consider the set of columns $\{\widehat{A}_{.,j} | j \in S_\lambda\}$; recall that they are orthogonal to each other (since $\widehat{A}^\mathsf{T}\widehat{A} = 1$). Now, for each $j \in S_\lambda$, we argued that $\widehat{A}_{.,j}$ is supported entirely on rows i such that $(\mathbf{\Sigma}_C)_{i,i} = \lambda$, i.e., on rows indexed by T_λ. Hence, $\widehat{A}$ restricted to rows T_λ and columns S_λ has full column rank. Hence $|T_\lambda| \geq |S_\lambda|$.

Mirroring Lemma. Pursuing the implications of the above arguments further, we uncover a surprising symmetry in the spectral images of a SNIR.

Consider any $\lambda \in \Lambda_D$ and $j \in S_\lambda$ as defined above. Consider the row j in the equation $\widehat{A}^{\mathsf{T}} \Sigma_C = \Sigma_D \widehat{B}^{\mathsf{T}}$ (from (4)). We have,

$$\left(\widehat{A}^{\mathsf{T}} \Sigma_C \right)_{j,i} = \begin{cases} \lambda \cdot \widehat{A}_{i,j} & \text{if } i \in T_\lambda, \\ 0 & \text{otherwise}, \end{cases}$$

since $\widehat{A}_{.,j}$ is supported only on rows in T_λ, and for $i \in T_\lambda$, we have $(\Sigma_C)_{i,i} = \lambda$. On the other hand, $\left(\Sigma_D \widehat{B}^{\mathsf{T}} \right)_{j,.}$ is the jth row of $\widehat{B}^{\mathsf{T}}$ scaled by $(\Sigma_D)_{j,j}$, or equivalently, it is $\lambda \widehat{B}^{\mathsf{T}}_{.,j}$. Thus, we obtain that for all $j \in S_\lambda$, and $i \in T_\lambda$, $\widehat{A}_{i,j} = \widehat{B}_{i,j}$, and for $i \notin T_\lambda$ whenever defined, $\widehat{A}_{i,j} = 0$ and $\widehat{B}_{i,j} = 0$. Note that here we may expand the range T_λ to $[\min(m_C, n_C)]$. Also, since this holds for any λ, we can consider j to be in the union of all S_λ, or equivalently, $j \in [\text{rank}(\Sigma_D)]$. This gives us the following result:

Lemma 3 (Informal). *Suppose a non-redundant correlation $D \in \mathbb{R}^{m_D \times n_D}$ has a perfect SNIR (A, B) to a correlation $C \in \mathbb{R}^{m_C \times n_C}$. Let $d = \text{rank}(\Sigma_D)$ and $r = \text{rank}(\Sigma_C)$. Then for each $(i, j) \in [d] \times [r]$, $\widehat{A}_{i,j} = \widehat{B}_{i,j}$. Further, for $i \notin [r]$ and $j \in [d]$, $\widehat{A}_{i,j} = 0$ and $\widehat{B}_{i,j} = 0$ (whenever defined).*

2.4   Effect of Common Information

An important aspect of correlations is the presence or absence of common information. We say that a correlation has (non-zero) common information if there is a bit of positive entropy on which Alice and Bob can non-interactively agree with probability 1 [13]. A correlation C has common information if and only if the bipartite graph G_C contains two (or more) connected components (the correlation corresponds to sampling an edge from the graph, and giving a node to each party; they can agree on which connected component the edge lies in, and nothing more). Equivalently, the matrix for C can be written as $C = \begin{bmatrix} \alpha C_0 & 0 \\ 0 & (1-\alpha)C_1 \end{bmatrix}$, where C_0, C_1 are two correlations and $0 < \alpha < 1$.

In the context of (non-secure) non-interactive reductions, common information is a *complete correlation*. That is, given common information in a source correlation, Alice and Bob can sample from any target correlation. Indeed, the tools for proving infeasibility in this area focus on how far source correlations are from having common information, measured using maximal correlation [3, 4, 18, 28, 30], or alternately, using the (reverse) hypercontractivity ribbon [3, 5, 8, 12, 21]. On the other hand, in the context of *interactive* secure reductions, common information is a trivial resource (against passive corruption) that does not help at all. Here we investigate the effect of common information in the source for secure and non-interactive reductions.

We note that $\widetilde{C} = \begin{bmatrix} \widetilde{C_0} & 0 \\ 0 & \widetilde{C_1} \end{bmatrix}$ (which remains invariant to α). Hence, $\Lambda_C = \Lambda_{C_0} \cup \Lambda_{C_1}$ (as multi-sets). By Theorem 2, D has a perfect SNIR to C only if $\Lambda_D \subseteq \Lambda_{C_0} \cup \Lambda_{C_1}$. But in fact, we can obtain the following (proven in Sect. 7):

Lemma 4. *Suppose* $C = \begin{bmatrix} \alpha C_0 & 0 \\ 0 & (1-\alpha)C_1 \end{bmatrix}$ *where* C_0, C_1 *are two correlations and* $0 < \alpha < 1$. *Then, a non-redundant correlation* D *devoid of common information has a perfect* SNIR *to* C *only if* D *has a perfect* SNIR *to* C_0 *as well as a perfect* SNIR *to* C_1; *in particular,* $\Lambda_D \subseteq \Lambda_{C_0} \cap \Lambda_{C_1}$.

2.5   Statistical SNIR

Perfectly secure SNIR can often be impossible even due to "uninteresting" reasons; e.g. it is impossible to realize a common random bit with bias $1/3$ using unbiased common random bits with perfect correctness, however, this can be realized with negligible error. As such it is important to extend our tools above to handle the case of statistical security. A significant part of the technical effort in this paper is directed towards this goal, as many of the several steps described above require a careful analysis to be applicable to statistical security.

For statistical security in cryptographic protocols, one usually asks for errors (in correctness and security) to be *negligible* in a security parameter k, while the protocol's complexity remains polynomial in k. A weaker security guarantee often considered settles for a protocol family where for any polynomial p, there is a protocol that achieves $1/p(k)$ error. Even weaker security guarantees are considered in the information-theory literature: the error can be $1/p(k)$ for a fixed polynomial p, or even any fixed function p such that $p(k) \to \infty$ as $k \to \infty$. It is this weakest form of security – security with (merely) vanishing error – that we shall rule out, thereby achieving a strong notion of impossibility. In this form, there is no restriction on the complexity of the protocol itself – which, in the case of a SNIR from D to C, corresponds to the *number of samples from* C used by the protocol. That is, we seek to show that there is an error lower bound ϵ such that for any $t \in \mathbb{N}$, D does not have a SNIR to $C^{\otimes t}$ (the tensor power notation indicating a correlation consisting of t independent samples from C).

In deriving our technical results, we lower bound the error in a SNIR from D to C, wherein only a single instance of C is allowed. Then, for this lower bound to be useful in the above sense, the error bound should be independent of the dimensions of C (but can depend on spectral properties that are invariant to tensor powering). As such, we keep track of the errors in our necessary conditions for a SNIR with an error ϵ in the form of $O_D(\epsilon)$, where the upper bound notation $O_D(\cdot)$ hides constants that can depend on D (but not on C).

We briefly sketch the arguments we need for extending our results to statistical SNIR.

- Firstly, the linear algebraic characterization of SNIR in (1) extends to the setting with statistical error, with a tight characterization in terms of the 1-norm of the error matrices (Theorem 3).
- Next, we extend (2) to the statistical setting, in Lemma 6. Recall that this was based on the non-redundancy of the correlation D; specifically, in the perfect security case, we relied on the fact that if $D = DT$ for a stochastic matrix T, then $T = I$. We show an analogous result that if $D \approx DT$, then

$T \approx I$, in terms of the 1-norm of the error matrices. The proof of this result (provided in the full version [1]) relies on a purely linear-algebraic technical observation which requires a careful application of Gaussian elimination.

- For the case of perfect security, we had argued that a SNIR for a non-redundant correlation D must be deterministic. Clearly, this is not the case any more for statistically secure SNIR, as a protocol can incur a small error by behaving arbitrarily with a small probability, and still remain secure. Nevertheless, we show that every (possibly randomized) SNIR protocol can be "rounded" to a deterministic protocol with an error of ϵ getting amplified to $O_D(\sqrt{\epsilon})$ (Lemma 7). The following steps are shown for a deterministic protocol.

- A robust version of Lemma 2 is proven as Lemma 10. Among other things, this requires a robust version of (5), which is proven as Lemma 8. Lemma 10 provides *multiple* error bounds in terms of the 1-norm of various matrices related to the error matrices (corresponding to $\theta \in \{0, 1\}$ in the lemma statement). The reason for this is that we cannot afford to multiply the bounds with quantities that relate to C; instead, the lemma gives bounds for matrix expressions that incorporate C in two different ways, as are required in the subsequent proofs.

- Theorem 4 extends the spectral criterion $\Lambda_D \subseteq \Lambda_{C^{\otimes t}}$ in Theorem 2 to the case of statistical security. While all other extensions result in statements that incorporate an error term, it is notable that the spectral criterion holds exactly! The reason for this is that if Λ_D is not exactly contained in $\Lambda_{C^{\otimes t}}$ for any t, then there must be an element in Λ_D that maintains a constant gap from all of $\Lambda_{C^{\otimes t'}}$, irrespective of how large t' is (Lemma 9). The proof of Theorem 4 also requires carefully keeping track of the how errors propagate in the spectral domain, using Lemma 10 mentioned above, as well as a technical bound proven as Lemma 11.

- Theorem 5 extends the Mirroring Lemma (Lemma 3) to the case of statistical security. For an ϵ-SNIR, the statement here incurs an error of the form $O_D(\sqrt{\epsilon})/\alpha^2$, where α denotes how close an element in Λ_C can approach an element in Λ_D without equaling it. Again, this proof relies on Lemma 10 and Lemma 11.

- Lemma 12 extends Lemma 4 to the case of statistical security. If a correlation D, devoid of common information, has an ϵ-SNIR to C, then, by Lemma 12, D has an SNIR to one of its component correlation with error $O_D(\epsilon)$. In the full version [1], we will also show that D has an SNIR to each of its component correlations, but with error scaled inversely with the probability of the component. Lemma 12 is used in Theorem 6 to show that common randomness does not aid in realizing SNIR; Theorem 7 uses this lemma to show that no correlation is *complete* in the SNIR setting.

2.6   Applications

We demonstrate the utility of the toolset we built for analyzing SNIR via a few fundamental examples.

Incompleteness in SNIR. Our first result addresses the question of completeness in the SNIR model and answers it in negative Theorem 7. There exist no finite correlation such that every target correlation has a statistical SNIR to possibly arbitrarily many copies of the correlation. This is in contrast with multiple other models of secure computation with simple complete primitives. Specifically, for interactive secure computation, all *non-trivial correlations* are complete (a trivial correlation is one in which the variables are independent conditioned on common information); in the case of (non-secure) non-interactive reduction (NIR), the complete correlations are exactly those which have non-zero common information.

Our incompleteness result is a consequence of the ineffectiveness of common information in SNIR. Lemma 12 shows that SNIR to a correlation C implies SNIR to one of its component correlations. A correlation D has no (non-secure) non-interactive reduction to a correlation C with strictly smaller maximal correlation; this implies that, given any correlation C, we can always choose a correlation D with a larger maximal correlation than all the component correlations of C.

Characterization of SNIR Between Binary Symmetric Correlations. A binary symmetric correlation with crossover probability p, denoted by BSC_p, is a symmetric Boolean correlation that corresponds to giving a uniform random bit to Alice, and then giving the same bit to Bob with probability $1-p$ and the opposite bit with probability p. Consider a protocol in which, given k instances of BSC_p, Alice and Bob each output the XOR of their k bits. It is not hard to show that this is in fact a (perfect) SNIR from BSC_q to BSC_p, where $q = p * \ldots * p$ (k times) with the operator $*$ defined by $p*p' = p(1-p') + p'(1-p)$. Surprisingly, these are the only values of q for which there is a (possibly statistical) SNIR from BSC_q to BSC_p. This result, which fully resolves the question of SNIR between BSCs, follows directly from analyzing the spectra of the correlations of the form BSC_p and applying our spectral criterion for SNIRs.

Characterization of SNIR Between Binary Erasure Correlations. BEC_p is a correlation which can be defined as picking a random bit for Alice, and sampling Bob's output based on it; here Bob gets an erasure symbol $\perp$ with probability p and the same bit as Alice got with probability $1 - p$. Consider a protocol in which, given k instances of BEC_p, Alice outputs the XOR of all her bits, and Bob outputs $\perp$ if at least one of the symbols he received is $\perp$ and otherwise outputs the XOR of all the bits. This is a SNIR from BEC_q to BEC_p, where $1 - q = (1 - p)^k$. Again, surprisingly, these are the only values of q for which there is a (possibly statistical) SNIR from BEC_q to BEC_p. Again, this result follows directly from our spectral criterion.

Necessary Conditions for SNIR Between OLE Correlations. We demonstrate the usefulness of spectral criterion by showing that it is impossible to obtain SNIR between OLE correlations over finite fields with different characteristics.

Application of Mirroring Lemma. We show that there is no statistical SNIR from binary erasure correlation or *oblivious transfer correlation* (OT) (see (6)) to binary symmetric correlation. These results do not follow from the spectral criterion, but can be based on the Mirroring Lemma. In this case, the source correlation C (BSC) has a certain symmetry ($\mathbf{\Psi}_C = \mathbf{\Phi}_C$) whereas the target correlation D (BEC and OT) have markedly different entries in $\mathbf{\Psi}_D$ and $\mathbf{\Phi}_D$; this, we show, makes it impossible for a spectral protocol to satisfy the Mirroring Lemma. Indeed, we provide a much more general implication of mirroring lemma for symmetric sources in Lemma 13.

We remark that our impossibility result rules out an error lower than a positive constant, no matter how many copies of BSC are used. In contrast, a quantitatively weaker result is implied by a known impossibility result for One-Way Secure Computation [14].

We remark that independently, [23] also considered these problems regarding SNIR between BSC and BEC correlations (using techniques tailored for these correlations). They obtain the above three results, with two caveats: their definition of a SNIR allowed only deterministic protocols, and required negligible security error. While the first caveat can be removed using our result in Lemma 7, the second one appears inherent to their techniques. We also remark that [23] also shows that BSC does not have a SNIR to BEC, using techniques similar to those in [14]; we have not obtained this result, as our approach relying on the mirroring lemma seems to require a tedious analysis for this example. This example gives a possible direction in which our toolkit could be expanded.

2.7   Future Directions

Our results and techniques suggest several exciting questions at the intersection of cryptography, linear-algebra and complexity of functions. We mention a few of these directions here.

1. As mentioned at the beginning, SNIR forms one part of a pair of questions about the feasibility of an (interactive) secure reduction from D to C. The question we do not address here is the (non-cryptographic) question regarding what correlations can be created as the views of two parties in an interaction. This is a purely "communication" problem, that fits in with the rich literature of communication complexity, which also studies the properties of communication protocols, albeit the goals are very different.
   Apart from this broad direction, our results open up some concrete questions. Consider Alice sending a single bit to Bob, based (probabilistically) on her sample from the correlation C. The resulting view is described by the following correlation, where Q encodes Alice's communication strategy as a diagonal matrix (with Q_{xx} being the probability of sending 0 on receiving x):

$$\begin{bmatrix} QC & 0 \\ 0 & (I - Q)C \end{bmatrix}.$$

   How is the spectrum of this new correlation related to that of C, over all possible choices of Q? If C corresponds to a (possibly noisy) string-OT, where

Bob receives two strings (y_0, y_1) and Alice receives (b, y_b), if Alice sends b to Bob, then the maximal correlation greatly increases. However, if C is of the form $C_1^{\otimes t}$ it would appear that sending a single bit will have only limited effect on the spectrum. Can this be quantified?

2. How "complex" can the spectrum of a correlation be, in terms of the complexity of sampling from it, or computing the probabilities? In particular, if a correlation is the tensor power of a smaller correlation, all the values in the spectrum can be computed as monomials of a few variables.

3. The correlation operator $\widetilde{M}$ essentially captures all the information about a correlation M (other than the distribution of the common information). However, the spectrum of a correlation discards the orthogonal transformations $\boldsymbol{\Psi}_M$ and $\boldsymbol{\Phi}_M$ that are part of the singular value decomposition of the correlation operator $\widetilde{M}$. Can we obtain tighter criteria for SNIR based on them?

4. The correlation operator is a tool worthy of study on its own. We have not explored some natural mathematical questions that would arise in such a study.

   – Which linear transformations correspond to valid correlation operators? In particular, given a valid correlation operator, can it be altered – say, by truncating the spectrum – to obtain the correlation operator of meaningfully "simpler" correlations? (Truncating the spectrum to retain only the top singular value yields the correlation operator corresponding to the product distribution with the same marginal.)

   – The correlation operator is quite symmetric in its definition (e.g., $\widetilde{M}^\intercal = \widetilde{M^\intercal}$). While not as versatile as the correlation operator, asymmetric variants of it does capture certain interesting details of a correlation. For instance, one can define $\boldsymbol{\Delta}_{M^\intercal}^{-\alpha} M \boldsymbol{\Delta}_M^{-(1-\alpha)}$ for any $0 \le \alpha \le 1$. We leave it to future work to explore such variants.

5. Finally, there are information-theoretic problems on SNIR that we have not explored. For instance, as pursued in [23], one may explore the exact constant rate at which a SNIR between specific correlations is possible. Also, as pursued in [22], one may consider the question of decidability (or even, efficient decidability) of the existence of SNIR between such a pair of correlations.

3 Preliminaries

In this section, we set up the notation and make the necessary definitions and formally define the notion of non-interactive secure reduction.

Notation. Throughout the paper, we only consider finite sets. Finite sets are denoted as $\mathcal{X}, \mathcal{Y}$, and so on; a random variable over set $\mathcal{X}$ is denoted as X and a member of $\mathcal{X}$ is denoted as x. For convenience, we consider vectors with elements indexed by elements $x \in \mathcal{X}$ for a arbitrary set $\mathcal{X}$; hence it makes sense to define an $\mathcal{X}$ dimensional column vector. For an $\mathcal{X}$ dimensional column (or row) vector $\boldsymbol{v}$, the entry at the position x is denoted by $(\boldsymbol{v})_x$. Similarly, for sets $\mathcal{X}$ and $\mathcal{Y}$, consider an $\mathcal{X} \times \mathcal{Y}$ dimensional matrix H. The row of H indexed by x and the column indexed by y are denoted as vectors $(H)_{x,\cdot}$ and $(H)_{\cdot,y}$, respectively, and the element indexed by (x, y) is denoted as $(H)_{x,y}$. The transpose is denoted by H^T. Finally, $|H|$ denotes the absolute value of H, i.e., $(|H|)_{i,j} = |(H)_{i,j}|$, for all $i \in [m]$ and $j \in [n]$. We remove the parentheses whenever there is no scope for confusion and the vector/matrix itself is subscripted; i.e., $(v)_x$, $(H)_{\cdot,x}$ and $(H)_{x,y}$ are simplified to v_x, $H_{\cdot,x}$ and $H_{x,y}$, respectively.

For $n \in \mathbb{N}$, an n dimensional column vector with all elements being 1 (resp. 0) is denoted by $\mathbf{1}^n$ (resp. $\mathbf{0}^n$). For $i \in [n]$, $\boldsymbol{\xi}_i^n$ denotes the n dimensional unit vector along the 'direction i'. That is, $(\boldsymbol{\xi}_i^n)_i = 1$ and $(\boldsymbol{\xi}_i^n)_j = 0$ for all $j \neq i$. We drop the superscript when there is no scope for confusion regarding the dimension of the vector. $n \times n$ dimensional identity matrix is denoted $I^{n \times n}$ and the 'zero matrix' (with all elements being 0) is denoted by $0^{n \times n}$.

We write $O_D(\epsilon)$ to denote an upper bound of the form $f(D) \cdot \epsilon$, for some fixed non-negative function f.

Definition 1 (Norms). For a $m \times n$ dimensional matrix H, 1-norm of the matrix, denoted by $\|H\|$, is the sum of the absolute value of all elements in H, i.e.,

$$\|H\| = \sum_{(i,j) \in [m] \times [n]} |H_{i,j}| = (\mathbf{1}^m)^\mathsf{T} |H| \mathbf{1}^n.$$

The 2-norm of an n dimensional vector v is defined as $\|v\|_2 = \left(\sum_{i \in [n]} v_i^2 \right)^{\frac{1}{2}}$. ◁

Definition 2. Let u and v be vectors of dimensions m and n, respectively. Then,

$$\delta(u, v) = \hat{u} - \hat{v},$$

where $\hat{u}$ and $\hat{v}$ are the $\max(m, n)$ dimensional zero-paddings of vector u and v, respectively.   ◁

Definition 3. A matrix T with non-negative entries is said to be *stochastic* if $T\mathbf{1} = \mathbf{1}$. A stochastic matrix in which every entry is either 0 or 1 is called a *deterministic* stochastic matrix or simply a *deterministic* matrix.   ◁

Definition 4. For an $m \times n$ dimensional matrix M, we define $\boldsymbol{\Delta}_M$ as the $n \times n$ diagonal matrix, such that

$$(\boldsymbol{\Delta}_M)_{i,j} = \begin{cases} (\mathbf{1}^\mathsf{T} M)_i & \text{if } i = j, \\ 0 & \text{otherwise.} \end{cases}$$

◁

Probability. Let X be a random variable distributed over a domain $\mathcal{X}$. Probability with which X takes on the value $x \in \mathcal{X}$ is denoted by $\mathrm{P}_X(x)$ or simply as $\mathrm{P}(x)$, when the distribution is apparent. Given two random variables X, X'

over the same domain, we write $\mathrm{SD}(X, X')$ to denote the statistical difference (a.k.a. total variation distance) between the two, which is computed as

$$\sum_{x \in \mathcal{X}} |\mathrm{P}_X(x) - \mathrm{P}_{X'}(x)|.$$

Throughout this paper, we would be interested in correlations, which are joint distributions over a product of two sets. For finite sets $\mathcal{X}$ and $\mathcal{Y}$, a $\mathcal{X} \times \mathcal{Y}$ dimensional matrix H with non-negative entries is a joint distribution matrix or simply a distribution matrix if

$$\sum_x \sum_y H_{x,y} = 1.$$

We write $(X, Y) \sim H$ to imply that the random variables (X, Y) are distributed according to the distribution law H; *i.e.*, $\mathrm{P}_{XY}(x, y) = H_{x,y}$ for all $(x, y) \in \mathcal{X} \times \mathcal{Y}$. In the sequel, we will always refer to a pair of random variables by its joint distribution matrix. We drop all-zero rows (and all-zero columns) from joint distribution matrices, i.e., elements in $\mathcal{X}$ (and $\mathcal{Y}$) which occur with zero probability are suppressed.

When we say Alice and Bob receive a correlation (X, Y), we mean Alice and Bob receive random variables X and Y respectively. The objective of non-interactive secure reductions is for Alice and Bob to *securely realize* a desired correlation among themselves using (potentially many copies) of the correlation at hand without communicating with each other.

Some Correlations of Interest. Below, we define some correlations that are extensively studied in information theory and cryptography which we use to illustrate the implications of our main results.

For $p \in [0, 1]$, the **Binary Symmetric Correlation** with crossover probability p over the alphabet $\{0, 1\} \times \{0, 1\}$, and the **symmetric Binary Erasure Correlation** with erasure probability p over the alphabet $\{0, 1\} \times \{0, 1, \bot\}$ are given by the following probability distribution matrices, respectively.

$$\mathsf{BSC}_p = \begin{bmatrix} \frac{1-p}{2} & \frac{p}{2} \\ \frac{p}{2} & \frac{1-p}{2} \end{bmatrix}. \quad \mathsf{BEC}_p = \begin{bmatrix} \frac{1-p}{2} & \frac{p}{2} & 0 \\ 0 & \frac{p}{2} & \frac{1-p}{2} \end{bmatrix}.$$

The **OLE correlation** (for Oblivious Linear-function Evaluation) over a finite field (or ring) $\mathbb{F}$ is the correlation $\mathsf{OLE}_\mathbb{F}$ over the domain $\mathbb{F}^2 \times \mathbb{F}^2$ such that, for all $a, b, x, y \in \mathbb{F}$,

$$(\mathsf{OLE}_\mathbb{F})_{(a,x),(b,y)} = \begin{cases} \frac{1}{|\mathbb{F}|^3} & \text{if } a \cdot b = x + y, \\ 0 & \text{otherwise.} \end{cases} \tag{6}$$

OLE correlation over $\mathbb{F}_2$ is alternately called the **Oblivious Transfer correlation** or OT for short.

Tensor Product. When G and H are $\mathcal{X} \times \mathcal{Y}$ and $\mathcal{X}' \times \mathcal{Y}'$ dimensional matrices, *tensor (Kronecker) product* of G and H, denoted as $G \otimes H$ is an $(\mathcal{X} \times \mathcal{X}') \times (\mathcal{Y} \times \mathcal{Y}')$ dimensional matrix such that, for all $(x, x') \in \mathcal{X} \times \mathcal{X}'$ and $(y, y') \in \mathcal{Y} \times \mathcal{Y}'$,

$$(G \otimes H)_{(x,x'),(y,y')} = G_{x,y} \cdot H_{x',y'}.$$

$G \otimes H$ is essentially the product distribution of G and H, *i.e.*, independent draws from distributions G and H. We will use the following well known result about Kronecker product [19].

Claim 1. *For matrices G, H and $t \in \mathbb{N}$, $(GH)^{\otimes t} = G^{\otimes t} H^{\otimes t}$.*

4   Definitions

We define the notion of secure non-interactive reduction (SNIR) in this section. Non-interactive reduction of a distribution to another without the security guarantee called non-interactive reduction (NIR) is well studied. We formally define NIR and discuss some of its properties before defining SNIR.

Definition 5. Let C and D be correlations over $\mathcal{X} \times \mathcal{Y}$ and $\mathcal{R} \times \mathcal{S}$, respectively. For any $\epsilon \geq 0$, an ϵ-*non-interactive reduction* (ϵ-NIR) from D to C is a pair of probabilistic algorithms $\mathfrak{A} : \mathcal{X} \to \mathcal{R}$ and $\mathfrak{B} : \mathcal{Y} \to \mathcal{S}$ such that, when $(X, Y) \sim C$ and $(R, S) \sim D$,

$$\mathrm{SD}\left((\mathfrak{A}(X), \mathfrak{B}(Y)), (R, S)\right) \leq \epsilon. \tag{7}$$

0-NIR is alternatively called a perfect NIR.   ◁

Definition 6. Let C and D be correlations over $\mathcal{X} \times \mathcal{Y}$ and $\mathcal{R} \times \mathcal{S}$, respectively. D is said to have a statistical NIR to C if for all $\epsilon > 0$, there exists a sufficiently large n for which, D has an ϵ-NIR to $C^{\otimes n}$.   ◁

Definition 7. Let C and D be correlations over $\mathcal{X} \times \mathcal{Y}$ and $\mathcal{R} \times \mathcal{S}$, respectively. For any $\epsilon \geq 0$, a ϵ-*secure non-interactive reduction* (ϵ-SNIR) from D to C is a pair of probabilistic algorithms $\mathfrak{A} : \mathcal{X} \to \mathcal{R}$ and $\mathfrak{B} : \mathcal{Y} \to \mathcal{S}$ such that, when $(X, Y) \sim C$ and $(R, S) \sim D$, in addition to condition (7), the following security conditions hold.

There exist a pair of probabilistic algorithms, $\mathsf{Sim}_A : \mathcal{R} \to \mathcal{X}$ and $\mathsf{Sim}_B : \mathcal{S} \to \mathcal{Y}$ such that,

$$\mathrm{SD}\left((X, \mathfrak{B}(Y)), (\mathsf{Sim}_A(R), S)\right) \leq \epsilon, \tag{8}$$

$$\mathrm{SD}\left((\mathfrak{A}(X), Y), (R, \mathsf{Sim}_B(S))\right) \leq \epsilon. \tag{9}$$

0-SNIR is alternatively called a perfect SNIR.   ◁

Definition 8. Let C and D be distributions over $\mathcal{X} \times \mathcal{Y}$ and $\mathcal{R} \times \mathcal{S}$, respectively. D is said to have a statistical SNIR to C if for all $\epsilon > 0$, there exists a sufficiently large n for which, D has an ϵ-SNIR to $C^{\otimes n}$.   ◁

We begin with a linear algebraic characterization of secure non-interactive reductions (SNIR). The following theorem is proved in the full version [1].

Theorem 3. *Let $\epsilon \geq 0$, and let C and D be correlations over $\mathcal{X} \times \mathcal{Y}$ and $\mathcal{R} \times \mathcal{S}$, respectively. D has a ϵ-SNIR to C if and only if there exist stochastic matrices A, B, U, and V of dimensions $\mathcal{X} \times \mathcal{R}$, $\mathcal{Y} \times \mathcal{S}$, $\mathcal{R} \times \mathcal{X}$, and $\mathcal{S} \times \mathcal{Y}$, respectively, such that*

$$A^\mathsf{T} C B = D + E \qquad A^\mathsf{T} C = D V + E_A \qquad C B = U^\mathsf{T} D + E_B,$$

where E, E_A, and E_B are matrices of dimensions $\mathcal{R} \times \mathcal{S}$, $\mathcal{R} \times \mathcal{Y}$, and $\mathcal{X} \times \mathcal{S}$, respectively, such that $\|E\|, \|E_A\|, \|E_B\| \leq \epsilon$.

Going forward, given distribution matrices C and D of dimensions $m_C \times n_C$ and $m_D \times n_D$, respectively, and stochastic matrices A and B of dimensions $m_C \times m_D$ and $n_C \times n_D$, respectively; we say that (A, B) is a ϵ-SNIR of D to C if the conditions in Theorem 3 are satisfied for some stochastic matrices U and V of dimensions $m_D \times m_C$ and $n_D \times n_C$, respectively.

5   Basic Properties of SNIR

In this section, we will establish some fundamental properties of SNIR that will be crucially used in arriving at the main results in the paper. In Lemma 5, we show that it is sufficient to study SNIR between correlations in which there are no redundant symbols (see Definition 9) in Alice's or Bob's side. Lemma 6 establishes a relation between SNIR protocols and their simulators (used for proving the security conditions) of a secure reduction. This relation is later used in Lemma 7 to show that protocols inducing SNIR are necessarily deterministic. This allows us to focus on SNIR with deterministic protocols in the sequel. Finally, the main result of this section characterizes the simulators (U and V) for a secure reduction in terms of the protocols (respectively, A and B).

We formally define redundant correlations and the core of a correlation.

Definition 9. *A distribution matrix H over $\mathcal{X} \times \mathcal{Y}$ is said to be redundant if there exist distinct $x, x' \in \mathcal{X}$ and $\alpha \in \mathbb{R}_{\geq 0}$ such that $H_{x,\cdot} = \alpha \cdot H_{x',\cdot}$ or there exist $y, y' \in \mathcal{Y}$ and $\beta \in \mathbb{R}_{\geq 0}$ such that $H_{\cdot,y} = \beta \cdot H_{\cdot,y'}$.*   ◁

By this definition, both the marginal distributions of a non-redundant distribution have full support since an all zero column (or row) is trivially a scalar multiple of any other column (or row).

Consider a (potentially redundant) distribution matrix H over $\mathcal{X} \times \mathcal{Y}$. Consider the partition $\mathcal{X}_1, \ldots, \mathcal{X}_m$ and $\mathcal{Y}_1, \ldots, \mathcal{Y}_n$ of $\mathcal{X}$ and $\mathcal{Y}$, respectively, such that $x, x' \in \mathcal{X}_i$ (resp. $y, y' \in \mathcal{Y}_j$) if and only if $H_{x,\cdot}$ and $H_{x',\cdot}$ (resp. $H_{\cdot,y}$ and $H_{\cdot,y'}$) are non-zero scalar multiples of each other. Additionally, we include all zero columns and rows in $\mathcal{X}_1$ and $\mathcal{Y}_1$, respectively. The distribution over such a partition induced by H is called the *core of the distribution H*. Formally, the non-redundant core of H, denoted by H_{core}, is the $m \times n$ dimensional matrix such that, for all $i \in [m]$ and $j \in [n]$,

$$(H_{\text{core}})_{i,j} = \sum_{x \in \mathcal{X}_i} \sum_{y \in \mathcal{Y}_j} H_{x,y}.$$

It is easy to verify that the core of any distribution is non-redundant and unique up to relabelling.

Lemma 5, Lemma 6 and Lemma 7 are formally proved in the full version [1].

Lemma 5. *Consider distributions C and D over $\mathcal{X} \times \mathcal{Y}$ and $\mathcal{R} \times \mathcal{S}$, respectively. For any $\epsilon \geq 0$, D has an ϵ-SNIR to C if and only if D_{core} has an ϵ-SNIR to C_{core}.*

Lemma 6. *Let C be a $m_C \times n_C$ dimensional distribution matrix and D be a $m_D \times n_D$ dimensional non-redundant distribution matrix. For any $\epsilon \geq 0$, if stochastic matrices A, B, U, V are such that*

$$\|A^\mathsf{T} C B - D\| \leq \epsilon \qquad \|A^\mathsf{T} C - DV\| \leq \epsilon \qquad \|CB - U^\mathsf{T} D\| \leq \epsilon,$$

then $\|VB - I\| \leq O_D(\epsilon)$ and $\|UA - I\| \leq O_D(\epsilon)$.

Lemma 7. *Let C and D be non-redundant distribution matrices of dimensions $m_C \times n_C$ and $m_D \times n_D$, respectively. For any $\epsilon \geq 0$, if there exist stochastic matrices A, B, U and V such that*

$$\|A^\mathsf{T} C B - D\| \leq \epsilon \qquad \|A^\mathsf{T} C - DV\| \leq \epsilon \qquad \|CB - U^\mathsf{T} D\| \leq \epsilon,$$

then there exist deterministic stochastic matrices $\bar{A}, \bar{B}$ such that,

$$\|\bar{A}^\mathsf{T} C \bar{B} - D\| \leq O_D(\sqrt{\epsilon}) \quad \|\bar{A}^\mathsf{T} C - DV\| \leq O_D(\sqrt{\epsilon}) \quad \|C\bar{B} - U^\mathsf{T} D\| \leq O_D(\sqrt{\epsilon}).$$

The following is the main result of this section that characterizes the simulators for a secure reduction in terms of the protocols.

Lemma 8. *Let C and D be non-redundant distribution matrices of dimensions $m_C \times n_C$ and $m_D \times n_D$, respectively. For any $\epsilon \geq 0$, if there exist deterministic stochastic matrices A and B, and stochastic matrices U and V such that*

$$\|A^\mathsf{T} C B - D\| \leq \epsilon \qquad \|A^\mathsf{T} C - DV\| \leq \epsilon \qquad \|CB - U^\mathsf{T} D\| \leq \epsilon,$$

then,

$$\|V - \Delta_D^{-1} B^\mathsf{T} \Delta_C\| \leq O_D(\epsilon) \qquad \|U - \Delta_{D^\mathsf{T}}^{-1} A^\mathsf{T} \Delta_{C^\mathsf{T}}\| \leq O_D(\epsilon).$$

Proof: For $i \in [n_C]$, define $j_i^* \in [n_D]$ as the unique index (since B is deterministic) such that $B_{i,j_i^*} = 1$. Define row vectors $\boldsymbol{c} = \mathbf{1}^\mathsf{T} C$ and $\boldsymbol{d} = \mathbf{1}^\mathsf{T} D$ of dimensions n_C and n_D, respectively. It can be verified that for all $i \in [n_C]$, for all $j \neq j_i^*$, $\left(\Delta_D^{-1} B^\mathsf{T} \Delta_C\right)_{j,i} = 0$, and $\left(\Delta_D^{-1} B^\mathsf{T} \Delta_C\right)_{j_i^*,i} = \frac{c_i}{d_{j_i^*}}$. Hence, for each $i \in [n_C]$,

$$\sum_{j \in [n_D]} \left| \left(\Delta_D^{-1} B^\mathsf{T} \Delta_C\right)_{j,i} - V_{j,i} \right| = \left| \frac{c_i}{d_{j_i^*}} - V_{j_i^*,i} \right| + \sum_{j \neq j_i^*} V_{j,i}. \tag{10}$$

Let $A^\mathsf{T}C - DV = E$; by our assumption, $\|E\| \leq \epsilon$. Define n_C dimensional row vector $e = \mathbf{1}^\mathsf{T}E$. Since A is a stochastic matrix, $\mathbf{1}^\mathsf{T}A^\mathsf{T} = \mathbf{1}^\mathsf{T}$. Consequently,

$$e = \mathbf{1}^\mathsf{T}E = \mathbf{1}^\mathsf{T}A^\mathsf{T}C - \mathbf{1}^\mathsf{T}DV = c - \sum_{j=1}^{n_D} d_j V_{j,\cdot}.$$

Hence, for all $i \in n_C$,

$$c_i - d_{j_i^*} V_{j_i^*,i} = e_i + \sum_{j \neq j_i^*} d_j V_{j,i}.$$

Since D is non-redundant all entries of d are non zero. Hence, for all $i \in [n_C]$,

$$\left| \frac{c_i}{d_{j_i^*}} - V_{j_i^*,i} \right| \leq \frac{1}{\min\limits_{j \in [n_D]} d_j} \left(|e_i| + \sum_{j \neq j_i^*} V_{j,i} \right).$$

Using this, along with (10), we get,

$$\|\Delta_D^{-1} B^\mathsf{T} \Delta_C - V\| = \sum_{i \in [n_C]} \sum_{j \in [n_D]} \left| \left(\Delta_D^{-1} B^\mathsf{T} \Delta_C - V \right)_{j,i} \right|$$

$$\leq \sum_{i \in [n_C]} \frac{|e_i|}{\min\limits_{j \in [n_D]} d_j} + \sum_{j \neq j_i^*} V_{j,i} \left(1 + \frac{1}{\min\limits_{j \in [n_D]} d_j} \right)$$

$$\leq \frac{1}{\min\limits_{j \in [n_D]} d_j} \cdot \left(\epsilon + \sum_{i \in [n_C]} \sum_{j \neq j_i^*} 2 V_{j,i} \right).$$

In the last inequality, we used $1 \leq \frac{1}{\min_i d_i}$, and since $\|E\| \leq \epsilon$, $\sum_{i \in [n_D]} |e_i| \leq \epsilon$. To bound the sum in the RHS, we proceed as follows. Since each row $i \in [n_C]$ of B has a unique non-zero entry (1 in the column j_i^*),

$$\sum_{j \in [n_D]} (VB)_{j,j} = \sum_{j \in [n_D]} \sum_{i \in [n_C]} V_{j,i} B_{i,j} = \sum_{i \in [n_C]} \sum_{j \in [n_D]} V_{j,i} \cdot B_{i,j} = \sum_{i \in [n_C]} V_{j_i^*,i}.$$

By Lemma 6, $\|VB - I\| = O_D(\epsilon)$. Furthermore, since V is stochastic matrix with n_D rows, all entries of V add up to n_D. Hence,

$$O_D(\epsilon) \geq \sum_{j \in [n_D]} (I - VB)_{j,j} = n_D - \sum_{j \in [n_D]} (VB)_{j,j} = n_D - \sum_{i \in [n_C]} V_{j_i^*,i}$$

$$= \sum_{i \in [n_C]} \sum_{j \in [n_D]} V_{j,i} - \sum_{i \in [n_C]} V_{j_i^*,i} = \sum_{i \in [n_C]} \sum_{j \neq j_i^*} V_{j,i}.$$

This concludes the proof. $\square$

6 Spectral Protocols

The properties of SNIR that were established in the previous section are used in this section to analyze the protocols in the so called *spectral domain*. We then show that these spectral protocols reveal more of the underlying structures in secure reductions that are not obvious when we analyze the protocols themselves. The properties of secure reductions revealed by analyzing the secure reductions in the spectral domain tend to be *robust*, in that, they easily extend to the statistical case. First, we make the following definitions.

Definition 10 (Spectrum of a Correlation). For any distribution matrix M of dimension $m \times n$, define[5]

$$\widetilde{M} = \Delta_{M^\intercal}^{-1/2} M \Delta_M^{-1/2}.$$

Further define Σ_M, Ψ_M and Φ_M to be given by a canonical singular value decomposition of $\widetilde{M}$, so that Σ_M is an $m \times n$ dimensional non-negative diagonal matrix with the diagonal sorted in descending order, Ψ_M and Φ_M are unitary matrices of dimensions $m \times m$ and $n \times n$, respectively, and

$$\widetilde{M} = \Psi_M^\intercal \Sigma_M \Phi_M.$$

The multi-set of *non-zero* singular values of $\widetilde{M}$ is called the *spectrum of M*, and is denoted by Λ_M.   ◁

We now describe the spectrum of the correlations of interest in this paper.

Binary Symmetric Correlation. For $0 < p < \frac{1}{2}$, $\mathsf{BSC}_p = \begin{bmatrix} \frac{1-p}{2} & \frac{p}{2} \\ \frac{p}{2} & \frac{1-p}{2} \end{bmatrix}$

$$\Sigma_{\mathsf{BSC}_p} = \begin{bmatrix} 1 & 0 \\ 0 & 1-2p \end{bmatrix} \qquad \Psi_{\mathsf{BSC}_p} = \begin{bmatrix} \frac{1}{\sqrt{2}} & \frac{1}{\sqrt{2}} \\ \frac{1}{\sqrt{2}} & -\frac{1}{2} \end{bmatrix} \qquad \Phi_{\mathsf{BSC}_p} = \begin{bmatrix} \frac{1}{\sqrt{2}} & \frac{1}{\sqrt{2}} \\ \frac{1}{\sqrt{2}} & -\frac{1}{2} \end{bmatrix}. \tag{11}$$

Binary Erasure Correlation. For $0 < p < 1$, when $q = 1-p$, $\mathsf{BEC}_p = \begin{bmatrix} \frac{q}{2} & \frac{p}{2} & 0 \\ 0 & \frac{p}{2} & \frac{q}{2} \end{bmatrix}$

$$\Sigma_{\mathsf{BEC}_p} = \begin{bmatrix} 1 & 0 & 0 \\ 0 & \sqrt{q} & 0 \end{bmatrix} \quad \Psi_{\mathsf{BEC}_p} = \begin{bmatrix} \frac{1}{\sqrt{2}} & \frac{1}{\sqrt{2}} \\ \frac{1}{\sqrt{2}} & -\frac{1}{2} \end{bmatrix} \quad \Phi_{\mathsf{BEC}_p} = \begin{bmatrix} \sqrt{\frac{q}{2}} & \sqrt{p} & \sqrt{\frac{q}{2}} \\ \sqrt{\frac{1}{2}} & 0 & -\sqrt{\frac{1}{2}} \\ \sqrt{\frac{p}{2}} & -\sqrt{q} & \sqrt{\frac{p}{2}} \end{bmatrix}. \tag{12}$$

Oblivious Transfer Correlation $\mathsf{OT} = \frac{1}{8} \cdot \begin{bmatrix} 1 & 0 & 1 & 0 \\ 1 & 0 & 0 & 1 \\ 0 & 1 & 1 & 0 \\ 0 & 1 & 0 & 1 \end{bmatrix}$

---

[5] Recall that we use the convention that a distribution matrix does not have an all-0 row or column, and hence the diagonal matrices $\Delta_{M^\intercal}$ and Δ_M have strictly positive entries in their diagonals.

$$\Sigma_{\text{OT}} = \begin{bmatrix} 1 & 0 & 0 & 0 \\ 0 & \frac{1}{\sqrt{2}} & 0 & 0 \\ 0 & 0 & \frac{1}{\sqrt{2}} & 0 \\ 0 & 0 & 0 & 0 \end{bmatrix} \quad \Psi_{\text{OT}} = \begin{bmatrix} \frac{1}{2} & \frac{1}{2} & \frac{1}{2} & \frac{1}{2} \\ 0 & \frac{-1}{\sqrt{2}} & \frac{1}{\sqrt{2}} & 0 \\ \frac{-1}{\sqrt{2}} & 0 & 0 & \frac{1}{\sqrt{2}} \\ \frac{1}{2} & \frac{-1}{2} & \frac{-1}{2} & \frac{1}{2} \end{bmatrix} \quad \Phi_{\text{OT}} = \begin{bmatrix} \frac{1}{2} & \frac{1}{2} & \frac{1}{2} & \frac{1}{2} \\ \frac{-1}{2} & \frac{1}{2} & \frac{1}{2} & \frac{-1}{2} \\ \frac{-1}{2} & \frac{1}{2} & \frac{-1}{2} & \frac{1}{2} \\ \frac{-1}{2} & \frac{-1}{2} & \frac{1}{2} & \frac{1}{2} \end{bmatrix}. \tag{13}$$

In the full version [1], we will show that the spectrum of the OLE correlation over a finite field $\mathbb{F}$ consists of only the values 1 and $\frac{1}{\sqrt{|\mathbb{F}|}}$.

Definition 11 (Spectral Image of SNIR). Given correlations $C \in \mathbb{R}^{m_C \times n_C}$ and $D \in \mathbb{R}^{m_D \times n_D}$, and a SNIR from D to C given by (A, B), where $A \in \mathbb{R}^{m_C \times m_D}$ and $B \in \mathbb{R}^{n_C \times n_D}$, we define its *spectral image* $(\widehat{A}, \widehat{B})$ (where $\widehat{A} \in \mathbb{R}^{m_C \times m_D}$ and $\widehat{B} \in \mathbb{R}^{n_C \times n_D}$) by

$$\widehat{A} = \Psi_C \, \Delta_{C^\intercal}^{1/2} \, A \, \Delta_{D^\intercal}^{-1/2} \, \Psi_D^\intercal, \qquad \widehat{B} = \Phi_C \, \Delta_C^{1/2} \, B \, \Delta_D^{-1/2} \, \Phi_D^\intercal.$$

◁

Note that above, for brevity we have suppressed C and D in the notation for $\widehat{A}$ and $\widehat{B}$, as they will be evident from context. Before turning to our main results, below we summarize a few properties of the spectrum of a correlation (see the full version [1] for the proof).

Lemma 9. *Let M be a distribution matrix of dimension $m \times n$. Then,*

(i) *Elements of Λ_M lie in the range $(0, 1]$, and $\max(\Lambda_M) = 1$. Furthermore, if M has no common information, then the second largest element of Λ_M is strictly less than 1.*

(ii) *For all $\ell \in \mathbb{N}$, $\Lambda_{M^{\otimes \ell}} \subseteq \Lambda_{M^{\otimes(\ell+1)}}$.*

(iii) *For all $\lambda \in (0, 1)$, there exists $\beta > 0$ such that for all $\ell \subset \mathbb{N}$ and for all $\sigma \in \Lambda_{M^{\otimes \ell}}$, either $\lambda = \sigma$ or $|\lambda - \sigma| > \beta$.*

Our goal in this section is to prove robust versions of the Spectral Criterion (Theorem 2) and the Mirroring Lemma (Lemma 3) as Theorem 4 and Theorem 5, respectively. Before proving those theorems, we state the following lemmas that are crucially used in the proofs of the theorems. The lemmas are formally proved in the full version [1].

The first lemma is the statistical equivalent of the results in Lemma 2 for perfect SNIR.

Lemma 10. *Suppose a non-redundant correlation $D \in \mathbb{R}^{m_D \times n_D}$ has a deterministic ϵ-SNIR (A, B) to a correlation $C \in \mathbb{R}^{m_C \times n_C}$, for $\epsilon \geq 0$. Then,*

(i). *There exist matrices E_1, E_2 such that $\|E_1\| = O_D(\epsilon)$ and $\|E_2\| = O_D(\epsilon)$, and*

$$\widehat{A}^\intercal \widehat{A} = I^{m_D \times m_D} + E_1 \qquad \widehat{B}^\intercal \widehat{B} = I^{n_D \times n_D} + E_2.$$

(ii). There exist matrices $\hat{E}, \hat{E}_A, \hat{E}_B$ such that

$$\hat{A}^{\mathsf{T}} \Sigma_C \hat{B} = \Sigma_D + \hat{E}, \quad \hat{A}^{\mathsf{T}} \Sigma_C = \Sigma_D \hat{B}^{\mathsf{T}} + \hat{E}_A, \quad \hat{B}^{\mathsf{T}} \Sigma_C^{\mathsf{T}} = \Sigma_D^{\mathsf{T}} \hat{A}^{\mathsf{T}} + \hat{E}_B,$$

where $\|\hat{E}\| = O_D(\epsilon)$, and for all $\theta \in \{0, 1\}$,

$$\|\hat{E}_A (\Sigma_C^{\mathsf{T}} \Sigma_C)^\theta \Sigma_C^{\mathsf{T}} \hat{A}\| = O_D(\epsilon), \|\hat{E}_A (\Sigma_C^{\mathsf{T}} \Sigma_C)^\theta \hat{B}\| = O_D(\epsilon),$$
$$\|\hat{E}_B (\Sigma_C \Sigma_C^{\mathsf{T}})^\theta \Sigma_C \hat{B}\| = O_D(\epsilon), \|\hat{E}_B (\Sigma_C \Sigma_C^{\mathsf{T}})^\theta \hat{A}\| = O_D(\epsilon).$$

Next is a technical lemma that will be needed in both the proofs.

Lemma 11. *Suppose a non-redundant correlation $D \in \mathbb{R}^{m_D \times n_D}$ has a deterministic ϵ-SNIR (A, B) to a correlation $C \in \mathbb{R}^{m_C \times n_C}$ for $\epsilon \geq 0$. Then, for all $i \in [m_D]$,*

$$\left\| \left(\Sigma_C \Sigma_C^{\mathsf{T}} - (\Sigma_D \Sigma_D^{\mathsf{T}})_{i,i} \cdot I \right) \hat{A}_{\cdot,i} \right\|_2 = O_D(\sqrt{\epsilon}).$$

Similarly, for $i \in [n_D]$,

$$\left\| \left(\Sigma_C^{\mathsf{T}} \Sigma_C - (\Sigma_D^{\mathsf{T}} \Sigma_D)_{i,i} \cdot I \right) \hat{B}_{\cdot,i} \right\|_2 = O_D(\sqrt{\epsilon}).$$

6.1   Spectral Criterion

Theorem 4. *A non-redundant correlation D has a statistically secure SNIR to C only if, there exists $\ell \in \mathbb{N}$ such that $\Lambda_D \subseteq \Lambda_{C^{\otimes \ell}}$.*

Proof: For all $\epsilon > 0$, there exist a large enough ℓ, and deterministic matrices A and B and stochastic matrices U and V such that,

$$\|A^{\mathsf{T}} C^{\otimes \ell} B - D\| \leq \epsilon, \quad \|A^{\mathsf{T}} C^{\otimes \ell} - DV\| \leq \epsilon, \quad \|C^{\otimes \ell} B - U^{\mathsf{T}} D\| \leq \epsilon. \quad (14)$$

If $\Lambda_D \not\subseteq \Lambda_{C^{\otimes t}}$ for all $t \in \mathbb{N}$, by Lemma 9 (ii), there exists $i \in [\min(m_D, n_D)]$ such that for all t, $(\Sigma_D)_{i,i} \notin \Lambda_{C^{\otimes t}}$. Then, by Lemma 9 (iii), there exists $\beta > 0$ such that for all $t \in \mathbb{N}$ and all $\lambda \in \Lambda_{C^{\otimes t}}$, $|(\Sigma_D)_{i,i} - \lambda| > \beta$. Hence, when $a = \hat{A}_{\cdot,i}$,

$$a^{\mathsf{T}} \cdot \left(\Sigma_C^{\otimes \ell} (\Sigma_C^{\otimes \ell})^{\mathsf{T}} - (\Sigma_D \Sigma_D^{\mathsf{T}})_{i,i} \cdot I \right)^2 \cdot a \geq \beta^4 (a^{\mathsf{T}} \cdot a). \quad (15)$$

But, (14) and Lemma 11 imply that

$$a^{\mathsf{T}} \cdot \left(\Sigma_C^{\otimes \ell} (\Sigma_C^{\otimes \ell})^{\mathsf{T}} - (\Sigma_D \Sigma_D^{\mathsf{T}})_{i,i} \cdot I \right)^2 \cdot a = O_D(\epsilon). \quad (16)$$

By (i) in Lemma 10, $a^{\mathsf{T}} \cdot a = 1 - O_D(\epsilon)$. This along with (15) and (16) imply that $\beta^4 = O_D(\epsilon)$. However, this yields a contradiction (since $\beta > 0$ is a constant while ϵ can be arbitrarily small), proving the theorem.   □

6.2   Mirroring Lemma

Theorem 5. *Suppose a non-redundant correlation $D \in \mathbb{R}^{m_D \times n_D}$ has a deterministic ϵ-SNIR (A, B) to a correlation $C \in \mathbb{R}^{m_C \times n_C}$ for $\epsilon \geq 0$. Then, for $i \in \min(m_D, n_D)$ such that $(\boldsymbol{\Sigma}_D)_{i,i} > 0$,*

$$\left\| \delta\left(\widehat{A}_{.,i}, \widehat{B}_{.,i} \right) \right\|_2 = \frac{O_D(\sqrt{\epsilon})}{\alpha_i^2},$$

where

$$\alpha_i = \min_{j:(\boldsymbol{\Sigma}_C)_{j,j} \neq (\boldsymbol{\Sigma}_D)_{i,i}} \left| (\boldsymbol{\Sigma}_C)_{j,j} - (\boldsymbol{\Sigma}_D)_{i,i} \right|.$$

Proof: By Lemma 10, we have matrix $\widehat{E}_A$ such that

$$\widehat{A}^{\mathsf{T}} \boldsymbol{\Sigma}_C = \boldsymbol{\Sigma}_D \widehat{B}^{\mathsf{T}} + \widehat{E}_A,$$

where $\|\widehat{E}_A \boldsymbol{\Sigma}_C^{\mathsf{T}} \widehat{A}\| = O_D(\epsilon)$ and $\|\widehat{E}_A \widehat{B}\| = O_D(\epsilon)$. Fix $i \in \min(m_D, n_D)$ such that $(\boldsymbol{\Sigma}_D)_{i,i} > 0$, and define $\lambda_i = (\boldsymbol{\Sigma}_D)_{i,i}$. Since $(\boldsymbol{\xi}_i)^{\mathsf{T}} \boldsymbol{\Sigma}_D = \lambda_i (\boldsymbol{\xi}_i)^{\mathsf{T}}$, denoting $\widehat{A}_{.,i}$ and $\widehat{B}_{.,i}$ by $\boldsymbol{a}$ and $\boldsymbol{b}$, respectively,

$$(\boldsymbol{\xi}_i)^{\mathsf{T}} \widehat{A}^{\mathsf{T}} \boldsymbol{\Sigma}_C - (\boldsymbol{\xi}_i)^{\mathsf{T}} \boldsymbol{\Sigma}_D \widehat{B} = \boldsymbol{a}^{\mathsf{T}} \boldsymbol{\Sigma}_C - \lambda_i \boldsymbol{b}^{\mathsf{T}} = (\boldsymbol{\xi}_i)^{\mathsf{T}} \widehat{E}_A. \tag{17}$$

Post-multiplying the above equation by the transpose of the LHS, we get,

$$(\boldsymbol{\Sigma}_C^{\mathsf{T}} \boldsymbol{a} - \lambda_i \boldsymbol{b})^{\mathsf{T}} \cdot (\boldsymbol{\Sigma}_C^{\mathsf{T}} \boldsymbol{a} \quad \lambda_i \boldsymbol{b}) = (\boldsymbol{\xi}_i)^{\mathsf{T}} \widehat{E}_A \boldsymbol{\Sigma}_C^{\mathsf{T}} \boldsymbol{a} - (\boldsymbol{\xi}_i)^{\mathsf{T}} \widehat{E}_A \lambda_i \boldsymbol{b} \tag{18}$$

But,

$$(\boldsymbol{\xi}_i)^{\mathsf{T}} \widehat{E}_A \boldsymbol{\Sigma}_C^{\mathsf{T}} \boldsymbol{a} - (\boldsymbol{\xi}_i)^{\mathsf{T}} \widehat{E}_A \lambda_i \boldsymbol{b} = (\boldsymbol{\xi}_i)^{\mathsf{T}} \widehat{E}_A \boldsymbol{\Sigma}_C^{\mathsf{T}} \widehat{A} \boldsymbol{\xi}_i + (\boldsymbol{\xi}_i)^{\mathsf{T}} \widehat{E}_A \widehat{B} \boldsymbol{\xi}_i$$

$$= \left(\widehat{E}_A \boldsymbol{\Sigma}_C^{\mathsf{T}} \widehat{A} \right)_{i,i} + \left(\widehat{E}_A \widehat{B} \right)_{i,i} \leq \|\widehat{E}_A \boldsymbol{\Sigma}_C^{\mathsf{T}} \widehat{A}\| + \|\widehat{E}_A \widehat{B}\| = O_D(\epsilon).$$

The above bound implies that, (18) can be written as,

$$(\boldsymbol{\Sigma}_C^{\mathsf{T}} \boldsymbol{a} - \lambda_i \boldsymbol{b})^{\mathsf{T}} \cdot (\boldsymbol{\Sigma}_C^{\mathsf{T}} \boldsymbol{a} - \lambda_i \boldsymbol{b}) = O_D(\epsilon). \tag{19}$$

Define the set $\mathcal{S} \subset [m_C]$ and the m_C dimensional vector $\boldsymbol{a}|_{\mathcal{S}}$ as follows.

$$\mathcal{S} = \{j \in [m_C] : (\boldsymbol{\Sigma}_C)_{j,j} = \lambda_i\}, \text{ and } (\boldsymbol{a}|_s)_j = \begin{cases} (\boldsymbol{a})_j & \text{if } j \in \mathcal{S}, \\ 0 & \text{otherwise.} \end{cases}$$

Let Σ be a $m_C \times n_C$ dimensional matrix such that,

$$(\Sigma)_{i,j} = \begin{cases} 1 & \text{if } i = j \in [\min(m_C, n_C)], \\ 0 & \text{otherwise.} \end{cases}$$

Define $\widehat{\boldsymbol{a}}^{\mathsf{T}} = \boldsymbol{a}^{\mathsf{T}} \Sigma$ and $(\widehat{\boldsymbol{a}}|_s)^{\mathsf{T}} = (\boldsymbol{a}|_s)^{\mathsf{T}} \Sigma$. We have $(\boldsymbol{a}|_s)^{\mathsf{T}} (\boldsymbol{\Sigma}_C - \lambda_i \Sigma) = 0$ since $(\boldsymbol{a}|_s)_j = 0$ if $(\boldsymbol{\Sigma}_C)_{j,j} \neq \lambda_i$. Hence,

$$\boldsymbol{a}^{\mathsf{T}} \boldsymbol{\Sigma}_C = \lambda_i \boldsymbol{a}^{\mathsf{T}} \Sigma + \boldsymbol{a}^{\mathsf{T}} (\boldsymbol{\Sigma}_C - \lambda_i \Sigma) = \lambda_i \widehat{\boldsymbol{a}}^{\mathsf{T}} + (\boldsymbol{a}^{\mathsf{T}} - (\boldsymbol{a}|_s)^{\mathsf{T}})(\boldsymbol{\Sigma}_C - \lambda_i \Sigma).$$

By Lemma 11, since $(a|_\mathcal{S})^\mathsf{T} \left(\mathbf{\Sigma}_C \mathbf{\Sigma}_C^\mathsf{T} - \lambda_i^2 I\right) = 0$,

$$(a - a|_\mathcal{S})^\mathsf{T} \left(\mathbf{\Sigma}_C \mathbf{\Sigma}_C^\mathsf{T} - \lambda_i^2 I\right) \left(\mathbf{\Sigma}_C \mathbf{\Sigma}_C^\mathsf{T} - \lambda_i^2 I\right)^\mathsf{T} (a - a|_\mathcal{S}) = a^\mathsf{T} \left(\mathbf{\Sigma}_C \mathbf{\Sigma}_C^\mathsf{T} - \lambda_i^2 I\right)^2 a$$
$$\overset{(a)}{=} O_D(\epsilon).$$

For all $j \notin \mathcal{S}$, $|(\mathbf{\Sigma}_C \mathbf{\Sigma}_C^\mathsf{T})_{j,j} - \lambda_i^2| \geq \alpha^4$. That is, for all j such that $(a - a|_\mathcal{S})_j \neq 0$, $|(\mathbf{\Sigma}_C \mathbf{\Sigma}_C^\mathsf{T})_{j,j} - \lambda_i^2| \geq \alpha^4$. Since $\alpha > 0$ by definition,

$$O_D(\epsilon) = (a - a|_\mathcal{S})^\mathsf{T} \cdot \left(\mathbf{\Sigma}_C \mathbf{\Sigma}_C^\mathsf{T} - \lambda_i I\right)^2 \cdot (a - a|_\mathcal{S}) \geq \alpha^4 \cdot (a - a|_\mathcal{S})^\mathsf{T} \cdot (a - a|_\mathcal{S})$$
$$\Rightarrow (a - a|_\mathcal{S})^\mathsf{T} \cdot (a - a|_\mathcal{S}) = \frac{O_D(\epsilon)}{\alpha^4} \Rightarrow \|a - a|_\mathcal{S}\|_2 = \frac{O_D(\sqrt{\epsilon})}{\alpha^2}.$$

$\mathbf{\Sigma}_C - \lambda_i \mathbf{\Sigma}$ is a $m \times n$ dimensional matrix with zero as non-diagonal entries and the absolute value of each diagonal entry is at most 1. This follows from Lemma 9, which established that each diagonal entry is at most 1. Hence,

$$\|(\mathbf{\Sigma}_C - \lambda_i \mathbf{\Sigma})^\mathsf{T}(a - a|_\mathcal{S})\|_2 \leq 2\|a - a|_\mathcal{S}\|_2 = \frac{O_D(\sqrt{\epsilon})}{\alpha^2}.$$

For brevity, denote $(\mathbf{\Sigma}_C - \lambda_i \mathbf{\Sigma})^\mathsf{T}(a - a|_\mathcal{S})$ by v. Then, by (19),

$$O_D(\epsilon) = (\mathbf{\Sigma}_C^\mathsf{T} a - \lambda_i b)^\mathsf{T} \cdot (\mathbf{\Sigma}_C^\mathsf{T} a - \lambda_i b) = (\lambda_i(\hat{a} - b) + v)^\mathsf{T} \cdot (\lambda_i(\hat{a} - b) + v)$$
$$\geq \lambda_i^2 (\hat{a} - b)^\mathsf{T} \cdot (\hat{a} - b) + 2\lambda_i v^\mathsf{T} \cdot (\hat{a} - b).$$

Using Cauchy's inequality,

$$\lambda_i^2 (\hat{a} - b)^\mathsf{T} \cdot (\hat{a} - b) \leq O_D(\epsilon) + 2\|v\|_2 \cdot \|\hat{a} - b\|_2 \leq O_D(\epsilon) + \frac{O_D(\sqrt{\epsilon})}{\alpha^2} \cdot \|\hat{a} - b\|_2.$$

By definition of $\hat{a}$, $\|\hat{a}\|_2 = \|a\|_2$. By the statement (i) of Lemma 10, $a^\mathsf{T} \cdot a = 1 - O_D(\epsilon)$ and $b^\mathsf{T} \cdot b = 1 - O_D(\epsilon)$. Hence $\|\hat{a} - b\|_2$ is upper bounded by 2. Using this bound,

$$(\hat{a} - b)^\mathsf{T} \cdot (\hat{a} - b) \leq O_D(\epsilon) + \frac{O_D(\sqrt{\epsilon})}{\alpha^2}.$$

This concludes the proof.   □

7   Common Information and SNIR

In this section, we study the role of common information in SNIR and establish that it does not aid in secure reductions. Intuition suggests that the common information available to both parties cannot be exploited to achieve SNIR. Specifically, having access to common randomness does not aid in SNIR; this is shown in the following theorem.

Theorem 6. *Let C_w be 1-bit common randomness correlation; i.e., $C_w = \begin{bmatrix} \frac{1}{2} & 0 \\ 0 & \frac{1}{2} \end{bmatrix}$. If a non-redundant correlation D without common information has a statistical SNIR to $C_w \otimes C_0$ for a correlation C_0, then D also has a statistical SNIR to C_0.*

In the full version [1], we state and prove a robust variant of Lemma 4, which shows that if a correlation D devoid of common information has an ϵ-SNIR to C, then it has a SNIR to each of its component distribution with error that depends inversely on the probability of the component. But when the reduction use arbitrarily large number of copies of common random bits, this dependence makes the lemma ineffective in proving the theorem. However, the following lemma (also proven in the full version [1]) implies that if D has an ϵ-SNIR to $C^{\otimes \ell}$, then it has a $O_D(\epsilon)$-SNIR to $C_0^{\otimes \ell}$ proving the theorem.

Lemma 12. *Consider a non-redundant correlation $D \in \mathbb{R}^{m_D \times n_D}$ with zero common information. For correlations $C_1, \ldots, C_k$ and positive numbers $\alpha_1, \ldots, \alpha_k$ such that $\alpha_1 + \ldots + \alpha_k = 1$, let*

$$
C = \begin{bmatrix}
\alpha_1 C_1 & 0 & 0 & \ldots & 0 \\
0 & \alpha_2 C_2 & 0 & \ldots & 0 \\
\vdots & & \ddots & & \vdots \\
\vdots & & & \ddots & \vdots \\
0 & 0 & \ldots & 0 & \alpha_k C_k
\end{bmatrix}.
\tag{20}
$$

If D has an ϵ-SNIR to C, then for some $1 \leq i \leq k$, D has a $O_D(\epsilon)$-SNIR to C_i.

8 Applications

In this section, we demonstrate the use of the results above in studying SNIR between various interesting classes of correlations.

Our first result shows that no finite correlation is complete for SNIR even when Alice and Bob share common information.

Theorem 7 [Incompleteness]. *For any correlation C, there exists a correlation D such that D does not have a statistical SNIR to C.*

Proof: We shall set D to be BSC_p for an appropriately chosen p.

For correlations $C_1, \ldots, C_k$ without common information and positive constants $\alpha_1, \ldots, \alpha_k$, suppose C can be represented as in (20). By Lemma 12, D has a ϵ-SNIR to $C^{\otimes \ell}$ only if it has a $O_D(\epsilon)$-SNIR to one of its component correlations; specifically, by Lemma 12, D has a $O_D(\epsilon)$-SNIR to $C_{a_1} \otimes C_{a_2} \otimes \ldots \otimes C_{a_k}$, for some $(a_1, \ldots, a_\ell) \in [k]^\ell$. This, trivially, implies that D has a $O_D(\epsilon)$-SNIR to $C_0^{\otimes \ell}$, where $C_0 = C_1 \otimes C_2 \otimes \ldots \otimes C_k$. Thus, D has a statistical SNIR to C_0 if it has a statistical SNIR to C. Choose $0 < p < \frac{1}{2}$ such that $1 - 2p > \max(\mathbf{\Lambda}_{C_0})$; by Lemma 9 (i), such a p exists since $C_1, \ldots, C_k$ have no common information. By (11), $\mathbf{\Lambda}_{\mathsf{BSC}_p} = \{1, 1 - 2p\}$; hence, by Theorem 4, BSC_p has no statistical SNIR to C_0 and hence to C; this proves the theorem. □

8.1 Applications of the Spectral Criterion

The spectral criterion in Theorem 4 can be used to analyze self-reductions of binary symmetric, binary erasure and OLE correlations.

The first couple of results *characterize* self-reductions of binary symmetric correlations and binary erasure correlations. Define the operator $*$ such that for $p, q \in [0, 1]$,

$$p * q = p(1 - q) + q(1 - p).$$

Naturally, for all $k \in \mathbb{N}$, we can extend this notion to define p^{*k} as $p * p * \ldots * p$ (k times). We prove the following two theorems in the full version [1].

Theorem 8. *For $p, q \in (0, \frac{1}{2})$, BSC_q has a statistical SNIR to BSC_p if and only if $q = p^{*\ell}$ for some $\ell \in \mathbb{N}$.*

The necessity of the condition is shown using the spectral criterion. As observed in (11), $\Lambda_{\mathsf{BSC}_p} = \{1, (1 - 2p)\}$. Hence, by Theorem 4, BSC_q has a statistical SNIR to BSC_p only if $(1 - 2q) = (1 - 2p)^\ell$ for some $\ell \in \mathbb{N}$. Necessity of the condition now follows from the fact that if $(1 - 2q) = (1 - 2p)^\ell$ then $q = p^{*\ell}$. The protocol for SNIR of $\mathsf{BSC}_{p^{*\ell}}$ to $\mathsf{BSC}_p^{\otimes \ell}$ described in Sect. 2.6 shows the sufficiency of the condition.

Theorem 9. *For $p, q \in (0, 1)$, BEC_q has a statistical SNIR to BEC_p if and only if $1 - q = (1 - p)^\ell$ for some $\ell \in \mathbb{N}$.*

The proof is similar to that of the previous theorem. As observed in (12), $\Lambda_{\mathsf{BEC}_p} = \{1, \sqrt{1 - p}\}$. Necessity of the condition follows from the fact that if $\sqrt{1 - q} = \sqrt{1 - q}^\ell$ then $q = p^\ell$. The protocol for SNIR of BEC_{p^ℓ} to $\mathsf{BEC}_p^{\otimes \ell}$ described in Sect. 2.6 shows the sufficiency of the condition.

Next, we show a necessary condition for self-reductions between OLE correlations over finite fields.

Theorem 10. *$\mathsf{OLE}_\mathbb{F}$ has a statistical SNIR to $\mathsf{OLE}_{\mathbb{F}'}$ only if both $\mathbb{F}$ and $\mathbb{F}'$ have the same characteristic.*

In the full version [1], we will show that the spectrum of the OLE correlation over a finite field $\mathbb{F}$ consists exclusively of the values 1 and $1/\sqrt{|\mathbb{F}|}$. Now, recall that $|\mathbb{F}| = p^k$ for some prime p and $k \in \mathbb{N}$, where p is the characteristic of the field. Hence, the only values in the spectrum of $\mathsf{OLE}_\mathbb{F}^{\otimes \ell}$, for a characteristic-$p$ field $\mathbb{F}$, are of the form $p^{t/2}$ for integers t. Hence, together with Theorem 4, this implies Theorem 10.

8.2 Applications of the Mirroring Lemma

In this section, we employ the mirroring lemma in Theorem 5 to argue impossibility of SNIR which cannot be inferred using only the spectral criterion. To this end, we derive a strong necessary condition for statistical SNIR to correlations with uniform marginals and positive semi-definite distribution matrices. A formal proof of the lemma is given in the full version [1].

Lemma 13. *Let C be a correlation with uniform marginals and $\Psi_C = \Phi_C$. A non-redundant distribution D over $m_D \times n_D$ has a statistical SNIR to C only if, there exist partitions $S_1 \sqcup S_2 \sqcup \ldots \sqcup S_l = [m_D]$ and $T_1 \sqcup T_2 \sqcup \ldots \sqcup T_l = [n_D]$ such that*

$$\sum_{i \in S_k} (D\mathbf{1})_i = \sum_{i \in T_k} (D^\mathsf{T}\mathbf{1})_i, \text{ for all } k \in [l],$$

and, for each $j \in [\min(m_D, n_D)]$ such that $(\Sigma_D)_{j,j} > 0$,

$$\left(\Delta_{D^\mathsf{T}}^{-1/2} \Psi_D^\mathsf{T} \right)_{i,j} = \left(\Delta_D^{-1/2} \Phi_D^\mathsf{T} \right)_{i',j} \text{ for all } k \in [l], i \in S_k, i' \in T_k.$$

As a direct consequence of this result, BEC does not have statistical SNIR to BSC. In the case of perfect SNIR, this impossibility is trivial to see: it is impossible to arrange for Bob to output only 0 or $\perp$, whenever Alice outputs 0 (perfect correctness).

Theorem 11. *For all values $p, q \in (0, 1)$, BEC_q has no statistical SNIR to BSC_p.*

Proof: We observe that, for all $0 < p < 1$, BSC_p has uniform marginal and, as described in (11), $\Psi_{\mathsf{BSC}_p} = \Phi_{\mathsf{BSC}_p}$. Furthermore, for $0 < q < 1$, it can be verified using (12) that

$$\left(\Delta_{\mathsf{BEC}_q^\mathsf{T}}^{-1/2} \Psi_{\mathsf{BEC}_q}^\mathsf{T} \right)_{\cdot,2} = \begin{bmatrix} 1 \\ -1 \end{bmatrix} \qquad \left(\Delta_{\mathsf{BEC}_q}^{-1/2} \Phi_{\mathsf{BEC}_q}^\mathsf{T} \right)_{\cdot,2} = \begin{bmatrix} \sqrt{\frac{1}{1-q}} \\ 0 \\ -\sqrt{\frac{1}{1-q}} \end{bmatrix}.$$

Impossibility follows directly from Lemma 13 as $(\Sigma_D)_{2,2} = \sqrt{1-q} > 0$ as given in (12). $\qquad \square$

Theorem 12. *OT has no statistical SNIR to BSC_p for any $0 < p < \frac{1}{2}$.*

Proof: Inspecting (13), $(\Sigma_{\mathsf{OT}})_{2,2} = \frac{1}{\sqrt{2}} > 0$ and

$$\left(\Delta_{\mathsf{OT}^\mathsf{T}}^{-1/2} \Psi_{\mathsf{OT}}^\mathsf{T} \right)_{\cdot,2} = \begin{bmatrix} 0 \\ -\sqrt{2} \\ \sqrt{2} \\ 0 \end{bmatrix} \qquad \left(\Delta_{\mathsf{OT}}^{-1/2} \Phi_{\mathsf{OT}}^\mathsf{T} \right)_{\cdot,2} = \begin{bmatrix} -1 \\ 1 \\ 1 \\ -1 \end{bmatrix}.$$

Impossibility follows directly from Lemma 13. $\qquad \square$

References

1. Agarwal, P., Narayanan, V., Pathak, S., Prabhakaran, M., Prabhakaran, V.M., Rehan, M.A.: Secure non-interactive reduction and spectral analysis of correlations. Cryptology ePrint Archive (2022)

826   P. Agarwal et al.

2. Agrawal, S., Prabhakaran, M.: On fair exchange, fair coins and fair sampling. In: Canetti, R., Garay, J.A. (eds.) CRYPTO 2013, Part I. LNCS, vol. 8042, pp. 259–276. Springer, Heidelberg (2013). https://doi.org/10.1007/978-3-642-40041-4_15

3. Ahlswede, R., Gacs, P.: Spreading of sets in product spaces and hypercontraction of the Markov operator. Ann. Probab. **4**(6), 925–939 (1976)

4. Anantharam, V., Gohari, A., Kamath, S., Nair, C.: On maximal correlation, hypercontractivity, and the data processing inequality studied by Erkip and Cover. CoRR. abs/1304.6133 (2013)

5. Beigi, S., Gohari, A.: On the duality of additivity and tensorization. In: ISIT, pp. 2381–2385. IEEE (2015)

6. Beimel, A., Ishai, Y., Kumaresan, R., Kushilevitz, E.: On the cryptographic complexity of the worst functions. In: Lindell, Y. (ed.) TCC 2014. LNCS, vol. 8349, pp. 317–342. Springer, Heidelberg (2014). https://doi.org/10.1007/978-3-642-54242-8_14

7. Beimel, A., Malkin, T.: A quantitative approach to reductions in secure computation. In: Naor, M. (ed.) TCC 2004. LNCS, vol. 2951, pp. 238–257. Springer, Heidelberg (2004). https://doi.org/10.1007/978-3-540-24638-1_14

8. Borell, C.: Positivity improving operators and hypercontractivity. Mathematische Zeitschrift **180**, 225–234 (1982)

9. Boyle, E., Couteau, G., Gilboa, N., Ishai, Y., Kohl, L., Scholl, P.: Efficient pseudorandom correlation generators: silent OT extension and more. In: Boldyreva, A., Micciancio, D. (eds.) CRYPTO 2019, Part III. LNCS, vol. 11694, pp. 489–518. Springer, Cham (2019). https://doi.org/10.1007/978-3-030-26954-8_16

10. Boyle, E., Couteau, G., Gilboa, N., Ishai, Y., Kohl, L., Scholl, P.: Efficient pseudorandom correlation generators from Ring-LPN. In: Micciancio, D., Ristenpart, T. (eds.) CRYPTO 2020, Part II. LNCS, vol. 12171, pp. 387–416. Springer, Cham (2020). https://doi.org/10.1007/978-3-030-56880-1_14

11. Chung, F.R.K.: Spectral Graph Theory. American Mathematical Society, USA (1997)

12. De, A., Mossel, E., Neeman, J.: Non interactive simulation of correlated distributions is decidable. In: SODA 2018, pp. 2728–2746. SIAM (2018)

13. Gács, P., Körner, J.: Common information is far less than mutual information. Probl. Control Inf. Theory **2**(2), 149–162 (1973)

14. Garg, S., Ishai, Y., Kushilevitz, E., Ostrovsky, R., Sahai, A.: Cryptography with one-way communication. In: Gennaro, R., Robshaw, M. (eds.) CRYPTO 2015, Part II. LNCS, vol. 9216, pp. 191–208. Springer, Heidelberg (2015). https://doi.org/10.1007/978-3-662-48000-7_10

15. Ghazi, B., Kamath, P., Sudan, M.: Decidability of non-interactive simulation of joint distributions. In: FOCS, pp. 545–554. IEEE Computer Society (2016)

16. Goldreich, O., Micali, S., Wigderson, A.: How to play ANY mental game. In: STOC, pp. 218–229 (1987). See [?, Chap. 7] Goldreich04book for more details

17. Goldrcich, O., Vainish, R.: How to solve any protocol problem - an efficiency improvement (extended abstract). In: Pomerance, C. (ed.) CRYPTO 1987. LNCS, vol. 293, pp. 73–86. Springer, Heidelberg (1988). https://doi.org/10.1007/3-540-48184-2_6

18. Hirschfeld, H.O., Wishart, J.: A connection between correlation and contingency. In: Proceedings of the Cambridge Philosophical Society, vol. 31, no. 4, p. 520 (1935)

19. Horn, R.A., Johnson, C.R.: Topics in Matrix Analysis. Cambridge University Press, Cambridge (1991)

20. Ishai, Y., Prabhakaran, M., Sahai, A.: Founding cryptography on oblivious transfer – efficiently. In: Wagner, D. (ed.) CRYPTO 2008. LNCS, vol. 5157, pp. 572–591. Springer, Heidelberg (2008). https://doi.org/10.1007/978-3-540-85174-5_32
21. Kamath, S., Anantharam, V.: On non-interactive simulation of joint distributions. IEEE Trans. Inf. Theory **62**(6), 3419–3435 (2016)
22. Khorasgani, H.A., Maji, H.K., Nguyen, H.H.: Decidability of secure non-interactive simulation of doubly symmetric binary source. Cryptology ePrint Archive, Report 2021/190 (2021). https://eprint.iacr.org/2021/190
23. Khorasgani, H.A., Maji, H.K., Nguyen, H.H.: Secure non-interactive simulation: feasibility & rate. In: CRYPTO (2022). To appear
24. Kilian, J.: Founding cryptography on oblivious transfer. In: STOC, pp. 20–31 (1988)
25. Kraschewski, D., Maji, H.K., Prabhakaran, M., Sahai, A.: A full characterization of completeness for two-party randomized function evaluation. In: Nguyen, P.Q., Oswald, E. (eds.) EUROCRYPT 2014. LNCS, vol. 8441, pp. 659–676. Springer, Heidelberg (2014). https://doi.org/10.1007/978-3-642-55220-5_36
26. Maji, H., Prabhakaran, M., Rosulek, M.: Complexity of multi-party computation functionalities, volume 10 of cryptology and information security series, pp. 249–283. IOS Press, Amsterdam (2013)
27. Narayanan, V., Prabhakaran, M., Prabhakaran, V.M.: Zero-communication reductions. In: Pass, R., Pietrzak, K. (eds.) TCC 2020, Part III. LNCS, vol. 12552, pp. 274–304. Springer, Cham (2020). https://doi.org/10.1007/978-3-030-64381-2_10
28. Rènyi, A.: On measures of dependence. Acta Mathematica Hungarica **10**(3–4), 441–451 (1959)
29. Sudan, M., Tyagi, H., Watanabe, S.: Communication for generating correlation: a unifying survey. IEEE Trans. Inf. Theory **66**(1), 5–37 (2020)
30. Witsenhausen, H.S.: On sequences of pairs of dependent random variables. SIAM J. Appl. Math. **28**(1), 100–113 (1975)
31. Wyner, A.D.: The common information of two dependent random variables. IEEE Trans. Inf. Theory **21**(2), 163–179 (1975)

Author Index